Preacher's
Sourcebook
of
Creative
Sermon
Illustrations

Preacher's Sourcebook

of

Creative

Sermon

Illustrations

ROBERT J. MORGAN

THOMAS NELSON
Since 1798

NASHVILLE DALLAS MEXICO CITY RIO DE JANEIRO BEIJING

Published in Nashville, Tennessee, by Thomas Nelson. Thomas Nelson is a trademark of Thomas Nelson, Inc.

Thomas Nelson, Inc. titles may be purchased in bulk for educational, business, fund-raising, or sales promotional use. For information, please email SpecialMarkets@ThomasNelson.com.

Scripture taken from the New King James Version. © 1982 by Thomas Nelson, Inc. Used by permission. All rights reserved.

The Author and the Publisher sincerely appreciate all those whose stories are retold or quoted in this book. We have made every effort to footnote and document each story. If we have inadvertently omitted anyone, please let us know.

This book was previously published as Nelson's Complete Book of Stories, Illustrations, and Quotes: The Ultimate Contemporary Resource for Speakers [*ISBN 0-7852-4479-4*].

ISBN-10: 1-4185-2803-X
ISBN-13: 978-1-4185-2803-4

Printed in the United States of America

12 13 QG 10 9 8 7

Preface

Someone Once Said . . .

- *Don't forget to give them a few anecdotes. Anecdotes are very much objected to by critics of sermons, who say they ought not be used in the pulpit. But some of us know better than that; we know what will wake a congregation up; we can speak from experience, that a few anecdotes here and there are first-rate things to get the attention of persons who won't listen to dry doctrine. Do try and learn as many anecdotes as possible.*—Charles Haddon Spurgeon[1]

Three short phrases have guided my pulpit ministry for nearly thirty years. They were spoken by Ruth Bell Graham in her log home astride a North Carolina mountain on May 13, 1972. I was a wide-eyed student visiting from Columbia Bible College with my friend Joe Medina. "Ruth," I asked, "I want to be a preacher one day, and your husband is one of the best-known in the world. What advice can you give me about pulpit ministry?"

Her simple reply has stayed with me ever since: *Preach expository sermons, keep them short, and use a lot of illustrations.*

It's too bad William Carey didn't have the opportunity to visit Ruth Graham. Though he eventually became the "Father of Modern Missions," he got off to a rough start. Seeking ordination from the Baptist Church in Olney, England, in 1785, he was turned down after the members heard him preach. They decided he needed a period of probation. Why?

Mr. Hall of Arnsby, criticising the attempt, said, "Brother Carey, you have no *likes* in your sermons. Christ taught that the Kingdom of Heaven was *like* to leaven hid in meal, *like* to a grain of mustard, and etc. You tell us what things are, but never what they are like."[2]

This book is intended to give you some *likes,* to provide a lot of illustrations. The right story, illustration, or quote, after all, is worth its weight in platinum. According to the *Wall Street Journal,* comedian Bob Hope has a walk-in vault located in an office compound on his estate which contains scores of large file drawers. The walls are cinder blocks, and the door is six-inch-thick steel with three one-inch dead bolts. The files contain yellowed sheets, mostly in all-cap type—original pages submitted by Hope's writers over the years, stretching back to 1934. A check or number in the margin tells when and where the gag was used. The jokes are referenced and cross-referenced under hundreds of topics and subtopics. Hope's collection of jokes is worth a fortune.[3]

Preachers, teachers, and public speakers should also be storing up a lifetime's worth of stories that inspire, enlighten, and motivate people to grasp and live truth. Jesus indicated as much by His frequent use of parables, and the Bible itself is partly an inspired book of true stories.

---

[1] Charles Haddon Spurgeon, *Sermons of Rev. C. H. Spurgeon of London: Volume 2* (New York: Robert Carter & Brothers, 1883), p. 355.

[2] Mary Drewery, *William Carey: A Biography* (Grand Rapids: Zondervan, 1978), p. 30.

[3] John McDonough, "Jokes of the Century," in *The Wall Street Journal,* November 6, 1997, p. A20.

I've found that illustrations serve three purposes. First, they wake people up who have drifted off during the more didactic portions of my message. Second, they keep the children tuned in. Third, illustrations enable people to see the practicality of what is being preached. Through the use of stories, illustrations, and quotes people see themselves as in a mirror and are better able to personalize the truth of Scripture.

When first beginning to preach, I asked Ed Young, who was then pastor of the First Baptist Church of Columbia, South Carolina, where he found all the marvelous stories he used week by week. He said simply, "I read a lot."

Taking that as my cue, I've spent thirty years reading a lot and carefully indexing stories, quotes, and illustrations for sermons and speeches. Some of the stories in this book are from Christian history—admittedly a taboo for some of today's preachers. But I've never yet found an audience who wasn't spellbound by the dramatic story of Polycarp's stand against his Roman persecutors in the second century, amused by Charles Spurgeon's one-hundred-year-old quips about faultfinders, or amazed by Charles Herbert Lightoller's escape from the *Titanic* in 1912. So I include my retelling of such events without hesitation.

There are many up-to-date illustrations here, too, of course; though *modern* illustrations sometimes become dated easier than the older ones. Often the best illustrations are found in the headlines of the morning newspaper or from the life experiences of the preacher. This book isn't intended to provide many of those kinds of stories—you can get those on your own. This volume is a supplement, a treasure trove of useable stories that are written to be spoken, and spoken to be heard.

I appreciate Phil Stoner and Teri Wilhelms of Thomas Nelson Publishers for their support and guidance in putting this collection from my own *vaults* into print. Special thanks to my wife, Katrina, for reading them all and making judicious comments.

Most of all, I want to thank the members of The Donelson Fellowship in Nashville, Tennessee, for listening to these stories for over twenty years. They know I've always tried to keep Ruth Graham's advice about sermons, although occasionally I've a little trouble with the "keep them short" part.

To them this book is dedicated.

Preacher's Sourcebook

of

Creative

Sermon

Illustrations

Someone Once Said . . .

- *How does the branch bear fruit? Not by incessant effort for sunshine and air; not by vain struggles . . . . It simply abides in the vine, in silent and undisturbed union, and blossoms and fruit appear as of spontaneous growth.*—Harriet Beecher Stowe, in her little booklet *How to Live on Christ*
- *Connected with Him in His love, I am more than conqueror; without Him, I am nothing. Like some railway tickets in America, I am "Not good if detached."*—Corrie Ten Boom

Date: _____ _____ _____
Place: _____ _____ _____
Occasion: _____ _____ _____

Abiding, Not Striving or Struggling

Missionary pioneer J. Hudson Taylor of China was working and worrying so frantically that his health was about to break. Just when his friends feared he was near a breakdown, Taylor received a letter from fellow missionary John McCarthy that told of a discovery McCarthy had made from John 15—the joy of abiding in Christ. McCarthy's letter said in part:

Abiding, not striving or struggling; looking off unto Him; trusting Him for present power . . . this is not new, and yet 'tis new to me . . . . Christ literally all seems to me now the power, the only power for service; the only ground for unchanging joy.

As Hudson Taylor read this letter at his mission station in Chin-kiang on Saturday, September 4, 1869, his own eyes were opened. "As I read," he recalled, "I saw it all. I looked to Jesus, and when I saw, oh how the joy flowed!" Writing to his sister in England, he said:

As to work, mine was never so plentiful, so responsible, or so difficult; but the weight and strain are all gone. The last month or more has been perhaps the happiest of my life, and I long to tell you a little of what the Lord has done for my soul . . . .

When the agony of soul was at its height, a sentence in a letter from dear McCarthy was used to remove the scales from my eyes, and the Spirit of God revealed the truth of our oneness with Jesus as I had never known it before. McCarthy, who had been much exercised by the same sense of failure, but saw the light before I did, wrote (I quote from memory): "But how to get faith strengthened? Not by striving after faith but by resting on the Faithful One."

As I read, I saw it all! . . . . As I thought of the Vine and the branches, what light the blessed Spirit poured into my soul!

Date: _____ _____ _____
Place: _____ _____ _____
Occasion: _____ _____ _____

Abide with Me

Henry Francis Lyte was of delicate health all his life, but that didn't stop him from working like an ox, year after year, pastoring among the seafaring folks around

Devonshire, England. But finally his strength gave out, and in 1847 his doctor suggested he move to the milder climate of southern France. It was a heartbreaking parting, and Lyte couldn't leave without one final sermon to his church of twenty-four years. His health was so frail that his friends advised against it, but Lyte was determined. Standing feebly, he said, "Oh, brethren, I stand here before you today, as alive from the dead, if I may hope to impress upon you and get you to prepare for that solemn hour which must come to all. I plead with you to become acquainted with the changeless Christ and His death."

After finishing his sermon, he served the Lord's Supper to his weeping flock and dismissed them. That evening, as his life's work drew to its close, he found comfort in pondering John 15: "Abide in Me, and I in you."

According to his gardener, Lyte wrote the following hymn after having walked down to the ocean and watched "the sun setting over Brixham Harbor like a pool of molten gold." Taking out a piece of paper, he wrote a poem and returned to his study to rewrite and polish it before giving it to his adopted daughter.

The next day he left for France. Reaching Nice, he had a seizure and passed away with the words, "Joy! Peace!" on his lips. His poem, however, lived on, becoming one of our most beloved hymns:

> *Abide with me—fast falls the eventide!*
> *The darkness deepens—Lord, with me abide;*
> *When other helpers fail and comforts flee,*
> *Help of the helpless, O abide with me!*

Date: _____   _____   _____
Place: _____   _____   _____
Occasion: _____   _____   _____

In the Twilight

On May 8, 1984, Benjamin M. Weir, veteran Presbyterian missionary to Lebanon, was kidnapped at gunpoint by Shiite Muslims in Beirut. During his sixteen-month imprisonment, he was constantly threatened with death. On his first night in captivity, one of his captors came to him and told him to face the wall, which he did. "Now take your blindfold off, and put this on." The man handed Weir a pair of ski goggles with the eye holes covered in thick plastic adhesive tape. He could see no light. In Weir's mind, the sun had set. He later wrote:

In the twilight there came to mind the hymn, "Abide with me—fast falls the eventide." I felt vulnerable, helpless, lonely. I felt tears in my eyes. Then I remembered the promise of Jesus, "If you abide in me and my words abide in you, ask what you will, and it shall be done unto you."

"Lord, I remember your promise, and I think it applies to me, too. I've done nothing to deserve it but receive it as a free gift. I need you. I need your assurance and guidance to be faithful

to you in this situation. Teach me what I need to learn. Deliver me from this place and this captivity, if it is your will. If it is not your will to set me free, help me to accept whatever is involved. Show me your gifts, and enable me to recognize them as coming from you. Praise be to you."

For the next sixteen months, his hope and joy was that he was not simply abiding in captivity, he was abiding in Christ and thus able to "bear much fruit."[1]

Date: _____ _____ _____
Place: _____ _____ _____
Occasion: _____ _____ _____

———— Abortion ————

Someone Once Said . . .

- *Unrestricted abortion is wrong, even if it's a right.*[2]
- *It has come to the time where the most dangerous place to be in America is not the inner city, where gangs threaten innocent lives, or in angry prisons, where only the fit survive, but in the womb of a mother who is being told that if she doesn't really want the baby, an abortion is the solution.*[3]
- *Since when does anyone's right to live depend on someone else wanting them? Killing the unwanted is a monstrous evil.*[4]
- *More than 95 percent of children killed by abortion are killed for reasons of convenience, not incest, not rape, not the physical condition of the unborn, and not the threatened health of the mother.*[5]
- *Worldwide, millions of unborn babies are killed each year. In the United States, over thirty-two million unborn babies have been killed in the twenty-one years since abortion was legalized, and more than 1.5 million are killed each year.*[6]

Date: _____ _____ _____
Place: _____ _____ _____
Occasion. _____ _____ _____

Definitions of Abortion

- *Death Before Birth*[7]
- *The Silent Holocaust*[8]

[1] Benjamin M. Weir and Dennis Benson, "Tough Faith," *Leadership Journal*, Winter 1989, 55.
[2] Roy Maynard, "Abortion: A Right That's Wrong," *World Magazine*, January 16, 1999, 14.
[3] Charles R. Swindoll, "Why I Stand For Life," *Focus on the Family*, August 1990, 18.
[4] Dr. John Willke, quoted by Charles R. Swindoll, "Why I Stand For Life," *Focus on the Family*, August 1990, 18.
[5] Alan Guttnacher Institute: research arm of Planned Parenthood, quoted by Charles R. Swindoll, "Why I Stand For Life," *Focus on the Family*, August 1990, 19.
[6] "National Right To Life" Web Page, http://www.nrlc.org.
[7] Harold O. J. Brown, *Death before Birth* (Nashville: Thomas Nelson Publishers, 1978).
[8] Attributed to Dr. C. Everett Koop.

- *Post-Conceptive Fertility Control*
- *Voluntary Miscarriage*
- *Every Woman's Right*

Date:	_____	_____	_____
Place:	_____	_____	_____
Occasion:	_____	_____	_____

One Woman's Answer to Abortion and Its Aftermath

After her divorce, Dot Huff met a well-to-do man who left his wife and children to marry her. This man owned a hotel and a yacht, and the two newly-re-weds enjoyed their *good* life. Then Dot became pregnant. They weren't ready for an end to their carefree lifestyle, for dirty diapers and babysitters and parenthood. An abortion seemed the easiest solution.

Dot arrived at the hospital feeling unexpectedly frightened and alone. A young woman in a nearby bed, trying to console her, said, "Don't worry—I've had four abortions. It's over real fast."

Dot wasn't consoled.

Shortly she was wheeled into another room and the procedure began. To her horror, she could hear, see, and feel everything that happened.

Returning home, Dot battled depression and guilt. She lashed out at her friends who had encouraged her to have the abortion, at her husband, at her doctors, and at herself. Her marriage broke up, and she moved home with her parents and twin sister.

Dot's sister, who had experienced two unplanned pregnancies herself, was now a Christian, and Dot noticed her reading the Bible every day. "If reading the Bible can help my sister," she said to herself, "maybe it can help me, too." She retrieved her grandmother's Bible from the bottom drawer of a chest and soon came to Genesis 9:6, a verse that stabbed at Dot like a knife: "Whoever sheds man's blood, by man his *blood* shall be shed; for in the image of God He made man" (NKJV).

Crying in anguish, Dot asked her sister, "What can I do? I'm going to hell. Please help me." In reply, her sister shared with her John 3:16, and Dot began to realize for the first time that Jesus Christ died on the cross to forgive and remove our sins. She quickly embraced Christ as her Savior, and her tears of shame became tears of relief.

In the days that followed, I found myself caring about the needs of others. I stopped griping when my mother asked for help around the house. I even stopped swearing, a habit that had been ingrained in me. I began attending a loving church, where I grew in my knowledge of Scripture. I came out from the black cloud of depression and was able to free myself and forgive those who had cooperated in the abortion.

The Lord has given Dot Huff many opportunities to share her story, both in private and in public, and her counsel has aided many women. *I am living proof,* she says, *that the Gospel of Christ is the power of God for the salvation of everyone who believes.*[1]

---

[1] Dot Huff, "Aftermath of Abortion: a *First Person* article," as told to Joan Brauning, *Moody Magazine,* May 1989, 80.

Date: _____   _____   _____
Place: _____   _____   _____
Occasion: _____   _____   _____

"Probably They Would Have Had Brown Eyes . . ."

Elaine Rotondo is a homemaker and a freelance writer. She and her husband, Ronald, have three daughters; they live in Sebastopol, California. In January, 1990, her poignant story appeared in *Decision* magazine:

Our third little girl completed our family, a special blessing. As I held her in my arms, I marveled at how God works his purpose in our lives.

But driving home from the supermarket one afternoon, I found myself thinking about two other children from my past. Those two I had never fussed over. In fact, I had tried to forget them entirely. Before now I had not even called them children. I had called them abortions.

When I became a Christian, I understood that abortion was a sin, and I had asked God to forgive me. But I had never felt sorry over the loss of those little ones.

Pulling my car to the shoulder of the road, I sat for some time, my moist fingers wrapped tightly around the steering wheel. Now I let my thoughts venture into a place they had never gone.

"How old would they be now?" I wondered. They probably would have had brown eyes, as their living sisters do.

I fought off the sickening reality that was rising in my mind. The full impact of what I had done so many years before was finally upon me. "They were alive," I said out loud. "They were real children!"

Shame washed over me like a dense, heavy wave. But as the tide of pain rose, I also felt the Lord's presence. This was too terrible for me to face alone; He would face it with me. God held me up in the moment of that horrible truth: I had taken life from my own children!

In my heart I cried out to the tiny souls who never had felt their mother's arms. I had never mourned these children. Now I longed for them. But it was too late. The pain was almost unbearable. I wept for a long time, wishing the very mountains would cover me and hide my guilt. Then I remembered Jesus. "The punishment that brought us peace was upon him, and by his wounds we are healed." (Isaiah 53:5, NIV).

This was why he had died, to pay the price of sin for me. Looking over the seat, I gazed intently at my three-month-old daughter sleeping soundly in her car seat. She was so fresh and alive!

"Thank you, Jesus," I whispered. "You are so good to me."[1]

Date: _____   _____   _____
Place: _____   _____   _____
Occasion: _____   _____   _____

Stages of Development

According to the National Right to Life, a pregnancy normally covers forty weeks, beginning at fertilization, when the sperm and the ovum meet to form a

---

[1] Elaine Rotondo, "They Were Children," *Decision,* January 1990, 10.

single cell. All the characteristics of each person—sex, eye color, shoe size, intelligence, etc.—are determined at fertilization by the baby's genetic code in the 46 human chromosomes. Every person begins as a separate single cell; nothing new is added except oxygen and nutrition. If the process is not interrupted, a human being will live approximately nine months in the mother's uterus and decades outside of it.

At Three Weeks: The baby's heart begins to beat and pump blood.

At Six Weeks: The baby has brain waves that can be measured with an electroencephalograph. (The end of human life can be defined as *the cessation of brain waves,* but many ignore the scientific evidence of brain waves in unborn babies).

At Seven Weeks: The baby is swimming in the amniotic sac with a natural swimmer's stroke and is already kicking.

At Eight Weeks: The baby begins swallowing.

At Nine Weeks: Parents can watch their baby moving around inside the uterus on an ultrasound scanner.

At Ten to Eleven Weeks: The baby can *breathe* amniotic fluid and urine, is sensitive to touch, and can seize an object placed in his or her hand.

At Eleven Weeks: All the baby's organ systems are functioning. Although still so small that the baby could stand on an adult's little fingertip, his or her little feet are perfectly shaped. The baby has a skeletal structure, nerves, and circulation, as well as eyelids, nails, and fingerprints.

At Fourteen Weeks: The baby's heart pumps several quarts of blood through his or her body every day.

At Eighteen Weeks: The child is perfectly formed.

At Nineteen Weeks: The baby can conceivably survive outside the womb. Kenya King was born in Florida on June 16, 1985, at nineteen weeks, or just a little more than 4½ months after her life began. She weighed eighteen ounces.[1]

Date:		
Place:		
Occasion:		

Interesting Case Studies

Would you consider abortion in any of the following four situations:

1. There's a preacher and wife who are very, very poor. They already have fourteen children, and now she finds out she's pregnant with the fifteenth. They're living in tremendous poverty. Considering their poverty and the excessive world population, would you consider recommending an abortion?

2. The father is sick with a bad cold, the mother has tuberculosis (TB). They have four children. The first is blind, second is dead, third is deaf, fourth has TB. She finds that she's pregnant again. Given their extreme situation, would you consider recommending an abortion?

---

[1] Adapted from material supplied by the National Right to Life Committee.

3. A white man has raped a thirteen-year-old black girl, and she became pregnant. If you were her parents, would you consider recommending an abortion?

4. A teenage girl is pregnant. She's not married. Her fiancé is not the father of the baby, and he's concerned. Would you consider recommending an abortion?

If you said *yes* to the first case, you just killed John Wesley, one of the great evangelists in the nineteenth century. If you said *yes* to the second case, you killed Ludwig van Beethoven. If you said *yes* to the third case, you killed Ethel Waters, the great black gospel singer who thrilled audiences for many years at Billy Graham Crusades around the world. And, if you said *yes* to the fourth case, you killed Jesus Christ.[1]

Date:			
Place:			
Occasion:			

When *Does* Life Begin?

A Roman Catholic priest was being interviewed on a radio call-in show, and the conversation focused on the point at which life begins. The priest believed that life begins at the moment of conception, though he acknowledged that some believe that life begins when the baby takes its first breath outside the womb.

One caller had a different opinion. "I believe," he said, "that life begins when the last kid leaves home, and the dog dies."

Date:			
Place:			
Occasion:			

Addictions/Alcohol

Someone Once Said . . .

• *If you drink before you drive, you are putting the quart before the hearse.*

Date:			
Place:			
Occasion:			

---

[1]This article has been circulating on the internet for some time without attribution.

Modern Society

Because we live in a very addict-prone culture, we must be more careful about our personal habits than those people in other ages did. Our society produces addicts more than any other in history. Why?

1. Our culture has a quick-fix, convenience-oriented mentality.
2. Our society stresses easy solutions.
3. Our era suffers from values confusion, confused morals. This is the first generation that hasn't passed its values on to its young. People don't have the kind of anchors they used to.
4. Our culture is heavily oriented toward entertainment.
5. Our culture suffers from disrupted family life. Children grow up in fragmented homes and experience internal abandonment.
6. There is an enormous loss of community. The average person moves about every three years. The sustained support of extended family members or ongoing close friendships is missing.
7. Ours is a high-stress culture; high anxiety.
8. Ours is a very abusive society.
9. There is a denial of limitations today; we don't deal with death very well.
10. The number of addicts tends to multiply. If you took all the various kids of addictions, the total figure would be about 131 million. Addicts produce addicts, so there is a multiplying effect.[1]

Date:	_____	_____	_____
Place:	_____	_____	_____
Occasion:	_____	_____	_____

Just the Two of Us

I first met her in high school. She was older than I was and exciting. She'd been around. My parents warned me to have nothing to do with her. They claimed that no good could come from our relationship.

But I kept meeting her on the sly. She was so sophisticated and worldly. It made me feel grown up just being with her. It was fun to take her to a party in those days. She was almost always the center of attention.

We began seeing more of each other after I started college. When I got a place of my own, she was a frequent guest. It wasn't long before she moved in with me. It may have been common law, but it was heartbreaking for my parents. I kept reminding myself I wasn't a kid anymore. Besides, it was legal.

We lived together right through college and into my early days in business. I seldom went anywhere without her, but I wasn't blind. I knew she was unfaithful to me. What's worse, I didn't care. As long as she was there for me when I needed her (and she always was), it didn't matter.

[1] My notes of a lecture by Dr. Patrick J. Carnes, Ph.D., C.A.S., Clinical Director of Sexual Disorder Services at The Meadows, a private multiple addiction/disorder treatment and recovery facility in Wickenburg, Arizona.

The longer we lived together, the more attached I became to her. But it wasn't mutual. She began to delight in making me look foolish in front of my friends. But I still couldn't give her up.

It became a love/hate relationship. I figured out that her glamour was nothing more than a cheap mask to hide her spite and cynicism behind. I could no longer see her beauty after I came to know her true character.

But old habits are hard to break. We had invested many years in each other. Even though my relationship with her made me lose a little respect for myself, she had become the center of my life. We didn't go anywhere. We didn't do anything. We didn't have friends over. It was just the two of us. I became deeply depressed and knew that she was largely responsible for my misery. I finally told her I was leaving her for good. It took a lot of guts, but I left.

I still see her around. She's still as beautiful as when we first met. I miss her now and then. I'm not boasting when I say she'd take me back in a minute. But by the grace of God, I will never take up with her again.

If you see her, just give her my regards. I don't hate her. I just loved her too much.

Chances are you know her family. The name's Alcohol.[1]

Date: _____   _____   _____
Place: _____   _____   _____
Occasion: _____   _____   _____

From the Diary of an Addict

Sunday, October 14: I'm living on borrowed time. I really don't know how long I'll make it. I can feel my heart beat; I just wonder how long my body can take this abuse. I'm sitting at a phone booth right now, not really sure who or why to call. I know exactly what they are going to tell me.

. . . This is so hard. It is worse than hard—when you know this is killing you and you keep on doing it. It is pure hell!!! What is so bad is that I try to think of all the people that love me and care for me. And believe me, I realize it's a lot of people. But I just can't quit right now.[2]

Date: _____   _____   _____
Place: _____   _____   _____
Occasion: _____   _____   _____

Drinking and Driving

- In 1997, 16,189 people were killed in crashes involving alcohol in the United States—an average of one every thirty-two minutes. These deaths constituted approximately 38.6% of all traffic fatalities.
- In 1997, about 1,058,990 people were injured in alcohol-related crashes—an average of one person injured approximately every 30 seconds.
- Every weekday night from 10 P.M. to 1 A.M., one in 13 drivers is drunk (BAC of .08 or more). Between 1 A.M. and 6 A.M. on weekend mornings, one in seven drivers is drunk.

---

[1] Clipping from my files.
[2] From the diary of the author's friend, Mark Sloan, who eventually overcame his addictions and is living for the Lord.

- About three of every five Americans will be involved in an alcohol-related crash at some time in their lives.
- Economic costs of alcohol-related crashes are estimated to be $45 billion yearly.
- In 1997, there were two alcohol-related traffic deaths per hour, forty-five per day and 315 per week. That is the equivalent of two jetliners crashing week after week.
- During the period 1982 through 1997, approximately 333,586 persons lost their lives in alcohol-related traffic crashes. (NHTSA, 1998).
- A driver with a BAC of 0.15 is more than three hundred times more likely to be involved in a fatal crash than a sober driver. (NHTSA, 1997)
- In the past decade, four times as many Americans died in drunk driving crashes as were killed in the Vietnam War.
- Drunk driving is the nation's most frequently committed violent crime.[1]

Date: _____   _____   _____

Place: _____   _____   _____

Occasion: _____   _____   _____

Just About Ruined My Life

America's worst drunk-driving disaster occurred on May 14, 1988, when Larry Mahoney, heavily intoxicated, drove his pickup truck the wrong way down Interstate 71 in Ohio and crashed into a church bus, causing a fiery crash that killed 27 people.

Mahoney, who was released from prison in 1999, has declined interviews with the media, but he did give *USA Today* a few words in 1992. With almost childlike simplicity, he said: "I'll tell you one thing. I'll never touch [alcohol] again. It's just about ruined my life."[2]

It has a way of doing that.

Date: _____   _____   _____

Place: _____   _____   _____

Occasion: _____   _____   _____

Aging

Someone Once Said . . .

- *It's attitude, not arteries, that determines the vitality of our maturing years.*—J. Oswald Sanders[3]

---

[1] Mothers Against Drunk Driving.

[2] Paul Hoversten, "A 'Quiet' Term in Prison, No Parole Requirements," *USA Today,* September 1, 1999, sec. 3A.

[3] J. Oswald Sanders, *Enjoying Your Best Years* (Grand Rapids: Discovery House, 1993), ch. 6.

- *The cure for age is interest and enthusiasm and work. Life's evening will take its character from the day which has preceded it.*—George Matheson, blind poet and hymnist
- *I have reached an honorable position in life, because I am old and no longer young. I am a far more useful person than I was fifty years ago, or forty years ago, or thirty, twenty, or even ten. I have learned so much since I was seventy.*—Pearl Buck[1]
- *There is a blessedness about old age that we young men know nothing of.*—Charles Spurgeon[2]
- *The time of old age, with all its infirmities, seems to me to be a time of peculiar blessedness and privilege to the Christian.*—Charles Spurgeon[3]
- *Old age can be delayed by a plentiful diet, regular sleep and short naps, and moderate exercise including [horseback] riding and dancing.*—Sir Francis Bacon[4]
- *The first half of our lives we are romantic. The last half we are rheumatic.*—Vance Havner[5]
- *The older we grow, the more we become like the place we're going.*[6]

Date: _____   _____   _____

Place: _____   _____   _____

Occasion: _____   _____   _____

Pony or Panther?

Two boys trudged the backroad, looping through the autumnal countryside as the setting sun diffused a final, lingering glow across the blue meadows and wooded hills. A few impatient stars twinkled in the blackening, and the shadows grew deeper and darker.

They were twins, these twelve-year-olds, and they had filled the day with rollicking fun—climbing trees, chasing rabbits, slashing through laurel thickets, splashing in the creek. But they had frolicked too long and now found themselves caught in the darkness as they drifted home.

Suddenly one of the boys stopped, thrusting out his hand to caution the other. A noise alarmed him—a dry, rattling noise, the sound of rustling bushes. He heard the padding of footsteps—an animal. A shadow passed near in the darkness.

"The panther," whispered Willie, the words freezing in his mouth. He knew well the stories of the stalking black panther that killed the cattle and terrified the residents of Little Creek. Once when nearly asleep, Willie had heard its squall, a heart-stopping wail that sounded like a tortured infant.

The boy's lungs tightened, his legs froze, the hair on his neck stood on end, and chill bumps coated his body.

But what was happening to his brother? Davie, knees collapsing, was rolling in the dirt, in a violent convulsion—of laughter. "What're you 'fraid of, Willie?" cackled Davie between heaves of laughter. "You ain't afraid of ol' Paint, are ya'?" At that

---

[1] Pearl Buck at age eighty-four.
[2] Charles Haddon Spurgeon, *Spurgeon's Sermons*, vol. 2 (Grand Rapids: Baker Book House, 1983), 373.
[3] Spurgeon, *Spurgeon's Sermons*, vol. 4, 286.
[4] Sir Francis Bacon, *History of Life and Death* (n.p., n.d.).
[5] Vance Havner, *Three Score & Ten* (Old Tappan, NJ: Fleming H. Revell Co., 1973), 72.
[6] Anonymous

moment their speckled pony stepped from the cowpath into the moonlight. She had gotten a whiff of the boys and had come to meet them.

"Willie," Davie scoffed, "don't you know the difference 'tween a panther and a pony?"

No, he didn't, and he isn't alone, for most of us also find that, in the shadows of autumn, panthers and ponies can look remarkably similar.

Many people fear the prospect of aging, believing it a panther. The suicide rate for people over sixty-five now accounts for 25% of reported self-inflicted deaths in America. Many other seniors live in silent depression. The popular British poet, Dylan Thomas, viewing age a panther, wrote:

> *Do not go gently into that good night.*
> *Old age should burn and rave at close of day.*
> *Rage, rage against the dying of the light.*

But another British poet, Robert Browning, looked into the same shadows and saw a pony:

> *Grow old with me!*
> *The best is yet to be,*
> *The last of life, for which the first was made:*
> *Our times are in His hand*
> *Who saith, "A whole I planned,*
> *Youth shows but half; trust God: See all,*
> *Nor be afraid."*

Date: _____ _____ _____
Place: _____ _____ _____
Occasion: _____ _____ _____

At His Age

Mischa Elman was a Russian-born violinist whose career spanned his entire life. He began performing when unusually young and continued into old age. Someone once asked him if he could tell any difference in audience reaction through the encircling years. "Not really," he replied. "When I was a boy, audiences would exclaim, 'Imagine playing the violin like that at his age!' Now, they're beginning to say the same thing again!"

Date: _____ _____ _____
Place: _____ _____ _____
Occasion: _____ _____ _____

"I Might Not See You Again"

Vance Havner told of a ninety-year-old who decided to travel around the world. His buddy came to him in distress, saying, "You shouldn't try a trip like this. I might not see you again."

"Maybe not," replied the man, suitcase in hand. "You may be dead when I get back!"

Date:			
Place:			
Occasion:			

Still Bearing Fruit

Dr. Charles McCoy never married, he devoted his years instead to pastoring a church and pursuing a plethora of educational goals. At age seventy-two, when his denomination required that he retire from ministry, he reluctantly left his Baptist pulpit in Oyster Bay, New York. He wasn't sure what to do with himself. Over the years, he had accumulated seven different college degrees, but now they all seemed futile: *I just lie on my bed thinking that my life's over, and I haven't really done anything yet. I've been pastor of this church for so many years, and nobody really wants me much—and what have I done for Christ? I've spent an awful lot of time working for degrees, but I haven't won very many people to the Lord.*

Getting Older

You know you're getting older when it takes more time to recover than it did to tire out.

—MILTON BERLE

But just a week after his retirement, he met a missionary who abruptly invited him to come to India to preach. Dr. McCoy deferred, citing his age. He had never been overseas, had never even traveled across America, had never flown in a plane. He couldn't imagine traveling to India. Furthermore, he hadn't the money.

The thought, however, nagged at him.

And so white-haired old Dr. Charles McCoy announced he was going to India. He sold his car and few possessions and bought a one-way plane ticket. "By yourself?" asked his horrified friends. "To India? What if you fall ill? What if you should die in India?"

"It's just as close to heaven from there as it is from here," he replied.

He arrived in Bombay with his billfold, his Bible, his passport—all of which were promptly taken by pickpockets. He was left with only the clothes on his back and the address of some missionaries that he had clipped from a magazine. The man who had originally invited him had remained in America, and when he showed up on the missionaries' doorstep, they weren't sure what to do with him.

After a day or so, McCoy declared he was going to visit the mayor of Bombay. *Don't waste your time,* advised his new friends. After several years of trying, they had never been able to see the mayor. McCoy prayed about it and went anyway. He presented his calling card to the receptionist, and she looked at it carefully, then disappeared through a door. Returning, she told him to come back at 3 o'clock.

McCoy returned that afternoon to find a reception in his honor attended by the most important civic leaders in Bombay. It seems the city fathers had been greatly impressed by McCoy's tall frame (he was 6'4"), his distinguished white hair, and especially by the long string of degrees after his name on his calling card. *He is a very important man,* they thought. *Perhaps even a representative of the President of the United States.*

Dr. McCoy spoke for a half-hour, giving his testimony about Jesus Christ. At the end, he was politely applauded by the assembled crowd, and afterward he was approached by a man in an impressive military uniform who invited him to speak to the students of his school. As it turned out, his school was India's equivalent to West Point. After his first address, McCoy was invited back repeatedly.

Invitations soon poured in from all over India, and he began an itinerant ministry of preaching the Gospel. In Calcutta he started a Chinese church. He was asked to do the same in Hong Kong. He was invited to Egypt and the Middle East, traveling everywhere on a shoestring but with an energy that he had seldom before felt. His evangelistic ministry stretched to sixteen years, and at age 88, he again found himself in India, in Calcutta.

His host dropped him off at the Grand Hotel, and as he stepped from the car he said, "You know I'm speaking tonight at the YMCA. I have time for a cup of tea and a bit of rest. I don't want to be late for the meeting." He ducked into the hotel, took the elevator to his floor, and suddenly the Lord called him home.

It was just as close to heaven from India, he had said, as from America. Dr. Charles McCoy had wonderfully embodied the final words of Psalm 92:

> *Those who are planted in the house of the Lord*
> *Shall flourish in the courts of our God.*
> *They shall still bear fruit in old age;*
> *They shall be fresh and flourishing,*
> *To declare that the Lord is upright;*
> *He is my rock, and there is no unrighteousness in Him.*[1]

```
Date:      _____    _____    _____
Place:     _____    _____    _____
Occasion:  _____    _____    _____
```

Seven Decades

The Seven Decades of Man: Spills, Drills, Thrills, Bills, Ills, Pills, and Wills.

```
Date:      _____    _____    _____
Place:     _____    _____    _____
Occasion:  _____    _____    _____
```

God, Grant Me . . .

> *God, Grant me the senility*
> *To forget the people*
> *I never liked anyway,*
> *The good fortune*

---

[1] *Parables, Etc.,* October 1983, 1–3. From: Franklin Graham, *This One Thing I Do.*

To run into the ones I do,
And the eyesight
To tell the difference.

Date: _____   _____   _____
Place: _____   _____   _____
Occasion: _____   _____   _____

Why Does God Let Us Get Old?

Robertson McQuilkin, former esteemed president of Columbia International University in Columbia, South Carolina, once drove an elderly friend on an errand. She moved slowly and painfully, being crippled with arthritis.

"Robertson," she asked as they drove along, "why does God let us get old and weak? Why must I hurt so?"

"I'm not sure," McQuilkin replied, "but I have a theory."

"What is it?"

He hesitated to share it, but she insisted. This is what he said: "I think God has planned the strength and beauty of youth to be physical. But the strength and beauty of age is spiritual. We gradually lose the strength and beauty that is temporary, so we'll be sure to concentrate on the strength and beauty which is forever."

Date: _____   _____   _____
Place: _____   _____   _____
Occasion: _____   _____   _____

You Know You're Getting Older When . . .

You know you're getting older when: Everything hurts, and what doesn't hurt, doesn't work. The gleam in your eyes is from the sun hitting your bifocals. You feel like the morning after, and you haven't been anywhere. Your little black book contains only names ending in M.D. Your knees buckle, and your belt won't.

You get winded playing cards. Your children begin to look middle-aged. You join a health club and don't go. You decide to procrastinate, but never get around to it.

Your mind makes contracts your body can't meet. You know all the answers, but nobody asks you the questions. You look forward to a dull evening at home. You're turning out lights for economic rather than romantic reasons.

Your favorite part of the newspaper is "Twenty-Five Years Ago Today."

You sit in a rocking chair and can't get it going.

You're 17" around the neck, 42" around the waist, and 106 around the golf course. Your pacemaker makes the garage door go up when you see a pretty girl.

The best part of your day is over when the alarm goes off. Your back goes out more than you do. A fortune-teller offers to read your face. The little gray-haired lady you help across the street is your wife. You've got too much room in the house and not enough room in the medicine cabinet. You sink your teeth in a steak, and they stay there.[1]

```
Date:      _____    _____    _____
Place:     _____    _____    _____
Occasion:  _____    _____    _____
```

What Age Can Do

- Commodore Vanderbilt built most of his railroads when he was well past seventy.
- Kant wrote some of his greatest philosophical works when he was past seventy.
- Goethe wrote the second part of *Faust* after the age of eighty.
- Tennyson was eighty-three when he wrote "Crossing the Bar."
- Benjamin Franklin most helped his country after his sixtieth birthday.
- Gladstone served as Prime Minister of England at age eighty-three.
- Bismarck oversaw the affairs of Germany in his mid-seventies.
- John Glenn returned to space at age seventy-five.
- Verdi wrote operas into his eighties.
- Titian painted his great work, *The Battle of Lepanto* at age ninety-five and his *Last Supper* at age ninety-nine.
- Michelangelo was still producing masterpieces at eighty-nine.
- Monet was doing the same at eighty-five.

```
Date:      _____    _____    _____
Place:     _____    _____    _____
Occasion:  _____    _____    _____
```

Prayer of an Aging Woman

Lord, you know better than I know myself that I am growing older and will some day be old. Keep me from getting talkative, particularly from the fatal habit of thinking that I must say something on every subject and on every occasion.

Release me from craving to straighten out everybody's affairs. Make me thoughtful, but not moody; helpful, but not bossy. With my vast store of wisdom it seems a pity not to use it all, but you know, Lord, that I want a few friends at the end. Keep my mind from the recital of endless details—give me wings to come to the point.

I ask for grace enough to listen to the tales of others' pains. Seal my lips on my own aches and pains—they are increasing, and my love of rehearsing them is becoming sweeter as the years go by. Help me to endure them with patience.

I dare not ask for improved memory, but for a growing humility and a lessening cocksureness when my memory seems to clash with the memories of others. Teach me the glorious lesson that occasionally it is possible that I may be mistaken.

Keep me reasonably sweet. I do not want to be a saint—some of them are so hard to live with—but a sour old woman is one of the crowning works of the devil.

---

[1] Accumulated from various sources.

Give me the ability to see good things in unexpected places, and talents in unexpected people. And give me, O Lord, the grace to tell them so.—Anonymous seventeenth-century nun

Date:	_____	_____	_____
Place:	_____	_____	_____
Occasion:	_____	_____	_____

Paul Harvey's "For What It's Worth"

Our *For What It's Worth Department* hears from Hershey, Pennsylvania—where the woman in the Mercedes had been waiting patiently for a parking place to open up.

The shopping mall was crowded.

The woman in the Mercedes zigzagged between rows—then up ahead she saw a man with a load of packages heading for his car.

She drove up, parked behind him and waited while he opened his trunk and loaded it with packages.

Finally he got in his car and backed out of the stall.

But before the woman in the Mercedes could drive into the parking space, a young man in a shiny new Corvette zipped past and around her and he pulled into the empty space, got out and started walking away.

"Hey!" shouted the woman in the Mercedes, "I've been waiting for that parking place!"

The college-ager responded, "Sorry, lady; that's how it is when you're young and quick."

At that instant she put her Mercedes in gear, floorboarded it, crashed into and crushed the right rear fender and corner panel of the flashy new Corvette.

Now the young man is jumping up and down shouting, "You can't do that!"

The lady in the Mercedes said, "That's how it is when you're old and rich!"[1]

Date:	_____	_____	_____
Place:	_____	_____	_____
Occasion:	_____	_____	_____

—————— Ambition/Desire for Greatness ——————

Someone Once Said . . .

- *From the desire of being great, good Lord deliver us!*—A Moravian Prayer[2]
- *I was never of any use until I found out that God did not intend to make me to be a great man.*[3]

---

[1] Paul Harvey, *For What It's Worth,* ed. By Paul Harvey, Jr. (New York: Bantam Books, 1991), 1.
[2] Mrs. Charles E. Cowman, *Springs in the Valley* (Los Angeles: Cowman Publications, Inc., 1939), 23.
[3] An anonymous pastor

- *Don't worry about doing something great. Be great by doing what you can where God has placed you. It will pay off after awhile.*[1]
- *Many, through wishing to be great, have failed to be good.*—Charles Spurgeon[2]
- *He is truly great who deemeth himself small, and counteth all height of honor as nothing.*—Thomas à Kempis
- *Lord, which of us is greatest?*—the Disciples
- *Seekest thou great things for thyself? Seek them not.*[3]
- *The famous Dr. Sigmund Freud of Vienna, one of the most distinguished psychologists of the twentieth century, says that everything you and I do springs from two motives: the sex urge and the desire to be great.*—Dale Carnegie, in *How to Win Friends and Influence People*
- *Hard studies, much knowledge, and excellent preaching are . . . hypocritical sins when they are done for our [own] glory.*—Richard Baxter, in *The Reformed Pastor*

Date: _____   _____   _____

Place: _____   _____   _____

Occasion: _____   _____   _____

Seekest Thou Great Things for Thyself?

When Charles Haddon Spurgeon was eighteen years old and seeking God's will for his life, he felt the need for theological training. Both his friends and his father advised him to attend college. So he made application to Regent's Park College, and an interview was set between the head of the college and young Spurgeon. The meeting was to be in Cambridge at the home of Mr. Macmillan, the publisher. Spurgeon rose early that morning and had special prayer, seeking God's guidance in the matter.

At just the appointed time, he showed up at Macmillan's house. He rang the bell, and a servant showed him into the parlor. There he sat for two hours until at last his patience could stand it no longer. He called for the servant and was horrified to discover that she had forgotten to announce his arrival, had not let anyone know he was there, had forgotten all about him.

Meanwhile the head of the college had sat waiting in an adjoining room until his patience, too, had been exhausted, and he had left Cambridge for London by train without the interview ever having taken place.

Spurgeon was deeply disturbed, and his first impulse was to run after the man, to chase him to London, to explain what had happened. But he took a long walk out in the country to calm down, and by-and-by a verse of Scripture came to his mind so forcibly that he almost seemed to hear it audibly—Jeremiah 45:5: "Seekest thou great things for thyself? Seek them not!"

The Lord seemed to be telling him not to worry about the misunderstanding, not to make extraordinary efforts to clear it up, but to take it as the Lord's will and

---

[1] Paul Robinson, veteran missionary to Uruguay, to fellow missionaries at his retirement reception, July 31, 1990.
[2] Charles Spurgeon, *Treasury of David* (n.p., n.d.), comment on Psalm 131:1
[3] Jeremiah 45:5

serve the Lord humbly where he was. As a result, Spurgeon never did make it to college, but it didn't matter. He became the most powerful, successful and fruitful minister in the history of Victorian England, and he later said that he "a thousand times thanked the Lord very heartily for the strange providence which forced his steps into another and far better path."

Date: _____ _____ _____
Place: _____ _____ _____
Occasion: _____ _____ _____

Seek Them Not!

J. Oswald Sanders, the missionary statesman and Bible teacher who for many years directed Overseas Missionary Fellowship, once wrote about a time when he wanted a particular position in the Christian world very much. Having friends in positions of influence, he was about to see if some strings could be pulled to turn the job in his direction. He was toying with the idea of doing a little lobbying.

But while walking down the main street in Auckland, New Zealand one day, turning the matter over in his mind, as he walked past His Majesty's Theatre, a verse of Scripture came to his mind with tremendous authority and powerful conviction: "Seekest thou great things for thyself? Seek them not!" (Jeremiah 45:5).

"The words came just as though it was God speaking. There were crowds all around me, and no one else heard the voice, but I heard it all right!" Sanders later said. "I believe that was a real turning point in my service to the Lord." As a result, he did not seek the position, but it later opened to him on its own in God's good timing.[1]

Date: _____ _____ _____
Place: _____ _____ _____
Occasion: _____ _____ _____

Yes, But I Am a Great Man

Winston Churchill was notoriously difficult to work for. One day a manservant, taking his life in his hands, decided to stand up to him. The men got into a blazing row, and when it was over Churchill, his lower lip jutting, said, "You were very rude to me, you know."

The servant, still seething, replied, "Yes, but you were rude, too."

Churchill grumbled, "Yes, but I am a great man."

The servant later said, "There was no answer to that. He knew, as I and the rest of the world knew, that he was right."[2]

[1] J. Oswald Sanders, "Lessons I've Learned," *Discipleship Journal*, Issue 15, 1983, 16.
[2] William Manchester, *The Last Lion: Winston Spencer Churchill: Alone* (Boston: Little, Brown and Company, 1988), 36.

Date: _____ _____ _____
Place: _____ _____ _____
Occasion: _____ _____ _____

China's First Emperor

The body of Ying Cheng, China's first emperor, was found resting in a copper coffin in a chamber sealed by a jade door, guarded by an army of 6,000 colorful, life-size terra-cotta soldiers.

He had became a warlord at age thirteen, and for twenty-five years had battled other warlords, amassing an army of a million men and achieving dominance with brutality. He once slaughtered 40,000 soldiers in a single campaign—after they had surrendered. He devoured his enemies, it was said, "as a silkworm devours the mulberry leaf."

━━━━━◇━━━━━
Lust of Praise

I have been too anxious to do great things. The lust of praise has ever been my besetting sin.
—ROBERT MURRAY
McCHEYNE
━━━━━◇━━━━━

At the height of his power he adopted a new title: *Ch'in Shih Huang Ti*—First Divine Emperor of China. It was because of this title that we call his land China today. He boasted that he was the head of a dynasty that would last ten thousand years.

Emperor Ch'in established a strong, central monarchy, developed a uniform code of law, launched massive public works—roads and canals—and built a shining new capital. His palace alone measured a mile and a half long and a half-mile wide, with thousands of rooms and an audience hall that could seat ten thousand people. It was connected via covered passageways with 270 other smaller palaces so that the Emperor could avoid assassination by sleeping in a different place every night.

But the Emperor's most enduring monument was his Great Wall built by tens of thousands of forced laborers. According to tradition tens of thousands of slaves died during its building, their bones being ground up and added to the mortar, making the Wall the "longest cemetery on earth." If it were in the United States, it would reach from Los Angeles to New York and back again to Chicago. At its top was a roadway wide enough for eight men marching abreast, and it was connected by twenty-five thousand towers. Signal messages could be sent across ancient China in twenty-four hours.

But Emperor Ch'in worried about dying, and he commanded his wise men, on pain of death, to find the Fountain of Youth.

They didn't.

His Prime Minister plotted against him, and the Divine Emperor was assassinated at age forty-one. The conspirators also forged a letter in the Emperor's name to his son and heir, bidding the son to commit suicide. He did.

Instead of enduring for ten thousand years the Emperor's dynasty was the shortest in Chinese history,

The Emperor's murderers tried to conceal his royal body, but it rotted and began to smell, forcing them to pull a cart of salted fish nearby in an effort to obscure the odor.

Those who appear as gods before men soon appear as men before God.[1]

---

[1] Stephen Bertman, *Doorways Through Time* (Los Angeles: Jeremy P. Tarcher, Inc., 1986), ch. 20.

Date: _____

Place: _____

Occasion: _____

Men As Gods

Once a man becomes a god to himself, he then becomes a devil to others.—Rev. William Secker, seventeenth century British clergyman[1]

Date: _____

Place: _____

Occasion: _____

What Does It Profit?

Charlemagne, it is said, gave instructions to be buried in the royal posture of a king upon his throne, with the Gospels opened on his knees, his sword beside him, and his crown upon his head.

When his tomb was later uncovered, there he was. The crown was still perched on his skull, and a bony finger rested on these words: "What will it profit a man if he gains the whole world and loses his own soul?"

Date: _____

Place: _____

Occasion: _____

Four Brothers

In *The Wounded Healer,* Henri Nouwen retells a tale from ancient India: Four royal brothers decided each to master a special ability. Time went by, and the brothers met to reveal what they had learned.

"I have mastered a science," said the first, "by which I can take but a bone of some creature and create the flesh that goes with it."

"I," said the second, "know how to grow that creature's skin and hair if there is flesh on its bones."

The third said, "I am able to create its limbs if I have the flesh, the skin, and the hair."

"And I," concluded the fourth, "know how to give life to that creature if its form is complete."

Thereupon the brothers went into the jungle to find a bone so they could demonstrate their specialties. As fate would have it, the bone they found was a lion's.

---

[1] William Secker, *The Nonsuch Professor in His Meridian Splendor* (Chicago: Fleming H. Revell Co., 1899), 86.

One added flesh to the bone, the second grew hide and hair, the third completed it with matching limbs, and the fourth gave the lion life.

Shaking its mane, the ferocious beast arose and jumped on his creators. He killed them all and vanished contentedly into the jungle.

We too have the capacity to create what can devour us. Goals and dreams can consume us. Possessions and property can turn and destroy us—unless we first seek God's kingdom and righteousness.[1]

Date:			
Place:			
Occasion:			

Pray for Felix

William Carey, who is called the father of modern missions, served the Lord in India for many years. He gradually became very concerned about the attitude of his son, Felix. The young man had promised to become a missionary, but he reneged on his vows when he was appointed ambassador to Burma by the Queen of England. Carey wrote to his friend, asking prayer for his son with these words: *Pray for Felix. He has degenerated into an ambassador of the British government when he should be serving the King of kings.*

Date:			
Place:			
Occasion:			

An Old Christian Hymn

What may be my future lot,
High or low concerns me not;
This doth set my heart at rest:
What my God appoints is best.

Date:			
Place:			
Occasion:			

One of the Drawbacks

Take the lady who was asked what positions her boys played on the football team. She replied, "I don't know, but I think John is one of the drawbacks."

---

[1]Nathan Castens, "To Illustrate," *Leadership Journal,* Winter 1985, 49.

Date:			
Place:			
Occasion:			

Fame

According to Fred Allen, "A celebrity is a person who works all his life to become well known, then wears dark glasses to avoid being recognized."[1]

Date:			
Place:			
Occasion:			

———— Angels ————

Someone Once Said . . .

- *I do not know how to explain it; I can not tell how it is, but I believe angels have a great deal to do with the business of this world.*—Charles H. Spurgeon[2]
- *The angels are near to us. [They] have long arms, and, although they stand before the face and in the presence of God and his son Christ, they are hard by and about us in those affairs which by God we are commanded to take in hand.*—Martin Luther[3]
- *It should be (but it is not) unnecessary to add that a belief in angels, whether good or evil, does not mean a belief in either as they are represented in art and literature. Devils are depicted with bats' wings and good angels with birds' wings, not because anyone holds that moral deterioration would be likely to turn feathers into membrane, but because most men like birds better than bats.*—C. S. Lewis[4]
- *However poor a preacher, I can preach the gospel better than Gabriel can, because Gabriel cannot say what I can say, "I am a sinner saved by grace."*—A. T. Pierson[5]

Date:			
Place:			
Occasion:			

Personal Stories by the Author

[A] A Meeting in an Elevator

Years ago, I popped into a hotel elevator and found myself standing beside the famous Christian writer and Nazi death-camp survivor, Corrie Ten Boom. I recog-

---

[1] John-Roger and Peter McWilliams, *Do It!* (Los Angeles: Prelude Press, 1991), 237.
[2] Charles Haddon Spurgeon, *Spurgeon's Sermons*, vol. 2 (Grand Rapids: Baker Book House, 1983), 191.
[3] Martin Luther, *The Table Talk of Martin Luther*, ed. Thomas S. Kepler (Grand Rapids: Baker, 1952), 279–280.
[4] C. S. Lewis, *Screwtape Letters* (New York: The Macmillan Company, 1961).
[5] A. T. Pierson, *The Gospel: Its Heart, Heights, and Hopes*, vol. 1 (Grand Rapids: Baker Book House, 1978), 9.

nized her at once, having read her books and seen her on television. When I introduced myself, instead of giving me a usual greeting she squinted at me as only an
old woman can squint and asked with a Dutch accent: "Young man, have you ever
seen an angel?"

"No," I replied, startled, "Not that I know of."

"Well, I have," she declared. And in the time our elevator took to reach the
bottom floor she told me of a time when she was smuggling Bibles into Communist
Eastern Europe. The border guard was checking everyone's luggage, and she knew
her load of Bibles would surely be discovered. In alarm she prayed, "Lord, you have
said that you would watch over your Word. Now, please watch over your Word that
I am smuggling."

Suddenly as she looked at her suitcase, it seemed to glow with light. No one
else saw it, but to her it was unmistakable. There was an aura of light wrapped
around that suitcase.

Her turn came at customs, and the guard, who had so vigilantly opened and
inspected every piece of everyone else's luggage, glanced at her bags, shrugged, and
waved her through.

It was an angel, she told me, who had helped her deliver God's Word behind
the Iron Curtain.

[B] Friends in Nigeria

On New Year's Day several years ago, my wife, Katrina, and I entertained
friends, Terry and Sue Hammack, who told us an amazing story. Terry and Sue are
missionaries with Sudan Interior Mission and lived on a compound in Kano, a large
city in northern Nigeria. On one occasion, the population of
Kano erupted in dangerous rioting against Christians. Terry
managed to smuggle his family to safety, but he felt compelled
to stay and help "hold down the fort," particularly as his job
included operating the radio equipment. For several days they
were trapped in the compound, surrounded by thousands of
angry Muslims. Day after day, the missionaries expected an
attack, and their lives were in jeopardy.

> ---✧---
> **Saved!**
>
> *Gabriel cannot say what I
> can say, "I am a sinner
> saved by grace."*
> —A. T. PIERSON
> ---✧---

Finally everything settled down, and the assault on the compound fizzled. Terry
wondered why. As he later talked to some of his contacts in Kano, he heard the
explanation. To the frenzied crowds, it appeared as if the compound had been ablaze.
Fire shot up from the walls, and these strange flames kept the rioters at bay.

Yet there had never been any fire in the compound or on the walls.

[C] At the Bedside of a Friend

Mrs. Agnes Frazier was the oldest member of our church. She was a woman of
deep piety and enthusiastic spirituality. At age ninety-five, her health failed, and I
received a call. "Mrs. Agnes is asking for you," said her nurse. When I entered her
bedroom, she was almost too weak to look up at me. Her words were indistinct at
times, but it soon became clear that she had wanted to see me because she was
curious about "these men."

"What men?" I asked.

"I keep seeing these two men," she said.

"What do they look like?"

"Two men, dressed in white from head to foot are standing at the foot of my bed. I don't know what to tell them. What should I say if they ask me something?"

"Tell them," I said at length, "that you belong to Jesus."

That seemed to satisfy her. "Yes," she said, "I'll tell them I belong to Jesus." And shortly afterward, she fell asleep in Christ and those two angels, I believe, ushered her to heaven.

Date:	_____	_____	_____
Place:	_____	_____	_____
Occasion:	_____	_____	_____

God's Dynamic Force

In her book, *Evidence Not Seen: A Woman's Miraculous Faith in the Jungles of World War II*, Darlene Deibler Rose tells of her experiences following the Japanese invasion of the island of New Guinea during World War II.

When the Japanese invaded the island, her husband was dragged away—she never saw him again—and she was left with another woman in a rat-infested house on the outskirts of the jungle. Japanese troops were everywhere and so were ruthless bandits.

One night her rest was disturbed by what she thought were rats. She heard them moving around in the living room, in the dining room, and along the halls. She tried to ignore them, but when she heard a book fall to the floor, that did it. "Margaret," she called to her fellow-worker. "Grab your dressing gown. We'll light the lamps and have another go at the rats. I've been hearing them from one end of the house to the other."

A hall ran the full length of the house. When she pulled open the bedroom door, in the dim light of a little night lamp, she saw someone swish past her. Stepping into the hall for a better look, she found herself face-to-face with a Boegis bandit.

He was wearing a black sarong that he flung over his shoulder to free his machete. With one fluid movement, the knife was extracted from his belt and held up in a striking position.

On impulse, Darlene rushed at him, and the man inexplicably turned and ran down the hall, through the bathroom, across the porch, and into the trees with Darlene hot on his heels. Other bandits appeared, and together they fled. Darlene stopped dead in her tracks and whispered, "Lord, what a stupid thing for me to do!"

Instantly a verse flashed into her mind: "The angel of the Lord encamps round about them that fear him and delivers them."

From that night on, Darlene slept with a club at the foot of her bed, but she never had to use it. The bandits returned several nights later, but never entered the house. She was not disturbed again. She suspected the gardener among the bandits, and, after the war, she asked him about it. Yes, he had been one of the culprits.

Darlene later wrote, "When I asked him why they had never entered the house again, he answered incredulously, 'Because of those people you had there—those people in white who stood about the house.' The Lord had put His angels around us. He had delivered."[1]

<table>
<tr><td>Date:</td><td>_____</td><td>_____</td><td>_____</td></tr>
<tr><td>Place:</td><td>_____</td><td>_____</td><td>_____</td></tr>
<tr><td>Occasion:</td><td>_____</td><td>_____</td><td>_____</td></tr>
</table>

Angel Beneath the Waves

Charles Herbert Lightoller was tall, sun-bronzed, and handsome, possessing a deep, pleasant speaking voice. His mother died during his infancy, his father abandoned him, and he ran off to sea at the age of thirteen. By 1912, he was a respected seaman for the White Star Line and was assigned to the maiden voyage of the greatest ocean liner ever built, the *Titanic*.

He was just drifting off to sleep on April 14th, when he felt a bump in the ship's forward motion. Hopping from his bunk, he soon learned that the *Titanic* had struck an iceberg. As the horrors of that night unfolded, Lightoller finally found himself standing on the roof of the officer's quarters, the water lapping at his feet, as he helped any and all around him into lifeboats. Finally, there was nothing left for Lightoller to do but jump from the roof into the freezing waters of the North Atlantic.

The shock of the 28-degree water against his sweating body stunned him. As he struggled to regain his bearing and swim away from the ship, he was suddenly sucked back and pinned against a ventilation grate at the base of a funnel that went all the way down to Boiler Room 6. He was stuck, drowning, and going down with the ship.

Suddenly Psalm 91:11 came clearly to his mind: *For He shall give His angels charge over you, To keep you in all your ways* . . . .

At that very moment, a blast of hot air exploded from the belly of the ship, shooting Lightoller like a missile to the surface of the ocean. At length, he managed to grab a piece of rope attached to the side of an overturned lifeboat and float along with it until he pulled himself on top of the upside-down boat.

He turned and watched the last moments of the *Titanic*. Her stern swung up in the air until the ship was in "an absolutely perpendicular position." Then she slowly sank down into the water, with only a small gulp as her stern disappeared beneath the waves.

There were about thirty men atop the lifeboat, and together they recited the Lord's Prayer, then Lightoller took command of the boat and guided them to safety.[2]

<table>
<tr><td>Date:</td><td>_____</td><td>_____</td><td>_____</td></tr>
<tr><td>Place:</td><td>_____</td><td>_____</td><td>_____</td></tr>
<tr><td>Occasion:</td><td>_____</td><td>_____</td><td>_____</td></tr>
</table>

---

[1] Darlene Deibler Rose, *Evidence Not Seen: A Woman's Miraculous Faith in the Jungles of World War II* (Carlisle, UK: OM Publishing, 1988), 46.

[2] Pieced together from several books and internet articles about the *Titanic*. His story also appeared in the *Congressional Record* of the investigation of the sinking of the *Titanic*. (Lightoller lived until December 8, 1952, and was an adherent of the Christian Science faith.)

D. L. Moody's Brush with Death in the Atlantic

Three days into D. L. Moody's voyage from Southampton, England, to America, he was resting on his bed, thanking God for traveling mercy when *"suddenly I was startled by a terrible crash and shock, as if the vessel had been driven on a rock . . . . My son jumped from his berth and rushed on deck. He was back again in a few moments, saying that the shaft was broken and the vessel was sinking. I did not at first believe it could be so bad but concluded to dress and go on deck. The report was only too true."*

Moody found himself consumed with panic, and as the day wore on, his fear deepened. Evening came. *"That was an awful night, the darkest in all our lives! Seven hundred men, women, and children waiting for the doom that was settling upon us! No one dared to sleep. We were all together in the saloon of the first cabin—Jews, Protestants, Catholics, and skeptics . . . . The agony and suspense were too great for words."*

The night passed, then another day. On the second evening of the crisis, Moody asked the captain for permission to hold a service. Nearly every passenger attended.

"With one hand clasping a pillar to steady myself on the reeling vessel, I tried to read the Ninety-first Psalm, and we prayed that God would still the raging of the sea and bring us to our desired haven. It was a new psalm to me from that hour. The eleventh verse touched me very deeply. It was like the voice of divine assurance, and it seemed a very real thing as I read: 'He shall give his angels charge over thee, to keep thee in all thy ways.' "

Surely He did it.

Moody went to his cabin, found relief in personal prayer, and fell asleep. About three o'clock in the morning, his son awoke him with the news that the steamer *Lake Huron* had seen their flares and was approaching to rescue them.[1]

Date: _____ _____ _____
Place: _____ _____ _____
Occasion: _____ _____ _____

Billy Graham's Comfort

"One of the most comforting truths in all the Bible to me as I travel from one part of the world to another," evangelist Billy Graham once said, "is to know that God has stationed His heavenly guards to protect, guide, and lead me through life's dangerous way. I cannot see these beings with my physical eyes, but I sense they are present every day."

Date: _____ _____ _____
Place: _____ _____ _____
Occasion: _____ _____ _____

The Unlikely Angel

Dobie Gadient, a schoolteacher for thirteen years, decided to travel across America and see the sights she had taught about. Traveling alone in a truck with

[1] A. P. Fitt, *The Life of D. L. Moody* (Chicago: Moody Press, n.d.), ch. 19.

camper in tow, she launched out. One afternoon, while she was rounding a curve on I-5 near Sacramento in rush-hour traffic, a water pump blew on her truck. She was tired, exasperated, scared, and alone. In spite of the traffic jam she caused, no one seemed interested in helping.

Leaning up against the trailer, she prayed, "Please, God, send me an angel, preferably one with mechanical experience." Within four minutes, a huge Harley drove up, ridden by an enormous man sporting long, black hair, a beard, and tattooed arms. With an incredible air of confidence, he jumped off and went to work on the truck, without even glancing at Dobie. Within another few minutes, he flagged down a larger truck, attached a tow chain to the frame of the disabled Chevy, and whisked the whole 56-foot rig off the freeway onto a side street, where he calmly continued to work on the water pump.

The intimidated schoolteacher was too dumbfounded to talk, especially when she read the paralyzing words on the back of his leather jacket: "Hell's Angels— California." As he finished his task, she finally got up enough courage to say, "thanks so much," and carry on a brief conversation. Noting her surprise at the whole ordeal, he looked her straight in the eye and advised, "Don't judge a book by its cover. You may not know who you're talking to." With that, he smiled, closed the hood of the truck, and straddled his Harley. With a wave, he was gone as fast as he had appeared.[1]

Date:			
Place:			
Occasion:			

Anger

Someone Once Said . . .

- *He that would be angry and not sin, must be angry at nothing but sin.*—Rev. William Secker, seventeenth century British minister[2]
- *Anyone can become angry. That is easy. But to be angry with the right person, to the right degree, at the right time, for the right purpose and in the right way—that is not easy.*—Aristotle
- *Quick, angry motions of the heart will sometimes force themselves into expression by the hand, though the tongue may be restrained. The very way in which we close a door or lay down a book may be a victory or a defeat . . . .*—Frances R. Havergal[3]
- *Anger is an acid that can do more harm to the vessel in which it is stored than to anything on which it is poured.*[4]
- *A fool gives full vent to his anger, but a wise man keeps himself under control.*—Proverbs 29:11 (NIV)

---

[1] Larry D. Wright, "To Illustrate," *Leadership Journal,* Spring Quarter, 1988. Attributed to a newsletter, *Our America.*
[2] William Secker, *The Nonsuch Professor in His Meridian Splendor* (Chicago: Fleming H. Revell Co., 1899), 149.
[3] Francis R. Havergal, *Kept for the Master's Use* (Philadelphia: The Rodgers Company, n.d.), 55.
[4] Copied from *The Baptist Beacon*

- *People who fly into a rage always make a bad landing.*
- Anger *is only one letter removed from* Danger.

```
Date:       _____   _____   _____
Place:      _____   _____   _____
Occasion:   _____   _____   _____
```

The Strange Looking Animal

Hercules, according to legend, grew increasingly irritated by a strange, menacing animal that kept blocking his path. In a fit of anger, he struck the animal with his club, killing it. As he continued his path, he kept encountering the same animal, each time larger and more menacing than before. At last a wise messenger appeared and warned Hercules to stop his furious assaults. "The monster is Strife, and you are stirring it up," said the messenger. "Just let it alone and it will shrivel and cease to trouble you."

```
Date:       _____   _____   _____
Place:      _____   _____   _____
Occasion:   _____   _____   _____
```

The Problem with Telling Someone Off

You may think you're better off when you tell someone off, but you're not, according to research compiled by psychologist-author Gary Emery. "Although a whole school of thought recommends that you verbally express your hostility," he reports in his book, Rapid Relief from Emotional Distress, *"a great deal of recent research has found the opposite to be the case. Researchers have found that freely venting your anger corrodes relationships and breeds more anger, not less. In one recent study . . . only one out of three hundred happily married couples reported that they yell at each other.*[1]

```
Date:       _____   _____   _____
Place:      _____   _____   _____
Occasion:   _____   _____   _____
```

How Arthur Ashe Dealt with Anger

In the 1975 Masters tennis tournament in Stockholm, Sweden, tennis star Arthur Ashe was winning a feverish battle with Romanian-born Ilie Nastase, sometimes dubbed "Nasty" Nastase for his flamboyant on-court antics. He was at his worst this day, stalling, cursing, taunting, and acting like a madman. Finally Arthur Ashe put down his racket and walked off the court, saying, "I've had enough. I'm at the point where I'm afraid I'll lose control."

---

[1] "Don't Get Angry," *USA Today,* November 1987.

"But Arthur," cried the umpire, "you'll default the match."

"I don't care," replied Ashe. "I'd rather lose that than my self-respect."

The next day the tournament committee came to a surprising solution. Refusing to condone Nastase's bullying tactics, they insisted that Nastase default the match for his unsportsman-like conduct.

Arthur Ashe won both in the game of tennis—and in the game of life.

Date: _____ _____ _____
Place: _____ _____ _____
Occasion: _____ _____ _____

How D. L. Moody Dealt with Anger

Evangelist D. L. Moody, the "Billy Graham" of the 19th century, had a sharp temper which he learned to control—usually. One evening Moody was conducting two evangelistic services back-to-back. After the first one, as Mr. Moody was standing near the door, welcoming the new crowd, a man approached him and delivered a highly offensive insult of some sort. Moody never later repeated it, but it must have been contemptible for in a sudden fit of anger, Moody shoved the man and sent him tumbling down a short flight of steps.

—◇—
The Measure of a Man

The size of a man can be measured by the size of the thing that makes him angry.
—J. K. MORLEY
—◇—

The man was not badly harmed, but Moody's friends wondered how he could now possibly preach the second service. "When I saw Mr. Moody give way to his temper," said an observer, "I said to myself, 'The meeting is killed.' The large number who have seen the whole thing will hardly be in a condition to be influenced by anything more Mr. Moody can say tonight."

But Moody called the meeting to order, stood, and with trembling voice spoke these words: *Friends, before beginning tonight I want to confess that I yielded just now to my temper, out in the hall, and have done wrong. Just as I was coming in here tonight, I lost my temper with a man, and I want to confess my wrong before you all, and if that man is present here whom I thrust away from me in anger, I want to ask his forgiveness and God's. Let us pray.*

Instead of a lost cause, the meeting seemed unusually touched that night, with many people deeply and eternally impressed with the Gospel.[1]

Date: _____ _____ _____
Place: _____ _____ _____
Occasion: _____ _____ _____

Counting It All Joy

• Thomas Jefferson said: *When angry, count ten before you speak; if very angry, one hundred.*

---

[1] William R. Moody, *The Life of Dwight L. Moody* (Murfreesboro, TN: Sword of the Lord Publishers, n.d.), 110–111.

- Mark Twain said: *When angry, count four; when very angry, swear.*
- Mrs. Fulton Oursler, whose husband wrote the classic book on the life of Christ, *The Greatest Story Ever Told,* once said she used to count to ten when becoming provoked. But one day she thought of the first ten words of the Lord's Prayer. Now instead of counting to ten, she slowly says: *Our Father which art in heaven, Hallowed be thy name.*

Date: _____ _____ _____
Place: _____ _____ _____
Occasion: _____ _____ _____

Beautiful Music But No Harmony

The names of Gilbert and Sullivan are well known by all lovers of music. They produced 14 operas together in the period from 1871 to 1896. Gilbert's words allied to Sullivan's music produced magic.

The tragedy, however, is that the two men detested each other. The problem arose because Sullivan ordered some carpet for the theater they had bought, and when Gilbert saw the bill he hit the roof. Neither could control his temper, and the two battled it out in court. They never spoke to one another again as long as they lived.

When Sullivan wrote the music for a new production, he mailed it to Gilbert. When Gilbert wrote the words, he mailed it back to Sullivan.

Once they were forced to be together during a curtain call, but they stood on opposite sides of the stage and bowed in different directions so they wouldn't see each other.

They knew how to make beautiful music, but they knew nothing about harmony.

Date: _____ _____ _____
Place: _____ _____ _____
Occasion: _____ _____ _____

Problems? Or Inconveniences?

In his book *Uh-Oh,* essayist Robert Fulghum wrote of the summer of 1959 when he was working at the Feather River Inn near Blairsden, California, in the Sierra Nevada Mountains. Just out of college, he was hot-headed and free with his opinions. One week he grew angry because the employees were being served the same thing for lunch every single day—two wieners, a mound of sauerkraut, and stale rolls. Furthermore, the cost of the meals was deducted from the employees' checks. On Friday night he learned that the same fare would be on the employee menu for two days more.

Fulghum, who had already taken a strong dislike to the hotel's owner, vented his anger to the night auditor, a man named Sigmund Wollman. *I declared that I have had it up to here; that I am going to get a plate of wieners and sauerkraut and go and wake up the owner and throw it on him. I am sick and tired of this crap and insulted and nobody is going to make me eat wieners and sauerkraut for a whole week and make me pay for it and who does he think he is anyway and how can life be sustained on wieners and sauerkraut and this is un-American . . .*

The whole hotel stinks anyhow. Fulghum continued in his tirade, *and the horses are all nags and the guests are all idiots and I'm packing my bags and heading for Montana where they never even heard of wieners and sauerkraut and wouldn't feed that stuff to pigs.*

Fulghum raved on for about twenty minutes, delivering his monologue at the top of his lungs and with much profanity.

Sigmund Wollman, who had spent three years in a German death camp during World War II, just sat, watching and listening. Finally he said, "Fulchum, are you finished?"

"No. Why?"

"Lissen, Fulchum. Lissen me, lissen me. You know what's wrong with you? It's not wieners and kraut and it's not the boss and it's not the chef and it's not this job."

"So what's wrong with me?"

"Fulchum, you think you know everything, but you don't know the difference between an inconvenience and a problem. If you break your neck, if you have nothing to eat, if your house is on fire—then you got a problem. Everything else is inconvenience. Life *is* inconvenient. Life *is* lumpy. Learn to separate the inconveniences from the real problems. You will live longer. And you will not annoy people like me so much. Good night."

And with those words, he waved the young man off to bed.

Before we lose our cool, it often helps to ask: Problem? Or inconvenience?[1]

> ──────◇──────
> **Good Anger**
>
> *A man that does not know how to be angry, does not know how to be good.*
> —HENRY WARD BEECHER
> ──────◇──────

Date:	_____	_____	_____
Place:	_____	_____	_____
Occasion:	_____	_____	_____

Righteous Indignation

"What is *righteous indignation?*" one child asked another.

"I don't know, but I think it means to get real mad and not cuss."

Date:	_____	_____	_____
Place:	_____	_____	_____
Occasion:	_____	_____	_____

---

[1] Robert Fulghum, *Uh-Oh* (New York: Villard Books, 1991), 143–146.

Atheism

Someone Once Said . . .

- *A little philosophy inclineth man's mind to atheism, but depth in philosophy bringeth men's minds about to religion.*—Francis Bacon
- *I think only an idiot can be an atheist.*—Professor Christian B. Anfinsen, Ph.D. in biochemistry, Harvard University and Nobel Prize winner for chemistry[1]
- *There is nothing in history to match the dire ends to which humanity can be led by following a political and social philosophy that consciously and absolutely excludes God.*—Ravi Zacharias[2]
- *I am thoroughly convinced that when the last chapter of humanity is written, we will find that the implications of atheism, i.e., living without God, if consistently carried through, will have made life plainly unlivable within the limits of reason or even of common sense.*—Ravi Zacharias[3]
- *Gratitude is the most awful moment in the life of an atheist. He feels thankful, but he has no one to thank.*—Peter Kreeft
- *Did you hear the one about the dyslexic, agnostic insomniac? He lay awake at night wondering if there really were a dog!*

Date:		
Place:		
Occasion:		

On the Air

Mark McGee, a confirmed atheist, hosted an afternoon radio talk show in central Florida that spouted forth a geyser of liberal opinions and atheistic diatribes. But imagine his agitation when the owner of the radio station decided to change the format from news/talk to Gospel music and religious programming. Mark hated the thought of continuing to work for the station, but, needing a job, he applied for the position of operations manager. His responsibilities included playing Gospel music and interviewing people on spiritual topics.

One of his first interviews was with a leading proponent of creationism. Other interviews followed with Bible teachers, pastors, and Christian scholars. Mark learned that, though the Bible was written over a period of about fifteen hundred years by forty-four authors, it all fit around a common theme: God's offer of salvation by grace through faith. He studied the evidence for the resurrection of Jesus Christ. For several months, he wrestled with the overwhelming evidence for Theism and Christianity. And at length he gave his heart and life to Jesus Christ.

---

[1] John Ankerberg and John Weldon, *Darwin's Leap of Faith* (Eugene, Oregon: Harvest House Publishers, 1998), 266.
[2] Ravi Zacharias, *Can Man Live Without God?* (Dallas: Word Publishing, 1994), xvii.
[3] Zacharias, *Can Man Live Without God?*, 17.

Shortly afterward, listeners in Central Florida were shocked to hear Mark McGee expounding the very Gospel he had previously sought to exterminate.[1]

Date: _____   _____   _____
Place: _____   _____   _____
Occasion: _____   _____   _____

If There Is No God . . .

In his book, *Reasonable Faith,* William Lane Craig puts it this way:

Man, writes Loren Eiseley, is the Cosmic Orphan. He is the only creature in the universe who asks, "Why?" Other animals have instincts to guide them, but man has learned to ask questions.

"Who am I?" man asks. "Why am I here? Where am I going?" Since the Enlightenment, when he threw off the shackles of religion, man has tried to answer these questions without reference to God. The answers that came back were not exhilarating, but dark and terrible. "You are an accidental by-product of nature, a result of matter plus time plus chance. There is no reason for your existence. All you face is death."

— ◇ —
Is God Dead?

If God is dead, then man is dead, too.
— ◇ —

Modern man thought that when he had gotten rid of God, he had freed himself from all that repressed and stifled him. Instead, he discovered that in killing God, he had also killed himself.

For if there is no God, then man's life becomes absurd.[2]

Date: _____   _____   _____
Place: _____   _____   _____
Occasion: _____   _____   _____

Atheism Unreasonable

Josh McDowell and Don Stewart, in *Answers to Tough Questions Skeptics Ask About the Christian Faith,* write:

Atheists affirm there is no God. Yet they cannot hold this position dogmatically. For us to be able to make this type of statement with authority, we would have to know the universe in its entirety and to possess all knowledge. If anyone had these credentials, then, by definition, he would be God.[3]

Date: _____   _____   _____
Place: _____   _____   _____
Occasion: _____   _____   _____

---

[1] Mark McGee, "Me? A Christian? Don't Count on It!," *Decision Magazine,* October 1991, 4–5.
[2] William Lane Craig, *Reasonable Faith: Christian Truth and Apologetics* (Wheaton, IL: Crossway Books, 1994), 57.
[3] Josh McDowell and Don Stewart, *Answers to Tough Questions Skeptics Ask About the Christian Faith* (San Bernardino: Here's Life Publishers, 1980), 106.

The Lord's Prayer Revisited

Lyman Abbot once paraphrased the Lord's Prayer to reflect the thinking of those who deny the Lord:

Our brethren, who art on earth,
Hallowed be our name.
Our kingdom come, our will be done
On earth, for there is no heaven.
We must get this day our daily bread;
We neither forgive nor are forgiven.
We fear not temptation,
For we deliver ourselves from evil.
For ours is the kingdom and the power
And there is no glory and no forever.
Amen.

Date: _____ _____ _____
Place: _____ _____ _____
Occasion: _____ _____ _____

The Atheist's Holiday

A 1999 study by the Barna Research Group shows that roughly seven percent of the American adult population—approximately fourteen million people—describe themselves as atheistic or agnostic. America has more atheists and agnostics than Mormons (by a three to one margin), Jews (by a four to one margin) or Muslims (by a fourteen to one margin.)[1]

An atheist complained that Christians had their special days such as Christmas, Easter, and so on. The Jews celebrate Passover. "But we atheists," he said, "have no recognized national holiday. It isn't fair."

"I have an idea," said the man's friend. "Why don't you celebrate April 1st?"

Date: _____ _____ _____
Place: _____ _____ _____
Occasion: _____ _____ _____

One Hundred Years

There is an old story of a Jewish rabbi who consented to take a weary traveler into his house for a night's rest. After they ate, the rabbi asked the gentleman, "How old are you?"

"Almost a century old," the old man replied.

"Are you a religious man?" asked the rabbi.

"No, I do not believe in God."

---

[1] Barna Research Group, October 15, 1999, www.barna.org.

The rabbi was infuriated. He opened the door and said, "I cannot keep an atheist in my house overnight."

The old man hobbled out into the cold darkness.

Later the Lord spoke to the rabbi. "Why did you let him go?"

The rabbi replied, "I turned him out because he was an atheist, and I cannot endure him overnight."

God replied, "Son, I have endured him for almost one hundred years. Don't you think you could endure him for one night?"[1]

Date: _____ _____ _____
Place: _____ _____ _____
Occasion: _____ _____ _____

Attitude

Someone Once Said . . .

- *The greatest discovery of my generation is that human beings can alter their lives by altering their attitudes of mind.*—William James
- *Think of it this way: Your total environment is a reflection of you as a person. The house and neighborhood in which you live, the car you drive, the clothes you wear, the job you do, the people with whom you regularly associate. Your total environment is an exact and merciless mirror of you as a human being. Now if you feel your environment can stand some improvement, you have only to improve your attitude. And your world will gradually change to reflect the changing person. Here's how to change your attitude: Beginning now, begin to act like the person you most want to become.*—Earl Nightingale[2]
- *If you keep on saying things are going to be bad, you have a good chance of being a prophet.*—Isaac Singer[3]
- *Everything can be taken away from a man but one thing: the last of the human freedoms—to choose one's attitude in any given set of circumstances.*—Viktor E. Frankl, Nazi Death Camp survivor[4]

Date: _____ _____ _____
Place: _____ _____ _____
Occasion: _____ _____ _____

Kids and Cats

Roland Hill used to say that he would not believe a man to be a true Christian if his wife, his children, the servants, and even the dog and cat, were not the better for it.

---

[1] Dan DeHaan, *The God You Can Know* (Chicago: Moody Press, 1982), 58.
[2] Based on the author's notes of a lecture by Mr. Nightingale
[3] Alan Loy McGinnis, *The Power of Optimism* (New York: Harper & Row, 1990), 131.
[4] Viktor E. Frankl, *Man's Search for Meaning* (New York: Washington Square Press, 1984), 86.

Date: _____ _____ _____
Place: _____ _____ _____
Occasion: _____ _____ _____

The Butterfly and the Caterpillar

I read once of a dashing knight who longed to rescue his princess, who was imprisoned by a cruel enemy in the palace tower. He devised a plan and recruited two small friends to send her a message. First there was Claude Caterpillar, who was a hard-working fellow but crusty and sour. He started inching his way up the wall toward the distant window, but it was hard work. He grumbled that the sun was hot, causing him to sweat. Then the sun withdrew behind a cloud, it started to rain, and he complained even louder about the raindrops. Finally he heaved himself onto the window ledge, looked at the fair maiden, and said, "Hey, you, come over here. Are you the lady in distress?" She nodded. Claude gave her the once-over and said, "You're kidding. You mean I climbed all the way up here for the likes of you? Well, the knight says to get ready, he's coming for you at 5 P.M. sharp. Think you can remember that, or should I repeat it?" And off he went.

Next, the knight sent Barney Butterfly. Barney, too, battled the rain and the contrary winds. He had almost made it to the window when a bird came by and nearly ate him alive. But finally he fluttered in, landing softly on the lady's finger. "Lovely and favored maiden," he said, "the white knight loves you dearly, and tonight he is coming to rescue you. He asks only that you be ready at 5 P.M."

The princess smiled and replied, "Thank you very much, Mr. Butterfly. You are very sweet, and I will be ready tonight when he comes. Claude Caterpillar already brought me the message, but tell me, why was he so disagreeable? He brought me the same news, but after he left, I felt worse than before he came."

The butterfly replied, "Oh, you mean Claude? Well, don't mind Claude. That's just the way he is. I used to be that way, too, until I was transformed."[1]

Date: _____ _____ _____
Place: _____ _____ _____
Occasion: _____ _____ _____

Two Buckets

In his book *Your Attitude: Key to Success,* John Maxwell says, *Our attitude determines our approach to life. The story of the two buckets underlies this truth. One bucket was an optimist, and the other was a pessimist.*

"There has never been a life as disappointing as mine," said the empty bucket as it approached the well. "I never come away from the well full, but what I return empty again."

"There has never been such a happy life as mine," said the full bucket as it left the well. "I never come to the well empty, but what I go away again full."[2]

---

[1] *Parables, Inc.,* January 1985, 6.
[2] John Maxwell, *Your Attitude: Key to Success* (San Bernardino, CA: Here's Life Publishers, 1984), 22.

Date: _____ _____ _____
Place: _____ _____ _____
Occasion: _____ _____ _____

Perspective

Sadie Smithson grew up in Johnson Falls, West Virginia. Her father kept a livery stable, Sadie herself contributed to the family income by sewing, and the family floated just above the poverty level. But Sadie craved respect. She wanted to mingle with the upper crust of Johnson Falls, and she had a plan for doing it. Her secret ambition was to join the Laurel Literary Society, an organization that represented all that was socially prestigious in her town. After high school graduation, she applied for admission into the Laurel Literary Society.

—◇—
Happiness Is Relative

A man is about as happy as he makes up his mind to be.
—ABRAHAM LINCOLN
—◇—

Nothing doing. She was rejected.

Well, she thought, perhaps they'll think better of me if I tour Europe. Few in Johnson Falls had ever been abroad. So she saved her money, daydreaming of the soft-gloved hands clapping after she had read her paper on "My Trip to Europe."

After many years she saved her money. Finally, she took her long-planned trip abroad, traveling with a professor and his wife, only to be caught in the opening shots of World War I. Sadie, in Belgium at the time, managed to get a ride to Paris; but the driver lost his way, and suddenly they found themselves crossing a battlefield.

Right beside the car lay one young soldier, badly wounded. He looked into Sadie's eyes and moaned, "Water, for God's sake!" Sadie immediately jumped out of the car with her drinking cup and made her way to a near-by spring. Then another dying soldier wanted a drink. Sadie refused to leave those boys, and finally the car drove off without her. All night long, she ran back and forth to the spring with her little cup, carrying water to injured men. She tore her skirt into bandages. She scribbled notes and messages for loved ones at home. And as she worked with each wounded man, she offered a prayer: "The Lord bless you and keep you and make his face to shine upon you."

It was a night of horror, of darkness, and of moaning, dying men. Finally, the darkness gave way to the dawn and with it an ambulance and young doctor. He was astonished to find a poor girl from West Virginia amid all the blood and carnage of war. "Who are you?" he asked, "and what in thunder are you doing here?"

"I'm Sadie Smithson," she said, "and I've been holding hell back all night."

"Well!" said the young doctor quietly, "Miss Sadie Smithson, I'm glad you held some of it back, for everybody else in the world was letting it loose last night."

As she was returning to America, she told her story to a fellow passenger on the ship. "I've never been married—never known what it was to have children—but that night all those men were my children, even the biggest and roughest of them, and I believe I could have died for any one of them."

"Well," said the friend, "the Laurel Literary Society will be glad enough to have you belong to it now."

"No," Sadie Smithson replied, "I've been face to face with war and death and hell and God. Now little things like the Laurel Literary Society don't matter to me any more."

"What does matter?" asked the friend.

"Nothing," Sadie said. "Nothing but God and love—and doing what I can do for those he sends me to."

Jesus Christ came in the darkness of night to a dying race of humanity. He loved us and gave himself for us. When we receive him, our perspective changes, and with it our attitude. The trivial and the important change places.[1]

Date:	_____	_____	_____
Place:	_____	_____	_____
Occasion:	_____	_____	_____

A Living Sacrifice

One Sunday in Copenhagen, Corrie ten Boom, eighty, spoke from Romans 12:1–2, urging her audience to present their bodies to Christ as living sacrifices. After church two young nurses invited her to their apartment for lunch, and Corrie went with them—only to discover they lived on the tenth floor, and there was no elevator.

She didn't think she could mount the stairs, but as the nurses were so eager for her visit she decided to try. By the fifth floor, Corrie's heart was pounding, her breath coming in gulps, her legs buckling. She collapsed in a chair on the landing thinking she could go no further, and she complained bitterly to the Lord. Looking upward, the stairs seemed to ascend to infinity, and Corrie wondered if she might die en route. "Perhaps I am leaving earth to go to heaven," she thought.

But the Lord seemed to whisper that a special blessing awaited her on the tenth floor, so she bravely pressed on, one nurse in front of her and another following.

Finally reaching the apartment, Corrie found there the parents of one of the girls. She soon discovered that neither parent was a Christian, but both were eager to hear the Gospel. Opening her Bible, Corrie carefully explained the plan of salvation. "I have traveled in more than sixty countries and have never found anyone who said they were sorry they had given their hearts to Jesus," she said. "You will not be sorry, either."

That day both prayed for Christ to enter their lives.

On her way down the steps, Corrie said, "Thank you, Lord, for making me walk up all these steps. And next time, Lord, help Corrie ten Boom listen to her own sermon about being willing to go anywhere you tell me to go—even up ten flights of stairs."[2]

Date:	_____	_____	_____
Place:	_____	_____	_____
Occasion:	_____	_____	_____

---

[1] William L. Stidger, *There Are Sermons in Stories* (New York: Abingdon, 1942), 11–13.
[2] Robert J. Morgan, *From This Verse* (Nashville: Thomas Nelson Publishers, Inc., 1998), October 16.

Rules for Dying

William Sangster was born in London in 1900 and started attending a Methodist church at age nine. At thirteen he became a Christian and immediately began sharing his faith with friends. After stints in the army and in college, he began pastoring a circuit of Methodist churches, working himself to exhaustion, frequently saying, "I just can't do enough!" His reputation as a powerful preacher and beloved pastor followed him from church to church.

In 1939, Sangster assumed leadership of Westminster Central Hall, a Methodist church near London's Westminster Abbey. During his first worship service he announced to his stunned congregation that Britain and Germany were officially at war. He quickly converted the church basement into an air-raid shelter, and for 1,688 nights Sangster ministered to the various needs of all kinds of people. At the same time, he somehow managed to write, preach gripping sermons, earn a Ph.D., and lead hundreds to Christ. He became known as Wesley's successor in London and was esteemed as the most beloved British preacher of his era.

After the war, Sangster headed Britain's Methodist Home Missions Department until he was diagnosed with progressive muscular atrophy. For three years he slowly died, becoming progressively more paralyzed, finally able to move only two fingers, but his attitude didn't falter. When he first learned of his illness, Sangster made four rules for himself. Many people have rules for living; Sangster composed four rules for dying: *I will never complain. I will keep the home bright. I will count my blessings. I will try to turn it to gain.* He did all those things. And thus the work of God was displayed in his life, and God's strength was made perfect in his weakness.[1]

Date:	_____	_____	_____
Place:	_____	_____	_____
Occasion:	_____	_____	_____

Attitude Makes All the Difference

Jim Smith went to church on Sunday morning. He heard the organist miss a note during the prelude, and he winced. He saw a teenager talking when everybody was supposed to "bow in prayer." He felt like the usher was watching to see what he put in the offering plate, and it made him boil. He caught the preacher making a slip of the tongue five times in the sermon by actual count. As he slipped out through the side door during the closing hymn, he muttered to himself, "Never again! What a bunch of clods and hypocrites!"

Ron Jones went to church on Sunday morning. He heard the organist play an arrangement of "A Mighty Fortress," and he was thrilled by the majesty of it. He heard a young girl take a moment in the service to speak her simple moving message of the difference her faith makes in her life. He was glad to see that his church was sharing in a special offering for the hungry children of Nigeria. He especially appreciated the sermon that Sunday—it answered a question that had bothered him for a

---

[1] Robert J. Morgan, *On This Day* (Nashville: Thomas Nelson Publishers, Inc., 1997), February 11th.

long time. He thought, as he walked out the doors of the church, "How can a man come here and not feel the presence of God?"

Both men went to the same church on the same Sunday morning. Each found what he was looking for.[1]

Date: _____   _____   _____
Place: _____   _____   _____
Occasion: _____   _____   _____

Backsliding

Someone Once Said . . .

- *No one is so empty as the man who has stopped walking with God and doesn't know it.*—Jerry White[2]
- *Backsliding starts in such a subtle way that most of us are not aware of it, and many of us may be backslidden and may not realize it.*—Theodore H. Epp[3]
- *We must not just take it for granted that we are in touch with God. Joseph and Mary lost a whole day of fellowship with Jesus because they "supposed him to be in the company." They took for granted something of which they should have made sure. "He [Samson] wist not that the Lord had departed from him" (Judges 16:20). He was out of touch with God and did not know it.*—J. Oswald Sanders[4]
- *Samson's last chapter was a sad story of binding, blinding, and grinding.*—Vance Havner[5]
- *Therefore we must give the more earnest heed to the things we have heard, lest we drift away.*—Hebrews 2:1
- *The captain gives earnest heed to the charts lest he drift unconsciously shorewards!*—F. W. Boreham[6]

Date: _____   _____   _____
Place: _____   _____   _____
Occasion: _____   _____   _____

Nibbling Away

Mike Yaconelli wrote on the Wittenburg Door: "I live in a small, rural community. There are lots of cattle ranches around here, and, every once in a while, a cow wanders off and gets lost. . . . Ask a rancher how a cow gets lost, and chances are he will reply, 'Well, the cow starts nibbling on a tuft of green grass, and when it finishes, it looks ahead to the next tuft of green

---

[1] Anonymous clipping in the author's files.
[2] Jerry White, *The Power of Commitment* (Colorado Springs: NavPress, 1985), 55.
[3] Theodore H. Epp, *The Backsliding Christian* (Lincoln, NE: Back to the Bible, 1956), 7.
[4] J. Oswald Sanders, *The Best That I Can Be* (Robesonia, PA: OMF Books, 1984), 37.
[5] Vance Havner, *In Times Like These* (Old Tappan, NJ: Fleming H. Revell Co., 1969), 37.
[6] F. W. Boreham, *Shadows On the Wall* (New York: Abingdon Press, 1922), 41.

grass and starts nibbling on that one, and then it nibbles on a tuft of grass right next to a hole in the fence. It then sees another tuft of green grass on the other side of the fence, so it nibbles on that one and then goes on to the next tuft. The next thing you know, the cow has nibbled itself into being lost.'"[1]

Most people don't deliberately set out to backslide, but following their appetites or desires from one tuft to the next, they nibble themselves through the fence and off the straight and narrow path.

> Date: _____   _____   _____
> Place: _____   _____   _____
> Occasion: _____   _____   _____

A Heart Warming

We need a heart warming. . . . The early Christians did not need a shot in the arm every Sunday to keep them going. They knew Jesus and they upset the world and worried the devil and gave wicked rulers insomnia and started something the jails couldn't lock up, fire couldn't burn, water couldn't drown, swords couldn't kill. . . .

You may belittle experience and speak of the dangers of emotion, but we are suffering today from a species of Christianity as dry as dust, as cold as ice, as pale as a corpse, and as dead as King Tut. We are suffering, not from a lack of correct heads but of consumed hearts.—Vance Havner[2]

> Date: _____   _____   _____
> Place: _____   _____   _____
> Occasion: _____   _____   _____

Sheep or Pigs

One difference between a sheep and a hog is that, when a sheep falls into a mudhole, it is uncomfortable and struggles to get out. When a hog falls into a mudhole, he wallows in it and enjoys it.—Charles Allen[3]

> Date: _____   _____   _____
> Place: _____   _____   _____
> Occasion: _____   _____   _____

Danger Zone

A foolish old farmer, so the story goes, concluded one day that the oats he had fed his mule for years were simply costing him too much. So he hatched a plan: he mixed a little sawdust in with the feed, and then a little more the next day, and even more the next, each time reducing the amount of oats in the mix.

---

[1] *Leadership Journal,* Fall 1988, 45.
[2] Vance Havner, *It Is Time* (Old Tappan, NJ: Fleming H. Revell Co., 1943), 77.
[3] Charles Allen, *Perfect Peace* (Old Tappan, NJ: Fleming H. Revell Co., 1979), 42.

B

The mule didn't seem to notice the gradual change, so the farmer thought things were fine and kept decreasing the proportion of oats. But weeks later, on the day he finally fed the poor beast nothing but sawdust, the mule finished the meal and fell over dead.

A silly tale, perhaps, but it serves as a parable of the back-slider—the Christian who slips further and further away from God through unrepented sin or neglect. Though we know our souls cannot survive on spiritual sawdust, we may well con-

> ◇
> **The Power of Prayer**
> *Backsliding starts when knee-bending stops.*
> ◇

vince ourselves that a little won't hurt too much, and a little less real spiritual food won't be missed. Then, over time, the proportion of sawdust increases while the oats gradually disappear. Before long, the change is complete, and our starved, sawdust-stuffed spiritual life has collapsed.[1]

Date: _____ _____ _____
Place: _____ _____ _____
Occasion: _____ _____ _____

The Way Back

With deep repentance and sincere faith, find your way back from your backsliding. It is your duty, for you have turned away from Him whom you professed to serve. It is your wisdom, for you cannot strive against Him and prosper. It is your immediate necessity, for what He has done is nothing compared to what He may do in the way of chastisement, since He is Almighty to punish.—Charles H. Spurgeon

Date: _____ _____ _____
Place: _____ _____ _____
Occasion: _____ _____ _____

Baptism

Someone Once Said . . .

- *[Baptism] signifies that the old Adam in us is to be drowned by daily sorrow and repentance, and perish with all sins and evil lusts, and that the new man should daily come forth again and rise, who shall live before God in righteousness and purity forever.*—Luther's Small Catechism

Date: _____ _____ _____
Place: _____ _____ _____
Occasion: _____ _____ _____

---

[1] Paul Thigpen, "Danger Zone," *Discipleship Journal*, July/August 1999, 22.

The Mockers

In his book, *The Holy Spirit in Missions,* nineteenth century author A. J. Gordon related an incident observed by Rev. Isaac D. Colburn, missionary to Burma. A group of Burmese Christians had gathered along the banks of a pool to witness the baptism of several new believers. Watching from a distance were many locals, some of them perched on rocky crags overlooking the water. Among these observers were two men, father and son, who detested the Gospel and had done everything in their power to dissuade those who were to be baptized.

As the Burmese pastor was opening the services by the pool, the father and son interrupted with blasphemous words, curses, and obscene gestures. The preacher rebuked them, but they continued all the more. Just as the pastor was about to plunge his first disciple into the water, the two antagonists stripped off their clothes and plunged naked into the water where they conducted their own malicious baptism, mocking the Christians by dipping each other in the water and uttering the name of the Trinity laced with profanities.

Standing on the bank was a native Korean evangelist named Sau Wah, who, before his conversion, had been a dreaded opponent of the Gospel. Now he rose and, his voice stern with authority, demanded silence. Turning to the old man in the water, he said, "O full of all deceit and all fraud, you son of the devil, you enemy of all righteousness, will you not cease perverting the straight ways of the Lord?"

As he spoke, the Holy Spirit seemed to fall on the assembly. The two blasphemers, suddenly thunderstruck, raced from the pool and up the bank, but before going many yards, they fell to the earth. The Christians proceeded with their baptism. Afterward, they found the father lying facedown on the ground, dead. The son recovered consciousness and was carried to the village, but within a few months he followed his father to the grave.

Date: _____   _____   _____
Place: _____   _____   _____
Occasion: _____   _____   _____

Drink Ye All of It

A young minister, fresh from the Baptist seminary, was conducting his first baptismal service. In his nervousness, he got his Scriptures confused concerning baptism and the Lord's Supper: *I now baptize you in the name of the Father and of the Son and of the Holy Spirit.* As he lowered the convert into the water, he added, *And now drink ye all of it.*

Date: _____   _____   _____
Place: _____   _____   _____
Occasion: _____   _____   _____

From *The Boston Globe*

The following article was ripped from *The Boston Globe,* Sunday, August 14, 1983 (Metro Section, p. 26): *Natick police yesterday ruled accidental the drowning Friday of an unemployed Dorchester man who apparently lost his balance and fell into deep water while being baptized in Lake Cochituate. John E. Blue, 37, who was living at the Jesus Nazareth Holiness Church at 3 Bowdoin St., was pronounced dead at Leonard Morse Hospital in Natick shortly after the 11:30 A.M. accident. Rev. Harold G. Branch of the church said he was baptizing Blue in waist-deep water near Rte. 9 when the two men lost their balance and fell backward. Police said the lake bottom drops off sharply immediately behind the spot where they were standing.*

Date: _____ _____ _____

Place: _____ _____ _____

Occasion: _____ _____ _____

Three Notorious Characters

I heard one of the funniest things to happen at church years ago from Dr. William Culbertson, president of Moody Bible Institute, when we were in a Bible Conference on the West Coast. As an Episcopalian, he enjoyed telling what happened once in a Baptist church in Indiana.

It seems that three rather notorious characters had been converted and were to be baptized. The whole community turned out. The little church had only one small dressing room which opened from the baptistery and was shielded from view only by a sheet hung over the entrance. The floor was covered with linoleum. On that not-to-be-forgotten night, the first candidate had been baptized and had gone up behind the sheet to change his clothes. The second man was then baptized, and joined his companion in the little dressing room. The third man was being baptized when the second man, wriggling out of his wet trousers, extricated one leg and gave a kick to free the other. His foot skidded on the wet linoleum floor, and into the baptistery he went—on top of the preacher and the third candidate. He grabbed the sheet in desperation as he went, and carried it with him into the pool. Meanwhile, the first man had removed all his wet clothes but had not yet put on any of his dry garments. When the sheet disappeared into the water, it left him standing before the congregation in his birthday suit. He grabbed a chair and tried to hide behind it. The lights had been turned low for the baptizing. Somebody yelled, "Turn out the lights!" An excited deacon turned them on full power.

It shouldn't have happened but it did. Anything can happen at church and usually does.[2]

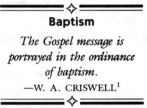

Baptism

The Gospel message is portrayed in the ordinance of baptism.
—W. A. CRISWELL[1]

---

[1] W. A. Criswell, *Ephesians* (Grand Rapids: Zondervan, 1974), 188.
[2] Vance Havner, *Threescore and Ten* (Old Tappan, NJ: Fleming H. Revell Co., 1973), 71–72.

Date: _____   _____   _____

Place: _____   _____   _____

Occasion: _____   _____   _____

——————————— **Beauty/Countenance** ———————————

Someone Once Said . . .

- *The gods we worship write their names on our faces.*—Ralph Waldo Emerson[1]
- *Oftentimes under silken apparel, there is a threadbare soul.*—Thomas Watson[2]
- *Wash your face every morning in a bath of praise.*—Charles Spurgeon[3]
- *I have seen more cheerful faces on iodine bottles than on some Christians.*—Vance Havner[4]
- *The man who is dejected and disquieted and miserable, who is unhappy and depressed always shows it in his face.*—Martyn Lloyd-Jones[5]
- *When a happy man comes into a room, it is as if another candle has been lighted.*—Robert Louis Stevenson
- *Even an old barn looks better with a fresh coat of paint.*—One woman's answer to the question, "Should Christians wear makeup?"

Date: _____   _____   _____

Place: _____   _____   _____

Occasion: _____   _____   _____

The Bible Says . . .

- *His face shone like the sun.*—Matthew 17:2
- *But we all, with unveiled face, beholding as in a mirror the glory of the Lord, are being transformed into the same image from glory to glory, just as by the Spirit of the Lord.*—2 Corinthians 3:18
- *They looked to Him and were radiant.*—Psalm 34:5
- *So when Aaron and all the children of Israel saw Moses, behold, the skin of his face shone. . . .*—Exodus 34:30
- *So the woman came and told her husband, saying, "A Man of God came to me, and His countenance was like the countenance of the Angel of God, very awesome."*—Judges 13:6
- *And all who sat in the council, looking steadfastly at [Stephen], saw his face as the face of an angel.*—Acts 6:15

---

[1] *The Book of Uncommon Prayer*, ed. Constance Pollock and Daniel Pollock (Dallas: Word Publishing, 1996), 61.

[2] Thomas Watson, *Gleanings From Thomas Watson* (Morgan, PA: Soli Deo Gloria Publications, 1995), 49.

[3] Charles Haddon Spurgeon, *Spurgeon's Sermons*, vol. 2 (Grand Rapids: Baker Book House, 1983), 184.

[4] Vance Havner, *Pepper 'N Salt* (Old Tappan, NJ: Flemming H. Revell Co., 1966), 27.

[5] David Martyn Lloyd-Jones, *Spiritual Depression* (Grand Rapids: Eerdmans Publishing Co., 1965), 13.

- *A merry heart makes a cheerful countenance. . . .*—Proverbs 15:13
- *A man's wisdom makes his face shine, / And the sternness of his face is changed.*—Ecclesiastes 8:1
- *Smiling faces make you happy.*—Proverbs 15:30.
- *Do not let your adornment be merely* outward—arranging the hair, wearing gold, or putting on *fine* apparel—rather *let it be* the hidden person of the heart, with the incorruptible *beauty* of a gentle and quiet spirit, which is very precious in the sight of God.—1 Peter 3:3–4
- *For this is the way the holy women of the past who put their hope in God used to make themselves beautiful.*—1 Peter 3:5
- *And Cain was very angry, and his countenance fell.*—Genesis 4:5
- *And Jacob saw the countenance of Laban, and indeed it was* not *favorable* toward him as before.—Genesis 31:2
- *The look on their countenance witnesses against them.*—Isaiah 3:9
- *Why are you cast down, O my soul? / . . . Hope in God; / For I shall yet praise Him, / The help of my countenance and my God.*—Psalm 43:5
- *. . . my face healer . . .*—Psalm 42:5 (Berkley)
- *He puts a smile on my face. He's my God.*—Psalm 43:5 (Peterson)

Date: _____ _____ _____
Place: _____ _____ _____
Occasion: _____ _____ _____

Depression and the Face

Of the five major categories of clinically depressive symptoms, the first is the sad affect. An example of the sad facial expression characteristic of a depressed person, is seen in reference to Cain's face downcast in Genesis 4:4–7. Depressed individuals may cry often, or at least feel like crying. Their eyes are downcast, the mouth droops, the forehead may be wrinkled. Their strained features make such individuals look tired, discouraged, and dejected. As depression worsens, they may lose interest in their personal appearance and even appear untidy. They may exhibit what is termed "smiling depression"—depression that shows even when they smile.[1]

Date: _____ _____ _____
Place: _____ _____ _____
Occasion: _____ _____ _____

Brighten Up!

When Paul said, in Philippians 4:4, *Rejoice in the Lord,* he was not coining a new phrase. He was simply quoting an Old Testament command that appears in Psalm 32, Psalm 64, Psalm 104, Joel 2, and Habakkuk 3. In these passages, the primary Hebrew word for *rejoice* is *simhah,* which has as its root meaning, *to shine, to be bright.*

---

[1] Paul D. Meier, Frank B. Minirth, Frank B. Wichern, *Introduction to Psychology and Counseling* (Grand Rapids: Baker Book House, 1982), 258.

Hebrew word for *rejoice* is *simhah*, which has as its root meaning, *to shine, to be bright.* So the biblical phrase *Rejoice in the Lord* could well be translated *Brighten up in the Lord always; and again I say brighten up!* In other words, *Put on a happy face. Smile. Lift up your countenance.*

```
Date:     _____    _____    _____
Place:    _____    _____    _____
Occasion: _____    _____    _____
```

An Invisible Sculptor

You can tell whether a man has been keeping up his life of prayer. His witness is in his face. There is an invisible sculptor that chisels the face into the upper attitude of the soul.—Dr. Joseph Parker (1830–1902), English Congregational preacher

```
Date:     _____    _____    _____
Place:    _____    _____    _____
Occasion: _____    _____    _____
```

Description of Missionary Henry Martyn (1781–1812)

His features were not regular, but the expression was so luminous, so intellectual, so affectionate, so beaming with Divine charity, that no one could have looked at his features and thought of their shape or form—the outbeaming of his soul would absorb the attention of every observer.[1]

```
Date:     _____    _____    _____
Place:    _____    _____    _____
Occasion: _____    _____    _____
```

Norman Vincent Peale's Recollection

How well I recall sitting beside my mother in church as a boy. Nearby sat old Brother Jones, a leading deacon and ostensibly a pillar of the church. This character always had a sad expression on his face. I used to whisper to my mother, "Why does Brother Jones have that sour look?"

"That is not sour. It's a pious look," my mother replied. My mother seemed to equate a pious look with saintliness. This did not impress me, for I and the kids around town knew a few things about Brother Jones that my mother did not. We boys had him realistically sized up.

But nowadays the genuine exponent of bona fide Christianity wears a happy face. And why not? He has been released from conflicts and misery. He has experienced victories.[2]

```
Date:     _____    _____    _____
Place:    _____    _____    _____
Occasion: _____    _____    _____
```

---

[1] Constance E. Padwick, *Henry Martyn* (Chicago: Moody Press, 1980), 162.
[2] Norman Vincent Peale, *Enthusiasm Makes the Difference* (Englewood Cliffs, NJ: Prentice-Hall, 1967), 136.

A Heavenly Glow

J. C. Maculay was born in Belfast, grew up in Scotland, and spent most of his ministry pastoring and teaching in Canada. In his book on personal evangelism, he tells this story: *I think, for instance, of an elderly German who lived a rough life in the Northern Ontario bush. His English was poor, his mind undeveloped, and his life one of very narrow limits. His countenance was dark and hard. But the Spirit of God stirred in his soul a sense of need, and he found his way to our services. One Sunday evening I took him into a little side room and tried to present the way of salvation. He did not seem to understand, and I almost despaired of his coming to the light. Finally I suggested that we kneel down and pray. I prayed that God would give light to the darkened mind. When we lifted our heads and arose from our knees, I saw something that startled me, and which I shall never forget. The darkness and the hardness had completely fallen away from my friend's countenance. Instead, his face was lit up with a heavenly glow, like a sunburst. His limited vocabulary made it impossible for him to say much, but his face spoke volumes. The presence of the Lord in that little room was so real, and the joy was unspeakable.*[1]

Date: _____   _____   _____
Place: _____   _____   _____
Occasion: _____   _____   _____

Mr. Glory-Face

Adoniram Judson went as a missionary to Burma. He so burned with the desire to preach the gospel before he had learned the language that he walked up to a Burman and embraced him. The man went home and reported that he had seen an angel. The living Christ was so radiant in Mr. Judson's countenance that men called him "Mr. Glory-Face."[2]

Date: _____   _____   _____
Place: _____   _____   _____
Occasion: _____   _____   _____

Just Looking at You

John Taylor Smith (1860–1907) was a British bishop and Chaplain general of British forces during World War I. He died on a ship in the Mediterranean and was buried at sea, but the stories of his ministry for Christ live to this day. Here is an incident, clipped from *Christianity Today*, January 21, 1977: *Bishop Taylor Smith was asked to preach at a jubilee celebration in Chicago. While he was crossing the Atlantic, he walked round on the promenade deck in the open air each day and lost his voice. He arrived in Chicago and preached in a whisper, with none of the modern electronic gadgets available for amplification. At the end of his address, someone came to him and said, "You have persuaded me that I must*

[1] J. C. Macaulay and Robert H. Belton, *Personal Evangelism* (Chicago: Moody Press, 1956), 99–100.
[2] Walter B. Knight, *Three Thousand Illustrations* (Grand Rapids: Eerdmans Publishing Co., 1947), 387.

become a Christian." The bishop asked, "What exactly was it that I said that brought you to this point?" The man answered, "I couldn't hear a word you said—it was just looking at you."

<table>
<tr><td>Date:</td><td></td><td></td><td></td></tr>
<tr><td>Place:</td><td></td><td></td><td></td></tr>
<tr><td>Occasion:</td><td></td><td></td><td></td></tr>
</table>

What Impressed Moody

Rev. William Pennefather was a prominent British clergyman who founded England's Mildmay Conference. D. L. Moody, who attended the conference, later said:

I well remember sitting in yonder seat looking up at this platform and seeing the beloved Mr. Pennefather's face illuminated as it were with heaven's light. I don't think I can recall a word that he said, but the whole atmosphere of the man breathed holiness, and I got then a lift and impetus in the Christian life that I have never lost. I thank God that I saw and spoke with that holy man; no one could see him without the consciousness that he lived in the presence of God.[1]

<table>
<tr><td>Date:</td><td></td><td></td><td></td></tr>
<tr><td>Place:</td><td></td><td></td><td></td></tr>
<tr><td>Occasion:</td><td></td><td></td><td></td></tr>
</table>

A Radiant Face

Alexander Maclaren (1826–1910), looking out over his congregation one Sunday, was shocked to see a well-known skeptic in the audience. As they chatted after the service, Maclaren persuaded the man to attend church for four more Sundays, for the sermons were on the main doctrines of the Christian faith. On the fourth Sunday, the man told Maclaren he had decided to become a Christian. The preacher asked which message had brought the man to that decision. The former skeptic replied:

Your sermons, sir, were helpful, but they were not what finally persuaded me to become a Christian. A few weeks ago, as I was leaving church, I noticed an elderly lady with a radiant face. Because she was making her way with difficulty along the icy street, I offered to help her. As we walked along together, she looked up at me and said, "I wonder if you know my Savior, Jesus Christ? He is everything in the world to me. I want you to love Him, too." Those few words touched my heart, and when I got home, I knelt down and received the Savior.

<table>
<tr><td>Date:</td><td></td><td></td><td></td></tr>
<tr><td>Place:</td><td></td><td></td><td></td></tr>
<tr><td>Occasion:</td><td></td><td></td><td></td></tr>
</table>

---

[1] William R. Moody, *The Life of Dwight L. Moody* (Murfreesboro, TN: Sword of the Lord Publishers, n.d.), 154.

Terrible Heresy

On one occasion Martin Luther had been brooding for several days. Reports had been and still were coming of groups of peasants in revolt, and of increased papal pressure on the nobles to renounce their stand for Luther. These conspired to make him feel that he had undertaken a hopeless task.

On the morning when he was most deeply melancholic, he came into the dining room for breakfast. His wife, Katie, greeted him, attired in a black dress which was as funereal in appearance as the costume that she had worn as a nun. Martin glanced at her quizzically. She usually greeted him with a cheerful, "Guten morgen, Herr Dokter," but this morning she said not a word.

"What is wrong, Katie?" Martin inquired.

"God is dead," she announced sadly.

"Woman, that is a terrible heresy. God is not dead, nor doth He sleep. Never say that The Eternal has died. When heaven and earth shall pass away God will remain," he affirmed.

"Then why do you waken each morning with such a doleful expression on your face? Why go through the day sighing like the north wind? In your university classes you claim to interpret the mind of God. You have appeared to know Him well, and I became certain, from the expression on your face, that God must surely have expired."

She made this statement without a change of expression. Suddenly Martin burst out laughing.

"You have convinced me, Katie, dear," he said. "So, if ever you see me again with a melancholy countenance, remind me that God is living, that He will live forevermore. I promise you that I shall try not to appear as dour as a shriveled turnip."[1]

> ═══ ◇ ═══
> **A Portrait of the Soul**
>
> *A person's face is the signature of his soul.*
> —WILLIAM L. STIDGER
> ═══ ◇ ═══

Date:	_____	_____	_____
Place:	_____	_____	_____
Occasion:	_____	_____	_____

Betraying the Secret

A group of prospectors set out from Bannock, Montana (then capital of the state) in search of gold. They went through many hardships, and several of their little company died en route. Finally, they were overtaken by Indians, who took their good horses, leaving them with only a few limping old ponies. They then threatened them, telling them to get back to Bannock and stay there; for if they overtook them again, they would murder the lot of them.

Defeated, discouraged and downhearted, the prospectors sought to make their way back to the capital city. As they tethered out the limping ponies on a creek side, one of the men casually picked up a little stone from the creek bed.

---

[1] Norman E. Nygaard, *A Mighty Fortress: The Life of Martin Luther* (Grand Rapids: Zondervan Publishing Co., 1964), 103.

He called to his buddy for a hammer and upon cracking the rock, he said, "It looks as though there may be gold here." The two of them panned gold the rest of the afternoon and managed to realize twelve dollars worth. The entire little company panned gold the next day in the same creek and realized fifty dollars, a great sum in those days.

They said to one another; "We have struck it!"

They made their way back to Bannock and vowed not to breathe a word concerning this gold strike, and they ever so carefully kept their promise. They secretively set about reequipping themselves with supplies for another prospecting trip.

When they got ready to go back, they were surprised to find three hundred men following them. Who had told them? No one! The writer of the book accounted thus for the incident: "Their beaming faces betrayed the secret!"

If we have been enamored with Him, whom, having not seen, we love, we should be unable to conceal the treasure: Our beaming faces should betray the secret![1]

Date: _____   _____   _____
Place: _____   _____   _____
Occasion: _____   _____   _____

How Much?

Americans spend over seven billion dollars a year on cosmetics alone.

Date: _____   _____   _____
Place: _____   _____   _____
Occasion: _____   _____   _____

Just in Time

There is the story of a woman who, early one morning, made a mad dash out of the house when she heard the garbage truck pulling away. She was still in her bathrobe. Her hair was wrapped in big curlers. Her face was covered with sticky cream. She was wearing a chin-strap and a beat-up old pair of slippers. In short, she was a frightful picture. When she reached the sidewalk, she called out, "Am I too late for the garbage?"

And the reply came back, "No, hop right in."[2]

Date: _____   _____   _____
Place: _____   _____   _____
Occasion: _____   _____   _____

---

[1] L.E. Maxwell, *The Prairie Overcomer,* May 1984, 34.
[2] *Parables, Etc.,* vol. 4, No. 11, January 1985, 5.

Captured by the Word

Origen of Alexandria wrote, *"As in the case of the fishes that fall into the net, some are found in one part of the net and some in another part, and each at the part at which it was caught, so in the case of those who have come into the net of the Scripture you would find some caught in the prophetic net; for example, of Isaiah, . . . or of Jeremiah or of Daniel; and others in the net of the law, and others in the gospel net, and some in the apostolic net; for when one is first captured by the Word or seems to be captured, he is taken from some part of the whole net."* (ANF 9:420)

Date: _____ _____ _____

Place: _____ _____ _____

Occasion: _____ _____ _____

The Only Book Saved

Alexander Duff, the first foreign missionary of the Church of Scotland, got off to a rough start. He was young, only twenty-three, and bright and innovative. But on his way to India in 1829 with his new wife, he was shipwrecked—not once but twice! The most serious wreck occurred when his ship, the *Lady Holland,* was within a few miles of India.

At ten o'clock P.M., Duff was half-undressed when a shock and shudder ran through the vessel. He rushed to the deck where the captain met him with terrifying words, "Oh, she's gone! She's gone!" The ship split apart, but a portion clung precariously to a reef. Through the night the passengers huddled in terror in the surviving portion, expecting every moment to be swept away. They were saved the next day, but their clothes and prized possessions were lost, including Duff's entire library of eight hundred volumes.

Later, standing on the shore and looking sadly toward the reef, Duff saw a small package bobbing atop the water. He watched and waited as it floated close enough for him to wade out and retrieve.

It was his Bible. Of all his precious books, it alone survived. His heart soared, for he took it as a sign from the Lord that this one book alone was worth more than all the others put together.

He assembled his fellow survivors and read Psalm 107, the Traveler's Psalm. Soon, using the same Bible, he began his first class with a little group of five boys under a banyan tree. Within a week the class had grown to three hundred, and it soon became a school that evangelized and educated the higher classes in India, producing a qualified generation of leaders for the nation's young church.

Date: _____ _____ _____

Place: _____ _____ _____

Occasion: _____ _____ _____

The *Bounty*'s Bible

The English ship *Bounty,* commanded by Lieutenant William Bligh, journeyed to the South Pacific in 1787 to collect plants of the breadfruit tree. Sailors signed on gladly, considering the voyage a trip to paradise. Having no second-in-command, Captain Bligh appointed his young friend Fletcher Christian to the post. The *Bounty* stayed in Tahiti six months, and the sailors, led by happy-go-lucky Fletcher Christian, enjoyed paradise to the full. When time came for departure, some of the men wanted to stay behind with their island girls. Three men, trying to desert, were flogged. The mood on ship darkened, and on April 28, 1789, Fletcher Christian staged the most famous mutiny in history. Bligh and his supporters were set adrift in an overloaded lifeboat (which they miraculously navigated 3700 miles to Timor).

The mutineers aboard the *Bounty* immediately began quarreling about what to do next. Christian returned to Tahiti, where he left some of the mutineers, kidnapped some women, took some slaves, and traveled with the remaining crew a thousand miles to uninhabited Pitcairn Island. There the little group quickly unraveled. They distilled whiskey from a native plant. Drunkenness and fighting marked their colony. Disease and murder eventually took the lives of all the men except for one, Alexander Smith, who found himself the only man on the island, surrounded by an assortment of women and children.

Then an amazing change occurred. Smith found the *Bounty's* neglected Bible. As he read it, he took its message to heart, then began instructing the little community. He taught the colonists the Scriptures and helped them obey its instructions. The message of Christ so transformed their lives that twenty years later, in 1808, when the ship *Topaz* landed on the island, it found a happy society of Christians living in prosperity and peace, free from crime, disease, murder—and mutiny. Years later the Bible fell into the hands of a visiting whaler who brought it to America, but in 1950 it was returned to the island. It now resides on display in the church in Pitcairn as a monument to its transforming message.[1]

Date:	_____	_____	_____
Place:	_____	_____	_____
Occasion:	_____	_____	_____

Find a Verse, and Put Your Name in It

Ruth Bell Graham vividly remembers September 2, 1933. She was thirteen. Her father, a missionary surgeon in China, and her mother were sending her to boarding school in what is now Pyongyang, North Korea. For Ruth, it was a brutal parting, and she earnestly prayed she would die before morning. But dawn came, leaving her prayers unanswered, and she gripped her bags and trudged toward the riverfront. She was leaving all that was loved and familiar: her Chinese friends, the missionaries, her parents, her home, her memories. The *Nagasaki Maru* carried her slowly down the Whangpoo River into the Yangtze River and on to the East China Sea.

---

[1] Robert J. Morgan, *On This Day* (Nashville: Thomas Nelson Publishers, 1997), April 28th.

B

A week later she was settling into her spartan dormitory. Waves of homesickness pounded her like a churning surf. Ruth kept busy by day, but evenings were harder. She would bury her head in her pillow and cry herself to sleep, night after night, week after week. She fell ill, and in the infirmary she read through the Psalms, finding comfort in Psalm 27:10—*When my father and my mother forsake me, Then the Lord will take care of me.*

The hurt and fear and doubt persisted. Finally, in desperation, she went to her sister Rosa, also enrolled in Pyongyang. "I don't know what to tell you to do," Rosa replied matter-of-factly, "unless you take some verse and put your own name in it. See if that helps." Ruth picked up her Bible and turned to a favorite chapter, Isaiah 53, and put her name in it: "But He was wounded for Ruth's transgressions; by His stripes Ruth is healed."

Her heart leaped, and the healing began.[1]

Date:			
Place:			
Occasion:			

Would It Make a Difference?

The well-known social critic Dennis Prager, debating the Oxford atheistic philosopher Jonathan Glover, raised this thorny question: *If you, Professor Glover, were stranded at the midnight hour in a desolate Los Angeles street, and if, as you stepped out of your car with fear and trembling, you were suddenly to hear the weight of pounding footsteps behind you, and you saw ten burly young men who had just stepped out of a dwelling coming toward you, would it or would it not make a difference to you to know they were coming from a Bible study?*[2]

Date:			
Place:			
Occasion:			

Revive Us Again

One day years ago, a teenager left home to attend college. His mother, worried about him, gave him a Bible and printed a verse of Scripture on the flyleaf. The young man soon discovered college life to be an endless series of parties, in which he spent all the money he could acquire on fleeting pleasures. On one occasion, he needed money for whiskey, and he pawned his Bible for it. Nevertheless, he eventually made it through college and became a doctor in a large hospital.

One day, Dr. Mackay treated a dying patient who knew that he was dying and asked for his "book." After the man passed away, Dr. Mackay noticed the man's "book" among his effects. He couldn't believe his eyes. It was the very Bible his

---

[1] Morgan, *On This Day,* September 2nd.
[2] Ravi Zacharias, *Can Man Live Without God?* (Dallas: Word Publishing, 1994), 41.

mother had given to him years before, with his name and the verse of Scripture still on the flyleaf.

He retreated to his office and began poring over the book. Several hours later he knelt and asked Jesus Christ to be his Savior and Lord. Dr. W. P. Mackay later became a minister and the writer of the old Gospel hymn "Revive Us, Again."

Date:	_____	_____	_____
Place:	_____	_____	_____
Occasion:	_____	_____	_____

Recalling the Bible

The biography of Geoffery Bull, a British missionary to Tibet who was captured and imprisoned by Chinese Communists, tells how his captors took his possessions from him, threw him in a series of prisons, robbed him of his Bible, and made him suffer terribly at their hands for three years. In addition to extreme temperatures and miserable physical conditions, bodily abuse and near starvation, Bull was subjected to such mental and psychological torture that he feared he would go insane.

How did he keep his mind at peace? He had no Bible now, but he had studied the Bible all his life. So he began to systematically go over the Scriptures in his mind. He found it took him about six months to go all the way through the Bible mentally. He started at Genesis and recalled each incident and story as best he could, first concentrating on the content and then musing on certain points, seeking light in prayer. He continued through the Old Testament, reconstructing the books and chapters as best he could, then into the New Testament, Matthew to Revelation. Then he started over again. He later wrote, "The strength received through this meditation was, I believe, a vital factor in bringing me through, kept by the faith to the very end."[1]

Date:	_____	_____	_____
Place:	_____	_____	_____
Occasion:	_____	_____	_____

———————— Bible: Scripture Memory ————————

Someone Once Said . . .

- *Like Joseph storing up grain during the years of plenty to be used during the years of famine that lay ahead, may we store up the truths of God's Word in our hearts as much as possible, so that we are prepared for whatever suffering we are called upon to endure.—* Billy Graham[2]

---

[1] Geoffrey T. Bull, *When Iron Gates Yield* (Chicago: Moody Press, n.d.).
[2] Billy Graham, *'Til Armageddon* (Minneapolis: WorldWide, 1981), 9.

- *[Memorizing Scripture is] the daily habit of supplying the subconscious with God's material to chew on.*—Bob Foster[1]
- *My mother stored my memory, which was then very retentive, with many valuable pieces, chapters, and portions of Scripture, catechisms, hymns, and poems. When the Lord at length opened my eyes, I found great benefit from the recollections of them.*—John Newton[2]

Date: _____ _____ _____

Place: _____ _____ _____

Occasion: _____ _____ _____

God Washed Her Brain

In his book *How To Be Born Again,* Billy Graham tells of a missionary who was imprisoned by the Japanese in China. At this concentration camp the penalty for owning even a portion of the Scriptures was death; however, a small Gospel of John was smuggled to her in a winter coat. At night when she went to bed she pulled the covers over her head and, with her flashlight in hand, read a verse and then put herself to sleep memorizing that verse. In this way, over a period of time, she memorized the entire Gospel of John.

When she went to wash her hands she would take one page at a time, dissolve it with the soap and water, and flush it down the drain. "And that is the way," she said, "that *John* and I parted company."

This little missionary was interviewed by a *Time* reporter just before the prisoners were released and he happened to be standing at the gates when the prisoners came out. Most of them shuffled along, eyes on the ground, little more than automatons. Then out came the little missionary, bright as a button. One of the reporters was heard to ask, "I wonder if they managed to brainwash her?"

The *Time* reporter overheard the remark and answered, "God washed her brain."[3]

Date: _____ _____ _____

Place: _____ _____ _____

Occasion: _____ _____ _____

Memorized Scripture at the Hanoi Hilton

When Howard Rutledge's plane was shot down over Vietnam, he parachuted into a little village and was immediately attacked, stripped naked, and imprisoned. For the next seven years he endured brutal treatment. His food was little more than a bowl of rotting soup with a glob of pig fat—skin, hair, and all. Rats the size of cats and spiders as big as fists scurried around him. He was frequently cold, alone, and tortured. He was sometimes shackled in excruciating positions and left for days

[1] Francis Cosgrove, "The Value of Scripture Memory," *Discipleship Journal,* Issue nine, 1982, 39.
[2] John Newton, "An Authentic Narrative," Letter 2, *Newton's Works* (Edinburgh, 1849), 3.
[3] Billy Graham, *How To Be Born Again* (Waco, TX: Word Publishing, 1977), 44–45.

in his own waste with carnivorous insects boring through his oozing sores. How did he keep his sanity?

In his book, *In the Presence of Mine Enemies,* Rutledge gives a powerful testimony as to the importance of Scripture memory. Some excerpts follow:

"Now the sights and sounds and smells of death were all around me. My hunger for spiritual food soon outdid my hunger for a steak. Now I wanted to know about that part of me that will never die. Now I wanted to talk about God and Christ and the church. But in Heartbreak solitary confinement there was no pastor, no Sunday-school teacher, no Bible, no hymnbook, no community of believers to guide and sustain me. I had completely neglected the spiritual dimension of my life. It took prison to show me how empty life is without God, and so I had to go back in my memory to those Sunday-school days in Tulsa, Oklahoma. If I couldn't have a Bible and hymnbook, I would try to rebuild them in my mind.

---◇---

God's Truth

May we store up the truths of God's Word in our hearts as much as possible.
—BILLY GRAHAM

---◇---

"I tried desperately to recall snatches of Scripture, sermons, gospel choruses from childhood, and hymns we sang in church. The first three dozen songs were relatively easy. Every day I'd try to recall another verse or a new song. One night there was a huge thunderstorm—it was the season of the monsoon rains—and a bolt of lightning knocked out the lights and plunged the entire prison into darkness. I had been going over hymn tunes in my mind and stopped to lie down and sleep when the rains began to fall. The darkened prison echoed with wave after wave of water. Suddenly, I was humming my thirty-seventh song, one I had entirely forgotten since childhood.

> *Showers of blessings,*
> *Showers of blessings we need!*
> *Mercy drops round us are falling,*
> *But for the showers we plead*

"I no sooner had recalled those words than another song popped into my mind, the theme song of a radio program my mother listened to when I was just a kid.

> *Heavenly sunshine, heavenly sunshine*
> *Flooding my soul with glory divine.*
> *Heavenly sunshine, heavenly sunshine,*
> *Hallelujah! Jesus is mine!*

"Most of my fellow prisoners were struggling like me to rediscover faith, to reconstruct workable value systems. Harry Jenkins lived in a cell nearby during much of my captivity. Often we would use those priceless seconds of communication in a day to help one another recall Scripture verses and stories.

"One day I heard him whistle. When the cell block was clear, I waited for his communication, thinking it to be some important news. 'I got a new one,' he said. 'I don't know where it comes from or why I remember it, but it's a story about Ruth and Naomi.' He then went on to tell that ancient story of Ruth following Naomi into a hostile new land and finding God's presence and protection there. Harry's urgent news was 2,000 years old. It may not seem important to prison life, but we lived off that story for days, rebuilding it, thinking about what it meant, and applying God's ancient words to our predicament.

"Everyone knew the Lord's Prayer and the Twenty-third Psalm, but the camp favorite verse that everyone recalled first and quoted most often is found in the Gospel of John, third chapter, sixteenth verse. . . . With Harry's help, I even reconstructed the seventeenth and eighteenth verses.

"How I struggled to recall those Scriptures and hymns! I had spent my first eighteen years in a Southern Baptist Sunday school, and I was amazed at how much I could recall. Regrettably, I had not seen then the importance of memorizing verses from the Bible, or learning gospel songs. Now, when I needed them, it was too late. I never dreamed that I would spend almost seven years (five of them in solitary confinement) in a prison in North Vietnam or that thinking about one memorized verse could have made the whole day bearable.

"One portion of a verse I did remember was, 'Thy word have I hid in my heart.' How often I wished I had really worked to hide God's Word in my heart. I put my mind to work. Every day I planned to accomplish certain tasks. I woke early, did my physical exercises, cleaned up as best I could, then began a period of devotional prayer and meditation. I would pray, hum hymns silently, quote Scripture, and think about what the verse meant to me.

"Remember, we weren't playing games. The enemy knew that the best way to break a man's resistance was to crush his spirit in a lonely cell. In other words, some of our POWs after solitary confinement lay down in a fetal position and died. All this talk of Scripture and hymns may seem boring to some, but it was the way we conquered our enemy and overcame the power of death around us."[1]

Date:		
Place:		
Occasion:		

20,000 Verses

In his book *Your Inner You*, pastor Leslie Flynn tells of his conversion to Christ during an evangelistic campaign led by Dr. Oscar Lowry, author of the book *Scripture Memorizing for Successful Soul-Winning.* Lowry admits that he entered Christian service as a young man with an undisciplined mind. Thinking he could not memorize Scripture, he filled the flyleaf of his Bible with references useful for counseling and evangelism, but it proved awkward to stop his conversations long enough to track down the right verse. Finally he determined to succeed at Scripture memory.

"If I can memorize one verse, I can memorize one more," he said, "and ten more, and even one hundred."

He rose early the next morning and chose what seemed to him a difficult passage, Romans 10:9–10. He paced the room, saying to himself, "I will do this thing." He struggled with this passage for half an hour, but finally succeeded in memorizing it completely. The next morning he reviewed and reinforced those verses in his memory, then added a new one. He kept reviewing his chosen passages and adding new ones until it dawned on him one day that he could repeat one hundred verses without looking in his Bible.

---

[1] Howard and Phyllis Rutledge and Mel and Lyla White, *In the Presence of Mine Enemies* (Old Tappan, NJ: Fleming H. Revell Co., 1973).

By the end of his life, he had learned over 20,000 verses, and he could locate each by chapter and verse without his Bible. No wonder his Christian life was full of joy, his mind full of wisdom, and his evangelistic efforts full of success.[1]

Date:	_____	_____	_____
Place:	_____	_____	_____
Occasion:	_____	_____	_____

So Full of the Bible . . .

Martin Seligman, noted psychologist at the University of Pennsylvania in Philadelphia, claims that most depressions are much simpler and more curable than commonly thought. The real disease, he says, is negative thinking. It isn't primarily childhood conflicts, unconscious anger, or faulty brain chemistry, but what Seligman calls "pessimistic explanatory style," being a negative "ruminator."

When the Word of God becomes engraved in our minds, it changes our perspective about life. That doesn't mean we'll live in constant euphoria, but it does provide an intellectual basis for optimistic thinking. One man called Scripture memory "the daily habit of supplying the subconscious with God's material to chew upon." The Apostle Paul said, "Fill your minds with those things that are good and that deserve praise: things that are true, noble, right, pure, lovely, and honorable . . . and the God of peace will be with you" (Philippians 4:8–9, TEV).

I recently read of a high-school student whose band performed on a Caribbean cruise. One night his buddies tried to entice him into the ship's bar, but Chad, whose mother was an alcoholic, had memorized verses from Proverbs about alcohol abuse. He explained to his friends that addiction ran in his family, then he had the courage to quote Scripture to them: "Wine is a mocker, strong drink is a brawler, and whoever is led astray by it is not wise." (20:1)

They replied, "Come on, Chad. Just one beer won't hurt."

He replied, "At the last it bites like a serpent and stings like a viper" (23:32). They accused him of rejecting their company, to which he said, "If sinners entice you, do not consent." (1:10)

"Leave him be," he heard one of the young men say to the others. "He's so full of Scripture we can't do a thing with him!"

Date:	_____	_____	_____
Place:	_____	_____	_____
Occasion:	_____	_____	_____

Ruth's Collection

"People are writing and talking about 'collectibles.' They can be a hedge against inflation, sort of a cushion in case of depression. They are small items that initially may have cost little or

---

[1] Leslie B. Flynn, *Your Inner You* (Wheaton, IL: Victor Books, 1984), 60.

B

nothing but that increase startlingly in value in a relatively short period of time. Included are old stamps, rare coins, old photographs, paintings, even certain cans and bottles.

"I got to thinking. What would be the best collectible for me? Something that would increase in value; something that would make me really wealthy; something I could share that would be a cushion in case of depression and could provide comfort in case of the death of a loved one or in old age.

"I had it! Bible verses. I had started long ago.

"In China, Miss Lucy Fletcher offered us, her students, $5.00 (a lot of money for a missionary's kid) if we would memorize the Sermon on the Mount. Hours and hours of going over and over Matthew 5, 6, 7. When the time came to recite it, I made one mistake so I got only $4.50. But I wouldn't take one thousand times that amount in place of having memorized it."[1]

Date: _____ _____ _____
Place: _____ _____ _____
Occasion: _____ _____ _____

What Scripture Memory Can Do for You

In his book, *How To Study the Bible for Yourself,* Tim LaHaye lists seven things that Scripture memory can do for you:

1. It will give you victory over sin.
2. It helps you overcome worry.
3. It will give you a confidence in sharing your faith.
4. It speeds up the transforming process.
5. It assists you in discovering God's will for your life.
6. It helps in your other Bible studies.
7. It outfits you for unlimited service to God.[2]

Date: _____ _____ _____
Place: _____ _____ _____
Occasion: _____ _____ _____

Bible Study

Someone Once Said . . .

- *There is dust enough on some of your Bibles to write "damnation" with your fingers.*— Charles Haddon Spurgeon[3]

---

[1] Ruth Bell Graham, *It's My Turn* (Old Tappan, NJ: Fleming H. Revell Co., 1982), 172.
[2] Tim LaHaye, *How To Study the Bible For Yourself* (Irvine, CA: Harvest House Publishers, 1976).
[3] Charles H. Spurgeon, *Spurgeon's Sermons,* vol. 1 (Grand Rapids: Baker Book House, 1983), 33.

- *If all the neglected Bibles were dusted simultaneously, we would have a record dust storm, and the sun would go into eclipse for a whole week.*—David F. Nygren
- *If we understood what happens when we use the Word of God, we would use it oftener.*—Oswald Chambers[1]
- *I have found that my spiritual growth is directly proportionate to the amount of time and effort I put into the study of Scripture.*—John MacArthur[2]
- *Other books were given for our information; the Bible was given for our transformation.*
- *Every study of the Bible is a study of the evidences of Christianity. The Bible itself is the greatest miracle of all.*—A. T. Pierson[3]
- *Those who know the Bible best find it ever new.*—attributed to D. L. Moody
- *The Bible that is falling apart usually belongs to someone who isn't.*
- *If you carry a Bible when you are young, it will carry you when you are old.*

Date:			
Place:			
Occasion:			

Reading Time

Half the books of the Bible can be read in ten to forty-five minutes each, and many of them can be read in less than twenty. The entire Old and New Testaments can be read aloud slowly and with expression in less than seventy-one hours.

Wilber M. Smith wrote, "It will probably astonish many to know that one single, normal issue of *The Saturday Evening Post* contains as much reading matter as the entire New Testament. Thousands of people read *The Saturday Evening Post* through every week. The number of Christians who read the New Testament through every week, or even one whole book of the New Testament every week, are so few that we need not talk about it."[4]

Date:			
Place:			
Occasion:			

Fathomless Bible Study

> My pail I'm often dropping
> Deep down into this well,
> It never touched the bottom,
> However deep it fell;

---

[1] Oswald Chambers, *Disciples Indeed* (London: Marshall, Morgan, & Scott, Ltd., 1955), 6.
[2] John F. MacArthur, Jr., *Why Believe the Bible* (Glendale, CA: Regal Books, 1980), 95.
[3] A. T. Pierson, *Many Infallible Proofs,* vol. 1 (Grand Rapids: Zondervan, n.d.), 90.
[4] Wilber M. Smith, *Profitable Bible Study* (Grand Rapids: Baker Book House, 1963), 61.

And though I keep on dipping
By study, faith and prayer,
I have no power to measure
The living water there.[1]

Date: _____ _____ _____
Place: _____ _____ _____
Occasion: _____ _____ _____

Cupboard of Neglect

Ah! You know more about your ledgers than your Bible; you know more about your daybooks than what God has written; many of you will read a novel from beginning to end, and what have you got? A mouthful of froth when you have done. But you cannot read the Bible; that solid, lasting, substantial, and satisfying food goes uneaten, locked up in the cupboard of neglect.—Charles Spurgeon[2]

Date: _____ _____ _____
Place: _____ _____ _____
Occasion: _____ _____ _____

Collecting Cookbooks

The *Wall Street Journal* reported that nearly one thousand different cookbooks are published each year in America, many of them glossy, full-color, and very expensive. But at the same time, fewer and fewer people are cooking, and increasing numbers are eating in restaurants. The reporter for the *Journal* interviewed one lady, a portfolio manager in New York; she has acquired sixteen cookbooks in the last four years and subscribes to two cooking magazines. But the last time she prepared a sit-down meal was four years ago, "and," she said, "it didn't turn out."

There are more Bible translations, study aids, and devotional books now than ever. Christian publishing is a big business in America. But for all that, people are reading and studying their Bible less and less.

Date: _____ _____ _____
Place: _____ _____ _____
Occasion: _____ _____ _____

Flake's Testimony

Arthur Flake, who inspired the Southern Baptist denomination to emphasize Sunday school work, shared this testimony in his book, *Life At Eighty as I See It:*

[1] J. Sidlow Baxter, *Explore the Book* (n.p., n.d.), 289.
[2] Spurgeon, *Spurgeon's Sermons*, vol. 1, 40.

When I first became a Christian, I lived in New York City, and did I feel lonely! I had to give up the crowd I was running with and form new friendships. I was advised by the man who led me to Christ to read the Bible. After business hours I would go to my room and read my Bible often for hours at a time. Though I did not understand all I read, and still do not, I did understand much that I read, and it made me feel that I was not alone but that I had a dear Friend who cared for me. Today I read the same identical verses and chapters I read then. Although I have read many of them hundreds of times, they are, I believe, sweeter today than they were then. What other book can one read with such results?[1]

Date: _____   _____   _____
Place: _____   _____   _____
Occasion: _____   _____   _____

Growing in the Word

[A] Augustine

Such is the depth of the Christian Scriptures that even if I were attempting to study them and nothing else from early boyhood to decrepit old age, with the utmost leisure, the most unwearied zeal, and talents greater than I have, I would still daily be making progress in discovering their treasures.—St. Augustine, in a letter to his son in A.D. 412.[2]

[B] Spurgeon

Nobody ever outgrows Scripture: the Book widens and deepens with our years.—Charles Spurgeon

Date: _____   _____   _____
Place: _____   _____   _____
Occasion: _____   _____   _____

Read It Some More

After passing through a period of skepticism, R. A. Torrey (1856–1928) yielded to Christ and studied in Germany. He was chosen in 1889 by D. L. Moody to oversee the fledgling Moody Bible Institute, and he also served as pastor of Moody Memorial Church. Between 1902 and 1906, he traveled around the world conducting evangelistic crusades with Charles M. Alexander, and from 1912 until 1924 he served as dean of the Bible Institute of Los Angeles (Biola)—all of this while speaking widely at Bible conferences and writing forty books.

His energy came from pouring himself into the Scripture.

Once a man approached him, a Dr. Congdon, complaining that he could get nothing out of his Bible study. The Scripture seemed to be dry as dust. "Please tell me how to study it so that it will mean something to me."

"Read it," replied Dr. Torrey.

---

[1] Arthur Flake, *Life At Eighty As I See It* (Nashville: Broadman Press, 1944), 97.
[2] Irving L. Jensen, *Enjoy Your Bible* (Minneapolis: World Wide Publications, n.d.), 25.

B

"I do read it."

"Read it some more."

"How?"

"Take some book and read it twelve times a day for a month."

"What book could I read that many times a day, working as many hours as I do?"

"Try 'Second Peter,'" replied Torrey.

The man later said, "My wife and I read 'Second Peter' three or four times in the morning, two or three times at noon, and two or three times at dinner. Soon I was talking 'Second Peter' to everyone one I met. It seemed as though the stars in the heavens were singing the story of 'Second Peter.' I read 'Second Peter' on my knees, marking passages. Teardrops mingled with the crayon colors, and I said to my wife, "See how I have ruined this part of my Bible."

"Yes," she said, "but as the pages have been getting black, your life has been getting white."[1]

Date: _____   _____   _____

Place: _____   _____   _____

Occasion: _____   _____   _____

Why Not Virgil?

In his biography of General Douglas MacArthur, *Rendezvous with History,* Major Courtney Whitney recounts an incident that occurred during the Korean War on the night preceding the Inchon landing. General MacArthur planned to encircle the North Korean forces that had driven south to Seoul and cut off their supply lines from the north. If successful, this stratagem might not only accelerate a drive toward victory, but more important, save the lives of some 100,000 U.N. troops.

It was a daring scheme. While encircling an enemy force was not a new strategy, it had never before been accomplished by way of the sea. Furthermore, the peculiar tides and unfavorable terrain at Inchon militated against an amphibious landing of troops. Yet that also contributed to MacArthur's decision to proceed; because of these impediments, the North Koreans would be caught unprepared for such a maneuver.

A Dusty Bible

The devil is not afraid of a Bible that has dust on it.

On the night before the landing, Courtney Whitney, who was aboard the flagship *Mount McKinley* with General Mac-Arthur, retired early in anticipation of the action at dawn. He'd been asleep only a short time when he was summoned to MacArthur's cabin. He found the General in bathrobe and slippers, pacing the floor. Whitney was told to be seated. MacArthur in a kind of self-debate talked as he walked the cabin, reviewing one by one the arguments against the proposed landing in the morning. MacArthur then countered with the reasons for the surprise assault.

---

[1] Robert J. Morgan, *From This Verse* (Nashville: Thomas Nelson Publishers, 1998), December 16th.

Finally at about 2:30 A.M., he concluded that his decision was a sound one. "Thanks, Court," the General said to Whitney. "Thanks for listening to me. Now let's get some sleep."

Then Courtney Whitney added these words: [*General MacArthur*] *threw off his robe, climbed into his bed and reached to the table alongside to pick up his Bible.*

Why the Bible? Why not Virgil or Shakespeare or Bunyan or Keats or Tennyson or Hemingway?

Can anyone live day-by-day, year-after-year, by Virgil? Is there life and power and comfort of temporal or eternal value in *The Divine Comedy?* What poetry or novel, however great, will hold its freshness when read again and again or committed to memory?

The Bible, on the other hand, possesses the power of life. It gives us teaching for conviction, for restoration, and for education in righteousness. It reveals God in His fullness through Jesus Christ. It strengthens; it encourages; it comforts; it challenges. It's a lamp to the feet, a light on our pathway. Not only day-by-day, but year-by-year, decade after decade, it can be read over and over again until its words become a part of life itself. Yet it never grows old or out of date.[1]

Date: _____ _____ _____
Place: _____ _____ _____
Occasion: _____ _____ _____

Coverdale's Plan of Bible Study

The English Bible translator, Miles Coverdale, whose version became the basis for the King James Version, listed his own Bible study techniques in the preface to his 1535 translation:

> *It shall greatly helpe ye to understand the Scripture,*
> *If thou mark*
> *Not only what is spoken or wrytten,*
> *But of whom,*
> *And to whom,*
> *With what words,*
> *At what time,*
> *Where,*
> *To what intent,*
> *With what circumstances,*
> *Considering what goeth before and what followeth.*

Date: _____ _____ _____
Place: _____ _____ _____
Occasion: _____ _____ _____

---

[1] Haddon Robinson, "On Target," *Focal Point: A Publication of Denver Seminary.*

George Mueller's Practice

The German Christian George Mueller, who developed highly successful ministries to homeless children in the nineteenth century, wrote this in his diary on May 9, 1841:

It has pleased the Lord to teach me a truth, the benefit of which I have not lost for more than fourteen years. The point is this: I saw more clearly than ever that the first great primary business to which I ought to attend every day was to have my soul happy in the Lord. The first thing to be concerned about was not how much I might serve the Lord, or how I might glorify the Lord; but how I might get my soul into a happy state, and how my inner man might be nourished. . . .

Before this time my practice had been, at least for ten years previously, as a habitual thing, to give myself to prayer after having dressed myself in the morning. Now, I saw that the most important thing I had to do was to give myself to the reading of the Word of God, and to meditation on it, that thus my heart might be comforted, encouraged, warned, reproved, instructed. . . .

The first thing I did, after having asked in a few words the Lord's blessing upon His precious Word, was to begin to meditate on the Word of God, searching as it were into every verse to get blessing out of it; not for the sake of public ministry of the Word, not for the sake of preaching on what I had meditated upon, but for the sake of obtaining food for my soul. The result I have found to be almost invariably this, that after a very few minutes my soul has been led to confession, or to thanksgiving, or to supplication; so that, though I did not, as it were, give myself to prayer, but to meditation, yet it turned almost immediately more or less into prayer. When thus I have been for a while making confession or intercession or supplication, or have given thanks, I go on to the next words or verse, turning all, as I go, into prayer for myself or others, as the Word may lead to it. . . .

By breakfast time, with rare exceptions, I am in a peaceful if not happy state of heart.

Date: _____   _____   _____

Place: _____   _____   _____

Occasion: _____   _____   _____

Ruth's Desk

In her autobiography, *It's My Turn*, Ruth Bell Graham wrote:

It could be merely a piece of plywood stretched across two sawhorses. But have a special place for Bible study that doesn't have to be shared with sewing or letter writing or the paying of bills. For years, mine was just an old wooden table between an upright chest of drawers and a taller desk. This year I fixed myself a permanent office upstairs, and my Bible study in the bedroom is now a big rolltop desk I have had for years.

But on this desk I have collected a number of good translations of the Bible for reference, a Bible dictionary, a concordance, and several devotional books. I also keep notebooks, a mug full of pens, and one particular Rapidograph pen, with a point like needle, that writes on India paper without smearing or going through.

When we were in school, we always kept a notebook handy to take notes on the professor's lecture. How much more important it is to take notes when God is teaching us.

If a busy housewife has to clear off a spot for Bible study during a crowded day, she is likely to put it off. But if she has a place where her Bible is always open and handy, whenever there is a lull in the storm she can grab a cup of coffee and sit down for a few minutes or more of pure refreshment and companionship.[1]

Date: _____ _____ _____

Place: _____ _____ _____

Occasion: _____ _____ _____

If It Be the Word of God . . .

G. Campbell Morgan had grown up in a Christian home, never questioning that the Bible was the Word of God. But in college, his faith was severely challenged and he began to entertain doubts. "The whole intellectual world was under the mastery of the physical scientists," he later said, "and of a materialistic and rationalistic philosophy. Darwin, Huxley, Tyndall, Spencer, Bain. There came a moment when I was sure of nothing."

In those days, opponents of the Bible appeared every Sunday in great lecture and concert halls across England, attacking Christianity and the Bible, and these brilliant atheists and agnostics troubled the young student. He read every book he could find, both for and against the Bible, both for and against Christianity, until he was so confused, so riddled with doubt that he felt he couldn't go on.

In desperation, he closed his books, put them in his cupboard and turned the lock. Going down to a bookshop, he bought a new Bible, returned to his room, sat down at his desk, and opened it. He said, *I am no longer sure that this is what my father claims it to be—the Word of God. But of this I am sure. If it be the Word of God, and if I come to it with an unprejudiced and open mind, it will bring assurance to my soul of itself.* As he looked into the book before him, studying its form and structure and unity and message, he was amazed. He later said, *That Bible found me. I began to read and study it then, in 1883, and I have been a student ever since.*[2]

Date: _____ _____ _____

Place: _____ _____ _____

Occasion: _____ _____ _____

——————————— Bitterness ———————————

Someone Once Said . . .

- *He that carries [bitterness] to bed with him will find the devil creep between the sheets.*— Rev. William Secker[3]

[1] Ruth Bell Graham, *It's My Turn* (Old Tappan, NJ: Fleming H. Revell Co., 1982), 170.

[2] Jill Morgan, *A Man of the Word: Life of G. Campbell Morgan* (Grand Rapids: Baker Book House, 1972), 38–41.

[3] William Secker, *The Nonsuch Professor In His Meridian Splendor* (Chicago: Fleming H. Revell Co., 1899), 150.

- *Wouldn't our enemies rub their hands with glee if they knew that our hate for them was exhausting us, making us tired and nervous, ruining our looks, giving us heart trouble, and probably shortening our lives?*—Dale Carnegie[1]
- *No matter how long you nurse a grudge, it won't get better.*—Anonymous

Date:			
Place:			
Occasion:			

Causes of Bitterness

The book *How To Beat Burnout* suggests that bitterness is "a hidden root of burnout," and isolates five reasons why people tend to grow bitter:

1. *Wrong motives or jealousy.* In counseling Christians, we frequently see bitterness associated with jealousy. The examples include successful attorneys who envy the abilities of their colleagues, Bible college and seminary students consumed with jealousy toward fellow students . . . pastors or missionaries envious of others who have seen more outward evidences of success.
2. *Wrong response to irritations; conditional love.* In Colossians 3:19 Paul instructs husbands to "love your wives and do not be bitter toward them." The Greek word *pikroi* used here (for the word *bitter*) demonstrates "resentment or an incensed and angry attitude of mind." Conditional love produces harshness and bitterness both in husbands and wives frequently, that can lead to marital burnout.
3. *Wrong response to adversity.* In Hebrews 12:15, we discover a warning against "any root of bitterness springing up," instead of enduring hardship as a discipline.
4. *Misplaced strife.* We have seen churches that have been crippled in their effectiveness for years because of bitter envying and strife on the part of church leaders.
5. *An unforgiving spirit.* Ephesians 4:31–32 draws a clear connection between bitterness and what is perhaps its most basic underlying cause, a refusal to forgive. "Let all bitterness be put away from you . . . Be kind to one another . . . forgiving one another. . . ."[2]

Date:			
Place:			
Occasion:			

"Charlie, It's Gone!"

One night in China, Southern Baptist missionary C. L. Culpepper stayed up late for devotions, but as he tried to pray he felt like stone. Finally he asked, "Lord, what is the matter?"

[1] Dale Carnegie, *How To Stop Worrying and Start Living* (New York: Simon and Schuster, 1948), 102.
[2] Frank Minirth, Don Hawkins, Paul Meier, Richard Flournoy, *How To Beat Burnout* (Chicago: Moody Press, 1986), ch. 4.

I had opened my Bible to Romans 2:17. It seemed the Apostle Paul were speaking directly to me when he said, "But if you call yourself a Christian and rely upon the Gospel, and boast of your relation to God, and know His will, and approve what is excellent; and if you are sure you are a guide to the blind, a light to those in darkness, a correction to the foolish, a teacher of children—you then who teach others, will you not teach yourself?"

The Holy Spirit used this verse like a sword to cut deeply into my heart. He said, "You are a hypocrite! You claim to be a Christian! What have you really done for Christ? The Lord said those who believed on Him would have rivers of living waters flowing from their inmost being! Do you have that kind of power?"

Culpepper awakened his wife, and they prayed into the night. The next morning at a prayer meeting with fellow workers, he confessed to pride and spiritual impotence, saying his heart was broken. The Holy Spirit began to so convict the others of sin that they could hardly bear it.

I watched their faces grow pale, then they began to cry and drop on their knees or fall prostrate on the floor. Missionaries went to missionaries confessing wrong feelings toward one another. Chinese preachers, guilty of envy, jealousy and hatred, confessed their sins to one another.

The revival spread through the seminary, the schools, the hospital, and the area churches. Perhaps the deepest impact was made on Culpepper's friend Wiley B. Glass, a much respected missionary. As Glass sat in the meetings, a man's face came before him and God seemed to be asking him about his attitude toward that man. Glass had hated the man for many years, and suddenly the Holy Spirit brought him under deep conviction.

In great anguish, Glass went to Culpepper, fell on his shoulder, and said, "Charlie, pray for me!" Both men went to their knees, but Glass was so distressed he couldn't express his problem. *He was pale as death and kept groaning in his anxiety. I prayed with him and for him several times during that day and the next. In the evening of the second day he came running to me and threw his arms around me.*

"Charlie, it's gone!" he exclaimed.

I said, "What's gone?" He replied, "That old root of bitterness."

He told me that thirty years earlier, before he came to China, a man had insulted his wife. The insult had made him so angry he felt he could kill the man if he ever saw him again. He realized a called servant of God should not feel that way, and it had bothered him for years. Finally he just turned the man over to God. When the Holy spirit began working in his heart during that week, the question came, "Are you willing for that man to be saved?"

He answered, "Lord, I'm willing for You to save him . . . just keep him on the other side of heaven!" Finally, he came to the place where he said, "Lord, if that man is alive, and if I can find him when I go on furlough, I will confess my hatred to him and do my best to win him to You." When he reached that decision, the Lord released the joys of heaven to his soul, and he was filled with love and peace. He became a more effective preacher for the Lord, and during the next few years he led hundreds to Christ.[1]

Bitter Heat

Heat not a furnace for your foe so hot that it do singe yourself.

—WILLIAM SHAKESPEARE

---

[1] C. L. Culpepper, "The Shantung Revival," *Spirit of Revival*, October 1991, 10–15. Also recorded in: Eloise Glass Cauthen, *Higher Ground: The Biography of Wiley B. Glass, Missionary to China* (Nashville: Broadman, 1978), 152.

Date: _____   _____   _____
Place: _____   _____   _____
Occasion: _____   _____   _____

Ahab and Anguish Lay Stretched Together

One of the most powerful pictures of the embittered heart is seen in Herman Melville's character Captain Ahab in *Moby Dick.* In a violent confrontation at sea, the great white whale dubbed Moby Dick had sliced off Ahab's leg. Ahab had been carried to his bunk in the bowels of the ship and there he lay, clinging to life, leg absent, during the return voyage.

For long months of days and weeks, Ahab and anguish lay stretched together in one hammock, rounding in midwinter that dreary, howling Patagonian Cape, then it was, that his torn body and gashed soul bled into one another and so interfusing, made him mad.

Ahab was eventually fitted with a peg leg, but there was no prosthesis for the soul. Obsessed with hate, Ahab set his face to search out and destroy Moby Dick, whatever the cost. He fitted a ship, hired a crew, and mounted a voyage of vengeance which led to his death, the destruction of his ship the *Pequod,* and the loss of all his men save one, Ishmael, who lived to tell the tale.

Date: _____   _____   _____
Place: _____   _____   _____
Occasion: _____   _____   _____

Just As I Am

She was an embittered woman, Charlotte Elliott of Brighton, England. Her health was broken, and her disability had hardened her. "If God loved me," she muttered, "he would not have treated me this way."

Hoping to help her, a Swiss minister named Dr. Cesar Malan visited the Elliotts on May 9, 1822. Over dinner, Charlotte lost her temper and railed against God and family in a violent outburst. Her embarrassed family left the room, and Dr. Malan, left alone with her, stared at her across the table.

"You are tired of yourself, aren't you?" he said at length. "You are holding to your hate and anger because you have nothing else in the world to cling to. Consequently, you have become sour, bitter, and resentful."

"What is your cure?" asked Charlotte.

"The faith you are trying to despise."

As they talked, Charlotte softened. "If I wanted to become a Christian and to share the peace and joy you possess," she finally asked, "what would I do?"

"You would give yourself to God just as you are now, with your fightings and fears, hates and loves, pride and shame."

"I would come to God just as I am? Is that right?"

Charlotte did come just as she was. Her heart was changed that day. As time passed she found and claimed John 6:37 as a special verse for her: ". . . the one who comes to Me I will by no means cast out."

Several years later, her brother, Rev. Henry Elliott, was raising funds for a school for the children of poor clergymen. Charlotte wrote a poem, and it was printed and sold across England. The leaflet said: *Sold For the Benefit of St. Margaret's Hall, Brighton: Him That Cometh To Me I Will In No Wise Cast Out.* Underneath was Charlotte's poem—which has since become the most famous invitational hymn in history:

> *Just as I am, without one plea,*
> *But that Thy blood was shed for me,*
> *And that Thou bidd'st me come to Thee,*
> *O Lamb of God, I come! I come!*[1]

Date: _____ _____ _____

Place: _____ _____ _____

Occasion: _____ _____ _____

Trash

Despite his great insights into the human mind, Sigmund Freud died at the age of eighty-three, a bitter and disillusioned old man who proved unable to sustain his friendships. He wrote in 1918, "I have found little that is good about human beings on the whole. In my experience most of them are trash. . . ."

Date: _____ _____ _____

Place: _____ _____ _____

Occasion: _____ _____ _____

Five Miles Ago

In his book *Guiding Your Family in a Misguided World,* Dr. Tony Evans tells of two monks walking through the countryside toward another village. As they came to the edge of a river, they saw an old woman sitting there, upset because there was no bridge. The first monk offered to carry her across, to the woman's great relief. So the two monks joined hands, lifted her between them and carried her across the river. When they got to the other side, they set her down, and she went on her way.

After they had walked another mile or so, the second monk began to complain. "Look at my clothes," he said. "They are filthy from carrying that woman across the river. And my back still hurts from lifting her. I can feel it getting stiff." The first monk just smiled and nodded his head.

A few minutes later, the second monk griped again, "My back is hurting me so badly, and it is all because we had to carry that silly woman across the river! I cannot

---

[1] Robert J. Morgan, *From This Verse* (Nashville: Thomas Nelson Publishers, 1998), September 4th.

B

go any farther because of the pain. Why is it you're not complaining about it, too? Doesn't your back hurt?"

"Of course not," the first monk replied. "You're still carrying the woman, but I set her down five miles ago."

We are often like that second monk who cannot let go of the pain of the past, and we still carry the burdens of things done years ago.

Date: _____ _____ _____
Place: _____ _____ _____
Occasion: _____ _____ _____

Blessings

Someone Once Said . . .

- *The Lord Jesus spreads a large table every day.*—Rev. William Secker[1]
- *The goodness of God is the drive behind all the blessings He daily bestows upon us.*—A. W. Tozer[2]
- *A hog will eat acorns under a tree day after day, never looking up to see where they came from. Some people are like that—but others are led through their blessings to realize the love of their heavenly Father.*—Charles Allen[3]

Date: _____ _____ _____
Place: _____ _____ _____
Occasion: _____ _____ _____

Two Kinds of Blessings

There are two blessings we often overlook: spiritual blessings and simple blessings. One man who came to appreciate the latter was Viktor Frankl, the renowned psychiatrist who endured years of unspeakable horror in Nazi death camps. In his classic book, *Man's Search for Meaning,* he wrote of the dreams often experienced by his fellow inmates at Auschwitz and Dachau:

What did the prisoner dream about most frequently? Of bread, cake, cigarettes, and nice warm baths. The lack of having these simple desires satisfied led him to seek wish-fulfillment in dreams.

Date: _____ _____ _____
Place: _____ _____ _____
Occasion: _____ _____ _____

---

[1] William Secker, *The Nonsuch Professor In His Meridian Splendor* (Chicago: Fleming H. Revell Co., 1899), 151.
[2] A. W. Tozer, *Knowledge of the Holy* (New York: Harper & Row, 1961), 88.
[3] Charles L. Allen, *Prayer Changes Things* (Westwood, NJ: Fleming H. Revell Co., 1964), 73.

Matthew Henry's Blessings

As to spiritual blessings, Matthew Henry was a master at recognizing them early in life. Henry died in 1714 when only fifty-two years of age, but his influence has spanned three centuries, chiefly through his *Bible Commentary*. He began the massive work in November 1704, and the first volume was published four years later. Four other volumes followed, and by his death he had completed his expositions through the book of Acts. After his death, thirteen scholars worked from his notes to finish the Epistles and Revelation. The complete edition of his great work appeared on bookstore shelves in 1811.

Matthew Henry's rich heart and mind were in evidence even at age thirteen. On October 18, 1675, he made this entry in his journal. He called it "A Catalogue of the Mercies of God." Recording his conversion three years earlier, he wrote:

For Spiritual Mercies; for the Lord Jesus Christ, his incarnation, Life, Death, Resurrection, Ascension and Intercession, for Grace, Pardon, Peace, for the Word, the means of Grace, for Prayer, for good Instructions, for the Good I have got at any time under the Word, for any Succour and Help from God under Temptation, for Brokenness of Heart, for an Enlightening. Lord Jesus, I bless thee for thy Word, for good Parents, for good Education, that I was taken into Covenant betimes at Baptism; and Lord, I give thee thanks, that I am thine and will be thine.

I think it was three years ago that I began to be convinced, hearing a Sermon by my Father on Psalm 51:17. "The Sacrifices of God are a broken Spirit; a broken and a contrite Heart, O God, thou wilt not despise." I think it was this that melted me, afterwards, I began to enquire after Christ.

Date: _____   _____   _____

Place: _____   _____   _____

Occasion: _____   _____   _____

Unsearchable Riches

A. T. Pierson (1837–1911), powerful preacher, educator, and missionary statesman, once tried to preach on God's blessings as described in Ephesians 1—3, a section of Scripture that continually talks about our unsearchable wealth and riches in Christ. Pierson said:

In the words of the text, "the unsearchable riches of Christ," "unsearchable" literally means riches that can never be explored. You not only cannot count or measure them, but you can form no estimate of them; and you not only can form no estimate of them, but you never can get to the end of your investigation. There is a boundless continent, a world, a universe of riches, that still lies before you, when you have carried your search to the limits of possibility. I feel as though I had a theme, about which no man ought to speak. An archangel's tongue could do no justice to it.

Pierson nevertheless tried to point out the truths about the believer's wealth as described in these three chapters. Then he told his congregation:

I sink back exhausted, in the vain attempt to set before this congregation the greatest mystery of grace that I ever grappled with. I cannot remember, in thirty years of Gospel preaching, ever

to have been confronted with a theme that more baffled every outreach of thought and every
possibility of utterance than the theme that I have now attempted in the name of God to present.[1]

Date: _____   _____   _____
Place: _____   _____   _____
Occasion: _____   _____   _____

Millionaire Unawares

In west Texas there is a famous oil field known as the Yates pool. During the depression this field was a sheep ranch, owned by a man named Yates. Mr. Yates was not able to make enough money on his ranching operation to pay the principal and interest on the mortgage, so he was in danger of losing his ranch. With little money for clothes or food, his family, like many others, had to live on a government subsidy. Day after day, as he grazed his sheep over those rolling west Texas hills, he was no doubt greatly troubled about how he would be able to pay his bills.

Then a seismographic crew from an oil company came into the area and told Mr. Yates that there might be oil on his land. They asked permission to drill a wildcat well, and he signed a lease.

The Father's Love

Some people are led through their blessings to realize the love of their heavenly Father.
—CHARLES ALLEN

At 1,115 feet they struck a huge oil reserve, giving 80,000 barrels a day. In fact, thirty years after the discovery, a government test of one of the wells showed that it still could flow 125,000 barrels of oil a day. And Mr. Yates owned it all. The day he purchased the land he received the oil and mineral rights. Yet, he was living on relief. A multimillionaire living in poverty: What was the problem? He did not know the oil was there. He owned it, but he did not possess it.

That is like many Christians today who don't realize how rich they are in Christ.[2]

Date: _____   _____   _____
Place: _____   _____   _____
Occasion: _____   _____   _____

Riches Unawares

Charles Spurgeon told a similar story. He said he was visiting an elderly woman in the almshouse. His attention was drawn to a framed document on the wall of her room, and he asked her about it. She said that years before, she had cared for an aged gentleman, and before he had died, he had written out a little note of appreciation to her followed by his signature. He had shortly afterwards died.

---

[1] A. T. Pierson, *The Gospel: Its Heart, Heights, and Hopes*, vol. 1 (Grand Rapids: Baker Book House, 1978), 220, 234.
[2] *Parables, Etc.,* vol. 3, No. 11, January 1984, 4.

After much persuasion Spurgeon was allowed to borrow the paper. When he took it to the bank, they exclaimed, "We've been wondering to whom the old gentleman left his money."

She was a wealthy woman, but she had been living like a beggar.[1]

Date: _____ _____ _____
Place: _____ _____ _____
Occasion: _____ _____ _____

Such As . . .

F. E. Marsh once listed some of God's blessings for his children:

- An acceptance that can never be questioned. (Ephesians 1:6).
- An inheritance that can never be lost (1 Peter 1:3–5).
- A deliverance that can never be excelled (2 Corinthians 1:10).
- A grace that can never be limited (2 Corinthians 12:9).
- A hope that can never be disappointed. (Hebrews 6:18, 19).
- A bounty that can never be withdrawn. (1 Colossians 3:21–23).
- A joy that need never be diminished (John 15:11).
- A nearness to God that can never be reversed (Ephesians 2:13).
- A peace that can never be disturbed (John 14:27).
- A righteousness that can never be tarnished (2 Corinthians 5:21).
- A salvation that can never be canceled (Hebrews 5:9).[2]

Date: _____ _____ _____
Place: _____ _____ _____
Occasion: _____ _____ _____

Blood of Christ

Someone Once Said . . .

- *The Bible is a book of blood . . . wholly distinct from all other books for just one reason, namely, that it contains blood circulating through every page and in every verse. From Genesis to Revelation we see the stream of blood.*—M. R. DeHaan[3]
- *Love is that liquor (liquid) sweet and most divine / Which my God feels as blood; but I as wine.*—George Herbert, Anglican priest and poet of "The Agonie"
- *Everything about the death of Christ was bloody—the slapping of his face must have cut his face; the scourge ripped apart his back; the crown of thorns pierced his brow; blood from his hands and ankles spurted with every blow of the hammer; blood likely oozed*

---

[1] Leslie B. Flynn, *19 Gifts of the Spirit* (Wheaton: Victor Books, 1975), 203–204.
[2] Clipped from my files.
[3] M. R. DeHaan, *The Chemistry of the Blood* (Grand Rapids: Zondervan, 1943), 13.

from his nose and mouth as he writhed on the cross; blood and water gushed from his side when the lance tore him open. It was not a bloodless death. It was a death designed to paint the cross crimson.

Date: _____ _____ _____

Place: _____ _____ _____

Occasion: _____ _____ _____

Delivery Trucks and Miniature Soldiers

Municipal areas require well-organized delivery and defense systems.

Almost every part of a city requires supplies, such as water, food, dry goods, and factory orders on a constant basis. These supplies must be delivered through a transportation system consisting of thousands of trucks with access to every part of the city through a complex of freeways, highways, streets, and alleys. The trucks transport supplies along city streets to stores and homes, while other trucks remove waste and allow the city to function and thrive.

Our bodies have a transportation system so complex and complete that it dwarfs that of a metropolis. The body's transportation system cuts through every tissue and organ by means of a network of sixty thousand miles of blood vessels. No cell of your body lies more than a hair's breadth from a blood capillary. The center of this vast system is a pump the size of an apple or a fist, that pumps two thousand gallons of blood through its chambers every day, sending blood to every part of the body. The blood carries vital, life-giving oxygen and nutrients to every cell in the body.

The body has twenty-five trillion red blood cells, which are like little UPS trucks carrying all sorts of packages (such as oxygen) that are needed by the cells in the body. Every cell in the body requires oxygen to remain alive. If the blood is cut off to any part of the body, it deprives that part of the body of oxygen, and that bodily part will die. If the brain is deprived of oxygen, the brain dies, and the body dies.

The white blood cells, meanwhile, are like billions of little tanks protecting the body. There are five different kinds of these white blood cells, and each one is trained to go after a different enemy. One drop of blood can contain anywhere from seven thousand to twenty-five thousand white blood cells, and the number of them increases when our body is fighting an illness, just like the government calling up the reserves.

As far as our skeletal structure is concerned, our bones do double duty. Not only do they support the body, keep us upright, and keep us from being amoeba-like blobs, but they are hollow. On the inside of these bones are marvelous little factories that operate day and night, producing these billions of little trucks and tanks.

The brain oversees the entire operation, and the heart keeps it functioning.

Thirty-five hundred years ago, God told us, "The life is in the blood."

And when Jesus Christ died, the life-giving blood drained from his body, providing forgiveness and life to all who believe.

Date: _____   _____   _____
Place: _____   _____   _____
Occasion: _____   _____   _____

Blood Under the Door

On the corner of the square in Rotterdam, Holland, there once stood a house known as the House of Terrors. The name comes from the sixteenth century when King Philip II of Spain, an arch-Roman Catholic, came against the Protestants of Holland, sending the Duke of Alva to slaughter them.

Spanish troops went house to house throughout Rotterdam, searching out Protestants and killing them. In this one particular house, a handful of men, women, and children heard the soldiers approaching. They heard the pounding of doors, the screams of victims, and the marching of feet coming toward them. Terror gripped their hearts.

But a young man suddenly got an idea. He took a goat in the house, killed it, and swept its blood under the doorway out onto the street. When the solders reached the house, they saw blood flowing from under the door, and, assuming their compatriots had already taken care of the job in that house, went their way.

Date: _____   _____   _____
Place: _____   _____   _____
Occasion: _____   _____   _____

Biblical Data

- Genesis 4:10–11—First reference to blood: *The voice of your brother's blood cries out to Me from the ground. So now you are cursed from the earth, which has opened its mouth to receive your brother's blood.* . . . This illustrates the reverential fear of the shedding of blood and its association with life.
- Genesis 9:4—*But you shall not eat flesh with its life, that is, its blood.*
- Genesis 49:11—*He washed his garments in wine, and his clothes in the blood of grapes.* Here Jacob is figuratively referring to grape juice as "the blood of grapes."
- Exodus 12:6–7, 13—*Keep [the lamb] until the fourteenth day of the same month. Then the whole assembly of the congregation of Israel shall kill it at twilight. And they shall take some of the blood and put it on the two doorposts and on the lintel of the houses where they eat it. . . . Now the blood shall be a sign for you on the houses where you are. And when I see the blood, I will pass over you. . . .*
- Leviticus 17:11—*For the life of the flesh is in the blood, and I have given it to you upon the altar to make atonement for your souls; for it is the blood that makes atonement for the soul.*
- Leviticus 17:13–14—*Whatever man of the children of Israel, or of the strangers who dwell among you, who hunts and catches any animal or bird that may be eaten, he shall pour out its blood and cover it with dust; for it is the life of all flesh. Its blood sustains its life.*

- Matthew 26:27–28—*Then He took from the cup, and gave thanks, and gave it to them, saying, "Drink from it, all of you. For this is My blood of the new covenant, which is shed for many for the remission of sins."*
- John 19:34—*But one of the soldiers pierced His side with a spear, and immediately blood and water came out.*
- Acts 20:28—*. . . take heed to yourselves and to all the flock . . . the church of God which He purchased with His own blood.*
- Romans 3:25—*. . . whom God set forth as a propitiation by His blood. . . .*
- Romans 5:9—*. . . having now been justified by His blood, we shall be saved from wrath through Him.*
- Ephesians 1:7—*In Him we have redemption through His blood, the forgiveness of sins, according to the riches of His grace.*
- Hebrews 9:7–22—*Into the [holy of holies] the high priest went alone once a year, not without blood, which he offered for himself and for the people's sins. . . . But Christ came as High Priest . . . not with the blood of goats and calves, but with His own blood He entered the Most Holy Place once for all, having obtained eternal redemption. For if the blood of bulls and goats and the ashes of a heifer, sprinkling the unclean, sanctifies for the purifying of the flesh, how much more shall the blood of Christ, who through the eternal Spirit offered Himself without spot to God, cleanse your conscience from dead works to serve the living God? . . . without shedding of blood there is no remission.*
- 1 Peter 1:18–19—*Knowing that you were not redeemed with corruptible things, like silver or gold, from your aimless conduct received by tradition from your fathers, but with the precious blood of Christ, as of a lamb without blemish and without spot.*
- 1 John 1:7—*. . . the blood of Jesus Christ His Son cleanses us from all sin.*
- Revelation 1:5—*To Him who loved us and washed us from our sins in His own blood. . . .*
- Revelation 5:9—*. . . For you were slain, / And have redeemed us to God by Your blood / Out of every tribe and tongue and people and nation.*

Date: _____   _____   _____

Place: _____   _____   _____

Occasion: _____   _____   _____

The Blood As a Cleansing Agent

William Cooper's hymn speaks of "a fountain filled with blood drawn from Emmanuel's veins, where sinners, plunged beneath that flood, lose all their guilty stains." The apostle John said that the blood of Jesus Christ "cleanses from all sin." The multitude in Revelation 7 had washed their robes and made them white in the blood of the Lamb.

But how is blood a cleaning agent? To us, blood is a soiling or staining agent, something we try to scrub *off*, not scrub *with*.

Dr. Henry Brand explained it this way in *Christianity Today:*

All that we have learned about physiology in recent years confirms the accuracy of the still-jarring juxtaposition of blood and cleansing. . . .

I suggest a simple experiment if you truly wish to grasp the function of blood as a cleansing agent. Find a blood pressure kit and wrap the cuff around your upper arm. When it is in position, have a friend pump it up to about 200 mm. of mercury, a sufficient pressure to stop the flow of blood in your arm. Initially your arm will feel an uncomfortable tightness beneath the cuff. Now comes the revealing part of the experiment: perform any easy task with your cuffed arm. Merely flex your finger and make a fist about ten times in succession, or cut paper with scissors, or drive a nail into wood with a hammer.

The first few movements will seem quite normal as the muscles obediently contract and relax. Then you will feel a slight weakness. Almost without warning a hot flash of pain will strike, after maybe ten movements. Your muscles will cramp. If you force yourself to continue this simple task, you will likely cry out in absolute agony. Finally, you cannot force yourself to continue; the pain overwhelms you.

======= ◇ =======
The Cleansing Blood

*He breaks the power of
    cancelled sin,
He sets the prisoner free;
His blood can make the
    foulest clean;
His blood availed for me.*
    —CHARLES WESLEY
======= ◇ =======

When your release the tourniquet and air escapes from the cuff, blood will rush into your aching arm and a wonderful sense of relief will soothe your muscles. . . . Physiologically, you have just experienced the cleansing of the blood.

While the blood supply to your arm was shut off, you forced your muscles to keep working. As they converted oxygen into energy, they produced certain waste products (metabolites) that are normally flushed away instantly in the bloodstream. Due to the constricted blood flow, however, these metabolites accumulated in your cells. They were not "cleansed" by the swirling stream of blood, and therefore in a few minutes you felt the agony of retained toxins.[1]

Date: _____   _____   _____
Place: _____   _____   _____
Occasion: _____   _____   _____

"Ahhh!"

In an article in *Christianity Today,* Dr. Paul Brand shares an experience from his early days in India as a missionary physician. He arrived as an orthopedic surgeon at the Christian Medical College in Vellore to work alongside a famous surgeon, Dr. Reeve Bretts from Boston. The doctors in Vellore were vexed over the unwillingness of most Indians to donate blood. "To them," Brand wrote, "blood is life, and who can tolerate the thought of giving up lifeblood, even to save someone else?" Sometimes, parents were unwilling to donate blood even to save the lives of their own children.

One day a twelve-year-old girl was admitted to the hospital, suffering from a very bad lung. Only the removing of her lung would save her life. The surgery required at least three pints of blood. Since the hospital had two pints, only one pint was required from the family. After huddling, the family pooled their money and offered to buy the additional pint.

With his patience running out, Dr. Bretts explained that there was no blood to

---

[1] Paul Brand and Philip Yancy, "Blood: The Miracle of Cleansing, Part 1," *Christianity Today,* February 18, 1983, 13.

be bought, and no other source for blood. The family might as well take the girl back home and let her die. The family huddled again and finally pushed forward a frail old woman, weighing perhaps ninety-five pounds, the smallest and weakest member of the family. Dr. Brand later recalled: *Reeve fixed a stare on the sleek, well-fed men who had made the decision, and then his anger took over. The bald spot atop his head turned blazing red. In halting but more-than-expressive Tamil* (the language of those people) *he blasted the dozen or so cowering family members. Few could understand his American accent, but everyone nearby caught the force of his torrent of words as he jabbed his finger back and forth from the husky men to the frail woman.*

Finally, with a melodramatic flourish, Reeve rolled up his own sleeves and called over to me, "Come on, Paul—I can't stand this! I won't let that poor girl die just because of these cowardly fellows. Bring the needle and bottle and take my blood." The family fell silent like birds before an eclipse, and watched in awe as I dutifully fastened a cuff around Reeve's upper arm, swabbed the skin, and plunged the needle into his vein. A rich red fountain spurted into the bottle and a great "Ahhh!" rustled through the family and spectators.

At once there was a great babel of voices. "Look, the sahib doctor is giving his own life!"[1]

Date: _____ _____ _____

Place: _____ _____ _____

Occasion: _____ _____ _____

The Broken Trail

Robert Bruce of Scotland was leading his men in a battle to gain independence from England. Near the end of the conflict, the English wanted to capture Bruce to keep him from assuming his position as next in line for the Scottish crown. So they put his own bloodhounds on his trail. When they got close, Bruce could hear them baying loudly. His attendant said, "We are done for. They are on your trail, and they will reveal your hiding place." Bruce replied, "It's all right." Then he headed for a stream that flowed through the forest. He plunged in and waded upstream a short distance. When he came out on the other bank, he was in the depths of the forest. Within minutes, the hounds, tracing their master's steps, came to the bank. But they went no farther. The English soldiers urged them on, but the trail was broken. The stream had carried the scent away. A short time later, the crown of Scotland rested on the head of Robert Bruce.

The memory of our sins, prodded on by Satan, can be like those baying dogs. But a stream flows, red with the blood of God's own Son. By grace through faith we are safe. No sin-hound can touch us. The trail is broken by the precious blood of Christ.[2]

Date: _____ _____ _____

Place: _____ _____ _____

Occasion: _____ _____ _____

---

[1] Brand and Yancy, "Blood: The Miracle of Cleansing, Part 3," *Christianity Today*, March 18, 1983, 20.
[2] From *Our Daily Bread*

Boredom

Someone Once Said . . .

- *Boredom is the vital problem of the moralist, since at least half the sins of mankind are caused by the fear of it.*—Bertrand Russell[1]
- *The best cure of boredom is finding what you enjoy doing and then doing it.*—Sam Keen, in his book *What To Do When You're Bored and Blue.*
- *One of the chief causes of fatigue is boredom.*—Dale Carnegie[2]

Date: _____ _____ _____

Place: _____ _____ _____

Occasion: _____ _____ _____

The Existential Vacuum

In his profound book, *Man's Search for Meaning,* Viktor Frankl wrote that phenomenally large numbers of modern men and women suffer from an "existential vacuum." He wrote: *The existential vacuum manifests itself mainly in a state of boredom. Now we can understand Schopenhauer when he said that mankind was apparently doomed to vacillate eternally between the two extremes of distress and boredom. In actual fact, boredom is now causing, and certainly bringing to psychiatrists, more problems to solve than distress. And these problems are growing increasingly crucial. . . .*[3]

Date: _____ _____ _____

Place: _____ _____ _____

Occasion: _____ _____ _____

The Bane of Boredom

It can give you a backache, a headache, insomnia, chronic fatigue—even impotence. Studies have shown it has a direct link to alcohol and drug abuse. It's also been associated with gambling, perverse sex, and hypochondria. And millions suffer from it.

It's boredom.

According to one study, more than twenty million Americans are afflicted. On top of that, a Lou Harris survey found that 40 percent of American workers are bored sick with their jobs.

No longer seen only as a complaint of the chronic malingerer, boredom has come to be recognized as one of America's most serious health problems. Scientists have discovered, that, in addition to causing psychological disorders, boredom is often at the root of many physical problems.

What are the most common causes of boredom? Psychologists list: unfulfilled expectations, unchallenging jobs, too much speculating, and too little participating.

---

[1] Donald W. McCullough, "Anything But Boredom!" *Christianity Today,* August 19, 1991, 30–31.
[2] Dale Carnegie, *How To Stop Worrying and Start Living* (New York: Simon and Schuster, 1948), 199.
[3] Viktor E. Frankl, *Man's Search for Meaning* (New York: Washington Square Press, 1984), 129.

Common phrases that signal a state of boredom include: "I'm frustrated," "I've had it up to here," and "I don't care anymore."[1]

Date: _____   _____   _____
Place: _____   _____   _____
Occasion: _____   _____   _____

Booooring!

Boring! It's the final condemnation, the complete put-down. Parents hear it after a concert or on a family vacation or in church. Actually, it's pronounced, "Booooring!" and it seems to emerge from the depths of disgust. It should be a four-letter word. The epithet never loses its power to terrify. Children, with blunt honesty, hurl the accusation like a hand grenade toward anything they consider undeserving of their presence, but adults, though perhaps more politely circumspect, fear it and feel it and flee it just as much.[2]

Date: _____   _____   _____
Place: _____   _____   _____
Occasion: _____   _____   _____

Reasons for Boredom

In her book, *Boredom: The Literary History of a State of Mind,* Patricia Meyer Spacks points out that, however ancient the feeling may in fact be, the words *bore* and *boredom* weren't used until the eighteenth century. Some of the reasons boredom arrived just then, she theorizes, were "the emergence of leisure," "the decline of orthodox Christianity," and "the newly elaborated notion of individual rights," implying, among other things, the right not to be bored.[3]

Date: _____   _____   _____
Place: _____   _____   _____
Occasion: _____   _____   _____

I Am Bored

Actor George Sanders was born in St. Petersburg, Russia, but his family was forced to flee to England during the Bolshevik Revolution. After graduating from college and working for a time at a tobacco company in Argentina, Sanders took to the London stage and debuted on-screen in 1936, in *Find the Lady.* Later in Hollywood, he signed a contract with 20th Century-Fox. He received an Academy Award

---

[1] Stephen Franzmeier, "Bored Sick," *The Nashville Tennessean,* September 4, 1988, sec. E-1.

[2] Donald W. McCullough, "Anything But Boredom!" *Christianity Today,* August 19, 1991, 30.

[3] Christopher Lehmann-Haupt, "Review of *Boredom: The Literary History of a State of Mind,* by Patricia Meyers Spacks," *The New York Times,* December 14, 1994.

for "Best Supporting Actor" for his role in *All About Eve* (1950). His career flagged after that, and his final role was as a drag queen in 1970's *The Kremlin Letter*. He was married four times—among his wives were sisters Zsa Zsa and Magda Gabor. His seven psychiatrists brought Sanders little comfort. He took his own life in 1972 with five tubes of Nembutal in a Barcelona hotel. His suicide note said: *Dear World, I am leaving because I am bored. I feel I have lived long enough. I am leaving you with your worries in this sweet cesspool. Good luck.*

Date: _____ _____ _____
Place: _____ _____ _____
Occasion: _____ _____ _____

Thank Heavens!

In 1958 the American writer Barnaby Conrad was badly gored in a bullfight in Spain. Eva Gabor and Noel Coward were overheard talking about the incident in a New York restaurant. "Noel, dahling," said Eva, "have you heard the news about poor Bahnaby? He vas terribly gored in Spain."

"He was *what?*" asked Coward in alarm.

"He vas gored!"

"Thank heavens. I thought you said he was bored."[1]

Date: _____ _____ _____
Place: _____ _____ _____
Occasion: _____ _____ _____

—————— Burden for Lost ——————

Someone Once Said . . .

- *I cared not where or how I lived, or what hardships I went through, so that I could but gain souls for Christ. While I was asleep, I dreamed of these things, and when I awoke, the first thing I thought of was this great work.*—David Brainerd
- *Lord, give me Scotland, or I die.*—John Knox
- *Father, give me these souls, or I die.*—John "Praying" Hyde
- *God, the sin of this city is breaking my heart.*—Samuel Hadley, about New York City
- *Lord, give me souls or take my soul.*—George Whitefield
- *Give me Lisu converts, and I can truly say I will be happy even in a pigsty.*—J. O. Fraser, missionary to the Lisu people of China
- *Here let me burn out for God.*—Henry Martyn, on the shores of India
- *I must open a way to the interior or perish.*—David Livingstone

[1]Donald W. McCullough, "Anything But Boredom!" *Christianity Today*, August 19, 1991, 30.

- *I feel as if I could not live if something is not done for China.*—Hudson Taylor
- *I am very tired, but must go on . . . A fire is in my bones . . . Oh God, what can I say? Souls! Souls! Souls! My heart hungers for souls!*—General William Booth
- *I would rather win souls than be the greatest king or emperor on earth; I would rather win souls than be the greatest general that ever commanded an army; I would rather win souls than be the greatest poet, or novelist, or literary man who ever walked the earth. My one ambition in life is to win as many as possible.*—R. A. Torrey
- *There is a power which lies at the center of all success in preaching, and whose influence reaches out to the circumference, and is essential everywhere. Without its presence we cannot imagine the most brilliant talents making a preacher of the Gospel in the fullest sense. Where it is largely present, it is wonderful how many deficiencies count for nothing . . . The power is the value of the human soul, felt by the preacher and inspiring all his work.*—Phillips Brooks, in Lectures on Preaching

Date: _____   _____   _____

Place: _____   _____   _____

Occasion: _____   _____   _____

"We Sang More Loudly . . ."

In a small church on the East Coast a pastor delivered a sermon on abortion, and after the service a German man who had lived in Nazi Germany told of his experience: *I lived in Germany during the Nazi Holocaust. I considered myself a Christian. We heard stories of what was happening to the Jews, but we tried to distance ourselves from it, because, what could anyone do to stop it?*

A railroad track ran behind our small church, and each Sunday morning we could hear the whistle in the distance and then the wheels coming over the tracks. We became disturbed when we heard the cries coming from the train as it passed by. We realized that it was carrying Jews like cattle in the cars!

> ◇
> **The Eternal Light**
> *We shall this day, my lord, light such a candle in England as shall never be extinguished!*
> —HUGH LATIMER
> ◇

Week after week the whistle would blow. We dreaded to hear the sound of those wheels because we knew that we would hear the cries of the Jews en route to the death camp. Their screams tormented us.

We knew the time the train was coming and when we heard the whistle blow we began singing hymns. By the time the train came past our church we were singing at the top of our voices. If we heard the screams, we sang more loudly and soon we heard them no more.

Years have passed and no one talks about it anymore. But I still hear that train whistle in my sleep. God forgive me; forgive all of us who called ourselves Christians and yet did nothing. . . .[1]

Date: _____   _____   _____

Place: _____   _____   _____

Occasion: _____   _____   _____

---

[1] Erwin W. Lutzer, *Hitler's Cross* (Chicago: Moody Press, 1995), 99–100.

Call To Ministry/Missions

Someone Once Said . . .

- *No generation in two thousand years of Church history has produced the task force necessary to reach the world. Is this because God has not called adequate numbers? Or is it because someone is not listening? The truth is, less than one percent of full-time Christian workers are engaged in evangelistic ministry among the unevangelized of the world. Is this the way the Commander-in-Chief would assign his troops? Or is someone not listening? With the need so vast and the laborers so few, why do we not go? Someone isn't listening!*—Robertson McQuilkin[1]
- *The Call is the inner motive of having been gripped by God—spoilt for every aim in life save that of discipling men to Jesus.*—Oswald Chambers[2]
- *One man or woman called to God is worth a hundred who have elected to work for God.*—Oswald Chambers[3]
- *If a man is called to preach the Gospel, God will crush him till the light of the eye, the power of the life, the ambition of the heart, is all riveted on Himself. That is not done easily. It is not a question of saintliness, it has to do with the Call of God.*—Oswald Chambers[4]
- *Many preachers are good tailors spoiled, and capital shoe makers turned out of their proper calling. When God means a creature to fly, he gives it wings, and when he intends men to preach he gives them abilities.*—Charles Spurgeon[5]
- *I knew an old minister once. . . . How I envy him. . . . I am listed as a famous home-runner, yet beside that obscure minister, who was so good and so wise, I never got to first base.*—Babe Ruth[6]

Date:	_____	_____	_____
Place:	_____	_____	_____
Occasion:	_____	_____	_____

How They Were Called into Ministry

"God's call does not come by any stereotyped method," wrote J. Oswald Sanders. "It will vary with the individual."[7] With that in mind, consider the following sampling of how God called certain ones to ministry:

Ambrose (c. A.D. 340–397) was born in Gaul, where his father was governor. His family shortly moved to Rome where Ambrose was raised to be a skilled poet,

---

[1] Excerpted from the pamphlet "Who's Calling? An Exploration of the Missionary Call" by Robertson McQuilkin.
[2] Oswald Chambers, *Disciples Indeed* (London: Morgan & Scott, Ltd., 1955), 10.
[3] Chambers, *Disciples Indeed,* 10.
[4] Chambers, *Disciples Indeed,* 11.
[5] Charles Spurgeon, *John Ploughman's Talks* (Grand Rapids: Baker, 1976), 59.
[6] Quoted by Kevin A. Miller in *Secrets of Staying Power* (Waco, TX: Word Books, 1988), 41.
[7] J. Oswald Sanders, *A Spiritual Clinic* (Chicago: Moody Press, 1961), 174.

orator, and lawyer. After practicing law in the Roman courts for a time, he was named governor of an Italian province and headquartered in Milan. A crisis arose there when Bishop Auxentius died in A.D. 374. The city was divided over who should replace him, and tensions were high. Ambrose assembled the people and used his oratorical powers to appeal for unity. But while he was speaking, a child cried out: "Let Ambrose be bishop!" The crowd took up the chant, and the thirty-five-year-old governor, to his dismay, was elected the city's pastor.

He set himself to study theology, soon becoming a great preacher and a deft defender of orthodox doctrine. He combated paganism and heresy with diligence, maintained the independence of the church against civil powers, and championed morality. He confronted political leaders, even emperors, when necessary. He wrote books and treatises, sermons, hymns, and letters. He tended Milan like a shepherd.

Perhaps none of that was more important than his influence on a hot-blooded infidel who slipped into town one Sunday to hear him preach. The skeptical Augustine found himself deeply impressed by the power of Ambrose's sermons, and he sought personal counseling from the bishop. But Ambrose was too busy. Visitors were allowed into his room, but he paid scant attention to them. He just went ahead reading. Several times Augustine sat watching him, but Ambrose remained unaware of it. His preaching, however, reached the prodigal, and shortly afterward Augustine was converted.

Ambrose continued preaching until he fell sick in A.D. 397. When distressed friends prayed for his healing, he said, "I have so lived among you that I cannot be ashamed to live longer, but neither do I fear to die; for we have a good Lord." On Good Friday, April 3, Ambrose lay with his hands extended in the form of the cross, moving his lips in prayer. His friends huddled in sadness and watched. Sometime past midnight, their beloved bishop passed to his good Lord.[1]

Charles Fuller (A.D. 1887–1968) pioneered Christian radio work, preaching for nearly thirty years each week to twenty million people on the "Old Fashioned Revival Hour," broadcast live from Long Beach Auditorium in California.

In 1919, Fuller was working in the orange groves of Southern California as manager of a fruit packing house. For some time, he had been restless, increasingly convinced that God wanted him to resign and go to the Bible Institute of Los Angeles (Biola) to train for ministry. He began to view his work in the packing house as "just a continuous whirligig and year-round race . . . and when it was all said and done, not much was accomplished for eternity. It was just a matter of getting the best prices."

One morning in April as Charles Fuller sat in his office in the packing house, the conviction that he should go into full-time service became so powerful that he had to leave his desk and find some place where he could be alone to pray. He went downstairs, through the packing house where men and women were working, and back to a storage room where the makings of orange boxes were stored. He knelt behind a stack of these.

He struggled with the fear that he didn't have the fluency and speaking ability needed for preaching, and he worried about the financial ramifications of leaving his

---

job, especially as he had recently made down payment on a twenty-acre orange grove of his own.

At first these obstacles seemed too great, and he rose to go back to his desk, but God's hand was so heavy upon him that he sank to his knees again and said, "Oh, Lord, I will walk in your path. I will even try to preach. I will resign my position and trust you to supply our needs as I prepare for ministry."

Peace came to his soul, and he soon notified the board members of the packing house that by the fall of that year he would be resigning so he could study at Biola. They took the news sadly, one even going so far as to say, "Charlie, you're too good a man for the ministry. You should stay here. Why, a minister only has to work one day a week—Sunday when he preaches. Furthermore, I don't think you're qualified for the ministry. You might well starve." But for Charles Fuller there was no turning back. From that day on he felt like Paul who said, "Woe is me if I preach not the Gospel."[1]

◇

The Woes of Preaching

If you can do anything other than preach, do it!

—attributed to CHARLES SPURGEON

◇

George Truett (1867–1944) was converted to Christ at age nineteen after hearing a sermon based on Hebrews 10:38: *Now the just shall live by faith.* The following Wednesday night, his pastor encouraged him to share his testimony, and the crowd was amazed at the power and passion of his words. From that time on, many people encouraged him to enter the ministry. His primary vocational interest, however, was teaching school.

Whenever asked to speak at church services or evangelistic meetings, he demonstrated remarkable ability. He was once introduced with the words, "Brethren, this is George Truett, and he can speak like Spurgeon. George, tell them what the Lord has done for you. . ." Still Truett worked at school, teaching, and toyed with the idea of studying law.

One Saturday, he heard that a special business meeting was going to be held at his church that night. He arrived to discover that the church was meeting to vote to ordain him into the ministry. The oldest deacon present rose to his feet and said, "I move that this church ordain brother Charles Truett to the full work of the Gospel ministry."

Truett, twenty-three, rose to protest, but the church would have none of it. He later recalled, "There I was, against a whole church, against a church profoundly moved. There was not a dry eye in the house . . . one of the supremely solemn hours in a church's life. I was thrown into the stream, and just had to swim."

W. A. Criswell, who followed Truett as pastor of the First Baptist Church of Dallas, followed a different route into ministry. He felt called to preach in childhood. When he was ten years old, he became intrigued with Rev. John Hicks, who stayed in the Criswell home while preaching at a local revival meeting. "I told him I had been thinking about being a preacher for years, since I was six," Criswell later recalled. "Yet I knew I wasn't even converted yet, hadn't been saved. But I knew God wanted me to be a preacher and had the same conviction then I have now. I cannot remember when I was not going to be a preacher." Criswell received Christ as his Savior, and he was baptized the following Sunday. His sense of God's calling on his life never wavered.[2]

---

[1] Adapted from Daniel P. Fuller, *The Story of Charles E. Fuller* (Waco, TX: Word Books, 1972), 37.
[2] Adapted from Billy Keith, *W. A. Criswell* (Old Tappan, NJ: Fleming H. Revell Co., 1973, 21.

C

Rodney (Gipsy) Smith (1860–1947) was one of the most remarkable and entertaining preachers of the twentieth century. He was also called to preach from almost the moment of his conversion. He and his family were gypsies in England, virtually homeless, but his father had experienced an unusual conversion. Shortly afterward, on November 17, 1876, Rodney attended a Primitive Methodist chapel and went forward following the sermon of Rev. George Warner. He heard someone whisper, "Oh, it's only a gypsy boy."

Rushing home, he told his father he had been converted. Though illiterate, he began carrying around a Bible, English dictionary and Bible dictionary, trying to learn to read them. People laughed at him, but he said, "Never you mind. One day I'll be able to read them, and I'm going to preach too. God has called me to preach."

As he worked on his reading, he began to practice preaching, going out into the fields and preaching to the turnips. At age seventeen, he stood on a small corner near his gypsy wagon and gave a brief testimony. It was his first attempt at preaching. But it wasn't his last. He became a worldwide evangelist, preaching to thousands at a time, and carrying on his phenomenal ministry for seventy years, until his death at age eighty-seven.

Stuart Briscoe, pastor of Elmbrook Church of Milwaukee, Wisconsin, described his call to preach like this: *I never intended to be a preacher. I was going to be a businessman. As a teenager in England, I'd just moved to a new town to start working, when a layman in the church I attended asked me how old I was.*

"Seventeen," I said.

"It's time you were preaching," he said, which was a total surprise to me. But two weeks later, I found myself preaching my first sermon in that small church. He had given me my topic: the church at Ephesus. So I studied everything I could find on the Ephesians.

In that first sermon, I went ten minutes over my allotted time—and only got through my first point. So he told me to come back the following week and finish. Which I did. Then he said, "There are lots of little churches around here that need preachers," and so he started sending me to different little congregations, preaching about Ephesians.

So I started preaching, and I discovered (1) I could do it, (2) I enjoyed doing it, and (3) people seemed to be blessed as I was doing it. Eventually the church affirmed my preaching, and I discovered a gifting. And I learned that where there's a gifting, often there's a calling. Over the years, that sense of calling has crystallized.

So after twelve years, I left the business world and went full time into the ministry.[1]

Date: _____   _____   _____
Place: _____   _____   _____
Occasion: _____   _____   _____

The Motivation of a Call

Ted Engstrom once wrote of a Christian businessman from America who was traveling to various mission fields of the world. One day he found himself in northern India near a leprosarium. Outside of the walls of this leprosarium he saw an unusual

---

[1] Stuart Briscoe, interviewed by *Leadership Journal,* Spring Quarter, 1990, 18.

sight: a lovely young missionary nurse who was attending the desperate needs of a filthy, wretched, leprous Indian beggar. There is nothing more distressing than that kind of a sight. Tenderly this young lady was ministering to this leprous beggar before he was admitted into the leprosarium. The businessman had his camera strung around his neck, but he couldn't shoot any film. He paused at the sight, then withdrew a few feet. Tears filled his eyes, and he said to the young nurse, "Young lady, I wouldn't do that for a million dollars."

Quickly she turned to him and said, "Sir, neither would I."[1]

Date: _____   _____   _____

Place: _____   _____   _____

Occasion: _____   _____   _____

A Raging Thirst

In his *Lectures To My Students,* Charles Spurgeon defines the call of ministry by listing several of its attributes:

1. The first sign of the heavenly calling is an intense, all-absorbing desire for the work. In order to be a true call to the ministry there must be an irresistible, overwhelming craving and raging thirst for telling others what God has done for our own souls.
2. In the second place, combined with the earnest desire to become a pastor, there must be aptness to teach and some measure of the other qualities needful for the office of a public instructor.
3. In order further to prove a man's call, after a little exercise of his gifts, such as I have already spoken of, he must see a measure of conversion-work going on under his efforts.
4. A step beyond all this is, however, needful in our inquiry. The will of the Lord concerning pastors is made known through the prayerful judgment of His church. It is needful as a proof of your vocation that your preaching should be acceptable to the people of God.[2]

Date: _____   _____   _____

Place: _____   _____   _____

Occasion: _____   _____   _____

Carey's Concern

William Carey, who is called the "Father of Modern Missions," served the Lord in India for many years. He gradually became very concerned about the attitude of his son, Felix. The young man had promised to become a missionary, but he reneged on his vows when he was appointed ambassador to Burma by the Queen of England.

---

[1] Ted W. Engstrom, *What in the World is God Doing?* (Waco: Word Books, 1978), 208.
[2] Charles H. Spurgeon, *Lectures to My Students* (Grand Rapids: Zondervan, 1954), 26–32.

Carey wrote to his friend, asking prayer for his son with these words: *Pray for Felix. He has degenerated into an ambassador of the British government when he should be serving the King of Kings.*

Date: _____ _____ _____
Place: _____ _____ _____
Occasion: _____ _____ _____

"I Am Called"

As her husband Jim made plans to reach the Auca Indians of South America, Elisabeth Elliot struggled with her willingness to let him go. Finally she confronted him, asking him the question that burned within her: "Jim, are you sure you are supposed to go?"

His simple reply: "I am called."

"So, it was all right," Elisabeth later wrote. "Scriptural principles, God-directed circumstances, and Jim's own inward assurance were consonant. I could share in it, then; I could happily help him plan."[1]

Date: _____ _____ _____
Place: _____ _____ _____
Occasion: _____ _____ _____

The Job Is Too Small

In her book, *It's My Turn,* Ruth Bell Graham recalls growing up as a missionary kid in China. Among her stories is this one. An oil company, about to open a new operation in China, wanted to find a man to manage the new division. They wanted someone young, a university graduate, a proven leader, and someone fluent in the Chinese language. They located a man who perfectly met this qualification. He was a twenty-eight-year-old missionary already living in the city where the company was planning to establish its office. When someone asked how much salary this young man was getting, the committee learned it was very modest. They set out to hire him.

The oil company offered the young missionary over ten times his current salary. He declined. They raised the offer. He declined again. They offered him even more, but yet again he turned them down.

Finally the agent asked, "What will you take?"

"It's not a question of salary," replied the missionary. "The salary is tremendous. The trouble is with the job. The job is too little. I feel that God has called me to preach the Gospel of Christ. I would be a fool to quit preaching in order to sell oil."

"Such were the giants," recalled Ruth Graham, "among whom we grew up."[2]

---

[1] Elisabeth Elliot, *Shadow of the Almighty* (Grand Rapids: Zondervan, 1958), 236.
[2] Ruth Bell Graham, *It's My Turn* (Old Tappan, NJ: Fleming H. Revell Co., 1982), 20–21.

Date: _____   _____   _____
Place: _____   _____   _____
Occasion: _____   _____   _____

How Do I Know?

John Newton, the converted slave trader who wrote "Amazing Grace," served churches in Olney, England, and in London. One day a young man wrote for counsel regarding God's call to the pastorate. Newton replied:

Dear sir:

I was long distressed, as you are, about what was or was not a proper call to the ministry. It now seems to me an easy point to solve, but perhaps will not be so to you until the Lord shall make it clear to you in your own case. In brief, I think [a true call] principally includes three things:

1. *A warm and earnest desire to be employed in this service. I apprehend [that] the man who is once moved by the Spirit of God to this work will prefer it, if attainable, to hoards of gold and silver, so that, though at times intimidated by a sense of its importance and difficulty compared with his own great insufficiencies, yet he cannot give up on it.*
2. *Besides this desire, there must, in due season, appear some competent sufficiency, gifts, knowledge, and utterance. Surely, if the Lord sends a man to teach others, he will furnish him with the means.*
3. *That which finally evidences a proper call is a correspondent opening in providence by a gradual train of circumstances pointing out the means, the times, and the place of actually entering upon the work.*

Date: _____   _____   _____
Place: _____   _____   _____
Occasion: _____   _____   _____

——————— Change Resisted by Clergy ———————

Someone Once Said . . .

- *One generation cannot do without the others. . . . The older generation is our link with the past, the younger generation is our link with the future, and we need both.*—John Maxwell[1]
- *If your horse is dead, for goodness sake—dismount.*—Eddy Ketchursid
- *Time makes more converts than reason.*—Thomas Paine

---

[1]John Maxwell, *Your Attitude* (San Bernardino, CA: Here's Life Publishers, Inc., 1984), 102.

Date: _____   _____   _____
Place: _____   _____   _____
Occasion: _____   _____   _____

The Shape of the Earth

Galileo Galilei was an Italian astronomer and physicist who made his first scientific discoveries while a student in Pisa. He dropped out of the university for lack of money, but returned at age twenty-five to teach mathematics. He formulated laws about gravity by conducting novel experiments like dropping weights from the leaning tower of Pisa. He devised the law of the pendulum by watching a lamp swing from the cathedral ceiling. His fame spread across Europe, drawing both students and criticism.

In 1609, he began building telescopes and making spectacular discoveries about the heavenly bodies. Galileo was a Christian who believed that God's world and God's Word were both valid objects for study. Using one of his telescopes, he even showed Pope Paul V some of his findings. But he was nonetheless attacked by the church, for his discoveries contradicted traditional teachings. Some clergymen condemned the whole study of astronomy by quoting Acts 1:13: "Why are you men from Galilee standing here and looking up into the sky?"

In 1632, Galileo was called before the leaders of the Inquisition to answer charges that his writings violated church teaching. Despite being seventy years old and infirm, he was forced to travel from Florence during the winter, arriving in Rome on a litter on February 13, 1633. Historians are unsure whether Galileo, during his trial, was tortured or simply threatened with torture. In any event, the old scientist was forced to read a statement renouncing his views—especially his observation that the earth moves around the sun—confessing them as "errors and heresies." A legend persists that having read his recantation, Galileo muttered, *E pur si muove—"But it moves after all."*

Galileo remained under house arrest, treated badly by church officials, until he became blind and feeble. He died on a winter's day in 1642 in the presence of his son and two of his pupils.[1]

Date: _____   _____   _____
Place: _____   _____   _____
Occasion: _____   _____   _____

The King James Version

When the King James Version of the Bible was issued in 1611, it was widely criticized and rejected by the clergy. Archbishop Richard Bancroft said, "Tell his

---

[1] Robert J. Morgan, *On This Day* (Nashville: Thomas Nelson Publishers, 1996), entry for February 13th.

majesty that I had rather be rent to pieces with wild horses than any such translation by my consent should be urged upon poor churches."[1]

Date: _____ _____ _____
Place: _____ _____ _____
Occasion: _____ _____ _____

Open-Air Evangelism

Immediately after evangelist George Whitefield (1714–1770) began preaching in the open air in the Moorfields near London, he attended morning services at Christ Church and found himself the object of the sermon. The preacher, Rev. Dr. Joseph Trapp, one of London's ablest clergymen, denounced the evangelist's activities, ridiculed his writing, and accused him of dishonesty.

In his biography of Whitefield, Arnold Dallimore wrote, "This attack confirmed Whitefield in his belief that he could expect nothing but opposition from the clergy and that God was thus thrusting him into the fields."[2]

Date: _____ _____ _____
Place: _____ _____ _____
Occasion: _____ _____ _____

Singing Hymns

When Isaac Watts was growing up in England, his Puritan father called him on the carpet for his lackluster participation in congregational singing. According to the common practice, the clerk would read the Psalm out line by line, with the congregation singing after him. Young Watts told his father bluntly that there was no music in the Psalms, and, furthermore, they didn't rhyme.

Old Deacon Watts, outraged, suggested that Isaac write his own songs if he thought he were smarter than King David.

Watts did.

Not everyone was happy with replacing the Psalms with hymns. Typical was this incident: When the first General Assembly of the Presbyterian Church in the United States of America met in Philadelphia's Second Presbyterian Church in May, 1789, Rev. Adam Rankin was granted permission to speak. "I have ridden on horseback all the way from my home in Kentucky," he said, "to ask this august body to refuse to allow the great and pernicious error of adopting the use of Isaac Watts' hymns in public worship in preference to Rouse's versifications of the Psalms of David."[3]

---

[1] Gustavus S. Paine, *The Men Behind the KJV* (Grand Rapids: Baker Book House, 1959), 106.
[2] Arnold Dallimore, *George Whitefield: Volume 1* (London: The Banner of Truth Trust, 1970), 288.
[3] Clint Bonner, *A Hymn is Born* (Nashville: Broadman, 1959), 8; and Ernest K. Emurian, *Living Stories of Famous Hymns* (Grand Rapids: Baker Book House, 1955), 17.

Date:			
Place:			
Occasion:			

Sunday School

When Robert Raikes started the Sunday School Movement, the Archbishop of Canterbury called together the bishops to see what could be done to stop him, for, he said, it was a violation of Exodus 20:8.

In the late 1700s, "Sabbath (Sunday) School Societies" were started here and there throughout the young United States of America. But at first, many members of the clergy were opposed to them, maintaining that it was a desecration of the Lord's Day to hold school on Sunday. A pastor in Connecticut said of a class held in his church on Sunday, "You imps of Satan, doing the devil's work. I'll have you set in the street."[1]

Date:			
Place:			
Occasion:			

Anesthesia

Imagine surgery before the day of anesthesia. Patients were strapped down while scalpel and saw cut through tissue and bone, every slice and turn of the knife causing unimaginable pain.

One Christian physician determined to do something about it. Sir James Young Simpson (1811–1870) practiced medicine in Scotland. He became Senior President of the Royal Medical Society of Edinburgh when only twenty-four, and in time received virtually every possible honor and position. He dreamed of finding a way of putting patients to sleep during surgery. On Monday evenings, Simpson periodically invited small groups of physicians to his home to experiment with chemicals, crystals, and powders, which were placed over a burning brazier while the doctors inhaled the fumes. Nothing worked until November 4, 1847. One of the men had purchased a crystal called chloroform in Paris. As the doctors sniffed the burning substance, they fell to the floor unconscious.

Like a Rock

In matters of style, swim with the current. In matters of principle, stand like a rock.

Simpson had his answer, but he soon encountered another problem. He was attacked by fellow Christians who claimed that pain was a God-ordained part of life. Freedom from pain comes only in heaven, and it is immoral to devise dangerous ways of escaping it on earth.

Sir James went to the Scriptures, seeking answers. He no sooner opened his Bible then he came to this verse: "And the Lord God caused a deep sleep to fall on

---

[1] C. B. Eavey, *History of Christian Education* (Chicago: Moody Press, 1964), 233.

Adam, and he slept; and He took one of his ribs, and closed up the flesh in its place." Carefully studying the text, Simpson wrote an article entitled, "Answer to the Religious Objections Advanced Against the Employment of Anesthetic Agents in Midwifery and Surgery." He ended his paper saying, "We may rest fully assured that whatever is true on point of fact or humane and merciful in point of practice, will find no condemnation in the Word of God."

His critics were silenced, and a new day dawned in medical science.[1]

Date:	_____	_____	_____
Place:	_____	_____	_____
Occasion:	_____	_____	_____

Subways

Marc Isambard Brunel (1769–1849) was a brilliant young man who, while fleeing the French Revolution, lost his passport, forged a replica from memory, and escaped to New York. He later moved to London, and at one point was confined to debtor's prison. He didn't stay there long. His engineering skills became legendary, and he planned the first tunnel under the Thames, a tunnel still in service; his underground digging machine made London's first "Tube" (subway) possible. But during its construction, he was hounded by clergymen who called it "flirtation with the Underworld."[2]

Date:	_____	_____	_____
Place:	_____	_____	_____
Occasion:	_____	_____	_____

Radio Evangelism

When the pioneers of radio evangelism started using the airways to proclaim the Gospel, they labored against a loud, persistent chorus of criticism. Clarence Jones, co-founder of missionary station HCJB in Equador, faced these questions: Will God prosper this new-fangled fad since it operates in the very realm of Satan—the air? Don't the Scriptures clearly portray the devil as the prince of the power of the air?[3]

Date:	_____	_____	_____
Place:	_____	_____	_____
Occasion:	_____	_____	_____

---

[1] Robert J. Morgan, *From This Verse* (Nashville: Thomas Nelson Publishers, 1998), entry for January 3rd. For more information, see *Chats from a Minister's Library* by Wilber M. Smith (Grand Rapids: Baker Book House, 1951), chapter 2: "Relation of a Verse in Genesis to the Early Use of Chloroform."
[2] Walter Clemons in "Tunnel Vision," in *Newsweek Magazine,* November 23, 1981, 111.
[3] Clarence W. Jones, *Radio: The New Missionary* (Chicago: Moody Press, 1946), 19.

Someone Once Said . . .

- *It is my firm belief that approximately eighty-five percent of one's adult personality is formed by the time he is six years old. Those first six years, therefore, are obviously the most crucial.*[1]
- *I believe some children can understand enough during the latter part of their first six years to know that they are frequently sinful, that they want God to forgive them, and that they want to live forever in heaven—and then put their simple faith in Christ.*—Paul D. Meier[2]
- *Give me a child until he is seven, and I don't care what you do with him.*—attributed to an unknown Roman Catholic educator
- *Give me a child of six to educate, and he will belong to me for life.*—attributed to the German National Socialist regime
- *Research on brain development is clear that the first three years are critical to a child's future success.*—Stand For Children
- *Save a man and you save a unit; save a boy and you save a multiplication table.*—Gipsy Smith

Date: _____ _____ _____

Place: _____ _____ _____

Occasion: _____ _____ _____

Landmines

According to "Save The Children," in the last decade alone, more than 1.5 million children have been killed during military conflicts. Millions more were injured. And one of every two hundred children—ten million children around the world—have been psychologically affected by war.

Much of the damage has resulted from the approximately one hundred million landmines that have been planted in sixty countries. These mines are often placed in areas frequented by children—schools, playgrounds, fields—and, with their natural curiosity, children are more likely to explore areas where mines have been laid. More than 26,000 people are killed or maimed by landmines each year; 90 percent of these victims are civilians, many of them children.

Satan has also permeated our society with spiritual landmines, many of them set to maim and mangle the souls and personalities of our children. That's why no ministry of the church is more important than "saving the children."

Date: _____ _____ _____

Place: _____ _____ _____

Occasion: _____ _____ _____

---

[1] Paul D. Meier, *Christian Child-Rearing and Personality Development* (Grand Rapids: Baker Book House, 1977), ix.

[2] Meier, *Christian Child-Rearing and Personality Development,* 95.

A Father's Plea

In the May 28, 1998, edition of *USA Today,* the following appeared among the letters to the editor:

Will somebody help me save my son?

My son is two years old and is a reflection of complete innocence. His vulnerability to this harsh, violent, ignorant and uncaring world just rips my heart apart. He knows nothing of the killing within the schools that are supposed to prepare children for the world. He knows nothing of the abuse that happens within the homes of children just his age. As he plays with his toys, he is oblivious to the tragedies that occur every day across the country. And as he clutches his blanket, sleeping soundly, dreaming of the mommy and daddy who love him, he has no idea of the complete social and moral decay of our country.

Does anyone care anymore? Will someone please, please help me save my son?—Edward Moats, Belleair Beach, Florida[1]

Date:	_____	_____	_____
Place:	_____	_____	_____
Occasion:	_____	_____	_____

Why Minister to Children?

In the first chapter of her classic book, *Children in the Bible School,* Dr. Lois E. LeBar listed eight reasons for emphasizing children's ministry:

1. The Bible clearly teaches that Christ Jesus calls the children to Himself (See Matthew 18:1–14 and 19:13–15). Jesus said about adults, "Compel them to come" (Luke 14:23), but he said of children, "Let them come unto me" (Matthew 19:14). Much more readily than adults, children feel the need of the Savior, and gladly come when they hear that He is near, if only parents and teachers are willing to take the time to lead them gently to Him.

2. The most favorable soil for sowing the seed of the Word is the plastic (pliable) heart of a child.

3. Early childhood's natural faith and dependency are soon outgrown. Faith is natural to a child, for complete physical dependence is accompanied by absolute emotional confidence.

4. Habits of the first seven years are indelibly established.

5. Less time and effort are necessary to win many children to Christ than one adult.

6. Children have their whole lives ahead of them for service. Suppose that Paul had been converted at seventy instead of twenty-five. There would have been no Paul in history. There was a Matthew Henry because he was converted at eleven and not at seventy; an Isaac Watts because he was converted at nine and not at sixty; a Jonathan Edwards because he was converted at eight and not eighty; a Richard Baxter because he was converted at six and not sixty.

---

[1] Letters to the editor in *USA Today,* Thursday, May 28, 1998, Page 12–A.

7. Children open many homes for personal work. Visiting children's homes furnishes a natural approach for conversation about spiritual things.

8. A teacher's own life is matured as he sees himself as God's child learning His higher ways. The disciples of old were amazed to discover not only that Christ gave children preference over adults, but also that adults had something to learn from children. One children's worker said, "Outside the Word itself, no other single factor has helped me grow spiritually as has work with children."[1]

C

Date:	_____	_____	_____
Place:	_____	_____	_____
Occasion:	_____	_____	_____

Two and a Half

Returning to his friend's home after conducting meetings in a town in England, D. L. Moody was asked by his host, "How many were converted tonight in the meeting?"

"Two and a half," replied Moody.

"What do you mean?" asked his friend. "Were there two adults and a child?"

"No," said the evangelist, "it was two children and one adult. The children have given their lives to Christ in their youth, while the adult has come with half of his life."[2]

Date:	_____	_____	_____
Place:	_____	_____	_____
Occasion:	_____	_____	_____

How Old Were They When They Were Saved?

Jesus said, "Let the little children come to me . . . for the kingdom of Heaven belongs to such as these." (Matthew 19:14, NIV) His words are being fulfilled in American society according to new data from the Barna Research Group of Ventura, California. The company's nationwide surveys have determined the probability of people accepting Christ as their savior in relation to a person's age. The data show that if a person does not accept Jesus Christ as savior before the age of 14, the likelihood of ever doing so is slim.

In God's Sight

I tell you that in God's sight he is no preacher who does not care for the children.
—CHARLES SPURGEON

Based on a nationwide representative sampling of more than 4200 young people and adults, the survey data show that people from ages 5 through 13 have a 32% probability of accepting Christ as their savior. Young people

[1] Lois E. LeBar, *Children in the Bible School* (Old Tappan, NJ: Fleming H. Revell Co., 1912), chapter one.
[2] LeBar, *Children in the Bible School*, 26.

from the ages of 14 through 18 have just a 4% likelihood of doing so, while adults (ages 19 through death) have only a 6% probability of making that choice.

While this information is consistent with other Barna studies over the years that have shown that a large majority of Christians accept Jesus Christ as their Savior before they reach the age of 18, this is the first study that has calculated people's probability of accepting Christ at different life stages. The data also challenge the widely-held belief that the teenage years are prime years for evangelistic activity.[1]

- Polycarp, church father, was nine
- Matthew Henry was eleven
- Jonathan Edwards was seven
- Isaac Watts was nine
- Henry Drummond was nine
- E. Stanley Jones, the great Methodist missionary statesman, was moved to be a missionary when he was eight years old. He saw a picture of a big tiger standing beside a small Indian boy, and underneath was the caption, "Who will tell me about Jesus?" And Stanley Jones said, "I will."
- Corrie ten Boom asked Christ to be her Savior at age five.
- W. A. Criswell, the famous Southern Baptist pastor, was saved when he was ten, but he felt God calling him into ministry even earlier. "I had been thinking about being a preacher for years, since I was six," he recalled. "I knew I wasn't converted yet, hadn't been saved. But I knew God wanted me to be a preacher."[2]
- Hymnist Philip Bliss was twelve years old when he made his public confession of Christ.
- William Booth, founder of the Salvation Army, was fifteen.
- Harry Ironside was thirteen.
- Count Nicholaus Ludwig Zinzendorf, who gave rise to modern Protestant missions, was saved at age four.

Date:			
Place:			
Occasion:			

Charles Spurgeon on the Conversion of Children

Let none despise the stirrings of the Spirit in the hearts of the young. Let not boyish anxieties and juvenile repentances be lightly regarded. I, at least, can bear my personal testimony to the fact that grace operates on some minds at a period almost too early for recollection.[3]

Date:			
Place:			
Occasion:			

[1] Source: Barna Research Group, November 15, 1999; website: www.barna.org
[2] Billy Keith, *W. A. Criswell* (Old Tappan, NJ: Fleming H. Revell Co., 1973), 21.
[3] W. Y. Fullerton, *Charles H. Spurgeon: London's Most Popular Preacher* (Chicago: Moody Press, 1966), 27.

Finding Pearls

Eliza Agnew (1807–1850) was called "The Mother of a Thousand Daughters." She was the first single female missionary to Ceylon, where she served as head of Central Boarding School for girls for forty years, never returning to her native land of America. During those years, more than 1,000 pupils came under her care and teaching, and 600 of her students became Christians. Agnew said that she was engaged in the ministry of "finding pearls."

How old was she when she determined in her heart that God was calling her to missionary service?

She was eight.

Date: _____ _____ _____

Place: _____ _____ _____

Occasion: _____ _____ _____

"That's a Cuss Word"

One morning years ago, I took a walking tour of Albany, New York, and finally stopped for lunch on a park bench. As I ate my sandwich, I felt someone staring at me. Turning around, I saw a little fellow watching me with intense interest. He appeared to be eleven or twelve, his eyes were big, and his face crinkled with curiosity.

A Good Start

The first six years of a child's life are the most crucial.

"What's your name?" he finally asked. Then, "What you eatin'? Where you from? Tennessee? Where's that? What're you doin' here?" To the last question, I told him I had come to Albany to preach at a church.

"What does it mean to preach?" he asked.

"It means to tell others about Jesus," I replied. When I said the word "Jesus," his eyes widened, and he cupped his hand over his mouth.

"'Jesus,'" he whispered, "Mister, Don't you know?"

"Know what?"

"That's a cuss word."

It dawned on me that the only time this boy had ever heard the name *Jesus* was as a profanity in his home and in his neighborhood haunts. Compare that little fellow's history with the Apostle Paul's description of Timothy's upbringing: *Now from childhood (from infancy—NIV), you have known the Holy Scriptures, which are able to make you wise for salvation through faith which is in Christ Jesus (2 Timothy 3:15).*

Date: _____ _____ _____

Place: _____ _____ _____

Occasion: _____ _____ _____

The Story of John Pounds

It was a terrible fall, and it sickened those who saw it. John Pounds, a tall, muscular teen laborer at the docks of Portsmouth, England, slipped and plunged from the top of a ship's mast, pitching headfirst into the bowels of the vessel. When fellow workers reached him, he was nothing but a mass of broken bones. For two years he lay in bed as his bones healed crookedly. His pain never ceased. Out of boredom, he began to read the Bible.

At length, John crawled from bed hoping to find something he could do with his life. A shoemaker hired him, and day after day, John sat at his cobbler's bench, a Bible open on his lap. Soon he was born again.

John ultimately gathered enough money to purchase his own little shoeshop, and one day he developed a pair of surgical boots for his crippled nephew Johnny, whom he had taken in. Soon John was making corrective shoes for other children, and his little cobbler's shop became a miniature children's hospital.

As John's burden for children grew, he began receiving homeless ones, feeding them, teaching them to read, and telling them about the Lord. His shop became known as "The Ragged School," and John would limp around the waterfront, food in his pockets, looking for more children to tend.

During his lifetime, John Pounds rescued five hundred children from despair and led every one of them to Christ. Moreover, his work became so famous that a "Ragged School Movement" swept England, and a series of laws were passed to establish schools for poor children in John's honor. Boy's homes, girl's homes, day schools, and evening schools were started, along with Bible classes in which thousands heard the Gospel.

When John collapsed and died on New Year's Day, 1839, while tending to a boy's ulcerated foot, he was buried in a churchyard on High Street. All England mourned, and a monument was erected over his grave, reading: "Thou shalt be blessed, for they could not recompense thee."[1]

Date: _____ _____ _____
Place: _____ _____ _____
Occasion: _____ _____ _____

A Child's Prayer

Overheard by a parent:

Now I lay me down to rest
I hope to pass tomorrow's test.
If I should die before I wake,
That's one less test I have to take.

Date: _____ _____ _____
Place: _____ _____ _____
Occasion: _____ _____ _____

---

[1] Robert J. Morgan, *From This Verse* (Nashville: Thomas Nelson Publishers, 1998), entry for August 13th.

Christlikeness

Someone Once Said . . .

- *Everything in the universe is good to the degree it conforms to the nature of God and evil as it fails to do so.*—A. W. Tozer[1]
- *I would suggest, first, that all of you Christians . . . begin to live more like Jesus Christ.*—Mahatma Gandhi, when asked by missionary E. Stanley Jones how Christianity could be more acceptable in India.
- *It would be well if there were as great a similarity between the life of Christ and the life of Christians, as there is between a just copy and the original. What He was by nature, we should be by grace.*—Rev. William Secker[2]
- *A Christian should be a striking likeness of Jesus Christ. . . . We should be pictures of Christ. . . . Oh! My brethren, there is nothing that can so advantage you, nothing can so prosper you, so assist you, so make you walk towards heaven rapidly, so keep your head upwards towards the sky, and your eyes radiant with glory, like the imitation of Jesus Christ.*—Charles Spurgeon[3]

Date: _____ _____ _____

Place: _____ _____ _____

Occasion: _____ _____ _____

Chipping Away

A sculptor once fashioned a magnificent lion out of solid stone. When asked how he had accomplished such a wonderful masterpiece, he replied, "It was easy. All I did was to chip away everything that didn't look like a lion." All God does is chip away everything in our lives that doesn't look like Christ.[4]

Date: _____ _____ _____

Place: _____ _____ _____

Occasion: _____ _____ _____

Conformed to the Image

The story is told of a heavyset woman who went to an exercise and diet clinic. The first thing the supervisor did was draw a silhouette on a mirror in the shape she wished to become. As she stood before the mirror, she bulged out over the silhouette. The instructor told her, "Our goal is for you to fit this shape."

For many weeks the woman dieted and exercised. Each week she would stand in front of the mirror, but her volume, while decreasing, still overflowed. And so

---

[1] A. W. Tozer, *A Treasury of A. W. Tozer* (Grand Rapids: Baker Book House, 1980), 22.
[2] William Secker, *The Nonsuch Professor In His Meridian Splendor* (Chicago: Fleming H. Revell Co., 1899), 37.
[3] From Spurgeon's Sermon, *Christ's People—Imitators of Him.*
[4] Carole Mayhall, *Filled to Overflowing* (Colorado Springs: NavPress, 1984), 97–107.

she exercised harder and dieted more rigidly. Finally one day, to everyone's delight, as she stood in front of the mirror she was conformed to the image of the silhouette.

It takes time and work to be conformed to the image of God's Son. The discipline of sorrow and suffering, the exercise of pain and trials conform us to His image.[1]

Date:			
Place:			
Occasion:			

More Like Jesus

William Howard Doane was a wealthy nineteenth-century industrialist who entered the business world at age sixteen and was president of his own manufacturing company by age twenty-nine. But his real love was music, and he sang solos and directed choirs at various churches around Cincinnati. At age thirty, Doane suffered a terrible heart attack which took him to the edge of the grave. As he recovered, he felt God wanted him to devote more of his time to the ministry of Christian music.

———◇———
A Likeness

A Christian should be a striking likeness of Jesus Christ.
———◇———

He began compiling and publishing hymn books, and writing musical scores for hymns and gospel songs. But Doane didn't feel he could compose words suitable to his melodies, and he was always looking for Christian poets who could write lyrics for the Gospel tunes. In November, 1867, in New York, he was asked by Rev. Dr. W. C. Van Meter to write a hymn in celebration of the anniversary of a rescue mission. Doane quickly came up with a melody, but could find no suitable words.

Kneeling in his New York hotel room, he asked God to send him a poem suitable for the anniversary celebration. He also prayed for a poet who could supply an ongoing stream of suitable verse. As he prayed, he heard a knock at the door. Opening it, he saw a messenger boy who handed him an envelope addressed to Mr. William Howard Doane. The letter read: *Mr. Doane: I have never met you, but I feel impelled to send you this hymn. May God bless it. Fanny Crosby.*

Thus began a relationship that gave the church some of its greatest Gospel hymns: "To God Be the Glory," "'Tis the Blessed Hour of Prayer," "Tho' Your Sins Be as Scarlet," "Pass Me Not," "Near the Cross," "Savior More Than Life To Me," "Rescue the Perishing," "Will Jesus Find Us Watching?," "Safe in the Arms of Jesus," and more.

The one enclosed in the letter that day was quickly embraced by congregations around the world:

More like Jesus would I be,
Let my Savior dwell in me,
Fill my soul with peace and love,
Make me gentle as the dove;

---

[1] Mayhall, *Filled to Overflowing,* 97–107.

More like Jesus while I go,
Pilgrim in this world below;
Poor in spirit would I be;
Let my Savior dwell in me.

More like Jesus when I pray,
More like Jesus day by day
May I rest me by His side,
Where the tranquil waters glide.

Date: _____ _____ _____
Place: _____ _____ _____
Occasion: _____ _____ _____

Family Likeness

After the death of Gustavus the Great, king of Sweden, in 1632, the chief statesmen of the country met to decide the future government. Some proposed a republic. Others suggested the vacant throne be offered to the king of Poland. In the midst of the deliberations the Chancellor suddenly rose. "Let there be no talk of a republic or of a Polish king," he wrote, "for the Great Gustavus has left an heir, a daughter six years of age." This was not generally known, and the statement was received with surprise.

"How do we know that this is not a trick of yours?" one inquired. "We have never seen this child; we were not aware that Gustavus had one."

"Wait a minute," replied the Chancellor, "and I will show you." Leaving the room, he returned with a little girl whom he placed upon the throne where only the rulers of Sweden might sit. The man who had expressed his disbelief pressed forward and gazed intently upon her face. Then, turning to the assembly, he said, "Comrades, I see in this child the features of the Great Gustavus. Look at her nose, her eyes, her chin; she is indeed the daughter of our king." This was enough. Young as she was, they acclaimed her, "Christina, Queen of Sweden."

As an heir of God and joint heir of Jesus Christ, you bear the image of our Lord . . . the family likeness.[1]

Date: _____ _____ _____
Place: _____ _____ _____
Occasion: _____ _____ _____

The Face of Christ

In his book, *When There Is No Miracle,* Robert Wise wrote about hearing a man named Cecil Henson tell his "death story" many times. In 1940, Cecil was pronounced dead for twenty or thirty minutes, and after his resuscitation and recovery,

---

[1] From *Our Daily Bread.*

he was a different man, no longer angry and now ready to pour himself into the raising of his young son Van (who later became a successful oral surgeon).

Cecil said that during his period of "twilight" he encountered Jesus in person. In those moments he looked fully into the face of the risen Christ and saw Him in all His glory.

Robert Wise said, *It is Cecil's description of His face that has gripped my imagination through the years. He saw the face of Jesus as a marvelous mosaic made up of a hundred small facets. Each piece added a shade or line to the total picture. So in looking into this composite face he could see the countenance of Christ. But as he looked, he could see a hundred parts.*

The startling realization was that the mosaic pieces were not tile, metal, or glass. Each small section was a clear, distinct, cameo of someone's face. As Cecil stared fixedly at the face there was a pulsating fluctuation between the total face and the cameo sections. One minute he could see the Face and then in the next he was aware of hundreds of faces.

In awe Cecil began to recognize what was revealed in each of those cameos. They were all people he knew. Moreover, they were all people who had loved him and given him kindness during his life. He could see an aunt and an uncle. And there was his mother and on the other side his father's face moved into focus. School teachers, friends, associates, people who had already become part of conveying the human picture of Christ.

Overwhelmed in worship and amazement, Cecil bowed before the risen Lord. In the lingering moments of that experience, anxieties, fears and doubts were healed. When Cecil "returned" to start his life again, the face of Jesus guided him through the years ahead. Christ and the Cross remained sufficient for him until, over twenty years later, he died.[1]

Date:	_____	_____	_____
Place:	_____	_____	_____
Occasion:	_____	_____	_____

Seeing His Face

One day missionary Amy Carmichael, who devoted her life to rescuing girls who had been dedicated to a life of slavery and shame in Indian Hindu Temples, took some of her children to see a goldsmith refining gold in the ancient manner of the Orient. The man sat beside a small charcoal fire. On top of the coals lay a common red curved roof-tile, and another tile over it like a lid. This was his homemade crucible. The man had a mixture of salt, tamarind fruit, and burnt brick dust which he called his "medicine" for the purifying of the gold. He dropped a lump of ore into the blistering mixture and let the fire "eat it." After awhile, the man lifted the gold out with a pair of tongs, let it cool, and studied it. Then he replaced the gold in the crucible and blew the fire hotter than it was before. This process went on and on, the fire growing hotter and hotter. "[The gold] could not bear it so hot at first," explained the goldsmith, "but it can bear it now; what would have destroyed it helped it."

As the children watched the gold being purified in the fire, someone asked the man, "How do you know when the gold is purified?"

The man's answer: "When I can see my face in it [the liquid gold in the crucible], then it is pure."

---

[1] Robert Wise, *When There Is No Miracle* (Hearthstone Publishing Company, 1998).

When the Great Refiner sees his own image reflected in us, He has brought us to purity and maturity.[1]

Date: _____ _____ _____

Place: _____ _____ _____

Occasion: _____ _____ _____

Offering Christ

In her book, *Legacy of a Pack Rat,* Ruth Graham tells of meeting a young Indian student named Pashi who was enrolled in a college near Ruth's North Carolina home. As she spoke with him about Christ, . . . *he replied devastatingly, "I would like to believe in Christ. We of India would like to believe in Christ. But we have never see a Christian who was like Christ."*

Come to think of it, neither have I.

We believers are all merely pilgrims in progress, encumbered with disagreeable genes, trying— and in the process being found "trying indeed." There are degrees of saintliness, but the very term Christ-like is confusing. Like Him in what way? His ability to heal? To cast out demons? To raise the dead? To cast the money changers out of the Temple? To teach? To face His accusers calmly, silently?

I think basically what is meant by the term Christ-like has got to do with His attitude toward His Father's will.

"Lo, I come to do Thy will . . . I delight to do Thy will."

Whatever the true meaning, I was feeling we had somehow let the Lord down rather badly.

So I decided to call our friend and longtime coworker, Dr. Akbar Haqq, a brilliant Christian who used to be President of the Henry Martyn School of Islamic Studies in New Delhi.

"Akbar," I asked when I got him on the phone and explained the problem, "what would you say? How would you answer Pashi?"

"That is quite simple," Akbar said decisively. . . . "I would tell him, 'I am not offering you Christians. I am offering you Christ.' "[2]

Date: _____ _____ _____

Place: _____ _____ _____

Occasion: _____ _____ _____

Christmas

Someone Once Said . . .

- *The incarnation is in itself an unfathomable mystery, but it makes sense of everything else that the New Testament contains.*—J. I. Packer[3]

---

[1] Adapted from Elizabeth Skoglund, *More Than Coping* (Minneapolis: World Wide Publications, 1987), 48.

[2] Ruth Bell Graham, *Legacy of a Pack Rat* (Nashville: Thomas Nelson Publishers, 1989), 180.

[3] J. I. Packer, *Knowing God* (Downers Grove, IL: InterVarsity Press, 1973), 47.

- *The hinge of history is on the door of a Bethlehem stable.*—Ralph W. Sockman, nineteenth-century Methodist pastor
- *Let us not flutter too high, but remain by the manger and the swaddling clothes of Christ, "in whom dwelleth all the fullness of the Godhead bodily.*—Martin Luther[1]
- *I wish we could put up some of the Christmas spirit in jars and open a jar of it every month.*—Better Homes and Gardens
- *God bless us, every one.*—Tiny Tim, from Charles Dickens' *A Christmas Carol*

Date:			
Place:			
Occasion:			

"You Will Recognize . . ."

In his book, *Hitler's Cross*, Erwin W. Lutzer analyzes the Nazi agenda for Germany and how the German church responded. Here is a paragraph from the book:

Since Germans had for centuries celebrated Christmas and Easter, Hitler had to reinterpret their meaning. Christmas was turned into a totally pagan festival; in fact, at least for the SS troops, its date was changed to December 21, the date of the winter solstice. Carols and Nativity plays were banned from the schools in 1938, and even the name Christmas was changed to "Yuletide." Crucifixes were eliminated from the classrooms, and Easter was turned into a holiday that heralded the arrival of spring.

You will recognize the same changes taking place in America today.[2]

Date:			
Place:			
Occasion:			

White Christmas?

Without Jesus to wash us whiter than snow, there can never be a genuinely White Christmas.

Consider Lindsay, for example. His father, a distant and severe man, worked him especially hard during the holidays. Lindsay was given extra chores at the family ranch, and his old man whipped him if he didn't work hard enough. Lindsay lived in fear of these beatings, which often drew blood. But even worse were the verbal floggings, the names, the insults, the belittling put-downs. They seemed especially harsh at Christmas.

The memories stayed with him all his life, tormenting him like demons every December. One friend said, "Lindsay was never able to find happiness. He became a hard-drinking hell-raiser who went from woman to woman and couldn't find peace or success."

---

[1] Martin Luther, *Table Talk* (Grand Rapids: Baker Book House, 1952), 75.
[2] Erwin W. Lutzer, *Hitler's Cross* (Chicago: Moody Press, 1995), 115.

Finally at age fifty-one, he angrily watched Bing Crosby's "White Christmas" one last time, then put a gun to his head and a bullet through his brain.

"I hated Christmas because of Pop, and I always will," he once said. "It brings back the pain and fear I suffered as a child. And if I ever do myself in, it will be at Christmastime. That will show the world what I think of Bing Crosby's 'White Christmas.'"

Ironically, sadly, he was Bing's son—Lindsay Crosby.

(That bizarre story is itself a parable of what happens when we gut Christmas of its true glory. If only Lindsay had really understood that Jesus Christ was born on Christmas day so that our sins, though they be as scarlet, shall be as white as snow. "Though they are red like crimson, They shall be as wool," Isaiah 1:18).[1]

Date: _____ _____ _____
Place: _____ _____ _____
Occasion: _____ _____ _____

That Masked Man

Black and white television was just taking off in the Tennessee mountains when I was born in the early 1950s, and I cut my teeth on some of the locally produced children's shows that were broadcast live from a nearby station. One show was hosted by a cowboy wearing a mask like the Lone Ranger's. He teased us about his true identity, and you can imagine our excitement when he announced one Monday that on Friday's program he would remove his mask.

Ratings must have soared that week, because all of us tuned in excitedly, waiting for the dramatic moment when our cowboy host would unmask and reveal himself. What did he really look like? Who was he in real life?

The day came, then the hour, then the moment. Reaching behind his head, he untied his mask. But to our consternation, just as the mask came off he turned his back to the camera, and we were left no wiser than before.

On Christmas evening, God took off His mask. He revealed Himself to us and allowed us to see Him as He really is. When we see Jesus Christ, we are seeing the very image of Almighty God. "No one has seen God at any time," says John 1:18. "The only begotten Son, who is in the bosom of the Father, He has declared Him." I once read of a great European cathedral whose ceiling was adorned with a painting of God, drawn in brilliant colors. But the ceiling was so high and the cathedral so narrow that it hurt visitors to crane their necks to view the painting. The ingenious rector place a mirror at ground level, tilted so that worshipers, by looking in the mirror, could study the image of the painting above.

Hebrews 1 says that Jesus Christ is the "express image" of God's person. Colossians 1:17 calls the Christ-child, "the image of the invisible God." Colossians 2:9 adds, "For in Him dwells all the fullness of the Godhead bodily."

---

[1] Clippings from my files.

Date: _____ _____ _____
Place: _____ _____ _____
Occasion: _____ _____ _____

The Oriental Manger

Britisher Geoffrey T. Bull, missionary to Tibet, was cold, exhausted, and hungry. He had been seized by Communists following their takeover of China in 1949, and his future was bleak. His captors drove him day and night across frozen mountains until he despaired of life. Late one afternoon, he staggered into a small village where he was given an upstairs room, swept clean and warmed by a small charcoal brazier.

After a meager supper, he was sent downstairs to feed the horses. It was very dark and very cold. He clambered down the notched tree trunk to find himself in pitch blackness. His boots squished in the manure and straw on the floor. The fetid smell of animals was nauseating. The horses sighed wearily, tails drooping, yet the missionary expected to be kicked any moment. Geoffrey, cold, weary, lonely, and ill, begin to feel sorry for himself.

"Then as I continued to grope my way in the darkness," he later wrote, "it suddenly flashed into my mind. What's today? I thought for a moment. In traveling, the days had become a little muddled in my mind. Suddenly it came to me. 'It's Christmas Eve.' I stood suddenly still in that Oriental manger. To think that my Savior was born in a place like this. To think that He came all the way from heaven to some wretched eastern stable, and what is more to think that He came for me. How men beautify the cross and the crib, as if to hide the fact that at birth we resigned Him to the stench of beasts and at death exposed Him to the shame of rogues.

"I returned to the warm, clean room which I enjoyed even as a prisoner, bowed to thankfulness and worship."[1]

Date: _____ _____ _____
Place: _____ _____ _____
Occasion: _____ _____ _____

Things You Probably Didn't Know About Christmas

- During the early days of Christianity, different parts of the world celebrated Christmas on different dates. If you traveled widely in the Roman world, you could conceivably enjoy six different Christmases in the span of a single year. It was Pope Julius I in the mid-fourth century who appointed a monk named Dionysius to set up a calendar standardizing a universal date, which came to be December 25.

---

[1] Geoffrey T. Bull, *When Iron Gates Yield* (Chicago: Moody Press, n.d.), 158–159.

- Christmas was outlawed in England by the Puritans under Oliver Cromwell (1599–1658) who thought of it as a "heathen celebration." It was illegal to celebrate the holiday until the British monarchy was restored in 1660.
- Christmas was also outlawed by the Puritans of New England. The following law was passed in Massachusetts in 1659: "Whoever shall be found observing any such day as Christmas and the like, either by forbearing labor, feasting or any other way, shall pay for any such offense five shillings as a fine to the country." The law remained on the books for 22 years, and Christmas was not made a legal holiday in Massachusetts until just before the Civil War.
- In Spain, Christmas gifts are not exchanged until January 6—for a very good reason. That is the date commemorating the visit of the Magi, who were the first to offer Christmas gifts—gold, frankincense, and myrrh. On that night, children set their shoes outside on the doorstep, filling them with straw for the camels. They believe the wise men will use the straw to feed their camels and in return fill the shoes with gifts and candy.
- The custom of sending Christmas cards began in 1843 when a wealthy Englishman, Sir Henry Cole, ran out of time to write personal letters to his friends at Christmas. He commissioned an artist, John Calcott Horsley, to design a card instead. Horsley drew a picture of a group of merry-wishers raising their glasses in toast. Underneath were the words, "A Merry Christmas and a Happy New Year to You." The card created much controversy, as critics complained it encouraged holiday drinking. But the custom of sending cards at Christmas caught on nonetheless.
- The Poinsettia is a Christmas tradition harkening from Mexico. According to legend, a boy named Pablo was headed to his village church to see its nativity scene. Realizing he had no gift for the Christchild, he hurriedly gathered some branches and weeds from the roadside. When he laid them before the manger, the other children laughed at him. But suddenly there appeared on each branch the brilliant, star-shaped flower of the Poinsettia.
- Candy canes were reportedly developed by a Christian candymaker in Indiana who built the story of Christmas into each piece. The hardness of the candy represents the solid rock of the Christian faith. The white represents the sinlessness of Christ, and the red stripes symbolize the bloody wounds caused by his flogging. The shape of the candy is that of a shepherd's staff, representing Christ as our Good Shepherd. Turned upside down, it forms the letter "J"—for Jesus.
- Our word *Christmas* comes from the English observance of the birth of Christ called *Christes masse (Christ's mass)*, because a special mass was celebrated on that day. In France, it's known as Noel; in Spain, *Navidad;* and in Italy, *Natale*—all those words meaning simply *birthday.* The Germans use the word *Weihnachten,* meaning *holy nights.*
- The word *Yule* comes from the Teutonic tribes of northern Europe. Because their winters were so long and harsh and their days so short, they always celebrated the winter solstice on December 22, the shortest day of the year. It was a time of great joy for them. From that point each year the days began to lengthen. They called the month *Yule,* or *Jol,* from which we get our English word *jolly.*

- The day after Christmas is commonly called "Boxing Day" in England, because of the custom of giving Christmas boxes containing gifts and money to the servants.

Date: _____ _____ _____
Place: _____ _____ _____
Occasion: _____ _____ _____

The Twelve Days of Christmas

Many historians believe the well-known song, *The Twelve Days of Christmas,* is actually a Christian hymn in disguise. During the reign of England's Queen Elizabeth I, a staunch Protestant, English Catholics were oppressed and persecuted. Priests met secretly with small groups of Catholics, risking their lives to conduct worship and observe mass.

Under such circumstances, it was difficult to train or catechize Catholic children. But an unknown, clever priest found a unique way of teaching the Gospel to children, using the theme of the twelve days between Christmas and Epiphany, when the Wise Men, according to tradition, arrived with their gifts for the Christchild.

The priest hid biblical truth in the symbols he used in his carol, beginning with the words *On the first day of Christmas my true love gave to me.* . . . The "True Love" referred to God the Father, and the "Me" represents the Christian who receives the gifts. The "Partridge in the Pear Tree" is Jesus. Why a partridge? Mother partridges are known for feigning injury to decoy predators from their babies. The children were thereby taught about Christ's sacrifice on our behalf.

The two turtle doves represented the Old and New Testaments.

The three French hens symbolized faith, hope, and love—the three great virtues we should display as we come to know Christ as Lord and read the Old and New Testaments. The other symbols:

- Four calling birds—the four Gospels
- Five golden rings—the first five books of the Bible, the Pentateuch
- Six geese a laying—the six days of creation
- Seven swans a-swimming—the seven gifts of the Holy Spirit
- Eight maids a-milking—the eight Beatitudes of Matthew 5
- Nine ladies dancing—nine choirs of angels
- Ten lords a-leaping—the Ten Commandments
- Eleven pipers piping—the eleven faithful apostles
- Twelve drummers drumming—the twelve articles of the Apostles' Creed[1]

Date: _____ _____ _____
Place: _____ _____ _____
Occasion: _____ _____ _____

[1] Clipping in my files

C

Angels from the Realms of Glory

When the Moravian Christians of Europe launched Protestant missions, they did it at a cost. Many of them had to leave their children behind in boarding schools across England and the Continent.

And so it was that the Montgomery family reluctantly placed six-year-old James in such an institution as they shipped off as foreign missionaries to the West Indies. When they later perished, James, left with nothing, spent his teenage years drifting from pillar to post, writing poetry and trying his hand at one thing then another.

In his early twenties, he began working for a British newspaper, the *Sheffield Iris,* and there he found his niche. When his editorials proved unpopular with the local officials, he was thrown into jail and fined twenty pounds. But he emerged from prison a celebrity, and he used his newly acquired fame to promote his favorite issues.

Chief among them was the Gospel. Despite the loss of his parents and all his hardships, James Montgomery remained devoted to Christ and the Scriptures.

As the years passed, he became the most respected leader in Sheffield, and his writings were eagerly read by its citizens. Early on Christmas Eve, 1816, James, forty-five, opened his Bible, and was deeply impressed by Luke 2:13. Pondering the story of the heralding angels, he took his pen and started writing. By the end of the day his new Christmas poem was being delivered to England in the pages of his newspaper. It was later set to music and was first sung on Christmas Day, 1821, in a Moravian Church in England.

> *Angels from the realms of glory,*
> *Wing your flight o'er all the earth;*
> *Ye who sang creation's story,*
> *Now proclaim Messiah's birth;*
> *Come and worship, Come and worship,*
> *Worship Christ the new-born King.*

His parents would have been proud.[1]

Date:			
Place:			
Occasion:			

How Children Hear Us Sing . . .

- Deck the Halls with Buddy Holly
- On the first day of Christmas my tulip gave to me
- Later on we'll perspire, as we dream by the fire.
- He's makin' a list, chicken and rice.
- Frosty the Snowman is a ferret elf, I say
- Sleep in heavenly peas

[1] Adapted from Robert J. Morgan, *From This Verse* (Nashville: Thomas Nelson, 1998), installment for August 2nd.

- In the meadow we can build a snowman, Then pretend that he is sparse and brown
- You'll go down in listerine
- Oh, what fun it is to ride with one horse, soap and hay
- Good tidings we bring to you and your kid

Date: _____   _____   _____
Place: _____   _____   _____
Occasion: _____   _____   _____

A Gift of Life

In 1910, a terrible plague swept through eastern Czechoslovakia during the Christmas season. It was diphtheria, and it devastated the little Czech village of Velky Slavhov. Nearly half the village contracted the infectious disease, and many of the victims were less than ten years of age. Whenever a member of a family would show symptoms, a large black "X" would be swabbed on the doorpost of the house as a warning that it had been quarantined.

There was an "X" painted on the doorpost of the home of Jano and Suzanna Boratkova. In little less than a week, the young couple, parents of three, found themselves childless. Their oldest child, a five-year-old daughter, had been the first to go. And even as Jano was working in the woodshed, pounding together a coffin for her, his two sons were dying.

A Charge Too Deep

Anyone who doesn't think Christmas doesn't last all year doesn't have a charge account.

—ANONYMOUS

As the two young boys breathed their last, Suzanna broke into agonizing sobs. She cleaned and wrapped the two boys for a final time and carefully laid them in handmade pine caskets. She and Jano lifted the coffins onto the wagon and started the slow journey through the biting December cold and the foot-high snow toward the graveyard. They passed by house after house marked with an "X", but they didn't have the strength to offer sympathy or encouragement. They were too wrapped up in their own grief.

The young couple laid their children in freshly-dug graves and struggled through the Lord's Prayer. Then they trudged back to the wagon and returned home. No one was there to meet them. It was too dangerous, for the house was quarantined. It was a frightening, dark little tomb. Little high-heeled brown leather shoes were still lined up against the wood stove, as they usually were when the children were tenderly in bed. But now the beds were empty, the house was cold, the shadows deep and cold.

Jano himself was sick. "I won't see another Christmas," he said, wheezing and coughing. "I don't think I'll see the New Year in, either." He pushed away the soup and bread, for it was too hard for him to swallow. The diphtheria had tied a noose around his neck, allowing neither food nor sufficient air to sustain him. Suzanna gathered some kindling and lit a fire for the night, sure that her husband was about to die. The snow was starting to fall again, and she paused to gaze through the window. Her mind went to a verse of Scripture—Psalm 121:1: *I will lift up mine eyes unto the hills from whence cometh my help. My help cometh from the Lord who made heaven and earth.*

Suddenly she saw someone approaching, a peasant woman tramping through the snow, a red and purple plaid shawl draped over her hunched shoulders. A kerchief was wrapped around her head, and her long skirt was a bright display of cotton and linen patchwork. In one hand, she held a jar of clear liquid. She approached the house and knocked on the door.

Suzanna cautiously opened the door. "We have the plague in our home," she said, "and my husband is in a fever right now." The old woman nodded and asked if she could step inside. She held out her little jar. "Take a clean, white linen and wrap it around your finger," she said. "Dip your finger into this pure kerosene oil and swab out your husband's throat, and then have him swallow a tablespoon of the oil. This should cause him to vomit the deadly mucous. Otherwise, he will surely suffocate. I will pray for you and your family."

Then, having left her folk remedy against diphtheria, she turned and left. Suzanna followed the woman's instructions, and early Christmas morning, Jano retched up the deadly phlegm. His fever broke, and Suzanna entertained a flicker of hope. There were no presents under the tree that year, but an old woman with her jar of oil was a gift of life. Jano recovered, in time the Lord gave the couple more children. In the 1920s Jano and Suzanna emigrated to America—with eight children, which included a set of triplets and two sets of twins.

It's a story that has been handed down through the generations of that family, the little peasant woman who came on Christmas Eve bearing the gift of life. Jesus, too, came on Christmas bearing the gift of life for hopeless, grieving, dying people. He came for Jew and Gentile. He came for you and me.[1]

Date:	_____	_____	_____
Place:	_____	_____	_____
Occasion:	_____	_____	_____

The Christmas Truce

This story has been told in a variety of ways, but this is the researched version that appeared in newspapers nationwide on December 25, 1994 from the Associated Press, dateline London. *Eighty years ago, on the first Christmas Day of World War I, British and German troops put down their guns and celebrated peacefully together in the no-man's land between the trenches.*

The war, briefly, came to a halt.

In some places, festivities began when German troops lit candles on Christmas trees on their parapets so the British sentries a few hundred yards away could see them.

Elsewhere, the British acted first, starting bonfires and letting off rockets.

Pvt. Oswald Tilley of the London Rifle Brigade wrote to his parents: "Just you think that while you were eating your turkey, etc., I was out talking and shaking hands with the very men I had been trying to kill a few hours before!! It was astounding."

---

[1] Kathleen R. Ruckman, "A Christmas Miracle" in *Focus on the Family Magazine*, December, 1988, 12–13.

Both armies had received lots of comforts from home and felt generous and well-disposed toward their enemies in the first winter of the war, before the vast battles of attrition began in 1915, eventually claiming 10 million lives.

All along the line that Christmas Day, soldiers found their enemies were much like them and began asking why they should be trying to kill each other.

The generals were shocked. High Command diaries and statements express anxiety that if that sort of thing spread it could sap the troops' will to fight.

The soldiers in khaki and gray sang carols to each other, exchanged gifts of tobacco, jam, sausage, chocolate and liquor, traded names and addresses and played soccer between the shell holes and barbed wire. They even paid mutual trench visits.

This day is called "the most famous truce in military history" by British television producer Malcolm Brown and researcher Shirley Seaton in their book "Christmas Truce," published in 1984.[1]

Date: _____   _____   _____

Place: _____   _____   _____

Occasion: _____   _____   _____

Gold, Frankincense, and Myrrh

In an article in the *Saturday Evening Post,* Donald Culross Peattie explained the significance of the gifts presented to the Christ-child by the Magi.

- Gold is one of the noble metals. No single acid can destroy it, nor will it rust away, like iron or tin . . . No one can successfully imitate or fake gold, so heavy and incorruptible is it. And it is a metal easily turned to the uses of beauty. It has been woven into fabrics at least since Biblical times (Exodus 39:2–3), for its ductility, as chemists say, is so great that a single grain of fine gold can be drawn out into a wire 1/1000 of an inch in diameter, extending for a length of about one mile. Pure, supple, almost indestructible, gold is indeed a royal metal . . . The expert hammer of the goldbeater, whose ancient art is referred to by Homer, can beat an ounce of gold into a sheet two hundred feet square, a mere shimmering film. . . . In the ancient world into which Christianity was born, gold was far rarer than now.
- [Incense] was made from an expensive and elaborate formula, containing sixteen different ingredients, with only priests allowed to concoct it. And the chief element in this holy recipe was frankincense, the second gift of the wise men to the Child. Frankincense is a resin, from a kind of tree held so sacred of old that in southern Arabia and Ethiopia, where it grew, only a few particularly pure persons were allowed even to approach it. . . . To obtain the precious frankincense itself, an Arab cuts a slash in the trunk, as a Vermonter cuts a maple, and then strips off a narrow piece of bark, about five inches long, below the cut. The sap slowly oozes out and is allowed to harden for about three months. At last it is collected in lumps, to be shipped from such strange

and faraway places as Berbera and Aden, near the mouth of the Red Sea, and Bombay. These lumps are yellow or colorless, dusty-looking, with a bitter taste. But they burn with a bright white flame, and then there arises to heaven that sweet, heavenly perfume of mystery the Wise Men thought pleasing to God.

- Myrrh [is] a shrub related to frankincense, of the genus *Commiphora*. The sap of myrrh is extracted in the same way as that of frankincense, and it comes in small lumps of reddish-brown resin. But its symbolism is more somber. The word myrrh comes from the Hebrew *mar,* meaning "bitter." The ancient Egyptians used this resin in embalming, and hence its connection with solemn occasion.[1]

Date: _____ _____ _____
Place: _____ _____ _____
Occasion: _____ _____ _____

The Old Monk

Corrie Ten Boom used to tell a story about an old monk who sang a Christmas song every Christmas Eve for his brothers in the monastery, and for visitors who would come from the village for the special services. His voice was very ugly, but he loved the Lord and sang from his heart. One year the director of the cloister said, "I'm sorry, Brother Don, we will not need you this Christmas. We have a new monk who has a beautiful voice."

The man did sing beautifully, and everyone was happy. But that night an angel came to the superior and said, "Why didn't you have a Christmas Eve song?"

The superior was very surprised. "We had a beautiful song," he replied. "Didn't you hear it?"

The angel shook his head sadly. "It may have been inspiring to you, but we didn't hear it in heaven."

"You see," Corrie would say, "the old monk with the raspy voice had a personal relationship with the Lord Jesus, but the young monk was singing for his own benefit, not for that of the Lord."[2]

Date: _____ _____ _____
Place: _____ _____ _____
Occasion: _____ _____ _____

Now It Was My Turn

Curtis Bradford, a pastor in Charleston, South Carolina, said that when he was seven years old he crawled into bed on Christmas Eve so excited he couldn't sleep.

---

[1] Donald Culross Peattie, "Gold, Frankincense and Myrrh," in *The Saturday Evening Post,* Nov./Dec., 1992, 56–60.

[2] Adapted from Corrie Ten Boom, *In My Father's House* (Old Tappan, NJ: Fleming H. Revel Company, 1976), 136–137.

Pretending to be asleep, he lay there until he was sure his parents were snoring. Then, about 2 A.M., he crept downstairs.

There under the Christmas trees were his presents. A drum set beckoned him to play it then and there, but he didn't dare. But he found other gifts he could play with. A cowboy outfit, a set of six-shooters, a puppet. Filled with excitement, he emptied his stocking, began eating the candy, the apple, the orange. . . . But suddenly, hearing a noise, he turned and saw his Dad looking sternly down at him.

For a fleeting moment, Curtis was afraid, but his dad broke into a smile, settled himself in the recliner, and listened while Curtis showed him everything, explaining how the six-shooters worked and how the puppet moved its mouth.

Sleep soon came over him, and his dad picked him up, carried him upstairs, and tenderly tucked him into bed. The next morning they had a wonderful Christmas, but, Curtis said, "I will never forget that Christmas Eve."

The years flew by, and on another memorable Christmas Curtis found himself again at his father's side. This time the older man lay paralyzed from an automobile accident and weak from cancer. Treatments, therapy, and experimental drugs had left him weighing less than one hundred pounds and in great pain. But despite his pain, he asked if Curtis would dress him so he could watch the family open presents. He wanted a cleanly shaven face. So Curtis lathered the shaving mug and brush and got out the razor to shave his dad. The old man told him how his beard grew this way and that, and how he needed to turn the razor up at one point and down at another.

After the shave, Curtis dressed him and carried him to the den where the family waited. He was able to sit there for almost fifteen minutes before the joy turned to almost unbearable pain. Then his eyes filled with tears, and he asked Curtis to carry him back to bed. Gently, the strong adult son gathered the frail man into his arms. Curtis later said, "As I made my way to his bedroom, I recalled the night many years before when he had carried me to my bedroom after our private Christmas showing. Now it was my turn to carry him."

Tears ran down Curtis' face as he nestled his dad into bed, and seeing the tears, the old man pointed to a tape recorder beside the bed. Curtis turned it on, and together they listened to the Bible being read. It was John 14: "In my father's house there are many mansions. . . ." Silently Curtis thanked God for saving him, for saving his father, for giving them those moments together, and for those times when the Lord had carried them both.

Two days later, Curtis' dad passed away. But the memories are precious rather than painful, says Curtis. "Because of Jesus, whose birth we celebrate on Christmas and who died to save those who believe in Him, I know I will see my father again. And what a family reunion that will be."[1]

Date:	_____	_____	_____
Place:	_____	_____	_____
Occasion:	_____	_____	_____

---

[1] Adapted from the article "Gifts From My Father" by Curtis Bradford in *Experiencing God* Magazine, December 1995, 16–17.

RATS

A minister once enlisted four children to help him preach his Christmas sermon on "The Star." He gave each child one of the four letters to hold up so he could make a point on each letter of the word "Star." When the children stepped forward and turned around, they were in reverse order. The congregation nearly fell out of their pews as they read: "RATS."

Date: _____ _____ _____
Place: _____ _____ _____
Occasion: _____ _____ _____

C

—————————————— **Church** ——————————————

Someone Once Said . . .

- *We leave comfortable homes to ride in comfortable cars to sit in comfortable churches to hear comfortable sermons. What do we know about the reproach of Christ?*—Vance Havner[1]
- *Too many church services start at eleven o'clock sharp and end at twelve o'clock dull.*—Vance Havner[2]
- *The world at its worst needs the church at its best.*—Anonymous

Date: _____ _____ _____
Place: _____ _____ _____
Occasion: _____ _____ _____

A Great Organization

In his book *Harvest of Humility,* John Seamands told of a wounded German soldier who was ordered to go to the military hospital for treatment. When he arrived at the large and imposing building, he saw two doors, one marked "For the slightly wounded" and the other, "For the seriously wounded."

He entered through the first door and found himself going down a long hall. At the end of it were two more doors, one marked "For officers" and the other "For non-officers." He entered the through the latter and found himself going down another long hall. At the end of it were two more doors, one marked "For party members" and the other "For non-party members." He took the second door, and when he opened it he found himself out on the street.

When the soldier returned home, his mother asked him, "How did you get along at the hospital?"

[1] Vance Havner, *Moments of Decision* (Old Tappan, NJ: Fleming H. Revell Co., 1979), 27.
[2] Vance Havner, *Pepper 'N Salt* (Old Tappan, NJ: Fleming H. Revell Co., 1966), 11.

"Well, Mother," he replied, "to tell the truth, the people there didn't do anything for me, but you ought to see the tremendous organization they have!"

Many churches have a superb organization. Their people are busy. But unless the Spirit of God is free to work through them, the church's ministry will be limited. The church at Sardis was organized—but dead. Don't let that happen in your church![1]

Date: _____ _____ _____
Place: _____ _____ _____
Occasion: _____ _____ _____

In the Name of Jesus

The medieval theologian John Duns Scotus was visiting Rome, and the Pope took him into the Vatican treasuries. Running his hands through the silver, the Pope said, "No longer does the church have to say, 'Silver and gold have I none.'" The theologian replied, "That's true, but also no longer can we say, 'In the name of Jesus Christ of Nazareth, rise up and walk.'"

Date: _____ _____ _____
Place: _____ _____ _____
Occasion: _____ _____ _____

From Catacombs to Cathedrals

Someone once said that Christianity has a way of beginning in a catacomb with nothing but a message and ending up in a cathedral with nothing but money.

Date: _____ _____ _____
Place: _____ _____ _____
Occasion: _____ _____ _____

The Original Staff

When the church began on earth, the Pastor was being executed as a criminal; the chairman of the board was out cursing and swearing that he had never even been a part it. The treasurer was committing suicide. Most of the rest of the board members had run away. And about the only ones who showed any signs of faithfulness were a few ladies from the woman's auxiliary.

Date: _____ _____ _____
Place: _____ _____ _____
Occasion: _____ _____ _____

---

[1] Clipped from *Our Daily Bread.*

God's Work

There are over sixty references to Ethiopia in the Bible, and Christianity there goes back to the days of Philip in Acts 8. But the modern story of the Ethiopian church also sounds like readings from the book of Acts, especially among the Wallamos. In 1927, the Sudan Interior Mission (SIM) sent missionaries to evangelize this wild tribe, worshipers of Satan. During its annual "Passover" the Wallamos sacrificed a bull to Satan, sprinkling its blood on the doorposts of their houses and serving its raw flesh to every member of their families. The atmosphere smelled of demons.

After several years a small church was established, but missionary labor was interrupted when Mussolini invaded Ethiopia in 1935. When Italian troops reached tribal areas, they demanded SIM leave. The missionaries met a final time with Wallamos believers. When they had arrived, not a single Wallamo had known of Christ. Now after nine years, forty-eight native believers gathered around them. The little church worshiped, wept, and shared the Lord's Supper. Then the twenty-six SIM missionaries boarded army trucks for evacuation. On April 17, 1937, their first day without missionary support, the little Wallamo church found itself having to stand on its own feet. "We knew God was faithful," wrote missionary Raymond Davis, "that he was able to preserve what he had begun among the Wallamos. But still we wondered—if we ever come back, what will we find?"

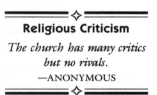

Religious Criticism

The church has many critics but no rivals.

—ANONYMOUS

The invasion of Ethiopia marked the beginnings of World War II, and it wasn't until July 4, 1943, that the missionaries returned. What they found almost defies belief. The Italian soldiers had tried to stamp out the small church. Church leaders were given one hundred lashes, and one in particular was given four hundred. They were unable to lie on their backs for months. Several had died. One of them, Wandaro, beaten in public, preached to the crowds between lashes. Another, Toro, stripped naked in the marketplace and flogged with a hippo-hide whip, bravely shouted out the Gospel. Conversions multiplied, and tribal villages began sending missionaries to other villages.

Instead of forty-eight believers, the returning missionaries now found eighteen thousand.[1]

```
Date:        _____    _____    _____
Place:       _____    _____    _____
Occasion:  _____    _____    _____
```

For the Sick

A little girl sitting in church with her dad suddenly felt sick. "Daddy," she whispered, "I have to vomit!" Her father told her to hurry to the restroom.

In just a moment she was back. "I didn't have to go too far," she explained. "There's a little box by the door that says, 'For the Sick.'"

---

[1] Robert J. Morgan, *On This Day* (Nashville: Nelson, 1997), entry for April 17th.

Date:			
Place:			
Occasion:			

God's Garden

In growing a healthy, fruit-bearing church, try this plan.
Plant three rows of squash:

- Squash gossip.
- Squash criticism.
- Squash indifference.

Plant seven rows of peas:

- Prayer
- Promptness
- Perseverance
- Politeness
- Preparedness
- Purity
- Patience

Plant seven heads of lettuce:

- Let us be unselfish and loyal.
- Let us be faithful to duty.
- Let us search the Scriptures.
- Let us not be weary in well-doing.
- Let us be obedient in all things.
- Let us be truthful.
- Let us love one another.

No garden is complete without turnips:

- Turn up for church.
- Turn up for meetings, in prayer, and Bible study.
- Turn up with a smile, even when things are difficult.
- Turn up with determination to do your best in God's service.

After planting, may you grow in grace and in the knowledge of our Lord and Savior Jesus Christ (2 Peter 3:18). And may you reap rich results.[1]

Date:			
Place:			
Occasion:			

---

[1] Clipped from my files.

Here's the Church . . .

During Vacation Bible School one year, a pastor's wife had an experience with her primary class that can teach us all a great lesson. About an hour before dismissal one evening, a new student was brought into the room. The little boy had one arm missing, and since the class was almost over, the teacher had no opportunity to learn the details of his situation, but she was nervous that one of the other children would say something insensitive to him, so she preceded cautiously with the lesson.

As the class time came to a close, she asked the children to join her in their usual closing ceremony. "Let's make our churches," she said, putting her hands together to form the "church."

"Here's the church and here's the steeple, open the doors and . . ." Suddenly the awful truth struck her. The very thing she had feared that the children would do, she had done.

As she stood there speechless, the little girl sitting next to the boy reached over with her left hand and placed it up to his right hand and said, "Josh, let's make the church together."[1]

Date: _____   _____   _____

Place: _____   _____   _____

Occasion: _____   _____   _____

The Perfect Church

A man reportedly came to the British pastor Charles H. Spurgeon looking for the perfect church. The famous preacher told him he had many saintly people in his congregation, but a Judas could also be among them. After all, even Jesus had a traitor in the company of His apostles. He went on to say that some might be walking disobediently, as had been the case among the believers at Rome, Corinth, Galatia, and Sardis.

"My church is not the one you're looking for," said Spurgeon. "But if you should happen to find such a church, I beg you not to join it, for you would spoil the whole thing."[2]

A survey by the Barna Research Group has pinpointed the top five reasons why Americans choose a church. A nationwide sampling of Americans were asked to respond to the following statement: "For most people there are a few key factors that determine whether or not they will return to a church they have visited. For each factor I mention please tell me if that factor would be extremely important, pretty important, somewhat important, not too important or not at all important in your decision of whether or not to return to a church you had visited." Of the 22 factors named, including worship styles and community outreaches, the top eight reasons for selecting a church, in order of importance, were:

- Theological beliefs
- How much people care

---

[1] Clipped from my files.
[2] From an *Our Daily Bread* clipping in my files.

- Quality of sermons
- Friendliness to visitors
- Help to poor and disadvantaged
- Quality of children's programs
- How much you like your pastor
- Denomination[1]

Date:			
Place:			
Occasion:			

Unique Perspectives

[A] A Matter of Sense

A preacher was in revival services in a town where a mental institution was located. One of the deacons employed at the institution asked the preacher to speak to the inmates at the chapel service. He agreed and after he had been preaching for a couple of minutes, one inmate stood up and said, "That's the worst preaching I've ever heard." This disturbed the preacher but he continued. After another five minutes the same inmate stood up and repeated, "I said, 'This is the worst preaching I've ever heard.'" Turning to the deacon who invited him, the preacher whispered, "Maybe I should stop. This man might get violent."

"Oh no, don't stop," said the deacon. "That man has been here four years, and that's the first sensible thing he has said."

[B] Future Publisher

The pastor, waiting at the door, inquired of a lady parishioner, "Was my sermon too long?"

"No," she said, "it just seemed long."

"I'm sorry to hear that," said the pastor.

"Oh, don't be," said the lady. "It was one of the best long speeches I ever heard. I just thought it was superfluous."

"Good. I intend to have it published posthumously."

"I hope you hurry," the woman said. "I want to read it."[2]

[C] A Bedtime Sermon?

One minister came home every evening in time to tuck in his little girl and tell her a bedtime story. One night he told her such a thrilling story that she sat up in bed, looked at her father, and asked, "Daddy, is that a true story or are you preaching?"

[D] Two-Minute Warning

One preacher's sermon was lasting so long that, at length, a restless little girl looked up at her mom and whispered, "Is it going into overtime?"

The mother hissed back, "Yes, and if you don't sit still, it'll be sudden death!"

---

[1] Source: Barna Research Group, November 18, 1998: website: www.barna.org

[2] Loyal Jones and Billy Edd Wheeler, *Laughter in Appalachia* (New York: Ivy Books, 1987), 25.

Date:			
Place:			
Occasion:			

Church Attendance

Someone Once Said . . .

- *Let us not hold aloof from our church meetings, as some do.*—Hebrews 10:25 (Phillips)
- *There is something wrong with our Christianity when we have to beg most of our crowd to come to church to hear about it.*—Vance Havner[1]
- *The great task of the church is not only to get sinners into heaven, but to get saints out of bed.*—Anonymous

Date:			
Place:			
Occasion:			

Eugene Peterson on "Church"

St. Paul talked about the foolishness of preaching; I would like to talk about the foolishness of congregations, God's choice of venue. Of all the ways in which to carry out the enterprise of church, this has to be the most absurd—a haphazard collection of people who somehow get assembled into pews on Sundays, half-heartedly sing a few songs most of them don't like, and tune in and out of a sermon according to the state of their digestion and the preacher's decibels, awkward in their commitments and jerky in their patterns.

But the people in those pews are also people who suffer deeply and find God in their suffering. They make love commitments, are faithful to them through trial and temptation, and bear fruits of righteousness, Spirit-fruits that bless the people around them. Babies, surrounded by hopeful and rejoicing parents and friends, are baptized in the name of the Father and the Son and the Holy Ghost. The dead are offered up to God in funerals that, in the midst of tears and grief, give solemn and joyful witness to the Resurrection. Sinners repent and take the body and blood of Jesus and receive new life.

And these two realities are mixed, impossible to separate.[2]

Date:			
Place:			
Occasion:			

---

[1] Vance Havner, *In Times Like These* (Old Tappan, NJ: Fleming H. Revell Co., 1969), 73.
[2] Eugene Peterson in "The Jonah Syndrome" in *Leadership Journal,* Summer 1990, 43.

How Would You Like It . . .

How would you like it if . . .

- Your watch ticked one time and missed the next?
- Your heart beat one time and missed the next?
- Your child missed every other day at school?
- The engine of your car only hit on half its cylinders?

Irregularity in any area of life causes problems. It was said about the early Christians, ". . . they continued steadfastly in the apostles, doctrine and fellowship, in breaking of bread and in prayer." If you are "on and off" in your church attendance, it hurts everybody.

Date: _____ _____ _____
Place: _____ _____ _____
Occasion: _____ _____ _____

Whether the Weather

In his book, *Pepper 'n Salt,* Vance Havner wrote: *My father was faithful to the house of God. When he felt like it and when he didn't, when the preaching was good and when it wasn't, my father was there.*

> *Whether the weather be good*
> *Or whether the weather be hot,*
> *Whether the weather be cold*
> *Or whether the weather be not,*
> *Whatever the weather, he weathered the weather,*
> *Whether he like it or not.*

Another thing I like about Dad at church: he did his sleeping at home. He never used the church for an adult nursery.[1]

Date: _____ _____ _____
Place: _____ _____ _____
Occasion: _____ _____ _____

Eight Reasons

Frances Ridley Havergal, British hymnist who wrote such classics as "Like a River Glorious," once made a list for herself of eight reasons for going to church, even on rainy days:

1. God has blessed the Lord's Day, making no exceptions for stormy days.
2. I expect my minister to be there. I'd be surprised if he stayed at home for the weather.

---

[1] Vance Havner, *Pepper 'n Salt* (Old Tappan, NJ: Fleming H. Revell Co., 1966), 26.

3. I might lose out on the prayers and the sermon that would have done me great good.
4. For any important business, rain doesn't keep me home; and church attendance is, in God's sight, very important.
5. Bad weather reveals on what foundation my faith is built; it will prove how much I love Christ. True love rarely fails to keep an appointment.
6. Those who stay at home from church because it's rainy frequently miss on fair Sundays, too. I must not take one step in that direction.
7. The Bible contains a special promise that where two or three meet together in Christ's name, He will be in the midst of them.
8. I don't know how many more Sundays God may give me, and it would be poor preparation for my first Sunday in Heaven to have slighted my last Sunday on earth.[1]

Date: _____ _____ _____
Place: _____ _____ _____
Occasion: _____ _____ _____

The House of Many Lamps

There is a legend of a village in Southern Europe that boasted of a church called "The House of Many Lamps." When it was built in the sixteenth century, the architect provided for no light except for a receptacle at every seat for the placing of a lamp. Each Sunday night, as the people gathered, they would bring their lanterns and slip them into the bracket at their seat. When someone stayed away, his place would be dark; and if very many stayed away, the darkness became greater for the whole. It was the regular presence of each person that lit up the church.[2]

Not a No-Show

Eighty percent of life is just showing up.
—WOODY ALLEN

Date: _____ _____ _____
Place: _____ _____ _____
Occasion: _____ _____ _____

The New Master

Missionary James King tells the true story of an African woman in one of his churches who attended every service accompanied by an old, mongrel dog. He would enter with the lady and sit beside her during the service. She always sat on an outside seat beside the aisle. At the conclusion of the service, when the invitation was given, the woman would always come and kneel at the altar for prayer, and the dog would faithfully take his place beside her.

---

[1] Clipping from my files.
[2] Clipping from my files.

The woman's husband was a cruel man who deeply resented her devotion to Christ, and one day he beat her so severely that she died, and he denied her a Christian funeral.

After the woman's death and burial, only the man and dog were left. But he noticed that the dog disappeared on Wednesday evening about 7:00 and didn't reappear for two hours. Every Sunday morning the dog likewise disappeared for a couple of hours.

One Sunday the man's curiosity was so aroused that he decided to follow and see where the dog went. Hurrying to keep up, the man followed the dog to the little church and watched as the dog took his seat on the aisle while the service went on. At the close of the service, the dog went to the altar and took his place where the wife had prayed.

The man was so touched in his spirit that he, too, went forward and gave his life to Christ.

Now the dog comes to church with a new master.[1]

Date: _____ _____ _____
Place: _____ _____ _____
Occasion: _____ _____ _____

——————————— Church Unity ———————————

Someone Once Said . . .

- *In the primitive times, there was so much love among the godly as set the heathen a-wondering, and now there is so little, as may set Christians a-blushing.*—Thomas Watson[2]
- *If Christ is amongst us, then it is necessary that we sometimes yield up our own opinion for the sake of peace. Who is so wise as to have perfect knowledge of all things? Therefore trust not too much to thine own opinion, but be ready also to hear the opinions of others.*— Thomas à Kempis

Date: _____ _____ _____
Place: _____ _____ _____
Occasion: _____ _____ _____

Tool Talk

Someone has imagined the Carpenter's tools holding a conference. Brother Hammer presided. Several suggested he leave the meeting because he was too noisy.

---

[1] *Parables, Etc.,* January, 1987, p. 4.
[2] Thomas Watson, *Gleanings From Thomas Watson* (Morgan, PA: Soli Deo Gloria Publications, 1995), p. 87.

Replied the Hammer, "If I have to leave this shop, Brother Screw must go also. You have to turn him around again and again to get him to accomplish anything."

Brother Screw then spoke up. "If you wish, I'll leave. But Brother Plane must leave too. All his work is on the surface. His efforts have no depth."

To this Brother Plane responded, "Brother Rule will also have to withdraw, for he is always measuring folks as though he were the only one who is right."

Brother Rule then complained against Brother Sandpaper, "You ought to leave too because you're so rough and always rubbing people the wrong way."

In the midst of all this discussion, in walked the Carpenter of Nazareth. He had arrived to start His day's work. Putting on His apron, He went to the bench to make a pulpit from which to proclaim the Gospel. He employed the hammer, screw, plane, rule, sandpaper, and all the other tools. After the day's work when the pulpit was finished, Brother Saw arose and remarked, "Brethren, I observe that all of us are workers together with the Lord."[1]

Date:			
Place:			
Occasion:			

Rooted Together

The huge redwood trees in California are considered the largest things on earth and the tallest trees in the world. Some of them are three hundred feet high and over 2,500 years old. One would think that trees so large would have a tremendous root system reaching down hundreds of feet into the earth. The redwoods actually have a very shallow system of roots, but they all intertwine. They are locked to each other. When the storms come or the winds blow, the redwoods stand. They are locked to each other, and they don't stand alone, for all the trees support and protect each other.[2]

Date:			
Place:			
Occasion:			

Chopsticks

Once there was a Chinese prince who died and was given a glimpse of both heaven and hell. First, he was escorted to hell, where he found tables laden with various foods and delicacies, but the people were sitting there angry and frustrated, quarreling with each other. They were not permitted to pick up the food with their fingers, and they couldn't feed themselves because the chopsticks they were given were ten feet long.

---

[1] Leslie B. Flynn, *19 Gifts of the Spirit* (Wheaton, IL: Victor Books, 1974), p. 28.
[2] Clipped from my files.

Then the prince was taken to heaven. Again he found a beautiful banquet, and again only ten-foot chopsticks. But here the people were happy and content, for they sat on opposite sides of the tables, each one feeding the person across from him.[1]

```
Date:        _____    _____    _____
Place:       _____    _____    _____
Occasion:    _____    _____    _____
```

Comfort

Someone Once Said . . .

- *Therefore ought a man to rest wholly upon God, so that he needeth not seek much comfort at the hands of men.*—Thomas à Kempis
- *Jesus went without comfort so that he could send us the Comforter.*—Edith Schaeffer

```
Date:        _____    _____    _____
Place:       _____    _____    _____
Occasion:    _____    _____    _____
```

"I Must Tell Jesus"

Elisha A. Hoffman was born May 7, 1839, in Orwigsburg, Pennsylvania. His father was a minister, and Elisha followed Christ at a young age. He attended Philadelphia public schools, studied science, then pursued the classics at Union Seminary of the Evangelical Association. He worked for eleven years with the Association's publishing house in Cleveland, Ohio. Then, following the death of his young wife, he returned to Pennsylvania and devoted thirty-three years to pastoring Benton Harbor Presbyterian Church.

Hoffman's pastime was writing hymns, many of which were inspired by pastoral incidents. One day, for example, while calling on the destitute of Lebanon, Pennsylvania, he met a woman whose depression seemed beyond cure. She opened her heart and poured on him her pent-up sorrows. Wringing her hands, she cried, "What shall I do? Oh, what shall I do?" Hoffman knew what she should do, for he had himself learned the deeper lessons of God's comfort. He said to the woman, "You cannot do better than to take all your sorrows to Jesus. You must tell Jesus."

Suddenly the lady's face lighted up. "Yes!" she cried, "That's it! I must tell Jesus." Her words echoed in Hoffman's ears, and he mulled them over as he returned home. He drew out his pen and started writing, *I must tell Jesus! I must tell Jesus! / I cannot bear my burdens alone; / I must tell Jesus! I must tell Jesus! / Jesus can help me, Jesus alone.*

Hoffman lived to be ninety, telling Jesus his burdens and giving the church such

---

[1] Clipped from my files. Attributed to Anne FitzPatrick.

hymns as *What A Wonderful Savior, Down at the Cross, Are You Washed in the Blood?, Leaning on the Everlasting Arms,* and a thousand more.[1]

Date:			
Place:			
Occasion:			

C

A Father's Comfort

Bible teacher Kay Arthur tells about getting out of the car one day, arms loaded down with books, and not wanting to go into her house. She was a young widow with two children, and it had been a bad day. She was hurting.

As she stared at the grass, her mind went back to a time in her childhood when she had been running through the grass toward her dad, terrified and screaming. He had scooped her up in his arms and given her comfort. She wished that she could be a little girl again. She wished that she had someone to hold her right then.

As she turned to go into the house, she suddenly saw herself in her mind's eye, a little girl in pigtails, flying down a vast marble corridor. Oil paintings bigger than life hung on the walls. She could hear her little shoes on the marble floor and see the tears that ran down her cheeks.

It was a long corridor. At the end, two huge gold doors glistened in the sunlight which filtered through beveled cathedral windows. On either side of the imposing doors stood two magnificently dressed guards holding huge spears and blocking the entrance into the room beyond.

Undaunted, the little girl ran straight toward the doors, still crying, "Abba!" She never broke her stride for, as she neared the doors, the guards flung them opened and heralded her arrival: "The daughter of the King! The daughter of the King!"

Court was in session. The cherubim and seraphim cried, "Holy, holy, holy!" and the elders sat on their thrones, dressed in white, wearing crowns of gold, and talking with the King of Kings. But none of this slowed his daughter!

Oblivious to everything going on about her, she ran past the seven burning lamps of fire and up the steps leading to the throne, and she catapulted herself into the King's arms. She was home and wrapped in the arms of his everlasting love. He reached up and, with one finger, gently wiped away her tears. Then He smoothed the sticky hair on her face back into her braids and said, "Now, now, tell your Father all about it."

Kay Arthur walked into the house, left her books on the table, walked through her house, and knelt down by her bedside. She told her Father all about it.[2]

Date:			
Place:			
Occasion:			

[1] Robert J. Morgan, *On This Day* (Nashville: Thomas Nelson Publishers, 1997), entry for May 7th.
[2] Kay Arthur, "Lessons on Love" in *What My Parents Did Right,* compiled and edited by Gloria Gaither (Nashville: StarSong Publishing Group, 1991), 16–18.

Lincoln's Friend

During the worst days of the Civil War, an old friend of Abraham Lincoln's, a Springfield, Illinois, shopkeeper named Billy Brown, decided he'd travel to Washington to see his old friend, the President of the United States. An aide to the president asked him if he had an appointment.

"No, sir," replied Billy. "I ain't, and it ain't necessary. Maybe it's all right and fitting . . . to have appointments, but I reckon Mr. Lincoln's old friends don't need them, so you just trot along . . . and tell him Billy Brown's here, and see what he says."

The aide frowned, but went. In about two minutes, the door popped open and out came Mr. Lincoln, face aglow. "Billy," he said, pumping his friend's hand, "now I am glad to see you. Come right in. You're going to stay to supper with Mary and me."

As soon as Mr. Lincoln could discharge his immediate responsibilities, the two men went to the back of the house and sat down on the stoop and, as Billy later put it, "talked and talked. He asked me about pretty nigh everybody in Springfield. I just let loose and told him about the weddings and the births and funerals and the buildings, and I guess there wasn't a yarn I'd heard in the three and a half years he'd been away that I didn't spin for him. Laugh—you'd ought to hear him laugh—just did my heart good, for I could see what they'd been doing to him. Always was a thin man, but Lordy, he was thinner than ever now, and his face was kind of drawn and gray—enough to make you cry."

Late that evening, Billy said goodbye. The President tried to get him to stay the night, but Billy, not wanting to impose, declined. As they parted, Lincoln said, "Billy, what did you come down here for?"

"I came to see you, Mr. Lincoln."

"But you ain't asked me for anything, Billy. What is it? Out with it."

"No, Mr. Lincoln, just wanted to see you—felt kind of lonesome—been so long since I'd seen you, and I was afraid I'd forget some of them yarns if I didn't unload them soon."

Lincoln gazed into his friend's eyes. "Do you mean to tell me you came all the way from Springfield, Illinois, just to have a visit with me; that you ain't got no complaints in your pockets or advice up your sleeve?"

"Yes, sir. That's about it."

Tears came into Lincoln's eyes and ran down his cheeks. "I'm homesick, Billy, just plumb homesick, and it seems as if this war would never be over. Many a night I can see the boys dying of the fields and can hear their mothers crying for them at home, and I can't help it, Billy. . . . You'll never know just what good you've done me."[1]

Date:	_____	_____	_____
Place:	_____	_____	_____
Occasion:	_____	_____	_____

[1] Keith W. Jennison, *The Humorous Mr. Lincoln* (New York: Bonanza Books, 1965), 125–126.

How Pain Unites the Body

Missionary surgeon Dr. Paul Brand tells of working for several years to bring physical rehabilitation to a leper named Sadan. The two men became dear friends, and Brand worked for years to help repair Sadan's wasted hands and fingers. At last Sadan felt he should return home to his family in Madras for a trial weekend to see if he, as a leper, would be accepted by family and friends.

Dr. Brand tried to prepare Sadan for the trip, reviewing especially all the dangers he might encounter since his body's extremities had no feeling and could sense no pain. Having learned to care for himself, Sadan boarded a train for Madras.

On Saturday night after an exuberant reunion dinner with his family, Sadan went to his old room, lay down on the pallet, and drifted off into a contented sleep. Imagine his horror upon awakening when, while checking himself as he had been trained to do, Sadan found part of his left index finger mangled. A rat had visited him during the night and gnawed his finger.

The next evening, he was afraid to go to sleep, so all evening he sat cross-legged on his pallet, his back against the wall, studying an accounting book by the light of a kerosene lantern. In the wee hours of the morning his eyes became so heavy he could no longer keep them open. The book fell onto his knees and his hand slid over against the hot glass of his lantern.

When Sadan awoke the next morning he saw instantly that a large patch of black skin had burned off the back of his right hand, and he soon returned to Dr. Brand, his two hands wrapped in bandages.

"When he met me, and I began to unroll the bandages, he wept," Dr. Brand later recalled. "I must confess that I wept with him. As he poured out his misery to me, he said, 'I feel as if I've lost all my freedom.' And then, a question that has stayed with me, 'How can I be free without pain?'"

Dr. Brand wrote: *Pain serves as vital a role in protecting and uniting that corporate membership as it does in guarding the cells of my own body. Deep emotional connections link human beings as certainly as dendrites link cells in our bodies . . .*

The body poorly protects what it does not feel.[1]

```
Date:      _____   _____   _____

Place:     _____   _____   _____

Occasion:  _____   _____   _____
```

Communication

Someone Once Said . . .

- *If I were to summarize in one sentence the single most important principle I have learned in the field of interpersonal relations, it would be this: Seek first to understand, then to be*

---

[1] Paul Brand and Philip Yancey in "Putting Pain To Work" in *Leadership Journal*, Fall, 1984, 121–124.

understood. This principle is the key to effective interpersonal communication.—Stephen Covey[1]

- *What do you mean we don't communicate? Just yesterday I faxed you a reply to the recorded message you left me on your answering machine.*—caption of a cartoon showing a husband and wife having breakfast, noses stuck in newspapers.

Date:	_____	_____	_____
Place:	_____	_____	_____
Occasion:	_____	_____	_____

Empathic Listening

In *The 7 Habits of Highly Effective People,* Stephen Covey tells of a father who came to him saying, "I can't understand my kid. He just won't listen to me." Covey patiently tried to get the dad to see the inconsistency of his statement. You don't understand people by getting them to listen to *you.* You understand them when you listen to them.

Covey suggests that there are five levels of *listening:*

- We may be ignoring another person, not really listening at all.
- We may be pretending to listen.
- We may be practicing selective listening, drifting in and out of the conversation and paying attention to only parts of what the other person is saying.
- We may be listening attentively.
- But very few of us ever practice the fifth level, the highest form of listening—empathic listening, listening with intent to understand, to get inside the other person's frame of reference, seeking to understand them emotionally as well as intellectually.[2]

Date:	_____	_____	_____
Place:	_____	_____	_____
Occasion:	_____	_____	_____

Levels of Communication

The authors of the book, *Who Cares About Love,* suggest that there are four levels of communication.

The first is the exchange of cliches: "Hi, how are you? Have a nice day."

The second level of communication shares data and information. Talk is about things that are impersonal and non-threatening—the weather, sports, world events.

The third level is when we begin to share something about who we are—our opinions and attitudes, our dreams, goals, and values.

---

[1] Stephen R. Covey, *The 7 Habits of Highly Effective People* (New York: Simon and Schuster, 237.
[2] Covey, *The 7 Habits of Highly Effective People,* 239–240.

The fourth and most intimate level of communication is when we share our feelings, emotions, joys, and fears with another person.

Sometimes we communicate very well when first beginning a loving relationship, when we are at the first or second level. But we can easily stagnate at one of these levels if we don't choose to go deeper and become more personal, open, and intimate.[1]

Date: _____ _____ _____
Place: _____ _____ _____
Occasion: _____ _____ _____

Communication in Marriage

There are five types of communication that make up the fabric of our relationships, and they play a special role in keeping our marriages from unraveling.

The first is **Small Talk.**

Sydney Smith, nineteenth-century English essayist, said, "One of the great pleasures of life is conversation."

Laurie Chock of Chock and Goldbert, a communications consulting firm in New York, said, "Small talk is a misnomer. Those little conversations probably have more impact than any other."

Another communications expert said, "For many of us, small talk is hard work. . . . [But] if you have comforted yourself by saying small talk doesn't matter, think again. It builds rapport and often leads to bigger things."

One of those bigger things is **Serious Talk.** There are times when we must broach difficult issues or have heart-to-heart talks about the things that we're about.

The third kind of talk is **Self Talk,** that is, talking about our problems, our fears, our hopes, our ambitions, our inner feelings.

A fourth kind of necessary communication is **Soul Talk,** talking about matters of the soul, talking about the Lord Jesus. Malachi 3:16 says: *Then those who feared the Lord talked with each other, and the Lord listened and heard. A scroll of remembrance was written in his presence concerning those who feared the Lord and honored his name. "They will be mine," says the Lord Almighty, "in the day when I make up my treasured possessions."*

The last kind of talk important for healthy marriages is **Sweet Talk.** This category includes things like: *I love you, Sugarbaby. You're the whipped cream on my sundae. You're the bubbles in my Pepsi. You're the feather in my cap.* Think of it as verbally snuggling.

Few marriages fail when these five kinds of communication are frequently practiced between husband and wife.

Date: _____ _____ _____
Place: _____ _____ _____
Occasion: _____ _____ _____

[1] Win Arn, Carroll Nyquist, and Charles Arn, *Who Cares About Love?* (Pasadena, CA: Church Growth Press, 1986), 92–93.

Dear Ann Landers

This column appeared in the Saturday, July 28, 1990, edition of the *Nashville Banner*:

Dear Ann Landers. Have you ever known a clam? Probably not. Well, I am married to one. This husband of mine cannot or will not carry on a conversation. I have tried hundreds of times to get him to talk to me. It is impossible. Here's the way it goes:

Me: What do you think about the government's plan to raise the price of postage stamps again?

The Clam: I have no idea.

Me: I read in the paper that there was a flood in the Sahara Desert.

The Clam: Oh, really?

His stock, all-purpose comments are: "Is that a fact?" "You can't win for losin'." "That's the way the ball bounces." "Well, ain't that one for the books!" His responses are a boring assortment of worn-out cliches and platitudes.

Half the time he tunes me out totally. For example, last night I said, "I just got back from a trip on the space shuttle." He replied, "That's nice."

Maybe it's genetic—not on his side of the family, but mine. My mother also married a clam. I remember one day when I came home after school, she was yelling (and I do mean yelling) at my father, "You never talk to me! Something must happen at work that you could tell me about!" He replied, innocently, "Why are you hollering? What do you want me to say?" Then he walked into the next room and plugged his eyes into the TV for the rest of the evening.

When I asked my mother why she married him, she said, "Because he was the quiet type."
I now know what she meant, because I made the same mistake. . . .

Date: _____ _____ _____
Place: _____ _____ _____
Occasion: _____ _____ _____

Important Words

- The five most important words are *You did a good job.*
- The four most important words are *What is your opinion?*
- The three most important words are *Let's work together.*
- The two most important words are *Thank you.*
- The single most important word is *We.*

Date: _____ _____ _____
Place: _____ _____ _____
Occasion: _____ _____ _____

Just Doesn't Know How To Communicate

A woman went to her pastor for marital counseling, and after a few preliminaries, the pastor said he had a few questions that would help identify the problems if she would just answer his questions as openly as possible. When the lady agreed, he began by saying, "Do you have any grounds?" To which the lady responded, "Why, yes we do, we have about ten acres just north of town."

"No, ma'am, that's not what I mean. What I mean is do you have . . . well, do you have a grudge?"

"Oh, no, but we do have a nice little carport."

"No, ma'am," said the pastor, "that's not what I mean. One more question: Does your husband ever beat you up?"

"Beat me up? Oh, no. I get up before he does just about every morning."

In complete exasperation the pastor said, "Lady, you're not listening to me. Why are you having trouble with your husband?"

"Well," replied the lady, "the man just doesn't know how to communicate."

Date:	_____	_____	_____
Place:	_____	_____	_____
Occasion:	_____	_____	_____

For What It's Worth . . .

Paul Harvey reported the following on his radio broadcast for January 15, 1982: The respected *American Medical News* confirms what our *For What It's Worth Department* is about to relay. A patient complained of an earache. His right ear. His doctor prescribed eardrops—an antibiotic. Are you with me to here?

The doctor prescribed eardrops for an earache. When the patient got the eardrops prescription filled the pharmacist wrote on the bottle. . . . Three drops in *r*—for *right*—ear. No space and no punctuation. For "right ear," the instructions on the bottle read: *r*—ear.

That spells *rear.*

The patient said later he knew it sounded like a strange remedy for an earache but he had dutifully applied the three drops to his rear for three days before the error was discovered.

Date:	_____	_____	_____
Place:	_____	_____	_____
Occasion:	_____	_____	_____

What the Church Needs . . .

A church was having its monthly business meeting. The treasury was in better shape than usual so the moderator asked if there were any special needs. One lady stood and said that she felt the church needed a chandelier.

A penny-pinching deacon jumped up and shouted, "I'm against it for three reasons. Number one, nobody would know how to spell it. Number two, nobody would know how to play it. And number three, what this church needs is more light.[1]

---

[1]Loyal Jones and Billy Edd Wheeler, *Laughter in Appalachia* (New York: Ivy Books, 1987), 26.

Date:	_____	_____	_____
Place:	_____	_____	_____
Occasion:	_____	_____	_____

The Great Debate

Many years ago in Russia, the Czar decided to take away land belonging to some Jewish peasants. The peasants sent a plea to the Czar that their land not be taken, but rather restored. Because of their persistence, the Czar agreed to restore their land on the condition that one of them should debate and win against his great, royal debater.

━━━━━◇━━━━━
Communication Cycle

Seek first to understand, then to be understood.
—STEPHEN COVEY
━━━━━◇━━━━━

This debater, who always represented the king, had never lost a debate. And he had an unusual characteristic. He never spoke a word. The debate was carried on by motions and pantomime.

When word came to the little Russian-Jewish village, they were crest-fallen and discouraged. None of them would dare face the great debater until finally one fellow in the village said, "Well, we have nothing to lose by trying. I'll go and debate him."

He was the town idiot, and the people sighed and threw up their hands in resignation, but he went anyway.

On the arranged day, the great debater started first. He waved his arms widely in the air in broad circles, then he sat down very smug and pleased with himself. The town idiot then got up and, with great vigor, pointed with one finger to the palm of the other hand. The audience was astonished to suddenly see a crestfallen look come over the face of the great debater. Everybody knew from the expression on his face he considered that he had lost the first round.

He got up again and this time enthusiastically pierced the air with three fingers as if to say, "Three, three, three." Again he sat down and smiled, looking very pleased—until the town idiot got up and waved one finger in the air and pierced the air with that finger. Another crest-fallen, discouraged look came over the face of the debater. He considered the second round lost.

Standing for a final round, he pulled out a loaf of bread and a glass of wine and solemnly partook of them. Then he sat down, very smug.

The town idiot then stood up and reached into a bag beside him and pulled out an apple and started chomping on it, standing there as he ate it. The great debater stood with despair on his face and threw his arms into the air, crying, "I give up! I have never met anyone so shrewd and wise as this gentleman is. He has beaten me on every round of the debate."

The Czar instantly told the town idiot to go back to his village with the news they could keep their land.

Afterward the Czar summoned the great debater and said, "What took place out there?"

"I have never seen anyone so wise as this poor Jewish peasant," came the reply. "I started the debate by waving my hands in the air to say, 'God is everywhere! God is everywhere,' but immediately this Jewish peasant pointed to his palm as if to say,

C

'Yes, but God is right here, too. God is right here with me.' And I had no answer for that.

"Then I help up three fingers to say, 'God is three. God is three.' But the Jewish peasant was too smart for me. He held up one finger to say, 'Yes, but He is also the One in Three. God is one.' And I had no answer for that.

Finally I stood up with the elements of the communion to show to the Jewish peasant that Jesus Christ is Messiah, the complete sacrifice for all the world. But my opponent reached in his sack for an apple, as though reminiscing of Eve and implying, 'Yes, but I am a sinner. I have sinned. I have partaken of what is forbidden, but the Lord has forgiven not only the whole world, but me.' I had no answer for that. He is a shrewd and wise man, and he won the debate fairly."

Meanwhile the peasant went back to his village and reported that he had won the debate. The people were thunderstruck, and they asked, "How did you do it? What took place in the debate?"

"Well," the Jewish peasant said, "The great debater waved his arms and said, 'You can't have your land. The Czar is going to take it.' But I pointed to my palm as though I had a deed there, 'But we have the rights to this property. We have the deed to it.'

"Then he stood up and flung his three fingers in the air, saying we had three days to get off this land. I told him we were not going to move one inch. Not one inch!

"Then he reached into his pouch and pulled out his lunch and started eating. I thought to myself, 'Well, if he is going to have his lunch, I'm going to have mine.' And I reached into my bag and pulled out my lunch, and suddenly they all said I had won the debate."

The message doesn't always come across as we think.

Date:	_____	_____	_____
Place:	_____	_____	_____
Occasion:	_____	_____	_____

Compassion

Someone Once Said . . .

- *If we could only read the secret history of our enemies, we would find in each man's life sorrow and suffering enough to disarm all hostility.*—Henry Wadsworth Longfellow

Date:	_____	_____	_____
Place:	_____	_____	_____
Occasion:	_____	_____	_____

The Antidote for Hatred

Compassion is the most powerful antidote for hatred and bitterness that the human heart can find. It's the one way to restore love to a broken relationship.

The most powerful story I've ever heard about this comes from Byron Deel, college basketball coach in Nashville, Tennessee, who grew up with an alcoholic and abusive father. Byron had two brothers and three sisters, a large family, but his dad spent the family income on alcohol, and he drank and ranted and raved and cursed and threatened and hit them. And then he left them. When Byron was twelve, his father walked away from the family, and did absolutely nothing to support them. There were no child care payments. No alimony. No cards at birthdays. No gifts at Christmas. Nothing but hardship and abandonment.

Six years later, he showed up again, two weeks after Byron had graduated from high school. It was an awkward meeting. He stayed about half an hour. And then he left again, and this time there was no contact for sixteen years. Byron told me, "My attitude toward my dad was everything that it shouldn't have been for a Christian. He had robbed me of a happy childhood. He had failed me at every point. He had abused me. I hesitate to say that I hated him, but perhaps hatred isn't too strong a word. There was a bitterness there that was almost a loathing. Whenever anyone asked me about my dad, I'd shut them off pretty fast. As I grew older, I put it all out of my mind, and there was just a blank spot there. I didn't think about it. I could go for years without once thinking about my father."

Then out of the blue Byron's aunt called him and said, "Your father is in Bristol, Virginia, very sick and close to death. It would mean something to him if he could see one of his children. He has cirrhosis of the liver." None of the other children wanted to see him, and Byron lived the closest to Bristol. So he got in his car and drove up there. He said, "I had a ton of thoughts. Not a lot of strong feelings, just a sense that someone should do this. I didn't want to, but it seemed like I should."

He walked into the Intensive Care Unit and there was a seventy-one-year-old man, connected to monitors, tubes inserted into his body, surrounded by medical equipment. Byron hadn't seen him for sixteen years, but he recognized the man. And something strange happened. As Byron saw his dad lying there helplessly, dying, strung about with wires and tubes and monitors and machines, all the years of hatred and anger melted away. He walked over and stood by the bedside. The man opened his eyes, saw Byron, and began to cry.

Byron said, "I wept, too. It was almost as though I could see going through his mind waves of regret for the wasted years." Byron spent that day and the next with his dad, and he was surprised to find that he had a lot of feeling for the man. "The burden that I had been carrying around for years, without realizing it, was gone. We were able to talk, and I was able to share the gospel with him."

Byron's father survived that stay in the hospital, and was able to return home briefly. During that time, Byron had a second visit, taking his wife and daughters with him. And during that visit, he grew convinced that his dad had trusted Jesus Christ as his Lord and Savior.

Later the call came that his father had died. But Byron was no longer bitter or estranged. The compassion of Jesus Christ had taken hold, and instead of seeing himself as an abused victim full of hatred and cold of heart, he saw something else. He saw his dad through the Lord's eyes, as a needy man who just needed Jesus Christ.

Instead of looking at your husband or wife and saying, "Why doesn't he treat me better? Why doesn't he do this or that? Why did I ever marry such a jerk?" look at him or her and say, "There is someone made in God's image who is hurting more than he knows, more than she realizes. How can the Lord enable me to help?"

C

Date: _____ _____ _____
Place: _____ _____ _____
Occasion: _____ _____ _____

Confession of Sin

Someone Once Said . . .

- *Unconfessed sin is unforgiven sin, and unforgiven sin is the darkest, foulest thing on this sin-cursed earth.*—D. L. Moody[1]
- *A child of God will confess sin in particular; an unsound Christian will confess sin by wholesale—he will acknowledge that he is a sinner in general.*—Thomas Watson[2]
- *Spit out the poison with all speed, hasten to take the remedy, and thou shalt feel thyself better than if thou didst long defer it.*—Thomas à Kempis

Date: _____ _____ _____
Place: _____ _____ _____
Occasion: _____ _____ _____

Under the Lights

In *How To Be Born Again*, Billy Graham wrote: *Several years ago I was to be interviewed at my home for a well-known television show and, knowing that it would appear on nationwide television, my wife took great pains to see that everything looked nice. She had vacuumed and dusted and tidied up the whole house but had gone over the living room with a fine-tooth comb since that was where the interview would be filmed. When the film crew arrived with all the lights and cameras, she felt that everything in the living room was spic and span. We were in place along with the interviewer when suddenly the television lights were turned on and we saw cobwebs and dust where we had never seen them before. In the words of my wife, "I mean, that room was festooned with dust and cobwebs which simply did not show up under ordinary light."*

Trash Talk

And forgive us our trashbaskets as we forgive those who put trash in our baskets.

—A FOUR-YEAR-OLD

The point is, of course, that no matter how well we clean up our lives and think we have them all in order, when we see ourselves in the light of God's Word, in the light of God's holiness, all the cobwebs and all the dust do show up.[3]

[1] D. L. Moody, *Prevailing Prayer* (Chicago: Moody Press, n.d.), 35.
[2] Thomas Watson, *Gleanings from Thomas Watson* (Morgan, PA: Soli Deo Gloria Publications, 1995), 7.
[3] Billy Graham, *How To Be Born Again* (Waco: Word Books, 1977), 118.

Help Me!

Taylor University President Jay Kesler once told of sitting with a young man who told him about his father, who had been raised as an orphan. When he had children of his own, he didn't seem to know how to handle them. He would alternately ignore them and discipline them in fits of anger. One day after a particularly embarrassing loss of temper, the father put his head in his hands and with desperation in his voice said, "Son, you don't understand. I've never had a father. I have never seen how fathers do it. I feel totally helpless. I don't know how to be a parent. I want to be a good parent, but I don't know how. Help me!" The boy took his father in his arms and the two of them wept together. From that point on, this son and his dad became the closest of friends.[1]

Conscience

Someone Once Said . . .

- *My conscience is captive to the Word of God. I will not recant anything, for to go against conscience is neither honest nor safe. Here I stand, I can do no other. God help me. Amen.*—Martin Luther, before the Diet of Worms
- *There are two sorts of sick consciences, those that are not aware enough of sin and those that are not aware enough of pardon.*—J. I. Packer
- *'Let your conscience be your guide' is only valid if God's Word is guiding your conscience.*—Anonymous
- *If it's doubtful, it's dirty.*—Advice of a wife to her husband who was trying to determine whether his shirt could be worn one more time before laundering.
- *It is important to cultivate an uneasy conscience. The good conscience is an invention of the Devil.*—Elton Trueblood[2]
- *A good conscience is the palace of Christ; the temple of the Holy Ghost; the paradise of delight; the standing Sabbath of the saints.*—St. Augustine[3]

---

[1] Jay Kesler, *Ten Mistakes Parents Make With Teenagers* (Brentwood, Tenn: Wolgemuth & Hyatt, Publishers, Inc.), 35.
[2] Elton Trueblood, *Foundation For Reconstruction* (New York: Harper & Brothers, 1946), 67–69.
[3] *The Encyclopedia of Religious Quotations,* ed. Frank Spencer Mead (Old Tappan, NJ: Fleming H. Revell Co., 1965), 84.

- *A good conscience is a continual Christmas.*—Benjamin Franklin, in *Poor Richard's Almanac*
- *Something that makes you tell your mother before your sister does.*—A little boy's definition of a conscience.

Date: _____ _____ _____
Place: _____ _____ _____
Occasion: _____ _____ _____

The Invisible Fence

We have an invisible fence around our yard to keep our Great Dane from running into the road. An invisible fence is a wire buried just under the ground around the parameter of the yard, and it emits a mild signal. The dog wears a special collar containing a beeper and two little prods. When he approaches the wire, the collar begins beeping, warning him he is near a forbidden boundary. If he keeps going, he'll get an unpleasant little electrical jolt.

A person's conscience is like the beeping sound of that collar. It is an inner voice that warns us that we're nearing a forbidden boundary. If we keep on going, we'll soon be at great risk on the broad highway.

If we ignore the beeping, we may soon effectively tune it out. We may even get to the point where we no longer feel the little jolts of warning, having become seared, calloused, and desensitized.

Date: _____ _____ _____
Place: _____ _____ _____
Occasion: _____ _____ _____

Aligned

Our consciences are not infallible, and they can become warped or weakened if not kept aligned by the infallible Word of God. When Robert Murray McCheyne lived in Dundee, Scotland, the clock in the bell tower was exceedingly accurate. Each day when passing on the street, McCheyne would set his watch by it.

Reading and studying the Bible is the best way for us to align our hearts to a trustworthy standard.

J. Oswald Sanders wrote, "Every conscience needs instruction. Its delicate mechanism has been thrown off balance by the Fall. Just as a bullet will reach the bull's-eye only if the two sights are in correct alignment, so correct moral judgments are delivered only when the conscience is correctly aligned with the Scriptures."[1]

Date: _____ _____ _____
Place: _____ _____ _____
Occasion: _____ _____ _____

---

[1] J. Oswald Sanders, *A Spiritual Clinic* (Chicago: Moody Press, 1958), 60.

How to Deaden the Conscience

In his book *Hitler's Cross*, Erwin W. Lutzer gives chilling details about the training of the dreaded SS troops in Nazi Germany. The head of the SS was Heinrich Himmler, who was faced with the problem of how to take decent young German men and deaden their consciences so that they would be willing to perform ghastly deeds of cruelty.

Both Hitler and Himmler believed that each of the SS troops had to perform some deed that violated their conscience and sense of decency. Only when they did what others found to be reprehensible would they break away from their old values. The conscience had to be deadened through these acts of barbarism; that would serve the dual purpose of cutting the recruit off from his past ties, his family and friends, and of bonding him to his new peers and his leader. The break would be so complete that he could never go back. An act of torture or murder would unite him with blood brothers who had crossed the same line, felt the same numbness, and sworn themselves to uphold the same cause.

The Nazis proved that ordinary people, if controlled with rigid discipline and the power of mass psychology, can be induced to carry out the most brutal and destructive crime the human mind can devise.

The troops could say with Hermann Goering, "I have no conscience! Adolf Hitler is my conscience!"[1]

Date: _____   _____   _____
Place: _____   _____   _____
Occasion: _____   _____   _____

The Still, Small Voice

In *Focus on the Family*, Rolf Zettersten wrote, "A good friend in North Carolina bought a new car with a voice-warning system. . . . At first Edwin was amused to hear the soft female voice gently remind him that his seat belt wasn't fastened. . . . He affectionately called this voice the 'little woman.'

"He soon discovered his little woman was programmed to warn him about his gasoline. 'Your fuel level is low,' she said one time in her sweet voice. Edwin nodded his head and thanked her. He figured he still had enough gas to go another fifty miles, so he kept on driving. But a few minutes later, her voice interrupted again with the same warning. And so it went over and over. Although he knew it was the same recording, Edwin thought her voice sounded harsher each time.

"Finally, he stopped his car and crawled under the dashboard. After a quick search, he found the appropriate wires and gave them a good yank. So much for the little woman.

---✧---
Condensation

Conscience is condensed character.
—ANONYMOUS
---✧---

"He was still smiling to himself a few miles later when his car began sputtering and coughing. He ran out of gas! Somewhere inside the dashboard, Edwin was sure he could hear the little woman laughing."

---

[1] Erwin W. Lutzer, *Hitler's Cross* (Chicago: Moody Press, 1995), 92–94.

People like Edwin learn before long that the little voice inside, although ignored or even disconnected, often tells them exactly what they need to know.[1]

Date:			
Place:			
Occasion:			

C

Contentment

Someone Once Said . . .

- *Discontent keeps a man from enjoying what he doth possess. A drop or two of vinegar will sour a whole glass of wine.*—Thomas Watson[2]
- *A little sprig of the herb called content put into the poorest soup will make it taste as rich as the Lord Mayor's turtle.*—Charles Spurgeon, in *John Ploughman's Talks*
- *It is not how much we have, but how much we enjoy, that makes happiness.*—Charles Spurgeon, in *John Ploughman's Talks*
- *I learned to look more upon the bright side of my condition, and less upon the dark side, and to consider what I enjoyed, rather than what I wanted; and this gave me sometimes such secret comforts, that I cannot express them; and which I take notice here, to put those discontented people in mind of it, who cannot enjoy comfortably what God has given them, because they see and covet something that He has not given them. All our discontents about what we want appeared to me to spring from the want of thankfulness for what we have.*— Robinson Crusoe, on his deserted island, after his heart had been changed by finding a Bible among the chests he had salvaged from his wrecked ship
- *Humility is like the lead to the net, which keeps the soul down when it is rising through passion [pride]; and contentment is like the cork, which keeps the heart up when it is sinking through discouragement.*—Thomas Watson[3]
- *What a foolish thing is this, that because I have not got what I want, I will not enjoy the comfort of what I have! There is a great deal of folly in a discontented heart.*— Jeremiah Burroughs, Puritan preacher
- *Contentment is realizing that God has already provided everything we need for our present happiness.*—Bill Gothard

Date:			
Place:			
Occasion:			

An Alternate Definition

Someone said that contentment was when your earning power equaled your yearning power.

---

[1] William J. Gestal, Jr. in "Conscience," *Leadership Journal,* Winter, 1991, 48.
[2] Thomas Watson, *Gleanings From Thomas Watson* (Morgan, PA: Soli Deo Gloria Publications, 1995), 37.
[3] Watson, *Gleanings From Thomas Watson,* 40.

Date: _____ _____ _____
Place: _____ _____ _____
Occasion: _____ _____ _____

Contented I Will Be

Fanny Crosby, the great writer of gospel songs, was blinded when only six weeks old by a country doctor who thought he was treating her with eyedrops. Yet her indomitable attitude soon manifested itself. At age eight, she wrote this little poem:

Oh, what a happy child I am,
Although I cannot see!
I am resolved that in this world
Contented I will be.

Date: _____ _____ _____
Place: _____ _____ _____
Occasion: _____ _____ _____

The Fisherman

Once a rich industrialist, disturbed to find a fisherman sitting idly by his boat, asked, "Why aren't you out there fishing?"

"Because I've caught enough fish for today," was the reply.

"Why don't you catch more fish than you need?" asked the rich man.

"What would I do with them?"

―✧―
Contented Desires

True contentment is found, not in having everything you want, but in not wanting to have everything.
―✧―

"You could earn more money and buy a better boat so you could go deeper and catch more fish. You could purchase nylon nets, catch even more fish, and make more money. Soon you'd have a fleet of boats and be rich like me."

"Then what would I do?" asked the fisherman.

"You could sit down and enjoy life."

"What do you think I'm doing now?" the fisherman replied.

Date: _____ _____ _____
Place: _____ _____ _____
Occasion: _____ _____ _____

The Power of Contentment

Once upon a time, a stonecutter lived all alone. Though he had acquired great skills, he was very poor. He lived in a tiny bamboo hut and wore tattered clothing.

One day as the stonecutter worked with his hammer and chisel upon a huge stone, he heard a crowd gathering along the streets. By their shouts he could tell that the king was coming to visit his humble village. Joining in the procession, the stonecutter gazed in awe as the king, dressed in marvelous silk, was greeted by his subjects.

Oh, how I wish I had the power and glory of the king, he thought. *He has soldiers at his command. There is no one more powerful.*

His cry was heard in the heavens, and immediately the humble stonecutter was transformed into a powerful king. He found himself riding on a great horse, waving at the crowds of people who had flocked to see him.

This is power, he thought.

As the summer progressed, however, the new king watched the effects of the heat upon his people. Men and animals became weary, and plants withered under the powerful rays of the sun. As he looked at the sky, the new king realized that the sun was more powerful than any earthly ruler.

How I wish I were as powerful as that, he thought. *I wish I were the sun.* Immediately, his wish was granted.

The stonecutter relished his new role as the sun. He gloried in the power he felt as he surveyed the kingdoms below. As he sent his bright rays to earth, he watched kings and princes hide under their parasols; he watched as powerful warriors became weak under his gaze. Even the crops in the field were under his command.

Then one day a tiny cloud moved over the land, shielding the earth from the sun's bright rays. Seeing that here was something more powerful, he thought, *I want very much to be a cloud.*

Again, his wish was granted. Now he blocked the sun's rays and felt important. He gathered all his strength, becoming a gigantic cloud, and began to pour down rain on the earth. Rivers formed where previously there were none, and water flooded the streets of the cities and the farmland. Everything—trees, animals, people—seemed to be awed by his power. Only the massive rocks were unswayed. Again he had discovered something more powerful.

There is nothing, he thought, *as powerful as a rock. How I wish I were a huge stone.* His wish was granted.

As a stone he remained motionless and powerful, unmoved by sun or wind or rain. He felt exempt from all the forces that shaped the existence of those around him.

Then one day a man approached, carrying a bag. When he stopped, he pulled out a chisel and a hammer and began to chip away at the rock. Realizing that the man with the tools was more powerful than any rock, he cried out, "Oh, I want to be a stonecutter."

Once again the heavens heard his cry, and he became a stonecutter. Once again he lived in a bamboo hut and made his living with hammer and chisel. And he was content.[1]

◇

Rich Satisfaction

Content makes poor men rich. Discontent makes rich men poor.

—BENJAMIN FRANKLIN

◇

---

[1] Martin Thielen, writing in *Leadership Journal.*

Date:	_____	_____	_____
Place:	_____	_____	_____
Occasion:	_____	_____	_____

————————— **Conversion Stories, Unusual** —————————

Someone Once Said . . .

- *The ark was a great ark, which held all kinds of creatures; and our Christ is a great Refuge, who saves all kinds of sinners.*—Charles Spurgeon[1]

Date:	_____	_____	_____
Place:	_____	_____	_____
Occasion:	_____	_____	_____

Saved by Smoking the Bible

Jacob Koshy grew up in Singapore with one driving ambition: to be a success in life, to gain all the money and possessions he could. That led him into the world of drugs and gambling, and eventually he became the lord of an international smuggling network. In 1980, he was arrested and placed in a government drug rehabilitation prison in Singapore.

He was frustrated beyond endurance. All his goals, purposes, dreams, and ambitions were locked up with him in a tiny cell, and his heart was full of a cold emptiness.

He was a smoker, and cigarettes weren't allowed in the center. Instead, he smuggled in tobacco and rolled it in the pages of a Gideon Bible. One day he fell asleep while smoking. He awoke to find that the cigarette had burned out, and all that remained was a scrap of charred paper. He unrolled it and read what was written: "Saul, Saul, Why do you persecute me?"

Jacob asked for another Bible and read the entire story of the conversion of Saul of Tarsus. He suddenly realized that if God could help someone like Saul, God could help him, too. There in his cell he knelt and prayed, asking Christ to come into his life and change him. He began crying and couldn't stop. The tears of a wasted life washed away his pain, and God redeemed him. He started sharing his story with the other prisoners, and as soon as he was released he became involved in a church. He met a Christian woman, married, and is now a missionary in the Far East where he tells people far and wide, "Who would have believed that I could find the truth by smoking the Word of God?"[2]

---

[1] Charles H. Spurgeon, *Spurgeon's Sermons, Vol. 4* (Grand Rapids: Baker Book House, 1983), 4.

[2] Jacob Koshy, "From Smoking the Word to Speaking the Word" in *Gideon Testimonies from International Extension Countries* (Nashville: The Gideons International, 1994), 59–60.

Date:			
Place:			
Occasion:			

The Keys to Life

In a prayer letter to his supporters, evangelist Billy Graham told this story: "I recently heard the story of a mother in an African nation who came to Christ and grew strong in her commitment and devotion to the Lord. As so often happens, however, this alienated her from her husband, and over the years he grew to despise and hate her new devotion to Christ.

"His anger and bitterness reached their climax when he decided to kill his wife, their two children and himself, unable to live in such self-inflicted misery. But he needed a motive. He decided that he would accuse her of stealing his precious keys— the keys were to the bank, the house, and the car. Early one afternoon he left his bank and headed for the tavern. His route took him across a footbridge extended over the headwaters of the Nile River. He paused above the river and dropped the keys. He spent all afternoon drinking and carousing.

"Later that afternoon, his wife went to the fish market to buy the evening meal. She purchased a large Nile perch. As she was gutting the fish, to her astonishment, in its belly were her husband's keys. How had they gotten there? What were the circumstances? She did not know; but she cleaned them up and hung them on the hook.

Sufficiently drunk, the young banker came home that night and pounded open the front door shouting, "Woman, where are my keys?" Already in bed, she got up, picked them off the hook in the bedroom, and handed them to her husband. When he saw the keys, by his own testimony he immediately became sober and was instantly converted. He fell on his knees sobbing, asked for forgiveness, and confessed Jesus Christ as his Lord and Savior."[1]

Date:			
Place:			
Occasion:			

The Prodigal

One of the most powerful personal evangelists of the nineteenth century was "Uncle" John Vassar, who grew up in his family's brewery in Poughkeepsie, New York. Following his conversion to Christ, he abandoned beer-making for soul-winning, and on May 15, 1850, he was commissioned as an agent for the American Tract Society of New York. Vassar took off across the country, never resting in his mission of selling Christian literature and asking everyone he met about their relationship with Christ.

---

[1] Billy Graham, Prayer Letter from the Billy Graham Evangelistic Association, July, 1989.

On one occasion, traveling in the West, he visited the home of a praying wife whose husband was an infidel. She begged for a Bible, and Vassar, giving her one, went his way. He had no sooner left when the husband, coming home, saw the book and was enraged. Seizing the Bible with one hand and the ax with the other, he hurried to the wood-pile where he placed it on the chopping block and hacked it crosswise in two. Returning to the house, he threw half of the destroyed Bible at his wife, saying, "As you claim a part of all the property around here, there is your share of this."

The other half he tossed into his tool shed. Months later on a wet winter's day, the man, wanting to get away from his Christian wife, retreated to his shed. The time passed slowly, and in boredom he looked around for something to read. Thumbing through the mutilated Bible, his attention was caught by the story of the prodigal son in Luke 15. He became absorbed in the parable only to discover that its ending belonged to his wife's section. He crept into the house and secretly searched for the bottom half of the book, but was unable to find where his wife had hidden it.

Finally he broke down, asked her for it, and read the story again and again. In the process he came to the Heavenly Father like a penitent prodigal returning home.[1]

Date:	_____	_____	_____
Place:	_____	_____	_____
Occasion:	_____	_____	_____

Converted by His Own Sermon

Quaint, bizarre, eccentric, peculiar—those words describe a little, wiry coal miner named Billy Bray, of Cornwell, England. Before his conversion in November, 1832, Billy lived a vile life. After finding Christ, he became a flaming evangelist and lay preacher.

On a mountain near his home lived a cluster of non-Christian families. Billy, after working underground all day, would emerge from the mines and set out for the mountain, where he visited door-to-door, evangelizing the families. Soon every inhabitant was converted, and a church house was built.

The Church of England sent Rev. W. Haslam to shepherd the families, but when Billy heard the new parson preach, he was upset. Haslam didn't seem to know the Gospel. Billy felt the pastor wasn't truly a Christian himself, and he told him so.

Haslam was shaken. The next Sunday as he stood to preach, he announced his text, Matthew 22:42: "What think ye of Christ?" As he began delivering his message, he felt himself trusting Christ as Savior. He was converted while preaching his own sermon.

Billy heard of it and came for a visit. When Haslam came to the door, Billy asked, "Converted, kind sir?" The man said, "Yes, thank God, I am." Billy was so happy, he threw his arms around him, lifted him up, and carried him around the room shouting, "Glory, glory, the parson's converted! Glory be to God."

Mrs. Haslam, hearing the commotion, entered the room, and Billy cried, "Be the missis converted?" She replied, "Yes, thank God." Billy started toward her, but

---

[1] Adapted from T. E. Vassar, *Uncle John Vassar; or, the Fight of Faith* (London: The American Tract Society, 1879), 146–148.

instead of picking her up, he just grinned ear to ear and said, "Oh, I be so happy I can hardly live. Glory! Glory be to God!"[1]

Date: _____ _____ _____
Place: _____ _____ _____
Occasion: _____ _____ _____

C

Courage

Someone Once Said . . .

- *I am immortal until my work is done.*—John Wesley
- *You can expect from me everything save fear or recantation. I shall not flee, much less recant. I will go to Worms if there were as many devils there as there are tiles on the roofs of the houses.*—Martin Luther
- *I have looked in the faces of many angry men, and yet have not been afraid above measure.*—John Knox[2]
- *Courage is that quality of mind which enables men to encounter danger or difficulty with firmness, or without fear or depression of spirits. . . . The highest degree of courage is seen in the person who is most fearful but refuses to capitulate to it.*—J. Oswald Sanders[3]
- *Lord, the task is impossible for me but not for Thee. Lead the way and I will follow. Why should I fear? I am on a Royal Mission. I am in the service of the King of Kings.*— Mary Slessor, beginning her remarkable missionary career in Calabar (now part of modern Nigeria)
- *When you're accustomed to standing before God, kings don't matter much. Big potentates are just small potatoes when you have been standing in the presence of the Most High.*— Vance Havner[4]
- *Another singular action of a sanctified Christian is to prefer the duty he owes to God to the danger he fears from man. Christians in all ages have prized their services above their safety. "The wicked flee when no man pursueth: but the righteous are bold as a lion." The fearful hare trembles at every cry; but the courageous lion is unmoved by the greatest clamors. Were believers to shrink back at every contrary wind that blows, they would never make their voyage to heaven.*—William Secker, seventeenth–century clergyman[5]
- *Courage is being the only one who knows you're afraid.*—Anonymous

Date: _____ _____ _____
Place: _____ _____ _____
Occasion: _____ _____ _____

---

[1] Robert J. Morgan, *From This Verse* (Nashville: Thomas Nelson, 1998), entry for July 15th.
[2] W. Stanford Reid, *Trumpeter of God: A Biography of John Knox* (Grand Rapids: Baker Book House, 1974), 227–228.
[3] J. Oswald Sanders, *Spiritual Leadership* (Chicago: Moody Press, 1967), 55.
[4] Vance Havner, *Just a Preacher* (Chicago: Moody Press, 1981), 131
[5] William Secker, *The Nonsuch Professor In His Meridian Splendor* (Chicago: Fleming H. Revell Co., 1899), 69.

The Boneless Wonder

Winston Churchill was famous for his occasional merciless attacks on his foes. Once, speaking before Parliament, he tore into England's titular Prime Minister Ramsay MacDonald, whom Churchill regarded as spineless and weak. Staring across the well at MacDonald, Churchill growled, "I remember when I was a child being taken to the celebrated Barnum's Circus which contained an exhibition of freaks and monstrosities, but the exhibit on the program which I most desired to see was the one described as 'The Boneless Wonder.' My parents judged that the spectacle would be too revolting and demoralizing for my youthful eyes, and I have waited fifty years to see the 'Boneless Wonder' sitting on the Treasury Bench."

We must never be "boneless wonders," for God has not given us a spirit of fear, but of power, love, and of a sound mind (2 Timothy 1:7).[1]

Date:	_____	_____	_____
Place:	_____	_____	_____
Occasion:	_____	_____	_____

Martin Neimoller's Courage

In 1934, Adolf Hitler summoned German church leaders to his Berlin office to berate them for insufficiently supporting his programs. Pastor Martin Niemoller explained that he was concerned only for the welfare of the church and of the German people. Hitler snapped, "You confine yourself to the church. I'll take care of the German people." Niemoller replied, "You said that 'I will take care of the German people.' But we too, as Christians and churchmen, have a responsibility toward the German people. That responsibility was entrusted to us by God, and neither you nor anyone in this world has the power to take it from us."

━━━━━◇━━━━━
Definition of Courage

Grace under pressure.
—ERNEST HEMINGWAY[2]
━━━━━◇━━━━━

Hitler listened in silence, but that evening his Gestapo raided Niemoller's rectory, and a few days later a bomb exploded in his church. During the months and years following, he was closely watched by the secret police, and in June 1937, he preached these words to his church: "We have no more thought of using our own powers to escape the arm of the authorities than had the apostles of old. We must obey God rather than man." He was soon arrested and placed in solitary confinement.

Dr. Niemoller's trial began on February 7, 1938. That morning, a green-uniformed guard escorted the minister from his prison cell and through a series of underground passages toward the courtroom. Niemoller was overcome with terror and loneliness. What would become of him? Of his family? His church? What tortures awaited them all?

The guard's face was impassive, and he was silent as stone. But as they exited a tunnel to ascend a final flight of stairs, Niemoller heard a whisper. At first he didn't

---

[1] William Manchester, *The Last Lion: Winston Spencer Churchill—Visions of Glory* (Boston: Little, Brown, & Co., 1983), 853.
[2] Quoted by John F. Kennedy, *Profiles in Courage* (New York: Pocket Books, Inc., 1957), 1.

know where it came from, for the voice was soft as a sigh. Then he realized that the officer was breathing into his ear the words of Proverbs 18:10: *The name of the Lord is a strong tower; the righteous run to it and are safe.*

Niemoller's fear fell away, and the power of that verse sustained him through his trial and his years in Nazi concentration camps.

Date:			
Place:			
Occasion:			

Who Said That?

During his years as premier of the Soviet Union, Nikita Khrushchev denounced many of the policies and atrocities of Joseph Stalin. Once, as he censured Stalin in a public meeting, Khrushchev was interrupted by a shout from a heckler in the audience.

"You were one of Stalin's colleagues. Why didn't you stop him?"

"Who said that?" roared Khrushchev. An agonizing silence followed as nobody in the room dared move a muscle. Then Khrushchev replied quietly, "Now you know why."[2]

Date:			
Place:			
Occasion:			

Creation

Someone Once Said . . .

- *The heavens declare the glory of God.*—David, King of Israel
- *The universe is not a chaos but a cosmos.*
- *This most beautiful system of the sun, planets, and comets could only proceed from the counsel and domain of an intelligent and powerful Being.*—Sir Isaac Newton[3]
- *The more I study physics, the more I am drawn toward metaphysics.*—Dr. Albert Einstein
- *The existence of the universe requires me to conclude that God exists.*—Robert A. Naumann, Professor of Chemistry and Physics at Princeton University[4]

[1] Robert J. Morgan, *On This Day* (Nashville: Thomas Nelson, 1997), entry for February 7th.
[2] From *SermonIllustrations.Com*
[3] Isaac Newton, *Mathematical Principles of Natural Philosophy*, in *The Great Books of the Western World*, Vol. 34 (Chicago: Encyclopedia Britannica, 1952), 369.
[4] Quoted in John Ankerberg and John Weldon's *Darwin's Leap of Faith* (Eugene, Oregon: Harvest House Publishers, 1998), 267. This book is packed with quotations and arguments in favor of creationism from leading scientists.

- *A common sense and satisfying interpretation of our world suggests the designing hand of a superintelligence. . . . There is, I shall argue, no contradiction between holding a staunch belief in supernatural design and being a creative scientist. . . . Just as I believe that the Book of Scripture illumines the pathway to God, so I believe that the Book of Nature, with its astonishing details . . . also suggests a God of purpose and a God of design. And I think my belief makes me no less a scientist.*—Dr. Owen Gingerich, professor of astronomy and the History of Science at Harvard University, and senior astronomer at the Smithsonian Astrophysical Observatory.[1]

Date: _____ _____ _____

Place: _____ _____ _____

Occasion: _____ _____ _____

Some Ideas Are So Bad . . .

- *Some ideas are so bad that it may be argued they should be rejected on the basis of their implications alone.*—John Ankerberg and John Weldon, discussing evolution[2]
- *False facts are highly injurious to the progress of science, for they often endure long.*—Charles Darwin, unwittingly describing his own hypothesis in *The Descent of Man*

Date: _____ _____ _____

Place: _____ _____ _____

Occasion: _____ _____ _____

What Scientists Think of Evolution

- *Ultimately the Darwinian theory of evolution is no more nor less than the great cosmogenic myth of the twentieth century.*—Michael Denton, molecular biologist and medical doctor[3]
- *It is becoming increasingly apparent that evolutionism is not even a good scientific theory.*—Dr. Willem J. Ouweneel, Research Associate in Developmental Genetics, Ultrech, Netherlands[4]
- *What I have learned in the past ten years of review of recent scientific knowledge of cellular morphology and physiology, the code of life (DNA), and the lack of supporting evidence for evolution in the light of recent scientific evidence is a shocking rebuttal to the theory of evolution.*—Dr. Isaac Manly of Harvard Medical School[5]
- *The human fossil record is strongly supportive of the concept of Special Creation. On the other hand, the fossil evidence is so contrary to human evolution as to effectively falsify*

[1] Owen Gingerich, "Dare a Scientist Believe in Design?" in *Evidence of Purpose,* ed. by John Marks Templeton (New York: Continuum, 1994), 25, 28, 32.

[2] Ankerberg and Weldon, *Darwin's Leap of Faith,* 18.

[3] Ankerberg and Weldon, *Darwin's Leap of Faith,* 11.

[4] Ankerberg and Weldon, *Darwin's Leap of Faith,* 58.

[5] Ankerberg and Weldon, *Darwin's Leap of Faith,* 77.

the idea that humans evolved.—Professor Marvin L. Lubenow, in his book *Bones of Contention*[1]

- *For the scientist who has lived by his faith in the power of reason, the story ends like a bad dream. He has scaled the mountains of ignorance; he is about to conquer the highest peak; as he pulls himself over the final rock, he is greeted by a band of theologians who have been sitting there for centuries.*—Robert Jastrow, Ph.D. Chief of the Theoretical Division of the National Aeronautics and Space Administration (1958–61) and Founder/Director of NASA's Goddard Institute; Professor of Geophysics at Columbia University; Professor of Space Studies—Earth Sciences at Dartmouth College, in his book *God and the Astronomers*[2]

- *Can all of life be fit into Darwin's theory of evolution? . . . If you search the scientific literature on evolution, and if you focus your search on the question of how molecular machines—the basis of life—developed, you find an eerie and complete silence. The complexity of life's foundation has paralyzed science's attempt to account for it. . . . I do not think [Darwin's mechanism] explains molecular life.*—Michael Behe, Associate Professor of Biochemistry at Lehigh University[3]

Date: _____   _____   _____

Place: _____   _____   _____

Occasion: _____   _____   _____

Who Made It?

Many years ago, Sir Isaac Newton had an exact replica of our solar system made in miniature. At its center was a large golden ball representing the sun, and revolving around it were smaller spheres attached at the ends of rods of varying lengths. They represented Mercury, Venus, Earth, Mars, and the other planets. These were all geared together by cogs and belts to make them move around the "sun" in perfect harmony.

One day as Newton was studying the model, a friend who did not believe in the biblical account of creation stopped by for a visit. Marveling at the device and watching as the scientist made the heavenly bodies move in their orbits, the man exclaimed, "Why, Newton, what an exquisite thing! Who made it for you?"

Without looking up, Sir Isaac said, "Nobody."

"Nobody?"

"That's right," replied Newton. "I said nobody. All of these balls and cogs and belts and gears just happened to come together, and wonder of wonders, by chance they began revolving in their set orbits and with perfect timing!"[4]

Date: _____   _____   _____

Place: _____   _____   _____

Occasion: _____   _____   _____

---

[1] Marvin L. Lubenow, *Bones of Contention* (Grand Rapids: Baker, 1992), 7.

[2] Quoted by Bill Durbin in "A Scientist Caught Between Two Faiths," *Christianity Today,* August 6, 1982, 14.

[3] Michael Behe, *Darwin's Black Box* (New York: The Free Press, 1996), 5.

[4] Clipped from *Our Daily Bread.*

How Large the Universe

How vast is God's universe? Pretend the earth were a grape or marble. In proportion, the sun would be the size of a beach ball and would be 163 yards away— a little less than the length of two football fields.

The largest planet in our solar system, Jupiter, would be about the size of a grapefruit, and it would be about five blocks up the road. What about the nearest star? In our scaled-down universe, the nearest star would still be 24,000 miles away.

If the earth were a grape, the Milky Way, reduced to a proportionate size, would still be 55 billion miles wide. And the universe is filled with other galaxies. Who can imagine the size of the universe?

Date: _____ _____ _____
Place: _____ _____ _____
Occasion: _____ _____ _____

Put Another Way . . .

"If we possessed an atlas of our galaxy that devoted but a single page to each star system in the Milky Way (so that the sun and all its planets were crammed in one page), that atlas would run to more than ten million volumes of ten thousand pages each. It would take a library the size of Harvard's to house the atlas, and merely to flip through it, at the rate of a page per second, would require over ten thousand years. . . . And there are a hundred million more galaxies."[1]

Date: _____ _____ _____
Place: _____ _____ _____
Occasion: _____ _____ _____

Deceived

In his book, *Bones of Contention,* professor Marvin Lubenow tells the sad story of Sir Arthur Keith, one of the greatest anatomists of the twentieth century. According to Keith's autobiography, as a young man he attended evangelistic meetings in Edinburgh and Aberdeen and watched students make their commitments to Jesus Christ. He himself often felt on "the verge of conversion," yet he resisted, rejecting the gospel because he felt that the Genesis account of Creation was just a myth and that the Bible was merely a human book.

Later, as a scientist, Keith became greatly intrigued by a famous discovery in England. In 1908, forty miles from downtown London, in a gravel pit near the village of Piltdown, some bones were "discovered," portions of a human skull, a molar, and a lower jaw. Soon it was announced to the Geological Society of London that these were the remains of the earliest known Englishman, *Eoanthropus dawsoni,*

---

[1] Timothy Farris, *Coming of Age in the Milky Way* (New York: William Morrow, 1988), 383.

C

otherwise known as Piltdown Man. The vast majority of paleoanthropologists worldwide hailed this as a great discovery of our potential human ancestors.

The literature produced on Piltdown man was enormous. It is said that more than five hundred doctoral dissertations were written about him. To Sir Arthur Keith, it was the validation of his evolutionary beliefs—the missing link—and he wrote more on Piltdown Man than anyone else. His famous work, *The Antiquity of Man,* centered on Piltdown. Much of his life was spent studying and proclaiming the wonders of this discovery.

Though the Piltdown fossils were discovered between 1908 and 1915, it was not until 1953 that the British Museum proclaimed the entire thing was a fraud. The jawbone was not much older than the year it was found. The bones had been treated with iron salts to make them appear old, and scratch marks were detected in the teeth, indicating that they had been filed.

Sir Arthur Keith was eighty-six years old when his colleagues visited him at his home to break the news that the fossil he had trusted in for forty years was a hoax. A great scholar had rejected the witness of both God's natural Creation and the Lord Jesus, whose resurrection validated everything He said and did, only to put a lifetime of misplaced faith in what proved to be a phony fossil.[1]

Date: _____   _____   _____

Place: _____   _____   _____

Occasion: _____   _____   _____

The Evidence at Hand

Paul Gentuso was a budding evolutionist until he studied the human hand in medical school. "In anatomy class," he said, "we dissected a human hand. In investigating the hand, I first removed the skin, then isolated the individual tendons and muscles as I worked my way to the bones. The tendons of the hand are aligned in tendon sheaths, like self-lubricating pulleys, allowing the hand to work in a tireless, noiseless, almost effortless fashion. It was perfectly designed to carry out all the work it was called to do, everything from lifting a small object to lugging a tree trunk."

The experience deeply affected Gentuso. Until then, he had entertained serious doubts about God's existence. "In seeing how each tendon was perfectly aligned along the axis of each finger and how each finger moved in a coordinated fashion when tugged by individual tendons," he said, "it became obvious to me that there was a Creator who had intelligently designed and created the human hand. This was the first time in my adult life that I could say with assurance that a Creator existed. It was really a spiritual experience for me. I went from doubt to certainty based on seeing God's creation."

Paul Gentuso later became a Christian, a missionary physician in Cote d'Ivoire, and a resident doctor in Nashville, Tennessee.[2]

---

[1] Marvin L. Lubenow, *Bones of Contention* (Grand Rapids: Baker, 1992), 44.
[2] Robert J. Morgan, *Beyond Reasonable Doubt* (Wheaton, IL: Evangelical Training Association, 1997), 19.

```
Date:        _____   _____   _____
Place:       _____   _____   _____
Occasion:    _____   _____   _____
```

Intelligent Design

In an article entitled "The Wonders of the Natural World: God's Design," university professor Gerald R. Bergman points out how advanced God's creation is over human invention:

- Before we ever discovered and harnessed electricity, electric eels have generated their own electricity at will, up to 700 volts.
- Before we ever invented electric lights, fireflies were flashing their signals to one another, and certain fish in the ocean depths produce light to guide their travels.
- Long before we learned to navigate the seven seas, birds traveled from the Arctic to the Antarctic, landing at the same nesting sites year after year.
- We take pride in our jet aircraft, but octopuses used jet propulsion long before us. In its bulbous body is a muscular "sack" with a small opening. When an octopus expands the sack, water is sucked in, and when it vigorously contracts it, the water spurts out in a jet. By alternate expansion and contraction of this muscular sack, the octopus can jet-propel its way through the water.
- Before we ever designed and built suspension bridges, God's spiders demonstrated engineering feats of amazing brilliance.
- Bird's nests display a high level of engineering skill in masonry, weaving, tunneling, and structural strength necessary to build them.
- Bees, with their wings, "air-condition" their hives.
- Beavers build large dams out of trees and mud.
- Wasps manufacture a type of paper.
- Man has developed radar and sonar systems, and this development is seen as a miracle of science. Yet bats can do the same thing. Scientists have blindfolded bats and set them loose in a room which has been strung with many thin threads. Scientists found that the bats can dart around the room without striking a single thread because in flight they emit supersonic sound pulses. These hit objects and bounce back to the bat's ears.

Why is it we attribute to blind chance that which we have accomplished only by intelligent design?[1]

```
Date:        _____   _____   _____
Place:       _____   _____   _____
Occasion:    _____   _____   _____
```

---

[1] Gerald R. Bergman, "The Wonders of the Natural World: God's Design," in *Decision Magazine,* April, 1981, 7.

The King of Creation

One of the most beautiful hymns about the creation is this one: *Praise ye the Lord, the Almighty / The King of Creation! / O my soul, praise Him, / For He is thy health and salvation!*

Its author would be horrified today to discover that his name has become better known in evolutionary circles than among Christians.

The hymn was written by an evangelical Lutheran theologian and school rector in the late 1600s, who was gifted in poetry and hymn writing. He would often take long walks in the country near Hochdal, Germany. As he strolled, he composed hymns and sang them in praise to God. One of his favorite spots was a beautiful gorge through which the Dussel River flowed, about ten miles east of Dusseldorf. He strolled in this valley so often that it became identified with him and eventually named after him. His name was Joachem Neander, and the valley became known as the Neanderthal, or the Neander Valley *(tal,* or *thal* in old German, means *valley).*

It was out of his love for the beauty of this valley and of God's matchless creation that Joachem Neander wrote, *Praise Ye the Lord, The King of Creation.*

But it was also in this valley two hundred years later, as limestone was being quarried for the manufacture of cement, that workmen came across some caves in the side wall of the gorge. One of the caves contained human bones, and the first Neanderthal had been discovered.

Professor Marvin L. Lubenow writes, "The typical Neanderthal does differ somewhat from the typical modern human. However, the two also overlap. In fact, there should never have been a question about Neanderthal's taxonomic status. When the first Neanderthal was discovered even 'Darwin's bulldog,' Thomas Huxley, recognized that Neanderthal was fully human and not an evolutionary ancestor. [Neanderthal is] a card-carrying member of the human family."

Nevertheless, the idea persists that Neanderthal Man is some sort of missing link in human evolution. As Lubenow puts it, "When Joachem Neander walked in his beautiful valley so many years ago, he could not know that hundreds of years later his name would become world famous, not for his hymns celebrating creation but for a concept that he would have totally rejected: human evolution."[1]

Date: _____   _____   _____

Place: _____   _____   _____

Occasion: _____   _____   _____

Not a Chance

In his book, *Not a Chance,* R. C. Sproul, a scholar with degrees from the Free University of Amsterdam, Geneva College, and Grove City College who lectures widely on apologetics, wrote: *For something to come from nothing it must, in effect, create itself. Self-creation is a logical and rational impossibility. For something to create itself it must be able to transcend Hamlet's dilemma, "To be or not to be." Hamlet's question assumed sound science. He understood that something (himself) could not both be and not be at the same time*

---

[1] Lubenow, *Bones of Contention,* chapter 6.

and in the same relationship. For something to create itself, it must have the ability to be and not be at the same time and in the same relationship. For something to create itself it must be before it is. This is impossible. It is impossible for solids, liquids, and gasses. It is impossible for atoms and subatomic particles. It is impossible for light and heat. It is impossible for God. Nothing anywhere, anytime, can create itself.[1]

Date: _____   _____   _____
Place: _____   _____   _____
Occasion: _____   _____   _____

I Do Know One Thing

Colin Patterson is a senior paleontologist at the British Natural History Museum and the author of the museum's general text on evolution. He gave a lecture at the American Museum of Natural History some time ago comparing creation with evolution, and this is part of what he said:

Can you tell me anything we know about evolution, any one thing . . . that is true? I tried that question on the geology staff at the Field Museum of Natural History and the only answer I got was silence. I tried it on the members of the Evolutionary Morphology seminar in the University of Chicago, a very prestigious body of evolutionists, and all I got there was silence for a long time and eventually one person said, "I do know one thing—it ought not to be taught in high school."[2]

━━━━◆━━━━
Creation and Science

A common sense and satisfying interpretation of our world suggests the designing hand of a superintelligence.

—DR. OWEN GINGERICH
━━━━◆━━━━

Patterson's quote is found in Phillip Johnson's book *Darwin on Trial*. Johnson, a graduate of Harvard and the University of Chicago, is a lawyer and a professor of law who served as a law clerk for Chief Justice Earl Warren of the United States Supreme Court and has taught law for over twenty years at the University of California at Berkeley. He decided to evaluate the evidence for evolution from the perspective of an attorney.

After exhaustive studies and research, he wrote *Darwin on Trial*, a book that rocked the scientific world. Johnson's conclusion in a nutshell—the confirmatory evidence for evolution is miserably lacking on every front, yet scientists continue to cling to this pseudo-science, as he calls it, because to abandon it would leave them with no explanation for the origin of life apart from a creating God which they refuse to consider.

Date: _____   _____   _____
Place: _____   _____   _____
Occasion: _____   _____   _____

Another Reason

One good reason for accepting divine creation of the cosmos is that it results in human dignity and happiness, whereas the results of the evolutionary hypothesis are

---

[1] R. C. Sproul, *Not A Chance* (Grand Rapids: Baker Book House, 1994), 12.
[2] Quoted in Phillip E. Johnson, *Darwin on Trial* (Downers Grove, IL: InterVarsity Press, 1991), 10.

dark, sinister, and deeply troubling. Scientists, after all, gather evidence for their theories by conducting experiments and finding out what works and what doesn't.

Does evolution then "work"? Does it result in psychological and sociological health and happiness? It is a well-known if seldom-mentioned fact of history that Darwin's survival-of-the-fittest and materialist evolutionary conjectures, seized upon by Karl Marx, provided the foundation for both Hitler's Holocaust and Stalin's genocide.[1]

In America, Darwin's influence has been more subtle, but think of it in this way: What would you expect of a generation that had been taught evolution from their earliest schooldays? If Darwin is right, we are nothing but accidental by-products of evolutionary dust on an insignificant world lost somewhere in the vastness of a hostile universe and doomed to perish in a short period of time. We are nothing more than a match that blazes for a moment, then is extinguished forever. We are without any divine guidance, without any moral absolutes. We have no spirit and no soul, therefore we become obsessed with our bodies, obsessed with pleasure. All we are, as the song says, is "dust in the wind."

What does such a belief do to optimism and hope? To moral values? To the sanctity of life? To human dignity? To the sacredness of home and family? To law and order?

Dostoevski once remarked that if God is dead, then everything is justifiable; philosopher Ravi Zacharias put it like this, "There is nothing in history to match the dire ends to which humanity can be led by following a political and social philosophy that consciously and absolutely excludes God."[2]

If, on the other hand, creation is true, then we are formed by a loving God in his own image, the crown of his creation and heirs of eternal life through his Son, Jesus Christ. We are people of dignity and worth, surrounded by a fantastic universe that he made for our enjoyment. We are guided by sound moral principles leading to human health and happiness, and we are comforted by all the promises in the book he has given. We have hope even during life's darkest hours, and we have value beyond that of any other living creatures.

Which option seems most sensible to you?[3]

Date:			
Place:			
Occasion:			

What Charles Spurgeon Had to Say About Evolution

If any of you shall live fifty years, you will see that the philosophy of today will be a football of contempt for the philosophy of that period. They will speak, amid roars of laughter, of evolution; and the day will come when there will not be a child but will look upon it as being the most

---

[1] For a more detailed study of this subject, see David Breese, *Seven Men Who Rule the World From the Grave* (Chicago: Moody Press, 1990).

[2] Ravi Zacharias, *Can Man Live Without God?* (Dallas: Word Publishing Co., 1994), xvii.

[3] Robert J. Morgan, *Beyond Reasonable Doubt* (Wheaton, IL: Evangelical Training Association, 1997), 30–31.

foolish notion that ever crossed the human mind.—from Spurgeon's sermon "God Justified, Though Man Believes Not," delivered Sunday evening, August 31, 1890

Date:	_____	_____	_____
Place:	_____	_____	_____
Occasion:	_____	_____	_____

Two Books and a Boy

In his little volume, *Peace in the Valley*, Vance Havner writes about his childhood:

The story of my early years might well be called 'Two Books and a Boy.' I grew up in the Carolina hills in an old-fashioned home with a Bible at the heart of it. Father read the Scriptures each evening at family devotions by the light of a kerosene lamp. I began to read the Book early, memorized portions of it, fed upon the stories of its heroes, Joseph and Moses and Samson and David and Daniel. Above all, there was the story of Jesus.

Another book came into my life as a lad. Living as I did in the country, I became interested in the bird life around me. We used to buy boxes of baking soda, each of which contained a card with the picture and description of a bird. I became fascinated with the subject and one day I secured a little bird guide. It opened a new world.

The Bible and the bird book did wonders for the boy. God has written his message to us in two books, the revelation of nature and the God-breathed Scriptures. The book of nature is not enough. By it we may know the art of God but not the heart of God. We may know the garden but not the Gardener. So God sent His Son and gave us the account of it in a Book.

I am glad that I grew up reading both books.[1]

Date:	_____	_____	_____
Place:	_____	_____	_____
Occasion:	_____	_____	_____

Flooded

There was once an old preacher who told some of his Sunday school boys the subject of his next Sunday's sermon. Wanting to trick him, the boys stole away with his Bible and glued some of the pages together. The next Sunday, the preacher stood to read his text. As he got to the bottom of the page he read, "When Noah was 120 years old he took unto himself a wife, who . . ." And turning the page he continued, ". . . was 140 cubits long, forty cubits wide, built of gopher wood, and covered with pitch inside and out."

The minister paused, a puzzled expression covering his face. He read it again, and then said, "My friends, this is the first time I have ever seen this in the Bible, but I take it as evidence of the assertion that we are fearfully and wonderfully made."[2]

---

[1] Vance Havner, *Peace in the Valley* (Old Tappan, NJ: 1962), 11–12.
[2] Adapted from W. C. Hewitt, *The Best After Dinner Stories and How To Tell Them* (Chicago: Charles T. Powner Co., 1946), 8.

Date:			
Place:			
Occasion:			

C

Criticism

Someone Once Said . . .

- *Fault-finding is dreadfully catching: one dog will set a whole kennel howling.*—Charles Spurgeon[1]
- *When you throw mud at someone, you're the one who is losing ground.*—Anonymous
- *When attacked by a dragon, do not become one.*—Marshall Shelley[2]
- *To thine own self be true.*—William Shakespeare
- *Doth the moon stay herself to lecture every dog that bayeth at her? Do not be in a hurry to set yourselves right. God will take care of you. Leave yourselves alone; only be very valiant for the Lord God of Israel.*—Charles Spurgeon[3]
- *O Lord, deliver me from this lust of always vindicating myself.*—St. Augustine

Date:			
Place:			
Occasion:			

Nine to One

In his book *The Youth Builder,* Jim Burns talks about the importance of building up young people with affirmation and trust. What he says about criticism applies to every age group: *For every critical comment we receive, it takes nine affirming comments to even out the negative effect in our life. Most young people receive more critical comments a day than encouraging ones. You can have a very positive, life-transforming effect when you develop a ministry of affirmation.*[4]

Date:			
Place:			
Occasion:			

Words to Hang Over the Desk

When Fiorello La Guardia was the mayor of New York City (1933–1945), he hung above his desk in City Hall a pronouncement by Abraham Lincoln. Interest-

---

[1] Charles Haddon Spurgeon, *John Ploughman's Talks* (Grand Rapids: Baker Book House, 1976), 23.
[2] Marshall Shelley, *Well-Intentioned Dragons* (Carol Stream, IL: Christianity Today, Inc., 1985), 61.
[3] Charles Haddon Spurgeon, *Spurgeon's Sermons, Vol. 1* (Grand Rapids: Baker Book House, 1983), 202.
[4] Jim Burns, *The Youth Builder* (Eugene, OR: Harvest House Publishers, 1988), 54.

ingly, General MacArthur had a copy of it hanging over his headquarters desk during World War II, and Winston Churchill had a framed copy of it on the walls of his study at Chartwell:

If I were to try to read, much less answer, all the attacks made on me, this shop might as well be closed for any other business. I do the very best I know how—the very best I can, and I mean to keep doing so until the end. If the end brings me out all right, what is said against me won't amount to anything. If the end brings me out wrong, ten angels swearing I was right would make no difference.

Date: _____ _____ _____

Place: _____ _____ _____

Occasion: _____ _____ _____

Good Advice

A minister named Bob Cook once came to Harry Ironside, asking the famous Bible teacher how he should respond to criticisms leveled against him. Ironside's advice: "Bob, if the criticism about you is true, mend your ways. If it isn't, forget about it!"

The same point was put this way by another man: "Never fear criticism when you're right; never ignore criticism when you're wrong."

Put yet another way: "Don't mind criticism. If it's untrue, disregard it; if it's unfair, keep from irritation; if it's ignorant, smile; if it's justified, learn from it."

Date: _____ _____ _____

Place: _____ _____ _____

Occasion: _____ _____ _____

Aesop on Criticism

One of Aesop's fables tells of an old man and his son bringing a donkey to market. Passing some people on the way, they hear one remark, "Look at that silly pair—walking when they could be riding comfortably."

The idea seemed sensible to the old man, so he and the boy mounted the donkey and continued on their way. Soon they passed another group. "Look at that lazy pair," said a voice, "breaking the back of that poor donkey, tiring him so that no one will buy him."

The old man slid off, but soon they heard another criticism from a passerby: "What a terrible thing, this old man walking while the boy gets to ride."

They changed places, but soon heard people whispering, "What a terrible thing, the big strong man riding and making the little boy walk."

The old man and the boy pondered the situation and finally continued their journey in yet another matter, carrying the donkey on a pole between them.

As they crossed the bridge, the donkey broke loose, fell into the river, and drowned.

Aesop's moral: You can't please everyone.

Date:			
Place:			
Occasion:			

Anonymous Wisdom

They're saying things that are not true;
O blessed Lord, what shall I do?
He answers, "What is that to thee?
Thy duty is to follow Me."

Date:			
Place:			
Occasion:			

Taking Criticism in Stride

Charles Spurgeon suffered a firestorm of criticism when beginning his ministry in London. A steady stream of articles trashed his sermons, and pamphlets appeared denouncing his methods, motives, mannerisms, and messages. He was vilified in cartoons and caricatures. Several writers questioned whether he was converted.

Barking Dogs

The dogs bark, but the caravan passes.

—ORIENTAL PROVERB

At first, this storm of cynicism and censure deeply hurt Spurgeon, who described himself as "broken in agony." But his wife prepared a plaque of Matthew 5:11–12 for the wall of their room where Charles would see it first thing every day: "Blessed are you when they revile and persecute you, and say all kinds of evil against you falsely for My sake. Rejoice and be exceedingly glad, for great is your reward in heaven."

The verse did its work, and in time Spurgeon learned to take criticism in stride. Not long before his death years later, a friend, visiting him in his study, said, "Do you know, Mr. Spurgeon, some people think you conceited?"

The great preacher paused a moment, then he smiled and said with a twinkle in his eye, "Do you see those bookshelves? They contain hundreds, nay, thousands of my sermons translated into every language under heaven. Well, now, add to this that ever since I was twenty years old there never has been built a place large enough to hold the numbers of people who wished to hear me preach, and, upon my honor, when I think of it, I wonder I am not more conceited than I am!"[1]

Date:			
Place:			
Occasion:			

[1] Adapted from Robert J. Morgan's *From This Verse* (Nashville: Thomas Nelson Publishers, 1998), entry for June 27th.

Hyde's Lesson

John Hyde (1865–1912) was a missionary to India who became so far-famed for his effective and powerful praying that he is known to history as Praying Hyde.

He once told of the "most salutary" lesson the Lord ever taught him about prayer. It occurred while he was praying for a national pastor in India, a man who was both having—and causing—problems.

Hyde began his prayer, "O God, Thou knowest this brother, how—" He was going to say "cold," when suddenly he was smitten in his spirit. A voice seemed to whisper sharply to him, "He that touches him touches the apple of my eye." A great horror swept over Hyde, and he felt he had been guilty before God of "accusing the brethren."

Falling to his knees, Hyde confessed his own sin, and he remembered the words of Paul, that we should think on things that are lovely and good. "Father," cried Hyde, "show me what things are lovely and of good report in my brother's life."

Like a flash, Hyde remembered the many sacrifices this pastor had made for the Lord, how he had given up all for Christ, how he had suffered deeply for Christ. He thought of the many years of difficult labor this man had invested in the kingdom and the wisdom with which he had resolved congregational conflict. Hyde remembered the man's devotion to his wife and family, and how he had provided a model to the church of godly husbanding.

John Hyde spent his prayer time that day praising the Lord for this brother's faithfulness.

Shortly afterward, Hyde journeyed into the plains to see this pastor, and he learned that the man had just received a great spiritual uplift, as if a personal revival had refreshed his heart like a springtime breeze.

While Hyde had been praising, God had been blessing.[1]

Date: _____ _____ _____
Place: _____ _____ _____
Occasion: _____ _____ _____

An Arabian Proverb

• If one person calls you an ass or a donkey, pay no attention to him. But if five people call you one, go out and buy yourself a saddle.

Date: _____ _____ _____
Place: _____ _____ _____
Occasion: _____ _____ _____

[1] Robert J. Morgan, *From This Verse* (Nashville: Thomas Nelson Publishers, 1998), entry for June 20th.

Someone Once Said . . .

- *Only one act of pure love, unsullied by any taint of ulterior motive, has ever been performed in the history of the world, namely the self-giving of God in Christ on the cross for undeserving sinners.*—John Stott
- *Christianity is a cross, and a cross is "I" crossed out.*—John Bisagno[1]
- *I saw that just as Christian came up to the Cross, his burden loosed from his shoulders and fell off his back and landed in the sepulcher. Then was Christian glad and lightsome and said with a merry heart, "He hath given me rest by His sorrow, and life by His death."*—John Bunyan, in *Pilgrim's Progress*
- *If Socrates died like a philosopher, Jesus Christ died like a God.*—Jean Jacques Rousseau

Date: _____ _____ _____

Place: _____ _____ _____

Occasion: _____ _____ _____

A Sack Full of Sparrows

Paul Harvey once told of a little boy, whom doting parents had spoiled into a brat. The boy carried with him a sack, and in the sack there was a most pitiful kind of stirring. He had captured some tiny birds. The sound of imprisoned wing-beats slapped hopelessly at the heavy manila walls. A pitiful chirping now and then issued from the little paper prison that he swung at his side. He met an old man as he walked along.

"Whatcha got in that sack?" asked the old man.

"I got a sack full of sparrows!" said the little boy.

"What are you going to do with them?" asked the old man.

"I'm going to take them out of the sack, one by one, and tease them—pull a feather out now and then, and then I'll release them to the cat for his dinner."

"How much would you sell the whole sack for?" asked the old man.

The little boy thought a moment and decided that he should put a lot of capital on the venture and dicker down if he had to, so he threw out the figure: "I'll take two dollars for the sack!"

"Done," said the old man; and he reached in his pocket, pulled out the two dollars, and gave them to the lad. The lad then handed him the sack. The old man held it far more kindly than the reckless youngster had.

In a moment he untwisted the coiled paper neck of the bag and pulled it open. In but a little bit, the sky connected brilliantly with the open inside of the bag and the birds were gone.

And so it happened one day that God met Lucifer with a huge bag. Inside the bag were the most hopeless sounds of life struggling to be free—the sounds of young and old alike wailing in pain.

───────────

[1] John Bisagno, *The Power of Positive Praying* (Grand Rapids: Zondervan, 1965), 27.

"What have you got in the bag?" asked the Father.

"People," smirked Lucifer.

"And what will you do with them?"

"I will torment them one by one, and when they are all worn out with trials, I will throw them into hell."

"And what will you take for all of them?"

"Your only Beloved."

"Done!" said the Father. And He reached down to earth and gave us the gift of His Son.

And in such a happy trade-off we come to hold the key to the resurrection and the life.[1]

Date:	_____	_____	_____
Place:	_____	_____	_____
Occasion:	_____	_____	_____

Seeing the Cross

[A] Raymond Lull

Raymond Lull was born in 1232 into a wealthy family on an island just off the coast of Spain. His early life was spent in debauchery and, as he later put it, "utter immorality." Yet he was recognized by his peers in Spain as a young man of brilliance and promise. During his early thirties, Lull was born again as a result of a dream or vision that he experienced. He saw "the Savior hanging on His cross, the blood trickling from His hands and feet and brow, look reproachfully at him." As a result, Lull soon gave his life to Christ and devoted himself to the ministry, becoming a missionary to the Muslims and eventually dying a martyr's death at age eighty by their hands.

[B] Count Nicholaus von Zinzendorf

Nicholaus Ludwig von Zinzendorf was born into one of Europe's leading families in the year 1700, and he grew up in an atmosphere of prayer, Bible-reading, and hymn-singing. He excelled in school, and seemed to possess all the qualities for national leadership. After finishing his university studies at Wittenberg, Germany, Zinzendorf embarked on a grand tour of Europe, attending lectures and visiting museums, palaces, and universities.

It was while visiting the art museum at Dusseldorf that the young count had a deeply moving experience that stayed with him the rest of his life. Seeing Domenico Feti's *Ecce Homo* ("Behold, the Man"), a portrait of the thorn-crowned Jesus, and reading the inscription below it—"I Did This For Thee! What Hast Thou Done For Me?" Zinzendorf said to himself, "I have loved Him for a long time, but I have never actually done anything for Him. From now on, I will do whatever He leads me to do."

---

[1] Calvin Miller, "Call in the Witnesses" in *Proclaim!*, Spring, 1999, 7

His life was never again the same, and he went on to found a spiritual community on his property, Herrnhut, which provided hundreds of Moravian missionaries over the next several decades and sparked the modern missionary movement.[1]

[C] Frances Havergal

Frances Ridley Havergal, the British musician and devotional writer, left us such classic hymns as *Like a River Glorious, Who is on the Lord's Side?, I Am Trusting Thee, Lord Jesus,* and *Take My Life and Let It Be.* One day in January, 1858, while visiting the art museum in Dusseldorf, Germany, she sat down wearily opposite Domenico Feti's picture of Christ under which was this caption: "I Did This For Thee! What Hast Thou Done For Me?" Deeply moved, Frances scribbled some lines that flashed into her mind, writing in pencil on a scrap of paper. Reading them over, they did not satisfy her so she tossed them into the fire, but they fell out untouched. Some months later she showed them to her father who encouraged her to preserve them. Being a musician himself, he even wrote a melody to accompany them. The resulting hymn, "I Gave My Life For Thee" was first published in 1860, and launched Frances Ridley Havergal as a serious composer of hymns:

> *I gave My life for thee,*
> *My precious blood I shed,*
> *That thou might'st ransomed be,*
> *And quickened from the dead.*
> *I gave, I gave my life for thee;*
> *What hast thou given for Me?*[2]

[D] John Newton

> *In evil long I took delight*
> *Unawed by shame or fear,*
> *Till a new object struck my sight*
> *And stopped my wild career.*
> *I saw One hanging on a tree,*
> *In agonies and blood,*
> *Who fixed his languid eyes on me,*
> *As near his cross I stood.*

[E] The Most Difficult Problem

Dr. Eric Frykenberg, veteran missionary to India, was a great storyteller, and he could vividly describe scenes and events from his fifty-plus years in Asia. One day someone asked him, "Dr. Frykenberg, what is the most difficult problem you ever faced?"

Without hesitation, he answered, "It was when my heart would grow cold before God. When that happened, I knew I was too busy. I also knew it was time to get away. So I would take my Bible and go off to the hills alone. I'd open my

---

[1] Adapted from *Christian History Magazine*, Vol. 1, No. 1, "The Rich Young Ruler Who Said Yes," 7ff.

[2] *Memorials of Frances Ridley Havergal* by her sister M. V. G. H. (New York: E. P. Dutton & Co, 1892), 65.

Bible to Matthew 27, the story of the Crucifixion, and I would wrap my arms around the cross.

"And then," Frykenberg said, "I'd be ready to go back to work."[1]

[F] No Answer

A man in Dundee, Scotland, was confined to bed for forty years, having broken his neck in a fall at age fifteen. But his spirit remained unbroken, and his cheer and courage so inspired people that he enjoyed a constant stream of guests. One day a visitor asked him, "Doesn't Satan ever tempt you to doubt God?"

"Oh, yes," replied the man. "He does try to tempt me. I lie here and see my old schoolmates driving along in their carriages and Satan whispers, 'If God is so good, why does He keep you here all these years? Why did he permit your neck to be broken?'"

"What do you do when Satan whispers those things?" asked the guest.

"Ah," replied the invalid, "I take him to Calvary, show him Christ, and point to those deep wounds, and say, 'You see, he *does* love me.' And Satan has no answer to that. He flees every time."[2]

[G] Stand at the Foot of the Cross

Charles Spurgeon once said, "Stand at the foot of the cross, and count the purple drops by which you have been cleansed: See the thorn-crown; mark His scourged shoulders, still gushing with encrimsoned rills. . . . And if you do not lie prostrate on the ground before that cross, you have never seen it."

Date:	_____	_____	_____
Place:	_____	_____	_____
Occasion:	_____	_____	_____

Two Evangelists

Billy Graham once recalled, *I remember preaching in Dallas, Texas, early in our ministry. It was 1953. About forty thousand people attended each night, but one evening only a few people responded to the appeal to receive Jesus Christ. Discouraged, I left the platform. A German businessman was there, a devout man of God. He put his arm around me and said, 'Billy, do you know what was wrong tonight? You didn't preach the cross.'*

The next night I preached on the blood of Christ, and a great host of people responded to receive Christ as Savior. When we proclaim the Gospel of Christ, when we preach Christ crucified and risen, there is a built-in power to it.[3]

One hundred years before, a reporter attending the great British evangelistic campaigns of evangelist D. L. Moody wrote something remarkably similar. Referring to the great crowds attending Moody's meetings, the London journalist wrote, "One cannot but ask the question, 'What is the magic power which draws together these

---

[1] Leslie B. Flynn, *Come Alive With Illustrations* (Grand Rapids: Baker Book House, 1987), 173.

[2] A similar story is told by Mark Guy Pearse in *Daniel Quorm & His Religious Notions,* as related by F. W. Boreham in *The Other Side of the Hill* (London: Epworth Press, 1954), 208-9.

[3] Billy Graham, "Go in His Power," in *Decision Magazine,* January, 1989, p. 1, taken from a message preached at the 1983 International Conference for Itinerant Evangelists.

mighty multitudes and holds them spellbound?' Is it the worldly rank or wealth of learning or oratory of the preacher? No, for he is possessed of little of these. It is the simple lifting up of the cross of Christ—the holding forth the Lord Jesus before the eyes of the people."[1]

Date: _____ _____ _____

Place: _____ _____ _____

Occasion: _____ _____ _____

A Physician Looks at Crucifixion

As Dr. Truman Davis contemplated the story of Christ, it dawned on him that he didn't know the actual immediate cause of death for a victim of crucifixion; so he began to study the ancient practice of torture and death by fixation to a cross.

The preliminary scourging was done with the victim naked, his arms tied to a post above his head. The heavy whip is brought down with full force again and again across Jesus' shoulders, back, and legs. At first the thongs cut through the skin only. Then, as the blows continue they cut deeper until the half-fainting victim is untied and allowed to slump to the pavement, wet in his own blood.

A heavy crossbeam is tied across his shoulders, but in spite of his efforts to walk erect, the weight of the heavy wooden beam, together with the shock produced by copious blood loss, is too much. He stumbles and falls. The rough wood gouges into the lacerated skin and muscles of the shoulders. He tries to rise, but human muscles have been pushed beyond their endurance.

A Pot of Gold

All of my life, I have been looking for a pot of gold at the foot of a rainbow, and I found it at the foot of the cross.

—DALE EVANS

At the site of execution, the crossbeam is thrown down, and the victim is pushed to the ground, his arms stretching over the wood. The legionnaire feels for the depression at the front of the wrist. He drives a heavy, square, wrought-iron nail through the wrist and into the wood. Quickly, he moves to the other side. Jesus is hauled up and lifted onto the upright post.

The left foot is now pressed backward against the right foot, and with both feet extended, toes down, a nail is driven through the arch of each, leaving the knees moderately flexed. The victim is now crucified. As he slowly sags down with more weight on the nails in the wrists excruciating pain shoots along the fingers and up the arms to explode in the brain—the nails in the wrists are putting pressure on the median nerves. As he pushes himself upward to avoid this stretching torment, he places his full weight on the nail through his feet. Again there is the searing agony of the nail tearing through the nerves between the metatarsal bones of the feet.

At this point, as the arms fatigue, great waves of cramps sweep over the muscles, knotting them in deep, relentless, throbbing pain. With these cramps comes the inability to push himself upward. Hanging by the arms, the pectoral muscles are

[1] Will Moody, *The Life of D. L. Moody by his Son* (Murfreesboro, TN: Sword of the Lord Publishers, n.d.), 212.

paralyzed and the intercostal muscles are unable to act. Air can be drawn into the lungs, but cannot be exhaled. The victim fights to raise himself up in order to get even one short breath. Finally carbon dioxide builds up in the lungs and in the blood stream and the cramps partially subside. Spasmodically, he is able to push himself upward to exhale and bring in the life-giving oxygen. It was undoubtedly during these periods that Jesus uttered the seven short sentences recorded.

The common method of ending a crucifixion was by crurifracture, the breaking of the bones of the legs. This prevented the victim from pushing himself upward; thus the tension could not be relieved from the muscles of the chest and rapid suffocation occurred. This was unnecessary for Christ, who died after six hours of crucifixion.

Apparently to make doubly sure of death, the legionnaire drove his lance through the fifth interspace between the ribs, upward through the pericardium and into the heart. There was an escape of water fluid from the sac surrounding the heart, giving postmortem evidence that our Lord died not the usual crucifixion death by suffocation, but of heart failure (a broken heart) due to shock and constriction of the heart by fluid in the pericardium.[1]

Date: _____   _____   _____
Place: _____   _____   _____
Occasion: _____   _____   _____

He Knows How It Feels

After a diving accident left Joni Eareckson Tada a quadriplegic, she became acquainted with Christ, but only gradually realized the full significance of the cross. One night in desperate depression, she begged a friend to give her some pills so she could die. When her friend refused, she thought, *I can't even die on my own!* Rage, bitterness, and emotional pain shook her spirit.

Joni's best friend, Cindy, came to visit and sat at the bedside struggling to some way be of encouragement. Suddenly she blurted out, "Joni, Jesus knows how you feel. You're not the only one who's been paralyzed. He was paralyzed too."

Joni glared at her. "Cindy, what are you talking about?"

"It's true. It's true, Joni. Remember, He was nailed to the cross. His back was raw from beatings like your back sometimes gets raw. Oh, He must have longed to move. To change His position, to redistribute His weight somehow, but He couldn't move. Joni, He knows how you feel."

Joni had never thought of it like that before. She later said, "God became incredibly close to me. I have seen what a difference the love shown me by friends and family had made. I began to realize that God also loved me."[2]

---

[1] Dr. C. Truman Davis, "A Physician Testifies About the Crucifixion," in *The Review of the News*, April 14, 1976.
[2] David A. Seamands, *Healing for Damaged Emotions* (Wheaton, IL: Victor Books, 1986), pp. 44–45, and adapted originally from Phillip Yancy's book, *Where is God When It Hurts?*

Date: _____ _____ _____
Place: _____ _____ _____
Occasion: _____ _____ _____

Paying the Price

In his book *More Than a Carpenter,* Josh McDowell uses a simple illustration to show what God was doing for us at the cross of Christ. He wrote: An incident that took place several years ago in California illuminates what Jesus did on the cross. . . . A young woman was picked up for speeding. She was ticketed and taken before the judge. The judge read off the citation and said, "Guilty or not guilty?" The woman replied, "Guilty." The judge brought down the gavel and fined her $100 or ten days. Then an amazing thing took place. The judge stood up, took off his robe, walked down around in front, took out his billfold, and paid the fine.

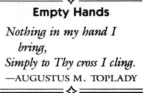

Empty Hands

Nothing in my hand I bring,
Simply to Thy cross I cling.
—AUGUSTUS M. TOPLADY

What's the explanation of this? The judge was her father. He loved his daughter, yet he was a just judge. His daughter had broken the law, and he couldn't just say to her, "Because I love you so much, I forgive you. You may leave." If he had done that, he wouldn't have been a righteous judge. . . . But he loved his daughter so much he was willing to take off his judicial robe and come down in front and represent her as her father and pay the fine.[1]

Date: _____ _____ _____
Place: _____ _____ _____
Occasion: _____ _____ _____

A Deeper Magic

In C. S. Lewis' book *The Lion, The Witch, and the Wardrobe,* Edmund had been enslaved by the White Witch. He had been foolish and rebellious and evil and traitorous. And he had fallen under her power.

When the Great Lion, Aslan, came to rescue him, the wicked witch reminded him of the Deep Magic that was written on the Table of Stone—that every traitor belongs to her and she has a right to the blood of every sinner.

But, to the amazement of all, after Aslan spoke to her privately she let the boy go. Later that night, Aslan surrendered himself into the witches' camp. They took him, shaved off his magnificent mane, ridiculed him, beat him, spat on him, and tied him to the Table of Stone. The witch whetted her knife, drew near him, and plunged it into the lion's heart, killing him.

In the distance, Aslan's dear friends, Lucy and Susan, cried and cried, and the next morning, they arrived sadly to recover his body. But they found the Stone Table broken, and the body of Aslan was nowhere to be seen. Suddenly they turned around

---

[1]Josh McDowell, *More Than a Carpenter* (Wheaton: Tyndale House Publishers, 1977), 114–115.

and found him larger than they had ever seen him, shaking his magnificent mane, fully and physically alive.

They hugged and kissed him, weeping for joy, then asked him, "But Aslan, what does it mean?"

This was Aslan's reply: "It means that though the witch knew the Deep Magic, there is a magic deeper still which she did not know. Her knowledge goes back only to the dawn of Time. But if she could have looked a little further back, into the stillness and darkness before Time dawned, she would have read there a different incantation. She would have known that when a willing victim who had committed no treachery was killed in a traitor's stead, the Table would crack and Death itself would start working backwards."

Date: _____ _____ _____

Place: _____ _____ _____

Occasion: _____ _____ _____

The Red Cross

Sir Arthur Conan Doyle, creator of Sherlock Holmes, wrote a book on the history of the Great Boer War in which he tells of a small detachment of British troops who, overwhelmed by enemy forces, fell back under heavy fire. Their wounded lay in a perilous position, facing certain death. One of them, a corporal in the Ceylon Mounted Infantry, later told that they all realized they had to come immediately under the protection of a Red Cross flag if they wanted to survive. All they had was a piece of white cloth, but no red paint. So they used the blood from their own wounds to make a large cross on that white cloth. The attackers respected that grim flag as it was held aloft, and the British wounded were brought to safety.

Date: _____ _____ _____

Place: _____ _____ _____

Occasion: _____ _____ _____

The Twisted Cross

In 1834, a German poet named Heinrich Heine made an astonishing prediction. He said that Germany was in an angry mood, and that only the cross of Christ was holding back the lust for war.

Heine had little understanding of the cross, and viewed it not theologically but superstitiously, calling it a talisman, an object with magical powers. He said, "That talisman is brittle, and the day will come when it will pitifully break. The old stone gods will rise from the long-forgotten ruin and rub the dust of a thousand years from their eyes, and Thor, leaping to life with his giant hammer, will crush the Gothic cathedrals."

Years later, a boy named Guido von List stood in St. Stefan's Cathedral in Vienna and vowed as an adult to build a temple to the ancient German gods. He chose a broken cross—a swastika—for his occult religion. He founded a secret blood society which substituted the swastika for the Cross in rituals involving sexual perversion and the practice of medieval magic.

In his early days in Vienna, Hitler knew and admired List, and when Hitler's Nazis were organized, they chose the broken cross as their symbol, and the German people found themselves standing between the two crosses with a choice to make.[1]

D

Date: _____   _____   _____
Place: _____   _____   _____
Occasion: _____   _____   _____

The Choice Behind *The Sound of Music*

Rosemaria Von Trapp, one of the famous "Sound of Music" children, has this to say about her famous parents, Baron Georg and Maria Von Trapp, who fled Nazi-occupied Austria instead of cooperating with the Nazis:

Only yesterday I talked to high school students—sophomores—who were doing research papers on the Holocaust of Hitler in Germany. They wanted me to talk about the Nazis. I told them that Hitler gave us a symbol of a cross with hooks on it. But our Christian faith gives us a symbol of a cross that brings freedom and resurrection. The world, you know, offers us a glossy cross with hooks in it. My father and mother had to make a choice. They chose the cross of Christ.[2]

Date: _____   _____   _____
Place: _____   _____   _____
Occasion: _____   _____   _____

Daily Devotions

Someone Once Said . . .

- *Maintain at all costs a daily time of Scripture reading and prayer. As I look back, I see that the most formative influence in my life and thought has been my daily contact with Scripture over sixty years.*—Frank Gaebelein, Christian educator, when asked what counsel he wished to pass on to the next generation of Christians
- *I have only missed my morning watch once or twice this term. . . . I can easily believe that it is next in importance to accepting Christ. For I know that when I don't wait upon God in prayer and Bible study, things go wrong.*—Bill Borden of Yale University
- *I must secure more time for private devotions. I have been living far too public for me. The shortening of private devotions starves the soul.*—William Wilberforce
- *When I miss a day of practice, I can always tell it. If I miss two days, the critics will pick it up. If I miss three days, the audience will notice it.*—Ignace Jan Paderewski, Polish pianist

---

[1] Adapted from chapter 3 of *Hitler's Cross* by Erwin W. Lutzer (Chicago: Moody Press, 1995).
[2] Author's interview with Maria Von Trapp, September, 1994.

```
Date:        _____    _____    _____
Place:       _____    _____    _____
Occasion:  _____    _____    _____
```

Morning Devotions

- *Wind up thy heart towards heaven in the beginning of the day, and it will go the better all the day after. He that loseth his heart in the morning in the world, will hardly find it again all the day. O! Christians, let God have your morning meditations.*—Thomas Watson[1]
- *The first hour of the morning is the rudder of the day.*—Henry Ward Beecher
- *If I have had any success in life, I attribute it to the habit of giving the first two hours of each day to Bible study and prayer.*—Lord Earl Cairns, Lord Chancellor of England[2]
- *The impressions of the morning are the deepest. Beginning the day with the Word of God, we begin on a high level. We begin with strength for the day's work, and power against the day's temptations.*—Wilber Smith[3]
- *Make it the first daily business to understand some part of [the Bible] clearly, and then the rest of the day to obey it.*—John Ruskin, to the students at Oxford University[4]
- *I ought to pray before seeing anyone. Often when I sleep long, or meet with others early, it is eleven or twelve o'clock before I begin secret prayer. This is a wretched system. It is unscriptural. Christ arose before day and went into a solitary place.*—Robert Murray McCheyne
- *The men who have done the most for God in this world have been early on their knees. He who fritters away the early morning, its opportunity and freshness, in other pursuits than seeking God will make poor headway.*—E. M. Bounds[5]
- *If God is not first in our thoughts and efforts in the morning, he will be in the last place the remainder of the day.*—E. M. Bounds[6]

```
Date:        _____    _____    _____
Place:       _____    _____    _____
Occasion:  _____    _____    _____
```

"In the Morning" by Ralph Cushman

I met God in the morning,
When my day was at its best
And His presence came like sunrise
Like a glory in my breast.

---

[1] Thomas Watson, *Gleanings From Thomas Watson* (Morgan, PA: Soli Deo Gloria Publications, 1995), 107.
[2] R. A. Torrey, *How To Succeed in the Christian Life* (Chicago: Moody Press, 1979), 50.
[3] Wilber M. Smith, *Profitable Bible Study* (Grand Rapids: Baker Book House, 1963), 59.
[4] Smith, *Profitable Bible Study,* 59.
[5] E. M. Bounds, *Preacher and Prayer* (Chicago: The Christian Witness Co., 1907), 55.
[6] Bounds, *Preacher and Prayer,* 55

All day long the Presence lingered,
All day long he stayed with me.
And we sailed in perfect calmness
O'er a very troubled sea.

Other ships were blown and battered
Other ships were sore distressed.
But the winds that seemed to drive them
Brought to us a peace and rest.

Then I thought of other mornings,
With a keen remorse of mind,
When I, too, had loosed the moorings
With the Presence left behind.

So I think I know the secret
Learned from many a troubled way.
You must seek God in the morning
If you want Him through the day.

Date: _____ _____ _____
Place: _____ _____ _____
Occasion: _____ _____ _____

Mueller's Secret

In his classic biography, *George Mueller of Bristol*, A. T. Pierson writes:

A "chance remark"—there is no chance in a believer's life!—made by the brother at whose house he was abiding at Plymouth, much impressed him. Referring to the sacrifices in Leviticus, he said that, as the refuse of the animals was never offered upon the altar, but only the best parts and the fat, so the choicest of our time and strength, the best parts of our day, should be especially given to the Lord in worship and communion. George Muller meditated much on this, and determined, even at the risk of damage to bodily heath, that he would no longer spend his best hours in bed. Henceforth he allowed himself but seven hours' sleep and gave up his after-dinner rest. This resumption of early rising secured long seasons of uninterrupted interviews with God, in prayer and meditation on the Scriptures, before breakfast and the various inevitable interruptions that followed. He found himself not worse but better, physically, and became convinced that to have lain longer in bed as before would have kept his nerves weak and, as to spiritual life, such new vitality and vigour accrued from thus waiting upon God while others slept, that it continued to be the habit of his afterlife.[1]

Date: _____ _____ _____
Place: _____ _____ _____
Occasion: _____ _____ _____

---

[1] Arthur T. Pierson, *George Mueller of Bristol* (Old Tappan, NJ: Fleming H. Revell Co., 1971), 163.

The Hollow Tree

In an old biography, *Yates the Missionary,* a pioneer Southern Baptist missionary to China tells how, as a student in a crowded dormitory, he found a way of having his daily devotions in peace:

As Mr. Fleming had three other boarders, who occupied the same large room with me, I found it necessary to resort to the woods again for an altar of prayer, without which I could not feel that my communion with God was satisfactory. And as the undergrowth about the academy was very sparse, I had some difficulty in finding a suitable place.

Finally I found in the midst of a majestic forest an immense hollow oak tree standing in a ravine. I cleaned out the hollow and made a plank floor to protect me from the dampness, for it was big enough for me to turn around in. Thither I went every morning just before daylight. This hollow tree, in the ravine and before daylight, was darker than Egypt. But I was afraid of neither snakes nor devils, for I knew that the Lord was with me there.

Date: _____ _____ _____

Place: _____ _____ _____

Occasion: _____ _____ _____

Remembering His Father

Missionary David Howard once described his father like this:

His thumbs were plugged in his ears, so he couldn't hear me tiptoe toward him. He was on his knees in his study, his back to the door. I peaked over his shoulder at the prayer list spread on the chair before him. My mother's name topped the list, followed by the names of his six children, then other people and projects he prayed for daily.

◆

Our Daily Bread

Maintain at all costs a daily time of Scripture reading and prayer.

—FRANK GAEBELEIN

◆

The light of dawn barely streaked the eastern sky. As a small boy, I sometimes enjoyed slipping downstairs before the bustle of the day began, but I never arrived there before my father.

A highly disciplined man, he believed the secret of a holy life lay in beginning each day alone with the Lord and His Word, and the secret of rising early was to get to bed at a reasonable hour. Before retiring he would spread out his Bible, Daily Light, notebook, carefully sharpened pencil, prayer list, and hymnal on his desk. In the kitchen he would set out the coffee pot and a cup. He resolved to lose no time in the quiet hours when he would meet with his Father.

For years this pattern remained unaltered, but it never became a meaningless routine. Convinced of its necessity and committed to holiness, my father eagerly looked forward to this early-morning rendezvous with God.[1]

Date: _____ _____ _____

Place: _____ _____ _____

Occasion: _____ _____ _____

---

[1] David M. Howard, "Profiles in Holiness: Phillip E. Howard," *Moody Magazine,* January 1985, 24.

Catching Up

An exploring party, with the help of national guides, was forcing its way at fast pace through the jungles. Still far from the day's agreed-upon destination, the national guides sat down.

"Are they sick?" the national leader was asked.

"No."

"Are they tired?"

"No."

"Then why are they stopping?"

The leader explained that they had a good reason. They had traveled so far and fast, that it was time for them to stop "until their souls catch up with their bodies."[1]

> **Devotional Hunger**
>
> *The shortening of private devotions starves the soul.*
>
> —WILLIAM WILBERFORCE

D

Date:			
Place:			
Occasion:			

Carey's Garden

In her biography of William Carey, *Young Man in a Hurry,* Lois Clinton tells of how the great missionary sustained his resilient spirit during the days of his greatest responsibilities and pressures:

He was still a gardener at heart. He found God especially near among the flowers and shrubs of a garden. In the walled garden of the mission house at Serampore, he built an arbour which he called his "bower." There at sunrise, before tea, and at the time of full moon when there was least danger from snakes, he meditated and prayed, and the Book which he ceaselessly translated for others was his own source of strength and refreshment.[2]

Date:			
Place:			
Occasion:			

How Do You Find the Time?

In a *Moody Magazine* article, Gigi Graham Tchividjian said that while small snatches of spiritual refreshment do not replace the need for careful, in-depth Bible study, they can be a lifesaver for busy moms. As a busy mother of seven small children, Gigi found herself unable to take an hour or a half-hour a day for sustained devotions, so she took stock of her own mother's example.

My mother had five children and often didn't have time for long devotions. But I remember her Bible always open in a convenient place—the kitchen counter, her bedside table, beside the sofa, or even on the ironing board. In this way, she could quickly glean a promise or memorize a verse as she continued her work

---

[1] Leslie B. Flynn, *Come Alive With Illustrations* (Grand Rapids: Baker Book House, 1987), 193–194.
[2] Lois Clinton, *Young Man in a Hurry* (Fort Washington, PA: Christian Literature Crusade, 1961), 55–56.

Following her example, I often pray for each child as I iron a dress or fold a shirt. I find myself thanking the Lord for their healthy bodies as I bathe them at night. I praise the Lord for their beds and hot running water as I change their sheets and scrub the tub.

I find I can worship Him as I sweep the terrace or trim the hedge or dust the living room. I can meditate as I take a walk or rake the leaves. . . .

These brief snatches of spiritual refreshment have often served as my spiritual lifeline. On days when my nerves are stretched to the limit and I feel myself drowning in confusion, slipping off for five minutes with the Lord buoys me like a life preserver.[1]

Date: _____ _____ _____

Place: _____ _____ _____

Occasion: _____ _____ _____

Commuting with Christ

In an article in *Discipleship Journal,* G. Ron Darbee tells how he turned his daily commute to work into an opportunity to meet with the Lord.

- He devotes Monday's drive time to prayer and praise, verbally praying and singing to the Lord. This helps him get a good start on the week.
- Tuesday's commute is devoted to a "Bible study on wheels." He listens to the Bible being read on cassette, or occasionally to the tape of a favorite Bible teacher.
- As he drives back and forth to work on Wednesday, Ron "makes a joyful noise," singing familiar hymns and praise songs or occasionally listening to taped Christian music.
- Thursday is devoted to Scripture memory. He keeps a memory verse on an index card clipped to his visor.
- Friday's drive time is devoted to contemplation. Ron praises God for the week behind, and he reflects on what took place. What went well? What requires more attention? He quietly prays, and seeks to hear anything the Lord is whispering to his spirit.[2]

Date: _____ _____ _____

Place: _____ _____ _____

Occasion: _____ _____ _____

——————————— Death ———————————

Someone Once Said . . .

- *Why do we have to die? As a kid you get nice little white shoes with white laces and a velvet suit with short pants and a nice collar and you go to college, you meet a nice girl*

[1] Gigi Graham Tchividjian, "How Do You Find the Time?," *Moody Magazine,* November 1991, 72–73.
[2] G. Ron Darbee, "Commuting With Christ," *Discipleship Journal,* Issue 79, 1994, 69–70.

and get married, work a few years and then you have to die! What is this? They never wrote that in the contract.—Mel Brooks, actor[1]

D

Appointment in Samarra

A fabled Baghdad merchant once asked his servant to run an errand. While at the marketplace, the servant rounded a corner and saw Lady Death. She terrified him so much that he returned with haste to his master.

"I am terrified," said the servant. "I want to take the fastest horse and ride toward Samarra." The master granted his request.

Later that afternoon the merchant visited the market and he, too, met Lady Death.

"Why did you startle my servant?" he asked.

Lady Death answered, "Frankly, it was I who was startled. I couldn't understand why your servant was in Baghdad, because I have an appointment with him tonight in Samarra."

The Winchester House

At the height of the Civil War, Oliver Winchester married Sarah Pardee of New Haven, Connecticut. Oliver Winchester was the man who invented the Winchester rifle, the first true repeating rifle, and it was put to great use by the Union Army during the War. Because of that, he amassed an incredible fortune, making the young couple rich beyond belief. Four years later, they gave birth to a little girl named Annie, but the baby died when about two weeks old, and Sarah was so shattered that she withdrew into herself and nearly lost her mind. Several years later, William himself developed tuberculosis and died. Sarah became heir of a vast fortune, but no amount of money would assuage her grief. She possessed no answer to the death or loneliness that overwhelmed her.

At a friend's suggestion, Sarah sought help from a spiritist. During the session, the medium said, "Your husband is here. He says there is a curse on your family which took his life and that of your child. It is a curse that has resulted from the terrible weapon created by the Winchester family. Thousands of persons have died because of it and their spirits are now seeking vengeance." Sarah was told that she, too, would soon die unless she sold out in New Haven and moved west. She would be guided by her husband who would tell her where to stop and build a house.

---

[1] John-Roger and Peter McWilliams, *Do It* (Los Angeles: Prelude Press, 1991), 65.

"You must build a home for yourself and for the spirits who have fallen from this terrible weapon. You can never stop building the house. If you continue building, you will live. Stop and you will die."

Sarah sold her home in New Haven, moved west with her boundless fortune, and finally reached a spot near San Jose where she found a seventeen-room house under construction on 162 acres of land. She purchased the house, tossed away the plans, and started building whatever she chose. For thirty-six years her workers built and rebuilt, altered and changed and constructed and demolished one section of the house after another. The sounds of hammers and saws sounded day and night. Railway cars brought in supplies, and every morning Sarah met with her foreman to sketch out new rooms. Rooms were added to rooms, wings were added to wings, levels were turned into towers and peaks. Staircases led nowhere. Doors opened to nothing. Closets opened to blank walls. Hallways doubled back upon themselves. The house became a vast, expensive maze, designed to confuse the evil spirits that tormented her.

Sarah Winchester depleted her fortune by building and rebuilding, remodeling and renovating her vast, confusing, sprawling, unplanned mansion. She believed that as long as she continued building, she would stay alive. But she didn't. On the night of September 4, 1922, after a conference session with the spirits in the séance room, Sarah went to her bedroom and died in her sleep at age eighty-three.

Breach of Contract

You go to college, you meet a nice girl and get married, work a few years and then you have to die! They never wrote that in the contract.

—MEL BROOKS

Date: _____   _____   _____
Place: _____   _____   _____
Occasion: _____   _____   _____

Helen of Troy

In his book about the world's greatest archaeological discoveries, *Doorways Through Time*, Dr. Stephen Bertman devotes a chapter to the excavations at ancient Troy. He ends his description with these words about the famous beauty of Helen of Troy.

A thousand years or more after the Trojan War, a Greek writer named Lucian wondered why so many men had given their lives in Helen's name. In a satiric dialogue, he made a dead philosopher named Menippus (who had newly arrived in Hades) ask the god Hermes for a guided tour. As Hermes pointed out the most distinguished residents of Hades, Menippus stood confused. "All I see are bones and naked skulls," he said, "and they all look alike."

"And yet," answered Hermes, "those are what all the poets admire, the things you call bones and despise."

"Perhaps," agreed Menippus, "but point Helen out to me. I can't find her myself."

"This skull," said Hermes, "is Helen."

Menippus stood there amazed. "Was this the reason," he asked, "why a thousand ships were manned by men from all over Greece, and Greek and Trojan armies died, and cities were laid waste?"

"Yes," Hermes said. "But you didn't see the woman when she was alive, or even you would have understood why 'for such a woman they suffered woe for so long.' Flowers, when they are dried out and faded, look ugly; but when they are in bloom and have color are beautiful indeed."

"Granted," said Menippus. "But didn't the Greeks know what a transient thing they were striving for, and how soon its bloom would fade?"[1]

Date: _____ _____ _____

Place: _____ _____ _____

Occasion: _____ _____ _____

Last Words

- *I am going to the great perhaps.*—Rabelais, French physician and humanist
- *Oh, God, here I go.*—Max Baer, boxer
- *I am about to—or I am going to—die. Either expression is used.*—Dominique Bouhours (1628–1702), a philosopher who worked endlessly to promote a high standard of grammar
- *Why, yes. I'd like a bulletproof vest.*—James Rogers, who was executed in 1960 in Nevada, upon being asked if he had a last request as he stood before the firing line
- *I wish the whole human race had one neck and I had my hands on it.*—Carl Panzram, who murdered twenty-three people
- *Just pull my legs straight, and place me as a dead man; it will save trouble for you shortly.*—Dr. Fidge, who had a boat converted into a coffin and stored under his bed
- *I am dying, as I have lived, beyond my means.*—Oscar Wilde
- *I've had eighteen straight whiskies. . . . I think that's the record.*—Dylan Thomas
- *It was a great game.*—Bing Crosby, who collapsed right after sinking a final putt on a golf course in Spain in 1977.
- *O my God! It is over. I have come to the end of it—the end, the end. To have only one life, and to have done with it! To have lived, and loved, and triumphed, and now to know it is over! One may defy everything else but this.*—Queen Elizabeth I[2]
- *I am as good as without hope, and without fear; a sad old man gazing into the final chasm.*—Thomas Carlyle
- *What's this?*—Leonard Bernstein, American composer who died in 1990
- *Don't turn down the light. I'm afraid to go home in the dark.*—O. Henry (William Sidney Porter), writer
- *That guy's got to stop. He'll see us.*—James Dean, just before his Porsche slammed into a car turning onto the highway
- *My God. What's happened?*—Princess Diana Spencer, in the Pont de l'Alma tunnel, as recorded in the official police files in Paris
- *That's obvious.*—John F. Kennedy, responding to the comment of Mrs. John Connally, the Texas governor's wife, who had said, "Mr. President, you can't say that Dallas doesn't love you."

---

[1] Stephen Bertman, *Doorways Through Time* (Los Angeles: Jeremy P. Tarcher, Inc., 1986), 73–74.
[2] Arthur W. Pink, *The Seven Sayings of the Savior on the Cross* (Grand Rapids: Baker Book House, 1958), 110.

Date: _____ _____ _____

Place: _____ _____ _____

Occasion: _____ _____ _____

Interesting Epitaphs

- This epitaph adorns the grave of Ellen Shannon, twenty-six, of Girard, Pennsylvania:

> *Who was fatally burned*
> *March 21, 1870*
> *by the explosion of a lamp*
> *filled with "R. E. Danforth's*
> *Non-Explosive*
> *Burning Fluid"*

- Epitaph of a dentist named John Brown:

> *Stranger! Approach this spot with gravity!*
> *John Brown is filling his last cavity.*

- These words are inscribed on the tomb of a watchmaker at St. Petrock's Church, Lyford, Devon, England:

> *Here lies in horizontal position the outside case of*
> *dear George Routleight, watchmaker,*
> *whose abilities in that line were an honour to his profession—*
> *integrity was the mainspring,*
> *and prudence the regulator of all the actions of his life.*
> *Humane, generous, and liberal, his hand never stopped*
> *until he had relieved distress.*
> *So nicely regulated were all his movements that he never went wrong,*
> *except when set agoing by people who did not know his key;*
> *even then he was easily set right again. He had the art of disposing*
> *his time so well that the hours glided away in one*
> *continued round of pleasure and delight,*
> *till an unlucky moment put a period to his existence.*
> *He departed this life November 14, 1802, aged fifty-seven.*
> *Wound up in hopes of being taken in hand by his Maker*
> *and being thoroughly cleansed, repaired,*
> *and set agoing in the world to come.*

- Inscribed on the tomb of Mel Blanc, creator of the cartoon characters Bugs Bunny and Porky Pig:

> *That's All, Folks!*

- The epitaph of Benjamin Franklin:

The Body of
B. Franklin, Printer
Like the Cover of an old Book
Its Contents torn out
And Stript of its Lettering & Gilding
Lies here. Food for Worms
For, it will as he believed
appear once more
In a new and more elegant Edition
corrected and improved
By the Author

Date: _____ _____ _____
Place: _____ _____ _____
Occasion: _____ _____ _____

The Hokey-Pokey

An undertaking firm in North Carolina was recently called on to conduct the funeral of the inventor of the Hokey-Pokey. Everything went well until they started to put the body in the coffin; then they had a serious problem. Every time they would put his right foot in, he'd put his right foot out.

Date: _____ _____ _____
Place: _____ _____ _____
Occasion: _____ _____ _____

Death for Christians

Someone Once Said . . .

- *Even in the best of health we should have death always before our eyes. We will not expect to remain on this earth forever, but will have one foot in the air, so to speak.*—Martin Luther
- *Who would fear the hissing serpent, if he knew it had no sting?*—Rev. William Secker, seventeenth-century British minister
- *We should teach our children to think no more of their bodies when dead than they do of their hair when cut off, or of their old clothes when they have done with them.*—George McDonald

Date: _____ _____ _____
Place: _____ _____ _____
Occasion: _____ _____ _____

The Hope of Dying

"Cheer up," said one man to his terribly seasick friend aboard ship, "seasickness never killed anybody."

"Don't tell me that," was the reply. "It's only the hope of dying that has kept me alive this long!"

Date: _____ _____ _____

Place: _____ _____ _____

Occasion: _____ _____ _____

Last Words of Famous Christians

- *You have been used to take notice of the sayings of dying men—this is mine: that a life spent in the service of God and communion with Him, is the most pleasant life that anyone can live in this world.*—Matthew Henry (1662–1714)
- *This night shall close the door and put my anchor within the veil, and I shall go away in a sleep by five of the clock in the morning. Glory! Oh, for a well-tuned harp! Glory! Glory dwelleth in Immanuel's land!*—Samuel Rutherford (1600–1661), who passed away just as he predicted, at 5 o'clock on the following morning, March 20, 1661
- *The waters are rising, but so am I. I am not going under, but over.*—Mrs. Catherine Booth
- *Glory!*—Billy Bray
- *This is life eternal, that they might know Thee! That is where I cast my first anchor!*—John Knox
- *Now, God be with you, my dear children. I have breakfasted with you and shall sup with my Lord Jesus Christ.*—Robert Bruce, King of Scotland (1274–1329)

Date: _____ _____ _____

Place: _____ _____ _____

Occasion: _____ _____ _____

Afraid? Of What?

The years leading up to World War II were very dangerous for missionaries to China. Political uproar, bandits, the Japanese Invasion, and the Communist Revolution caused many of them to fear for their lives.

One of the missionaries, Jack Vinson, was seized by bandits and carried off in the night. He was eventually shot and beheaded. A witness later described how earlier she had seen Vinson threatened by a bandit with a revolver who said, "I'm going to kill you! Aren't you afraid?"

"No, I am not afraid," Vinson had replied. "If you kill me, I will go right to God."

The news of Vinson's martyrdom deeply moved the Christians in China. When missionary E. H. Hamilton heard the story after emerging from another bandit-infested area, he wrote a poem that became the watchword for the missionary community during the dark days that followed. It was this poem that strengthened John and Betty Stam before their martyrdom.

> *Afraid? Of What?*
> *To feel the spirit's glad release?*
> *To pass from pain to perfect peace,*
> *The strife and strain of life to cease?*
> *Afraid—of that?*
>
> *Afraid? Of What?*
> *Afraid to see the Savior's face*
> *To hear his welcome, and to trace*
> *The glory gleam from wounds of grace?*
> *Afraid—of that?*
>
> *Afraid? Of What?*
> *A flash, a crash, a pierced heart;*
> *Darkness, light, O Heaven's art!*
> *A wound of His a counterpart?*
> *Afraid—of that?*
>
> *Afraid? Of What?*
> *To do by death what life could not—*
> *Baptized with blood a stony plot,*
> *Till souls shall blossom from the spot?*
> *Afraid—of that?*[1]

Date: _____   _____   _____
Place: _____   _____   _____
Occasion: _____   _____   _____

What Thomas Watson Thought of Death

The Puritan giant Thomas Watson made these comments about the death of Christians:

- *The world is but a great inn, where we are to stay a night or two, and be gone; what madness is it to set our heart upon our inn, as to forget our home.*[2]
- *What a wicked man fears, a godly man hopes for.*[3]
- *The apostles had three great desires, and they were all centered in Christ. One was to be found in Christ (Philippians 3:9); the other was to magnify Christ (Philippians 1:20); the third was to be with Christ (Philippians 1:23).*[4]

---

[1] Mrs. Howard Taylor, *The Triumph of John and Betty Stam* (Philadelphia: China Inland Mission, 1935), 104–105.
[2] Thomas Watson, *Gleanings From Thomas Watson* (Morgan, PA: Soli Deo Gloria Publications, 1995), 115.
[3] Watson, *Gleanings From Thomas Watson*, 116.
[4] Watson, *Gleanings From Thomas Watson*, 117.

- *Death to a child of God is like the whirlwind to the prophet Elijah; it blew off his mantle, but carried the prophet up to heaven.*[1]
- *A Christian's best things are to come.*[2]

Date: _____ _____ _____

Place: _____ _____ _____

Occasion: _____ _____ _____

No Unqualified Dying

The ninetenth-century Bible teacher A. T. Pierson had this interesting observation: "It is a remarkable fact that in the New Testament, so far as I remember, it is never once said, after Christ's resurrection, that a disciple died—that is, without some qualification.

- Stephen *fell asleep.*
- "Knowing that I must shortly *put off this my tabernacle,* as the Lord showed me," Peter says.
- Paul says, "The *time of my departure* is at hand." The figure here is taken from a vessel that, as she leaves a dock, throws the cables off the fastenings, and opens her sails to the wind to depart for the haven.
- The only time where the word "dead" is used, it is with qualification: *the dead in Christ, the dead which die in the Lord.*

"Christ abolished death," said Pierson, "and the term *death.*"[3]

Date: _____ _____ _____

Place: _____ _____ _____

Occasion: _____ _____ _____

D. L. Moody's Deathbed Scene

D. L. Moody, badly overweight, grew ill in Kansas City, canceled his engagements, and returned home to Northfield, Massachusetts. He lugged himself up to his bedroom to dress for dinner but felt so exhausted that he took to bed. He declined quickly, and it became clear he was dying of "fatty degeneration of the heart." On December 22, he suddenly opened his eyes and spoke clearly: "Earth recedes! Heaven opens before me." His son, sitting near him, suggested he was dreaming. "This is no dream, Will," Moody replied. "It is beautiful! It is like a trance! If this is death, it is sweet! God is calling me, and I must go!"

The family gathered around. "This is my triumph!" said Moody. "This is my coronation day! I have been looking forward to it for years." His face suddenly lit up. "Dwight! Irene! I see the children's faces!" (Dwight and Irene were his recently

---

[1] Watson, *Gleanings From Thomas Watson,* 118.
[2] Watson, *Gleanings From Thomas Watson,* 123.
[3] Arthur T. Pierson, *The Gospel,* vol. 3 (Grand Rapids: Baker Book House, 1978), 136.

deceased grandchildren.) Moody closed his eyes and appeared unconscious. Then he spoke again. "No pain! No valley! If this is death, it's not bad at all! It's sweet!"

A little later, he raised himself on an elbow and exclaimed, "What does all this mean? What are you all doing here?" His wife explained he had not been well. Moody fell back on the bed, and said, "This is very strange! I've been beyond the gates of death to the very portals of Heaven, and here I am back again. It is very strange."

Then he said, "I'm not at all sure but that God may perform a miracle and raise me up. I'm going to get up and sit in that chair. If God wants to heal me by a miracle, all right; if not, I can meet death in my chair as well as here." To everyone's shock, Moody rose, walked across the room, and sat in an easy chair. But he soon returned to bed exhausted, spoke tenderly to them some more, and finally slipped on to heaven. His funeral was conducted at 10 A.M. on December 26, 1899 by C. I. Scofield, and he was laid to rest atop Northfield's Mount Hermon.[1]

D

Date: _____ _____ _____

Place: _____ _____ _____

Occasion: _____ _____ _____

Frances Ridley Havergal's Deathbed Scene

Frances R. Havergal was the famous hymn-writer who penned such poems as *Another Year is Dawning, Take My Life and Let It Be,* and *Like a River Glorious.* In 1879, despite recurring bouts of illness, she toured, sang, wrote, and traveled. She visited local schools all across England, offering free Bibles to all the children who would memorize Isaiah 53. She was planning another missionary tour of Ireland, and she became very involved in the Total Abstinence campaign, encouraging people to sign pledge cards against personal use of alcohol.

As part of that campaign, Frances set a goal of personally talking to every young person in her village about the Lord and about total abstinence, and on May 21, she went to meet some boys. As heavy clouds blew in from the English Channel, the day grew cold and wet. Frances returned home chilled.

She became ill and was confined to bed, writing to a friend: *I am in bed again with another of these tryingly frequent feverish attacks, and I am writing on the back of your own letter, not having other paper within reach! The fact is, I have knocked myself up with this Temperance work, but having got the whole rising generation of the village into my Temperance regiment, except four naughty black sheep, seems to me quite worth being knocked up for!*

Her fever grew worse, and friends and family members grew alarmed. It gradually became apparent that, at age forty-two, Frances Ridley Havergal was dying. On Whit Sunday, as one of her doctors left her room, he told her, "Good-bye, I shall not see you again." She said, "Then you really think I am going?" He replied, "Yes."

"Today?"

"Probably."

"Beautiful," she said, "too good to be true."

---

[1] Robert J. Morgan, *On This Day* (Nashville: Thomas Nelson Publishers, 1997), December 26th.

Soon afterward she looked up smiling and said, "Splendid to be so near the gates of heaven!" She asked her brother to sing some hymns to her, then he said to her, "You have talked and written a great deal about the King, and you will soon see Him in his beauty."

"It's splendid!" she replied. "I thought He would have left me here a long while; but He is *so* good to take me now."

A little later she whispered, "Come, Lord Jesus, come and fetch me." Then she said to her sisters, "Do you think I shall be disappointed?" (Meaning, "Do you think I may recover?") They said, "No, dearest, we are quite sure you are going to Him now."

She continued to decline, but when someone near her bed repeated Isaiah 41:10 incorrectly, she roused enough to correct them. She dozed for a few minutes, then suddenly awakened, saying, "I am lost in amazement." She began singing faintly but clearly, a song to one of her own tunes, "Hermas"—

> *Jesus, I will trust Thee,*
> *Trust Thee with my soul:*
> *Guilty, lost, and helpless,*
> *Thou hast made me whole:*
> *There is none in heaven,*
> *Or on earth, like thee;*
> *Thou has died for sinners,*
> *Therefore, Lord for me.*

A terrible rush of convulsions seized her, and when they ceased, the nurse gently laid her back on her pillows. Frances' sister later wrote: *Then she looked up steadfastly, as if she saw the Lord. Surely nothing less heavenly could have reflected such a glorious radiance upon her face. For ten minutes we watched that almost visible meeting with her King, and her countenance was so glad, as if she were already talking to Him! Then she tried to sing, but after one sweet, high note, "HE—," her voice failed and her brother commended her soul into the Redeemer's hand.*

Date: _____ _____ _____
Place: _____ _____ _____
Occasion: _____ _____ _____

Churchill's Funeral

Winston Churchill arranged his own funeral. There were stately hymns in St. Paul's Cathedral and an impressive liturgy. When they said the benediction, he had arranged for a bugler high in the dome of St. Paul's Cathedral on one side to play "Taps," the universal signal that the day is over. But when that was finished, there was a long pause and then a bugler on the other side played "Reveille," the signal of a new day beginning. It was Churchill's way of communicating that while we say "Good night" here, it's "Good morning" up there!

Jesus Christ said, "I am the resurrection, and the life; he that believeth in me, though he were dead, yet shall he live" (John 11:25). When a man steps out of his own grave, he is anything that he says that he is and he can do anything that he says he can do![1]

Date: _____ _____ _____
Place: _____ _____ _____
Occasion: _____ _____ _____

Either Way, I Win

When Rev. J. Reford Wilson, former director of Free Will Baptist Foreign Missions, entered the hospital for the last time, the doctors told him that his chances of survival were small. But, they said, surgery might help. Even so, the surgery itself contained risk and his chances were marginal. With the steady eye-to-eye contact and disarming, twinkling smile so familiar to his friends, Reford said, "Either way, Doc, I win."

Date: _____ _____ _____
Place: _____ _____ _____
Occasion: _____ _____ _____

John Todd's Letter

Todd was born in Rutland, Vermont in October of 1800, and shortly afterward his family moved to Connecticut. When John was six years old, both parents died, and a kindly aunt agreed to give John a home. There he lived until he left to study for the ministry. By and by his aunt became seriously ill and feared she would die. In her alarm, she wrote her nephew with questions about death. Here is a portion of John Todd's reply:

Death in the Forefront

Even in the best of health we should have death always before our eyes.

—MARTIN LUTHER

It is now thirty-five years since I, as a little boy of six, was left quite alone in the world. You sent me word that you would give me a home and be a kind mother to me. I will never forget the day when I made the long journey of ten miles to your house in North Killingworth. I can still remember my disappointment when instead of coming for me yourself, you sent Caesar to fetch me.

I well remember my tears and anxiety as, perched high on your horse and clinging tight to Caesar, I rode off to my new home. Night fell before we finished the journey, and, as it grew dark, I became lonely and afraid. "Do you think she'll go to bed before we get there?" I asked Caesar anxiously. "Oh, no," he said reassuringly. "She'll stay up for you. When we get out of this here woods, you'll see her candle shinin' in the window."

Presently we did ride out into the clearing, and there, sure enough, was your candle. I remember you were waiting at the door, that you put your arms close about me and that you lifted me—a tired and bewildered little boy—down from the horse. You had a fire burning on

---

[1] Robert Russell, "If A Man Dies, Will He Live Again?" *Proclaim!*, Spring 1999, 9.

the hearth, a hot supper waiting on the stove. After supper you took me to my room, heard me say my prayers and then sat beside me till I fell asleep.

You probably realize why I am recalling all of this to your memory. Someday soon God will send for you to take you to a new home. Don't fear the summons, the strange journey or the dark messenger of death. God can be trusted to do as much for you as you were kind enough to do for me so many years ago. At the end of the road you will find love and a welcome awaiting, and you will be safe in God's care. I shall watch you and pray for you till you are out of sight and then wait for the day when I shall make the journey myself and find my Savior and you waiting at the end of the road to greet me.

Date: _____ _____ _____
Place: _____ _____ _____
Occasion: _____ _____ _____

Death of Children

Someone Once Said . . .

- *I shall go to him, but he shall not return to me.*—2 Samuel 12:23
- *Even so it is not the will of your Father who is in heaven that one of these little ones should perish.*—Matthew 18:14
- *If any righteous person of their number passes away from the world, they rejoice and thank God, and escort his body as if he were setting out from one place to another nearby. When a child is born to one of them, they praise God. If it dies in infancy, they thank God the more, as for one who has passed through the world without sins.*—Marcianus Aristides, to the Roman Emperor Hadrian, from an A.D. 125 document describing Christians

Date: _____ _____ _____
Place: _____ _____ _____
Occasion: _____ _____ _____

D. L. Moody and His Grandchildren

[A] Little Dwight

While D. L. Moody was ministering in Colorado, his only grandson and namesake, Dwight, died when only one year old. From Colorado Springs, the great evangelist wrote this letter:

I know Dwight is having a good time, and we should rejoice with him. What would the mansions be without children? And he has gone to help get things ready for his parents. You know the Master said: "The last shall be first." He was the last to come into our circle, and he is the first to go up there! So safe, so free from all the sorrow that we are passing through! I do thank God for such a life. It was nearly all smiles and sunshine. What a glorified body he will have, and with what joy he will await your coming! God does not give us such strong love for each other for a few days or years, but it is going to last forever, and you will have the dear little man with you for ages and ages, and love will keep increasing. The master had need of him, or He would never have called him, and you should feel highly honored that you had anything in your home that He wanted.

I could not wish him back, if he could have all earth could give him. And then the thought that the Savior will take such good care of him! No going astray; no sickness; no death. Dear, dear little fellow. . . .

I believe the only thing he took away from earth was that sweet smile, and I have no doubt that when he saw the Savior he smiled as he did when he saw you. My heart goes up to God often for you, and the word that keeps coming to my mind is this: "It is well with the child."[1]

[B] Irene

Not long after the death of little Dwight, another grandchild died. Irene followed her baby brother to the grave, dying of pneumonia two days past her fourth birthday. At the funeral, her grandfather rose and spoke these words:

Is It Well?

"Is it well with the child?"
And she answered,
"It is well."

—2 KINGS 4:26

I would like to say a few words, if I can trust myself. I have been thinking this morning about the aged prophet waiting in the valley of the Jordan, so many years ago, for the chariot of God to take him home. The chariot of God came down to the Connecticut valley yesterday morning about half-past six, and took our little Irene home . . .

Irene has finished her course. Her work was well wrought on earth. She has accomplished more than many in their threescore years and ten. We would not have her back, although her voice was the sweetest voice I ever heard on earth. She never met me once since she was three months old, until the last few days of pain, without a smile. But Christ had some service for her above. My life has been made much better by her ministry here on earth. She has made us all better. . . . She was too fair for this earth.

I thank God this morning for the hope of immortality. I know I shall see her in the morning, more beautiful in her resurrection glory than she was here.[2]

Date:	_____	_____	_____
Place:	_____	_____	_____
Occasion:	_____	_____	_____

The Lamb

One of the oldest sermon illustrations regarding the death of children involves a couple who were so distraught over the death of a little girl they took a period abroad in order to process their grief. One day, walking through the fields, the two noticed a shepherd leading his flock. There was a brook there, but the sheep seemed too frightened to hop across it. Taking a lamb in his arms, the shepherd jumped over the stream and placed it about fifty yards on the other side.

Presently it began bleating for its mother. The mother, hearing the call, raised her head and bolted toward the brook, leaping over it with no problem. The other sheep followed, and soon the entire flock was on the other side.

---

[1] A. P. Fitt, *The Life of D. L. Moody* (Chicago: Moody Press, n.d.), 139–140.
[2] Fitt, *The Life of D. L. Moody*, 141–142.

"Now, I understand," said the wife, watching from a distance. "The Lord has taken my lamb that I myself may meet her on the other side."

Date:	_____	_____	_____
Place:	_____	_____	_____
Occasion:	_____	_____	_____

Tears in Eyes, Joy in Heart

During their years as medical missionaries to China, Dr. and Mrs. L. Nelson Bell faced many challenges, including civil war, bandits, and Japanese occupations. But none was so difficult as the death of their infant son, little Nelson Bell, Jr. In a letter dated 1925, Dr. Bell wrote:

Virginia and I realized that he was going and we were with him alone when the end came. It was so sweet and so peaceful, no struggle and no evidence of pain, just quietly leaving us and going back to Him.

His going has left an ache in our hearts and our arms feel very empty, but oh the joy of knowing he is safe. It has but drawn us closer to Him and given us a new tie and joy to look forward to in Heaven. We would not have him back for we know it was His will that he should go. There is no repining, wishing we had used other medicines, etc. We feel that everything that could have possibly been done was done. We had the joy of caring for him ourselves while he was sick, and the memory is very sweet. He had been such a perfectly healthy baby, in some ways one of the best developed children I have ever seen and so full of life that he was a favorite with the foreigners and Chinese alike.

Virginia and I had the privilege of fixing him ourselves when he died, and then Virginia immediately went to the Talbots where Rosa and Ruth were at school. She wanted to tell them herself, rather than have them hear the news through the Chinese. They were nearly heartbroken, but it was a wonderful opportunity to bring the great hope that is ours very close and plain to them.

We laid him to rest just at sunset, and the service was such a sweet one, and we pray was a blessing to the large number of Chinese friends who came. Virginia expressed my feelings exactly as we were leaving the little cemetery (owned by the hospital) when she said, "I have a song in my heart, but it is hard to keep the tears from my eyes." At the grave we sang "Praise God from Whom All Blessings Flow" for this had made the wonderful hope of eternity doubly precious to us. Were it not for that hope we would not be here in China.[1]

Date:	_____	_____	_____
Place:	_____	_____	_____
Occasion:	_____	_____	_____

More Love to Thee

All her life, Elizabeth Payson was frail and sickly, but her spirit was strong, and her ability to compose inspirational poems was striking. Her father had been one

---

[1] Clipping in my file. The original letter by Dr. Bell belongs to his daughter, Ruth Bell Graham.

of New England's best-loved preachers, and from him she inherited empathy and eloquence.

In 1845, at age twenty-seven, she married the pastor of Mercer Street Presbyterian Church in New York City, Dr. George L. Prentiss. She was loved by both the congregation at Mercer Street Church and the wider population in New York City. Despite physical infirmities, she cheerfully fulfilled her role as pastor's wife and mother to the couple's three beloved children.

But disaster struck in 1856 during an epidemic. Two of the couple's children died within a few weeks of the other, and for months Elizabeth was inconsolable. The members of the church did all they could, comforting the couple, bringing by food, and helping with the running of the household. But Elizabeth was devastated.

In her diary, she wrote, "Empty hands, a worn-out, exhausted body, and unutterable longings to flee from a world that has so many sharp experiences." During this time, she wrote a simple poem:

> *I thought that prattling boys and girls*
> *Would fill this empty room;*
> *That my rich heart would gather flowers*
> *From childhood's opening bloom:*
> *One child and two green graves are mine,*
> *This is God's gift to me;*
> *A bleeding, fainting, broken heart,*
> *This is my gift to Thee.*

But the Lord directed Elizabeth's heart to the Old Testament story of Jacob, the man who had so many sorrows related to his children, yet God had met him in his distress and in the end it all worked for good. She prayed earnestly for a similar experience. The old hymn "Nearer, My God, to Thee," occupied her thoughts, and she made it the prayer of her heart.

One night, pondering these things, she composed her own poem, writing all four stanzas in one evening. Though it gave her great comfort, she didn't think her poem worthy of publication and didn't show it to anyone for thirteen years. It has since become a classic:

> *More love to Thee, O Christ, More love to Thee!*
> *Hear Thou the prayer I make On bended knee;*
> *This is my earnest plea: More love, O Christ, to Thee,*
> *More love to Thee, More love to Thee.*
>
> *Once earthly joy I craved, sought peace and rest;*
> *Now Thee alone I seek—Give what is best;*
> *This all my prayer shall be: More love, O Christ, to Thee,*
> *More love to Thee, More love to Thee.*

Date: _____ _____ _____

Place: _____ _____ _____

Occasion: _____ _____ _____

Demons

Someone Once Said . . .

- *Millions of unseen creatures walk the earth unseen both when we wake and when we sleep.*—John Milton, in *Paradise Lost*
- *And though this world with devils filled should threaten to undo us, / We will not fear for God has willed his truth to triumph through us.*—Martin Luther
- *There are two equal and opposite errors into which our race can fall about the devils. One is to disbelieve in their existence, the other is to believe and to feel an unhealthy interest in them.*—C. S. Lewis

Date: _____ _____ _____
Place: _____ _____ _____
Occasion: _____ _____ _____

From Martin Luther's *Table Talk*

A woman at Eisenach lay very sick, having endured horrible paroxysms, which no physician was able to cure, for it was directly a work of the devil. She had had swoonings and four paroxysms, each lasting three or four hours. Her hands and feet bent in the form of a horn; she was chill and cold; her tongue was rough and dry; her body was much swollen. She, seeing Luther, who came to visit her, was much rejoiced thereat, raised herself up, and said: "Ah! My loving father in Christ, I have a heavy burden upon me, pray to God for me," and so fell down in her bed again. Whereupon Luther sighed and said: "God rebuke thee, Satan, and command thee that thou suffer this, his divine creature, to be at peace." Then turning himself towards the standers-by, he said: "She is plagued of the devil in the body, but the soul is safe, and shall be preserved; therefore let us give thanks to God, and pray for her"; and so they all prayed aloud the Lord's Prayer. After which, Luther concluded with these words: "Lord God, heavenly Father! Who hast commanded us to pray for the sick, we beseech thee, through Jesus Christ, thy only Son, that thou wouldst deliver this thy servant from her sickness, and from the hands of the devil. Spare, O Lord, her soul, which, together with her body, thou hast purchased and redeemed from the power of sin, of death, and of the devil." Whereupon the sick woman said, "Amen." The night following she took rest, and the next day was graciously delivered from her disease and sickness.[1]

Date: _____ _____ _____
Place: _____ _____ _____
Occasion: _____ _____ _____

---

[1] Martin Luther, *The Table Talk of Martin Luther,* Ed. Thomas S. Kepler (Grand Rapids: Baker Book House, 1952), 292–293.

From Nineteenth-Century China

Rev. John L. Nevius, nineteenth-century missionary to China, encountered so many cases of demon possession during his forty years there that he recorded his experiences in a book entitled *Demon Possession and Allied Themes,* published by Fleming H. Revell in 1894. Here is one example, which he records in the second chapter.

One day Nevius received a letter telling him of a man in the village of Hingkia who was suffering from an evil spirit. "It is true and most humiliating," said the man, Mr. Kwo, "that I, a man in the full vigor of health, should be a slave to this demon, is the trial of my life; but there is no help for it." And yet, being told of Christ, Mr. Kwo agreed to tear down the demon shrine in his house and seek more information about the Lord Jesus.

In March of 1879, while traveling through the area, John Nevius paid a visit to Mr. Kwo. He discovered the thirty-eight-year-old man to be illiterate, but bright and entertaining. With the help of his wife and a Christian from the next village, Mr. Kwo had been studying a copy of the Scriptures and a Chinese catechism they had received. Nevius determined that the little family was sincerely trusting Christ as Savior and Lord, and, upon their request, he baptized them.

> **Victory!**
>
> *Jesus is Victor.*
>
> —CORRIE TEN BOOM

Later he asked Mr. Kwo more about this prior demon possession. The Chinese gentleman explained that, in 1877, he had purchased some pictures of Chinese gods, and while displaying them in the house, he had had a vivid dream. In his dream, a demon told him, "I have taken up abode in your house." Afterward, disturbing things happened. Seized by an impulse, Kwo had suddenly risen one night from bed and gone to a gambler's den where he had lost a large sum of money.

Soon he was losing more money, large sums for the small family, to gambling. Sometimes, after a night of gaming, he would come home, frothing at the mouth, staggering around nearly unconscious. He grew violent, attacking all who ventured near him. His father, hearing these alarming reports, came to visit, but Mr. Kwo took a gun from under his bed and fired it at him, missing.

He was bound in chains and taken to a doctor who gave him large doses of medicine without effect. For several days, Mr. Kwo raved wildly as the evil spirit spoke through Mr. Kwo's mouth, commanding the family to burn incense and to submit to the demon world. A shrine was built in the house, and there the family, in great fear, worshipped Satan. The evil spirit told the family how to perform miracles of healing on others, and soon people from neighboring villages were flocking to the Kwo house.

"The demon said he had many inferior spirits subject to him," Kwo told John Nevius. "He also frequently indicated his plan for my future life and employment. It was through his assistance that I should become more and more skilled in healing diseases."

It was at this point, when Mr. Kwo was miserable and desperate, that he heard of Jesus Christ and tore down his demon shrine. Soon afterward, his little girl died. Mrs. Kwo was much distressed, believing it was in consequence of having offended the demon. But Mr. Kwo replied that no matter what might happen, he was going to follow Christ.

A few days later the demon returned for what proved to be the last time. "I have returned but for one visit," came the voice through Mr. Kwo's throat, speaking to the wife. "If your husband is determined to be a Christian, this is no place for me. But I wish to tell you I had nothing to do with the death of your child."

"What do you know of Jesus Christ?" she asked.

"Jesus Christ is the great Lord over all, and now I am going away and you will not see me again."

That was the last visit. The Kwo family was never plagued by evil spirits again. He became a most effective evangelist in his area, and his home became a center for Bible teaching and fellowship.[1]

Date:	_____	_____	_____
Place:	_____	_____	_____
Occasion:	_____	_____	_____

From Twentieth-Century China

One day as missionary Dick Hillis preached in a Chinese village, his sermon was suddenly interrupted by a piercing cry. Everyone rushed toward the scream, and Dick's coworker, Mr. Kong, whispered that an evil spirit had seized a man. "That is heathen superstition," said Dick, who had not previously encountered demon possession.

A woman pushed through the crowd toward them. "I beg you help me!" she cried. "An evil spirit has again possessed the father of my children and is trying to kill him."

Kong stepped over a filthy old dog lying in the doorway and faced the madman. The room was charged with a sense of evil. "An evil spirit has possessed Farmer Ho," Kong told the onlookers. "Our God, the 'Nothing-He-Cannot-Do One' is more powerful than any spirit, and He can deliver this man. First, you must promise you will burn your idols and trust in Jesus, son of the Supreme Emperor."

The people nodded. Kong asked Dick to begin singing the hymn "There is Power in the Blood." With great hesitation, Dick began to sing, "Would you be free from your burden of sin. . . ."

"Now," continued Kong, "in the name of Jesus we will command the evil spirit to leave this man." Kong began praying fervently. Suddenly, the old dog in the doorway vaulted into the air, screeching, yelping, whirling in circles snapping wildly at his tail. Kong continued praying, and the dog abruptly dropped over dead.

Instantly Dick remembered Luke 8, the demons of the Gadarenes who invisibly flew into the herd of swine. As Kong finished praying, Farmer Ho seemed quiet and relaxed, and soon he was strong enough to burn his idols. At his baptism shortly afterward, he testified, "I was possessed by an evil spirit who boasted he had already killed five people and was going to kill me. But God sent Mr. Kong at just the right moment, and in Jesus I am free."[2]

---

[1] John L. Nevius, *Demon Possession and Allied Themes* (Chicago: Fleming H. Revell, 1894).

[2] Robert J. Morgan, *From This Verse* (Nashville: Thomas Nelson Publishers, 1998). August 7th. Originally: Jan Winebrenner, *Steel in His Soul, The Dick Hillis Story* (Chicago: Moody Press, 1985), Chapter 6.

From Indonesia

Roy Rosedale has served with Campus Crusade for Christ both here and abroad for twenty-nine years and currently teaches at the International School of Theology. Once while he and his wife Eleanor were serving in Indonesia, they faced a strange and dangerous situation. He writes:

I was away on a ministry trip when this occurred, as such attacks usually did. Eleanor had noticed earlier in the day that a former helper walked into our yard, around the back and then out again, without speaking to anyone. We had dismissed her because Eleanor had repeatedly caught her stealing. Later the same day, at the edge of our lawn by the street, Eleanor noticed something ugly that was also part of the curse ritual, though she wasn't aware of the significance of either one at the time. But late that evening, as she stepped out into our living room she was overwhelmed by a sudden chilling awareness that she was surrounded by a circle of malevolent, invisible adversaries, focusing on her. Filled with fear, she whispered "Jesus!" Then, "In Jesus' Name get out of here, whatever you are, in Jesus' name get out!" But nothing changed. Filled with terror, she whispered, "Oh God, show me what to do." She got down on her face on the tile floor before Him, arms covering her head, and He caused her to say what no one had ever taught her to say, the thing that drove the adversary back: "The blood, Lord, the Blood . . . over me, over the children, over Roy wherever he is, this house, oh I don't know what's happening, but the blood, Lord, the blood." Whatever forces were arrayed against her began to recede until they were gone. She sat up and wept and thanked God for delivering her. We learned later, from the evidence, that the dismissed employee had bought a death curse from a black witch. It was intended to stop her heart in fear. Eleanor could understand how that could occur, particularly if the victim had to see what surrounded him—which mercifully God did not permit. Those who are not Christians have no way to dispel such forces. They literally are frightened to death. But to my knowledge, no Christians have died. Invariably they cry out for their King, and He saves them. (I heard their inability to kill Christians so frustrates Indonesian witches that some of them will no longer attempt it.) It is my belief that just as witches call on Satan and gain demonic assistance, when Christians call on Jesus, God's angels come to their aid.[1]

From Brazil

Ken Eagleton, veteran Free Will Baptist missionary in Brazil, told of several encounters he has had over the years with demon-possessed individuals. In one case,

---

[1] Roy Rosedale, "We Learned How To Overcome the Adversary in Jesus' Name." *International School of Theology.* Spring 1998, < http://www.leaderu.com/isot/docs/overadvers.html >

members of his church asked him to visit someone who was having trouble. Entering the woman's bedroom, Ken found her literally stiff as a board, lying like a piece of lumber, unable to move anything but her eyes. The room was small, but Ken squeezed into a little chair near her bed and tried to talk to her.

He learned from her family that she had recently visited a famous witch in the next village who had given her some medicines to take and rituals to perform to make her feel better. Now she was lying there, unable to talk and unable to open her mouth. The only sound she could make was a faint grunting sound from her throat. As Ken tried to work with her, all at once as fast as lightning, she drew up her knees, spun around as if on a lazy-susan, and slammed her feet into his stomach, pressing him against the wall. Others in the room rushed to restrain her.

Finally Ken stopped trying to talk to the woman, and he addressed instead the demons, asking them their names. To Ken's surprise, the demons started giving the names of people.

"This is the only time demons ever identified themselves to me using human-like names," he later explained. "Usually they called themselves things like Lust, Suicide, Nicotine, Alcohol, Immorality. But this time, they gave personal names."

Ken worked and prayed a long time, but he was never able to get the demons to leave the woman. Why? He explained that he and his coworkers in Brazil had little real success with people who didn't really want to be delivered.

When asked why we hear and read more about demon possession overseas than in America, Ken's answer is that in nations like Brazil and Haiti, the people openly seek out evil spirits. They overtly interact with the demonic world.

"But," Ken continued, "as witchcraft and the occult become more and more a part of the American culture, we're going to see more and more cases of demon possession here in the United States."

"We'd all be terribly surprised," he said, "if we knew just how deeply our current society is being influenced by demons."[1]

Demons Among Us

There is a devil, and there are demons. They may be more sophisticated in America than they are in some parts of the world, but they are demons nevertheless.

—BILLY GRAHAM

Date: _____   _____   _____

Place: _____   _____   _____

Occasion: _____   _____   _____

Denominations

Someone Once Said . . .

- *Today in the United States alone, there are almost 2,000 denominations and associations representing 385,000 churches.* —Bruce Shelley[2]

---

[1] Interview with the author, Spring 1999.
[2] Bruce Shelley, "Denominations—Divided We Stand," *Christianity Today*, September 7, 1998, 90.

- *A true denomination does not . . . make exclusive claims upon its members. It frees them to cooperate with Christians from other denominations in various specialized ministries.*—D. G. Tinder[1]
- *I belong to the same denomination that David did. I am a companion of all them that fear Thee and keep Thy precepts.*—Harry A. Ironside[2]
- *Whatever may be the denominational flags that are raised, let them all be lowered when the blood-stained banner of the cross appears.*—A. T. Pierson[3]
- *It is better to unite with a live church of some other denomination that to unite with a dead church of your own.*—R. A. Torrey[4]

Date: _____ _____ _____
Place: _____ _____ _____
Occasion: _____ _____ _____

Whitefield on Denominations

When evangelist George Whitefield preached from the balcony of the Philadelphia Courthouse to thousands who gathered on Market and Second Streets, he cried out:

"Father Abraham, whom have you in Heaven? Any Episcopalians?"

"No."

"Have you any Independents or Seceders?"

"No."

"Have you any Methodists?"

"No, no, no!"

"Whom have you there?"

"We don't know those names here! All who are here are Christians—believers in Christ—men [and women] who have overcome by the blood of the Lamb and the Word of His Testimony."

"Oh, is this the case? Then God help me, God help us all, to forget party names and to become Christians in deed and in truth."[5]

Date: _____ _____ _____
Place: _____ _____ _____
Occasion: _____ _____ _____

Spurgeon's Mixed Feelings

- *I bless God that there are so many denominations. If there were not men who differed a little in their creeds, we should never get so much gospel as we do. . . . God has sent different men to defend different kinds of truths.*[6]

---

[1] Ed. Walter A. Elwell, *Evangelical Dictionary of Theology* (Grand Rapids: Baker Book House, 1984), 311.
[2] E. Schuyler English, *H. A. Ironside: Ordained of the Lord* (East Stroudsburg, PA: Pinebrook Book Club, 1946), 157.
[3] Arthur T. Pierson, *The Gospel,* vol. 2 (Grand Rapids: Baker Book House, 1978), 132.
[4] R. A. Torrey, *How to Succeed in the Christian Life* (Chicago: Moody Press, 1979), 44.
[5] This story has been attributed to John Wesley.
[6] Charles Haddon Spurgeon, *Spurgeon's Sermons,* vol. 2 (Grand Rapids: Baker Book House, 1983), 224.

- *Denomination! A plague upon denominationalism! There should be but one denomination: We should be denominated by the name of Christ, as a wife is named by her husband's name. As long as the Church of Christ has to say, "My right arm is Episcopalian, and my left arm is Wesleyan, and my right foot is Baptist, and my left foot is Presbyterian or Congregational," she is not ready for marriage. She will be ready when she has washed out these stains, when all her members have "one Lord, one faith, one baptism."*[1]

- *When I read [Genesis 6:14, about rooms in Noah's ark] I thought it would serve for a point in the parable. . . . Those who lived in one room did not stand or sit with those who lived in another, but they were all in the same ark. So I have sometimes thought, There are our Wesleyan friends, some of them love the Lord; I have no doubt they are in the ark, though they do not occupy the same apartment as we do. There are our Baptist friends, who love the Lord; we welcome them in our room. Then there are our Independent friends, those also love the Lord; they are in another room. And our Presbyterian and Episcopalian brethren—in all these various sections are some who are called of God and brought into the ark, though they are in different rooms. But, beloved, they are all in one ark.*[2]

- *Two men . . . were walking from opposite directions on a foggy night! Each saw what he thought was a terrible monster moving towards him and making his heart beat with terror; as they came nearer to each other, they found that the dreadful monsters were brothers. So, men of different denominations are often afraid of one another, but when they get close to each other and know each other's hearts, they find out they are brethren after all.*[3]

Date: _____ _____ _____
Place: _____ _____ _____
Occasion: _____ _____ _____

Another Way of Putting It

California pastor Jack Hayford once put it this way: *Yes, we are all a part of the whole body of Christ, but as Israel camped around the Tabernacle in tribes, so we need to, every once in a while, be with our tribe and accept the ministry given to our tribe.*[4]

Date: _____ _____ _____
Place: _____ _____ _____
Occasion: _____ _____ _____

Principles of Denominationalism

Church historian Bruce Shelley suggests that the denominational theory of the church that arose in England in the 1600s was based on the following principles:

[1] Charles Haddon Spurgeon, *Messages of Hope and Faith* (Cleveland, Ohio: Publishing House of the Evangelical Association, n.d.), 308.
[2] Spurgeon, *Spurgeon's Sermons,* vol. 4, 10.
[3] C. H. Spurgeon, *Lectures to My Students* (Grand Rapids: Zondervan, 1972), 384.
[4] Quoted in the newsletter of Christ's Church Fellowship, Cincinnati, Ohio, December 14, 1988.

1. Considering the human inability always to see the truth clearly, differences of opinion about the outward form of the church are inevitable.
2. Even though these differences do not involve fundamentals of the faith, they are not matters of indifference.
3. Since no church has a final and full grasp of divine truth, the true church of Christ can never be fully represented by any single ecclesiastical structure.
4. The mere fact of separation does not itself constitute schism. It is possible to be divided at many points and still be united in Christ.[1]

Date: _____ _____ _____
Place: _____ _____ _____
Occasion: _____ _____ _____

Elton Trueblood on Denominations

There is no vital religion in the world today that is not sectarian, and there cannot be. The reason for this is rooted deeply in human nature. We naturally form into groups and find our best life in reasonably small fellowships. Like-minded fellowships in different committees strengthen one another in conscious loyalty to a heritage. Such groups are called denominations. There is nothing very dangerous or surprising about this and certainly there is nothing about it that is unique to religion. We do it in everything else, as the existence of lodges, political parties and service clubs so abundantly testifies. It is very curious, indeed, that a man who takes for granted the existence of separate organizations for Rotary, Kiwanis, and Lions Clubs should profess to be shocked by the fact that Christians are organized in a similar way.[2]

Date: _____ _____ _____
Place: _____ _____ _____
Occasion: _____ _____ _____

Warren Wiersbe's Philosophy

I had decided to be a Christian first, a pastor second, and a Baptist third. I wasn't going to make denominational affiliation a test of spirituality or fellowship. My ecclesiastical home has been with the Baptists, and I've tried to live apart from anything that dishonors the Lord, but I don't think there's a drop of denominational blood in my veins. In more than four decades of ministry, I've preached in Christian churches of many denominations and no denomination; I've discovered that Bob Cook was right when he said, "I've learned that God blesses people I disagree with."[3]

Date: _____ _____ _____
Place: _____ _____ _____
Occasion: _____ _____ _____

[1] Bruce Shelley, "Denominations—Divided We Stand," *Christianity Today,* September 7, 1998, 90.
[2] Elton Trueblood, *Foundations for Reconstruction* (New York: Harper & Brothers, 1946), 54–55.
[3] Warren Wiersbe, *Be Myself: The Memoirs of One of America's Most Respected Bible Teachers* (Victor Books, 1994), 89.

Cheering the Lutherans

Three Lutheran pastors were invited by a Catholic priest to attend Mass one Sunday at his church. They arrived a bit late. All the pews were filled, and they had to stand in the back of the church. The priest noticed them as he began the Mass, and he whispered to one of the altar boys, "Get three chairs for our Lutheran friends." The altar boy didn't hear, so the priest spoke a bit louder, motioning to the rear of the congregation: "Three chairs for the Lutherans." Dutifully the boy arose, stepped to the altar rail, and loudly proclaimed to the congregation: "Three cheers for the Lutherans!"

Date: _____ _____ _____

Place: _____ _____ _____

Occasion: _____ _____ _____

——— Depression ———

Someone Once Said . . .

- *Depression affects more people in our culture than any other emotional disorder.*—Armand Mayo Nicholi II[1]
- *Americans, on average, may be more depressed, and at a younger age, than they have ever been: unprecedented psychological misery in a nation with unprecedented prosperity and material well-being.*—Psychologist Martin Seligman[2]
- *Unhappy Christians are, to say the least, a poor recommendation for the Christian faith. . . . A depressed Christian is a contradiction in terms.*—D. Martyn Lloyd-Jones[3]
- *The devil's one object is so to depress God's people that he can go to the man of the world and say: There are God's people. Do you want to be like that?*—D. Martyn Lloyd-Jones[4]

Date: _____ _____ _____

Place: _____ _____ _____

Occasion: _____ _____ _____

Depression in the Workplace

According to the September 10, 1999 issue of *USA Today*, depression is so pervasive it is having an economic impact on the American work force. The article said: *Depression among workers poses problems in most American offices and factories, according to human-resource managers who responded to a questionnaire. Among those human-resource managers for 406 U.S. companies, more than half—56 percent—said employees suffering from depression have had a negative impact on productivity at their companies in the past three years.*

---

[1] Armand Mayo Nicholi II, "Why Can't I Deal With Depression," *Christianity Today*, November 11, 1993, 39.
[2] Martin E. P. Seligman, *Learned Optimism* (New York: Alfred A. Knopf, 1990), 65.
[3] D. Martyn Lloyd-Jones, *Spiritual Depression* (Grand Rapids: Eerdmans, 1965), 5, 11.
[4] Lloyd-Jones, *Spiritual Depression*, 19.

Nearly four in ten said depression among workers is a moderate or large problem for their companies. The survey, faxed to 2,300 companies, was conducted in July by the Society for Human Resource Management and the National Foundation for Brain Research.

About seventeen million Americans experience serious depression each year. Symptoms that can indicate depression that human resource managers said they most often recognized among workers include tiredness or lethargy, poor concentration, a decline in productivity, overall sadness and an increase in unexplained absences.[1]

Date:		
Place:		
Occasion:		

Signs of Depression

According to the National Institute of Mental Health, one out of four Americans will suffer a major episode of depression. Those exhibiting four of the following symptoms may need help now:

- Loss of interest in usual activities
- Feelings of guilt, worthlessness, hopelessness
- Weight gain or loss
- Sleep disturbances
- Depressed mood
- Hyperactivity
- Lethargy
- Anxiety
- Crying
- Slow thinking
- Suicidal thoughts

Date:		
Place:		
Occasion:		

Great Christians Who Suffered From Depression

- *You seem to imagine I have no ups and downs but just a level and lofty stretch of spiritual attainment with unbroken joy. . . . By no means! I am often perfectly wretched and everything appears most murky.*—John Henry Jowett, pastor of New York's Fifth Avenue Presbyterian Church and later Westminster Chapel in London, to a friend in 1920[2]
- *There are dungeons beneath the castles of despair.*—Charles Spurgeon, who suffered debilitating bouts of depression all his life

---

[1] *USA Today*, 10 September 1999, sec. D.
[2] Kent Hughes, *Liberating Ministry from the Success Syndrome* (Wheaton, IL: Tyndale House Publishers, 1987), 143.

- *Lord Jesus, receive my spirit and put an end to this miserable life.*—John Knox
- *I had my temptations attending me. . . . Sometimes I should be assaulted with great discouragement therein, fearing that I should not be able to speak the Word at all . . . at which times I should have such a strange faintness and strengthlessness seize upon my body that my legs have scarce been able to carry me.*—John Bunyan[1]
- *Resolute as was Dr. Whyte's character, he had seasons of deep depression regarding the results of his work in the pulpit or among his people.*—G. F. Barbour, biographer of Alexander Whyte, Scotland's greatest preacher since John Knox[2]
- *God is to me the Great Unknown. I believe in him, but I find him not.*—Adoniram Judson, America's first foreign missionary, suffering from a deep depression following the death of his wife, Nancy[3]
- *With the last of her savings drawn out of her small bank account Lottie [Moon, the great Southern Baptist missionary to China] lapsed into a period of deep depression. She quit eating, and her mental and physical health declined. A doctor was sent for, and only then was it discovered that she was starving to death. In hopes of saving her life, her colleagues made arrangements for her to return home in the company of a nurse, but it was too late. She died aboard ship while at port in Kobe, Japan, on Christmas Eve, 1912.*—Ruth Tucker, in *From Jerusalem to Irian Jaya*[4]
- *Cursed be the day in which I was born!*—Jeremiah
- *It is enough! Now, Lord, take my life.*—Elijah
- *Conflicts without, fears within . . . depressed.*—Paul the apostle, in 2 Corinthians 7:6 (NASV)

Date:			
Place:			
Occasion:			

Strange Comfort

- *It is not without its comfort that the two men who conversed with the Lord on the Mount of Transfiguration both broke under the strain of their ministry and prayed that they might die.*—J. Oswald Sanders[5]

Date:			
Place:			
Occasion:			

God Moves in a Mysterious Way

The hymns *There is a Fountain Filled with Blood* and *God Moves in a Mysterious Way* were written by William Cowper (pronounced Cooper), close friend of John Newton

---

[1] John Bunyan, *Grace Abounding to the Chief of Sinners* (Grand Rapids: Baker Book House, 1986), 129.
[2] Hughes, *Liberating Ministry from the Success Syndrome,* 143.
[3] Ruth Tucker, *From Jerusalem to Irian Jaya* (Grand Rapids: Academie Books, 1983), 129.
[4] Tucker, *From Jerusalem to Irian Jaya,* 238.
[5] J. Oswald Sanders, *A Spiritual Clinic* (Chicago: Moody Press, 1958), 113.

and one of England's greatest poets. Despite his many uplifting hymns, Cowper suffered from severe depression all his life, spending eighteen months in an insane asylum and trying on several occasions to take his own life.

He was born in a preacher's home in 1731, but his childhood was marred by the death of his mother, a bad case of shyness, and the psychological terrors of being bullied at boarding school.

His conversion to Christ was the turning of the corner, allowing Cowper to cast away ultimate despair and giving him long stretches of sunny confidence. Nevertheless, periods of formidable gloom dogged him the rest of his life. According to E. E. Ryden's account of his life in *The Story of Our Hymns:*

In 1773, two years after the two friends (John Newton and Cowper) had begun "The Olney Hymns," Cowper passed through a mental crisis that almost ended in tragedy. Obsessed with the idea that it was the divine will that he should offer up his life by drowning himself in the Ouse river, the afflicted poet ordered a post chaise, and instructed the driver to proceed to a certain spot near Olney, where he planned to leap into the river. When he reached the place, Cowper was diverted from his purpose when he found a man seated at the exact place where he had intended to end his life. Returning home, he is said to have thrown himself on his knife, but the blade broke. His next attempt was to hang himself, but the rope parted.

After his recovery from this dreadful experience, he was so impressed by the realization of God's overruling providence that he was led to write the hymn, "God Moves in a Mysterious Way." It is regarded by many critics as the finest hymn ever written on the theme of God's providence.[1]

> God moves in a mysterious way,
> His wonders to perform:
> He plants His footsteps in the sea,
> And rides upon the storm.

Date: _____ _____ _____

Place: _____ _____ _____

Occasion: _____ _____ _____

Lincoln's Depression

In a letter to his law partner, Abraham Lincoln, who suffered from depression all his life, wrote: *I am now the most miserable man living. If what I feel were equally distributed to the whole human family, there would not be one cheerful face on earth. Whether I shall ever be any better, I cannot tell. I awfully forebode that I shall not. To remain as I am is impossible. I must die or be better it seems to me.*[2]

Date: _____ _____ _____

Place: _____ _____ _____

Occasion: _____ _____ _____

[1] E. E. Ryden, *The Story of Our Hymns* (Rock Island, IL: Augustana Book Concern, 1930), 254.

[2] Dale Carnegie, *Little Known Facts About Well Known People* (New York: Blue Ribbon Books, Inc., 1934), 163.

Churchill's Depression

Winston Churchill was another of history's greatest leaders who was tormented by what he called his "Black Dog"—periodic moods of soul-crushing depression. William Manchester wrote that all his life Churchill suffered "spells of depression, sinking into the brooding depths of melancholia."

One friend said of him, "What a creature of strange moods he is, always at the top of the wheel of confidence or at the bottom of an intense depression."

Often feelings of disappointment and hopelessness simply overwhelmed him, and thoughts of self-destruction were never far away. Churchill once told his doctor, "I don't like standing near the edge of a platform when an express train is passing through. I don't like to stand by the side of a ship and look down into the water. A second's action would end everything."

—◇—
Mental Sniffles?

Depression is the common cold of the mind.
—◇—

To another, he admitted, "I've no desire to quit this world, but thoughts, desperate thoughts, come into the head."

Manchester points out depression is common among the great; it may balance their moods of omnipotence. Among its sufferers have been Goethe, Lincoln, Bismarck, Schumann, Tolstoy, Robert E. Lee, and Martin Luther.

Churchill coped with his depression through cultivating zestful companionship, avoiding hospitals, and incessant activity. He told one friend that unless he was perpetually active he relapsed into "dark moments of impatience and frustration."[1]

Date: _____ _____ _____
Place: _____ _____ _____
Occasion: _____ _____ _____

Maria Theresa's Depression

Maria Theresa (1717–1780), Empress of Austria and once the most powerful woman in the world, was crippled by depression following the deaths of her son Karl, her sister Johanna, and her husband, Emperor Francis. In *To the Scaffold*, historian Carolly Erickson tells of Maria Theresa's grief at the death of her husband:

The grieving widow had her rooms painted black, the windows draped with black velvet and her person veiled and swathed in somber widow's weeds. By nature energetic and affirmative, though plagued by periods of depression, the Empress now seemed to lose heart completely, sitting alone in her darkened apartments, her hair shorn, her thoughts increasingly morbid. . . .

[She] ordered her own coffin prepared and placed beside her husband's in the burial vault of the Capucin church. The Empress spent a large part of each afternoon in the vault, sitting beside Francis's coffin and the empty one waiting for her, praying and weeping. . . .

"Emperor Francis I, my husband," she wrote in her prayer book, "died on the evening of the eighteenth of August at half past nine o'clock. He lived 680 months, 2,958 weeks, 20,778

---

[1] William Manchester, *The Last Lion: Winston Spencer Churchill: Visions of Glory, 1874–1932* (Boston: Little, Brown, & Co., 1983), 23–24.

days, or 496,992 hours. Our happy marriage lasted twenty-nine years, six months, and six days—1,540 weeks, 10,781 days, or 258,744 hours."[1]

Date: _____ _____ _____
Place: _____ _____ _____
Occasion: _____ _____ _____

Charles Spurgeon's Depression

It is no secret that the Prince of Preachers, Charles Haddon Spurgeon, suffered black periods of anguishing depression. His congregation at the Metropolitan Tabernacle was once amazed to hear Spurgeon once begin a sermon from Isaiah 41:14 with these words in his introduction: *I have to speak today to myself, and whilst I shall be endeavoring to encourage those who are distressed and downhearted, I shall be preaching, I trust to myself, for I need something which shall cheer my heart—why I cannot tell, wherefore I do not know, but I have a thorn in the flesh, a messenger of Satan to buffet me; my soul is cast down within me; I feel as if I had rather die than live; all that God hath done by me seems to be forgotten, and my spirit flags and my courage breaks down . . . I need your prayers.*[2]

Date: _____ _____ _____
Place: _____ _____ _____
Occasion: _____ _____ _____

Satan's Tool

A medieval legend tells of an angel being sent to strip Satan of all his favorite temptations with which he seduces mankind. After much argument, the devil agreed. But he begged to be allowed to keep the least important of all his temptations.

"Which is . . . ?" asked the angel.

Satan shrugged. "Depression," he said.

He got his wish, and the angel returned to heaven, leaving depression behind.

"Good!" laughed Satan in glee. "In this one gift I have secured all."

Date: _____ _____ _____
Place: _____ _____ _____
Occasion: _____ _____ _____

Grimaldi

Joseph Grimaldi (1778–1837) is remembered as history's greatest clown. He was exclusively a theatrical clown, and is considered the "Father of Modern Clowning" because he is the entertainer who elevated the whiteface clown to a starring role. He

---

[1] Carolly Erickson, *To The Scaffold: The Life of Marie Antoinette* (New York: William Morrow and Company, Inc., 1991), 35.

[2] Charles Haddon Spurgeon, *Spurgeon's Sermons*, vol. 4 (Grand Rapids: Baker Book House, 1983), 351.

played for the King of England among others, and he made the world laugh. So great was his reputation that a doctor once gave a patient who complained of depression this simple prescription: "You must go to the music hall and see Grimaldi."

The patient bowed and said, "I'm sorry, doctor, but with me that will not work. You see, I am Grimaldi."[1]

Date:	_____	_____	_____
Place:	_____	_____	_____
Occasion:	_____	_____	_____

Wrong Thinking

In his book, *Learned Optimism*, Professor Martin Seligman refers to depression as "the ultimate expression of pessimism," and claims that many depressed people can talk their way out of pessimism by changing the way they think. As Seligman puts it, we can change our "explanatory style." After studying optimists and pessimists for twenty-five years, Seligman writes:

The defining characteristic of pessimists is that they tend to believe bad events will last a long time, will undermine everything they do, and are their own fault. The optimists, who are confronted with the same hard knocks of this world, think about misfortune in the opposite way. They tend to believe defeat is just a temporary setback, that its causes are confined to this one case. The optimists believe defeat is not their fault: Circumstances, bad luck, or other people brought it about. Such people are unfazed by defeat. Confronted by a bad situation, they perceive it as a challenge and try harder.[2]

Seligman claims that we can change from pessimistic thinking to optimistic thinking. *One of the most significant findings in psychology in the past twenty years is that individuals can choose the way they think.*[3]

Depression is nothing more than its symptoms. It is caused by negative thoughts. There is no deep underlying disorder to be rooted out: not unresolved childhood conflicts, not our unconscious anger, and not even our brain chemistry. Emotion comes directly from what we think. . . .

Depression results from lifelong habits of conscious thought. If we change these habits of thought, we will cure depression.[4]

Date:	_____	_____	_____
Place:	_____	_____	_____
Occasion:	_____	_____	_____

Martyn Lloyd-Jones' Advice

We must talk to ourselves instead of allowing "ourselves" to talk to us! Do your realize what that means? I suggest that the main trouble in this whole matter of spiritual depression in a sense is this, that we allow our self to talk to us instead of talking to our self. . . .

[1] Erik Brady, "Crown Prince of Baseball's Reign of Pain," *USA Today*, 31 July 1992, sec. C1.
[2] Martin E. P. Seligman, *Learned Optimism* (New York: Alfred A. Knopf, 1990), 4–5.
[3] Seligman, *Learned Optimism*, 8.
[4] Seligman, *Learned Optimism*, 74–75.

Most of your unhappiness in life is due to the fact that you are listening to yourself instead of talking to yourself. . . .

The main art in the matter of spiritual living is to know how to handle yourself. You have to take yourself in hand, you have to address yourself, preach to yourself, question yourself. You must say to your soul: "Why art thou cast down"—what business have you to be disquieted? You must turn on yourself, upbraid yourself, condemn yourself, exhort yourself, and say to yourself: "Hope thou in God"—instead of muttering in this depressed unhappy way. And then you must go on to remind yourself of God. . . .[1]

D

Date:			
Place:			
Occasion:			

Giant Despair

John Bunyan, author of *Pilgrim's Progress,* suffered from bouts of depression, and we may view as partly autobiographical his account of Christian's falling into the clutches of Giant Despair.

In the seventh stage of their journey, as Christian and Hopeful grow weary with their trip and wish for an easier way, they notice a little meadow on their left called By-path Meadow, with a stile leading over the fence. They detour in this way, but soon night overtakes them and they find themselves lost in a terrible storm. At last, weary and worried, they fall asleep under a tree and are captured the next day by Giant Despair who beats them cruelly and throws them into the dungeon of Doubting Castle. It was "a very dark dungeon, nasty and stinking to the spirit," and here the two men lay in misery from Wednesday morning till Saturday night, without one bit of bread or drink of water or light.

Finally, having reduced them to miserable depression, Giant Despair leaves a knife, a rope, and poison in their cell, and the two men are sorely tempted to end their lives. But remembering the commandment, "Thou shalt not kill," they resign themselves to the continued tortures of Giant Despair.

Early on a Sunday morning, Christian suddenly sits up *as one half amazed, and says, "Why a fool, thus to lie in a stinking dungeon when I may as well walk at liberty! I have a key in my bosom called Promise that will, I am persuaded, open any lock in Doubting Castle." Then said Hopeful, "That is good news; good brother, pluck it out of thy bosom and try."*

Then Christian pulled it out of his bosom, and began to try at the dungeon-door, whose bolt, as he turned the key, gave back and the door flew open with ease, and Christian and Hopeful both came out.

Date:			
Place:			
Occasion:			

[1]Lloyd-Jones, *Spiritual Depression,* 20–21.

You Stink!

On one uncharacteristically awful afternoon during the 1950s, the Yankee super-star Mickey Mantle struck out three times in a row, and he was badly depressed. "When I got back to the clubhouse," he remembered, "I just sat down on my stool and held my head in my hands, like I was going to start crying. I heard someone come up to me, and it was little Tommy Berra, Yogi's boy, standing there next to me. He tapped me on the knee, nice and soft, and I figured he was going to say something nice to me, like 'You keep hanging in there' or something like that. But all he did was look at me, and then he said in his little kid's voice, 'You stink.' "[1]

Date: _____   _____   _____
Place: _____   _____   _____
Occasion: _____   _____   _____

Despair

Someone Once Said . . .

- *We stand on the shore of an ocean, crying to the night and the emptiness; sometimes a voice answers out of the darkness. But it is the voice of one drowning; and in a moment the silence returns.*—Bertrand Russell, in his autobiography
- *I live in a vacuum that is as lonely as a radio tube when the batteries are dead and there is no current to plug into.*—Ernest Hemingway[2]
- *We are orphans, you and I. Every soul in this vast corpse-trench of the universe is utterly alone.*—Jean Paul Richter, eighteenth-century German author and philosopher[3]
- *My days are in the yellow leaf; / The flowers and fruits of love are gone; / The worm, the canker, and the grief / Are mine alone.*—Lord Byron, in his poem "On This Day I Complete My Thirty-Sixth Year"
- *The prisoner who had lost faith in the future—his future—was doomed.*—Viktor E. Frankl, describing his observations while interred in a Nazi death camp[4]

Date: _____   _____   _____
Place: _____   _____   _____
Occasion: _____   _____   _____

From Shakespeare's *Macbeth*

To-morrow, and to-morrow, and to-morrow,
Creeps in this petty pace from day to day,
To the last syllable of recorded time;

---

[1] Greggery C. Ward and Ken Burns, *Baseball: An Illustrated History* (New York: Alfred A. Knoph, 1994), 311.
[2] Daniel Pawley, "Ernest Hemingway: Tragedy of an Evangelical," *Christianity Today.*
[3] W. A. Criswell, *Great Doctrines of the Bible*, vol. 2 (Grand Rapids: Zondervan, 1982), 174.
[4] Viktor E. Frankl, *Man's Search for Meaning* (New York: Washington Square Press, 1959), 95.

And all our yesterdays have lighted fools
The way to dusty death. Out, out, brief candle!
Life's but a walking shadow, a poor player,
That struts and frets his hour upon the stage,
And then is heard no more; it is a tale
Told by an idiot, full of sound and fury,
Signifying nothing.

Date: _____ _____ _____
Place: _____ _____ _____
Occasion: _____ _____ _____

Two Explanations

- For if there's no God, what's so special about human beings? They're just accidental by-products of nature which have evolved relatively recently on an infinitesimal speck of dust called Planet Earth, lost somewhere in a hostile and mindless universe, and which are doomed to perish individually and collectively in a relatively short time.—William Lane Craig
- The average person in the world today, without faith and without God and without hope, is engaged in a desperate personal search throughout his lifetime. He does not really know where he has been. He does not really know what he is doing here and now. He does not know where he is going. The sad commentary is that he is doing it all on borrowed time and borrowed money and borrowed strength—and he already knows that in the end will he surely die.—A. W. Tozer[1]

Date: _____ _____ _____
Place: _____ _____ _____
Occasion: _____ _____ _____

From Thoreau's Journal

This is man, and one wonders why he wants to live at all. A third of his life is lost and deadened under sleep; another third is given to sterile labor; a sixth is spent in all his goings and comings, in the [toil] and shuffle of the streets, in thrusting, shoving, pawing. How much of him is left, then, for a vision of the tragic stars? How much of him is left to look upon the everlasting earth? A few snatched moments only from the barren glut and suck of living.—Henry D. Thoreau, in his *Journal*

Date: _____ _____ _____
Place: _____ _____ _____
Occasion: _____ _____ _____

[1] A. W. Tozer, *Whatever Happened to Worship* (Camp Hill, PA: Christian Publications, 1985), 65.

Graffiti Philosophy

- *We are beautiful drunkards, comets wandering alone, looking at the stars, waiting for a future that doesn't come.*—graffiti, written in Portuguese on a wall in Porto Alegre, Brazil
- *All things are transient. The sun after the splendor of the day sinks into the ocean, the moon after showing us her full light wanes. In the same way the anguish of love ends in but a breath of wind.*—found under the ashes of Pompeii, scribbled on a wall on the "Street of Abundance"[1]

Date: _____ _____ _____
Place: _____ _____ _____
Occasion: _____ _____ _____

Observer in an Airport

"You stand here and watch the world go by, don't you?"

I had ducked into a newsstand at Chicago's O'Hare for a paper, and the small, gray-haired lady who took my money had perceptive eyes and oversized glasses. She only glanced at me, her attention barely leaving the mass of humanity that was coming and going in a blur of motion. I was intrigued by her absorption in the flowing crowd, so I asked her, "You just stand here and watch the world go by, don't you?"

"Yes . . ." she said, her eyes still on the humanity. "Yes, and much of it is sad."

She turned briefly to me, gave me my change and my paper, and nodded toward the men's bathroom across the concourse. "You wouldn't believe the suicides they take out of that washroom. Many men go in there and kill themselves, and the paramedics take them out one after another, all the time."

With that observation, she dismissed me from her attention, her eyes transfixed again by humanity.[2]

Date: _____ _____ _____
Place: _____ _____ _____
Occasion: _____ _____ _____

We Wonder

Thomas Hardy, the English novelist and poet, asked this question in his pessimistic and agnostic poem, "Nature's Questioning":

> *We wonder, ever wonder, why we find us here!*
> *Has some Vast Imbecility,*
> *Mighty to build and blend*
> *But impotent to tend,*
> *Framed us in jest, and left us now to hazardry?*[3]

---

[1] Stephen Bertman, *Doorways Through Time* (Los Angeles: Jeremy P. Tarcher, Inc., 1986), 89.
[2] Conversation with the author, February 17, 1995.
[3] Warren W. Wiersbe, *Why Us?* (Old Tappan, NJ: Fleming H. Revell Co., 1984), 29.

Date: _____ _____ _____

Place: _____ _____ _____

Occasion: _____ _____ _____

D

Friedrich Nietzsche

Few have suffered a sadder story than the German philosopher Friedrich W. Nietzsche. Nietzsche grew up in a Christian home. Both his grandfathers had been Christian ministers, and his father was a Lutheran pastor. But Nietzsche rejected Christianity, and formulated his famous "Death of God" philosophy.

When Nietzsche said that God was dead, he didn't mean that a literal God had literally died. He meant that, in Western civilization, belief in God was dead. Western philosophers no longer accepted God or sought to obey him. In other words, as far as Western philosophy is concerned, God just doesn't exist anymore. Christianity has been replaced by humanism as the cornerstone of Western thought.

Nietzsche's famous parable about this is called the *Madman*.

A madman appeared in the marketplace one morning, holding a lighted lantern in the bright daylight. He startled everyone by crying, "I'm looking for God! I'm looking for God!" The people made fun of him, saying, "Do you think God is lost? Is he hiding?" The madman leaped among the people, his eyes wild with alarm, crying, "Where is God? I'll tell you where he is. We have killed him—you and I. All of us are his murderers. We have cut ourselves off from God as though we had unchained the earth from the sun, and we are wobbling out of control, plunging backward, sideward, forward, in all directions. We're becoming cold and dark and empty. Don't you feel it?"

Then Nietzsche asked a profound question: "How shall we, the murderers of all murderers, comfort ourselves?"

The philosopher understood the implication of what he was advocating. In removing God from our lives, we were removing our source of comfort and stripping ourselves of hope and peace. We were crossing the line of despair.

Nietzsche thought that after an initial time of chaos and despair, his God-is-dead philosophy would pave the way for a great superman to come and take charge of the human race, someone who could lead humanity to its zenith. But the insanity he predicted for the world came upon himself. Apparently unable to live with his own beliefs, Nietzsche became increasingly irrational. One day he collapsed on a street in Turin and was taken to an asylum. For the last twelve years of his life he was insane, becoming himself a madman, being cared for by his mother, a devoted Christian.

Furthermore, the superman he predicted for the world was personified in the person of one of his greatest disciples—Adolf Hitler.

Ravi Zacharias, in his book *Can Man Live Without God?* wrote, "There is nothing in history to match the dire ends to which humanity can be led by following a political and social philosophy that consciously and absolutely excludes God. . . . I, for one, see Nietzsche's life and death as a blueprint for where we are headed inexorably as a nation."[1]

---

[1] Ravi Zacharias, *Can Man Live Without God?* (Dallas: Word Publishing, 1994).

Date: _____ _____ _____
Place: _____ _____ _____
Occasion: _____ _____ _____

Nevermore or Evermore?

Edgar Allan Poe was a tragic figure in American literature. His parents were penniless actors who died when he was very young. He went to live with strangers in an unhealthy home atmosphere, and, as a young man, his one true love died and left him a broken, alcohol-addicted man. And so it is no wonder that his writings are filled with despair. Shortly after his wife's death, he wrote his most famous poem, *The Raven.*

Once upon a midnight dreary, while I pondered weak and weary
Over many a quaint and curious volume of forgotten lore—

The story told in this incredible poem is of a depressed man, filled with grief, going mad in his study because of the death of his beloved Lenore. And the word that echoes through almost every verse of this poem is the haunting word *nevermore.*

Is there anything beyond the grave? Will I live after death? Will I ever again see my Lenore? Will I ever again have hope?

No! Nevermore! Nevermore! Nevermore! And the poem ends:

And my soul
from that shadow that lies floating on the floor
Shall be lifted—nevermore!

Compare that to a poem written by Virgil Brock earlier in this century. Mr. Brock was a Christian, a poet, and a writer of hymns. One day he went out at twilight, and he saw the sun setting in the West. Night was creeping over him, and he thought about death and eternity. He thought of those his loved ones who walked no more on this earth. And he wrote:

Beyond the sunset, O glad reunion,
With our dear loved ones who've gone before;
In that fair homeland we'll know no parting,
Beyond the sunset, forevermore!

The soul without Jesus cries, "Nevermore!" But the Christian sings, "Evermore!" And that makes all the difference.

Date: _____ _____ _____
Place: _____ _____ _____
Occasion: _____ _____ _____

Into the Dark

Columba was a sixth-century missionary, born in Ireland, who harbored a passion and vision for all the world. He established a missionary training school on the island of Iona, off the coast of Scotland, and kept the burden of missions alive at the onset of the medieval age. One of Columba's missionaries, according to an ancient story, took the gospel to Northumbria, and there the local tribal king called together his wise men and chiefs to consider the matter. "Should we hear the gospel or not?" he asked. There was great debate, but one of the wise men finally brought the discussion around to this. He said, "Our life is like the flight of a bird through our lighted hall. In comes the bird out of the dark, flies about a little while in the light of our torches, and flies out again into the dark. So we come out of the dark, and go into the dark. If these strangers can tell us anything better, let us listen."

That pagan chieftain of 1,400 years ago put his finger on a great apologetic for Christianity. How do we know Christianity is true? Because if it isn't, we're nothing more than frightened little birds who come from the dark and flutter around frantically before returning to a cold and blackened void.

The well-known Calvinist apologist Cornelius Van Til bases his defense of Christianity on this very thing—all other theologies and philosophies lead inexorably to darkness and despair. All other philosophies, if followed to their logical ends, lead to chaos and irrationality. Only Christianity gives meaning to life. One can be both consistent in mind and happy in spirit only with theism in general and Christianity in particular.

Serious Despair

There is but one truly serious philosophical problem, and that is suicide.
—ALBERT CAMUS

Francis Schaeffer's approach was similar. As a young man he grew up in a very liberal church, a church that believed nothing of substance in the Bible. He decided on the basis of what he was hearing that the only logical philosophy in life was agnosticism, or perhaps atheism. As an agnostic, he started to read the Bible for the first time. He wanted to compare it to the Greek philosophers he was reading. He had no thought of ever becoming a Christian, but as he read through the Bible, he saw the logical consistency of it and the way in which Scripture alone answered the problems of life. He became a Christian, and years later he wrote a book entitled *He Is There and He Is Not Silent.* In that book, he said,

There is no other sufficient philosophical answer. You can search through university philosophy, underground philosophy, filling station philosophy—it does not matter which—there is no other sufficient philosophical answer to existence. There is only one philosophy, one religion, that fills this need in all the world's thought, whether the East, the West, the ancient, the modern, the new, the old. Only one fills the philosophical need of existence, of being, and it is the Judaeo-Christian God—not just an abstract concept, but rather that this God is really there. He really exists. It is not that this is the best answer to existence; it is the only answer. That is why we may hold our Christianity with intellectual integrity.[1]

Date:			
Place:			
Occasion:			

Who Is in Charge of this Clattering Train?

Throughout the 1930s, Winston Churchill grew increasingly frustrated with the British government's failure to take Adolf Hitler and the Nazi threat seriously. He

---

[1] Robert J. Morgan, *Beyond Reasonable Doubt* (Wheaton, IL: Evangelical Training Association, 1997), ch. 12.

finally concluded that Prime Minister Baldwin was hopelessly unable to face the challenges of leading England. In trying to awaken the British public, Churchill quoted a little poem from an 1883 issue of *Punch,* lines he had memorized as a schoolboy in Brighton. The words vividly describe the plight of the human race without Christ:

> *Who is in charge of this clattering train?*
> *The axles creak and the couplings strain;*
> *And the pace is hot, and the points are near,*
> *And Sleep has deadened the driver's ear;*
> *And the signals flash through the night in vain,*
> *For Death is in charge of this clattering train.*[1]

Date: _____ _____ _____
Place: _____ _____ _____
Occasion: _____ _____ _____

Details

Someone Once Said . . .

- *God cares about details. If you comb out some hairs in the morning, the record in Heaven is changed.*—John R. Rice
- *Once you start ignoring [details], you won't be ready on game day.*—Don Shula, known for his detailed planning of every football game[2]
- *Effort is what ultimately separates journeyman players from impact players. Knowing how well a player executes all these little things is the key to unlocking his career.*—Pat Riley, basketball coach
- *I spare no pains whatever, even in the minutest trifles.*—Claude Monet, French painter, when asked his secret for becoming one of the world's greatest painters[3]
- *The difference between the right word and the almost-right word is the difference between the lightning and the lightning bug.*—Mark Twain

Date: _____ _____ _____
Place: _____ _____ _____
Occasion: _____ _____ _____

For Want of a Nail

For want of a nail, the horse was lost. For want of a horse, a General was lost. For want of a General, a battle was lost. For want of a battle, a war was lost. For want of a war, a nation was lost. And all for the want of a nail.

---

[1] William Manchester, *The Last Lion: Winston Spencer Churchill: Alone, 1932–1940* (Boston: Little, Brown and Company, 1988), 148.

[2] Brian White, "Wife's Death Gives Shula New Focus," *USA Today,* 9 July 1991, sec. 3C.

[3] Charles Spurgeon, *Lectures To My Students* (Grand Rapids: Zondervan, 1954), 287.

Date: _____ _____ _____

Place: _____ _____ _____

Occasion: _____ _____ _____

For Want of a Comma

A wealthy woman who was traveling overseas saw a bracelet she thought was irresistible, so she sent her husband this cable: "Have found wonderful bracelet. Price $75,000. May I buy it?" Her husband promptly wired back this response: "No, price too high." But the cable operator omitted the comma, so the woman received the message: "No price too high."

She bought it.

What a difference a comma made.

Date: _____ _____ _____

Place: _____ _____ _____

Occasion: _____ _____ _____

Trifles

There is a story that Michelangelo was working on a statue one afternoon when some friends visited him. A month later they returned and found him still working on the same statue.

"What have you done since our last visit?" asked one of them.

"Oh, I've smoothed a line here and polished an arm, taken a few flakes of marble from the forehead, and so on," replied the great artist.

"But those are only trifles! Is that all you've done?"

"True, they are but trifles," replied Michelangelo. "But trifles make perfection, and perfection is no trifle."

Date: _____ _____ _____

Place: _____ _____ _____

Occasion: _____ _____ _____

On the Other Hand . . .

• *Our life is frittered away by detail. . . . Simplify, simplify.*—Henry David Thoreau

Date: _____ _____ _____

Place: _____ _____ _____

Occasion: _____ _____ _____

Who Can See?

The story is told of a craftsman who had traveled to America from Europe to dedicate his life to some of the detail work in one of this country's grandest places of worship. One day a sightseer was touring the edifice and observed the workman meticulously laboring near the high ceiling on a symbol which could hardly be seen from the floor. What is more, he seemed to be occupied with a detail on the top, even out of view of the most carefully observant worshipper. The sightseer said, "Why are you being so exact; no one can even see the detail you care creating from this distance?"

The busy artist replied, not missing a stroke, "God can."[1]

Date:			
Place:			
Occasion:			

Disappointment

Someone Once Said . . .

- *Disappointments: His Appointments.*
- *Disappointment: God's way of dimming the glamour of the world and deepening our ability to enjoy Him (Psalm 119:37).*—Bill Gothard
- *Have you ever thought that our disappointments are God's way of reminding us that there are idols in our lives that must be dealt with?*—Erwin Lutzer[2]
- *Why art thou disquieted; because it happeneth not to thee according to thy wishes and desires? Who is he that hath everything according to his will? Neither I, nor thou, nor any man upon the earth.*—Thomas à Kempis
- *All I can say in this affair is that, however mysterious the leadings of Providence are, I have no doubt but they are superintended by an infinitely wise God.*—William Carey, after he and his luggage were put ashore and he was denied passage aboard the ship that was to take him as a missionary to India[3]

Date:			
Place:			
Occasion:			

Sovereign Arms

Kay Arthur was bitterly disappointed when she contracted a heart infection that forced her removal from the mission field. She and her family, serving in Mexico, were forced to return home. "I felt like a failure," she wrote. "Depression set in until I cried, 'Father, whatever you want.'"

"It would be several years before I'd see how He'd use those formative years of

[1] Ronald Allen and Gordon Borror, *Worship: Rediscovering the Missing Jewel* (Portland, OR: Multnomah Press, 1982), 29.
[2] Erwin Lutzer, *Managing Your Emotions* (Wheaton, IL: Victor Books, 1988), 109.
[3] Mary Drewery, *William Carey: A Biography* (Grand Rapids: Zondervan, 1978), 49.

study in Mexico to prepare me to write inductive Bible studies that would eventually reach fifty-two countries."

"My disappointments aren't over," Kay admits. "Pain and trials are almost constant companions, but never enemies. They drive me into His sovereign arms. There He takes my disappointments and works everything together for good."[1]

D

Date: _____ _____ _____

Place: _____ _____ _____

Occasion: _____ _____ _____

A Really Bitter Blow

In 1874, hymn writer Frances Ridley Havergal wrote a poem for the New Year and printed it on specially designed greeting cards for friends. The stanzas said:

> *Another year is dawning:*
> *Dear Father, let it be,*
> *In working or in waiting,*
> *Another year with Thee;*
> *Another year of progress,*
> *Another year of praise,*
> *Another year of proving*
> *Thy presence all the days.*

As it turned out, she *needed* that prayer, because just a few days later she suffered a stunning disappointment. She was hoping to be launched in America as an author, and her agent in New York had made reassuring promises and claims. Then came a letter that she thought would bear the first of many royalty checks. Instead it reported that her publisher had gone bankrupt in the New York Stock Market crash of 1873.

But as Frances had only recently turned all her affairs over to the Lord, she bore the crisis with peace, writing to a friend:

Heartsick

Hope deferred makes the heart sick.

—PROVERBS 13:12

I have just had such a blessing in the shape of what would have been only two months ago a really bitter blow to me. . . . I was expecting a letter from America, enclosing thirty-five pounds now due to me, and possibly news that [my book] was going on like steam. The letter has come, and, instead of all this, my publisher has failed in the universal crash. He holds my written promise to publish only with him as the condition of his launching me, so this is not simply a little loss, but an end of all my American prospects of either cash, influence, or fame, at any rate for a long time to come. I really had not expected that He would do for me so much above all I asked, as not merely to help me to acquiesce in this, but positively not to feel it at all, and only to rejoice in it as a clear test of the reality of victorious faith which I do find brightening almost daily. Two months ago this would have been a real trial to me, for I had built a good deal on my American prospects; now "thy will be done" is not a sigh but only a song.[2]

---

[1] Kay Arthur, "In Person: My Disappointments, His Appointments," *Moody Magazine,* January 1992, 30.
[2] *Memorials of Frances Ridley Havergal by her Sister M. V. G. H.* (New York: E. P. Dutton & Co., 1892), 134–135.

```
┌─────────────────────────────────────────────────────────────────┐
│  Date:      _____   _____   _____        │
│  Place:     _____   _____   _____        │
│  Occasion:  _____   _____   _____        │
└─────────────────────────────────────────────────────────────────┘
```

The Discipline of Disappointment

In his excellent little book, *The Disciplines of Life,* V. Raymond Edman devotes a chapter to "The Discipline of Disappointment."

Disillusionment, despair, defeat, and degrading self-pity do not meet nor mend disappointment. Going onward does. An excellent example is found in the experience of the Apostle Paul as recorded in 2 Corinthians 12:12–14. He had anticipated meeting Titus in the old city of Troas, but Titus did not put in an appearance. There is no indication in the sacred record as to why he did not come, only that Paul was restless in spirit. How did he react to that disappointment? He kept right on going. . . .

Edman continues by saying that several things help deal with disappointment:

- Thankfulness helps. Habakkuk saw no outward prospect of prosperity, only utter desolation and disappointment, yet a thankful heart lifted him to high places of victory. (Habakkuk 3:17–19)
- Assurance helps. Paul was certain that although he had been disappointed, he could be satisfied in whatever provision the Master made for him.
- Going on helps. Rather than sulk by life's roadside, Paul went to the next place of service.

There is a disciple of disappointment that would destroy us, unless we cause it to lift us into a new sphere of usefulness and devotion.[1]

```
┌─────────────────────────────────────────────────────────────────┐
│  Date:      _____   _____   _____        │
│  Place:     _____   _____   _____        │
│  Occasion:  _____   _____   _____        │
└─────────────────────────────────────────────────────────────────┘
```

Paul Harvey's "For What It's Worth . . ."

Our "For What It's Worth Department" hears that Speedy Morris—basketball coach for La Salle University—was shaving when his wife called out to tell him he was wanted on the phone by Sports Illustrated.

Speedy Morris was so excited by the prospect of national recognition that he nicked himself with his razor and ran—with a mixture of blood and lather on his face—and fell down the steps.

But he got to the phone.

And the voice on the other line said:

"For just seventy-five cents an issue you can get a one-year trial subscription. . . ."[2]

---

[1] V. Raymond Edman, *The Disciples of Life* (Minneapolis: World Wide Publications, 1948), 159–165.
[2] Paul Harvey, *Paul Harvey's For What It's Worth,* ed. Paul Harvey, Jr. (New York: Bantam Books, 1991), 118.

Date: _____ _____ _____
Place: _____ _____ _____
Occasion: _____ _____ _____

Discipleship/Mentoring

Someone Once Said . . .

- *The word "disciple" occurs 269 times in the New Testament. "Christian" is found three times, and was first introduced to refer precisely to the disciples.*—Dallas Willard[1]
- *The disciple of Jesus is not the deluxe or heavy-duty model of the Christian—especially padded, textured, streamlined, and empowered for the fast lane on the straight and narrow way. He stands on the pages of the New Testament as the first level of basic transportation in the kingdom of God.*—Dallas Willard[2]
- *Everyone who makes it has a mentor.*—*The Harvard Business Review*[3]
- *You've got to have mentors along the way.*—Lee Iacocca[4]

Date: _____ _____ _____
Place: _____ _____ _____
Occasion: _____ _____ _____

Where Would We Be Without Staupitz?

In a thought-provoking article in *Christianity Today,* historian Bruce Shelley pointed out that we would not have some of our greatest heroes of church history had there not been mentors who loved and discipled them. Behind the great leaders of the church stood others who, through their lives and teaching, provided instruction. He gives five examples:

- Behind Augustine, there was Monica, his mother, a devout Christian and a tireless prayer warrior who prayed for her wandering prodigal until he was at last converted. Augustine later called Monica his mother both in the flesh and in the Lord.
- Behind Martin Luther was Johann Von Staupitz, professor of Bible at the university in Wittenberg. When Luther became an Augustinian monk, Staupitz became his spiritual director and counselor. "If it had not been for Dr. Staupitz," Luther later said, "I should have sunk in hell." It was Staupitz who taught Luther about grace and who directed him into the study of theology.

[1] Dallas Willard, "Discipleship: For Super Christians Only?" *Christianity Today,* 10 October 1980, 24.
[2] Dallas Willard, "Discipleship: For Super Christians Only?" *Christianity Today,* 10 October 1980, 24.
[3] Clipping in my files.
[4] Clipping in my files.

- Behind John Calvin was William Farel, who spurred Calvin on to courage and devotion, and who, when Calvin was dying, left his own sickbed to come from afar to encourage him.
- Behind John Wesley was Peter Boehler, who belonged to the Moravians, a group of German Christians who seemed to possess what Wesley seemed to lack—a personal, restful trust in God. It was by following Boehler's counsel that Wesley eventually found his heart "strangely warmed" at a midweek meeting on Aldersgate Street.
- Behind William Carey was Andrew Fuller, who had broken with the hyper-Calvinistic Baptists of his day and was appealing for people to be converted to Christ. Spurred on by Fuller's evangelistic zeal, Carey asked the logical question, "What about the people beyond our shores? Don't they, too, need the gospel?" The two men became soul-mates in missions, Carey in India, and Fuller, his mentor and supporter, cheering from the stands back home.[1]

Date: _____   _____   _____
Place: _____   _____   _____
Occasion: _____   _____   _____

Little Bilney

Behind Hugh Latimer (1485–1555), the "Preacher of the English Reformation," was his mentor Thomas Bilney.

Bilney, a quiet scholar at Cambridge University, acquired a Greek New Testament from the famous Erasmus. As he pored over it, one verse of Scripture seemed to be written in letters of light, and it led to his conversion: *Christ Jesus came into the world to save sinners!*

Bilney wanted to share his experience with others, but this was Reformation truth, and the Reformation had not yet reached England. Teachers such as Luther were being fiercely attacked by English churchmen like Hugh Latimer.

But as Bilney listened to young Latimer rail against the Reformation, he prayed this unusual prayer: "O God, I am but 'little Bilney,' and shall never do any great thing for Thee. But give me the soul of that man, Hugh Latimer, and what wonders *he* shall do in Thy most holy name."

One day Bilney pulled Latimer aside. Using his own conversion verse—1 Timothy 1:15—he led the great Latimer to simple faith in Christ, and the English Reformation was born.

Date: _____   _____   _____
Place: _____   _____   _____
Occasion: _____   _____   _____

---

[1]Bruce L. Shelley, "Where Would We Be Without Staupitz?" *Christianity Today,* 16 December 1991, 29–31.

The Navigator and the Hitchhiker

The name Dawson Trotman, founder of the Navigators, will forever be associated with discipleship, because discipling others became the passion of his life. It happened like this. One day early in his ministry Dawson was driving along and he saw a young man walking down the street on his way to caddy at the golf course. Trotman often picked up hitchhikers, for it gave him a chance to witness.

Student or Disciple?

A student learns what his teacher knows, but a disciple becomes what his master is.

The hitchhiker on this day swore as he got into the car; Dawson reached into his pocket for a gospel tract and handed it to him. The man glanced at the tract, then looked at Dawson and said, "Haven't I seen you somewhere before?"

Dawson looked at him closely. As it turned out, the two men had met on the same road the previous year. Dawson had witnessed to him, led him to Christ, and had "sped on my merry way" confident that another soul had entered the kingdom.

But now, a year later, there was no more evidence of the new birth in this young man than if he had never heard the gospel.

"After I met this boy the second time on the way to the golf course, I began to go back and find some of my 'converts.' I want to tell you, I was sick at heart."

Motivated by that experience, Dawson Trotman began working on follow–up, on developing ways of mentoring those whom he was winning to Christ.

"Before I had forgotten to follow up on the people God had reached through me," he later said. "But from then on I began to spend time helping them. . . . You can lead a soul to Christ in anywhere from twenty minutes to a couple of hours. But it takes from twenty weeks to a couple of years to get him on the road to maturity."[1]

Date: _____ _____ _____
Place: _____ _____ _____
Occasion: _____ _____ _____

Discouragement

Someone Once Said . . .

- *All discouragement is of the devil. Discouragement is to be resisted just like sin. To give way to the one is just as bad and weakens us as much as to give way to the other.*—J. O. Fraser, missionary to China[2]
- *No, I do not become discouraged. You see, God has not called me to a ministry of success. He has called me to a ministry of mercy.*—Mother Teresa, when asked if she ever grew fainthearted while working among the poor.

[1] Dawson Trotman, *Born to Reproduce* (Colorado Springs: NavPress, 1975).
[2] Geraldine Taylor, *Behind the Rangers: The Life-Changing Story of J. O. Fraser* (Singapore: OMF International, 1998), 111.

Date: _____ _____ _____

Place: _____ _____ _____

Occasion: _____ _____ _____

Learning What Doesn't Work

Thomas Edison, probably the greatest inventor in history, only had three months of formal schooling. Yet his 1,093 inventions transformed the world, including motion pictures, mimeograph machines, the phonograph, and the electric light. His secret? He defined genius as "one percent inspiration and ninety-nine percent perspiration," and he proved his definition by working for days at a time, obsessed with his projects, stopping only for short catnaps. Failure never discouraged him. When about 10,000 experiments with a storage battery failed to produce results, a friend tried to console him. "Why, I have not failed," Edison said. "I've just found 10,000 ways that won't work."[1]

Date: _____ _____ _____

Place: _____ _____ _____

Occasion: _____ _____ _____

"I've Failed . . ."

W. A. Criswell was perhaps the best-known pastor in the world during his long tenure at the First Baptist Church of Dallas, Texas. His sermons, personal efforts, and multiple books have been the means of winning untold numbers to Christ.

But in Criswell's biography, author Billy Keith tells an interesting story about the man who led Criswell to the Lord. It was when W. A. was ten years old, and Rev. John Hicks came to his small Texas town to conduct a revival meeting. Hicks stayed in the Criswell home during his two-week campaign. Young W. A. was greatly taken with John Hicks, and one day he asked permission to leave school to attend the 10 o'clock service at the church. Entering the chapel, he sat directly behind his mother and drank in every word that Hicks spoke. When Hicks gave the invitation, the lad went forward and, with tears, took Jesus Christ as his Savior.

Years later, when Criswell was a world-renowned pastor, he recounted his conversion to a friend of his, Wallace Basset.

"Would you repeat that, W. A.?" Basset asked.

He repeated the story.

"I just can't imagine that," Basset said. "Johnny Hicks was a dear friend of mine, and he was here in Baylor Hospital in his last illness of which he died. I went often to see Johnny and one day as I sat beside him, he said, 'Wallace, my life is over, my preaching days are done, and I've never done anything for Jesus. I've failed, Wallace, I've failed.'"

---

[1] Clipping in my files.

Those were the last words the old preacher ever spoke. He didn't realize how successful he had been in just that one conversion.[1]

Date:			
Place:			
Occasion:			

A Wing and a Prayer

In the book, *A Home Forum Reader,* Glenn Wasson related a simple experience that had a profound effect on him. He had been clearing brush in the mountains for several hours when he took a lunch break, sat on a log, and bit into his sandwich. The scenery was beautiful—by a rushing stream, woods all around him, a canyon close by.

But his contemplations were broken by a persistent bee that started tormenting him, buzzing around his head, its stinger threatening. Glenn waved it off, but it returned. This time he swatted it to the ground and stepped on it. But to his amazement, the bee emerged from the sand to renew its attack.

This time Glenn ground the insect into the sand, bringing all his 210 pounds to bear. The deed being done, he returned to his log to resume his lunch. But eventually the corner of his eye noticed movement in the sand near his feet. The bee was dragging itself back into the land of the living.

Glenn, intrigued, bent over to watch. The bee's right wing seemed all right, but the left one was "crumpled like a piece of paper." Nonetheless, the bee stretched and tried his wing, moving it slowly up and down. It ran its legs along the length of the damaged wing, trying to straighten it. At the same time, the bee groomed and doctored itself as well as it could, trying to recover from the disaster.

Finally it tried using its wing, but the left one seemed hopelessly crippled.

Glenn knelt in the sand and bent over for a closer look. Being a veteran pilot, he knew a good deal about wings. He concluded that the bee would never fly again.

The bee, however, had other ideas, and it kept working with its wing, furiously trying to press out the crinkled spots, stretch out the torn spots, and increase the tempo of its fluttering. As Glenn, still on his knees, watched, the bee attempted to fly. It managed an elevation of three inches before crashing back to earth. Undeterred, it tried again, and again. Each effort was a little more successful, though sometimes the bee would fly erratically this way or that. At last, the bee took off, buzzed over the stream, and was gone.

"As the bee disappeared," Glenn later wrote, "I realized that I was still on my knees, and I remained on my knees for some time."[2]

> ◆
> **Definition of
> Discouragement**
>
> *The result of failing a test
> that we know God brought
> into our lives.*
> *(Proverbs 19:3)*
> —BILL GOTHARD
> ◆

---

[1] Billy Keith, *W. A. Criswell* (Old Tappan, NJ: Fleming H. Revell Co., 1973), 21, 124.
[2] "A Wing and a Prayer," *Reader's Digest.*

Date: _____ _____ _____

Place: _____ _____ _____

Occasion: _____ _____ _____

Discouragement in Ministry

Someone Once Said . . .

- *Discouragement is the occupational hazard of the Christian ministry.*—John Stott[1]
- *Could we but see the smallest fruit, we could rejoice midst the privation and toils which we bear, but, as it is, our hands do often hang down.*—Mary Moffat, missionary[2]
- *If I should write of the heavy burden of a godly preacher, which he must carry and endure, as I know from my own experience, I would scare every man from the office of preaching.*—Martin Luther[3]
- *Sometimes I am quite dejected when I see the impenetrability of the heart of those with us. They hear us preach on the Lord's Day, but we are forced to witness their disregard to God all through the week.*—William Carey, of his fellow passengers aboard the ship taking him to India[4]
- *Every day, almost every hour, the consciousness of failure and sin oppressed me.*—J. Hudson Taylor[5]
- *Discouragement . . . creeps over my heart and makes me go with heaviness to my work. . . . It is dreadfully weakening.*—Charles H. Spurgeon[6]
- *There may be long seasons of darkness [in ministry]—the chariot wheels of God's Gospel may seem to drag heavily, but here is the promise and yonder is the throne, and when omniscience has lost its eyesight, and omnipotence falls back impotent, and Jehovah is driven from His throne, then the Church of Jesus Christ can afford to be despondent, but never until then.*—T. DeWitt Talmage[7]
- *It has been my experience in working with many ministers, Christian workers, and their families that not only is depression the most common emotional problem, but it is also the most destructive.*—Archibald Hart[8]
- *The belief that your actions will be futile.*—Martin Seligman, psychologist, giving the underlying cause of depression[9]
- *Remember you are only accountable for your labor, and not for your success. So still toil on!*—Charles Haddon Spurgeon[10]

---

[1] Kevin A. Miller, *Secrets of Staying Power* (Waco: Word Books, 1988), 9.

[2] Ruth Tucker, *From Jerusalem to Irian Jaya* (Grand Rapids: Zondervan, 1983), 145.

[3] Martin Luther, *The Table Talk of Martin Luther,* ed. Thomas S. Kepler (Grand Rapids: Baker Book House, 1952), 245.

[4] Mary Drewery, *William Carey: A Biography* (Chicago: Moody Press, 1978), 57.

[5] Tucker, *From Jerusalem to Irian Jaya,* 182.

[6] Charles Haddon Spurgeon, *Messages of Hope and Faith* (Cleveland, Ohio: Publish House of the Evangelical Association, n.d.).

[7] John Rusk, *The Authentic Life of T. DeWitt Talmage* (n.c.: L. G. Stahl, 1902), 370–371.

[8] "Review of *Coping With Depression in the Ministry and Other Helping Professions,*" *Leadership Journal,* Fall 1984, 55.

[9] Martin E. P. Seligman, *Learned Optimism* (New York: Alfred A. Knopf, 1990), 70.

[10] Charles Haddon Spurgeon, *Spurgeon's Sermons,* vol. 2 (Grand Rapids, Mich: Baker Book House, 1983), 238.

- Be steadfast, immovable, always abounding in the work of the Lord, knowing that your labor is not in vain in the Lord.—1 Corinthians 15:58
- Discouragement is not in the dictionary of the kingdom of Heaven.—Melinda Rankin, first Protestant missionary to Mexico[1]

Date: _____ _____ _____
Place: _____ _____ _____
Occasion: _____ _____ _____

John Calvin's Discouragements

John Calvin was not immune to discouragement. Here are some of his observations:

- Today hardly one in a hundred considers how difficult and arduous it is faithfully to discharge the office of pastor.
- The crushing effect of a general though false consensus against us is a hard temptation and one almost impossible to resist.
- I am entangled in so many troublesome affairs that I am almost beside myself.
- You can scarcely believe what a burden of troublesome business I am weighed down and oppressed by here.
- In addition to the immense troubles by which I am so sorely consumed, there is almost no day on which some new pain or anxiety does not come.
- The wisest servants of God sometimes weaken in the middle of the course, especially when the road is rough and obstructed and the way more painful than expected. How much more, then, should we ask God that he never withdraw the aid of his power among the various conflicts that harass us, but rather that he instill us continually with new strength in proportion to the violence of our conflicts.[2]

Date: _____ _____ _____
Place: _____ _____ _____
Occasion: _____ _____ _____

William Carey's Discouragement

Few Christian workers have ever been so overwhelmed as William Carey, the "Father of Modern Missions," during his first years in India. Everything seemed against him. His wife, who had never wanted to come to India to begin with, was hostile and sinking into insanity. His four children were continually contracting tropical diseases. His coworker, John Thomas, squandered all their money, leaving Carey virtually destitute. The local authorities opposed him, and there was no fruit to show for his attempts to preach and evangelize. He spouted his anger and frustra-

---

[1] Julia H. Johnston, *Fifty Missionary Heroes* (New York: Fleming H. Revell, 1913), 136.
[2] William J. Bouwsma, *John Calvin: A Sixteenth Century Portrait* (New York: Oxford University Press, 1988), 26–27.

tion into his journal, and there, too, he verbalized his trust in God. One entry during those early months read:

When I first left England, my hope of the conversion of the heathen was very strong, but among so many obstacles, it would entirely die away, unless upheld by God. Nothing to exercise it, but plenty to obstruct it, for now a year and nineteen days, which is the space since I left my dear charge [church] at Leicester. Since that I have had hurrying up and down; a five months' imprisonment with carnal men on board the ship; five more learning the language; my colleague separated from me; long delays and few opportunities; no earthly thing to depend on, or earthly comfort, except food and raiment. Well, I have God, and His word is sure.[1]

Date:			
Place:			
Occasion:			

The Man Who Overcame Discouragement

The beginnings of Sudan Interior Mission (SIM) were marked by failure, discouragement, death, and despair. Yet one man, Rowland Bingham, would not give up. In 1893, Bingham along with Walter Gowans and Thomas Kent arrived in Lagos with a passion to evangelize Sub-Saharan Africa. But they were told, "Young men, you will never see the Sudan; your children will never see the Sudan; your grandchildren may." They nevertheless began an 800-mile trek into the interior, but in less than a year Gowans and Kent were both dead. Bingham returned to England, stunned and uncertain. "My faith was being shaken to the very foundation," he later wrote. "Why should those most anxious to carry out the Lord's commands and to give His gospel to millions in darkness be cut off right at the beginning of their career? Many questions faced me."

> **No Christian Despondency**
>
> *When omniscience has lost its eyesight, and omnipotence falls back impotent . . . then the Church of Jesus Christ can afford to be despondent, but never until then.*
>
> —T. DeWITT TALMAGE

Seven years passed, but eventually Rowland Bingham established the Sudan Interior Mission, and in 1900 he once again started for Africa. This time he was stopped by a life-threatening bout of malaria. His companions, daunted, sailed back home, and Rowland himself had no choice but to return to England.

It would have been easier for me, perhaps, had I died in Africa, for on the homeward journey I died another death. Everything seemed to have failed. . . . I went through the darkest period of my whole life.

But he wouldn't give up. In 1901, he made his third attempt. This one was more successful, and it resulted in the first SIM station in Africa.

Today SIM is an international mission organization with more than 1,800 missionaries serving in more than forty-three countries on five continents and three islands in the Indian Ocean.[2]

---

[1] Mary Drewery, *William Carey: A Biography* (Chicago: Moody Press, 1978), 74
[2] Tucker, *From Jerusalem to Irian Jaya*, 295–300.

Date: _____ _____ _____
Place: _____ _____ _____
Occasion: _____ _____ _____

D

Not One Convert

Allen Francis Gardiner grew up in a Christian home, took to the sea, and achieved a successful British naval career with little thought for God. But in 1822, he fell ill and reevaluated his life. He scribbled in his journal: *After years of ingratitude, unbelief, blasphemy and rebellion, have I at last been melted? Alas, how slow, how reluctant I have been to admit the heavenly guest who stood knocking without!*

Traveling around the world had given Captain Gardiner a glimpse of the need for missionaries, and he gave himself for the task. Leaving England for South America, he hoped to minister among the Araucanian (or Mapuche) Indians of Southern Chile. Government interference and intertribal fighting forced him back to England. Three years later he was at it again, visiting the Falklands and investigating the possibility of taking the gospel to the islands of Patagonia and Tierra del Fuego. Sensing opportunity at hand, Gardiner returned to England and on July 4, 1844, established a small organization called the Patagonian Missionary Society. He wrote, *I have made up my mind to go back to South America and leave no stone unturned, no effort untried, to establish a mission among the aboriginal tribes. While God gives me strength, failure will not daunt me.*

Gardiner visited South America a third time, but his efforts were again thwarted by intertribal fighting and governmental interference, the land being strongly Catholic, intolerant to Protestant missions. He returned to England, recruited six missionaries, and set sail for Tierra del Fuego. But all seven men died of disease, starvation, and exposure on Picton Island. Gardiner, the last to die, dated his final journal entry September 5, 1851: *Good and marvelous are the loving kindnesses of my gracious God unto me. He has preserved me hitherto and for four days, although without bodily food, without any feelings of hunger or thirst.*

Captain Allen Gardiner died without seeing a single soul saved among those for whom he was most burdened. But he lit a fire which has never gone out. His South American Missionary Society (as it came to be called) has been sending missionaries and saving souls for over 150 years.[1]

Date: _____ _____ _____
Place: _____ _____ _____
Occasion: _____ _____ _____

Words on a Blackboard

Jonathan and Rosalind Goforth were among the most effective missionaries to China during the late 1800s and early 1900s. But their early ministry showed little promise, and Rosalind nearly gave up. In her book, *Climbing*, she writes:

---

[1] Robert J. Morgan, *On This Day* (Nashville: Thomas Nelson Publishers, 1997), September 5th.

Those very earliest days and weeks at Changte were indeed times of testing. Often it seemed, at least to me, all useless, hopeless, like casting bread upon the waters. But one little thing helped me more than I could ever tell. I had a Chinese carpenter make a good sized blackboard. It was really intended for the children, for the drawing of letters, pictures, and so on. One day when feeling discouraged and in need of help I opened my Bible and was led (I know) to 2 Corinthians 9:6: "He who sows sparingly will also reap sparingly, and he who sows bountifully will also reap bountifully." So impressed was I with the latter clause that I went to the blackboard and printed in large letters, high up out of the children's reach, the words:

HE WHO SOWS BOUNTIFULLY
WILL ALSO REAP BOUNTIFULLY

For more than two years, until our new home was built, this promise remained constantly before me, an ever-present incentive to sow bountifully the gospel seed, as I have endeavored to picture it, even though it often seemed the seed was being cast on stony ground. The day came, however, when my husband and I were permitted to see bountiful harvests of souls reaped for our Master in that region.[1]

Date:			
Place:			
Occasion:			

Work by Faith

In an article written for the newsletter *Prokope*, Warren Wiersbe wrote: *Ministers are human beings, made of dust, subject to the same forces that discourage and destroy the men and women who sit in the pews. For some reason, many church members have the idea that their pastor is exempt from personal pressures and problems—or that he has a secret system for overcoming the difficulties of life and ministry. He does not.*

Wiersbe goes on to list several things that most discourage ministers:

- Unreachable Goals
- Unmanageable Schedules
- Uncomfortable Situations
- Unbearable Problems

George Morrison has said, continues Wiersbe, *that God rarely allows His servants to see how much good they are doing, so you will have to work by faith and leave the results to Him. We'll get the report and the reward when we stand before Him in glory, not one minute before. Meanwhile, let's not permit these four "frustration factors" to add to our burdens and rob us of joy and power in our ministry.*[2]

Date:			
Place:			
Occasion:			

---

[1] Rosalind Goforth, *Climbing* (Wheaton, IL: Sword Book Club, 1946), 52–53.
[2] Warren W. Wiersbe, "Formula for Frustration," *Prokope*, May-June 1987, 1–2.

"The Minister's Fainting Fits"

Charles Spurgeon devoted a chapter ("The Minister's Fainting Fits") about ministerial discouragement in his *Lectures to My Students*. He said: *Knowing by most painful experience what deep depression of spirit means, being visited therewith at seasons by no means few or far between, I thought it might be consolatory to some of my brethren if I gave my thoughts thereon, that young men might not fancy that some strange thing had happened to them when they become for a season possessed by melancholy.*

Spurgeon goes on to list several reasons for discouragement in ministry, including:

- We are mere humans and, as such, compassed with infirmity and heirs of sorrow.
- Most of us are in some way or other physically unsound.
- Our work, when earnestly undertaken, lays us open to attacks in the direction of depression. Who can bear the weight of souls without sometimes sinking to the dust?
- Our position in the church gives a sense of loneliness and isolation.
- There can be little doubt that sedentary habits have a tendency to create despondency.

The great preacher went on to warn that discouragement can hit us in the hour of our greatest success, before any great achievement, in the midst of a long stretch of unbroken labor, or when suddenly hit by "one crushing stroke."

What should we do? *Be not dismayed by soul-trouble. Count it no strange thing, but a part of ordinary ministerial experience. . . . Cast the burden of the present, along with the sin of the past and the fear of the future, upon the Lord, who forsaketh not His saints. Live by the day—aye, by the hour. Put no trust in frames and feelings. . . . Continue with double earnestness to serve the Lord when no visible result is before you.*

Come fair or come foul, the pulpit is our watchtower and the ministry our warfare; be it ours, when we cannot see the face of our God, to trust under the shadow of His wings.[1]

Date: _____   _____   _____
Place: _____   _____   _____
Occasion: _____   _____   _____

Sign on a Minister's Desk

An anonymous pastor wrote the following: *In the first five years of my ministry, I had a sign on my desk that read, "Win the World for Christ!" In my second five years of ministry, I put up a new sign that read, "Win One or Two for Christ!" Since that time I have this sign on my desk: "Try Not to Lose Too Many!"*[2]

Date: _____   _____   _____
Place: _____   _____   _____
Occasion: _____   _____   _____

[1] Charles Haddon Spurgeon, *Lectures to My Students* (Grand Rapids: Zondervan, 1972), ch. 11.
[2] Paul W. Thomton, *Leadership Journal*, Winter 1985, 117.

Divorce

Someone Once Said . . .

- *There are no winners when a marriage begins to unravel.*—James Dobson[1]
- *In every marriage more than a week old, there are grounds for divorce. The trick is to find, and continue to find, grounds for marriage.*—Robert Anderson[2]
- *Commitment is not a cage; it is a safety net.*—William Coleman[3]
- *I have married hundreds of couples and counseled hundreds of others, and I have never yet known a marriage to fail where the couples had—or had acquired—the habit of praying aloud together.*—Norman Vincent Peale[4]
- *Each divorce is the death of a small civilization.*—Pat Conroy[5]
- *"I hate divorce," says the Lord God of Israel.*—Malachi 2:16 (NIV)

Date: _____ _____ _____

Place: _____ _____ _____

Occasion: _____ _____ _____

Elton Trueblood's Thoughts:

In an almost prophetic book written at the end of World War II, Elton Trueblood anticipated the decline of American society that would take place during the remaining half of the twentieth century. Here is what he said about divorce:

Divorce, though sometimes justified, must always be looked upon as failure. A divorced couple must see that they have failed in the most important undertaking of their lives. Divorce may sometimes be the lesser of two evils, but in any case it is evil, and we dare never look upon it with complacency. In short, if our society is to be strong and the lives of our children protected, the marriage vow must be taken with complete seriousness. It must become a matter of conviction. It is interesting to note that there is some progress in the Bible in regard to divorce, but that the movement is not, as we might suppose, toward greater looseness; it is a movement toward greater strictness.[6]

Date: _____ _____ _____

Place: _____ _____ _____

Occasion: _____ _____ _____

Not All That Well

When Joseph Stowell, president of Moody Bible Institute, was ministering in the Ukraine, a church leader there asked him this question over dinner: "What do

---

[1] *Focus on the Family Newsletter,* June 1991, 1.

[2] Alan Loy McGinnis, *The Power of Optimism* (New York: Harper & Row, 1990), 113.

[3] William Coleman, *What Makes a Marriage Last* (San Bernardino, CA: Here's Life Publishers, 1990), 25.

[4] Clipped from my files, from an article that originally appeared in *Readers' Digest.*

[5] *Focus on the Family Newsletter,* June 1991, 1.

[6] Elton Trueblood, *Foundations for Reconstruction* (New York: Harper & Brothers, 1946). 78.

you believe about divorce and remarriage, and how does the church in America handle it?"

The honest response from Stowell's heart was, "We don't handle it all that well."[1]

Date: _____   _____   _____

Place: _____   _____   _____

Occasion: _____   _____   _____

Stowell's Advice

One of the most balanced treatments of divorce comes from the pen of Joseph Stowell, president of Moody Bible Institute. Admitting that he has struggled mightily on how to apply the Bible's teachings on this subject, he wrote, *Frankly, at times I have wished that God had written one more chapter in the Bible detailing the proper application point by point. But He has not. Instead, He desires that we study diligently and prayerfully, seeking both wisdom and compassion.*

Diverse Families

Fifty years ago parents were apt to have a lot of kids. Nowadays kids are apt to have a lot of parents.

—ANONYMOUS

In summary, Stowell says we must *keep our commitment to strong families and still provide welcome and support to those who have been damaged by divorce.* This means maintaining a proper balance between grace and truth. *Grace that threatens truth is not grace at all,* he writes. *And truth apart from grace requires the impossible goal of perfection. God's nature combines grace and truth without compromising either. This is our challenge, too, if we are to display His character in our day when broken homes are so common. This means:*

- *Truth demands that the biblical teachings about marriage and divorce must never be lost or weakened. Family is God's first and foremost institution. It is true that God hates divorce and that the Bible emphasizes that marriage is an indissoluble contract between two people and a sacred commitment sanctioned by God and sealed by vows spoken in His name.*
- *Grace demands that we apply biblical requirements with tender compassion. Grace seeks to help. Grace is remedial. Grace finds godly, gifted people in the church to stand beside the victims of divorce, including the children. Grace recognizes that some who have experienced the wrenching trauma of divorce still have a heart for God and a desire to grow in Him.*

It is a difficult issue, admits Stowell, *but in today's world it is a vitally important issue. We can find the solution only in an uncompromised combination of that divine blend of grace and truth.*[2]

Date: _____   _____   _____

Place: _____   _____   _____

Occasion: _____   _____   _____

---

[1] Joseph M. Stowell, "The Divorce Dilemma," *Moody Magazine,* November 1991, 15.
[2] Joseph M. Stowell, "The Divorce Dilemma," *Moody Magazine,* November 1991, 12–15.

Key Scriptures

Here are the Bible's major texts relating to the subject of divorce:

- Genesis 2:24
- Deuteronomy 24:1–4
- Malachi 2:11–16
- Matthew 5:31–32
- Matthew 19:3–9
- Mark 10:2–12
- Luke 16:18
- Romans 7:1–3
- 1 Corinthians 7:13–15

Date: _____ _____ _____

Place: _____ _____ _____

Occasion: _____ _____ _____

One Pastor's Advice

Gary Richmond, minister to single parents at a church in California, is often asked hard questions about divorce, such as "Is Divorce Ever Appropriate?" and "Am I sinning if I file for divorce?" Writing in *Focus on the Family*, he made some well-thought-through comments: *I tremble when I answer because I know, as a pastor, I am speaking on God's behalf.*

—◇—
Prayer and Marriage

I have never yet known a marriage to fail where the couples had—or had acquired—the habit of praying aloud together.
—NORMAN VINCENT PEALE
—◇—

What matters is what God thinks. He has promised His Holy Spirit to convict us of sin if we're sinning. A good rule concerning sin is: "When in doubt, don't." If there is a shred of doubt that you are violating God's will, then you will lose nothing by waiting to make the decision. You will certainly win God's approval, not to mention peace of mind. Don't make this decision quickly. Give God the time to move in your situation or make His will clear to you.

Now let me commit myself, realizing that no matter what I say I will have critics. I believe there are three legitimate causes for divorce:

- *Adultery*
- *Abuse (physical, to spouse or children)*
- *Abandonment*

I believe that persons whose mates have abandoned them, abused them or committed adultery would be permitted to divorce if they desired to do so.

You may ask, "Is there a Scripture substantiating your position that physical abuse is a legitimate reason to divorce your mate?" No direct Scripture exists, but consider . . . Ephesians 5:25–33. This passage allows no room for physical abuse. I believe Lewis Smedes spoke rightly when he said, "This is not to say that God approves of divorce; it is only to say that He sometimes disapproves of its alternatives more than he disapproves of divorce."[1]

---

[1] Gary Richmond, "When Families Break Up: The Human Toll," *Focus on the Family*, August 1989, 4.

Date: _____ _____ _____

Place: _____ _____ _____

Occasion: _____ _____ _____

Statistics

Nearly 1.2 million American marriages were dissolved by the courts in 1994—triple the 1960 figure. Experts predict that nearly half of all new marriages will end in divorce.[1]

Americans for Divorce Reform, Inc., of Arlington, Virginia, have compiled the following statistics regarding divorce in America:

1. There is consensus that the overall U.S. divorce rate had a brief spurt after World War II followed by a decline; then it started rising in the 1960s and even more quickly in the 1970s. It leveled off in the 1980s and has declined slightly since.
2. Defining what number the "Divorce Rate" is, however, is elusive and perhaps impossible. There are many different valid measurements. Probably forty or even fifty percent of marriages will end in divorce if current trends continue. But this is only a projection and does not reflect current reality or the recent past, and things certainly could turn out differently.
3. No-fault divorce laws were one of the principal causes of increasing divorce in the 1970s and since.
4. Divorce greatly increases two- or three-fold the incidence of all kinds of bad effects on children of divorce, including psychological problems, juvenile delinquency, suicide, under-education, and teen motherhood. Problems arise from conflict during and after divorce more than from conflict during the marriage, and there is an increased incidence of detriment even if the divorce is low-conflict. Problems persist into early adulthood and affect the marriage and mating choices of children of divorce.
5. Marriage is better than divorce or bachelorhood for the health, wealth, and happiness of adults of all ages and genders.
6. Pre-marital counseling helps reduce the risk of divorce somewhat and can prevent many bad marriages.[2]

Date: _____ _____ _____

Place: _____ _____ _____

Occasion: _____ _____ _____

Divorce Rate for Christians

According to Richard Fowler of the Minirth-Meier Counseling Clinic, the divorce rate for Christians is only ten percent below that for non-Christians.[3]

---

[1] *Los Angeles Times*, 27 May 1996, sec. A16.
[2] *Americans for Divorce Reform*, <www.divorcereform.org>
[3] H. Wayne House, "The Bible and Divorce: Three Views," *Discipleship Journal*, Issue 75, 33.

Date:	_____	_____	_____
Place:	_____	_____	_____
Occasion:	_____	_____	_____

Telling the Children

In his book, *Death of a Marriage,* Pat Conroy writes:

There are not metaphors powerful enough to describe the moment when you tell the children about the divorce. Divorces without children are minor-league divorces. To look into the eyes of your children and to tell them that you are mutilating their family and changing all their tomorrows is an act of desperate courage that I never want to repeat. It is also their parents' last act of solidarity and the absolute sign that the marriage is over. It felt as though I had doused my entire family with gasoline and struck a match.

Date:	_____	_____	_____
Place:	_____	_____	_____
Occasion:	_____	_____	_____

Bolting the Doors

Jill Briscoe, author, speaker, and pastor's wife, writes that one of the things her parents did right was to maintain their commitment to each other without ever considering divorce as an option. She writes, "My sister and I knew that Mom and Dad enjoyed being married, would stay married, and hoped we'd do the same. Differences they had were kept between them and worked out in the context of the promises they made to each other and to God on their wedding day. There was no option out! As someone has said, when the doors on a marriage are shut and bolted and a fire breaks out, all your time and energy goes to putting out the flames."[1]

Date:	_____	_____	_____
Place:	_____	_____	_____
Occasion:	_____	_____	_____

James Dobson's Parents

Marriage vows are inviolable, and by entering into them, I am binding myself absolutely for life. The idea of estrangement from you through divorce for any reason at all (although God allows one—infidelity) will never at any time enter into my thinking.—Commitment made by James Dobson, Sr., to his wife before their marriage, as quoted by their son, James Dobson, Jr.[2]

---

[1] Jill Briscoe, "A Foundation for Faith," *What My Parents Did Right,* comp. and ed. Gloria Gaither (Nashville: StarSong Publishing Group, 1991), 33.

[2] James Dobson, "A Lifetime of Friendship," *What My Parents Did Right,* comp. and ed. Gloria Gaither (Nashville: StarSong Publishing Group, 1991), 70–71.

Date:			
Place:			
Occasion:			

Incompatibility

On his April 2, 1979, radio broadcast, Paul Harvey, amazement in his voice, reported that Romeo Bitencourt of Porto Alegre, Brazil, had just been granted a divorce.

Romeo was a Brazilian farmer.

He was ninety years old, had been married sixty-five years, had twelve children, fifty grandchildren, and thirty-six great-grandchildren.

The reason given for the divorce?

"Incompatibility."

Date:			
Place:			
Occasion:			

———— Doctrine, Importance of ————

Somebody Once Said . . .

- *Great saints have always been dogmatic.*—A. W. Tozer[1]
- *There can be no spiritual health without doctrinal knowledge.*—J. I. Packer[2]
- *We cannot have the benefits of Christianity if we shed its doctrines.*—D. Martyn Lloyd-Jones[3]
- *The truth is, no preacher ever had any strong power that was not the preaching of doctrine.*—Phillips Brooks[4]
- *The time will come when they will not endure sound doctrine.*—2 Timothy 4:3
- *Contend earnestly for the faith. . . .*—Jude, verse 3

Date:			
Place:			
Occasion:			

More Quotes

- *Theology means "the science of God," and I think any man who wants to think about God at all would like to have the clearest and most accurate ideas about Him that are available.*—C. S. Lewis[5]

[1] A. W. Tozer, *A Treasury of A. W. Tozer* (Grand Rapids: Baker Book House, 1980), 174.
[2] J. I. Packer, *Knowing God* (Downers Grove, IL: InterVarsity Press, 1973), 17.
[3] D. Martyn Lloyd-Jones, *I Am Not Ashamed* (Grand Rapids: Baker Book House, 1986), 92.
[4] Phillips Brooks, *Lectures on Preaching* (Grand Rapids: Zondervan, n.d.), 129.
[5] C. S. Lewis, *Mere Christianity* (New York: The Macmillan Company, 1952), 119.

- *The West remembers enough about Christianity to feel guilty for its sins, but not enough to recall where forgiveness comes from.*—Dave Breese[1]

> Date: _____ _____ _____
> Place: _____ _____ _____
> Occasion: _____ _____ _____

What Joseph Parker Said

They may be old-fashioned doctrines, but they created missionary societies, Sunday schools, hospitals, orphanages, and refuges for penitence; they gave every child a new value, every father a new responsibility, every mother a new hope, and constituted human society into a new conscience and a new trust. We cannot first sneer at the doctrine and then claim its infinite beneficence, nor can we borrow its socialism that we may quench its inspiration. Let us be very careful how we give up trees that have borne such fruit, and in whose leaves there has been such healing.—Joseph Parker, London pastor (1830–1902)[2]

> Date: _____ _____ _____
> Place: _____ _____ _____
> Occasion: _____ _____ _____

What D. L. Moody Said

A man once said to Dwight L. Moody, "Sir, the doctrine you preach is absurd. You say that you only have to believe on Christ to change the entire course of your life and make sure of Heaven. In my opinion, that's ridiculous. I can't accept such a theory." Moody replied, "Let's see if I understand you. Are you contending that what a man believes won't change his course of action?" "That's right!" Moody continued, "Suppose a man should suddenly cry out right now that your house was on fire. If the flames leaped up and blocked your door, what would you do? If you believed that man, I'm sure you'd try to escape through that large open window, wouldn't you?" "Yes, but I didn't think about faith in that light!" "No, I guess you didn't," said the evangelist. "But that's what true believing will do every time—it will change your course of action!"[3]

Present Needs

The chief need of the present age is great theology.
—DR. LORAINE BOETTNER

> Date: _____ _____ _____
> Place: _____ _____ _____
> Occasion: _____ _____ _____

---

[1] Dave Breese, *Seven Men Who Rule the World From the Grave* (Chicago: Moody Press, 1990), 89.
[2] Joseph Parker, *A Preacher's Life: An Autobiography and an Album* (London: Hodder and Stoughton, n.d.), 99.
[3] Clipped from *Our Daily Bread.*

What A. W. Tozer Said

It would be impossible to overemphasize the importance of sound doctrine in the life of a Christian. Right thinking about all spiritual matters is imperative if we would have right living. As men do not gather grapes of thorns nor figs of thistles, so sound character does not grow out of unsound teaching.[1]

Date: _____ _____ _____
Place: _____ _____ _____
Occasion: _____ _____ _____

C. S. Lewis Said

In *Mere Christianity*, C. S. Lewis makes a great analogy. *Doctrines*, he says, *are like maps. They are not the reality and may not be as exciting as reality, but they chart reality for us in a vital way. Just as studying a map of the shore of the Atlantic is not as exciting as walking along the Atlantic coast itself, so studying the doctrine of atonement is not exactly the same as the experiencing the cross itself. But the purpose of a map is to represent, graph, and explain the reality. If you want to find your way, you need to have a reliable map, and we should consult it frequently.*[2]

Date: _____ _____ _____
Place: _____ _____ _____
Occasion: _____ _____ _____

What Vance Havner Said

When we have room enough for any and every brand of doctrine, that's too much room. Can the same fountain send forth both bitter water and sweet? Can two walk together unless they be agreed? One scholar says that the early Christians condemned false doctrine in a way that sounds almost unchristian today.[3]

Date: _____ _____ _____
Place: _____ _____ _____
Occasion: _____ _____ _____

Doubt

Someone Once Said . . .

- *Believe your beliefs and doubt your doubts.*—Anonymous
- *Every other crime touches God's territory, but unbelief aims a blow at his divinity, impeaches his veracity, denies his goodness, blasphemes his attributes, maligns his character;*

---

[1] Tozer, *A Treasury of A. W. Tozer*, 174.
[2] Lewis, *Mere Christianity*, 119–120.
[3] Vance Havner, *Just a Preacher* (Chicago: Moody Press, 1981), 121.

therefore, God, of all things, hates first and chiefly, unbelief, wherever it is.—Charles Haddon Spurgeon[1]

Date: _____ _____ _____
Place: _____ _____ _____
Occasion: _____ _____ _____

Side by Side

G. Campbell Morgan had grown up in a Christian home, never questioning that the Bible was the Word of God. But in college, his faith was severely challenged, and he began to entertain doubts. "The whole intellectual world was under the mastery of the physical scientists," he later said, "and of a materialistic and rationalistic philosophy. Darwin, Huxley, Tyndall, Spencer, Bain. There came a moment when I was sure of nothing."

Date: _____ _____ _____
Place: _____ _____ _____
Occasion: _____ _____ _____

Pyrrho

Pyrrho of Elis, Greece, was a young man who, joining the forces of Alexander of Macedon, journeyed through places like Egypt, Babylon, Persia, and India. During his travels his ponderings led him to conclusions that produced the Greek philosophical school of Skepticism.

Pyrrho maintained that no knowledge could be known for certain, whether scientific, moral, religious or metaphysical. On all questions of truth, we must suspend judgment, which will lead us, according to Pyrrho, to a state of mind known as Ataraxia—a complete calmness of the soul.

This philosopher is remembered as the ultimate anxious doubter who was not sure of anything, who did not know anything, and was not sure he did not know—who even doubted whether the world itself were not an illusion, and whose friends accompanied him in his walks lest he should doubt the reality of a precipice and walk over its edge to his own ruin.

This is the man whose shadow falls over our dark and doubting age.

Date: _____ _____ _____
Place: _____ _____ _____
Occasion: _____ _____ _____

C. S. Lewis on Doubt

Now Faith . . . is the art of holding on to things your reason has once accepted, in spite of your changing moods. For moods will change, whatever view your reason takes. I know that by

---

[1] Charles Haddon Spurgeon, *Spurgeon's Sermons*, vol. 2 (Grand Rapids: Baker Book House, 1983), 61.

experience. Now that I am a Christian I do have moods in which the whole thing looks very improbable: but when I was an atheist I had moods in which Christianity looked terribly probable. This rebellion of your moods against your real self is going to come anyway. That is why Faith is such a necessary virtue: unless you teach your moods "where they get off," you can never be either a sound Christian or even a sound atheist, but just a creature dithering to and fro, with its beliefs really dependent on the weather and the state of its digestion.[1]

D

Date: _____ _____ _____
Place: _____ _____ _____
Occasion: _____ _____ _____

Henry Drummond on Doubt

In 1887, Henry Drummond preached a sermon in Northfield, Massachusetts, entitled *Dealing With Doubt.* Here is one of his observations:

Christ never failed to distinguish between doubt and unbelief. Doubt is can't *believe; unbelief is* won't *believe. Doubt is honest; unbelief is obstinacy. Doubt is looking for light; unbelief is content with darkness. Loving darkness rather than light—that is what Christ attacked and attacked unsparingly. But for the intellectual questioning of Thomas, and Philip, and Nicodemus, and the many others who came to Him to have their great problems solved, He was respectful and generous and tolerant.*

But how did He meet their doubts? The church, as I have said, says "Brand him!" Christ said, "Teach him."

When Thomas came to Him, denied His very resurrection, and stood before Him waiting for the scathing words and lashing for his unbelief, they never came. They never came. Christ gave him fact—facts.[2]

Date: _____ _____ _____
Place: _____ _____ _____
Occasion: _____ _____ _____

Martyn Lloyd-Jones on Doubt

In his book, *Spiritual Depression,* Martyn Lloyd-Jones writes: *Doubts are not incompatible with faith. . . .*

Some people seem to think that once you become a Christian you should never be assailed by doubts. But that is not so, Peter still had faith (as he panicked in the storm in Matthew 14). . . . His faith was not gone, but because it was weak, doubt mastered him and overwhelmed him and he was shaken. . . .

Doubts will attack us, but that does not mean that we are to allow them to master us.[3]

[1] C. S. Lewis, *Mere Christianity* (New York: Macmillan Co., 1952), 109.
[2] Warren W. Wiersbe, *Listening to the Giants* (Grand Rapids: Baker Book House, 1980), 115–116.
[3] D. Martyn Lloyd-Jones, *Spiritual Depression* (Grand Rapids: Eerdmans, 1965), 154.

Date: _____ _____ _____

Place: _____ _____ _____

Occasion: _____ _____ _____

Dying to Self

Someone Once Said . . .

- *When James Calvert went out as a missionary to the cannibals of the Fiji Islands, the captain of the ship sought to turn him back. "You will lose your life and the lives of those with you if you go among such savages," he cried. Calvert only replied, "We died before we came here."*—David Augsburger[1]
- *There came a day when George Mueller died, utterly died! No longer did his own desires, preferences, and tastes come first. He know that from then on Christ must be all in all.*— George Mueller, when asked the secret of his victorious Christian life
- *A communist is a dead man on furlough.*—Vladimir Lenin
- *We dye to live, we live to dye; the more we dye, the more we live; and the more we live, the more we dye.*—sign in the window of a dry-cleaning and dyeing business

Date: _____ _____ _____

Place: _____ _____ _____

Occasion: _____ _____ _____

Bonhoeffer

Dietrich Bonhoeffer recognized the evil of Adolf Hitler and the Nazi movement from the beginning, even in the early days of the movement when most of the Protestants in Germany were Hitler supporters. As a result, he found himself unpopular, even with other Christians. As restrictions and then persecutions came in waves upon European Jews, Bonhoeffer cried against it and warned the church and the German people of the emerging evil. But no one listened. Finding himself in danger, he fled to America, but he felt all the while that his place was with the believers in Germany, and in the early 1940s he returned to the fatherland, only to be arrested and taken to the extermination camp at Flossenburg, where he was stripped and hanged at age thirty-nine.

Bonhoeffer had to make the ultimate sacrifice with inner tranquillity and resignation because of his conviction that there are five different deaths every Christian should die:

1. Death to Natural Relationships. During the days of the Third Reich, many pastors said that they would be willing to endure imprisonment or death, but they could not do so because of their families. It is one thing for a

---

[1] Charles W. Colson, *Life Sentence* (Minneapolis: World Wide Publications, 1979), 154.

husband or a father to be persecuted; it is quite another to see children suffer a similar fate. Hitler always used a man's family as an inducement for absolute obedience. Bonhoeffer answered that our commitment to Christ should be so all-consuming that all natural affection must come under its authority. (Matthew 10:37)

2. Death to success. Bonhoeffer said, "Success is a veneer that covers only the emptiness of the soul."
3. Death to the flesh. The Christian should have no fear of suffering, for he is already dead to self.
4. Death to the love of money.
5. Physical death for Christ, should a person be thus called.[1]

Date: _____ _____ _____
Place: _____ _____ _____
Occasion: _____ _____ _____

The Supreme Weapon

Joseph Tson, the evangelical dissident in Communist Romania, was often summoned before government officers who used every tactic to break his faith in Christ. Once, being interrogated at Ploiesti, an officer threatened to kill him.

God's Calling

When God calls a man, he bids him come and die.
—DIETRICH BONHOEFFER

"Sir," replied Tson, "let me explain how I see this issue. Your supreme weapon is killing. My supreme weapon is dying.

"Here is how it works. You know that my sermons on tape have spread all over the country. If you kill me, those sermons will be sprinkled with my blood. Everyone will know I died for my preaching. And everyone who has a tape will pick it up and say, 'I'd better listen again to what this man preached, because he really meant it; he sealed it with his life.'

"So, sir, my sermons will speak ten times louder than before. I will actually rejoice in this supreme victory if you kill me."

The officer sent Tson home.[2]

Date: _____ _____ _____
Place: _____ _____ _____
Occasion: _____ _____ _____

What Can You Do with a Man Like That?

When the fifth-century bishop of Constantinople, Chrysostom, was driven from the city into exile, he wrote a friend, *When I was driven from the city, I felt no anxiety, but said to myself, "If the empress wishes to banish me, let her do so; the earth is the Lord's. If*

---

[1] Erwin W. Lutzer, *Hitler's Cross* (Chicago: Moody Press, 1995), 182–186.
[2] Josef Tson, "Thank You for the Beating," *Christian Herald*, April 1988.

she wants to have me sawn asunder, I have Isaiah for an example. If she wants me to be drowned in the ocean, I think of Jonah. If I am to be thrown into the fire, the three men in the furnace suffered the same. If cast before wild beasts, I remember Daniel in the lions' den. If she wants me to be stoned, I have before me Stephen, the first martyr. If she demands my head, let her do so; John the Baptist shines before me. Naked I came from my mother's womb; naked shall I leave this world."

Date: _____ _____ _____
Place: _____ _____ _____
Occasion: _____ _____ _____

"I Am Willing"

Chet Bitterman, graduate of Columbia Bible College in Columbia, South Carolina, entered Colombia, South America with his wife and daughters to translate the Bible into the Carijona language. He was kidnapped by terrorists on January 19, 1981, and seven weeks later shot dead, a single bullet to the chest.

Eight months before entering Colombia, he penned this in his journal: *Maybe this is just some kind of self-inflicted martyr complex, but I find this recurring thought that perhaps God will call me to be martyred for Him in his service in Colombia. I am willing.*

Date: _____ _____ _____
Place: _____ _____ _____
Occasion: _____ _____ _____

Easter

Someone Once Said . . .

- *The bodily resurrection of Jesus Christ from the dead is the crowning proof of Christianity. If the resurrection did not take place, then Christianity is a false religion. If it did take place, then Christ is God and the Christian faith is absolute truth.*—Henry Morris[1]
- *It is fitting that a supernatural person should enter and leave the earth in a supernatural way. This is in fact what the New Testament teaches and the Church believes. His birth was natural, but His conception was supernatural. His death was natural, but His resurrection was supernatural.*—John Stott[2]

Date: _____ _____ _____
Place: _____ _____ _____
Occasion: _____ _____ _____

---

[1] Henry M. Morris, *Many Infallible Proofs* (San Diego: CLP Publishers, 1974), 88.
[2] John R. W. Stott, *Basic Christianity* (Grand Rapids: Eerdman's Publishing Company, 1958), 45.

Easter Is Coming

During morning worship on Palm Sunday, 1994, a tornado struck the Goshen United Methodist Church in Piedmont, Alabama. It happened during a dramatic presentation. The electricity failed, and the congregation was trying to get along without its sound system. A window broke, people screamed, and the building exploded, injuring scores of members and killing twenty. Among the fatalities was Hannah Clem, four-year-old daughter of Pastor Kelly Clem.

The night after the tragedy, Kelly was trying to sleep, tossing and turning through the pain of her own injuries. An unusual dream came to her. She saw herself trying to lift bricks and toss them aside, clearing away rubble, trying to rescue the victims. She kept doing the same thing over and over. Everything was gray and dull. But as her dream progressed, she stepped back from the scene and saw right in the spot where Hannah had been buried, children, dressed in beautiful, bright colors. They seemed oblivious to the onlookers, and were playing and laughing with each other. They were standing on grass of the greenest green. When Kelly awoke, a peace settled over her and strengthened her for the funerals ahead.

The next day, a reporter asked Kelly if the disaster had shattered her faith. "It hasn't shattered my faith," she replied. "I'm holding on to my faith. It's holding me. All of the people of Goshen are holding on to each other, along with the hope they will be able to rebuild. Easter is coming."[1]

Date: _____ _____ _____
Place: _____ _____ _____
Occasion: _____ _____ _____

Black Easter

Nearly a thousand missionary personnel for the China Inland Mission (CIM) were trapped in China when the Communists took over in the 1940s. CIM ordered a total evacuation in January, 1951, but was it too late? Communists are not adverse to killing.

Arthur and Wilda Mathews applied for exit visas on January 3. Their living conditions had deteriorated to a bare kitchen where, in the corner, Wilda had converted a footlocker into a prayer nook. Days passed with no action on their requests. Meanwhile, citizens were executed every day, and from her kitchen Wilda could hear the shots. The strain grew unbearable. "The imagination is what jumps around into all sorts of places it ought to keep out of," Arthur wrote to his parents.

He was told at last that his wife and child could leave if he would secretly work for the Communists. Arthur refused. Day after day he was summoned and grilled. Day after day he said good-bye to Wilda, wondering if he would ever see her again. Finally Arthur bluntly told the authorities, "I am not a Judas. If you expect me or anyone else in the China Inland Mission to do that kind of thing, you had better not try because we cannot do it."

---

[1] Adapted from Dale Clem, "Winds of Fury, Glimpses of Grace," *Christian Reader*, May/June 1998, 88–100.

Wilda was utterly overcome by fear and doubt. Sunday, March 21, 1951, was, as she called it later, Black Easter. Wilda sneaked into an Easter church service, but when she opened her mouth to sing "He Lives!" no words came out. Returning home, she fell at the trunk and her trembling fingers found 2 Chronicles 20:17: *You will not need to fight in this battle. Position yourselves, stand still and see the salvation of the Lord, who is with you . . . Do not fear or be dismayed. . . .* Wilda clamped onto that verse, and two weeks later she wrote, "The conflict has been terrible, but peace and quiet reign now."

It was two years before she exited the country, and even longer for Arthur who became the last CIM missionary to leave China. But miraculously, all of them got out without a single one being martyred. It was the greatest exodus in missionary history.[1]

Date:			
Place:			
Occasion:			

The Church Behind Bars

Chuck Colson, exhausted from an over-booked schedule, arrived in rain and fog at a prison in remote Montana on the day before Easter, 1988. He was to speak at two services that morning, and the first went badly.

———◇———
Easter Ministry

Easter is the truth that turns a church from a museum into a ministry.
—WARREN WIERSBE
———◇———

Dog-tired and dry, his preaching lacked enthusiasm, and he sensed that he wasn't reaching the men at all. Between services, he went to the chaplain's office, sank to his knees beside the desk, and earnestly asked the Lord to take away his frustration, exhaustion, and despair. But as he rose from his knees, he felt no different and was too tired to greet the inmates as they began assembling. Waiting as long as possible to enter the service, he was surprised to find the room packed. As he took his seat, one of the inmates rose to give a testimony.

"Ten years ago when Chuck Colson came to this prison," the man said, "I was in my cell. I had no intention of coming to the chapel to hear him. I knew he was a phony, and I wanted nothing to do with Christianity. But everyone in the prison seemed to be talking about the visit. The governor was coming with Colson, as well as a lot of television and newspaper reporters. *If Colson can get the governor to come to prison,* I thought, *I might as well see what he is all about.*"

Then the man turned to Colson and said, "I listened to you preach, and I was impressed, but I wasn't buying it. When the meeting ended, I headed for the door. Somehow you were there before me, and you cut me off at the pass. You looked right at me and asked, 'Do you know Jesus Christ as your Savior?' I looked back at you and said, 'No.'

"I'll never forget—" the man continued. "You looked me straight in the eye and said, 'Well, why are you here, then? You'd better get with it.'

---

[1] Robert J. Morgan, *On This Day* (Nashville: Thomas Nelson Publishers, 1997), March 21st.

"That exchange haunted me. It was the beginning of my spiritual journey. Soon after I gave my life to Jesus, and everything has been different ever since."

The inmate, having given his own heart to Christ, had begun to evangelize inside the prison. One after another, prisoners had come to Christ.

"You see all these men, Chuck? This is the body of Christ that has grown up as a result of that meeting ten years ago. The church is alive inside this prison."

Amid thunderous applause, the inmate proceeded to give Chuck a collection taken in the prison for Prison Fellowship's ministry.

"I felt their vitality flood into me," Chuck later recalled. "I had come to them weary and worn out, and the church inside the prison—planted without my knowledge ten years earlier—replenished me with its love and faithfulness. Just at the point of need, the power of the resurrected Christ flowed from one part of His body into another.

"That Easter I had proof once again, in His living presence among a band of Christian inmates, that Jesus Christ is risen again."[1]

Date: _____   _____   _____
Place: _____   _____   _____
Occasion: _____   _____   _____

A Most Excellent Day

It was Good Friday, and Lois Neely of Ontario was struggling with the blues. She had expected to spend Easter with friends in Florida, but a serious illness had cancelled her plans. She was bitterly disappointed, and as she sat gazing through a frosted window at the cold, barren landscape her thoughts went to the swimming pool and tall palm trees she was missing. Several problems confronted her, and she was worried and weary.

Finally she prayed. "Lord," she said, "if you could gladden the hearts of those sad followers who had been walking to Emmaus, You are able to do it for me."

Remembering that the Emmaus disciples in Luke 24 had invited a friend to dinner, she decided to do the same. The friend came, and the two women had a lovely time. Then, remembering the women who visited the tomb on Easter Sunday, she called the chaplain in her retirement center, and the two began planning an Easter Sunrise service.

To her surprise, forty seniors showed up, and the whole group seemed energized to sing, *Christ the Lord Is Risen Today, Alleluia!*

That evening, Lois wrote in her diary, "A most excellent day!"

And isn't that, after all, what Easter is![2]

Date: _____   _____   _____
Place: _____   _____   _____
Occasion: _____   _____   _____

[1] Adapted from Chuck Colson, "Empty at Easter," *Moody Magazine,* February 1990, 13–14.
[2] Adapted from Lois Neely, "Unexpected Delights at Easter," *Decision Magazine,* April 1998, 25.

Why Can You Refute Christianity?

Josh McDowell entered university as a young man looking for a good time and searching for happiness and meaning in life. He tried going to church, but found religion unsatisfying. He ran for student leadership positions but was disappointed by how quickly the glamour wore off. He tried the party circuit, but he woke up Monday mornings feeling worse than ever.

He finally noticed a group of students engaged in Bible study, and he became intrigued by the radiance of one of the young ladies. He asked her a reason for it. She looked him straight in the eye, smiled, and said, "Jesus Christ."

"Oh, for heaven's sake," he retorted, "don't give me that garbage about religion."

She replied, "I didn't say religion; I said Jesus Christ."

The students invited him to intellectually examine the claims of Christ and the evidence supporting Christianity. He accepted their challenge, and after much study and research, finally admitted that he couldn't refute the body of proof supporting Christianity. McDowell received Christ as his Savior, and his research became the background for his book *Evidence That Demands a Verdict.*

One of the major factors in his conversion to Christianity was his inability to ignore the historical resurrection of Jesus Christ, a point he made later to a student at the University of Uruguay who asked him, "Professor McDowell, why can't you intellectually refute Christianity?"

"For a very simple reason," replied McDowell. "I am not able to explain away an event in history—the resurrection of Jesus Christ."[1]

Date:			
Place:			
Occasion:			

Evidence for the Resurrection

John Stott suggests, "Perhaps the transformation of the disciples of Jesus is the greatest evidence of all for the resurrection. It was the resurrection which transformed Peter's fear into courage and James' doubt into faith. It was the resurrection which changed the Sabbath into Sunday and the Jewish remnant into the Christian Church. It was the resurrection which changed Saul the Pharisee into Paul the apostle and turned his persecuting into preaching."[2]

Date:			
Place:			
Occasion:			

Because of Easter

- Because of Good Friday you can look back and not be afraid.
- Because of Easter you can look ahead and not be afraid.

[1] Josh McDowell, *The Resurrection Factor* (San Bernardino: Here's Life Publishers, Inc., n.d.), 2–7.
[2] John R. W. Stott, *Basic Christianity* (Grand Rapids: Eerdman's Publishing Company, 1969), 57–59.

- Because of Ascension Day you can look up and not be afraid.
- Because of Pentecost you can look inward and not be afraid.[1]

Date:			
Place:			
Occasion:			

The Canoe-Shaped Coffin

Herman Melville's great classic, *Moby Dick,* is packed with biblical themes and allusions. For example, there is a character aboard ship named Queequeg, who was beloved by the crew. When he was seized by a serious fever, everyone tended him carefully and he recovered, but the illness left him worried about his future. Calling the ship's carpenter, Queequeg requested a coffin be made for him in the shape of a canoe. The carpenter took Queequeg's measurements, marshaled his planks and tools, and set to work. Soon it was finished.

Little more is said of the strange coffin, and, as the book progresses, the story returns to Captain Ahab and his fatal obsession with the great whale, Moby Dick.

In the novel's dramatic climax, Captain Ahab finds Moby Dick, but the great whale overcomes the captain, smashing the boat to pieces, killing Ahab and tossing the crew into the sea to be eaten alive by sharks.

Ishmael, the storyteller, finds himself floundering in the water, being sucked into the vortex of the sinking ship, circling in a fatal eddy, prey for the sharks. Suddenly a "black bubble" burst from the water, liberated from the depths by its own buoyancy. It shoots up with great force and lands near Ishmael. It is the canoe-shaped coffin. Climbing into it, Ishmael floats for a day and night until he is rescued by a passing ship.

Because of Easter, our coffins are nothing more than canoes bearing us across the Jordan River to fairer worlds on high.

Date:			
Place:			
Occasion:			

All You Have to Do . . .

The French mathematician Auguste Comte was talking about religion one day with the Scottish essayist Thomas Carlyle. Comte suggested they start a new religion to replace Christianity, based on positive thinking and mathematical principles. Carlyle thought about it a moment and replied, "Very good, Mr. Comte, very good. All you will need to do will be to speak as never a man spoke, and live as never a man lived, and be crucified, and rise again the third day, and get the world to believe that you are still alive. Then your religion will have a chance to get on."

---

[1] From my notes of a sermon by Warren Wiersbe.

Date:	_____	_____	_____
Place:	_____	_____	_____
Occasion:	_____	_____	_____

Satan's Waterloo

From an old clipping, here is the way the news of the victory at Waterloo arrived in England. There were no telegrams or telephones in those days, of course, but everyone knew that Wellington was facing Napoleon in a great battle, and that the future of England was in great uncertainty. A sailing ship semaphored (signaled with coded flags) the news to the signalman on top of Winchester Cathedral. He signaled to another man on a hill, and thus news of the battle was relayed by semaphore from station to station to London and all across the land. When the ship came in, the signalman on board semaphored the first word: *Wellington*. The next word was *defeated,* and then the fog came down and the ship could not be seen. "Wellington Defeated" went across England, and there was great gloom all over the countryside. After two or three hours, the fog lifted, and the signal came again: *Wellington Defeated the Enemy.* Then all England rejoiced.

—◇—
Crowning Proof

The bodily resurrection of Jesus Christ from the dead is the crowning proof of Christianity.
—HENRY MORRIS
—◇—

There was that day, when they put the body of the Lord in the tomb, that the message appeared to be *Christ Defeated.* . . . But three days later, the fog lifted.[1]

Date:	_____	_____	_____
Place:	_____	_____	_____
Occasion:	_____	_____	_____

How Terrible

William Sangster, the great Methodist leader who helped guide Londoners through the horrors of the World War II bombings, fell ill to a disease that progressively paralyzed his body, and eventually his vocal cords. On the Easter just before he died, he managed to scribble this short note to his daughter: *How terrible to wake up on Easter and have no voice to shout, "He is Risen!" Far worse, to have a voice and not want to shout.*

Date:	_____	_____	_____
Place:	_____	_____	_____
Occasion:	_____	_____	_____

The Sacrificial Skins

Wilfred Grenfell, famous missionary doctor to Labrador, had many hair-raising adventures, but one is told more than any of the others. On Easter Sunday in 1908,

[1] From a clipping in my notebook from college days, source unknown.

he received an urgent call to come and treat a gravely ill youth in a village sixty miles away. He harnessed his dog team and set out for the village as quickly as possible. This was the time of the Spring thaw, but to save time Grenfell decided to risk crossing the ice on the bay instead of winding around the rugged shoreline. It was an unwise decision, for the ice was breaking and shifting, and Grenfell and his dogs suddenly plunged into the icy water.

He managed to pull himself and three of his dogs onto a large chunk of ice, but the wind, bitterly cold, was driving the ice out to sea. To avoid freezing to death, Grenfell killed his three dogs and wrapped himself in their bloody skins. There he shivered through the long night. The following morning he was near death, but his friends, risking their lives, maneuvered between the surging ice chunks, to rescue him.

The story of his courage spread widely, leading many others to come serve with him in Labrador.

Even so, it was on Good Friday that we were wrapped in the righteousness of the Lamb who was slain for our salvation, and it was on Easter Sunday that we were rescued from a cold death by the sudden appearance of the Risen Lord.[1]

Date: _____ _____ _____
Place: _____ _____ _____
Occasion: _____ _____ _____

Full of Emptiness

There's a beautiful old story about a Sunday school teacher who asked the children in his class to bring plastic eggs on Easter Sunday, each one filled with something that symbolized the meaning of the resurrection. The day came, and the teacher took each child's egg in turn, opening it and making a point of amplifying and reinforcing its meaning. One child had a tiny flower, and the teacher spoke of the new life that springs forth at Easter. Another egg contained a crayoned picture of Christ, and the teacher spoke of that. Another had a small nail, and the point was made about the nails of the cross. Another had a round pebble that represented the stone that had guarded the tomb.

But the teacher was dumbfounded when he opened the egg of seven-year-old Brian, a mentally-challenged boy, and found nothing there. But not to worry, Brian himself spoke up and announced: "It's full of emptiness—just like the tomb of Jesus."

His was the best lesson of all.

Date: _____ _____ _____
Place: _____ _____ _____
Occasion: _____ _____ _____

---

[1] Ruth Tucker, *From Jerusalem to Irian Jaya* (Grand Rapids: Zondervan, 1983), 331–332.

What's So Special About Easter?

A group of four year olds were gathered in a Sunday school class in Chattanooga. The teacher, looking at her class enthusiastically, asked, "Does anyone know what today is?"

One little girl knew. "It's Palm Sunday!" she said.

"Very good," said the teacher. "And does anyone know what next Sunday is?"

The same little girl lifted her hand again. "Yes, next Sunday is Easter," she announced.

The teacher was very pleased with this little girl, and she complimented her effusively before asking a third question. "Now, does anyone know what makes Easter so special."

It was the same little girl who again raised her hand and offered this answer: "Yes, next Sunday is Easter because Jesus rose from the dead . . ."

Before the teacher could compliment her, she kept on talking: ". . . but if he sees his shadow, he has to go back in for seven weeks."

Date:			
Place:			
Occasion:			

Empathy

Someone Once Said . . .

- *Know all and you will pardon all.*—Thomas à Kempis
- *If there is any one secret of success, it lies in the ability to get the other person's point of view and see things from his angle as well as your own.*—Henry Ford[1]
- *I sat where they sat, and remained there astonished among them seven days.*—Ezekiel 3:15
- *If you would sell John Smith what John Smith buys, you must see John Smith through John Smith's eyes.*—Old proverb among sales representatives

Date:			
Place:			
Occasion:			

Helped Her Cry

Methodist preacher Charles Allen tells of a little child who went on an errand for her mother. She was late coming back, and her mother asked for an explanation. The child explained that a playmate of hers down the street had fallen and broken her doll and that she had helped her. The mother wondered what she could do to

---

[1] Dale Carnegie, *How To Win Friends and Influence People* (New York: Simon and Schuster, 1936), 42–43.

help mend the broken doll. The little girl made a marvelous reply, "I just sat down and helped her cry."[1]

Date: _____ _____ _____
Place: _____ _____ _____
Occasion: _____ _____ _____

The Whiteskin Cries

Bob and Carolyn Thomas served as missionaries in Papua New Guinea. Among Bob's stories is this one: *It was Sunday morning in the village. I started a fire in the fireplace while Carolyn fixed cheese omelets. As soon as I finished breakfast, I turned on our short-wave and picked up the Kentucky Derby on a U.S. station. It was exciting to hear, but afterwards I was flooded with homesick memories of our springtime family ritual of watching the Derby together. I was surprised when the tears came.*

Looking back, I realize the Lord was preparing my heart for another sorrow. A village leader had just died. I planned to spend Sunday on the mountain where my village friends were mourning, so I hiked to the top of the mountain and joined my adopted village brothers. In this area of New Guinea, people kick the bamboo-woven walls off the house of someone who dies. It is a release for their enormous grief. The walls of this dead man's house had already been kicked off and nailed back three times.

I felt so sorry for them. I thought again how I missed my family back home. I couldn't hold them back, so a few tears trickled down. Then I heard whispers through the crowd, "Lala siacma" ("The Whiteskin cries!"). Suddenly two men leapt on top of me, knocking my glasses off. They held me tightly, and the whole crowd wailed.

Afterwards they told me they didn't think Whiteskins cried. In their culture, if someone is sad and only cries a little, they jump on him to help the mourner cry hard and get it all out. They say it is no good if the sorrow stays inside you and kills you. I thought, "Wow, they are wiser than we are about mourning."

So the story went out over the mountains that the Whiteskins really love us; they share our deep sorrow.

It was good to be in the house of mourning.

Date: _____ _____ _____
Place: _____ _____ _____
Occasion: _____ _____ _____

Old Crittingden

The popular writer F. W. Boreham once lost patience with a difficult man named Crittingden, who said and wrote many critical words. Boreham, angered beyond endurance, finally wrote a flaming letter designed to sting and rebuke the complainer. He walked to the mailbox to post the letter. It was a lovely night for a walk, and he

[1] Charles Allen, *Perfect Peace* (Old Tappan, NJ: Fleming H. Revell Co., 1979), 134.

passed by the mailbox without dropping the letter in. He said to himself, "I'll mail it on the way back."

A quarter of a mile further on, he met a friend who said, "Poor old Crittingden is dead."

Boreham was shocked. "Is he, indeed? When did this happen?"

"Oh, he died suddenly—early this afternoon. It's really for the best, you know. He's had a hard time. You know all about it, I suppose?"

"No, I don't."

"Oh, I thought everybody knew. He only had two children, a son and a daughter. The son was killed soon after his wife died, and the daughter lost her mind and is in the asylum. Poor old Crittingden never got over it. It soured him."

Boreham returned to his fireside that night, humbled and ashamed. He tore the letter into small fragments and burned them one by one. And as he knelt before the blaze, he prayed that he, in days to come, might find the grace to deal gently and lovingly with difficult people, even as he wished they might have the grace to treat him.

Date:	_____	_____	_____
Place:	_____	_____	_____
Occasion:	_____	_____	_____

Paradigm Shift

Stephen Covey writes in his *Seven Habits of Highly Effective People* about an experience he had on a subway in New York. It was Sunday morning, and the passengers were sitting quietly, napping, reading the paper, lost in thought. But the peaceful scene changed when a man and his children suddenly boarded. The children were loud and rambunctious, and they disrupted the entire car.

The man sat down beside Covey, seemingly oblivious to the situation. The children were yelling, throwing things, and even grabbing people's papers. It was very disturbing, and yet the man did nothing.

Covey fought the feelings of irritation that rose in him, but as the confusion grew worse he finally turned and said, "Sir, your children are really disturbing a lot of people. I wonder if you couldn't control them a little more?"

The man lifted his gaze as if coming to himself, then he said softly, "Oh, you're right. I guess I should do something about it. We just came from the hospital where their mother died about an hour ago. I don't know what to think, and I guess they don't know how to handle it either."

Covey later wrote, *Can you imagine what I felt at that moment? My paradigm shifted. Suddenly I saw things differently, and because I saw differently, I thought differently, I felt differently, I behaved differently. My irritation vanished . . . my heart was filled with the man's pain. Feelings of sympathy and compassion flowed freely. "Your wife just died? Oh, I'm so sorry! Can you tell me about it? What can I do to help?" Everything changed in an instant.*[1]

---

[1] Stephen R. Covey, *The 7 Habits of Highly Effective People* (New York: Simon and Schuster, 1989), 30–31.

Hard Living People

In his book *Hard Living People and Mainstream Christians,* Professor Tex Sample tells about interviewing Don Bakely, executive director of Crosslines, an urban mission in Kansas City, Kansas, for twenty-five years. Bakely told Sample this graphic story from his early days of pastoring a church in urban Camden, New Jersey. It had to do with the church secretary, Ella, and a neighborhood thug known as "Big Mart."

Bakely tried hard to connect with the toughs and street people in Camden, and he especially wanted to reach Big Mart. One day he was sitting in his office, and he heard a commotion outside, profanity, shouting, a loud argument. It was between Ella and Big Mart. He was calling her a vile and obscene name.

About that fast, Ella comes tearing into my office. "Did you hear what that young man called me out there?"

"Yes," I said.

"Well, what are you going to do about it?"

"That's a good question, Ella," I says, "a really good question. But the real question is what are you going to do about it?"

Stopped momentarily, and a bit exasperated she says, "I guess I want you to go out there and throw him out."

"Ella," I said, "I've been working for six weeks to get him in here. You want me to throw him out on the first day? . . . Ella, let me tell you a story; it's a true story; then I want you to go home and think about it. . . .

"When Big Mart was a little boy, his dad came home one night in a rage and began to beat up Big Mart's mother. He became so furious and so violent that he brought the children into the room, closed the door and forced them to watch while he killed her. He then took a paring knife and cut her head off in front of those children. When Big Mart could not stand it anymore he broke for the door and got out, but when he reached the top of the stairs, his father threw his mother's head and hit him in the back pitching him down the entire flight to the bottom floor. It knocked him out, but when he woke up on the landing, he was lying on his mother's head. That's Big Mart. He's the guy you met out there, the guy who . . . uh . . . called you that name."

Ella didn't say a word. She just turned and walked out the door . . . She was back in twenty minutes. I was worried. I wanted her to think about it longer than that, but she walked over to my desk and just looked at me.

"Well?" I finally asked, not really wanting to know what I expected to hear.

She says, "I guess I am going to have to learn how to get cussed out."

"And," said Don Bakely, "the ministry of that church began right there, right then."[1]

---

[1] Tex Sample, *Hard Living People and Mainstream Christians* (Nashville: Abingdon Press, 1993), 160–162.

Date: _____ _____ _____
Place: _____ _____ _____
Occasion: _____ _____ _____

Incarnation

In 1873, a Belgian Catholic priest named Joseph Damien De Veuster was sent to minister to lepers on the Hawaiian Island of Molokai. When he arrived, he immediately began to meet each one of the lepers in the colony in hopes of building a friendship. But wherever he turned, people shunned him. It seemed as though every door was closed. He poured his life into his work, erecting a chapel, beginning worship services and pouring out his heart to the lepers. But it was to no avail. No one responded to his ministry. After twelve years Father Damien decided to leave.

Laughter and Tears

Rejoice with those who rejoice, and weep with those who weep.

—ROMANS 12:15

Dejectedly, he made his way to the docks to board a ship to take him back to Belgium. As he stood on the dock, he wrung his hands nervously, recounting his futile ministry among the lepers. As he did he looked down at his hands, he noticed some mysterious white spots and felt some numbness. Almost immediately he knew what was happening to his body. He had contracted leprosy.

It was then that he knew what he had to do. He returned to the leper colony and to his work. Quickly the word about his disease spread through the colony. Within a matter of hours everyone knew. Hundreds of them gathered outside his hut, they understood his pain, fear, and uncertainty about the future.

But the biggest surprise was the following Sunday. As Father Damien arrived at the Chapel, he found hundreds of worshipers there. By the time the service began, there were many more with standing room only, and many gathered outside the chapel. His ministry became enormously successful. The reason? He was one of them. He understood and empathized with them.[1]

Date: _____ _____ _____
Place: _____ _____ _____
Occasion: _____ _____ _____

The Other Team

In the comic strip *Peanuts,* Linus was watching a football game on television, cheering "Go! Go! Go!" When the game ended victoriously, he jumped up in a surge of emotion and ran out to find Charlie Brown.

"What a comeback!" he exclaimed. "The home team was behind six to nothing with only three seconds to play. They had the ball on their own one-yard line. The quarterback took the ball, faded back behind his own goal and threw a perfect pass to the left end who whirled away from four guys and ran in for the touchdown!

---

[1] Author unknown, *Parables, Etc.,* June 1984, 5–6.

The fans went wild! You should have seen them! And when they kicked the extra point, thousands of people ran onto the field laughing and screaming and rolling on the ground and hugging each other and everything!"

Charlie Brown turned to him and asked, "How did the other team feel?"[1]

Date:			
Place:			
Occasion:			

Emptiness

Someone Once Said . . .

- *I'm shocked by the hole in America's heart.*—Norman Lear, television producer
- *Everybody basically has an empty hole inside of them that they try to fill with money, drugs, alcohol, power—and none of the material stuff works.*—Robert F. Kennedy, Jr.[2]
- *I had won Wimbledon twice before, once as the youngest player. I was rich. I had all the material possessions I needed. . . . It's the old song of movie stars and pop stars who commit suicide. They have everything, and yet they are so unhappy. I had no inner peace. I was a puppet on a string.*—Boris Becker, tennis star
- *I live in a vacuum that is as lonely as a radio tube when the batteries are dead and there is no current to plug into.*—Ernest Hemingway
- *The existential vacuum is a widespread phenomenon of the twentieth century.*—Viktor Frankl[3]
- *I used to say: "There is a God-shaped hole in me." For a long time I stressed the absence, the hole. Now I find it is the shape which has become more important.*—Salman Rushdie, Indian-English novelist
- *Just consider the mass neurotic syndrome so pervasive in the younger generation: there is ample empirical evidence that the three facets of this syndrome—depression, aggression, addiction—are due to what is called in logotherapy "the existential vacuum," a feeling of emptiness and meaninglessness.*—Viktor Frankl[4]
- *The world is fading, not filling.*—Thomas Watson[5]
- *I'd like to know / what this show / is all about / before its out.*—Piet Hein, Danish poet[6]

Date:			
Place:			
Occasion:			

---

[1] Charles Schulz, *Parables, Etc.*, November 1985, 5.

[2] Daniel Chu and Vicki Sheff, "Toxic Avenger," *People*, July 22, 1991, 74.

[3] Viktor E. Frankl, *Man's Search for Meaning* (New York: Washington Square Press, 1984), 128.

[4] Frankl, *Man's Search for Meaning*, 166.

[5] Thomas Watson, *Gleanings From Thomas Watson* (Morgan, PA: Soli Deo Gloria Publications, 1995), 31.

[6] John Archibald Wheeler, "Understanding How the Universe Came Into Being," *Science Digest*, October 1979, 38.

Empty at the Top

[A] Edmund Hillary

The great Israeli statesman, Abba Eban, wrote in his autobiography about a conversation he once had with Edmund Hillary, the first man to climb Mount Everest. Eban asked Hillary what exactly he felt when he reached the peak. He replied that the first sentiment was one of ecstatic accomplishment. But then there came a sense of desolation. What was there now left to do?[1]

[B] Jon Krakauer

In May, 1996, journalist Jon Krakauer was part of an expedition that reached the top of Mount Everest. Twelve of his compatriots were killed in the highly publicized descent, a story that Krakauer records in his book *Into Thin Air*. But he begins his account by describing his feelings on May 10, 1996, as he reached the highest spot on earth:

> Straddling the top of the world, one foot in China and the other in Nepal, I cleared the ice from my oxygen mask, hunched a shoulder against the wind and stared absently down at the vastness of Tibet. I understood on some dim, detached level that the sweep of earth beneath my feet was a spectacular sight. I'd been fantasizing about this moment, and the release of emotion that would accompany it, for many months. But now that I was finally here, actually standing on the summit of Everest, I just couldn't summon the energy to care. . . .

I snapped four quick photos . . . then turned and headed down. My watch read 1:17 P.M. All told, I'd spent less than five minutes on the roof of the world.[2]

◆

An Empty Heart

There is a God-shaped vacuum in the heart of every man, which cannot be filled by any created thing but only by God the Creator, made known through Jesus Christ.

—PASCAL

◆

Date:		
Place:		
Occasion:		

Comedian Jackie Gleason

The late comedian Jackie Gleason was described in *Reader's Digest* as "a lonely and suffering soul given to late-night drinking sessions, looking for answers to life and death, with a terrible emptiness in him that he couldn't fill."[3]

Date:		
Place:		
Occasion:		

Novelist Jack Higgins

Jack Higgins, the renowned author of *The Eagle Has Landed,* has said that the one thing he knows now, at this high point in his career, that he wished he

---

[1] Abba Eban, *Abba Eban: An Autobiography* (New York: Random House, 1977), 609.
[2] Jon Krakauer, *Into Thin Air* (New York: Doubleday/Anchor Books, 1997), 3–4.
[3] "The Unforgettable Jackie Gleason," *Reader's Digest,* July 1988, 48.

had known as a small boy is this: "When you get to the top, there's nothing there."[1]

Date: _____ _____ _____
Place: _____ _____ _____
Occasion: _____ _____ _____

——————— Encouragement ———————

Someone Once Said . . .

- *For every critical comment we receive, it takes nine affirming comments to even out the negative effect in our life.*—Jim Burns[2]
- *Many of our daily conversations are actually mutual counseling sessions whereby we exchange the reassurance and advice that help us deal with routine stresses.*—from a National Institute Mental Health Report[3]

Date: _____ _____ _____
Place: _____ _____ _____
Occasion: _____ _____ _____

Holding Each Other Up

In *Guideposts* magazine Donald Vairin of Oceanside, California, told of serving as a young hospital corpsman in the invasion of Guam during World War II. Suddenly his boat came to a grinding halt. They had hit a coral reef, and the commanding officer ordered everyone off the ship.

Donald jumped into the ocean and sank like a rock, his carbine rifle, medical pack, canteen, and boots dragging him down. He forced himself to the surface, gasping for air, only to sink again. He tried to pull off his boots, but the effort exhausted him, and he suddenly realized he wasn't going to make it.

Just then he saw a man thrashing in the water next to him, and in desperation he clutched onto him. That proved enough to hold him up and get him to the reef where he was picked up by a rescue boat. But Donald felt so guilty about grabbing the drowning man to save himself that he never told anyone what had happened.

About six months later, on shore leave in San Francisco, he stopped in a restaurant. A sailor in uniform waved him over to sit with him, and as he did so he announced to his friends, "This is my buddy. He saved my life."

"What are you talking about?" asked Donald.

---

[1] Ravi Zacharias, *Can Man Live Without God?* (Dallas: Word Publishing, 1994), xvii.
[2] Jim Burns, *The Youth Builder* (Eugene, OR: Harvest House Publishers, 1988), 54.
[3] Dr. Julius Segal, *Winning Life's Toughest Battles* (New York: Ivy Books, 1896), 18.

"Don't you remember," said the man. "We were in the water together at Guam. You grabbed on to me. I was going down, and you held me up."[1]

Date: _____ _____ _____
Place: _____ _____ _____
Occasion: _____ _____ _____

We Take Turns

A young mother was sick in bed when her nine-year-old daughter walked in from school. Thinking her mother was asleep, she quietly unfolded the blanket at the foot of the bed and gently tucked it around her mom. The mother stirred, then whispered, "It wasn't too long ago that I was tucking you in. And now you're covering me."

The little girl, bending over her mother, replied, "We take turns."

Date: _____ _____ _____
Place: _____ _____ _____
Occasion: _____ _____ _____

Reflectors

Author Robert Fulghum sometimes, when attending lectures, would respond in an unusual way to the speaker's final, routine words: "Are there any questions?"

"Yes," Fulghum sometimes says. Then he asks, "What is the meaning of life?"

People generally laugh and gather their notes, prepared to leave as the speaker smiles and shrugs off the question. But one day, to his surprise, Fulghum got a serious answer. It was from Dr. Alexander Papaderos, a Greek philosopher and the founder of an institute on the island of Crete. At the end of a lecture one day, Dr. Papaderos asked, "Are there any questions?"

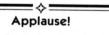
Applause!

Find the good and applaud.
—ZIG ZIGLAR

"Yes," said Fulghum, "what is the meaning of life?"

The other attendees whispered and chuckled and prepared to leave, but Dr. Papaderos held up his hand. "I will answer your question," he said. He drew from his pocket a small round mirror, about the size of a quarter. As he was growing up during the war, his family was very poor, and he had few toys. One day he found the broken pieces of a mirror, left over from the wreck of a German motorcycle. He tried in vain to piece the bits together, but finally ended up discarding all but the largest piece.

"This one," he said, holding it higher. "And by scratching it on a stone I made it round. I began to play with it as a toy and became fascinated by the fact that I could reflect light into dark places where the sun would never shine—in deep holes and crevices and dark closets. It became a game for me to get light into the most inaccessible places I could find.

---

[1] Donald Vairin, "His Mysterious Ways," *Guideposts*, September 1999, 39.

"I kept the little mirror, and as I went about my growing up, I would take it out in idle moments and continue the challenge of the game. As I became a man, I grew to understand that this was not just a child's game but a metaphor for what I might do in my life. . . .

"With what I have I can reflect light into the dark places of this world—into the black places in the hearts of men—and change some things in some people."

Having said that, Dr. Papaderos took his small mirror and, holding it carefully, caught the rays of daylight streaming through the window and reflected them in Robert Fulghum's face.[1]

E

Date:			
Place:			
Occasion:			

The Encouragement of the Word

It was the encouragement of the Word that sustained young William Carey during his first months as pioneer missionary in India. Everything seemed to conspire against him. No one was responding to his message. His coworker, John Thomas, was in constant danger of being arrested in Calcutta due to indebtedness, and he was dragging William down with him. The Carey family was ill-housed and nearly destitute. Two of the four children suffered from severe dysentery. Worst of all, his own wife Dorothy was hostile, unhappy, and appeared to be losing her mind.

But this is what he wrote:

If my family were but hearty in the work, I should find a great burden removed, but the carnal discourse of the passage, and the pomp and grandeur of Europeans here, have intoxicated their minds, so as to make them unhappy in one of the finest countries of the world, and lonely in the midst of a hundred thousand people. These are burdens and afflictions for me, but I bless God that I faint not, and when my soul can drink her fill at the word of God, I forget all. . . .[2]

Date:			
Place:			
Occasion:			

A Few Kind Words

The late Bishop Fulton Sheen once entered a greasy-spoon restaurant for breakfast, and when the waitress, groggy and disinterested, took his order, he replied, "Bring me some ham and eggs and a few kind words."

When she returned fifteen minutes later, she set the food before him and said, "There."

"What about the kind words?"

---

[1] Robert Fulghum, *It Was on Fire When I Lay Down on It* (New York: Villard Books, 1990), 173–177.
[2] Mary Drewery, *William Carey: A Biography* (Chicago: Moody Press, 1978), 70.

The server looked him over a moment, then replied, "I'd advise you not to eat them eggs!"[1]

Date:			
Place:			
Occasion:			

A Little Better

Cliff Barrows, associate and music director for the Billy Graham Crusades, said that when he was younger he was once asked to lead the singing at his church. It was his first opportunity to do such a thing, and the people didn't sing very well. Cliff scolded them, saying something like, "This is about the worst singing I've ever heard. I'm ashamed of you. Now, come on and let's do better."

Returning home, his father pulled him aside and told him something he never forgot. "Cliff, you'll never get people to sing better by scolding them and telling them how badly they're doing. You have to tell them that they're doing pretty well, and that you think they can do a little better."

Cliff never forgot that advice, and through the years he has been known for his smile, his encouragement, and his positive approach.

Date:			
Place:			
Occasion:			

Of Course You Can

Author Muriel Anderson says that four of the most important words in her life are "Of course you can."

"I was fortunate," she wrote, "to have had a father who was good at shouting *of course you can* at just the right moments."

Once when she was in high school her family had moved to a city from a small town. She loved the place and wrote an article about it, wanting more than anything to have the article published in the small-town, weekly paper. She didn't expect to be successful, though, because the paper was a weekly with a tight budget who bought practically no freelance material.

"I don't think I can get it published," I said.

"Of course you can," said my dad. And she did—launching her career as a writer.[2]

Date:			
Place:			
Occasion:			

---

[1] James Dobson, *Straight Talk to Men and Their Wives* (Waco: Word Publishing, 1980), 171.
[2] *Handbook of Short Story Writing* (Cincinnati: Writer's Digest Books, 1970), 1.

By and By

Joseph Webster walked wearily into the little drugstore in Elkhorn, Wisconsin. It was a lovely day in the late fall of 1867, but Webster looked as though he had lost his best friend. His problems had gotten the best of him, and his mood was heavy.

The proprietor of the little shop was Samuel Bennett, thirty-one, who not only filled prescriptions—he sometimes wrote them. On this day, he had just the prescription for his discouraged friend.

After listening carefully to Webster's accumulated burdens, he picked up his pen and began writing on a 5 x 7 piece of paper. In a few minutes he handed his friend a poem, one he had composed on the spot.

Webster read the poem, picked up his fiddle, and began improvising a simple melody. "Hand me some paper," he said, "so I can jot down the notes before I forget them."

He played the tune two or three times, then, recruiting a couple of customers who had walked into the store, they formed a makeshift quartet and sang it. Thus the world was given the popular gospel tune:

> *There's a land that is fairer than day, And by faith we can see it afar*
> *For the Father waits over the way, To prepare us a dwelling place there.*
> *In the sweet by and by, We shall meet on that beautiful shore.*
> *In the sweet by and by, We shall meet on that beautiful shore.*

Date: _____ _____ _____
Place: _____ _____ _____
Occasion: _____ _____ _____

Bear Bryant's Secret

The legendary coach of Alabama's Crimson Tide, Bear Bryant, once said: *I'm just a plowhand from Arkansas, but I have learned how to hold a team together. How to lift some men up, how to calm others down, until finally they've got one heartbeat together, a team. There's just three things I'd ever say:*

- *If anything goes bad, I did it.*
- *If anything goes semi-good, then we did it.*
- *If anything goes real good, then you did it.*[1]

Date: _____ _____ _____
Place: _____ _____ _____
Occasion: _____ _____ _____

---

[1] Clipping in my files

Enemies, Treatment of

Someone Once Said . . .

- *To do evil for good is human corruption; to do good for good is civil retribution, but to do good for evil is Christian perfection.*—Rev. William Secker[1]
- *Kindness is the ability to treat your enemy decently.*—Anonymous
- *Our friends love us in spite of our faults, but our enemies hate us in spite of our virtues.*—Anonymous
- *If all people, when they feel the first approaches of resentment, envy, or contempt, towards others; if in all disagreements and misunderstandings, they should, instead of indulging their minds with low reflections, have recourse, at such times, to a more particular and extraordinary intercession with God, for such persons as had raised their envy, resentment, or discontent; this would be a certain way to prevent the growth of all uncharitable tempers.*—William Law, in *A Serious Call to a Devout and Holy Life*, published in 1728

Date:			
Place:			
Occasion:			

Teach Me to Love

It wasn't easy for Corrie Ten Boom to forgive the Nazi captors who had tormented her at Ravensbrück. They had caused her to suffer horribly. Even worse, they had caused the death of her sister, Betsy.

Ten years after her release, Corrie ran into a lady who wouldn't look her in the eyes. Asking about her, Corrie was told the woman had been a nurse at a concentration camp. Suddenly the memories flashed back. Corrie recalled taking Betsy to the infirmary to see this woman. Betsy's feet were paralyzed, and she was dying. The nurse had been cruel and sharp-tongued.

Corrie's hatred now returned with vengeance. Her rage so boiled that she knew of but one thing to do. "Forgive me," she cried out to the Lord, "Forgive my hatred, O Lord. Teach me to love my enemies."

The blood of Jesus Christ seemed to suddenly cool her embittered heart, and Corrie felt the rage being displaced with a divine love she couldn't explain. She began praying for the woman, and one day shortly afterward she called the hospital where the nurse worked and invited the woman to a meeting at which she was speaking.

"What!" replied the nurse. "Do you want *me* to come?"

"Yes, that is why I called you."

"Then I'll come."

That evening the nurse listened carefully to Corrie's talk, and afterward Corrie sat down with her, opened her Bible, and explained 1 John 4:9: "In this the love of

---

[1] William Secker, *The Nonsuch Professor in His Meridian Splendor* (Chicago: Fleming H. Revell Co., 1899), 153.

God was manifested toward us, that God has sent His only begotten Son into the world, that we might live through Him." The woman seemed to thirst for Corrie's quiet, confident words about God's love for us, his enemies. And that night, a former captive led her former captor to "a decision that made the angels sing."

God had taken Corrie's subconscious feelings of hatred, she later explained, and transformed them, using them as a window through which His light could shine into a darkened heart.

E

Date:			
Place:			
Occasion:			

Lessons to Unlearn

Roy Anthony Borges is a prison inmate who, becoming a Christian, had some hard lessons to unlearn. All his life he had been taught to hate his enemies, particularly within prison walls. One of his most vexing enemies was Rodney, who stole his radio and headphones one day while Roy was playing volleyball in the prison yard. It was an expensive radio, a gift from his mother. The earphones had been a Christmas present from his sister. Roy was angry and wanted revenge, but as he prayed about it, it seemed to him that God was testing him.

Day after day, Roy wanted to respond violently, to knock the wisecrack grin off Rodney's face, but Romans 12:20–21 kept coming to mind: Paul's instruction to avoid vengeance, leaving it to God to settle the score. Roy began to look at Rodney through God's eyes and have compassion on him. He began praying for him. He began trusting God to accomplish something in Rodney's life.

By and by, Roy's hatred for Rodney began fading, and he found himself helping his enemy and telling him about Jesus. Then one day, Roy later wrote, "I saw Rodney kneeling down next to his bunk reading his Bible, and I knew that good had overcome evil."[1]

Date:			
Place:			
Occasion:			

The Holy Man

There's an old story of a holy man who, while meditating in the countryside, noticed a scorpion struggling to get out of the swirling water of a rapid brook. Its efforts to climb onto a rock were futile, for the water was too strong. The holy man, taking pity on the creature, tried to help it, but the scorpion kept striking back at him.

---

[1] Roy Anthony Borges, "Love Your Enemies: One Prisoner's Story of Risky Obedience," *Discipleship Journal*, Issue 107, 42–43.

A friend, passing by, said to the holy man, "Don't you realize that it is the nature of a scorpion to attack and sting?"

"Yes," said the holy man, "but it is my nature to save and rescue. Why should I change my nature just because the scorpion doesn't change his?"

Date:			
Place:			
Occasion:			

Not an Enemy in the World

A reporter, interviewing an old man on his 100th birthday, asked, "What are you most proud of?"

"Well," said the old man, pondering the question, "I don't have an enemy in the world."

"That's wonderful!" said the reporter.

"Yep," added the centenarian, "I've outlived every last one of them."

Date:			
Place:			
Occasion:			

———————— Enthusiasm ————————

Someone Once Said . . .

- *Nothing is so contagious as enthusiasm; it moves stones, it charms brutes.*—Edward Bulwer-Lytton
- *When you're discouraged, it is remarkable how you can change your mood if you act enthusiastic.*—Alan Loy McGinnis[1]
- *To have enthusiasm, simply act enthusiastic.*—Normal Vincent Peale[2]
- *"Enthusiasm" is from the word "entheos," meaning "God within." Enthusiastic, exuberant people, rare as they are, are the ones who make the difference.*—Earl Nightingale
- *A blacksmith can do nothing when his fire is out.*—Charles Spurgeon, in *Lectures to My Students*
- *Whenever enthusiasm for any reason declines, tension seems to increase.*—Norman Vincent Peale[3]

Date:			
Place:			
Occasion:			

---

[1] Alan Loy McGinnis, *The Power of Optimism* (San Francisco: Harper & Row Publishers, 1990), 91.
[2] Norman Vincent Peale, *Enthusiasm Makes the Difference* (Englewood Cliffs, NJ: Prentice-Hall, Inc., 1967), 66.
[3] Peale, *Enthusiasm Makes the Difference*, 106.

What Is Enthusiasm?

- Enthusiasm is a kind of faith that has been set afire.—George Matthew Adams
- Enthusiasm is the mother of effort, the sustaining power of all great action.
- Enthusiasm is being fully absorbed in your dream.
- Enthusiasm is the sparkle in your eyes; it is the swing in your gait, the grip of your hand, the irresistible surge of your will, and your energy to execute your ideas.—Henry Ford
- Earnestness is enthusiasm tempered by reason.

Date: _____ _____ _____

Place: _____ _____ _____

Occasion: _____ _____ _____

Two Panels

A European artist once drew a powerful cartoon in which the first panel showed a group of small school children entering a street level subway station. They're the picture of exuberant joy; laughing, playing, tossing their hats in the air. But in the next panel, a group of middle aged adults are emerging from the subway station, wearing the facial expressions of zombies; dull, void of enthusiasm.

There is no caption, but none is needed. The question shouts from the pictures: "What happened to those people in the years since childhood that has removed every vestige of zest from their lives?"[1]

> **Unlimited Success**
>
> *A man can succeed at almost anything for which he has unlimited enthusiasm.*
>
> —ANDREW CARNEGIE

Date: _____ _____ _____

Place: _____ _____ _____

Occasion: _____ _____ _____

Lesson of the Raspberries

Harry Emerson Fosdick wrote about growing up in upstate New York, where one summer's day his mother sent him out to pick a quart of raspberries. "I dragged my feet in rebellion," he said, "and the can was filling very slowly. Then a new idea came: it would be fun to pick two quarts of raspberries and surprise her. I had so interesting a time picking two quarts to the utter amazement of the household, and they never forgot it. But alas, I have often forgotten the philosophy of it: we can change any situation by changing our attitude toward it."[2]

Date: _____ _____ _____

Place: _____ _____ _____

Occasion: _____ _____ _____

[1] Notes in my file from a lecture by Earl Nightingale.
[2] Alan Loy McGinnis, *The Power of Optimism* (San Francisco: Harper & Row Publishers, 1990), 151.

Ten Ways to Cultivate Enthusiasm

In his old book, *Stay Alive All Your Life,* Norman Vincent Peale suggests ten still-practical steps for cultivating the essential quality of enthusiasm in our lives:

1. Look for interest and romance in the simplest things about you.
2. Enlarge your view of your own God-given capacities. Within the limit of humility develop a good opinion of yourself.
3. Diligently practice eliminating all dull, dead, unhealthy thoughts so that your mind may be freshened up and capable of developing enthusiasm.
4. Daily affirm enthusiasm. As you think it, talk it, and live it, you will have it.
5. Practice daily relaxation to keep your mind and spirit from getting tired.
6. Act enthusiastic, for as you act you tend to be.
7. Allow no sense of guilt to take the luster off your spirit. It's the greatest of all causes of ennui.
8. Keep the creative channel open between God and yourself, remember that enthusiasm is "entheos" meaning "God within."
9. Keep spiritually virile and alive.
10. Give all you've got to life and it will give its fullest gifts to you. It will never grow dull.[1]

```
Date:      _____   _____   _____
Place:     _____   _____   _____
Occasion:  _____   _____   _____
```

———————————— Envy/Jealousy ————————————

Someone Once Said . . .

- *Envy is rebellion against God's leading in the lives of his children. It's saying that God has no right to bless someone else more than you.*—Erwin Lutzer
- *[Envy is] one of the most cancerous and soul-destroying vices there is. . . . It is terribly potent, for it feeds and is fed by pride, the taproot of our fallen nature.*—J. I. Packer[2]
- *Envy can ruin reputations, split churches, and cause murders. Envy can shrink our circle of friends, ruin our business, and dwarf our souls. . . . I have seen hundreds cursed by it.*—Billy Graham
- *Criticism is often nothing more than low-grade envy.*
- *One of the major causes of stress is combative competition—more accurately, envy. Rooted in a lack of self-esteem, it grows in the soul-soil of comparisons and blossoms in noxious thorns of desire for what others have or achieve.*—Lloyd John Ogilvie

---

[1] Norman Vincent Peale, *Stay Alive All Your Life* (Carmel, NY: Guideposts Associates, Inc., 1957), 43–44.
[2] J. I. Packer, *Knowing God* (Downers Grove, IL: InterVarsity Press, 1973), 151, 153.

- *The envious man feels other's fortunes are his misfortunes; their profit, his loss; their blessing, his bane; their health, his illness; their promotion, his demotion; their success, his failure.*—Leslie Flynn
- *Jealousy, the jaundice of the soul.*—John Dryden, quoted by Coach Pat Riley[1]

Date: _____ _____ _____
Place: _____ _____ _____
Occasion: _____ _____ _____

Destroyed by Envy

According to an ancient Greek legend, a certain athlete ran well but placed second in the race. The winner was encompassed with praise, and eventually a statue was erected in his honor. Envy ate away at the man who had placed second. He resented the winner, and he could think of little else. Eventually he decided to destroy the statue of the winner.

Night after night, he went to the statue under cover of darkness, chiseling away at the base to weaken the foundation. But one night as he chiseled in violent anger, he went too far. The heavy marble statue teetered on its base and crashed down on the disgruntled athlete. He died beneath the weight of the marble replica of the man he had grown to hate.

His own envy had destroyed him.

> **Fiery Enthusiasm**
>
> *If you aren't fired with enthusiasm, you will be fired with enthusiasm.*
>
> —VINCE LOMBARDI

Date: _____ _____ _____
Place: _____ _____ _____
Occasion: _____ _____ _____

Near-Sighted

We should have 20/20 vision, as in John 20:20—*Then the disciples were glad when they saw the Lord.* Instead we often have 21/21 vision, as in John 21:21—*But Lord, what about this man?*

Date: _____ _____ _____
Place: _____ _____ _____
Occasion: _____ _____ _____

Crabs

Fishermen know that one never needs a top for crab baskets. If one of the crabs starts to climb up the side of the basket, the other crabs will reach up and pull it back down.

---

[1] Pat Riley, *The Winner Within* (New York: Berkley Books, 1994), 59.

Date: _____ _____ _____
Place: _____ _____ _____
Occasion: _____ _____ _____

Meyer and Morgan

The famous Bible teacher F. B. Meyer often ministered at D. L. Moody's Northfield Bible Conference in Northfield, Massachusetts, and he always drew great crowds. But when the equally famous G. Campbell Morgan began preaching at Northfield, his stirring Bible studies attracted larger audiences. Meyer confessed to some of his close friends that he was tempted to feel envious of Morgan. "The only way I can conquer my feelings," Meyer said, "is to pray for him daily, which I do."[1]

Date: _____ _____ _____
Place: _____ _____ _____
Occasion: _____ _____ _____

Unless His Grace Give Me Victory

Henry Varley is best known as the man who said to D. L. Moody, *The world has yet to see what God will do with a man who is fully committed to him.* That statement so challenged Moody that he resolved to be that man, with world-changing results.

What isn't so well known is that Varley was himself a powerful evangelist and pastor. But in Ralph Turnbull's biography of him, *Henry Varley's Life Story,* we learn that one of Varley's most difficult battles concerned his jealousy of another preacher. A neighborhood pastor began drawing some of Varley's members, and Varley felt deep resentment toward the man. Writing later, he admitted:

I shall never forget the sense of guilt and sin that possessed me over that business. I was miserable. Was I practically saying to the Lord Jesus, "Unless the prosperity of Thy church and people comes in this neighborhood by me, success had better not come"? Was I really showing inability to rejoice in another worker's service? I felt that it was a sin of a very hateful character. I never asked the Lord to take away my life either before or since, but I did then, unless his grace would give me victory over this foul image of jealousy.[2]

Date: _____ _____ _____
Place: _____ _____ _____
Occasion: _____ _____ _____

Lord, Take Away This Envy

This day twenty years ago I preached for the first time as an ordained minister. It is amazing that the Lord has spared me and used me at all. I have no reason to wonder that He used others

[1] Warren W. Wiersbe and Lloyd M. Perry, *The Wycliffe Handbook of Preaching and Preachers* (Chicago: Moody Press, 1984), 195.
[2] Gordon MacDonald, *Restoring Your Spiritual Passion* (Nashville: Thomas Nelson Publishers, 1986), 100.

far more than He does me. Yet envy is my hurt, and today I have been seeking grace to rejoice exceedingly over the usefulness of others, even where it cast me into the shade. Lord, take away this envy from me!—entry in the diary of Andrew Bonar (1810–1892), famous Scottish minister

Date: _____   _____   _____
Place: _____   _____   _____
Occasion: _____   _____   _____

Behind the Stage

Gordon MacDonald warns of the danger of the world's competitive spirit filtering into the hearts of Christian workers—pastors and preachers and writers—who become envious of one another's success. MacDonald, citing a passage from Henri Nouwen, describes an actor who noticed the terrible hypocrisy of his compatriots during a particular play in which he had a role. While rehearsing the most moving scenes of love, tenderness, and intimacy, the actors were so jealous of each other and so apprehensive about their chances of "making it" that the back stage scene was one of hatred,

Envious Friends

Love is the glue that cements friendships, but jealousy is the slime that keeps it from sticking.

harshness, and mutual suspicion. Those who kissed each other on the stage were tempted to hit each other behind it, and those who displayed such love before an audience felt nothing but hostile rivalry as soon as the footlights were dimmed.[1]

Date: _____   _____   _____
Place: _____   _____   _____
Occasion: _____   _____   _____

Number One

A bright, ambitious young student at Stanford was given a summer trip to the Far East by his parents, and while he was there he came under the influence of a group of Buddhists. They criticized his ambitious ways, telling him that he studied so hard, not to learn, but to get a better grade than his friend. He worked so hard, not to better society, but to purchase more than his peers. He dated the most beautiful girls, not to find true love, but to be seen with the most admired women. The young man admitted that it was true, and from Tokyo he called his parents and told them he was dropping out of school and entering a Buddhist monastery.

Six months later, his parents received this letter: *Dear dad and mom. I know you weren't happy with my decision to stay here, but I want to tell you how happy I now am. I am at peace for the first time in my life, living in an environment without competition or envy. Here we all share and life is equal. This way of life is so much in harmony with the inner essence of*

---

[1] MacDonald, *Restoring Your Spiritual Passion*, 99–100.

my soul that in only six months I've become the Number Two disciple in the monastery, and I think I can be Number One by June![1]

> Date: _____ _____ _____
> Place: _____ _____ _____
> Occasion: _____ _____ _____

Example

Someone Once Said . . .

- *We unconsciously imitate what pleases us and approximate to the characters we most admire.*—Christian Nestell Bovee (1820–1904), U.S. author and lawyer
- *I talk and talk and talk, and I haven't taught people in fifty years what my father taught by example in one week.*—Mario Cuomo, former governor of New York

> Date: _____ _____ _____
> Place: _____ _____ _____
> Occasion: _____ _____ _____

Let Us Go and Preach

One day St. Francis of Assisi said to one of the young monks at the Portiuncula, "Let us go down to the town and preach!" The novice, delighted at being singled out to be the companion of Francis, obeyed with alacrity. They passed through the principal streets, turned down many of the byways and alleys, made their way into the suburbs, and at great length returned by a circuitous route to the monastery gate. As they approached it, the younger man reminded Francis of his original intention.

"You have forgotten, Father, that we went to the town *to preach!*"

"My son," Francis replied, "we *have* preached. We were preaching while we were walking. We have been seen by many; our behavior has been closely watched; it was thus that we preached our morning sermon. It is of no use, my son, to walk anywhere to preach unless we preach everywhere as we walk."[2]

> Date: _____ _____ _____
> Place: _____ _____ _____
> Occasion: _____ _____ _____

I'd Rather See a Sermon

> *I'd rather see a sermon than hear one any day.*
> *I'd rather one would walk with me than merely show the way.*

---

[1] Adapted from a clipping in my files which indicates a version of this story first appeared in a book entitled *Who Needs God* by Kushner.

[2] F. W. Boreham, *The Crystal Pointers* (London: The Epworth Press, 1925), 19.

EXAMPLE 275

> *The eye's a better pupil and much sharper than the ear.*
> *Fine counsel can confuse me, but example's always clear.*
> *The lectures you deliver may be very wise and true,*
> *But I'd rather get my lesson by observing what you do.*—Author unknown

Date: _____ _____ _____
Place: _____ _____ _____
Occasion: _____ _____ _____

E

According to You

> *You are writing a gospel,*
> *A chapter each day,*
> *By the deeds that you do,*
> *By the words that you say;*
> *Men read what you write,*
> *Whether faithless or true.*
> *Say—what is the gospel,*
> *According to you?*—Paul Gilbert

Date: _____ _____ _____
Place: _____ _____ _____
Occasion: _____ _____ _____

The Model

G. Campbell Morgan once received a letter from a man who was converted under his ministry. The man spoke of coming into the church as a boy, neglected and hungry, and as he listened to the great preacher he resolved that he, too, would like to become a preacher of the gospel. Not only did he become a minister, but in the course of time his son also went into the ministry. In the letter the man said: "From that night you became my great human ideal. . . . I think I have read every book you have written. I placed your picture on the fly-leaf of my Bible, and I have never stood up to preach without first turning to look upon it. It somehow helps me more than anything else."[1]

Date: _____ _____ _____
Place: _____ _____ _____
Occasion: _____ _____ _____

The Example

Christians are always on display, whether they realize it or not. In his book, *Ten Mistakes Parents Make With Teenagers,* Jay Kesler describes a conversation he had with a young lady at a Youth for Christ summer camp.

---

[1] Jill Morgan, *A Man of the Word: Life of G. Campbell Morgan* (Grand Rapids: Baker Book House, 1972), 378.

This particular camp was in Ohio, and after one of the services some kids had come forward to the altar. One young woman was having a difficult time, so the counselors asked me if I would speak to her.

We sat down in the front row of the chapel, and through many tears her heartbreaking story began to unfold. She'd been molested by her own father about three times a week since she was four years old. She'd never told anyone about this and carried a great sense of guilt, as though she were to blame for her father's actions.

---◆---

The Silent Influence

Into the hands of every individual is given a marvelous power for good or evil—the silent, unconscious, unseen influence of his life.

—WILLIAM GEORGE
JORDAN

---◆---

As she told me the story, I noticed that both of her wrists were scarred. (If you work with youth today, you see those marks often.) "Tell me about your wrists," I said.

"Well, I tried to kill myself."

"Why didn't you do it?" I asked. Killing yourself is a relatively simple thing if you really want to do it. If it is just a bid for attention, the attempt is usually feeble.

She said, "Well, I got to thinking . . . we have a youth pastor at our church—"

Oh no, *I thought,* now I'm going to hear an ugly story *about her getting involved with some youth pastor. But that wasn't it at all. She said, "He'd just gotten married before he came to our church, and I've been watching him. When he's standing in line in church behind his wife, he squeezes her right in church. They look at each other, and they hug each other right in our church. One day I was standing in the pastor's study, looking out the window, and the youth pastor walked his wife out into the parking lot. Now there was only one car in the parking lot; nobody was around; nobody was looking. And that guy walked all the way around the car and opened the door and let her in. Then he walked all the way around and got in himself. And there was nobody even looking."*

That was a nice story, but I couldn't make a connection between that and her problem of incest or attempted suicide. So I asked why this seemed so significant to her. She said, "Well, I just got to thinking that all men must not be like my dad, huh?"

I said, "You're right. All men are not like your father."

"Jay, do you suppose our youth pastor's a Christian?"

"Yes," I said, "I think he probably is."

"Well, that's why I came tonight. I want to be a Christian, too."

Why did she want to be a Christian? Because she saw a man being affectionate and respectful to his wife—when he thought nobody was looking. That's the power of a consistent life.[1]

Date:			
Place:			
Occasion:			

Influence

Leslie Flynn points out that the Italian word for *influence* is *influenza*. The word *influenza* was introduced into English in the mid-1700s, apparently coming from the

---

[1] Jay Kesler, *Ten Mistakes Parents Make With Teenagers* (Brentwood, TN: Wolgemuth & Hyatt Publishers, Inc., 1988), 29–30.

EXAMPLE 277

Italian phrase which attributed the origin of this malady to an *influenza di freddo* (influence of the cold).

We are, by our very natures, very contagious people—our example tends to spread to others as easily as the flu. Everyone exerts influence.[1]

Date:			
Place:			
Occasion:			

E

Pippa Passes

Robert Browning once wrote a poem entitled "Pippa Passes" about an Italian girl. Because of her poverty and destitute family, she was forced to work every day during the entire year in the silk mills, but on New Year's Day she was given the day off. In sheer joy, she walked through the streets of her town in northeast Italy, singing a song of faith with words that said:

> The year's at the spring,
> And day's at the morn;
> Morning's at seven;
> The hill-side's dew-pearled;
> The lark's on the wing;
> The snail's on the thorn;
> God's in his Heaven—
> All's right with the world!

As she walked down the narrow streets, her thankful heart free and overflowing, her song reached people just at a crucial moment in their lives. An unwed couple were moved to make some changes in their lives. An artist on the verge of losing his temper was calmed. An anarchist intent on assassinating the Austrian emperor was halted. A churchman planning to murder a child for money was smitten with remorse.

Pippa returned home from her walk later in the day, unaware of the unseen effects of her attitude and song.

Date:			
Place:			
Occasion:			

Learning by Example

The comedian Sam Levenson once recalled that his over-protective mother went with him on his very first day of school and insisted on talking to the teacher before leaving him. Levenson said that, among other things, his mother told the teacher

---

[1] Leslie Flynn, *Your Influence is Showing* (Nashville: Broadman Press, 1967), 11.

that if he misbehaved she should punish the boy *next* to him. Why? "My little boy learns *by example*," she said.

```
Date:       _____   _____   _____
Place:      _____   _____   _____
Occasion:   _____   _____   _____
```

Failure

Someone Once Said . . .

- *Success is never final; failure is never fatal; it is the courage to continue that counts.*—Winston Churchill
- *I have always felt that although someone may defeat me, and I strike out in a ball game, the pitcher on the particular day was the best player. But I know when I see him again, I'm going to be ready for his curve ball. Failure is a part of success.*—Hank Aaron
- *We failed, but in the good providence of God apparent failure often proves a blessing.*—Robert E. Lee
- *I honestly think it is better to be a failure at something you love than to be a success at something you hate.*—George Burns
- *It is better to fail in a cause that will ultimately succeed, than to succeed in a cause that will ultimately fail.*—Peter Marshall[1]
- *It is a mistake to suppose that men succeed through success; they much oftener succeed through failures. Precept, study, advice, and example could never have taught them so well as failure has done.*—Samuel Smiles (1812–1904), Scottish author

```
Date:       _____   _____   _____
Place:      _____   _____   _____
Occasion:   _____   _____   _____
```

The Thin Line Between Success and Failure

Paul Tournier, Swiss physician and counselor, suggests that it is not easy to tell the difference between success and failure, or to know where the line between the two is drawn. Take technology, for example. We take great pride in our technological advances, but it may well be that our successes in technology will lead to the destruction of the human race—humanity's ultimate failure. Tournier writes, . . . *it is often difficult to say which side has really won a war—sometimes not the one with the military victory, but in fact the vanquished, who have bequeathed to their vanquishers the fundamental principles of their civilization.*

It is, then, extremely difficult to define failure and success, the line of demarcation between them is so elusive. Is the atomic bomb a success or a failure? Today's success will be revealed

---

[1] Erwin W. Lutzer, *Hitler's Cross* (Chicago: Moody Press, 1995), 155.

tomorrow to have been a failure. I am often struck that so few rich people really enjoy the fortune they have amassed. They have succeeded in life, but they have not made a success of their lives.

Drawing from his own experience, Tournier gives an interesting illustration:

I have given many lectures, and I do not deny that it gives me pleasure when the lecture goes well. One of my most vivid memories is of a lecture I gave many years ago, one of my worst failures. It was at a university. I felt right from the first word that I was not going to make contact with my audience. I clung to my notes and laboriously recited, with growing nervousness, what I had to say. As the audience left I could see my friends slipping hurriedly away, to spare themselves and me the embarrassment of a meeting. On the way home in my car with my wife, I burst into tears.

But the next day a professor of philosophy called me on the telephone. He told me he had listened in his life to a large number of remarkable lectures. . . . He had never heard one as bad as mine, he added, and this was what intrigued him and made him want to see me. This incident was the beginning of a wonderful friendship between us. I was the witness of his conversion to the Christian faith, and that was the source of more lasting joy to me than could ever have been procured by success in delivering a lecture.[1]

Heightened Resolve

Failure always made me try harder next time.

—MICHAEL JORDAN

F

> Date: _____ _____ _____
>
> Place: _____ _____ _____
>
> Occasion: _____ _____ _____

A Short Biography of Abraham Lincoln

Difficult childhood
Less than one year formal schooling
Failed in business in 1831
Defeated for the legislature, '32
Again failed in business, '33
Elected to the legislature, '34
Fiancée died, '35
Defeated for Speaker, '38
Defeated for Elector, '40
Married, wife a burden, '42
Only one of his four sons lived past age 18
Defeated for Congress, '43
Elected to Congress, '46
Defeated for Congress, '48
Defeated for Senate, '55
Defeated for Vice-President, '56
Defeated for Senate, '58
Elected President, 60[2]

---

[1] Paul Tournier, *The Adventure of Living* (San Francisco: Harper & Row, Publishers, 1965), 125–127.
[2] John Maxwell, *Your Attitude: Key to Success* (San Bernardino, CA: Here's Life Publishers, 1984), 80.

Date: _____ _____ _____
Place: _____ _____ _____
Occasion: _____ _____ _____

More Accomplished in Failure Than Success

In his award-winning *Profiles in Courage,* John F. Kennedy tells the story of George W. Norris of Nebraska. Norris began his career as a country teacher on the plains of Nebraska, then a small-town lawyer, a local prosecuting attorney and judge. In 1903, he entered the House of Representatives, and he was later elected to the Senate. Kennedy describes him as a "chunky figure" clothed in "drab black suits, white shirts, and little shoestring ties."

—◇—
Fleeting Success

Success is never final. Failure is never fatal.
—JOE PATERNO
—◇—

Norris was an independent-thinking Republican who sometimes took up unpopular causes and fought uphill battles, saying, "I would rather go down to my political grave with a clear conscience than ride in the chariot of victory."

Interestingly, he lost many of his most anguishing political fights. But years later, looking back over his life and career, Norris made this observation to a friend: *It happens very often that one tries to do something and fails. He feels discouraged, and yet he may discover years afterward that the very effort he made was the reason why somebody else took it up and succeeded. I really believe that whatever use I have been to progressive civilization has been accomplished in the things I failed to do rather than in the things I actually did do.*[1]

Date: _____ _____ _____
Place: _____ _____ _____
Occasion: _____ _____ _____

Successful Failures

John Maxwell points out that most successful people begin as failures:

- Ignace Paderewski, the great Polish pianist, was once told by his music teacher that his hands were much too small to master the keyboard.
- The great Italian tenor, Enrico Caruso, was told by his teacher that his voice sounded like the wind whistling through the window.
- When the British statesman, Benjamin Disraeli, attempted to speak in Parliament for the first time, members hissed him into silence and laughed when he said, "Though I sit down now, the time will come when you will hear me."
- Henry Ford forgot to put a reverse gear in his first car.
- In 1902, the poetry editor of *The Atlantic Monthly* sent a sheaf of poems back to a 28–year-old poet with this curt note: "Our magazine has no room for your vigorous verse." The poet was Robert Frost.

---

[1]John F. Kennedy, *Profiles in Courage* (New York: Pocket Books, Inc., 1956), 178.

- In 1905, the University of Bern turned down a Ph.D. dissertation as being irrelevant and fanciful. Its author was Albert Einstein.
- The rhetoric teacher at Harrow School in England wrote this on sixteen-year-old Winston Churchill's report card: "A conspicuous lack of success."
- Thomas Edison once spent $2,000,000 on an invention that proved to be a flop.[1]

Date: _____ _____ _____
Place: _____ _____ _____
Occasion: _____ _____ _____

F

The Back Door to Success

In his little book, *Failure: The Back Door To Success*, Pastor Erwin Lutzer makes these points:

- We forget that God is a specialist; He is well able to work our failures into His plans.
- Heaven will be filled with surprises! Many "successful" Christians will be nobodies, and some whose lives were strewn with the wreckage of one failure after another will be great in the kingdom.
- If money is a basis of judging success or failure; it is obvious that Jesus Christ was a failure!
- The reason we think there are great differences among Christians is that we compare our lives with those of other believers. When we compare ourselves with God, those differences are negligible. One molehill is nearly the height of another, if you measure them all against the Himalayas.[2]

Date: _____ _____ _____
Place: _____ _____ _____
Occasion: _____ _____ _____

The Rabbi's Wisdom

A troubled man went to see a wise and good rabbi.

"Rabbi," he said, wringing his hands, "I am a failure. More than half the time I do not succeed in doing what I must do."

"Oh?" said the Rabbi.

"Please say something wise, rabbi."

After much pondering the rabbi spoke as follows: "Ah, my son, I give you this wisdom. Go and look on page 930 of the *New York Times Almanac* for the year 1970, and you will find peace of mind maybe."

---

[1] John Maxwell, *Your Attitude: Key to Success* (San Bernardino, CA: Here's Life Publishers, 1984). 79–80.
Robert Frost, Albert Einstein, and Winston Churchill stories—*Parables, Etc.*, August 1996, 1–2.
[2] Erwin W. Lutzer, *Failure: The Back Door to Success* (Chicago: Moody Press, 1975), 16, 17, 21, 35.

This is what he found: the listing of the lifetime batting averages of all the greatest baseball players. Ty Cobb, the greatest slugger of all, had a lifetime average of only .367.

The man went back to the rabbi and said, "Ty Cobb—.367. That's it?"

"That's it," said the rabbi. "Ty Cobb got one hit out of every three times at bat. He failed twice as often as he succeeded. So what do you expect already?"

"Ah," said the man, who thought he was a wretched failure because he failed only half the time.[1]

Date: _____ _____ _____
Place: _____ _____ _____
Occasion: _____ _____ _____

His First Sermon Flopped

The world-famed Methodist missionary E. Stanley Jones candidly shared how his very first sermon flopped:

"The little church was filled with my relatives and friends, all anxious that the young man should do well. I had prepared for three weeks, for I was to be God's

═══════◇═══════
No Failure in Christ

In His will there is no failure; out of His will, there is no success.
═══════◇═══════

lawyer and argue His case well. I started on rather a high key and after a half dozen sentences used a word I had never used before and I have never used since: indifferentism. Whereupon a college girl smiled and put down her head.

"Her smiling so upset me that when I came back to the thread of my discourse it was gone. My mind was an absolute blank. I stood there clutching for something to say. Finally I blurted out 'I am very sorry, but I have forgotten my sermon,' and I started for my seat in shame and confusion.

"As I was about to sit down, the Inner Voice said: 'Haven't I done anything for you? If so, couldn't you tell that?' I responded to this suggestion and stepped down in front of the pulpit—I felt I didn't belong behind it—and said, 'Friends, I see I can't preach, but you know what Christ has done for my life, how He has changed me, and though I cannot preach I shall be his witness the rest of my days.'

"At the close a youth came up to me and said he wanted what I had found. It was a mystery to me then, and it is a mystery to me now that, amid my failure that night, he still saw something he wanted. As he and I knelt together he found it. It marked a profound change in his life, and today he is a pastor, and his daughter is a missionary in Africa. As God's lawyer, I was a dead failure; as God's witness, I was a success. That night marked a change in my conception of the work of the Christian minister—he is to be, not God's lawyer to argue well for God, but God's witness, to tell what Grace has done for an unworthy life."[2]

[1] Alan Loy McGinnis, *The Power of Optimism* (San Francisco: Harper & Row, Publishers, 1990), 29–30.
[2] Ruth Tucker, *From Jerusalem to Irian Jaya* (Grand Rapids, MI: Zondervan, 1983), 282–283.

Ultimate Failure

In 1978 during the firemen's strike in England, the British army took over emergency fire-fighting. On January 14 they were called out by an elderly lady in South London to retrieve her cat. They arrived with impressive haste, very cleverly and carefully rescued the cat, and started to drive away. But the lady was so grateful she invited the squad of heroes in for tea. Driving off later with fond farewells and warm waving of arms, they ran over the cat and killed it.

Date: _____ _____ _____
Place: _____ _____ _____
Occasion: _____ _____

———————————————— Faith ————————————————

Someone Once Said . . .

- *Faith is like muscle which grows stronger and stronger with use, rather than rubber, which weakens when it is stretched.*—J. O. Fraser, missionary to China
- *Faith is the Samsonian lock of the Christian; cut it off, and you may put out his eyes— and he can do nothing.*—Charles Haddon Spurgeon[1]
- *Not a great faith we need, but faith in a great God.*—J. Hudson Taylor
- *Little faith will bring your soul to heaven, but great faith will bring heaven to your soul.*— Anonymous

Date: _____ _____ _____
Place: _____ _____ _____
Occasion: _____ _____ _____

Definitions of Faith

- The art of holding on to things your reason has once accepted, in spite of your changing moods.—C. S. Lewis[2]
- Faith is to believe what you do not see; the reward of this faith is to see what you believe.—St. Augustine
- Faith is voluntary anticipation.—Clement of Alexandria

Date: _____ _____ _____
Place: _____ _____ _____
Occasion: _____ _____ _____

[1]Charles Spurgeon, *Spurgeon's Sermons*, vol. 2 (Grand Rapids, MI: Baker Book House, 1983), 59.
[2]C. S. Lewis, *Mere Christianity* (New York: Macmillan Co., 1948), 109.

Biblical Definitions of Faith

- Believing there will be a fulfillment of those things that are told us by the Lord—Luke 1:45
- Believing that it will be just as was told us—Acts 27:25
- Not wavering at the promise of God, but being fully convinced that what He has promised He is able to perform—Romans 4:20–21
- Judging Him faithful who has promised—Hebrews 11:11
- The substance of things hoped for, the evidence of things not seen—Hebrews 11:1

Date: _____ _____ _____

Place: _____ _____ _____

Occasion: _____ _____ _____

Spurgeon on Faith

Look at the faith of the master mariner! He looses his cable, he streams away from the land. For days, weeks, even months, he sees neither sail nor shore, yet on he goes day and night without fear, till one morning he finds himself exactly opposite the desired haven toward which he has been steering.

How has he found his way over the trackless deep? He has trusted his compass, his nautical almanac, his glasses, and the heavenly bodies; and obeying their guidance, without sighting land, he has steered so accurately that he has not changed a point to enter port.

It is a wonderful thing. . . . It is glorious to be so far out on the ocean of Divine love, believing in God, and steering for Heaven straight away, by the direction of the Word of God.[1]

Date: _____ _____ _____

Place: _____ _____ _____

Occasion: _____ _____ _____

Manning's Faith in God

Henry Edward Cardinal Manning (1808–1892) began his ministry in the Anglican Church, but after his conversion to Rome, he became Archbishop of Westminster, and a popular writer. During a period of great depression and a darkening of his faith, he went into a well-known bookstore for a copy of one of his own books, entitled *Faith in God*. As he waited for the book to be sent up from the storeroom, he heard a man's voice call up saying, "Manning's *Faith in God* is all gone."

That was all the lesson he needed to hear.

Date: _____ _____ _____

Place: _____ _____ _____

Occasion: _____ _____ _____

---

[1] Mrs. Charles E. Cowman, *Springs in the Valley* (Los Angeles: Cowman Publications, Inc., 1939), 338–339.

"But I Believe God . . ."

In her book *It's My Turn* Ruth Bell Graham tells a story about her growing up days in Tsingkiang, China, where her father was a missionary physician. The business manager at the local hospital told about a jolly gentleman named Mr. Kao Er. One day as he attended prayer meeting, bandits broke into his house and kidnapped his two children, an eight-year-old son and a baby daughter.

As word spread, the local Christians and missionaries gathered in earnest prayer.

Never one to miss an opportunity to witness, Mr. Kao Er had a large sign painted and posted in front of the hospital gate. It said, in effect: *The bandits have kidnapped our children and have demanded a thousand yuan ransom. I am not a wealthy man. I cannot pay a thousand yuan. I cannot pay five hundred yuan. I cannot even pay fifty yuan. But I believe God. If it is His will, He is able to bring my children back without any ransom.*

Passerbys were amazed by his message, and it was widely expected that the children would be quickly killed.

Weeks passed, and in the course of time a band of soldiers broke in upon the hive of bandits. As they pursued them, they heard a sound from the ditch beside the road. One soldier stopped to look, and there he found a skeleton-like child lying in the ditch where the bandits had hastily thrown him. It was Mr. Kao Er's son. He had been imprisoned under a large overturned vessel, and was on the brink of starvation. But he was alive, and he recovered.

But what of the baby girl?

Later there was another battle between the bandits and the soldiers. This time, the wife of the bandit chief was captured, and she was found nursing two babies—not twins—too near in age to both be her own. The daughter, too, was returned to her parents.

Ruth recalls, "Sitting one Sunday in the little gray-brick Chinese church, I watched as Mr. Kao Er, carrying his still-too-weak-to-walk son, and his wife, carrying the now healthy, chubby baby girl, walked forward to publicly give thanks to God and to dedicate both children to Him.[1]

Date:			
Place:			
Occasion:			

Why God Responds to Faith

Houston pastor John Bisango describes a time when his daughter Melodye Jan, age five, came to him and asked for a doll house. John promptly nodded and promised to build her one, then he went back to reading his book. Soon he glanced out the study window and saw her arms filled with dishes, toys, and dolls, making trip after trip until she had a great pile of playthings in the yard. He asked his wife what Melodye Jan was doing.

---

[1] Ruth Bell Graham, *It's My Turn* (Old Tappan, NJ: Fleming H. Revell Co., 1982), 30–32.

"Oh, you promised to build her a doll house, and she believes you. She's just getting ready for it."

"You would have thought I'd been hit by an atom bomb," John later said. "I threw aside that book, raced to the lumber yard for supplies, and quickly built that little girl a doll house. Now why did I respond? Because I wanted to? No. Because she deserved it? No. Her daddy had given his word, and she believed it and acted upon it. When I saw her faith, nothing could keep me from carrying out my word."[1]

Date:	_____	_____	_____
Place:	_____	_____	_____
Occasion:	_____	_____	_____

The Communion Set

Faith honors God, and God honors faith! A story from the life of missionaries Robert and Mary Moffat illustrates this truth. For ten years this couple labored faithfully in Bechuanaland (now called Botswana) without one ray of encouragement to brighten their way. They could not report a single convert.

—◇—
Free Checking

Faith makes cash out of God's checks.
—JOHN R. RICE
—◇—

Finally the directors of their mission board began to question the wisdom of continuing the work. The thought of leaving their post, however, brought great grief to this devoted couple, for they felt sure that God was in their labors, and that they would see people turn to Christ in due season. They stayed, and for a year or two longer, darkness reigned.

One day a friend in England sent word to the Moffats that she wanted to mail them a gift and asked what they would like. Trusting that in time the Lord would bless their work, Mrs. Moffat replied, "Send us a communion set; I am sure it will soon be needed." God honored that dear woman's faith. The Holy Spirit moved upon the hearts of the villagers, and soon a little group of six converts was united to form the first Christian church in that land. The communion set from England was delayed in the mail, but on the very day before the first commemoration of the Lord's Supper in Bechuanaland, the set arrived.[2]

Date:	_____	_____	_____
Place:	_____	_____	_____
Occasion:	_____	_____	_____

Has He Said, and Will He Not Do It?

The Protestant Reformation, which began in 1517, produced virtually no church-sent missionaries until two Moravians, Leonard Dober and David Nitschmann, were commissioned on August 18, 1732, in an unforgettable service in which

---

[1] John Bisango, *The Power of Positive Praying* (Grand Rapids, MI: Zondervan, 1965), 24.
[2] "faith," < www.sermonillustrations.com >

100 hymns were sung. The two soon left Herrnhut for Copenhagen, seeking passage to the islands.

But Copenhagen proved unfriendly, and the two men were pelted with obstacles. One disappointment followed another, and much opposition arose to their mission. No one would help them. No ship would take them. Their morale sank. At that critical moment, Numbers 23:19 turned up in their daily devotional book: *Has He said, and will He not do? Or has He spoken, and will He not make it good?* Inspired by these words, Dober and Nitschmann determined to persevere, believing that God would fulfill what he had started through them.

A handful of people in Copenhagen began helping them, and the tide of public opinion turned. Two royal chaplains lent their support, and even the Queen of Denmark encouraged them. Princess Charlotte contributed financially. A court official secured passage for them on a Dutch ship, and on October 8, 1732, they sailed for the West Indies, opening the modern era of missions. The Lord had spoken to them, and they had believed that He would make it good.

F

Date:			
Place:			
Occasion:			

More Moravians

Not long after the first Moravian missionaries had left for the West Indies, John Wesley, unconverted at the time, found himself aboard ship alongside another group of them. It was January 25, 1736, and the weather was rough. Three storms had already battered the boat, and a fourth was brewing. Wesley scribbled in his journal, "Storm greater: afraid!" But the Moravians were trusting God so simply and so completely that they evidenced no signs of fear, and they even persevered in their plans for a worship service. In the middle of their singing, a gigantic wave rose over the side of the vessel, splitting the main-sail, covering the ship, pouring water like Niagara Falls between decks "as if the great deep had already swallowed us up."

The English passengers screamed as the ship lurched and pitched between towering waves. A terrified Wesley clung on for dear life. But the German missionaries didn't miss a note. Wesley, awestruck by their composure, later went to the leader and asked, "Weren't you afraid?"

"I thank God, no."

"Were not your women and children afraid?"

"No," replied the man. "Our women and children are not afraid."

Back in London, Wesley was so struck by their sturdy faith that he attended a Moravian meeting on Aldersgate Street on May 24, 1738. He later said, "I felt my heart strangely warmed. I felt I did trust in Christ, Christ alone for salvation, and an assurance was given to me that He had taken away my sins, even mine."

Wesley became a famous evangelist and social reformer, with the world as his parish. But he himself was won to Christ by the power of a small group whose faith in Christ was strong enough to keep them unflappable in a storm.

Date:	_____	_____	_____
Place:	_____	_____	_____
Occasion:	_____	_____	_____

Faith, Mighty Faith

Charles Wesley, studying Abraham's faith as described in Romans 4:13, wrote a hymn of eleven stanzas about faith. The most popular stanza has provided a watchword for the Victorious Christian Life movement for a hundred years:

> *Faith, mighty faith, the promise sees,*
> *And looks to that alone;*
> *Laughs at life's impossibilities,*
> *And cries, It shall be done!*

Date:	_____	_____	_____
Place:	_____	_____	_____
Occasion:	_____	_____	_____

An Old Story

One of our oldest sermon illustrations still provides a powerful illustration of the personal nature of faith. A far-famed tightrope walker came to Niagara Falls and stretched his rope across the thunderous currents from Canada to the United States. Before the breathless multitudes, he walked, then ran, across the falls. He did the same blindfolded, with drums rolling. Then, still blindfolded, he pushed a wheelbarrow across the falls.

The crowds went wild, and the aerialist shouted to them, "Who believes I can push a man in this wheelbarrow across these falls?"

A gentleman in the front waved his hands, shouting, "I do! I believe!"

"Then," said the walker, "come and get in the wheelbarrow."

To no surprise, the man's intellectual assent failed to translate into personal belief.

Date:	_____	_____	_____
Place:	_____	_____	_____
Occasion:	_____	_____	_____

Anyone Else?

A man slipped and fell off a cliff while hiking on a mountaintop. Luckily he was able to grab a branch on his way down. Holding on for dear life, he looked down only to see a rock valley some fifteen hundred feet below. When he looked up it was twenty feet to the cliff where he had fallen.

Panicked, he yelled, "Help! Help! Is anybody there? Help!"

A booming voice spoke up. "I am here, and I will save you if you believe in me."

"I believe! I believe!" yelled back the man.

"If you believe me, let go of the branch and then I will save you."

The young man, hearing what the voice said, looked down again. Seeing the rock valley below, he quickly looked back up and shouted, "Is there anybody else up there!"[1]

Date:			
Place:			
Occasion:			

F

Faithfulness

Someone Once Said . . .

- *Faithfulness to principle is only proved by faithfulness in detail.*—Frances Ridley Havergal
- *My dear Senator, I am not called to be successful, but faithful.*—Mother Teresa, to Senator Mark Hatfield who, while touring her work in Calcutta, asked, "How can you bear the load without being crushed by it?"
- *Dependability: Fulfilling what I agreed to do even though it requires unexpected sacrifices. (Proverbs 15:4)*—Bill Gothard
- *I meant what I said, and I said what I meant. An elephant's faithful, one hundred percent.*—Dr. Seuss, in *Horton Hears a Who*
- *She Hath Done What She Could.*—Inscription on the tombstone of the blind hymnist Fanny J. Crosby

Date:			
Place:			
Occasion:			

Old Faithful

Old Faithful is not the largest geyser in Yellowstone National Park, nor does it reach the greatest height. But it is by far the most popular one. Why? It is regular and dependable, hence its name, "Old Faithful."

Date:			
Place:			
Occasion:			

---

[1] Kenneth Blanchard and Robert Lorber, *Putting the One Minute Manager to Work* (New York: Berkley Books, 1985), 20.

First Converts

- William Carey, the "Father of Modern Missions," labored for seven years in India before baptizing his first convert. Mary Drewery, in her biography of Carey, said, "The number of actual conversions directly attributable to him is pathetically small; the number indirectly attributable to him must be legion."[1]
- America's first missionary, Adoniram Judson, labored for seven years in Burma before seeing his first convert.
- Robert Morrison, the founder of Protestant missions in China, labored for seven years before his first convert was won to Christ.
- On May 16, 1819, Pomare II was baptized—the first convert on the island of Tahiti after twenty-two years of tears and toil by missionaries Mr. and Mrs. Henry Nott.
- Missionary Allen Gardiner traveled repeatedly to South America, trying to evangelize the islands of Patagonia and Tierra del Fuego. He eventually died of starvation without seeing a single soul saved, but the South American Missionary Society he founded has been sending missionaries and saving souls for over 150 years.
- Jimmy Aldridge and his colleagues with Free Will Baptist Foreign Missions worked for nine years in Bondoukou in the Ivory Coast of West Africa before seeing their first converts in the villages.
- In 1939 the first Sudan Interior Mission (SIM) workers went to Doro in southern Sudan to share the gospel with the Mabaan people, who had never heard of Christ. Years passed, and three SIM workers were buried at Doro, and more than fifty worked there diligently from 1939 to 1964 when they had to leave because of civil war. When they left there were less than a handful of baptized believers in good standing. But when they were able to later return to the Sudan, they were amazed to find large groups of witnessing believers with nearly three hundred waiting to be baptized.

Date: _____ _____ _____
Place: _____ _____ _____
Occasion: _____ _____ _____

In Lowly Paths

Washington Gladden was a New England pastor who grew very discouraged with the apparent fruitlessness of his work. One day, downhearted, he climbed up to the church belfry to think. From his high perch, it seemed tempting to jump off, and had he been an unconverted man, he might have considered it, so low were his spirits. Instead he poured out his heart to God, and from that experience wrote out a prayer which later became a powerful hymn:

[1] Mary Drewery, *William Carey: A Biography* (Grand Rapids, MI: Zondervan, 1978), 90.

O Master, let me walk with Thee
In lowly paths of service free;
Tell me Thy secret; help me bear
The strain of toil, the fret of care.

Date: _____ _____ _____

Place: _____ _____ _____

Occasion: _____ _____ _____

F

Faithful Despite . . .

Chuck Colson writes of being invited to preach at tough old San Quentin Prison, an opportunity he greatly anticipated and carefully planned for. Three hundred of the 2,200 inmates had agreed to come to the chapel to hear him. But just days before his arrival, officials uncovered a hidden cache of weapons, and the prison was immediately locked down with inmates confined to their cells.

When Colson arrived at the prison chapel, he was disheartened to find that only a handful of men were able to be present, and they were mostly Christians. His spirits flagged, for he had so hoped to preach the gospel to the unsaved. Struggling with a lack of enthusiasm, he thought *Maybe I'll just give a short devotional, ten minutes or so. I can't really preach my heart out to this crowd.*

> **Presidential Duties**
>
> *No president who performs his duties faithfully and conscientiously can have any leisure.*
> —JAMES K. POLK

But spotting a video camera in the far end of the room, he said to himself, *Maybe this is being recorded for the chapel library. Maybe I'd better give it my all.* He felt convicted for basing his morale and mood on the outer circumstances rather than the inner impulse of the Spirit, and so he preached with great fervor, as though a thousand inmates were listening.

Later he mentioned to the prison chaplain how disappointed he had been to have missed sharing the gospel with the three hundred men who had originally signed up to attend. "Didn't you know?" asked the chaplain. "Because of the lockdown, the administration agreed to videotape your sermon. They'll be showing it to all the inmates tomorrow on closed-circuit television in the morning and again in the afternoon."

In fact, the sermon was aired not just twice, but nearly a dozen times over the following weeks. Because of the lockdown, not just three hundred but all 2,200 prisoners heard the gospel.

Colson said that he learned three lessons from the incident:

- Mother Teresa is right. God calls us to faithfulness, not to success.
- When our goal is to change society, we often fail. When it is simple obedience to God, He blesses our efforts more than we can envision.
- We should not grow weary in well-doing, for we shall reap a harvest if we faint not.[1]

---

[1] Charles Colson, "A Way of Escape at San Quentin," *Christianity Today,* 72.

Date: _____ _____ _____
Place: _____ _____ _____
Occasion: _____ _____ _____

A Poem by John Oxenham

> *Is your place a small place?*
> *Tend it with care!—*
> *He set you there.*
>
> *Is your place a large place?*
> *Guard it with care!—*
> *He set you there.*
>
> *Whate'er your place, it is*
> *Not yours alone, but His*
> *Who set you there.*[1]

Date: _____ _____ _____
Place: _____ _____ _____
Occasion: _____ _____ _____

Vance Havner on Faithfulness

God is faithful, and He expects His people to be faithful. God's Word speaks of faithful servants, faithful in a few things, faithful in the least, faithful in the Lord, faithful ministers. And all points up that day when He will say, "Well done, thou good and faithful servant."

What terrible times we have in our churches trying to keep people faithful in attendance and loyalty! How we reward and picnic and coax and tantalize church members into doing things they don't want to do but which they would do if they loved God! The only service that counts is faithful service.

True faith shows up in faithfulness. Not everyone one can sing or preach, but all can be faithful.[2]

Date: _____ _____ _____
Place: _____ _____ _____
Occasion: _____ _____ _____

The Influence of a Very Average Life

In her little book, *Kept for the Master's Use,* hymn-writer Frances Ridley Havergal says: *Of ourselves we may have but little weight, no particular talents or position or anything*

---

[1] John Oxenham, *Bees in Amber;* quoted by V. Raymond Edman, *The Disciplines of Life* (Minneapolis, Minnesota, 1948), 202.

[2] Vance Havner, *Hearts Afire* (Old Tappan, NJ: Fleming Revell Co., 1952).

else to put into the scale, but let us remember that again and again God has shown that the influence of a very average life, when once really consecrated to Him, may outweigh that of almost any number of merely professing Christians. Such lives are like Gideon's three hundred, carrying not even the ordinary weapons of war, but only trumpets and lamps and empty pitchers, by whom the Lord wrought great deliverance, while He did not use the others at all. For He hath chosen the weak things of the world to confound the things that are mighty.[1]

Date: _____ _____ _____

Place: _____ _____ _____

Occasion: _____ _____ _____

F

Semper Fi

One of the most tragic events during the Reagan presidency was the Sunday morning terrorist bombing of the Marine barracks in Beirut, in which hundreds of Americans were killed or wounded as they slept. Many of us can still recall the terrible scenes as the dazed survivors worked to dig out their trapped brothers from beneath the rubble.

A few days after the tragedy, I recall coming across an extraordinary story. Marine Corps Commandant Paul Kelly visited some of the wounded survivors then in a Frankfurt, Germany, hospital. Among them was Corporal Jeffrey Lee Nashton, severely wounded in the incident. Nashton had so many tubes running in and out of his body that a witness said he looked more like a machine than a man, yet he survived.

> ⬥
> ### Great Faith
> *A little thing is a little thing, but faithfulness in a little thing is a great thing.*
> —J. HUDSON TAYLOR
> ⬥

As Kelly neared him, Nashton, struggling to move and racked with pain, motioned for a piece of paper and a pen. He wrote a brief note and passed it back to the Commandant. On the slip of paper were but two words—"Semper Fi"—the Latin motto of the Marines meaning "forever faithful." With those two simple words Nashton spoke for the millions of Americans who have sacrificed body and limb and their lives for their country—those who have remained faithful.[2]

Date: _____ _____ _____

Place: _____ _____ _____

Occasion: _____ _____ _____

Keep Kicking

Two frogs fell into a tub of cream. The one looked at the high sides of the tub which were too difficult to crawl over and said, "It is hopeless." So he resigned himself to death, relaxed, and sank to the bottom. The other one determined to keep swimming as long as he could. "Something might happen," he said. And it did. He

---

[1] Frances Ridley Havergal, *Kept for the Master's Use* (Philadelphia: The Rogers Company, n.d.), 162.

[2] J. Dobson and Gary Bauer, *Children at Risk* (Word Publishers 1990), 187–188. <www.sermonillustrations. com>

kept kicking and churning, and finally he found himself on a solid platform of butter and jumped to safety.

Date: _____ _____ _____
Place: _____ _____ _____
Occasion: _____ _____ _____

Fear

Someone Once Said . . .

- *Fear is that little darkroom where negatives are developed.*—Michael Pritchard[1]
- *Fear is pain arising from the anticipation of evil.*—Aristotle
- *To him who is in fear, everything rustles.*—Sophocles
- *When a man is defeated by life it is always due, ultimately, to the fact that he is suffering from [a] spirit of fear. . . . The spirit of fear is the real, the ultimate cause of all failure in life, and of all unhappiness.*—Dr. Martyn Lloyd-Jones[2]
- *Fear is a conglomeration of sinister shadows, and a shadow that has no substance.*—Norman Vincent Peale[3]
- *There is nothing like suspense and anxiety for barricading a human's mind against the Enemy.*—Screwtape to Wormwood, in C. S. Lewis' *Screwtape Letters*, (the "Enemy" here being God)[4]
- *Why should I fear? I am on a Royal Mission. I am in the service of the King of kings.*—Mary Slessor, missionary hero[5]
- *And though this world with devils filled should threaten to undo us / We will not fear for God has willed His truth to triumph through us.*—Martin Luther

Date: _____ _____ _____
Place: _____ _____ _____
Occasion: _____ _____ _____

Variations of a Theme

- *The only thing we have to fear is fear itself.*—Franklin D. Roosevelt
- *The thing I fear most is fear.*—Michel Eyquem De Montaigne, 1580
- *Nothing is terrible except fear itself.*—Francis Bacon, 1623
- *The only thing I am afraid of is fear.*—Duke of Wellington, 1831
- *Nothing is so much to be feared as fear.*—Henry David Thoreau, 1841

---

[1] John-Roger and Peter McWilliams, *Do It!* (Los Angeles: Prelude Press, 1991), 36.
[2] D. Martyn Lloyd-Jones, *I Am Not Ashamed* (Grand Rapids, MI: Baker Book House, 1986), 162.
[3] Norman Vincent Peale, *Stay Alive All Your Life* (Carmel, NY: Guideposts Associates, Inc., 1957), 76.
[4] C. S. Lewis, *The Screwtape Letters* (New York: The Macmillan Company, 1961), 34.
[5] Eugene Myers Harrison, *Blazing the Missionary Trail* (Wheaton, IL: Van Kampen Press, 1949), 113.

Date: _____ _____ _____
Place: _____ _____ _____
Occasion: _____ _____ _____

F

Fear Creates What It Fears

Dr. Paul Tournier observes that "fear creates what it fears. Fear of war impels a country to take the very measures which unleash war. The fear of losing the love of a loved one provokes us to just that lack of frankness which undermines love. The skier falls as soon as he begins to be afraid of falling. Fear of failing in an examination takes away the candidate's presence of mind and makes success more difficult."[1]

Date: _____ _____ _____
Place: _____ _____ _____
Occasion: _____ _____ _____

F.E.A.R.

Someone once described fear in an acronym: False Expectations Appearing Real.

Date: _____ _____ _____
Place: _____ _____ _____
Occasion: _____ _____ _____

What Americans Are Afraid Of

The Sunday supplement magazine, *USA Weekend,* ran a cover story in its August 22–24, 1997 issue, entitled "Fear: What Americans Are Afraid of Today." In a scientific poll, the magazine uncovered the things Americans fear most:

- 54% are "afraid" or "very afraid" of being in a car crash.
- 53% are "afraid" or "very afraid" of having cancer.
- 50% are "afraid" or "very afraid" of inadequate Social Security.
- 49% are "afraid" or "very afraid" of not having enough money for retirement.
- 36% are "afraid" or "very afraid" of food poisoning from meat.
- 35% are "afraid" or "very afraid" of getting Alzheimer's.
- 34% are "afraid" or "very afraid" of pesticides on food.
- 33% are "afraid" or "very afraid" of being a victim of individual violence.
- 32% are "afraid" or "very afraid" of being unable to pay current debts.
- 30% are "afraid" or "very afraid" of exposure to foreign viruses.
- 28% are "afraid" or "very afraid" of getting AIDS.
- 25% are "afraid" or "very afraid" of natural disasters.

[1] Paul Tournier, *The Adventure of Living* (San Francisco: Harper & Row, 1965), 123.

Other findings:

- Is the world a safer place than when you were growing up? No, say 9 in 10 Americans.
- 4 in 10 people feel unsafe taking a walk alone at night within a half-mile of home.
- 1 in 4 women thinks she has been followed by a stranger in the past year.
- 1 in 5 fears being caught in a bombing in a public place.[1]

Date: _____ _____ _____
Place: _____ _____ _____
Occasion: _____ _____ _____

Fearful of Footprints

The destructive effect of fear and worry on our Christian faith is vividly illustrated by Daniel DeFoe's character Robinson Crusoe. Rejecting his father's pleas, Crusoe had left home in search of wealth and adventure. His life was one of recklessness and godlessness until, following a terrible storm and shipwreck, he found himself stranded on a deserted island in the Caribbean. There his soul began to respond to the Lord, and finding a Bible among the effects salvaged from the ship, he was converted and grew into a thankful, devout, hard-working Christian. His life, though missing human companionship, was peaceful and prayerful. His faith grew strong.

But one day Crusoe found a footprint in the sand, and he suddenly realized that he was not alone on the island. Knowing the fierce, cannibalistic practices of the native tribes, he grew into a fearful man. He looked over his shoulder with every step. He no longer slept peacefully. He altered his habits and patterns. He visualized himself being captured, boiled, and devoured.

Thus my fear banished all my religious hope. All that former confidence in God, which was founded upon such wonderful experience as I had had of His goodness, now vanished, as if He that had fed me by miracle hitherto could not preserve, by His power, the provision which He had made for me by His goodness. . . .

That is what fear does to us—it is diametrically opposed to our faith.

Date: _____ _____ _____
Place: _____ _____ _____
Occasion: _____ _____ _____

Fear of Dentists

When I was a child, my dentist had his office at the end of a long dark hallway on the sixth floor of an old downtown building. It was a terrifying trip filled with ominous dread that lingers to this day.

---

[1] *USA Weekend,* August 22–24, 1997, 5.

My dread, however, was nothing compared to the panic attacks that seized Elva Minette Martin before her dentist appointments. *I would worry and get an upset stomach, lie in bed with my mind racing and awaken in the clutches of terror. I was sure that I wouldn't be able to swallow or move when I sat in the dentist's chair.*

One week shortly before a routine visit, Elva was preparing to teach her Sunday school class from John 6, about the storm on the Sea of Galilee. Just as the disciples' panic reached its worst, Jesus came walking on the water and saying, "It is I; do not be afraid."

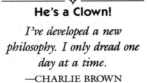

He's a Clown!

I've developed a new philosophy. I only dread one day at a time.

—CHARLIE BROWN

As she studied those words, Elva was suddenly convicted about her own fears.

That night I went to bed, but not to sleep. My mind knew that God was able to help me, yet I was still afraid. Acknowledging his Lordship in my life, I finally gave up my hold on fear. I prayed, "OK, Lord. Even when I go to the dentist, I will remember your promise."

As Elva headed toward her appointment, she was nervous yet excited, sensing the Lord would give her a breakthrough. *He calmed me, even relieved my grasp on the arms of the dentist's chair. Each time I began to worry, I remembered his promise: "It is I; do not be afraid."*

What a joyous time! God suspended my fear. I had never thought that I could ever say that going to the dentist was a wonderful experience—but it was. Not because of what went on around me or what happened to me, but because of what was in my heart. With his help, I am learning to say, "God is in control; I will not be afraid."[1]

Date:			
Place:			
Occasion:			

The Coyote's Wail

When businessman Allen Emery was in the wool business, he once spent an evening with a shepherd on the Texas prairie. During the night, the long wail of coyotes pierced the air. The shepherd's dogs growled and peered into the darkness. The sheep, which had been sleeping, lumbered to their feet, alarmed, bleating pitifully. The shepherd tossed more logs onto the fire, and the flames shot up. In the glow, Allen looked out and saw thousands of little lights. He realized those were reflections of the fire in the eyes of the sheep.

"In the midst of danger," he observed, "the sheep were not looking out into the darkness but were keeping their eyes set in the direction of their safety, looking toward the shepherd. I couldn't help but think of Hebrews 12: 'looking unto Jesus, the author and finisher of our faith. . . .'"[2]

---

[1] Robert J. Morgan, *From This Verse* (Nashville: Thomas Nelson Publishers, 1998), September 3rd.
[2] Morgan, *From This Verse*, December 4th.

Date: _____ _____ _____
Place: _____ _____ _____
Occasion: _____ _____ _____

He Was Never Fearful

Dr. L. Nelson Bell was serving as a medical missionary when the Japanese invaded China, and his family was at great risk. It was November 1938, and Sutsien, his neighbor station a few miles away, had fallen. Rumors of missionary casualties were rampant. On Christmas Day, Nelson wrote to his mother in America: *This past Thursday it was my time to lead foreign prayer meeting, and I talked about the place of physical fear in the life of the Christian. Last week it dawned on me that our Lord, tempted in all points the same as we are, yet without sin, hungered, thirsted, was tired, became angry, and gave every evidence of his humanity, but He was never fearful. Fear, therefore, must come from lack of faith—sin. Just as we never become sinless, so we never entirely lose fear, but it surely is His will for His children to live with peace in their hearts, trusting in Him and His promises.*[1]

Years later, his daughter, Ruth Bell Graham, said this in describing her growing-up years in China: *I can never recall going to sleep at night without hearing gunshots in the countryside around the house. I remember one tremendous fire over in the city. We went up to the third-story attic window where we could see it and hear the explosions. We thought the city was being invaded. The whole skyline was lit up. . . . I think the greatest tribute to mother's courage is that we children never sensed fear and we ourselves never had any fear. Now this is bound to reflect your parents. If they had been nervous, we would have been nervous.*[2]

Date: _____ _____ _____
Place: _____ _____ _____
Occasion: _____ _____ _____

Needless Fear

The early American Indians had a unique practice of training young braves. On the night of a boy's thirteenth birthday, after learning hunting, scouting, and fishing skills, he was put to one final test. He was placed in a dense forest to spend the entire night alone. Until then, he had never been away from the security of the family and tribe. But on this night, he was blindfolded and taken several miles away. When he took off the blindfold, he was in the middle of a thick woods, and he was terrified. Every time a twig snapped, he visualized a wild animal ready to pounce. After what seemed like an eternity, dawn broke and the first rays of sunlight entered the interior of the forest. Looking around, the boy saw flowers, trees, and the outline of a path. Then to his utter astonishment, he beheld the figure of a man standing just a few feet away, armed with bow and arrow. It was his father. He had been there all night long.[3]

---

[1] John C. Pollock, *A Foreign Devil in China* (Minneapolis: World Wide Publications, 1971), 191.
[2] Pollock, *A Foreign Devil in China*, 81.
[3] From *Our Daily Bread*.

```
Date:        _____    _____    _____
Place:       _____    _____    _____
Occasion:  _____    _____    _____
```

Luther on Fear

Martin Luther made this interesting observation in his *Table Talk*. God and the devil take opposite tactics in regard to fear. The Lord first allows us to become afraid, that he might relieve our fears and comfort us. The devil, on the other hand, first makes us feel secure in our pride and sins, that we might later be overwhelmed with fear and despair.

```
Date:        _____    _____    _____
Place:       _____    _____    _____
Occasion:  _____    _____    _____
```

Men and Their Fears

"Strange fears possess the souls of many. Even some great ones of the earth have not been free from them. Dr. [Samuel] Johnson, with all his philosophy, was very careful not to enter a room with his left foot foremost. If by any chance he did so, he would immediately step back and reenter with his right foot foremost. He was terribly afraid of death, too, and would not suffer it to be mentioned in his presence. Julius Caesar, to whom the shouts of thousands of the enemy were but sweet music, was mortally afraid of the sound of thunder and always wanted to be underground to escape the dreadful noise. Marshal Saxe, who loved to look upon the ranks of opposing armies, fled and screamed in terror at the sight of a cat. Peter the Great could scarcely be persuaded to cross a bridge, and whenever he placed his foot on one he would cry out with fear."[1]

```
Date:        _____    _____    _____
Place:       _____    _____    _____
Occasion:  _____    _____    _____
```

John Knox

Scotland's Queen Mary once asked John Knox to come to her privately if she did anything of which he did not approve. Knowing this would inhibit his freedom to preach, Knox pointed out that he was called to a public ministry, not to wait at princes' doors to whisper in their ears. If she wished to hear his views on any matter she could do so by attending the services in St. Giles.

---

[1] James Smith and Robert Lee, *Handfuls on Purpose: Series XII* (Grand Rapids, MI: Eerdmans Publishing Co., 1971), 100–101.

As he left the royal court, some were surprised by his lack of fear. His reply: *I have looked in the faces of many angry men, and yet have not been afraid above measure.*[1]

Knox understood Proverbs 29:25: "The fear of man brings a snare, but whoever trusts the Lord shall be safe."

Date:			
Place:			
Occasion:			

"I'm a Christian Lady"

One February evening, Louise Degrafinried heard the rustling of leaves outside her secluded Tennessee home, and she cautiously peered out the window. She knew that five men had escaped from the nearby Fort Pillow State Prison, less than twenty-five miles away. They were armed and considered dangerous. "Nathan," she said to her husband, "what would we do if those men came here?"

"Honey, we'd do just what they said."

Louise didn't like that idea at all, but she wasn't afraid. She had learned about God as a child and firmly believed her grandfather had been right in saying, "If you trust in the Lord, then he will take care of you."

Nevertheless she was glad the next morning when the sun rose. But as she was cooking breakfast and chatting with a friend on the phone, she heard Nathan shout. Louise quickly told her friend to call the police, then she hung up the phone and went to the door. There stood a tall man, covered with mud, jabbing a shotgun into Nathan's side. They stumbled into the kitchen, and the man threatened to shoot them if they didn't let him use their truck.

Nathan went outside to crank the truck as the escapee kept the shotgun trained on Louise. As soon as her husband was out the door, Louise took a few steps forward and said, "Young man!" He pointed his shotgun at her, but she seemed unafraid.

"Young man," she said again, "I'm a Christian lady. We don't have any violence in this house. This is God's house. Put down that gun." The man hesitated. "I said to put the gun down!"

Slowly he bent over and leaned the gun against the couch. Then he slumped on the couch himself and said, "Lady, I'm so hungry. I haven't eaten in three days."

"Then I will fix you breakfast," she said, cracking some more eggs into a bowl. She began talking to him, learning his name (Riley), age, and background. After saying grace over the food, she fixed a solution to help his ailing throat.

"You sound like my grandmother," said Riley, and over breakfast he started talking sadly to Louise about his dead grandmother who had loved him.

"Well, I love you," said Louise, "and I'm not dead. Jesus loves you, too. He died for us all. That's the way I know he loves you." Riley didn't say much. He just kept eating, and Louise kept giving him the Bible. Finally she said, "Young man, you'd like to give yourself up, wouldn't you?"

---

[1] W. Stanford Reid, *Trumpeter of God: A Biography of John Knox* (Grand Rapids, MI: Baker Book House, 1974), 227–228.

"Oh, lady," he replied, "They'd kill me in a minute."

"No, they won't. Not here. There won't be any violence in this house, by anyone."

Riley paused. Slowly he nodded his head. "Okay."

Within minutes, Riley was in handcuffs and headed back to prison, having gained a new prayer partner. As for Louise, she reports, "Things are pretty much back to normal now, except that I've gotten a little more attention than an old country woman should expect."[1]

Date: _____   _____   _____

Place: _____   _____   _____

Occasion: _____   _____   _____

Biting Angels

Little Hannah had never spent a night in the country before, and she was nervous about the sounds of the crickets, frogs, and insects outside the door of their vacation cabin. Her little voice whined in the darkness, "Mommy, everything buzzes, and I'm afraid."

"Don't be afraid," said her mother. "Remember the angels are right here watching over you."

A few minutes later, the air was pierced with an "Aough!"

"What is it now, Hannah?" asked her weary mother.

"I don't know," said Hannah, voice trembling. "But I think one of the angels just bit me."

Date: _____   _____   _____

Place: _____   _____   _____

Occasion: _____   _____   _____

Fear of God

Someone Once Said . . .

- *When you fear God, you have nothing else to fear.*—Anonymous
- *He feared man so little, because he feared God so much.*—inscription to Lord Lawrence in Westminster Abbey
- *This phrase "the fear of the Lord" occurs over and over and over. I was really surprised to find more than three hundred references in the Old Testament that speak of the fear of the Lord. The fear of the Lord is reverential trust and hatred of evil, and there you have the whole thing.*—William Anderson[2]

---

[1] Louise Degrafinried and Jeffery Japinga, "The Woman Who Wasn't Afraid," *Reader's Digest,* February 1985, 105–108. Original article in *Guideposts Magazine.*

[2] William Anderson, *The Faith That Satisfies* (New York: Loizeaux Brothers, Inc., 1948), 23–27.

- *The fear of God is . . . astonished reverence. I believe that the reverential fear of God mixed with love and fascination and astonishment and admiration and devotion is the most enjoyable state and the most satisfying emotion the human soul can know.*—A. W. Tozer[1]
- *Christian, let God's distinguishing love to you be a motive to you to fear Him greatly. Remember that this fear of the Lord is His treasure, a choice jewel.*—John Bunyan, in The Fear of God
- *The fear of the Lord: The continual awareness that God is watching and weighing every one of my thoughts, words, actions, and attitudes. (Proverbs 9:10)*—Bill Gothard

Date: _____   _____   _____

Place: _____   _____   _____

Occasion: _____   _____   _____

Waterfalls and Canyons

When I was a boy, my parents took us to Niagara Falls. We rode the boat *Maid of the Mist* right out into the basin of the falls, and we also tramped down the steps to the edge of the bottom of the falls, and my dad even took me into the caves behind the falls where openings had been cut out. It is a terrifying thing to stand

—◇—
Trusting God

The fear of the Lord is reverential trust and hatred of evil.

—WILLIAM ANDERSON
—◇—

there, only inches from such power and from possible death, deafened by a thunderous roar, the ground trembling from six million cubic feet of water bursting over the falls every minute and falling 170 feet into the basin below.

On another vacation, we traveled to the Grand Canyon, and I still remember the overwhelming sense of awe, majesty, dizziness, and downright terror as I stood near the edge and gazed into the chasm.

This is akin to the fear of God. It isn't an unhealthy fear, but an overwhelming sense of God Himself.

If we feel a kind of fear and awe over a mere waterfall or chasm, how much more should we feel that way about the Lord, who is a million times more powerful than a cataract, a billion times more pure, and a trillion times more overwhelming and all-engulfing than a canyon?

It is that fear of God that keeps sin at bay in our lives and gives us a foothold for wisdom.[2]

Date: _____   _____   _____

Place: _____   _____   _____

Occasion: _____   _____   _____

A Fountain of Life

In his book, *Knowledge of the Holy*, A. W. Tozer writes: *In olden days men of faith were said to "walk in the fear of God" and to "serve the Lord with fear." However intimate*

---

[1] A. W. Tozer, *Whatever Happened to Worship* (Camp Hill, PA: Christian Publications, 1985), 30–31.
[2] From a sermon by Robert J. Morgan.

their communion with God, however bold their prayers, at the base of their religious life was the conception of God as awesome and dreadful. This idea of God transcendent runs through the whole Bible and gives color and tone to the character of saints. This fear of God was more than a natural apprehension of danger; it was a nonrational dread, an acute feeling of personal insufficiency in the presence of God the Almighty.

Wherever God appeared to men in Bible times the results were the same—an overwhelming sense of terror and dismay, a wrenching sensation of sinfulness and guilt. When God spoke, Abraham stretched himself upon the ground to listen. When Moses saw the Lord in the burning bush, he hid his face in fear to look upon God. Isaiah's vision of God wrung from him the cry, "Woe is me!" Daniel's encounter with God was probably the most dreadful and wonderful of them all.

Conversely, the self-assurance of modern Christians, the basic levity present in so many of our religious gatherings, the shocking disrespect shown for the Person of God, are evidence enough of deep blindness of heart. Many call themselves by the name of Christ, talk much about God, and pray to Him sometimes, but evidently do not know who He is. "The fear of the Lord is a fountain of life," but this healing fear is today hardly found among Christian men.[1]

Date: _____   _____   _____

Place: _____   _____   _____

Occasion: _____   _____   _____

Never! And Yet . . .

C. S. Lewis, speaking of the awesomeness of God, found a modern example in the children's story *The Wind in the Willows.* Rat and Mole approach Pan on the island:

"Rat," he found breath to whisper, shaking, "Are you afraid?"

"Afraid?" murmured the Rat, his eyes shining with unutterable love. "Afraid? Of Him? O, never, never. And yet—and yet—O Mole, I am afraid."[2]

Date: _____   _____   _____

Place: _____   _____   _____

Occasion: _____   _____   _____

The Zeal of the Lord

David McCullough's biography of Teddy Roosevelt, *Mornings On Horseback,* includes this story of young Teddy as a child in New York City:

Mittie [his mother] had found he was so afraid of the Madison Square Church that he refused to set foot inside if alone. He was terrified, she discovered, of something called the "zeal." It was crouched in the dark corners of the church ready to jump at him, he said. When she asked what a zeal might be, he said he was not sure, but thought it was probably a large animal like an alligator or a dragon. He had heard the minister read about it from the Bible. Using a concordance, she read him those passages containing the word zeal until suddenly, very excited,

---

[1] A. W. Tozer, *The Knowledge of the Holy* (New York: Harper & Row, 1961), 78.

[2] Elizabeth Skoglund, *More Than Coping* (Minneapolis: World Wide Publications, 1979), 73.

he told her to stop. The line was from the Gospel of John 2:17: "And his disciples remembered that it was written, 'The zeal of thine house hath eaten me up.'"

Date:	_____	_____	_____
Place:	_____	_____	_____
Occasion:	_____	_____	_____

Flattery

Someone Once Said . . .

- *One who extremely exaggerates in his opinion of your qualities, so that it may come nearer to your opinion of them.*—Oscar Wilde, when asked his definition of a flatterer
- *Flattery is like cologne water, to be smelt of, not swallowed.*—Josh Billings, nineteenth-century writer
- *Praise, like gold and diamonds, owes its value to its scarcity.*—Dr. Samuel Johnson
- *Flattery corrupts both the receiver and the giver.*—Edmund Burke
- *Flatter me, and I may not believe you. Criticize me, and I may not like you. Ignore me, and I may not forgive you. Encourage me, and I will not forget you.*—William Ward, college administrator
- *A little flattery will support a man through great fatigue.*—James Monroe

Date:	_____	_____	_____
Place:	_____	_____	_____
Occasion:	_____	_____	_____

Churchill's Assessment

When Adolf Hitler sought to placate Austrian minister Kurt von Schuschnigg by complimenting and praising him publicly, a disgusted Winston Churchill muttered, "When a snake wants to eat his victims he first covers them with saliva."[1]

Date:	_____	_____	_____
Place:	_____	_____	_____
Occasion:	_____	_____	_____

Lentils

In ancient Greece, the politically crafty philosopher Aristippus had learned to get along in court by flattering the tyrant Denys. Aristippus looked down his nose

---

[1] William Manchester, *The Last Lion: Winston Spencer Churchill—Alone* (Boston: Little, Brown, & Co., 1988), 250.

at some of his less prosperous fellow philosophers and wise men who would not stoop that low. One day he saw his old colleague Diogenes washing some vegetables, and he said to him disdainfully, "If you would only learn to flatter King Denys you would not have to be washing lentils."

Diogenes looked up slowly and in the same tone replied, "And you, if you had only learned to live on lentils, would not have to flatter King Denys."[1]

Date: _____ _____ _____
Place: _____ _____ _____
Occasion: _____ _____ _____

On the Other Hand . . .

Andrew DuBrin, a professor of management at Rochester Institute of Technology, writes favorably of flattery in his book *Personal Magnetism:*

"Call it graciousness, charm, politeness, good human relations, positive reinforcement, office politics, obsequiousness, making others feel good, or sucking up—whatever the name, magnetic people do it consistently. A notable characteristic of personally magnetic people is their ability and willingness to flatter others. If you can learn to flatter others effectively, you will substantially augment your ability to attract and retain supporters.

"Flattery works well with about 95 percent of the people who have sufficient mental ability to comprehend the compliments. The young, the old, the rich, the poor, the famous, the unknown, the sick and the well all respond to sensible flattery. The other 5 percent are people with low self-esteem, the callused and the jaundiced. The people who do not respond to flattery ward off compliments, preferring to let their good deeds speak for themselves."[2]

Date: _____ _____ _____
Place: _____ _____ _____
Occasion: _____ _____ _____

Forgiving Oneself

Someone Once Said . . .

- *There is no forgiveness from God unless you freely forgive your brother from your heart. And I wonder if we have been too narrow in thinking that "brother" only applies to someone else. What if YOU are the brother or sister who needs to be forgiven, and you need to forgive yourself?*—David Seamands[3]

---

[1] *Parables, Etc.,* November 1983, 3.
[2] Quoted from an unattributed clipping in my files.
[3] David Seamands, *Healing for Damaged Emotions* (Wheaton, IL: Victor Books, 1981), 31–32.

- *But now, do not therefore be grieved or angry with yourselves because you sold me here; for God sent me before you to preserve life.*—Joseph, in Genesis 45:5, to his brothers regarding the sins they committed against him years before
- *You come to a point when you've prayed, you've asked forgiveness, you've done everything you can do. And you just decide you have to forgive yourself, stop brooding over it, and get on with life. That's all you can do.*—a school bus driver who accidentally ran over a child, killing her

Date:	_____	_____	_____
Place:	_____	_____	_____
Occasion:	_____	_____	_____

The Knife and the Scalpel

The knife sliced through the man's shirt like a razor, entering his back at the shoulder and cutting diagonally toward the spine. Skin and muscle melted like mutton before a cleaver. The shock paralyzed him, and searing pain tore through his body like currents of fire. He tried to scream, but the knife had punctured a lung. Being withdrawn, it was plunged in again. And again. The third plunge was most cruel, stabbing, carving, nicking spinal cord and puncturing heart. The victim twisted toward his attacker, seeing through anguished eyes the face of his betrayer.

Three times the scalpel lacerated the man's chest, scoring the skin, cutting along carefully drawn lines. Its surgical steel grew red. Flesh and fat separated, the chest opened. Soon the heart was bared.

Two knives. One in the hand of a killer, the other in the hand of a healer. One cut into the back, the other into the chest. Three stabs for the betrayal. Three for the surgery. The surgeon, being healed, was operating on the man who had attacked him.

This is the story found in Luke 22 and John 21.

Three times Peter stabbed Jesus in the back. And three times, Jesus cut Peter to the heart. The Lord knew that Peter's guilt and his sense of shame were blacker than coal. But he also knew that Peter would never become the bold and brilliant leader of the early church if he spent his days groping in the coal mines of guilt and moping in his mineshafts of shame. So he told him, in effect, to get over it. To put it behind him. To renew his love for his Master, and to get busy feeding the sheep.[1]

Date:	_____	_____	_____
Place:	_____	_____	_____
Occasion:	_____	_____	_____

Phantom Pain

Dr. Paul Brand, writing with Philip Yancey, told a story about his medical school administrator, a man named Mr. Barwick, who had a serious and painful circulation

---

[1] From a sermon by the author.

problem in his leg, but who refused to allow amputation. But finally, the pain became too great for him to bear, and Barwick cried at last, "I'm through with that leg. Take it off."

Surgery was scheduled immediately, but before the operation Barwick asked the doctor, "What do you do with legs after they're removed?"

"We may take a biopsy or explore them a bit, but afterwards we incinerate them."

"I would like you to preserve my leg in a pickling jar," said Barwick, to the surprise of all. "I will install it on my mantle shelf. Then, as I sit in my armchair, I will taunt that leg, 'Hah! You can't hurt me anymore!'"

Ultimately Barwick got his wish, but the despised leg had the last laugh.

Barwick suffered phantom limb pain of the worst degree. Somehow locked in his memory were the sensations associated with that leg. Even after the wound healed, Barwick could feel the torturous pressure of the swelling as the muscles cramped and itched and throbbed.

"He had hated the leg with such intensity that the pain had unaccountably lodged permanently in his brain," wrote Brand, who then added, "To me, phantom limb pain provides wonderful insight into the phenomenon of false guilt. Christians can be obsessed by the memory of some sin committed years ago. It never leaves them, crippling their ministry, their devotional life, their relationships with others. . . .

"Unless they experience the truth of 1 John 3:19–20 that 'God is greater than our conscience,' they become as pitiful as poor Mr. Barwick, shaking his fist in fury at the pickled leg on the mantel."[1]

F

Date:			
Place:			
Occasion:			

Roots

In his book, *Healing for Damaged Emotions,* David Seamands writes about a young minister who once came to see him. He was having a lot of problems getting along with other people, especially his wife and family. Seamands recalls: "I had already talked privately with his wife; she was a fine person—attractive, warm, affectionate, loving—and totally supported him in his ministry. But he was continually criticizing her, scapegoating her. Everything she did was wrong. He was sarcastic and demanding, and withdrew from her advances, rejecting her love and affection. Slowly but surely it began to dawn on him: he was destroying their marriage.

"Then he realized that in his weekend pastorate he was hurting people through sermons which were excessively harsh and judgmental. . . .

"Finally, in his desperation, he came to see me. At the beginning of our interview, he met trouble like a real man: he blamed it on his wife! But after a while, when be became honest, the painful root of the matter came to light.

---

[1] *Leadership Journal,* Summer 1984, 55.

"While he was in the armed forces in Korea, he had spent two weeks of R&R in Japan. During that leave, walking the streets of Tokyo, feeling empty, lonely, and terribly homesick, he fell into temptation and went three or four times to a prostitute.

"He had never been able to forgive himself. He had sought God's forgiveness, and with his head, believed he had it. But the guilt still plagued him, and he hated himself. Every time he looked in the mirror, he couldn't stand what he was seeing. He had never shared this with anyone, and the burden was becoming intolerable.

"When he returned home to marry his fiancée, who had faithfully waited for him all those years, his emotional conflicts increased because he still could not accept complete forgiveness. He couldn't forgive himself for what he had done to himself and to her; so he couldn't accept her freely offered affection and love. He felt he had no right to be happy.

"As A. W. Tozer put it, the young minister was living in 'the perpetual penance of regret.'

"How beautiful it was to see him receive full, free forgiveness from God, then from his wife, and perhaps best of all, from himself."[1]

Date:			
Place:			
Occasion:			

To Win As Many As He Had Killed

One of the earliest missionaries in Christian history was Columba, born in Ulster, Ireland, on December 7, A.D. 521. His grandfather had been baptized by St. Patrick himself, and Columba's parents were believers of royal stock. He possessed a powerful presence with strong features and an authoritative voice, but Columba was strong-willed and combative. His fiery temper and iron will caused problems.

———◆———
Godly Forgiveness

There is no forgiveness from God unless you freely forgive your brother from your heart.
—DAVID SEAMANDS
———◆———

One day, Columba copied the contents of a book without permission, and when the owner requested the copy Columba refused. The argument took on a life of its own, involving more and more people. Eventually a war erupted in which three thousand men lost their lives.

Full of remorse, Columba sought and found the forgiveness of God. Then he committed himself to win as many to Christ as had died in the war. Thus he left Ireland at age forty-two to become a missionary to Scotland. With twelve companions, he established himself on Iona, a bleak, foggy island just off the Scottish coast, three miles long and a mile and a half wide. He built a crude monastery which soon became a training center for missionaries, one of the most venerable and interesting spots in the history of Christian missions. It was a lighthouse against heathenism.

From Iona, Columba made missionary forays into Scotland, converting large numbers. An entire tribe of pagans, the Picts, were won to the faith. He confronted

---
[1] Seamands, *Healing for Damaged Emotions,* 30–31.

the Druids, contesting with them over their alleged magical arts and demonic powers. He spent the rest of his life as the apostle to Scotland and as a trainer of missionaries.

What motivated him? He considered himself a debtor. He felt obligated to win as many as he had destroyed.

Date:			
Place:			
Occasion:			

F

Ashamed of Daddy

Mary Anna Martin grew up during the depression, but her family, despite its poverty, was rich in love and happiness. Her dad and mom were caring and tender parents, and laughter filled their home. Her father always whistled, and her mother sang while doing her housework. Her father was a baker, but he lost his bakery shop in the first years of the depression. He had to take any job he could to pay the family's rent and keep food on their table. He worked at the local YMCA for awhile, then with the WPA. When that job ran out, he found a job as a janitor. He was an older man, small and gray, and it was hard work. But he did his best and whistled as he worked.

Mary Anna said, "My life was happy and carefree until the year I left elementary school and started junior high. I was thirteen, and soon became part of a new group of friends. I knew that Daddy was a janitor, but I didn't know where, until that awful day during lunch break." Mary Anna was seated at a table with her new friends when she heard a teacher call her father's name in a loud voice. Someone had dropped their tray, and food and milk covered the table and floor. She saw him walk toward the table, carrying a mop and old rags. One of the girls said to Mary Anna, "That janitor has the same last name as yours. Do you know him?"

Mary Anna slowly raised her head and looked at the little, gray man cleaning up the spilled food. She hesitated, then said, "I've never seen him before in my life." A wave of intense embarrassment swept over her, and she instantly felt ashamed of denying her dearest friend on earth. She hated herself for those words and tried to make up for what she had done by showing her father that she loved him more than ever. He loved for someone to brush his hair as he sat in his easy chair. She would do it. She sang to him and read to him and spent time with him. But regardless of how hard she tried, nothing made her feel better.

The years passed, and her father developed Alzheimer's disease. One day when he was ill and she was sitting with him, she started crying. Her mother asked her what was wrong, and Mary Anna poured out her heart and told her what had been bothering her for more than fifteen years. She said, "I have been asking God to forgive me, but I can't get over what I had done."

Her mother drew her close and held her tightly as she wept. "Honey," she said, "your daddy knew you loved him, and he would have loved you even if he had known about your being ashamed of him when you were so young. You know Simon Peter denied that he knew our beloved Jesus before he was crucified on the cross, and Jesus loved him just the same." Suddenly Mary Anna felt at peace with herself for the first time since she was in junior high. She knew that because of the love of Christ, it was time to turn the corner.[1]

Date: _____ _____ _____
Place: _____ _____ _____
Occasion: _____ _____ _____

Guilt and Shame

In terms of sheer numbers, using the King James Version, the words *shame, ashamed,* and their derivatives far outdo *guilt* and *guilty.* The former are mentioned 224 times in the Bible, and the latter 23 times.

Date: _____ _____ _____
Place: _____ _____ _____
Occasion: _____ _____ _____

The Door

In *Decision Magazine,* Mark Strand tells of an experience that occurred following his first year of college. His dad and mom had left for vacation, and Mark wrecked their pickup truck, crumpling the passenger-side door. Returning home, he parked the truck. When his dad returned home and saw the damage, Mark acted surprised and denied any knowledge of the accident. Mr. Strand then asked the hired man about it, and to Mark's delight, the man admitted he was responsible. He had heard a loud noise while passing the truck with the wings of the cultivator up, and now he assumed he had caused the damage.

But the weeks that followed were torturous as Mark struggled with his guilty conscience. He repeatedly considered telling the truth, but was afraid. Finally one day he impulsively blurted it out.

"Dad, there's something I need to tell you."

"Yes?"

"You know that pickup door? I was the one who did it."

Dad looked at me. I looked back at him. For the first time in weeks I was able to look him in the eyes as the topic was broached. To my utter disbelief, Dad calmly replied, "I know."

Silent seconds, which seemed like hours, passed. Then dad said, "Let's go eat." He put his arm around my shoulder, and we walked to the house, not saying another word about it. Not then, not ever.[2]

Date: _____ _____ _____
Place: _____ _____ _____
Occasion: _____ _____ _____

[1] Mary Anna Martin, "I Was Ashamed of My Daddy," *Mature Living,* February 1996, 36–38.
[2] Mark Strand, "I Couldn't Forget That Door," *Decision,* December 1996, 19.

Lord of the Compost Heap

Joseph Bayly wrote the following in *Psalms for My Life:*

> Lord of the compost heap
> you take garbage
> and turn it into
> soil good soil
> for seeds to root
> and grow
> with wildest increase
> flowers to bloom
> with brilliant beauty.
> Take all the garbage
> of my life,
> Lord of the compost heap,
> turn it into
> soil good soil
> and then plant seeds
> to bring forth
> fruit and beauty
> in profusion.[1]

Date: _____ _____ _____

Place: _____ _____ _____

Occasion: _____ _____ _____

Forgiving Others

Someone Once Said . . .

- *Everyone says forgiveness is a lovely idea, until they have something to forgive.*—C. S. Lewis[2]
- *A Christian will find it cheaper to pardon than to resent. Forgiveness saves the expense of anger, the cost of hatred, the waste of spirits.*—Hannah More
- *It is a great thing to be a really good forgiver.*—F. W. Boreham[3]
- *When you bury the hatchet, don't bury it in your neighbor's back.*—Anonymous
- *The sin of unforgiveness is a cancer that destroys relationships, eats away at one's own psyche, and—worst of all—shuts us off from God's grace.*—Robertson McQuilkin[4]
- *Doing an injury puts you below your enemy; revenging one, makes you even with him; forgiving it sets you above him.*—Anonymous

---

[1] Joseph Bayly, "Psalms of My Life," *Christianity Today*, January 15, 1988, 35.
[2] C. S. Lewis, *Mere Christianity* (New York: The Macmillan Company, 1958), 89.
[3] F. W. Boreham, *The Other Side of the Hill* (London: Epworth Press, 1917), 240.
[4] Robertson McQuilkin, *The Two Sides of Forgiveness*, (Columbia International University), 1

- *Real forgiveness means looking steadily at the sin, the sin that is left over without any excuse, after all allowances have been made, and seeing it in all its horror, dirt, meanness and malice, and nevertheless being wholly reconciled to the man who has done it.*—C. S. Lewis
- *Every cat knows some things need to be buried.*—Ruth Bell Graham[1]

Date:	_____	_____	_____
Place:	_____	_____	_____
Occasion:	_____	_____	_____

Climbing

In her autobiographical book *Climbing,* missionary Rosalind Goforth tells of the internal rage she harbored against someone who had greatly harmed her and her husband, Jonathan. It was a serious injury which the couple would never afterward talk about, but while Jonathan seemed to easily forgive the offender, Rosalind refused to do so.

For more than a year, she would not talk to nor recognize that person who lived near them on their missionary station in China; four years passed and the matter remained unresolved and, to an extent, forgotten.

One day the Goforths were traveling by train to a religious meeting elsewhere in China. For months, Rosalind had felt a lack of power in her Christian life and ministry, and in her train compartment she bowed her head and cried to God to be filled with the Holy Spirit.

Unmistakably clear came the Inner Voice, "Write to (the one toward whom I felt hatred and unforgiveness) and ask forgiveness for the way you have treated him." My whole soul cried out "Never!" Again I prayed as before, and again the Inner Voice spoke clearly as before. Again I cried out in my heart, "Never; never. I will never forgive him!" When for the third time this was repeated, I jumped to my feet and said to myself, "I'll give it all up, for I'll never, never forgive!"

One day afterward, Rosalind was reading to the children from *Pilgrim's Progress.* It was the passage in which a man in a cage moans, "I have grieved the Spirit, and He is gone: I have provoked God to anger, and He has left me." Instantly a terrible conviction came upon her, and for two days and nights she felt in terrible despair.

Finally, talking late at night with a fellow missionary, a young widower, she burst into sobs and told him the whole story. "But Mrs. Goforth," he said, "are you willing to write the letter?"

At length she replied, "Yes."

"Then go at once and write it."

Rosalind jumped up, ran into the house, and wrote a few lines of humble apology for her actions, without any reference to his. The joy and peace of her Christian life returned.

---

[1] Ruth Bell Graham, *Legacy of a Pack Rat* (Nashville: Oliver Nelson, 1989), 172.

"From that time," Rosalind wrote in her autobiography, "I have never dared *not to forgive*."[1]

Date: _____ _____ _____

Place: _____ _____ _____

Occasion: _____ _____ _____

Carrying a Grudge

The great Methodist pastor Charles Allen wrote that, when he was in the fourth grade, the superintendent of the school mistreated him. There was no doubt about it. It was a deliberate wrong which the man committed because he had fallen out with Charles' father.

The Allens moved from that town, and the years passed.

One day during Charles' first pastorate, he heard that his old antagonist was seeking a job with the schools in the area. Charles knew that as soon as he told his friends on the school board about the man, they would not hire him.

I went out to get in my car to go see some of the board members and suddenly it came over me what I had done. Here I was out trying to represent Him who was nailed to the Cross and me carrying a grudge. That realization was a humiliating experience. I went back into my house, knelt by my bedside, and said, "Lord, if you will forgive me of this, I will never be guilty any more." That experience and that promise are among the best things that ever happened in my life.[2]

Date: _____ _____ _____

Place: _____ _____ _____

Occasion: _____ _____ _____

What Does It Mean to Forgive Another?

In his book *Caring Enough To Forgive / Caring Enough To Not Forgive*, David Augsburger suggests that forgiveness is a "journey of many steps" taken carefully and thoughtfully, the steps including:

1. To see the other as having worth again, regardless of wrongdoing;
2. To see the other as equally precious again, in spite of the pain felt;
3. To cancel demands on the past, recognizing that changing the unchangeable is impossible;
4. To work through the anger and pain felt by both in reciprocal trusting and risking until genuineness in intention is perceived and repentance is seen by both to be authentic;
5. To drop the demands for an ironclad guarantee of future behavior;

---

[1] Rosalind Goforth, *Climbing: Memories of a Missionary's Wife* (Wheaton, IL: Sword Book Club, 1940), 99–102.
[2] Charles Allen, *The Miracle of Love* (Old Tappan, NJ: Fleming H. Revell Co., 1972), 38.

6. To touch each other deeply, to feel moved by warmth, love, compassion, to celebrate it in mutual recognition that right relationships have been achieved.[1]

Date:	_____	_____	_____
Place:	_____	_____	_____
Occasion:	_____	_____	_____

To Send Away

Matthew, in recording a section of the Lord's Prayer, "Forgive us our debts as we forgive our debtors," used the word *aphiemi* for *forgive*. It means *to send away*. This is the same word used in Luke 4:39 when Jesus rebuked the fever in Peter's mother-in-law. That is the kind of forgiveness Psalm 103:12 describes as God removing our transgressions "as far as the East is from the West."

Date:	_____	_____	_____
Place:	_____	_____	_____
Occasion:	_____	_____	_____

The Hidden Root of Burnout

According to the Minirth and Meier book *How To Beat Burnout,* resentment is far more responsible for burnout than overwork. "In our counseling ministries, we have seen literally hundreds of examples that verify a close connection between bitterness and resentment and the experience of symptoms that we call burnout. . . . Bitterness leads to burnout . . . and freedom from bitterness is necessary for effective recovery from burnout."[2]

Date:	_____	_____	_____
Place:	_____	_____	_____
Occasion:	_____	_____	_____

Clara Barton's Attitude

Clara Barton never harbored resentments. One time a friend recalled to her a cruel thing that had happened to her some years previously, but Clara seemed not to remember it.

"Don't you remember the wrong that was done to you?" asked the friend.

"No," answered Clara. "I distinctly remember forgetting that."

---

[1] David Augsburger, *Caring Enough To Forgive / Caring Enough To Not Forgive* (Ventura, CA: Regal Books, 1981), 31.

[2] Frank Minirth, Don Hawkins, Paul Meier, and Richard Flournoy, *How To Beat Burnout* (Chicago: Moody Press, 1986), 48.

Date: _____ _____ _____

Place: _____ _____ _____

Occasion: _____ _____ _____

Forgiving His Son's Murderer

Rev. Walter H. Everett answered the phone, unprepared for the words he heard: "Scott was murdered last night." Walter's anger toward his son's killer raged through him like a violent riptide, growing even worse when a plea bargain resulted in a reduced sentence for the attacker.

My rage was affecting my entire life. "How am I going to let go of this anger?" I wondered. The answer came the first time I saw Mike, almost a year after Scott's death. Mike stood in court prior to his sentencing and said he was truly sorry for what he had done.

Three-and-a-half weeks later, on the first anniversary of Scott's death, I wrote to Mike. I told him about my anger and asked some pointed questions. Then I wrote, "Having said all that, I want to thank you for what you said in court, and as hard as these words are for me to write, I forgive you." I wrote of God's love in Christ and invited Mike to write to me if he wished.

Three weeks later his letter arrived. He said that when he had read my letter, he couldn't believe it. No one had ever said to him, "I forgive you." That night he had knelt beside his bunk and prayed for, and received, the forgiveness of Jesus Christ.

Additional correspondence led to regular visits during which we spoke often of Mike's (and my) growing relationship with Christ. Later I spoke on Mike's behalf before a parole board, and he was given an early release. In November 1994, I was the officiating minister at his wedding.

When asked about his early release, Mike says, "It felt good, but I was already out of prison. God had set me free when I asked for his forgiveness."

Can I truly forgive? I had wondered if it were possible. But I've discovered the meaning of the Apostle Paul's words: "For freedom Christ has set us free."[1]

> ⬥
> ### Burning Bridges
> *He that doth not forgive burns the bridge over which he himself must needs pass.*
> —ANONYMOUS
> ⬥

Date: _____ _____ _____

Place: _____ _____ _____

Occasion: _____ _____ _____

The Unfrozen Hand

Writing in *Christianity Today*, Professor Lewis B. Smedes relates a story about Corrie Ten Boom to illustrate the power of forgiveness:

She was stuck for the war years in a concentration camp, humiliated and degraded, especially in the delousing shower where the women were ogled by the leering guards. But she made it through that hell. And eventually she felt she had, by grace, forgiven even those fiends who guarded the shower stalls.

---

[1] Walter H. Everett, "Forgiving The Man Who Killed My Son," *Decision*, December 1996, 32.

So she preached forgiveness, for individuals, for all of Europe. She preached it in Bloemendaal, in the United States, and, one Sunday, in Munich. After the sermon, greeting people, she saw a man come toward her, hand outstretched: "Ja, Fräulein, it is wonderful that Jesus forgives us all our sins, just as you say." She remembered his face; it was the leering, lecherous, mocking face of an SS guard of the shower stall.

Her hand froze by her side. She could not forgive. She thought she had forgiven all. But she could not forgive when she met a guard, standing in the solid flesh in front of her. Ashamed, horrified at herself, she prayed, "Lord, forgive me, I cannot forgive." And as she prayed she felt forgiven, accepted, in spite of her shabby performance as a famous forgiver.

Her hand was suddenly unfrozen. The ice of hate melted. Her hand went out. She forgave as she was forgiven.[1]

Date:	_____	_____	_____
Place:	_____	_____	_____
Occasion:	_____	_____	_____

As Reported on CNN

Never before, say some experts, has there been such a need to forgive what seems to be the unforgivable.

Studies funded by the Templeton Forgiveness Research Campaign are trying to monitor and measure the physiological effects of forgiveness and its benefits, taken from the pulpit into the lab.

Everett Worthington is the director of the campaign. One day after mailing off his manuscript outlining a step-by-step process of forgiveness, his own ability was sorely tested when his mother was murdered.

"I remember looking down at the wall, seeing a baseball bat and saying, 'I wish that whoever did this was here right now. I would beat his brains out,'" Worthington said.

Instead, Worthington took his own medicine, focusing on what he considers the most important component of forgiveness—empathy. In this case, for the burglar who killed his mother.

"I can imagine what it must have been like for this kid to hear behind him a voice saying something like, 'What are you doing here?'" he said.

By understanding how it might have happened, Worthington says he's been able to forgive his mother's murderer.

"I cannot imprison him by holding unforgiveness towards him," he said.

Researchers say there is a physiological reason for forgiveness—health.

At Hope College in Michigan, researchers measure heart rates, sweat rates, and other responses of subjects when asked to remember past slights.

"Their blood pressure increases, their heart rate increases, and the muscle tensions are also higher," said professor Charlotte van Oyen Witvliet. This suggests their stress responses are greater during their unforgiving than forgiving conditions.

Scientists also find that forgiveness has a lot to do with genetics. Research in chimpanzees shows it might even be crucial for survival of the species.

---

[1] Lewis B. Smedes, "Forgiveness: The Power to Change the Past," *Christianity Today*, January 7, 1983, 26.

"In a cooperative system, it is possible that your biggest rival is someone who you will need tomorrow," said Frans De Waal of Emory University's Yerks Primate Center.[1]

Date: _____ _____ _____
Place: _____ _____ _____
Occasion: _____ _____ _____

Forgive Everyone of Everything?

F

In his excellent work, *The Two Sides of Forgiveness,* Robertson McQuilkin questions the common conventional wisdom that we should forgive everyone of everything. He writes:

God's love is unlimited, for everyone. Ours ought to be. But God's forgiveness is strictly limited to those who repent. Confusion and guilt overwhelm many of God's people who demand that we do what God does not do—pardon everyone for everything.

We can justify this distinction by returning to the two basic meanings of forgive: to remit the guilt and to relinquish resentment. In the sense of remitting guilt, God, in love, forgives a specified few and, in love, does not forgive the majority of humankind. In the sense of relinquishing resentment, however, God forgives everyone. He never for a moment felt bitterness or ill-will against anyone. . . .

Love should also shape the way we relate to people, whether friend or enemy. Does love cancel the debt? Sometimes. Does love let go of the resentment? Always.[2]

Date: _____ _____ _____
Place: _____ _____ _____
Occasion: _____ _____ _____

Forgiveness Unclogs a Pipeline

Victor Guaminga, an Ecuadorian Christian, is a World Vision project coordinator in his own country. Wanting to eradicate water-borne diseases in his home village, Laime Chico, Victor developed a plan for building a pipeline to supply the villagers with clean, drinkable water from a source some distance away.

Unfortunately, the best path for such a pipeline was right through Laime San Carlos, a rival village—one with which Victor's village had a long-lasting feud.

When certain implacable enemies in the rival village heard about the proposed water line, they made it known that they would destroy any pipes laid for that purpose. Therefore, the whole plan was stymied.

In spite of their neighbors' hostility, however, Christians in Victor's village, knowing that the other village had no church, decided to conduct an evangelistic effort there.

---

[1] Eileen O'Connor, "Forgiveness Heals the Heart, Research Hints," *CNN,* May 20, 1999.
[2] McQuilkin, *The Two Sides of Forgiveness,* (2–3.

Doing so was both difficult and dangerous. Not many of the rival village's people paid any attention to the evangelizers. But four did respond to the gospel message and became believers in Christ.

After being spiritually nurtured by believers from Victor's church, the four converts became faithful witnesses to others in their own village. Slowly, a church formed there also.

Eventually the very man who had most vehemently opposed the water project became a believer himself. Seeing, then, how wrong his attitude had been, he asked forgiveness and gave his cooperation to the project.

Five years after that project in Ecuador was proposed, clean, drinkable water flowed through dependable pipes not only to Victor's village but to the formerly hostile one, plus two other nearby villages. And now there are growing churches in all four places.[1]

Date: _____   _____   _____

Place: _____   _____   _____

Occasion: _____   _____   _____

Bats Out of Hell

Mitsuo Fuchida, commander of the Japanese Air Force, led the squadron of 860 planes that attacked Pearl Harbor on December 7, 1941.

American bomber Jacob DeShazer was eager to strike back, and the following April 18th, he flew his B-25 Bomber, the *Bat Out of Hell,* on a dangerous raid over Japan. After dropping his bombs on Nagoya, DeShazer lost his way in heavy fog and ejected as his plane ran out of fuel. He was taken prisoner, tortured by the Japanese, and threatened with imminent death. For almost two years, DeShazer suffered hunger, cold, and dysentery.

In May of 1944, he was given a Bible. "You can keep it for three weeks," said the guard. DeShazer grabbed it, clutched it to his chest, and started reading in Genesis. Scarcely sleeping, he read the Bible through several times, memorizing key passages. On June 8, after reading to Romans 10:9, Jacob prayed to receive Jesus Christ as his Savior.

Immediately Matthew 5:44 became a critical text for DeShazer as he determined to treat his Japanese guards differently. His hostility toward them evaporated, and every morning he greeted them warmly. He prayed for them and sought to witness to them. He noticed their attitude toward him also changed, and they would often slip him food or supplies.

After the war, DeShazer returned to Japan as a missionary. Copies of his testimony, "I Was a Prisoner of the Japanese," flooded the country, and thousands wanted to see the man who could love and forgive his enemies. DeShazer settled down to establish a church in Nagoya, the city he had bombed.

One man in particular, deeply affected by DeShazer's testimony, was led to Christ by Glenn Wagner of the Pocket Testament League. Shortly afterward, the

---

[1] "Example in Ecuador: Forgiveness Unclogs a Pipeline," *World Vision,* February-March 1986, 18.

man paid a visit to Jacob DeShazer at his home, and the two became dear friends and brothers. It was Mitsuo Fuchida, who had led the Pearl Harbor attack. As DeShazer served as missionary in Japan, Fuchida became a powerful evangelist, preaching throughout Japan and around the world.[1]

Date:			
Place:			
Occasion:			

Good and Bad Forgivers

In his delightful volume, *The Other Side of the Hill,* F. W. Boreham calls forgiveness "one of the highest arts of life," and he suggests that some people are good forgivers, and others are poor forgivers. He gives an example of both from history:

[A] The Poor Forgiver

When John Wesley was traveling by ship to America he heard an unusual noise in the cabin of General Oglethorpe, the Governor of Georgia. Wesley stepped in to inquire. It turned out that Grimaldi, the Governor's servant, had devoured the entire stock of the great man's favorite wine. "But I will be avenged!" cried the Governor, who ordered the poor man tied hand and foot to be carried away for severe punishment. "For you know, Mr. Wesley," stormed Oglethorpe, "I never forgive!"

"In that case, sir," replied Wesley, "I hope you never sin!"

The General was quite confounded at the reproof, and putting his hand into his pocket book, took out a bunch of keys, which he threw at Grimaldi, saying, "There, villain, take my keys and behave better in the future."

His forgiveness, such as it was, was poor indeed.

[B] The Good Forgiver

Boreham contrasts that with the example of William Gladstone, Prime Minister of England. Once, when Gladstone was Chancellor of the Exchequer, he sent down to the Treasury office for a sheaf of statistics on which he based his budget proposals. Now it happened that, in compiling the statistics, the clerk had made a mistake that vitally affected the entire situation. The blunder was only discovered after Gladstone had elaborated his proposals and made his budget speech in the House of Commons. The papers immediately exposed the fallacy, and for a moment the Chancellor was overwhelmed with embarrassment. He was made to appear ridiculous before the entire nation.

He sent down to the Treasury for the clerk to come to him at once. The clerk duly arrived, trembling with apprehension, and expecting instant dismissal. He began to stammer out his apologies, and his entreaty for forgiveness. Mr. Gladstone stopped him. "I sent for you," he said, "because I could imagine the torture of your feelings. You have been for many years dealing with the bewildering intricacies of the national accounts, and you have done your work with such conscientious exactness that this is your first mistake. It was because of your splendid record that I did not trouble

---

[1] Robert J. Morgan, *From This Verse* (Nashville: Thomas Nelson Publishers, 1998), June 28th.

to verify your calculations. I have sent for you to compliment you on that record and to set you at ease."

"If the New Testament means anything," commented F. W. Boreham, "it means that a man who can forgive with such gallantry and chivalry is a very great Christian indeed."[1]

Date:			
Place:			
Occasion:			

The Investment

The manager of an IBM project that lost $10 million before it was scrapped was called into a meeting at the corporate office.

"I suppose you want my resignation?" he asked.

"Resignation nothing!" replied his boss. "We've just spent $10 million *educating* you."[2]

Date:			
Place:			
Occasion:			

Forgive Us

A four-year-old was praying one night, having been listening at church: "And forgive us our trashbaskets as we forgive those who put trash in our baskets."

Date:			
Place:			
Occasion:			

———— Friendship/Fellowship ————

Someone Once Said . . .

- *I would rather be chained in a dungeon, wrist to wrist with a Christian, than to live forever with the wicked in the sunshine of happiness.*—Charles Haddon Spurgeon[3]
- *He who would be good must either have a faithful friend to instruct him or a watchful enemy to correct him.*—Rev. William Secker[4]
- *A man, sir, should keep his friendships in a state of constant repair.*—Samuel Johnson

---

[1] Boreham, *The Other Side of the Hill*, 242–243.

[2] Alan Loy McGinnis, *The Power of Optimism* (San Francisco: Harper & Row Publishers, 1990), 128.

[3] Charles Haddon Spurgeon, *Spurgeon's Sermons*, vol. 2 (Grand Rapids, MI: Baker Book House, 1983), 90.

[4] William Secker, *The Nonsuch Professor In His Meridian Splendor* (Chicago: Fleming H. Revell Co., 1899), 154.

- *The man who has learned how to keep his friendships in perfect repair is a very wise workman indeed.*—F. W. Boreham
- *The only way to have a friend is to be one.*—Ralph Waldo Emerson
- *You can make more friends in two months by becoming interested in other people than you can in two years by trying to get other people interested in you.*—Dale Carnegie[1]
- *To be interesting, be interested.*—Mrs. Charles Northam Lee
- *A man that hath friends must show himself friendly.*—Proverbs 18:24

Date: _____ _____ _____
Place: _____ _____ _____
Occasion: _____ _____ _____

F

More Quotes

- *A friend is anybody who forgives our good points.*—Anonymous
- *A real friend is a guy who walks in when everybody else walks out.*—Anonymous
- *Our American culture produces people who more closely identify with characters on a weekly TV series than with their next-door neighbors.*—Steven A. Hamon[2]

Date: _____ _____ _____
Place: _____ _____ _____
Occasion: _____ _____ _____

One Last Quote

- *You know, the only thing I miss is the fellowship I used to have with all the guys down at the tavern. We used to sit around, laugh, and drink a pitcher of beer, tell stories, and let our hair down. I can't find fellowship like that with Christians.*—a recently converted Christian[3]

Date: _____ _____ _____
Place: _____ _____ _____
Occasion: _____ _____ _____

"I Could Not Stay Away"

It was "fellowship" that brought the village tinker John Bunyan, the future writer of *Pilgrim's Progress*, to Christ. In his book *Grace Abounding to the Chief of Sinners*, he recalls being a lost and profane young man who was first pricked for Christ by overhearing the conversation of a group of village women enjoying sweet fellowship.

But upon a day, the good providence of God did cast me to Bedford, to work on my calling;

---

[1] Dale Carnegie, *How To Win Friends and Influence People* (New York: Simon and Schuster, 1936), 58.
[2] Steven A. Hamon, "Closer Than a Brother," *Christianity Today*, January 1, 1982, 30.
[3] Win Arn, Carroll Nyquist, and Charles Arn, *Who Cares About Love?* (Pasadena, CA: Church Growth, 1986), 122.

and in one of the streets of that town, I came where there were three or four women sitting at a door in the sun, and talking about the things of God; and being now willing to hear them discourse, I drew near to hear what they said. . . . But I understood not; for they were far above, out of my reach, for their talk was about a new birth, the work of God on their hearts, also how they were convinced of their miserable state by nature; they talked how God had visited their souls with His love in the Lord Jesus, and with what words and promises they had been refreshed, comforted, and supported against the temptations of the devil. Moreover, they reasoned of the suggestions and temptations of Satan in particular; and told to each other by which they had been afflicted, and how they were borne up under his assaults. . . .

And methought they spake as if joy did make them speak; they spake with such pleasantness of Scripture language, and with such appearance of grace in all they said, that they were to me as if they had found a new world. . . .

At this I felt my own heart began to shake, as mistrusting my condition. . . .

Thus, therefore, when I had heard and considered what they said, I left them, and went about my employment again, but their talk and discourse went with me; also my heart would tarry with them, for I was greatly affected with their words. . . .

Therefore I should often make it my business to be going again and again into the company of these poor people, for I could not stay away. . . .[1]

Date: _____   _____   _____

Place: _____   _____   _____

Occasion: _____   _____   _____

From Vance Havner

Christian fellowship has almost become a lost art. I recall how, as a boy, I sat before the open fire on a Saturday night while father and the visiting minister talked long and late about the things of God. I remember John Brown, deacon in my first country charge, who used to visit my room and talk until midnight. There was time in those days, but who can take time off today to meditate at the Master's feet, like Mary of old, or to share His fellowship with other Christians? Fellowship has come to mean a noisy after-session at church with coffee and cookies and a lot of idle chatter about everything on earth but spirit things. How many Christian homes know how to converse about Jesus Christ? Bunyan was helped by overhearing two godly women talk about the things of God. Would anybody listening in on your conversation be helped in his soul?[2]

Date: _____   _____   _____

Place: _____   _____   _____

Occasion: _____   _____   _____

Advice from Pros

John D. Rockefeller once said, "The ability to deal with people is as purchasable a commodity as sugar or coffee. And I will pay more for that ability than for any other under the sun."

[1] John Bunyan, *Grace Abounding to the Chief of Sinners* (Grand Rapids: Baker Book House, 1986), 29–30.
[2] Vance Havner, *Pepper 'N Salt* (Old Tappan, NJ: Fleming H. Revell Co., 1967), 69.

Roger Ailes, the political consultant who directed President George Bush's media campaign, gave similar advice:

The only advice some of my clients need when they come to see me can be summed up in two words: "Lighten up!" It's ironic, but your career can depend on whether you get serious about taking yourself less seriously.

According to executive recruiters, for seven out of ten people who lose their jobs, the cause isn't a lack of skill—it's personality conflicts. The management newsletter Bottom Line / Personal *reports a similar finding: "As an executive reaches middle management and beyond, the primary criteria for advancement are communication and motivation skills, rather than job performance. Relations with superiors and peers are also critical." The bottom line: "Top management promotes people it likes."*

What's the most common reason someone isn't liked in business? He takes himself too seriously. He has no sense of humor.

. . . It's important to take your job seriously. But people who take themselves too seriously tend to believe that their title or their intelligence makes them more important than others.

. . . According to researchers at the Center for Creative Leadership, "insensitivity to others, abrasiveness, and aloofness" often seem to be the factors that derail the careers of otherwise talented executives.

Ailes goes on to suggest asking ourselves these questions:

- *When someone comes to me with a problem . . . do I shift gears and listen—or put him off and hope he'll go away?*
- *How often do I find myself complaining about something?*
- *Do I take a lot of satisfaction in lecturing people or being tough with them?*
- *When someone tells me a new idea, do I look for an objection to puncture his balloon?*
- *How often do I use the word "I"?*[1]

Date: _____ _____ _____

Place: _____ _____ _____

Occasion: _____ _____ _____

Ten Rules

In his book, *The Power of Positive Thinking,* Norman Vincent Peale lists ten rules for becoming the kind of person whom others enjoy being around:

1. Learn to remember names.
2. Be a very comfortable person so there is no strain in being with you—be an old-shoe, old-hat kind of individual. Be homey.
3. Acquire the quality of relaxed, easy-goingness so that things don't ruffle you.
4. Don't be egotistical. Guard against giving the impression that you know it all. Be normal and naturally humble.
5. Cultivate the quality of being interesting so that people will want to be with you and get something of stimulating value from their association with you.

---

[1] Clippings from my files.

6. Study to get the "scratchy" elements out of your personality.
7. Sincerely attempt to heal, on an honest Christian basis, every misunderstanding you have had and now have. Drain off your grievances.
8. Practice liking people.
9. Never miss an opportunity to say a word of congratulation upon anyone's achievement, or express sympathy in sorrow or disappointment.
10. Get a deep spiritual experience so that you have something to give people that will help them to be stronger and meet life more effectively. Give strength to people and they will give affection to you.[1]

> Date: _____ _____ _____
> Place: _____ _____ _____
> Occasion: _____ _____ _____

Queen Victoria's Two Prime Ministers

Queen Victoria once shared her impressions of her two most famous prime ministers. Of William Gladstone, she said, "When I am with him, I feel I am with one of the most important leaders in the world." On the other hand, she confessed that when she was with Disraeli, he made her feel "as if I am one of the most important leaders of the world."[2]

That reminds me of something my father once said. He was a school teacher in a rural district. Over the years he served under a number of county school superintendents, two of whom (I'll call them Jones and Johnson) he once compared in this way. "When I went to Mr. Jones with a request, he could turn it down and make me feel good. But when I went to Johnson with a request, he could agree with it but make me feel bad."

> Date: _____ _____ _____
> Place: _____ _____ _____
> Occasion: _____ _____ _____

Around the Corner

Around the corner I have a friend,
In this great city that has no end;
Yet days go by and weeks rush on,
And before I know it, a year is gone,
And I never see my old friend's face.
For life is a swift and terrible race.
He knows I like him just as well
As in the days when I rang his bell
And he rang mine. We were younger then,

---

[1] Norman Vincent Peale, *The Power of Positive Thinking* (New York: Prentice-Hall, Inc., 1952), 210–211.
[2] Haddon Robinson, "On Target," *Focal Point,* quoting from David Smith, *The Friendless American Male.*

And now we are busy, tired men:
Tired of playing a foolish game,
Tired of trying to make a name.
"Tomorrow," I say, "I will call on Jim
just to show that I am thinking of him."
But tomorrow comes—and tomorrow goes,
And the distance between us grows and grows.
Around the corner!—yet miles away . . .
"Here's a telegram, Sir," . . . "Jim died today."
And that's what we get and deserve in the end:
Around the corner, a vanished friend.
—Charles Hanson Towne[1]

F

Date: _____ _____ _____
Place: _____ _____ _____
Occasion: _____ _____ _____

Sent Out Two by Two

When God promised to meet the needs of His children, we may safely assume that includes our need for meaningful friendships. As we love Him and seek to love others, He will send to us those who can meet our needs for fellowship and intimacy.

In his book *To China With Love* missionary J. Hudson Taylor told of being in Shanghai and feeling the Lord wanted him to enter the Swatow region of China, an area rife with opium and slave trafficking without a single British missionary to preach the gospel.

But Taylor didn't want to go, for he didn't want to leave his mentor, Rev. William Burns, an English Presbyterian on whose friendship Taylor was depending for his spiritual and emotional well-being. He and Burns had become very close, and the thought of separation was more than Taylor could bear.

Like It or Not!

Good old friends are worth keeping whether you like them or not.

—ANDY ROONEY

Then one day while taking afternoon tea at the American Presbyterian Mission House in Shanghai, a missionary sang a hymn entitled, "The Missionary Call." The words spoke of being willing to give up friends and "every tie that binds the heart" for the sake of the Kingdom. Taylor was deeply smitten, and that evening he invited his friend William Burns for a talk.

"With many tears I told him how the Lord had been leading me, and how rebellious I had been and unwilling to leave him for this new sphere of labor. He listened with a strange look of surprise, and of pleasure rather than pain; and answered that he had determined that very night to tell me that he had heard the Lord's call to Swatow, and that his one regret had been the prospect of severance of our happy fellowship. We went together; and thus we recommenced missionary work in that part of China, which in later years has been so abundantly blessed."[2]

[1] Haddon Robinson, "On Target," *Focal Point.*
[2] J. Hudson Taylor, *To China With Love* (Minneapolis, Minnesota: Dimension Books, n.d.), 89–91.

Date: _____ _____ _____
Place: _____ _____ _____
Occasion: _____ _____ _____

Paul's Address Book

Gordon MacDonald points out in *Restoring Your Spiritual Passion* that the apostle Paul, strong as he was, had a great need and a great capacity for friendship:

The apostle Paul was clearly a man committed to raising up a band of special friends. He knew who they were, and he regularly recognized them for their contribution to his spiritual passion. His friends were a resource upon which he obviously depended and without which he would not have survived.

His address book of special friends would have included Aquila and Priscilla, with whom he occasionally worked and lived (see Acts 18:3), Onesiphorus ("for he oft refreshed me" 2 Tim. 1:16—KJV), Philemon ("I have derived much joy and comfort from your love" Philem. 1:7—RSV), Luke, and a host of others. Paul's friends came in all ages and backgrounds, and he seems to have taken great care to cultivate them.[1]

Date: _____ _____ _____
Place: _____ _____ _____
Occasion: _____ _____ _____

"Blest Be the Tie That Binds"

John Fawcett was converted as a teenager listening to George Whitefield. He joined the Baptists and was ordained on July 31, 1765. He began pastoring a poor church in Wainsgate, finding time here and there for writing. His writings spread abroad, and the little church feared they would lose their pastor to a larger place. Fawcett wondered the same thing, lamenting in his diary that his family was growing faster than his income.

The call came from London's famous Carter's Lane Church. "Think of it!" Fawcett told his wife. "They want us in London to take the place of the late Dr. Gill at that great church! It's almost unbelievable!" The following Sunday he broke the news to his church, then began packing. Books, dishes, pictures, and furniture were crated for the overland journey to the world's largest city. When the day of departure came, church members assembled and bravely tried to hold their tears. Finally everything was loaded but one box, and Fawcett entered the house to retrieve it. There he found his wife deep in thought. "John," she said, voice breaking, "do you think we're doing the right thing? Will we ever find a congregation to love us and help us with the Lord's work like this group here?"

"Do you think we've been too hasty in this?" John asked.

"Yes. I think we should stay right here and serve these people."

---

[1] Gordon MacDonald, *Restoring Your Spiritual Passion* (Nashville: Oliver Nelson, 1986), 176–177.

John was silent a moment, for his heart, too, had been breaking. He nodded. "I was so overjoyed when the call came that I never really prayed about it like a minister should."

They walked onto the porch, called the people together, revealed their change of heart, and amid joyous tears unloaded their wagons. Fawcett stayed at Wainsgate the rest of his life. But not in obscurity. Out of this experience, he wrote the world-famous hymn:

> *Blest be the tie that binds*
> *Our hearts in Christian love.*
> *The fellowship of kindred minds*
> *Is like to that above.*[1]

Date: _____ _____ _____
Place: _____ _____ _____
Occasion: _____ _____ _____

Making Coffee

Mr. Sam Rayburn was Speaker of the United States House of Representatives longer than any other man in our history. There is a story about him that reveals the kind of man he really was.

The teenage daughter of a friend of his died suddenly one night. Early the next morning the man heard a knock on his door, and, when he opened it, there was Mr. Rayburn standing outside.

The Speaker said, "I just came by to see what I could do to help."

The father replied in his deep grief, "I don't think there is anything you can do, Mr. Speaker. We are making all the arrangements."

"Well," Mr. Rayburn said, "have you had your coffee this morning?"

The man replied that they had not taken time for breakfast. So Mr. Rayburn said that he could at least make coffee for them. While he was working in the kitchen, the man came in and said, "Mr. Speaker, I thought you were supposed to be having breakfast at the White House this morning."

"Well, I was," Mr. Rayburn said, "but I called the President and told him I had a friend who was in trouble, and I couldn't come."[2]

Date: _____ _____ _____
Place: _____ _____ _____
Occasion: _____ _____ _____

Your Best Friend

Once Henry Ford was having lunch with a man when suddenly he asked him, "Who is your best friend?" The man started naming certain people. "No," said Mr.

---

[1] Robert J. Morgan, *On This Day* (Nashville: Thomas Nelson Publishers, 1997), July 31st.
[2] Charles L. Allen, *Perfect Peace* (Old Tappan, NJ: Fleming H. Revell Co., 1979), 137–138.

Ford, "I will tell you who your best friend is." He took out a pencil and wrote on the tablecloth this sentence: "Your best friend is he who brings out the best that is within you."[1]

Date: _____ _____ _____
Place: _____ _____ _____
Occasion: _____ _____ _____

The Hidden Value of Fellowship

- *Many of our daily conversations are actually mutual counseling sessions whereby we exchange the reassurance and advice that help us deal with routine stresses.*—Reported by the National Institute of Mental Health[2]
- *Often when people are really given the chance to open up, they unravel their own problems and the solutions become clear to them in the process. At other times, they really need additional perspective and help. The key is to genuinely seek the welfare of the individual, to listen with empathy, to let the person get to the problem and the solution at his own pace and time. . . . When people are really hurting and you really listen with a pure desire to understand, you'll be amazed how fast they will open up.*—Stephen R. Covey, in *The 7 Habits of Highly Effective People*[3]

Date: _____ _____ _____
Place: _____ _____ _____
Occasion: _____ _____ _____

Staying with the Gang

In his book, *The Art of the Leader*, William A. Cohen, professor of marketing at California State University, Los Angeles, and the director of the Small Business Institute at Cal State, draws on his military background to explain the importance of cohesion in human relationships:

During the 1958 Lebanon crisis, an Air Force fighter pilot who had very limited training on his type of aircraft was ordered to fly from his base in South Carolina to Adana, Turkey.

He ran into bad weather. He considered aborting the flight and turning back. Instead, he pressed on. His inexperience led to difficulty in locating his tanker aircraft. Over the middle of the Atlantic Ocean with only four minutes of fuel left, he was desperate. He thought about ejecting from his aircraft and leaving it to crash. Then just in time he found his aerial tanker and took on the necessary fuel.

Some hours later, he landed at Adana. When he was asked about his experience, he said, "In my worst moment, I suddenly realized that staying with my gang meant more than anything in the world."

---

[1] Charles L. Allen, *Prayer Changes Things* (Old Tappan, NJ: Fleming H. Revell Co., 1964), 95–96.
[2] Julius Segal, *Winning Life's Toughest Battles: Roots of Human Resilience* (New York: Ivy Books, 1986), 18.
[3] Stephen R. Covey, *The 7 Habits of Highly Effective People* (New York: Simon and Schuster, n.d.), 251–252.

Other studies of men in combat confirm the feelings of this young airman. Army historian Brigadier General S. L. A. Marshall, who conducted more than four hundred interviews with American infantrymen immediately after combat in both the European and Pacific theaters of war, concluded that the main motivation for a soldier to fight is a sense of psychological unity with other members of his immediate combat unit. Said General Marshall: "I hold it to be one of the simplest truths of war that the thing which enables an infantry soldier to keep going with his weapons is the near presence or presumed presence of a comrade."

Patriotism, religion, and ideology are surely strong motivators. However, "staying with the gang," a good description of cohesion, is even stronger.

F

Date: _____ _____ _____
Place: _____ _____ _____
Occasion: _____ _____ _____

"GBUJS"

Dr. Julius Segal, the distinguished psychologist who worked with the Iran Hostages, Vietnam POWs, and other survivors, wrote a book entitled *Winning Life's Toughest Battles* in which he shared his observations of those who had overcome terrible trauma in their lives. His first chapter is devoted to the importance of having friends, a circle of comrades with whom to communicate. He wrote, "Few individuals can cope with trauma alone. Even the most powerful figures in the world need contact with others in the face of crisis."

He related the experience of Vice Admiral James B. Stockdale, heroic survivor of 2,714 days as a POW in Vietnam.

On one occasion, the North Vietnamese handcuffed Stockdale's hands behind his back, locked his legs in heavy irons, and dragged him from his dark prison cell to sit in an unshaded courtyard so other prisoners could see what happened to anybody who refused to cooperate.

Stockdale remained in that position for three days. Since he had not been in the sun for a long time, he soon felt weak, but the guards would not let him sleep. He was beaten repeatedly. After one beating, Stockdale heard a towel snapping out in a prison code the letters: GBUJS. It was a message he would never forget: "God bless you, Jim Stockdale."

In every episode of captivity in recent American history, POWs and hostages have been sustained by ingeniously improvised lifelines of communication. In Vietnam, a clever tap code, in which the number and sequence of taps spelled out letters of the alphabet, became the prisoners' chief means of communication. It was this code that sustained Jim Stockdale.

At first the prisoners had trouble remembering the letter codes long enough to put them together to form coherent messages. Soon, however, their proficiency improved, and the system became second nature. The lonely prisoners tapped on the walls, the ceilings, or the floor. . . .

Eventually the POWs developed sophisticated extensions of the tapping routine. An especially effective ploy was to sweep through a prison compound using the broom movement to "talk" to an entire group. If one man walked by another's cell, he could drag his sandals in code. Some men sent messages to their comrades through the noises they made while shaking out their blankets, others by belching, blowing their noses, or, for a few prisoners who had the talent to do so at will, passing gas. One POW feigned sleep for a couple of hours each day during the siesta period and through his snoring managed to report how everyone was doing and what was going on in his cellblock.

Segal quotes former POW Everett Alvarez who later said, "We really got to know each other through our silent conversations across the brick walls. Eventually, we learned all about each other's childhood, background, experiences, wives and children, hopes and ambitions."

Segal goes on to report a study of over two thousand who had suffered trauma, including physical abuse, rape, or the death of a loved one. Survivors were healthier if they managed to confide in someone about the event. Those who hadn't discussed their experiences developed more illness of various sorts—from headaches to lung disease.[1]

Date:	_____	_____	_____
Place:	_____	_____	_____
Occasion:	_____	_____	_____

Amen and Alleluia!

"Amen" and "Alleluia" are words that unite Christians around the world, for they are virtually the same in every language, as illustrated by a gripping story that Daniel Christiansen tells about a relative, a Romanian soldier in World War II, named Ana Gheorghe.

It was 1941, and Russian troops had overrun the Romanian region of Bessarabia and entered Moldavia. Ana and his comrades were badly frightened. Bullets whizzed around them, and mortar shells shook the earth. By day, Ana sought relief reading his Bible, but at night he could only crouch close to the earth and recall verses memorized in childhood.

One day during a spray of enemy fire, Ana was separated from his company. In a panic, he bolted deeper and deeper into the woods until, huddling at the base of a large tree, he fell asleep from exhaustion. The next day, trying to find his comrades, he moved cautiously toward the front, staying in the shadows of the trees, nibbling a crust of bread, drinking from streams. Hearing the battle closing in, he unslung his rifle, pulled the bolt, and watched for the enemy, his nerves near the breaking point. Twenty yards away, a Russian solider suddenly appeared.

All my mental rehearsals of bravery served me nothing. I dropped my gun and fell to my knees, then buried my face in my sweating palms and began to pray. While praying, I waited for the cold touch of the Russians rifle barrel against my head.

I felt a slight pressure on my shoulder close to my neck. I opened my eyes slowly. There was my enemy kneeling in front of me, his gun lying next to mine among the wildflowers. His eyes were closed in prayer. We did not understand a single word of the other's language, but we could pray. We ended our prayer with two words that need no translation: "Alleluia . . . Amen!"

Then, after a tearful embrace, we walked quickly to opposite sides of the clearing and disappeared beneath the trees.[2]

---

[1] Segal, *Winning Life's Toughest Battles: Roots of Human Resilience,* Ch. 1.
[2] Robert J. Morgan, *From This Verse* (Nashville: Thomas Nelson Publishers, 1998), December 29th.

Date:			
Place:			
Occasion:			

Alexander and Hephaestion

Alexander the Great is a meteor that flashed through the darkened skies of history. Young, handsome, driven, and idealistic, he virtually conquered the world, yet like David with Jonathan, he was utterly dependent on the companionship of a friend. Unlike David, Alexander never recovered from the loss of that friend.

Alexander and Hephaestion had grown up together, each knew all the secrets of the other. The two men were the same age. They shared one tent, drank from one cup, and fought in battle side by side. They were inseparable.

Hephaestion was taller, thus was sometimes mistaken for Alexander. On one occasion, when Darius' queen entered their tent, she bowed before Hephaestion, thinking him Alexander. She was alarmed to discover her error, but the young king simply smiled and said, "Hephaestion is also Alexander," as if to indicate that the two men were one.

When Hephaestion died, Alexander was broken in spirit. According to historian Will Durant, he *broke down in uncontrolled grief. He lay for hours upon the corpse, weeping; he cut off his hair in mourning, and for days refused to take food. He sentenced to death the physician who had left the sick youth's side to attend the public games. He ordered a gigantic funeral pile to be erected in Hephaestion's memory, at a cost, we are told, of ten thousand talents [$60,000,000], and sent to inquire of the oracle of Ammon whether it was permitted to worship Hephaestion as a god. In his next campaign a whole tribe was slain, at his orders, as a sacrifice to Hephaestion's ghost. . . .*

Back in Babylon, he abandoned himself more and more to drink. One night, reveling with his officers, he proposed a drinking. . . . Shortly afterward, at another banquet, Alexander drank heavily again; and cold weather suddenly setting in, he caught a fever, and took to his bed. The fever raged for ten days, during which Alexander continued to give orders to his army and his fleet. On the eleventh day he died, being in the thirty-third year of his age.[1]

Date:			
Place:			
Occasion:			

How to Differ

Friends learn to appreciate their disagreements. In 1920, Dr. J. B. Gambrell, a leader of the Southern Baptist Convention, was traveling through Europe with his colleague, Dr. E. Y. Mullins. They made great traveling companions. Dr. Mullins later wrote: "We discussed everything you can think of. We agreed on the great

---

[1] Will Durant, *The Story of Civilization: Part II: The Life of Greece* (New York: Simon and Schuster, 1966), 551.

things. We did not always agree on other things. It was a good arrangement, because while we agreed enough to be congenial, we differed enough to make it interesting."[1]

Date: _____ _____ _____

Place: _____ _____ _____

Occasion: _____ _____ _____

How to Ruin a Good Friendship

Ernest Hemingway had an extraordinary talent for making friends. Gerald Murphy, an American he met in Paris, recalled his "enveloping personality, so physically huge and forceful. He overstated everything and talked so rapidly and so graphically that you found yourself agreeing with him." He was by no means easy to get along with, and another friend and helper, Robert McAlmon, described him as "the hurt, sensitive boy, deliberately young and naive, wanting to be brave and somehow on the defensive." His flair for making friends was coupled with a tendency to fall out with them. He was jealous of other men's success and often abused and betrayed other writers, like Ford Madox Ford and John Dos Passos, who had been generous and welcoming to him. The force of his personality was such that, despite his ingratitude and his mean streak, he never lacked company. Even his malice had a certain charm. His obsession with courage drove him to prove himself by humiliating others. He one by one knocked off the best friendships he ever had.[2]

Date: _____ _____ _____

Place: _____ _____ _____

Occasion: _____ _____ _____

The Porcupine Syndrome

Chuck Swindoll suggests that many Christian groups are like a pack of porcupines on a frigid wintry night. The cold drives us closer together in a tight huddle to keep warm. As we begin to snuggle really close, our sharp quills cause us to jab and prick each other—a condition which forces us apart. But before long we start getting cold, so we move back to warm again, only to stab and puncture each other once more.

> To dwell above with saints we love,
> That will be grace and glory.
> To live below with saints we know;
> That's another story.

"How can we break ye olde porcupine syndrome?" asks Swindoll. "The answer in one word is involvement. Or, to use the biblical term, it is *fellowship*."[3]

---

[1] E. C. Routh, *The Life Story of Dr. J. B. Gambrell* (Oklahoma City: Routh, 1929), 153.
[2] Nicholas McDowell, *Hemingway* (East Sussex, England: Wayland Publishers Ltd, 1988), 30.
[3] Charles R. Swindoll, *Strengthening Your Grip* (Waco: Word Books, 1982), 32.

Date:			
Place:			
Occasion:			

Gambling

Someone Once Said . . .

- *A young gambler is sure to be an old beggar if he lives long enough.*—Charles Spurgeon[1]
- *Gambling: unnecessarily risking the possessions which God has entrusted to us in games of chance or skill in the hope of gaining something from our neighbor without giving him a fair service or product in return whether for the sake of profit or thrills.*—John Mark[2]
- *No one gambles with another in order to give away to the other what is his own (for he could do that without gambling), nor in order to lose what is his own, nor in order to seek the gain of the other man as though it were his own. This is why gambling is always contrary to love and is motivated by greed because a man seeks, to the harm of another, what does not belong to him.*—Martin Luther
- *The safest bet is the one you didn't make.*
- *Horse sense is what keeps horses from betting on what people will do.*—Oscar Wilde
- *The urge to gamble is so universal and its practice so pleasurable that I assume it must be evil.*—Heywood Hale Broun, broadcaster

Date:			
Place:			
Occasion:			

Facts from *Christianity Today*

Americans can make a legal wager of some sort in every state except Utah, Hawaii, and Tennessee.

In 42 states, pari-mutuel betting, including horse and dog races, is legal, although that has been in decline for 15 years as other less skill-oriented forms of risk-taking grew more popular. Lotteries are conducted by 37 states, but new games must constantly be introduced—or existing games repackaged—to keep sales from falling.

The vast acceleration lately has been due to casinos, with 600 operating in 26 states, from economically depressed river towns to isolated Native American reservations.

According to *International Gaming and Wagering Business,* Americans lost $50.9 billion in legal games in 1997, $27.2 billion of that in casinos and $16.6 billion in lotteries.[3]

---

[1] Charles Haddon Spurgeon, *John Ploughman's Talks* (New York: Sheldon & Company, n.d.), 106.
[2] John Mark, "Wanna Bet? A Christian View on Gambling," <www.pastornet.net>.
[3] John W. Kennedy, "Gambling Away the Golden Years," *Christianity Today,* May 24, 1999, 45.

Date: _____ _____ _____
Place: _____ _____ _____
Occasion: _____ _____ _____

More Stats

The National Gambling Impact Study Commission reported in 1999 that:

- More than 20 million Americans have or could develop gambling problems.
- More than 5 million Americans are pathological or problem gamblers.
- More than 15 million Americans are at risk of becoming pathological gamblers.
- Over 1 million American teens engage in severe pathological gambling each year.

Date: _____ _____ _____
Place: _____ _____ _____
Occasion: _____ _____ _____

Gambling and the Elderly

The May 24, 1999 issue of *Christianity Today* carried a frightening article about the way the gambling industry is targeting senior citizens. Here are some excerpts:

According to John Eades, fifty-seven, author of a new recovery book, *Gambling Addiction: The Problem, the Pain, and the Pathway to Recovery* (Thistle Press), increased gambling among the elderly comes at a huge cost to themselves, their families, and their churches. "As older persons become addicted, they use Sunday as a gambling day, not a church day. Once they're hooked, they're ashamed to come back to church. They need to have a spiritual transformation to change."

Don't Bet on It!

Gambling is a great way of getting nothing for something.

Compulsive gambling causes people who have no past criminal behavior to suddenly write bad checks or steal money from relatives. Out-of-control bettors lose their jobs, gamble away cars and homes, file for bankruptcy, divorce, go to prison, or kill themselves—all because the addiction becomes paramount in their lives.

Gambling enterprises make it easy and affordable for the elderly to bet. Casinos commission tour companies to arrange low-cost trips to gather senior citizens from specified sites and bus them to the site.

"These trips are sponsored by everybody: church groups, banks, senior centers, retirement centers," says Dennis P. McNeilly, a forty-five-year-old Jesuit priest who is a psychologist at the University of Nebraska Medical Center in Omaha.

Pat Fowler, fifty-two, executive director of the Florida Council on Compulsive Gambling in Orlando, asks, "Who else will pick you up at your home, take you to engage in an exciting activity in a safe environment, give you lunch, call you by your name, and make you feel important? Our society sees seniors primarily as disposable, and this industry has picked up on that."[1]

Several recent studies confirm that more senior citizens are gambling, and losing control. For instance:

- A February University of Chicago National Opinion Research Center (NORC) nationwide study of 2,400 adults comparing data between 1974 and now shows the highest increase among gamblers has been among those sixty-five and older.
- Research conducted by Linda Bradley of 235 gambling senior citizens from Westerly, Rhode Island, shows that the third and the fourth are the busiest days of the month at casinos, as retirement checks arrive in the mail. More than half who gambled had an annual income of less than $20,000; 31 percent gambled with money from pensions, 20 percent from social security.
- "We found a disproportionate number of gamblers are elderly," says J. Terrence Brunner, sixty-one, executive director of the watchdog Chicago-based Better Government Association. "Of that group, women tend to play the slots and veg-out, sometimes for hours."
- Valerie Lorenz, sixty-two, whose Compulsive Gambling Center in Baltimore is connected with the longest-running residential treatment program for pathological gamblers in the country, says more elderly married couples are becoming addicted. "We're seeing more husbands and wives addicted, first one and then the other, invariably on slots."
- Technological developments could result in more elderly addicts. Since 1995, Internet users have been able to gamble on interactive Web sites. About 140 unregulated sites exist, based primarily in the Caribbean. In a few years, though it faces legislative challenges from the casino industry fearful of losing business, shut-ins could gamble via their television sets.
- Recovering addict Eades says senior centers are unwittingly sending more and more undiagnosed Alzheimer's patients to gamble. "You don't have to function at a high level to play slot machines."[2]

Date:	_____	_____	_____
Place:	_____	_____	_____
Occasion:	_____	_____	_____

One Woman's Experience

At one time, her faith and family were the most important things in Maxi Chamber's life. She was an elected city council member, business owner, and an outspoken witness for Christ.

But one day she won a simple game of bingo. Since she and her husband David were having some financial problems, the $500 enabled them to pay some bills. She didn't realize that gambling was wrong and had never heard a sermon about it.

[1] John W. Kennedy, "Gambling Away the Golden Years," *Christianity Today*, May 24, 1999, 42.
[2] John W. Kennedy, "Gambling Away the Golden Years," *Christianity Today*, May 24, 1999, 43.

Over the course of a year, what began as a once-a-week activity developed into an every-night habit.

Soon she was betting a hundred dollars here, and two hundred there. David grew ashamed and hurt, but Maxi couldn't stop. She began frequenting a nearby Indian reservation casino, and on every trip to the grocery store she would spend twenty or thirty dollars on lottery tickets.

The children grew distant and depressed, and David grew increasingly angry. Because Maxi was gambling away the money needed for necessities, the family went without new shoes, clothes, or food.

Two years into her gambling, Maxi began to feel suicidal. She cried constantly, seldom slept, and began taking tranquilizers and antidepressants. Her losses became greater, and she began writing checks for much more than was in her account. She took out a loan, forging her husband's name, to cover her losses.

Finally she lost the last of her last borrowed $10,000 at a casino table, and as she turned away the dealer shouted, "Better luck next time!" But Maxi's luck was gone, and as she drove home she cried out to God for help. The next morning she cleaned the house of anything that suggested gambling, and, sitting down with her checkbook, she totaled up her damages. At length, she had to confess to David.

"David," she said, "I have something to tell you." His body tensed. "You have every reason to divorce me," she continued. "No one would have put up with what you've endured over the last three years. There are no excuses for what I'm about to tell you."

David wrapped his arms around Maxi, and they sobbed together. But the injuries were too great, and the couple divorced with the three sons choosing to live with their father. Slowly Maxi Chambers is rebuilding her life, reading the Scriptures and staying close to the Lord and to her church. And she has a mission in life now—to warn everyone she can of the subtle dangers of the habit that almost destroyed her.[1]

Date:	_____	_____	_____
Place:	_____	_____	_____
Occasion:	_____	_____	_____

Nothing New

Gambling can take a man's shirt off his back, but Christ can clothe him with hope. Camillus de Lellis learned both lessons. He was an Italian, born in 1550 to a mother nearly sixty. By seventeen, he stood six-and-a-half feet tall, big boned, well-muscled, quick-tempered, and unchaste. He enlisted in the army, was sent to war, but on the battlefield contracted a leg disease that afflicted him the rest of his life.

The hospital for incurables in Rome, San Giacomo, admitted him, but he was soon ejected for quarreling. That wasn't his worst fault. Camillus relished betting, and by 1574 his addiction had taken his last penny. That autumn in the streets of Naples he gambled with his last possession, the shirt on his back. Losing the wager, he stripped it off and limped away both broke and broken.

---

[1] Maxi Chambers, "Gambling With My Life," *Christian Reader,* July/August 1997, 69–73.

Camillus secured a construction job, and one day a friar came along preaching. The message hit home, and Camillus fell to his knees, crying to God for mercy. He was twenty-five years old when he became a Christian. He returned to San Giacomo and offered himself a volunteer. He ministered intently to the suffering, and in time he was promoted, then promoted again. He eventually became hospital superintendent.

With a friend's endowment, he organized a small army of male nurses to serve the sick in Christ's name. He also mobilized volunteers to travel with troops in Hungary and Croatia, thus forming the first "military field ambulance." He sent nurses aboard galley ships to attend slaves suffering from pestilence. In all, Camillus organized eight hospitals, pioneered medical hygiene and diet, and successfully opposed the prevailing practice of burying patients alive.

All the while, Camillus' leg was worsening, and he began suffering ruptures elsewhere on his body. Sometimes on his rounds, he crawled from sickbed to sickbed. On July 14, 1614, after a final tour of his works, Camillus de Lellis died at age sixty-four. He was canonized in 1746 and declared patron saint of the sick by Pope Leo XIII, and of nurses and nursing by Pope Pius XI.[1]

Date: _____ _____ _____

Place: _____ _____ _____

Occasion: _____ _____ _____

Gamblers Anonymous

Gambler's Anonymous has twenty questions that it asks new members. Compulsive gamblers usually answer "yes" to at least seven of the twenty questions.

1. Do you lose time from work due to gambling?
2. Does gambling make your home life unhappy?
3. Does gambling affect your reputation?
4. Do you ever feel remorse after gambling?
5. Do you ever gamble to get money with which to pay debts or to otherwise solve financial difficulties?
6. Does gambling cause a decrease in your ambition or efficiency?
7. After losing, do you feel you must return as soon as possible to win back your losses?
8. After a win, do you have a strong urge to return and win more?
9. Do you often gamble until your last dollar is gone?
10. Do you ever borrow to finance your gambling?
11. Do you ever sell anything to finance gambling?
12. Are you reluctant to use "gambling money" for normal expenditure?
13. Does gambling make you careless about the welfare of your family?
14. Do you ever gamble longer than you planned?
15. Do you ever gamble to escape worry or trouble?
16. Do you ever commit, or consider committing, an illegal act to finance your gambling?

---

[1] Robert J. Morgan, *On This Day* (Nashville: Thomas Nelson, 1997), July 14th.

17. Does gambling cause you to have difficulty sleeping?
18. Do arguments, disappointments, or frustrations create within you an urge to gamble?
19. Do you have an urge to celebrate good fortune by a few hours of gambling?
20. Do you ever consider self-destruction as a result of your gambling?

Date: _____ _____ _____
Place: _____ _____ _____
Occasion: _____ _____ _____

Gentleness

Someone Once Said . . .

- *Hearts are flowers; they remain open to the softly falling dew, but shut up in the violent downpour of rain.*—Jean Paul Richter[1]
- *John Knox did much, but he might perhaps have done more if he had had a little love. Luther was a conqueror—peace to his ashes, and honor to his name!—still, we who look upon him at a distance, think that if he had sometimes mixed a little mildness with it . . . he might have done more good than he did.*—Charles Haddon Spurgeon[2]

Date: _____ _____ _____
Place: _____ _____ _____
Occasion: _____ _____ _____

Lesson of the Goldfish

Richard L. Dunagin of Denton, Texas, writing in *Leadership Journal,* said that his children won four free goldfish at the school carnival, necessitating a Saturday morning family outing to find an aquarium. The first several they found were too expensive, but then he spotted a used one right in the middle of the aisle: A discarded ten-gallon tank complete with gravel and filter. It was five dollars.

"Of course, it was nasty dirty, but the savings made the two hours of cleanup a breeze. Those four new fish looked great in their new home, at least for the first day. But by Sunday one had died. Too bad, but three remained. Monday morning revealed a second casualty, and by Monday night a third goldfish had gone belly up.

"We called in an expert, a member of our church who had a 30-gallon tank. It didn't take him long to discover the problem: I had washed the tank with soap, an absolute no-no. My uninformed efforts had destroyed the very lives I was trying to protect.

---

[1] Zig Ziglar, *Top Performance.*
[2] Charles Haddon Spurgeon, *Spurgeon's Sermons,* vol. 1 (Grand Rapids: MI: Baker Book House, 1983), 258.

"Sometimes in our zeal to clean up our own lives or the lives of others, we unfortunately use "killer soaps"—condemnation, criticism, nagging, fits of temper. We think we're doing right, but our harsh, self-righteous treatment is more than they can bear."[1]

Date:			
Place:			
Occasion:			

Five Ways to Be Gentle

Jerry Bridges suggests these five strategies for obeying the biblical injunctions about gentleness:

- Actively seek to make others feel at ease. Be sensitive to other's opinions and ideas, welcoming opinion.
- Show respect for the personal dignity of the other person. When you need to change a wrong opinion, do so with persuasion and kindness rather than domination or intimidation.
- Avoid blunt speech and abrupt manner. Be sensitive to how others react to your words, considering how they may feel. When it is necessary to wound, also include encouragement.
- Don't be threatened by opposition; gently instruct, asking God to dissolve the opposition.
- Do not belittle or degrade or gossip about a brother who has fallen—instead grieve and pray for his repentance.[2]

Date:			
Place:			
Occasion:			

——————————— Giving ———————————

Someone Once Said . . .

- *The basic question is not how much of **our** money we should give to God, but how much of **God's** money we should keep for ourselves.*—J. Oswald Sanders[3]
- *There is a blessed kind of giving, which, though it makes the purse lighter, makes the crown heavier.*—Thomas Watson[4]
- *The interest comes to infinitely more than the principal.*—Thomas Watson[5]

---

[1] Richard L. Dunagin, "Gentleness," *Leadership Journal*, Summer 1985, 68.
[2] Jerry Bridges, *The Practice of Godliness* (Colorado Springs: NavPress, 1996), < www.primenet.com. >
[3] J. Oswald Sanders, *A Spiritual Clinic* (Chicago: Moody Press, 1958), 85.
[4] Thomas Watson, *Gleanings From Thomas Watson* (Morgan, PA: Soli Deo Gloria Publications, 1995), 26.
[5] Watson, *Gleanings From Thomas Watson*, 26.

- *Tithing is the solution no one talks about. . . . If every Christian tithed, every congregation would be free of financial worries and could begin truly to be the salt of the earth. If every Christian would tithe, the church would begin to make an impact on the world that would change it. The church instead is paralyzed.*—R. T. Kendall[1]
- *Be faithful with what you receive; be prayerful about what you need; be open about what you are doing.*—E. Brandt Gustavson
- *I just don't see how I can give as much as a tenth, pastor. Would it be all right if I just gave a fourth.*—apologetic member to pastor

Date: _____   _____   _____
Place: _____   _____   _____
Occasion: _____   _____   _____

Spurgeon on "Giving"

Earn all you can, save all you can, and then give all you can. Never try to save out of God's cause; such money will canker the rest. Giving to God is no loss; it is putting your substance into the best bank. Giving is true having, as the old gravestone said of the dead man, "What I spent I had, what I saved I lost, what I gave I have."[2]

Date: _____   _____   _____
Place: _____   _____   _____
Occasion: _____   _____   _____

Different Audiences

It's easier to make a paying audience laugh. They get dressed up and they put on a tie and they get in their cars and they pay so much that they like your act. An audience that doesn't pay is very critical.—George Burns

Date: _____   _____   _____
Place: _____   _____   _____
Occasion: _____   _____   _____

Determined Giving

In stories of survivors of the Nazi death camps, an attitude of determined giving was one of the things that distinguished the survivors from those who perished. If a prisoner was on the verge of starvation, but he had a crust of bread or a scrap of a potato that he could share with his comrade in suffering, he was psychologically and spiritually capable of surviving.

---

[1] R. T. Kendall, *Tithing: A Call to Serious, Biblical Stewardship* (Grand Rapids: Zondervan, 1982), 13.
[2] Charles Haddon Spurgeon, *John Ploughman's Talks* (New York: Sheldon & Company, n.d.), 139.

A survivor of Treblinka described it this way: "In our group we shared everything, and the moment one of the group ate something without sharing it, we knew it was the beginning of the end for him."[1]

Date: _____ _____ _____
Place: _____ _____ _____
Occasion: _____ _____ _____

A Hundred Times Over

The following is the testimony of Fred Green of Nashville, Tennessee: "When I was sixteen years old, my father ran a labor camp for the city of Springdale, Arkansas. I was given the job of picking up the trash and cleaning the restrooms, and for that job I was paid three dollars a day and, even more importantly, I was allowed to drive a very old, beat-up pick-up truck. I can remember my first paycheck. My parents and I were sitting around the dining room table, and I was discussing how I was going to spend all that money. After I finished my dad said, "What about the Lord?" I sat down and refigured my budget, and it was at that time that I first laid aside ten percent of my income for the Lord. To the best of my knowledge I have given ten percent or more of every dollar I have ever earned to the Lord. The Lord has blessed me a hundred times over and is still blessing me and my family for this effort."

Date: _____ _____ _____
Place: _____ _____ _____
Occasion: _____ _____ _____

You Have the First Piece

Give as an act of worship. Honor the Lord with your money and with the firstfruits of all of your income. Two little boys were each given a box of chocolates by their grandfather. The first boy took the package into his bedroom, tore into it, and stuffed the candies into his mouth until he was one big mess of smeared chocolate. The other boy unwrapped his package there in front of his grandfather. He opened the box and looked at all the candies. Then he raised the box to his grandfather and said, "Thank you for giving me this candy. Here. You have the first piece."

Date: _____ _____ _____
Place: _____ _____ _____
Occasion: _____ _____ _____

A Ray of Light

R. T. Kendall, longtime minister at Westminster Chapel, London, wrote that shortly after he and his wife were married they found themselves hopelessly in debt.

---

[1] Julius Segal, *Winning Life's Toughest Battles* (New York: Ivy Books, 1986), 105.

Tithing seemed utterly impossible to them. Some of the bills could not be helped, and others were the consequence of imprudence. Kendall was engaged in secular work at the time, and one day he came home very, very discouraged. He fell on his knees in a sense of desperation, hoping that God would give him a ray of light that would help him through. There on the dining room table lay the large, white Bible his grandmother had given to him. He picked it up and opened it at random. Instantly his eyes fell on these words: "Will a man rob God?"

He didn't like what he found one bit, so he closed his Bible and sat down to watch the television (for which he still owed). But he was perfectly miserable. He knew that God wanted him to begin tithing, but he postponed it for a while longer; and in the meantime things went from bad to worse. "Although my wife and I were both working, it seemed that paying our bills was like dipping a cup into the ocean of debt."

Then one day they made a turn. They took 10 percent of their income right off the top, making tithing the number one priority. He paid their bills with the remaining 90 percent.

"We were not out of debt in weeks, but we were completely out of debt in less than two years, and those days became the happiest we have known."[1]

Date:	_____	_____	_____
Place:	_____	_____	_____
Occasion:	_____	_____	_____

A Little Bit of Prayer and 19 Cents

Lyle Eggleston served as a missionary for many years in a little town on the rocky coast of northern Chile. In time, the congregation grew to about eighty adults, but Eggleston was concerned that the Christians in that area didn't seem able to support their own national pastor. The people were very poor, and the church's offerings amounted to no more than six dollars a month.

One day, Eggleston brought the problem to the Lord during a definite time of prayer. A few weeks later he stopped to visit a middle-aged couple, new converts who had begun the habit of reading their Bibles every day.

"What does the word tithing mean?" asked Manuel. "We ran into that in our reading, and we don't understand it."

Eggleston didn't really want to answer the question, for he knew that Manuel and his wife were unemployed and on the verge of destitution. They were somehow managing to feed themselves and their twenty-five Rhode Island hens on the income from the eggs laid each day.

Nevertheless they insisted he explain the concept of tithing to them, so he turned to 1 Corinthians 16 and 2 Corinthians 8 and 9 where Paul urged believers to lay aside each week a portion of their income to the Lord.

The following Sunday Manuel handed Lyle an envelope and, smiling, said, "That's our tithe!" Inside were a few bills amounting to about 19 cents.

[1] R. T. Kendall, *Tithing: A Call to Serious, Biblical Stewardship* (Grand Rapids, MI: Zondervan, 1982), 25.

The next Sunday afternoon, the couple flagged down Lyle as he rode his bicycle past their house. They had some exciting news. The Tuesday morning after they had given their tithe, there's wasn't a bite for breakfast, nor any money. Their first impulse was to take the few pesos that had accumulated in their "tithe box," but on second thought they said, "No. That's God's money. We will go without breakfast this morning."

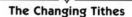

The Changing Tithes

If every Christian would tithe, the church would begin to make an impact on the world that would change it.

—R. T. KENDALL

G

There was nothing to do but tend the hens. Much to their surprise, there were eggs in the nests that had usually at that hour been empty. Later in the day, a little man came along with a pushcart wanting fertilizer. They cleaned out their hen house, and the manure brought a good price. After buying groceries, there was enough money left over for the wife to purchase a pair of shoes, so she rode the bus 12 kilometers around the bay into a larger town. There she bumped into a nephew she had not seen in five years, and who, to her utter surprise, owned a shoe store. After she had found just the pair she wanted, he wrapped them for her and handed her the package with these words, "Oh no, Aunt, I can't take your money. These shoes are a gift from me."

The following week, Manuel got a job on a project that would last for two years, and soon the little couple was tithing on a much larger salary. Word got around the church, and others began experimenting with giving. Soon the church's income begin to rise dramatically, and they were able to pay their own rent and utility bills, support a national pastor who was working with Indians, and, in a short time, they were able to call and finance a pastor of their own.

Lyle Eggleston and his wife were able to move to a new location and start a new work as the little church grew in numbers, size, property, and faith. "We had offered up a bit of prayer and 19 cents," Lyle later said, "and God did the rest."[1]

Date: _____   _____   _____
Place: _____   _____   _____
Occasion: _____   _____   _____

Tithing from Bread and Dirty Soup

In the book *Tortured for Christ,* Richard Wurmbrand tells of his many years in and out of miserable Communist prisons because of his faith in Christ. He was often tortured, and on some occasions nearly starved to death. But the principle of tithing was so internalized in his heart that when he was given one slice of bread a week and dirty soup every day, he faithfully tithed from it. Every tenth day he gave his soup to a weaker brother, and every tenth week he took his slice of bread and gave it to one of his fellow prisoners in Jesus' name.

Date: _____   _____   _____
Place: _____   _____   _____
Occasion: _____   _____   _____

---

[1] Lyle Eggleston, "The Church That Learned to Give," *Moody,* July/August 1988, 31–32.

Colgate

The Colgate-Palmolive Company is one of the oldest in America, going back nearly two hundred years. It was started by a young man named William Colgate. He left home at sixteen years of age to seek his fortune, and everything that he owned in this world was tied in a bundle that he carried in his hand. But as he walked along on his way to the city, he met an old neighbor, the captain of a canal boat, and the words the old man spoke to him on that day stayed with him his entire life.

"Well, William, where are you going?" asked the canal-boat captain.

"I don't know. Father is too poor to keep me at home any longer, and says I must make a living for myself now." William went on to say that he had no skills, that he didn't know how to do anything except make soap and candles.

"Well," said the old man, "let me pray with you and give you a little advice."

There in the pathway, the two of them—a teenager and an old man—knelt down and the man prayed earnestly for William. Then, rising up, the boat captain said this: "Someone will soon be the leading soapmaker in New York. It can be you as well as anyone. I hope it may. Be a good man; give your heart to Christ; give the Lord all that belongs to Him of every dollar you earn; make an honest soap; give a full pound; and I am certain you will yet be a prosperous and rich man."

When William arrived in New York, he had trouble finding a job, but he followed the old man's advice. He dedicated himself to Christ, joined a church, and began worshiping there. The first thing he did with the first dollar he earned was to give 10 percent of it to the Lord's work. From that point on, he considered ten cents of every dollar as sacred to the Lord. In fact, he soon began giving 20 percent of his income to the Lord, then he raised it to 30 percent, then to 40 percent, then to 50 percent. And late in his life, he had become so successful that he devoted the whole of his yearly income—100 percent of it—to the Lord.

And even today, this very morning, nearly two hundred years later, some of you brushed your teeth or washed your faces with products from that young man's factory.

Date:	_____	_____	_____
Place:	_____	_____	_____
Occasion:	_____	_____	_____

What Those Oats Can Do

Henry Crowell, founder of the Quaker Oats Company and a significant contributor to the work of Moody Bible Institute knew how to use money wisely. As a young man, he received Christ as his Savior. When he began his business career in a little Ohio factory, he promised God that he would honor Him in his giving. God's blessing was upon him; and, as his business grew, he increased his giving. After more than forty years of giving 60 percent of his income to God, Crowell testified, "I've never gotten ahead of God. He has always been ahead of me in giving."[1]

---

[1] George Sweeting, "Money: Blessing or Curse?," *Moody,* April 1981, 1.

Date:			
Place:			
Occasion:			

Other Business Leaders

- *The only investments I ever made which have paid constantly increasing dividends is the money I have given to the Lord.*—J. L. Kraft, head of Kraft Cheese, who for many years gave 25 percent of his income to Christian causes
- *I have tithed every dollar God has entrusted to me: And I want to say, if I had not tithed the first dollar I made, I would not have tithed the first million dollars I made.*—John D. Rockefeller, Sr.
- *I am totally dependent on God for help in everything I do. Otherwise I honestly believe I would start to fall apart in months.*—Wallace Johnson, founder of Holiday Inn and a Christian steward

Date:			
Place:			
Occasion:			

Proving God

In his book *Proving God,* Al Taylor tells the story of Arlie Rogers of Selma, California, who came to be known as the "Sweet Potato King" because of his vast farming operations in the San Joaquin Valley. Arlie and his brother first arrived in California with little money. By scraping and saving, they finally managed to purchase a farm. At that time, the money crop was cotton, so the two brothers invested every penny they could get in sowing cotton.

> **Right Again!**
>
> *Give God what is right, not what is left.*
>
> —ANONYMOUS

When the cotton plants were just out of the ground, a great sandstorm blew through the valley, destroying everyone's crops. The Rogers brothers were disconsolate.

Arlie called the church and asked their pastor to visit. As Pastor Burnham walked across the devastated fields, the brothers poured out their troubles. "Everything we had was in that crop. We don't have any money or credit left to replant. We are completely ruined. Now we will lose everything."

Pastor Burnham knew these brothers as dedicated Christians, active in their church, and faithful in giving their tithes to the Lord. Squinting at them, he replied, "No, fellows, it's really not that bad. The God we serve raised His own Son from the dead after three days. I know He can raise cotton."

With that, the pastor sank to his knees in the dirt and prayed a simple little prayer. "Father," he said, "these men are tithers. You said You would rebuke the devourer for a tither. I am asking You to manifest the power of Your Word and fulfill that promise right here in this cotton field. Bring this cotton back and give these men a good crop in Jesus' name. Amen."

He rose, brushed the dust from his knees, and said, "That ought to take care of it."

It did. A few days later the Rogers brothers called him back. There before his eyes a good crop was rising from the ground. God had rebuked the devourer.[1]

Date:			
Place:			
Occasion:			

John Rascus' $300

Venerable W. A. Criswell used to preach from Matthew 6:19–21, ending his sermon with these words: *John Rascus put $300 in the collection plate when it passed, and he said softly, "I'll see you in heaven." Those around him said, "Old John is getting senile. He says he is going to see that $300 in heaven. He may meet his Maker over there, but he certainly won't meet his money."*

Now, the church treasurer used some of that $300 to pay the electric bill. He gave some of it to the preacher to buy gasoline. Some went to ministerial students, and some to the mission field.

Early one morning John Rascus died in his sleep. On that first Lord's Day in glory, he walked down the golden streets and a young fellow came up and said, "Thank you, brother John. I was cold and lonely and it was a dark night. I saw the lights of the church. Just to get out of the dark, I went in. While there, the darkness left my soul and I found Jesus."

Another came to him saying, "The preacher came to the filling station. As I filled his tank, he told me about Jesus and I gave my heart to the Lord."

Next John met a throng of people who said, "I want to thank you for those students you helped. They preached the gospel to my family, and we found the Lord."

He next met those of strange tongues who said, "Thank you, brother, for sending us the gospel across the seas." Finally old John came to Hallelujah Square and, turning to an angel, he said, "I feel sorry for you angels. You have never known what it is to be saved by the blood of Jesus, My Lord."

John Rascus mused a moment, then added, "And you do not know what it is to transform the possessions of earth into the treasures of heaven."

"Sir," replied the angel, "all we do is just watch it from the streets of glory."[2]

Date:			
Place:			
Occasion:			

More Criswell

A man was asked, "What did you do yesterday?"

He replied, "Yesterday I taught a class in the Criswell College. On Tuesday I was down in the Rio Grande Valley working in Vacation Bible School. On Wednesday I was operating in our Baptist hospital in Nigeria. On Thursday I was teaching the Word of God in the Amazon jungle. On Friday I was building a church house in the Philippines. On Saturday I was preaching on the streets in the Japanese capital of Tokyo."

[1] Al Taylor, *Proving God* (Cleveland, TN: Pathway Press, 1991), 102–103.
[2] W. A. Criswell, *Great Doctrines of the Bible*, vol. 6 (Grand Rapids, MI: Zondervan, 1986), 118–120.

The friend exclaimed, "Man, even in the jet age you cannot do that!"

The fellow said, "But I do it every day. I dedicate to the Lord a gift in the First Baptist Church of Dallas, and it goes all over the earth doing good for Jesus."[1]

Date:			
Place:			
Occasion:			

Sending It on Ahead

A sailor, shipwrecked on a South Sea island, was seized by the natives, carried, shoulder-high to a rude throne and proclaimed king. He learned that according to custom a king ruled for a year. The idea appealed to the sailor until he began to wonder what had befallen previous kings. He learned that when a king's reign ended, he was banished to a lonely island where he starved. Knowing he had power of kingship for a year, the sailor began issuing orders. Carpenters were to make boats. Farmers were to go ahead to the island and plant crops. Builders were to erect a sturdy home. When his reign finished, he was exiled, not to a barren isle, but to a paradise of plenty.[2]

Date:			
Place:			
Occasion:			

Too Many One-Dollar Bills

Among the CNN headlines for April 6, 1999, was this one: *Armed Robber Holds Up Church During Easter Service*. It happened in a Louisiana church of about one hundred worshipers. A gunman wearing a ski mask entered a suburban New Orleans church fifteen minutes into the morning service. Holding a gun to one member's head, he ordered most of the members to lie on the floor while the remaining handful were forced to walk through the room taking the "offering."

But he was disappointed with the results. He left grumbling that there were too many one-dollar bills.[3]

Date:			
Place:			
Occasion:			

Giving and Maturity

Robertson McQuilkin writes that the maturity of Christians can be measured by both the way and the attitude with which they give to the Lord's work. He suggests these classifications:

---

[1] Criswell, *Great Doctrines of the Bible*, vol. 6, 140.
[2] Leslie B. Flynn, *Come Alive with Illustrations* (Grand Rapids, MI: Baker Book House, 1987), 27–28.
[3] *CNN Custom News*, April 6, 1999.

- Infancy is marked by non-giving, illustrated by the man in Luke 12:16–18 who hoarded his wealth.
- Kindergarten is characterized by Impulse Giving, such as Zacchaeus in Luke 19:8.
- Elementary: Legalistic Giving, as is described in Luke 11:42.
- Christians at a "Secondary Level" of maturity—high school—give in keeping with honest management, like the steward in Luke 16.
- Higher levels mature into Love Giving, as is seen in the poor widow in Luke 21:1–4.
- The Graduate Level of giving is Faith Giving, based on Luke 12:28. These people give sacrificially, gladly, and by faith, trusting God to meet their needs.[1]

Date: _____ _____ _____
Place: _____ _____ _____
Occasion: _____ _____ _____

I Could Have Done More

The film *Schindler's List* chronicled the heroic efforts of a German industrialist named Oskar Schindler. Through his unselfish activities, over a thousand Jews on the trains to Auschwitz were saved. Although the film, even on television, has some very graphic and disturbing scenes, the message itself is profound.

After Schindler found out what was happening at Auschwitz, he began a systematic effort to save as many Jews as he could. For money, he could buy Jews to work in his factory which was supposed to be a part of the military machine of Germany. On one hand he was buying as many Jews as he could, and on the other hand he was deliberately sabotaging the ammunition produced in his factory. He entered the war as a wealthy industrialist; by the end of the war, he was basically bankrupt.

When the Germans surrendered, Schindler met with his workers and declared that at midnight they were all free to go. The most emotional scene of the film was when Schindler said good-bye to the financial manager of the plant, a Jew and his good and trusted friend. As he embraced his friend, Schindler sobbed and said, "I could have done more." He looked at his automobile and asked, "Why did I save this? I could have bought 10 Jews with this." Taking another small possession he cried, "This would have saved another one. Why didn't I do more?"

One day Jesus is going to split the eastern sky and come for His own. It will not matter then how much money we have in a mutual fund or how many bedrooms we have in our homes. The temporary satisfaction we have in vacations and nice cars will be gone. Only what we have done for the cause of Christ will matter.[2]

Date: _____ _____ _____
Place: _____ _____ _____
Occasion: _____ _____ _____

---

[1] Robertson McQuilkin, *Measuring Maturity* (Columbia, SC: Columbia International University, n.d.).
[2] James Forlines, *Men's Beat of Free Will Baptist Foreign Missions*, April 1999, 4.

A Little Poem by John Bunyan

There was a man,
Some called him mad;
The more he gave,
The more he had.

Date: _____ _____ _____
Place: _____ _____ _____
Occasion: _____ _____ _____

Ten Apples

Once upon a time there was a man who had nothing, and God gave him ten apples.

- He gave him the first three apples to eat.
- He gave him the second three apples to trade for shelter from the sun and rain.
- He gave him the third three apples to trade for clothing to wear.
- He gave him the last apple so that he might have something to give back to God to show his gratitude for the other nine.
- The man ate the first three apples.
- He traded the second three for a shelter from the sun and rain.
- He traded the third three for clothing to wear.
- Then he looked at the tenth apple. It seemed bigger and juicer than the rest. He knew that God had given him the tenth apple so that he might return it to Him out of the gratitude for the other nine. But the tenth apple looked bigger and juicier than the rest. And he reasoned that God had all the other apples in the world. So the man ate the tenth apple—and gave back to God the core.[1]

Date: _____ _____ _____
Place: _____ _____ _____
Occasion: _____ _____ _____

Credit for One

Early in their marriage, Billy and Ruth Graham were visiting a church where Billy was preaching. During the offering, an usher came to the platform and pushed the offering plate in front of the guest evangelist. Billy reached for his wallet and pulled out what he thought was a dollar bill. As it dropped into the plate, he saw it was his one and only ten-dollar bill. His heart sank as he saw the bulk of his financial resources disappearing into the church coffers.

---

[1] Unattributed, in a clipping from the pastor's column of the newsletter of the First Baptist Church of Dallas, Texas.

To further complicate matters, the church treasurer failed to give him an honorarium for his services that evening.

On the way home he told Ruth what had happened. Instead of sympathizing, she said, "And just think—the Lord will give you credit only for the *one*. That's all you meant to give!"[1]

Date:	_____	_____	_____
Place:	_____	_____	_____
Occasion:	_____	_____	_____

The Offering

I would like to remind you that what you are about to give is deductible, cannot be taken with you, is referred to in the Bible as filthy lucre, the love of which is the root of all evil.— One pastor's way of introducing the regular Sunday morning offering

Date:	_____	_____	_____
Place:	_____	_____	_____
Occasion:	_____	_____	_____

John Wesley's Three Rules for Managing Money

1. Gain all you can.
2. Save all you can.
3. Give all you can.

Date:	_____	_____	_____
Place:	_____	_____	_____
Occasion:	_____	_____	_____

God

Someone Once Said . . .

- *What kind of guy is God?*—college student to Billy Graham
- *God is not like anything.*—A. W. Tozer[2]
- *Without God, God cannot be known.*—Irenaeus (about A.D. 175)
- *Were we able to extract from any man a complete answer to the question, "What comes into your mind when you think about God?" we might predict with certainty the spiritual future of that man.*—A. W. Tozer[3]

[1] Lee Fisher, *A Funny Thing Happened on the Way to the Crusade* (Carol Stream, IL: Creation House, 1974), 64.
[2] A. W. Tozer, *The Knowledge of the Holy* (New York: Harper & Row, Publishers, 1961), 14.
[3] Tozer, *The Knowledge of the Holy*, 9.

- *Disregard the study of God, and you sentence yourself to stumble and blunder through life blindfolded, as it were, with no sense of direction. . . .*—J. I. Packer[1]
- *If we would bring back spiritual power to our lives, we must begin to think of God more nearly as He is.*—A. W. Tozer[2]
- *For in glory He is incomprehensible, in greatness unfathomable, in height inconceivable, in power incomparable, in wisdom unrivaled, in goodness inimitable, in kindness unutterable.*—Theophilus of Antioch, 2nd century A.D.
- *God is a Spirit, infinite, eternal, and unchangeable in His being, wisdom, power, holiness, justice, goodness and truth.*—answer to the fourth question of the Westminster Shorter Catechism, a statement that the theologian Charles Hodge described as "probably the best definition of God ever penned by man."[3]
- *It is perilously possible to make our conceptions of God like molten lead poured into a specially designed mould, and when it is cold and hard we fling it at the heads of the religious people who don't agree with us.*—Oswald Chambers[4]
- *A little knowledge of God is worth more than a great deal of knowledge about Him.*—J. I. Packer[5]

Date: _____ _____ _____
Place: _____ _____ _____
Occasion: _____ _____ _____

The Study of God

James Denney, the saintly Scotch preacher/teacher/theologian used to warn his students against thinking they could learn all there was to know about God during their university and seminary studies. "Gentlemen," he would tell them, "to study infinity requires eternity."

Date: _____ _____ _____
Place: _____ _____ _____
Occasion: _____ _____ _____

Baffling

John Calvin liked to tell his students Cicero's story about Simonides, the ancient Greek poet, who was asked by Hiero the Tyrant what God was. Simonides requested a day to consider the question, then another day, then another day. Finally he concluded that the question only became more baffling the longer he thought about it.[6]

[1] J. I. Packer, *Knowing God* (Downers Grove, IL: InterVarsity, 1973), 14–15.
[2] Tozer, *The Knowledge of the Holy*, 7.
[3] Packer, *Knowing God*, 16.
[4] Oswald Chambers, *Disciples Indeed* (London: Oswald Chambers Publications Association, and Marshall, Morgan, & Scott, Ltd., 1955), 14.
[5] Packer, *Knowing God*, (Downers Grove, IL: InterVarsity, 1973), 21.
[6] William J. Bouwsma, *John Calvin: A Sixteenth Century Portrait* (New York: Oxford University Press, 1988), 155.

> Date: _____ _____ _____
> Place: _____ _____ _____
> Occasion: _____ _____ _____

Helen Keller

When Helen Keller was ten years old, her father asked the famous Boston minister, Phillips Brooks, to tell her about God. He gladly did so. After their first conversation, Brooks was profoundly moved by Helen's response. She said that she had always known there was a God, but had not before known His name.

> Date: _____ _____ _____
> Place: _____ _____ _____
> Occasion: _____ _____ _____

Fleas and a Dog

Robert Fulghum once sat beside an Australian carpenter on an airplane, and they struck up a conversation about theology. The carpenter declared that his theology had a lot to do with fleas and a dog. How so? Arguing whether or not God exists, he said, is like fleas arguing whether or not the dog exists.

That reminds me of an old story that, I believe, first appeared in a British newspaper, about a family of mice who lived inside a large piano. All the dark spaces of their world were filled with sound and harmony. At first the mice were impressed by it. They drew comfort and wonder from the thought that there was Someone who made the music—though invisible to them—above, yet close to them. They loved to think of the Great Player whom they could not see.

—◇—
A Worm's Comprehension

Bring me a worm that can comprehend a man, and then I will show you a man who can comprehend God.

—JOHN WESLEY
—◇—

Then one day a daring mouse climbed up part of the piano and returned very thoughtful. He had discovered how the music was made. Wires were the secret; tightly stretched wires of graduated lengths which trembled and vibrated. They must revise all their old beliefs: None but the most conservative could any longer believe in the Unseen Player.

Later another explorer carried the explanation further. Hammers were now the secret, numbers of hammers dancing and leaping on the wires. This was a more complicated theory, but it all went to show that they lived in a purely mechanical and mathematical world. The Unseen Player came to be thought of as a myth.

But the pianist continued to play.[1]

> Date: _____ _____ _____
> Place: _____ _____ _____
> Occasion: _____ _____ _____

---

[1] From a sermon by the author. Robert Fulghum, *Uh-Oh* (New York: Villard Books, 1991), 133.

Great or Small?

A well-known English deist, Anthony Collins of the seventeenth century, was walking one day when he crossed paths with a commoner. "Where are you going?" asked Collins.

"To church, sir."

"What are you going to do there?"

"To worship God, sir."

"Is your God a great or a little God?" asked Collins.

"He is both, sir."

"How can He be both?"

"He is so great, sir, that the heaven of heavens cannot contain Him; and so little that He can dwell in my heart."

Collins later declared that this simple answer had more effect on his mind than all the volumes he had ever read about God, and all the lectures he had ever heard.

Date: _____ _____ _____
Place: _____ _____ _____
Occasion: _____ _____ _____

Man's Best Friend

Edwin Arlington Robinson wrote, "The world is a kind of spiritual kindergarten where bewildered infants are trying to spell God with the wrong blocks."

Two men were traveling together by plane. While one napped, the other remained busy working a crossword puzzle. He nudged his friend in the ribs and asked, "What is a word of three letters, with the letter O in the middle, meaning, man's best friend?"

His friend mumbled, "Dog."

But dog didn't fit the puzzle. The man kept working at it and finally said, "The last letter is D." But they never did come up with the right answer, that the first letter was G.

And in the puzzles of life, many people never realize that their best friend is God.

Date: _____ _____ _____
Place: _____ _____ _____
Occasion: _____ _____ _____

Letting God Take Over

"Suppose I try to run a store. I know nothing about it, I get the books mixed up, I do not know how to buy or sell, things are in a dreadful mess. I turn the whole business over to another to own and manage and I become only a clerk in the same store I used to run. Mind you, I am as busy as ever but I have changed my responsibility. The care, the upkeep, the management, all that now is the owner's concern; my part is just to be a faithful clerk.

"This Christ life is simply turning the little shop of life, so woefully perplexing, over to another. Christ becomes owner, manager, overseer; his is the responsibility, the upkeep. Your part is to be a faithful clerk, steward of the grace of God. . . .

"And one day, if you have been faithful over a few things, he will give you a heavenly shop in the city of the King!"—Vance Havner[1]

Date: _____ _____ _____
Place: _____ _____ _____
Occasion: _____ _____ _____

A Picture of God

There's a story about a kindergarten teacher who asked a boy what he was drawing. Without pausing to look up, he said, "A picture of God." The teacher smiled and responded, "But nobody knows what God looks like." The boy carefully put down his crayon, looked her squarely in the eye, and declared, "They will when I'm finished."

Date: _____ _____ _____
Place: _____ _____ _____
Occasion: _____ _____ _____

Kids' Letters to God

- Dear GOD, Instead of letting people die and having to make new ones, why don't You just keep the ones You have?—Jane
- Dear GOD, Maybe Cain and Abel would not kill each other so much if they had their own rooms. It works with my brother.—Larry
- Dear GOD, If You watch me in church on Sunday, I'll show You my new shoes.—Mickey
- Dear GOD, In school they told us what You do. Who does it when You are on vacation?—Jane
- Dear GOD, I read the Bible. What does "begat" mean? Nobody will tell me. Love, Alison
- Dear GOD, Are You really invisible or is it just a trick?—Lucy
- Dear GOD, Is it true my father won't get in Heaven if he uses his bowling words in the house?—Anita
- Dear GOD, Did You mean for the giraffe to look like that or was it an accident?—Norma
- Dear GOD, Who draws the lines around the countries?—Nan
- Dear GOD, I went to this wedding and they kissed right in church. Is that okay?—Neil

[1] Vance Havner, *Consider Jesus* (Grand Rapids: Baker Book House, 1987), 51.

- Dear GOD, Thank you for the baby brother, but what I prayed for was a puppy.—Joyce
- Dear GOD, Please send me a pony. I never asked for anything before. You can look it up.—Bruce
- Dear GOD, I want to be just like my Daddy when I get big but not with so much hair all over.—Sam
- Dear GOD, You don't have to worry about me. I always look both ways.—Dean
- Dear GOD, I think the stapler is one of your greatest inventions.—Ruth M.
- Dear GOD, I think about You sometimes even when I'm not praying.—Elliott
- Dear GOD, Of all the people who work for You I like Noah and David the best.—Rob
- Dear GOD, My brother told me about being born but it doesn't sound right. They're just kidding, aren't they?—Marsha
- Dear GOD, I would like to live nine hundred years like the guy in the Bible.—Love, Chris
- Dear GOD, We read Thomas Edison made light. But in Sunday school they said You did it. So I bet he stole your idea.—Sincerely, Donna
- Dear GOD, I didn't think orange went with purple until I saw the sunset You made on Tuesday. That was cool.—Eugene[1]

G

Date:		
Place:		
Occasion:		

Call It a Day

After creating a period of night and day, an angel asked God, "So what are we gonna do now?" and God replied "I guess we'll call it a day."

Date:		
Place:		
Occasion:		

God's Care

Someone Once Said . . .

- *With the goodness of God to desire our highest welfare, the wisdom of God to plan it, and the power of God to achieve it, what do we lack?*—A. W. Tozer[2]

---

[1] Original source unknown. Circulating on the Internet.
[2] A. W. Tozer, *The Knowledge of the Holy* (New York: Harper & Row, Publishers, 1961), 70.

- *This is the victory that overcomes the world when we are shipwrecked on God and stranded on Omnipotence!*—Vance Havner[1]

Date: _____ _____ _____
Place: _____ _____ _____
Occasion: _____ _____ _____

Cords of Love

Our Daily Bread once referred to naturalist S. L. Bastian who told of a certain kind of spider that builds its nest in the branch of a small tree or bush. In this delicate enclosure the baby spiders are hatched. If the nest is disturbed in any way, the little spiders will all rush out in fright. At once the mother goes to their side. She is alerted to their potential danger in a most unique manner. Each of the young ones has a thin silky strand attached to it, and all of these threads are joined to the body of the mother. When the babies are threatened by an enemy, they naturally scurry off, giving their lines a sharp tug. This is instantly felt by the adult spider. Within seconds she pulls them back to the nest where they are protected from harm.

That reminds me of something I once read about Mary Slessor, missionary hero to Calabar (Nigeria). She would often rescue babies who were in danger and dying, and often the infants filled her home by the dozens. How to care for them through the night became a problem, especially when one of them stirred and cried. Mary learned to tie a string to each little hammock, lay in bed at night, and pull the strings as each baby needed soothing.

The prophet Hosea says that we are linked to God with cords of love, cords that cannot be broken. The gentle cords of His eternal love bind all our hearts and hurts to Him.

Date: _____ _____ _____
Place: _____ _____ _____
Occasion: _____ _____ _____

Love That Will Not Let Go

George Matheson was only fifteen when he was told he was losing what little poor eyesight he had. Not to be denied, Matheson continued straightaway with his plans to enroll in the University of Glasgow, and his determination led to his graduating at age nineteen. But as he pursued graduate studies in theology for Christian ministry he did become blind. His sisters joined ranks beside him, learning Greek and Hebrew to assist him in his studies. He pressed faithfully on.

But his spirit collapsed when his fiancée, unwilling to be married to a blind man, broke their engagement and returned his ring. He never married, and the pain of that rejection never totally left him. Years later, as a well-loved pastor in Scotland, his sister came to him, announcing her engagement. He rejoiced with her, but his

[1] Vance Havner, *Though I Walk Through the Valley* (Old Tappan, NJ: Fleming H. Revell Co., 1974), 20.

mind went back to his own heartache. He consoled himself in thinking of God's love which is never limited, never conditional, never withdrawn, and never uncertain. Out of this experience he wrote the hymn, *O Love That Wilt Not Let Me Go*.

> *O love that wilt not let me go,*
> *I rest my weary soul in thee;*
> *I give thee back the life I owe,*
> *That in thine ocean depths it flow*
> *May richer, fuller be.*

Date: _____ _____ _____
Place: _____ _____ _____
Occasion: _____ _____ _____

The Weather Vane

One day C. H. Spurgeon was walking through the English countryside with a friend. As they strolled along, the evangelist noticed a barn with a weather vane on its roof. At the top of the vane were these words: "GOD IS LOVE." Spurgeon remarked to his companion that he thought this was a rather inappropriate place for such a message. "Weather vanes are changeable," he said, "but God's love is constant."

"I don't agree with you about those words, Charles," replied his friend. "You misunderstood the meaning. That sign is indicating a truth: Regardless of which way the wind blows, God is love."

Date: _____ _____ _____
Place: _____ _____ _____
Occasion: _____ _____ _____

God's Changelessness

Someone Once Said . . .

- *God never changes moods or cools off in His affections or loses enthusiasm. His attitude toward sin is now the same as it was when He drove out the sinful man from the eastward garden, and His attitude toward the sinner the same as when He stretched forth His hands and cried, "Come unto me, all ye that labour and are heavy laden, and I will give you rest.*—A. W. Tozer[1]

Date: _____ _____ _____
Place: _____ _____ _____
Occasion: _____ _____ _____

[1] A. W. Tozer, *A Treasury of A. W. Tozer* (Grand Rapids: Baker Book House, 1980), 18.

The Changelessness of God

In his classic *Knowing God,* J. I. Packer says, "God does not change. Let us draw out this thought." He then proceeds with these points:

- God's love does not change. He is from everlasting to everlasting.
- God's character does not change. Strain, or shock, or a leukotomy can alter the character of a man, but nothing can alter the character of God.
- God's truth does not change. It is forever settled in the heavens.
- God's ways do not change. He still deals with people today as He did in the Scriptures.
- God's purposes do not change. The Lord is not a man that He should repent.
- God's Son does not change. He is the same yesterday, today, and forever.[1]

Date: _____ _____ _____
Place: _____ _____ _____
Occasion: _____ _____ _____

From the Vanishing Point to the Vanishing Point

"From everlasting to everlasting, thou art God," said Moses in the Spirit. "From the vanishing point to the vanishing point" would be another way to say it. . . . The mind looks backward in time till the dim past vanishes, then turns and looks into the future till thought and imagination collapse from exhaustion; and God is at both points, unaffected by either.—A. W. Tozer[2]

Date: _____ _____ _____
Place: _____ _____ _____
Occasion: _____ _____ _____

No Change with Regard to God

"The Christian knows no change with regard to God. He may be rich today and poor tomorrow; he may be sickly today and well tomorrow; he may be in happiness today, tomorrow he may be distressed; but there is no change with regard to his relationship to God. If he loved me yesterday he loves me today. I am neither better nor worse in God than I ever was. Let prospects be blighted, let hopes be blasted, let joy be withered, let mildews destroy everything. I have lost nothing of what I have in God."—Charles Spurgeon[3]

Date: _____ _____ _____
Place: _____ _____ _____
Occasion: _____ _____ _____

[1] J. I. Packer, *Knowing God* (Downers Grove, IL: InterVarsity, 1973), Ch. 7.
[2] A. W. Tozer, *The Knowledge of the Holy* (New York: Harper & Row Publishers, 1961), 45
[3] Charles Haddon Spurgeon, *Spurgeon's Sermons,* vol. 2 (Grand Rapids, MI.: Baker Book House, 1983), 6.

Thou Changest Not . . .

Faithful: *Steadfast; firm in adherence to promises; conscientious; given with strong assurance; true to the facts. Faithful implies unswerving adherence to a person or to a promise (Dictionary). God is faithful . . . Your faithfulness reaches to the clouds. Your faithfulness also surrounds You.*

- *Your faithfulness endures to all generations. All your commands are faithful . . . Your testimonies . . . are righteous and very faithful. These words are faithful and true.*
- *By faith Sarah herself also received strength to conceive seed, and she bore a child when she was past the age, because she judged Him faithful who had promised. He who calls you is faithful. The Lord is faithful, who will establish you and guard you from the evil one. Therefore know that the Lord your God, He is God, the faithful God. Faithfulness [is] the belt of His waist.*
- *Judah still walks with God, Even with the Holy One who is faithful. If his sons forsake My law And do not walk in My judgments, If they break my statutes and do not keep My commandments, Then I will punish their transgression with the rod, And their iniquity with stripes. Nevertheless My lovingkindness I will not utterly take from him, Nor allow my faithfulness to fail. If we are faithless, He remains faithful. . . . He is faithful and just to forgive us our sins . . . a merciful and faithful High Priest . . . Jesus Christ, the faithful witness.*
- *Through the Lord's mercies we are not consumed, Because His compassions fail not. They are new every morning; Great is Your faithfulness.*
- *No temptation has overtaken you except such as is common to man; but God is faithful, who will not allow you to be tempted beyond what you are able, but with the temptation will also make the way of escape, that you may be able to bear it.*
- *Now I saw heaven opened, and behold, a white horse. And He who sat on him was called Faithful and True.*
- *With my mouth I will make known your faithfulness.*
- *Let us hold fast the confession of our hope without wavering, for He who promised is faithful.*[1]

G

> *Great is Thy faithfulness, O God my Father,*
> *There is no shadow of turning with Thee;*
> *Thou changest not, Thy compassions they fail not;*
> *As Thou hast been Thou forever wilt be.*[2]

Date: _____ _____ _____

Place: _____ _____ _____

Occasion: _____ _____ _____

Great Is Thy Faithfulness

The hymn "Great is Thy Faithfulness" was written by Thomas Chisholm, who was born Lincoln-like in a log cabin in Kentucky. As a young adult, he was converted

---

[1] 1 Corinthians 1:9; Psalm 36:5; Psalm 86:8; Psalm 119:90; Psalm 119:86, 138; Revelation 21:5; Hebrews 11:11; 1 Thessalonians 5:14; 2 Thessalonians 3:3; Deuteronomy 7:9; Isaiah 11:5; Hosea 11:12; Psalm 89:30–33; 2 Timothy 2:13; 1 John 1:9; Hebrews 2:17; Revelation 1:5; Lamentations 3:22–23; 1 Corinthians 10:13; Revelation 19:11; Psalm 89:1; Hebrews 10:23.
[2] Thomas O. Chisholm.

by the evangelist H. C. Morrison. Chisholm's health was unstable, and he alternated between bouts of illness and gainful employment in which he did everything from journalism to insurance to evangelistic work. Through all the ups and downs, he discovered new blessings from God every morning. Lamentations 3 became precious to him, and he wrote this hymn after thirty years of serving Christ.

It was relatively unknown until popularized around the world by George Beverly Shea and the choirs at the Billy Graham Crusades.

================◇================
Mood Change

God never changes moods or
cools off in His affections or
loses enthusiasm.
—A. W. TOZER

================◇================

At Graham's 1954 Harringay Crusade, Wilber Konkel first heard "Great Is Thy Faithfulness," and a flood of memories coursed through his mind. He recalled the dark nights of World War II, when London was nearly bombed to oblivion. "Each night as the enemy planes came over," Konkel wrote, "we cast our care upon Him. I quoted (this Scripture) to myself. I used it in my prayers. Those were dark days. At times they seemed hopeless. It was in those darkest hours that God proved His faithfulness to me. We were so near death. Yet it is the Lord's mercies that we are not consumed, because his compassions fail not. They are new every morning."[1]

Date:	_____	_____	_____
Place:	_____	_____	_____
Occasion:	_____	_____	_____

"But God Was Faithful . . ."

Ruth and I found out that for us, worrying and praying were not mutually exclusive. We trusted the Lord to bring the children through somehow in His own way in due time. On a day-to-day basis, however, we muddled through. But God was faithful. Today each of them is filled with faith and fervor for the Lord's service.—Billy Graham, recalling the difficult years when his sons were away from the Lord[2]

Date:	_____	_____	_____
Place:	_____	_____	_____
Occasion:	_____	_____	_____

Higher Still

A. T. Pierson (1837–1911) was a brilliant Bible teacher from New York City who filled in for the great Charles Spurgeon during the latter's illness. These insights regarding the immutability of God provide terrific preaching material, but it isn't necessary to read and quote them verbatim. Put them in your own words:

That which is "most high" is lifted up above all else. The lower down we are the more perishable everything is. The grass under your foot in the summer is one of the frailest things in nature; it grows and blooms today, it withers and decays tomorrow. You ascend a little higher and

---

[1] Wilbur Konkel, *Living Hymn Stories* (Minneapolis: Bethany Fellowship, Inc., 1971), 69–73.
[2] Billy Graham, *Just As I Am* (San Fransico: Harper/Zondervan, 1977), 711.

you find the trees that last not only for one season but many seasons, till you come to great trees like the Sequoia Gigantea in the Californian forests, that have been standing for three thousand or thirty-five hundred years, but even these decay and fall by-and-by. You rise above the level of the trees, and come to the hills that last for ages, though they are worn away by rains and snows, and are shaken by storms and upheaved by earthquakes until sometimes they disappear altogether as hills and become the beds of lakes. You mount still above the hills, and there are what are called in the Bible "everlasting mountains" that have stood ever since the world began. You soar above the mountains, and you come to the planets that are constantly changing their places in the sky as they move around the sun in their annual journeys; but far beyond the planets stand the fixed stars that never have changed their place since time began. So you see that the farther up you go, the nearer you come to that which does not change, and beyond all these is He who is "the same yesterday, and today, and forever." He is the unchanging God and the unchanging friend of His people.[1]

Date: _____   _____   _____

Place: _____   _____   _____

Occasion: _____   _____   _____

The Same Sky

A sailor serving in the South Pacific during World War II was frightened and homesick. His way of life and all that had been familiar to him was gone, and he found himself living a strange life among strangers, unsure of his fate from moment to moment. Standing on the deck of his ship one night, he spotted the Big and Little Dippers, Scorpio, and Gemini—the same constellations he had studied in the blackened sky nights without number back home in Ohio. Suddenly he felt at home and at peace, realizing the same sky as always was above him—and the same God as always was beside him.

Date: _____   _____   _____

Place: _____   _____   _____

Occasion: _____   _____   _____

God Cannot Change

As A. W. Tozer points out, God cannot change, for all change must be in one of three directions: (1) From better to worse; (2) From worse to better; (3) From one order of being to another. God's perfections rule out all three possibilities.

"The law of mutation," writes Tozer, "belongs to a fallen world, but God is immutable, and in Him men of faith find at last eternal permanence.

"In coming to Him at any time we need not wonder whether we shall find Him in a receptive mood. He is always receptive to misery and need, as well as to love and faith. He does not keep office hours nor set aside periods when He will see no one. Neither does He change His mind about anything. Today, this moment, He

---

[1] Arthur T. Pierson, *The Gospel*, vol. 2 (Grand Rapids, MI: Baker Book House, 1972), 75–76.

feels toward His creatures, toward babies, toward the sick, the fallen, the sinful, exactly as He did when He sent His only-begotten Son into the world to die for mankind.

"God never changes moods or cools off in His affections or loses enthusiasm. . . .

"'I am the Lord, I change not.'"[1]

Date: _____ _____ _____

Place: _____ _____ _____

Occasion: _____ _____ _____

Naught Changeth Thee

We blossom and flourish as leaves on the tree
And wither and perish—but naught changeth Thee
—Walter Chalmers Smith, "Immortal, Invisible"

Date: _____ _____ _____

Place: _____ _____ _____

Occasion: _____ _____ _____

Vance Havner Weighs In

We need not worry for fear the faith of our fathers will have no relevance today. Times have changed, they tell us, but time makes no difference to the great I AM. He outlasts all our little systems; they have their day and cease to be. With Him a thousand years are as a day and a day as a thousand years. It would be amusing if it were not so pathetic, the concern of those who are afraid the Gospel will be out of date. It is never out of date, for it is dateless, it bares the postmark of no age or time. "The Old-Time Religion" is a misnomer for it is not merely old-time, but new-time, any-time, all-the-time.[2]

Date: _____ _____ _____

Place: _____ _____ _____

Occasion: _____ _____ _____

Just a Second

A man met God and asked, "What is a million years to you?" "Like a second," God answered. "What is ten million dollars to you?" was the next question. "Like a dime," came the answer. "Well then," the man continued, "Can I borrow a dime?" God responded, "Just a second."

[1] A. W. Tozer, *The Knowledge of the Holy* (New York: Harper & Brothers, 1961), Ch. 9.

[2] Vance Havner, *Though I Walk Through the Valley* (Old Tappen, NJ: Fleming H. Revell Co., 1974), 118–119.

Date: _____ _____ _____
Place: _____ _____ _____
Occasion: _____ _____ _____

God's Forgiveness

Someone Once Said . . .

- *It is indeed amazing that in as fundamentally irreligious a culture as ours, the sense of guilt should be so widespread and deeply-rooted as it is.*—Erich Fromm, psychologist
- *When I bring my sins to the Lord Jesus He casts them into the depths of the sea—forgiven and forgotten. He also puts up a sign, "No Fishing Allowed!"*—Corrie ten Boom[1]
- *The word "grace" is a kind of shorthand for the whole sum of unmerited blessings which come to men through Jesus Christ.*—Alexander Maclaren

G

Date: _____ _____ _____
Place: _____ _____ _____
Occasion: _____ _____ _____

Regrets

The frustrating thing about time is that is always moves forward. There is no "R" on the stickshift, no reverse in the gears. Time never moves backward, not an inch, not a step, never. The hands of the clock always move clockwise, and the pages of the calendar are torn off in only one direction. Therefore a deed once done can never be undone. A word once spoken can never be unsaid. An opportunity missed can not be reclaimed in exactly the same way. As a result, all of us live with certain regrets.

Only the blood of Christ can remove them from our hearts and send them as far from us as the East is from the West.[2]

Date: _____ _____ _____
Place: _____ _____ _____
Occasion: _____ _____ _____

Erased

There is a story that one night Martin Luther went to sleep troubled about his sin. In a dream he saw an angel standing by a blackboard, and at the top of the board was Luther's name. The angel, chalk in hand, was listing all of Luther's sins, and the

---

[1] Corrie ten Boom, *Not Good if Detached* (Fort Washington, PA: Christian Literature Crusade, 1957), 19.
[2] From a sermon by the author.

list filled the blackboard. Luther shuddered in despair, feeling that his sins were so many that he could never be forgiven. But suddenly in his dream he saw a pierced hand writing above the list these words: "The blood of Jesus Christ His Son cleanses us from all sin." As Luther gazed in amazement, the blood flowed from the wounded hand and washed the record clean.[1]

Date: _____ _____ _____
Place: _____ _____ _____
Occasion: _____ _____ _____

What I Envy Most . . .

The well-known secular humanist and novelist in England, Marghanita Laski, said just before she died in 1988, "What I envy most about you Christians is your forgiveness; I have nobody to forgive me."

Date: _____ _____ _____
Place: _____ _____ _____
Occasion: _____ _____ _____

Rosalind's List

Rosalind Goforth was a well-known missionary to China who, along with her husband Jonathan, enjoyed an illustrious career and ministry. But for many years, even having labored for the Lord in China, Rosalind often felt oppressed by a burden of sin. She felt guilty and dirty, nursing an inward sense of spiritual failure. Finally one evening when all was quiet, she settled at her desk with Bible and concordance, determined to find out God's attitude toward the failures, the faults, the sins of his children. She put these words at the top of the page: *What God Does With Our Sins.* Then as she searched through the Scriptures, she compiled this list of seventeen truths:

1. He lays them on his Son—Jesus Christ. Isaiah 53:6
2. Christ takes them away. John 1.29
3. They are removed an immeasurable distance—as far as East is from West. Psalm 123:12
4. When sought for, they are not found. Jeremiah 50:20
5. The Lord forgives them. Ephesians 1:7
6. He cleanses them ALL away by the blood of his son. 1 John 1:7
7. He cleanses them as white as snow or wool. Isaiah 1:18; Psalm 51:7
8. He *abundantly* pardons them. Isaiah 55:7
9. He tramples them under foot. Micah 7:19 (RV)
10. He remembers them no more. Hebrews 10:17
11. He casts them behind his back. Isaiah 38:17

---

[1] W. Hershel Ford, *Simple Sermons for Saints and Sinners* (Grand Rapids, MI: Baker Book House, 1954), 9.

12. He casts them into the *depths* of the sea. Micah 7:19
13. He will not impute us with sins. Romans 4:8
14. He covers them. Romans 4:7
15. He blots them out. Isaiah 43:25
16. He blots them out as a thick cloud. Isaiah 44:22
17. He blots out even the proof against us, nailing it to His Son's Cross. Colossians 2:14[1]

Date:			
Place:			
Occasion:			

G

Rain, Wind, Blood

Frank I. Stanton wrote:

> *The rain beat on my window pane;*
> *I said, Come in, O rain, O rain;*
> *Come in out of the dark, deep night,*
> *And wash my soul and make it white.*
> *But the rain replied,*
> *For the soul that died,*
> *There is only One, the Crucified.*

> *The wind beat on my window pane,*
> *I said, Come in, O wind, O wind;*
> *Come in out of the wild stormy night*
> *And waft my soul to realms of light.*
> *But the wind replied,*
> *For the soul that died,*
> *There is only One, the Crucified.*

To those two verses, D. E. E. Barton of Montgomery, Alabama, added another:

> *The blood beat on my window pane;*
> *I said, Come in, O blood, O blood;*
> *The blood came in from Calvary's night,*
> *And washed my soul and made it white.*
> *And the blood replied,*
> *For the soul that died,*
> *I am thine own, the Crucified.*[2]

Date:			
Place:			
Occasion:			

[1] Rosalind Goforth, *Climbing* (Wheaton, IL: Sword Book Club, 1940), 90.
[2] Robert G. Lee, *Heart to Heart* (Nashville: Broadman Press, 1977), 66.

A Father's Letter

In November 1991, Jerry Jenkins wrote a bizarre true story about a man awakened in the middle of the night by a phone call. He was groggy. The girl on the other end was weeping. "Daddy," she said, "I'm pregnant."

Though stunned beyond belief, he forgave her and prayed with her. The next day he and his wife wrote her two letters of counsel and love.

Three days later the man received another phone call. His daughter was shocked by the letters. She was not the one who had called earlier. . . . Apparently some other girl had dialed a wrong number.

"These letters are my treasure," the daughter later said, "real love letters written by a godly father who never imagined he would have to write them to his own daughter."

Here are a few excerpts:

Part of me seemed to die last night. Not because of what it means to me as much as what it means to you. You were free to make all kinds of choices. Now you are shut up to a few, and none of them to your liking. But God will see you—and us—through.

Though I weep inside, I can't condemn you, because I sin too. Your transgression here is no worse than mine. It's just different. Even if my heart did not shout out to love and defend and protect you—as it does—the New Testament tells me I can't take forgiveness myself and withhold it from others.

We think of sin as acts. But sin is a package, an attitude that expresses itself in different ways and to different degrees. But it all comes from the same sin package you inherited through us. Christ is the only difference.

Portrait in White

God paints in many colors, but he never paints so gorgeously as when he paints in white.

—G. K. CHESTERTON

God forgives this sin as well as others—really forgives and cleanses. David was a man of God when he went into his experience with Bathsheba and in the grace of God he came out a man of God. And his sin included murder!

Satan has no doubt tried to tell you that this affects your standing before God. It doesn't, but it will affect your relationship till you bring the whole matter to Him. There will be a coolness, a separation, an estrangement, until you open the problem by confessing and asking forgiveness.

I will not reproach you or [your boyfriend]. I will not even dare to look down at you in my innermost heart, but it is not because the issue doesn't matter. The responsibility is his no less than yours. This is not an ideal basis for marriage. You want a husband who takes you by choice. But if you face the issue and God so leads, He could build a solid marriage. We stand ready to do whatever we can.

We're praying much. We love you more than I can say. And respect you, too, as always.

Saturday I was very downcast. I tried to sing as I worked outside, and then, increasingly, I seemed to see a calm and loving face I knew was Jesus. It was no vision—I didn't see details— but it was a strong reminder that He is with us and waiting for us to remember this. He loves us and will help us through, especially you. It's great to know Jesus is walking with you.

While we can't say that God causes failures, He does permit them, and I think it's clear He uses them to build character and beauty that we'd never have without them. Remember, God's love is in even this, maybe especially in this.

We're glad that in a measure, at least, we can help the daughter we love so much. This is a day of testing, but hold our ground we must. God will give us the victory. That's wonderful. We're looking forward to your being at home. Love, Dad.[1]

Date:			
Place:			
Occasion:			

Fished from the Trash

In his book, *How To Be Born Again*, Billy Graham refers to a story that Corrie ten Boom used to tell of a little girl who broke one of her mother's treasured demitasse cups. The little girl came to her mother sobbing, "Oh, mama, I'm so sorry I broke your beautiful cup."

The mother replied, "I know you're sorry, and I forgive you. Now don't cry any more." The mother then swept up the pieces of the broken cup and placed them in the trash can. But the little girl enjoyed the guilty feeling. She went to the trash can, picked out the pieces of the cup, brought them to her mother and sobbed, "Mother, I'm so sorry I broke your pretty cup."

This time her mother spoke firmly to her. "Take those pieces and put them back in the trash can and don't be silly enough to take them out again. I told you I forgave you so don't cry any more, and don't pick up the broken pieces any more."[2]

Date:			
Place:			
Occasion:			

What to Do with Guilt

Many people deal with guilt by **drowning it.** Some drown it in alcohol and drug abuse. Marijuana use among teenagers increased 37% between 1994 and 1995. The use of LSD and other hallucinogens was up 54%. And the use of cocaine increased by 166%. Over fourteen million Americans are in 12-step programs. Why are Americans drinking and drugging themselves to death? We're trying to escape ourselves and drown the pangs of our own guilt. Marlon Brando was once young, trim, and handsome. A million girls dreamed of having him. But now he weighs over four hundred pounds, and he told someone, "I'm sorry for all the harm I've done and for all the troubles I've brought to others in my life. I've never been a good parent or a good husband. I've been too busy with my own life to have time for others. Now I'm a guilty old man who's ashamed of the kind of life I've led. There's nothing left for me except eating."

Other people deal with guilt by **denying it.** As our society has become increasingly secular, it has lost respect for the authority of the Word of God, and that has

[1] Jerry B. Jenkins, "Treasure By Mistake," *Moody Magazine,* September 1991, 6.
[2] Billy Graham, *How To Be Born Again* (Waco: Word Books, 1977), 129.

led to a dangerous and destructive moral and spiritual chain reaction. If there is no authoritative Word of God, then there are no moral absolutes. If there are no moral absolutes, there are no ultimate standards of right and wrong. If there are no ultimate standards of right and wrong, then we can base our rules and standards on societal consensus. If we base our rules on societal consensus, then we can adjust them to our own shape and size. We can adjust them downward. We can live any way we want to, and there is no such thing as genuine guilt before God. Guilt is just a nagging relic of Puritanism, a Victorian antique, a psychosis to be denied.

Some people deal with guilt by **deflecting it.** They blame other people for their failures and faults and shortcoming. They blame their parents or their environments. This technique goes all the way back to the garden of Eden when Adam blamed Eve and Eve blamed the serpent.

But sooner or later, all these techniques fail, and we find we can't escape the consequences of our own sinfulness and guilt. Jeremiah 2:22 says, " 'Although you wash yourself with soda and use an abundance of soap, the stain of your guilt is before me,' declares the Sovereign Lord."

Guilt is the corrosion of the soul. How can we get rid of it? We can't drown it, deny it, or deflect it. We can only **dissolve it** in the blood of Jesus Christ.[1]

Date: _____ _____ _____

Place: _____ _____ _____

Occasion: _____ _____ _____

God's Guidance

Someone Once Said . . .

- *In His will is our peace.*—Dante
- *To know the will of God is the greatest knowledge. To do the will of God is the greatest achievement.*—George Truett
- *To go as I am led, to go when I am led, to go where I am led . . . it is that which has been for twenty years the one prayer of my life.*—A. T. Pierson[2]
- *God generally guides [us] by the exercise of [our] sanctified judgment.*—J. Oswald Sanders
- *The man or woman who is wholly and joyously surrendered to Christ can't make a wrong choice—any choice will be the right one.*—A. W. Tozer[3]
- *Has it ever struck you that the vast majority of the will of God for your life has already been revealed in the Bible? That is a crucial thing to grasp.*—Paul Little, in *Affirming the Will of God*

---

[1] From a sermon by the author.
[2] Arthur T. Pierson, *The Gospel,* vol 2 (Grand Rapids, MI: Baker Book House, 1978), 8.
[3] A. W. Tozer, "Four Ways To Find God's Will," *HIS Magazine,* May 1969.

- *Belief that divine guidance is real rests upon two foundation-facts: first, the reality of God's plan for us; second, the ability of God to communicate with us. On both these facts the Bible has much to say.*—J. I. Packer[1]
- *Never doubt in the darkness what God has shown you in the light.*
- *The will of God—nothing more, nothing less.*

Date: _____   _____   _____

Place: _____   _____   _____

Occasion: _____   _____   _____

F. B. Meyer's Formula

One night as the famous Bible teacher F. B. Meyer stood on the deck of a ship approaching land, he wondered how the crew knew when and how to safely steer to the dock. It was a stormy night, and visibility was low. Meyer, standing on the bridge and peering through the window, asked "Captain, how do you know when to turn this ship into that narrow harbor?"

"That's an art," replied the captain. "Do you see those three red lights on the shore? When they're all in a straight line I go right in!"

Later Meyer said: *When we want to know God's will, there are three things which always occur: the inward impulse, the Word of God, and the trend of circumstances. . . . Never act until these three things agree.*

Date: _____   _____   _____

Place: _____   _____   _____

Occasion: _____   _____   _____

George Mueller's Six Steps

Evangelist and philanthropist George Mueller, born in Germany, became one of the most powerful evangelical leaders in nineteenth-century England and is particularly remembered for his work with orphans. He once articulated six principles he followed when seeking the Lord's will:

1. I seek at the beginning to get my heart into such a state that it has no will of its own in regard to a given matter. Nine-tenths of the trouble with people is just here. Nine-tenths of the difficulties are overcome when our hearts are ready to do the Lord's will, whatever it may be. When one is truly in this state, it is usually but a little way to the knowledge of what his will is.
2. Having done this, I do not leave the result to feeling or simple impression. If I do so, I make myself liable to great delusions.
3. I see the will of the Spirit of God through, or in connection with, the Word of God. The Spirit and the Word must be combined. If I look to the Spirit alone without the Word, I lay myself open to great delusions also. If the

---

[1] J. I. Packer, *Knowing God* (Downers Grove, IL: InterVarsity, 1973), 210.

Holy Spirit guides us at all, He will do it according to the Scriptures and never contrary to them.

4. Next I take into account providential circumstances. These often plainly indicate God's will in connection with His Word and Spirit.

5. I ask God in prayer to reveal His will to me aright.

6. Thus, through prayer to God, the study of the Word, and reflection, I come to a deliberate judgment according to the best of my ability and knowledge; and if my mind is thus at peace, and continues so after two or three more petitions, I proceed accordingly. In trivial matters, and in transactions involving more important issues, I have found this method always effective.

Date: _____ _____ _____

Place: _____ _____ _____

Occasion: _____ _____ _____

J. Oswald Sanders on Guidance

I try to gather all the information and all the facts that are involved in a decision, and then weigh them up and pray them over in the Lord's presence, and trust the Holy Spirit to sway my mind in the direction of God's will. And God generally guides by presenting reasons to my mind for acting in a certain way.[1]

Date: _____ _____ _____

Place: _____ _____ _____

Occasion: _____ _____ _____

Willing to Wait

In his booklet *Getting to Know the Will of God,* Dr. Alan Redpath tells about trying to decide whether he should enter the ministry or stay in his present profession as a chartered accountant of the staff of Imperial Chemical Industries, Ltd. He made a list on paper of all the reasons for staying in business, and each morning during his devotions, he asked the Lord to show him particular Bible verses that would counter or affirm the reasons listed. "Lord," he prayed, "I am not here to evade you. I am here because I want to know your will."

What happened? *Day by day I turned to my Bible. Almost every day a verse seemed to speak to me and I began to write that verse against one of the arguments. At the end of a year, every argument in favor of staying in business had been wiped out. It took over a year, but I was not in a hurry. I was willing to wait; I wanted it to be in God's time. Too much was at stake to dash into the thing. I wanted to intelligently find the will of God. And I found it as I sought the Lord through my daily reading and meditation.*[2]

[1] J. Oswald Sanders, "Lessons I've Learned," *Discipleship Journal,* Issue 15, 1983, 14.

[2] Alan Redpath, *Getting to Know the Will of God* (Chicago: InterVarsity Press, 1954), 13–14.

Date:			
Place:			
Occasion:			

Thy Way, Not Mine, O Lord

Thy way, not mine, O Lord,
However dark it be!
Lead me by Thine own hand;
Choose Thou the path for me.
Smooth let it be or rough,
It will be still the best;
Winding or straight, it leads
Right onward to Thy rest.
I dare not choose my lot;
I would not if I might;
Choose Thou for me, my God:
So shall I walk aright.
Take Thou my cup, and it
With joy or sorrow fill,
As best to Thee may seem;
Choose Thou my good and ill.
Choose Thou for me my friends,
My sickness and my health;
Choose Thou my cares for me,
My poverty or wealth.
Not mine, not mine the choice,
In things or great or small;
Be Thou my guide, my strength,
My wisdom and my all.—Horatius Bonar[1]

Date:			
Place:			
Occasion:			

Guide Me, O Thou Great Jehovah

In eighteenth-century Wales, a young man named William Williams graduated from the university as a physician, but quickly changed professions to become a physician of the soul—a clergyman. Being warned against the "fanatical dissenters" such as Wesley and Whitefield, Williams decided to become one himself, becoming a Calvinistic Methodist.

During his forty-three years of itinerant ministry, Williams traveled over 95,000 miles, and his impassioned preaching drew crowds of 10,000 or more. Once he

[1] V. Raymond Edman, *The Disciplines of Life* (Minneapolis: World Wide Publication, 1948), 100.

spoke to an estimated crowd of 80,000, noting in his journal, "God strengthened me to speak so loud that most could hear."

William Williams is best remembered, however, for his hymns, becoming in Wales what Isaac Watts was in England. In all, he composed over eight hundred hymns, his best known being an autobiographical prayer. Williams had lived as a pilgrim, pressing on through the snow of winter, the rains of springtime, and the heat of fall. He was beaten by mobs (once within an inch of his life) and cheered by crowds, but in all his travels he sought only to do the will of God, saying:

> Guide me, O Thou great Jehovah
> Pilgrim through this barren land;
> I am weak, but Thou art mighty;
> Hold me with Thy powerful hand.[1]

Date: _____ _____ _____

Place: _____ _____ _____

Occasion: _____ _____ _____

God's Guidance System

On autumn nights as we sleep peacefully in our beds, millions of songbirds are quietly traveling under cover of darkness, heading south for warmer climates. Take Baltimore orioles, for example. Every fall, they pack their bags, close up their homes, leaving the key under the mat, and like senior citizens head south. It's the weather patterns that tell the birds that it is time to move. "As cold fronts move across eastern North America," wrote one expert, "they're sending waves of orioles, along with warblers and other songbirds, on their way to wintering grounds in Mexico and Latin America." As cold fronts pass, clear skies and north winds usually follow. These conditions are ideal for migration, allowing the birds to travel with no risk of storms, the wind at their backs and a clear view of the stars to help them find their way.

Reasonable Presentation

God generally guides me by presenting reasons to my mind for acting in a certain way.

—JOHN WESLEY

They fly over thousands of houses and highways, shopping centers and parking lots, passing state after state. If a particular oriole opts for a direct flight home, it will fly over the Gulf of Mexico in a single night, crossing six hundred miles of open water.

The entire trip from Baltimore (for example) to Mexico, Panama, or Costa Rica takes about two weeks. But the oriole knows exactly where it is going. God planted within its little brain a perfect guidance system that tells it exactly where to go, and when, and how.

The Bible says that we are more valuable to the Lord than all the birds in the sky. We are worth more than many sparrows. If the Lord is pleased to guide the birds in their migrations, it's a safe bet that He also wants to guide our lives.

---
[1] Albert Edward Bailey, *The Gospel in Hymns* (New York: Charles Scribner's Sons, 1950), 107–110.

He who, from zone to zone,
Guides, through the boundless sky, thy certain flight,
In the long way that I must tread alone,
Will lead my steps aright![1]

Date: _____ _____ _____
Place: _____ _____ _____
Occasion: _____ _____ _____

God's Holiness

Someone Once Said . . .

- *As I read the Bible, I seem to find holiness to be His supreme attribute.*—Billy Graham[2]
- *It does not seem proper to speak of one attribute of God as being more central and fundamental than another; but if this were permissible, the scriptural emphasis on the holiness of God would seem to justify its selection.*—Louis Berkhof, in *Systematic Theology*
- *Lower our sense of holiness, and our sense of sin is lowered.*—Dan DeHaan[3]

Date: _____ _____ _____
Place: _____ _____ _____
Occasion: _____ _____ _____

Holy, Holy, Holy

Philadelphia pastor James Montgomery Boice once spoke to a discipleship group on the attributes of God. He began by asking them to list God's qualities in order of importance. They put love first, followed by wisdom, power, mercy, omniscience, and truth. At the end of the list they put holiness.

"That did surprise me," Boice later wrote, "because the Bible refers to God's holiness more than any other attribute."

The Bible doesn't generally refer to God as *Loving, Loving, Loving!* Or *Wise, Wise, Wise!* Or *Omniscient, Omniscient, Omniscient!* But over and over we read the cry of the angels, *Holy, Holy, Holy!*[4]

Date: _____ _____ _____
Place: _____ _____ _____
Occasion: _____ _____ _____

---

[1] Clint Bonner, *A Hymn is Born* (Nashville: Broadman Press, 1959), 14–16.
[2] Billy Graham, *Till Armageddon* (Minneapolis: World Wide Publications, 1981), 41.
[3] Dan DeHaan, *The God You Can Know* (Chicago: Moody Press, 1982), 67.
[4] James Montgomery Boice, "Holy, Holy, Holy," *Moody,* January 1985, 14.

Tozer on the Knowledge of the Holy

Neither the writer nor the reader of these words is qualified to appreciate the holiness of God. Quite literally a new channel must be cut through the desert of our minds to allow the sweet waters of truth that will heal our great sickness to flow in. We cannot grasp the true meaning of the divine holiness by thinking of someone or something very pure and then raising the concept to the highest degree we are capable of. God's holiness is not simply the best we know infinitely bettered. We know nothing like the divine holiness. It stands apart, unique, unapproachable, incomprehensible and unattainable. The natural man is blind to it. He may fear God's power and admire his wisdom, but His holiness he cannot even imagine.—A. W. Tozer[1]

=====◇=====
Holy Attribution

Holiness is the central nature of the being of God from which such attributes as love, justice, and mercy emanate.
—GEORGE ALLEN TURNER
=====◇=====

Date: _____ _____ _____
Place: _____ _____ _____
Occasion: _____ _____ _____

Simple Yet Profound

One man described his observations of the concept of holiness like this: *There is a simple yet profound word which occurs nine hundred times in the Bible. You see it first in Genesis, as we are told how God created heaven and earth. You see it last in the closing chapter of Revelation where we are told about God's creation of a new heaven and a new earth. But except for a few grand old hymns of the faith, you do not see this word much today . . . This word is "Holy." We get our words "saint," "sanctify," and "sanctification" from the same root words. All these terms carry the idea of being "set apart. . . ."*

Just as all the colors of the spectrum come together to form the pure white light which illuminates our world, so all the attributes of God come together into His holiness.[2]

Date: _____ _____ _____
Place: _____ _____ _____
Occasion: _____ _____ _____

———— God's Presence ————

Someone Once Said . . .

- *His center is everywhere, His circumference is nowhere.*—Henry Law[3]
- *God is non-material, non-corporeal, and therefore non-localized.*—J. I. Packer[4]

[1] A. W. Tozer, *The Knowledge of the Holy* (New York: Harper & Row Publishers, 1961), 111.
[2] Jim Killion, "Set Apart."
[3] Henry Law, *The Gospel in Exodus* (London: Banner of Truth Trust, 1967), 11.
[4] J. I. Packer, *Knowing God* (Downers Grove, IL: InterVarsity, 1973), 109.

- *The humble heart is His throne in regard to His gracious presence, and heaven is His throne in regard to His glorious presence, and yet neither of these thrones will hold Him, for the heaven of heavens cannot contain Him.*—Thomas Watson[1]
- *"The practice of the presence of God" consists not of projecting an imaginary object from within his own mind and then seeking to realize its presence; it is rather to recognize the real presence of the One whom all sound theology declares to be already there.*—A. W. Tozer[2]

Date: _____ _____ _____
Place: _____ _____ _____
Occasion: _____ _____ _____

G

D. L. Moody's Habit

Someone once asked evangelist Dwight Moody how he managed to remain so intimate in his relationship with Christ. He replied, *I have come to Him as the best friend I have ever found, and I can trust Him in that relationship. I have believed He is Savior; I have believed He is God; I have believed His atonement on the cross is mine, and I have come to Him and submitted myself on my knees, surrendered everything to Him, and gotten up and stood by His side as my friend, and there isn't any problem in my life, there isn't any uncertainty in my work but I turn and speak to Him as naturally as to someone in the same room, and I have done it these years because I can trust Jesus.*[3]

Date: _____ _____ _____
Place: _____ _____ _____
Occasion: _____ _____ _____

God Is Present Everywhere

Those who seek the throne of grace
Find that throne in every place;
If we live a life of prayer,
God is present everywhere.

In our sickness and our health,
In our want, or in our wealth,
If we look to God in prayer,
God is present everywhere.

When our earthly comforts fail,
When the woes of life prevail,
'Tis the time for earnest prayer;
God is present everywhere.

Then, my soul, in every strait,
To thy Father come, and wait;

[1] Thomas Watson, *Gleanings From Thomas Watson* (Morgan, PA: Soli Deo Gloria Publications, 1995), 35.
[2] A. W. Tozer, *The Knowledge of the Holy* (New York: Harper & Row, Publishers, 1961), 83.
[3] William M. Anderson, *The Faith That Satisfies* (New York: Loizeaux Brothers, 1948), 165.

He will answer every prayer:
God is present everywhere.
—Oliver Holden, 1765–1844[1]

```
Date:      _____    _____    _____
Place:     _____    _____    _____
Occasion:  _____    _____    _____
```

He Is Here Present

John Marrant, a fourteen-year-old in Colonial Charleston, was converted through the preaching of George Whitefield, but his family disapproved of his new faith. John, dispirited, left home with only a small Bible and a little hymnbook in his pocket. He wandered through the wilderness several days, eating little and sleeping in trees for fear of beasts.

At length, he was seized by a Cherokee hunter. *He asked me how I did live. I said I was supported by the Lord. He asked me how I slept. I answered that the Lord provided. He inquired what preserved me from being devoured by wild beasts? I replied, the Lord Jesus kept me from them. He stood astonished, and said, "You say the Lord Jesus Christ does this, and does that, and does everything for you; He must be a fine man; where is He?" I replied, "He is here present." To this he made no answer.*

Back in the hunter's village, John was promptly condemned to death. *The executioner showed me a basket of turpentine wood stuck full of small skewers. He told me I was to be stripped naked and laid down in the basket, and these sharp pegs were to be stuck into me, then set on fire, and when they burnt to my body, I was to be thrown into the flame, which was to finish my execution.*

John immediately burst into prayer, and his pitiful words so moved the executioners they took him to the chief. Opening his little Bible to Isaiah 53, John read: "All we like sheep have gone astray; We have turned, every one to his own way; And the Lord has laid on Him the iniquity of us all." Turning here and there in the Bible, John preached the gospel, converting among others the chief himself. For the next two years, the teenager remained among the Cherokees, preaching and teaching and making disciples.[2]

```
Date:      _____    _____    _____
Place:     _____    _____    _____
Occasion:  _____    _____    _____
```

When I Am with My Preacher

Methodist pastor Charles Allen had a golfing buddy who was, according to others, easily frustrated on the golf course and, after bad shots, very foul-mouthed.

---

[1] *The Christian Book of Mystical Verse*, comp. and ed. A. W. Tozer (Harrisburg, PA: Christian Publications, Inc., 1963), 59.
[2] Robert J. Morgan, *From This Verse* (Nashville: Thomas Nelson Publishers, 1998), May 10th.

Yet Allen himself had never heard the man utter a profane word. One day he asked him about it. The man simply replied, "When I am with my preacher I control myself."

Later Allen used this as a sermon illustration.

"Suppose one realized that he or she is in God's presence at all times," he said. "What a marvelous difference that would make!"[1]

Date: _____   _____   _____

Place: _____   _____   _____

Occasion: _____   _____   _____

G

A Reflection of the Divine Presence

Missionary John Paton never forgot his father's deeply ingrained habits of daily devotions. Day after day, he would hear his father praying in the next room of the little cottage where he lived, and even as a boy of six, he noticed the bright countenance his father perpetually wore. He later said that while the outside world might not understand the light on his father's face, "we children knew that it was a reflection of the Divine Presence in which his life was lived."

Paton recalled, "Never in temple or cathedral, on mountain or in glen, can I hope to feel that the Lord God is more near, more visibly walking and talking with men, than under that humble cottage roof of thatch and oaken wattles. Though everything else in religion were by some unthinkable catastrophe to be swept out of memory, my soul would wander back to those early scenes, and would shut itself up once again in that sanctuary closet, and, hearing still the echoes of those cries to God, would hurl back all doubt with the victorious appeal: *He walked with God; why may not I?*"

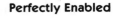

Perfectly Enabled

I was enabled to go on because I had the word of a perfect Gentleman, never known to break a promise, that He would be with me always.

—DAVID LIVINGSTONE

Later John Paton experienced grave difficulties and breathtaking dangers as a missionary in the South Pacific. "Without the abiding consciousness of the presence and power of my Lord and Savior," he wrote, "nothing in the world could have preserved me from losing my reason and perishing miserably. His words *Lo, I am with you always, even unto the end* became to me so real that it would not have startled me to behold Him, as Stephen did, gazing down upon the scene. It is the sober truth that I had my nearest and most intimate glimpses of the presence of my Lord in those dread moments when musket, club, or spear was being leveled at my life.[2]

Date: _____   _____   _____

Place: _____   _____   _____

Occasion: _____   _____   _____

[1] Charles Allen, *The Miracle of Love* (Old Tappan, NJ: Fleming H. Revell Co., 1972), 36.
[2] *A Frank Boreham Treasury* (Chicago: Moody Press, 1984), Ch. 16.

St. Patrick's Prayer

Christ be with me, Christ within me,
Christ behind me, Christ before me,
Christ beside me, Christ to win me;
Christ to comfort and restore me;
Christ beneath me, Christ above me,
Christ in quiet, Christ in danger,
Christ in hearts of all that love me,
Christ in mouth of friend and stranger.

Date: _____ _____ _____
Place: _____ _____ _____
Occasion: _____ _____ _____

Not Far Away

Dr. Tony Compolo says that when he was a boy growing up in a congested and bustling city, his mother arranged for a teenage girl who lived nearby to walk home with him at the end of the day. For this, she was paid a nickel a day. But Tony rebelled in the second grade and told his mother, "I'll walk myself to school, and, if you give me a nickel a week, I will be extra careful. You can keep the other twenty cents and we'll all be better off."

After a period of pleading and begging, little Tony finally got his way. For the next two years he walked himself back and forth to school. It was an eight-block walk with many streets to cross, but he was careful and didn't talk to strangers or get distracted along the way.

Years later at a family party, he bragged about his independence and reminded his family of how he had taken care of himself as a boy. His mother laughed and added the rest of the story. "Did you really think you were alone?" she said. "Every morning when you left for school, I left with you. I walked behind you all the way. When you got out of school at 3:30 in the afternoon, I was there. I always kept myself hidden, but I was there and I followed you all the way home. I just wanted to be there for you in case you needed me."[1]

Date: _____ _____ _____
Place: _____ _____ _____
Occasion: _____ _____ _____

Expedient for Me to Go Away

Jesus told His disciples that it was expedient for him to go away, otherwise the Spirit would not come. Robert Hall Glover, in *The Bible Basis of Missions,* writes, "By Christ's ascension and the Holy Spirit's descent, Christ exchanged His bodily pres-

---

[1] Dr. Anthony Campolo, "A Dreamer for the Kingdom," *What My Parents Did Right,* comp. and ed. Gloria Gaither (Nashville: StarSong Publishing Group, 1991), 36–37.

ence with His then disciples in Jerusalem for His spiritual omnipresence with His disciples everywhere."[1]

Another writer suggests that our Lord's post-resurrection appearances to his apostles, with their sudden appearances and departures, were his way of weaning them from depending upon His physical presence and introducing them to the omni-nature of His spiritual presence.

Date:			
Place:			
Occasion:			

G

Abiding in the Presence

Jacqueline was an elderly woman who lived to take care of her daughter, who was wheelchair bound. When her daughter died, Jacqueline not only lost her purpose for living, she lost her living companion. Her cottage in the country seemed as empty as an eggshell. Occasionally a friend would call or a note would arrive, but most of her time was spent in oppressive, ongoing solitude. Her health didn't allow her to circulate very much, and her best friends were now all in heaven.

One day Jacqueline's Bible opened to Philippians 4:5 and four words struck her forcibly: *"The Lord is near."* If so, thought Jacqueline, *I should be more aware of it.*

"Lord," she said, "I'm going to pretend you're here all the time. No, forgive me for using that word; there is no pretending to be done. I'm going to use my God-given imagination to visualize how very present You really are. Help me ever *remind myself* of the reality of Your nearness."

That evening as she retired, she said, "I'm going on to bed now, Lord. Will You please watch over me as I sleep." The next morning on awakening, she said, "Good morning, Lord. This is the day You have made." Sitting down with her hot tea, she read through the book of Philippians again, underlining verse 5, then she prayed aloud for a very long time. At noon, she said, "Now, Lord, let's watch the news on television, so you can show me things in this world I can pray for." Jacqueline and the Lord watched the news together, then she prayed for flood victims in the Delta, a newly-installed president in an African country, and for a man sentenced to life imprisonment.

At supper, she bowed her head and thanked the Lord for her food, but she didn't feel her prayers were traveling up to heaven. She felt instead she was talking to someone sitting across the table from her.

Gradually her attitude was transformed. The loneliness lessened, her joy increased, her fears diminished, and she never afterwards felt she was alone in the house. Jacqueline was learning how to abide in the Presence.

Date:			
Place:			
Occasion:			

---

[1] Robert Hall Glover, *The Bible Basis of Missions* (Chicago: Moody Press, 1946), 56.

When Christ Came to Church

A. J. Gordon (1836–1895), converted at age fifteen, was a Baptist minister and author, for many years pastor of the Clarendon Street Baptist Church in Boston. The secret of his powerful ministry is described in his delightful, moving, and hard-to-find book, "When Christ Came to Church."

In this book, he relates a dream that came to him early in his ministry at Clarendon Street. In this dream he came into his pulpit and stood there at the start of the service. As he began the service, the door opened at the back, and the usher admitted a very fine looking gentleman, brought him down the aisle, and showed him a seat. The man had a very refined face, and there was something very elegant about it. Through the whole service, Gordon couldn't help noticing him and wondering who he was.

After the service when all the people had gone home, Gordon sought out an usher and asked about the man: "Who is that gentleman you showed in tonight?"

"Oh," came the reply, "didn't you know, that was Jesus Christ. He came into the service and asked that He might sit there. Didn't you realize that?"

Gordon suddenly awoke from his dream, but his ministry was turned upside down from that day. The next time he went into his pulpit, he seemed transformed, refreshed, renewed. He was aware that Jesus was there, in the pew, in the pulpit, in that place.

Date:	_____	_____	_____
Place:	_____	_____	_____
Occasion:	_____	_____	_____

A Life-Long Experiment

Frank Laubach (1884–1970) became a missionary to the illiterate, pouring his life into the task of teaching the unlettered how to read so they could discover for themselves the truths of the Word of God. His career touched millions, and by his death his techniques were known on almost every continent. On January 30, 1930, he decided to begin a life-long experiment.

- *Can we have that contact with God all the time? All the time awake, fall asleep in His arms, and awaken in His presence? Can we attain that? Can we do His will all the time? Can we think His thoughts all the time? . . . Can I bring the Lord back to my mind flow every few seconds so that God shall always be on my mind? I choose to make the rest of my life an experiment answering that question.*
- *March 1, 1930: This sense of being led by an unseen hand which takes mine while another hand reaches ahead and prepares the way, grows on me daily. . . . Sometimes it requires a long time early in the morning. I determine not to get out of bed until that mind, set upon the Lord, is settled.*
- *April 18, 1930: I have tasted a thrill in fellowship with God which has made everything discordant with God disgusting. This afternoon the possession of God has caught me up with such sheer joy that I thought I never had known anything like it. God was so close and so amazingly lovely that I felt like melt all over. . . . After an hour of close fellowship with God, my soul feels clean, as newly fallen snow.*

- *May 34, 1930: The concentration upon God is strenuous, but everything else has ceased to be so. I think more clearly. I forget less frequently. Things which I did with a strain before, now I do easily and with no effort whatsoever. I worry about nothing and lose no sleep. . . . Even the mirror reveals a new light in my eyes.*[1]

Date: _____ _____ _____

Place: _____ _____ _____

Occasion: _____ _____ _____

Is God Here?

While my young son Doug was looking at a full moon, he asked, "Mom, is God in the moon?" I explained that God is everywhere. "Is he in my tummy?" Doug wanted to know. "Well, sort of," I responded, not sure where these questions were leading. Then Doug declared, "God wants a banana."—Buff Spies[2]

Date: _____ _____ _____

Place: _____ _____ _____

Occasion: _____ _____ _____

—————— God's Protection ——————

Someone Once Said . . .

- *Plagues and deaths around me fly / Till he pleases, I cannot die.*—Anonymous
- *When Jesus takes your hand, He keeps you tight. When Jesus keeps you tight, He leads you through your whole life. When Jesus leads you through your life, He brings you safely home.*—Corrie ten Boom[3]

Date: _____ _____ _____

Place: _____ _____ _____

Occasion: _____ _____ _____

Everlasting Arms, Overshadowing Wings

The best way to handle danger is simply to be where God tells you to be. When physician L. Nelson Bell and his wife Virginia felt God calling them to China as missionaries, they gave scant thought to danger. It came upon them nonetheless in the form of the Japanese invasion of China. The Bells were in Tsingkiangpu, the provincial capital of Kiangsu, and the enemy advanced against them from all four directions. Older missionaries urged the Bells to flee, for the Japanese were known for their cruelty.

But Dr. Bell had been studying the Old Testament, especially Psalms, Proverbs,

---

[1] Max Lucado, "Keeping Company with God," *Discipleship Journal,* Issue 106, July/August 1998, 23–24.

[2] Clipped from my files.

[3] Corrie ten Boom, *In My Father's House* (Old Tappan, NJ: Fleming H. Revell Co., 1976), 147.

and Isaiah, and he developed a strong conviction that it was God's will for them to remain in Tsingkiangpu. Virginia agreed, writing to her mother in America, "The children are just as happy as can be, and if things come to worst here, I'm going to stick right with them and keep them happily engaged. Our God is able, and that 'Restraining Hand' is all-loving and all-powerful."

Dr. Bell later wrote that the decision to remain "deepened and confirmed our sense of the closeness of God. He was right there with us. Underneath with everlasting arms, over us with overshadowing wings—we were conscious of His peace and presence in a way that I don't think we would ever have been otherwise. There was prayer, constant prayer, in our heart. And also constant thanksgiving and praise for the consciousness of His presence. You had no one else to depend on. It was a sense of safety within His keeping."

Date: _____ _____ _____
Place: _____ _____ _____
Occasion: _____ _____ _____

These Forty Years

Solomon Ginsburg, a Polish Jew, became a flaming evangelist across both Europe and South America. In 1911, needing rest, he decided to head to America on furlough. His route took him to Lisbon where he planned to cross the Bay of Biscay to London, then on to the States.

Arriving in Lisbon, Ginsburg found the bulletin boards plastered with weather telegrams warning of terrific storms raging on the Bay of Biscay. It was dangerous sailing, and he was advised to delay his trip a week. His ticket allowed him to do that, and he prayed about it earnestly.

But as he prayed, he turned to his W.M.U. prayer calendar and found the text for that day was Deuteronomy 2:7—"For the Lord your God has blessed you in all the work of your hand. He knows your trudging through this great wilderness. These forty years the Lord your God has been with you; you have lacked nothing." The Lord seemed to assure him that his long, worldwide travels were under divine protection. Ginsburg boarded ship at once, crossed without incident, and caught the *Majestic* in London. His transatlantic voyage was smooth and restful.

Only after arriving in the United States did Solomon learn that had he delayed his trip in Lisbon, he would have arrived in London just in time . . .

. . . just in time to board the *Titanic*.

Date: _____ _____ _____
Place: _____ _____ _____
Occasion: _____ _____ _____

A Very Present Help

In 1947, missionaries Dick and Margaret Hillis settled with their four children by the Mule River in the Honan province of China. Nearby, a mission church swelled with nearly a thousand Chinese every Sunday. It would have been a happy time but for the impending war between Chiang kai-Shek and the forces of Mao Tse-tung.

One day, Nationalist Captain Hwang urgently told Mr. Hillis, "The Communists are marching on Mule River Market. You had better take your family and flee." But it was too late. The Reds had blown up all railroad bridges. That evening the Hillises heard the first shots, and soon the battle raged around them. There was no sleep as they spent the night in prayer. The city soon fell, and the streets filled with Communist troops.

Then a new danger arose. Captain Hwang, outside the city walls, was lobbing shells at the rebels. The bombing reached a crescendo one night as each shell dropped closer to the Hillis' home. The house next door exploded, killing all the inhabitants, and it appeared the Hillis' home would be next. The family huddled in the corner as another shell exploded, sending dirt, glass, and bricks through windows and walls. The house quaked. The children screamed, momentarily deafened. The family prepared for death. But the shelling abruptly stopped, and the Hillises cautiously emerged from their corner. The room was filled with debris, but no one was hurt.

Immortal Life

My life is immortal until my work on earth is done.
—JOHN WESLEY

By and by, as Dick tucked each child into bed, he knelt beside Margaret Anne and noticed a dirty scrap of paper stuffed under her pillow. On it was printed in big, childlike letters these words: "God is our refuge and strength, a very present help in trouble."

During the Chinese nights of terror, little Margaret Anne had been resting on a very big verse from a very faithful God.[1]

Date: _____ _____ _____

Place: _____ _____ _____

Occasion: _____ _____ _____

Chickens, Dogs, and Spiders

Emperor Charles V was trying to assassinate John Brenz, friend of Martin Luther. Hearing of the plot, Brenz barely had time to grab a loaf of bread and duck into his neighbor's hayloft. There he hid fourteen days. The bread was quickly gone, but the Lord sent a hen who showed up and laid an egg each day for fourteen days. In this way, Brenz was kept alive. On the fifteenth day the chicken didn't come, and the reformer wondered what he would do. But from the street below came the cries, "The cavalrymen are gone at last."

In a similar way, a dog provided for the needs of another reformer, John Craig, who was arrested during the Inquisition. On the eve of his scheduled execution, Craig escaped, but while fleeing through the Italian backcountry, he ran out of food and money. Suddenly a dog approached him, a purse in its mouth. Craig tried to drive the animal away, but it dog persisted in bringing the purse to Craig. In it was enough money to take him to freedom.

---

[1] Jan Winebrenner, *Steel in His Soul: The Dick Hillis Story* (Mukilteo, WA: OC International, 1996), 105–114.

Similarly, Robert Bruce of Scotland was running for his life, fleeing persecutors. He ducked into a small cave, and a spider immediately appeared and spun a web over the opening. Bruce's pursuers fanned across the landscape, knowing he was near. Two of them approached the cave, and one of the men started to go in. The other one stopped him, saying, "He could never have gotten in there without breaking that spider's web."

Bruce breathed this prayer, "O God, I thank Thee that in the tiny bowels of a spider you can place for me a shelter."[1]

Date: _____ _____ _____
Place: _____ _____ _____
Occasion: _____ _____ _____

"Peter!"

In *A Man Called Peter*, the biography of Senate Chaplain Peter Marshall, his wife, Catherine Marshall, recounts a strange incident that happened to Peter early in his life. He was working in the English village of Bamburgh, sixteen miles from the Scottish border. One dark and starless night, walking from a nearby village, Peter was making his way through moorlands. He was having great trouble seeing the path, for the blackness was inky and eerie. Suddenly he heard his name: "Peter!" There was urgency in the voice. "Yes," Peter replied, stopping and listening. There was no reply, and he resumed his walking.

Suddenly the voice came again, even more urgently: "Peter!" He stopped dead still, trying to peer into the impenetrable darkness, and he stumbled and fell to his knees. Putting out his hand to catch himself, he found nothing there. As he cautiously investigated, feeling around in a semicircle, he found himself to be on the very brink of an abandoned stone quarry. Just one step more would have sent him plummeting into space and to certain death.

The incident made an unforgettable impression on Peter. There was never any doubt in his mind about the source of the voice. He felt that God must have some great purpose in his life to have intervened so specifically.

Date: _____ _____ _____
Place: _____ _____ _____
Occasion: _____ _____ _____

———————— God: Trinity ————————

Somebody Once Said . . .

- *Our sincerest effort to grasp the incomprehensible mystery of the Trinity must remain forever futile, and only by deepest reverence can it be saved from actual presumption.*—A. W. Tozer[2]

---

[1] Robert J. Morgan, *From This Verse* (Nashville: Thomas Nelson, 1998), February 14th.
[2] A. W. Tozer, *The Knowledge of the Holy* (New York: Harper & Row Publishers, 1961), 25.

- *This* [doctrine of the Trinity] *is the teaching of Scripture and this has been the historic view of the Church in all of its branches down through the centuries.*—D. James Kennedy
- *Apart from* [the doctrine of the Trinity], *doctrines such as the Deity of Christ, the incarnation, the personality of the Holy Spirit, regeneration, justification, sanctification, the meaning of the crucifixion, and the resurrection cannot be understood.*—Dr. Loraine Boettner
- [*The Trinity is*] *a mystery indeed, yet one which explains many other mysteries, and which sheds a marvelous light on God, on nature, and on man.*—Robert Flint

Date: _____ _____ _____
Place: _____ _____ _____
Occasion: _____ _____ _____

G

Creeds and Formulas

- *The Father is made of none, neither created nor begotten. The Son is of the Father alone, not made, nor created, but begotten. The Holy Spirit is of the Father and the Son: not made, nor created, nor begotten, but proceeding.*—The Athanasian Creed
- *There is but one living and true God. In the unity of the Godhead, there be three persons of one substance, power, and eternity: God the Father, God the Son, and God the Holy Ghost. The Father is of none, neither begotten nor proceeding; The Son is eternally begotten of the Father; the Holy Ghost eternally proceeding from the Father and the Son.*—The Westminster Confession of Faith
- *There is but one living and true God. And in the unity of the Godhead there are three Persons of one substance, power and eternity: the Father, the Son, and the Holy Ghost.*—The Thirty-Nine Articles of the Church of England

Date: _____ _____ _____
Place: _____ _____ _____
Occasion: _____ _____ _____

Two Great Mysteries

The two greatest mysteries of Christianity are: (1) The Trinity of God; and, (2) The Duality of Christ. How can God be three Persons, yet one God? How can Jesus Christ be two Natures, yet one Man?

J. I. Packer wrote, "Here are two mysteries for the price of one—the plurality of persons within the unity of God, and the union of Godhead and manhood in the person of Jesus."[1]

On these two mysteries, all else hangs.

---

[1]J. I. Packer, *Knowing God* (Downers Grove, IL: InterVarsity, 1973), 46.

Date:			
Place:			
Occasion:			

The Ocean in a Hole

W. A. Criswell, in a sermon on the Trinity, said, "In reading the life of Augustine, I note that one day, when he was walking along the seashore, he saw a little boy digging a trench in the sand. He walked over to the lad and asked him what he was doing. The little fellow replied, 'Sir, I am making a trench.' 'Why are you doing it?' asked Augustine. The little lad replied, 'I am going to empty the sea into my trench.' The great thinker, the greatest of the Latin Fathers, continued his walk and mused: 'So the lad thinks that he is going to empty the sea into the little trench he has made in the sand. Sometimes we are like that. We propose to encompass the infinitude of God in the small limits of our mind.' "[1]

Date:			
Place:			
Occasion:			

Verse

> Timeless, spaceless, single, lonely,
> Yet sublimely Three,
> Thou art grandly, always, only
> God in Unity!
> Lone in grandeur, lone in glory
> Who shall tell Thy wondrous story,
> Awful Trinity?—Frederick W. Faber

Date:			
Place:			
Occasion:			

Light

In his book, *The Chemistry of the Blood*, M. R. DeHaan, founder of the Radio Bible Class, notes that in saying "God is light," the biblical authors are telling us something about the Trinity. A scientific analysis of sunlight reveals that it consists of three kinds of rays:

1. Chemical rays or actinic. These rays are invisible and can neither be seen or felt.
2. Light rays. These rays can be seen but never felt.
3. Heat rays. These rays are felt but never seen.

---

[1] W. A. Criswell, *Great Doctrines of the Bible*, vol. 3 (Grand Rapids, MI: Zondervan, 1982), 69.

DeHaan writes, "God is light and in Him is no darkness at all. We know the Godhead consists of Three Persons: The Father, the Son, and the Holy Spirit. The Father corresponds to the chemical rays of sunlight; No man hath seen God at any time. The Son, who is the light of the world, corresponds to the light rays, the One whom we can see but not feel. The Holy Spirit corresponds to the heat rays, since He is felt in the lives of believers but never seen."[1]

Date: _____ _____ _____
Place: _____ _____ _____
Occasion: _____ _____ _____

G

Music

In *Worship: Rediscovering the Missing Jewel,* Ronald Allen and Gordon Borror write: "Consider the biblical teaching about the essence of God. He is one God, three persons. Throughout the ages this concept has caused no end of confusion and frustration to theologian and layman alike. Much has been written and said about this eternal truth. But by no available means is it more beautifully expressed than in the music of Bach's trio sonatas for organ. Musicians through the years have marveled at the artistic excellence of these works. They have one melody in the right hand, one melody in the left, and yet another in the pedal line—all sounding at once, each retaining its own identity, yet together forming beautiful harmony. The composer intended this to be an expression, a tonal picture, of the eternal mystery of the Godhead."[2]

Date: _____ _____ _____
Place: _____ _____ _____
Occasion: _____ _____ _____

—————————— Grandparents ——————————

Someone Once Said . . .

- *Do, I beseech you, my venerable friends, try to be of a happy temperament and cheerful spirit, for a child will run away from a surly old man; but there is not a child in the world but loves his grandpapa if he is cheerful and happy.*—Charles Spurgeon[3]
- *Grandparents are meant for kisses and hugs. For watching rainbows and catching bugs. For baking all of your favorite things. For books to read and songs to sing.*—Anonymous
- *The nicest possible place to hear a story is on grandmother's lap.*—Elizabeth Faye
- *Children's children are a crown to the aged.*—Proverbs 17:6

---

[1] M. R. DeHaan, *The Chemistry of the Blood* (Grand Rapids: Zondervan, 1943), 66.
[2] Ronald Allen and Gordon Borror, *Worship: Rediscovering the Missing Jewel* (Portland, OR: Multnomah Press, 1982), 28.
[3] Charles Haddon Spurgeon, *Spurgeon's Sermons,* vol. 2 (Grand Rapids, MI: Baker Book House, 1983), 379.

- *I call to remembrance the genuine faith that is in you, which dwelt first in your grandmother Lois.*—Paul to Timothy, in 2 Timothy 1:5
- *Teach [these things] to your children and your grandchildren*—Deuteronomy 4:9
- *A life thoroughly committed to Christ, lived and tested over time, seasoned with experience and humility, is more powerful than most people ever imagine. People who have a heritage of godly grandparents carry this influence in their lives sometimes without recognizing its source.*—Jay Kesler[1]
- *Children and grandparents are natural allies.*

Date: _____ _____ _____
Place: _____ _____ _____
Occasion: _____ _____ _____

Over the Mountains

Several years ago, after one of my daughters returned from a week at my mother's house, I asked her what she had best liked about the experience. She furrowed her brow, thought about it, and said, "Waking up in the morning. I'd open my eyes, and for a moment I wouldn't know where I was; then I'd look around at the room and remember that I was at Grandma's."

"Over the mountains," the old poem says, "and through the woods, to grandmother's house we go."

"The bond between a child and a grandparent is the purest, least psychologically complicated form of human love," says Dr. Arthur Kornhaber, author of several books on grandparenting. He claims that grandparents can offer an emotional safety net when parents falter. They pass on traditions in the form of stories, songs, games, skills, and crafts. And they have another magical ingredient that parents often lack—time. What many grandchildren appreciate most is the relaxed rhythm of life at Grandma's and Grandpa's.

Kornhaber has found that children who are close to at least one grandparent are more emotionally secure than other children; and they have more positive feelings about older people and about the process of aging. Grandparents are, after all, *grand* parents. And in the dictionary the word *grand* means: *having more importance than others; foremost; having higher rank; large and striking in size, scope, extent, or conception; lavish, marked by regal form and dignity; intended to impress; very good; wonderful.*[2]

Date: _____ _____ _____
Place: _____ _____ _____
Occasion: _____ _____ _____

Statistics

- In the year 1900 the average life span in the United States was 47.3 years. Life expectancy now is even greater. A large percentage of people in the United

---

[1] Jay Kesler, "Grandparents in the Gap," *Focus on the Family,* March 1999, 3.
[2] From a sermon by the author.

States are living longer each year, and opportunities for long-lasting, high-impact grandparenting are greater than ever.

- The average age in America at which a woman becomes a grandmother is 46; and many in America become grandparents at 29 or 30.
- Half of adults aged 45 to 59, and 83 percent of those aged 60 and older are grandparents.
- There are 60 million grandparents in America today, and the number is accelerating rapidly because baby boomers are entering the grandparenting years. The number of grandparents in America will swell 26% in the first years of the twenty-first century.
- By 2005, 76 million Americans will be grandparents.
- Increasing numbers of grandparents are going to court for the right to visit their grandchildren. Twelve states now allow grandparents to petition for visitation rights without prerequisites. Support groups exist to give grandparents advice on legal actions.
- According to statistics from the U.S. Census Bureau (1998), 4 million children (6% of all children) were living in their grandparents' homes in 1996. Of that number, 1.4 million did not have a parent also living in the home, which means that these children's grandparents were solely responsible for parenting their grandchildren.

Date: _____   _____   _____
Place: _____   _____   _____
Occasion: _____   _____   _____

History of "National Grandparents Day"

In 1973, West Virginia began a statewide campaign to set aside a special day just for grandparents. The first Grandparents Day was set by Governor Arch Moore.

Through concerted efforts on the part of individuals interested in preserving their heritage, this campaign was headed by Marian McQuade of Fayette County, mother of fifteen children.

Divine Ingenuity

Blessed be the divine ingenuity that invented grandfathers and grandmothers.

—F. W. BOREHAM

Senator Jennings Randolph (D-WV) was especially instrumental in this project. In 1973, Senator Randolph introduced a resolution in the United States Senate and in 1978, five years after its inception, Congress passed legislation proclaiming the first Sunday after Labor Day as National Grandparents Day.

September was the month chosen, signifying the "autumn years" of life, and today this event, begun by only a few, is observed by thousands throughout the United States.

Date: _____   _____   _____
Place: _____   _____   _____
Occasion: _____   _____   _____

The Role of Grandparents

In their book, *Grandparenting by Grace,* Irene M. Endicott and C. Ferris Jordan suggest that grandparents are the "central core of the family."

- We are teachers of God's plan of salvation to our children and grandchildren. (see Isaiah 12:2–6)
- We are witnesses of how God has proven faithful to His people and to our family specifically. (see Deuteronomy 3:9)
- We are the family historian, holding the keys to learning about family roots and experiences for the generations to come.
- We have fun with our grandchildren and shape their self-esteem.
- We are a safe refuge for our grandchildren in times of trouble.
- We are a soft shoulder in sorrow and encourager of new beginnings.
- We are wise, non-judgmental counselors to our grandchildren.
- We bless our grandchildren by honoring their achievements and showing compassion for their losses.
- We represent stability to young families in dealing with change.
- We undergird our grandchildren with faithful prayer (see Matthew 21:22).[1]

Date: _____   _____   _____

Place: _____   _____   _____

Occasion: _____   _____   _____

The Need for Grandparents

Writing in *Focus on the Family Magazine,* Jay Kesler presented this probing assessment of children's need for grandparents:

"Young Timothy needed the strong spiritual roots provided by his mother and grandmother. And young people today, facing those same tensions, need godly parents and grandparents to help their own roots go deep so that they might withstand the storms of everyday life.

"To meet that need, God, in His divine wisdom, ordained that each child should have six adults to provide care and backup. In ancient times, because of disease and accident, life expectancy was short. Families were often broken up as fathers went off to war or mothers were sold into slavery. The involvement of the extended family, especially grandparents, was crucial to the survival of children.

"In a similar way in the United States, matriarchs in the African-American community often proved to be the social strength to enable family life to continue amid the havoc wreaked by slavery. These grandparents, who gave their grandchildren a foundation of moral character, often persevered with the strength gleaned from prayer and deep faith in the ultimate justice of God.

"As we draw to the close of the twentieth century, many families will face similar challenges—not because of slavery, but because of the breakdown of the moral and

---

[1] Irene M. Endicott and C. Ferris Jordan, *Grandparenting by Grace* (Nashville: Lifeway Press, 1994), 8–9.

social fabric of society. In single-parent families and in homes where both parents work, grandparents are becoming increasingly important. . . .

"I'm making a passionate call for a recommitment to Christian grandparents. The whole weight of responsibility cannot rest on an individual set of grandparents or a single grandmother or grandfather, but we can stand in the gap in our particular situations, as God asked in Ezekiel 22:30."[1]

Date: _____   _____   _____

Place: _____   _____   _____

Occasion: _____   _____   _____

G

A Second Chance

F. W. Boreham, the Australian Christian of a century ago, wrote, "Grandfatherism gives every man a second chance. If his parents fail him, his grandparents may yet prove his salvation."

Perhaps history's most dramatic illustration of that truth is King Manasseh in 2 Chronicles 33. Manasseh was the son of good King Hezekiah, but even good men can have prodigal sons, and Manasseh was a twelve-year-old terror. When Hezekiah died, Manasseh assumed the throne, a teenage tyrant, horribly wicked. The parallel account in 2 Kings 21 also tells us that Manasseh slaughtered many of his own people, establishing a reign of terror in Jerusalem.

How would you like this man as your grandfather? Don't answer too soon for there's more to this story. After a lifetime of violence, demonism, bloodshed, immorality, and the worst moral pollution the world had ever seen, Manasseh came to the Lord.

When he died at age sixty-seven, having served as Judah's king for fifty-five years, his son Amon, age twenty-two, took over. He did such evil in the sight of the Lord that his own people assassinated him after only two years, and his eight-year-old son Josiah became king, and he was among Judah's best kings—a godly man who repaired the temple and reestablished the worship of Jehovah among the people.

How can we explain Josiah's passion for godliness? His grandfather had died two years before, but he had enjoyed his grandfather during his first six years. In other words, the last six years of Manasseh and the first six years of Josiah overlap; and the last six years of Manasseh were his repentant years, his godly years, his years of reform and contrition.

It was too late for him to influence his own son Amon, but it wasn't too late for Josiah. We can easily picture the old king spending long hours with his small grandson saying, "Josiah, someday you'll be king of this land; and you must never do the things that I did. You must serve the Lord Jehovah. . . ." The story of Josiah is the story of a grandfather's influence.

---

[1] Jay Kesler, "Grandparents in the Gap," *Focus on the Family*, March 1999, 3.

Nothing But Gout?

"Charles," said Grandfather Spurgeon, "I have nothing to leave you but rheumatic gout; and I have left you a great deal of that."

But Rev. James Spurgeon left his grandson a great deal more than that.

Charles went to live with his grandparents at age one. James, pastor of an Independent Church, had a "large head and large voice." He wore breeches, buckled shoes, and silk stockings. He was a great preacher, and under his tutelage young Charles fell in love with the message and the ministry of preaching.

As a teenager, Charles was once asked to preach at a church in Suffolk. His train being delayed, James began a sermon for him. When the old man saw Charles enter, he interrupted himself. "Here comes my grandson," he said. "He may preach the gospel better than I can, but he cannot preach a better gospel—can you, Charles?" Young Charles took up the sermon from Ephesians 2, right where his grandfather had left off.

Nor did Charles ever forget Grandmother Spurgeon, sitting by the fire, an open Bible on her lap, speaking of the Lord. She taught him many lessons, and she was goodhearted and kind. She kept a little shelf over the kneading trough where she placed bits of sweet pastry, low enough for the boy's plump fingers.

The old couple's grandparenting ministry became the most important thing they ever did for the Lord, for it produced England's greatest preacher.

What Is a Grandmother?

An eight-year-old wrote, "A grandmother is a lady who has no children of her own, so she likes other people's boys and girls. Grandmas don't have anything to do except be there. If they take us for walks, they slow down past pretty leaves and caterpillars. They never say 'Hurry up.' Usually they are fat but not too fat to tie shoes. They wear glasses, and sometimes they can take their teeth out. They can answer questions like why dogs hate cats and why God isn't married. They don't talk like visitors do which is hard to understand. When they read to us, they don't skip words or mind if it is the same story again. Everybody should try to have a grandma, especially if you don't have television, because grandmas are the only grownups who always have time."

Grumbling

Someone Once Said . . .

- *You Christians seem to have a religion that makes you miserable. You are like a man with a headache. He does not want to get rid of his head, but it hurts him to keep it.*—A candid friend, to Hannah Whitall Smith
- *When one's flesh and bones are full of aches and pains, it is as natural for us to murmur as for a horse to shake his head when the flies tease him . . . but nature should not be the rule with Christians, or what is their religion worth?*—Charles H. Spurgeon[1]
- *A person who has a negative attitude toward himself will also be quite critical of others.*—Paul D. Meier[2]
- *Those who wish to sing always find a song.*—A Swedish Proverb

G

Date: _____ _____ _____
Place: _____ _____ _____
Occasion: _____ _____ _____

The Grumbling Israelites

The Children of Israel were forever grumbling about one thing or another. Just check out these four consecutive chapters as they began their journeys toward the Promised Land:

- Exodus 14:11: *Then they said to Moses, "Because there were no graves in Egypt, have you taken us away to die in the wilderness?"*
- Exodus 15:24: *And the people complained against Moses, saying, "What shall we drink?"*
- Exodus 16:2: *Then the whole congregation of the children of Israel complained against Moses and Aaron. . . .*
- Exodus 17:3: *. . . and the people complained.*

"[Do not] complain, as some of them also complained, and were destroyed by the destroyer," says 1 Corinthians 10:10. Their complaining demonstrated both a lack of gratitude for past blessings and a lack of confidence in God's wisdom, will, and ways.

Perhaps the unknown author of "Grumble Tone" had the Israelites in mind when he wrote:

> *There was a boy named Grumble Tone who ran away to sea,*
> *"I'm sick of things on land," he said, "as sick as I can be;*
> *A life upon the bounding wave will suit a lad like me!"*

---

[1] Charles H. Spurgeon, *John Ploughman's Talks* (New York: Sheldon & Company, n.d.), 38.
[2] Paul D. Meier, *Christian Child-Rearing and Personality Development* (Grand Rapids, MI: Baker Book House, 1977), 25.

The seething ocean billows failed to stimulate his mirth,
For he did not like the vessel, nor the dizzy, rolling berth,
And he thought the sea was almost as unpleasant as the earth.

He wandered into foreign lands, he saw each wondrous sight,
But nothing that he heard or saw seemed just exactly right;
And so he journeyed on and on, still seeking for delight.

He talked with kings and ladies fair; he dined in courts, they say,
But always found the people dull, and longed to get away
To search for that mysterious land where he would like to stay.

He wandered over all the world, his hair grew white as snow;
He reached that final bourne at last where all of us must go,
But never found the land he sought. The reason you would know?

The reason was that north or south, where'er his steps were bent,
On land or sea, in court or hall, he found but discontent;
For he took his disposition with him everywhere he went.

Date: _____ _____ _____
Place: _____ _____ _____
Occasion: _____ _____ _____

It's You

A woman left her house and went down to the plaza to do her errands. To her disgust, she found every shop malodorous. "Phew," she said to the clerk in the grocery store, "it stinks in here." Going next door to the dry-cleaners, she frowned at the odor. She stepped into the bank to make a deposit, and found a sewer-like smell, which she complained about as she cashed a small check.

Returning home, she discovered she had stepped in something earlier in the day, and she herself had been carrying the smell around with her everywhere she went.

Date: _____ _____ _____
Place: _____ _____ _____
Occasion: _____ _____ _____

You Idiot

In *Discipleship Journal*, Don McCullough wrote: "John Killinger tells about the manager of a minor league baseball team who was so disgusted with his center fielder's performance that he ordered him to the dugout and assumed the position himself.

"The first ball that came into center field took a bad hop and hit the manager in the mouth. The next one was a high fly ball, which he lost in the glare of the sun—until it bounced off his forehead. The third was a hard line drive that he charged with outstretched arms; unfortunately, it flew between his hands and smacked his eye.

"Furious, he ran back to the dugout, grabbed the center fielder by the uniform, and shouted, 'You idiot! You've got center field so messed up that even I can't do a thing with it!' "[1]

Date:			
Place:			
Occasion:			

A Contentious People

Jonathan Edwards, America's greatest theologian and the man who helped spark the greatest revival in American history, was dismissed by his church over a dispute. His members would not accept his position that unbelievers should not be allowed to participate in the Lord's Supper. In his farewell message, Edwards said:

As you would seek the future prosperity of this society, it is of vast importance that you should avoid contention.

A contentious people will be a miserable people. The contentions which have been among you, since I first became your pastor, have been one of the greatest burdens I have labored under in the course of my ministry—not only the contentions you have had with me, but those which you have had with one another, about your lands, and other concerns—because I knew that contention, heat of spirit, evil speaking, and things of the like nature, were directly contrary to the spirit of Christianity, and did, in a peculiar manner, tend to drive away God's Spirit from a people, and to render all means of grace ineffectual, as well as destroy a people's outward comfort and welfare.

Let me therefore earnestly exhort you, as you would seek your own future good, hereafter to watch against a contentious spirit . . .

Date:			
Place:			
Occasion:			

Me? Grumble?

Beverly Bush Smith was shocked when her husband finally spoke his mind. "It's hard to come home from work," he said, "and listen to you complain."

"Me? Complain?" thought Beverly. She had never thought of herself as a complainer. But her husband continued: "I listen to you grumble that you were caught in traffic, or that your editor trashed the lead on which you worked so hard, or that my mother demanded your time, or that the washing machine overflowed."

"I though I was just telling you about my day," Beverly replied.

"But it comes through in your tone of voice and body language."

For several weeks Beverly tried very hard to utter no grumbling sounds, but at length on a particularly bad day, the complaints poured out like a torrent. The next morning in her Bible study she looked up the word "murmuring"—which means

---

[1] "Let's Illustrate," *Leadership Journal*, Fall 1989, 51.

to grumble. She read of how the Israelites had grumbled in their wanderings, and how it was displeasing to God. She read Philippians 2:14 which says, "Do all things without complaining and disputing."

All things.

Beverly later wrote, "Now evening conversations with my husband are more pleasant. I hear a lot more about his concerns by encouraging him to tell me his feelings before I leap in with my problems.

"When I am tempted to launch into a monologue of the day's woes, I remind myself that I do not want to quench the Holy Spirit with my complaining. And I pray that God will help me reflect His love."[1]

Date:			
Place:			
Occasion:			

Negative Talk

Alan Loy McGinnis is a business consultant and author who had been called in to help change the negative trends in many large companies and corporations. In his book, *The Power of Optimism,* McGinnis writes:

"Corporations occasionally ask me to work with their low-producing managers and salespersons, the people who are failing, but whom they'd like to reclaim. As I sit with these men and women and listen to their conversation, I'm always struck by how pessimistic and cynical their talk is. One might say, 'Of course, they're negative; they know they're in trouble in their company.' But I suspect that it may have worked the other way—the one reason they became losers was their habit of negative talk. At some point they evidently got into the habit of commenting on bad circumstances, the bad working conditions, the bad state of their business. Maybe it originally got them some sympathy and attention, or maybe they picked up the habit from other workers. In any event, they became negative, and their work suffered."

Row, Row, Row Your Boat

The person who rows the boat usually doesn't have time to rock it.

—ANONYMOUS

McGinnis suggests several ways to reverse this, but one of the most powerful is to monitor and change the way we talk. When people began talking more positively, they begin thinking or acting more so. He suggests watching every conversation to see the direction of the comments and attitudes it contains.

"In almost every situation," he writes, "it is possible to give the conversation an optimistic spin."[2]

Date:			
Place:			
Occasion:			

[1] Beverly Bush Smith, "Me? Grumble?," *Decision,* July/August 1989, 6.
[2] Alan Loy McGinnis, *The Power of Optimism* (New York: Harper & Row, 1990), 134–141.

Dragon's Teeth

In mythology we read about Cadmus, who slew a dragon. Then he took the dragon's teeth and sowed them broadcast in a fertile field. When he returned later, he found that each seed had sprung up into a giant. He was afraid of what they might do to him so he decided to employ a clever ruse to cause the giants to fight each other. He threw a stone and struck one of the giants on the ear. This giant thought another giant had struck him, so a fight ensued. Soon all the giants were fighting each other and before long all of them were killed while Cadmus looked on and laughed.

Our churches are full of potential spiritual giants, but Satan often sows discord among the members and they end up as spiritual pygmies, fighting one another.[1]

G

Date: _____ _____ _____
Place: _____ _____ _____
Occasion: _____ _____ _____

A Nonsquawking Flight

A writer in a recent edition of *Our Daily Bread* told of being on a flight in which two children were argumentative and quarrelsome. The flight attendant, however, knew how to handle them. "What is all this squawking up here?" she asked, coming to their seats and smiling. The children grew quiet. Leaning over them she said in a serious tone, "I must remind you, this is a nonsquawking flight." The children remained quiet thereafter.

It's a long journey when you have to sit in the squawking section.[2]

Date: _____ _____ _____
Place: _____ _____ _____
Occasion: _____ _____ _____

The Monk

A certain monastery enforced a vow of silence. Each monk could utter only two words every five years, and those two words had to be spoken in the presence of the abbot. One of the monks, when given his opportunity to speak, said, "Bad food!" Five years later, his two words were, "Bed hard." When given his third opportunity to speak five years later, he said, "I quit."

"Well," said the abbot, "you might as well quit. All you've done since you got here is complain!"

Date: _____ _____ _____
Place: _____ _____ _____
Occasion: _____ _____ _____

[1] W. Herschel Ford, *Simple Sermons on Prayer* (Grand Rapids, MI: Baker Book House, 1985), 31.
[2] David C McCasland, *Our Daily Bread*, May 9, 1996.

Habits

Someone Once Said . . .

- *Thoughts produce acts, acts produce habits, and habits produce character.*—Anonymous
- *If we realize the extent to which we are mere walking bundles of habits, we would give more heed to their own formation.*—William James[1]
- *First we form habits, then they form us. Conquer your bad habits, or they'll eventually conquer you.*—Dr. Rob Gilbert[2]
- *You keep on doing it, and you try to stop, but you can't.*—a six-year-old's definition of a habit
- *Approximately 90 percent of what we do every day is governed by the habits in our lives.*—Dr. Michael Mitchell, author of *Building Strong Families*[3]
- *It is a hard thing to break through a habit and a yet harder thing to go contrary to our will. Yet if thou overcome not slight and easy obstacles, how shalt thou overcome greater ones? Withstand thy will at the beginning, and unlearn an evil habit, lest it lead thee little by little into worse difficulties.*—Thomas à Kempis
- *The Christian must see that bad habits are ultimately spiritual issues.*—Erwin Lutzer
- *Small habits, well pursued betimes / May reach the dignity of crimes.*—Hannah Moore
- *A bad habit takes twenty-one days to break; a good habit takes twenty-one days to make.*
- *Habits are the best of servants—and the worst of masters.*—Anonymous

Date: _____ _____ _____

Place: _____ _____ _____

Occasion: _____ _____ _____

Saplings

The *Heidelberg Herald* published this thought-provoking story: *An elderly teacher, with a pupil by his side, took a walk through a forest. Suddenly he stopped and pointed to four plants close at hand. The first was just beginning to peep above the ground, the second had rooted itself pretty well into the earth, the third was a small shrub, while the fourth was a full-sized tree. The tutor said to his young companion, "Pull up the first plant." The boy did so, eagerly, using only his fingers. "Now pull up the second." The youth obeyed but found the task more difficult. "Do the same with the third," he urged. The boy had to use all his strength to uproot it. "Now," said the instructor, "try your hand with the fourth." The pupil put his arms around the trunk of the tall tree and couldn't even shake its leaves. "This, my son, is just what happens with our bad habits. When they are young, we can remove them readily; but when they are old, it's hard to uproot them, though we pray and struggle ever so sincerely."*[4]

---

[1] William James, "Making Habits Work for You," *Getting the Most Out Of Life* (New York: Pleasantville, New York, 1946), 108.

[2] Quoted by John-Roger and Peter McWilliams, *Do It!* (Los Angeles: Prelude Press, 1991), 414.

[3] Michael A. and William Mitchell, "Habits—They Can Make or Break Your Child," *ParentLife*, March 1998, 6.

[4] Clipped from my files.

Date: _____ _____ _____
Place: _____ _____ _____
Occasion: _____ _____ _____

Threads

Horace Mann, the great educator, once said, "Habits are like a cable. We weave a strand of it everyday and soon it cannot be broken."

Michael and William Mitchell, in an article in *ParentLife Magazine*, tell of a teacher who wanted to show her pupils the power of habits, and how they are formed through repeated acts or thoughts. Taking a roll of thread, she wrapped it one time around a student's wrists when placed together. "That," she said, "represents your doing something one time. Can you break the thread?" The student easily did so.

Then she wrapped the thread around his wrists, two, three, four, five or more times. The effort to break the thread became more and more difficult until finally the child was unable to free his hands at all.

"That," she said, "is what happens when acts are repeated until they become habits."[1]

William James said that by allowing separate acts to reoccur until they become habits *we are spinning our own fates, good or evil, and never to be undone. . . . As we become permanent drunkards by so many separate drinks, so we become saints in the moral, and experts in the practical and scientific spheres, by so many separate acts and hours of work.*[2]

Date: _____ _____ _____
Place: _____ _____ _____
Occasion: _____ _____ _____

Ropes

Jay Adams says about habits: *"Proverbs" plainly warns against the slavery of sinful habits: "For directly before the eyes of the Lord are man's ways, and all his paths are well considered. His own iniquities seize the wicked, and he is held fast by the ropes of his own sin. He dies for lack of discipline" (Proverbs 5:21,22—Berkeley). Sinful habits are hard to break, but if they are not broken they will bind the client even more tightly. He is held fast by these ropes of his own sin.*[3]

Date: _____ _____ _____
Place: _____ _____ _____
Occasion: _____ _____ _____

---

[1] Michael A. and William Mitchell, "Habits—They Can Make or Break Your Child," *ParentLife*, March 1998, 6.

[2] William James, "Making Habits Work for You," *Getting the Most Out Of Life* (New York: Pleasantville, New York, 1946), 108.

[3] Jay E. Adams, *Competent to Counsel* (Grand Rapids: Zondervan, 1970), 145.

William James' Advice

William James, philosopher and pioneer American psychologist, wrote about habits in his classic book *Psychology: Briefer Course.*

In the acquisition of a new habit, or the leaving off of an old one, there are four great maxims to remember: First, we must take care to launch ourselves with as strong an initiative as possible. . . .

Second, never suffer an exception to occur till the new habit is securely rooted in your life. Each lapse is like letting fall a ball of string which one is carefully winding up; a single slip undoes more than a great many turns will wind up again. . . .

The third maxim is: Seize the first possible opportunity to act on every resolution you make. It is not in the moment of their forming, but in the moment of their producing motor effects that resolutions communicate a new "set" to the brain. . . . A tendency to act becomes effectively ingrained in us only in proportion to the frequency with which the actions actually occur, and the brain "grows" to their use. . . .

As the fourth practical maxim, we may, then, offer something like this: Keep the faculty of effort alive in you by a little gratuitous exercise every day. That is, be systematically ascetic or heroic in little unnecessary points, do every day or two something for no other reason than that you would rather not do it, so that when the hour of dire need draws nigh it may find you nerved and trained to stand the test.

Habitual Chains

The chains of habit are generally too small to be felt until they are too strong to be broken.
—SAMUEL JOHNSON

Date:	_____	_____	_____
Place:	_____	_____	_____
Occasion:	_____	_____	_____

The First Days Are the Hardest

In his book *The 7 Habits of Highly Effective People,* Stephen Covey describes the breaking and making of habits to the launch of a spacecraft like Apollo 11. To get to the moon, writes Covey, those astronauts "literally had to break out of the tremendous gravity pull of the earth. More energy was spent in the first few minutes of lift-off, in the first few miles of travel, than was used over the next several days to travel half a million miles.

"Habits, too, have tremendous gravity pull—more than most people realize or would admit. Breaking deeply imbedded habitual tendencies such as procrastination, impatience, criticalness, or selfishness that violate basic principles of human effectiveness involves more than a little willpower and a few minor changes in our lives. 'Lift off' takes a tremendous effort, but once we break out of the gravity pull, our freedom takes on a whole new dimension."[1]

---

[1] Stephen R. Covey, *The Seven Habits of Highly Effective People* (New York: Simon and Schuster, 1989), 46–47

Date: _____ _____ _____
Place: _____ _____ _____
Occasion: _____ _____ _____

How to Say No to a Stubborn Habit

In his book *How to Say No to a Stubborn Habit,* Erwin Lutzer writes: "We are responsible for our own sin—including those sins 'which so easily beset us.' The fact that we do something wrong habitually does not relieve us of responsibility. On the contrary, it may make the sin all the worse. So we must take personal responsibility for our own habits and not shrink from calling them sin.

"Sinful habits are not insurmountable problems for the Christian. After all, the Holy Spirit indwells us and is working to conform us to the image of Christ. And if God be for us, who can be against us? (Romans 8:31) Furthermore, Galatians 5:16 says that if we "walk by the Spirit [we] will not carry out the desire of the flesh." And 1 Corinthians 10:13 is a promise that God will not permit us to be tempted beyond our ability. If we make use of the resources provided by God through His Spirit and His Word, we can attack any habit knowing that we can win."

Lutzer goes on to offer these suggestions for overcoming bad habits:

1. Remember that sin begins in the mind. If we can stop the sin in our mind, we can stop it in our actions.
2. Defeating a habit also requires changes in lifestyle. We are to make no provision for the flesh (Romans 13:14), avoiding the company, for example, of those who have the same problem, and the places and circumstances which tempt us.
3. We can't battle the bad habit alone. We should develop relationships with more mature Christians who will encourage us and hold us accountable.
4. Focus on developing good habits. Do not just stop sinning, start doing right. The good habits will replace the sinful ones.[1]

Date: _____ _____ _____
Place: _____ _____ _____
Occasion: _____ _____ _____

An Eleven-Step Program

Dr. Stan O'Dell, professor of psychology at the University of Mississippi, suggests the following ingredients in the breaking of bad habits:

1. Make sure the change is for you, not to please someone else. Resolutions that are made to please a spouse, friend, or parent rarely succeed.
2. Make a list of the reasons why you want to change.

---

[1] Summarized in a news clipping in my files.

3. Be firm, but don't expect too much too soon. Break down your goal into small steps.
4. Announce your plan. Make a public commitment to it.
5. Make the old habit as unpleasant or inconvenient as possible, while making the new habit easy to achieve.
6. Plan strategies for special situations, and have a backup plan ready in case you slip.
7. Recruit help from friends. Promising to meet a friend at exercise class makes you less likely to skip class.
8. Consult an expert if necessary. Such serious problems as alcoholism, smoking, or drug abuse often require professional help.
9. Reward yourself for small successes.
10. Hold on for ninety days—the average time it takes to establish a new habit.
11. Once you have established the habit, take it a day at a time. Don't panic if you have an off day; just be sure to get right back in your routine the next day.[1]

Date: _____ _____ _____

Place: _____ _____ _____

Occasion: _____ _____ _____

Dear Ann Landers

Advice columnist Ann Landers passed along these suggestions for those wanting to give up cigarettes:

- Make the decision to quit. Set yourself a quit date and prepare yourself for the transition.
- Become aware of your pattern of use, identifying trigger places, people, and activities.
- Explore on paper your motivations for quitting. Carry a list with you of your top three reasons.
- Start an exercise program.
- Set up a social support system.
- Commit to doing what it takes to get through the short-term discomfort.
- Smoke your last cigarette and say good-bye.
- Dispose of all tobacco products and paraphernalia.
- Drink lots of water to help eliminate nicotine from your system.
- Take deep breaths to keep you centered.
- Take action whenever an urge presents itself. Call your support people. Pray. Take a walk. Stretch. The urge **will** pass.
- Envision yourself already smoke-free.
- Modify your lifestyle to support your smoke-free status.
- Change your daily routines to avoid old triggers.
- Develop a system of rewards for yourself.

---

[1] Robin Street, "Plan for Success in Breaking Bad Habits," *Cooking Light Magazine.*

• Develop new interests to give your life a positive focus, and redirect your energy.[1]

Date: _____ _____ _____
Place: _____ _____ _____
Occasion: _____ _____ _____

How Franklin Graham Licked Cigarettes

After Franklin Graham committed himself to Christ, he was surprised to find his taste for cigarettes was strong as ever. He determined to quit smoking, but three days later, he awoke with *an absolutely overwhelming—almost terrifying—desire for a cigarette. I wanted to smoke so badly that I couldn't think of anything else. It intensified with each passing minute. Throughout the day, the yearning for a cigarette grabbed me like the jaws of a junkyard dog.*

He finally shared his struggle with his friend Roy Gustafson. "Roy, I quit smoking, but I don't think I can hold out. I just don't think I have the power to say no any longer."

"Oh, you don't, huh?" replied Roy, looking up from a hamburger. "Why don't you just get down on your knees and tell God He's a liar?"

"What? I can't do that!"

Roy quoted 1 Corinthians 10:13 to him, then said, "You need to tell God He's a liar. You claimed that verse and it didn't work."

"I'm not going to call God a liar," said Franklin. "Besides, I haven't claimed that verse yet!"

"You haven't?" said Roy, sounding shocked. "Why don't you, then?"

Franklin did claim that verse. And it did work.[2]

Date: _____ _____ _____
Place: _____ _____ _____
Occasion: _____ _____ _____

Dear Abby . . .

Dear Abby:

I am engaged to be married to a wonderful young lady. Although I am usually well-behaved, I have a terrible temper and sometimes swear and use bad language—a habit I want very much to break.

"Cheryl" and I consulted a psychologist about this problem, and she suggested that I wear an elastic band around my wrist, and every time I start to lose my temper, I should snap it.

I tried it a few times, but Cheryl said I wasn't snapping it hard enough, so at our next session, the therapist suggested that Cheryl snap it whenever I started to get nasty. And snap it hard enough to make it sting.

---

[1] Clipped from my files.
[2] Robert J. Morgan, *From This Verse* (Nashville: Thomas Nelson Publishers, 1998), October 28th.

I know this may sound funny or even childish, but the rubber band treatment worked for me! The therapist said that this technique is used to stop smoking, drinking, and obsessive thoughts.

Pass this on to your readers if you think it will help. It helped me.—John M. in Bridgeport, Connecticut

Dear John:

The rubber-band-snapping technique has been used successfully for a number of years for people who are compulsive about scratching itches or itching scratches, picking at pimples, and biting, picking, or tearing fingernails. It's simple: Snap the rubber band instead of yielding to the compulsive behavior.[1]

Date:	_____	_____	_____
Place:	_____	_____	_____
Occasion:	_____	_____	_____

Happiness

Someone Once Said . . .

- *Whoever is happy will make others happy, too.*—Anne Frank, in *The Diary of a Young Girl*
- *A man is about as happy as he makes up his mind to be.*—Abraham Lincoln
- *A man is happy so long as he chooses to be happy and nothing can stop him.*—Alexander Solzhenitsyn
- *Happiness is a habit.*—Anonymous
- *It's not your position that makes you happy; it's your disposition.*—Anonymous
- *Happiness is not a destination; it is a manner of traveling. Happiness is not an end in itself. It is a by-product of working, playing, loving and living.*—Dr. Haim Ginott
- *So I'm happy tonight. I'm not worried about anything. I'm not fearing any man. Mine eyes have seen the glory of the coming of the Lord!*—Martin Luther King, Jr., on the night before his assassination in Memphis
- *Happiness is an imaginary condition, formerly attributed by the living to the dead, now usually attributed by adults to children and by children to adults.*—Thomas Szasz, psychiatrist
- *Let us all be happy, and live within our means, even if we have to borrow the money to do it with.*—Artemus Ward (1834–1867), U.S. humorist

Date:	_____	_____	_____
Place:	_____	_____	_____
Occasion:	_____	_____	_____

---

[1] *Nashville Tennessean*, July 23, 1994, sec. 2-D.

What a Happy Child!

Fanny Crosby, one of America's favorite writers of gospel music, was blinded when she was six weeks old by a doctor who put an incorrect solution on her inflamed eyes. But her attitude grew strong as the years passed, leading to a lifetime of uplifting music. One of her first poems expressed remarkable wisdom for a child of only eight:

Oh, what a happy child I am,
Although I cannot see!
I am resolved that in this world,
Contented I will be.

Date: _____ _____ _____
Place: _____ _____ _____
Occasion: _____ _____ _____

Happiness and Holiness

The writer and preacher A. T. Pierson once spoke these insightful words in a sermon. "He who thinks duty and delight are opposed lives a comparatively low life. If he gets high enough up for a true view, he will see that all opposition between happiness and holiness is only apparent. The roads of duty and delight never cross each other."

Date: _____ _____ _____
Place: _____ _____ _____
Occasion: _____ _____ _____

Viktor Frankl's Advice

In *Man's Search for Meaning*, Nazi death camp survivor Viktor E. Frankl writes, "Don't aim at success—the more you aim at it and make it a target, the more you are going to miss it. For success, like happiness, cannot be pursued; it must ensue, and it only does so as the unintended side-effect of one's personal dedication to a cause greater than oneself or as the by-product of one's surrender to a person other than oneself."[1]

Date: _____ _____ _____
Place: _____ _____ _____
Occasion: _____ _____ _____

In the Manufacturing Business

In his famous book *The Power of Positive Thinking,* Norman Vincent Peale includes a chapter entitled, "How to Create Your Own Happiness."

[1] Viktor E. Frankl, *Man's Search for Meaning* (New York: Washington Square Press, 1959), 16–17.

"Who decides whether you shall be happy or unhappy?" he asks. "The answer—you do!"

Peale then relates a conversation he had with a couple over dinner in a railway dining car during a trip. The woman was expensively dressed in furs, diamonds, and an expensive dress. But she seemed to be having a most unpleasant time with herself. Rather loudly she declared that the car was dingy and drafty, the service bad, the food terrible.

Her husband, in contrast, was genial, affable, easy-going, and pleasant.

During dinner, Peale asked the man what business he was in. He said he was a lawyer, then he added, "My wife is in the manufacturing business."

This was surprising, for she did not seem to be the industrial or executive type. So Peale asked, "What does she manufacture?"

"Unhappiness," replied the man. "She manufactures her own unhappiness."

An icy chill descended over the table, but, reflecting on the conversation later, Dr. Peale wrote, "I was grateful for his remark, for it describes exactly what so many people do—they manufacture their own unhappiness.[1]

Date: _____ _____ _____
Place: _____ _____ _____
Occasion: _____ _____ _____

Sutter's Gold

Sometimes the sources of our happiness contain the seeds of our own destruction. Consider General John A. Sutter. On January 24, 1848, one of his workmen, building a grist mill on the south fork of the American River, found a small yellow stone that appeared to be gold. The next morning at daybreak, the man rushed forty miles down the canyon to Sutter's ranch house with the exciting news. Sutter was elated, his heart filled with ultimate happiness. Gold on his land! Pure, yellow nuggets that would make him literally the richest man on earth.

Sutter tried to keep his discovery a secret, but within a day all his ranch hands had left their tasks in a mad frenzy, digging and panning and scratching for gold. Within a week, the whole countryside was in turmoil as ranches, towns, and villages were abandoned, everyone rushing to Sutter's ranch in search of gold.

Telegraph wires hummed, and soon soldiers were deserting from the army, fathers from their families, employees from their jobs, farmers from their ranches. By 1848, it seemed that half the country was camping on Sutter's ranch, digging for gold. Ships had no sooner docked in San Francisco Bay before the sailors jumped ship and headed for the hills.

John Sutter could only look on in helpless rage as his ranch was ransacked, his barns torn down, his crops trampled, and his cattle slaughtered. In time, he fought

---

Pursuit of Happiness

The Constitution only gives people the right to pursue happiness. You have to catch it yourself.
—BENJAMIN FRANKLIN

---

[1]Norman Vincent Peale, *The Power of Positive Thinking* (New York: Prentice-Hall, Inc., 1952), 63–64.

back by filing what was, at that time, the biggest lawsuit in history. He claimed that both San Francisco and Sacramento had been built on his property. He won the suit, but never received a penny. Mobs, enraged by the decision, burned the courthouse with its records and blew up Sutter's houses and barns with dynamite. They murdered one of his sons and drove another to commit suicide. A third son, attempting to flee the madness by going to Europe, drowned. John A. Sutter himself, staggering under these cruel blows, lost his reason.

For twenty years after that, he haunted the Capitol in Washington, trying to persuade Congress to recognize his rights. Dressed in rags, the poor, old, demented man went from one senator to another pleading for justice, and the children in the street laughed and jeered him as he passed.

In the Spring of 1880, he died alone in a furnished room in Washington, alone and despised. He didn't have a dollar when he passed away, though he did possess a legal deed to the greatest fortune on earth.[1]

H

Date:			
Place:			
Occasion:			

The Witness of Happy Hearts

Christiana Tsai was born into a wealthy home in China and raised in a deeply devout Buddhist home. As her parents sent her to a Christian high school run by missionaries, her father told her, "Just be sure you don't eat [fall for] Christianity!"

But that is exactly what happened. She went on to become one of the most famous Christians in China, largely due to her fascinating autobiography, *Queen of the Dark Chamber,* in which she gives two illustrations of true happiness:

- When Christiana told her family of her conversion to Christ, they reacted with fury and horror, persecuting her. They snatched her Bible, tore it to pieces, and threw it in her face. Yet some time later, her "Eighth Brother" approached her. "Tell me about Christianity and why you became a Christian," he asked. "I have noticed that in spite of the way we treat you now, you seem much happier than you used to. I think I would like to believe, too." In time, Christiana's happiness paved the way for her sharing the Good News of Christ with her entire family.
- Christiana's closest friend was Mary Leaman, the principal of her school and her mentor. In 1944 during the Japanese occupation of China, Miss Leaman, by then elderly and sick, was forced into a concentration camp. She paid a final visit to Christiana on the day she was to be interred, and afterward souls were saved because of her attitude, which Christiana describes in no more than a dozen words: *Not to cry! Not to faint! Just a smile and a prayer!* That was all. But that was enough to make the Chinese ask, "What religion is this that gives such power to Miss Leaman and Miss Tsai, to enable them to smile

[1] Dale Carnegie, *Little Known Facts About Well Known People* (New York: Blue Ribbon Books, Inc., 1934), 6–10.

under such conditions?" Happy hearts are a powerful witness in unhappy times.[1]

```
Date:      _____    _____    _____
Place:     _____    _____    _____
Occasion:  _____    _____    _____
```

Healing

Someone Once Said . . .

- *It is as wrong to say that the church has no part in the ministry of healing as it is to say that the only thing that prevents people from being healed is their lack of faith.*—Colin Brown[2]
- *Ultimate healing and the glorification of the body are certainly among the blessings of Calvary for the believing Christian. Immediate healing is not guaranteed. God can heal any disease, but He is not obligated to do so.*—Warren Wiersbe[3]
- *Because we are the handiwork of God, it follows that all our problems and their solutions are theological.*—A. W. Tozer[4]
- *One thing I know: that though I was blind, now I see.*—the man in John 9

```
Date:      _____    _____    _____
Place:     _____    _____    _____
Occasion:  _____    _____    _____
```

Quotes Throughout Church History

- *Numberless demonics throughout the whole world and in your city, many of our Christian men, exorcising them in the name of Jesus Christ, who was crucified under Pontius Pilate, have healed, and do heal, rendering helpless and driving the possessing devils out of the men.*—Justin Martyr, second century
- *Others still heal the sick by laying their hands on upon them, and they are made whole.*—Irenaeus, second century
- *And how many men of rank, to say nothing of the common people, have been delivered from devils and healed of disease.*—Tertullian, second and third centuries
- *And some give evidence of their having received through their faith a marvelous power by the cures that they perform, invoking no other name over those who need their help than that of the God of all things and of Jesus.*—Origen, second and third centuries

---

[1] Christiana Tsai, *Queen of the Dark Chamber* (Chicago: Moody Press, 1953), 73, 173–175.
[2] Colin Brown, "The Other Half of the Gospel?" *Christianity Today,* April 21, 1989, 29.
[3] Warren W. Wiersbe, *Why Us?* (Old Tappan, NJ: Fleming H. Revell, 1984), 152.
[4] A. W. Tozer, *The Knowledge of the Holy* (New York: Harper & Row, Publishers, 1961), 34.

- *Let them, therefore, with fasting and prayer, make their intercessions, and not with the well arranged and fitly ordered words of learning, but as men who have received the gift of healing confidently, to the glory of God.*—Clement, second and third centuries
- *Therefore, concerning this anointing of the sick, we hold it as an article of faith, and profess sincerely from the heart that sick persons, when they ask it, may lawfully be anointed with the anointing oil by one who joins with them in praying that it may be efficacious to the healing of the body.*—Waldensian Confession, fifteenth century
- *How often has it happened and still does that devils have been driven out in the name of Christ, also by calling on his name and prayer that the sick have been healed?*—Martin Luther, sixteenth century
- *How many times have I known the prayer of faith to save the sick when all physicians have given them up as dead.*—Richard Baxter, seventeenth century[1]
- *We have had undeniable proofs thereof . . . in the healing of maladies in themselves incurable, such as cancers, consumptions, when the patient was in the agonies of death, etc., all by means of prayer, or of a single word.*—Count Nicholaus Zinzendorf, eighteenth century

H

Date: _____   _____   _____

Place: _____   _____   _____

Occasion: _____   _____   _____

Climbing into God

"Prayer," said Martin Luther, "is a climbing up of the heart into God. None can believe how powerful prayer is, and what it is able to effect, but those who have learned it by experience."

Luther spoke from his *own* experience, for he received many interesting answers to prayer. One of them occurred when his dearest friend and associate, Philip Melancthon, fell ill. According to an ancient biography, Luther arrived to find Philip about to "give up the ghost. His eyes were set; his consciousness was almost gone; his speech had failed, and also his hearing; his face had fallen; he knew no one, and had ceased to take either solids or liquids."

Luther, beside himself with grief, exclaimed, "Blessed Lord, how has the devil spoiled me of this instrument!" He turned toward the window and began praying aloud earnestly. Almost instantly Philip began to move, and he was soon completely restored. Melancthon later said, "I should have been a dead man had I not been recalled from death itself by the coming of Luther."

A similar event in 1541 involved Friedrich Myconius, another of Luther's friends, who was found in the last stages of tuberculosis and was almost speechless. Luther was unable to visit Myconius' bedside, so he wrote a prayer and sent it to him by courier, saying: *May God not let me hear so long as I live that you are dead, but cause you to survive me. I pray this earnestly, and will have it granted. Amen.*

Myconius later said, "I was so horrified when I read what the good man had written, that it seemed to me as though I had heard Christ say, 'Lazarus come forth!' "

---

[1] A. J. Gordon, *The Ministry of Healing* (n.p., n.d.).

And it so happened as Luther prayed. Myconius recovered and was kept from the grave until a short time after Luther's death in 1546.

Date: _____ _____ _____

Place: _____ _____ _____

Occasion: _____ _____ _____

Excerpts from John Wesley's Diary

Here are three entries from John Wesley's journal, taken from incidents years apart, that shows that Wesley believed that God could heal in response to prayer. The three incidents involved healing for himself, a friend—and a horse.

- 1741, May 10. Sunday, pain in back and head, with fever; had to lie down most of day; only easy in one position. At night tried to preach; pain, and seized with cough, etc. There came to mind strongly, "These signs shall follow them that believe." Prayed; called on Jesus aloud to increase my faith and to confirm the Word of His grace. While I was speaking my pain vanished away, the fever left me, my bodily strength returned, and for many weeks I felt neither sickness nor pain. Unto Thee, O Lord, do I give thanks!
- 1745, Jan. 14. On way to Bristol. Was earnest desired to turn aside and call at the house of a poor man, William Shalwood. I found him and his wife sick in one bed, and with small hopes of the recovery of either. Yet (after prayer) I believed they would not die, but live and declare the loving kindness of the Lord. The next time I called he was sitting below stairs, and his wife able to be abroad.
- 1781, Sept. 5. On Wednesday noon I preached at Taunton. I believe it my duty to relate here what some will esteem a most notable instance of enthusiasm (fanaticism). Be it so or not, I aver the plain fact. In an hour after we left Taunton, one of the chaise horses was on a sudden so lame that he could hardly set his foot to the ground. It being impossible to procure any human help, I knew no remedy but prayer. Immediately the lameness was gone, and he went just as he did before.

Date: _____ _____ _____

Place: _____ _____ _____

Occasion: _____ _____ _____

Joni Eareckson Tada on Healing

Joni Eareckson Tada, paralyzed from the neck down in a swimming accident, wrote in a best-selling book about her experiences. Afterward, she received many calls and letters telling her that God had both the power and the desire to heal her. She became convinced of it and, in a little oak chapel near her home, several elders and ordained ministers anointed her head with olive oil and offered fervent, believing prayers for her healing. She fully expected God to heal her.

"A week went by," she later wrote, "then another, then another. My body still hadn't gotten the message that I was healed. Fingers and toes still didn't respond to the mental command. . . .

"You can image the questions that began popping into my mind. Is there some sin in my life? . . . Had we done things right? . . . Did I have enough faith?

Joni spent the next six years searching in the Bible for answers about divine healing, finally coming to this conclusion:

"God certainly can, and sometimes does, heal people in a miraculous way today. But the Bible does not teach that He will always heal those who come to Him in faith. He sovereignly reserves the right to heal or not to heal as He sees fit."

Joni continues, "From time to time God, in His mercy, may grant us healing from disease as a gracious glimpse, a 'sneak preview' of what is to come. It is my opinion that He sometimes does. But, in view of the fact that the kingdom has not yet come in its fullness, we are not to automatically expect it."[1]

Date:			
Place:			
Occasion:			

Auf Wiedersehen

Dr. Effie Jane Wheeler was a longtime and beloved professor at Wheaton College. The following letter was written by her on Memorial Day of 1949, and read in chapel by Wheaton's president, Dr. V. Raymond Edman, on May 31, 1949:

My beloved Wheaton family everywhere, but most especially those of you who are on campus:

I greatly appreciate the moment in Chapel that may be given to reading this, for before you leave for the summer I should like to have you know the truth about me as I learned it myself only last Friday.

My doctor at last has given what has been his real diagnosis of my illness for weeks—an inoperable case of cancer of the pancreas.

Now if he had been a Christian he wouldn't have been so dilatory or shaken, for he would have known, as you and I do, that life or death is equally welcome when we live in the will and presence of the Lord.

If the Lord has chosen me to go to Him soon, I go gladly. On the other hand, I remember that Christ is still the Great Physician. And so in simple faith and trust I say to Him, "Lord, if thou wilt, thou canst make me whole." I await His answer utterly at peace.

Please do not give a moment's grief to me. Think of me only happily, gaily, as I do of you. My interest is as keen as ever in everything over there—Student Memorial Center and the buildings that are to follow, commencement affairs with all the joy and lightheartedness.

I do not say a cold goodbye, but rather a warm auf Wiedersehen, "till I see you again"— by God's power and grace on campus this fall or later in the Blessed Land, where I may be allowed to draw aside a curtain when you enter.

With a heart full of love for every individual of you, Effie Jane Wheeler.[2]

---

[1] Joni Eareckson and Steve Estes, *A Step Further* (Grand Rapids, MI: Zondervan, 1982), 123–133.
[2] A clipping in my files.

```
Date:      _____   _____   _____
Place:     _____   _____   _____
Occasion:  _____   _____   _____
```

The Sixty-Six Cent Solution

Missionaries Dick Hillis and Margaret Humphrey were married on April 18, 1938, in a little house in Hankow, China. The only wedding music was the percussion of Japanese bombs in the distance. They moved into a drab mud-brick house and settled into a flurry of missionary activity.

━━━━◇━━━━
Obligatory Health

God can heal any disease, but He is not obligated to do so.
—WARREN WIERSBE
━━━━◇━━━━

Seven months later, Margaret showed symptoms of fever. It rapidly worsened, and Dick anguished as it rose to 103 degrees, then to 105 degrees. With no doctor in the village and no adequate transportation to the distant hospital, he felt helpless. He prayed, but sensed no response from God. *Why? Why doesn't God answer? He couldn't take her from me. He knows I need her, not just for myself, but for the work also.*

As he knelt by Margaret's bed gripping her torrid hand, a sentence came to mind from a letter his father had written before his marriage: "Remember, Dick, if you are really in love, you will face the danger of loving the gift more than the giver."

"Oh, God," Dick cried, "You have given me so much to love in Margaret. Is it possible I have loved her too much?" The closing words of 1 John flashed to mind: "Little children, keep yourselves from idols."

Knowing the Lord was working deeply in his heart, Dick knelt a long time, praying. "Lord, I give Margaret back to you. If you require it, I will walk to her grave, still trusting you. But if you will raise her up, I will always seek to put you first."

Peace came over him, allowing him to rest. The next morning when Margaret's temperature still hovered at 105 degrees, Dick decided to visit the local Chinese herb shop. The aged proprietor there found a small glass vial that a traveling medicine man had sold him two years previously. It was supposed to reduce fever. Dick purchased the solution for sixty-six cents, then hurried home and gave Margaret the injection. Her temperature began going down, and two weeks later she was good as new.[1]

```
Date:      _____   _____   _____
Place:     _____   _____   _____
Occasion:  _____   _____   _____
```

"I'm Healed"

Russell and Darlene Deibler were welcomed as missionaries to New Guinea in 1938 by an old and distinguished British missionary, Dr. Robert Alexander Jaffray.

---

[1] Jan Winebrenner, *Steel in his Soul* (Chicago: Moody Press, 1985), 60–62.

When, during World War II, the Japanese invaded the island, Dr. Jaffray was with them. The Japanese seized Russell and the other male missionaries, hauling them to concentration camps. Darlene never saw her husband again. But Dr. Jaffray, being aged and ill, was allowed to remain with the women, which included Margaret Jaffray, his daughter.

Margaret was extremely careful about the foods she prepared for her father, because of Dr. Jaffray's diabetic condition. She and Darlene had stockpiled as much saccharin as they could, for use in recipes calling for sugar. But the supplies were very limited, for the war had cut them off from all external provisions.

One afternoon after a tiring walk, Dr. Jaffray, Margaret, and Darlene collapsed into chairs for tea. Margaret prepared tea and set the tray on a small table near her father. He helped himself to milk, and, instead of taking saccharin, he picked up the sugar bowl and spooned one, two, three teaspoons of sugar into his tea. The women couldn't believe their eyes, and Margaret was horrified. "Daddy," she pleaded, "please don't do that. You know you aren't supposed to have sugar."

Remembering that he had recently been in a diabetic coma and understanding her fears, he tried to reassure her. "Muggie," he said, "I'm healed. I need this sugar for strength." He continued to use sugar, and when she begged that he not use so much, he patted her hand, saying, "It's all right, Muggie. I'm healed."

Not too many days later, the women were able to smuggle a urine specimen to a local Dutch doctor with a message: "For several days now Dr. Jaffray has been using sugar. He believes the Lord has healed him, but we would like confirmation."

A few days later a letter was smuggled back. The doctor had examined the specimen and found not a trace of sugar. Dr. Jaffray had indeed been healed.

Darlene later wrote, "We had a time of praising and thanking the Lord. He was preparing Dr. Jaffray for a time when there would be no saccharin, only scant rations of sugar. The Lord is very good to those who put their trust in Him."[1]

Date: _____ _____ _____
Place: _____ _____ _____
Occasion: _____ _____ _____

Good Medicine

Faith, prayer, and Christianity do a body good. Over two hundred clinical studies have confirmed that faith reduces depression, hypertension, and stroke. Dr. Mark Houston of Nashville's St. Thomas hospital said, "The data is impressive. If you have those ingredients of religious commitment—faith, prayer, worship attendance, and other things—you are better off in all aspects of health." Here are some recent discoveries:

- In 1995, researchers asked 232 elderly patients undergoing elective heart surgery how religious they were. Those who described themselves as deeply religious were more likely to be alive six months later than others.

[1]Darlene Deibler Rose, *Evidence Not Seen: One Woman's Miraculous Faith in a Japanese P.O.W. Camp* (Carlisle, UK: OM Publishing, 1988), 48–49.

- Another study found that repetitive prayer and the rejection of negative thoughts can benefit treatment of a number of diseases.
- Heart patients who had someone praying for them without their knowledge suffered 10% fewer complications, according to research done by the Mid America Heart Institute, the heart program of St. Luke's Hospital in Kansas City, Missouri.
- A major study of church attendance and mortality reveals that people who attend church weekly live an average of seven years longer than people who never attend church. The findings were announced by sociologists from the University of Texas, the University of Colorado at Boulder, and Florida State University. The study, funded partly by the National Science Foundation, involved a nationally representative sample of over twenty-two thousand people.
- Dr. Dale Matthews, a medical researcher with degrees from Duke and Princeton and an assistant professor at Georgetown University Medical School, has done extensive research into the relationship between faith and health. His book, *The Faith Factor,* has landed him on television programs like *Oprah, Larry King Live,* and *Good Morning America.* Matthews cites a landmark study published in 1997 by the *American Journal of Public Health* which looked at 5,200 patients in California for 28 years and found that those people who were regular churchgoers, who attended church once or more per week, had significantly lower mortality rates. The men had a 25% lower mortality rate and the women had a 33% lower mortality rate. "The research tells us that people of faith reap benefits in dealing with alcoholism, drug abuse, depression, high blood pressure, heart disease and cancer," says Dr. Matthews. "We tend to stay healthier, to recover faster, and even when recovery does not happen, we cope better with disease. The secular world seems surprised to hear about the link between religion and well-being, but I'm not," says Matthews, whose belief in Jesus Christ is the foundation of his life. The physician started reading the Bible at age twelve, following the death of his one-year-old brother, Douglas, who had cancer. "I believe God gave me a hunger for the Bible to help me heal from the grief of losing my little brother," he says. "I took a Bible from the pew in our church and started reading. Even though I didn't understand everything I read, I fell in love with the Bible." And now, Matthews' patients hear more about the Bible. "When patients tell me they are Christians or that they are open about faith, I will ask if it's all right to share Bible verses with them. If they say yes, I pull out my Bible and read some passages to them. Sometimes I'll give Bible 'prescriptions'—assignments of Scripture for my patients to read on their own. We'll talk about how the Bible passages relate to their lives and their illnesses, and this seems to make a big difference to a lot of people."
- More than half of all medical schools in the United States now offer courses or forums on spirituality and health.
- A poll in 1997 said 63% of people want to talk to their doctors about faith, and 40% want their doctors to pray with them.

Date: _____   _____   _____
Place: _____   _____   _____
Occasion: _____   _____   _____

The Touch of the Master's Hand

One of the most famous musicians of the nineteenth-century was a self-taught Norwegian violinist named Ole Bull (1810–1880). He was a composer and artist of amazing skill who toured Europe and America with enormous success. During his lifetime, he was the world's most renowned violinist.

But he wasn't known by everyone. One day while traveling in the forests of Europe, he became lost and in the dark of night stumbled upon a log hut, the home of a hermit. The old man took him in, fed and warmed him, and after supper they sat in front of a blazing fireplace and the old hermit picked some crude tunes on his screechy, battered violin.

"Do you think I could play on that?" asked Ole Bull.

"I don't think so," replied the hermit. "It took me years to learn."

Ole Bull replied, "Let me try." Taking the old marred violin, he drew the bow across the strings and suddenly the hermit's hut was filled with music so beautiful the hermit sobbed like a child.

We are battered instruments; life's strings have been snapping; life's bow has been bent. Yet if we will only let Him take us and touch us, from this old battered, broken, shattered, marred instrument, He will bring forth music fit for the angels.[1]

Date: _____   _____   _____
Place: _____   _____   _____
Occasion: _____   _____   _____

—————————— **Heaven** ——————————

Someone Once Said . . .

- *If you read history you will find that the Christians who did most for the present world were precisely those who thought most of the next.*—C. S. Lewis[2]
- *Aim at Heaven and you will get earth "thrown in": aim at earth and you will get neither.*—C. S. Lewis[3]
- *Heaven is now nearer to me than Britain.*—Mary Slessor, pioneer missionary to Calabar, West Africa, upon hearing of the deaths of her mother and sister
- *Heaven: where questions and answers become one.*—Elie Wiesel

[1] Mrs. Charles E. Cowman, *Springs In the Valley* (Los Angeles: Cowman Publications, Inc., 1939), 238.
[2] C. S. Lewis, *Mere Christianity* (New York: The Macmillan Company, 1943), 104.
[3] Lewis, *Mere Christianity.* 104.

- *We can't travel over all of London in two weeks, nor explore Rome or Venice in a month. Nor do I believe we will see all of the great city of God in a day.*—T. DeWitt Talmage
- *Heaven does not float around. It is not made of air, thin air. It is real, a country, a clime.*—E. M. Bounds[1]
- *Earth is but a pilgrim's stay, a pilgrim's journey, a pilgrim's tent. Heaven is a city, permanent, God-planned, God-built, whose foundations are as stable as God's throne.*— E. M. Bounds[2]
- *Drawing near to the city, they had yet a more perfect view thereof. It was built of pearls and precious stones, also the streets thereof were paved with gold; so that, by reason of the natural glory of the city, and the reflection of the sunbeams upon it, Christian with desire fell sick; Hopeful also had a fit or two of the same disease.*—John Bunyan, in *Pilgrim's Progress*

Date: _____ _____ _____
Place: _____ _____ _____
Occasion: _____ _____ _____

More Insights

- *There is no more comparison to be made between heaven and earth than there is between a piece of rusty iron and refined gold.*—Rev. William Secker, seventeenth-century British minister
- C. S. Lewis wrote of his "inconsolable longing . . . for news from a country we have never visited."
- Malcolm Muggeridge, journalist and author, and at one time a strong atheist, said that from the time he was a boy, he had a sense of being a stranger in this world. He always felt there was a world beyond this to which he was moving.

Date: _____ _____ _____
Place: _____ _____ _____
Occasion: _____ _____ _____

The Neglected Subject

Philip Yancey, writing in *Christianity Today*, noted that although 71 percent of Americans believe in an afterlife, no one talks about it much. "Percentages don't apply to eternity, of course; but for the sake of argument, assume that 99 percent of our existence will take place in heaven. Isn't it a little bizarre that we simply ignore heaven, acting as if it doesn't matter?"

He points out that year after year, the *Reader's Guide to Periodical Literature* contains few if any articles devoted to the subject of heaven. There are many articles devoted

---

[1] Edward M. Bounds, *Heaven: A Place, A City, A Home* (Grand Rapids, MI: Baker Books House, 1975), 13.
[2] Bounds, *Heaven: A Place, A City, A Home*, 16.

to old age, death, and out-of-body experiences. But unlike previous eras, few books or magazine articles are appearing about heaven.

Why? Yancey suggests three reasons:

1. Affluence has given us in this life what former generations longed for in anticipation of heaven.
2. A creeping paganism invites us to accept death as the culmination of life on earth.
3. Older images of heaven, the biblical ones, have lost their appeal. Walls of emerald, sapphire, and jasper, streets of gold, and pearly gates may have inspired Middle Eastern peasants, but they don't mean much to the world of Bauhaus.

Yancey concludes, "To people who are trapped in pain, in economic chaos, in hatred and fear—to these, heaven offers a promise of a time, far longer and more substantial than this time on earth, of health and wholeness and pleasure and peace. If we do not believe that, then, as the apostle Paul noted, there is not much reason for being a Christian in the first place."[1]

Date:			
Place:			
Occasion:			

How Very Little Has Been Written

The great evangelical scholar Wilber M. Smith wrote that any careful student of Christian doctrine will soon discover "how very little has been written on the subject of heaven. . . . Almost all Systematic Theologies devote infinitely more space to Hell than Heaven as, for instance, Shedd, who assigns two pages in his *Dogmatic Theology* to Heaven, and eighty-seven pages to Eternal Punishment!"[2]

Date:			
Place:			
Occasion:			

From *Newsweek*

Newsweek devoted its March 17, 1989, issue to the subject "Heaven." Here are some fascinating excerpts:

- Easter is the one Sunday in the year when Christians can anticipate a sermon about life after death. But out of principle, many Christian clergy are loath to mention heaven—or, for that matter, hell. For some pastors, it's a question of rhetorical modesty: after centuries of cajoling listeners with overly graphic

---

[1] Philip Yancey, "Heaven Can't Wait," *Christianity Today,* September 7, 1984, 53.
[2] Wilber M. Smith, *Biblical Doctrine of Heaven* (Chicago: Moody Press, 1980), 11–12.

sermons on the pleasures of heaven and the horrors of hell, preachers today are hesitant to describe places that no one has actually seen. For others it's a matter of intellectual integrity. "The problem is that the [mainstream Protestant] clergy simply don't believe in an afterlife themselves, either the Biblical view or any view," says Douglas Stuart, an evangelical theologian at Gordon-Conwell Theological Seminary.

- While the pulpit may be full of agnostics, the pews are filled with believers. . . . In fact, public opinion polls show that most Americans not only believe in God but also anticipate some kind of heaven. According to a recent *Newsweek* poll, 94 percent of Americans believe that God exists and 77 percent believe in heaven. Among these believers, three out of four rate their chance of getting there *good* or *excellent.*
- Recent polling data suggest that "those who believe in life after death lead happier lives and trust people more."
- Meantime, observes American church historian Martin Marty, "Hell disappeared. And no one noticed." For liberal Protestants, hell began to fade in the nineteenth century along with Calvinism's stern and predestining God. . . . Today, hell is theology's H-word, a subject too trite for serious scholarship.
- At Harvard Divinity School, theologian Gordon Kaufman traces four centuries of decline in the concepts of heaven and hell; what is left is intellectually empty baggage. "It seems to me we've gone through irreversible changes," Kaufman declares. "I don't think there can be any future for heaven and hell."
- The studied evasions emanating from most American pulpits leave a real void for laymen seeking some assurance that being human has more than transitory significance. . . .
- In rejecting heaven and hell, the rationalistic modern consciousness also rejects the awesome seriousness of moral and immoral behavior.[1]

Date: _____   _____   _____

Place: _____   _____   _____

Occasion: _____   _____   _____

From *Time*

Time devoted its March 14, 1997, cover story to the subject, "Does Heaven Exist?" Some excerpts:

- It used to be that the hereafter was virtually palpable, but American religion now seems almost allergic to imagining it. Is paradise lost?
- In a curious way, heaven is AWOL. This is not to say that Americans think death ends everything or even that they doubt heaven's existence. People still believe in it: it's just that their concept of exactly what it is has grown foggier, and they hear about it much less frequently from their pastors.
- David Wells, a theology professor at Massachusetts' Gordon-Conwell Theological Seminary, notes, "We would expect to hear of [heaven] in the Evangeli-

[1] Kenneth L. Woodward, "Heaven," *Newsweek,* March 27, 1989, 52–53.

cal churches, but I don't hear it at all. I don't think heaven is even a blip on the Christian screen, from one end of the denominational spectrum to the other."

- Rev. J. Philip Wogaman, whose Foundry Methodist Church is up the street from the White House, explains bluntly, "I'm not interested in speculating on the architecture or the geography. I don't think of heaven as a specified place in the universe to which we could somehow go if we could find the right galaxy. . . . I preach on trust in God."
- In the more liberal congregations, heaven is found mostly in hymns, preserved like a bug in amber.[1]

Date: _____ _____ _____

Place: _____ _____ _____

Occasion: _____ _____ _____

Polling Data

A telephone poll of 1,018 American adults, conducted the week of March 11–12 by Time/CNN and Yankelovich Partners, Inc., asked these questions:

- Do you believe in the existence of heaven, where people live forever with God after they die?
    Yes: 81%
    No: 13%
- Do you believe in hell, where people are punished forever after they die?
    Yes: 63%
    No: 30%
- Do people get into heaven based mostly on the good things they do or on their faith in God, or both (asked of 809 who believe in heaven):
    Good things they do: 6%
    Faith in God: 34%
    Both: 57%
- Immediately after death, which of the following do you think will happen to you? (asked of 809 who believe in heaven):
    Go directly to heaven: 61%
    Go to purgatory: 15%
    Go to hell: 1%
    Be reincarnated: 5%
    End of existence: 4%
- Which of the following do you believe are in heaven? (asked of 809 who believe in heaven):
    Angels: 93%
    St. Peter: 79%
    Harps: 43%
    Halos: 36%

[1] David Van Biema, "Does Heaven Exist?" *Time*, March 24, 1997, 70–78.

- Does only a person's soul live in heaven, or does a person have both a soul and body? (asked of 809 who believe in heaven):
    Only soul: 66%
    Body and soul: 26%
- Do you believe you will meet friends and family members in heaven when you die? (asked of 809 who believe in heaven):
    Yes: 88%
    No: 5%[1]

Date: _____ _____ _____
Place: _____ _____ _____
Occasion: _____ _____ _____

Just Passing Through

An American tourist visited the nineteenth-century Polish rabbi, Hofetz Chaim. Astonished to see that the rabbi's home was only a simple room filled with books, plus a table and a bench, the tourist asked, "Rabbi, where is your furniture?"

"Where is yours?" replied the rabbi.

"Mine?" asked the puzzled American. "But I'm a visitor here. I'm only passing through."

"So am I," said Hofetz Chaim.[2]

Date: _____ _____ _____
Place: _____ _____ _____
Occasion: _____ _____ _____

Home Before Dark

Vance Havner once painted a powerful picture of heaven with these words:

"When I started out as a boy preaching, Father went along. Then when I got old enough to go by myself, he'd meet me at the little railroad station in Newton, North Carolina. I can see him standing there by that old Ford roadster, in that old blue serge suit that hadn't been pressed since the day he bought it.

"When I'd go up to him, the first thing he'd asked me would be, 'How did you get along?'

"It's been a long time, and one of these days when my train rounds into Grand Central Station in glory, I think he'll be there—not in the old blue serge suit, but in the robes of glory. I wouldn't be surprised if the first thing he'd say would be, 'How did you get along?'

"I think I'll say, 'Pretty well, and I owe a lot to you for it.' Then I think I'd say, 'You remember back in the country when I was a little boy, no matter where I was

[1] David Van Biema, "Does Heaven Exist?" *Time,* March 24, 1997, 70–78.
[2] Clipping in my files.

in the afternoon I was supposed to be back by sundown. It's been a long trip, Dad, but here I am by the grace of God, home before dark.'"[1]

Date:			
Place:			
Occasion:			

Two Men

Two men were dying across town from one another. One was a very wealthy man who had amassed and enjoyed a fortune. His Victorian house was lavishly furnished with antiques and expensive paintings. A stylish car sat outside the door, and a boat was on the nearby lake. The second man had never flourished financially, but he had loved the Lord and worked faithfully in the village church.

The first, as he died, moaned, "I'm leaving home. . . . I'm leaving home."

The second died with a glow on his face, saying, "I'm going home. I'm going home."

Date:			
Place:			
Occasion:			

Shall We Gather at the River?

Rev. Robert Lowry, thirty-eight, ministered in New York City during that terrible period in 1864 when the plague was sweeping away multitudes of citizens. When he wasn't visiting sick members of his Hanson Place Baptist Church, he was conducting funerals. One hot July day, Lowry himself was near collapse, exhausted, dispirited. Reaching for a scrap of paper, he began composing a poem; then, at his organ, he composed the music for it. It spoke of his hope to meet his suffering and dying parishioners in heaven, down by the River of Life.

> *Shall we gather at the river,*
> *Where bright angel feet have trod?*
> *With its crystal tide forever*
> *Flowing by the throne of God?*
>
> *Yes, we'll gather at the river,*
> *The beautiful, the beautiful river;*
> *Gather with the saints at the river*
> *That flows by the throne of God.*

Date:			
Place:			
Occasion:			

[1] *Christianity Today*, November 7, 1986, 45.

Walls and Domes and Spires

In his book on Heaven, evangelist D. L. Moody quotes "an eminent living divine" as saying: "When I was a boy, I thought of heaven as a great, shining city, with vast walls and domes and spires, and with nobody in it except white-robed angels, who were strangers to me. By and by my little brother died, and I thought of a great city with walls and domes and spires, and one little fellow that I was acquainted with. He was the only one I knew at that time. Then another brother died, and there were two that I knew. Then my acquaintances began to die, and the flock continually grew. But it was not till I had sent one of my little children to his Heavenly Parent—God—that I began to think I had a little in myself. A second went; a third went; a fourth went, and by that time I had so many acquaintances in heaven, that I did not see any more walls and domes and spires. I began to think of the residents of the celestial city as my friends. And now so many of my acquaintances have gone there, that it sometimes seems to me that I know more people in heaven than I do on earth."[1]

Date: _____ _____ _____

Place: _____ _____ _____

Occasion: _____ _____ _____

The Hope of Dying

Every winter, just when it seems the deep freeze is here to stay, the garden catalogs begin arriving, and those of us with green thumbs enjoy every page of them. We study the rose catalogs and make lists of new roses we'd like to try, and new varieties of vegetables, new floral introductions. And sure enough, the Spring-time comes, the rose bushes arrive, the soil warms up, and all of creation comes back to life. It's the anticipation of the Springtime that gets us through the winter. And it's the anticipation of Heaven that moves us victoriously through the overcast days and years on earth. Poet John Oxenham, wrote:

> *Wish me "Bon Voyage!"*
> *As you do a friend*
> *Whose joyous visit finds its happy end.*
> *And bid me both "a Dieu!"*
> *And "au revoir!"*
> *Since, though I come no more,*
> *I shall be waiting there to greet you,*
> *At His door.*

Date: _____ _____ _____

Place: _____ _____ _____

Occasion: _____ _____ _____

[1]D. L. Moody, *Heaven* (Chicago: Moody Press, n.d.), 32.

My Father's House

Among America's greatest orators was John Jasper, a former slave, who once began a funeral sermon, saying, *Let me say a word about this William Ellyson. I say it the first and get it off my mind. Ellyson was no good man—didn't say he was; didn't try to be good, and they tell me he died as he lived, without God and without hope in the world. It's a bad tale to tell on him, but he fixed the story hisself.*

Faithful Souls

Little faith will bring your soul to heaven; great faith will bring heaven to your soul.

—ANONYMOUS

Jasper then shifted gears and took his audience on a breath-taking tour of heaven. *I loves to go down to the old muddy James, mighty red and muddy, but it goes along so grand and quiet like it was tending to business. But that ain't nothing to the river which flows by the throne. I longs for its crystal waves, and the trees on the banks, and all manners of fruits. This old head of mine often gets hot with fever and rolls on the pillow, and I has many times desired to cool it in that blessed stream as it kisses the banks of that upper Canaan. The thought of seeing that river, drinking its water and resting under those trees . . . Oh, to be there!*

After that, I'd stroll up them avenues where the children of God dwell, and view their mansions. Father Abraham, I'm sure he got a great palace. And David. And Paul, the mighty scholar who got struck down in the Damascus Road, I want to see his mansion. Then I cut round to the back streets and looks for the little home where my Savior set my mother up to housekeeping. I expect to know the house by the roses in the yard and the vine on the porch.

At that point, Jasper dramatically sprang back, clapped his hands, and shouted, *Look there! See that one! Hallelujah, it's John Jasper's. Said He was going to prepare a place for me. There it is! Too good for a poor sinner like me, but He built it for me, a turn-key job, and mine forever!*

Jasper waxed on like this for an hour and a half, but to the listeners it seemed like only a moment. That day, they glimpsed glory.[1]

Date:			
Place:			
Occasion:			

"And I Shall See"

The famous blind hymnist Fanny Crosby attended a mid-week prayer meeting service in 1891 at which Dr. Howard Crosby spoke from the Twenty-third Psalm. Later that week, Fanny was stunned when Dr. Crosby suddenly died. Pondering the suddenness of death, she asked herself, "I wonder what my first impression of heaven will be." A moment later she answered her own question with sudden insight: "Why, my eyes will be opened and I will see my Savior face to face." A few days later, she wrote one of her most famous hymns:

> *Some day the silver cord will break,*
> *And I no more as now shall sing;*
> *But oh, the joy when I shall wake*
> *Within the palace of the King!*

---

[1]Robert J. Morgan, *From This Verse* (Nashville: Thomas Nelson Publishers, 1998), September 15th.

And I shall see Him face to face,
And tell the story—Saved by grace;
And I shall see Him face to face,
And tell the story—Saved by grace.

Date: _____ _____ _____
Place: _____ _____ _____
Occasion: _____ _____ _____

The Saint's Everlasting Rest

The greatest treatment on Heaven to ever appear, according to scholar Wilber M. Smith, is Richard Baxter's *The Saint's Everlasting Rest,* published in 1649. Baxter, the great English Puritan, was frail of body, and at age thirty-five suffered a total collapse. Expecting to die and wanting to prepare himself for leaving the world, he began to meditate on heaven and on heaven's joys. He wrote out his thoughts for his own benefit, and after his recovery those notes became the basis for his massive *Saint's Everlasting Rest.* He suggested his readers follow his example of meditating on heaven for a half-hour each day. "For want of this recourse to heaven," he wrote, "thy soul is as a lamp not lighted."

Baxter wrote that God could have withheld information from us about heaven, the New Jerusalem, and eternal life. But He didn't. The Bible is filled with information about the saints' everlasting rest. This, then, should color the way we view everything in life.

Baxter wrote: "It hath pleased our Father to open his counsel, and to let us know the very intent of his heart, and to acquaint us with the eternal extent of his love; and all this that our joy may be full, and we might live as the heirs of such a kingdom. And shall we now overlook all, as if he had revealed no such matter? Shall we live in earthly cares and sorrows, as if we knew of no such thing? And rejoice no more in these discoveries, than if the Lord had never written it? O that our hearts were as high as our hopes, and our hopes as high as these infallible promises!"

Date: _____ _____ _____
Place: _____ _____ _____
Occasion: _____ _____ _____

What Will We Be Doing in Eternity?

In his book on Heaven, Wilber Smith suggests that the Bible gives us five different occupations that will engage believers throughout eternity.

1. Worship. The book of Revelation contains more songs than any other in the Bible, with the exception, of course, of the Psalter—fourteen of them, all sung by groups appearing in heaven.

2. Service. One of the most significant statements regarding the activity of the redeemed in glory is the short but pregnant sentence, "His servants shall service him" (Revelation 22:3).
3. Authority. In two of His eschatological parables, our Lord speaks of assigning certain authority to His faithful servants upon His return (Luke 19, Matthew 25; also see Revelation 19:8, 11–16 and Matthew 19:28).
4. Fellowship. Many passages in the New Testament speak of the ultimate fellowship that all believers will have in glory (for example, Hebrews 12:23; Revelation 19:19).
5. Learning. None other than Sir William Robertson Nicoll, along with others, has frankly confessed his own conviction regarding Christ being our great Instructor in heaven: "May we not suppose that He teaches the redeemed to love God as they have never loved Him before?"
6. Resting.[1]

Date: _____ _____ _____
Place: _____ _____ _____
Occasion: _____ _____ _____

C. S. Lewis on the Reasonableness of Heaven

Discussing heaven and hope in his book *Mere Christianity*, C. S. Lewis wrote, "Creatures are not born with desire unless satisfaction for those desires exists. A baby feels hunger: well, there is such a thing as food. A duckling wants to swim: well, there is such a thing as water. Men feel sexual desire: well, there is such a thing as sex. If I find myself a desire which no experience in this world can satisfy, the most probable explanation is that I was made for another world. If none of my earthly pleasures satisfy it, that does not prove that the universe is a fraud. Probably earthly pleasures were never meant to satisfy it, but only to arouse it, to suggest the real thing. If that is so, I must take care, on the one hand, never to despise, or be unthankful for, these earthly blessings, and on the other, never to mistake them for the something else of which they are only a kind of copy, or echo, or mirage. I must keep alive in myself the desire for my true country, which I shall not find till after death; I must never let it get snowed under or turned aside; I must make it the main object of life to press on to that other country and to help others to do the same."[2]

Date: _____ _____ _____
Place: _____ _____ _____
Occasion: _____ _____ _____

Will We Know Each Other?

John Evans, the great Scottish minister, was seated in his study. His wife came in and said, "My dear, do you think we will know each other in heaven?" He turned

[1] Wilber M. Smith, *Biblical Doctrine of Heaven* (Chicago: Moody Press, 1980), Ch. 11.
[2] Lewis, *Mere Christianity*, 106.

to her and said, "My dear, do you think we will be bigger fools in heaven than we are here?"[1]

Date:			
Place:			
Occasion:			

Where Has He Gone?

The stunning news flew like arrows through the corridors and chambers of the palace: The king was dead. He had been found in his bed, having died a natural death in his sleep.

"Where has he gone?" asked one of the king's shrewdest advisors.

"Why, to heaven!" replied the others.

"No," said the one gravely. "I served this king for many years and traveled with him extensively. He loved to travel, and would talk about his trips extensively beforehand. Every detail was planned and anticipated. But I have never heard him say a word about traveling to heaven. It was a journey for which I saw no preparation. I am quite sure that he has not gone to heaven."

Date:			
Place:			
Occasion:			

Too Much Oat Bran

Two Christians lived very healthy lives. When they died, they went to heaven. As they walked along, marveling at the paradise around them, one of the men turned to the other and said, "Wow. I never imagined heaven was would be good as *this!*"

"Yeah," agreed the other. "And just think, if we hadn't eaten all that oat bran we could have gotten here ten years sooner."

Date:			
Place:			
Occasion:			

The Happy Ending

Young Jonathan had been promised a new puppy for his tenth birthday, but had a tough time choosing between a dozen likely candidates at the neighborhood pet shop. Finally he decided upon one nondescript shaggy pup who was wagging his tail furiously.

Why that one? Jonathan explained: "I want the one with the happy ending."[2]

---

[1] Robert G. Lee, *Heart to Heart* (Nashville: Broadman Press, 1977), 107.
[2] Clipping in my files.

Date: _____ _____ _____
Place: _____ _____ _____
Occasion: _____ _____ _____

Pavement

Once upon a time, there was a man who spent half of his life getting rich. Hearing he could take none of it into heaven, he was greatly distressed. The man pleaded in many prayers that God would make an exception.

Finally God said to the man, "Look, whatever you can fit into a black garbage sack you can bring into heaven."

The man joyfully spent the second half of his life accumulating gold, then he died. As he approached the pearly gates dragging his garbage sack, two angels stopped him. "Excuse me sir," said one angel, clearing his throat. "Nobody's allowed to bring anything into heaven."

The man straightened up and proudly announced, "I have received special permission from God to do so."

The angels, being surprised, inquired of St. Peter who said, "Yes, God has okayed this sack."

The angels were understandably very curious as to what could be so important. "Excuse me, sir," said one. "Could we see what you brought?"

The man nodded and opened his sack. Both angels peeked down into the bag, but quickly looked up with expressions of bewilderment as if they'd just seen the most preposterous thing.

Then one of them sputtered: "Pavement!"

Date: _____ _____ _____
Place: _____ _____ _____
Occasion: _____ _____ _____

When Did This Happen?

Fred arrived at the Pearly Gates ready for his interview with St. Peter. As Pete ran down the questions on his clipboard, he came to this one: "Can you share any experience in your life on earth when you did anything that was purely unselfish?"

Fred answered quickly. "Yes, I have something you might be interested in. One day I was walking along when I saw a little old lady being attacked by a group of motorcycle thugs. I ran toward her and jerked her from the grasp of a huge, burly, bearded brute. Then I kicked over his Harley to distract him while I hustled her into the arms of another passerby for safety. Then I turned back to the gang and started fighting the whole bunch of them, tooth and nail. I got in some terrific punches. I kicked the ringleader in the shins and gave another a great shot right in the gut with my fist."

St. Peter was impressed. "Tell me," he asked, "when did this happen?"

Fred looked at his watch. "Oh, about two minutes ago."

Date:			
Place:			
Occasion:			

Children's Ideas of Heaven

How do children picture heaven? Here are some contributions as given in the *Pastor's Story File:*

- It is a place where there is a lot of money lying around. You could just pick it up, play with it, and buy things. I think I am going to buy a basketball, and I am going to play basketball with my great-great grandmother.—Eric, age eight
- Heaven is up in the sky, and you could look down at circuses for free if you want to, except you have to ask God for permission first.—Scott
- Heaven is kind of big and they sit around playing harps. I don't know how to play a harp, but I suppose I should learn how to play that dumb thing pretty soon.—David, age seven
- I know what heaven is, but I don't want to go there. I want to go to North Carolina instead.—Tommy, age seven[1]

Date:			
Place:			
Occasion:			

Hell

Someone Once Said . . .

- *There is no doctrine which I would more willingly remove from Christianity than this (hell) if it lay in my power. But it has the full support of Scripture and, especially, of our Lord's own words; it has always been held by Christendom, and has the support of reason.*—C. S. Lewis[2]
- *Wisdom directs us to admit that there is no biblical alternative to the biblical doctrine of eternal punishment; to settle in our minds that Jesus, chief exponent of the doctrine, surely knew what he was talking about, and never to forget or conceal the inevitability of hell for those who will not lay hold of eternal life.*—J. I. Packer[3]
- *As the Lord liveth, sinner, thou standest on a single plank over the mouth of hell, and that plank is rotten. Thou hangest over the pit by a solitary rope, and the strands of that rope are breaking.*—Charles Spurgeon[4]

---

[1] Rick Gabelman, "The Shepherd's Voice," *The Pastor's Story File,* February, 1987.
[2] Kenneth S. Kantzer, *Christianity Today,* February 21, 1986, 12.
[3] J. I. Packer, "Is Hell Out of Vogue?" *Action,* September–October 1989, 11.
[4] Charles Haddon Spurgeon, *Spurgeon's Sermons,* vol. 1 (Grand Rapids, MI: Baker Book House, 1983), 294.

- *If once you fall into hell, after millions of ages are elapsed, you will be as far from coming out as you were at going in.*—Rev. William Secker[1]
- *That which makes hell so full of horror, is that it is below all hopes; and that which makes heaven so full of splendor is that it is above all fears.*—Rev. William Secker, seventeenth-century British minister
- *A hard look at this doctrine should first change our view of sin. Most believers do not take sin as seriously as God does.*—John Thomas[2]
- *As hell was becoming for many no more than a swear word, sin was also an accepted way of life. . . . If people can ignore what the Bible calls sin, then they can quite logically discount what it says about the reality of hell.*—Billy Graham
- *The last sermon on hell I heard I preached myself. And that was nearly thirty years ago.*—Kenneth S. Kantzer[3]
- *My congregation would be stunned to hear a sermon on hell.*—Rev. Mary Kraus, pastor of Dumbarton United Methodist Church in Washington, D.C.[4]
- *We cannot, of course, form any adequate notion of hell, any more than we can of heaven, and no doubt it is good for us that this is so; but perhaps the clearest notion we can form is that derived from contemplating the cross.*—J. I. Packer[5]

Date: _____ _____ _____

Place: _____ _____ _____

Occasion: _____ _____ _____

From *Newsweek*

Newsweek devoted its March 27, 1989 issue to the subject of Heaven. In the process, the writer, Kenneth L. Woodward, also made some interesting comments about hell:

- American church historian Martin Marty [observes], "Hell disappeared. And no one noticed." For liberal Protestants, hell began to fade in the nineteenth century along with Calvinism's stern and predestining God. . . . Today, hell is theology's H-word, a subject too trite for serious scholarship.
- At Harvard Divinity School, theologian Gordon Kaufman traces four centuries of decline in the concepts of heaven and hell; what is left is intellectually empty baggage. "It seems to me we've gone through irreversible changes," Kaufman declares. "I don't think there can be any future for heaven and hell."
- The studied evasions emanating from most American pulpits leave a real void for laymen seeking some assurance that being human has more than transitory significance. . . .
- In rejecting heaven and hell, the rationalistic modern consciousness also rejects the awesome seriousness of moral and immoral behavior.[6]

[1] William Secker, *The Nonsuch Professor In His Meridian Splendor* (Chicago: Fleming H. Revell Co., 1899), 231.
[2] John Thomas, "That Hideous Doctrine," *Moody Magazine*, September 1985, 92.
[3] Kenneth S. Kantzer, "Do You Believe in Hell?" *Christianity Today*, February 21, 1986, 12.
[4] *U. S. News and World Report*, March 25, 1991, 60.
[5] J. I. Packer, *Knowing God* (Downers Grove, IL: InterVarsity, 1973), 175–176.
[6] Kenneth L. Woodward, "Heaven," *Newsweek*, March 27, 1989, 52–53.

From *U.S. News and World Report*

The magazine *U.S. News and World Report* devoted its March 25, 1991, cover story to the subject, "Hell's Sober Comeback." Here are some interesting excerpts:

- Hell is every believer's worst nightmare. And its presence is being felt more acutely today than it has in decades.
- For much of the twentieth century, hell didn't fare well. Attacked by modern intellectualism and paled by the flames of Hiroshima and the Holocaust, hell's frightful imagery lost much of its fury. By most accounts, it has all but disappeared from the pulpit rhetoric of mainline Protestantism. And it has fared only marginally better among evangelicals.
- A recent Gallup Poll showed more Americans believe in hell today than did in the generally more wholesome and pious 1950s.[1]

The Gallup Poll for *U.S. News and World Report*

- Percentage of Americans who say they believe in—

	Heaven	Hell
1990	78%	60%
1981	71%	53%
1965	68%	54%
1952	72%	58%

- Chances in heaven and hell: Excellent or good chance of going to—
  Heaven: 78%
  Hell: 4%[2]

Plain Words

"There are some ministers who never mention anything about hell. I heard of a minister who once said to his congregation, 'If you do not love the Lord Jesus Christ,

---

[1] "Hell's Sober Comeback," *U.S. News and World Report,* 56.
[2] "Hell's Sober Comeback," *U.S. News and World Report,* 57.

you will be sent to that place which it is not polite to mention.' He ought not to have been allowed to preach again, I am sure, if he could not use plain words. Now, if I saw that house on fire over there, do you think I would stand and say, 'I believe the operation of combustion is proceeding yonder?' No; I would call out, 'Fire! Fire!' and then everybody would know what I meant."—Charles Haddon Spurgeon[1]

Date: _____ _____ _____
Place: _____ _____ _____
Occasion: _____ _____ _____

Did You Mean Hell?

C. S. Lewis once went to hear a young parson deliver a sermon. Very much in earnest, the young man ended his message like this: "And now, my friends, if you do not believe these truths, there may be for you grave eschatological consequences."

Lewis later visited the young minister and asked him, "Did you mean that they would be in danger of hell?"

"Why, yes," said the parson.

"Then why in the world didn't you say so?" Lewis replied.[2]

Date: _____ _____ _____
Place: _____ _____ _____
Occasion: _____ _____ _____

That's Where I Got My Information

When North Carolina evangelist Vance Havner was beginning his ministry, he pastored a country church where a farmer didn't like the sermons he preached on hell. The man said, "Preach about the meek and lowly Jesus."

"That's where I got my information about hell," replied Havner.[3]

Date: _____ _____ _____
Place: _____ _____ _____
Occasion: _____ _____ _____

What Is Hell Like?

Several years ago, writer John Thomas wrote an article in *Moody* magazine in which he fleshed out the picture behind the New Testament words describing hell as a bottomless pit of pain, weeping, wailing, gnashing of teeth, and endless darkness:

[1] Charles Haddon Spurgeon, *Spurgeon's Sermons,* vol. 1 (Grand Rapids, MI: Baker Book House, 1983), 309.
[2] Frank E. Gaebelein, "The Bible: Both the Source and Setting for Learning," *Christianity Today,* February 6, 1981, 23.
[3] Vance Havner, *Just a Preacher* (Chicago: Moody Press, 1981), 26.

Imagine the person who just entered hell—a neighbor, relative, co-worker, friend. After a roar of physical pain blasts him, he spends his first moments wailing and gnashing his teeth. But after a season, he grows accustomed to the pain, not that it's become tolerable, but that his capacity for it has enlarged to comprehend it. Though he hurts, he is now able to think, and he instinctively looks about him. But as he looks, he sees only blackness.

In his past life he learned that if he looked long enough, a glow of light somewhere would yield definition to his surroundings. So he blinks and strains to focus his eyes, but his efforts yield only blackness. He turns and strains his eyes in another direction. He waits. He sees nothing but unyielding black ink. It clings to him, smothering and oppressing him.

Realizing that the darkness is not going to give way, he nervously begins to feel for something solid to get his bearings. He reaches for walls or rocks or trees or chairs; he stretches his legs to feel the ground and touches nothing.

Hell is a bottomless pit; however, the new occupant is slow to learn. In growing panic, he kicks his feet and waves his arms. He stretches and he lunges. But he finds nothing. After more feverish tries, he pauses from exhaustion, suspended in black. Suddenly, with a scream he kicks, twists, and lunges until he is again too exhausted to move.

He hangs there, alone in his pain. Unable to touch a solid object or see a solitary thing, he begins to weep.

His sobs choke through the darkness. They become weak, then lost in hell's roar.

As time passes, he begins to do what the rich man did—he again starts to think. His first thoughts are of hope. You see, he still thinks as he did on earth, where he kept himself alive with hope. When things got bad, he always found a way out. If he felt pain, he took medicine. If he was hungry, he ate food.

. . . [But] the awful truth spreads before him like endless, overlapping slats: "When I put in ten thousand centuries of time here, I will not have accomplished one thing. I will not have one second less to spend here.

The smoke of [his] torment goes up forever and ever . . .[1]

Ignoring Sin

If people can ignore what the Bible calls sin, then they can quite logically discount what it says about the reality of hell.
—BILLY GRAHAM

Date: _____ _____ _____

Place: _____ _____ _____

Occasion: _____ _____ _____

To Hell and Back

Dr. Maurice Rawlings, M.D., cardiologist and professor of medicine at the University of Tennessee College of Medicine in Chattanooga, was a devout atheist who considered all religion "hocus-pocus." To him, death was nothing more than a painless extinction.

But in 1977, Rawlings was resuscitating a man who came back from the edge of death. The man was terrified and screaming. Rawlings wrote: *Each time he regained heartbeat and respiration, the patient screamed, "I am in hell!" He was terrified and pleaded*

---

[1] John Thomas, "That Hideous Doctrine," *Moody*, September 1985, 91–92.

with me to help him. I was scared to death. . . . Then I noticed a genuinely alarmed look on his face. He had a terrified look worse than the expression seen in death! This patient had a grotesque grimace expressing sheer horror! His pupils were dilated, and he was perspiring and trembling— he looked as if his hair was on end.[1]

There are many stories of near-death experiences in which people report moving down a peaceful tunnel toward a gentle light, but Dr. Rawlings' research, which appeared in *Omni* magazine, demonstrated that about 50 percent of near-death victims report seeing lakes of fire, devil-like figures, and other sights reflecting the darkness of hell.

"Just listening to these patients has changed my whole life," claims Dr. Rawlings. "There is a life after death, and if I don't know where I'm going, it's not safe to die." Through these experiences, Dr. Rawlings began studying what the Bible had to say about hell and other subjects, and he became a Christian. Two of his books are: *Beyond Death's Door* and *To Hell and Back.*

Date: _____ _____ _____
Place: _____ _____ _____
Occasion: _____ _____ _____

A Picture of Hell

Carl Steinman was fascinated by volcanoes, and, going against the advice of his guide, he ventured to the edge of an active volcano while visiting Mount Hecla, Iceland. The volcano was showing every sign of erupting, and as Steinman leaned over the edge, the earth grumbled and quaked, throwing him forward. He fell into the crater, his feet lodging themselves in blocks of lava; and there he hung, suspended over the yawning gulf. He later wrote:

"Oh, the horrors of that awful realization! There, over the mouth of a black and heated abyss, I was held suspended, a helpless and conscious prisoner, to be hurled downward by the next great throe of trembling nature!

"'Help! Help! Help!—for the love of God, help!' I shrieked, in the very agony of my despair.

"I had nothing to rely upon but the mercy of heaven, and I prayed to God as I had never prayed before, for the forgiveness of sins, that they might not follow me to judgment." More tremors sent rocks tumbling down the sides of the crater and rolling into the caldron below. But Steinman's terrified pleas were answered by his guide, who, risking his life, scrambled to rescue him, shouting, "I warned you!"

"You did," cried Steinman, "but forgive me, and save me, for I am perishing!"[2]

Date: _____ _____ _____
Place: _____ _____ _____
Occasion: _____ _____ _____

---

[1] Maurice Rawlings, *Beyond Death's Door* (Nashville: Thomas Nelson Publishers, 1979), 3.
[2] D. L. Moody, *Prevailing Prayer* (Chicago: Moody Press, n.d.), 81.

The Lowin', Bleezin' Fire

Most of us would recoil at frightening children into receiving Jesus Christ by threatening them with hell. But listen to this account of the conversion of the great pioneer missionary, Mary Slessor, in her biography, *The Missionary Heroine of Calabar* by Esther E. Enock:

She was born in Aberdeen, on December 2, 1848. When first she came to Dundee with her parents and brothers and sisters, she was, as she says, "a wild lassie," and ran about the streets with other children as wild as herself.

An old widow who used to watch these children and felt concern for their souls would often call them into her room and tell them of their need of salvation.

One dark winter afternoon she had gathered them round her fire, and suddenly, with that fire for her text, she showed the children in a few forcible words what is the fate of those who reject God's offer of salvation in the Lord Jesus Christ.

"If ye dinna repent, and believe on the Lord Jesus Christ, your soul will burn in the lowin', bleezin' fire for ever and ever," she said.

No paring down of the awful truth of eternal punishment here, no shaping it to please our weak, shrinking, easy-going nature. These children, young as they were, were in need of salvation; they were in danger of eternal destruction through neglect of it, and warn them she must, and did.

Dear, faithful old woman, what a wonderful thing she did for Africa when she spoke those words. Mary Slessor was then and there convinced of her need, and in a little while was rejoicing in the fact that she was saved. "For God so loved the world that He gave His only begotten Son, that whosoever believeth in Him should not perish, but have eternal life."

Henceforth, she lived not unto herself, but unto Him who died for her and rose again.[1]

Date: _____ _____ _____

Place: _____ _____ _____

Occasion: _____ _____ _____

You Don't Have to Go

One day when Vice President Calvin Coolidge was presiding over the Senate, one senator angrily told another to go "straight to hell." The offended senator complained to Coolidge as presiding officer. The vice president looked up from a book he had been leafing through while listening to the debate. "I've been looking through the rule book," he said. "You don't have to go."

Date: _____ _____ _____

Place: _____ _____ _____

Occasion: _____ _____ _____

[1] Esther E. Enock, *The Missionary Heroine of Calabar* (Fort Washington, PA: Christian Literature Crusade, 1937), 8.

History, Value of

Someone Once Said . . .

- *The longer you look back, the farther you can look forward.*—Winston Churchill[1]
- *If we don't know our own history, we will simply have to endure all the same mistakes, sacrifices, and absurdities all over again.*—Aleksandr Solzhenitsyn
- *Those who cannot remember the past are condemned to repeat it.*—George Santayana, philosopher
- *To be ignorant of what happened before you were born is to remain a child forever.*—Cicero
- *It is not the remembered but the forgotten past that enslaves us.*—C. S. Lewis
- *How shall we labor with any effect to build up the church if we have no thorough knowledge of her history? History is, and must ever continue to be, next to God's word, the richest foundation of wisdom, and the surest guide to all successful practical activity.*—Philip Schaff
- *As a rule, history seems to repeat itself and the experience of the past is a valuable support to reason.*—Quintilian
- *Histories are a true school for learning how to order our lives.*—John Calvin[2]
- *History is a vast early warning system.*—Norman Cousins
- *The past is prologue.*

Date:	_____	_____	_____
Place:	_____	_____	_____
Occasion:	_____	_____	_____

Lost Heritage

The October 22, 1996, headlines of the *London Times* cried: *Lost Forever: A Nation's Heritage Looted By Its Own People.* "Afghanistan's National Museum in Kabul is rubble," said the newspaper. "It once held one of earth's greatest multicultural antique collections: Persian, Indian, Chinese, Central Asian, and beyond. But Mujahidin rebels blasted into vaults and shattered display cases, looted the relics, and sold them here and there around the world for quick cash. Rockets slammed into the museum's roof, burying ancient bronzes under tons of debris. Pottery from prehistory was thrown into bags like cheap china. The Bagram collection, one of the greatest archaeological finds of the twentieth century, disappeared. Nearly forty thousand coins, some of the world's oldest, vanished. The museum, once a repository for Afghan history, became a military post, and the storied past has now been ruined by the unbridled present. A nation has lost its history. With no history, there is no heritage. And with no heritage from the past there is no legacy for the future."

---

[1] William Manchester, *The Last Lion: Winston Spencer Churchill: Visions of Glory* (Boston: Little, Brown, & Co., 1983), 12.

[2] William J. Bouwsma, *John Calvin: A Sixteenth-Century Portrait* (New York: Oxford University Press, 1988), 90.

The same could happen to the church of Jesus Christ. Contemporary Christianity is interested in recent trends, current challenges, and modern methods. So am I. But nothing braces me to face these days like visiting the cloud of witnesses that comprise church history.[1]

Date:			
Place:			
Occasion:			

Heritage Stew

There is a story about the French farmers who were nearly starving early in the 1800s. They were kept alive by what came to be called "The One Hundred Year Old Soup." Each week, to a pot which always simmered on the back of the kitchen stove, the farmer's wife would add whatever was available: sometimes it would be a carrot, sometimes an onion, sometimes no more than dandelions. But each week something would be added with a little more water. The soup never stopped simmering. It was always there.

When the oldest daughter left to set up housekeeping, included in her dowry was a little pot of that soup, taken from the back of the stove and shared. When French immigrants arrived on these shores, those from the southeast rural area of France carried their little pot of "one hundred year old soup." Some soup eaten today in South Carolina among those of French descent derives from that one hundred year old soup.

The church of Jesus Christ has been boiling for two thousand years. Many ingredients have been added and many people have been fed. It is ever old, yet ever new. It is a constant, life-giving gift from those generations that have preceded us, but it needs constant replenishing that those who follow may also be fed.[2]

Date:			
Place:			
Occasion:			

Remember

Haddon Robinson, observing that the Old and New Testaments were full of history and peppered with the word "remember," wrote: "Unfortunately, many of us ignore history. We have not read the minutes of the previous meetings. Graham Wallas, in *Our Social Heritage,* imagines what would happen if every human being instantly lost all knowledge and all habits acquired from previous generations and, at the same time, retained every power of the mind except memory. The result would wipe out civilization and culture and threaten the annihilation of the human race."

Robinson goes on to quote Hendrik Rookmaaker, the Christian art critic, who warned his students: "You cannot begin as though there was nothing before you.

---

[1] Robert J. Morgan, *On This Day* (Nashville: Thomas Nelson Publishers, 1997).
[2] Jack E. Snider, Executive Vice President of King College, Bristol, Tennessee.

There have been many who have struggled before you. Learn from them; be humble. You stand on the shoulders of those others, and you can maybe take their ideas a little further; that is all. Then one day, someone will go beyond you; only be sure that you take your ideas and your work deeper into the Christian way of seeing reality."[1]

Date:			
Place:			
Occasion:			

Holy Spirit

Someone Once Said . . .

- *To be filled with the Holy Spirit is to be filled with Christ. The Holy Spirit came to glorify Christ. Therefore, if I am filled with the Spirit, I am abiding in Christ. . . . And if I am controlled and empowered by Christ, He will be walking around in my body, living His resurrection life in and through me.*—Bill Bright[2]
- *The ministry of the Spirit is Christo-centric. The test of any professed movement of the Spirit whether in personal or corporate experience is the place it gives to Christ.*—J. Oswald Sanders[3]
- *Think of God in His foraging, invading, energizing, vitalizing, renewing, enlightening, convicting, and strengthening aspects, and we shall come somewhere near the Holy Spirit.*—Sam Shoemaker
- *We have become preoccupied today with the extraordinary, sporadic, non-universal ministries of the Spirit to the neglect of the ordinary, general ones.*—J. I. Packer[4]
- *It is stark tragedy that the doctrine which is intended to produce "the unity of the Spirit," becomes a fruitful source of disunity.*—J. Oswald Sanders, about the doctrine of the Holy Spirit[5]

Date:			
Place:			
Occasion:			

The Honorable Bird

Dorothy Sayers tells of a Japanese convert struggling to grasp Christian theology. "Honorable Father, very good," he said to his missionary teacher. "Honorable Son, very good. But Honorable Bird, I do not understand at all."[6]

---

[1] Haddon Robinson, "On Target," *Focal Point.*
[2] Bill Bright, *How To Be Filled With the Spirit* (Arrowhead Springs, CA: Campus Crusade for Christ, 1971), 12–13.
[3] J. Oswald Sanders, *The Holy Spirit and His Gifts* (Grand Rapids, MI: Zondervan Publishing Co., 1970), 72.
[4] J. I. Packer, *Knowing God* (Downers Grove, IL: InterVarsity, 1973), 107.
[5] Sanders, *The Holy Spirit and His Gifts,* 7.
[6] Philip Yancy, foreword of Robertson McQuilkin's *Life in the Spirit.*

The Heavenly Dove

Gordon Brownville's *Symbols of the Holy Spirit* tells about the great Norwegian explorer Roald Amundsen, the first to discover the magnetic meridian of the North Pole and to discover the South Pole. On one of his trips, Amundsen took a homing pigeon with him. When he had finally reached the top of the world, he opened the bird's cage and set it free.

◇
Glorifying Christ

The Holy Spirit glorifies Christ, and when the Holy Ghost works most, you do not think about the Holy Ghost, but you think about our dear Lord.

—F. W. MEYER
◇

Imagine the delight of Amundsen's wife, back in Norway, when she looked up from the doorway of her home and saw the pigeon circling in the sky above. No doubt she exclaimed, "He's alive! My husband is still alive!"

So it was when Jesus ascended. He was gone, but the disciples clung to His promise to send them the Holy Spirit. What joy, then, when the Holy Spirit descended at Pentecost. The disciples had with them the continual reminder that Jesus was alive and victorious at the right hand of the Father. This continues to be the Spirit's message.[1]

The Spotlight

In his writing on the victorious Christian life, Robertson McQuilkin suggests we imagine the following: the President of the United States comes to speak at your local high school auditorium and the band strikes up "Hail to the Chief" as the president strides to the microphone. The spotlight follows his every step. Suddenly the crowd, as one, rises and—what's this? They turn their backs to the stage and, pointing to the balcony, erupt in applause for the fine performance of the spotlight operator! Absurd? Of course, but it illustrates a truth about the Spirit. The Spirit glorifies—shines the spotlight on—the Son . . . We must not focus so completely on the person and work of the Spirit that we lose sight of the central figure of time and eternity, the Lord Jesus Christ.[2]

---

[1] Thomas Lindberg, "Holy Spirit," *Leadership Journal,* Summer 1986, 39.
[2] Robertson McQuilkin, *Life in the Spirit.*

The Same Verse

Leighton Ford tells of a visit his brother-in-law, Billy Graham, made to a very large and influential church. His guide told him of an unfortunate experience. One of the officers in that church had repeatedly gotten drunk, and so they had to discipline him and put him out of the church fellowship. Mr. Graham asked, "How long has it been since you put somebody out of the church for not being filled with the Spirit?" His guide looked startled. So Mr. Graham continued, "The Bible says, 'Don't get drunk with wine,' but the very same verse says, 'Be filled with the Spirit.'" You see, the positive command to be filled with the Spirit is just as binding on us as a negative command not to be drunk with wine.

Date: _____ _____ _____

Place: _____ _____ _____

Occasion: _____ _____ _____

H

From A. W. Tozer

One quality belonging to the Holy Spirit, of great interest and importance to every seeking heart, is penetrability. He can penetrate matter, such as the human body; He can penetrate mind; He can penetrate another spirit, such as the human spirit. He can achieve complete penetration of and actual intermingling with the human spirit. He can invade the human heart and make room for Himself without expelling anything essentially human. The integrity of the human personality remains unimpaired. Only moral evil is forced to withdraw.

The metaphysical problem involved here can no more be avoided than it can be solved. How can one personality enter another? The candid reply would be simply that we do not know, but a near approach to an understanding may be a simple analogy borrowed from the old devotional writers of several hundred years ago. We place a piece of iron in a fire and blow up the coals. At first we have two distinct substances, iron and fire. When we insert the iron in the fire we achieve the penetration of the fire by the iron. Soon the fire begins to penetrate the iron and we have not only the iron in the fire but the fire in the iron as well. They are two distinct substances, but they have co-mingled and interpenetrated to a point where the two have become one.[1]

Date: _____ _____ _____

Place: _____ _____ _____

Occasion: _____ _____ _____

Music Within

In her *Dear Abby* newspaper column, Abigail Van Buren shares a letter from R. T. Holland of Los Angeles who tells of an article from the medical section of

[1] A. W. Tozer, *The Divine Conquest*, in *A Treasury of A. W. Tozer* (Grand Rapids, MI: Baker Book House, 1980), 43.

Time magazine. The magazine cited a man who went to a psychiatrist complaining that he was always hearing radio broadcasts. Thinking to humor him, the psychiatrist asked what he was hearing right then. The man replied that he was hearing Rudy Vallee broadcasting from the Steel Pier in Atlantic City.

After much questioning he discovered that the man worked in a glass bottle factory and had gotten some silica crystals in dental cavities. The combination of the silica, saliva and some bridgework in his mouth had literally transformed him into a walking crystal radio receiver!

The psychiatrist referred the patient to a dentist who gave his teeth a thorough cleaning, filled the cavities and redid the bridgework. As a result, the patient "went off the air," was able to concentrate, and lived happily ever after.

The Bible says that those who are filled with the Spirit are tuned into the heavenly frequency and carry a song around with them everywhere they go—speaking to themselves in songs, hymns, and spiritual songs, singing and making music to the Lord in their hearts.[1]

Date:			
Place:			
Occasion:			

The Illumination of the Holy Spirit

"The Holy Ghost does not reveal anything fresh now. He brings old things to our remembrance. . . . The canon of revelation is closed, there is no more to be added; God does not give a fresh revelation, but he rivets the old one. When it has been forgotten, and laid in the dusty chamber of our memory, he fetches it out and cleans the picture, but does not paint a new one. There are no new doctrines, but the old ones are often revived."—Charles Haddon Spurgeon[2]

Date:			
Place:			
Occasion:			

Oswald Chambers

As a young man, Oswald Chambers, of *My Utmost For His Highest* fame, battled a persistent sense of barrenness in his Christian life. He finally wrote: *I was getting desperate. I knew no one who had what I wanted; in fact I did not know what I did want. But I knew that if what I had was all the Christianity there was, the thing was a fraud.*

Then Luke 11:13 got hold of me.

At a little meeting in Dunoon, a well known lady was asked to take the after meeting. She did not speak, but set us to prayer, and then sang, "Touch me again, Lord." I felt nothing, but

---

[1] From an undated "Dear Abby" clipping in my files.
[2] Charles Haddon Spurgeon, *Spurgeon's Sermons*, vol. 1 (Grand Rapids, MI: Baker Book House, 1983), 79.

I knew emphatically my time had come. I rose to my feet. Then and there I claimed the gift of the Holy Spirit in dogged committal on Luke 11:13.

I had no vision of heaven or of angels; I had nothing. I was as dry and empty as ever, no power or realization of God, no witness of the Holy Spirit. Then I was asked to speak at a meeting and forty souls came out to the front! I came to realize that God intended me, having asked, to simply take it by faith, and that power would be there. I might see it only by the backward look, but I was to reckon on the fact that God would be with me.

From that point on, Oswald Chambers ministered with unusual power. His words and writings touched people around the world, especially when he taught, as he frequently did, from his favorite verse, Luke 11:13. And when Oswald died at an early age in Egypt during World War I, an old Australian soldier whom he had led to Christ had a Bible carved in stone for his grave. Its pages were turned to Luke 11:13.[1]

Date: _____   _____   _____

Place: _____   _____   _____

Occasion: _____   _____   _____

H

The Sawmill

Bible teacher F. B. Meyer once had a firewood factory that employed prisoners. Meyer would give them a job to do, good wages, a place to live, and, when possible, spiritual encouragement. In exchange, he expected them to render good employment. They didn't, and he lost money. Finally he fired them all and purchased a circular saw powered by a gas engine. In one hour, it turned out more work than the combined efforts of all the men covered in the course of a whole day. One day, Meyer had a little conversation with his saw. "How can you turn out so much work?" he asked. "Are you sharper than the saws my men were using? No? Is your blade shinier? No? What then? Better oil or lubrication against the wood?"

The saw's answer, could it speak, would have been, "I think there is a stronger driving power behind me. Something is working through me with a new force. It is not I, it is the power behind."

Meyer later observed that many Christians and many ministers are working in the power of the flesh, in the power of their intellect, their energy, their enthusiastic zeal, but with poor effect. They need to become linked to the power of God through the Holy Ghost.[2]

Date: _____   _____   _____

Place: _____   _____   _____

Occasion: _____   _____   _____

The Power of Water

The famous Boston pastor Dr. A. J. Gordon visited the World's Fair in Chicago. In the distance he saw a man robed in bright, gaudy Oriental clothes who appeared

---

[1] Robert Morgan, *From This Verse* (Nashville: Thomas Nelson Publishers, 1998), August 11th.

[2] F. B. Meyer, *The Christ Life for Your Life* (Chicago: Moody Press, n.d.), 86.

to be laboriously turning the crank of a pump and thereby making a mighty flow of water. Gordon was impressed with the man's energy, his smooth motions, and his obvious physical conditioning. He was pumping a tremendous amount of water.

Drawing closer, Gordon was surprised to discover that the man was actually made of wood. Instead of turning the crank and making the water flow, the flow of water was actually turning the crank and thereby making him go!

Thus it is with those in the Lord's work. It isn't our efforts for him that achieve the results. The flowing river of the Holy Spirit, channeled through our lives and lips, keeps us going and yields infinite results through our ministries.[1]

Date:			
Place:			
Occasion:			

Honesty

Someone Once Said . . .

- *A person who is dishonest in little things isn't really honest in anything.*—Charles Finney
- *He was a man of integrity and feared God more than most men do.*—Nehemiah 7:2 (NIV)

Date:			
Place:			
Occasion:			

Cheating 101

Victoria Benning wrote a story in *The Washington Post* on Sunday, October 11, 1998, headlined "Computer Cheating on Rise at Colleges." The article began:

George Mason University instructor Anne Marchant calls them "patchwork plagiarists"— the students who copy and paste together passages from various articles they have found on the Internet and then turn in the work as their own.

She catches at least one such student every semester in her computer science classes, she said. She even discovers such plagiarism in her computer ethics course.

"Certainly, cheating is pervasive," Marchant said. "It's usually deadly obvious. The introduction will be written in broken English. Then it will have this flawlessly written, almost doctoral-quality body. Then a conclusion that goes back to broken English."

Teachers and administrators at several Washington-area colleges agree that cheating is on the rise—because the computer has made cheating so easy.

---

[1] Robert L. Sumner, *Biblical Evangelism* (Murfreesboro, Tenn: Sword of the Lord Publishers, 1966), 102.

The high-tech offenses include using information from the Internet without proper attribution, buying term papers from on-line paper mills, and sharing answers and course work via e-mail or diskette. Dozens of websites are dedicated to helping students cheat more easily and successfully. . . . The computer has made cheaters out of students who otherwise would never have considered such trickery, some educators say.

"In the olden days, a student had to go to the library, dig up the information and retype it," said Leon Geyer, a Virginia Tech professor and an adviser to the school's student-run undergraduate honor system. "Now you can sit in your dorm room and just reach out, point, and click."

Date: _____ _____ _____
Place: _____ _____ _____
Occasion: _____ _____ _____

Your Cheatin' Heart

According to *Psychology Today*, a survey of 2,153 juniors and seniors from colleges across the nation found that 70 percent of men and women confessed to cheating during high school. Nearly half of all college students surveyed cheated.[1]

Date: _____ _____ _____
Place: _____ _____ _____
Occasion: _____ _____ _____

More Numbers

According to polls reported by *USA Today*, Americans lie—and are lied to—much more than we realize. Citing statistics from the book *The Day America Told the Truth*, the newspaper reported that 91 percent of Americans lie routinely.

- 36% of those tell dark, important lies
- 86% lie regularly to parents
- 75% lie to friends
- 73% lie to siblings
- 69% to spouses
- 81% lie about feelings
- 43% lie about income
- 40% lie about sex[2]
- According to a study by the American Management Association, U.S. businesses annually lose over $10 billion to employee pilferage and commercial bribery, over $4 billion to embezzlement, over $2.5 billion to burglary, over $2 billion to shoplifting, over $1.3 billion to arson, and over $500,000 per incident of computer fraud.

---

[1] *Psychology Today*, December 1992, 9.
[2] "Numbers Tell the Story," *USA Today*, January 9, 1992, sec. 4D.

Employee Theft

The September 2, 1996, issue of the *Wichita Business Journal* carried a disturbing front page article on employee theft that began: "Everyone is honest and trustworthy, right? That's what some clients thought when they started their small business. In just a short time they were out of business because of an employee skimming from the cash register and theft of warehouse goods.

"A little here and a little there . . . who's going to notice? You should take notice. According to the U.S. Department of Commerce, approximately a third of all business failures each year can be traced to employee theft and other employee crime.

"While managers and owners would like to think their employees are all trustworthy and honest, large-scale anonymous surveys have shown almost half of employees admitted to stealing."[1]

The Royal Path

In nineteenth-century America, a book called *The Royal Path of Life,* became popular, being sold house-to-house by salesmen going door-to-door carrying sample books with beautiful bindings. It contained the homespun wisdom of Christian businessman Thomas L. Haines and his neighbor, L. W. Yaggy. So beloved was the book that it was endorsed by preachers, priests, and rabbis alike. One Baptist newspaper editor even went so far as to say, "Next to the Bible, [*The Royal Path of Life*] is the most valuable book ever printed in the English language."

Nevertheless, it is an almost forgotten book today. For those who can find a copy, however, its words still ring true. Here is some of what *The Royal Path of Life* has to say on the subject of honesty:

- *The first step toward greatness is to be honest, says the proverb. But the proverb fails to state the case strong enough. Honesty is not only the first step toward greatness, it is greatness itself.*
- *He who says there is no such thing as an honest man, you may be sure is dishonest himself. When any one complains as Diogenes did, that he has to hunt the street with candles at noon-day to find an honest man, we are apt to think that his nearest neighbor would have the same difficulty.*

---

[1] Frank Saeks, "Employee Theft Happens Much More Often Than You Think," *Wichita Business Journal,* September 2, 1996, 1.

- *In the long run, character is better than capital.*
- *Some, in their passion for sudden accumulation, practice secret frauds and imagine there is no harm in it, so long as they are not detected. But in vain will they cover up their transgressions. For God sees it to the bottom. Let them not hope they will always keep it from man. The birds of the air sometimes carry the tale abroad. In the long web of events, "be sure your sin will find you out."*

Date: _____ _____ _____

Place: _____ _____ _____

Occasion: _____ _____ _____

The Influence of a Father's Honesty

[A] Allan Emery

Allen C. Emery was a successful businessman who also served as an officer for many evangelical organizations, such as board chairman of the Billy Graham Evangelistic Association. For years he and his wife have hosted a Bible club at their Massachusetts church that draws up to one hundred young people each week. In his book *A Turtle on a Fencepost*, Emery writes, "Today I find myself still asking myself, 'What would daddy do?' when confronted with those decisions in business and in life that are so often not black and white, but gray. I am in debt to the memory-making efforts that my father made to imprint indelibly upon my mind the meaning of integrity."

Emery remembers his dad as a man who valued honesty in all the affairs of life. "Once [my dad] lost a pair of fine German binoculars. He collected insurance only to find the binoculars a year later. Immediately he sent a check to the company and received a letter back stating that this seldom occurred and that they were encouraged. It was a small thing, but children never forget examples lived before them."[1]

[B] Don Wyrtzen

In the book, *What My Parents Did Right,* musician Don Wyrtzen tells how his father, Jack Wyrtzen, founder of *Word of Life*, taught him a hard lesson about honesty. Don writes of attending his father's evangelistic rallies in New York's Times Square. "One time a Jewish friend named Jimmy and I decided that we would ride the subways. Instead of buying a 15-cent token to get on the subway, we went underneath the turnstiles. Later that night in the car, Jimmy and I were bragging to my dad how we had ridden all over New York City without paying for our subway tokens. Becoming very serious, Dad explained to us that that was cheating. He had me write a letter to the New York City Port of Authority, apologize to them, and tape some change to a card to pay what I owed. That memory sticks out in my mind. Dad felt that being honest in little things was exceedingly important, and he wasn't going to let an opportunity to teach me this slip by. I have been grateful for his tough lessons since."[2]

---

[1] Allan C. Emery, *A Turtle on a Fencepost* (Waco: Word Books, 1979), 27–31.
[2] Don Wyrtzen, "Caught Rather Than Taught," *What My Parents Did Right,* comp. and ed. Gloria Gaither (Nashville: StarSong Publishing Group, 1991), 257–258.

[C] Henry Bosch

Devotional writer Henry G. Bosch once wrote in *Our Daily Bread* that when he was a boy he would often work with his father during the summer months. Leaving home each morning, they would stop at a particular store for a newspaper which

they read at coffeebreak. One day, arriving at work, Henry's dad discovered that he had taken two papers by mistake because they were so thin. After a moment's thought, he decided to return to the store immediately to pay for the extra paper. "I don't want the owner, who isn't a Christian, to think I'm dishonest," said Mr. Bosch.

About a week later, some expensive items were shoplifted from the same store. The police calculated that at the time of the robbery only two men had been shopping in the store—Mr. Bosch and another man. "I know John is honest," said the storekeeper. "Just last week he came all the way back here to return a newspaper he'd taken by mistake."

The police questioned the other man instead and, in so doing, apprehended the culprit who made a full confession.

"Father's honesty and Christian character . . . not only made a deep impression on the storekeeper," Henry later wrote, "but his actions also left an indelible mark upon my young and pliable mind."

[D] Robert I. Brandt

Robert Brandt is a doctor in Pennsylvania who took his sons camping one night and by the campfire told them this story: About a hundred years ago there was a man who worked in a stone quarry who was injured by a sliding boulder. His foot was crushed. He was dirt poor, and he feared losing his job for he had children in diapers and a pregnant wife. Because he couldn't afford a horse, he had to walk everywhere; so his injured foot was a constant, throbbing trial.

A few days later, on payday, he limped to the general store for groceries, then hobbled home. When he pulled his receipt from his pocket, he discovered that he had been given too much change. What should he do? As his worried wife watched from the kitchen doorway, he began limping every searing step back to the store to return the change.

After Dr. Brandt had told that story to his children, he asked them, "What do you think, guys? Did he do the right thing? Was that trip necessary?"

The boys quickly offered several alternatives, but after a spirited discussion they concluded that he had done the right thing. Then the boys slid down into their sleeping bags as the fire died down. Only then did Dr. Brandt tell them the rest of the story.

"The young father who worked in the stone quarry never became rich, but he lived a long, happy and honorable life. Before he died, he had passed his values in honesty to his children and his grandchildren. Even his great-grandchildren still hear about his honesty."

"Where did you hear that stone-man story anyway, Dad?" asked Roger.

"When I was just a boy about your age, I heard it from a kind old man sitting in a rocking chair with a cane between his knees. I sat spellbound as he rocked, slowly spinning his cane as he told me that story—about himself. He was my grandfather, and your great-grandfather!"[1]

Date:			
Place:			
Occasion:			

No Pacifiers

In her book *In My Father's House,* Corrie Ten Boom explains why she was never given a pacifier as a baby. She writes:

"Achievement and honesty were such basic ingredients in Papa's personality that there were times when we had to hide the giggles he disliked so much. One of the stories Mama told about him was, 'My husband is so honest that when the children were babies, he wouldn't allow me to give them a pacifier, no matter how loud or how long they cried. He would say, "They think they are getting a drink. That is fooling a child to put something in her mouth which is a lie."'"

"Mama would sigh with amused resignation and say, 'So my babies never had a pacifier, because my husband was so honest.'"[2]

Date:			
Place:			
Occasion:			

How Close?

"Ken," the teacher asked a struggling student during an exam, "how close are you to the right answer?"

"About two seats," he replied.

Date:			
Place:			
Occasion:			

Hope

Someone Once Said . . .

- *A continual looking forward to the eternal world.*—C. S. Lewis, giving his definition of hope[3]

---

[1] Robert I. Brandt, "A Heritage of Honesty," *Decision Magazine,* July–August 1991, 8–9.
[2] Corrie Ten Boom, *In My Father's House* (Old Tappan, NJ: Fleming H. Revell Co., 1976), 59
[3] C. S. Lewis, *Mere Christianity* (New York: The Macmillan Company, 1943), 104.

- *Most of the important things in the world have been accomplished by people who have kept on trying when there seemed to be no hope at all.*—Dale Carnegie
- *Hope is never ill when faith is well.*—John Bunyan
- *"Hope" is the thing with feathers / That perches in the soul / And sings the tunes without the words / And never stops—at all.*—Emily Dickinson
- *While there's life, there's hope.*—Cicero
- *The mighty hope that makes us men.*—Tennyson, *In Memoriam*

Date: _____ _____ _____
Place: _____ _____ _____
Occasion: _____ _____ _____

Thomas à Kempis, in *The Imitation of Christ*

In Thee, therefore, O Lord God, I put all my hope. . . . *For many friends shall not profit, nor strong helpers be able to succour, nor prudent counselors to give a useful answer, nor the books of the learned to console, nor any precious substance to deliver, nor any secret and beautiful place to give shelter, if Thou Thyself do not assist, help, strengthen, comfort, instruct, keep in safety . . .*

To hope in Thee above all things is the strongest solace of Thy servants.

Date: _____ _____ _____
Place: _____ _____ _____
Occasion: _____ _____ _____

A Note of Hope

Church growth guru Lyle E. Schaller suggests that if we want our churches to grow we will offer people a "note of hope." He writes, "Perhaps the most common characteristic of churches that are attracting increasing numbers of people today is not where the minister is on the theological spectrum or the denominational affiliation, but on what people hear and feel during the worship experience. This is a note of hope. . . . The one theme that is common to churches that are attracting more people is the theme of hope. . . . That note of hope and optimism about the future is a powerful factor in determining the size of the crowd."[1]

Date: _____ _____ _____
Place: _____ _____ _____
Occasion: _____ _____ _____

Faith and Hope

John Maxwell tells about a small town in Maine that was proposed for the site of a great hydro-electric plant. A dam would be built across the river and the town

---

[1] Lyle E. Schaller, *44 Ways to Increase Church Attendance* (Nashville: Abingdon Press, 1988), 23–24.

submerged. When the project was announced, the people were given many months to arrange their affairs and relocate.

During those months, a curious thing happened. All improvements ceased. No painting was done. No repairs were made on the buildings, roads, or sidewalks. Day by day the whole town got shabbier and shabbier. A long time before the waters came, the town looked uncared for and abandoned, even though the people had not yet moved away. One citizen explained: "Where there is no faith in the future, there is no power in the present." That town was cursed with hopelessness because it had no future.[1]

Date:			
Place:			
Occasion:			

New Beginnings

Proverbs 24:16 says, "No matter how often an honest man falls, he always gets up again" (TEV). The first person to invent the wheel only discovered what God had already designed, for the Lord created things in circles. The stars and planets are round, they move in orbital circuits, and life, as a result, moves in cycles. Every one hundred years, we have a new century; every 365 days, we have a new year; every 24 hours we have a new day; every 60 minutes we have a new hour. God created the potential for new beginnings into the very design of our universe.

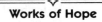
Works of Hope

Everything that is done in the world is done by hope.
—MARTIN LUTHER

And for good reason. Every hero of Scripture needed new beginnings: Adam and Eve after they ate the forbidden fruit; Moses after he killed the Egyptian; David after his adulterous relationship; Elijah after an emotional breakdown in the desert; the disciples after Good Friday . . .

And maybe you.[2]

Date:			
Place:			
Occasion:			

Surviving on Hope

In his book, *Man's Search for Meaning*, Viktor Frankl tells of his years trapped in the indescribable horrors of Auschwitz and Dachau. He was transported there like a despised animal, given two minutes to strip naked or be whipped, every hair was shaved from his body, and he was condemned to a living death. His father, mother, brother, and wife died in the camps or were sent to the gas ovens. His existence was

---

[1] John Maxwell, *Your Attitude* (San Bernardino, CA: Here's Life Publishers, 1984), 120.
[2] From a sermon from the author.

full of cold, fear, starvation, pain, lice and vermin, dehumanization, exhaustion, and terror.

Frankl wrote that he was able to survive because he never lost the quality of hope. Those prisoners who lost faith in the future were doomed. When a prisoner lost hope, Frankl said, he let himself decline, becoming subject to mental and physical decay. He would die from the inside out.

Frankl said that this usually happened quite suddenly. One morning a prisoner would just refuse to get up. He wouldn't get dressed or wash or go outside to the parade grounds. No amount of pleading by his fellow prisoners would help. No threatening by the captors would have any effect. Losing all hope, he had simply given up. He would lay there in his own excrement till he died. American soldiers later told Frankl that this behavior pattern existed also among prisoners of war, and was called "give-up-itis."

When a prisoner lost hope, said Frankl, "he lost his spiritual hold."[1]

Date: _____ _____ _____
Place: _____ _____ _____
Occasion: _____ _____ _____

POWs

In his book *Winning Life's Toughest Battles,* psychologist Julius Segal wrote about the 25,000 American soldiers who were held by the Japanese in POW camps during World War II. "Forced to exist under inhumane conditions, many of them died. Others, however, survived and eventually returned home. There was no reason to believe there was a difference in the stamina of these two groups of soldiers. The survivors, however, were different in one major respect: They confidently expected to be released someday. As described by Robins Readers in *Holding On to Hope,* 'They talked about the kinds of homes they would have, the jobs they would choose, and even described the kind of person they would marry. They drew pictures on the walls to illustrate their dreams. Some even found ways to study subjects related to the kind of career they wanted to pursue.'"

Segal goes on to point out that researchers have found that a hopeful attitude can lead to physiological changes that improve the immune system—the body's defense against toxins and disease.[2]

Date: _____ _____ _____
Place: _____ _____ _____
Occasion: _____ _____ _____

The String of Hope

G. F. Watt has a famous painting entitled *Hope.* It pictures a poor woman against the world. Her eyes are bandaged so that she cannot see ahead. In her hands is a

[1] Viktor E. Frankl, *Man's Search for Meaning* (New York: Washington Square Press, 1984), 95, 163.
[2] Dr. Julius Segal, *Winning Life's Toughest Battles* (New York: Ivy Books, 1896), 95–97.

harp, but all the strings are broken save one. Those broken strings represent her shattered expectations, her bitter disappointments. That one last unbroken string is the string of hope. She strikes that string and a glorious melody floats out over the world; it fills her dark skies with stars. The artist painted a great truth: Even when all else is gone, you still can have hope.[1]

Date:		
Place:		
Occasion:		

Saved by Hope

An interesting item appeared in a Nashville newspaper, datelined Memphis (UPI): A woman named Hope pulled a man from chilly harbor waters after watching him drive his car off the bank in an apparent suicide attempt.

Hope Phillips, thirty-eight, said Monday she was sitting in her car with her husband and son Sunday afternoon when she saw the man drive down Riverside Drive into Wolf River Harbor.

Phillips said she saw the man climb on top of the sinking car. "His face was like, 'I'm so desperate, please help me.' All I could do was run into the water," she said.

Phillips said she swam toward the man, who was about twenty-five feet off the bank, and used a tree branch to pull him toward the bank. Her husband helped drag him out of the water. The man said he was a student at the University of Tennessee.

She said: "He kept telling us he wasn't worth anything. I said, 'You are worth something, you're here, aren't you?'

"Then he asked my name. I said 'Hope,' and he said, 'What's your name?' He repeated it twice. He had a smile on his face. You knew he didn't want to die."

The police took the man to the Regional Medical Center.[2]

Date:		
Place:		
Occasion:		

Hopeful

A man approached a little league baseball game one afternoon. He asked a boy in the dugout what the score was. The boy responded, "Eighteen to nothing—we're behind."

"Boy," said the spectator, "I'll bet you're discouraged."

"Why should I be discouraged?" replied the little boy. "We haven't even gotten up to bat yet!"

[1] Charles L. Allen, *The Miracle of Love* (Old Tappan, NJ: Fleming H. Revell Co., 1972), 71.
[2] Newspaper clipping in my files.

Date: _____ _____ _____

Place: _____ _____ _____

Occasion: _____ _____ _____

Hospitality

Someone Once Said . . .

- *Nothing is more pleasant than the tie of host and guest.*—Aeschylus, fifth century Greek writer

Date: _____ _____ _____

Place: _____ _____ _____

Occasion: _____ _____ _____

Entertainment or Hospitality

Karen Maines has pointed out that entertainment and hospitality are two different kinds of events. Writing in *Moody* magazine, she observes:

- *Entertaining says, "I want to impress you with my home, my clever decorating, my gourmet cooking." Hospitality, seeking to minister, says, "This home is a gift from my Master. I use it as He desires. . . ." Hospitality aims to serve.*
- *Entertainment subtly declares, "This home is mine, an expression of my personality. Look, please, and admire." Hospitality whispers, "What is mine is yours."*
- *Entertaining looks for a payment—the words, "My, isn't she a remarkable hostess. . . ." With no thought of reward, hospitality takes pleasure in giving, doing, loving, serving*
- *The model for entertaining is the slick women's magazines with their alluring pictures of foods and rooms. The model for hospitality is the Word of God. Christ sanctifies our simple fare and makes it holy, useful.*[1]

Date: _____ _____ _____

Place: _____ _____ _____

Occasion: _____ _____ _____

The Ten Booms

Corrie Ten Boom's family was torn apart by the Nazis, with most of her immediate relatives perishing in concentration camps due to their harboring of Jews in their home. It was a sacrifice they were willing to make, for God had given them a heart for hospitality. In her book *In My Father's House*, Corrie writes about her family's penchant for taking in guests as she remembered it from childhood: "Many lonesome

---

[1]Karen Maines, "Hospitality Means More Than a Party," *Moody*, December 1976, 38–39.

people found a place with us, where there was music, humor, interesting conversations, and always room for one more at the oval dinner table. Oh, it's true, the soup may have been a bit watery when too many unexpected guests came, but it didn't matter.

"Mother loved guests. Her lovely blue eyes would brighten, and she would pat her dark hair into place when she knew we would be squeezing another visitor around the table—already bursting with four children, three aunts, herself, and Papa. With a flourish she would place a little box on the table, and spreading her arms wide, she would say to our visitor, 'You are welcome in our house, and because we are grateful for your coming, we will add a penny to the blessing box for our missionaries.'

"Years afterward on my trips around the world, when I have been dependent upon the hospitality of others, I believe that I have enjoyed the reward for the open doors and hearts of our home."[1]

H

Date:			
Place:			
Occasion:			

The Criswells

W. A. Criswell, arguably the most powerful Southern Baptist preacher of his generation, was converted because of his parent's hospitality. When W. A. was ten years old, a preacher came to their church to hold a revival. Anna Criswell invited him to make his lodgings with them during his two-week stay. Young W. A. was greatly impressed by the visiting evangelist, Rev. John Hicks, and would walk beside him back and forth to the church. At home during meals, the boy pulled his chair close so he could listen to the adult conversation. Rev. Hicks took time to talk to him about his thoughts and aspirations, and by the time Rev. Hicks left town, W. A. Criswell had asked Jesus Christ to be his Savior.

Date:			
Place:			
Occasion:			

The Goforths

Jonathan and Rosalind Goforth were among the most successful missionaries who ever served in China. Part of their secret was their hospitality skills, which, on some occasions, got quite a workout. They practiced what they called "Open-House Evangelism." Since the Chinese were very curious to see the interior of the Goforth's house, with its European furniture and fashions (including a kitchen stove, a sewing machine, and an organ), the Goforths opened their home for tours. Visitors came

---

[1] Corrie Ten Boom, *In My Father's House* (Old Tappan, NJ: Fleming H. Revel Company, 1976), 40.

from miles around. Jonathan would give a brief presentation of the gospel at the beginning of the tour, then Rosalind would often speak with the women afterward.

On one single day alone, more than two thousand people showed up, and during one particular five-month period, some twenty-five thousand people came to visit. Rosalind later said, "Some may think that receiving visitors is not real mission work, but I think it is. I put myself out to make friends with the people and I reap the results when I go to their villages to preach. Often the people of a village will gather around me and say, 'We were at your place and you showed us through your house, treating us like friend.' Then they almost always bring me a chair to sit on, a table to lay my Bible on, and some tea."

According to missionary historian Ruth Tucker, "It was this type of evangelism that paved the way for Goforth's future ministry."[1]

Date: _____   _____   _____
Place: _____   _____   _____
Occasion: _____   _____   _____

Francis and Edith Schaeffer

The ministry of Francis and Edith Schaeffer drew swarms of students to their Swiss home in the mid-1950s, and thus their L'Abri Fellowship was born. But in the early days, Edith worried about things like funding and strength and privacy. She later wrote:

I was sitting at my typewriter, feeling the heaviness that went with the uncertainties ahead. I propped my Bible up on the typewriter, and asked God to give me help and comfort. My reading took me to the Book of Isaiah. Now I believe the Bible is, to the spiritual life of a Christian, what warm fresh wheat bread is to the physical life—both nourishing and appetizing! There are also times when God speaks to some of His children in the very words of the Bible, written hundreds of years ago, yet seemingly written as a message for the situation of the moment.

Let me tell you what happened that day. (As I read Isaiah 2:2–3) I reached for my pencil and wrote in the margin: "Jan '55 promise . . . Yes, L'Abri." For I had the tremendous surge of assurance that although this had another basic meaning, it was being used by God to tell me something. I did not feel that "all nations" were literally going to come to our home for help, but I did feel that it spoke of people from many different nations coming to a house that God would establish for the purpose of making His ways known to them. It seemed to me that God was putting his hand on my shoulder in a very real way and saying that there would be a work which would be His work, not ours. I felt that this work was going to be L'Abri.[2]

Date: _____   _____   _____
Place: _____   _____   _____
Occasion: _____   _____   _____

---

[1] Ruth Tucker, *From Jerusalem to Irian Jaya* (Grand Rapids, MI: Zondervan, 1983), 190.
[2] Edith Schaeffer, *L'Abri* (Wheaton, IL: Tyndale House Publishers, 1969), 75–76.

Haven for Guests

Leslie B. Flynn points out that the main part of *hospitality* is *hospital*. He writes, "Ancient travelers, whether pilgrims or businessmen, fared poorly when venturing beyond their own country. Thus, religious leaders established international guest houses in the fifth century. These havens were called "hospice" from *hospes,* Latin for "guests." With the coming of the Crusades, the importance of the hospice increased greatly. Pilgrims, crusaders, and other travelers found hospices, by this time run by religious orders, the only reputable guest houses of the era. Soon after the Crusades most of these institutions began to specialize in the care of the poor, sick, aged, and crippled. During the fifteenth century, secular interests took over most entertaining of travelers, so the *hospital* restricted its function to care and treatment of the sick and handicapped. But originally it meant *a haven for guests.*"[1]

Date: _____ _____ _____
Place: _____ _____ _____
Occasion: _____ _____ _____

A Final Thought

- *When I sell liquor, it's called bootlegging; when my patrons serve it on silver trays on Lake Shore Drive, it's called hospitality.*—Al Capone

Date: _____ _____ _____
Place: _____ _____ _____
Occasion: _____ _____ _____

Humility

Someone Once Said . . .

- *Humility does not consist simply in thinking cheaply of oneself, so much as in not thinking of oneself at all—and of Christ more and more.*—Keith Brooks
- *Genuine humility is unconscious. . . . God's workmen must be so emptied of self that they are unconsciously humble.*—Watchman Nee[2]
- *Humility is like the lead to the net, which keeps the soul down when it is rising through passion (pride); and contentment is like the cork, which keeps the heart up when it is sinking through discouragement.*—Thomas Watson[3]
- *The more humble a man is in himself, and the more obedient towards God, the wiser will he be in all things, and the more shall his soul be at peace.*—Thomas à Kempis

---

[1] Leslie B. Flynn, *19 Gifts of the Spirit* (Wheaton: Victor Books, 1975), 109.
[2] Watchman Nee, *The Normal Christian Worker* (Hong Kong: Church Book Room, n.d.), 39
[3] Thomas Watson, *Gleanings From Thomas Watson* (Morgan, PA: Soli Deo Gloria Publications, 1995), 40.

- *The humble man feels no jealously or envy. He can praise God when others are preferred and blessed before him. He can bear to hear others praised while he is forgotten because . . . he has received the spirit of Jesus who pleased not himself, and who sought not His own honor.*—Andrew Murray
- *Should you ask me: What is the first thing in religion? I should reply: the first, second, and third thing therein is humility.*—Augustine
- *It is not a great thing to be humble when you are brought low, but to be humble when you are praised is a great and rare attainment.*—St. Bernard of Clairvaux

Date:			
Place:			
Occasion:			

What They Thought of Themselves

- *I've never yet read of a crime but what I, too, might have committed that crime.*—Dr. Samuel Johnson
- *There, but for the grace of God, go I.*—Anonymous
- *I see nothing but hell.*—John Wesley, about looking into his own heart
- *When I saw John Bunyan as God saw John Bunyan, I did not say I was a sinner; I said that I was sin from the top of my head to the soles of my feet.*—John Bunyan
- *I think God was looking for a little man, little enough so that He could show Himself strong through him. A man can receive nothing, except it be given him from heaven.*—Hudson Taylor, explaining his success

Date:			
Place:			
Occasion:			

Magnanimous People

Warren Bennis, well-known management consultant and leadership guru, wrote in *Why Leaders Can't Lead:* "Magnanimous and/or humble people are notable for their self-possession. They know who they are, have healthy egos, and take more pride in what they do than in who they are. They take compliments with a grain of salt and take intelligent criticism without rancor. Such people learn from their mistakes and don't harp on the mistakes of others. They are gracious winners and losers. Tennis star John McEnroe is neither magnanimous nor humble. Albert Schweitzer and Albert Einstein were. Today there are far more McEnroes than there are Schweitzers and Einsteins, and self-possession declines as self-impertinence rises. True leaders are, by definition, both magnanimous and humble."[1]

Down Under

Humility is like underwear. We should have it but not let it show.

---

[1] Warren Bennis, *Why Leaders Can't Lead* (San Francisco: Jossey-Bass Publishers, 1989), 118.

Date:			
Place:			
Occasion:			

The Apostle Paul Once Said . . .

J. Oswald Sanders once noted that the "humility of the leader, as his spirituality, will be an ever-increasing quality." He points out the progression we see over time with the Apostle Paul in regard to his self-assessment:

- *I am the least of the apostles*—1 Corinthians 15:9
- [I am] *the least of all the saints*—Ephesians 3:8
- [I am] *the chief of sinners*—1 Timothy 1:15[1]

H

Date:			
Place:			
Occasion:			

Charles Spurgeon Once Said . . .

- *We have plenty of people nowadays who could not kill a mouse without publishing it in the Gospel Gazette. Samson killed a lion and said nothing about it: the Holy Spirit finds modesty so rare that He takes care to record it. Say much of what the Lord has done for you, but say little of what you have done for the Lord. Do not utter a self-glorifying sentence!*[2]

Date:			
Place:			
Occasion:			

Jonathan Blanchard

As a student, Jonathan Blanchard, who later would establish both Wheaton and Knox Colleges, prayed this simple prayer: *O my Savior God, deliver me from sluggishness on the one hand and from ambition on the other. May I do all I can do, and feel no more lifted up than if I did nothing.*[3]

Date:			
Place:			
Occasion:			

---

[1] J. Oswald Sanders, *A Spiritual Clinic* (Chicago: Moody Press, 1958), 109.

[2] Richard Ellsworth Day, *The Shadow of the Broad Brim* (Valley Forge: The Judson Press, 1934), 182.

[3] Clyde S. Kilby, *Minority of One: A Biography of Jonathan Blanchard* (Grand Rapids, MI: Eerdmans Publishing House, 1959), 38.

I Am Clay

"I am clay," wrote Missionary author Elisabeth Elliot as she mused over Isaiah 59:9–11, the passage that pictures us as vessels in the Potter's hand. "The word *humble* comes from the root word *humus,* earth, clay," she wrote.

Date: _____   _____   _____
Place: _____   _____   _____
Occasion: _____   _____   _____

The Little Servant

Warren Wiersbe and Lloyd Perry tell this story about missionary Hudson Taylor in *The Wycliffe Handbook of Preaching and Preachers:* Taylor was scheduled to speak at a large Presbyterian church in Melbourne, Australia. The moderator of the service introduced the missionary in eloquent and glowing terms. He told the large congregation all that Taylor had accomplished in China, and then presented him as "our illustrious guest."

Taylor stood quietly for a moment, and then opened his message by saying, "Dear friends, I am the little servant of an illustrious Master."[1]

Date: _____   _____   _____
Place: _____   _____   _____
Occasion: _____   _____   _____

The Great Dr. Brengle

On one occasion Samuel Brengle, longtime revered leader of the Salvation Army, was introduced as "the great Dr. Brengle." In his diary he wrote:

"If I appear great in their eyes, the Lord is most graciously helping me to see how absolutely nothing I am without Him, and helping me to keep little in my own eyes. He does use me. But I am so concerned that *He* uses me and that it is not of me the work is done. The axe cannot boast of the trees it has cut down. It could do nothing but for the woodsman. He made it, he sharpened it, and he used it. The moment he throws it aside, it becomes only old iron. O that I may never lose sight of this."[2]

Date: _____   _____   _____
Place: _____   _____   _____
Occasion: _____   _____   _____

---

[1] Warren W. Wiersbe and Lloyd M. Perry, *The Wycliffe Handbook of Preaching and Preachers* (Chicago: Moody Press, 1984), 243.
[2] Oswald Sanders, *Spiritual Leadership* (Chicago: Moody Press, 1967), 58.

Your Place by John Oxenham

Is your place a small place?
Tend it with care!—
He set you there.

Is your place a large place?
Guard it with care!—
He set you there.

Whate'er your place, it is
Not yours alone, but His
Who set you there.[1]

Date: _____ _____ _____
Place: _____ _____ _____
Occasion: _____ _____ _____

H

A Small Place

"Father, where shall I work today?"
And my love flowed warm and free.
Then He pointed me out a tiny spot,
And said, "Tend that for me."
I answered quickly, "Oh, no, not that.
Why, no one would ever see,
No matter how well my work was done.
Not that little place for me!"
And the word He spoke, it was not stern,
He answered me tenderly,
"Ah, little one, search that heart of thine;
Art thou working for them or me?
Nazareth was a little place,
And so was Galilee."[2]

Date: _____ _____ _____
Place: _____ _____ _____
Occasion: _____ _____ _____

"I Wasn't God's First Choice"

A British parlor maid named Gladys Aylward grew up among the poor of England, and because of a learning disability, dropped out of school and became a domestic servant for a well-to-do British family. Her job demanded long hours, hard work, and low pay. When she was in her late twenties, she was riding a bus, reading a newspaper. There was an article about the need for missionaries in China. From

---

[1] V. Raymond Edman, *The Disciplines of Life* (Minneapolis: World Wide Publications, 1948), 202.
[2] Edman, *The Disciplines of Life*, 209.

that moment on, Gladys' heart was broken for China, and she resolved to go herself. She applied to the board of the China Inland Mission, but they turned her down. Crushed with disappointment, she returned to her small upstairs room, opened her purse, and turned it upside down. Two pennies fell onto her Bible. She said, "O God, here's my Bible! Here's my money! Here's me! Use me, God." She started scrimping and saving every penny she earned, and she finally determined that while she could never save enough to travel to China by ship, she could scrape together enough for a train ticket across Europe and Asia, a dangerous crossing because of a war blazing on the Manchurian border.

The day finally came when a few bewildered friends and family members gathered at London's Liverpool Station to see her off. She traveled from England across the Channel to The Hague, across Europe to Moscow, and across Siberia toward China. Bundled in an overcoat and orange frock, Gladys carried her bedroll, two suitcases (one stocked with food), and a bag clanking with pots and pans. Day and night the train pressed on into the frigid, Siberian wasteland, and finally it stopped in the dead of night in the middle of the wasteland, at the war zone. The other passengers, all soldiers, disembarked and headed in the direction of gunfire. Gladys got off and started trudging back, suitcases in hand, the way the train had come and nearly died before she found the nearest station.

By sheer determination Gladys Aylward finally arrived in China and moved in with an older single missionary woman—who, as it turned out, didn't quite know what to do with her.

To make a long story short, Gladys Aylward, parlor maid from England, became one of the most famous missionaries of the twentieth century, a woman that has been called "the most noted single woman missionary in modern history." A popular biography about her was made into a movie starring Ingrid Bergman. She was featured in an episode of television's "This Is Your Life." She dined with Queen Elizabeth and Prince Philip. She traveled the world, speaking in some of America's greatest churches.

But the most notable thing about Gladys was her brokenness, her humility, and her willingness to be available to God. She once said, "I wasn't God's first choice for what I've done for China. There was somebody else . . . I don't know who it was—God's first choice. I don't know what happened. Perhaps he died. Perhaps he wasn't willing . . . And God looked down . . . and saw Gladys Aylward."

"Think of what you were when you were called," said Paul. "Not many of you were wise, influential, or of noble birth. But God chose the lowly things . . ." (1 Cor. 1:26–27 NIV)

Date:			
Place:			
Occasion:			

Second Fiddle

- A famous conductor was once asked which instrument he considered the most difficult to play. His reply: "Second fiddle."[1]

---

[1] From *Our Daily Bread.*

- Robert Morrison of China wrote, "The great fault, I think, in our missions is that no one likes to be second."
- Vance Havner wrote in his devotional book, *Day by Day: Blessed are the Saints of the Second Fiddle!*
- After Abraham Lincoln had defeated Stephen A. Douglas for the presidency, the two were together on the east portico of the Capitol for Lincoln's inauguration. The President-elect was introduced by Senator Edward E. Baker of Oregon. Lincoln stood beside him, carrying the manuscript of his speech, a cane, and his tall silk hat. As he made ready to speak, he looked around for a place to put the hat. Stephen Douglas quickly stepped forward, took the hat, and returned to his seat. "If I can't be President," he said to a cousin of Mrs. Lincoln, "I can at least hold his hat."[1]
- British pastor George Duncan says that one of the most important lessons in Christian service is that of learning to play the second fiddle well. "Think for a moment," he writes, "how often we come across those whose worth is seldom recognized by men, but I am sure will never be overlooked by God, and will certainly not go unrewarded. Many are prepared to recognize the prominent part played by Simon Peter among the disciples, but forget that if there had not been an Andrew who 'brought him to Jesus' there would never have been a Peter! The church universal gives thanks to God for Paul, the greatest Christian who ever lived, but forget that if there had not been a Barnabas there might never have been a Paul!" Duncan goes on to ask his readers how many of them recognize the name of Albert McMakin. But Albert was the young man who invited and took sixteen-year-old Billy Graham to the evangelistic services in which he accepted Christ as his Savior. "So before there could be a Billy there had to be an Albert!"[2]

Date:			
Place:			
Occasion:			

How Can We Tell?

There is a story by Venerable Bede, the "Father of Church History" (c. 673–735) in which Augustine, missionary to England under Pope Gregory I, was trying to convert the English to Christianity. Despite much success, Augustine had trouble converting the Celtics to Rome. The Celtic leaders asked a wise man whether they should submit to Augustine or not.

"Yes," the old man said, "if he is a man of God."

"How can we tell?"

"If he is gentle and humble of heart."

"How can we discern that about him?"

---

[1] Keith W. Jennison, *The Humorous Mr. Lincoln* (New York: Bonze Books, 1965), 76.
[2] George Duncan, *Marks of Christian Maturity* (Hants, UK: Marshall Pickering, 1986), 145–146.

"Arrange it so that Augustine and his men arrive first at your meeting place," replied the wise man. "If he stands up when you arrive, it will prove that he is a servant of Christ. In that case, do as he bids you."

Unfortunately, Augustine failed to rise as he greeted the Celts, and they refused to accept his leadership.

Date: _____ _____ _____
Place: _____ _____ _____
Occasion: _____ _____ _____

Screwtape's Advice

In his classic novel *The Screwtape Letters,* C. S. Lewis composes advice coming from Screwtape, a high-ranking demon, to his nephew Wormword on how to trip up a young Christian. Chapter 14 is devoted to trying to inflate the subject's pride. Screwtape writes: *Your patient has become humble; have you drawn his attention to the face? All virtues are less formidable to us once the man is aware that he has them, but this is specially true of humility. Catch him at the moment when he is really poor in spirit, and smuggle into his mind the gratifying reflection, "By jove! I'm being humble," and almost immediately pride— pride at his own humility—will appear. If he awakes to the danger and tries to smother this new form of pride, make him proud of his attempt—and so on, through as many stages as you please.*[1]

Date: _____ _____ _____
Place: _____ _____ _____
Occasion: _____ _____ _____

More Screwtape

In *The Screwtape Letters,* C. S. Lewis has a high demonic personage mentoring a young demon about how to defeat a young Christian convert. Screwtape tells Wormwood to have his human subject think of pride, not as pride, but as having a low opinion of himself. *Fix in his mind the idea that humility consists in trying to believe [his] talents to be less valuable than he believes them to be. . . .*

Referring to God as the "Enemy" Screwtape goes on to provide Wormwood with an insightful and surprising elucidation of genuine humility: *The Enemy wants to bring the man to a state of mind in which he could design the best cathedral in the world, and know it to be the best, and rejoice in the fact, without being any more (or less) or otherwise glad at having done it than he would be if it had been done by another.*[2]

Date: _____ _____ _____
Place: _____ _____ _____
Occasion: _____ _____ _____

---

[1] C. S. Lewis, *The Screwtape Letters* (New York: The Macmillan Company, 1961), 71–75.
[2] Lewis, *The Screwtape Letters,* 71–75.

Two Goats

Martin Luther reportedly told of two mountain goats who met each other on a narrow ledge just wide enough for one of the animals to pass. On the left was a sheer cliff, and on the right a steep wall. The two were facing each other, and it was impossible to turn or to back up.

How did they solve their dilemma? If they had been people, they would have started butting each other until they plunged into the chasm together. But according to Luther, the goats had more sense than that. One of them lay down on the trail and let the other literally walk over him—and both were safe.

Date: _____ _____ _____
Place: _____ _____ _____
Occasion: _____ _____ _____

H

Perspective

If you can start the day without caffeine . . . If you can always be cheerful, ignoring aches and pains . . . If you can resist complaining and boring people with your troubles . . . If you can eat the same food everyday and be grateful for it . . . If you can understand when your loved ones are too busy to give you any time . . . If you can take criticism and blame without resentment . . . If you can resist treating a rich friend better than a poor friend . . . If you can face the world without lies and deceit . . . If you can overlook it when those you love take it out on you when, through no fault of yours, something goes wrong . . . If you can conquer tension without medical help . . . If you can say honestly that deep in your heart you have no prejudice against creed, color, religion or politics . . .

Then, my friend, you are almost as good as your dog.[1]

Date: _____ _____ _____
Place: _____ _____ _____
Occasion: _____ _____ _____

Under Oath

Henry Augustus Rowland, professor of physics at Johns Hopkins University, was once called as an expert witness at a trial. During cross-examination a lawyer demanded, "What are your qualifications as an expert witness in this case?"

The normally modest and retiring professor replied quietly, "I am the greatest living expert on the subject under discussion."

Later a friend well-acquainted with Rowland's disposition expressed surprise at the professor's uncharacteristic answer.

Rowland answered, "Well, what did you expect me to do? I was under oath."[2]

---

[1] Source unknown. From a clipping in my files.
[2] From *The Pastor's Story File*.

Date:			
Place:			
Occasion:			

"The Honor of the Thing"

Abraham Lincoln was once asked by a friend back home, "How does it feel to be President of the United States?" Lincoln reportedly replied that it was like the man who was tarred and feathered and run out of town on a rail. When someone in the crowd asked how he enjoyed it, he replied, "If it were not for the honor of the thing, I'd just as soon walk."

Date:			
Place:			
Occasion:			

Nothing Very Wonderful About It

Once, when an acquaintance praised Johann Sebastian Bach for his wonderful skill as an organist, he replied with characteristic humility and wit: "There is nothing very wonderful about it. You have only to hit the right notes at the right moment and the instrument does the rest."[1]

Date:			
Place:			
Occasion:			

Hymns/Singing

Someone Once Said . . .

- *I don't care who writes a nation's laws if I can write its songs.*—ancient poet
- *Let me write the hymns and the music of the church, and I care very little who writes the theology.*—R. W. Dale[2]
- *Luther has damned more souls with his hymns than with all his sermons.*—complaint of a sixteenth-century Jesuit priest[3]
- *I think that life is not too long / and therefore I determine, That many people read a song / who will not read a sermon.*—Fanny Crosby

---

[1] Patrick Kavanaugh, *The Spiritual Lives of Great Composers* (Nashville: Sparrow Press, 1992), 13.
[2] R. W. Dale, *Nine Lectures on Preaching, Delivered at Yale* (Cincinnati: Jennings & Graham, n.d.), 271.
[3] Richard D. Dinwiddie, "When You Sing Next Sunday, Thank Luther," *Christianity Today*, October 21, 1983, 18.

- *After the sacred Scriptures, the next best companion for the soul is a good hymnal.—* A. W. Tozer[1]
- *Next to the Word of God, music deserves the highest praise. The fathers and prophets wanted nothing else to be associated as clearly with the Word of God as music. I am quite of the opinion that next to theology, there is no art which can be compared to music; for it alone, after theology, gives us rest and joy. . . . Music is the handmaiden of theology.—* Martin Luther[2]
- *Isaac Watts and Charles Wesley . . . were able to marry the harp of David to the Epistles of Paul and to give us singing doctrine.—*A. W. Tozer[3]
- *There are two types of unfamiliar hymns. One is the hymn that we have never heard or sung before. However, another hymn that is unfamiliar is the one we have sung so many times that we sing it and never think about it.—*Charles Allen[4]
- *The Christian life is simply God's life vibrating through us*
- *Be sure and sing early in the morning and in the night season.—*Thomas Ken, author of the Doxology, to his students at Winchester College

H

Date:			
Place:			
Occasion:			

The Song Within

Our minds can sing, if not our mouths. Edith Schaeffer wrote, "I awakened yesterday morning with music and words surging through my head: 'Great is thy faithfulness; great is thy faithfulness; morning by morning new mercies I see. . . .' It was as if a full orchestra and choir were in my room; yet no sound could be heard by anyone else. What a fantastic detail of God's creation—people can sing aloud, and can sing within. . . . We don't need to waken the whole household by bursting forth in song; we can rejoice in song in our heads at night, or start the day or the year that way."[5]

Ruth Graham tells of a musician who lived in a land where "God's music" was not allowed to be played. Daily he took out his score on Handel's *Messiah* and placed it on the dining room table. Then, on the table, his fingers silently and diligently played through the entire score. He was making music that only God could hear.[6]

Date:			
Place:			
Occasion:			

[1] A. W. Tozer, *We Travel an Appointed Way* (Camp Hill, PA: Christian Publications, 1988), 63.

[2] Richard D. Dinwiddie, "When You Sing Next Sunday, Thank Luther," *Christianity Today*, October 21, 1983, 21.

[3] Tozer, *We Travel an Appointed Way*, 65.

[4] Charles L. Allen, *Perfect Peace* (Old Tappan, NJ: Fleming H. Revell Co., 1979), 57.

[5] Edith Schaeffer, "Christians Are Singing People," *Christianity Today*, January 7, 1977, 24.

[6] Ruth Bell Graham, *Legacy of a Pack Rat* (Nashville: Thomas Nelson Publishers, 1989), 204.

Lifted by Song

In his book, *Songs That Lift the Heart,* Gospel singer George Beverly Shea tells of his friend Burt Frizen of Wheaton, Illinois. While attending college in Wheaton, Burt distinguished himself with his fine baritone voice. But his college studies were interrupted by the war. Serving in Germany, he was seriously wounded and lay dying for six hours. He passed in and out of consciousness, aware at each wakening that his life was ebbing faster and faster.

To face that moment, he began singing a hymn his mother had taught him:

> *There is a name to me so dear*
> *Like sweetest music to my ear;*
> *For when my heart is troubled, filled with fear,*
> *Jesus whispers peace.*

As he sang, a German soldier came upon him, his bayonet fixed. Burt anticipated the worst but kept singing. As he sang he felt himself being lifted up. He was carried to a nearby stone ledge. There the enemy soldier left Burt unharmed. A few minutes later, he was discovered and rescued by his own medics.[1]

Date: _____ _____ _____
Place: _____ _____ _____
Occasion: _____ _____ _____

The Healing Balm

Author and Counselor Alan Loy McGinnis instructs his readers to take charge of their feelings, and choose to be optimists. This can be done, in part, by employing "uplifting music to lift your mood. . . . Music can be an important stimulant to optimistic thinking. Churches have always included singing in worship, and music is far more effective when the whole congregation sings rather than when they listen to a choir perform. Singing reinforces one's beliefs.

"Horace spoke of music as 'the healing balm of troubles.' Congreve in *The Morning Bride* said, 'Music hath charms to soothe the savage breast.' Coleridge said, 'I feel physically refreshed and strengthened by it.' And Goethe, who was not particularly musical, said music made him unfold 'like the fingers of a threatening fist which straighten amicably.' "[2]

Date: _____ _____ _____
Place: _____ _____ _____
Occasion: _____ _____ _____

The Second Best Book

A. W. Tozer wrote, "I say without qualification, after the Sacred Scriptures, the next best companion for the soul is a good hymnal. . . . After the Bible, the hymnbook

---

[1] George Beverly Shea, *Songs That Lift the Heart* (Minneapolis: World Wide Publications, 1972), 66–67.
[2] Alan Loy McGinnis, *The Power of Optimism* (New York: Harper & Row, 1990), 98–99.

is next. And remember, I do not say a songbook or a book of gospel songs, but a real hymnal containing the cream of the great Christian hymns left to us by the ages.

"A great hymn embodies the purest concentrated thoughts of some lofty saint who may have long ago gone from the earth and left little or nothing behind him except that hymn.

"Sometimes our hearts are strangely stubborn and will not soften or grow tender no matter how much praying we do. At such times, it is often found that the reading or singing of a good hymn will melt the ice jam and start the inward affections flowing.

"Every Christian should have lying beside his Bible a copy of some standard hymnbook. He should read out of one and sing out of the other, and he will be surprised and delighted to discover how much they are alike."[1]

Date: _____ _____ _____
Place: _____ _____ _____
Occasion: _____ _____ _____

Singing His Own Inspired Words

Scripture songs are nothing new. What else is the book of Psalms? The nineteenth-century hymnist Frances Ridley Havergal once said, "I believe there is nothing like singing His own words. The preacher claims the promise, 'My word shall not return unto Me void,' and why should not the singer equally claim it? Why should we use His own inspired words, with faith in their power, when speaking or writing, and content ourselves with human words put into rhyme (and sometimes very feeble rhyme) for singing?"[2]

Date: _____ _____ _____
Place: _____ _____ _____
Occasion: _____ _____ _____

Music Can Lift Our Hearts

"A hymnal is one of the most remarkable aids to participatory worship a lay person can utilize. Within its binding and pages are contained the doctrines of the faith culled through the ages and saturated with the devotion of those saints who have been members of the church triumphant. Music by its very nature evokes the soul's response. If we allow it, music can lift our hearts to attend to God."—Karen Maines, in the Introduction of the hymnal, *Sing Joyfully*[3]

Date: _____ _____ _____
Place: _____ _____ _____
Occasion: _____ _____ _____

[1] Tozer, *We Travel an Appointed Way*, 63–65.
[2] Frances Ridley Havergal, *Kept for the Master's Use* (Philadelphia: The Rodgers Co. n.d.), 75.
[3] Karen Maines, *Sing Joyfully* (Carol Stream, IL: Tabernacle Publishing Co., 1989), 5.

The God Who Sings

Warren Wiersbe points out that all three members of the Godhead sing:

- God the Father sings, according to Zephaniah 3:17: "The Lord your God in your midst, The Mighty One, will save; He will rejoice over you with gladness, He will quiet you with His love, He will rejoice over you with singing."
- God the Son sings, for we read in Matthew 26:30 that after he and his disciples had sung a hymn, they went to the Mount of Olives.
- But how does the Holy Spirit sing? He sings through His church! Ephesians 5:18ff: "Be filled with the spirit, speaking to one another in psalms and hymns and spiritual songs, singing and making melody . . ."[1]

Date: _____ _____ _____
Place: _____ _____ _____
Occasion: _____ _____ _____

They Have Sung Their Creed

R. W. Dale, in his Yale lectures on preaching, spent most of one session on the power of music in the life of a congregation, saying, "The congregations that always leave the singing to the choir, and never sing at all, or that sing very rarely, or that sing languidly and without any vigor and heartiness, do not know what they miss. In nearly all great revivals of religion the common people themselves have been inspired with a passion for singing. They have sung their creed: it seemed the freest and most natural way of declaring their triumphant belief in the great Christian truths."[2]

Date: _____ _____ _____
Place: _____ _____ _____
Occasion: _____ _____ _____

The Power of Song

In a recent article in the Wheaton College alumni magazine, Larry Eskridge asked a good question: "How many of you can remember much about the sermons we heard during childhood? And try as we might, it's likely that few of us could put together even the most skeletal three-point sermon outline from a message we heard just a month ago.

"But almost without effort we can remember every word of the hymns we sang decades ago. Hymns like *Amazing Grace, Leaning on the Everlasting Arms, I Love to Tell the Story, O, For a Thousand Tongues to Sing, How Firm a Foundation,* and *Just As I Am . . .*

---

[1] Dr. Warren Wiersbe, sermon at Cedarville College, 1998.
[2] R. W. Dale, *Nine Lectures on Preaching, Delivered at Yale* (Cincinnati: Jennings & Graham, n.d.), 273.

seemed to tie our hearts together in ways no sermon or Sunday school lesson possibly could."[1]

Date: _____ _____ _____
Place: _____ _____ _____
Occasion: _____ _____ _____

Music Evangelism

In 1735 aboard a windjammer crossing the Atlantic, John Wesley was terrified. The storm was so fierce that the mainsail split and the mast broke in two. The seas pounded the deck. Passengers ran, screaming, all except for a group of twenty-six German Christians—Moravians—who were singing above the howling of the wind. Despite the fierceness of the storm, they didn't miss a note. Wesley, who wasn't a Christian at the time, later asked one of them, "Weren't you afraid?"

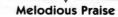

Melodious Praise

Next to the Word of God, music deserves the highest praise.

—MARTIN LUTHER

"Thank God, no," came the reply.

The faith and confidence of these Christians—their song in the storm—so impressed Wesley that later, at a Moravian meeting house in London, he too gave himself fully to Jesus Christ.

Date: _____ _____ _____
Place: _____ _____ _____
Occasion: _____ _____ _____

Wesley's Rules for Singing

John Wesley's rules for singing were published as part of his 1780 hymnal. They include the following:

1. Learn these tunes before you learn any others; afterwards learn as many as you please.
2. Sing them exactly as they are printed here, without altering or mending them at all.
3. Sing all. See that you join with the congregation as frequently as you can.
4. Sing lustily and with a good courage. Beware of singing as if you were half dead, or half asleep.
5. Sing modestly. Do not bawl, so as to be heard above or distinct from the rest of the congregation.
6. Sing in tune. Whatever time is sung, be sure to keep with it. Do not run before or stay behind it. Take care not to sing too slow.

---

[1] Larry Eskridge, "O Sing Unto the Lord an Old Song," *Wheaton*, Autumn 1999, 18.

7. Above all sing spiritually. Have an eye to God in every word you sing. Aim at pleasing him more than yourself, or any other creature. In order to do this attend strickly to the sense of what you sing.

In addition, Wesley wrote something interesting in his Journal on July 3, 1764, about learning new hymns: "I seldom relish verses at first hearing. Till I have heard them over and over, they give me no pleasure, and they give me next to none when I have heard them a few times more, so as to be quite familiar."

Date:	_____	_____	_____
Place:	_____	_____	_____
Occasion:	_____	_____	_____

Music's Power to Heal

According to an article in *Reader's Digest*, music is being touted by many doctors as an aid in healing. Many times, soft classical music is played in operating rooms to calm the patient and surgical team, and sometimes the patient is given earphones to hear soothing music while under anesthesia. "We've seen confirmation of music's benefits in helping to avoid serious complications during illness, enhancing patients' well-being, and shortening hospital stays," said one physician.

Another doctor said, "Half an hour of music produced the same effect as ten milligrams of Valium."

Some studies show that music can lower blood pressure, basal-metabolism and respiration rates, thus lessening physiological responses to stress. Other studies suggest music may help increase production of endorphins.

Clinical researchers at the UCLA School of Nursing in Los Angeles, and at Georgia Baptist Medical Center in Atlanta, found that premature babies gained weight faster and were able to use oxygen more efficiently when they listened to soothing music mixed with voices or womb sounds.

Music therapy is proving especially effective in three key medical areas:

1. Pain, anxiety, and depression. Cancer patients often brood in their hospital rooms, refusing to talk with doctors and nurses. The music therapist can give them a positive outlook.
2. Mental, emotional, and physical handicaps.
3. Neurological disorders. Some patients who cannot talk or move are often able to sing.

"Music is not magic," said one therapist. "But in a hospital or at home, for young people or older ones, it can be a potent medicine that helps us all."[1]

There is nothing new here. In a book published in 1925, Christian writer Henry H. Jowett described how music was being used in London in the ministry of healing, saying, "At the Maudesley Hospital it has passed far beyond the experimental stage, and is in confident and constant practice. It is being used in nervous disorders and in restoring mental powers to ex-Service men. . . . The holy, healing Spirit of God

[1] David M. Mazie, "Music's Surprising Power to Heal," *Reader's Digest*, August 1992, 174–178.

is brooding over the stricken spirits of men and is restoring their broken estate through the seductive and mollifying ministry of music and song."[1]

Yet we can trace the therapeutic use of music even earlier, to 1 Samuel 16: "David would take a harp and play it with his hand. Then Saul would become refreshed and well, and the distressing spirit would depart from him." (1 Samuel 16:23)

Date: _____ _____ _____

Place: _____ _____ _____

Occasion: _____ _____ _____

For Pets, Too

According to an article in the *Nashville Tennessean,* veterinarians in Tokyo are recommending music for house pets who are restless, tense, or irritable. "Cheerful but serene music is good for dogs, and romantic music is good for cats," said Morito Aoki, a forty-nine-year-old vet who has experimented with music on more than one hundred dogs and cats. He has created a compact disc, using professional musicians, that contains six slow and calm instrumental tunes for dogs and seven cat numbers that are bouncier and more rhythmic.[2]

Date: _____ _____ _____

Place: _____ _____ _____

Occasion: _____ _____ _____

Spurgeon's Songs

Anyone who has read many of the sermons of Charles Spurgeon knows that they are constantly punctuated with the verses of hymns that he seemingly plucks out of thin air and incorporates into his message at powerful junctures. How did he come to learn the words to so many hymns? In *The Essex Lad,* a 1892 biography of Spurgeon, we read that as a child, Spurgeon lived with his grandparents for some years, and even afterward would pay frequent and prolonged visits to them in Stambourne.

"It was during these periodical visits that his grandmother offered him a farthing each for every hymn he could correctly repeat to her from memory. At once he set to work, and so quickly did he learn them that his grandmother said: 'Charlie, I see danger of becoming bankrupt, and I must reduce the price to a penny a dozen.' Even at this price he committed to memory almost the whole of Dr. Watts' hymns."

Spurgeon later said, "No matter on what subject I preach, I can even now, in the middle of any sermon, quote some verse of a hymn in harmony with the subject; the hymns have remained with me."

---

[1] J. H. Jowett, *Life in the Heights* (Grand Rapids, MI: Baker Book House, 1925), 138.
[2] "CDs soothe Japanese House Pets," *The Nashville Tennessean,* Sunday, November 17, 1991, sec. 6-A.

Date: _____ _____ _____
Place: _____ _____ _____
Occasion: _____ _____ _____

Singing I Go

In his autobiography, *Then Sings My Soul,* George Beverly Shea, longtime soloist for the Billy Graham Crusades, tells of growing up in a pastor's home in Canada. Every morning of his childhood, Bev Shea awoke in the same way. His mother, a gifted musician, would sit down at the piano, hit the cords, and begin singing in a sweet soprano voice the old gospel song:

> *Singing I go along life's road,*
> *Praising the Lord, praising the Lord,*
> *Singing I go along life's road,*
> *For Jesus has lifted my load.*

The way we are awakened in the morning has a big impact on our attitude all day long; so no wonder George Beverly Shea came to be called "America's beloved gospel singer."

Date: _____ _____ _____
Place: _____ _____ _____
Occasion: _____ _____ _____

That's Okay

A man once complained to the minister following church, "I don't like the hymns you chose today."

"That's okay," came the reply. "We weren't singing them for you."

Date: _____ _____ _____
Place: _____ _____ _____
Occasion: _____ _____ _____

Interruptions

Someone Once Said . . .

- *There's something in the role of a pastor that says the pastor should always be available.*—Ed Bratcher, pastor and author[1]
- *If you're always available, you're never available.*—Ed Young, pastor[2]

---

[1] Kevin A. Miller, *Secrets of Staying Power* (Waco, TX: Word Books, 1988), 55.
[2] Personal conversation with author.

- *Interruptions, ranked as the number one source of discouragement on the "Leadership" survey, arise because pastors are on emergency call twenty-four hours a day.*—Kevin A. Miller[1]
- *What gives the manager's job its nightmarish quality are the interruptions.*—George Berkwitt[2]
- *It is difficult to produce a television documentary that is both incisive and probing when every twelve minutes one is interrupted by twelve dancing rabbits singing about toilet paper.*—Rod Serling, writer and television producer
- *Today, the degradation of the inner life is symbolized by the fact that the only place sacred from interruption is the private toilet.*—Lewis Mumford, U.S. urban planner and historian

Date: _____ _____ _____

Place: _____ _____ _____

Occasion: _____ _____ _____

Interruptions in the Workplace

A new study, believed to be the first published research in the world to focus on interruptions at work, found that school principals spend around one-third of their day attending to interruptions. The study showed that most principals were interrupted, on average, between twenty-five and twenty-eight times a day. Dr. Ross Thomas, who oversaw the project, said, "I don't see that there is anything wrong with principals being interrupted because it is part-and-parcel of the job—schools are people-oriented organizations. Much of the time-management literature implies that interruptions are to be avoided at all costs, but this is absurd. Very few time-management authors concede that there is value in the interruptions, but they should realize that a lot of fun lies in the challenge of everyday interruptions." He suggests that principals try, not to avoid interruptions, but to manage them better.[3]

Date: _____ _____ _____

Place: _____ _____ _____

Occasion: _____ _____ _____

Another Study

A recent study reported by Brid O'Conaill and David Frohlich of Hewlett Packard Labs in England found that on average their managers were being interrupted just over four times every hour. The average duration of an interruption was two minutes eleven seconds. Approximately ten minutes in every hour was being spent engaged in an interruption, and in just over 55 percent of the cases the recipient returned to their original activity.

---

[1] Kevin A. Miller, *Secrets of Staying Power* (Waco, TX: Word Books, 1988), 55.

[2] R. Alec Mackenzie, *The Time Trap* (New York: McGraw-Hill Book Company, 1972), 85.

[3] "Research Shows Impact of Interruptions at Work," *Smiths Online* Vol. 39, Number 4. 27 March 1998, < www.une.edu >.

Date: _____ _____ _____
Place: _____ _____ _____
Occasion: _____ _____ _____

The Interruptions Are the Ministry

A minister once observed that sometimes "interruptions *are* the ministry." In the book, *Before Burnout,* the authors point out that Mark's Gospel provides many examples of Jesus handling interruptions well. After he healed a man with an unclean spirit (Mark 1:21–26), Jesus was suddenly interrupted by an entire city who demanded his attention (1:33). He was then interrupted in the midst of his teaching by four men carrying a paralyzed man (2:1–5). . . . Later Jesus was pursued and interrupted by a large multitude (3:7–9). At one point, after being interrupted by Jairus, Christ was almost immediately interrupted again by a woman with a long-term illness. The Savior compassionately handled all of those interruptions well.

A study of the way Jesus handled these kinds of interruption can teach us several things:

1. Christ always responded graciously. He never conveyed the attitude that people did not have a right to interrupt Him.
2. He made people a priority. For the most part, those who interrupted Him were not prominent individuals, yet Christ treated them as important.
3. Although frequently interrupted, Christ did not allow those interruptions to deflect Him from His ultimate purpose. For example, after dealing with the woman with the issue of blood, Jesus immediately went on to raise Jairus' daughter.
4. On occasion, the Savior actually initiated an interruption himself. He interrupted His teaching of the multitude to call Levi the tax collector to follow Him.
5. Fifth, when important priorities made it necessary, Christ isolated Himself from interruptions.

"Learning to handle interruptions in a Christlike fashion," say the authors, "will take us a significant distance down the road of handling life's circumstances."[1]

Date: _____ _____ _____
Place: _____ _____ _____
Occasion: _____ _____ _____

Saved by an Interruption

It was Saturday night of Thanksgiving weekend, and the Coconut Grove was packed. Waiters were setting up extra tables to handle the diners. The overflow from

---

[1] Frank Minirth, Don Hawkins, Paul Meier, Chris Thurman, *Before Burnout* (Chicago: Moody Press, 1990), 151–152.

the dining room surged down a narrow stairway to the Melody Lounge. This dimly lit basement bar offered a South Seas ambiance, with artificial palm trees, driftwood, rattan and a ceiling draped in blue satin. The only illumination came from behind the bar, supplemented by low-wattage bulbs hidden in the palms. Even this was too bright for one young man. He reached up, unscrewed a bulb and settled back in his date's arms. Like many others there, he was in uniform. It was 1942; the U.S. had been fighting WWII for nearly a year. Dr. Vincent Senna was having dinner that night in the Grove and was paged because one of his patients had gone into labor. Grumbling, Senna rushed to the hospital in time to deliver the baby . . . and save his life. Because after he left, for still unknown reasons, the Coconut Grove burst into flames, and over 490 people died in the smoke and flames. The interruption that ruined his evening also saved his life![1]

Date: _____ _____ _____
Place: _____ _____ _____
Occasion: _____ _____ _____

Interruption at 2 A.M.

While facing one of the great crises of his political life, the great prime minister of England, William Gladstone, sat writing one morning at two o'clock on a speech with which he hoped to win a great political victory in the House of Commons the next day. At that hour there came to his door the mother of a poor, dying cripple, asking him to come and bring some message of hope and cheer to her hopeless boy. Without hesitation, the great Commoner left the preparation of his speech and spent the night leading the child to Christ. Staying till the early dawn, he closed the eyes of the dead child and went back to his home and faced his day with a smile of confidence, peace, and power.

Later that morning Gladstone said to a friend, "I am the happiest man in the world today." A few hours later he made the greatest speech of his life in the House of Commons, carrying his cause to a triumphant success.[2]

Date: _____ _____ _____
Place: _____ _____ _____
Occasion: _____ _____ _____

"But There Were Interruptions!"

And the Lord spoke to Noah and said: "In six months I'm going to make it rain until the whole earth is covered with water and all the evil people are destroyed. But, I want to save a few good people, and two of every kind of living thing on the earth. I am ordering you to build an Ark." And in a flash of lightning he delivered the specifications for an Ark.

---

[1] *Reader's Digest*, November 1992, <www.sermonillustrations.com>.
[2] George Sweeting, *Love is the Greatest* (Chicago: Moody Press, 1974), 123.

"Ok," said Noah, trembling in fear and fumbling with the blueprints.

"Six months, and it starts to rain," thundered the Lord. "You'd better have my Ark completed, or learn to swim for a very long time."

Six months passed. The skies began to cloud up and rain began to fall. The Lord saw Noah was sitting in his front yard weeping, and there was no Ark.

"Noah," shouted the Lord, "Where is my Ark?" A lightning bolt crashed into the ground next to Noah.

"Lord, please forgive me!" begged Noah. "I did my best, but there were interruptions!"

"First I had to get a building permit for the Ark construction project, and your plans did not meet code. So I had to hire an engineer to redraw the plans. Then I got into a big fight over whether or not the Ark needed a fire sprinkler system. My neighbors objected, claiming I was violating zoning by building the Ark in my front yard, so I had to get a variance from the city planning commission.

> ━━━━◇━━━━
> **Uninterrupted Success**
>
> *The man who says it cannot be done, should not interrupt the man who is doing it.*
> —CHINESE PROVERB
> ━━━━◇━━━━

"Then I had a big problem getting enough wood for the Ark because there was a ban on cutting the trees, to save the Spotted Owl. I had to convince the U.S. Forest Service that I needed the wood to save the owls. But, they wouldn't let me catch any owls. So no owls. Then the carpenters formed a union and went out on strike. I had to negotiate a settlement with the National Labor Relations Board before anyone would pick up a saw or hammer. Now we have sixteen carpenters going on the boat and still no owls.

"Then I started gathering the animals, and got sued by an animal rights group. They objected to me taking only two of each kind. Just when I got the suit dismissed, EPA notified me that I couldn't complete the Ark without filing an environmental impact statement on your proposed flood. They didn't take kindly to the idea that they had no jurisdiction over the conduct of a Supreme Being. Then the Army Corps of Engineers wanted a map of the proposed new flood plain. I sent them a globe.

"Right now I'm still trying to resolve a complaint from the Equal Employment Opportunity Commission over how many Croatians I'm supposed to hire. The IRS has seized all my assets, claiming I'm trying to avoid paying taxes by leaving the country, and I just got a notice from the state about owing some kind of use tax.

"I really don't think I can finish your Ark for at least another five years," Noah wailed.

The sky began to clear. The sun began to shine. A rainbow arched across the sky. Noah looked up and smiled. "You mean you're not going to destroy the earth?" Noah asked hopefully.

"No" said the Lord sadly, "The government already has. . . ."[1]

> Date: _____ _____ _____
> Place: _____ _____ _____
> Occasion: _____ _____ _____

---

[1] Source unknown.

The Interrupter

Lee Fisher, longtime associate of evangelist Billy Graham, tells of a time when Mr. Graham was preaching on Trans World Radio through his German interpreter, Peter Schneider. All went well, except for a listener in Cologne, Germany, who wrote to complain. She said that she was impressed with Billy Graham's power and authority. "But there is only one thing wrong," she stated. "There's a man speaking English who keeps interrupting him."[1]

Date:			
Place:			
Occasion:			

Jesus Christ

Someone Once Said . . .

- *I believe that Christ died for me because it is incredible; I believe that He rose from the dead because it is impossible.*—A. W. Tozer[2]
- *Christ is the central figure in biblical revelation. The cross is the central factor in biblical revelation.*—Dan DeHaan[3]
- *Jesus Christ: the meeting place of eternity and time, the blending of deity and humanity, the junction of heaven and earth.*—Anonymous
- *Jesus is God spelling Himself out in language that man can understand.*—S. D. Gordon
- *Most men are notable for one conspicuous virtue or grace. Moses for meekness, Job for patience. John for love. But in Jesus you find everything.*—J. Oswald Sanders[4]
- *He stands absolutely alone in history; in teaching, in example, in character, an exception, a marvel, and He is Himself the evidence of Christianity.*—A. T. Pierson[5]
- *He authenticates Himself.*—Bishop Clark[6]
- *He comes forth from the carpenter's shop, where like all other well-trained Hebrew youth, He had learned His father's trade, and His first public utterance is the most original and revolutionary address on practical morals which the world ever heard.*—A. T. Pierson[7]
- *No other God have I but Thee; born in a manger, died on a tree.*—Martin Luther

Date:			
Place:			
Occasion:			

[1] Lee Fisher, *A Funny Thing Happened on the Way to the Crusade* (Carol Stream, IL: Creation House, 1974), 28.
[2] A. W. Tozer, *The Knowledge of the Holy* (New York: Harper & Row, Publishers, 1961), 27.
[3] Dan DeHaan, *The God You Can Know* (Chicago: Moody Press, 1982), 67.
[4] J. Oswald Sanders, *The Incomparable Christ* (Chicago: Moody Press, 1971), 13.
[5] Arthur T. Pierson, *Many Infallible Proofs*, vol. 2 (Grand Rapids, MI: Zondervan, n.d.), 48.
[6] Pierson, *Many Infallible Proofs*, vol. 2, 48.
[7] Pierson, *Many Infallible Proofs*, vol. 2, 88.

Classic Summations

The life of Jesus Christ is so intensely beautiful and powerful that verbal descriptions of it have moved audiences for centuries. Here are some favorites:

- **Attributed to John Chrysostom (c. A.D. 347–407), Bishop of Constantinople**

  I do not think of Christ as God alone, or man alone, but both together. For I know He was hungry, and I know that with five loaves He fed five thousand. I know He was thirsty, and I know that He turned the water into wine. I know he was carried in a ship, and I know that He walked on the sea. I know that He died, and I know that He raised the dead. I know that He was set before Pilate, and I know that He sits with the Father on His throne. I know that He was worshipped by angels, and I know that He was stoned by the Jews. And truly some of these I ascribe to the human, and others to the divine nature. For by reason of this He is said to have been both God and man.

- **Augustine (A.D. 354–430)**

  He it is by whom all things were made, and who was made one of all things; who is the revealer of the Father, the creator of the Mother; the Son of God by the Father without a mother, the Son of man by the Mother without a father; the Word who is God before all time, the Word made flesh at a fitting time, the maker of the sun, made under the sun; ordering all the ages from the bosom of the Father, hallowing a day of to-day from the womb of the Mother; remaining in the former, coming forth from the latter; author of the heaven and the earth, sprung under the heaven out of the earth; unutterably wise, in His wisdom a babe without utterance; filling the world, lying in a manger.

- **The Council of Chalcedon, A.D. 451**

  We . . . confess one and the same Son, our Lord Jesus Christ; the same perfect in Manhood; truly God and truly Man, in all things like unto us without sin; . . . and in these latter days for us and for our salvation, born of Mary the Virgin Mother of God according to the Manhood . . . existing in two natures without mixture, without change, without division, without separation; the diversity of the two natures not being at all destroyed by their union, but the peculiar properties of each nature being preserved . . . not parted or divided into two persons, but one Lord Jesus Christ.

- **John Donne (A.D. 1573–1631), English poet and clergyman**

  The whole life of Christ was a continual Passion; others die martyrs but Christ was born a martyr. He found a Golgotha even in Bethlehem, where he was born; for to his tenderness then the straws were almost as sharp as thorns after, and the manger as uneasy at first as his cross at last. His birth and death were but one continual act, and his Christmas Day and his Good Friday are but the evening and morning of one and the same day.[1]

- **Attributed to Phillips Brooks (A.D. 1835–1893), American Episcopal minister**

  He was born in an obscure village, the child of a peasant woman. He worked in a carpenter shop until he was thirty. Then for three years he was an itinerant preacher. He never wrote a book. He never held an office. He never had a family or owned a house. He never went to college. He never traveled two hundred miles from the place where he was born. He never did one of the things that usually accompany greatness. He had no credentials but himself. He was only thirty-three when the tide of public opinion turned

---

[1] Constance and Daniel Pollock, *The Book of Uncommon Prayer* (Dallas: Word Publishing Co., 1996), 49.

against him. His friends ran away. He was nailed to a cross between two thieves. When he was dead, he was laid in a borrowed grave through the pity of a friend. Nineteen centuries have come and gone, and today he is the central figure of the human race, and the leader of the column of progress. I am far within the mark when I say that all the armies that ever marched, all the navies that ever sailed, all the parliaments that ever sat, all the kings that ever reigned, put together, have not affected the life of man on earth as has that One Solitary Life.

• J. Sidlow Baxter, British Bible teacher

Fundamentally, our Lord's message was Himself. He did not come merely to preach a Gospel; He himself is that Gospel. He did not come merely to give bread; He said, "I am the bread." He did not come merely to shed light; He said, "I am the light." He did not come merely to show the door; He said, "I am the door." He did not come merely to name a shepherd; He said: "I am the shepherd." He did not come merely to point the way; He said, "I am the way, the truth, and the life."[1]

• Philip Schaff, church historian

A catalog of virtues and graces, however complete, would merely give us a mechanical view. It's the spotless purity and the sinlessness of Jesus as acknowledged by friend and foe that raises His character high above the reach of all others. In Him we see the even harmony and symmetry of all graces: His love for God and man, His dignity and humility, His strength and tenderness, His greatness and simplicity, and His self-control and submission. It's the absolute perfection of Christ's character that makes Him a moral miracle in History. It's futile to compare Him with saints and sages, ancient or modern. Even the skeptic Jean Jacques Rousseau was compelled to remark, "If Socrates lived and died like a sage, Jesus lived and died like a God."

• Will Durant, historian

The historian Will Durant, author of the massive *Story of Civilization*, devoted an entire volume of 751 pages to the years surrounding the life of Christ, and he entitled it "Caesar and Christ." In it he noticed the stylistic differences between the Gospels, but he concluded, *The contradictions are of minutiae, not substance; in essentials the synoptic gospels agree remarkably well, and form a consistent portrait of Christ. No one reading these scenes can doubt the reality of the figure behind them. That a few simple men should in one generation have invented so powerful and appealing a personality, so lofty an ethic and so inspiring a vision of human brotherhood, would be a miracle far more incredible than any recorded in the Gospels. After two centuries of Higher Criticism the outlines of the life, character, and teachings of Christ, remain reasonably clear, and constitute the most fascinating feature in the history of Western man.*[2]

• A. T. Pierson, Bible teacher

This precious Book tells us of one who resigned the throne and crown of heaven, exchanged the radiant robe of the universal King for the garment of a servant, descended to death, condescended to human want and woe and wickedness, lay in a lowly cradle in a cattle stall at Bethlehem, and hung upon a cross of shame of Calvary, that even those

[1] J. Sidlow Baxter, *Explore the Book*, vol. 5 (Grand Rapids, MI: Zondervan, 1960), 308.
[2] Will Durant, *The Story of Civilization: Volume III—Caesar and Christ* (New York: Simon and Schuster, 1972), 557.

who crucified Him might be forgiven. Can you span the chasm between the throne of a universe and that cross? A crown of stars and a crown of thorns? The worship of the host of heaven and the mockery of an insulting mob? . . . There is nothing like it in history, not even in fable.

How can we understand . . . ? A man with human infirmities, without human sin or sinfulness; poor, yet having at His disposal universal riches; weak and weary, yet having the exhaustless energy of God; unable to resist the violence and insults of His foes, yet able to summon legions of angels at a word or wish; suffering, yet incapable of anything but perfect bliss; dying, yet Himself having neither beginning of days or end of years?[1]

• Dr. Porter

In his book, *Many Infallible Proofs:* volume 2, A. T. Pierson, having alluded to the raw, brutal nature of the Roman Empire, quotes this paragraph from a Dr. Porter: *How, then, can it be explained that forth from that generation came the loftiest and loveliest, the simplest, yet the most complete ideal of a master, friend, example, Savior of human kind, that the world has ever conceived? An ideal that, since it was furnished to man in the record, has never been altered except for the worse; a picture that no genius can retouch except to mar; a gem that no polisher can try to cut, except to break it; able to guide the oldest and to soothe the youngest of mankind; to add luster to our brightest joys, and to dispel our darkest fears? Whether realized in fact or regarded only as an ideal, the conception of Jesus is the greatest miracle of the ages!*

• An Unknown Author

Buddha never claimed to be God. Moses never claimed to be Jehovah. Mohammed never claimed to be Allah. Yet Jesus Christ claimed to be the true and living God.

Buddha simply said, "I am a teacher in search of the truth."

Jesus said, "I am the Truth."

Confucius said, "I never claimed to be holy."

Jesus said, "Who convicts me of sin?"

Mohammed said, "Unless God throws his cloak of mercy over me, I have no hope."

Jesus said, "Unless you believe in me, you will die in your sins."

• Attributed to Napoleon

You speak of Caesar, Alexander, of their conquests; of the enthusiasm they enkindled in the hearts of their soldiers, but can you conceive of a dead man making conquests with an army faithful and entirely devoted to His memory? My army has forgotten me while living. Alexander, Caesar, Charlemagne and myself have founded empires. But on what did we rest the creations of our genius? Upon force! Jesus Christ alone founded His empire upon love: and at this hour millions of men would die for Him. I have so inspired multitudes that they would die for me—but, after all, my presence was necessary—the lighting of my eye, my voice, a word from me—then the sacred fire was kindled in their hearts. Now that I am at St. Helena, alone, chained upon this rock, who fights and wins empires for me? What an abyss between my deep misery and the eternal reign of Christ who is proclaimed, loved, adored, and whose reign is extending over all the earth.[2]

• Thomas, the disciple of Jesus

My Lord and My God!

---

[1] Pierson, *Many Infallible Proofs,* vol. 2, 44, 55.
[2] Pierson, *Many Infallible Proofs,* vol. 2, 49.

Date: _____ _____ _____
Place: _____ _____ _____
Occasion: _____ _____ _____

The Childhood of Christ

In Summer days, like you and me
He played about the door,
Or gathered, when the father toiled,
The shavings from the floor.
Sometimes He lay upon the grass
The same 'as you and I,
And saw the hawks above Him pass
Like specks against the sky;
Or clinging to the gate, He watched
The stranger passing by.
And when the sun at break of day
Crept in upon His hair
I think it must have left a ray
Of unseen glory there—
A kiss of love on that little brow,
For the thorns that it must wear.
—A. B. Paine[1]

Date: _____ _____ _____
Place: _____ _____ _____
Occasion: _____ _____ _____

The Hidden Years

"It is a challenging thought . . ." writes J. Oswald Sanders, "that our divine Lord spent six times as long working at the carpenter's bench, as he did in His world-shaking ministry. . . .

"He saw no incongruity in the Lord of glory standing in the saw pit laboriously cutting the thick logs into planks, or using plane and hammer. . . .

"Justin Martyr, who lived shortly after the death of John the apostle, wrote of Jesus, 'When He was among men He made ploughs and yokes and other farm implements.'

"One writer suggests that there was one shop in Nazareth where benches were made to stand on four legs, and doors to open and shut properly, for no second-rate work ever left His bench—near enough was not good enough for our Great Exemplar."[2]

---

[1] J. Oswald Sanders, *The Incomparable Christ* (Chicago: Moody Press, 1971), 35.
[2] Sanders, *The Incomparable Christ*, 46–47.

Date: _____   _____   _____
Place: _____   _____   _____
Occasion: _____   _____   _____

The God-Man

> Our blessed Lord combined in one, two natures, both complete;
>   A perfect manhood all sublime, in Godhead all replete.
>
> As man He entered Cana's feast, a humble guest to dine;
>   As God He moved the water there, and changed it into wine.
>
> As man He climbed the mountain's height, a suppliant to be;
>   As God He left the place of prayer and walked upon the sea.
>
> As man He wept in heartfelt grief, beside a loved one's grave;
>   As God He burst the bands of death, Almighty still to save.
>
> As man He lay within a boat o'erpowered by needful sleep;
>   As God He rose, rebuked the wind and stilled the angry deep.
>
> Such was our Lord in life on earth, in dual nature one;
>   The woman's seed in very truth and God's eternal Son.
>
> O Child, O Son, O Word made flesh, may Thy high praise increase:
>   Called Wonderful, the Mighty God, Eternal Prince of Peace[1]

Date: _____   _____   _____
Place: _____   _____   _____
Occasion: _____   _____   _____

Liar, Lunatic, or Lord?

In *Mere Christianity*, C. S. Lewis wrote, "A man who was merely a man and said the sort of things Jesus said wouldn't be a great moral teacher. He would either be a lunatic on the level with a man who says he's a poached egg—or else he would be the devil of hell; you must take your choice. Either this was, and is, the Son of God, or else a mad man or something worse. You can shut Him up for a demon, or you can fall at His feet and call Him Lord and God. But don't come up with any patronizing nonsense about His being a great moral teacher. He hasn't left that alternative open to us. He did not intend to."[2]

Date: _____   _____   _____
Place: _____   _____   _____
Occasion: _____   _____   _____

---

[1] W. A. Criswell, *Great Doctrines of the Bible*, vol. 2 (Grand Rapids, MI: Zondervan Publishing House, 1982), 122.

[2] C. S. Lewis, *Mere Christianity* (New York: The MacMillan Co., 1960), 41.

The Prince

Soren Kierkegaard, the Danish theologian, told a story about a certain kingdom wherein there was a handsome prince, searching for a woman worthy enough to be his wife and to become queen of the land. One day while running an errand for his father he passed through a poor village. As he glanced out the window of his carriage his eyes fell on a beautiful peasant maiden. During ensuing days, he often passed by the young lady and soon fell in love with her by sight. But he had a problem. How could he seek her hand?

He could command her to marry him, but the prince wanted someone who would marry him out of love, not coercion. He could show up at her door in his splendid uniform in a gold carriage drawn by six horses, attendants in tow, and bearing a chest of jewels and gold coins. But then how would he know if she really loved him or if she was just overawed and overwhelmed with his splendor? Finally he came up with another solution.

He stripped off his royal robes, put on common dress, moved into the village, and got to know her without revealing his identity. As he lived among the people, the prince and the maiden became friends, shared each other's interests, and talked about their concerns. By and by, the young lady grew to love him for who he was and because he had first loved her.

This is exactly the Gospel. The Prince of Peace Himself, Jesus Christ, laid aside the robes of his glory, garbed himself as a peasant, became a human being, and moved into our village, onto our planet, to woo us to himself. Both the one who makes us holy and those who are being made holy are of the same family. So Jesus is not ashamed to call us brothers.

He who was shadowed out in Eden, He to whom Abel looked, He who was Abraham's seed and David's offspring and the sweet theme of every prophet's word, He who was pierced on Calvary and laid in the grave, is the same Jesus who shall shortly come again. No sinner escapes death, but through one victim, one righteousness, one faith, one hope, one clinging to the cross, one cleaving to one Lord, one journeying in one blood-stained path. There is one only Savior of all the saved, one only door of heaven, one only plea before the judgment seat, one only ransom of a guilty soul.[1]

Date:			
Place:			
Occasion:			

Peace Child

In Don Richardson's best-selling book, *Peace Child,* he tells of going, accompanied by his wife Carol and seventeen-month-old child, to the Sawi, a headhunting tribe in Netherlands' New Guinea. There savagery was a way of life. The tribesmen considered headhunting, cannibalism, and treachery as virtues. As these savages heard

---

[1] Henry Law, *The Gospel in Exodus* (London: First Banner of Truth Trust, 1967), 33.

the story of the Gospel, they considered Judas—not Jesus—the hero, and Don almost despaired of ever reaching them.

At last, the warfare and barbarism between the Sawi and their neighbor tribes grew so intense that the Richardsons decided to pack their bags and leave. But when the Sawi heard of it, they were deeply disturbed. They had come to love and trust the Richardsons. To prevent their leaving, the Sawi met in a special session and decided to make peace.

The next day as Don watched with mounting curiosity, the peace ritual began. Young children from the warring villages were to be exchanged, and as long as any of those children were alive, the peace would continue.

It was an anguishing ritual, for every mother feared her child would be taken. But after a period of emotional indecision, the chief himself grabbed his only son and rushed toward the enemy tribe, literally giving the tribe to his enemies. In return, he received a son from the other side. Peace descended across the mountains.

As Don pondered the significance of the ceremony, he realized there was a powerful Redemptive Analogy. Shortly afterward, gathering the elders together, he told them how God the Heavenly Father sent Jesus to earth as His Peace Child to make peace between God and man.

It was a lesson they understood and embraced at last.[1]

Date: _____ _____ _____

Place: _____ _____ _____

Occasion: _____ _____ _____

Very Good, Mr. Comte

Auguste Comte, the French philosopher, and Thomas Carlyle, the Scottish essayist were deeply engaged in conversation. Comte said he was going to start a new religion that would supplant the religion of Christ. It was to have no mysteries and was to be as plain as the multiplication table; its name was to be positivism. "Very good, Mr. Comte," Carlyle replied, "very good. All you will need to do will be to speak as never a man spake, and live as never a man lived, and be crucified, and rise again the third day, and get the world to believe that you are still alive. Then your religion will have a chance to get on."[2]

Date: _____ _____ _____

Place: _____ _____ _____

Occasion: _____ _____ _____

As to Jesus of Nazareth

A few weeks before he died, Benjamin Franklin responded to an inquiry by President Ezra Stiles of Yale University concerning his religious faith. Said Franklin:

---

[1] Don Richardson, *Peace Child*, (Regal Publishers, 1975).
[2] Billy Graham, *How To Be Born Again* (Waco: Word Books, 1977), 136.

"As to Jesus of Nazareth . . . I have . . . some doubts as to his Divinity, tho' it is a question I do not dogmatize upon, having never studied it, and think it needless to busy myself with it now, when I expect soon an opportunity of knowing the truth with less trouble. I see no harm, however, in its being believed, if that belief has the good consequences . . . of making his doctrines more respected and observed."[1]

Date: _____ _____ _____
Place: _____ _____ _____
Occasion: _____ _____ _____

The Greatest Question

Television talk-show host Larry King made a very perceptive comment when he was asked who he would most like to have interviewed from across history. One of those he named was Jesus Christ. "What would you have asked Him?" Came the rejoinder to Mr. King. "I would like to ask Him if He was indeed virgin born, because the answer to that question would define history."[2]

Date: _____ _____ _____
Place: _____ _____ _____
Occasion: _____ _____ _____

The Collector

Recently, someone sent me the story of a very wealthy man who, with his devoted son, shared a passion for art collecting. They traveled around the world together, adding only the finest paintings to their collection. Included among them were works by Picasso, Van Gogh, and Monet. The old man was a widower, but his son filled up the void in his life, and this was their common bond.

But war erupted, and the young man enlisted and was sent overseas. Day after day, the old father prayed, held his breath, and waited for news. One autumn day near Thanksgiving the dreaded telegram came, bordered in black. The young man had died bravely in combat, trying to evacuate those caught under fire. Distraught and lonely, the old man faced the upcoming holidays with anguish and sorrow. On Christmas morning, a knock sounded at the door. The father opened it to find a soldier there, carrying a small package. As they talked, the soldier said, "Your son and I became very close, and he told me all about your joint art collection. I myself am an artist, and I wanted to give you this."

The man took this package in his feeble hands, unwrapped it, and there was a portrait of his son in striking detail. It wasn't a masterpiece, but it was the most precious work of art the man had ever seen. As he gazed at it, he wept. And as the young soldier left, the lonely father pushed aside thousands of dollars worth of art and hung the portrait of his son in the prized spot over the fireplace.

[1] Bruce Shelley, *Church History in Plain Language* (Waco: Word Books, 1982), 329.
[2] Ravi Zacharias, *Can Man Live Without God?* (Dallas: Word Publishing, 1994), xvii.

As the months passed, the old man received letter after letter, telling him of his son's bravery and selflessness, and of how many lives he had saved and how many more he had touched. With each passing day the portrait over the fireplace became more precious, and he told his friends that it was the greatest gift he had ever received.

The following Spring, the old man grew ill and passed away. The art world was full of anticipation, wanting to get its hands on this man's fabulous collection. A day was set to auction it all off, and according to the old man's instruction the first painting was one that was not on any museum's list—the painting of the man's son. When the auctioneer asked for an opening bid, the room was silent.

⬦
Historical Jesus

The name of Jesus is not so much written as ploughed into the history of the world.
—EMERSON

⬦

"Who will open the bidding at $100?" he asked. "The moments stretched on awkwardly, and finally someone in the back of the room said, "Let's go on to the next piece."

"No," replied the auctioneer. "We have to sell this one first."

Finally a neighbor of the man spoke. "Will you take fifty dollars for the painting? That's all I have, but I knew the boy and I liked him, so I'd like to have it."

"Fifty dollars, we have fifty dollars," shouted the auctioneer. "Will anyone go higher?" No one did. "Going once, going twice, gone." And the gavel fell.

Everyone breathed a deep sigh of relief, thankful that now they could proceed with the "real" auction and get their hands on the masterpieces. But imagine their shock when the auctioneer suddenly declared that the proceedings were over. A loud clamor arose. Stunned disbelief. "What do you mean it's over?" the people shouted. "What about all the masterpieces?"

The auctioneer replied, "It's very simple. According to the will, whoever takes the son gets it all."

The Bible says, "God has given us eternal life, and this life is in His Son. He who has the Son has life; he who does not have the Son of God does not have life." (1 John 5:11–12)[1]

Date:			
Place:			
Occasion:			

The Way It Should Be

Pastor D. James Kennedy said in a sermon, "I remember years ago talking to a man in his home about Christ and asking him who he thought Jesus was. He said, 'Oh, He's a wonderful man. He was the greatest man who ever lived, the most loving and gracious person who ever walked upon this earth.'

"I said, 'Let me tell you something I believe will startle you. According to the Scriptures, and the historic Christian faith, Jesus of Nazareth, the carpenter of Galilee was and is the eternal Creator of the universe, the omnipotent, omniscient, and Almighty God.'

---
[1] Circulating on the internet

"Instantly, his eyes filled with tears and this man of about fifty-five or sixty said, 'I have been in church all of my life and I never heard that before. But I have always thought that is the way it ought to be—that God ought to be like Jesus.'"[1]

Date: _____ _____ _____
Place: _____ _____ _____
Occasion: _____ _____ _____

A Max Lucado Story

Longing to leave her poor Brazilian neighborhood, Christina wanted to see the world. Discontent with a home having only a pallet on the floor, a washbasin, and a wood-burning stove, she dreamed of a better life in the city. One morning she slipped away, breaking her mother's heart.

Knowing what life on the streets would be like for her young, attractive daughter, Maria hurriedly packed to go find her. On her way to the bus stop she entered a drugstore to get one last thing. Pictures. She sat in the photograph booth, closed the curtain, and spent all she could on pictures of herself. With her purse full of small black-and-white photos, she boarded the next bus to Rio de Janeiro.

Maria knew Christina had no way of earning money. She also knew that her daughter was too stubborn to give up. When pride meets hunger, a human will do things that were before unthinkable. Knowing this, Maria began her search. Bars, hotels, nightclubs, any place with the reputation for street walkers or prostitutes. She went to them all. And at each place she left her picture—taped on a bathroom mirror, tacked to a hotel bulletin board, fastened to a corner phone booth. And on the back of each photo she wrote a note. It wasn't too long before both the money and the pictures ran out, and Maria had to go home.

The weary mother wept as the bus began its long journey back to her small village. It was a few weeks later that young Christina descended the hotel stairs. Her young face was tired. Her brown eyes no longer danced with youth but spoke of pain and fear. Her laughter was broken. Her dream had become a nightmare. A thousand times over she had longed to trade these countless beds for her secure pallet. Yet the little village was, in too many ways, too far away.

As she reached the bottom of the stairs, her eyes noticed a familiar face. She looked again, and there on the lobby mirror was a small picture of her mother. Christina's eyes burned and her throat tightened as she walked across the room and removed the small photo. Written on the back was this compelling invitation. "Whatever you have done, whatever you have become, it doesn't matter. Please come home."

She did.[2]

Date: _____ _____ _____
Place: _____ _____ _____
Occasion: _____ _____ _____

[1] D. James Kennedy, "Is Jesus God," (Coral Ridge Ministries, P. O. Box 40, Fort Lauderdale, FL 33302).
[2] Max Lucado, *No Wonder They Call Him Savior* (Multnomah Press, 1986), 158–159.

Looking Unto Jesus

Bible teacher A. T. Pierson tells about a new convert to Christ who had a strange dream in which he was trapped down in a very deep well in the night. He looked up and saw a single star shining far above him, and it seemed to let down lines of silver light that took hold upon him and lifted him up. Then he looked down, and he began to go down. He looked up, and he began to go up; he looked down, and he began to go down again. He found that by simply keeping his eye on that star, he rose out of the well until his foot stood on the firm ground.

The dream was a parable, said Dr. Pierson. "Get your eyes off yourself and on your Savior, get them off your disease and on your physician. . . . Now and here, turn your eyes to the Lord Jesus."[1]

"Satan, the Hinderer, may build a barrier about us," Hudson Taylor once said, "but he can never roof us in so that we cannot look up."

Date: _____   _____   _____

Place: _____   _____   _____

Occasion: _____   _____   _____

The Incarnation

Perhaps you saw the movie about her starring Sigourney Weaver, or read of her exploits in *National Geographic*. Maybe you saw her book or heard of her death. Dian Fossey was an unusual woman, a California-born zoologist who left the comforts of home to move to Africa. There she lived among the rare, gentle mountain gorillas of Rwanda who were threatened with extinction due to the cruelty of poachers who were tracking them down, one-by-one, and slaughtering them.

She began her mission in 1963 on the sides of a 14,000 foot tall, rain-shrouded volcano, and after several years they came to accept her as one of their own. Fossey named them, cradled their babies, cried with them when then mourned their dead. She once wrote: "These powerful but shy and gentle animals accepted and responded to my attentions when I acted like a gorilla. So I learned to scratch and groom and beat my chest. I imitated my subjects' vocalizations (hoots, grunts, and belches), munched the foliage they ate, kept low to the ground and deliberate in movement."

After eighteen years with the gorillas, she became like them, dwelling among them, and they were her friends. When faced with the danger, she bravely defended them.

In the early hours of December 27, 1985, she was knifed and murdered, apparently by poachers whose trade she had sought to destroy. She died for those she came to live among and to save.

Two thousand years ago, Christ left the comforts of His home for the fog-shrouded volcano of earth. He identified with us, learned our names, wept with us. And He, too, died for those he came to live among and to save.

---

[1] Arthur T. Pierson, *The Gospel: Its Heart, Heights, and Hopes,* vol. 1 (Grand Rapids, MI: Baker Book House, 1978), 192–3.

He once observed: "Greater love has no one than this, than to lay down one's life for his friend." (John 15:13)

```
Date:       _____   _____   _____
Place:      _____   _____   _____
Occasion:   _____   _____   _____
```

Journaling

Someone Once Said . . .

- *I believe it [keeping a journal] is a very useful method to take some account of every day, however unprofitable.*—John Newton
- *A journal is an aid to concentration, a mirror for the soul, a place to generate and capture ideas, a safety valve for the emotions, and a powerful tool for spiritual growth.*—Ron Klug[1]
- *It is a healing experience simply to put our feelings into words.*—Dr. Julius Segal[2]
- *Life always sees at least a step or two ahead of us. It's easy to lose control. I often turn to my journal as the key to unlock the shackles of the time trap. Reflection enables me to sort out what is important.*—Douglas J. Rumford, pastor of the Presbyterian Church of Old Greenwich, Connecticut[3]

```
Date:       _____   _____   _____
Place:      _____   _____   _____
Occasion:   _____   _____   _____
```

A Private Dialogue

In an interview with *Leadership Journal,* educator Roberta Hestenes was asked what other spiritual practices besides prayer can promote spiritual growth in a pastor. She replied, in part, "One spiritual discipline that's been present from the first centuries is journaling, which is a private dialogue between you and God. Augustine's *Confessions* is a journal. John Wesley kept one, as did Jim Elliot. But Christians today don't realize this is a resource to help them reflect on faith, to make space for God in their lives."

Dr. Hestenes continued, "I rediscovered journaling when I had cancer and needed to reflect on the meaning of that experience. I had spontaneously kept a journal as a young Christian. I don't remember that anyone taught me, though all of us in our parachurch movement were taught to keep a prayer list, which is a form of it.

---

[1] Ron Klug, "How To Keep a Spiritual Journal," *Decision Magazine,* January 1983, 5.
[2] Dr. Julius Segal, *Winning Life's Toughest Battles* (New York: Ivy Books, 1896), 28.
[3] Ron Klug, "How To Keep a Spiritual Journal," *Decision Magazine,* January 1983, 5.

"But when I was struggling with cancer, I found journaling an enormously beneficial aid to prayer, a time to quiet the noise externally and internally and pour everything out to God."[1]

Date:	_____	_____	_____
Place:	_____	_____	_____
Occasion:	_____	_____	_____

Jotted in his Journal

Ray Palmer, in his early twenties, burned the candle at both ends, working himself often to exhaustion. He sometimes wondered if he could go on, teaching at a girls' school, clerking at a store, studying for the ministry, and working in the church. He kept a little morocco-bound notebook, and one night in his boarding house, he opened it and wrote out his prayers in the form of a poem. Doing so gave him renewed encouragement.

═══════◇═══════
Waste-Free Thoughts

*My journal is that of me
which would else spill over
and run to waste.*
—HENRY DAVID THOREAU
═══════◇═══════

One day in 1832, he met Lowell Mason in front of a store in Boston. Mason was a banker and church musician who was compiling a church songbook. Mason asked Palmer for a poem to go into it, and Palmer opened his little notebook and showed Mason the poem. After reading it, Mason said, "Mr. Palmer, you may do many good things, but posterity will remember you as the author of 'My Faith Looks Up to Thee.'"

That night, Lowell Mason set Palmer's poem to music, and Dr. Ray Palmer has indeed gone down in church history because of that one poem jotted in his journal:

*My Faith looks up to Thee,
Thou Lamb of Calvary,
Savior divine!
Now hear me while I pray,
Take all my guilt away,
O let me from this day
Be wholly Thine!*[2]

Date:	_____	_____	_____
Place:	_____	_____	_____
Occasion:	_____	_____	_____

Through the Centuries

Michael Frank, writing in the *New York Times* on the 1997 exhibition "Private Histories: Four Centuries of Journal Keeping" at the Pierpont Morgan Library in

---

[1] Roberta Hestenes, "Can Spiritual Maturity be Taught," *Leadership Journal*, Fall 1988, 15.
[2] Clint Bonner, *A Hymn is Born* (Nashville: Broadman, 1959), 63–64.

New York, reports that no one is quite sure when or where diaries were first kept, although none seem to have come down to us from before the Renaissance. Leonardo's notebooks may be a sort of forerunner to the diary, but the earliest richly textured diary was kept between 1660 and 1669 by Samuel Pepys, a pioneer and progenitor of the form. The diary came into its own in the West in the eighteenth and nineteenth centuries.

Frank observes, "It is one of the curious practices of journal keepers that they tend to fall into the habit of writing when they are in a particular, and often a particularly distressed, state of mind. . . . Diarists are often at their most animated when the basic routines and rhythms of their lives are disrupted. Grief is just one powerful disrupter; war and travel are two others."[1]

Date: _____ _____ _____

Place: _____ _____ _____

Occasion: _____ _____ _____

Henry Martyn's Journal

J

Henry Martyn's strange and effective career as a missionary to India and Persia would have been largely lost to us had he not begun keeping a journal while in college. He wrote: *My object in making this journal is to accustom myself to self-examination, and to give my experience a visible form, so as to leave a stronger impression on the memory, and thus to improve my soul in holiness; for the review of such a lasting testimony will serve the double purpose of conviction and consolation.*[2]

Date: _____ _____ _____

Place: _____ _____ _____

Occasion: _____ _____ _____

Eric Liddell's Notebook

Eric Liddell, the Flying Scotsman, was an Olympic national hero who gave himself as a missionary to China. He was imprisoned at the beginning of the War in a Japanese internment camp, but his attitude kept all around him refreshed. He glided from person to person and from group to group, giving comfort and care, sharing the Scriptures, and leading in worship. He spoke of the fragrance of a God-enfolded life. Some in the camp wanted to know his secret. One of his fellow internees came up with her own answer about it:

"What was his secret? Once I asked him, but I really knew already, for my husband was in his dormitory and shared the secret with him. Every morning about 6 A.M., with curtains tightly drawn to keep in the shining of our peanut-oil lamp, lest the prowling sentries would think someone was trying to escape, he used to

---

[1] Michael Frank, "Telling It All To a Friend: Dear Diary . . ." *The New York Times*, May 16, 1997.

[2] Constance E. Padwick, *Henry Martyn: The Pioneer Translator Who Opened the Scriptures to the Muslim and Hindu Worlds* (Chicago: Moody Press, 1980), 65.

climb out of his top bunk, past the sleeping forms of his dormitory mates. Then, at the small Chinese table, the two men would sit close together with the light just enough to illumine their Bibles and notebooks. Silently they read, prayed, and thought about the day's duties, noted what should be done. Eric was a man of prayer . . ."[1]

Date: _____ _____ _____
Place: _____ _____ _____
Occasion: _____ _____ _____

Moody's Notebook

A personal notebook can be an "idea catcher." William Moody once wrote this about his famous father, evangelist D. L. Moody: "With what keenness he listened to other preachers for good thoughts and illustrations, and how his face lit up as he took out the notebook which he kept in his hip pocket! He urged the habit of making notes of all the good things one read and heard, believing that it would make the Bible more deeply interesting day by day."[2]

Date: _____ _____ _____
Place: _____ _____ _____
Occasion: _____ _____ _____

Kathryn Koob's Journal

Kathryn Koob, one of the Americans held hostage for over a year during the Carter administration's crisis with Iran, kept a journal. Writing on the backs of envelopes, she jotted down a record of her days in captivity. She said, "My journal helped me remember my reactions and some things I had read. It also reminded me of things I wanted to think about more deeply and helped me crystallize my thinking."[3]

Date: _____ _____ _____
Place: _____ _____ _____
Occasion: _____ _____ _____

Gordon MacDonald's Journal

In his book, *Ordering Your Private World,* Gordon MacDonald writes: "When I studied some of the mystic and contemplative Christians, I found that one practical way to learn to listen to God speak in the garden of my private world was to keep

[1] Sally Magnusson, *The Flying Scotsman* (New York: Quartet Books, 1981), 165.
[2] William Moody, *The Life of D. L. Moody by his Son* (Murfreesboro, Tenn: Sword of the Lord Publishers, n.d.), 441.
[3] Ron Klug, "How To Keep a Spiritual Journal," *Decision Magazine,* January 1983, 5.

a journal. With a pencil in hand ready to write, I found that there was an expectancy, a readiness to hear anything God might wish to whisper through my reading and reflection.

"The discovery came almost twenty years ago, while I was reading a biography. The subject of the book had maintained a lifelong habit of recording his spiritual pilgrimage. I was now benefiting from that discipline, even though he had been writing more for his own benefit than for mine. . . .

"I became impressed by the fact that many, many godly men and women down through the centuries had also kept journals, and I began to wonder if they had not put their fingers upon an aid to spiritual growth. To satisfy my curiosity, I decided to experiment and began keeping one for myself. . . .

"Today after twenty years of journal keeping, I have acquired a habit. Hardly a morning passes that I do not open the journal and record the things I hear God saying through my reading, meditation, and daily experience. When the journal opens, so does the ear of my heart."[1]

When asked, "How do you keep a journal? How do you begin?" MacDonald replies: "My own journals are spiral bound notebooks, which I purchase at an office supply store. They are rather unimpressive in appearance. I can complete one of these notebooks in about three months. The virtue of their smaller size lies not only in portability but in the fact that, should one ever be lost, I would not have misplaced a year or more of writing.

"I write in my journal almost every day, but I am not overly disturbed if an occasional day passes without an entry.

"I include prayers if I feel like writing them down, insights that come from reading the Bible and other spiritual literature, and concerns I have about my own personal behavior. . . .

"Journal keeping becomes a habit for most people if they will stick with it for the better part of a year. Most people quit too quickly, never achieving the habit pattern, and that is unfortunate."[2]

Date:			
Place:			
Occasion:			

Bill Hybels' Journal

Pastor Bill Hybels discusses his journaling in his book *Too Busy Not To Pray.* Saying that most Christians are too busy—too many RPMs—he writes: "The first step toward RPM reduction is called *journaling.* . . . It involves writing down your experiences, observations, and reflections; looking behind the events of the day for their hidden meanings; recording ideas as they come to you. . . .

---

[1] Gordon MacDonald, *Ordering Your Private World* (Nashville: Thomas Nelson, 1985), 130–132.
[2] MacDonald, *Ordering Your Private World,* 133–135.

"Over the years, I found myself drawn to the writings of a wide variety of people—mystics, Puritans, contemporary authors rich in their devotional handing of Scripture—who seemed to have one thing in common. Most of them journaled."

Hybels says that, inspired by Gordon MacDonald's example, he turns every day in his journal to the next blank page and writes the same first word: *Yesterday*, followed by a paragraph or two of recounting yesterday's events. He has found that this is an important first step in slowing him down to pray. "It gives the body a rest. It focuses the mind. It frees the spirit to operate."

Then Hybels uses the next space to write out a prayer for each day. He limits both the *yesterday* segment and the prayer to one page each. "Once I write out the prayer, I put the notebook on my credenza and kneel down. Not everyone is like me in this respect, but I find I pray much more effectively on my knees. I read the prayer aloud, adding other comments or concerns as I go through it."[1]

Date: _____ _____ _____
Place: _____ _____ _____
Occasion: _____ _____ _____

Ruth Graham's Journal

"Cultivate the notebook habit," advises Ruth Bell Graham. She has had an old, loose-leaf leather notebook for years which she has bound and re-bound. As she fills it up, she transfers the pages to newer notebooks on her shelf, and keeps using the old leather one. She records her thoughts, prayers, observations, feelings, and insights from Scripture. On that shelf is a lifetime of wisdom, stored away in her journals.[2]

Date: _____ _____ _____
Place: _____ _____ _____
Occasion: _____ _____ _____

"It Stirs Me Up Much . . ."

Jim Elliot, who perished while trying to reach the Auca Indians in 1956, left behind a journal that has deeply moved multitudes and been the means of many young people giving their lives to missions. Interestingly, Elliot's own interest in missions was whetted while reading another journal. In *Shadow of the Almighty*, Elisabeth Elliot quotes from Jim's journal, dated October 24, 1949: *I see the value of Christian biography tonight, as I have been reading Brainerd's* Diary *much today. It stirs me up much to pray and wonder at my nonchalance while I have not power from God. I have considered Hebrews 13:7 just now, regarding the remembrance of certain ones who spake the word of God, "consider the outcome of their life, and imitate their faith."*

---

[1] Bill Hybels, *Too Busy Not to Pray* (Downers Grove, IL: InterVarsity Press, 1988), 101–105.
[2] Based on an interview with the author.

Date: _____   _____   _____
Place: _____   _____   _____
Occasion: _____   _____   _____

Another Benefit

ABC News reported on April 14, 1999, about a new study that found that patients with arthritis or asthma often got better after writing about terrible experiences in their lives such as a car wreck or the death of a loved one. A group of 112 patients spent a total of just one hour writing. Four months later, nearly half of those who wrote about stressful events had improved significantly.

The study is believed to be the first to examine how writing about stressful events affects specific illnesses. It was conducted at the State University of New York at Stony Brook and published in *The Journal of the American Medical Association,* and it reinforces similar studies that have shown the health benefits for healthy people who wrote about stressful events.[1]

Date: _____   _____   _____
Place: _____   _____   _____
Occasion: _____   _____   _____

From *Newsweek*

In its April 26, 1999, edition, *Newsweek* carried a story entitled "Pen, Paper, Power!" by Claudia Kalb. "Confessional writing has been around at least since the Renaissance," she wrote, "but new research suggests that it's far more therapeutic than anyone ever knew. Since the mid-1980s, studies have found that people who write about their most upsetting experiences not only feel better but visit doctors less often and even have stronger immune responses. Last week, scientists reported findings that make the link even clearer. A study published in *The Journal of the American Medical Association (JAMA)* showed that writing exercises can help alleviate symptoms of asthma and rheumatoid arthritis. 'It's hard to believe,' says James Pennebaker, a psychology professor at the University of Texas at Austin and a pioneer in the field of expressive writing, but 'being able to put experiences into words is good for your physical health.'

"Even the best-adjusted and healthiest people acquire emotional baggage in the course of a lifetime—be it childhood angst over parental divorce, conflicts with friends and family or remorse over missteps and lost opportunities. In the scientific studies, researchers ask participants to write about a disturbing experience for fifteen to twenty minutes a day for three or four consecutive days. Forget polish and politeness, they say. The point is not to craft a perfect essay but to dig deeply into one's emotional junkyard, then translate the experience into language on the page.

[1] <http://journals.about.com/arts/journals/gi/dynamic/offsite.htm?site = htt p://abcnews.go.com/sections/living/DailyNews/writing-health990413.html>

"In one study . . . published last year, researchers found direct physiological evidence: writing increased the level of disease-fighting lymphocytes circulating in the bloodstream. And preliminary research shows that writing can cause modest declines in blood pressure."[1]

Date:			
Place:			
Occasion:			

Joy

Someone Once Said . . .

- *We are half-hearted creatures, fooling about with drink and sex and ambition, when infinite joy is offered to us, like an ignorant child who wants to go on making mud pies in the slum because he cannot imagine what is meant by the offer of a holiday at the sea.*—C. S. Lewis
- *Happiness is an emotion, and joy is an attitude. Emotions come and go, but attitudes come and grow.*[2]
- *If you have no joy in your religion, there's a leak in your Christianity somewhere.*—Billy Sunday
- *Holy joy will beautify you.*—Charles Spurgeon

Date:			
Place:			
Occasion:			

Serve the Lord with Joy

- *Preaching ought to be a joy, and yet it may become a task. Constant preaching should be constant enjoyment.*—Charles Spurgeon
- *If ministers only saw the preciousness of Christ, they would not be able to refrain from clapping their hands with joy and exclaiming, "I am a minister of Christ."*—Robert Murray McCheyne
- *Let us rejoice with one another that in a world where there are a great many good and happy things for men to do, God has given us the best and happiest and made us to be preachers of this truth.*—Phillips Brooks, in his *Yale Lectures*
- *I might have entered the ministry if certain clergymen I knew had not looked and acted so much like undertakers.*—Oliver Wendell Holmes
- *Thank God for the joy of ministry.*—Warren Wiersbe

---

[1] Claudia Kalb, "Pen, Paper, Power!" *Newsweek*, April 26, 1999.
[2] From a sermon by the author.

Date:			
Place:			
Occasion:			

JOY

Many people have heard that JOY means Jesus first, Others next, and Yourself last. But in a Christmas sermon in 1998, Pastor Phil Toole of Mountain Valley Community Church of Scottsdale, Arizona, put it different.

Jesus
O
You

"The 'J' stands for Jesus," said Pastor Toole. "The 'Y' stands for you. Do you know what the 'O' stands for? It stands for zero. Just what it says—nothing. What I am saying here is the way to stay close to Jesus and keep joy in your heart is let nothing between Jesus and you."

J

Date:			
Place:			
Occasion:			

Looking in the Wrong Places

Comedian Lenny Bruce once shared his philosophy of life like this: "Look, you have only sixty-five years to live. Before you're twenty, you can't enjoy anything because you don't know what's going on. After you're fifty, you can't enjoy it either, because you don't have the physical energies. So you only have around twenty-five years, and I'm going to *swing.*"

He died of an overdose of morphine at age forty.

Date:			
Place:			
Occasion:			

When the King Is Home

The king of a particular country traveled often, but one day a man living near the palace remarked to a friend, "Well, it looks like the king is home tonight."

"How do you know?" asked the other.

The man pointed up toward the royal house. "Because when the king is home," he said, "the castle is all lit up."

Date:			
Place:			
Occasion:			

Serving Too Cheerfully

Composer Franz Joseph Haydn, recalling his struggles while working on a certain sacred work, wrote, "I prayed to God—not like a miserable sinner in despair—but calmly, slowly. In this I felt that an infinite God would surely have mercy on his finite creature, pardoning dust for being dust. These thoughts cheered me up. I experienced a sure joy so confident that as I wished to express the words of the prayer, I could not express my joy, but gave vent to my happy spirits and wrote above the *Miserere,* 'Allegro.'"

———◇———
Make-Up Artist
Joy . . . is a woman's best cosmetic.
—ROSALIND RUSSELL
———◇———

His music was so ebullient in temperament that it was actually criticized by the sterner members of the church. His reply: "Since God has given me a cheerful heart, He will forgive me for serving Him cheerfully."

When Haydn pondered the reality of a God who really cared for him, he said his heart "leapt for joy." He could not prevent his music from expressing the same exuberance—even when the music was conveying Christianity's more somber themes.[1]

Date:			
Place:			
Occasion:			

This Is the Day

James Guthrie, Scottish Worthy, went to the scaffold because of his faith in Christ. In telling his story, Jock Purves, writes, "James Guthrie ever kept through his busy life his own personal fellowship with Christ in the fresh joyous bloom of his new birth, as if he had been but a young convert."

Waking about 4 A.M. on the day he was to be executed, Guthrie spent time in personal worship, and was asked by his friend James Cowie how he felt. "Very well," replied Guthrie. "'This is the day that the Lord has made; let us rejoice and be glad in it.'"[2]

Date:			
Place:			
Occasion:			

---

[1] Patrick Kavanaugh, *The Spiritual Lives of Great Composers* (Nashville: Sparrow Press, 1992), 21.
[2] Jock Purves, *Fair Sunshine* (London: Banner of Truth Trust, 1968), 17.

"You're a Lucky Dog"

The famous missionary C. T. Studd once traveled to China on a ship whose captain was an embittered opponent of Christianity and who often studied the Bible for the sole reason of arguing with the missionaries who frequently sailed on his ship. When he learned that Studd was aboard his ship, the captain lit into him. But instead of arguing with him, Studd put his arm around the captain and said, "But, my friend, I have a peace that passeth all understanding and a joy that nothing can take away."

The captain finally replied, "You're a lucky dog," and walked away. Before the end of the voyage, he became a rejoicing believer in Jesus Christ.[1]

Date: _____ _____ _____
Place: _____ _____ _____
Occasion: _____ _____ _____

From a Sermon by Vance Havner

J

- *The Church suffers today from a saddening lack of old-fashioned, simple-hearted, overflowing, Christian joy. We have plenty of knowledge, plenty of enthusiasm and denominational zeal, but Christians and churches that started out in revival fires are living in the smoke.*
- *When one recalls that we are to rejoice in the Lord always—and then looks in on the average Sunday congregation, he realizes that something has happened to us since Pentecost.*
- *Although the New Testament centers on the cross . . . its note from beginning to end is one of triumphant joy. It begins with an angel chorus and ends with rejoicing around the throne.*
- *Today the same church member who yells like a Comanche Indian at a football game sits like a wooden Indian in the house of God on Sunday.*
- *In John 20:20 we read: "Then were the disciples glad, when they saw the Lord." Here we have the secret of Christian joy: it turns upon those two words, "then" and "when." It does not read, "Then were the disciples glad when they saw themselves . . ." or their circumstances. . . . We do not even read that the disciples were glad when they saw a particular doctrine about the Lord. . . . We are glad only when and as we see the Lord.*[2]

Date: _____ _____ _____
Place: _____ _____ _____
Occasion: _____ _____ _____

From a Sermon by Charles Spurgeon

On Sunday night, March 24, 1895, Charles Spurgeon prepared this sermon for his congregation at the Metropolitan Tabernacle.

---

[1] Norman P. Grubb, *C. T. Studd, Cricketer and Pioneer* (London: Religious Tract Society, 1933), 52–53.
[2] Vance Havner, *The Secret of Christian Joy* (Old Tappan, NJ: Fleming H. Revell Co., 1938), 9–16.

- *There is a marvelous medicinal power in joy. Most medicines are distasteful; but this, which is the best of all medicines, is sweet to the taste, and comforting to the heart.*
- *This blessed joy is very contagious. One dolorous spirit brings a kind of plague into the house; one person who is wretched seems to stop all the birds from singing wherever he goes. . . . [But] the grace of joy is contagious.*
- *Holy joy will oil the wheels of your life's machinery. Holy joy will strengthen you for your daily labor. Holy joy will beautify you and give you an influence over the lives of others.*

Date: _____ _____ _____
Place: _____ _____ _____
Occasion: _____ _____ _____

That Little Book

Norman Vincent Peale once visited a friend in the hospital. He had previously had one leg amputated and now he had lost his other one. Nevertheless, he seemed happy and enthusiastic.

"Everyone tells me you are the happiest person in the hospital," said Dr. Peale. "You are not putting it on, are you?"

"No, no, I am as happy as can be."

"Let me in on your secret," Peale asked.

"Do you see that little book lying over there on the table?" the man replied, pointing to the Bible. "There is where I get my medicine. When I feel a little low, I just read that Book."[1]

Date: _____ _____ _____
Place: _____ _____ _____
Occasion: _____ _____ _____

——————————— Judgment ———————————

Someone Once Said . . .

- *There are few things stressed more strongly in the Bible than the reality of God's work as Judge.* —J. I. Packer[2]
- *God's anger was seen to be not a passion, but a principle—the eternal hatred of wrong, which corresponds with the eternal love of right, and which is only another aspect of love. The magnetic needle swings on its delicate axis; it attracts at one end; it repels at the other.* —A. T. Pierson[3]
- *The vague and tenuous hope that God is too kind to punish the ungodly has become a deadly opiate for the consciences of millions. It hushes their fears and allows them to*

---

[1] Norman Vincent Peale, *Enthusiasm Makes the Difference* (Englewood Cliffs, NJ: Prentice-Hall, Inc., 1967), 182.
[2] J. I. Packer, *Knowing God* (Downers Grove, IL: InterVarsity, 1973), 125.
[3] Arthur T. Pierson, *Many Infallible Proofs*, vol. 2 (Grand Rapids, MI: Zondervan, n.d.), 98.

practice all pleasant forms of iniquity while death draws every day nearer and the command to repent goes unheeded.—A. W. Tozer[1]

- *The entire New Testament is overshadowed by the certainty of a coming day of universal judgment, and by the problem thence arising: how may we sinners get right with God while there is yet time?*—J. I. Packer[2]
- *His wrath is not an impetuous and changeable passion, but an eternal and unchangeable principle.*—A. T. Pierson[3]

Date: _____ _____ _____
Place: _____ _____ _____
Occasion: _____ _____ _____

Doomed

The 1999 crash of golfer Payne Stewart's plane was a bizarre incident. He and five companions boarded a twin-engine, $2.4 million Learjet which left the runway at 9:19 A.M. There were two pilots, and all seemed fine when they checked in with air traffic controllers a few minutes later.

But for unknown reasons, the pilots apparently lost consciousness shortly before they were to turn west toward Dallas, and when they couldn't be raised by air traffic controllers, two Air Force jets went aloft to investigate.

No one was at the controls. There was no movement in the cockpit, and the windows were fogged, suggesting that the cabin had depressurized and become chilled with stratospheric air some 45,000 feet above the earth.

One of the Air Force pilots said, "It's a very helpless feeling to pull alongside another aircraft and realize the people inside that aircraft potentially are unconscious or in some other way incapacitated. And there's nothing I can do physically from my aircraft even though I'm fifty to one hundred feet away, to help them at all."

When one of its two engines finally ran out of fuel, the plane roller-coastered through the clouds, heading toward final, cataclysmic destruction.

One air safety investigator said that airplane depressurization can be "very insidious." He explained that the problem could slowly deprive the crew of its ability to know what was happening. "It could be one of those things where you're feeling good, you're feeling happy, and you don't know what's going on."

Picture humanity on a runaway airplane, on a collision course, with only moments of time remaining. Yet people are so caught up in their pleasures and pressures and pursuits that they don't realize the urgency of their plight.

Date: _____ _____ _____
Place: _____ _____ _____
Occasion: _____ _____ _____

---

[1] A. W. Tozer, *The Knowledge of the Holy* (New York: Harper & Row, Publishers, 1961), 95.
[2] J. I. Packer, *Knowing God* (Downers Grove, IL: InterVarsity, 1973), 127.
[3] Pierson, *Many Infallible Proofs*, vol. 2, 90.

Two Columns

The Bible presents a God who is the absolute of perfection, who is a God of love, and yet who is simultaneously a God of wrath. A. T. Pierson compares it to an arch. You have the love of God supporting one side and the wrath of God supporting the other side, and without either of them the entire thing would fall down.

God would not be God if he didn't have the capacity of wrath. Why? I was reading the other day about a young, handsome, dapper fellow, a medical doctor, who always wore crisp and well-tailored clothing. He handled himself with polish and smoothness. He always bore the fragrance of expensive cologne. But his very demeanor made him all the more fiendish, for his name was Josef Mengele, the Angel of Death at Auschwitz. With a flick of his well-washed and perfumed hand he personally selected 400,000 prisoners to die in the gas chamber. He conducted horrible experiments on people, hoping to produce a superior race. One observer said, "He would spend hours bent over his microscope while the air outside stank with the heavy odor of burning flesh from the chimney stacks of the crematoria."

He had a special fascination for children who were twins. He would give them horrible injections, operate on their spine to paralyze them, then begin removing parts of their body one at a time for observation.

Now, what would you think of a person—or, for that matter, a God—who could see that sort of indescribable evil without feeling any anger? If God could watch the hurt and the evil in this universe with no feelings of indignation and fury, he would be defective in his character. He wouldn't be God at all.

So I submit that rather than apologizing for the doctrine of the wrath of God, or ignoring it, we should appreciate it as a vital and wonderful part of God's divine character.[1]

Date:			
Place:			
Occasion:			

Spiders Over the Fire

America's greatest theologian is often identified as Jonathan Edwards, a New England pastor of the 1700s. Edwards was brilliant. At age six he studied Latin. He entered Yale when not quite thirteen and graduated when barely fifteen. He was ordained at age nineteen, taught at Yale by twenty, and later became president of Princeton. Harvard granted him both a bachelor's and a master's degree on the same day.

But he is best known for *Sinners in the Hands of an Angry God*—the most famous sermon in American history.

He preached it on Sunday, July 8, 1741, while ministering in tiny Enfield, Connecticut. A group of women had spent the previous night praying for revival. When Edwards rose to speak, he quietly announced that his text was Deuteronomy 32:35, ". . . their foot shall slide in due time." This "hellfire and brimstone" approach

---

[1] From a sermon by the author.

was somewhat a departure for Edwards. Of his one thousand written sermons, less than a dozen are of this type.

Edwards neither gestured nor raised his voice. He spoke softly and simply, warning the unconverted that they were dangling over hell like a spider over the fire. *O sinner! consider the fearful danger. The unconverted are now walking over the pit of hell on a rotten covering, and there are innumerable places in this covering so weak that it will not bear their weight, and these places are not seen.*

Edwards' voice was suddenly lost amid cries and commotion from the crowd. He paused, appealing for calm. Then he concluded: *Let everyone that is out of Christ, now awake and fly from the wrath to come. The wrath of Almighty God is now undoubtedly hanging over a great part of this congregation. Let every one fly out of Sodom.*

Strong men held to pews and posts, feeling they were sliding into hell. Others shook uncontrollably and rolled on the floor. Throughout the night cries of men and women were heard throughout the village, begging God to save them. Five hundred were converted that evening, sparking a revival that swept thousands into the kingdom.

The Great Awakening had come.[1]

Date: _____ _____ _____
Place: _____ _____ _____
Occasion: _____ _____ _____

Judgment Day

In the history of New England, May 19, 1780, has become known for its supposed foreshadowing of the Judgment Day. At noon the skies were turned from blue to gray, and by mid-afternoon they had become so black that men fell on their knees and cried out to God for mercy ere they went to their doom. On that day the Connecticut House of Representatives was in session. When darkness fell by day, some began to shout and plead for mercy. Others demanded an immediate adjournment. The speaker of the House, Colonel Abraham Davenport, called for silence. Then he spoke: "The Day of Judgment is either approaching or it is not. If it is not, there is no cause for adjournment. If it is, I choose to be found doing my duty. I wish, therefore, that candles be brought."[2]

Date: _____ _____ _____
Place: _____ _____ _____
Occasion: _____ _____ _____

The Times Are Waxing Late

We have little information about the life of Bernard of Morlaix (or Cluny) who lived in the middle of the twelfth century, but he left behind a poem of three thousand

[1] Robert J. Morgan, *On This Day* (Nashville: Thomas Nelson Publishers, 1997), July 8th.
[2] Andrew W. Blackwood, *Expository Preaching for Today* (Grand Rapids, MI: Baker Book House, 1975), 112.

lines, *De Contemptu Mundi*. The theme of this huge composition is expressed in the opening lines of one of the stanzas:

> *The world is very evil*
> *The times are waxing late*
> *Be sober and keep vigil*
> *The judge is at the gate.*

Date: _____ _____ _____
Place: _____ _____ _____
Occasion: _____ _____ _____

J. I. Packer on Judgment

"Why," asks J. I. Packer, "do men fight shy of the thought of God as a Judge? Why do they feel the thought to be unworthy of Him? The truth is that part of God's moral perfection is His perfection in judgment. Would a God who did not care about the difference between right and wrong be a good and admirable Being? Would a God who put no distinction between the beasts of history, the Hitlers and Stalins (if we dare use names), and His own saints, be morally praiseworthy and perfect? Moral indifference would be an imperfection of God, not a perfection. But not to judge the world would be to show moral indifference. The final proof that God is a perfect moral being, not indifferent to questions of right and wrong, is the fact that He has committed Himself to judge the world."[1]

Date: _____ _____ _____
Place: _____ _____ _____
Occasion: _____ _____ _____

Vesuvius

When the Apostle Paul was being transported as a missionary prisoner to Rome, his ship docked to the south of Rome in the Italian port city of Puteoli. This was a holiday resort for fashionable Roman society, a spa with nearby hot sulfur springs. Many of the Roman emperors had villas there.

Puteoli lay in the shadow of a great and rugged mountain—a volcano, though it hadn't erupted in a thousand years—Vesuvius. Shortly after Paul's time, Vesuvius exploded like an atomic bomb. It erupted for forty hours, and while Puteoli was spared, another nearby city was flooded by molten lava, buried before the inhabitants could escape. They were killed by the gasses and the ash, then preserved by the molten lava which rolled over them and hermetically sealed them in a gigantic tomb of pumice.

That city was Pompeii, and for many years it remained buried under twenty feet of hardened lava. Excavations have given us a perfectly preserved Roman city, frozen in time, caught in the act of being itself.

---

[1] Packer, *Knowing God*, 130.

The twenty thousand people of Pompeii, it seems, worshipped two gods: Venus, the love goddess, and Mercury, the god of commerce. They worshipped, in other words, money and pleasure. Their worship of Mercury is evidenced by their economic prosperity. Pompeii was a thriving city, a neat grid-pattern of shop-lined streets wrapped in a gated wall. It pulsed with industry, many of its people working in a winery, Pompeii being world-famous for its wine.

But they also loved pleasure. The city walls were filled with advertisements by prostitutes. Prices indicate that the average girl cost about the price of a modest dinner at a Pompeiian tavern. On one hotel, a sign said, "If you sit down here, read this first: If you're looking for a girl, ask for Attica—four bucks, high class."

> ◆
> **Judgmental Principle**
> *God's anger was seen to be not a passion, but a principle.*
> —A. T. PIERSON
> ◆

On the walls of brothels were testimonies by satisfied customers. Everywhere were models and carvings of the phallus—the male sexual organ—which in ancient Pompeii was considered the symbol of success. It was carved on sidewalks and houses, drawn on walls and posts.

The statues and sculptures of Pompeii, excavated by archaeologists, were hidden for many years in the "off limits" rooms of Italian museums because they were so obscene. On one Pompeiian wall, someone with a knowledge of the Old Testament had written some graffiti—just three words: *Sodom and Gomorrah!*

And, like Sodom and Gomorrah, Pompeii perished suddenly by fire. Judgment came swiftly and without warning, and there was no escape.

And, like Sodom and Gomorrah, our world today is awash in corruption and confusion, awaiting the judgment. We don't know when the volcano of judgment and retribution will erupt, but the Apostle Peter said, *The end of all things is near . . . For the day of the Lord will come like a thief. The heavens will disappear with a roar; the elements will be destroyed by fire, and the earth and everything in it will be laid bare. That day will bring about the destruction of the heaven by fire, and the elements will melt in the heat.*

Date: _____ _____ _____
Place: _____ _____ _____
Occasion: _____ _____ _____

The Water Will Boil

David Marks was one of the most powerful evangelists in early American history. He was born to godly Connecticut parents in 1805, and his awareness of God began early in life. The incident that started him thinking about the Savior was a day when he was watching some flax burn. He had heard of the fires of hell, and as he watched the flames, he thought how exceedingly dreadful even one moment in hell would be.

"What would I do if the wrath of God fell on the earth?" he asked himself. After serious thought, he decided that should the Day of Judgment come, he would descend into the well and hide there. Running to his mother, he shared his plan; but she replied, "Ah, my son, the water will boil and the earth will burn."

He then told her that he would run to a spot he knew in the rocks where he could hide. She said, "But the rocks will melt." He was so overwhelmed with dread that he told her he would just die and escape the wrath of God in the grave. But she replied, "My child, your hope is in vain; for the dead will awake and come out of their graves."

Young David went outside and walked through the fields, pondering at length the reality of that coming day and his being unprepared for it. Putting his hand over his heart, he looked toward heaven and said, "God, be merciful to me a sinner."[1]

Date:		
Place:		
Occasion:		

Where the Fire Has Been

Many years ago, a father and his daughter were walking through the grass on the Canadian prairie. In the distance, they saw a prairie fire; eventually, they realized, it would engulf them. The father knew there was only one way of escape: they would quickly begin a fire right where they were and burn a large patch of grass. When the huge fire drew near, they then would stand on the section that had already burned. When the fire actually did approach them, the girl was terrified by the raging flames. But her father assured her, "The flames can't get to us. We are standing where the fire has already been."

Are you afraid of God's judgment? If you have trusted Christ as Savior, you can never come under His wrath. When we depend on Him, we are secure; we are where the wrath of God has already been.[2]

Date:		
Place:		
Occasion:		

The Dump

Senior Pastor Joel Eidsness of Walnut Hill Community Church in Bethel, Connecticut, once took his seven-year-old daughter on an unusual date. They visited the town dump. Backing his Oldsmobile up against the mound of refuse, he placed his daughter on the roof, and, with pencil and paper, they began listing all the items they could identify. There was a plastic swimming pool, a barbecue, and several old lawn chairs. There were Barbie dolls, bicycle frames, skateboards, play refrigerators and stoves, radios, televisions—everything that a young girl dreams of and more.

Returning home, they pulled alongside a double trailer truck, piled high with hunks of scrap—cars that had been crushed. He leaned over to his daughter and reminded her that the beautiful car they were riding in would someday end up in a scrap heap like that.

---

[1] Pat Thomas, *David Marks* (Antioch, Tenn: The Home Missions Department of the National Association of Free Will Baptists, 1994), 3.

[2] Erwin W. Lutzer, *Failure: The Back Door to Success* (Chicago: Moody Press, 1975), 53.

He later wrote, "That was a day Kristen and I will never forget. It was a powerful reminder that someday everything we own will be junk. In city dumps the things that have captivated our attention and dominated our lives will smolder beneath a simmering flame, amidst stinking mounds of rotting garbage. But the picture portrays not only the end of our lives and that of our children. It also portrays the ultimate collapse of human history as we now know it. History is not destined to grind on forever. It awaits—wittingly or unwittingly—the awesome and terrible judgment of God."[1]

Date: _____ _____ _____
Place: _____ _____ _____
Occasion: _____ _____ _____

But Few Listened

Winston Churchill, his wary eye fixed on Hitler, was a lone voice in the years preceding World War II. He continually warned his nation and the world of the impending disasters about to befall Europe, but few listened. In 1936, he embarked on a strenuous campaign to awaken England with his cries of alarm. In one article, published in the most prominent newspapers of fourteen countries, he warned that the peoples of Europe were *chattering, busy, sporting, toiling, amused from day to day by headlines and from night to night by cinemas, slipping, sinking, rolling backward to the age when the earth was void and darkness moved upon the face of the waters.*

Surely, he argued, *it is worth a supreme effort . . . to control the hideous drift of events and arrest calamity on the threshold. Stop it! Stop it! Stop it!!! NOW is the appointed time.*

But few listened.[2]

Date: _____ _____ _____
Place: _____ _____ _____
Occasion: _____ _____ _____

Two Soldiers

Walter B. Knight tells about two soldiers traveling by train at the end of World War II. One had spent more than three years in the South Pacific, and now was returning to his father, mother, friends, and sweetheart. All were waiting for him at the station in Chicago, and his eagerness could hardly be contained. "How fast are we traveling?" he asked the porter. "How far are we from Chicago? We can't get there too quickly for me."

On the same train another serviceman sat in the same coach. His face looked

[1] Bill Hybels, Stuart Brisco, and Haddon Robinson, *Mastering Contemporary Preaching* (Portland, OR: Multnomah, 1989), 138–139.
[2] William Manchester, *The Last Lion: Winston Spencer Churchill—Alone* (Boston: Little, Brown, & Co., 1988), 205.

like a blown-out lamp, a picture of gloom and dejection. He was in handcuffs and in the charge of military police. He was not eager to reach his destination, for nothing awaited him but judgment and punishment.

Two men on the same train bound for the same destination—one eager for reunion, the other dreading judgment.[1]

Date:			
Place:			
Occasion:			

From Paul Harvey

For What It's Worth Department hears of a great escape! Gary Tindle was in a California courtroom charged with robbery. He asked and got from Judge Armando Rodriguez permission to go to the bathroom. While the bathroom door was guarded—Mr. Tindle climbed up onto the plumbing and opened a panel in the ceiling.

Sure enough, a dropped ceiling with space between. He climbed up—and into the crawlspace—and headed south. He'd gone thirty-some feet when the ceiling panels broke from under him and dropped him to the floor . . .

Right back in Judge Rodriguez's courtroom.[2]

Date:			
Place:			
Occasion:			

Both Days

The following conversation was heard between an old farmer in the country and the new parson.

"Do you belong to the Christian family?" asked the minister.

"No, they live two farms down," replied the farmer.

"No, no, I mean are you lost?"

"Lost? Why, I've lived here thirty years."

"I mean are you ready for the Judgment Day?"

"When is it?" asked the farmer.

"Well, it could be today or tomorrow."

"Well," said the farmer, "when you find out for sure when it is, you let me know. My wife will probably want to go both days."

Date:			
Place:			
Occasion:			

---

[1] From a clipping in my files.
[2] Paul Harvey, *For What It's Worth*, ed. By Paul Harvey, Jr. (New York: Bantam Books, 1991), 129.

Kindness

Someone Once Said . . .

- *Kindness: Love in Action.*—Charles Allen[1]
- *I expect to pass through life but once. If therefore, there be any kindness I can show, or any good thing I can do to any fellow-being, let me do it now, and not defer or neglect it, as I shall not pass this way again.*—William Penn[2]
- *He who sows courtesy reaps friendship, and he who plants kindness gathers love.*—Saint Basil (A.D. 330–379)
- *The nicest thing we can do for our Heavenly Father is to be kind to one of his children.*—St. Teresa of Avila[3]
- *Constant kindness can accomplish much. As the sun makes ice melt, kindness causes misunderstanding, mistrust, and hostility to evaporate.*—Albert Schweitzer

Date: _____ _____ _____
Place: _____ _____ _____
Occasion: _____ _____ _____

Random Acts of Kindness

K

If you don't think the world is hungry for kindness, consider this. In 1982, Berkeley writer and activist Anne Herbert coined a simple phrase: *Random Acts of Kindness* (RAOK). The idea took root, then took off. In 1992, a book by that title was published promoting this thought: "Imagine what would happen if there were an outbreak of kindness in the world, if everybody did one kind thing on a daily basis." The book became an instant best-seller, spawning such things as:

- An annual RAOK Week—Participants are encouraged to do things like paying the toll of the person on the road behind them, shovel their neighbor's driveway, offer flowers to a co-worker with whom they normally clash. (In 1997, more than 500 communities in five countries celebrated Random Acts of Kindness Week).
- RAOK Clubs that hand gifts to strangers on the subway and deliver 'baskets of joy' to nursing homes, hospitals, and rehab centers.
- A RAOK World movement, spreading through classrooms, churches, hospitals, businesses, municipalities, web sites, and service clubs.
- RAOK emphases in schools. Some principals now give deserving students certificates saying "Caught Ya Being Kind."
- RAOK foundations, magazines, and newsletters.
- An endorsement from Princess Diana: "Perhaps we're too embarrassed to change or too frightened of the consequences of showing that we actually care. But why not risk it anyway? Begin Today. Carry out a random act of seemingly

---

[1] Charles Allen, *The Miracle of Love* (Old Tappan, NJ: Fleming H. Revell Co., 1972), 19.
[2] Allen, *The Miracle of Love*, 19–20.
[3] Ruth Bell Graham, *Legacy of a Pack Rat* (Nashville: Thomas Nelson Publishers, 1989), 26.

senseless kindness, with no expectation of reward or punishment, safe in the knowledge that one day, someone somewhere might do the same for you."
- A special edition of *The Oprah Winfrey Show.*
- Thousands of suggestions for RAOK, such as: *Adopt a stray animal. Smile at the bus driver. Just really listen to someone. Compliment a stranger sincerely. Return shopping carts to the store. Write a thank you note to someone. Buy biscuits for your neighbor's dog. Paint flowers on the envelopes you mail. Treat your local police officer to coffee. Give up your place in line at the grocery store to the person with just one item.*

Date:	_____	_____	_____
Place:	_____	_____	_____
Occasion:	_____	_____	_____

A Warm Coat

In his book *The 7 Habits of Highly Effective People,* Stephen Covey tells of spending an evening with his two sons. They did a variety of things, ending with a movie. Four-year-old Sean fell asleep during the movie, and when it was over Covey picked him up in his arms, carried him to the car, and laid him in the back seat. It was very cold that evening, so he took off his coat and gently arranged it around the boy.

Later that evening it came time to "tuck in" six-year-old Stephen. Covey tried to talk to him about the evening, to find out what he had liked the most, but there was little response. Suddenly Stephen turned over on his side, facing the wall, and started to cry.

"What's wrong, honey? What is it?" asked Covey.

The boy turned back, chin quivering, eyes wet. "Daddy," he asked, "if I were cold, would you put your coat around me, too?"

Covey wrote, "Of all the events of that special night out together, the most important was a little act of kindness—a momentary, unconscious showing of love to his little brother."[1]

Date:	_____	_____	_____
Place:	_____	_____	_____
Occasion:	_____	_____	_____

The Second Mile

Methodist preacher Charles Allen, who grew up in a minister's home, often heard his father preach about "The Second Mile." But later, in adulthood, all Allen could remember about the sermon was this illustration, which he frequently used in his own messages. A man rented a house. There were no trees around it, and his wife suggested they set some out. It would have been easy to walk down to the woods, dig up a few small trees, and set them out in the yard. But he refused; he said it was his duty to pay the rent and that was all.

---

[1] Stephen R. Covey, *The 7 Habits of Highly Effective People* (New York: Simon and Schuster, 1989), 192–193.

The years went by but the man never set out any trees. Every month for twenty-five years he paid the rent. Then one day he bought the house and it belonged to him—but there were no trees in the yard.

If the man had gone just a little beyond his duty, if he had shown some generosity and kindness, if he had gone the second mile, he would have ended up with nice trees of his own to give him cooling shade. But he didn't.[1]

Date: _____ _____ _____
Place: _____ _____ _____
Occasion: _____ _____ _____

Martin Avdeitch

At about age fifty, Russian novelist Leo Tolstoy developed a profound interest in spiritual things and began studying the Gospels in earnest. Unfortunately, he rejected more than he accepted, repudiating belief in miracles, the deity of Christ, the personality of God, and the plan of salvation. Tolstoy reduced Christianity to little more than charity and good works.

Thankless Acts

The best portion of a good man's life is his little, nameless, unremembered acts of kindness and of love.

—WILLIAM WORDSWORTH

He nonetheless wrote about it beautifully, and nothing sums up his philosophy better than this story which Tolstoy based on one of his favorite passages, Matthew 25:31–40:

One night Martin Avdeitch, a humble shoemaker, dozing over his open Bible, suddenly seemed to hear a voice saying, "Martin! Look thou into the street tomorrow, for I am coming to visit thee." Convinced the Lord Jesus was going to visit him, Martin awoke the next morning with nervous excitement. But no one showed up that day except a succession of penniless and pitiful souls: an aged veteran, a shivering mother and newborn, an old peddler woman and a frightened boy who had filched one of her apples.

With a kind heart, Martin cared for each person, but as evening fell, he was disappointed that Jesus had not visited that day. Putting on his spectacles, he took up his Bible with a sigh, and it opened to Matthew 25. Martin read: "For I was hungry and you gave Me food; I was thirsty and you gave Me drink; I was a stranger and you took Me in."

"Lord, when did we do these things?"

Looking on down the page, Martin read: "Assuredly, I say to you, inasmuch as you did it to one of the least of these My brethren, you did it to Me."

Then Avdeitch understood that the vision had come true, and that his Savior had in very truth visited him that day, and that he had received Him.

Date: _____ _____ _____
Place: _____ _____ _____
Occasion: _____ _____ _____

[1] Charles L. Allen, *Prayer Changes Things* (Westwood, NJ: Fleming H. Revell Co., 1964), 117.

Sometimes Kindness Can Make You Cry

Allan Emery, who has not only been successful in business but has devoted much of his time to providing leadership to many Christian organizations, is highly respected as a shrewd, yet kind, man. Credit his father.

Allan recalls taking an extended train trip as a youngster. One morning in the dining car, he heard his father, himself an important businessman, comment that the porter seemed to be in pain and walked with a limp. The poor man, it turned out, was suffering from an infected ingrown toenail.

Later in the morning, Allan was surprised to see the porter coming from his parent's sleeping car. There was a distressed look on his face, and as he passed by big tears fell from his eyes and cascaded down his cheeks. Going into the men's lounge, the man put his hands over his face and cried. Allen sat down on the bench beside him and at length asked, "Are you crying because your toe hurts?"

"No," said the man, "it was because of your daddy."

With great concern, Allen pressed for the story. His parents had returned from breakfast and immediately approached the porter, asking about his toe. Mr. Emery explained that he wasn't a doctor, but he might be able to help him. He removed the man's shoe and sock, and carefully lanced the infected toe, cleaned it, and carefully bandaged it. "It doesn't hurt at all now," said the porter through his tears. "It feels fine."

"Then why are you crying?"

"Well, while he was dressing my toe, your daddy asked me if I loved the Lord Jesus. I told him my mother did but that I did not believe as she did. Then he told me that Jesus loved me and had died for me. As I saw your daddy carefully bandaging my foot, I saw a love that was Jesus' love and I knew I could believe it. We got down on our knees and we prayed and, now, I know that I am important to Jesus and that he loves me."

With that, the porter burst into tears again. When his sobs subsided, he looked over at Allen and said, "You know, boy, kindness can make you cry."[1]

Date: _____ _____ _____
Place: _____ _____ _____
Occasion: _____ _____ _____

Laziness

Someone Once Said . . .

- *Laziness is nothing more than the habit of resting before you get tired.*—Jules Renard
- *Some people stand on the promises; others just sit on the premises.*

Date: _____ _____ _____
Place: _____ _____ _____
Occasion: _____ _____ _____

---

[1] Allan C. Emery, Jr., *A Turtle on a Fencepost* (Waco, Texas: Word Books, 1979), 43–46.

Some Clippings from *U.S. News and World Report*

- **October 27, 1998:** BEAVER, Pa. (AP)—On your mark. Get set. Loaf! This year's Couch Potato Marathon got off in true sedentary style with contestants relaxing on a well-worn couch and watching a videotape of the course they did not run. . . . Participants in Sunday's non-marathon collected pledges for each of the 26 miles of open highway none would ever jog. The proceeds will help finance Beaver's first homeless shelter.

  Two couches—one a tweedy brown, one a floral chartreuse—were parked in front of a television set. On the screen was the course video, with a red arrow pointing to the center of the screen that said, "You are not here."

  Mary Hamilton, program coordinator for Housing Enterprises and Local Programs, came up with the idea while driving. . . . "We were trying to think of something novel to help the homeless," she said. Her first thought was to run a marathon, but as Ms. Hamilton put it, "That's too much work for us."

- **April 6, 1998:** Boys and girls who watch four or more hours of TV a day are significantly fatter than children who watch two hours a day or less, researchers at Johns Hopkins University reported last week in the *Journal of the American Medical Association.* 26 percent of American children watch the tube more than four hours a day. For black children it's 43 percent; for Mexican-American children it's 31 percent. Such inactivity is troubling, since childhood obesity sets the stage for a fat adulthood, and with it, increased risks of high blood pressure, diabetes, and heart disease.

- **September 14, 1998:** Americans are used to being admonished for their self-destructive fondness for cheese-flavored snacks and La-Z-Boys. But citizens of developing countries are also falling prey to the perils of the First World's fat-rich diet and couch-potato ways. At last week's 8th International Congress on Obesity, held in Paris, researchers warned that the planet's expanding waistlines threaten "to become the curse of the next millennium."

- **September 9, 1997, in an article titled, "Even Less to Admire":** To the list of Adolf Hitler's many negative qualities we can now add laziness. New evidence reveals that in the years leading up to the war, for example, he would go off on holiday for six months at a stretch, leaving no one in charge of Germany. A documentary, *The Nazis: A Warning from History,* being televised in Britain this week, draws a stark contrast between his public image as the hard-working Führer and the reality of his leadership. The documentary features interviews with Hitler's SS bodyguard, Herbert Dohring, and a former Nazi foreign office aide, Günter Lohse, who both testified to the Führer's extreme laziness. Dohring says Hitler often overslept, refused to write down his policies, and rarely issued written orders. Hitler's aides would listen to his stream-of-consciousness monologue and create policy out of it. The Führer refused to look at state documents and hated making decisions. The result, according to Lohse, was "total chaos." As far as Hitler was concerned, problems sorted themselves out.

L

"If It's All the Same to You, Mr. President"

Pastor Peter Wilkes of San Jose, California, includes President Theodore Roosevelt among his heroes, saying that Roosevelt was an interesting combination of St. Vitus and St. Paul. "He fired aphorisms at people: Get action, do things, be sane, don't fritter your time away, create, act, be somebody."

Once after two sets of tennis with the French Ambassador, TR suggested jogging. After the jogging there was an intense workout with a medicine ball. The president, not even panting, slapped the suffering ambassador on the back and asked heartily, "What would you like to do next?"

"If it's all the same to you, Mr. President," replied the ambassador, "I would like to lie down and die."

Wesley's Diligence

John Wesley averaged three sermons a day for fifty-four years. In his work of evangelism he traveled by horseback or by carriage more than 200,000 miles. His published works include a four-volume commentary on the whole Bible, a four-volume work on church history, six books on church music, and seven volumes of sermons. He also edited a set of fifty books known as *The Christian Library*. He was greatly devoted to pastoral work, taking on himself the care of all the Methodist churches, never rising later than 4 A.M. and seldom concluding his labors before 10 P.M.[1]

"Thou Wicked and Slothful Servant"

In his book *The Normal Christian Worker*, the Chinese teacher Watchman Nee listed the character qualities needed for effective Christian service. Chapter one is devoted to "Diligence." Noting that our Lord criticized the man in his parable in Matthew 25:24–30 as being both "wicked" and "slothful," Nee warns his readers

---

[1] From *Our Daily Bread.*

about laziness, saying: *Look at the apostles. How diligent they were! Think of the colossal amount of work Paul accomplished in a life-time. See him traveling from place to place, preaching the gospel wherever he goes, or reasoning intently with individuals; even when he is put in prison he is still buying up opportunities—preaching to all who come in contact with him and writing to those from whom he has been cut off. Read what he writes to Timothy from prison: "Preach the word; be instant in season, out of season." Imprisonment might restrict Paul's outward movements, but it could not limit the effectiveness of his ministry. What spiritual wealth he ministered through his prison epistles! There was not a shred of laziness about Paul; he was always taking time by the forelock.*[1]

Date: _____ _____ _____

Place: _____ _____ _____

Occasion: _____ _____ _____

John Ploughman

Charles Spurgeon is arguably Christian history's best-selling author with more words in print than anyone else, living or dead. In all, he wrote 135 books and edited another twenty-eight. If we include pamphlets, the total number of Spurgeon's volumes rises to two hundred. His collected sermons stand as the largest set of books by a single author in the history of Christianity.

Distinguished Ambition

The person who can distinguish between being tired and being lazy will go far.

L

He did all this while suffering debilitating bouts of gout and depression, caring for an invalid wife, reading an average of six books a week, preaching as many as ten times Sunday-to-Sunday, and he once said he counted eight sets of thoughts passing through his mind at the same time while preaching. He oversaw the work of dozens of charitable organizations.

He was seldom heard by fewer than six thousand people, and on one occasion his audience numbered nearly 24,000—all this before the days of microphones and mega-churches.

In 1865, Spurgeon launched a magazine called *The Sword and The Trowel* in which he regularly included maxims under the penname of John Ploughman. The character was actually based on an old farmer, Will Richardson, in Spurgeon's hometown of Stambourne. As a boy, Spurgeon had spent many an hour in the furrows behind Richardson's plow, listening to the man's homespun quips, quotes, comments, and common sense. Years later, in his garden house where *The Sword and the Trowel* was edited, Spurgeon's mind wandered back to those scenes as he composed Ploughman's proverbs.

John Ploughman quickly became for Spurgeon what Poor Richard had been for Benjamin Franklin—his most popular character. When the proverbs were collected and issued as *John Ploughman's Talks*, it became his best-selling book.

The first chapter of *John Ploughman's Talks* is entitled "To the Idle." Here are some of Ploughman's maxims:

---

[1] Watchman Nee, *The Normal Christian Worker* (Hong Kong: Church Book Room, 1968), 12.

- *Idle men are common enough, and grow without planting. . . . Laziness is in some people's bones.*
- *The ugliest sight in the world is one of those thorough-bred loafers who would hardly hold up his basin if it were to rain with porridge. . . . Perhaps if the shower would turn to beer, he might wake himself up a bit.*
- *I have heard men say, "Better do nothing than do mischief," but I am not even sure of that.*
- *The rankest weeds on earth don't grow in the minds of those who are busy at wickedness, but in foul corners of idle men's imaginations, where the devil can hide away unseen like an old serpent as he is.*
- *Idle men tempt the devil to tempt them.*
- *The Lord Jesus tells us himself that when men slept the enemy sowed the tares; and that hits the nail on the head, for it is by the door of sluggishness that evil enters the heart more often, it seems to me, than by any other.*[1]

Date: _____ _____ _____
Place: _____ _____ _____
Occasion: _____ _____ _____

"Let's Call the Dog"

An old mountaineer and his wife were sitting in front of the fireplace one evening just whiling away the time. After a long silence, the wife said: "Jed, I think it's raining. Get up and go outside and see."

The old mountaineer continued gazing absently at the fire, then sighed and said, "Aw, Ma, why don't we just call in the dog and see if he's wet."

Date: _____ _____ _____
Place: _____ _____ _____
Occasion: _____ _____ _____

Loneliness

Someone Once Said . . .

- *It seems my tragic destiny that in all the important moments of my life I find myself alone.*—Benito Mussolini
- *Sometimes I think the only people who stay with me and really listen are people I hire, people I pay.*—Marilyn Monroe[2]
- *Sometimes I get so lonely I could scream.*—Inger Stevens, actress and star of the TV series *The Farmer's Daughter,* who took her own life

[1] Charles Spurgeon, *John Ploughman's Talks* (Grand Rapids, MI: Baker, 1976), ch. 1.
[2] William J. Weatherby, *Conversations with Marilyn.*

- *It is strange to be known so universally, and yet to be so lonely.*—Albert Einstein[1]
- *I live in a vacuum that is as lonely as a radio tube when the batteries are dead and there is no current to plug into.*—Ernest Hemingway[2]
- *We are orphans, you and I. Every soul in this vast corpse-trench of the universe is utterly alone.*—Jean Paul Richter, eighteenth-century German author and philosopher[3]
- *O that I had . . . an earthly friend on whom I could unbosom my soul.*—William Carey, the "Father of Modern Missions" in India[4]
- *I think we are a very lonely populace; we are cut apart from each other.*—George Gallup[5]
- *Loneliness becomes our "friend" when it forces us to enjoy the friendship of God as much as we would the friendship of others.*—Bill Gothard
- *When you are lonely, too much stillness is exactly the thing that seems to be laying waste your soul. Use that stillness to quiet your heart before God. Get to know Him.*—Elisabeth Elliot
- *Loneliness is an opportunity for Jesus to make Himself known.*—F. B. Meyer[6]

Date:	_____	_____	_____
Place:	_____	_____	_____
Occasion:	_____	_____	_____

Bill Gothard on Loneliness

In one of his "birthday card" mailings some years back, Bill Gothard made three observations about loneliness:

1. Loneliness is the anguish I feel when I sense that I am being cut off from the spirit of others. ("I am full of heaviness: and I looked for someone to lament with me; but there was none, and for comforters, but I found none."—Psalm 69:20)
2. Loneliness is the evidence that I was expecting others to meet my needs as only God can. ("My soul wait thou only upon God. For my expectation is from Him."—Psalm 62:5)
3. Loneliness means that at that very moment, God feels the same anguish toward me because my basic delight is not in Him. ("I will delight myself in the Lord and He shall give me the desires of my heart."—Psalm 37:4)

Then Gothard adds, "Read Psalms when lonely; quote 73:25," which says: "Whom have I in heaven but You? And there is none upon earth that I desire besides You."

[1] Timothy Ferris, *Science 83,* October 1983, 39.
[2] Daniel Pawley, "Ernest Hemingway: Tragedy of an Evangelical," *Christianity Today.*
[3] A. W. Criswell, *Great Doctrines of the Bible,* vol. 2 (Grand Rapids, MI: Zondervan, 1982), 174.
[4] Mary Drewery, *William Carey: A Biography* (Chicago: Moody Press, 1978), 74.
[5] Gerhard and LB Gschwandtner, "The Gallup Survey on Success," *Personal Selling Power,* May/June 1987, 7.
[6] Warren W. Wiersbe, *Listening to the Giants* (Grand Rapids, MI: Baker, 1980), 101.

Date: _____ _____ _____

Place: _____ _____ _____

Occasion: _____ _____ _____

His Very Special Day

It was Grandfather's birthday. He was seventy-nine. He got up early, shaved, showered, combed his hair and put on his Sunday best so he would look nice when they came.

He skipped his daily walk to the town café where he had coffee with his cronies. He wanted to be home when they came.

He put his porch chair on the sidewalk so he could get a better view of the street when they drove up to help celebrate his birthday.

At noon he got tired but decided to forgo his nap so he could be there when they came. Most of the rest of the afternoon he spent near the telephone so he could answer it when they called.

He has five married children, thirteen grandchildren, and three great-grandchildren. One son and daughter live within ten miles of his place. They hadn't visited him for a long time. But today was his birthday, and they were sure to come.

At suppertime he left the cake untouched so they could cut it and have dessert with him.

After supper he sat on the porch waiting.

At 8:30 he went to his room to prepare for bed. Before retiring he left a note on the door which read, "Be sure to wake me up when they come."

It was Grandfather's birthday. He was seventy-nine.[1]

Date: _____ _____ _____

Place: _____ _____ _____

Occasion: _____ _____ _____

Loneliness and Longevity

According to a study reported by *Reader's Digest*, lonely people seem more likely to die of heart disease than do the socially active, according to a study conducted by doctors in Sweden. The study allowed for medical and life-style risk factors—age, smoking, physical inactivity, and signs of heart disease—and found that the subjects with few social contacts had a 40 percent greater risk of dying from cardiovascular disease than the rest did.[2]

"Loneliness," said *Newsweek* magazine in reporting a similar study, "can speed your demise no matter how conscientiously you care for your body." One study of elderly heart-attack patients found that those with two or more close associates enjoyed twice the one-year survival rate of those who were completely alone. "We

---

[1] Ann Landers column, clipped, undated, in my files.
[2] Dr. Kristina Orth-Gomer and Professor Jeffrey Johnson, *Reader's Digest*, April 1987, 36.

go through life surrounded by protective convoys of others," says Robert Kahn, a University of Michigan psychologist who has studied the health effects of companionship. "People who manage to maintain a network of social support do best."[1]

Date: _____ _____ _____

Place: _____ _____ _____

Occasion: _____ _____ _____

Lonely on the Worldwide Web

A paper by six researchers at Carnegie Mellon University, published in *The American Psychologist,* reported the startling news that the Internet, the very touchstone of the new American capitalism, is actually bad for some people's psychological well-being. Across the board, the researchers found a small but statistically significant trend: the more time the subjects spent at their keyboards, the more depressed and lonely they were at the end of the experiment.

> **Laying Waste**
>
> *When you are lonely, too much stillness is exactly the thing that seems to be laying waste your soul.*
> —ELISABETH ELLIOT

This result wasn't just surprising, it was paradoxical, according to the study's lead author, Robert Kraut of Carnegie Mellon's Human-Computer Interaction Institute. Unlike people who watch a lot of television, who generally know they're wasting time and despise themselves for it, the Internet users reported enjoying the time they spent online. And they did commendably useful things with it, like the woman who sent a pair of mittens to someone she met through an online knitting group, or the teenager who met a girl online and took her to the prom. Far-flung family members stayed in closer touch with e-mail, and some casual acquaintances graduated to friendships. Hence the paradox, says Kraut: "They're using it socially, they're enjoying the use of it socially, yet [the Internet] seems to be associated with symptoms of social isolation, such as depression and loneliness."[2]

Date: _____ _____ _____

Place: _____ _____ _____

Occasion: _____ _____ _____

Loneliness in Three Stages

The following testimony appeared in the newsletter of Nashville's Crisis Pregnancy Support Center:

"I got pregnant when I was sixteen, and the only thing lonelier than being sixteen and pregnant is knowing you have to make an adoption plan for your baby.

---

[1] Geoffrey Cowley, "How To Live to 100," *Newsweek,* June 30, 1997.

[2] Jerry Adler, "Online and Bummed Out: One Study says the Internet can be Alienating," *Newsweek,* September 14, 1998.

"Loneliness gradually became a part of my life as my pregnancy progressed. In the beginning my friends still dropped by and sometimes I would still go out with them. Before long, however, my pregnancy became obvious, and I was always tired. They still wanted me to do things with them, but most of the time I just didn't feel like it. I began to amuse myself by reading, watching TV, and thinking about the baby that was to come. This was the first stage of my loneliness when I learned to do everything alone.

"When watching TV and reading got old, I spent a lot of time crying in my room. I was alone and confused, and I knew I couldn't keep my baby. As I decided on adoption, I thought my heart would break. The decision was made out of love for my baby, but it was the hardest decision I will ever make in my whole life. This was the second stage of my loneliness when I cried alone.

"The third stage of my loneliness was the shortest because this is where the Lord found me. My mother told me to trust in the Lord and He would give me the strength to do what I had to do. I began to spend a lot of time praying, and I found that I was no longer alone. I had a friend who was always there to listen. That friend was Jesus Christ, and He was the cure for all my loneliness."[1]

Date:			
Place:			
Occasion:			

Lord's Supper

Someone Once Said . . .

- *Is there anything more sorrowful, more deserving of tears than that [the Lord's Supper] should be used as a subject of strife and division?*—Philip Melanchthon[2]
- *If Melanchthon were alive today, he might not weep because of controversies that surround the Lord's Supper, but he might well sorrow because of our indifference to its meaning and importance.*—Erwin Lutzer[3]
- *The Lord's Supper should be the crowning service in the church, and thus be earth's nearest approach to heaven.*—Andrew W. Blackwood[4]
- *The link between the cross and the crown is the Table of the Lord. Do not forget, when you sit down at the Communion, that the bread and the cup point back to Christ's accomplished work, and forward to your accomplished salvation.*—A. T. Pierson

Date:			
Place:			
Occasion:			

---

[1] "Lonely," in Crisis Pregnancy Support Center, Nashville, Tennessee Newsletter, Summer 1990.
[2] Erwin W. Lutzer, "Deserving of Tears," *Moody*, February 1984, 127.
[3] Erwin W. Lutzer, "Deserving of Tears," *Moody*, February 1984, 128.
[4] Andrew W. Blackwood, *The Fine Art of Public Worship* (Nashville: Abingdon, 1939), 204.

Thomas à Kempis on the Lord's Supper

Oh admirable and hidden grace of the sacrament, which only Christ's faithful ones know, but the faithless and those who serve sin cannot experience! In this Sacrament is conferred spiritual grace, and lost virtue is regained in the soul, and the beauty which is disfigured by sin returneth again. So great sometimes is this grace that out of the fullness of devotion given, not only the mind but also the weak body feeleth that more strength is supplied unto it.[1]

Date:	_____	_____	_____
Place:	_____	_____	_____
Occasion:	_____	_____	_____

Every Three Minutes

Legendary sports broadcaster Jon Miller, who provided the play-by-plays for the Baltimore Orioles for many years, was considered one of the best sports announcers in the nation. His sense of drama and his voice of authority could make even an 8–1 blowout sound exciting.

In broadcasting a game, Miller never forgot the most important thing. He always kept an egg-timer to remind him to give the score every three minutes.

The Lord's Supper is, in a way, like that. Amid all the vigor, drama, and disappointment of life, it reminds us on a regular basis, every week or every month, of the most important thing.

Date:	_____	_____	_____
Place:	_____	_____	_____
Occasion:	_____	_____	_____

The Mangled Bicycle

Roger Rose faced deep sorrow as a child. His young brother was fatally injured in a tragic accident. A dirt road ran alongside their home, and only on rare occasions would an automobile be seen on it. But one day as his brother was crossing on his bicycle, a car came roaring over a nearby hill, and he was run over and killed.

Roger said, "Later, when my father picked up the mangled, twisted bike, I heard him sob out loud for the first time in my life. He carried it to the barn and placed it in a spot we seldom used. Father's terrible sorrow eased with the passing of time, but for many years whenever he saw that bike, tears began streaming down his face.

"Since then I have often prayed, 'Lord, keep the memory of your death that fresh to me! Every time I partake of Your memorial supper, may my heart be stirred as if it occurred only yesterday. Never let the communion service become a mere formality, but always a tender and touching experience.'"[2]

---

[1] Thomas à Kempis, *The Imitation of Christ*, Fourth Book, ch. 1, segment 11.
[2] From *Our Daily Bread*.

Date:			
Place:			
Occasion:			

Package from Home

Writing in *Leadership Journal,* Pastor Martin Thielen of Honolulu wrote about a service in which he had presided over the observance of the Lord's Supper. He said that a few weeks earlier, he had read a Lord's Supper sermon by John Claypool in which he told the story of Dietrich Bonhoeffer, a brilliant young pastor and seminary teacher who opposed Hitler's policies in the 1930s. On April 5, 1943, the Germans arrested Bonhoeffer and put him in prison. Two years later the Nazis executed him, hanging him on the gallows just days before the Allies swept in to liberate Germany.

> ——————◆——————
> **The Cross and
> the Crown**
>
> *The link between the cross
> and the crown is the Table
> of the Lord.*
> —A. T. PIERSON
> ——————◆——————

About ten weeks after his arrest, Bonhoeffer ended a letter to his parents with these words:

"It is Monday, and I was just sitting down to a dinner of turnips and potatoes when a parcel you sent me by Ruth arrived. Such things give me greater joy than I can say. Although I am utterly convinced that nothing can break the bonds between us, I seem to need some outward token or sign to reassure me. In this way, material things become the vehicles of spiritual realities. I suppose it is rather like the felt need in our religion for sacraments."

Bonhoeffer knew his parents loved him. Yet he still hungered for that love to be reaffirmed. He needed to be reminded of their love in a tangible way. His package from home served that purpose, and Bonhoeffer saw the Lord's Supper doing the same.

"I decided to use Bonhoeffer's analogy," Thielen wrote, "along with some of John Claypool's insights, in my Lord's Supper sermon. I did not preach an informational, three-point message on the meaning of the Supper. Instead I told stories.

"I began by recounting how much I enjoyed receiving packages from home during my college years—especially if they included a check! I told my congregation that the contents of the package—cookies, socks, money, whatever—served as powerful reminders that my parents loved and were thinking of me.

"I then told the story about Dietrich Bonhoeffer and his package from home. With the help of some biblical passages, I drove home the point that the Lord's Supper is a package from our heavenly home, a tangible expression of God's love for us.

"I concluded the sermon by walking to the Communion table and saying, 'Come, brothers and sisters in Christ, let us partake. A package from home has arrived. Let us eat and drink and be reminded of God's awesome love for his children.'

"After the service," concluded Pastor Thielen, "people didn't say, 'Nice service, Pastor.' Several commented, 'That was the most moving Lord's Supper service I have ever experienced.'"[1]

---

[1] Martin Thielen, *Leadership Journal,* Winter 1994, 39–40.

Date: _____   _____   _____
Place: _____   _____   _____
Occasion: _____   _____   _____

Luther and Zwingli

Unity is essential among Christians, but unity does not mean uniformity, and one of the most remarkable patterns in Church history is that God uses his church and blesses his children even when, for various reasons, they sometimes disagree. History's first missionary team, Paul and Barnabas, split up over the John Mark issue in Acts 15. Wesley and Whitefield were at odds over various points of their theologies. And the Reformers themselves, strong-willed men, crossed swords over, among other things, the nature of the Lord's Supper.

The Swiss Reformers, led by Ulrich Zwingli, insisted that the Lord's Supper was a memorial service, while the German Reformers, led by Martin Luther, insisted that Christ is actually present in the consecrated bread and wine, although Luther was never able to explain exactly how that happens.

The conflict was so sharp that a local political leader invited the men to his beautiful castle in Marburg on this date in church history: October 1, 1529. The discussions took place in the banquet hall where a long table, covered with a velvet runner, was set in the middle of the room. Before the proceedings began, Luther took a piece of chalk and, on the cloth in front of him, wrote the words, "This is my body."

The debate raged for three days. Zwingli insisted that the verb "is" in the phrase "This is my body" should be interpreted as "represents." Luther said, "Where in the Bible does the verb 'is' ever mean 'represent'?" Zwingli showed him several places.

But Luther wouldn't budge. At the end of the three-day conference, the delegates had agreed on fourteen of fifteen areas of former division. But on the fifteenth—the Lord's Supper—they failed to reach agreement and the Reformers were unable to join the German and Swiss factions into one powerful whole. As a result, Zwingli lost the support of the German princes. The five Catholic Cantons of Switzerland sent an army against him, and he died in the battle of Kappel.

But nothing could stop the Reformer's fire, and despite the failure of the Marburg meetings, the doctrine of justification by grace through faith spread across the continent.

Date: _____   _____   _____
Place: _____   _____   _____
Occasion: _____   _____   _____

My Elder Brother Died

In his book *Spiritual Depression,* Dr. Martyn Lloyd-Jones tells about a young girl in the days of the Covenanters in Scotland. She was going to attend a Communion

Service held by the Covenanters on a Sunday afternoon, a service that was absolutely prohibited under the law.

The soldiers of the King of England were looking everywhere for people who were going to meet together and partake in this Communion Service, and as this girl turned a corner on her way she came face to face with a band of soldiers, and she knew she was trapped.

For a moment she wondered what she was going to say. She was unwilling to lie, but it would be deadly to tell the truth. But immediately on being questioned, she found herself answering: "My Elder Brother has died and they are going to read His will this afternoon, and He has done something for me and has left something for me, and I want to hear them read the will."

And they allowed her to go on.[1]

Date: _____ _____ _____
Place: _____ _____ _____
Occasion: _____ _____ _____

That Is My Mother

Dr. W. A. Criswell, longtime pastor of the First Baptist Church of Dallas, was once invited into the palatial home of one of his wealthier members. As they stood in the beautiful walnut-paneled library, Criswell saw an oval picture of an old-fashioned girl on the wall. The host, pointing to the picture, said, "That is my mother." Then, as tears came to his eyes, he continued, "I never saw her. She died in childbirth when I was born. Someday, when I get to heaven, after seeing my Savior, I want first of all to see the face of my mother."

Criswell later wrote, "I could have exclaimed, 'That is your *mother?* That is nothing but a piece of paper and cardboard covered with ink!' But I did nothing of the kind. I knew what he meant. 'That picture represents my angel mother. I never saw her, but some day in heaven I shall see her face to face and love her aboundingly for giving her life for me.' "

Criswell continued, "It is exactly so with our own Lord Jesus. This is his body, and this is his blood, and it pictures our lovely Lord until that preciously beautiful day in heaven when we see him face-to-face and thank him for giving his life for us."[2]

Date: _____ _____ _____
Place: _____ _____ _____
Occasion: _____ _____ _____

The Meaning of the Lord's Supper

Andrew W. Blackwood suggests that the Lord's Supper is an act with ten different meanings:

---

[1] D. Martyn Lloyd-Jones, *Spiritual Depression* (Grand Rapids, MI: Eerdmans, 1965), 104–105.
[2] W. A. Criswell, *Criswell's Guidebook for Pastors* (Nashville: Broadman, 1980), 202.

1. It is a memorial of Christ's redeeming grace: "This do in remembrance of Me." Like the Passover out of which it grew, the Christian Supper teaches us to look back upon the meaning of our redemption.
2. It is a symbol of Christ's death for us sinners: "This is my body, which is broken for you."
3. It is our mightiest means of grace. Grace is the sum of all that we know about God. It is the attraction of his goodness, supremely in the cross. The means of grace, as we use the term, include the reading of the Bible, private prayer, public worship, and the Lord's Supper.
4. It is a thanksgiving feast. Such is the literal meaning of that stately title, the Eucharist. In the Greek the original word means thanksgiving.
5. It is likewise a family meal. As such, it has among Christians the place which the Passover filled in the religious experience of the ancient Hebrews. The Passover was preeminently a family meal.
6. This family meal is at the same time the Holy Communion with the Church of all the ages, on earth, and in glory. This is no small part of what we mean when we stand to say in the Apostle's Creed, "I believe . . . in the holy communion of saints." The word "communion" literally refers to that which we have in common. Another word which means almost the same as communion is fellowship.
7. It is likewise a Sacrament. Theologically the word sacrament means an outward and visible sign of God's inward and spiritual grace.
8. The Sacrament is also a Covenant of Grace: "This cup of the New Covenant in my blood . . ."
9. There is a sermon in the Supper, the most powerful and moving sermon in the history of the church: "Ye do show the Lord's death till He come." The verb translated "show" literally means to preach.
10. The Lord's Supper is a symbol of Christian hope: ". . . till He comes."[1]

Date: _____ _____ _____

Place: _____ _____ _____

Occasion: _____ _____ _____

A Memorial

W. A. Criswell once wrote that the Lord's Supper is, first of all, a memorial to the atoning death of our Savior. He said, "There are many kinds of memorials on the earth. If you have ever been to Washington, D.C., you have seen there the tall, monolithic marble monument to the Father of our country—the Washington Monument. In Egypt, you can see many towering obelisks. Sometimes a monument will take the form of a mausoleum. In India, you will see the most beautiful mausoleum in the world—the Taj Mahal—built by Shah Jahan in memory of a beloved wife.

---

[1] Blackwood, *The Fine Art of Public Worship*, Ch. 12.

"But our Lord did not create a monument out of marble to bring to us the memory of our Savior's suffering in our behalf. In fact, this memorial is not in the form of any kind of structure. He did it in a primeval, fundamental, and basic way— by eating and drinking—and this simple memorial is to be repeated again and again and again. The broken bread recalls for us His torn body, and the crimson of the cup reminds us of the blood poured out upon the earth for the remission of sins."[1]

Date: _____   _____   _____
Place: _____   _____   _____
Occasion: _____   _____   _____

The Longest Communion Service

On May 8, 1984, Benjamin M. Weir, veteran Presbyterian missionary to Leba-non, was kidnapped at gunpoint by Shiite Muslims in Beirut. On Saturday night of his first week of captivity, having decided to observe communion the next day, he set aside a piece of bread from his sandwich.

The next morning, he awoke thinking of all the places of worship around the world that would be celebrating the Lord's Supper that day. He wrote:

"I unwrapped my piece of bread and began the Presbyterian order of worship: *We are now about to celebrate the sacrament of the Lord's Supper.* For me the *we* had special meaning. . . . First Corinthians 11, with its account of the meal with Jesus, took me back to apostolic times.

"I ate the bread behind closed doors with the fearful disciples of the risen Lord on that first Easter. When it came to sharing the cup, I had no visible wine, but that didn't seem to matter. I knew that others were taking the cup for me elsewhere at this universal table.

"As others prayed for me, so I prayed for them and their ministry and mission. It was the longest Communion service I had ever attended.

"As night came, I recalled how Carol and I had listened to hymns on the BBC's *Evensong* every Sunday evening before dropping off to sleep. So I proceeded to have my own quiet evensong. The hymns came tumbling out one after the other. . . .

"I was finally able to settle down for the night with a feeling of trust, comfort, and praise."[2]

Date: _____   _____   _____
Place: _____   _____   _____
Occasion: _____   _____   _____

After 11 Years

John Paton's life was molded by his childhood in a little cottage in Kirkmahoe, Scotland. The cottage had ribs of oak, stone walls, a thatched roof, and three rooms filled with eleven children. The front room served as bedroom, kitchen, and parlor.

---

[1] W. A. Criswell, *Great Doctrines of the Bible,* vol. 3 (Grand Rapids, MI: Zondervan, 1983), 83.
[2] Benjamin M. Weir with Dennis Benson, "Tough Faith," *Leadership Journal,* Winter 1989, 57.

The rear room was his father's stocking-making shop. The middle room was a closet where John's father retired each day for prayer and Bible study. The sound of his father's prayers through the wall made a powerful impression on young John.

Years later, when Scotland's Reformed Church issued a plea for missionaries for the South Pacific, John went to his parents for advice. They told him something they had never before disclosed—he had been dedicated to foreign missions before birth.

John sailed from Scotland April 16, 1858, landing on the islands in November. He found himself among cannibals, endangered again and again. "They encircled us in a deadly ring," he wrote of one incident, "and one kept urging another to strike the first blow. My heart rose up to the Lord Jesus; I saw him watching all the scene. My peace came back to me like a wave from God. I realized that my life was immortal till my Master's work with me was done."

The turning point came when Paton decided to dig a well to provide fresh water for the people. The islanders, terrified at bringing "rain from below," watched with deepest foreboding. Paton dug deeper and deeper until finally, at thirty feet, he tapped into a stream of water. Opposition to his mission work ceased, and the wide-eyed islanders gave him their full respect. Chief Mamokei accepted Christ as Savior, then a few others made the daring step. On October 24, 1869, nearly eleven years after his arrival, Paton led his first communion service. Twelve converted cannibals partook of the Lord's Supper. "As I put the bread and wine into those hands once stained with the blood of cannibalism, now stretched out to receive and partake the emblems of the Redeemer's love," he wrote, "I had a foretaste of the joy of Glory that well nigh broke my heart to pieces."[1]

Date: _____ _____ _____
Place: _____ _____ _____
Occasion: _____ _____ _____

"I Can't"

In his book *The Body,* Charles Colson tells about Pat Novak, a pastor in a nonsacramental denomination, who was serving as a hospital chaplain intern just outside of Boston several years ago. Pat was making his rounds one summer morning when he was called to visit a patient admitted with an undiagnosed ailment. John, a man in his sixties, had not responded to any treatment; medical tests showed nothing; psychological tests were inconclusive. Yet he was wasting away; he had not even been able to swallow for two weeks. The nurses tried everything. Finally they called the chaplain's office.

When Pat walked into the room, John was sitting limply in his bed, strung with IV tubes, staring listlessly at the wall. He was a tall, grandfatherly man, balding a little, but his sallow skin hung loosely on his face, neck, and arms where the weight had dropped from his frame. His eyes were hollow.

Pat was terrified; he had no idea what to do. But John seemed to brighten a bit as soon as he saw Pat's chaplain badge and invited him to sit down. As they talked, Pat sensed that God was urging him to do something specific: He knew he was to

[1] Robert J. Morgan, *On This Day* (Nashville: Thomas Nelson Publishers, 1996), October 24th.

ask John if he wanted to take Communion. Chaplain interns were not encouraged to ask this type of thing in this public hospital, but Pat did.

At that John broke down. "I can't!" he cried. "I've sinned and can't be forgiven."

Pat paused a moment, knowing he was about to break policy again. Then he told John about 1 Corinthians 11 and Paul's admonition that whoever takes Communion in an unworthy manner eats and drinks judgment to himself. And he asked John if he wanted to confess his sin. John nodded gratefully. To this day Pat can't remember the particular sin John confessed, nor would he say if he did, but he recalls that it did not strike him as particularly egregious. Yet it had been draining the life from this man. John wept as he confessed, and Pat laid hands on him, hugged him, and told John his sins were forgiven.

Then Pat got the second urging from the Holy Spirit: Ask him if he wants to take Communion. He did. Pat gave John a Bible and told him he would be back later. Already John was sitting up straighter, with a flicker of light in his eyes.

Pat visited a few more patients and then ate some lunch in the hospital cafeteria. When he left he wrapped an extra piece of bread in a napkin and borrowed a coffee cup from the cafeteria. He ran out to a shop a few blocks away and bought a container of grape juice. Then he returned to John's room with the elements and celebrated Communion with him, again reciting 1 Corinthians 11. John took the bread and chewed it slowly. It was the first time in weeks he had been able to take solid food in his mouth. He took the cup and swallowed. He had been set free.

Within three days John walked out of that hospital.[1]

Date:			
Place:			
Occasion:			

Marriage

Someone Once Said . . .

- *The ever-living Christ is here to bless you. The nearer you keep him, the nearer you will be to one another.*—Geoffrey Francis Fisher, Archbishop of Canterbury, at the wedding of Queen Elizabeth II
- *To keep your marriage brimming / With love in the loving cup / Whenever you're wrong, admit it / Whenever you're right, shut up!*—Ogden Nash
- *My wife and I were happy for twenty years. Then we met.*—Rodney Dangerfield

Date:			
Place:			
Occasion:			

---

[1] Charles W. Colson, *The Body* (Nashville: Word Publishing, 1992), 139–140.

Working on It

- The simplest prescription for a good marriage contains only two points:
  1. Walk with the Master—1 John 1:7: "But if we walk in the light as He is in the light, we have fellowship with one another."
  2. Work on the Marriage—Colossians 3:23 (NIV): "Whatever you do, work at it with all your heart."
- *Couples who do not expect to work at their relationship often have the roughest ride on the back roads of matrimony.*—William L. Coleman[1]
- *In physics, the law of entropy says that all systems, left unattended, will run down. Unless new energy is pumped in, the organism will disintegrate. Entropy is at work in many areas other than physics. I see it, for instance, when I work with couples whose marriages are in trouble. A marriage will not continue to be good simply because two people love each other, are compatible, and get off to a fine start. To the contrary, marriages left to their own devices tend to wear out, break down, and ultimately disintegrate. This is the law of entropy. So to keep our relationships working, we must constantly pump new energy into them.*—Alan Loy McGinnis[2]
- *Marriages are made in heaven, but we are responsible for the maintenance work.*

Date:	_____	_____	_____
Place:	_____	_____	_____
Occasion:	_____	_____	_____

M

Just a Piece of Paper?

In *Mere Christianity*, C. S. Lewis answers those who claim that a marriage license is just a piece of paper: *Those who are in love have a natural inclination to bind themselves by promises. Love songs all over the world are full of vows of eternality and constancy. The Christian law is not forcing upon the passion of love something which is foreign to that passion's own nature: it is demanding that lovers should take seriously something which their passion itself impels them to do.*[3]

Date:	_____	_____	_____
Place:	_____	_____	_____
Occasion:	_____	_____	_____

More Advice from C. S. Lewis

Although C. S. Lewis wasn't married at the time he wrote *Mere Christianity*, he described marital oneness and love with amazing insight:

---

[1] William L. Coleman, *What Makes a Marriage Last* (San Bernardino, CA: Here's Life Publisher, 1990).
[2] Alan Loy McGinnis, *The Power of Optimism* (New York: Harper & Row Publishers, San Francisco, 1990), 45.
[3] C. S. Lewis, *Mere Christianity* (New York: The Macmillan Company, 1958), 83.

The Christian idea of marriage is based on Christ's words that a man and wife are to be regarded as a single organism—for that is what the words "one flesh" would be in modern English. And the Christians believe that when He said this He was not expressing a sentiment but stating a fact—just as one is stating a fact when one says that a lock and its key are one mechanism, or that a violin and a bow are one musical instrument. The inventor of the human machine was telling us that its two halves, the male and the female, were made to be combined together in pairs, not simply on the sexual level, but totally combined. . . .

What we call "being in love" is a glorious state, and, in several ways, good for us . . . It is a noble feeling, but it is still a feeling. Now no feeling can be relied on to last in its full intensity, or even to last at all. Knowledge can last; principles can last; habits can last, but feelings come and go. And in fact, whatever people say, the state called "being in love" usually does not last. If the old fairy-tale ending "They lived happily ever after" is taken to mean "They felt for the next fifty years exactly as they felt the day before they were married," then it says what probably never was nor ever could be true, and would be highly undesirable if it were. Who could bear to live in that excitement for even five years? What would become of your work, your appetite, your sleep, your friendships? But, of course, ceasing to be "in love" need not mean ceasing to love. Love in this second sense—love as distinct from "being in love" is not merely a feeling. It is a deep unity, maintained by the will and deliberately strengthened by habit, reinforced by (in Christian marriages) the grace which both parties ask, and receive, from God. They can have this love for each other even at those moments when they do not like each other, as you love yourself even when you do not like yourself. They can retain this love even when each would easily, if they allowed themselves, be "in love" with someone else. "Being in love" first moved them to promise fidelity: this quieter love enables them to keep the promise. It is on this love that the engine of marriage is run: being in love was the explosion that started it.[1]

Night Light

Marriage is an institution that turns a night owl into a homing pigeon.

Date: _____ _____ _____

Place: _____ _____ _____

Occasion: _____ _____ _____

The Guest List

Some time ago a young man—let's call him Joe—began thinking of marriage. He was nervous about the whole thing, but he knew what he wanted in a wife, and he started looking. He went out of his way to meet new girls, but only one stole his heart—let's call her Jo Beth. He worked his way into a relationship with her, and to his great joy, she returned his affection. They fell in love and one evening he proposed. Their families were thrilled, and word quickly spread among their friends. Joe and Jo Beth couldn't hide their joy as they started planning their wedding. They chose the date. They contacted the minister. They talked about the flowers and the candles and the ceremony and the food. Then the guest list: who to invite? They started compiling names. Their parents and grandparents and relatives, of course. Their friends. Their work associates. And then Joe said something interesting, or perhaps

---

[1] Lewis, *Mere Christianity*, (New York: The Macmillan Company, 1958), 81, 84–85.

it was Jo Beth. "What would you think of inviting Jesus Himself? Let's add him to the wedding list just as we'd invite anyone else. Let's send Him a formal invitation to be a part of our marriage."

So they did—and Jesus Christ came. Now, when Jesus attends a wedding, you never know what will happen. What happened on this occasion is recorded in the Gospel of John, chapter 2. Jesus took the occasion to perform his first miracle—the turning of water into wine.

This young couple was evidently well known to Mary and Jesus. The Lord had undoubtedly sold wood products to people in Cana, for He was a carpenter, and Cana was near Nazareth. Mary evidently felt responsible to see that things went well at the wedding banquet, so there could have been family connections. At any rate, the young couple didn't hesitate to invite Jesus to their wedding.

Jesus wants to attend our weddings, live in our homes, and help us build our marriages. He wants to turn water into wine, that is, to transform ordinary relationships into very special ones. Charles Erdman put it this way: "All the signs wrought by our Lord were symbolic of the experiences which would result from faith in him. It is most significant, therefore, that his first miracle, which was an index to his whole ministry, was so related to the joy of a wedding feast."

A Christian marriage has the presence of Jesus Christ in it, filling the house, casting his glow on the home, and making the relationships spiritual and special. And that makes all the difference.[1]

Date: _____   _____   _____

Place: _____   _____   _____

Occasion: _____   _____   _____

M

Nice Night in June

Nice night in June. Stars shine. Big moon.
In park with girl. Heart pound. Head swirl.
Me say love. She coo like dove.
Me smart. Me fast. Me don't let chance pass.
Get hitched me say. She say okay.
Wedding bells ring. Honeymoon. Everything.
Settle down. Happy life. Happy man. Happy wife.
Another night in June. Stars shine. Big moon.
Me not happy anymore. Carry baby. Walk the floor.
Wife mad. She stew. Me mad. Stew too.
Life one big spat. Nagging wife. Bawling brat.
We realize at last, we moved too fast.

Date: _____   _____   _____

Place: _____   _____   _____

Occasion: _____   _____   _____

[1] From a sermon by the author.

Ivan Ilyich

In Leo Tolstoy's *The Death of Ivan Ilyich,* the key character of the book, Ivan, a lawyer, married his sweetheart. Tolstoy wrote: *The preparations for marriage and the first period of married life, with its conjugal caresses, new furniture, new dishes, new linen—the period up to his wife's pregnancy—went very well . . .*

But then, things seemed to change. It seemed to Ivan that his wife became moody and irritable. Ivan, frustrated, didn't enjoy her as much as before, so he began seeking ways to avoid being at home so much. He found his diversion at work.

Tolstoy wrote: *To the degree that his wife became more irritable and demanding, Ivan Ilyich increasingly made work the center of gravity in his life. He grew more attached to his job and more ambitious than ever. Very soon, within a year after his wedding, Ivan Ilyich realized that married life, though it offered certain conveniences, was in fact a very complex and difficult business . . .*

Then Tolstoy offered this interesting paragraph: *Of married life, [Ivan] demanded only the conveniences it could provide—dinners at home, a well-run household, a partner in bed, and, above all, a veneer of respectability which public opinion required. As for the rest, he tried to find enjoyment in family life, and if he succeeded, was very grateful, but, if he met with resistance and quarrelsomeness, he immediately withdrew into his separate, entrenched world of work and found pleasure there. . . . [Finally] all they had left were the rare periods of amorousness that came over them, but these did not last long. They were merely little islands at which the couple anchored for a while before setting out again on a sea of veiled hostility, which took the form of estrangement from each other.*

Tolstoy possessed the ability to creep into homes and take snapshots of marriage and show people their own hearts. Many couples can identify with the home of Ivan Ilyich. The missing link in their marriage is communication. Ivan and his wife didn't sit down and talk through things. They ran into stresses and just withdrew from each other. They didn't do those things necessary for keeping the lines open.

When I was a boy, I used to watch my mother sew. She drew a needle from a pin cushion, took it to the window, put the end of a piece of string into her mouth to wet it, and threaded it through the eye of the needle. Then she joined two pieces of cloth, inserted the needle through them both at once, and began stitching them together, winding the thread back and forth in a pattern guaranteed to make a tight seam. The more stitches, the tighter the union.

Communication is the needle and thread of marriage. Without it, you have only two pieces of cloth that may live in the same house and occasionally touch one another or rub against each other, but without actually being joined as one. But if there is communication, the stitching process begins, and the more communication, the tighter the seam. Every meaningful conversation is like a stitch holding the two together.

Communication, in other words, is the only means by which two people become one.

Date: _____   _____   _____

Place: _____   _____   _____

Occasion: _____   _____   _____

"I Mean Everything"

Sinclair Lewis once received a letter from a very young and very pretty woman who wished to become his secretary. She said she could type, file, and anything else, and concluded, "When I say anything, I mean *anything.*" Lewis turned the letter over to his wife, Dorothy Thompson. She wrote to the young woman saying, "Mr. Lewis already has an excellent secretary who can type and file. I do everything else, and when I say everything, I mean *everything.*"[1]

Date: _____ _____ _____
Place: _____ _____ _____
Occasion: _____ _____ _____

Where Are Our Manners?

The most consistent research finding about what is different in the communication of strangers and people married to each other is that married people are ruder to each other than they are to strangers. They interrupt their spouses more, put their spouses down more, and are less complimentary to each other.[2]

Date: _____ _____ _____
Place: _____ _____ _____
Occasion: _____ _____ _____

M

Express Affection Every Day

Dr. Nathaniel Branden is a California psychologist whose advice about marriage has appeared in several national magazines. When couples come to him asking, "Are there specific ways in which couples who remain happily in love behave differently from couples who don't?" Branden says, "Yes!" He points out that couples who stay in love never take their relationship for granted, but they express their affection for each other every day in various ways.

- They frequently say "I love you."
- They are physically affectionate, holding hands, hugging, cuddling.
- They express their love sexually.
- They verbalize their appreciation and admiration.
- They share their thoughts and feelings, learning to self-disclose what's on their minds and hearts to each other, confiding in each other.
- They express their love materially, giving little gifts to each other.
- They create time alone together.[3]

---

[1] McGinnis, *The Power of Optimism,* 12.
[2] John Gottman, *A Couple's Guide to Communication* (Champaign, IL: Research Press, 1976). 45.
[3] Dr. Nathaniel Branden, "Advice That Could Save Your Marriage" *Reader's Digest.*

Date:	_____	_____	_____
Place:	_____	_____	_____
Occasion:	_____	_____	_____

Toilet-Seat Theory of Marriage

In the May 28, 1997, edition of the *New York Times,* writer Hara Estroff Marano reported on a study by Dr. John Gottman, professor of psychology at the University of Washington in Seattle, that it is the mundane events of everyday life that build love in marriage. Call it the toilet-seat theory of romance. For example, whether a man puts the toilet seat down holds a major clue to the success of a marriage: it is a sign that he understands and respects his wife's needs and is open to the kind of giving and taking of influence that leads to long-term marital stability.

With the aid of videotape and sensors that monitor people's bodily responses, Gottman has spent twenty-five years scrutinizing what actually goes on in marriage. He has followed 670 couples, from newlyweds to retirees, and has found that only 20% of divorces are caused by an affair. "Most marriages die with a whimper," he says, "as people run away from one another, slowly growing apart."[1]

Date:	_____	_____	_____
Place:	_____	_____	_____
Occasion:	_____	_____	_____

Choosing to Love

[A] A Missionary Wife

One missionary wife sent this testimony to Charles Shepson following a visit to Fairhaven, a marriage and counseling ministry in Roan Mountain, Tennessee:

I felt trapped between my feelings and my Christian convictions. I hated my husband and wanted to leave him. I honestly did not know how I could go on living with him, feeling the way I did. I knew that to leave him was wrong and would have far-reaching consequences for my family. And we were missionaries!

I knew what was right. I could quote all the verses, yet I had myself convinced at times that it was more cowardly to stay in the marriage than it would be to leave it. My whole life was misery. I was rejecting everything I believed in.

My husband and I were given an opportunity to go to your retreat center for counsel, and in agreeing to go, I made my first tentative choice to work on our marriage. My first day there, I made a deliberate choice to commit myself to my husband and to our marriage. It was a decision based upon what I knew to be right, but it in no way reflected my feelings at the time. I still felt rebellious and bitter. I felt no love, and these feelings stayed with me. Each positive step I took was a response to my choice as I ignored my feelings.

We started to rebuild our marriage. Our first aim was friendship, since we felt this was a measurable, reachable goal. I had no expectations, but I stuck with it, knowing only that I was

---

[1] Hara Estroff Marano, "Rescuing Marriages Before They Begin," *The New York Times,* May 28, 1997.

doing the right thing. My miracle happened—slowly, very slowly. As I acted on my choice and built on it, my feelings began to change. Over the months I began to feel respect, then tenderness, and finally love for my husband. I saw his weakness, and I saw his strength. I saw him through entirely different eyes, and I loved him.[1]

[B] Campolo's Advice

Dr. Tony Campolo once wrote: I challenge those who come to me for marriage counseling this way: "If you do what I tell you to do for an entire month, I can promise you that by the end of the month, you will be in love with your mate. Are you willing to give it a try?" When couples accept my challenge, the results are invariably successful. My prescription for creating love is simple: do ten things each day that you would do if you really were in love. I know that if people do loving things, it will not be long before they experience the feelings that are often identified as being in love. Love is not those feelings. Love is what one wills to do to make the other person happy and fulfilled. Often, we don't realize that what a person does influences what he feels.

[C] "As If"

William James, the father of American psychology concluded that we become how we act . . . so if we wish to conquer undesirable emotional tendencies in ourselves, we must go through the outward movements of the kind of tendencies we wish to cultivate—Zig Ziglar

William James himself put it like this: *By regulating the action . . . we can indirectly regulate the feeling.*

[D] Married to a Goddess

In his book, *The Fine Art of Friendship,* Ted W. Engstrom tells of a man named Joe who "had just about had it with his wife of three years. He no longer thought of her as attractive or interesting; he considered her to be a poor housekeeper who was overweight, someone he no longer wanted to live with. Joe was so upset that he finally decided on divorce. But before he served her the papers, he made an appointment with a psychologist with the specific purpose of finding out how to make life as difficult as possible for his wife.

"The psychologist listened to Joe's story and then gave this advice, 'Well, Joe, I think I've got the perfect solution for you. Here's what I want you to do. Starting tonight when you get home, I want you to start treating your wife as if she were a goddess. That's right, a goddess. I want you to change your attitude toward her 180 degrees. Start doing everything in your power to please her. Listen intently to her when she talks about her problems, help around the house, take her out to dinner on weekends. I want you to literally pretend that she's a goddess. Then, after two months of this wonderful behavior, just pack your bags and leave her. That should get to her!'

"Joe thought it was a tremendous idea. That night he started treating his wife as if she were a goddess. He couldn't wait to do things for her. He brought her breakfast in bed and had flowers delivered to her for no apparent reason. Within three weeks the two of them had gone on two romantic weekend vacations. They read books to each other at night, and Joe listened to her as never before. It was

[1] James D. Berkley, "Rebuilding Marriages in Crisis," *Leadership Journal,* Spring 1989, 62.

M

incredible what Joe was doing for his wife. He kept it up for the full two months. After the allotted time, the psychologist gave Joe a call at work.

" 'Joe,' he asked, 'how's it going? Did you file for divorce? Are you a happy bachelor once again?'

" 'Divorce?' asked Joe in dismay. 'Are you kidding? I'm married to a goddess. I've never been happier in my life!' "[1]

Date: _____ _____ _____
Place: _____ _____ _____
Occasion: _____ _____ _____

Love Stories of Great Christians

[A] William and Anne Grenfield

William Grenfield was born in England in 1865 and educated at Oxford. While completing his medical training, he stumbled one night into a revival campaign conducted by D. L. Moody. A man was praying, and his prayer stretched so long that Grenfield, in boredom, started to leave. But Moody suddenly rose and interrupted the prayer, inviting the audience to sing a song "while our brother finishes his prayer." Grenfield stayed, and shortly after was soundly converted to Christ. He later became one of the most noted missionary physicians in modern history, laboring for forty-two years among the fishing villages on the coasts of Labrador and Newfoundland.

How did he meet his wife? Once while aboard a ship he met a beautiful lady—a total stranger. He fell violently in love with her and immediately proposed. She protested that he did not even know her name, but the doctor informed her that he knew what it would soon be. His prediction came true, and he and Anne MacClanahan were married on November 18, 1909, in Chicago, devoting themselves to working side by side in the cause of Christ.

[B] James and Emily Gilmore

When James Gilmore sailed for China in 1870, he was young, strong, and in need of a wife. He plunged into re-opening the London Missionary Society's work in Mongolia, but with no one to lean on. "Companions I can scarcely hope to meet," he wrote, "and the feeling of being alone comes over me." As labors increased, so did loneliness. "Today I felt a good deal like Elijah in the wilderness," he told his journal. "He prayed that he might die . . . I felt drawn towards suicide. Two missionaries should always go together. Oh! the intense loneliness . . ."

The pain deepened when his proposal to a Scotch girl was rejected. "I then put myself and the direction of this affair—I mean the finding of a wife—into God's hands, asking Him to look me out one, a good one, too."

In 1873, Gilmore visited friends in Peking, a Mr. and Mrs. Meech. Seeing a picture of Mrs. Meech's sister, Emily Prankard, James asked about her. As his hostess described Emily, James found himself falling in love. He gazed at her picture, saw some of her letters, and asked more and more questions.

---

[1] Ted W. Engstrom, *The Fine Art of Friendship* (Nashville: Thomas Nelson, 1985), 128–129.

Early next year, James wrote to Emily, proposing marriage in his first letter. By the same mail he informed his parents in Scotland: "I have written and proposed to a girl in England. It is true I have never seen her, and I know very little about her, but I have put the whole matter into the hands of God, asking Him, if it be best, to bring her, if it be not best, to keep her away, and He can manage the whole thing well."

Receiving Gilmore's letter, Emily took it at once to the throne of grace. Later Gilmore recalled, "The first letter I wrote her was to propose, and the first letter she wrote me was to accept." By autumn, Emily was in China, arriving on November 29, 1874. A week later, they were married. Gilmore acquired both wife and colleague, and they labored faithfully side by side for years, reaching northern China for Christ.[1]

[C] Robert and Mary Moffat

Robert Moffat was a strong, healthy, young man who loved working outdoors. He was hired by James Smith, owner of Dukinfield Nurseries, but Smith had a misgiving, for he knew two things: first, that Robert's good looks would appeal to his only daughter Mary, and second, that Robert wanted to be a missionary.

It happened just as Smith feared. As Robert worked in the gardens, he met Mary and discovered that she, too, was a Christian with an interest in missions (having been educated in a Moravian school). Unknown to her parents, she had secretly prayed two years before that God would send her to Africa.

An intense attachment formed quickly, but when the young couple announced to family members their plans to marry and leave England as missionaries to South Africa, the reaction was violent. Robert's parents seemed resigned, but the Smiths refused to give their consent. All pleading and imploring failed. At last, with his heart breaking, Robert decided to abandon hope of marriage and leave for the field alone. "From the clearest indications of his providence," he wrote his parents, "he bids me go out alone. It is the Lord, let him do what seemeth Him good." So on October 18, 1816, Robert Moffat sailed for South Africa, leaving his heart behind.

He arrived on the field suffering deep loneliness. "I have many difficulties to encounter, being alone," he wrote his parents. Meanwhile in England, Mary, too, was miserable. Three long years passed, and she finally told Robert in a letter that she had given up all prospect of joining him.

But her next letter a month later contained different news: "They both yesterday calmly resigned me into the hands of the Lord," she wrote, "declaring they durst no longer withhold me." Mary quickly packed her trunks, told her anguished parents goodbye with no expectation of ever seeing them again, and left for South Africa. There she and Robert were married before a handful of friends on December 27, 1819. And there they labored side-by-side for fifty-three years, becoming one of the greatest husband–wife teams in missionary history.[2]

[D] John and Idelette Calvin

Churchmen had been celibate for centuries, and John Calvin wondered if he, a first-generation Protestant, should break tradition. "I am not yet married," he wrote.

---

[1] Robert J. Morgan, *On This Day* (Nashville: Thomas Nelson Publishers, 1997). November 29th.
[2] Morgan, *On This Day,* December 27th.

"Whether I shall ever marry I do not know. In any case, if I take a wife it will be that, freed from cares, I can consecrate myself to the Lord."

He fell in love at age thirty, but the marriage was called off. His friend William Farel suggested another woman, but Calvin was unimpressed. A third prospect looked promising, but Calvin was cautious. "I will look very foolish if my hope again falls through."

It did. "I have not found a wife," he lamented, "and frequently hesitate as to whether I ought any more to seek one." Suddenly he noticed a widow in his congregation, Idelette de Bure, who had been converted through his preaching. He made frequent pastoral visits to her, and was smitten. They quickly married.

Idelette proved an ideal pastor's wife. She visited the sick, poor, and distressed. She entertained visitors who came consulting her famous husband. She furnished her table with vegetables from her own garden. She bore patiently the loss of the couple's three infants. She softened Calvin's hard edge and provided him joy.

When Idelette fell ill, Calvin anguished. As the hour of death drew near, they talked about "the grace of Christ, the hope of everlasting life, our marriage, and her approaching departure." Then he turned aside to pray. Idelette suddenly cried, "O glorious resurrection! O God of Abraham and of all our fathers, the believers of all the ages have trusted on Thee and none has hoped in vain. And now I fix my hope on Thee." Having thus spoken, she died. Calvin wrote to Farel on April 2, 1549, "Intelligence of my wife's death has perhaps reached you. I do what I can to keep myself from being overwhelmed with grief. My friends also leave nothing undone that may administer relief to my mental suffering."

John and Idelette enjoyed nine years together. Never again did John Calvin seek a wife, for no one could replace his ideal Idelette.[1]

Date:	_____	_____	_____
Place:	_____	_____	_____
Occasion:	_____	_____	_____

And Then, There Was Isobel Kuhn

Isobel Kuhn, popular author and missionary to China, was married to John, a man just as strong willed and stubborn as she was. The two had many conflicts. John, for example, had a cook in China to whom he was devoted but whom Isobel couldn't stand. Tensions grew, and Isobel sulked and stewed and finally exploded. She and John had a blazing argument.

Stuffing her hat on her head, Isobel stalked from the house, through town, and onto the plain boiling with rage. She said to herself, "I am not going to live with a man who gives a lazy servant preference over his wife." She walked for hours, enraged, not caring where she went. She finally returned home, but the situation remained tense although John told Isobel she could dismiss the servant. When the local church leaders visiting wanting to know why the cook had been fired, John

---

[1] Morgan, *On This Day,* April 2nd.

wouldn't back Isobel. And he didn't hire anyone else, sending all the domestic duties on her.

Other issues soon arose. For a long time the marriage was painful and stressed. But John and Isobel were committed to the Master. They were committed to personal spiritual maturity and to working and maintaining the relationship, however difficult it seemed. Furthermore, Isobel admitted that she had nowhere to go. She often walked out on John, but in that remote region on the Chinese-Thai border, there was nowhere for her to go. The two finally built a satisfying, fulfilling marriage.

Near the end of her life, Isobel wrote these words: *I feel many modern marriages are wrecked on just sharp shoals as this. A human weakness is pointed out. The correction is resented. Argument grows bitter. Young people are not ready to forgive, not willing to endure. Divorce is too quickly seized upon as the way out. [But] to pray God to awaken the other person, to be patient until he does so—this is God's way out. And it molds the two opposite natures into one invincible whole.*

Date: _____ _____ _____
Place: _____ _____ _____
Occasion: _____ _____ _____

The Golden Secret

On her golden wedding anniversary, my grandmother revealed the secret of her long and happy marriage. "On my wedding day, I decided to choose ten of my husband's faults which, for the sake of our marriage, I would overlook," she explained.

A guest asked her to name some of the faults. "To tell the truth," she replied, "I never did get around to listing them. But whenever my husband did something that made me hopping mad, I would say to myself, 'Lucky for him that's one of the ten.'"[1]

Date: _____ _____ _____
Place: _____ _____ _____
Occasion: _____ _____ _____

Till We Meet Again

A new widow was agonizing about what slogan to have inscribed on her husband's tombstone. Should it say this, or should it say that? Finally she decided on these two: *Rest in Peace—Until We Meet Again*

Date: _____ _____ _____
Place: _____ _____ _____
Occasion: _____ _____ _____

[1] Roderick McFarlane, *Reader's Digest,* December 1992.

A Better Plan

When in college, I came across a poem written by a teenage girl looking for a husband. It was written as a prayer, and this is what she said:

Dear God, I pray all unafraid / As girls are wont to be
I do not want a handsome man / But make him, Lord, like Thee.
I do not need one big and strong / nor yet so very tall,
Nor need he be some genius / or wealthy, Lord, at all;
But let his head be high, dear God, / and let his eye be clear,
His shoulders straight, whate'er his fate / whate'er his earthly sphere.
And let his face have character, / a ruggedness of soul,
And let his whole life show, dear God, / a singleness of goal.
And when he comes / as he will come
With quiet eyes aglow / I'll know, dear Lord,
That he's the man / I prayed for long ago.

That girl's name was Ruth Bell, and she later met and married—Billy Graham. I found her poem while a college student, shy and wondering if I would ever find anyone to marry. So following her example I wrote a prayer to the Lord as my request for a life partner. It said:

I stumble, Lord, when I should think / Of finding one for me.
But to Thy throne I come to claim / That prudent wife from Thee.
She need not be a beauty, Lord, / The queen crowned at the fair;
Nor need she have a made-up face / Beneath embellished hair.
But let her eyes contain Thy strength, / Her smile announce Thy grace;
Her body kept within Thy realm, / Thy sheen upon her face.
Lord, give her hands that make each day / An innovative art,
And grant her feet to always serve / The progress of Thy heart.
She need not be a scholar, Lord, / But warm like Thee, and wise;
And with Thy wit, Thy word prepared / To teach and empathize.
And when the throbs of life shall come, / The trials that we shall see,
May she both find in Thee her peace / And be a strength to me.
So as I wait on Thee, dear Lord, / And in Thy dictates lean
Make me to be your man, and hers / And her to be my queen.[1]

Date:	_____	_____	_____
Place:	_____	_____	_____
Occasion:	_____	_____	_____

"Without My Glasses"

Soon after our last child left home for college, my husband was resting next to me on the couch with his head in my lap. I carefully removed his glasses. "You know, honey," I said sweetly, "without your glasses you look like the same handsome

---

[1] From a sermon by the author.

young man I married." "Honey," he replied with a grin, "without my glasses, you still look pretty good too!"—Valerie L. Runyan, in *Reader's Digest*[1]

Date: _____ _____ _____
Place: _____ _____ _____
Occasion: _____ _____ _____

Agreeing on Things

- *If two people agree on everything, one of them is unnecessary.*—Ruth Graham
- *If two people agree on everything, they double their chances of being wrong.*
- "As much as possible the dad and mom need to be united in their approach to discipline. My wife is stricter than I am with our girls, and we often become frustrated with one another. We may air our disagreements in private and try to reach common ground, but in front of the kids we try hard to be as one. Even if I disagree with the way Katrina handles a situation, I never undercut her. (After all, she's probably right.) Marital disagreements on issues like discipline have actually strengthened our marriage, for they've enabled us both to become more balanced. Katrina has tended to strengthen my resolve in discipline, and perhaps I've helped her be more relaxed in dealing with problems."[2]

Date: _____ _____ _____
Place: _____ _____ _____
Occasion: _____ _____ _____

M

Elton Trueblood on Marriage and Love

It may seem a gratuitous paradox, but the truth is that marriage is more important than love. Marriage is more important than love because it is the normal situation out of which true and abiding love arises. The popular notion, much encouraged by light fiction and the motion picture, is that love is primary, marriage being a dull anticlimax. But this is vast error.

Real love hardly exists outside marriage. How could it? Real love is a slow growth coming from unity of life and purpose. Love is a product. It is a thing to be created by mutual service and sacrifice. Normally this service and sacrifice can exist only between married people and only if the bond is accepted as a permanent one.

Love outside of marriage or before marriage is largely romantic fiction. Before marriage there is a certain amount of passion and the mutual attraction which is the possibility of love. This is a good starting point, but it would be a very weak conclusion. The Hollywood mentality is in error because it supposes that this weak thing is love and that it is of primary worth.[3]

---

[1] Valerie L. Runyan, *Reader's Digest*, December 1992.
[2] From a sermon by the author.
[3] Elton Trueblood, *Foundations for Reconstruction* (New York: Harper and Brothers, 1946), 76.

Date: _____ _____ _____
Place: _____ _____ _____
Occasion: _____ _____ _____

Martin and Katie

When Martin Luther married, neither he nor his bride, Katherine von Bora, felt "in love." Katherine was still getting over a broken engagement to a man she truly loved. And Martin admitted, "I am not 'in love' or burning with desire." Yet their love for each other blossomed throughout their twenty-year marriage.[1]

Date: _____ _____ _____
Place: _____ _____ _____
Occasion: _____ _____ _____

Hostile Start Makes for Divorce

According to *USA Today,* experts can predict, within three minutes of the onset of a quarrel, which couples will divorce. "The biggest lesson to be learned from this study is that the way couples begin a discussion about a problem—how you present an issue and how your partner responds to you—is absolutely critical," says pioneering researcher and psychologist John Gottman of the University of Washington in Seattle.

Newlyweds heading for divorce start an argument by sending out hostile vibes through their tone of voice, facial gestures, and what they say, the six-year study finds.

The biggest problems occur when the woman brings up an issue "harshly" and critically, and the man responds with great negativity, say Gottman and study co-author Sybil Carrere. (Gottman's earlier research showed that women initiate discussions about problems about 80% of the time.)

In a lab setting, the research team taped 124 prescreened couples who had agreed to discuss an issue they found troublesome.

The team coded five positive emotions and 10 negative ones, including disgust, contempt, belligerence, whining and stonewalling. Communication problems were the most frequently chosen topic.

In stable couples, both spouses expressed fewer negative and more positive emotions at the start of discussions than those who eventually divorced. Study results will be published in the . . . journal Family Process.[2]

Date: _____ _____ _____
Place: _____ _____ _____
Occasion: _____ _____ _____

---

[1] "Little Known Facts about Luther," *Christian History Magazine,* America Online.
[2] Karen S. Peterson, "Hostile Start Makes for Divorce," *USA Today,* September 29, 1999, sec. D-1

Kissing the Bride

The wedding went off without a hitch and the preacher wound up with, "I now pronounce you man and wife." The flustered bridegroom, however, was still in a nervous fog. "Isn't it kisstomary," he sputtered, "to cuss the bride?"

The preacher smiled and said, "Not until you've been married a little while."

Date: _____ _____ _____
Place: _____ _____ _____
Occasion: _____ _____ _____

Joe White's Looks

Archie Campbell enjoyed telling about a friend of his, Joe White, who was in a car accident and had to be taken to the hospital. His wife stayed outside until the doctor came out. The doctor said, "Mrs. White, I don't like the looks of your husband." She said, "I don't either, but he's good to the kids."

Date: _____ _____ _____
Place: _____ _____ _____
Occasion: _____ _____ _____

M

The Dog Ate It

A new husband came home one evening to find his wife in tears. "You know the dinner I cooked for you tonight?" she said. "The dog ate it."

"Don't worry about it, sweetheart," replied the man. "I'll get another dog."

Date: _____ _____ _____
Place: _____ _____ _____
Occasion: _____ _____ _____

No Good Thing

At a three-day retreat for pastors and their wives, one session consisted of testimonies about how the Lord had blessed our lives and ministries. One young preacher's wife stood up and began nervously, "The Bible promises, 'No good thing does the Lord withhold from them that walk uprightly.' Well," she said sincerely, "my husband is one of those 'no good things'!"

Date: _____ _____ _____
Place: _____ _____ _____
Occasion: _____ _____ _____

Meditation

Someone Once Said . . .

- *Meditation is the skeleton key that unlocks the greatest storeroom in the house of God's provisions for the Christian.*—from "A Primer on Meditation"[1]
- *The heart is hard and the memory slippery, and without meditation all is lost; meditation imprints and fastens a truth in the mind. Without meditation the truths which we know will never affect our hearts.*—Thomas Watson[2]
- *Meditation is simply thought prolonged and directed to a single object. Your mystic chambers where thoughts abide are the secret worship of an unseen Sculptor chiseling living forms for a deathless future. Personality and influence are modeled here.*—A. T. Pierson
- *Churches today are failing to teach and preach biblical meditation. As a result, Christians are weak, anemic. . . . Biblical meditation must become an integral part of a Christian's life if he is to be a radiant and victorious Christian.*—Eddie Dobson[3]
- *We should be careful not to give all our time just to reading the Word, to see how much we can cover, but, after reading a portion, we should carefully, prayerfully turn it over in our minds, and appropriate it in our hearts.*—Wilber M. Smith[4]
- *The very word "meditation" suggests something about healing. It's not very far from the word "medicine" or "medication."*—Bill Moyers[5]
- *Reading without meditation is unfruitful; meditation without reading is dangerous.*—Thomas Watson[6]

Date: _____ _____ _____
Place: _____ _____ _____
Occasion: _____ _____ _____

J. I. Packer

J. I. Packer writes in his classic *Knowing God:* "How can we turn our knowledge *about* God into knowledge *of* God? The rule for doing this is demanding, but simple. It is that we turn each truth that we learn *about* God into matter for meditation *before* God, leading to prayer and praise *to* God."

He adds, "Meditation is a lost art today, and Christian people suffer grievously from their ignorance of the practice. Meditation is the activity of calling to mind, and thinking over, and dwelling on, and applying to oneself, the various things that one knows about the works and ways and purposes and promises of God. It is an activity of holy thought, consciously performed in the presence of God, under the eye of God, by the help of God, as a means of communion with God. Its purpose is to clear one's mental and spiritual vision of God, and to let His truth make its full

---

[1] *A Primer on Meditation* (Colorado Springs: The Navigators, n.d.), 2.
[2] Thomas Watson, *Gleanings From Thomas Watson* (Morgan, PA: Soli Deo Gloria Publications, 1995), 106.
[3] Eddie Dobson, "The Secret of Meditation," *Faith Aflame,* July-August 1978, 5.
[4] Wilber M. Smith, *Profitable Bible Study* (Grand Rapids, MI: Baker Book House, 1963), 63.
[5] Bill Moyers, *Healing and the Mind* (New York: Doubleday, 1993), 129.
[6] Watson, *Gleanings From Thomas Watson,* 112.

and proper impact on one's mind and heart. It is a matter of talking to oneself about God and oneself; it is, indeed, often a matter of arguing with oneself, reasoning oneself out of moods of doubt and unbelief into a clear apprehension of God's power and grace. Its effect is ever to humble us, as we contemplate God's greatness and glory, and our own littleness and sinfulness, and to encourage and reassure us—'comfort' us in the old, strong Bible sense of the word—as we contemplate the unsearchable riches of divine mercy displayed in the Lord Jesus Christ."[1]

Date: _____ _____ _____
Place: _____ _____ _____
Occasion: _____ _____ _____

Muse or Amuse

"Muse" was the name given to an ancient Greek god who spent much time in solitude and thinking. It has become a word which means to ponder, think, consider, meditate, reflect. The letter "a" used as a prefix renders a word into the negative (theist/atheist). The whole entertainment industry is built on the principle of a-musement, of not thinking, of letting the producers and directors and actors and athletes think for us. It is an industry the Enemy wants to use to keep us from thinking, especially from thinking about God and His Word.

Date: _____ _____ _____
Place: _____ _____ _____
Occasion: _____ _____ _____

M

Chewing the Cud

In the Navigators little booklet on meditation, we read: "Meditation is *chewing*. It is like the graphic picture of a cow and her process of mastication. Bringing up previously digested food for renewed grinding and its preparation for assimilation. Meditation is pondering various thoughts by mulling them over in the mind and heart. It is the processing of mental food. We might call it 'thought digestion.' 'Chewing' upon a thought deliberately and thoroughly, thus providing a vital link between theory and action. What metabolism is to the physical body of a cow, meditation is to your mental and spiritual life."[2]

Date: _____ _____ _____
Place: _____ _____ _____
Occasion: _____ _____ _____

[1] J. I. Packer, *Knowing God* (Downers Grove, IL: InterVarsity, 1973), 18–19.
[2] *A Primer on Meditation* (Colorado Springs: The Navigators, n.d.), 3.

Three Steps

In his Basic Youth Conflicts seminary, Bill Gothard suggests three steps to meditation:

- **Memorize**—It is easier to meditate on Scripture that has been committed to memory. It allows the mind to mull over passages while walking, driving, showering, or falling asleep.
- **Visualize**—See the passage. Let it come alive. Visualize the green pastures, the still waters, and the resting sheep of the Twenty-third Psalm.
- **Personalize**—Put yourself in the picture, pondering the application of the passage to your own life.[1]

Date: _____ _____ _____
Place: _____ _____ _____
Occasion: _____ _____ _____

Mull, Mill, and Meal

The words mull, mill, and meal all come from an Old English word meaning the pulverizing of corn in a grinder. To mull over a subject is to ponder it, to pulverize it in the millstones of the mind.

In October of 1920, Dr. Frederick Banting was working on his lecture for the following day. His medical practice was too new to be lucrative, so he supplemented his income by teaching. He worked far into the night on the problem of diabetes, but medical science provided scant data on the dreaded disease, and no cure had yet been discovered.

Effective Meditation

Holding the Word of God in your heart until it has affected every phase of your life . . . This is meditation.
—ANDREW MURRAY

He fell asleep. At two in the morning, he awoke with a start. Grabbing a notebook, he penned three short sentences, then collapsed again in sleep. But those three sentences led to the discovery of insulin.[2]

A century earlier, Elias Howe's fertile mind had imagined the sewing machine. He worked and worked on his invention, but its stitches were jagged and uneven. One night, he dreamed that a tribe of savages had kidnapped him. They threatened to kill him if he didn't invent a sewing machine in twenty-four hours. He failed, but as the spears flew at him, he noticed they had holes near their tips. He awoke with an idea: put the eye of the needle near the tip.

He patented his sewing machine in 1846.[3]

Date: _____ _____ _____
Place: _____ _____ _____
Occasion: _____ _____ _____

[1] David Seamands, *Putting Away Childish Things* (Wheaton, IL: Victor Books, 1986), 18.
[2] Robert J. Morgan, "The Well-Fed Imagination," *Leadership Journal*, Summer 1993, 33.
[3] The story about Elias Howe is from a clipping in my files.

Napoleon

When he was Emperor, Napoleon would sometimes stretch out on the settee near the fireplace and appear to be dozing. But his aides soon learned that he was meditating. He explained to them, "If I always seem to be ready for everything, to face up to anything, it is because I never undertake anything at all without first having meditated for a long time and foreseen what might happen. It is not a genie, but meditation, that suddenly reveals to me, in secret, what I must say or do under circumstances not anticipated by others."[1]

Date: _____ _____ _____
Place: _____ _____ _____
Occasion: _____ _____ _____

Abraham Lincoln

Abraham Lincoln learned the art of pondering and meditating early in life. He once said: "Among my earliest recollections I remember how, when a mere child, I used to get irritated when anybody talked to me in a way I could not understand. I can remember going into my little bedroom, after hearing the neighbors talk of an evening with my father, and spending no small part of the night trying to make out what was the exact meaning of some of their, to me, dark sayings. I could not sleep, although I tried to, when I went on such a hunt for an idea, until I had caught it, and when I thought I had got it I was never satisfied until I had repeated it over and over again, until I had put it in language plain enough, as I thought, for any boy I knew to comprehend."[2]

Date: _____ _____ _____
Place: _____ _____ _____
Occasion: _____ _____ _____

Jonathan Edwards

In his little booklet on the life of Jonathan Edwards, Ed Reese writes: "One of the secrets of [Edwards'] success was that he always thought through his subject matter. Even on walks and while riding horseback through the woods, he would jot down items and pin them to his coat. When he returned to the parsonage, he wrote out the fuller explanation of the bits noted on the scraps. It is said that at times the whole of his coat front would sometimes be covered with bits and pieces of paper."[3]

Date: _____ _____ _____
Place: _____ _____ _____
Occasion: _____ _____ _____

[1] Notes in my files made from Andre Castelot's biography of Napoleon.
[2] Keith W. Jennison, *The Humorous Mr. Lincoln* (New York: Bonanza Books, 1965), 4.
[3] Ed Reese, *The Life and Ministry of Jonathan Edwards* (Glenwood, IL: Fundamental Publishers, 1975), 12.

Visualizers

In his bestselling book, *The 7 Habits of Highly Effective People,* Stephen Covey writes, "Expand your mind. Visualize in rich detail. Involve as many of the senses as you can."

He observes, "Almost all of the world-class athletes and other peak performers are visualizers. They see it; they feel it; they experience it before they actually do it. . . . There is an entire body of literature and audio and video tapes that deals with this process of visualization."

Covey then adds that much of this literature is fundamentally sound, and most of it appears to have come from people who were students of the Bible.[1]

Date: _____   _____   _____
Place: _____   _____   _____
Occasion: _____   _____   _____

Images in the Mind

Do you remember the classic fright scene in Alfred Hitchcock's movie, *Psycho?* If you saw the movie, you no doubt can still relive how you reacted when Janet Leigh was stabbed to death in the shower. Does just thinking about it or picturing it in your mind cause you to tense up? Did you know that thousands of people reported being unable to take a shower after they saw that movie unless someone else was home? When people saw the movie in the theater for the first time they jumped or screamed or cried or ran out of the theater because it was portrayed so vividly that their minds reacted to it as though it were real. The stabbing was dramatized so realistically in pictures that it had a dramatic effect on viewers for years to come.

If a movie producer can cause such an intense reaction in our minds, think about the power we have over our own minds. Thoughts and mental images control the body. The Russians have a proverb that says, "The brain is capable of holding a conversation with the body that ends in death."[2]

Date: _____   _____   _____
Place: _____   _____   _____
Occasion: _____   _____   _____

The Power of Imagination

Marie Dalloway has worked with top-level athletes and coaches (including those connected with the Olympic Training Centers in Lake Placid, New York, and in Colorado Springs, Colorado), teaching them the power of visualization. In her book, *Visualization: The Master Skill in Mental Training,* she writes:

---

[1] Stephen R. Covey, *The 7 Habits of Highly Effective People* (New York: Simon and Schuster, 1989), 131–134.
[2] From a clipping in my files.

- *Peak performers visualize more and better than do others. They may have learned spontaneously to visualize events in vivid detail. Others can learn to visualize the way peak performers do. The athlete who hones the basic skills for visualization and consistently applies them is assured of enhanced performance.*
- *An excellent example is Jack Nicklaus, who has used this skill throughout his career in golf. Before he hits a golf ball, whether in practice or in competition, Nicklaus mentally rehearses the shot in detail. He pictures the address of the ball, the swing, the trajectory of the flight of the ball, the landing, the roll of the ball, and the final lay of the ball. Interestingly, he then backs up the action and sees it occur in reverse, like a slow rewind of a video tape.*
- *In the early 1950's, ex-Celtic center Bill Russell discovered the benefits of mentally previewing defensive moves on the court. At eighteen, Russell traveled by bus throughout the Northeast with basketball players from California. On these long rides from one small town to another, Russell visualized his defensive responses to the offensive plays of centers he would be opposing. The mental practice paid off. On the court Russell was exceptionally effective at blocking shots. He responded with defensive plays exactly as he had pictured in his mind. "It seemed natural, almost as if I were stepping into a film and following the signs. I was so elated I thought I'd float right out of the gym."*[1]

Date: _____ _____ _____
Place: _____ _____ _____
Occasion: _____ _____ _____

"I Talk'd to Myself"

As I walk'd by myself
I talk'd to myself
and myself replied to me;
And the questions myself
then put to myself,
with their answers I gave to thee.
—Attributed to Bernard Barton, 1826

Date: _____ _____ _____
Place: _____ _____ _____
Occasion: _____ _____ _____

Meditate During the Night Watches

"Psychologists tell us the subconscious mind works while we sleep," observes Leslie Flynn. "Dawson Trotman, founder of the Navigators, believed that the last prevailing thought in one's conscious mind before going to sleep should be some portion of God's Word. He called this his H.W.L.W. principle (His Word the Last

---

[1] Marie Dalloway Optimal, *Visualization: The Master Skill in Mental Training* (Phoenix: Performance Institute, 1992).

Word). Associates with whom he traveled said that at the close of day, with lights out and conversation ended, someone would quote a verse or short passage from the Bible. The theory was that this last dominate idea would simmer in the subconscious and become the first thought on rising."[1]

Date: _____   _____   _____
Place: _____   _____   _____
Occasion: _____   _____   _____

Excerpts from a Spurgeon Sermon

In the summer of 1857, Charles Spurgeon preached a sermon entitled "Meditation on God." Here are some excerpts:

- *Meditation furnishes the mind somewhat with rest. It is the couch of the soul. The time that a man spends in necessary rest, he never reckons to be wasted, because he is refreshing and renovating himself for further exertion. Meditation, then, is the rest of the spirit.*
- *Meditation is a word that more than half of you, I fear, do not know how to spell. You know how to repeat the letters of the word, but I mean to say, you can not spell it in the reality of life. You do not occupy yourselves with any meditation.*
- *He is not the best student who reads the most books, but he who meditates the most upon them; he shall not learn most of divinity who hears the greatest number of sermons, but he who meditates the most devoutly upon what he does hear; nor shall he be so profound a scholar who takes down ponderous volumes one after the other, as he who, reading little by little, precept upon precept, and line upon line, digests what he learns, and assimilates each sentiment to his heart by meditation.*
- *The best and most saintly of men have been men of meditation. Isaac went out into the fields at eventide to meditate. David says, "As for me, I will meditate on thy statutes." Paul, who meditated continually, says to Timothy, "Give thyself to meditation." To the Christian meditation is most essential. . . . Meditation and prayer are twin sisters, and both of them appear to me equally necessary to a Christian life.*

Date: _____   _____   _____
Place: _____   _____   _____
Occasion: _____   _____   _____

Midlife

Someone Once Said . . .

- *In the middle of the journey of our life / I came to myself within a dark wood / Where the straight way was lost.*—Dante

[1] Leslie B. Flynn, *Your Inner You* (Wheaton, IL: Victor Books, 1984), 47.

- *My wife told me that swimming was good for my figure, and I asked her if she had ever looked at a duck's figure.*—Warren Wiersbe[1]
- *I'm somewhere between estrogen and death.*—Erma Bombeck, when asked her age

Date: _____ _____ _____
Place: _____ _____ _____
Occasion: _____ _____ _____

Changes at Midlife

Many psychologists believe that we alternate in life between periods of tranquility and consolidation on the one hand, and periods of instability on the other. Infants are calm and given to sleep. Toddlers are "terrible twos." Middle childhood, a period of relative calm, gives way to the turbulence of the adolescent years. Early adulthood is a period of settling down, becoming established, growing roots, but then comes midlife.

"We have only recently begun to recognize that adulthood is also characterized by predictable periods of tranquility and stress," writes James Dobson. "It is now apparent that the mature years continue to be characterized by alternating periods of equilibrium and disequilibrium."[2]

What is it about the middle years? It was at midlife that King David destabilized spiritually, and many factors often complicate this period, especially for men, including:

- The decline of physical health and vigor
- The aging of one's spouse
- Growing, grudging awareness that goals set in earlier years are beyond reach
- Job dissatisfaction or termination—a man in midlife often feels "trapped" in the field he has chosen
- Care-giving for elderly parents while, at the same time, raising teenagers
- The loss of parents, aunts, and uncles
- The financial stresses of educating children while preparing for retirement
- The departure of children from the home
- Hormonal changes that may be occurring

Date: _____ _____ _____
Place: _____ _____ _____
Occasion: _____ _____ _____

And Yet . . .

CNN carried this story entitled "Middle Age is Prime Time to Many," by its health correspondent, Al Henmin, on June 1, 1999:

---

[1] Warren Wiersbe, *Be Myself: The Memoirs of One of America's Most Respected Bible Teachers* (Victor Books, 1994), 273.

[2] James Dobson's *Straight Talk to Men and Their Wives* (Waco: Word Publishing, 1980), 173.

"Midlife: a time when hairlines recede and waistlines expand. Is middle age really as bad as we've been led to believe? Not according to a recent major study. Instead of dreading life after 40, researchers said most people consider midlife to be "prime time." Researchers say midlife can begin as early as 30, but those questioned believe midlife hits between 44 and 72.

The majority of the nearly 8,000 questioned for the MacArthur Foundation say they're convinced their lives are better at midlife. They are healthier, happier and more in control of their lives than a decade earlier.

So what about the much-hyped midlife crisis? It never happened for nine out of ten who say they've never felt the overwhelming dread that life's half over, and never felt compelled to escape behind the wheel of a flashy sports car.

Women told researchers the bad side effects of menopause are "overrated." And so, too, may be the issue of sex or lack thereof as we age. Although the study shows sex goes from weekly at age 30 to less than once a month after 70, the vast majority believe their marriages are strong.[1]

Date:			
Place:			
Occasion:			

Wanting to Run Away

Just as he reached mid-life, Jim Conway fell into vicious depression. *Repeatedly I had fantasies of getting on a sailboat and sailing off to some unknown destination.* He was a pastor, a husband, a father, and an author. But he wanted to run away like a prodigal and start a new life. He later wrote:

The mid-life crisis is a time of high risk for marriages. It's a time of possible career disruption and extramarital affairs. There is depression, anger, frustration, and rebellion.

At mid-life, a man begins to realize his body is not as strong as it used to be, nor his wife as young. He often feels like a failure at work because his accomplishments fall short of previous expectations. He's caught between generations, having to care for aged parents just as his children are lurching through the teen years. When the kids graduate and fly the coop, it sometimes hits the father harder than the mother. Then come the college bills. All of this hit Conway like a sucker punch.

No Young Men

There is no such thing as a young man, for he is not a man until he is middle aged.

—ANTHONY TROLLOPE

I had literally come to the end of my rope. I was ready to leave everything and run away. I crawled into bed that November night and hardly slept as I made my plans. I was awake through most of the night, detailing specific steps I would take as I left my present life and ran away to start another life . . .

But the next morning, as he starting reading his Bible where he had left off the day before, in Psalm 18, he found these words (or they found him): "In my distress I called upon the Lord, And cried out to God; He heard my voice from His temple . . .

---

[1] Al Henmin, "Middle Age is Prime Time to Many," *CNN*, June 1, 1999.

He drew me out of many waters . . . You will light my lamp; the Lord my God will enlighten my darkness."

He closed his Bible.

The healing had begun.[1]

Date: _____ _____ _____
Place: _____ _____ _____
Occasion: _____ _____ _____

Malcolm Muggeridge

Malcolm Muggeridge, the British writer and social critic, once wrote:

I may, I suppose, regard myself or pass for being a relatively successful man. People occasionally stare at me in the streets—that's fame. I can fairly easily earn enough to qualify for admission to the higher slopes of the Internal Revenue—that's success. Furnished with money and a little fame even the elderly, if they care to, may partake of trendy diversions—that's pleasure. It might happen once in a while that something I said or wrote was sufficiently heeded for me to persuade myself that it represented a serious impact on our time—that's fulfillment. Yet I say to you—and I beg you to believe me—multiply these tiny triumphs by a million, add them all together, and they are nothing—less than nothing, a positive impediment—measured against one draught of that living water Christ offers to the spiritually thirsty, irrespective of who they are.[2]

Date: _____ _____ _____
Place: _____ _____ _____
Occasion: _____ _____ _____

Middle Age Is . . .

- *Middle age is that time of life when your age starts to show around your middle.*—Bob Hope
- *Midlife is when actions creak louder than words.*
- *Middle age is when everything starts to click . . . your knees, your elbows, your neck.*— Robert Orben
- *Middle age is when you're faced with two temptations and you choose the one that gets you home by nine o'clock.*—Ronald Reagan
- *Middle age is when you're warned to slow down by a doctor rather than a policeman.*
- *Middle age is that difficult period between adolescence and retirement when you have to take care of yourself.*

Date: _____ _____ _____
Place: _____ _____ _____
Occasion: _____ _____ _____

[1] Jim Conway, *Men in Midlife Crisis* (Elgin, IL: David C. Cook Publishing Co., 1986).
[2] Muggeridge's Obituary, *Christianity Today.*

Mind

Someone Once Said . . .

- *The most important things in life are the thoughts you choose to think.*—Marcus Aurelius
- *I think, therefore I am.*—Decartes[1]
- *We are what we think. All that we are arises with our thoughts. With our thoughts, we make the world.*—Buddha
- *It doubtless is true that people become what they think about.*—Gary R. Collins
- *All mortals tend to turn into the thing they are pretending to be.*—C. S. Lewis
- *If I knew what you think, I would know what you are. Our thoughts make us what we are.*—Dale Carnegie
- *A man is what he thinks about all day long.*—Ralph Waldo Emerson
- *Our life is what our thoughts make it.*—Marcus Aurelius
- *For as he thinks in his heart, so is he.*—Proverbs 23:7

Date: _____ _____ _____
Place: _____ _____ _____
Occasion: _____ _____ _____

The Battleground

- *Every temptation comes to us via our thoughts.*—Erwin Lutzer[2]
- *The mind of man is the battleground on which every moral and spiritual battle is fought.*—J. Oswald Sanders[3]
- *Our defeat or victory begins with what we think, and if we guard our thoughts we shall not have much trouble anywhere else along the line.*—Vance Havner[4]
- *Self-control is primarily mind-control.*—John Stott
- *Every kidnapping was once a thought. Every extramarital affair was first a fantasy.*—Leslie Flynn

Date: _____ _____ _____
Place: _____ _____ _____
Occasion: _____ _____ _____

More Quotes

- *It is not enough to have a good mind; the main thing is to use it well.*—Descartes
- *For 2,400 years, ever since Hippocrates located the seat of the intellect inside the skull, the mind has been forced to admit that its greatest achievements, its loftiest thoughts, its*

---

[1] *Cogito, ergo sum.* Decartes' point was that consciousness is the only sure evidence that we actually exist.
[2] Erwin Lutzer, "Those Sins that Won't Budge," *Moody*, March 1978, 48.
[3] J. Oswald Sanders, *A Spiritual Clinic* (Chicago: Moody Press, 1961), 20.
[4] Vance Havner, *Pleasant Paths* (Grand Rapids, MI: Baker Book House, 1945), 72.

deepest emotions all arise from something with the consistency of Jell-O and the color of day-old slush.—Newsweek[1]
- *A bookstore is one of the only pieces of evidence we have that people are still thinking.*—Jerry Seinfeld

Date: _____ _____ _____
Place: _____ _____ _____
Occasion: _____ _____ _____

Depression and the Mind

In his book *Learned Optimism*, Professor Martin Seligman makes a case for considering depression as arising, not from misplaced chemicals or lingering childhood trauma, but from negative thinking. Summarizing the research of Joseph Wolpe and Tim Beck, Seligman explained how cognitive therapy began to be considered a treatment for mental illness.

"Depression is nothing more than its symptoms," writes Seligman. "It is caused by conscious negative thoughts. There is no deep underlying disorder to be rooted out: not unresolved childhood conflicts, not our unconscious anger, and not even our brain chemistry. Emotion comes directly from what we think: Think 'I am in danger' and you feel anxiety. Think 'I am being trespassed against' and you feel anger. Think 'loss' and you feel sadness. . . .

"Depression results from lifelong habits of conscious thought. If we change these habits of thought, we will cure depression."[2]

Date: _____ _____ _____
Place: _____ _____ _____
Occasion: _____ _____ _____

M

Martin Luther King, Jr.'s Seat

In the *Autobiography of Martin Luther King, Jr.,* Dr. King tells of growing up in Atlanta, Georgia:

I remember another experience I used to have in Atlanta. I went to high school on the other side of town—to the Booker T. Washington High School. I had to get the bus in what was known as the Fourth Ward and ride over to the West Side. In those days, rigid patterns of segregation existed on the buses, so that Negroes had to sit in the backs of buses. Whites were seated in the front, and often if whites didn't get on the buses, those seats were still reserved for whites only, so Negroes had to stand over empty seats. I would end up having to go to the back of that bus with my body, but every time I got on that bus I left my mind up on the front seat. And I said to myself, "One of these days, I'm going to put my body up there where my mind is."[3]

And he did.

Our bodies always end up where our minds are.

---

[1] Sharon Begley, "How the Brain Works," *Newsweek,* February 7, 1983, 40.
[2] Martin E. P. Seligman, *Learned Optimism* (New York: Alfred A. Knopf, 1990), 74–75.
[3] *The Autobiography of Martin Luther King, Jr.,* ed. Clayborne Carson. (New York: Warner Books, Inc., 1998), 9.

> Date: _____ _____ _____
> Place: _____ _____ _____
> Occasion: _____ _____ _____

Spurgeon's Confession

Charles Spurgeon once made a remarkably honest confession to his congregation. In a sermon entitled "The Power of the Holy Ghost," he said: *I hope that my will is managed by Divine Grace. But I am afraid my imagination is not at times. Those who have a fair share of imagination know what a difficult thing it is to control. You cannot restrain it. . . . My imagination has taken me down to the vilest kennels and sewers of earth. It has given me thoughts so dreadful that, while I could not avoid them, yet I was thoroughly horrified by them. These thoughts will come; and when I feel in the holiest frame, the most devoted to God, and the most earnest in prayer, it often happens that that is the very time when the plague breaks out the worst.*[1]

> Date: _____ _____ _____
> Place: _____ _____ _____
> Occasion: _____ _____ _____

Garbage

Leslie Flynn tells of a mother who was peeling vegetables for a salad when her daughter, home from college, casually mentioned she was going to a questionable movie that evening. The mother suddenly picked up a handful of garbage and threw it in the salad. "Mother!" said the shocked girl. "You're putting garbage in the salad."

"I know," replied the mother, "but I thought that if you didn't mind garbage in your mind, you certainly wouldn't mind a little in your stomach."[2]

> Date: _____ _____ _____
> Place: _____ _____ _____
> Occasion: _____ _____ _____

The Power of Suggestion

Franz Anton Mesmer was the talk of Paris in the 1780s. In spite of his training as a physician, he held the unorthodox view that a mysterious magnetic power permeates the universe and resides in human bodies. Treatment of disease, he proposed, could best be done by using magnetic forces from the environment to restore the patient's "magnetic equilibrium." Such view put Mesmer into conflict with the medical profession in his native Vienna, but laypeople were intrigued with the theory.

---

[1] Charles Haddon Spurgeon, *Spurgeon's Sermons,* vol. 1 (Grand Rapids, MI: Baker Book House, 1983), 126–127.
[2] Leslie B. Flynn, *Your Inner You* (Wheaton, IL: Victor Books, 1984), 39.

When the doctor moved to France, his reputation preceded him and soon patients were flocking to experience magnetic treatments.

It wasn't easy to treat so many people on a one-to-one basis, so Mesmer developed a group technique. As many as thirty people would come at a time and sit around a large wooden tub known as a "baquet." The baquet was filled with water, ground glass, iron filings, and long metal rods that extended from the tub and were grabbed at one end by the patients. According to Mesmer, the magnetic fluid in the baquet somehow came to the people through the rods and led to all kinds of physical cures.

> **A Word on Words**
>
> *You are not what you think you are, but what you think, you are.*
>
> —NORMAN VINCENT PEALE

Mesmer did what he could to make the healing sessions impressive and emotionally powerful. Soft music played in the background. The room was dimly lit and thickly draped. Mesmer himself demanded silence when he entered the room. Often he wore a long flowing lilac silk robe, and walked about, touching the afflicted body parts with a long iron wand and making magnetic "mesmeric passes" as he waved his free hand through the air.

A few people had no response to this dramatic treatment, but many thought they felt forces moving through their bodies, and some went into prolonged convulsions. These involved jerking of the body, apparent dreaminess or stupor, and sometimes piercing cries. Mesmer's followers called this experience "the crisis" and claimed that it brought great healing.

But King Louis XVI wasn't so easily convinced and undoubtedly His Majesty's interest in Mesmer was sparked by secret reports that some mesmerites had radical political ideas. To investigate, the king appointed a Royal Commission and declared that it would be chaired by the American ambassador to France, a man named Benjamin Franklin.

The commissioners went to work with enthusiasm, conducting experiments and interviewing Mesmer's patients. After careful study, it was concluded that body magnetism did not exist, that the baquet fluid had no power, and that convulsions and proclaimed cures came as a result of the creative imagination of Mesmer and his highly suggestible followers. Shortly after the report was issued, Mesmer left France and the mesmerites went underground, but a half-century later mesmerism re-emerged in a more sophisticated form and with a new name—hypnosis.[1]

Date:			
Place:			
Occasion:			

As a Man Thinks . . .

One of history's sharpest minds belonged to Thomas Edison, the great inventor. Despite only three months of formal schooling, Edison and his inventions changed the world forever.

[1] Gary R. Collins, *The Magnificent Mind* (Waco: Word Publishers, 1985), 163–164.

His secret? "One percent inspiration and 99 percent perspiration," as he put it; and he proved his definition by working days at a time, obsessed with his projects, neglecting family and friends, and stopping only for short catnaps. Failure never seemed to discourage him. When about ten thousand experiments with a storage battery failed to produce results, a friend tried to console him. "Why, I have not failed," Edison quipped. "I've just found 10,000 ways that won't work."

Of all his inventions, perhaps the most famous is the electric light. He devised the prototype, then spent two years looking for the right filament, sending associates to the jungles of the Amazon and to the forests of Japan. He even tried strands of red hair from a friend's beard. Finally, he utilized carbonized thread, and it worked! The world gained electric lights.

Our light bulbs today have three parts to them. There is the glass itself—the bulb surrounding the filament. Inside the bulb is a mixture of gases, commonly argon and nitrogen. Finally, in the very center of the bulb, is the filament. Most filaments today are made of a very tough metal, and when electricity flows through them, they become very hot—about 4,500 degrees—making them glow and give off light.

Light bulbs bear a fascinating resemblance to you and me. There is the outside covering, the glass bulb, the body—the part people see. Inside, like invisible gases within the bulb, are our personalities. And at the very center of it all is that part of us that glows and enlightens—the human mind.

The mind is the sum and substance, the axis and pivot, of our existence. It is the base of operations, the core of our humanity. Our minds are the most important things about us, and our lives are simply the overflow of our thoughts.

Dale Carnegie was once asked on a radio program, "What is the biggest lesson you have ever learned?" He quickly replied, "By far the most vital lesson I have ever learned is the importance of what we think. If I knew what you think, I would know what you are. Our thoughts make us what we are. Our mental attitude is the X-factor that determines our fate. Emerson said: 'A man is what he thinks about all day long.' How could he possibly be anything else?"

Why? An old maxim states: "Thoughts produce acts, acts produce habits, and habits produce character." The Roman philosopher Marcus Aurelius said, "Our life is what our thoughts make it." Or as the Bible puts it, "For as he thinks in his heart, so is he." (Proverbs 23:7)[1]

Date:			
Place:			
Occasion:			

The Cauliflower Jewel

Each of us owns a jewel far more valuable than any displayed in the window of Cartier's or Tiffany's. It's a three-pound blob of gray pulp resembling a rotting cauliflower.

Unimpressed?

---

[1] From a sermon by the author.

This jewel is the most incredible creation in God's universe, a fabulous, living supercomputer with unfathomable circuitry and unimaginable complexity. It is the human mind—a collection of billions of neurons, each as complex as a small computer. Imagine having 100 billion computers inside your skull!

Each of these neurons consists of a central nerve-cell core attached to a long tail and several thousand wispy dendrites. These dendrites reach out to make contact with other dendrites, and the number of connection points between these dendrites is perhaps one quadrillion in every human brain. According to one writer, the number of connections within one human brain rivals the number of stars and galaxies in all the universe.

That's not all, for each of these connection points is itself a marvel of complexity. The dendrites don't actually touch each other, but they efficiently and rapidly pass messages to each other through the form of electrical and chemical impulses in a series of processes that takes less than one-thousandth of a second.

"All of this is so complex," said one scientist, "that the brain cannot even begin to comprehend its own complexity."

What a jewel![1]

Date: _____   _____   _____
Place: _____   _____   _____
Occasion: _____   _____   _____

I Was Just Thinking About You

M

When Harry Truman became president, he worried about losing touch with common, everyday Americans, so he would often go out and be among them. Those were in simpler days when the President could take a walk like everyone else. One evening, Truman decided to take a walk down to the Memorial Bridge on the Potomac River. When there, he became curious about the mechanism that raised and lowered the middle span of the bridge. He made his way across the cat walks and through the inner workings of the bridge, and suddenly he came upon the bridge tender, eating his evening supper out of a tin bucket.

The man showed absolutely no surprise when he looked up and saw the best-known and most powerful man in the world. He just swallowed his food, wiped his mouth, smiled, and said, "You know, Mr. President, I was just thinking of you."

It was a greeting that Truman adored and never forgot.

Wouldn't it be wonderful, if Jesus Christ were to suddenly appear before us physically or come suddenly in the cloud, if we could say, "You know, Lord, I was just thinking of you."[2]

Date: _____   _____   _____
Place: _____   _____   _____
Occasion: _____   _____   _____

[1] From a sermon by the author.
[2] David McCullough, *Truman* (New York: Simon & Schuster, 1992), 623.

The Harbor

The Bible describes our minds by using the figure of a ship looking for a harbor. Though you may be unable to keep disease-ridden ships from sailing back and forth on the ocean, you *can* refuse them docking privileges in the harbor of your mind.

- Jeremiah 4:14 says, "How long will you harbor your evil thoughts?" (NLT)
- Deuteronomy 15:9 says, "Be careful not to harbor this wicked thought." (NIV)
- Job talks about those who harbor resentment in their hearts.
- The Psalmist talks about those who harbor malice in the minds.
- James talks about those who allow bitter envy and selfish ambition to harbor within them.
- Jesus conveyed the same basic idea when asking, "Why do you *entertain* evil thoughts in your minds?" (Matthew 9:4—NIV)
- Paul had the same thought in mind when he said, "Clothe yourselves with the Lord Jesus Christ, and do not think about how to gratify the desires of the sinful nature." (Romans 13:14—NIV)

Date: _____ _____ _____
Place: _____ _____ _____
Occasion: _____ _____ _____

From Charles Spurgeon's *John Ploughman*

Some will say they cannot help having bad thoughts; that may be, but the question is, do they hate them or not? Vain thoughts will knock at the door, but we must not open to them. Though sinful thoughts rise, they must not reign. He who turns a morsel over and over in his mouth, does so because he likes the flavor, and he who meditates upon evil, loves it, and is ripe to commit it. Snails leave their slime behind them, and so do vain thoughts.

Good thoughts are blessed guests, and should be heartily welcomed, well fed, and much sought after. Like rose leaves, they give out a sweet smell if laid up in the jar of memory. They cannot be too much cultivated; they are a crop which enriches the soil.

Date: _____ _____ _____
Place: _____ _____ _____
Occasion: _____ _____ _____

Pepsi or Seven-Up?

Suppose you have a sponge and a pitcher of Pepsi Cola. If you dip your sponge into Pepsi and squeeze it, what's going to come out? Seven-up? No, when you squeeze a sponge soaked in Pepsi, Pepsi is going to gush out of it.

If you saturate your mind with questionable movies, videos, magazines, novels, music, and entertainments, do you think that holiness and happiness and godliness will flow out?

Date: _____ _____ _____

Place: _____ _____ _____

Occasion: _____ _____ _____

Glass Hives

When I was child my parents took me to the Tennessee Valley Fair to ride the rides and see the exhibits. One of the most interesting displays was the honeybees in glass hives. There appeared to be thousands of bees, all of them hustling and bustling in frantic activity beneath the pane of glass that covered their colony. The bee keeper showed us the queen and explained about the workers, the guards, and the drones, every one of them oblivious to the fact that their every move was being observed by a higher intelligence.

In the same way, our heads, are like glass hives and God sees every hustling, bustling thought buzzing through our brains. None are hidden from him.

- 1 Chronicles 28:9—*The Lord searches all hearts and understands all the intents of the thoughts.*
- Psalm 7:9—*The righteous God tests the hearts and minds.*
- Psalm 94:11—*The Lord knows the thoughts of man.*
- Psalm 139:1—*O Lord, You have searched me and known me. You know my sitting down and my rising up; You understand my thought afar off.*
- Jeremiah 11:20—*O Lord of hosts, You who judge righteously, testing the mind and the heart. . . .*
- Jeremiah 12:3—*But You, O Lord, know me; You have seen me, and You have tested my heart toward you.*
- Jeremiah 17:9—*The heart is deceitful above all things, and desperately wicked; who can know it? I, the Lord, search the heart, I test the mind. . . .*
- Jeremiah 20:12—*O Lord of hosts, You who test the righteous and see the mind and heart . . .*
- Ezekiel 11:5—*Thus says the Lord: . . . I know the things that come into your mind. . . .*
- Revelation 2:23—*I am He who searches the minds and hearts.*
- Hebrews 4:12–13—*For the word of God is living and powerful, and sharper than any two-edged sword, piercing even to the division of soul and spirit, and of joints and marrow, and is a discerner of the thoughts and intents of the heart. And there is no creature hidden from His sight, but all things are naked and open to the eyes of Him to whom we must give account.*
- Matthew 12:25—*But Jesus knew their thoughts. . . .*

Date: _____ _____ _____

Place: _____ _____ _____

Occasion: _____ _____ _____

Missions

Someone Once Said . . .

- *If God has called you to be a missionary, don't stoop to be a king.*—Charles Spurgeon

Date: _____ _____ _____

Place: _____ _____ _____

Occasion: _____ _____ _____

How Christianity Spread

Philip Schaff, the great church historian, wrote an eight-volume set of books covering the entire sweep of church history. In referring to the growth of the Kingdom in the post-apostolic era, this is what he says:

Christianity once established was its own best missionary. It grew naturally from within. It attracted people by its very presence. It was a light shining in darkness and illuminating the darkness. And while there were no professional missionaries devoting their whole life to this specific work, every congregation was a missionary society, and every Christian believer a missionary, inflamed by the love of Christ to convert his fellow men. The example had been set by Jerusalem and Antioch, and by those brethren who, after the martyrdom of Stephen, were scattered abroad and went about preaching the Word. Justin Martyr was converted by a venerable old man whom he met walking on the shore of the sea. "Every Christian laborer," says Tertullian, "both finds out God and manifests him. . . ." Celsus scoffingly remarks that fullers and workers in wool and leather, rustic and ignorant persons, were the most zealous propagators of Christianity, and brought it first to women and children. Women and slaves introduced it into the home circle. . . . Every Christian told his neighbor, the laborer to his fellow laborer, the slave to his fellow slave, the servant to his master and mistress, the story of his conversion as a mariner tells the story of the rescue from shipwreck.[1]

Date: _____ _____ _____

Place: _____ _____ _____

Occasion: _____ _____ _____

Lost Opportunity

In her classes on the history of missions, Yvonne Wood of the U. S. Center for World Missions, describes what she calls "the biggest lost opportunity in missionary history."

There was a thirteen-year-old in Mongolia who inherited a bit of land from his father. This boy was a precocious warrior with instinctive brilliance as a military strategist; he was also ruthless, and he formed fighting bands that went from village to village until he was ruling over two million people in a Mongolian Empire that

---

[1] Philip Schaff, *History of the Christian Church, Vol 2: Ante-Nicene Christianity* (Grand Rapids, MI: Eerdmans Publishing Co., 1910), 20–21.

stretched from China to India, and from Siberia to edges of Western Europe. They gave this young man the title of Genghis Khan and he ruled over more territory than any man has ever ruled.

Meanwhile, at the same time in Western Europe, a great revival was occurring under the preaching of men like St. Francis of Assisi, and thousands were becoming Christians.

Following Khan's death, the bulk of his empire eventually went to his grandson, Kublai Khan, who established his capital city in Beijing. He had two Italians in his court named Polo, the father and the uncle of famed explorer Marco Polo. They began to tell Kublai Khan about Christianity, and the great ruler became very interested. He sent the Polo brothers back with a request for 100 missionaries to tell the Mongolians and the Chinese about Christianity. "When we learn about Christianity, there will be more Christians in my empire than in all Europe," he said.

The Polos returned with the message, but no one was interested in going. Finally two friars agreed to go with the Polos (and Marco Polo accompanied them) but along the way the friars got fainthearted and turned around and went home.

When they got back to Kublai Khan, he said, "Where are the missionaries?" No one came. Eventually the church did send a small handful of missionaries, but by that time the opportunity had passed.[1]

Date:	_____	_____	_____
Place:	_____	_____	_____
Occasion:	_____	_____	_____

M

The Moravians

The Protestant Reformation, which began in 1517, produced virtually no church-sent missionaries until two Moravians, Leonard Dober and David Nitschmann, left the warmth of their community of Herrnhut and ventured to St. Croix in 1732.

It was Herrnhut's leader, Count Nicholaus Ludwig von Zinzendorf, who spurred their going. Zinzendorf had visited Copenhagen the previous year on political business. While there, he had met a black man from St. Thomas, who pleaded with him to send someone to share the gospel with his enslaved family members in the Danish West Indies.

Back at Herrnhut, Zinzendorf shared this burden, and it took root. A year later, on August 18, 1732, two young men were commissioned as missionaries in an unforgettable service in which a hundred hymns were sung. Leonard Dober and David Nitschmann soon left Herrnhut for Copenhagen, seeking passage to the islands.

But Copenhagen proved unfriendly, and the two men were pelted with obstacles. One disappointment followed another, and much opposition arose to their mission. No one would help them. No ship would take them. Their hearts sank.

---

[1] Based on notes taken from Yvonne Wood's lecture on the history of missions at the Perspectives on the World Missions Course.

At that critical moment, Numbers 23:19 turned up in their daily devotional book: *Has He said, and will He not do? Or has He spoken, and will He not make it good?* Inspired by these words, Dober and Nitschmann determined to persevere, believing that God would fulfill what he had started through them.

A handful of people in Copenhagen began helping them, and the tide of public opinion turned. Two royal chaplains lent their support, and even the Queen of Denmark encouraged them. Princess Charlotte contributed financially. A court official secured passage for them on a Dutch ship, and on October 8, 1732, they sailed for the West Indies, opening the modern era of missions.

The Lord had spoken to them, and he had made it good.[1]

Date:			
Place:			
Occasion:			

A Brief Life of Carey

William Carey was a cobbler who lived, as one historian put it, "in a forgotten village in the dullest period of the dullest of all centuries." He was born in 1761 in Paulerspury, a rural village of eight hundred inhabitants north of London. His father was a poor weaver, working at a loom in his own cottage.

William was a sickly child, afflicted by numerous allergies and sensitive to the sun. He was also poorly educated. Entering adolescence, William frequently got into trouble, swearing, lying, and running with an undesirable group. At length, he was apprenticed to a shoemaker.

William found himself working alongside a senior apprentice named John Warr, who was a dedicated Christian and who began faithfully to witness to William, but the young man wanted nothing to do with religion.

Those were the days of the American Revolution, and King George III, hoping for divine assistance in his war efforts, proclaimed a day of national prayer for Sunday, February 10, 1779. Warr persuaded his young friend to join him for a church service.

The preacher spoke from Hebrews 13:13, urging his listeners to give their lives to Christ. The text spoke directly to William, seventeen, and from that day, the direction of his life changed. He was baptized and became a member of the local Baptist Church. In time, he began to do some preaching and pastoral work in nearby Baptist churches.

In 1781, William married Dorothy (Dolly) Plackett, and within a year they bore a daughter, Ann. But fever swept through the Carey household. Their little girl died, and William nearly died also. He recovered at last, but the disease left him bald; for many years he wore a wig.

One day William acquired a book that had become a best seller in England—Captain Cook's *Voyages*. Reading the accounts of the famous sailor's travels, William began thinking of overseas evangelism. On the wall of his cobbler's shop, he hung a homemade world map, jotting down facts and figures beside the countries.

---

[1] Robert J. Morgan, *From This Verse* (Nashville: Thomas Nelson Publishers, 1998), January 20th.

During those days, most Protestants believed the Great Commission had been given only to the original Apostles. Except for the Moravians, there was virtually no thought about missions in the church.

But William Carey began preaching about it. At meetings of Baptist ministers, he continually brought up the subject until they wearied of it. In one famous exchange, Dr. John C. Ryland, the man who had baptized him, said, "Young man, sit down! When God pleases to convert the heathen, he'll do it without consulting you or me."

Carey, deeply disturbed, authored a book justifying and explaining the imperative of Gospel evangelism. Published on May 12, 1792 it has become a classic in Christian history: *An Enquiry into the Obligations of Christians, to use means for the Conversion of the Heathens in which the Religious State of the Different Nations of the World, the Success of Former Undertakings, and the Practicability of Further Undertakings, are Considered.*

William was invited to preach to his fellow ministers on Wednesday, May 31, 1792, at the Baptist Associational Meeting in Nottingham. He spoke on the imperative of world evangelization from Isaiah 54:2–3, and it was in this sermon that he is quoted as having said: *Expect great things from God; Attempt great things for God.*

The following morning there was a business meeting among the ministers, and William expected a resolution that would lead to establishing a missionary society. When no action was taken, William turned to fellow minister Andrew Fuller, gripping his arm, and asking "Is nothing again going to be done?"

Before the Assembly dispersed at noon, it had been resolved on a proposition from Fuller "that a plan be prepared against the next Minister's Meeting at Kettering, for forming a Baptist Society for propagating the Gospel among the Heathens."

On Tuesday, October 2, 1792, fourteen men huddled in the back-parlor of widow Wallis' house in Kettering. Carey, thirty-one, reviewed the achievements of the Moravians and recounted the Bible's missionary mandate. By and by, a resolution was worded: *Humbly desirous of making an effort for the propagation of the Gospel amongst the Heathen, according to the recommendations of Carey's Enquiry, we unanimously resolve to act in Society together for this purpose; and as, in the divided state of Christendom, each denomination, by exerting itself separately, seems likeliest to accomplish the great end, we name this the Particular Baptist Society for the Propagation of the Gospel among the Heathen.*

Andrew Fuller passed around his snuff box with its picture of Paul's conversion on the lid, taking up church history's first collection of pledges for organized, home-supported Protestant missions. And Carey immediately began planning to go to India.

That's when his problems began. . . .

But the end of the story is this: William Carey did go to India. He never took a furlough and never returned to England. He stayed for forty-one years, dying there at age seventy-three. When all was said and done, he had translated the complete Bible into six languages, and portions of the Bible into twenty-nine others. He had founded over one hundred rural schools for the people of India. He had founded Serampore College, which is still training ministers to this day.

He introduced the concept of a savings bank to the farmers of India. He published the first Indian newspaper. He wrote dictionaries and grammars in five different languages. He so influenced the nation of India that, largely through his efforts, the practice of sati (the burning of widows) was outlawed.

Most importantly, he launched the modern era of missions and laid the foundations for the modern science of missiology. One biographer, Mary Drewery, wrote: "The number of actual conversions attributed to him is pathetically small; the number indirectly attributable to him must be legion."

> Date: _____ _____ _____
> Place: _____ _____ _____
> Occasion: _____ _____ _____

Support Base

In his book, *The Great Omission,* Robertson McQuilkin points out that in the days before William Carey, the father of the modern Protestant missionary movement, the Moravians from Herrnhut considered a support base of four adequate to keep one missionary at the front. Using that formula, America's forty million evangelicals could support ten million overseas workers.

Using a more modern standard, it was said that during World War II fifteen personnel were needed to keep one man at the front. Using that as a basis, the American evangelical church could support a missionary force of 2,666,666.

But evangelical churches of the United States, perhaps the wealthiest group of Christians in history, now have about 37,000 career foreign missionaries, about 9,000 of whom are engaged in full-time evangelism.

"The truth is," says McQuilkin, "less than 1 percent of full-time Christian workers are engaged in evangelistic ministry among the unevangelized of the world. Is this the way the Commander-in-Chief would assign His troops? Or is someone not listening?"[1]

> Date: _____ _____ _____
> Place: _____ _____ _____
> Occasion: _____ _____ _____

Willing to Stay

George Murray, missionary to Italy, missiologist, and president of Columbia International, once said that for years he was *willing to go but planning to stay.* Not until he became *planning to go but willing to stay* did God send him out to Italy.

> Date: _____ _____ _____
> Place: _____ _____ _____
> Occasion: _____ _____ _____

---

[1] Robertson McQuilkin, *The Great Omission* (Grand Rapids, MI: Baker Book House, 1984).

World Population

According to *Encyclopaedia Britannica:*

- At the time of King David (1000 B.C.), there were approximately **150 million** people on earth.
- By the time of Christ, the figure had doubled to **300 million.**
- Due to wars and plagues, the population increased very little for the next 1,500 years. By the 1600s when the Pilgrims emigrated to the New World, there were about **500 million** people on the planet—one-half billion.
- By 1750, conventionally the beginning of the Industrial Revolution in Britain, world population may have been as high as **800,000,000.**
- The world reached **1 billion** about 1800.
- By 1930, the population reached **2 billion.**
- By 1960, **3 billion.**
- By 1974, **4 billion.**
- In 1999, **6 billion.**
- By 2025, the world's population is projected to be **7.8 billion.**
- By 2050, nearly **9 billion.**
- According to the Population Reference Bureau, every minute 101 people in the world die—and 261 people are born.

Date: _____   _____   _____
Place: _____   _____   _____
Occasion: _____   _____   _____

M

More Stats

According to Bob Sjogren, it took from the beginning of church history until the year 1900 for committed believers to become 2.5% of the world population. It took only 70 more years for that percentage to double. By 1970, committed believers were 5% of a much larger world population. Then it took just 22 years to double again. In 1992, committed believers grew to become 10% of a still larger world population.

According to George Otis of the Sentinel Group, about 70% of all the church's outreach since its beginning until today has been accomplished in this century alone, and about 70% of what has been accomplished in this century has taken place since 1945. And 70% of what has happened since 1945 has happened in this decade of the 1990s.

According to missionary statistics, over 260,000 people every day are now being presented the plan of salvation, and there is a growing sense of excitement among missiologists that we could actually be within striking distance of seeing the gospel presented to every known people group within the lifetime of some who are in his great hall tonight.

But the greatest areas of harvest are outside of North America. Only about 15% of the worldwide body of Christ lives in North America, and we aren't doing so well. Eighty-five percent of our churches are plateaued or declining.

Date: _____ _____ _____

Place: _____ _____ _____

Occasion: _____ _____ _____

The Role of Prayer

J. O. Fraser was a missionary to China in the early 1900s. He credited the conversion of hundreds of Lisu families to the prayers of his very earnest little prayer group back in England. He said, *Christians at home can do as much for foreign missions as those actually on the field. It will only be known on the Last Day how much has been accomplished in missionary work by the prayers of earnest believers at home.*

Date: _____ _____ _____

Place: _____ _____ _____

Occasion: _____ _____ _____

How Long?

Don Curry serves in the Sind desert region of Pakistan with the Bible and Medical Missionary Fellowship. He is a physician with a keen interest in community health and tribal evangelism. With his wife, Nancy, he recently visited a village of animists and told them the story of Jesus. They were intrigued with Christ's teaching about love and forgiveness, deeply moved by his compassionate ministry, stirred at the mention of our Lord's death and resurrection. Someone asked Don, "When did this happen? Ten or fifteen years ago?"

Don replied, "No, it took place almost two thousand years ago."

Saddened, the man asked, "What terrible thing have we done, that God should have kept this wonderful story from us for so long?"[1]

Date: _____ _____ _____

Place: _____ _____ _____

Occasion: _____ _____ _____

Those of You Who Know

At an old seminary, there was a custom that the president could call on any student on any day for that morning's chapel sermon. One young man was petrified, and each day he dreaded going to chapel for fear he would be called upon. Sure enough, one day the president rose, looked over the audience, pointed directly at him, and said, "Young man, you are to preach our sermon today."

The student rose, but as he ascended the platform he was a nervous wreck. Looking over the congregation, he couldn't speak. His mouth was dry, his knees

---

[1] Clipped from *Eternity* Magazine.

were knocking together, his hands were shaking, him mind was reeling, and he felt he had a biscuit stuck in his throat. Finally he stammered, "How many of you know what I am going to say today?"

Nobody raised a hand.

"Then neither do I," he said, and sat down.

The next day as the students filed into chapel, the president again pointed to the young man, giving him a second time. But again, the young man was gripped with stage fright, his hands and knees shaking. With a tremor in his voice, he finally stammered, "How many of you know what I am going to say today?"

This time everyone raised their hand.

"Then if you already know, I don't need to tell you," the young man said and promptly sat down.

The president of the seminary was angry, but he decided to give the young man one last chance. The next day, he again called on the student, and this time the student was even more nervous than before. His mouth was thick and dry, and he felt he was going to faint. At last he muttered, "How many of you know what I am going to say today?"

This time, half the students raised their hands and the other half didn't.

"Then those of you who know," he said, "please tell those of you who don't!" And . . .

And that is what a missionary is. Those of us who know telling those who don't.[1]

Date: _____ _____ _____
Place: _____ _____ _____
Occasion: _____ _____ _____

M

Mistakes

Someone Once Said . . .

- *To confess that you were wrong yesterday is only to acknowledge that you are a little wiser today.*—Charles Haddon Spurgeon[2]
- *Who doesn't make mistakes! But the greatest error of all is to let any mistake destroy your faith in yourself. The only sensible course is to study and analyze why you made the mistake. Learn all you can from it, then forget it and go ahead. Figure on doing better next time.*—Norman Vincent Peale[3]
- *God can give a straight blow with a crooked stick. He blesses us in spite of our blunders.*—Corrie ten Boom

---

[1] This story was told to me in the 1970s by an elderly gentleman with whom I shared a few minutes on the patio of the Pocket Testament League in Pennsylvania.

[2] Charles Haddon Spurgeon, *Spurgeon's Sermons*, vol. 2 (Grand Rapids, MI: Baker Book House, 1983), 67.

[3] Norman Vincent Peale, *Stay Alive All Your Life* (Carmel, NY: Guideposts Associates, Inc., 1957), 138.

- *Our God is a God who not merely restores, but takes up our mistakes and follies into His plan for us and brings good out of them. This is part of the wonder of his gracious sovereignty.*—J. I. Packer[1]
- *If you don't learn from your mistakes, there's no sense making them.*

Date:			
Place:			
Occasion:			

Count It All Joy

Joy Ridderholf, founder of Gospel Recordings, Inc., once wrote: *Count it all joy—even when you feel stupid.* Someone had written her asking, "Can a person rejoice in his own blunders?" Her answer: "Being notoriously absent minded, I have made some bad ones! But I do not mean to, and each time I hope to do better. However, I immediately begin to rejoice in it. Furthermore, I thank God for permitting me to make the mistake."

Joy went on to say that on one occasion she had forgotten a speaking engagement. When it came to her mind, she was horrified and felt very stupid. But it was too late to correct it, so all she could do was to rejoice and to comfort herself in the realization that God would cause it to work out for good. The result was that the person who suddenly had to fill in for her discovered the gift of speaking and a new area of ministry.

"Some people say the only good they get out of such mistakes is to learn not to do it again," added Joy. "Very well, but most of us find that we still are apt to forget things and make mistakes, even though we have tried hard to improve. No rejoicing Christian is purposely careless. So why not turn it to something that will delight God's heart? Rejoice! When we, by rejoicing, place the case in His hands, Jesus takes the 'tangled strands that we have spun in vain,' and by the skill of His dear hands, only beauty shall remain. Remember—even when you feel stupid, count it all joy."

Date:			
Place:			
Occasion:			

"Aren't You Afraid We'll Make Mistakes?"

Several years ago, at a political briefing for religious leaders in Washington, a group of ministers chatted with Jennings Randolph, the senior senator from West Virginia, who had first been elected to Congress in 1933. He was the only remaining member of the Senate or House of Representatives who had been elected in the great landslide that swept Franklin D. Roosevelt into office during the Great Depression.

---

[1]J. I. Packer, *Knowing God* (Downers Grove, IL: InterVarsity Press, 1973), 219.

During the course of the briefing, Senator Randolph recalled that just after the election of 1933, he was called to the White House. There, in the president's private quarters, sat FDR. The lights were low, and a fire was roaring in the fireplace. About a dozen or so leaders of the Congress had come at FDR's request. Jennings Randolph couldn't believe he had been included, as young and unknown and inexperienced as he was. But Roosevelt had his eye on Jennings Randolph.

The young congressman didn't say much that night. He just sat there in awe as Franklin Roosevelt began to speak. Roosevelt told the congressional leaders what he had in mind, and how quickly he wanted to move during the first one hundred days of his administration.

He said he intended to declare a bank holiday, which was a positive-sounding phrase that really meant closing all the nation's banks indefinitely until bankers and the government could regain control of the situation. He wanted to send Congress a record number of bills quickly and furiously, including the creation of the Civilian Conservation Corps, the Tennessee Valley Authority, and the Federal Emergency Relief Administration.

He went on and on, speaking confidently, but in such low tones that Randolph had to strain to hear him. But when FDR was finished the group was stunned and speechless until one of the senators said, "Mr. President, if we move that quickly aren't you afraid we'll make mistakes?"

Roosevelt, paused, looked at the man, considered his reply, and said, "Senator, if we *don't* move that quickly, we'll soon find that we no longer have the opportunity even of making mistakes."[1]

M

Date: _____ _____ _____
Place: _____ _____ _____
Occasion: _____ _____ _____

Experience

An old, successful business leader was asked one day by his young protégé for the secret of success. The old man said, "I can give it to you in two words: Right Decisions!"

"But how does one go about making right decisions?" asked the young man.

"Experience!" came the reply.

"But how does one gain experience?"

"Wrong Decisions!" replied the man.

Date: _____ _____ _____
Place: _____ _____ _____
Occasion: _____ _____ _____

[1] Based on my notes from a question/answer session with Sen. Jennings.

Date:			
Place:			
Occasion:			

Tea on the Wall

In his book, *How To Be Born Again,* Billy Graham writes: "There is a well-known story of some men in Scotland who had spent the day fishing. That evening they were having tea in a little inn. One of the fishermen, in a characteristic gesture to describe the size of the fish that got away, slung out his hands just as the little waitress was getting ready to set the cup of tea at his place. The hand and the teacup collided, dashing the tea against the whitewashed walls. Immediately an ugly brown stain began to spread over the wall. The man who did it was very embarrassed and apologized profusely, but one of the other guests jumped up and said, "Never mind." Pulling a pen from his pocket, he began to sketch around the ugly brown stain. Soon there emerged a picture of a magnificent royal stag with his antlers spread. That artist was Sir Edwin Landseer, England's foremost painter of animals.

—◇—

Learning Curve

To make no mistakes is not in the power of man, but from their errors and mistakes the wise and good learn wisdom for the future.

—PLUTARCH

—◇—

"This story has always beautifully illustrated to me that fact that if we confess not only our sins but our mistakes to God, He can make out of them something for our good and His glory. Sometimes it's harder to confess our mistakes and stupidities to God than it is our sins. Mistakes and stupidities seem so dumb, whereas sin seems to more or less to be an outcropping of our human nature. But Romans 8:28 tells us that if they are committed to God He can make them work together for our good and His glory."[1]

Date:			
Place:			
Occasion:			

Good Advice

The GMP Institute of Cincinnati is a company that helps organizations integrate the government's Good Manufacturing Practice requirements into their systems. In its material, the GMP suggests this philosophy for helping companies deal with employee or employer mistakes:

It's good mental health to believe:

1. All people make mistakes. Expect mistakes.
2. People don't intend to make mistakes.
3. People don't like to make mistakes.
4. People want to "make up" for mistakes made.
5. People want to learn from their mistakes.

[1] Billy Graham, *How To Be Born Again* (Waco: Word, 1977), 129–130

6. People are hurt more by self-regarding feelings than criticism from others when they make mistakes.
7. People improve performance after working out correction of mistakes.[1]

Date: _____ _____ _____

Place: _____ _____ _____

Occasion: _____ _____ _____

Speech Goofs

- *This is a great day for France!*—Richard Nixon, while attending Charles De Gaulle's funeral
- *For seven and a half years I've worked alongside President Reagan. We've had triumphs. Made some mistakes. We've had some sex . . . uh . . . setbacks.*—George Bush
- *I believe we are on an irreversible trend toward more freedom and democracy. But that could change.*—Dan Quayle
- *What a waste it is to lose one's mind—or not to have a mind. How true that is.*—Dan Quayle, addressing the United Negro College Fund
- *My fellow Americans, I've signed legislation that will outlaw Russia forever. We begin bombing in five minutes.*—Ronald Reagan, about to go on the air for a radio broadcast, unaware that the microphone was already on.
- *Nixon has been sitting in the White House while George McGovern has been exposing himself to the people of the United States.*—Frank Licht, governor of Rhode Island, campaigning for McGovern in 1972
- *Winfield goes back to the wall. He hits his head on the wall and it rolls off! It's rolling all the way back to second base! This is a terrible thing for the Padres!*—Jerry Coleman, Padres radio announcer
- *I would not live forever, because we should not live forever, because if we were supposed to live forever, then we would live forever, but we cannot live forever, which is why I would not live forever.*—Miss Alabama, in the 1994 Miss Universe contest, when asked "If you could live forever, would you and why?"
- *Smoking kills. If you're killed, you've lost a very important part of your life.*—Brooke Shields, during an interview on being named spokesperson for a federal anti-smoking campaign
- *Outside of the killings, Washington has one of the lowest crime rates in the country.*—Mayor Marion Barry, Washington, D.C.
- *The doctors X-rayed my head and found nothing.*—Dizzy Dean, explaining how he felt after being hit on the head by a ball in the 1934 World Series
- *I am a jelly donut.*—John F. Kennedy, addressing a German-speaking audience in German, attempting to say, "I am a Berliner!"

Date: _____ _____ _____

Place: _____ _____ _____

Occasion: _____ _____ _____

[1] <www.gmplst.com/manartI.htm>

Church Newsletter Goofs

- Low Self-Esteem Support Group will meet Thursday at 7 P.M. Please use the back door.
- The pastor will preach his farewell message, after which the choir will sing, "Break Forth In Joy."
- Due to the Rector's illness, Wednesday's healing services will be discontinued until further notice.
- The eighth-graders will be presenting Shakespeare's *Hamlet* in the church basement on Friday at 7 P.M. The congregation is invited to attend this tragedy.
- The concert held in Fellowship Hall was a great success. Special thanks are due to the minister's daughter who labored the whole evening at the piano which, as usual, fell upon her.
- Twenty members were present at the meeting held at the home of Mrs. Marsha Crutchfield last evening. Mrs. Crutchfield and Mrs. Rankin sang a duet, The Lord Knows Why.
- A songfest was hell at the Methodist church Wednesday.
- Scouts are saving aluminum cans, bottles, and other items to be recycled. Proceeds will be used to cripple children.
- The pastor is on vacation this week. Massages can be given to the church secretary.

Date: _____ _____ _____
Place: _____ _____ _____
Occasion: _____ _____ _____

———————————— Money ————————————

Someone Once Said

- *Getting riches brings care; keeping them brings trouble; abusing them brings guilt; and losing them brings sorrow. It is a great mistake to make so much of riches as we do.*—D. L. Moody[1]
- *The trouble is that too many people are spending money they don't have for things they don't need to impress people they don't like.*—Anonymous
- *It is almost impossible to develop true worshippers in affluent surroundings.*—Erwin Lutzer[2]
- *Christians have never worn the clothes of affluence well.*—Jerry White[3]
- *Money won't buy happiness, but it will pay the salaries of a huge research staff to study the problem.*—Bill Vaughan

[1] D. L. Moody, *Heaven* (Chicago: Moody Press, n.d.), 87.
[2] Erwin W. Lutzer, *Failure: The Back Door to Success* (Chicago: Moody Press, 1975), 108.
[3] Jerry White, *The Power of Commitment* (Colorado Springs: NavPress, 1985), 46.

Date: _____ _____ _____
Place: _____ _____ _____
Occasion: _____ _____ _____

From the Lips of Millionaires

- *I have made many millions, but they have brought me no happiness.*—Rockefeller
- *The care of $200,000,000 is enough to kill anyone. There is no pleasure in it.*—Vanderbilt
- *I am the most miserable man on earth.*—John Jacob Astor
- *What can I say? I only know I am desolate.*—J. Paul Getty
- *I was happier when doing a mechanic's job.*—Henry Ford
- *Millionaires seldom smile.*—Andrew Carnegie

Date: _____ _____ _____
Place: _____ _____ _____
Occasion: _____ _____ _____

Money Will Buy . . .

- *a bed but not sleep*
- *books but not brains*
- *food but not appetite*
- *finery but not beauty*
- *a house but not a home*
- *medicine but not health*
- *luxuries but not culture*
- *amusements but not happiness*
- *a crucifix but not a Savior*
- *religion but not salvation*
- *a good life but not eternal life*
- *a passport to everywhere but heaven*

Date: _____ _____ _____
Place: _____ _____ _____
Occasion: _____ _____ _____

M

Remember Lot's Wife

In his book of sermons, *Feminine Faces,* Clovis Chappell says that when Pompeii was being excavated, there was found a body that had been embalmed by the ashes of Vesuvius. It was that of a woman. Her feet were turned toward the city gate, but her face was turned backward toward something that lay just beyond her outstretched hands. The prize for which those frozen fingers were reaching was a bag of pearls.

Maybe she herself had dropped them as she was fleeing for her life. Maybe she had found them where they had been dropped by another. But, be that as it may, though death was hard at her heels, and life was beckoning to her beyond the city gates, she could not shake off their spell. She had turned to pick them up, with death as her reward . . . frozen in an attitude of greed.[1]

Date:			
Place:			
Occasion:			

Open Hands

My parents consistently taught us that all we had must be held in an open hand, that when we closed our fingers tightly over anything placed in our trust, we lost the joy and the blessing. Things acquired as an end in themselves became idols and possessed us.—Allan Emery[2]

Date:			
Place:			
Occasion:			

What Robinson Saw

Bud Robinson, the well-known Holiness preacher, was taken by friends to New York and shown around the city. That night in his prayers he said, "Lord, I thank You for letting me see all the sights of New York. And I thank You most of all that I didn't see a thing that I wanted!"[3]

Date:			
Place:			
Occasion:			

The Truest Indicator

The way we handle our money is perhaps the truest indicator of the spiritual condition of our heart . . .

The Bible contains more than five hundred references to prayer and almost five hundred references to faith, but there are more than two thousand references to money and possessions. Out of thirty-eight parables that Jesus told in the Gospels, sixteen deal with how we handle our money. Jesus said more about money and possessions than about heaven and hell combined. One out of every ten verses in the Gospels deals with money or possessions—288 verses in the four Gospels.[4]

---

[1] *Leadership Journal,* Fall, 1989, 51.
[2] Allan C. Emery, *A Turtle on a Fencepost* (Waco: Word Books, 1979), 34–35.
[3] Vance Havner, *Pepper 'N Salt* (Old Tappan, NJ: Fleming H. Revell Co., 1966), 98.
[4] *Spirit of Revival,* November 1987, 13.

Date: _____ _____ _____
Place: _____ _____ _____
Occasion: _____ _____ _____

Good News and Bad News

A minister stood one Sunday with an announcement for his congregation. "I've got good news and bad news," he said. "The good news is, we have enough money to pay for our new building program. The bad news is, it's still out there in your pockets."

Date: _____ _____ _____
Place: _____ _____ _____
Occasion: _____ _____ _____

A Family of Writers

A man was telling his friend, "I come from a family of writers. My sister wrote books that no one would read. My brother wrote songs that no one would sing. My mother wrote plays that no one would see, and my father wrote checks that no one would cash."

Date: _____ _____ _____
Place: _____ _____ _____
Occasion: _____ _____ _____

M

The Answer

When the preacher's car broke down on a country road, he walked to a nearby roadhouse to use the phone. After calling for a tow truck, he spotted his old friend, Frank, drunk and shabbily dressed at the bar. "What happened to you, Frank?" asked the good reverend. "You used to be rich."

Frank told a sad tale of bad investments that had led to his downfall. "Go home," the preacher said. "Open your Bible at random, stick your finger on the page and there will be God's answer."

Some time later, the preacher bumped into Frank, who was wearing a Gucci suit, sporting a Rolex watch and had just stepped out of a Mercedes. "Frank," said the preacher, "I am glad to see things really turned around for you."

"Yes, preacher, and I owe it all to you," said Frank. "I opened my Bible, put my finger down on the page and there was the answer—Chapter 11."

> **A Fool and His Money . . .**
>
> *When your outgo exceeds your income, your upkeep will be your downfall.*
>
> —ANONYMOUS

Mothers

Someone Once Said . . .

- *People are what their mothers make them.*—Ralph Waldo Emerson
- *All that I am or hope to be I owe to my angel mother.*—Abraham Lincoln
- *Give me a generation of Christian mothers, and I will undertake to change the whole face of society in twelve months.*—Lord Shaftesbury

A History of Mother's Day

Mother's Day, in one form or another, has been around a long time. In ancient Greece, a celebration honoring mothers occurred every Spring.

In the Middle Ages, a custom called *Mothering Sunday* began when children, who often left home early to learn a trade or become apprentices, would be released from work every year on the forth Sunday of Lent to attend church with their families. As they returned home, they often took cakes or little gifts to their mothers. This was termed "going a-mothering." To this day, Mother's Day in the United Kingdom is celebrated on the fourth Sunday of Lent.

It was in 1872 that Julia Ward Howe (author of *The Battle Hymn of the Republic*) suggested the idea of Mother's Day in the United States.

The cause was taken up by Anna Jarvis, daughter of a Methodist pastor. Jarvis felt the scars of the Civil War could be healed by mothers—and by honoring mothers. She died in 1905 before her dream of establishing a holiday could be fulfilled. But her daughter, also named Anna Jarvis, took up the crusade.

Anna had been deeply influenced by her mother, and she often recalled hearing her mother say that she hoped someone would one day establish a memorial for all mothers, living and dead.

Anna had been particularly touched at age twelve while listening to her mother teach a Sunday school class on the subject "Mothers in the Bible." Mrs. Jarvis closed the lesson with a prayer to this effect: *I hope and pray that someone, sometime, will found a memorial mother's day. There are many days for men, but none for mothers.*

Anna never forgot that moment, and at their mother's graveside service, Anna's brother Claude heard her say ". . . by the grace of God, you shall have that Mother's Day."

Anna thus began a campaign to establish a national Mother's Day. She and her supporters began to write a constant stream of letters to ministers, businessmen, politicians and newspaper editors. She spent a fortune trying to attract attention to her idea, and took every opportunity to give speeches, send telegrams, or write articles promoting her cause.

On the second anniversary of her mother's death, May 12, 1907, Anna led a small tribute to her mother at Andrews Methodist Episcopal Church in Gafton, West Virginia. She donated five hundred white carnations, her mother's favorite flower, to be worn by everyone in attendance. On this first Mother's Day service, the pastor used the text, "Woman, behold thy son; Son, behold thy mother." (John 19:26) That same day a special service was held at the Wanna-maker Auditorium in Philadelphia, which could seat no more than a third of the fifteen thousand people who showed up.

After that, things begin to take off. Various states jumped on the bandwagon, officially proclaiming a Mother's Day each year, and, in 1914, President Woodrow Wilson officially established Mother's Day a national holiday to be held on the second Sunday of May.

Rocking Destiny

The hand that rocks the cradle rules the nation and its destiny.

—SOUTH AFRICAN PROVERB

But having succeeded at last, Anna Jarvis soon became embittered by the commercialization of the holiday and turned against it, actually filing a lawsuit to stop a 1923 Mother's Day festival. She was even arrested for disturbing the peace at a mother's convention where women sold white carnations.

"This is not what I intended," Jarvis growled. "I wanted it to be a day of sentiment, not profit!"

"A printed card means nothing except that you are too lazy to write to the woman who has done more for you than anyone in the world," she said on another occasion. "And candy! You take a box to Mother—and then eat most of it yourself. A pretty sentiment."

Shortly before her death in 1948, Anna Jarvis, living in a nursing home, received Mother's Day cards from all around the world. But she told a reporter she was sorry she had ever started the whole thing.

We aren't.

Date:			
Place:			
Occasion:			

O Susanna!

What a difficult life. She was the twenty-fifth child in a dissenter's family. Though brilliant, she procured little education. Though strong-willed, she lived in a male-dominated age. She married an older man and bore him nineteen children. Nine of them died. Her house burned up, her barn fell down, her health failed, and she lived with the wolf at the door.

She was Susanna Wesley.

Samuel and Susanna, married in 1689, began pastoring in dreary little Epworth in 1697. They served there forty years, enduring hardships like these:

- Samuel's salary was so small (and he was so incapable of managing it) that he was thrown into debtor's prison, leaving Susanna to fend for herself.
- The two were strong-willed and argumentative. Samuel once prayed for the King and waited for Susanna's "Amen." She didn't say it. "I do not believe the Prince of Orange to be the King," she said spiritedly. "Then you and I must part," replied Samuel, "for if we have two kings we must have two beds." They separated, to be reunited only after the King's death.
- They also disagreed about Susanna's ministry, for her Bible lessons drew more listeners than his sermons.
- Susanna gave birth to a daughter during the election of 1705. The nurse, exhausted by overnight revelry, slept so heavily the next morning that she rolled on the baby and smothered it.
- Susanna herself was often bedfast, having to delegate home duties to the children. But several of her children were so wayward that she called them "a constant affliction."
- Her brother, having promised her a sizable gift, disappeared mysteriously and was never heard from again.
- Finally, on July 21, 1731, Susanna described an accident in which her horses stampeded, throwing Samuel from their wagon and injuring him so that he was never well from that day.

A difficult life. And yet the parsonage at Epworth was destined to become the most celebrated in English history, for from it came two of the greatest evangelists of all time, John and Charles Wesley. And the mother who raised them shook the world.[1]

Date:	_____	_____	_____
Place:	_____	_____	_____
Occasion:	_____	_____	_____

Last Letter to Mother

One of the most beautiful letters ever written was addressed by the Scottish essayist and historian, Thomas Carlyle, to his mother Margaret Carlyle. The letter was found when Mr. Froude went over Carlyle's papers after his death, and bore the inscription, "My last letter to my mother."

> *My dear, good mother,*
> *Let it be ever a comfort to you, however weak you are, that you did your part honorably and well while in strength, and were a noble mother to me and to us all. I am now myself grown old, and have had various things to do and suffer for so many years, but there is nothing I ever had to be so much thankful for as the mother I had.*

[1] Robert J. Morgan, *On This Day* (Nashville: Thomas Nelson Publishers, 1997), July 21st.

That is a truth which I know well, and perhaps this day again it may be some comfort to you. Yes, surely, for if there has been good in the things I have uttered in the world's hearing, it was your voice essentially that was speaking through me; essentially what you and my brave father meant and taught me to mean, this was the purport of all I spoke and wrote. And if in the few years that may remain to me I am to get any more written for the world, the essence of it, so far as it is worthy and good, will still be yours. May God reward you, my dearest mother, for all you have done for me! I never can.[1]

Date: _____ _____ _____

Place: _____ _____ _____

Occasion: _____ _____ _____

A Ruth Bell Graham Poem

Had I been Joseph's mother
I'd have prayed / protection from his brothers
"God, keep him safe. / He is so young,
so different from / the others."
Mercifully, / she never knew
there would be slavery / and prison, too.

Had I been Moses' mother
I'd have wept / To keep my little son:
praying she might forget / the babe drawn
from the water / of the Nile.
Had I not kept / him for her / nursing him the while,
was he not mine?—and she / but Pharaoh's daughter?

Had I been Daniel's mother
I should have pled / "Give victory!
—this Babylonian horde / godless and cruel—
Don't let him be a captive—better dead,
Almighty Lord!"

Had I been Mary, / Oh, had I been she,
I would have cried / As never mother cried,
"Anything, O God, / Anything . . .—but / crucified."

With such prayers importunate
My finite wisdom would assail
Infinite Wisdom. God, how fortunate
Infinite Wisdom / should prevail.[2]

Date: _____ _____ _____

Place: _____ _____ _____

Occasion: _____ _____ _____

[1] George Jackson, *The Ten Commandments* (Edinburgh: Oliphant, Anderson, & Ferrier, 1898), 107–108.
[2] Ruth Bell Graham, *Prodigals and Those Who Love Them* (Colorado Springs: Focus on the Family, 1991), 69.

The Oldest Mother

The following item appeared in newspapers and magazines in May of 1997:

For most 63-year-old women, their children's first steps are distant memories. But for one senior citizen, that precious parental milestone is still to come. Last November, aided by in vitro fertilization provided by the University of Southern California, an anonymous 63-year-old became the world's oldest known mother. Her daughter entered the world at a healthy 6 pounds, 4 ounces.

The case, which came to light last week in the May issue of the journal *Fertility and Sterility,* raises thorny issues. The woman claimed to be 10 years younger in order to meet USC's under-55 criteria for assisted reproduction candidates; by the time doctors learned the truth, she was already into the second trimester. The successful pregnancy, says Paul Root Wolpe, a senior faculty associate at the University of Pennsylvania's Center for Bioethics, may spell the end for arbitrary age limits. "This is going to force the medical community to defend why a 54-year-old woman can have a baby and a 56-year-old woman can't," he says. "They won't have a good answer."

Some are concerned by the ethical propriety of raising a child at such an advanced age. But others think the concern over an older woman's fitness for motherhood reflects deeply entrenched prejudices. Says Dr. Donna Pratt of Chicago's Center for Human Reproduction: "No one argues if a 63-year-old man wants to be a father."[1]

Date: _____ _____ _____
Place: _____ _____ _____
Occasion: _____ _____ _____

The Mother Load

By the early 1990s, more than half of the mothers of infants under one year of age were in the labor force, and the majority of America's infants now spend time in "nonmaternal child care." Researchers are scrambling to determine what, if any, impact that will have on the mental/emotional well-being of the next generation.

In the November 1999 issue of *Developmental Psychology,* a major new study found that young children who were placed in daycare are slightly less likely to bond well with their mothers than stay-at-home children. But researchers, hoping parents won't be alarmed unnecessarily, caution the results are preliminary and say there's no way to judge how much time in day care may be too much.

Researchers for the National Institute of Child Health and Human Development (NICHD) Study of Early Child Care began tracking nearly 1,300 young subjects and their mothers in 1991 when the infants were six months old. It found a "small but significant" link between time spent in daycare and how positively a child interacts with his/her mother.

"The more hours a child spends in child care, the slightly less positive mother-child interaction is," said Margaret Tresch Owen, a psychologist at the University

[1] Brendan I. Koerner, "Baby Talk: A 63-Year-Old Mother," *U.S. News and World Report,* May 5, 1997.

of Texas at Dallas who helped collect the data. But she conceded that researchers can't tell parents at what point the bonding begins to deteriorate.[1]

According to CNN, this latest daycare report "contradicts more positive information about day care in years past. And with three out of five U.S. preschoolers already in some form of child care, the findings may reinforce the concerns of millions of parents worried that having their children in daycare may not be a wise decision.

"But researchers emphasize they see no cause for alarm or any lasting impact on overall child development. In short, working mothers don't need to quit their jobs, Owen said. Child care providers say parents should be more concerned about the quality of care than the quantity of time a child spends away from home.

"'I think you could probably get a study to say just about anything you wanted it to,'" said Cheryl Smith, director of the Downtown Child Development Center, a daycare facility in Atlanta. "'I think the bonding between mother and child does not have to be interrupted because of the child care arrangements that you choose.'"[2]

Time, reporting about the same study in a commentary written by Karen Dickenson entitled "The Mother Load," observed:

"Show me a study about children in daycare, and I'll show you a study that's bound to make mothers feel bad. . . . We moms get caught in the tension between academic studies (and our own fears) telling us that daycare breeds ear infections and bad habits, and equally compelling research showing that if we rear our kids at home, we retard their social development. We worry when our toddler clings to us in the morning—and when she doesn't."[3]

Date: _____ _____ _____
Place: _____ _____ _____
Occasion: _____ _____ _____

Erma Bombeck's Tribute to Her Mom

When the good Lord was creating mothers He was into His sixth day of overtime when the angel appeared and said, "You're doing a lot of fiddling around on this one."

And the Lord said, "Have you read the specs on this order? She has to be completely washable, but not plastic; have 180 moveable parts, all replaceable; run on black coffee and leftovers; have a lap that disappears when she stands up; a kiss that can cure anything from a broken leg to a disappointed love affair; and six pairs of hands."

The angel shook her head slowly and said, "Six pairs of hands . . . no way!"

"It's not the hands that are causing me problems," said the Lord, "It's the three pairs of eyes that mothers have to have."

[1] "Child Care and Mother/Child Interaction in the First 3 Years of Life" *Developmental Psychology,* November 1999, Vol. 35, No. 6, 1399/1413.
[2] "Study: Day care slightly weakens child-mother bond," *CNN,* November 8, 1999
[3] Karen Dickenson, "The Mother Load," *Time,* November 15, 1999.

"That's on the standard model?" asked the angel.

The Lord nodded. "One pair that sees through closed doors when she asks, 'What are you kids doing in there?' when she already knows; another here in the back of her head that sees what she shouldn't but what she has to know; and, of course, the ones here in front that can look at a child when he goofs up and say, 'I understand and I love you' without so much as uttering a word . . .

"I can't quit now . . . Already I have one who heals herself when she is sick, can feed a family of six on one pound of hamburger, and can get a nine-year-old to stand under a shower."

The angel circled the model of the mother very slowly. "It's too soft," she sighed. "But tough!" said the Lord excitedly. "You cannot imagine what this mother can do or endure."

"Can it think?"

"Not only can it think, but it can reason and compromise and dream," said the Creator.

Finally the angel bent over and ran her finger across the cheek. "There's a leak," she pronounced. "I told you you were trying to put too much into this model."

"It's not a leak," said the Lord, "It's a tear."

"What's it for?"

"It's for joy, sadness, disappointment, pain, loneliness and pride."

"You're a genius," said the angel.

The Lord looked somber, "I didn't put it there."[1]

Date: _____   _____   _____
Place: _____   _____   _____
Occasion: _____   _____   _____

She's Just Perfect

A small boy invaded the lingerie section of a big department store and shyly presented his problem to the salesclerk. "I want to buy my mom a present of a slip," he said, "but I'm darned if I know what size she wears."

The clerk said, "It would help to know if your mom is short or tall, fat or skinny."

"She's just perfect," beamed the little boy, so the clerk wrapped up a size thirty-four for him.

Two days later Mom came to the store herself and changed it to a size fifty-two.[2]

Date: _____   _____   _____
Place: _____   _____   _____
Occasion: _____   _____   _____

[1] <http://people.ce.mediaone.net/dalbec/momsday.html>
[2] From a clipping in my files.

New Year's Day

Someone Once Said

- *A.D.—The Year of our Lord*
- *You crown the year with Your goodness.*—Psalm 65.1
- *On the thirty-second day of the thirteenth month / on the eighth day of the week we will find the things we seek.*—Sam Walter Foss
- *Time has no divisions to mark its passage; there is never a thunderstorm to announce the beginning of a new year. It is only we mortals who ring bells and fire off pistols.*—Thomas Mann, in *The Magic Mountain*
- *A New Year's Resolution usually goes in one year and out the next.*—Anonymous

Date: _____ _____ _____
Place: _____ _____ _____
Occasion: _____ _____ _____

Two-Faced

The month of January is named after the Roman god Janus, who was pictured as a man with two faces, one looking backward and the other forward. New Year's Day provides a valuable time to ponder the past while anticipating the future.

Date: _____ _____ _____
Place: _____ _____ _____
Occasion: _____ _____ _____

N

New Year's Customs

Not all countries celebrate the New Year at the same time or in the same way because of different calendars and customs.[1]

- In **Ancient Egypt,** the holiday was celebrated when the Nile flooded, usually near the end of September. This flooding made it possible to grow crops in the desert, and the people celebrated by taking statues of the god Amon, his wife and son, up the Nile by boat. Singing, dancing, and feasting was done for a month, then the statues were returned to the temple.
- **Babylonia's** New Year was in the Spring. During the festival, the king was stripped of his clothes and sent away, and for a few days there was a relaxation of laws. Then the king returned in grand procession, dressed in fine robes. Everyone returned to work and behaved properly. Thus the New Year gave people a new start to their lives.
- The **Roman** New Year festival was called the *Calends,* and people decorated their homes and gave each other gifts. It was Emperor Julius Caesar who

[1] Jausten, < www.geocities.com/Heartland/Plains/7214/newyear.htm >

began the calendar system in which the first month is named for the two-faced god Janus.

- The **Celtic** New Year festival took place at the end of October, at summer's end. The Celts gathered mistletoe to keep ghosts at bay, for this was the time when the dead were thought to return to haunt the living.
- The **Jewish** New Year, *Rosh Hashanah,* is a holy time when people consider things they have done wrong in the past and promise to do better in the future. Special services are held in synagogues and the *Shofar* is blown.
- The **Muslim** Calendar is based on the movements of the moon, so the date of New Year is eleven days earlier each year. In some Islamic nations, people put grains of wheat or barley in a little dish to grow. By New Year's the grains have produced shoots, reminding the people of a new year of life.
- **Hindus** do not all celebrate New Year in the same way or at the same time. The people of West Bengal wear flowers of pink, red, purple, or white. In Kerala, mothers put food, flowers, and little gifts on a special tray to surprise their children. In central India, orange flags are flown from buildings. In Gujarat in western India, small oil lamps are lit along the roofs of buildings.
- In **Vietnam,** the New Year is called *Tet Nguyen Dan,* or *Tet* for short. It begins between January 21 and February 19, the exact date changing from year to year. The Vietnamese believe there is a god in every home who travels to heaven (traditionally on a carp) to report how good or bad each family member has been in the past year. Live carp are often purchased and set free in a river.
- In Shinto families in **Japan,** a rope of straw is often placed across the front of houses to keep out evil spirits and bring happiness during the coming year.
- The **Chinese** New Year is celebrated some time between January 17 and February 19, at the time of the new moon, and is call *Yuan Tan.* It is a time of parades and street processions involving large costumes and thousands of lanterns which light the way for the New Year. Firecrackers are used to frighten the spirits away.
- In **Greece,** New Year's Day is also the Festival of Saint Basil, who was famous for his kindness. Greek children leave their shoes by the fire on New Year's Day with the hope that he will come and fill them with gifts.
- In some villages in **Scotland,** barrels of tar are set afire and rolled through the streets, signifying the burning of the old year.
- In the **United States,** New Year's Eve is celebrated with parties and champagne by some, and by prayer and worship by others in traditional "watch night" services. January 1st is devoted to parades, football games, and for some, black-eyed peas.
- **All over the world,** Robert Burns's poem *Auld Lang Syne* is sung at midnight on New Year's Eve. The words *auld lang syne* mean *old, long time.*

Date: _____   _____   _____

Place: _____   _____   _____

Occasion: _____   _____   _____

A. W. Tozer's New Year's Message

A. W. Tozer, long-time editor of the *Alliance Witness*, once penned this greeting for the cover of the January 1, 1938, edition of his magazine, and it was reprinted on the cover for the New Year's edition in 1979. It read in part:

While all the promises of God are true and precious, yet it is good to take them one by one and especially commit ourselves to them. If you ask God to give you a special message for the opening year, one that will be made seasonable and real in every exigency of the unknown future, you will be surprised how faithfully He will fulfill His Word, and how fittingly the Holy Spirit will speak to you of things to come, and anticipate the real needs and exigencies of your life.

Date: _____   _____   _____
Place: _____   _____   _____
Occasion: _____   _____   _____

Another Year Is Dawning

Hymnist Frances Ridley Havergal took New Year's Day very seriously, always using it as a time of reflection and often composing a poem to send to friends expressing her feelings about the new day and year. The one she wrote in 1874 has become immortal. She was thirty-six at the time, and she dashed off this poem and had it printed on a specially designed greeting card to be sent to friends. The card was captioned: "A Happy New Year! Ever such may it be!" The inside said:

> *Another year is dawning:*
> *Dear Father, let it be,*
> *In working or in waiting,*
> *Another year with Thee;*
> *Another year of progress,*
> *Another year of praise,*
> *Another year of proving*
> *Thy presence all the days.*

Date: _____   _____   _____
Place: _____   _____   _____
Occasion: _____   _____   _____

N

Matthew Henry's New Year

The famous Bible commentator Matthew Henry wrote this resolution in his journal on January 1, 1705: *Not renouncing, but repeating and ratifying all my former Covenants with God, and lamenting it, that I have not lived up more closely to them; I do in the beginning of this New Year solemnly make a fresh surrender of myself, my whole self, body, soul, and spirit, to God the Father, Son, and Holy Ghost, my Creator, Redeemer, and Sanctifier, covenanting and promising, not in any strength of my own, for I am very weak, but in the strength of the grace of Jesus Christ, that I will endeavour this year to stand complete in all the Will of God.*

I know this is the Will of God, even my sanctification; Lord grant that this year I may be more holy, and walk more closely than ever in all holy conversation; I earnestly desire to be filled with thy holy thoughts, to be carried out in holy affections, determined by holy aims and intentions, and governed in all my words and actions by holy principles. O that a golden thread of holiness may run through the whole web of this year.

Date: _____   _____   _____

Place: _____   _____   _____

Occasion: _____   _____   _____

Time

> *When I was a child, I laughed and wept,*
> *Time crept;*
> *When as a youth, I dreamed and talked,*
> *Time walked;*
> *When I became a full grown man,*
> *Time ran;*
> *When older still I daily grew,*
> *Time flew;*
> *Soon I shall be traveling on,*
> *Time gone.*[1]

Date: _____   _____   _____

Place: _____   _____   _____

Occasion: _____   _____   _____

Obedience

Someone Once Said . . .

- *Our Lord bade us go not merely to teach them "all things whatsoever I have commanded you," but to teach them to observe these things.*—Vance Havner[2]
- *You have not really learned a commandment until you have obeyed it . . . . The church suffers today from Christians who know volumes more than they practice.*—Vance Havner[3]

Date: _____   _____   _____

Place: _____   _____   _____

Occasion: _____   _____   _____

---

[1] Author unknown. Clipping in my files.
[2] Vance Havner, *Consider Jesus* (Grand Rapids, MI: Baker Book House, 1987), 61.
[3] Havner, *Consider Jesus,* 61.

The Problem with Samson

My daughter Hannah and I had a Great Dane named Samson that we dearly loved, and Samson, as it turns out, was well named, for he was big and strong and muscular—and, like his namesake, he also had a penchant for wandering. We built fences, we tried chains and dog runs, we tried everything to keep Samson at home. But he'd dig under the fence or climb over it, and it drove us to distraction.

So we bought the best-selling book on the market on the subject of training dogs. *No Bad Dogs* was written by the famous British dog trainer Barbara Woodhouse, who raises Great Danes herself. One night when I went upstairs to tuck in Hannah, she had a sad expression on her face, and she said, "Dad, I know now what Samson's real problem is. Let me read you this paragraph." This is what she read me out of *No Bad Dogs* by Barbara Woodhouse:

In a dog's mind, a master or a mistress to love, honor, and obey is an absolute necessity. The love is dormant in the dog until brought into full bloom by an understanding owner. Thousands of dogs appear to love their owners, they welcome them home with enthusiastic wagging of the tail and jumping up, they follow them about their houses happily and, to the normal person seeing the dog, the affection is true and deep. But to the experienced dog trainer this outward show is not enough. The true test of real love takes place when the dog has got the opportunity to go out on its own as soon as the door is left open by mistake and it goes off and often doesn't return home for hours. That dog loves only its home comforts and the attention it gets from its family; it doesn't truly love the master or mistress as they fondly think. True love in dogs is apparent when a door is left open and the dog still stays happily within earshot of its owner. For the owner must be the be-all and end-all of a dog's life.

The real test of our Christianity isn't seen in our work or activity, or even in our theological purity. It's found in this: when we have an opportunity to wander away, to disobey, to leave his presence, do we choose instead to stay close to him, to abide in Christ, to obey?[1]

Date:			
Place:			
Occasion:			

All Right, Loving

Aretta Loving, Wycliffe missionary, was washing her breakfast dishes when she saw Jimmy, the five-year-old neighbor, headed straight toward the back porch. She had just finished painting the back-porch handrails, and she was proud of her work.

"Come around to the front door, Jimmy," she shouted. "There's wet paint on the porch rails."

"I'll be careful," Jimmy replied, not turning from his path.

"No, Jimmy! Don't come up the steps," Aretta shouted, knowing of Jimmy's tendency to mess things up.

"I'll be careful," he said again, by now dangerously close to the steps.

---

[1] From a sermon by the author.

"Jimmy, stop!" Aretta shouted. "I don't want carefulness. I want obedience!" As the words burst from her mouth, she suddenly remembered Samuel's response to King Saul: *To obey is better than sacrifice.*

How would Jimmy respond, Aretta wondered. To her relief, he shouted back, "All right, Loving, I'll go around to the front door." He was the only one who called her by her last name like that, and it had endeared him to her from the beginning. As he turned around the house, Aretta thought to herself, "How often am I like Saul or like Jimmy, wanting to go my own way? I rationalize, 'I'll be careful, Lord' as I proceed with my own plans."

But He doesn't want carefulness. He wants obedience.[1]

Date:			
Place:			
Occasion:			

Walls

The dictionary provides several definitions for *discipline*. The first is *punishment,* but the dictionary's second definition is richer: *Training that corrects, molds, or perfects the mental faculties or moral character.*

Discipline, in other words, is training in virtue and self-control. If we say that someone is a disciplined person, we mean he is self-controlled. How important is self-control? Proverbs 25:28 says: *Like a city whose walls are broken down is a man who lacks self-control (NIV).*

A strong, safe, well-guarded city in biblical times had high, thick walls to thwart invaders. Enemies had to camp in the vulnerable open and send troops rushing toward the gates with battering rams. The city's defensive forces could shoot well-aimed arrows and repulse the enemy. The population felt safe, because the walls were unassailable.

But if the walls collapsed like those of Jericho, the enemy could waltz right in, rape the women, loot the stores, kill the men, massacre the children, and burn the town.

Proverbs 25 says that a person's self-discipline is his defense in life. The devil can't touch a self-controlled, well-disciplined person. But if we're undisciplined, prone to indulge our appetites, doing what we feel like doing, exercising little self-control, then Satan doesn't even have to fire a shot. He can stroll into our lives and do whatever he wishes. That's why Peter wrote: *Be self-controlled and alert. Your enemy the devil prowls around like a roaring lion looking for someone to devour. Resist him, standing firm in the faith.*[2]

Spiritual Ecstasy

The best measure of the spiritual life is not its ecstasies, but its obedience.
—OSWALD CHAMBERS

Date:			
Place:			
Occasion:			

---

[1] Adapted from Aretta Loving, "Obedience is Better," *Decision,* September 1990, 15.
[2] From a sermon by the author

Parenting

Someone Once Said . . .

- *Before I was married I had three theories about raising children. Now I have three children and no theories.*—John Wilmot, the Earl of Rochester[1]
- *A father's first responsibility to his child is to love his wife. The most favored children in the world are those whose parents love each other.*—Charles Shedd
- *To our forefathers the Christian faith was an experience. To our fathers it was an inheritance. To our generation it is a convenience. And to our children it is a nuisance.*—an anonymous speaker, emphasizing the importance of raising children in a genuine, glowing Christian environment

Date: _____ _____ _____

Place: _____ _____ _____

Occasion: _____ _____ _____

Keep on Singing

Like any good mother, when Karen found out that another baby was on the way, she did what she could to help her three-year-old son, Michael, prepare for a new sibling. They find out that the new baby is going to be a girl, and day after day, night after night, Michael sings to his sister in Mommy's tummy. The pregnancy progressed normally for Karen, an active member of the Panther Creek United Methodist Church in Morristown, Tennessee. Then the labor pains come. Every 5 minutes . . . every minute. But complications arise during delivery. Hours of labor. Would a C-section be required? Finally, Michael's little sister is born. But she is in serious condition. With sirens howling in the night, the ambulance rushes the infant to the neonatal intensive care unit at St. Mary's Hospital, Knoxville, Tennessee.

The days inch by. The little girl gets worse. The pediatric specialist tells the parents, "There is very little hope. Be prepared for the worst."

Karen and her husband contact a local cemetery about a burial plot. They had fixed up a special room in their home for the new baby, but now they plan a funeral. Michael keeps begging his parents to let him see his sister, "I want to sing to her," he says.

Week two in intensive care. Things don't look good. Michael keeps nagging about singing to his sister, but kids are never allowed in Intensive Care. Karen makes up her mind. She will take Michael whether they like it or not. If he doesn't see his sister now, he may never see her alive. She dresses him in an oversized scrub suit and marches him into ICU. He looks like a walking laundry basket, but the head nurse recognizes him as a child and bellows, "Get that kid out of here now! No children are allowed in ICU." The mother rises up strong in Karen, and the usually mild-mannered lady glares steel-eyed into the head nurse's face, her lips a firm line. "He is not leaving until he sings to his sister!"

[1] John-Roger and Peter McWilliams, *Do It!* (Los Angeles: Prelude Press, 1991), 175.

591

Karen tows Michael to his sister's bedside. He gazes at the tiny infant losing the battle to live. And he begins to sing. In the pure-hearted voice of a three-year-old, Michael sings: "You are my sunshine, my only sunshine, you make me happy when skies are gray . . ."

Instantly the baby girl responds. The pulse rate becomes calm and steady.

"Keep on singing, Michael." "You never know, dear, how much I love you. Please don't take my sunshine away . . ."

The ragged, strained breathing becomes as smooth as a kitten's purr. "Keep on singing, Michael." "The other night, dear, as I lay sleeping, I dreamed I held you in my arms . . ." Michael's little sister relaxes as rest, healing rest, seems to sweep over her. Tears conquer the face of the bossy head nurse. Karen glows. "You are my sunshine, my only sunshine. Please don't take my sunshine away."

The baby is well enough to go home! *Woman's Day Magazine* called it "The Miracle of a Brother's Song." The medical staff just called it a miracle. Karen called it a miracle of God's love. A few weeks later, Michael's little sister was baptized at the Panther Creek Church.[1]

Date:	_____	_____	_____
Place:	_____	_____	_____
Occasion:	_____	_____	_____

Why Children Love God

The minister asked a group of children in Sunday School class, "Why do you love God?" He got a variety of answers, but the one he liked best was from a boy who said, "I guess it just runs in our family."

Date:	_____	_____	_____
Place:	_____	_____	_____
Occasion:	_____	_____	_____

How to Raise a Happy Child

When John and Peter were growing up, other kids felt sorry for them. Their parents always had them doing chores: weeding the garden, running errands, carrying out the trash. When they grew older, they delivered newspapers or mowed lawns. Sometimes other parents shook their heads and remarked that all work and no play made a dull boy.

But when the boys reached adulthood, they were better off than their childhood playmates who had been less industrious. They earned more money and had more job satisfaction. They had better marriages and closer relationships with their children. They were healthier and lived longer. Most of all, they were happier. *Far* happier.

---

[1] This story, which has been circulating on the Internet, has been verified for the author by employees at St. Mary's Hospital.

These are the remarkable findings of a 40-year study that began in the 1940s— a study that may help you raise happier children today. Started in an effort to understand juvenile delinquency, the study followed the lives of 456 teenage boys from inner-city Boston, many from impoverished or broken homes. When they were compared at middle age, one fact stood out: regardless of intelligence, family income, ethnic background or amount of education, those who had worked as boys, even at simple household chores, enjoyed happier and more productive lives than those who had not.[1]

Date: _____ _____ _____

Place: _____ _____ _____

Occasion: _____ _____ _____

Fences

A kindergarten in one town sat right on a corner by a busy highway. Although the school had a nice yard in which the children could play, at recess they would huddle right up against the building. The cars whizzing by frightened them.

One day, workmen erected a steel fence around the school yard. From that point on, the children used the entire playground. The fence did not limit their freedom; it actually expanded it.

Children need fences, for they feel more secure having the discipline of clear boundaries.[2]

Date: _____ _____ _____

Place: _____ _____ _____

Occasion: _____ _____ _____

P

A Father's Advice

Heinrich Bullinger was a good pastor and a better father. He was born in 1504 to a priest who, in his old age, embraced Reformation views. Though it cost him his church, it gained him his son. Young Heinrich fell in love with Luther's writings, Melanchthon's books, and the study of the Bible. At the remarkably young age of twenty-seven, he was asked to take the place of slain Swiss Reformer Ulrich Zwingli as pastor of the Grossmunster of Zurich. He ascended the pulpit there on December 23, 1531.

Bullinger continued Zwingli's practice of preaching through books of the Bible, verse by verse. His home, like his Bible, was open from morning till night, and he freely distributed food, clothing, and money to the needy. His wisdom and influence spread across Europe.

---

[1] Edwin Kiester, Jr., and Sally Valente Kiester, "How To Raise a Happy Child," *Reader's Digest,* January 1986, 95.

[2] Larry Burkett, "Are Allowances Scriptural?" *Moody,* May 1982, 61.

No one was more affected than his own son, Henry. When the young man packed his bags and set out for college in Strassburg, Heinrich gave him ten rules for living:

1. Fear God at all times, and remember that the fear of God is the beginning of wisdom.
2. Humble yourself before God, and pray to him alone through Christ, our only Mediator and Advocate.
3. Believe firmly that God has done all for our salvation through his Son.
4. Pray above all things for a strong faith active in love.
5. Pray that God may protect your good name and keep you from sin, sickness, and bad company.
6. Pray for the fatherland, for your dear parents . . . for the spread of the Word of God.
7. Be reticent, be always more willing to hear than to speak, and do not meddle with things you do not understand.
8. Study diligently. . . . Read daily three chapters of the Bible.
9. Keep your body clean and unspotted, be neat in your dress, and avoid above all things intemperance in eating and drinking.
10. Let your conversation be decent, cheerful, moderate.

The advice was taken, and Henry Bullinger later became, like his father and grandfather, a minister of the Gospel of Jesus Christ.

Date:	_____	_____	_____
Place:	_____	_____	_____
Occasion:	_____	_____	_____

The Family Altar

Before her death, Morrow Coffey Graham wrote a little book about her experiences as the mother of the man who would preach the Gospel to more people than any other in history.

My husband and I established a family altar the day we were married and we carried that through. In the breakfast room I always kept a Scripture calendar with a verse for the day. Each morning we read that, too, and prayed to the Lord. As we gathered at the breakfast table, everyone would bow his head and fold his hands as my husband asked the blessing. Often as I packed the children's school lunches, I could hear my husband talking to the children. He helped them memorize literally hundreds of Bible verses.

I looked forward to our evenings together as a family. Everyone gathered in the family room. We did this right after the dinner dishes were put away. It was the most important thing in our life, this time of Bible reading and prayer. I know that today Billy recalls those instructional periods as among the most important in his life, helping him to become saturated with the Bible.

Since my children have married and gone their separate ways, and since my husband's death, I have found myself with more time to devote to prayer. I pray without ceasing for Billy Frank.

In the early days of Billy's ministry, his mother accompanied him on a trip. Seeing his busy schedule, the throngs of people, and the stresses he encountered, she grew alarmed. But the Lord gave her Jeremiah 23:23, and it became her theme-verse in praying for him: "'Am I a God near at hand,' says the Lord, 'And not a God afar off?'"

I knew God had a long arm; He was wholly trustworthy. I have always had great confidence in the Lord's watchcare over Billy, and I have not feared, therefore, for his life.[1]

Date:			
Place:			
Occasion:			

Baxter and Boston

Richard Baxter was one of England's greatest ministers. In early life, he went into a large parish that was composed almost entirely of rich, cultured people. He found that the congregation was cold, and all was not as he had hoped. He was disappointed, but he determined that the way to save the church was to establish a warm and living faith inside the walls of family homes. Baxter therefore spent three years in visiting the homes of his community and helping establish family altars—a daily time of prayer and Bible reading—in every home. He succeeded amazingly, and the condition of the home was the fountainhead that filled his church to over-flowing and revived Christianity in his parish.

Thomas Boston was likewise a great minister, but, unlike Baxter, he spent the years of his early ministry in the slums of a city among the poor. There he discovered the same condition—the church was cold and empty. He had no influence, and he grew disheartened and discouraged. He determined that the only way to save the church was to save the family, and so he went through that poor community, establishing family altars. It took him three years, but Thomas Boston's church sparked a revival of Christianity in his region.[2]

Date:			
Place:			
Occasion:			

Ruth Graham on the Family Altar

In a 1975 interview with *Family Life Today*, Ruth Bell Graham was asked about conducting a daily family altar. She first spoke of how her own interest in the Bible had been piqued at an early age: *Each morning when I went downstairs to breakfast, my father—a busy missionary surgeon—would be sitting reading his Bible. At night, her work behind her, my mother would be doing the same. Anything that could so capture the interest and*

---

[1] Morrow Coffey Graham, *They Call Me Mother Graham* (Old Tappan, New Jersey: Fleming H. Revell Co., 1977).

[2] Old clipping in my files. Source unknown.

devotion of those I admired and loved the most, I reasoned, must be worth investigating. So at an early age, I began reading my Bible and found it to be, in the words of the old Scotsman, "sweet pasturage."

Then she gave these suggestions about leading children in a family worship time: *I believe it is important to keep the Scripture reading and prayer relatively brief and to vary it from time to time. . . .*

It pays to start young and give it in small doses. For "a child's mind," said John Trapp in the seventeenth century, "is like a small-necked bottle: pour in the wine too rapidly and much of the liquid spills over and is wasted.

Bear in mind the words of Isaiah 28:9, 10, "Whom shall he teach knowledge? And whom shall he make to understand doctrine? Them that are weaned from the milk, and drawn from the breasts. For precept must be upon precept, . . . line upon line . . . , here a little, and there a little."[1]

Date:			
Place:			
Occasion:			

Birth Order

The impact on a child's personality of the order of birth has intrigued psychologists since the early twentieth century, and over two thousand studies have been published on the subject.

In a front page story of the *Wall Street Journal,* David Stipp wrote about the newest research regarding birth order:

"Historian Frank Sulloway says it is only natural that he has spent twenty-four years plotting to overthrow the reigning ideas in his field. After all, he's a later-born.

"Based on a massive statistical analysis of many of those who shaped the past, Dr. Sulloway has detected a grand pattern. Forget Adam Smith's invisible hand, Karl Marx's class struggles and Sigmund Freud's Oedipal clashes. Radical change in human affairs is wrought by the perennial rivalry between the eldest children and their younger siblings.

"Later-borns are more open-minded than firstborns," says Dr. Sulloway. "They are 'born to rebel,' take risks and explode accepted wisdom. Charles Darwin, Igor Stravinsky and Rachel Carson were later-borns. So was Victorian novelist George Eliot, who renounced religion and lived adulterously with her married mentor." Some others: Marx, Lenin, Castro, Ho Chi Minh, Ralph Nader, Marlon Brando, Anita Hill, and Bill Gates.

"Firstborns tend to stiffly support the status quo," says Dr. Sulloway, a guest scholar at Massachusetts Institute of Technology. "They are status-conscious and often emerge as leaders. But when faced with revolutionary change, they try to slam on the brakes. John Adams, Calvin Coolidge, and Ayn Rand were firstborns. So are Chief Justice William Rehnquist and radio host Rush Limbaugh."[2]

---

[1] Ruth Bell Graham, "Start Young . . . Give Small Doses," *Family Life Today,* January 1975, 3–5.
[2] David Stipp, "Family Matters: Blame the Birth Order for History's Revolt This MIT Scholar Says," *The Wall Street Journal,* August 23, 1994, 1.

Date: _____ _____ _____
Place: _____ _____ _____
Occasion: _____ _____ _____

Making Sacrifices

Martha Scarborough celebrated Independence Day, July 4, 1870, by giving birth to a son, Lee. When the boy was eight, Martha and her husband George, a part-time Baptist preacher, moved to Texas to raise cattle and share Christ. A dugout shelter served as home, then a log cabin near Clear Fork Creek. George and Martha dreamed of a beautiful house atop a nearby hill. They saved frugally, but times were lean, and years passed before they accumulated enough to proceed with the long-discussed house. Lee, meanwhile, grew into a brawny sixteen-year-old cowboy.

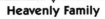

Heavenly Family

A happy family is but an earlier heaven.

—ANONYMOUS

One day, their work behind them, George said to Martha, "Let's go up the hill and select a suitable place for the home. We have saved money for that purpose, so we had as well begin plans to build." Arm in arm, the couple strolled to the grassy crest of the hill behind their cabin. This was a moment long anticipated. At the top of the hill, he said, "Here is the place. This is the most suitable location we can find." But Martha turned toward him, her eyes filling with tears. "My dear," she said, "I do appreciate your desire to build me a new, comfortable home on this place of beauty, but there is another call for our money which is far greater. Let's live on in the old house and put this money in the head and heart of our boy. I fear that if we use this money to build a home we shall never be able to send Lee to college. I would rather a thousand times that we should never build this house if we can invest the money in our boy."

George was disappointed, and he said little for several days. Finally one evening past midnight he yielded. The house was never built, but Lee Scarborough left home on January 8, 1888, for Baylor College in Waco, Texas. He eventually became a powerhouse for Christ, a Southern Baptist leader, a writer, a seminary president, a pastor, an evangelist, and a business leader who built colleges, seminaries, churches, hospitals, and mission stations around the world. And it was from a book of his sermons that young Billy Graham, a student in Florida, found the material for his first sermon.[1]

P

Date: _____ _____ _____
Place: _____ _____ _____
Occasion: _____ _____ _____

Friendship

Many years ago, British pastor John Patton gave his Sunday night congregation this advice about becoming "pals" with their children: "Thirty years divide a father

---

[1] Robert J. Morgan, *On This Day* (Nashville: Thomas Nelson Publishers, 1997), July 4th.

and son. Each looks out on the world with his own eyes, and sees things from his own view-point. Is it any wonder that misunderstandings sometimes arise? The remedy lies along the lines of forbearance and sympathy. Be the pal of your boy. Let father and son cultivate the spirit of comradeship, and in every event of life there will be a chance of complete understanding between them."[1]

Date: _____   _____   _____

Place: _____   _____   _____

Occasion: _____   _____   _____

Too Young to Date?

Paul Harvey once delighted his radio listeners with this story. "Our *For What It's Worth Department* reads *The Washingtonian* . . .

About the nine-year-old boy who announced to his parents that he had a date. A date with a girl at the age of nine? His parents were taken aback. But the lad had already telephoned the girl they'd met last summer and invited her to his house for dinner. He had lured her with the promise his mom would make popovers. And his dad would get a VCR tape of *Thriller* at the video store.

So—the pretty little girl was delivered by her mother.

After dinner the two youngsters went down to the rec room and watched Michael Jackson. At ten P.M. his father delivered them to her front door. Her four older sisters rushed out to hug and greet her. It was her first date also.

Back home, before the dying fire, dad sat soberly thinking about how fast babies grow up. His young son, misinterpreting his father's mood, walked over, put his hand on dad's shoulder and said, "Don't worry, Dad; nothing happened!"[2]

Date: _____   _____   _____

Place: _____   _____   _____

Occasion: _____   _____   _____

Another Young Dater

Young people are starting to date too young nowadays. The other day one mother was overheard telling her son, "Now remember, Tommy, I want you back in this house when the big hand is on twelve and the little hand is on nine.

Date: _____   _____   _____

Place: _____   _____   _____

Occasion: _____   _____   _____

---

[1] John A. Patton, *Faces Through the Mist* (London: James Clark & Co., Limited, n.d.), 18.
[2] Paul Harvey, *For What It's Worth*, ed. By Paul Harvey, Jr. (New York: Bantam Books, 1991), 91.

Murphy's Laws of Parenting

1. The tennis shoes you must replace today will go on sale next week.
2. Leakproof thermoses—will.
3. The chances of a piece of bread falling with the grape-jelly side down are directly proportional to the cost of the carpet.
4. The garbage truck will be two doors past your house when your teen remembers it's his turn to take out the trash.
5. The shirt your child must wear today will be the only one that needs to be washed or mended.
6. Gym clothes left at school in lockers mildew at a faster rate than other clothing.
7. The item your child lost, and must have for school within the next ten seconds, will be found in the last place you think to look.
8. Sick children recover miraculously when the pediatrician enters the treatment room.
9. Refrigerated items, used daily, will gravitate toward the back of the refrigerator.
10. Your chances of being seen by someone you know dramatically increase if you drive your child to school in your robe and curlers.[1]

Date: _____ _____ _____
Place: _____ _____ _____
Occasion: _____ _____ _____

———— Patience/Waiting on the Lord ————

P

Someone Once Said . . .

- *Patience means living out the belief that God orders everything for the spiritual good of his children.*—J. I. Packer
- *Grin and bear it is old-fashioned advice, but sing and bear it is a great deal better.*—Charles Spurgeon[2]
- *Patience does not just grin and bear things, stoic-like, but accepts them cheerfully as therapeutic workouts planned by a heavenly trainer who is resolved to get you up to full fitness.*—J. I. Packer
- *Are we prepared to take the awful patient ways of God? We must not be infected by the world's valuation of either speed or success.*—John B. Phillips[3]
- *The trouble is that I'm in a hurry, but God isn't.*— Phillips Brooks, Boston pastor when asked, one day, the reason for his agitation

---

[1] Circulating on the Internet.
[2] Charles H. Spurgeon, *John Ploughman's Talks* (New York: Sheldon & Company, n.d.), 35.
[3] Ruth Bell Graham, *Legacy of a Pack Rat* (Nashville: Oliver Nelson, 1989), 52.

- *Beware the barrenness of busyness.*—Slogan on a bumper sticker
- *I'm extraordinarily patient provided I get my own way in the end.*—Margaret Thatcher

Date:	_____	_____	_____
Place:	_____	_____	_____
Occasion:	_____	_____	_____

Patience Is Strength

- *Patience is a weapon.*—Anonymous
- *Patience and passage of time do more than strength and fury.*—Jean de la Fontaine, (1621–1695) French poet
- *The two most powerful warriors are patience and time.*—Leo Tolstoy, Russian novelist
- *Our patience will achieve more than our force.*—Edmund Burke
- *With time and patience the mulberry leaf becomes satin.*—Oriental proverb

Date:	_____	_____	_____
Place:	_____	_____	_____
Occasion:	_____	_____	_____

The Twentieth Time

"I wonder at your patience. You have told the same thing to that child twenty times," said Rev. Samuel Wesley.

"Had I satisfied myself by saying the matter only nineteen times," Susanna Wesley replied, "I should have lost all my labor. You see, it was the twentieth time that crowned the whole."[1]

Date:	_____	_____	_____
Place:	_____	_____	_____
Occasion:	_____	_____	_____

Richard Nixon on Patience

In a Christmas interview in 1986, Richard Nixon spoke of peace efforts under way throughout the world during the Reagan administration. He was asked, "Is the USA better off this Christmas than it was at this time last year?" The former president answered:

As Americans, we have many great strengths, but one of our weaknesses is impatience. The Russians think in terms of decades, the Chinese in terms of centuries. Americans think in terms

---

[1] Clint Bonner, *A Hymn is Born* (Nashville: Broadman Press, 1959), 16.

of years, months, and even days. But if in the quest for a realistic, lasting peace, we expect overnight success—instant gratification—we are bound to be disappointed.

Date: _____ _____ _____
Place: _____ _____ _____
Occasion: _____ _____ _____

Waiting on the Lord

- *He who waits on God loses no time.*—Vance Havner
- *To be impatient with God, chronically, habitually impatient with Him because things are not to our liking, makes the Christian life a dreadful burden.*—Eileen L. Guder
- *We hear a great deal about "Go ye," but not much about "Tarry ye." We preach about urgency but not about patience.*—A. W. Tozer
- *O, tarry thou the Lord's leisure.*—Psalm 27:14 from the Prayer Book

Date: _____ _____ _____
Place: _____ _____ _____
Occasion: _____ _____ _____

Oaks or Squash

Before James Garfield became President of the United States, he was principal of Hiram College in Ohio. A father once asked him if a particular course of study couldn't be simplified so that his son could go through by a shorter route.

"Certainly," replied Garfield. "But it all depends upon what you want to make of your boy. When God wants to make an oak tree, he takes a hundred years. When he wants to make a squash, he requires only two summers."

Date: _____ _____ _____
Place: _____ _____ _____
Occasion: _____ _____ _____

Growing Bamboo

Have you heard about the Chinese bamboo tree? The Chinese plant the seed; they water and fertilize it, but the first year nothing happens. The second year they water and fertilize it, and still nothing happens. The third and fourth years they water and fertilize it, and nothing happens. Then the fifth year they water and fertilize it, and sometime during the course of the fifth year, in a period of approximately six weeks, the Chinese bamboo trees grows roughly ninety feet.

The question is, Did it grow ninety feet in six weeks or did it grow ninety feet in five years? The obvious answer is that it grew ninety feet in five years, because had they not applied the water and fertilizer each year there would have been no Chinese bamboo tree.

All of us have had these "Chinese bamboo tree" experiences . . ."[1]

Date: _____ _____ _____
Place: _____ _____ _____
Occasion: _____ _____ _____

JFK's Story

One of John F. Kennedy's favorite stories concerned French General Louis Lyautey. After World War I, the general asked his gardener to plant an oak tree in a particular part of his estate. The gardener noted that the tree the general had chosen was slow-growing and wouldn't reach maturity for nearly a century. The general replied, "In that case, there is no time to lose. Plant it this afternoon."

Date: _____ _____ _____
Place: _____ _____ _____
Occasion: _____ _____ _____

By J. J. Lynch

His wisdom is sublime,
His heart profoundly kind;
God never is before His time,
And never is behind.[2]

Date: _____ _____ _____
Place: _____ _____ _____
Occasion: _____ _____ _____

Not a Blast of Hurry

Missionary J. O. Fraser who worked among the Lisu peoples of China, once commented about the necessity of waiting on the Lord to do His work without the frantic, panicked rushing about that characterizes much of our labor. He said:

In the biography of our Lord nothing is more noticeable than the quiet, even poise of His life. Never flustered whatever happened, never taken off His guard, however assailed by men or demons in the midst of fickle people, hostile rulers, faithless disciples—always calm, always collected. Christ the hard worker indeed—but doing no more, and no less, than God had appointed

[1] Zig Ziglar, *Raising Positive Kids in a Negative World* (Nashville: Thomas Nelson, 1985), 225.
[2] V. Raymond Edman, *The Disciples of Life* (Minneapolis: World Wide Publications, 1948), 78.

Him, and with no restlessness, no hurry, no worry. Was ever such a peaceful life lived, under conditions so perturbing?[1]

Date: _____ _____ _____
Place: _____ _____ _____
Occasion: _____ _____ _____

If Thou But Suffer God to Guide Thee

Be patient and await His leisure
In cheerful hope with heart content,
To take whate'er Thy Father's pleasure
And His discerning love hath sent;
Nor doubt our inmost wants are known
To Him who chose us for His own.

Date: _____ _____ _____
Place: _____ _____ _____
Occasion: _____ _____ _____

An Almost Forgotten Fanny Crosby Hymn

Wait on the Lord, wait cheerfully,
And He will thy youth renew;
Wait on the Lord obediently,
Whatever He bids thee do.

Wait on the Lord, for whom hast thou
On earth or in heaven but He?
Over thy soul a watch He keeps,
Whatever thy path may be.

Date: _____ _____ _____
Place: _____ _____ _____
Occasion: _____ _____ _____

P

"I Wouldn't Have Hurried"

Madeline Rockwell wrote the following story for *Reader's Digest:* My Grandmother was a ball of fire, while Grandpa was slow and deliberate. One night they were awakened by a commotion in the chicken house. Grandma sprang out of bed, ran to the chicken house and found the cause of the racket, a large black snake. Having nothing to dispatch it with, she clamped her bare foot down on its head.

---

[1] Geraldine Taylor, *Behind the Rangers: The Life-Changing Story of J. O. Fraser* (Singapore: OMF International, 1998), 191.

There she stood, until Grandpa finally arrived, a good fifteen minutes later. He was fully dressed, and even his pocket watch in place. "Well," he said cheerfully to my disheveled and enraged grandma, "If I'd known you had him, I wouldn't have hurried so."[1]

Date: _____ _____ _____
Place: _____ _____ _____
Occasion: _____ _____ _____

Peace

Someone Once Said . . .

- *There was in him an inner calm hard to explain.*—an unnamed officer, describing British General William George Shedden Dobbie
- *The peace of God is that eternal calm which lies far too deep in the praying, trusting soul to be reached by any external disturbances.*—A. T. Pierson
- *Do you know what it is, when you are tossed on the waves, to go down into the depths of Godhead, there rejoicing that not a wave of trouble ruffles your spirit, but that you are serenely at home with God your own Almighty Father?*—Charles Haddon Spurgeon[2]
- *Here I am at sixty-five, still seeking for peace.*—H. G. Wells[3]

Date: _____ _____ _____
Place: _____ _____ _____
Occasion: _____ _____ _____

The Age of Anxiety

A wife called the doctor one morning, saying, "Doctor, come quick! It's my husband!"

"What's the matter?" he calmly replied.

"Well, he got up this morning and took his vitamin pill. Then he took his appetite suppressant, his anti-depressant, and his tranquilizer. He also took an antihistamine and some Benzedrine. Then he lit a cigarette, and there was this explosion!"

Date: _____ _____ _____
Place: _____ _____ _____
Occasion: _____ _____ _____

---

[1] Clipped from my files.
[2] Charles Haddon Spurgeon, *Spurgeon's Sermons*, vol. 2 (Grand Rapids, MI: Baker Book House, 1983), 4.
[3] Wilber M. Smith, *Chats from a Minister's Library* (Grand Rapids, MI: Baker Book House, 1951), 190.

The Rock

A ship was wrecked in a furious storm and the only survivor was a little boy who was swept by the waves onto a rock. He sat there all night long until, the next morning, he was spotted and rescued.

"Did you tremble while you were on the rock during the night?" someone later asked him.

"Yes," said the boy. "I trembled all night—but the rock didn't."

Date: _____ _____ _____
Place: _____ _____ _____
Occasion: _____ _____ _____

Urgent Need

Missionary Tom Willey, twenty-seven, a graduate of Asbury College, was serving in the interior of Peru in the Amazon Basin. It had taken many treacherous days to trek into the jungle by train, car, mule, boat, and on foot, to work among the Campa Indians. He had been accepted out of curiosity if for no other reason, but he had high hopes for a harvest of souls. Tom had little difficulty adjusting to jungle life, and he plunged into his work with relish. He seemed to maintain an attitude of contented joy.

One day a radiogram arrived, informing Tom that his father was gravely ill and not expected to live. Tom's father was not a Christian, and the young missionary, who had been deeply burdened for him, felt he must return home at once in the hope of speaking one more time to his dad about the Lord Jesus.

Tom boarded a boat and headed upstream toward a trail out of the jungle. But once on the trail, his Indian guides became lost and Tom found himself winding around and around inside the jungle on trails leading nowhere. At every junction, hopeless decisions were made regarding the best fork to take, but the guides had lost all sense of direction. Hours passed, a night passed, then another day.

A powerful anxious surge of fear turned Tom's mind into a whirling turmoil. The physical hardships of the previous months, the loneliness, the spiritual drain he had experienced—all of it fed his fears and stretched his soul to the breaking point. His father, who needed him more than ever, was dying, and Tom was hopelessly lost in the Peruvian jungles.

Tom stalked back and forth like a tiger, ready to explode. The guides urged him to sit down, but he couldn't. He had lost his spiritual poise.

But he hadn't forgotten how to pray. As he prayed, relief came and his mind was suddenly filled with various promises from the Scripture: "I will never leave you nor forsake you." "Fear thou not; for I am with thee: be not dismayed; for I am thy God." "Come unto me, all ye that labor and are heavy laden, and I will give you rest."

Tom felt as though a warm blanket of peace were being draped around his shivering soul, the fear retreated, and he sensed that someone somewhere must have been praying for him. He was later to learn that at that precise hour, two dear praying

---

Promissory Note

God has not promised an easy way, but peace at the center of the hard way.

—DALE EVANS

P

women at Asbury had been strangely burdened to pray for "young Tom Willey. He must be in danger somewhere."

Tom Willey did make it out of the Peruvian jungles, and eventually won to Christ his father on his deathbed.[1]

Date: _____ _____ _____

Place: _____ _____ _____

Occasion: _____ _____ _____

Thomas Watson

The Puritan Thomas Watson put it this way: *God the Son is called the Prince of Peace. He came into the world with a song of peace: "On earth peace. . . ." He went out of the world with a legacy of peace, "Peace I leave with you, My peace I give unto you." Christ's earnest prayer was for peace; He prayed that His people might be one. Christ not only prayed for peace, but bled for peace: "Having made peace through the blood of His cross." He died not only to make peace between God and man, but between man and man. Christ suffered on the cross, that He might cement Christians together with His blood; as He prayed for peace, so He paid for peace.*[2]

Date: _____ _____ _____

Place: _____ _____ _____

Occasion: _____ _____ _____

Like a Cyclone

F. B. Meyer describes the Christ-life as: *A rest which is full of work, but like the cyclone, all the atoms of which revolve in turbulent motion around the central cavity of rest, so do all the activities of God revolve around His deepest heart which is tranquil and serene. And so it is possible, if you and I learn the lesson amid anxiety and sorrow and trial and pressure of work, always to carry a heart so peaceful, so still, so serene as to be like the depth of the Atlantic which is not disturbed by the turbulent winds that sweep its surface.*[3]

Date: _____ _____ _____

Place: _____ _____ _____

Occasion: _____ _____ _____

An Old Poem

> *In the center of the whirlpool, while the waters rush around,*
> *There's a space of perfect stillness, though with turmoil it is bound;*
> *All is calm, and all is quiet, scarcely e'en a sense of sound.*
> *So with us—despite the conflict—when in Christ His peace is found.*[4]

---

[1] Jerry Ballard, *Never Say Can't* (Carol Stream, IL: Creation House, 1971), 56–58.
[2] Thomas Watson, *Gleanings From Thomas Watson* (Morgan, PA: Soli Deo Gloria Publications, 1995), 86.
[3] F. B. Meyer, *The Christ Life for Your Life* (Chicago: Moody Press, n.d.), 115–116.
[4] Mrs. Charles E. Cowman *Springs in the Valley* (Los Angeles: Cowman Publications, Inc., 1939), 148.

Date: _____   _____   _____
Place: _____   _____   _____
Occasion: _____   _____   _____

Frozen in Ice

In 1680, after soldiers had dragged away her husband, William, because of his outspoken preaching, Marion Veitch said: *It bred some new trouble and fear to my spirit; but He was graciously pleased to set home that word 'He does all things well; Trust in the Lord and fear not what man can do'; which brought peace to me in such a measure that I was made to wonder; for all the time the officers were in the house He supported me so that I was not in the least discouraged before them.*

Shortly afterward news arrived that William was to be hanged. Marion rode horseback through a blinding January snowstorm to Morpeth jail, arriving at midnight. At daybreak, she was given a few moments with her husband, "then I went to a friend's house and wept my fill." That day, prosecutor Thomas Bell announced, "Veitch will hang tomorrow as he deserves."

But that evening, Mr. Bell tarried at a friend's house, drinking and talking until past ten. The night was dark and cold when he left for home. He never arrived. Two days later, his body was found in the river, frozen up to his arms in a solid block of ice.

William Veitch was released, and he and Marion lived to ripe old age, passing their godly heritage on to their children and grandchildren.

The Lord's peace had, as usual, been followed by His providence.[1]

Date: _____   _____   _____
Place: _____   _____   _____
Occasion: _____   _____   _____

P

The Good War

In his oral history of World War II, *The Good War*, author/historian Studs Terkel related the experience of David Milton who was an eighteen-year-old merchant seaman aboard ship in 1942. Milton told of one time when his ship was transporting Sherman tanks across to Europe. *In the middle of the Atlantic, these tanks broke loose in a big storm. They were Sherman tanks, twenty, thirty tons. As the ship would roll, these tanks would just slide through the hole and bang up against the bulkhead. Then they'd roll the other way, just shaking the ship apart. So we pulled out of the convoy. We headed into the sea, while the deck seaman went down below to secure those tanks. They were riding them like cowboys, trying to hook cables through. Finally, they got the tanks lashed down. . . .*[2]

---

[1] G. M. Alexander, *Changes for the Better* (Yorks, England: Zoar Publications, 1976), 7–9.
[2] Studs Terkel, *The Good War: An Oral History of World War II* (New York, NY: Pantheon, 1984), 104.

The great danger to Milton's ship came, not from the storm on the outside, but by the disturbance on the inside. We can handle the stresses without only when we are battened down within.

Date: _____   _____   _____

Place: _____   _____   _____

Occasion: _____   _____   _____

Master, the Tempest Is Raging

President James A. Garfield had been in office only four months when he was shot in a train station in Washington, D.C., enroute to a class reunion. For weeks as he hovered between life and death, the worried nation discovered an old hymn titled, "Master, the Tempest is Raging." It was sung from coast to coast, over and over, and it gave comfort to America.

The hymn had been written by a woman at the end of her rope. Mary Ann Baker's family had been devastated by a certain disease. Her father and mother had died from it, she herself was bedridden, then her beloved brother fell ill. Hoping to find a cure, he left Chicago and traveled to a warmer climate. For weeks, the telegrams flew back and forth between brother and sister, until the last telegram came, telling her of his death.

"I have always tried to believe on Christ," she said, "and give the Master a consecrated life, but this is more than I can bear. What have I done to deserve this? God does not care for me or mine."

But gradually, the Lord brought relief and understanding into Mary Ann's heart, and she acquiesced to His will. A great peace filled her soul, one she could hardly describe. Shortly afterward, in 1874, a friend, Rev. H. R. Palmer, asked Mary Ann to write a song to go along with a Sunday school lesson from Mark 4:37–39, about Christ calming the sea.

Mary Ann hesitated at first, for she was familiar with the superb fourteenth-century hymn on this text, the words of which were still popular in her day:

> *Fierce was the wild billow, Dark was the night;*
> *Oars labored heavily, Foam glimmered white.*
> *Trembled the mariners, Peril was nigh;*
> *Then saith the God of God, "Peace! It is I!"*

But she very much wanted an opportunity to express the inner peace that God had given her. She had learned that sometimes God stills the frightened disciple even more than He stills the raging elements. And so out of her own experience and from her study of Mark 4 came the words which, a few years later, comforted a nation:

> *Master, the tempest is raging, The billows are tossing high;*
> *The sky is o'ershadowed with blackness, No shelter or help is nigh.*
> *Carest thou not that we perish? How canst thou lie asleep,*
> *When each moment so madly is threat'ning, A grave in the angry deep?*

The winds and the waves shall obey Thy will: Peace, be still.
Whether the wrath of the storm-tossed sea Or demons or men or whatever it be,
No waters can swallow the ship where lies The Master of ocean and earth and skies.
They all shall sweetly obey thy will: Peace, be still; peace, be still.[1]

Date: _____ _____ _____
Place: _____ _____ _____
Occasion: _____ _____ _____

Resting in Peace

Count Nicholas Ludwig von Zinzendorf has been called the "rich young ruler who said YES." Born into one of Europe's leading families, he gave his life to Christ, established a Christian community at his Herrnhut estate, and oversaw the sending of the first missionaries in Protestant history. Then late in life, Zinzendorf married his beloved Anna.

Three years later, his strength ebbed. He pushed himself to finish some writing projects, but he noticed that Anna, too, was growing weaker. On Sunday, May 4, 1760, they attended church together, but with difficulty. Anna returned to her bed. The next day Nicholas was unable to eat much lunch, and he complained of thirst. He visited Anna's sickbed, then fell into bed himself. Speech became difficult, and it grew apparent he and Anna were both dying in rooms next to each other.

About midnight on May 8, Zinzendorf was seized by a coughing spasm, and at nine o'clock the next morning, he said, "I am about to go to the Savior. I am ready. I am resigned to his will, and he is satisfied with me . . . I am ready to go to him. Nothing more stands in my way." His eyes lingered another hour, then they closed. A friend by his bed began praying, "Lord, now lettest thou thy servant depart in peace. The Lord bless thee, and keep thee. . . . The Lord lift up his countenance upon thee and give thee peace." At the word "peace" Zinzendorf stopped breathing.

When Anna was told, she said, "I have the happiest prospect of you all. I will soon be going to him." She watched his burial from her window, then thirteen days later joined him.

Date: _____ _____ _____
Place: _____ _____ _____
Occasion: _____ _____ _____

Persevering in Difficulty

Someone Once Said . . .

- *Great works are performed not by strength but by perseverance.*—Samuel Johnson[2]
- *We can do anything we want as long as we stick to it long enough.*—Helen Keller

---

[1] Ernest K. Emurian, *Living Stories of Famous Hymns* (Grand Rapids, MI: Baker Book House, 1955), ch. 28.
[2] Pat Riley, *The Winner Within* (New York: Berkley Books, 1994), 120.

- *By perseverance the snail reached the ark.*—Charles Spurgeon
- *There is nothing so fatal to character as half-finished tasks.*—David Lloyd George
- *There are very few problems that pure, dogged persistence won't eventually solve.*—Zig Ziglar[1]
- *I can plod. I can persevere in any definite pursuit. To this I owe everything.*—William Carey
- *The optimistic individual perseveres. In the face of routine setbacks, and even of major failures, he persists. When he comes to the wall at work, he keeps going, particularly at the crucial juncture when his competition is also hitting the wall and starting to wilt.*—Martin Seligman[2]
- *The ability to concentrate—to persevere on a course without distraction or diversion—is a power that has enabled men of moderate capability to reach heights of attainment that have eluded the genius. They have no secret formula other than to persevere.*—R. Alec Mackenzie.[3]
- *I have God, and his Word is sure . . . and though the superstition of the heathen were a million times worse than they are, if I were deserted by all, and persecuted by all, yet my hope, fixed on that sure Word, would rise superior to all obstructions. . . . I shall come out of all trials as gold purified by fire.*—William Carey[4]
- *There is no means of escaping from tribulation and sorrow, except to bear them patiently.*—Thomas à Kempis

Date: _____   _____   _____
Place: _____   _____   _____
Occasion: _____   _____   _____

Per-severe

We must never forget that the word persevere comes from the prefix *per*, meaning *through*, coupled with the word *severe*. It means to keep pressing on, trusting God, looking up, doing our duty—even through severe circumstances.[5]

Date: _____   _____   _____
Place: _____   _____   _____
Occasion: _____   _____   _____

Landing Well

Helen Hayes once made a shrewd observation that is as pertinent to business leadership as it is to her own profession of acting. Talent and ability are not enough, she said. "Nothing is any good without endurance."

---

[1] Zig Ziglar, *Raising Positive Kids in a Negative World* (Nashville: Thomas Nelson, 1985), 229.
[2] Martin E. P. Seligman, *Learned Optimism* (New York: Alfred A. Knopf, 1990), 255.
[3] R. Alec Mackenzie, *The Time Trap* (New York: McGraw-Hill Book Company, 1972), 37.
[4] Mary Drewery, *William Carey: A Biography* (Chicago: Moody Press, 1978), 75.
[5] From a sermon by Robert J. Morgan..

During World War II, the Royal Air Force psychologists observed that pilots made the most errors as they flew their planes in for a landing on returning to their base from hazardous raids. The cause, said the analysts, was an "almost irresistible tendency to relax."

The ultimate source of a manager's ability to stay the course must be self-discipline. Only then can he share the boast of a genius like Louis Pasteur: "My greatest strength lies solely in my tenacity."[1]

Date: _____ _____ _____

Place: _____ _____ _____

Occasion: _____ _____ _____

Lacking Perseverance

Author A. J. Cronin was a medical doctor at age thirty-three in London's West End, and, he says, "I wasn't a bad doctor." But he was frustrated by a certain character flaw that inhibited everything that he did. He didn't stick with any one thing for long. He lacked perseverance.

One day he developed indigestion and at length consulted a colleague who diagnosed gastric ulcers and, to Cronin's shock, prescribed six months complete rest in the country on a milk diet.

Cronin retreated to a small farmhouse near the village of Tarbert in the Scottish Highlands. After a week of forced idleness, Cronin felt himself going crazy, bored, and reduced to feeding chickens and learning the names of cattle. Casting round for something to do, he recalled that for years he had considered being a writer.

> **Ever-New Beginnings**
>
> *The perseverance of the saints consists in ever new beginnings.*
>
> —ALEXANDER WHYTE

"By heavens!" Cronin said to himself, "This is my opportunity. Gastric ulcer or no gastric ulcer, I will write a novel." Going straight into the village, he bought himself two dozen tablets of paper. Upstairs in his cold, clean bedroom, he sat at a small table and tried to think of something to write. After three hours, the page was still blank, but eventually he began to write a few sentences.

For three months, he wrote down sentences and wadded up discarded sheets of paper. Finally he sent a batch of material to his secretary in London who typed and returned it. Reading it over, Cronin was appalled. It was utter nonsense, and he decided to abandon the whole thing. He abruptly bundled up the papers, went out, threw them in the ash can, and went for a walk in the drizzling rain.

Halfway down the shoreline of the lake, he came to old Angus, the farmer, patiently and laboriously ditching a patch of heath. As the two men talked, Cronin told the farmer of his decision to abandon writing. The old man was silent a long while before speaking.

"No doubt you're the one that's right, doctor, and I'm the one that's wrong. My father ditched this bog all his days and never made a pasture. I've dug it all my

---

[1] Mortimer R. Feinberg and Aaron Levenstein, "Building Endurance," *The Wall Street Journal on Management.*

days and I've never made a pasture. But pasture or no pasture, I can not help but dig. For my father knew and I know that if you only dig enough a pasture can be made here."

Cronin, understanding the old man's words, tramped back to the farm, drenched and cold, and he picked up the soggy bundle from the ash can. He dried the pages at the kitchen oven, then flung it onto the table and began to work with a kind of frantic desperation. *I would not be beaten, I would not give in. I wrote harder than ever. At last, toward the end of the third month, I wrote "finis." I had created a book.*

He sent his manuscript to a publisher at random and promptly forgot about it.

On the last day of his stay, Cronin went around the village to say good-bye to those who had befriended him. Entering the post office, he was handed a telegram—an urgent invitation to meet the publisher. His novel, *Hatter's Castle,* was chosen by the Book Society, dramatized and serialized, translated into nineteen languages, bought by Hollywood, and went on to sell millions of copies.

I had altered my life radically, beyond my wildest dreams. And all because of a timely lesson in the grace of perseverance.[1]

Date: _____ _____ _____
Place: _____ _____ _____
Occasion: _____ _____ _____

Truman and Korea

Having successfully driven Communists from the south of Korea, President Harry Truman decided to press beyond the 38th parallel and liberate the entire peninsula, calculating that the Chinese wouldn't intervene. But on the day after Thanksgiving in 1950, China launched a furious counterattack, sending over a quarter-million troops against American forces. As Truman gathered his advisors at the White House, the mood was silent and grim. The president began to speak, and suddenly his mouth drew tight, his cheeks flushed. It appeared to the men that Truman would sob. But when he spoke again, his voice was strangely calm and quiet. He said, "This is the worst situation we have had yet. We'll just have to meet it as we've met all the rest . . . Let's go ahead now and do our jobs as best we can."[2]

Date: _____ _____ _____
Place: _____ _____ _____
Occasion: _____ _____ _____

His Secret

In a 1992 *Reader's Digest* article titled "The Ultimate Key to Success," Suzanne Chazin wrote:

---

[1] A. J. Cronin, "The Turning Point of My Career," *Getting the Most out of Life,* (Pleasantville, NY: The Reader's Digest Association, Inc., 1946), 1–6.
[2] David McCullough, *Truman* (New York: Simon & Schuster, 1992), 816.

Every day, a fatherless boy gazed at the fence separating his family's ramshackle cabin from the Glen Lakes Country Club golf course on the outskirts of Dallas. What chance did a poor Chicano boy with a seventh-grade education have of being welcomed into that world?

Yet the boy was determined. First, he gained entrance to the grounds as a gardener. Then he began caddying and playing a few holes at dusk. He honed his putting skills by hitting balls with a soda bottle wrapped in adhesive tape.

Today no fence keeps Lee Trevino, two-time U.S. Open winner, from being welcomed into any country club in the nation.

Sure, Trevino had talent. But talent isn't what kept him from quitting after he placed an embarrassing fifty-fourth in his first U.S. Open. His secret was perseverance.

Persistent people know they can succeed where smarter and more talented people fail. . . . Successful people understand that no one makes it to the top in a single bound. What truly sets them apart is their willingness to keep putting one step in front of the other—no matter how rough the terrain.[1]

Date:			
Place:			
Occasion:			

The Spider and the King

In the thirteenth century, there was a disagreement between Scottish leaders about which of them should be king. England's King Edward I stepped in and took the honor for himself, stripping Scotland of its crown, its royal regalia, and even the sacred Stone of Scone on which the kings of Scotland had always been crowned. The latter he placed in Westminster Abbey in London.

The outraged Scots secretly crowned Robert Bruce their king, but they seemed no match for the English army. Scottish troops were scattered, living in the mountains, living on eels and salmon and deer, and under constant attack from their enemy. Robert Bruce himself was wounded, and his capture seemed imminent. The English had even captured one of his bloodhounds and were using it to search for him.

After madly careening through the Scottish woods, exhausted, frightened, and bleeding, Bruce suddenly came to a stream. Plunging in, he waded alongside the bank until hoisting himself onto the limb of a tree. There he stayed, and the dog lost the scent.

Bruce spent the ensuing winter hidden away in a hovel in the mountains, keeping himself alive on a bag of old potatoes. One cold, gray afternoon, he felt almost hopeless, spirits badly draining. But he noticed a spider trying to weave a web in the corner of the window. The creature was having a hard time of it, because the wind kept blowing away his threads. Time after time, the spider gave another effort until finally the thread held.

---

[1] Suzanne Chazin, "The Ultimate Key to Success," *Reader's Digest*, April 1992, 21–26.

"I might be that spider," said Bruce. "I, too, have failed. Like those threads, my lines have been broken and blown away. But you have shown me that there is always one more time—a time for one more attempt and, with persistence, a winning one!"

Bruce left the hovel to gather his scattered troops, and by the Spring he had an army that was tougher than ever. Battle after battle raged until their lines finally held and they drove the English out of Scotland.

Ever since that time no one by the name of Bruce, it is said, has ever killed a spider.[1]

Date: _____ _____ _____
Place: _____ _____ _____
Occasion: _____ _____ _____

Holding On

Greg Asimakoupoulos tells of a commuter flight from Portland, Maine, to Boston. The pilot, Henry Dempsey, heard an unusual noise near the rear of the small aircraft. He turned the controls over to his co-pilot and went back to investigate.

As he reached the tail section, the plane hit an air pocket, and Dempsey was tossed against the rear door. He quickly discovered the source of the mysterious noise. The rear door had not been properly latched prior to takeoff, and it flew open. He was instantly sucked out of the jet.

The co-pilot, seeing the red light that indicated an open door, radioed the nearest airport, requesting permission to make an emergency landing. He reported that the pilot had fallen out of the plane, and he requested a helicopter search of that area of the ocean.

After the plane landed, they found Henry Dempsey—holding onto the outdoor ladder of the aircraft. Somehow he had caught the ladder, held on for ten minutes as the plane flew 200 mph at an altitude of 4,000 feet, and then, at landing, kept his head from hitting the runway. It took airport personnel several minutes to pry Dempsey's fingers from the ladder.

"Things in life may feel turbulent," said Asimakoupoulos, "and you may not feel like holding on. But have you considered the alternative?"[2]

Date: _____ _____ _____
Place: _____ _____ _____
Occasion: _____ _____ _____

——— Prayer Before Meals ———

Someone Once Said . . .

• *For the people will not eat until he comes, because he must bless the sacrifice . . .*
—1 Samuel 9:13

---

[1] Louis Untermeyer, *The World's Great Stories* (New York: M. Evans and Company, Inc., 1964), 199–201.
[2] Greg Asimakoupoulos, "Holding On," *Leadership Journal,* Summer 1991, 49.

- *Give us this day our daily bread.*—Matthew 6:11
- *Then He commanded the multitudes to sit down on the grass. And He took the five loaves and the two fish, and looking up to heaven, He blessed and broke and gave the loaves to the disciples, and the disciples gave to the multitudes.*—Matthew 14:19; also see Mark 6:41, John 6:11
- *And He took the seven loaves and the fish and gave thanks, broke them and gave them to His disciples, and the disciples gave to the multitudes.*—Matthew 15:36; also see Mark 8:6–7
- *And while they were eating, He took a loaf [of bread], praised God and gave thanks and asked Him to bless it to their use. [Then] He broke [it] and gave to them. . . .* —Mark 14:22 (Amplified Bible); also see Matthew 26:26 and 1 Corinthians 11:24.
- *Now it came to pass, as He sat at the table with them, that He took bread, blessed and broke it, and gave it to them. Then their eyes were opened and they knew Him, and He vanished from their sight.*—Luke 24:30
- *And as day was about to dawn, Paul implored them all to take food, saying, "Today is the fourteenth day you have waited and continued without food, and eaten nothing. Therefore I urge you to take nourishment, for this is for your survival. . . ." And when he had said these things, he took bread and gave thanks to God in the presence of them all, and when he had broken it he began to eat.*—Acts 27:33–35
- *He who eats, eats to the Lord, for he gives God thanks . . .*—Romans 14:6
- *But if I partake with thanks, why am I evil spoken of for the food over which I give thanks?*—1 Corinthians 10:30

Date: _____   _____   _____
Place: _____   _____   _____
Occasion: _____   _____   _____

Before and After

Missionary Henry Martyn had a habit of praying both before and after meals. One acquaintance later wrote of his first impressions of Martyn. "He seems to be a mild and benevolent enthusiast—a sort of character with which I am always half in love. We had the novelty of grace before and after dinner, all the company standing."

Another acquaintance wrote a letter introducing him to the British ambassador in Persia, saying, ". . . I am satisfied that if ever you see him, you will be pleased with him. He will give you grace before and after dinner, and admonish such of your party as take the Lord's name in vain, but his good sense and great learning will delight you, whilst his constant cheerfulness will add to the hilarity of your party."[1]

Date: _____   _____   _____
Place: _____   _____   _____
Occasion: _____   _____   _____

P

[1] Constance E. Padwick, *Henry Martyn* (Chicago: Moody Press, 1980), 210–212.

Where Did This Come From?

At supper one night, seven-year-old Brad asked why his dad thanked God before eating food that had come from the grocery store. The father picked up a roll and asked, "Where did this come from?"

"From the store," Brad said.

"Where did they get it?"

"I dunno. From the bakery?"

"Where did they get it?"

"They made it."

"From what?" asked the father.

"From flour."

"Where did that come from?"

"From wheat."

"Where did the wheat come from?"

"The farmers."

"And where did the farmer get it?"

"He grew it," said Brad.

"From what?"

"Seed."

"And who made the seed?"

"God, I guess," said Brad.

"And that," said the father, "is why we thank Him."

Date: _____   _____   _____

Place: _____   _____   _____

Occasion: _____   _____   _____

Back of the Loaf

Back of the loaf is the snowy flour,
And back of the flour the mill,
And back of the mill are the wheat and the shower,
And the sun, and the Father's will.[1]

Date: _____   _____   _____

Place: _____   _____   _____

Occasion: _____   _____   _____

Learning to Pray

In his book *Home: Where Life Makes Up Its Mind,* Charles Swindoll says:

Most of us did not learn to pray in church. And we weren't taught it in school, or even in pajamas beside our bed at night. If the truth were known, we've done more praying around the

---

[1] Anonymous.

kitchen table than anywhere else on earth. From our earliest years we've been programmed: if you don't pray, you don't eat. It started with Pablum in the high chair, and it continues through porterhouse at the restaurant. Right? Like passing the salt or doing the dishes, a meal is incomplete without it.

Swindoll goes on to offer several suggestions for saying grace before meals, including:

- *Think before you pray. What's on the table? Call the food and drink by name. "Thank you, Lord, for the hot chicken-and-rice casserole in front of us. Thank you for the cold lemonade."*
- *Involve others in prayer: Try some sentence prayers around the table.*
- *Sing your family blessing.*
- *Keep it brief, please.*
- *Occasionally pray after the meal.*[1]

Date: _____ _____ _____
Place: _____ _____ _____
Occasion: _____ _____ _____

Ungrateful Beggars

According to *Our Daily Bread*, when King Alfonso XII of Spain learned that the attendants of his court were neglecting to pray before eating, he determined to teach them a lesson. A huge banquet was prepared, and all the king's guests plowed in, none of them pausing to give thanks to God. But by pre-arrangement, a filthy beggar wandered into the banquet hall, seated himself at the head table, and chowed down.

The guests waited for the guards to seize the man, but, to their amazement, he continued gobbling up the food without hindrance. Then the beggar wiped his mouth, rose and stalked out without a word.

Someone near the king said, "What a despicable fellow! He didn't even say 'thank you.'"

Rising, King Alfonso said to them all: "Do you realize that you've been bolder and more ungrateful than that beggar? Every day you sit down at a table abundantly supplied by your Heavenly Father, yet you neither ask His blessing nor express your gratitude!"

It was a lesson none of them ever forgot.[2]

Date: _____ _____ _____
Place: _____ _____ _____
Occasion: _____ _____ _____

[1] Charles R. Swindoll, *Home: Where Life Makes Up Its Mind* (Portland, Oregon: Multanomah Press, 1979).
[2] From *Our Daily Bread*.

God's Provision

Rev. and Mrs. G. Christian Weiss lived entirely by faith when they were engaged in home missionary work in northern Minnesota. One winter, when the snows were unusually thick and their supplies unusually thin, Mrs. Weiss set a bowl of boiled potatoes on the table.

"This is it!" she said. It was their last provisions.

Without complaining, they bowed their heads and her husband gave thanks, asking God to supply their future needs. Suddenly they heard a sharp knock. At the door was the wife of the manager of the nearby ranger station. After stammering a moment in seeming embarrassment, she said, "We were expecting a crew of workers today, but they phoned to say they weren't able to get through. I had a big dinner prepared for them, and my husband and I will never be able to eat all that food before it spoils. Could you come over and have dinner with us?"

The Weisses quickly consented, and shortly they sat down for a second time that night, but now they said grace over a feast of roast duck, vegetables, pie, and all the trimmings.[1]

Date:			
Place:			
Occasion:			

Food for All

George Mueller, born into a German tax collector's family, was often in trouble. He learned early to steal and gamble and drink. As a teenager, he learned how to stay in expensive hotels, then sneak out without paying the bill. But at length he was caught and jailed. Prison did him little good, for upon release he continued his crime spree until, on a Saturday night in 1825, he met Jesus Christ.

———◆———
Thankful Acceptance

Nothing is to be refused if it is received with thanksgiving.

—1 TIMOTHY 4:14
———◆———

Mueller married and settled down in Bristol, England, growing daily in faith and developing a burden for the homeless children running wild and ragged through the streets. At a public meeting in Bristol on December 9, 1835, he presented a plan for an orphanage. Several contributions came in. Mueller rented Number 6 Wilson Street, and on April 11, 1836, the doors of the orphanage opened. Twenty-six children were immediately taken in. A second house soon opened, then a third.

From the beginning, Mueller refused to ask for funds or even to speak of the ministry's financial needs. He believed in praying earnestly and trusting the Lord to provide. And the Lord *did* provide, though sometimes at the last moment. The best-known story involves a morning when the plates and bowls and cups were set on the tables, but there was no food or milk. The children sat waiting for breakfast while Mueller led in prayer for their daily bread. A knock sounded at the door. It was the baker. "Mr. Mueller," he said, "I couldn't sleep last night. Somehow I felt you didn't have bread for breakfast, so I got up at 2 A.M. and baked some fresh

---
[1] From *Our Daily Bread.*

bread." A second knock sounded. The milkman had broken down right in front of the orphanage, and he wanted to give the children his milk so he could empty his wagon and repair it.

Such stories became the norm for Mueller's work. During the course of his ninety-three years, Mueller housed more than ten thousand orphans, "prayed in" millions of dollars, traveled to scores of countries preaching the Gospel, and recorded fifty thousand answers to prayer.[1]

Date:			
Place:			
Occasion:			

Your Bread Will Be Given You

Sophia's husband John, an ardent soul-winner, spent his short life preaching on the streets, in the parks, in halls and theaters, wherever he could. But at age twenty-seven, he contracted typhoid and quickly died, leaving Sophia Ironside with two small boys and no income.

One of the boys, Harry (later the world-famous pastor of Moody Memorial Church), watched his mother closely. On one occasion, he recalled company coming for supper. Sophia's cupboard was nearly bare, but she scraped together a meal with the little that remained. After the visitors left, she found under one of their plates a ten-dollar bill—a vast sum in those days. With eyes full of tears, she offered thanks to God.

Some time later, the cupboard was again empty. Sophia gathered her two sons to the table for breakfast, but their plates were empty, and there was only water to drink. "We will give thanks, boys," she said. Closing her eyes, she prayed, quoting Isaiah 33:16, "Father, Thou hast promised in Thy Word, 'Your bread shall be given you, and your water shall be sure.' We have the water, and we thank Thee for it. And now, we trust Thee for the bread, or for that which will take its place."

Just as she finished praying, the doorbell rang, and the boys ran to the door to find a man there. "Mrs. Ironside," he said, "I feel very bad. We have been owing you for months for that dress you made for my wife. We've had no money to pay you. But just now we're harvesting our potatoes, and we wondered if you would take a bushel or two on account of the old bill."

"Indeed, I'll be glad to," replied Sophia.

In a few minutes, the potatoes were sizzling in the frying pan, and the boys had answered prayer for breakfast.

Date:			
Place:			
Occasion:			

---

[1]Robert J. Morgan, *On This Day* (Nashville: Thomas Nelson Publishers, 1997), April 11th.

Never Again

Charles Colson, former special assistant to President Richard Nixon, went to prison for his role in the Watergate scandal and was converted to Christ through reading C. S. Lewis' *Mere Christianity.*

He wrote of his conversion in *Born Again,* a book that was launched with a backbreaking tour that ended up in California. Arriving late at his hotel, he and his friend Fred Denne went to the coffee shop for a snack. The room had a Spanish motif; red tile on the floor, wrought iron tables and chairs. A waitress in a pink uniform waited on them. The men noticed she looked like a young starlet, blondish hair and pleasant-faced.

"Two cheese omelets, one milk, and one iced tea," said Fred.

After she left, the two men reviewed the next day's schedule a few minutes, then decided to ask the Lord's blessings on their anticipated meal. They bowed their heads, and, as blessings go, it was fairly long. When they raised their heads, the waitress was standing nearby, omelets in hand.

"Hey," she said loudly, "were you guys praying?" Everyone in the small room turned to look at them.

"Yes, we were," said Colson.

"Hey, that's neat," said the waitress. "I've never seen anybody do that in here before. Are you preachers?"

They said no, but she persisted in asking questions. Then she said, "I'm a Christian. At least I was once."

"What happened?" the men asked.

"I accepted Jesus as my Savior at a rally when I was a teenager. Then I went to live in Hawaii. Well, I just lost interest, I guess. Forgot about it."

"I don't think you lost it," Colson said gently. "You just put it aside for a while."

The waitress seemed thoughtful. "It's funny, but the moment I saw you guys praying I felt excited all over again."

They talked to her at some length about returning to the Lord, about the prodigal son, and about the Lord's love and forgiveness.

Later during their stay at the hotel they saw her again. "Hey, you guys," she shouted. She told them she had already called a Christian friend and was joining a Bible study the next day. "And I'm going to find a church, too. I've come back."

Colson later wrote, "Until that night, I had felt awkward at times praying over meals in crowded restaurants. Never again."[1]

Date:		
Place:		
Occasion:		

I Wasn't Addressing You

There is a story that when Bill Moyers was a special assistant to President Lyndon B. Johnson, he was asked to say grace before a meal in the family quarters

---

[1] Charles W. Colson, *Life Sentence* (Minneapolis: World Wide, 1979), 105–106.

of the White House. As Moyers began praying softly, the President interrupted him with "Speak up, Bill! Speak up!" The former Baptist minister from east Texas stopped in mid-sentence and without looking up replied steadily, "I wasn't addressing you, Mr. President."

Date: _____ _____ _____
Place: _____ _____ _____
Occasion: _____ _____ _____

Hello . . .

Hello. This is Emily. I'm fine, how are you? Thanks for the sky and birds and stuff.
Actually I'm having a pretty good week.
And thanks for the mashed potatoes, but not for the lima beans.
I thank you really much for the meatloaf.
And thanks for the chairs, and the tables, and the doors, and the couch and the television and the walls and the roof and the bed and the bathroom and the towels and the grass and the clouds and the street and . . .
. . . Take care. Amen, from Emily.—Prayer of a five-year-old, reported by Robert Fulghum[1]

Date: _____ _____ _____
Place: _____ _____ _____
Occasion: _____ _____ _____

What He Feeds Me . . .

Missionary Nathan Snow said while trying to adjust to the rather curious food on his Asian mission field: *Where He leads me, I will follow. What He feeds me, I will swallow.*

Date: _____ _____ _____
Place: _____ _____ _____
Occasion: _____ _____ _____

And Give Us This Day

• *. . . and give us our daily low calorie, high protein, vitamin-enriched bread.*

Date: _____ _____ _____
Place: _____ _____ _____
Occasion: _____ _____ _____

P

---

[1] Robert Fulghum, *Uh-Oh* (New York: Villard Books, 1991), 140–141.

Prayer

Someone Once Said . . .

- *It is a good thing to let prayer be the first business of the morning and the last in the evening.*—Martin Luther, in a forty-page letter to his barber who had asked him about the Christian life
- *Prayer is the key to the morning and the bolt of the evening.*—Anonymous
- *A day hemmed in prayer is less likely to come unraveled.*—Anonymous
- *The one concern of the devil is to keep Christians from praying. He fears nothing from prayerless studies, prayerless work, prayerless religion. He laughs at our toil, mocks at our wisdom, but trembles when we pray.*—Samuel Chadwick[1]
- *Prayer is a mighty instrument, not for getting man's will done in Heaven, but for getting God's will done on earth.*—Robert Law
- *I never prayed sincerely for anything but it came, at some time . . . somehow, in some shape.*—Adoniram Judson[2]
- *Prayer delights God's ear, it melts His heart, it opens His hand: God cannot deny a praying soul.*—Thomas Watson[3]
- *I must talk to Father about this.*—Billy Bray
- *Prayer bathes the soul in an atmosphere of the divine presence.*—Charles Finney[4]
- *When life knocks you to your knees—well, that's the best position in which to pray, isn't it?*—Ethel Barrymore
- *Daniel would rather spend a night with the lions than miss a day in prayer.*—Anonymous

Date: _____   _____   _____

Place: _____   _____   _____

Occasion: _____   _____   _____

When You Don't Feel Like Praying

- *When thou feelest most indisposed to pray, yield not to it. But strive and endeavor to pray even when thou thinkest thou canst not pray.*—an old divine[5]
- *Pray when you feel like it, for it is a sin to neglect such an opportunity. Pray when you don't feel like it, for it is dangerous to remain in such a condition.*—quoted by Ruth Bell Graham
- *It is a good thing to let prayer be the first business in the morning and the last in the evening. Guard yourself against such false and deceitful thoughts that keep whispering: Wait a while. In an hour or so I will pray. I must first finish this or that. Thinking such thoughts we get away from prayer into other things that will hold us and involve us till*

---

[1] Cameron V. Thompson, *Master Secrets of Prayer* (Lincoln, Nebraska: Back to the Bible, 1959), 8.

[2] Thompson, *Master Secrets of Prayer*, 8.

[3] Thomas Watson, *Gleanings From Thomas Watson* (Morgan, PA: Soli Deo Gloria Publications, 1995), 99.

[4] Charles Finney, *Prevailing Prayer* (Grand Rapids, MI: Kregel, 1965), 45.

[5] J. Oswald Sanders, *Effective Prayer* (Chicago: Moody Press, 1969), 9.

the prayer of the day comes to naught.—Martin Luther, in a forty-page letter to his barber, Peter Beskendorf, who had asked, "Dr. Luther, how do you pray?"

Date: _____ _____ _____
Place: _____ _____ _____
Occasion: _____ _____ _____

Who Prays?

Newsweek Magazine devoted its cover-story on January 6, 1992, to the subject of prayer, saying, "This week, if you believe in all the opinion surveys, more of us will pray than will go to work, or exercise, or have sexual relations. According to the recent studies at NORC, a research center, by Andrew M. Greeley, the sociologist-novelist-priest, more than three quarters (78 percent) of all Americans pray at least once a week; more than half (57 percent) report praying at least once a day. Indeed, Greeley finds that even among the 13 percent of Americans who are atheists or agnostics, nearly one in five still prays daily. . . .

"Indeed, the current edition of *Books in Print* lists nearly two thousand titles on prayer, meditations, and techniques for spiritual growth—more than three times the number devoted to sexual intimacy and how to achieve it."

The article goes on to talk about the benefits that are experienced by couples who pray together in marriage, saying, "As some young couples have found, praying together is the tie that really binds. . . . Greeley's surveys show that spouses who pray together report greater marital satisfaction than those who don't, and that frequent sex coupled with frequent prayer make for the most satisfying marriages."[1]

Date: _____ _____ _____
Place: _____ _____ _____
Occasion: _____ _____ _____

P

What We Pray For

According to a Yankelovich Poll reported in *USA Today* commissioned for the Lutheran Brotherhood, nine out of ten adults in America say they pray. What do they pray for most often?

- 98%—Our own families
- 81%—World's Children
- 77%—World Peace
- 69%—Co-workers

Date: _____ _____ _____
Place: _____ _____ _____
Occasion: _____ _____ _____

---

[1] Kenneth L. Woodward, "Talking to God," *Newsweek,* January 6, 1992, 39–42.

How John Hyde Learned to Pray

One translation of Isaiah 62:6–7 says, "They must remind the Lord of his promises . . . They must give him no rest until he restores Jerusalem."

We should remind God of his promises and give him no rest until he answers. That is a passage that taught John (Praying) Hyde to pray with persistence. Hyde grew up in Carthage, Illinois, in a minister's home. At McCormick Theological Seminary, he committed himself to overseas evangelism, and following graduation he went to India. His itinerant ministry took him from village to village, but his preaching produced few converts until he discovered the truth of Isaiah 62:6–7, and took these words literally.

At the beginning of 1908, he prayed to win at least one soul to Christ every day. By December 31, he had recorded over four hundred converts. The following year, the Lord laid two souls per day on his heart, and his prayer was again answered. The next year he prayed for four souls daily with similar results.

Once, stopping at a cottage for water, Praying Hyde pleaded with God for ten souls. He presented the Gospel to the family, and by the end of his visit all nine members of the family had been saved. But what of number ten? Suddenly a nephew who had been playing outside ran into the room and was promptly converted.

Date: _____ _____ _____
Place: _____ _____ _____
Occasion: _____ _____ _____

How Oral Roberts Learned to Pray

Evangelist Oral Roberts says that his mother's advice is the best he has ever heard on the subject of prayer. He was very ill, a seventeen-year-old invalid, when his mother said, "Oral, you must give your life to God. Only God can help you now. And you must pray."

"I don't know how to pray," the young man responded.

"Oral, you don't have to know how to pray. Just talk to God out of your heart. Tell him what you feel inside. That's what it takes to pray."

Oral Roberts later said, "After all these years I have not been able to improve on my mother's advice: Just talk to God out of your heart. I can only add: Talk to God as a person. . . . Do not think of him as being hundreds of miles away, although you know he is everywhere at the same time . . . To think of Christ as a person makes it easy for you to see him in your mind's eye. You see him walking the hills of Judea. You see him beside the waters of the Sea of Galilee. You see him standing on the hillside, preaching to the people. You see him laying his hands on the sick. You see him blessing little children. You see him on the cross. You see him rising from the dead. You see him ascending to Heaven. And you see him sitting on God's right side. You can see the Lord in your mind's eye. And so, when you pray, pray to God as a person."[1]

---

[1] Oral Roberts, *Best Times and Best Ways to Pray* (Tulsa: Oral Roberts Evangelistic Association, n.d.), 9–11.

Date:			
Place:			
Occasion:			

The Prayer of Faith

I once spent the night in a crumbling hotel in Porto Alegre, Brazil. A friend and I ascended to our room, high in the building, in a tiny, creaking elevator. From our window I saw slums spreading out far beneath me, and I felt uneasy. That evening I prayed, "Lord, please save me from any danger of fire. You can see we're at the top of a dilapidated hotel, which is nothing but a firetrap. There isn't a fire station near, and I can't see any fire escapes outside the building. Lord, you know that this building would go up in flames in a second, and at this very moment it is probably full of people falling asleep with Marlboros in their mouths . . ."

By the time I finished praying, I was a nervous wreck, and I hardly slept a wink all night. The next morning, as I evaluated my evening, I realized that my bedtime prayer had focused on my negative feelings rather than on God's assurances and promises, and learned an important truth: Unless we plead in faith, our prayers can do more harm than good.[1]

Date:			
Place:			
Occasion:			

The 100-Year Prayer Meeting

In 1722, Count Nicholas Ludwig von Zinzendorf, troubled by the suffering of Christian exiles from Bohemia and Moravia, allowed them to establish a community on his estate in Germany. The center became known as Herrnhut, meaning "Under the Lord's Watch." It grew quickly, and so did its appreciation for the power of prayer.

On August 27, 1727, twenty-four men and twenty-four women covenanted to spend an hour each day in scheduled prayer, praying in sequence around the clock. Soon others joined the prayer chain. More signed on, then others still. Days passed, then months. Unceasing prayer rose to God twenty-four-hours a day as someone—at least one—was engaged in intercessory prayer each hour of every day. The intercessors met weekly for encouragement and to read letters and messages from their brothers in different places, giving them specific needs to pray about. A decade passed, the prayer chain continuing nonstop. Then another decade. It was a prayer meeting that lasted over one hundred years.

Undoubtedly this prayer chain helped birth Protestant missions. Six months into it, Zinzendorf, twenty-seven, suggested the possibility of attempting to reach others for Christ in the West Indies, Greenland, Turkey, and Lapland. Twenty-six Moravians

P

---

[1] From a sermon by the author.

stepped forward the next day to volunteer. The first missionaries, Leonard Dober and David Nitschmann, were commissioned during an unforgettable service on August 18, 1732, during which one hundred hymns were sung. The two men reached the West Indies in December of that year, beginning the "Golden Decade" of Moravian Missions, 1732–1742. During the first two years, twenty-two missionaries perished and two more were imprisoned, but others took their places. In all, seventy Moravian missionaries flowed from the six hundred inhabitants of Herrnhut, a feat unparalleled in missionary history.

By the time William Carey became the "Father of Modern Missions" over three hundred Moravian missionaries had already gone to the ends of the earth. And that's not all. The Moravian fervor sparked the conversions of John and Charles Wesley and indirectly ignited the Great Awakening that swept through Europe and America, sweeping thousands into the kingdom. The prayer meeting lasted one hundred years. The results will last for eternity.[1]

Date: _____ _____ _____

Place: _____ _____ _____

Occasion: _____ _____ _____

Prayer, Unanswered

The following was an unpublished poem of hymn-writer Fanny Crosby, recently discovered by Donald Hustad. The manuscript carried several notations, including the initials "M. S." and the name "H. P. Main." There is also a question, "Is this O.K.?" signed by "I.A.S."—Ira Allan Sankey—and the further notes "O.K." and "This is fine." At the upper right the paper is embossed with the name "HAMILTON." The poem is entitled, "For What His Love Denies."

God does not give me all I ask,
Nor answer as I pray;
But, O, my cup is brimming o'er
With blessings day by day.
How oft the joy I thought withheld
Delights my longing eyes,
And so I thank Him from my heart
For what His love denies.

Sometimes I miss a treasured link
In friendship's hallowed chain,
And yet His smile is my reward
For every throb of pain.
I look beyond, where purer joys
Delight my longing eyes;
And so I thank Him from my heart
For what His love denies.

[1] Robert J. Morgan, *On This Day* (Nashville: Thomas Nelson Publishers, 1997), August 27.

How tenderly He leadeth me
When earthly hopes are dim;
And when I falter by the way,
He bids me lean on Him.
He lifts my soul above the clouds
Where friendship never dies;
And so I thank Him from my heart
For what His love denies.
—Fanny Crosby, Jan. 6, 1899[1]

Date: _____ _____ _____
Place: _____ _____ _____
Occasion: _____ _____ _____

God's Four Answers

In talking with people who are concerned because God doesn't seem to be answering their prayers, Pastor Bill Hybels uses a little outline he borrowed from a pastor friend of his:

- If the request is wrong, God says: *No*
- If the timing is wrong, God says: *Slow*
- If you are wrong, God says: *Grow*
- But if the request is right, the timing is right, and you are right, God says: *Go!*[2]

Date: _____ _____ _____
Place: _____ _____ _____
Occasion: _____ _____ _____

P

Awakened to Pray

His nightmares began each day when he awoke.

James Stegalls was nineteen. He was in Vietnam. Though he carried a small Gideon New Testament in his shirt pocket, he couldn't bring himself to read it. His buddies were cut down around him, terror was building within him, and God seemed far away. His twentieth birthday passed, then his twenty-first. At last, he felt he couldn't go on.

On February 26, 1968, he prayed for it all to end, and his heart told him he would die before dusk. Sure enough, his base came under attack that day and Jim heard a rocket coming straight toward him. Three seconds to live, he told himself, then two, then . . .

---

[1] *Fanny Crosby Speaks Again,* ed. Dr. Donald P. Hustad (Carol Stream, Ill: Hope Publishing Co., 1977), 93.
[2] Bill Hybels, *Too Busy Not To Pray* (Downers Grove, IL: InterVarsity Press, 1988), 74.

A friend shoved him into a grease pit, and he waited for the rocket to explode, but there was only a surreal silence. The fuse malfunctioned.

For five hours James knelt in that pit, and finally his quivering hand reached into his shirt pocket and took out his Testament. Beginning with Matthew, he continued through the first 18 chapters.

"When I read Matthew 18:19–20," he said, "I somehow knew things would be all right."

Long after Jim returned home, as he visited his wife's grandmother, Mrs. Harris, she told him a night years before when she had awakened in terror. Knowing Jim was in Vietnam, she had sensed he was in trouble. She began praying for God to spare his life. Unable to kneel because of arthritis, she lay prone on the floor, praying and reading her Bible all night.

Just before dawn she read Matthew 18:19–20: *If two of you agree down here on earth concerning anything you ask, my Father in heaven will do it for you. For where two or three gather together because they are mine, I am there among them.*

She immediately called her Sunday school teacher, who got out of bed and went to Mrs. Harris' house where together they claimed the Lord's promise as they prayed for Jim until reassured by God's peace.

Having told Jim the story, Mrs. Harris opened her Bible to show him where she had marked the passage.

In the margin were the words: *Jim, February 26, 1968.*[1]

Date:			
Place:			
Occasion:			

Urgent Impression

Archibald Gracie relished his swim on April 14, 1912. The ship's pool was a "six-foot tank of salt water, heated to a refreshing temperature. In no swimming bath had I ever enjoyed such pleasure before." But his account went on to say, "How near it was to being my last plunge. Before dawn of another day I would be swimming for my life in mid-ocean in a temperature of 28 degrees!"

After his swim that Sunday night aboard ship, Colonel Archibald Gracie retired to his cabin and fell asleep, only to be awakened by "a sudden shock and noise." Dressing quickly, he ascended to the deck and learned the ship had collided with an iceberg.

During the same moments in New York, his wife's sleep was also disturbed. Seized by sudden anxiety, she sank to her knees holding her prayerbook, "which by chance opened to the prayer 'For Those At Sea.'" She prayed earnestly until about 5 A.M. when the burden lifted. She rested quietly until eight when her sister "came

---

Hand in Hand

To clasp hands in prayer is the beginning of an uprising against the disorder in the world.

—KARL BARTH

---

[1] Jim L. Stegall, "Hardly a Coincidence," *Changed Lives: USA Testimonies.*

softly to the door, newspaper in hand, to gently break the tragic news that the *Titanic* had sunk."

What had happened meantime to her husband? *I was in a whirlpool, swirling round and round, as I still tried to cling to the railing as the ship plunged to the depths below. Down, down, I went: it seemed a great distance . . . (Ascending back to the surface) I could see no Titanic. She had entirely disappeared beneath the surface of the ocean without a sign of any wave. A thin light-gray smoky vapor hung like a pall a few feet above the sea. There arose the most horrible sounds ever heard by mortal man, the agonizing cries of death from over a thousand throats . . .*

Col. Archibald Gracie later wrote: *I know of no recorded instance of Providential deliverance,* he wrote, *more directly attributable to . . . prayer.*[1]

Date: _____ _____ _____
Place: _____ _____ _____
Occasion: _____ _____ _____

A Mother's Impression

On a day I shall never forget, recalled Hudson Taylor, the famous missionary to China, *when I was about fifteen years of age, because my mother was absent from home, I had a holiday, and in the afternoon looked through my father's library to find some book with which to while away the hours. I turned over a basket of pamphlets, and selected from among them a Gospel tract which looked interesting. I sat down to read the little book in an utterly unconcerned state of mind.*

Little did I know at the time what was going on in the heart of my mother, eighty miles away. She rose from dinner with an intense yearning for the conversion of her boy, and she went to her room and turned the key in the door, resolved not to leave until her prayers were answered. Hour after hour did she plead for me, until at length she was constrained to praise God for that which His Spirit taught her had been accomplished.

In the meantime I had taken up this little tract, and while reading was struck with the sentence, "The finished work of Christ." The thought passed through my mind, "Why does the author use this expression?" Immediately the words "It is finished" came to mind. What was finished? I replied, "A full and perfect atonement for sin: Christ died for our sins." As light flashed into my soul by the Spirit, that there was nothing to be done but to fall down on one's knees, and accepting this Savior and His salvation, to praise Him forever.

When mother came home a fortnight later, I was the first to meet her at the door to tell her I had glad news. I can almost feel her arms around my neck, as she said, "I know, my boy; I have been rejoicing for a fortnight."

You will agree with me that it would be strange indeed if I were not a believer in the power of prayer.

Date: _____ _____ _____
Place: _____ _____ _____
Occasion: _____ _____ _____

[1] Colonel Archibald Gracie, *Titanic: A Survivor's Story* (Gloucestershire, the United Kingdom, 1985).

Praying for Jabez

In his nineteenth-century book, *The Holy Spirit in Missions,* A. J. Gordon relates a powerful story from an earlier book by Rev. Dr. Cox on the history of missionary work by English Baptists. It involves England's first missionary, William Carey, who sailed for India in 1793.

It was while Carey was almost alone in India, and greatly distressed for lack of another missionary, that the annual meeting of the Baptist Missionary Society was held in London. During the session, Carey's friends Andrew Fuller and John Ryland had preached. In his discourse, Ryland mentioned that two of Carey's sons, Felix and William, were devoted to the Lord and to the work of missions. "But," he said, "there is a third who gives him pain; he is not yet turned to the Lord." Then Ryland's voice failed as he wept from grief and concern. Finally "in a voice which seemed to exhaust a whole soul of feeling" he said, "Brethren, let us send up a united, universal and fervent prayer to God in solemn silence for the conversion of Jabez Carey."

As though the Holy Spirit had suddenly fallen upon the assembly, the whole congregation of two thousand persons pleaded in silent intercession.

The result? One of the first letters afterward received bore news of the conversion of this son who had greatly pained his father by his apparent disregard for Christianity. And the time of his awakening was found to accord almost exactly with the hour of this memorable intercession. Almost immediately, he applied for missionary service, and soon Dr. Carey and the other two sons united in laying hands on the third, ordaining him to ministry.

"I trust," wrote Dr. Carey, "that this will be a matter of everlasting praise. Oh, praise the Lord with me, and let us exalt His name together! To me the Lord has been very gracious. I trust all my children love the Lord; and three out of four are actually engaged in the important work of preaching the Gospel among the heathen."

Date:			
Place:			
Occasion:			

The Options

- *Praying will make you leave off sinning, or sinning will make you leave off praying.*— Charles Haddon Spurgeon

Date:			
Place:			
Occasion:			

"Because You Ask Not"

Evangelist John R. Rice once wrote, "I once imagined I was in Heaven. Walking along with the Angel Gabriel I said, 'Gabe, what is that big building there?'

" 'You'll be disappointed,' he answered. 'I don't think you want to see it.' But I insisted, and he showed me floor after floor of beautiful gifts, all wrapped and ready to be sent.

" 'Gabriel, what are all these?'

"He said, I thought rather sadly, 'We wrapped these things, but people never called for them.' "[1]

Date:			
Place:			
Occasion:			

Coming to a King

Thou art coming to a King
Large petitions with thee bring;
For His grace and power are such
None can ever ask too much.—John Newton

Date:			
Place:			
Occasion:			

Power, Pennies

In his delightful little booklet, *Master Secrets of Prayer,* Cameron V. Thompson has several excellent illustrations, including these two:

- Trams and trolleys and some buses have long poles which reach up and bring electricity and power to the motors from overhead wires. The pole may be within an inch of the wire, yet no power can pass; the bus or trolley stays in the same place. The people inside can sing and shout and preach and hold a great meeting, but when they get out they are still at the same place.
- Our baby Joy set her heart on a certain present. She asked her sisters how many pennies it would take to buy it. Then she prayed for 1,400 pennies. A few days later some friends came by with a jar of money they were saving for us. In it were slightly more than 1,400 pennies.[2]

Date:			
Place:			
Occasion:			

---

[1] John R. Rice, "Go Ahead and Ask!" Moody Magazine, January 1977, 61.
[2] Cameron V. Thompson, *Master Secrets of Prayer* (Lincoln, Nebraska: Back to the Bible, 1959). 33–34, 55–56.

Three Times a Day at 91

Several years ago, Mrs. Flooie Cassel, ninety-one, wrote an article in *Alliance Witness,* describing the various ministries she conducts for the Lord from her room in the nursing home. One was that of prayer.

"Missionaries give me prayer requests which I remember before God's throne three times a day. This practice began a number of years ago at a women's missionary meeting. We had a speaker who talked about tithing our time as well as our money. That evening I knelt and asked the Lord how much time I should spend in prayer. He definitely told me three hours a day. I began spending one hour each morning, afternoon and evening in prayer.

"But then I got very busy with child evangelism classes, giving demonstrations on the use of flannelgraph material, speaking at women's meetings. I began to slip up on my prayer time in the afternoon. Soon I was too ill to teach or speak.

"I had heard a sermon on how Daniel waited twenty-one days to learn something from the Lord. So I began waiting for the Lord to reveal to me why I was no longer able to draw upon 'His supernatural strength for my supernatural tasks,' as Dr. A. B. Simpson so ably expressed it.

"After several nights of waiting on the Lord in prayer, I understood. The Lord said, 'I will not let you teach again until you get back to your three hours a day in prayer.'

"I asked forgiveness for my neglecting prayer and promised, with the help of the Holy Spirit, never to forget this important lesson. Now in my ninety-first year, I still have this ministry of prayer three times a day."[1]

Date:			
Place:			
Occasion:			

City of Everywhere

In Hugh Price Hughes' story, the "City of Everywhere," a man arrived in a city one cold morning. As he got off the train, the station was like any other station with the crowds and redcaps, except that everybody was barefooted. They wore no shoes. He noticed the cab driver was barefooted. "Pardon me," he asked the driver, "I was just wondering why you don't wear shoes. Don't you believe in shoes?"

"Sure we do," said the driver.

"Why don't you wear them?"

"Ah, that's the question," came the reply. "Why don't we wear shoes? Why don't we?"

At the hotel it was the same. The clerk, bell boys, everybody was barefooted. In the coffee shop he noticed a nice-looking fellow at a table opposite him who was also barefooted. He said, "I notice you aren't wearing any shoes. I wonder why? Don't you know about shoes?"

The man replied, "Of course I know about shoes."

---

[1] Flossie Cassel, "Fourscore and Eleven is No Time To Quit," *The Alliance Witness,* March 8, 1978, 10–12.

"Then why don't you wear them?"

"Ah, that's the question. Why don't we? Why don't we?"

After breakfast he walked out on the street in the snow but every person he saw was barefooted. He asked another man about it, and pointed out how shoes protect the feet from cold. The man said, "We know about shoes. See that building yonder? That is a shoe factory. We are proud of that plant and every week we gather there to hear the man in charge tell about shoes and how wonderful they are."

"Then why don't you wear shoes?"

"Ah, that's the question."

Don't we believe in prayer? Don't we know what it could mean in our lives? Then why don't we pray? Ah, that's the question . . . Why don't we?[1]

Date: _____ _____ _____
Place: _____ _____ _____
Occasion: _____ _____ _____

Pride

Someone Once Said . . .

- *Pride is the only disease known to man that makes everyone sick except the one who has it.*—"Uncle" Bud Robinson
- *Some persons are like hens, which no sooner drop their eggs, than they begin to chatter.*—Rev. William Secker[2]
- *The worm of pride is always injurious to celestial plants.*—Rev. William Secker[3]
- *It is out of self-love that all other evil passions spring.*—Alexander Whyte
- *Pride is the ground in which all other sins grow.*—William Barkley
- *I will not say a good man is never proud, but I will say a proud man is never good.*—Rev. William Secker[4]
- *Pride is essentially competitive—is competitive by its very nature—while the other vices are competitive only, so to speak, by accident. Pride gets no pleasure out of having something, only out of having more of it than the next man.*—C. S. Lewis[5]
- *None are so empty as those who are full of themselves.*—Benjamin Whichcote
- *A man wrapped up in himself makes a pretty small package.*—Anonymous
- *An egoist is someone who is always me-deep in conversation.*—Milton Berle
- *An egoist is a man who talks about himself so much that you don't have a chance to talk about yourself.*—Vance Havner
- *Did you notice how we shook that bridge?*—a flea to the elephant he was riding, after crossing an old bridge

---

[1] Charles Allen, *All Things are Possible Through Prayer* (Westwood, NJ: Fleming H. Revell Co., 1963), 52–53.

[2] William Secker, *The Nonsuch Professor In His Meridian Splendor* (Chicago: Fleming H. Revell Co., 1899), 57.

[3] Secker, *The Nonsuch Professor In His Meridian Splendor*, 134,

[4] Secker, *The Nonsuch Professor In His Meridian Splendor*, 135.

[5] C. S. Lewis, *Mere Christianity* (New York: The Macmillan Company, 1958), 95.

Date: _____ _____ _____
Place: _____ _____ _____
Occasion: _____ _____ _____

Magic Johnson

Basketball coach Pat Riley in his book *The Winner Within* tells about the 1980 World Championship Los Angeles Lakers. They won the NBA Championship that year, and they were recognized as the best basketball team in the world. They began their 1980–1981 season considered likely to win back-to-back championships. But within weeks of the season opener, Magic Johnson tore a cartilage in his knee, and he needed a three-month recuperation period. The team and the fans rallied, and the remaining players played their hearts out. They determined to make it through that period without losing their rankings. They were winning seventy percent of their games when the time began to draw near for Magic Johnson to return to action.

As his return grew closer, the publicity surrounding him increased. During time-outs at the games, the public address announcer would always say, "And don't forget to mark your calendars for February 27th. Magic Johnson returns to the lineup of your World Champion Los Angeles Lakers!" During that announcement, the other players would look up and curse. They'd say, "We're winning now. What's so great about February 27th?" As the day approached, fewer and fewer things were written or said about the players who were putting out so much effort. All the media attention was focused on the one player who hadn't been doing a thing. Finally the 27th came, and as they clicked through the turnstiles every one of the 17,500 ticket holders was handed a button that said, "The Magic Is Back!" At least fifty press photographers crowded onto the floor while the players were introduced. Normally only the starters were introduced, and Magic Johnson was going to be on the bench when the game began. But he was nevertheless included in the introductions. At the mention of his name, the arena rocked with a standing ovation. Flashbulbs went off like popcorn. Magic Johnson was like a returning god to the crowd that night.

Meanwhile the other players who had carried the team for three months and who were totally ignored, were seething with jealousy, resentment, anger, and envy. They were so resentful that they barely won the game that night against a bottom-of-the-bucket team, and eventually the morale of the entire team collapsed. The players turned on each other. The coach was fired. And they eventually lost their opening game of the play-offs, having one of the most disastrous records ever.

Riley said, "Because of greed, pettiness, and resentment, we executed one of the fastest falls from grace in NBA history. It was the Disease of Me."[1]

Date: _____ _____ _____
Place: _____ _____ _____
Occasion: _____ _____ _____

---

[1] Pat Riley, *The Winner Within* (New York: Berkley Books, 1994), ch. 2.

Only God Is Great

In 1717 when France's Louis XIV died, his body lay in a golden coffin. He had called himself the "Sun King," and his court was the most magnificent in Europe. To dramatize his greatness, he had given orders that during his funeral the cathedral would be only dimly lighted with only a special candle set above the coffin. As thousands waited in hushed silence, Bishop Massilon began to speak. Then slowly reaching down, he snuffed out the candle, saying, "Only God is great!"

Date: _____ _____ _____
Place: _____ _____ _____
Occasion: _____ _____ _____

On All My Pride

When I survey the wondrous cross,
On which the Prince of glory died,
My richest gain I count but loss,
And pour contempt on all my pride.—Isaac Watts

Date: _____ _____ _____
Place: _____ _____ _____
Occasion: _____ _____ _____

Three Tests

"Pride," says Oswald Sanders, "is a sin of whose presence its victim is least conscious. There are, however, three tests by means of which it can soon be discovered:

- *The test of precedence.* How do we react when another is selected for the assignment we expected, or for the office we coveted? When another is promoted and we are overlooked? When another outshines us in gifts and accomplishments.
- *The test of sincerity.* In our moments of honest self-criticism we will say many things about ourselves, and really mean them. But how do we feel when others, especially our rivals, say exactly the same things about us?
- *The test of criticism.* Does criticism arouse hostility and resentment in our hearts, and cause us to fly into immediate self-justification?[1]

Date: _____ _____ _____
Place: _____ _____ _____
Occasion: _____ _____ _____

P

---

[1]J. Oswald Sanders, *Spiritual Leadership* (Chicago: Moody Press, 1967), 143.

The Great Sin

In *Mere Christianity*, C. S. Lewis writes this about Pride: *There is one vice of which no man in the world is free; which every one in the world loathes when he sees it in someone else; and of which hardly any people, except Christians, ever imagine that they are guilty themselves. I have heard people admit that they are bad-tempered, or that they cannot keep their heads about girls or drink, or even that they are cowards. I do not think I have ever heard anyone who was not a Christian accuse himself of this vice. And at the same time I have very seldom met anyone, who was not a Christian, who showed the slightest mercy to it in others. There is no fault which makes a man more unpopular, and no fault which we are more unconscious of in ourselves. And the more we have it in ourselves the more we dislike it in others.*[1]

Date: _____   _____   _____
Place: _____   _____   _____
Occasion: _____   _____   _____

The Veiled Prophet

When Robert Louis Stevenson arrived in Samoa, he was invited by the head of the Malau Institute for training native pastors to address the students. He willingly consented. His address was based on the Mohammedan story of the veiled prophet. This prophet, a burning and shining light among the teachers of his people, wore a veil over his face because, he said, the glory of his countenance was so great that no one could bear the sight.

But at last the veil grew old and fell into decay. Then the people discovered that he was only an ugly old man trying to hide his own ugliness. Stevenson went on to enforce the need for sincerity on the ground that, however high the truths the teacher taught, however skillfully he might excuse blemishes of character, the time comes when the veil falls away, and a man is seen by people as he really is. It is seen whether beneath the veil is the ugly face of unmortified egotism or the transformed glory of Christlike character.[2]

Date: _____   _____   _____
Place: _____   _____   _____
Occasion: _____   _____   _____

But Jesus . . .

- We take pride in birth and rank, but it's said of Jesus, He was a carpenter's son.
- We take pride in possessions, but it's said of Jesus, "The Son of man hath no place to lay His head."
- We take pride in our respectability, but it's said of Jesus, "Can anything good come out of Nazareth?"

---

[1] Lewis, *Mere Christianity*, 94.
[2] Sanders, *Spiritual Leadership*, 143–144.

- We take pride in our personal appearance, but it's said of Jesus, "He hath no form nor comeliness."
- We take pride in our reputation, but it's said of Jesus, "Behold a man gluttonous and a winebibber."
- We take pride in our friendships, but it's said of Jesus, "He was a friend of publicans and sinners."
- We take pride in our independence, but Jesus gave himself to people and had the woman at the well draw water for him.
- We take pride in our degrees and learning, but Jesus never went to college and it's said of Him, "How knows this man letters having never learned to read?"
- We take pride in our position, but Jesus said, "I am among you as one who serves."
- We take pride in our success, but it's said of Jesus, "His own did not receive Him or believe on Him. He was despised and rejected."
- We take pride in our self-reliance, but it's said of Jesus, "He went down to Nazareth and was subject to His parents."
- We take pride in our abilities, but Jesus said, "I can of mine own self do nothing."
- We take pride in our self-will, but Jesus said, "I seek not my own will but the Father's." And "If thou be willing, remove this cup from me, nevertheless not my will but thine be done."
- We take pride in our intellect, but Jesus said, "As the Father has taught me, I speak these things."
- We take pride in our resentment and justifiable pride, but Jesus said, "Father, forgive them."
- We take pride in our holiness, but it's said of Jesus, "He receiveth sinners and eateth with them."
- We take pride in the fact we're the righteousness of God, but it's said of Jesus, "He who knew no sin became sin on our behalf in order that we might become the righteousness of God in Him."[1]

Date:			
Place:			
Occasion:			

P

Fatal Words

Two ducks and a rather egotistical frog developed a friendship. When their pond dried up, the ducks knew they could easily fly to another location, but what of their friend the frog? Finally they decided to fly with a stick between their two bills, and with the frog hanging onto the stick by his mouth. All went well until a man looked up and saw them in the sky. "What a clever idea," said the man. "I wonder who thought of that?"

"I did," said the frog.

---

[1] Clipping in my files, attributed to Rev. Milton Hubbard.

Date:			
Place:			
Occasion:			

—————————— Profanity ——————————

Someone Once Said . . .

- *What aileth the man so sinfully to swear.*—Chaucer, in *Canterbury Tales*
- *If my mom walked the halls of my high school, she wouldn't believe it.*—Tighe Herren, seventeen, high school junior from Louisville, KY, about profanity at school[1]
- *What is required in the third commandment? The third commandment requireth the holy and reverent use of God's names, titles, attributes, ordinances, Word, and works. What is forbidden in the third commandment? The third commandment forbiddeth all profaning or abusing of anything whereby God maketh himself known.*—The Westminster Shorter Catechism, questions 54 and 55

Date:			
Place:			
Occasion:			

John Bunyan

Profanity has plagued society for as long as people have had tongues in their mouths. John Bunyan, author of *Pilgrim's Progress*, prior to his conversion, was so profane he could hardly speak a word without attaching a curse to it. But one thing cured him. He was standing one day before a shop window, cursing and swearing freely, and a woman passed by. She herself was a "very loose and ungodly wretch," yet she rebuked him, saying that he was "the ungodliest fellow for swearing that ever she heard in all her life," and she further declared that he was "able to spoil all the youth in a whole town, if they but came into his company."

Bunyan later wrote, "I wished with all my heart that I might be a little child again, that my father might learn me to speak without this wicked way of swearing; for, thought I, I am so accustomed to it that it is vain for me to think of a reformation, for I thought it never could be. I knew not how to speak unless I put an oath before and another behind, to make my words have authority."

But the Lord so cleaned up his English language that he wrote the greatest English classic—and the most printed book outside the Bible—ever written: *Pilgrim's Progress*.

Date:			
Place:			
Occasion:			

---

[1] Nanci Hellmich, "Kids Often Cuss for Emphasis," *USA Today,* Jan 20, 1997, sec. D1.

John Newton

As a teenager and as a young man, John Newton was a profane sailor who used such vulgar and filthy obscenities and profanities that even the salty sailors were embarrassed. But then he became a Christian, a clergyman, and a hymnwriter. He not only wrote "Amazing Grace" but this hymn about the very name of the Lord which he previously had profaned day and night:

How sweet the name of Jesus sounds
In a believer's ear!
It soothes his sorrows, heals his wounds,
And drives away his fear.

Jesus, my Shepherd, Brother, Friend,
My Prophet, Priest, and King,
My Lord, my Life, my Way, my End,
Accept the praise I bring.

Till then I would Thy love proclaim
With every fleeting breath;
And may the music of Thy name
Refresh my soul in death.

The same name—Jesus. The same word—God. But now a praise instead of a profanity. He traded his salty tongue in for words seasoned with salt.

Date: _____ _____ _____
Place: _____ _____ _____
Occasion: _____ _____ _____

George Washington

General George Washington issued the following on August 3, 1776: *I am sorry to be informed that the foolish and wicked practice of profane swearing, a vice heretofore little known in an American army, is growing into fashion. I hope that the officers will, by example and influence, endeavor to check it, and that both they and their men will reflect, that we have but little hope of the blessing of heaven in our arms, if we insult Him by our impiety and folly. Added to this it is a vice so mean and low, without any temptation, that every man of sense and character detests and despises it.*

Date: _____ _____ _____
Place: _____ _____ _____
Occasion: _____ _____ _____

Richard Nixon

When transcripts of the famous Watergate tapes were released, Americans were stunned to read of the unrestrained filthiness of language used by President Richard

Nixon and his associates. Nixon's every sentence seemed soiled with both profanities and obscenities of the rawest kind.

It seems all the more ironic, then, to watch videotapes of the televised campaign debate between Nixon and John F. Kennedy on October 13, 1960, when Nixon sanctimoniously criticized the crusty language of Harry Truman. Nixon said: *It makes you realize that whoever is President is going to be a man that all the children of America will either look up to or will look down to. And I can only say that I'm very proud that President Eisenhower restored dignity and decency and, frankly, good language to the conduct of the presidency of the United States. And I only hope that should I win this election, that I could [see] to it that whenever any mother or father talks to his child, he can look at the man in the White House and say: "Well, there is a man who maintains the kind of standards personally that I would want my child to follow."*

Date: _____ _____ _____
Place: _____ _____ _____
Occasion: _____ _____ _____

Branch Rickey

Branch Rickey, a member of Baseball's Hall of Fame and long-time manager of several major league teams, was a Christian. When he had been head of the Brooklyn Dodgers, he was at a meeting negotiating a ballplayer's contract in a deal involving thousands of dollars. Suddenly Rickey threw down his pencil, pushed back his chair, and growled, "The deal's off."

The other men were astonished. "Why?" they asked. "We're coming along well with these negotiations."

"Because," said Rickey, "you've been talking about a friend of mine, and I don't like it."

"But what friend do you mean? I haven't been talking about anyone, let alone a friend of yours."

"Oh, yes, you have," replied Rickey. "You've mentioned him in almost every sentence." And he referred them to their constant profane use of the name of Jesus Christ. The men quickly apologized, stopped their profanity, and the negotiations continued.

Date: _____ _____ _____
Place: _____ _____ _____
Occasion: _____ _____ _____

Harland Sanders

The late Colonel Sanders, founder of Kentucky Fried Chicken, once said that his conversion to Christ cost him half of his vocabulary.

Date: _____ _____ _____
Place: _____ _____ _____
Occasion: _____ _____ _____

How Many Swear Words

Number of swear words in vocabulary of average American male: 58; Of average American female: 29.

Date: _____ _____ _____
Place: _____ _____ _____
Occasion: _____ _____ _____

Profanity in Movies

In an article titled, "Curses! A Run of Cussing in New Movies," *USA Today* reported, "Hollywood's hits are running a blue streak. With the holiday blitz of movie releases, it has become more common to hear foul language emanating from the screen. And more often than ever it seems to be coming from characters we're supposed to admire. . . .

"Richard Heffner, chairman of the nine-member board of the Motion Picture Association of America's Classification and Rating Administration, which assigns ratings on USA films, says that there seems to be more swearing in USA movies than at any time in his fourteen years on the board—and that more profanity is being used by 'nice' characters. . . .

"Yet we're becoming increasingly desensitized to cussing as we hear and use it more in real life, says New York cultural sociologist Donna Gaines. "Saying something 'sucks' was once shocking," she says. "Now it's mainstream."[1]

P

Date: _____ _____ _____
Place: _____ _____ _____
Occasion: _____ _____ _____

Matured?

In an article titled "Networks Turn Up Volume on Foul Words," *USA Today* reported: "Parents who don't allow swear words to be uttered at home may want to channel surf this fall with the volume down. . . ."

"I am concerned [about the coarsening of language]. We do have to look at that," says CBS chief Leslie Moonves. But he, like others in Hollywood, believes that TV is reflecting the country's behavior, not causing it. "America has matured and we have to accept that."[2]

---

[1] Donna Britt, "Curses! A Run on Cussing in New Movies," *USA Today*, January 4, 1988.
[2] Alan Bash, "Networks Turn Up Volume on Foul Words," *USA Today*, July 28, 1995, sec. 3D.

> Date: _____ _____ _____
> Place: _____ _____ _____
> Occasion: _____ _____ _____

Curses

In an article titled "Today's Schools Cursed by an Increase in Swearing," *USA Today* reported: "A generation ago, kids who swore ran the risk of having their mouths washed out with soap. How times have changed. Today the halls of the nation's schools echo with language that would stand a sailor's hair on end. Teachers and principals say kids are cursing more often than they used to, and usually it's done without even thinking.

"In a recent poll of high school principals, 89% said they face profane language and provocative insults toward teachers or other students on a regular basis."[1]

> Date: _____ _____ _____
> Place: _____ _____ _____
> Occasion: _____ _____ _____

Birth of the Sunday School

Many years ago a young newspaper publisher went for a walk in one of the lower-class neighborhoods of Gloucester, England. He was on his way to interview a man to be his gardener. But as publisher Robert Raikes walked through the slums, he was surrounded by children, and he was horrified at the language they used. Even in their playing, these children swore and cussed and profaned the Lord's name and the Lord's words. His soul was so deeply disturbed by what he saw and heard on that day that he resolved to do something about it. And he did. He started a new institution, a new kind of school, a new ministry that, to this day, we call—Sunday school.

> Date: _____ _____ _____
> Place: _____ _____ _____
> Occasion: _____ _____ _____

Revivals

Travelers said that if one passed through the Northwest in 1799, he could hear on every side only swearing and profanity and obscenity. But a great revival swept through the area in the year 1800, and in 1801 travelers could hear on every hand the Gospel being preached to multitudes and songs of praise to God along the highways. The Great Revival had come.

---

[1] Nanci Hellmich, "Today's Schools Cursed by an Increase in Swearing," *USA Today*, Jan 20, 1997, sec. D1.

The same thing was true of the Welsh Revival of the early 1900s. Many of the coal miners used pony-drawn carts to haul the coal out of the mines. After the revival they had a great deal of trouble, for the ponies were no longer able to understand them. The ponies, they told one another with a smile, had evidently not been converted.

Date: _____ _____ _____
Place: _____ _____ _____
Occasion: _____ _____ _____

Cuss Control Academy

Jim O'Conner of Chicago, who could swear a blue streak himself, realized one day that he couldn't even attend a movie without hearing a cuss word. He determined to clean up his language and to help others clean up theirs. So he started "Cuss Control Academy," offering seminars for businesses and schools, and a pending book. "Did swearing ever help you win an argument?" he asks. "Did it make you pleasant to be with? Did it make you articulate or eloquent? Did it demonstrate your ability to deal with a difficult situation? By cleaning up your language, you can gain respect, have more influence, and feel better about yourself." A 10-step program for stopping the cussing habit:

1. Recognize that swearing does damage. It won't win friends, dates, or jobs.
2. Eliminate casual swear words. If you're telling a funny story and think a little f-word will throw in emphasis, pretend your granny's listening.
3. Think positive.
4. Practice patience.
5. Cope. Consider an annoyance a challenge.
6. Stop complaining.
7. Use alternate words.
8. Make your point politely.
9. Think of what you should have said.
10. Work at it. Plan ahead for stressful situations or those in which you often swear and develop tricks to stop yourself.[1]

Date: _____ _____ _____
Place: _____ _____ _____
Occasion: _____ _____ _____

I Won't Do It!

Robert Schuller admits that he doesn't know if the following story is truth or legend, but it makes a good point nonetheless.

---

[1] Mike Kilen, "Stop the Dadgum Profanity," *The Nashville Tennessean,* January 30, 1999, sec. 1D.

It was during the days of the French Revolution that King Louis XVI and his queen were condemned to death. They were escorted to the guillotine in a public square in Paris and beheaded. Then the frenzied mob called for the prince, the dauphin: "Bring out the prince," they cried. "He's next."

The six-year-old was terrified. According to the storytellers, he stood on the platform trembling in his black velvet coat and patent leather shoes. Long golden curls tumbled down over his shoulders. The mob screamed, "Down with royalty! Kill him! Death to the prince!"

Suddenly a shout came out of the crowd. "Don't kill him. You'll only send his soul to heaven. That's too good for royalty. I say, turn him over to Meg, the old witch. She'll teach him filthy words. She'll teach him to be a sinner. And then, when he dies his soul will go to hell!"

So according to the story, that's what happened. The officials turned the young prince over to old Meg. The vile woman of the back alleys began to teach him dirty words. But every time the wicked woman prompted the prince to be profane he would stubbornly stamp his little feet, clench his fists, declaring, "I will not say it. I will not say those dirty words. I was born to be a king, and I won't talk that way!"

Which is exactly the attitude we should have towards the devil when he tempts us to do the same.[1]

---◇---

Unholy Retribution

The kid who used to get spanked for writing obscenities in rest rooms is now cleaning up as a writer in Hollywood.

—ANONYMOUS

---◇---

Date:			
Place:			
Occasion:			

Noah's Chickens

• *Why did Noah almost not let the chickens on the ark? Because they used fowl language.*

Date:			
Place:			
Occasion:			

Promises

Someone Once Said . . .

• *We have twenty-five cents—and all the promises of God.*—Hudson Taylor, in a letter to his wife during a trying time in the work of China Inland Mission[2]

---

[1] Robert H. Schuller, *Self-Esteem* (Waco: Word Books, 1982), 60–61.

[2] Warren W. Wiersbe and Lloyd M. Perry, *The Wycliffe Handbook of Preaching and Preachers* (Chicago: Moody Press, 1984), 242.

- *I have thumbed my Bible many a year; I have never yet thumbed a broken promise. The promises have all been kept to me; not one good thing has failed.*—Charles H. Spurgeon[1]
- *I can say myself, I have lived on one promise for weeks, and want no other. I want just simply to hammer that promise out into gold-leaf and plate my whole existence from it.*—Charles Spurgeon[2]
- *God never gives his children a promise which he does not intend them to use. There are some promises in the Bible which I have never yet used, but I am well assured that there will come times of trial and trouble when I shall find that that poor despised promise, which I thought was never meant for me, will be the only one on which I can float.*—Charles Spurgeon[3]

Date: _____ _____ _____

Place: _____ _____ _____

Occasion: _____ _____ _____

How Many Promises in the Bible?

Dr. Everek R. Storms of Ontario spent a vast amount of time studying the promises of Scripture. Writing in *Contact* Magazine, he said:

"The Holy Scriptures contain a grand total of 8,810 promises. How do I know? I counted them.

"All my life I have seen various figures quoted as to the number of promises in the Bible. The one most generally given is 30,000. Since this is a round number with four zeroes in it, I have always been a little suspicious about it. Furthermore, since there are only 31,101 verses in the Bible, it would mean that there would be practically one promise in every verse. I do not guarantee my count to be perfect, but it is the most accurate I know of."

Dr. Storms goes on to classify the promises found in Scripture into eight kinds:

- There are 7,487 promises from God to man (about 85 percent of all the Bible's promises).
- There are 991 instances of one person making a promise to another person.
- There are 290 promises from man to God.
- There are promises made by the angels, most of them found in Luke.
- There are nine promises made by "that old liar, the devil." (For example, his promise to give Jesus all the kingdoms of the world if he would fall down and worship him.)
- Two promises are made by an evil spirit.
- Two are made by God the Father to God the Son.

Dr. Storms additionally found that one book of the Bible contains no promise at all—Titus. Ephesians has only six promises. On the other hand, Isaiah, Jeremiah, and Ezekiel have over 1,000 promises each.

---

[1] Charles H. Spurgeon, *Spurgeon's Sermons*, vol. 4 (Grand Rapids, MI: Baker Book House, 1983), 287.
[2] Charles H. Spurgeon, *Spurgeon's Sermons*, vol. 2 (Grand Rapids, MI: Baker Book House, 1983), 172.
[3] Spurgeon, *Spurgeon's Sermons*, vol. 2, 404.

What section of Scripture most impressed Dr. Storms? He wrote, "The most outstanding chapter as far as promises are concerned in Psalm 37. Practically every verse is a most wonderful promise."[1]

Date: _____   _____   _____
Place: _____   _____   _____
Occasion: _____   _____   _____

The Value of God's Promises

We never face any life-situation for which God has not supplied specific promises that give us mercy and grace to help in time of need. The old Puritan Thomas Watson put it very quaintly in a sermon to his little congregation in England on

===◇===
Useful Promises

God never gives his children a promise which he does not intend them to use.
—CHARLES SPURGEON
===◇===

Sunday, August 17, 1662: *Trade much in the promises. The promises are great supports to faith. Faith lives in a promise, as the fish lives in the water. The promises are both comforting and quickening, the very breast of the gospel; as the child by sucking the breasts gets strength, so faith by sucking the breast of a promises gets strength and revives. The promises of God are bladders (flotation devices) to keep us from sinking when we come to the waters of affliction. O! trade much in the promises; there is no condition that you can be in, but you have a promise.*

J. I. Packer comes round to the same point in his book *Knowing God: In the days when the Bible was universally acknowledged in the churches as "God's Word written," it was clearly understood that the promises recorded in Scripture were the proper, God-given basis for all our life of faith, and that the way to strengthen one's faith was to focus it upon particular promises that spoke to one's condition.*[2]

Date: _____   _____   _____
Place: _____   _____   _____
Occasion: _____   _____   _____

The Handwriting of God

Missionaries Dick and Margaret Hillis found themselves caught in China during the Japanese invasion. The couple lived with their two children in the inland town of Shenkiu. The village was tense with fear, for every day brought terrifying reports of the Japanese advance. At the worst possible time, Dick developed appendicitis, and he knew his life depended on making the long journey by rickshaw to the hospital. On January 15, 1941, with deep foreboding, Margaret watched him leave.

Soon the Chinese colonel came with news. The enemy was near and townspeople must evacuate. Margaret shivered, knowing that one-year-old Johnny and two-month-old Margaret Anne would never survive as refugees. So she stayed put. Early

---

[1] Everek R. Storms, *Standing on the Promises, Contact,* March 1978, 13–14.
[2] J. I. Packer, *Knowing God* (Downers Grove, IL: InterVarsity Press, 1973), 103.

next morning she tore the page from the wall calendar and read the new day's Scripture. It was Psalm 56:3—*What time I am afraid, I will trust in thee.*

The town emptied during the day, and next morning Margaret arose, feeling abandoned. The new verse on the calendar was Psalm 9:10—*Thou, Lord, hast not forsaken them that seek thee.*

The next morning she arose to distant sounds of gunfire and worried about food for her children. The calendar verse was Genesis 50:21—*I will nourish you and your little ones.* An old woman suddenly popped in with a pail of steaming goat's milk, and another straggler arrived with a basket of eggs.

Through the day, sounds of warfare grew louder, and during the night Margaret prayed for deliverance. The next morning she tore the page from the calendar to read Psalm 56:9—*When I cry unto Thee, then shall my enemies turn back.* The battle was looming closer, and Margaret didn't go to bed that night. Invasion seemed imminent. But the next morning, all was quiet. Suddenly, villagers began returning to their homes, and the colonel knocked on her door. For some reason, he told her, the Japanese had withdrawn their troops. No one could understand it, but the danger had passed. They were safe.

Margaret glanced at her wall calendar and felt she had been reading the handwriting of God.[1]

Date: _____ _____ _____
Place: _____ _____ _____
Occasion: _____ _____ _____

The Key of Promise

In one memorable scene from Bunyan's *Pilgrim's Progress,* Christian, finding the pathway difficult, climbed over a stile to walk in a meadowy bypath. Eventually the ground grew soggy and covered with poisonous vines. The sky became black, and Christian spent the night huddled at the foot of an oak tree, caught in a downpour. Next morning, Giant Despair came upon him, captured him, beat him, and imprisoned him in the dungeon of Doubting Castle with its grim battlements and thick, black walls. Christian tried to sing, but couldn't. His mood was dungeon-dark. Giant Despair beat him mercilessly, and he grew weaker each day. At length he found in his cell a rope, a knife, and a bottle, the tools of suicide, and for a moment he was tempted to end his misery.

But one evening about midnight he began to pray, and . . .

. . . *a little before day, good Christian, as one half amazed, brake out into this passionate speech: What a fool am I, thus to lie in a stinking dungeon, when I may as well walk at liberty! I have a key in my bosom, called Promise, that will, I am sure, open any lock in Doubting Castle.*

It did. Using the key of God's promises, Christian escaped, never again to fall into the clutches of Giant Despair or Doubting Castle.

[1]Jan Winebrenner, *Steel in His Soul, The Dick Hillis Story* (Chicago: Moody Press, 1985), ch. 10.

Date:			
Place:			
Occasion:			

Providence

Someone Once Said . . .

- *History is HIS STORY.*
- *Providence: The Hand behind the headlines.*—Anonymous
- *Despots may plan and armies may march, and the congresses of the nations may seem to think they are adjusting all the affairs of the world, but the mighty men of the earth are only the dust of the chariot wheels of God's providence.*—T. Dewitt Talmage[1]
- *The longer I live, the more convincing proofs I see of this truth, that God governs in the affairs of man.*—Benjamin Franklin, quoted by Ronald Reagan in his address to the National Association of Evangelicals, March, 1983.
- *The Most High rules in the kingdom of men.*—Daniel 4:25
- *Statesmanship is the art of finding out in what direction the Almighty God is going, and in getting things out of His way.*—Frank Gunsaulus, in *Monk and King*[2]
- *If you know how to read between the lines of secular history, you will see that God is writing another history.*—Vance Havner[3]
- *We believe in the providence of God, but we do not believe half enough in it.*—Charles Spurgeon[4]
- *Life must be lived forward; it can only be understood backwards.*—Søren Kierkegaard
- *All my days I have been aware of One going before me and with me, of doors ajar that I never could have opened.*—Vance Havner[5]
- *I thank God for the Unseen Hand, sometimes urging me onward, sometimes holding me back; sometimes with a caress of approval, sometimes with a stroke of reproof; sometimes correcting, sometimes comforting. My times are in His hand.*—Vance Havner[6]
- *The Unseen Hand may be obscured at times by the fogs of circumstance but just because we can't see the sun on a cloudy day doesn't mean that it isn't there.*—Vance Havner[7]
- *He knows, and foreknows, all things, and His foreknowledge is foreordination; He, therefore, will have the last word, both in world history and in the destiny of every man.*—J. I. Packer[8]
- *The more we trust the sovereignty of heaven, the less we fear the calamities of earth.*—Anonymous

---

[1] Rev. John Rusk, *The Authentic Life of T. DeWitt Talmage* (L. G. Stahl, 1902), 371.
[2] G. Campbell Morgan, *The Minor Prophets* (Old Tappan, NJ: Fleming H. Revell, 1960), 144.
[3] Vance Havner, *In Times Like These* (Old Tappan, NJ: Fleming H. Revell Co., 1969), 113.
[4] Mrs. Charles E. Cowman, *Springs in the Valley* (Los Angeles: Cowman Publications, Inc., 1939), 223.
[5] Vance Havner, *Though I Walk Through the Valley* (Old Tappan, NJ: Fleming H. Revell Co., 1974), 23.
[6] Vance Havner, *Fourscore* (Old Tappan, NJ: Fleming H. Revell Co., 1982), 23.
[7] Havner, *Fourscore*, 23.
[8] J. I. Packer, *Knowing God* (Downers Grove, IL: InterVarsity, 1973), 25.

- *You meant evil against me; but God meant it for good.*—Joseph, in Genesis 50:20
- *All things work together for good to those who love God.*—Romans 8:28

Date: _____ _____ _____
Place: _____ _____ _____
Occasion: _____ _____ _____

Providential Orderings at the English Channel

- **The Spanish Armada**—King Philip II of Spain, a Catholic, wanting to topple Protestantism in England, readied his navy, the largest and strongest on earth, for invasion. He was trusting God, he said, to send him favorable weather, as he would be fighting a divine cause. On May 30, 1588, he fell to his knees before his "Invincible Armada," prayed for victory, and watched it disappear over the horizon. But providence sided with the English. The Spanish Armada was quickly hurled in every direction by a violent storm. The beleaguered fleet regrouped, pressed on, and was spotted by the British on July 19. Winds turned against the Armada, slowing its progress. When the battle was joined on July 21, weather again aided the English. Heavy winds favored their smaller, more manageable ships. The English outmaneuvered the Spanish, and at just the right moments the weather shifted, always in England's favor. By July 31, the Duke of Parma had informed Philip of likely defeat: "God knows how grieved I am at this news at a time when I hoped to send Your Majesty congratulations. I will only say that this must come from the hand of the Lord, who knows well what He does . . ."
- **The Miracle of Dunkirk**—Poland, Denmark, Norway, Holland, Belgium, France—all had fallen to the Nazi blitzkrieg, forcing the British Expeditionary Force to the sea and trapping them for apparent, inevitable annihilation. England's King George VI called for a national day of prayer as a risky evacuation began on May 26, lasting for ten days. The weather behaved oddly. When the dikes were opened to hinder the German advance, the wind blew in from the sea, aiding this strategic move. But had it continued to blow in from the sea, it would have wrecked many of the tiny boats and small vessels transporting soldiers. Instead, the wind blew as needed, where needed, and when needed to facilitate the retreat. And when not needed, it didn't blow. Thousands of troops escaped in an improvised flotilla of tiny vessels only because, through the entire evacuation, the waters of the English Channel were still as a pond, despite the fact that at the end of May the channel is normally rough and stormy. As an added advantage, the fog rolled in at critical moments, covering the rescue of the troops.

P

Date: _____ _____ _____
Place: _____ _____ _____
Occasion: _____ _____ _____

Thomas Watson on Providence

The quaint Puritan, Thomas Watson, wrote: *There is no such thing as blind fate, but there is a Providence that guides and governs the world.* "*The lot is cast into the lap, but the whole disposing thereof is of the Lord (Proverbs 16:33) . . . Providence is God's ordering all issues and events of things, after the counsel of His will, to His own glory . . . The wheels of the clock seem to move contrary one to the other, but they help forward the motion of the clock, and make the alarum [sic] strike; so the providences of God seem to be cross wheels; but for all that they shall carry on the good of the elect.*[1]

> Date: _____ _____ _____
>
> Place: _____ _____ _____
>
> Occasion: _____ _____ _____

John Calvin on Providence

When the light of divine providence has once shone upon a godly man, he is then relieved and set free not only from the extreme anxiety and fear that were pressing him before, but from every care. . . . Ignorance of providence is the ultimate misery; the highest blessedness lies in knowing it. . . . [It gives] incredible freedom from worry about the future.[2]

> Date: _____ _____ _____
>
> Place: _____ _____ _____
>
> Occasion: _____ _____ _____

Which Way Flows the Mississippi?

"Ask any school boy, 'Which way does the Mississippi River flow?' He will say, 'From north to south.' If you have flown over the Mississippi there are times and places where the Mississippi River will flow north. There are times and places where the Mississippi River will flow due west, but it ultimately and finally flows south. So the elective purpose of God in Christ Jesus is frustrated, turned, twisted, but it is God's purpose of the ages that the reign and kingdom shall belong to Him."
—W. A. Criswell[3]

> Date: _____ _____ _____
>
> Place: _____ _____ _____
>
> Occasion: _____ _____ _____

Who Caused the Pit to Hold No Water?

The English divine, Henry Law (1686–1761) wrote this about Jesus Christ's extended hand of Providence:

---

[1] Thomas Watson, *Gleanings From Thomas Watson* (Morgan, PA: Soli Deo Gloria Publications, 1995), 33.
[2] William J. Bouwsma, *John Calvin: A Sixteenth Century Portrait* (New York: Oxford UP, 1988), 171–172.
[3] W. A. Criswell, *Ephesians* (Grand Rapids, MI: Zondervan, 1974), 131.

"He moves the ever-moving wheels of circumstances. No sparrow falls, no leaf decays, but in accordance with His ordering mind. He wills, and things occur. Chance is a figment of a dreaming pillow. It never was. It never can be. Thus to the child of God there is no trifle or unimportant event. Momentous issues often hang on rapid words, on sudden looks, on unintended steps. . . .

"When Joseph's brethren thirsted for his blood, who caused the pit to hold no water? Who brought the Ishmaelites to bear him into Egypt? Who gave the sleepless night to Persia's King? Who brought the aged Simeon, the pious Anna, at the fit moment, to the temple? Who led Onesimus to hear Paul's saving words at Rome?"[1]

---◇---

Appointed Travel

We travel an appointed way.

—A. W. TOZER

---◇---

Date:			
Place:			
Occasion:			

Providence, Rhode Island

He was an Anglican, then a Puritan, then a Separatist, then a Baptist, then a "Seeker." He quarreled with civil leaders, frustrated church leaders, and loved the Indians. He founded an American colony and established the first Baptist church on American soil. Most of all, he trusted the overruling providence of God so much that he named a city in honor of it.

Who was he? He was Roger Williams, born circa 1603 in England. He grew up in London near a square in front of Newgate Prison, famous as the site of execution for condemned heretics. Young Roger witnessed many such executions, and he developed an abhorrence for the persecution of those with differing religious beliefs. His convictions deepened when, as an eighteen-year-old, he worked as recording secretary in a British courtroom, transcribing the cases of heretical prosecution. By the time Williams graduated from Cambridge, he was a powerful preacher and a relentless advocate of religious liberty.

In 1630 under King Charles I, the campaign against non-Anglicans was at fever pitch, and Williams was infuriated by the treatment given his friend, Dr. Alexander Leighton, a Puritan—life imprisonment, heavy fine, defrocking, public whipping, ears cut off, nose split on both sides, and branding of a double SS (for "Sower of Sedition") on his face.

With righteous wrath, Williams began preaching and writing against the church/state unions and their resulting policies of coercion and persecution. Finding himself at risk, he accepted an invitation from Puritans in Boston and embarked secretly on a ship for America December 8, 1630. But he found Puritan leaders in America also intolerant. They, too, sought to impose their beliefs through legal constraint. One night, news reached him that authorities were plotting to seize him and return him in chains to England. Bundling himself against the cold, he fled

---

[1] Henry Law, *The Gospel in Exodus* (London: The Banner of Truth Trust, 1967), 36.

through the snow into Indian country. On the shores of Narragansett Bay, he purchased land from the Indians and there he founded a settlement, naming it Providence, where all could worship in freedom. There he established the first Baptist church in America. And there he established the colony of Rhode Island.[1]

Date: _____ _____ _____
Place: _____ _____ _____
Occasion: _____ _____ _____

However Mysterious the Leadings of Providence

William Carey had been working for years to fulfill his burning desire to go as a missionary to India. Having overcome one obstacle after another, he finally found himself aboard the *Oxford,* bound for Asia. But before the ship could overcome contrary winds and leave the shorelines of England, he was suddenly deposited back on land by the ship's captain who had received an anonymous letter against Carey. There the would–be missionary stood, his luggage piled up beside him, his hopes dashed.

But William Carey was a plodder, and he took setbacks in stride, trusting God's overruling plan. To his friend Andrew Fuller, he wrote: "All I can say in this affair is that, however mysterious the leadings of Providence are, I have no doubt but they are superintended by an infinitely wise God."

And it proved to be so.[2]

Date: _____ _____ _____
Place: _____ _____ _____
Occasion: _____ _____ _____

God Moves in a Mysterious Way

The grand old hymn *God Moves in a Mysterious Way* was written by William Cowper (pronounced Cooper), the English poet, friend of John Newton, who struggled all his life with melancholy. According to Ernest Emurian in *Living Stories of Famous Hymns,* William Cowper wrote this hymn following a period of almost suicidal depression. Calling for a carriage, he ordered the driver to take him to the Ouse River, three miles away, where he planned to kill himself. The driver, knowing the state of mind of his passenger, breathed a prayer of thanks when a thick fog enveloped the area. He purposely lost his way in the dense fog, jogging up one road and down another as Cowper fell into a deep sleep. Several hours passed, the driver going in circles, letting his passenger rest. Finally he returned him to his home.

"We're back home," said Cowper. "How is that?"

"Got lost in the fog, sir. Sorry."

---

[1] Robert J. Morgan, *On This Day* (Nashville: Thomas Nelson Publishers, 1997), December 8th.
[2] Mary Drewery, *William Carey: A Biography* (Grand Rapids, MI: Zondervan, 1978), 49.

Cowper paid his fare, went inside, and pondered how he had been spared from harming himself by the merciful providence of God. That same evening in 1774, his forty-third year, reflecting on his narrow escape, he wrote this autobiographical hymn[1]:

> *God moves in a mysterious way his wonders to perform;*
> *He plants his footsteps in the sea, and rides upon the storm.*
>
> *Deep in unfathomable mines of never-failing skill,*
> *He treasures up his bright designs and works his sovereign will.*
>
> *You fearful saints, fresh courage take; the clouds you so much dread*
> *Are big with mercy and shall break in blessings on your head.*
>
> *Judge not the Lord by feeble sense, but trust him for his grace;*
> *Behind a frowning providence he hides a smiling face*
>
> *His purposes will ripen fast, unfolding every hour;*
> *The bud may have a bitter taste, but sweet will be the flower.*
>
> *Blind unbelief is sure to err and scan his work in vain:*
> *God is his own interpreter, and he will make it plain.*

Date: _____ _____ _____

Place: _____ _____ _____

Occasion: _____ _____ _____

That's Good News

A wise old Chinese gentleman lived on the troubled Mongolian border. One day his favorite horse, a beautiful white mare, jumped the fence and was seized on the other side by the enemy. His friends came to comfort him. "We're so sorry about your horse," they said. "That's bad news."

"How do you know it's bad news?" he asked. "It might be good news."

A week later, the Chinaman looked out his window to see his mare returning at breakneck speed, and alongside her was a beautiful stallion. He put both horses into the enclosure, and his friends came to admire the new addition. "What a beautiful horse," they said. "That's good news."

"How do you know it's good news?" replied the man. "It might be bad news."

The next day, the man's only son decided to try riding the stallion. It threw him, and he landed painfully, breaking his leg. The friends made another visit, all of them sympathetic, saying, "We're so sorry about this. It's such bad news."

"How do you know it's bad news?" replied the man. "It might be good news."

Within a month, a terrible war broke out between China and Mongolia. The Chinese recruiters came through the area, pressing all the young men into the army. All of them perished—except for the Chinaman's son, who couldn't go off to war because of his broken leg.

---

[1] Ernest K. Emurian, *Living Stories of Famous Hymns* (Grand Rapids, MI: Baker Book House, 1955), 51–52.

"You see," said the gentleman, "the things you considered good were actually bad, and the things that seemed to be bad news were actually for our good."

Or, as Hudson Taylor once put it:

> *Ill that God blesses is our good,*
> *And unblest good is ill.*
> *And all is right that seems most wrong*
> *If it be His sweet will.*

Date: _____ _____ _____
Place: _____ _____ _____
Occasion: _____ _____ _____

Within the Shadow

> *Careless seems the great Avenger; history's pages but record*
> *One death-grapple in the darkness 'twixt old systems and the Word;*
> *Truth forever on the scaffold, Wrong forever on the throne,—*
> *Yet that scaffold sways the future, and, behind the dim unknown,*
> *Standeth God within the shadow, keeping watch above his own.*
> —J. R. Lowell, *The Present Crisis*

Date: _____ _____ _____
Place: _____ _____ _____
Occasion: _____ _____ _____

Over the Falls

Seven-year-old Roger Woodward along with his seventeen-year-old sister was enjoying a boat ride on the Niagara River. They were guests of a man from Niagara Falls, New York, and were boating above the falls. But when the boat developed motor trouble and capsized, all three were thrown into the river. The man went over the falls and was killed. Roger's sister was plucked from the river about twenty feet from the edge of the falls by two tourists. But Roger went over the falls wearing nothing but his swimming trunks and an orange life preserver.

The "Maid of the Mist" tourist boat was just turning away from the falls when the crew spotted him, floating in the basin. Pulling him from the water, they rushed him to the hospital where he remained three days with a slight concussion and was released.

Thirty years passed and Roger Woodward returned to Niagara Falls to give his testimony at the Glengate Alliance Church. The audience was hushed as he told his miraculous story, the panic he felt as he drifted helpless toward the precipice, the anger he felt because no one on the shoreline could help him, the flashbacks he experienced as he inwardly said goodbye to his parents and his dog and his toys.

He said, "It wasn't the hand of fate [that saved me]. It wasn't the hand of luck. It was the Spirit of the Living God that saved my life that day and saved my sister and gave us hope that one day we could come to know Him."

Date: _____ _____ _____
Place: _____ _____ _____
Occasion: _____ _____ _____

Blown Off Course

Sometimes when our plans don't work out as hoped, it's because God is detouring us, leading us elsewhere, in his overruling providence. Thomas Coke, a sophisticated Oxford-educated Welshman, left his ministry in the Anglican Church in 1777 to become John Wesley's chief assistant in the new and quickly-growing Methodist movement. On September 24, 1785, he packed his books and bags and sailed out of England, down the Channel, and into the Atlantic, leaving for Nova Scotia where he wanted to establish a group of missionaries who accompanied him. But the voyage was ill-fated and grew more perilous by the day, the ship being caught in mountainous waves and mast-splitting winds. The ship's captain determined that Coke and his missionaries, like biblical Jonah, were bringing misfortune on his ship, and he considered throwing them overboard. He did, in fact, gather up some of Coke's papers and toss them into the raging ocean. The voyage took three months rather than the expected one, and instead of landing in Nova Scotia, the damaged ship ended up in the Caribbean, limping into St. John's harbor on the island of Antigua on Christmas Day.

Coke knew that at least one Methodist lived somewhere on Antigua, a missionary named John Baxter. Hoping to find him, Coke and his three missionaries asked to be rowed ashore from their shattered ship in the predawn morning. They started down the street in St. John's and stopped the first person they found, a fellow swinging a lantern in his hand, to inquire of Baxter.

It was John Baxter himself. He was on his way to special Christmas morning services he had planned for the island, and the sudden appearance of Coke and his missionaries out of the darkness—out of nowhere—seemed too good to be true. It took three services that day to accommodate the crowds. And after it was over, Coke and his associates abandoned any idea of going to Nova Scotia. They planted the missionary team instead on Antigua and on neighboring islands, and by the time of Coke's death in 1814 there were over seventeen thousand believers in the Methodist churches there.[1]

Date: _____ _____ _____
Place: _____ _____ _____
Occasion: _____ _____ _____

[1] Robert J. Morgan, *On This Day* (Nashville: Thomas Nelson Publishers, 1997), September 24th.

Reading

Someone Once Said . . .

- *We are what we read.*—Anonymous
- *Leaders are readers and readers are leaders.*—Anonymous
- *Bring . . . the books. Especially the parchments.*—the Apostle Paul, during his final imprisonment
- *Can you imagine, Paul has been to heaven and back. He wrote most of the New Testament. He has seen the Lord, and yet he wants books.*—Charles Spurgeon[1]
- *[Send] a warmer cap, a candle, a piece of cloth to patch my leggings. . . . But above all, I beseech and entreat your clemency to be urgent with the Procureur that he may kindly permit me to have my Hebrew Bible, Hebrew Grammar and Hebrew Dictionary, that I may spend time with that in study.*—William Tyndale, during his final imprisonment
- *An ordinary man can . . . surround himself with two thousand books . . . and thenceforward have at least one place in the world in which it is possible to be happy.*—Augustine Birrell, English politician and man of letters
- *Reading aloud is one of the best-kept secrets of good parenting.*—Barbara Bush
- *Read, read, read! Use the Bible as home base, but vary your diet. I usually have several books going at once, tucked around here and there for easy access.*—Ruth Bell Graham[2]
- *Read to refill the wells of inspiration.*—Harold J. Ockenga, who took a suitcase full of books on his honeymoon
- *Read, not to contradict or confute, nor to believe and take for granted, nor to find talk and discourse, but to weigh and consider. Some books are to be tasted, others to be swallowed, and some few to be chewed and digested.*—Francis Bacon

Date: _____   _____   _____

Place: _____   _____   _____

Occasion: _____   _____   _____

On the Reading of Old Books

- *Many Christians are so busy trying to keep up with the books of the hour that they never catch up with the past to meet the people who belong to the ages.*—Warren Wiersbe[3]
- *Whenever a new book comes out, I read an old one.*—John Ruskin[4]
- *If [one] must read only the new or only the old, I would advise him to read the old . . . It is a good rule, after reading a new book, never to allow yourself another new one till you have read an old one in between.*—C. S. Lewis[5]

---

[1] Warren Wiersbe, "Let's Get Back to Reading," *Moody Magazine,* July/August 1983, 72.

[2] Personal conversation with the author.

[3] Warren Wiersbe, *Be Myself: The Memoirs of One of America's Most Respected Bible Teachers* (Victor Books, 1994), 242.

[4] David A. Seamands, *Leadership Journal,* Fall 1994, 35.

[5] C. S. Lewis, *God in the Dock* (Grand Rapids, MI: Eerdmans, 1970), 201–202.

- *If I have not read a book before, it is, for all intents and purposes, new to me whether it was printed yesterday or three hundred years ago.*—William Hazlitte (b. 1778), English writer
- *A book that people praise, but don't read.*—Mark Twain, his definition of a literary classic

Date: _____ _____ _____

Place: _____ _____ _____

Occasion: _____ _____ _____

How Many Books?

Some literary sources advise to read *fewer* books, but to read them with greater care. Matthew Arnold gave it as his opinion that the best literature was to be found within the covers of five hundred books. Daniel Webster preferred to master a few books rather than to read indiscriminately. It was his contention that reading a few great writers who have built up the permanent literature of the English language, well mastered, was better than skimming a multitude of ephemeral works. Hobbs, the English philosopher, once said, "If I had read as many books as other people, I would know as little."

A Whole New Life

When you sell a man a book, you don't sell him twelve ounces of paper and ink and glue—you sell him a whole new life.
—CHARLES MORLEY

Spurgeon counseled his students: "Master those books you have. Read them thoroughly. Bathe in them until they saturate you. Read and reread them, masticate them and digest them. . . . A student will find that his mental constitution is more affected by one book thoroughly mastered than by twenty books he has merely skimmed.

Cannon Yates suggested that when one has found a book really worth digesting, that three readings are required to absorb its contents. The first reading should be rapid and continuous. The second reading should be careful, slow, and detailed, making notes. After an interval, the third reading should be fairly rapid and continuous, and a brief analysis should be written in the back of the book.[1]

Date: _____ _____ _____

Place: _____ _____ _____

Occasion: _____ _____ _____

The Joys of Reading

Warren Wiersbe gives three reasons why he enjoys reading: "First, there's the joy of meeting people I've always wanted to meet. If it were announced that Hudson Taylor or Charles Spurgeon or Campbell Morgan was speaking at a particular church, Christians from all over the world would show up. But we forget that when we open up a book by Hudson Taylor, for example, that man is speaking to us.

---

[1] Oswald Sanders, *Spiritual Leadership* (Chicago: Moody Press, 1967), 99–102.

"Another joy is visiting great periods of history. I would like to have lived in London from 1835 to about 1895, the Victorian era. . . . I could have traveled from place to place, hearing some of the greatest people who ever walked the face of God's earth—F. B. Meyer, D. L. Moody, Charles Haddon Spurgeon, Joseph Parker, Alexander Maclaren . . .

"A third joy I have in reading is grappling with great issues. . . . Everyone is a philosopher because everyone has some view of life."[1]

Date: _____ _____ _____
Place: _____ _____ _____
Occasion: _____ _____ _____

The Man Most Pitied

Someone once asked Benjamin Franklin what sort of person he most pitied. Franklin replied, "A lonesome man on a rainy day who does not know how to read."

Date: _____ _____ _____
Place: _____ _____ _____
Occasion: _____ _____ _____

Who Reads?

According to statistics published by Denver Conservative Baptist Seminary in their magazine *Focal Point* and attributed to a Gallup poll:

- 58% of Americans have never finished reading a book.
- While book sales are increasing from year to year, 80% of these books are read by 12% of the American people.
- Only 1% of all Christians ever visit Christian bookstores.

Date: _____ _____ _____
Place: _____ _____ _____
Occasion: _____ _____ _____

Thirty Minutes a Day

According to Warren Wiersbe, "If you spent thirty minutes a day studying any subject—veterinary medicine, for example—within ten years you'd have the equivalent of a Ph.D. in that subject.[2]

[1] Warren Wiersbe, "Let's Get Back to Reading," *Moody Magazine,* July/August 1983, 76–77.
[2] Warren Wiersbe, "Let's Get Back to Reading," *Moody Magazine,* July/August 1983, 76.

Date:			
Place:			
Occasion:			

Wesley and His Reading

"John Wesley had a passion for reading and most of it was done on horseback. He rode sometimes ninety and often fifty miles in a day. He read deeply on a wide range of subjects. It was his habit to travel with a volume of science or history or medicine propped on the pommel of his saddle, and in that way he got through thousands of volumes. . . . He told the younger ministers of the Wesleyan societies either to read or get out of the ministry!"[1]

Date:			
Place:			
Occasion:			

That's the Trouble

Major John Skidmore, one of Oswald Chamber's closest friends, came to see Chambers, complaining of being drained. Oswald asked what he had been reading, to which Skidmore said, "Only the Bible and books directly associated with it."

"That's the trouble," said Chambers. "You have allowed part of your brain to stagnate for want of use."

Reaching for a nearby pen and paper, Oswald began listing more than fifty books dealing with philosophy, psychology, theology, and every phase of current life.

"When people refer to a man as 'a man of one book,' meaning the Bible, he is generally found to be a man of multitudinous books, which simply isolates the one Book to its proper grandeur," said Oswald. "The man who reads only the Bible does not, as a rule, know it or human life."

Chambers love for books came in part from his sitting at the feet of the Scottish preacher Alexander Whyte, who taught a series of classes that Oswald attended as a young man. Many times, Oswald saw Whyte hold up a battered old book, telling the students, "Sell your beds and buy it."

Afterward, Oswald never went anywhere without a book. Once, while traveling, he wrote his sister Florence saying, "My box has at last arrived. My books! I cannot tell you what they mean to me—silent, wealthy, loyal lovers. To look at them, to handle them, and to re-read them! I do thank God for my books with every fiber of my being. Why, I could have almost cried for excess of joy when I got hold of them again. I see them all just at my elbow now—Plato, Wordsworth, Myers, Bradley, Halyburton, St. Augustine, Browning, Tennyson, Amiel, etc. I know them. I wish you could see how they look at me, a quiet, calm look of certain acquaintance."[2]

R

---

[1] Sanders, *Spiritual Leadership,* 95.
[2] David McCasland, *Oswald Chambers: Abandoned to God* (Oswald Chambers Publications Association, Ltd., 1993), 156–157, 50, 108–9.

Date:			
Place:			
Occasion:			

The Value of Biography

- *Next to the Holy Scriptures, the greatest aid to the life of faith may be Christian biography. It is indeed notable that a large part of the Bible itself is given over to the life and labors of prophets, patriarchs and kings—who they were, what they did and said, how they prayed and suffered and triumphed at last.*—A. W. Tozer
- *History is but the lengthy shadow of great men.*—Emerson
- *Biography transmits personality. . . . Who can gauge the inspiration to the cause of missions of great biographies like those of William Carey, Adoniram Judson, Hudson Taylor, Charles Studd, or Albert Simpson.*—J. Oswald Sanders[1]
- *The reading of good biography forms an important part of a Christian's education. It provides him with numberless illustrations for use in his own service. He learns to assess the true worth of character, to glimpse a work goal for his own life, to decide how best to attain it, what self-denial is needed to curb unworthy aspirations, and all the time he learns how God breaks into the dedicated life to bring about his own purposes.*—Ransome W. Cooper[2]

Date:			
Place:			
Occasion:			

It Stirs Me Up Much

Jim Elliot, who gave his life while trying to reach the Auca Indians, was largely shaped through the reading of Christian biography. "I see the value of Christian biography tonight," he wrote in his journal, "as I have been reading Brainerd's Diary much today. It stirs me up much to pray and wonder at my nonchalance while I have not power from God. I have considered Hebrews 13:7 just now, regarding the remembrance of certain ones who spake the word of God, 'consider the outcome of their life, and imitate their faith.' I recall now the challenge of Goforth's *Life* and *By My Spirit,* read in the summer of 1947, the encouragement of Hudson Taylor's *Spiritual Secret,* and *The Growth of a Soul.* There are incidents which instruct me now from the reading of J. G. Paton's biography, read last winter. And now this fresh Spirit-quickened history of Brainerd. O Lord, let me be granted grace to 'imitate their faith.'"

It has since been through the reading of Elliot's journals that scores of young people have given their lives to the service of the Gospel.[3]

---

[1] Sanders, *Spiritual Leadership,* 99.
[2] Sanders, *Spiritual Leadership,* 100.
[3] Elisabeth Elliot, *Shadow of the Almighty* (Grand Rapids, MI: Zondervan, 1958), 108

Date:	_____	_____	_____
Place:	_____	_____	_____
Occasion:	_____	_____	_____

The Royal Path of Life

In the late 1800s, a publishing sensation swept over America. A six-hundred-page book entitled, *The Royal Path of Life,* written by two Chicagoans, became popular both in the refined East and in the pioneer West. It was filled with quaint maxims, observations, and homespun wisdom. Here are some segments from the chapter entitled "Reading":

- There are four classes of readers. The first is like the hour-glass. With their reading being like the sand, it runs in and runs out and leaves no vestige behind. A second is like a sponge which imbibes everything, and returns it in the same state, only a little dirtier. A third is like a jelly bag, allowing all that is pure to pass away, retaining only the refuse and dregs. The fourth are like workers in the diamond mines of Golconda, who, casting aside all that is worthless, obtain only pure gems.
- One's reading is usually a fair index of his character.
- "A man is known," it is said, "by the company he keeps." It is equally true that a man's character may be to a great extent ascertained by knowing what books he reads.
- You cannot afford to read a bad book, however good you are. You say, "The influence is insignificant." I tell you that the scratch of a pin has sometimes produced the lockjaw.
- Inferior books are to be rejected, in an age and time when we are courted by whole libraries. And no man's life is long enough to compass even those which are good and great and famous. Why should we bow down at puddles?
- To read with profit, the books must be of a kind calculated to inform the mind, correct the head, and better the heart. These books should be read with attention, understood and remembered, and their precepts put in practice. It depends less on the number than quality. One good book well understood and remembered, is of more use than to have a superficial knowledge of fifty, equally sound.

R

Date:	_____	_____	_____
Place:	_____	_____	_____
Occasion:	_____	_____	_____

Successful People Read

Some years ago, George and Alec Gallup set out to discover what makes some people more successful than others. Using the polling techniques that have made them famous, the brothers researched and wrote a book titled, *The Great American*

Success Story. One of their findings: Successful people read. George Gallup said he discovered that reading was essential because it "makes a person ready to converse. It seems to be a key to feeling confident. These people have a broad knowledge and feel they can shift over to another field or chain of thought. . . . I think reading would be a very big boost to self-esteem because then you have more information with which to make evaluations and decisions."[1]

Date: _____ _____ _____
Place: _____ _____ _____
Occasion: _____ _____ _____

Repentance

Someone Once Said . . .

- *Repentance: That mighty change in mind, heart, and life, wrought by the Spirit of God.*—Richard Trench, archbishop of Dublin
- *It is a change of mind about sin and self and the Savior.*—Vance Havner
- *A thousand years of remorse over a wrong act would not please God as much as a change of conduct and a reformed life.*—A. W. Tozer, in *The Divine Conquest*
- *I think there is little doubt that the teaching of salvation without repugnance has lowered the moral standards of the Church and produced a multitude of deceived religious professors who erroneously believe themselves to be saved when in fact they are still in the gall of bitterness and the bond of iniquity.*—A. W. Tozer[2]
- *Justification is the truly dramatic transition from the status of a condemned criminal awaiting a terrible sentence to that of an heir awaiting a fabulous inheritance.*—J. I. Packer[3]
- *Does "repent and believe the gospel" imply that the sinner must do two things to be saved, and not one only? The exhortation is really only one requirement. The instruction, "Leave London and go to Los Angeles," sounds like a two-fold request, but it really is only one; it is impossible to go to Los Angeles without leaving London.*—J. Edwin Orr[4]

Date: _____ _____ _____
Place: _____ _____ _____
Occasion: _____ _____ _____

You Didn't Tell Me That!

J. Edwin Orr, the revivalist and historian, was with Billy Graham when the evangelist addressed a meeting in Beverly Hills attended by the notorious gangster

[1] George Gallup, Jr., *Personal Selling Power,* May/June 1987, 7–8.
[2] A. W. Tozer, *A Treasury of A. W. Tozer* (Grand Rapids, MI: Baker Book House, 1980), 116–117.
[3] J. I. Packer, *Knowing God* (Downers Grove, IL: InterVarsity, 1973), 121.
[4] Edwin Orr, "Playing the Good News Off-Key," *Christianity Today,* January 1, 1982, 27.

Mickey Cohen. "He expressed some interest in the message," Orr later wrote, "so several of us talked with him, including Dr. Graham, but he made no commitment until some time later when another friend urged him—with Revelation 3:20 as a warrant—to invite Jesus Christ into his life.

"This he professed to do, but his life subsequently gave no evidence of repentance, 'the mighty change of mind, heart, and life.' He rebuked our friend, telling him, 'You did not tell me that I would have to give up my work!' He meant his rackets. 'You did not tell me that I would have to give up my friends!' He meant his gangster associates.

"He had heard that so-and-so was a Christian cowboy, so-and-so was a Christian actress, so-and-so was a Christian senator, and he really thought he could be a Christian gangster. . . .

"The fact is, repentance is the missing note in much modern evangelism."[1]

Date: _____ _____ _____
Place: _____ _____ _____
Occasion: _____ _____ _____

Avoiding the "R"

Jimmy had trouble pronouncing the letter "R" so his teacher gave him a sentence to practice at home: "Robert gave Richard a rap in the rib for roasting the rabbit so rare."

Some days later the teacher asked him to say the sentence for her. Jimmy rattled it off like this: "Bob gave Dick a poke in the side for not cooking the bunny enough."

He had evaded the letter "R."

There are a lot of people today—including Christians—who go to great lengths to avoid the "R" word of "Repentance."

Date: _____ _____ _____
Place: _____ _____ _____
Occasion: _____ _____ _____

R

Is It Repentance?

- *Regret* is being sorry—mentally (King Saul, for example).
- *Remorse* is being sorry—mentally and emotionally (like Judas).
- *Repentance* is being sorry—mentally, emotionally, and volitionally (like Matthew, among others).

Date: _____ _____ _____
Place: _____ _____ _____
Occasion: _____ _____ _____

[1] Edwin Orr, "Playing the Good News Off-Key," *Christianity Today*, January 1, 1982, 24–25.

Metanoia

The Greek word for repentance, *metanoia*, is composed of two parts: *meta*, meaning change, and *noia*, meaning mind.

```
Date:     _____   _____   _____
Place:    _____   _____   _____
Occasion: _____   _____   _____
```

Fifty Times

The word "repentance" or "repent" is used in the writings of Paul to the Romans, the Corinthians, and to Timothy, and by the writer to the Hebrews as well as by Peter. It occurs ten times in the Book of the Revelation of John. In all of the New Testament it appears more than fifty times. Hebrews lists it as an elementary doctrine of Christ, a foundation. How serious then is the condition of a professing church where repentance is missing from its elementary evangelism or church growth?—J. Edwin Orr

```
Date:     _____   _____   _____
Place:    _____   _____   _____
Occasion: _____   _____   _____
```

Who Is General Jackson?

In his excellent biography of Andrew Jackson, Marquis James tells of a Sunday morning in 1818 when the General traveled from his home, the Hermitage, into downtown Nashville to attend a Methodist Conference. The famous circuit-riding preacher, Peter Cartwright, was to speak that day.

---◇---

The Last Word

Our Lord's last word to the church was not the Great Commission, but a plea for repentance.
—VANCE HAVNER

---◇---

The pastor of the church had invited Cartwright with misgivings, for the evangelist was unpredictable. He had been known to knock a sinner down and literally drag him to the throne of grace. But interest had been high, and it seemed that everyone in Nashville had come to church that Sunday to see the eccentric Cartwright. His text was: "What shall it profit a man if he gains the whole world and loses his own soul?"

Cartwright had just read his text and had paused to let the words sink in when General Jackson entered the church and slowly walked down the aisle. Every seat was taken, and he stood for a moment, leaning against a pillar.

Peter Cartwright felt a tug at the tail of his coat. "General Jackson has come in!" the Nashville pastor whispered excitedly. "General Jackson has come in."

The whisper was audible to most of the church. Peter Cartwright's jaw tightened, and he gave the minister a look of scorn.

"Who is General Jackson?" shouted Cartwright. "If he doesn't repent and get his soul converted," he continued, saying in effect, "God will damn his soul to hell as quick as an unconverted pagan."

After the sermon, Rev. Cartwright was advised to leave town immediately, for Jackson was known for his fiery temper and his deadly duels. Instead, the evangelist accepted an invitation to preach at a church right next to the Hermitage.

Jackson invited him to dinner.[1]

Date: _____ _____ _____
Place: _____ _____ _____
Occasion: _____ _____ _____

Weeping with an Onion

Some have tears enough for their outward losses, but none for their inward lusts; they can mourn for the evil that sin brings, but not for the sin which brings the evil. Pharaoh more lamented the hard strokes which were upon him, than the hard heart that was within him. Esau mourned not because he sold the birth-right, which was his sin, but because he lost the blessing, which was his punishment. This is like weeping with an onion, the eye sheds tears because it smarts.—Rev William Secker, seventeenth-century British minister[2]

Date: _____ _____ _____
Place: _____ _____ _____
Occasion: _____ _____ _____

Repentance Is a Process

In their book discussing the tragedy of domestic violence and battered women, the husband/wife team of psychologist James Alsdurf and former *Family Life Today* editor Phyllis Alsdurf, discuss the need for repentance on the part of those who abuse their spouses. Their strong, yet true, words have applications to other areas of shortcoming in our lives: *The victim of abuse can choose to forgive her batterer, both for his sake and for her own, but the work of reconciliation cannot begin until the batterer repents. And repentance is a process. It starts when the batterer spiritually and psychologically faces the awfulness of his actions. There must come that loathing of oneself for one's sins as Ezekiel exhorts: "Then you will remember your evil ways and wicked deeds, and you will loathe yourselves for your sins and detestable practices" (Ezekiel 36:31, NIV). The horrors of the past must be named, not left vague and undefined. Here sin and sickness move from the abstract to the concrete. And, most importantly, the batterer takes responsibility for what he has done.*[3]

Date: _____ _____ _____
Place: _____ _____ _____
Occasion: _____ _____ _____

---

[1] Marquis James, *The Life of Andrew Jackson* (Indianapolis: The Bobbs-Merrill Co., 1937), 296–297.

[2] William Secker, *The Nonsuch Professor In His Meridian Splendor* (Chicago: Fleming H. Revell Co., 1899), 124–125.

[3] James and Phyllis Alsdurf, *Battered into Submission* (Downers Grove, IL: InterVarsity Press, 1989), 104.

———————— Resilience ————————

Someone Once Said . . .

- *The Spring-Back Factor.*—Definition of resilience from a self-help brochure
- *Resilience is the capacity for recovery. It's your capability to retain a positive self-image, a positive view of the world, even after you've been tested by difficult or traumatic circumstances. Think of it like the elasticity of a new rubber band. When the band is stretched very tightly, it springs right back into its former shape.*—Sherry Lowry, business consultant

Date: _____ _____ _____

Place: _____ _____ _____

Occasion: _____ _____ _____

The New Buzz Word

USA Weekend recently featured a cover story on the subject of *resilience,* asking the question: "Why do some people bounce while others break?"

The writer defined *resilience* as "the ability to get through, get over, and thrive after trauma, trials, and tribulations." A simpler definition just refers to resiliency as the ability to "bounce back."

The article said that while self-esteem was the buzz word the latter part of the twentieth century, resilience is going to be the new emphasis. President Bill Clinton demonstrated such a remarkable ability to bounce back from adversity that he was dubbed the "Come-Back Kid."

But it isn't just a skill for successful politicians.

- Many major corporations now offer their employees training in *resilience* techniques, and job placement firms are now sponsoring seminars in career resilience.
- Prominent psychologists are writing books now on the subject, and the self-improvement gurus are talking about "bounce-back" skills.
- One of Oprah Winfrey's most popular shows was devoted to the theme of resiliency, as she interviewed people who had survived unbelievable disasters and come back stronger than ever.
- In sports, more and more experts are studying why some athletes and teams perform better than others after suffering a defeat, an area of enquiry that has been dubbed "athletic resilience."
- The National Cancer Institute is studying why some patients seem more physically resilient than others.
- Researchers from major universities across America are engaged in studying why some people are more emotionally resilient than others.
- "Resilience [is] the ability to get through, get over and thrive after trauma, trials, and tribulations," said the magazine. "Instead of asking *why* bad things happen to good people, researchers are now focusing on *how* good people can

666

best overcome bad events and situations. Some go so far as to call resilience the 'it' skill of the next millennium."[1]

Date: _____ _____ _____

Place: _____ _____ _____

Occasion: _____ _____ _____

A Little Brown Cork

A little brown cork fell in the path of a whale
Who lashed it down with his angry tail.
But in spite of its blows it quickly arose,
And floated serenely before his nose.
Said the cork to the whale:
"You may flap and sputter and frown,
But you never, never, can keep me down;
For I'm made of the stuff
That is buoyant enough
To float instead of to drown.[2]

Date: _____ _____ _____

Place: _____ _____ _____

Occasion: _____ _____ _____

How to Develop Resiliency

Al Siebert, Ph.D., in his book, *The Survivor Personality,* claims that emotional resilience comes from developing the following attributes:

- Be curious, play, and laugh. Life's best survivors have a child-like curiosity.
- Learn from unpleasant experiences. Treat difficult situations like a workout at the gym. You do your very best, pause afterward to reflect on what happened, and ask, "What can I learn from this?" Then imagine yourself doing better next time.
- Develop strong self-esteem. Self-esteem works like a thick skin or blanket of energy around you.
- Value your paradoxical traits. Interviews and surveys show that life's best survivors value being flexible, resilient, and adaptable above any other quality. Appreciate your inborn ability to be both one way and the opposite. It is healthy to be both serious and playful, self-appreciating and self-critical, optimistic and pessimistic, angry and forgiving, trusting and cautious. Paradoxical traits are, at the psychological level, like the opposing muscles in your body that contract and extend.

R

---

[1] Monika Guttman, "Resilience," *USA Weekend,* March 5–7, 1999, 4–5.
[2] Clipping from my files. Author unknown.

- Practice empathy for difficult people.
- Expect good outcomes.

Date:			
Place:			
Occasion:			

Life at Two Levels

Corrie Ten Boom was at the Nazi death camp Ravensbruck where roll call came at 4:30 every morning. Most mornings were cold, and sometimes the women would be forced to stand without moving for hours in the bone-chilling pre-dawn darkness.

━━━━━◇━━━━━
Calm Resolve

Resilience is the capacity for recovery.
—SHERRY LOWRY
━━━━━◇━━━━━

Nearby were the punishment barracks where all day and far into the night would come the sounds of cruelty: blows landing in regular rhythm and screams keeping pace.

But Corrie and her sister Betsie had a Bible, and at every opportunity they would gather the women together like orphans around a blazing fire, and read Romans 8: "Who shall separate us from the love of Christ? Shall tribulation, or distress, or persecution, or famine, or nakedness, or peril, or sword? . . . In all these things we are more than conquerors through Him who loved us."

Corrie later said: *I would look about us as Betsie read, watching the light leap from face to face. More than conquerors. It was not a wish. It was a fact. We knew it, we experienced it minute by minute in an ever widening circle of help and hope. Life at Ravensbruck took place on two separate levels. One, the observable, external life, grew every day more horrible. The other, the life we lived with God, grew daily better, truth upon truth, glory upon glory.*[1]

Date:			
Place:			
Occasion:			

Steps

Fay Goddard, missionary with OMF in the Philippines, had just returned to the field following her first furlough when she awoke feeling "really rotten." She had almost no strength for the simplest of daily chores. The next day her weakness was joined by a pounding head and a strange burning sensation on her lower spine. On the following day, her whole body throbbed. Her condition became so grave she was airlifted to Manila where the examining doctors told her she had polio.

Fay was stunned. At only twenty-nine, she had been vigorous and strong. Just a week before she had been hiking through the mountains; now she was all but helpless, unable even to hold a full glass of water.

Back in Seattle she was fitted for a wheelchair and told that she would be severely handicapped the rest of her life. How did she bounce back?

---

[1] Corrie Ten Boom, *The Hiding Place.*

The first thing that helped her, she later wrote, was remembering that when she had returned to the Buhid tribe following her furlough, she had taken time to kneel down in her little bedroom and reaffirm the Savior's lordship over her life. She told God she was willing to be used by Him however he chose.

Her second help came from God's word. *His promises hadn't changed. The grace was still there for the taking.*

Fay's third strength came from visiting a fellow missionary who had previously contracted polio in the Philippines, but who exhibited a determined and uplifting attitude.

Fourth, she realized she could still minister wherever she was. During her nine months in rehabilitation at the University of Washington Hospital, *I was aware that God had just changed my mission field. Instead of g-stringed, barefoot Buhid, He had put me right in the middle of a group of people whose lives had been shattered by accidents, crippling disease . . . teenage boys paralyzed from the neck down in falls on ski slopes or in twisted auto wrecks . . .*

After being released from her extended stay in the hospital, she was invited to join the home staff of OMF at their headquarters in Philadelphia. "We'll find something for you to do," they said. That's when depression hit. The "something to do" turned out to be stuffing envelopes, licking stamps, and trying to find enough to do to fill the day. Her life began to lose its purpose, and the devil attacked her spirit.

But the Lord spoke to her: "If I want you to stuff envelopes and lick stamps, what is that to you. Just follow me." Fay replied, "Okay, Lord. I'll do it." She made up her mind to obey. Within days she was given the job of producing the mission's magazine, *East Asia Millions.*

Now, more than twenty years later, I am still putting the magazine together—editing the material, doing the layout, and seeing that it is properly ready for printing. The joy is still there.[1]

Date:			
Place:			
Occasion:			

R

Therefore We Must Go Forward

William Carey, the "Father of Modern Missions," wanted to translate the Bible into as many Indian languages as possible. He established a large printshop in Serampore where translation work was continually being done. Carey spent hours each day translating Scripture, often while his insane wife ranted and raved in the next room.

Carey was away from Serampore on March 11, 1812. His associate, William Ward, was working late. Suddenly Ward's throat tightened, and he smelled smoke. He leaped up to discover clouds belching from the printing room. He screamed for help, and workers passed water from the nearby river until 2 A.M., but everything was destroyed.

[1] Fay Goddard, "In Any Way He Chooses," *When the Roof Caves In* (Republic of Singapore: Overseas Missionary Fellowship, 1985), 27–34.

On March 12, 1812, missionary Joshua Marshman entered a Calcutta classroom where William was teaching. "I can think of no easy way to break the news," he said. "The printshop burned to the ground last night." Carey was stunned. Gone were his massive polyglot dictionary, two grammar books, and whole versions of the Bible. Gone were sets of type for 14 eastern languages, 1,200 reams of paper, 55,000 printed sheets, and 30 pages of his Bengal dictionary. Gone was his complete library. "The work of years—gone in a moment," he whispered.

He took little time to mourn. "The loss is heavy," he wrote, "but as traveling a road the second time is usually done with greater ease and certainty than the first time, so I trust the work will lose nothing of real value. We are not discouraged, indeed the work is already begun again in every language. We are cast down but not in despair."

When news of the fire reached England, it catapulted Carey to instant fame. Thousands of pounds were raised for the work, and volunteers offered to come help. The enterprise was rebuilt and enlarged. By 1832, complete Bibles, New Testaments, or separate books of Scripture had issued from the printing press in 44 languages and dialects.

The secret of Carey's success is found in his resiliency. "There are grave difficulties on every hand," he once wrote, "and more are looming ahead. Therefore we must go forward."[1]

Date: _____ _____ _____
Place: _____ _____ _____
Occasion: _____ _____ _____

Thank God We Can Start Anew

In December 1914, a great, sweeping fire destroyed Thomas Edison's laboratories in West Orange, New Jersey, wiping out two million dollars' worth of equipment and the record of much of his life's work.

Edison's son Charles ran about frantically trying to find his father. Finally he came upon him, standing near the fire, his face ruddy in the glow, his white hair blown by the winter winds. "My heart ached for him," Charles Edison said. "He was no longer young, and everything was being destroyed. He spotted me. 'Where's your mother?' he shouted. 'Find her. Bring her here. She'll never see anything like this again as long as she lives.'"

The next morning, walking about the charred embers of so many of his hopes and dreams, the sixty-seven-year-old Edison said, "There is great value in disaster. All our mistakes are burned up. Thank God we can start anew."[2]

Date: _____ _____ _____
Place: _____ _____ _____
Occasion: _____ _____ _____

[1] Robert J. Morgan, *On This Day* (Nashville: Thomas Nelson Publishers, 1997).
[2] Alan Loy McGinnis, *The Power of Optimism* (New York: Harper & Row, 1990), 15–16.

Optimism

Proverbs 15:30 says: *A cheerful look brings joy to the heart, and good news gives life to the bones.*

In other words, when you look at other human beings with cheerfulness, it brings joy and life to their own spirits. They're lifted up and encouraged. The Amplified Bible translates this verse: *The light of the eyes of him whose heart is joyful rejoices the heart of others,* and the Good News Bible simply says, *Smiling faces make you happy.*

This is the real meaning behind the famous children's book *Pollyanna,* written by Eleanor Porter in 1913. It sold over a million copies and spawned a whole line of books. It was dramatized in 1916 and later made into a movie with Mary Pickford. It was later remade by Disney, starring Hayley Mills, and into a BBC production a few years later. The word *Pollyanna* even became a part of the American vocabulary, being listed in *Webster's* as "someone who is excessively happy."

That's where the problem lies. When we think of a *Pollyanna* now, we think of someone who is foolishly optimistic or excessively happy, someone who denies reality. But the book doesn't really present Pollyanna in that light. It tells of a little girl whose father, a minister, died, leaving her orphaned. Her only relative was an unpleasant and severe aunt in Vermont who took her in. But Pollyanna was an optimist who somehow managed to find a bright side to everything. Her favorite word was "glad," and she enjoyed her "Glad Game," in which she tried to find something in every situation, no matter how bad, to be glad about.

For example, when she arrived in Vermont, she thought that the servant who met her was her aunt. "Oh, Aunt Polly, I'm so glad you've come to meet me!"

"But I'm not your Aunt Polly," said the servant. "She stayed home." After taking a moment to absorb that, Pollyanna beamed and replied, "Well, I'm glad Aunt Polly didn't come to meet me—because now I can still look forward to meeting *her* and I have *you* for a friend besides!"

Pollyanna's cheerfulness eventually began to transform her aunt into a pleasant and loving person, and, in fact, the whole town became a different place because of Pollyanna, just like the verse says: *A cheerful look brings joy to the heart.*

But the real question of the book is—what was behind Pollyanna's optimism?

Like so much of earlier fiction, *Pollyanna* was written from a Christian perspective, and there's a very tender chapter in the middle of the book in which the town minister is discouraged to the point of resignation. Things hadn't gone well at church, and people were critical and divided. He rode into the forest to ponder things, and his spirits were lower than they'd ever been. Pollyanna, playing in the woods, saw him and noticed his depressed expression.

'I know how you feel,' she said as they talked. *'Father used to feel like that too, lots of times. I reckon ministers do—most generally. [My father] grew mighty discouraged until he found his rejoicing texts.'*

'His what?'

'Well, that's what father used to call 'em. Of course, the Bible didn't name 'em that. But it's all those that begin,"Be glad in the Lord," or "Rejoice greatly," or "Shout for joy," and all that, you know—such a lot of 'em. Once, when father felt specially bad, he counted 'em. There were eight hundred of 'em.'

'Eight hundred!"

'Yes—that told you to rejoice and be glad, you know; that's why father named 'em the "rejoicing texts." Father said that if God took the trouble to tell us eight hundred times to be glad and rejoice, He must want us to do it. And father felt ashamed that he hadn't done it more. After that, they got to be such a comfort to him, you know, when things went wrong, like the time the Ladies' Aiders got in a fight. Why, it was those texts, too, father said, that made him think of the Glad Game.'

Thus we learn that Pollyanna's cheerfulness wasn't really an air-headed escape from reality into the fanciful world of positive thinking. It was instead a simple childlike faith, learned from her father, trusting God and rejoicing in all life's ins-and-outs, and ups-and-downs.

Date:	_____	_____	_____
Place:	_____	_____	_____
Occasion:	_____	_____	_____

Revival

Someone Once Said . . .

- *They tell me a revival is temporary; so is a bath, but it does you good.*—Billy Sunday
- *When I was a boy, preachers used to talk about "holding a revival." What we really need is somebody who will turn a revival loose.*—Vance Havner[1]
- *A revival is the church remembering, the church repenting, the church repeating.*—Vance Havner, commenting on Revelation 2:5: "Remember therefore from whence thou art fallen, and repent, and do the first works."[2]

Date:	_____	_____	_____
Place:	_____	_____	_____
Occasion:	_____	_____	_____

What Is Revival?

One of the best summary descriptions of "Revival" is found at the beginning of an article titled "Seasons of the Spirit," in *Christian History Magazine:*

"The Scriptures show us that God's people go through periods of spiritual renewal, and periods of spiritual decline. We might think of these times like waves and troughs, or like mountains and valleys.

"During a renewal, or awakening, there will be not only a great reviving of Christians, but also a large impact on the problems of society. The period of God's

---

[1] Vance Havner, *Pepper 'n Salt* (Old Tappan, NJ: Fleming H. Revell Co., 1966), 46.
[2] Vance Havner, *Day by Day* (Old Tappan, NJ: Fleming H. Revell Co., 1953), 200.

blessing may last for many years, as did the Second Great Awakening in America, or be rather brief, as was the Third Awakening of the late 1850s.

"When the winds of a renewal have passed, the Church may enter a period of lethargy, possibly for many years. Such cycles have already been repeated many times during the 2,000 years of Christian history. It is not that the Spirit of God cannot sustain the higher life for Christians; rather, the Spirit allows times of decline to cause His people to pray for growth and for power."[1]

Date:	_____	_____	_____
Place:	_____	_____	_____
Occasion:	_____	_____	_____

Revivals in the Bible

- The Revival under King Jehoash in 2 Kings 11—12
- The Revival under King Hezekiah in 2 Kings 18
- The Revival under King Asa in 2 Chronicles 15
- The Revival under King Josiah in 2 Kings 22—23
- The Revival in the time of Zerubbabel in Ezra 5—6
- The Revival under Nehemiah in Nehemiah 8—9 and 13
- The Revival at Pentecost in Acts 2—3

Date:	_____	_____	_____
Place:	_____	_____	_____
Occasion:	_____	_____	_____

The Pietist Movement, Germany—Late 1600s

The Protestant Movement, begun by Luther in 1517, had lost much of its steam by the 1600s. All three major Protestant communions—Anglican, Reformed, and Lutheran—had chosen national churches closely tied to the political structures of their respective countries, and church life tended to be formal and shallow. Among the Anglicans in England, the desire for religious renewal led to the emergence of the Puritans. Among the Reformed Churches in Holland and elsewhere, a movement called Precicianism developed, spurred on by English Puritanism. It is sometimes referred to as Reformed Pietism.

Within Lutheranism, the tide began to turn toward revival with the publication of a devotional book called *True Christianity*, by John Arndt, who stated in the preface that he wrote the book to show Christians "wherein true Christianity consists, namely, in the proving of true, living, active faith through a genuine godliness." Arndt was much concerned about true repentance, renewal of the individual from the inside out, and about union with Christ which results in dying to self and living a Christlike life.

R

---

[1] "Seasons of the Spirit," *Christian History Magazine*, Issue 23, p. 6.

The embers of revival were whipped into flame by the preaching of Philip Jacob Spener whose controversial Christian renewal groups transformed congregational life among the Lutherans.

Among the results of this revival: Count Nicholaus Ludwig von Zinzendorf, deeply influenced by pietistic preaching, gave refuge on his estate to a group of inflamed Moravian Christians. Out of this community known as Herrnhut came the first great wave of missionaries in Protestant history. It was under the influence of the Moravians that John and Charles Wesley were moved to the Lord and began their earth-shaking ministries.[1]

> Date: _____ _____ _____
> Place: _____ _____ _____
> Occasion: _____ _____ _____

Second Great Awakening—Mid-1790s to 1840

The Second Great Awakening lasted much longer than the one in the 1740s, and had a profound influence on America and the world. In Great Britain, John Erskine of Edinburgh published a fervent plea for prayer, and two pastors took him up—John Sutcliffe and Andrew Fuller. Their personal prayers and the prayers of others whom they influenced paved the way for the Second Great Awakening. Yorkshire begin to feel the effects of these "concerts of prayer," and soon the revival spread to rural Britain. In America, Boston's Isaac Backus took up the same call to prayer.

In the region around Kentucky, the Second Great Awakening began with James McGready. Camp Meetings held by men like James McGready, Barton Stone, and, later, Peter Cartwright swept thousands into the kingdom.

In New England and the East, the awakening began at Hampden-Sydney College and spread up from Virginia into New England. In Lee, Massachusetts, in 1792, Rev. Alvan Hyde wrote: *A marvelous work was begun, and it bore the most decisive marks of being God's work. So great was the excitement though not yet known abroad, that into whatever section of the town I now went, the people in that immediate neighborhood, would leave their worldly employments, at any hour of the day, and soon fill a large room. . . . All our religious meetings are very much thronged. . . .*

Timothy Dwight, president of Yale University, became the unofficial leader of the Awakening in the Northeast as the awakening spread through the great colleges and universities that dotted the landscape.

Later, the revival was continued under the dynamic ministry of a converted lawyer-turned-preacher, Charles Grandison Finney.

> Date: _____ _____ _____
> Place: _____ _____ _____
> Occasion: _____ _____ _____

---

[1] *Christian History Magazine*, Vol. V, No. 2.

More on the Second Great Awakening

J. Edwin Orr, foremost authority on revivals, writes, "Nowhere in the world have evangelical awakenings occurred so frequently as on the campuses."

In his book, *Campus Aflame*, he describes the impact of the Second Great Awakening on American college campuses.

"During the last decade of the eighteenth century, the typical Harvard student was atheist. Students at Williams College conducted a mock celebration of Holy Communion. When the Dean at Princeton opened the chapel Bible to read, a pack of playing cards fell out, some radical having cut a rectangle out of each page to fit the pack. Christians were so unpopular that they met in secret and kept their minutes in code. The radical leader of deist students led a mob in burning the Bible of a Raritan valley Presbyterian Church. Students disrupted worship services with both profanity and sputum. They burned down buildings, and they forced the resignation of college presidents.

Rejuvenation

Revival rejuvenates the family of God; an awakening rocks the surrounding community.

—J. EDWIN ORR

"Many historians have agreed that conditions on campus and in society were deplorable. The last two decades of the eighteenth century were the darkest period, spiritually and morally, in the history of American Christianity."

Then came the Awakening.

"So far as can be ascertained," writes Orr, "the first of a series of college awakenings occurred as early as 1787. At Hampden Sydney College in Virginia, a few students, none of them active Christians but all of them concerned about the moral state of the college, met for prayer. They locked themselves in a room, for fear of the other students. One of them said, 'We tried to pray, but such prayer I never heard the like of.' He added, 'We tried to sing, but it was in the most suppressed manner, for we feared the other students.'

"The ungodly students created a disturbance, and their President came to investigate. He rebuked the rowdies and invited the intercessors to his study for continued prayer. They continued in power, until an awakening was felt at last. Within a short space of time, more than half the number of students professed conversion in a movement that stirred the local churches also."[1]

Date: _____   _____   _____

Place: _____   _____   _____

Occasion: _____   _____   _____

The Cain Ridge Revival—1801

As the Second Great Awakening flickered to life around at the end of the eighteenth century, scattered revivals erupted like geysers in the backlands of Kentucky. People gathered under makeshift arbors while the Gospel was preached, sometimes accompanied by emotional outbursts. Barton Stone, pastor of the Presbyterian church at Cain Ridge (near Lexington), hearing of the camp meetings, wit-

[1] J. Edwin Orr, *Campus Aflame* (Glendale, CA: Regal Books, 1971), iv, 19–20, 25.

nessed one for himself—*The scene was passing strange. Many fell down as slain in battle and continued for hours in an apparently motionless state—sometimes for a few moments reviving and exhibiting symptoms of life by a deep groan or by a prayer for mercy most fervently uttered.*

His church at Cain Ridge immediately planned a camp meeting for the first weekend of August, 1801. The church could hold five hundred, but workers, fearing an oversized crowd, threw up a large tent. Church families opened homes, barns, and cabins to the expected visitors.

But they didn't expect twenty thousand! Hoards arrived by horse, carriage, and wagon. Prayer and preaching continued around the clock on Friday, Saturday, and Sunday. Excitement mounted; cries and screams pierced the hazy summer air; men swooned; women were seized by spasms; children fell into ecstasy; so many fainted that the ground was covered with bodies like a battlefield. Then the "jerks" broke out. *Their heads would jerk back suddenly, frequently causing them to yelp. I have seen their heads fly back and forward so quickly that the hair of females would crack like a whip.*

On Monday, August 9, 1801, food and supplies were exhausted, and so were the worshipers. Many left, but others came to take their places. Four more days of singing, preaching, shrieking, and jerking continued before the geyser died down. Between one thousand and three thousand had been converted, and the news was the buzz of the region. People across the new nation began discussing the revival of Christianity, and church historians view the Cane Ridge Revival as among the most important religious gathering in American history.[1]

Date:			
Place:			
Occasion:			

The Fulton Street Revival and the Third Great Awakening—Late 1850s

Jeremiah C. Lanphier, a layman, accepted the call of the North Reformed Dutch Church in New York City to begin a full-time program of evangelism. He visited door-to-door, placed posters in boarding houses, and prayed. But the work languished and Lanphier grew discouraged.

As autumn fell over the city, Lanphier decided to try noontime prayer meetings, thinking that businessmen might attend during their lunch hours. He announced the first one for September 23, 1857, at the Old Dutch Church on Fulton Street. When the hour came, Lanphier found himself alone. He sat and waited. Finally, one man showed up, then a few others.

But the next week, twenty came. The third week, forty. Someone suggested the meetings occur daily, and within months the building was overflowing. Other churches opened their doors. The revival spread to other cities. Offices and stores closed for prayer at noon. Newspapers spread the story, even telegraph companies set aside certain hours during which businessmen could wire one another with news of the revival.

---

[1] Robert J. Morgan, *On This Day* (Nashville: Thomas Nelson Publishers, 1997) August 9th.

The revival—sometimes called "The Third Great Awakening"—lasted nearly two years, and between 500,000 and 1,000,000 people were said to have been converted. Out of it came the largest outlay of money for philanthropic and Christian causes America had yet experienced.

Date: _____   _____   _____
Place: _____   _____   _____
Occasion: _____   _____   _____

Revivals in the Union and Confederate Armies—Early 1860s

Major revivals broke out in the Civil War armies. In the Union Army, between 100,000 and 200,000 soldiers were converted. Among Confederate forces, approximately 150,000 troops converted to Christ. Sometimes preaching and praying continued twenty-four hours a day, and chapels couldn't hold the soldiers who wanted to get inside.

A "Great Revival" occurred among Robert E. Lee's forces in the fall of 1863 and winter of 1864. Some 7,000 soldiers were converted.[1]

Date: _____   _____   _____
Place: _____   _____   _____
Occasion: _____   _____   _____

The Fourth Great Awakening and the Welsh Revival—1904–1905

Another awakening occurred around the world in the early 1900s. It was most prominently observed in Wales. Evan Roberts was a coal miner there, tall, blue-eyed, young and thin. His dark hair curled over forehead and ears. He harbored a deep burden for souls, and he prayed earnestly for revival. At age twenty-five, having just begun studying for the ministry, he asked his pastor for permission to hold some evening meetings. Only a few people came at first, but within days village shops were closing early for the services. People left work to secure seats at church. The building was packed and roadways clogged with would-be attenders. Services often lasted till 4:30 A.M. Sins were confessed, sinners converted, homes restored.

In neighboring towns Roberts saw similar results. All across Wales, theaters closed, jails emptied, churches filled, and soccer matches were canceled to avoid conflicting with the revival. Welsh miners were so converted that their pit ponies had to be retrained to work without the prodding of curse words.

On March 29, 1905, Evan Roberts opened a series of meetings at Shaw Street Chapel in Liverpool—out of Wales into England, out of the country into the city. Thousands thronged around the church, and people poured in from all parts of England, Scotland, Ireland, the Continent, and America. Multitudes were converted or found new joy in Christ. Often Roberts didn't even preach. The very sight of him sent rivers of emotion flowing through the crowds. When he did speak his

R

---

[1] *Christian History Magazine,* Issue 33, Vol. XI, No. 1, p. 2.

message was quiet and simple: "Obedience to Jesus, complete consecration to his service, receiving the Holy Spirit and allowing ourselves to be ruled by him."

The Liverpool meetings left Roberts exhausted, needing weeks to recover. On his next preaching tour, a whirlwind of revival again swirled around him; but yet again, the young man returned home drained and exhausted. Roberts spoke four times more, then he retired to a friend's home for a week's recovery. He stayed seventeen years, and he never preached again. He spent his remaining forty-five years in secluded ministry and prayer, here and there, with friends. He died in 1951.

His public ministry had lasted only months, but it had shaken Wales and England to the foundations.[1]

Date: _____ _____ _____
Place: _____ _____ _____
Occasion: _____ _____ _____

The Shantung Revival

As an example of an incidence of localized, spontaneous revival, consider this story: One night in China, Southern Baptist missionary C. L. Culpepper stayed up late for devotions, but as he tried to pray he felt like stone. Finally he asked, "Lord, what is the matter?"

I had opened my Bible to Romans 2:17. It seemed the Apostle Paul was speaking directly to me when he said, "But if you call yourself a Christian and rely upon the Gospel, and boast of your relation to God, and know His will, and approve what is excellent; and if you are sure you are a guide to the blind, a light to those in darkness, a correction to the foolish, a teacher of children—you then who teach others, will you not teach yourself?"

The Holy Spirit used these verse like a sword to cut deeply into my heart. He said, "You are a hypocrite! You claim to be a Christian! What have you really done for Christ? The Lord said those who believed on Him would have rivers of living waters flowing from their inmost being! Do you have that kind of power?"

Culpepper awakened his wife, and they prayed into the night. The next morning at a prayer meeting with fellow workers, he confessed to pride and spiritual impotence, saying his heart was broken. The Holy Spirit began to so convict the others of sin that they could hardly bear it.

I watched their faces grow pale, then they began to cry and drop on their knees or fall prostrate on the floor. Missionaries went to missionaries confessing wrong feelings toward one another. Chinese preachers, guilty of envy, jealously and hatred, confessed their sins to one another.

The revival spread through the seminary, the schools, the hospital, and the area churches.

The impression that the Shantung Revival wrote upon my soul lingers with me even today. Throughout the breadth and depth of Shantung Province, I discovered signs of revival. The churches were crowded as never before. Attendance multiplied. Countless people gave up their idols.

Still today, my heart often returns to Shantung.[2]

---

[1] Robert J. Morgan, *On This Day* (Nashville: Thomas Nelson Publishers, 1997), March 29th.
[2] C. L. Culpepper, "The Shantung Revival," *Spirit of Revival,* October 1991, 10–15.

Date: _____ _____ _____
Place: _____ _____ _____
Occasion: _____ _____ _____

Revival Patterns

According to a sidebar in *Christian History Magazine,* spiritual awakenings, whether in biblical or church history, manifest patterns that are similar, often strikingly so. Usually the following elements are seen:

1. Awakenings are usually preceded by a time of spiritual depression, apathy and gross sin, in which a majority of nominal Christians are hardly different from the members of secular society, and the churches seem to be asleep.

2. An individual or small group of God's people becomes conscious of their sins and backslidden condition, and vows to forsake all that is displeasing to God.

3. As some Christians begin to yearn for a manifestation of God's power, a leader or leaders arise with prophetic insights into the causes and remedies of the problems, and a new awareness of the holy and pure character of the Lord is present.

4. The awakening of Christians occurs: many understand and take part in a higher spiritual life.

5. An awakening may be God's means of preparing and strengthening His people for future challenges or trials.[1]

Date: _____ _____ _____
Place: _____ _____ _____
Occasion: _____ _____ _____

How to Bring About Revival

The world's foremost authority on the subject of revivals and awakenings was Dr. J. Edwin Orr. In the early 1970s when Dr. Orr was presenting a series of lectures on revival at Columbia Bible College, a student approached him.

"Dr. Orr," said the student, "besides praying for revival to occur, what can I do to help bring it about?"

Without a moment's pause, Dr. Orr glanced at the student and replied, "You can let it begin with you."[2]

Date: _____ _____ _____
Place: _____ _____ _____
Occasion: _____ _____ _____

R

---

[1] "Patterns of Spiritual Renewal," *Christian History Magazine,* Issue 23, p. 7.
[2] Personal interview with the author.

Revive Us Again

Here in his own words is the story of a Scottish medical doctor named W. P. Mackay.

My dear mother . . . had been a godly, pious woman, quite often telling me of the Savior, and many times I had been a witness to her wrestling in prayer for my soul's conversion. But nothing had made a deep impression on me. The older I grew the more wicked I became. . . . I was in danger of becoming an infidel . . .

One day a seriously injured [laborer] had fallen a considerable distance while climbing a ladder. The case was hopeless; all we could do was ease the pains of the unfortunate man. He seemed to realize his condition, for he was fully conscious, and asked me how long he would last. . . .

The patient was alone in the world. His only wish was to see his landlady, because he owed her a small sum, and also wished to bid her farewell. He also requested his landlady send him, "The Book."

"What book?" I questioned.

"Oh, just ask her for the book, she will know," was his reply.

After a week of such suffering he died. I went to see him on my regular visits at least once a day. What struck me most was the quiet, almost happy expression which was constantly on his face. I knew he was a Christian, but about such matters I cared not to talk with him or hear.

After the man had died, some things about the deceased's affairs were to be attended to in my presence.

"What shall we do with this?" asked the nurse, holding up a book in her hand.

"What kind of book is it?" I asked.

"The Bible of the poor man. His landlady brought it on her second visit. As long as he was able to read it he did so, and when he was unable to do so any more, he kept it under his bed cover."

I took the Bible and—could I trust my eyes? It was my own Bible! The Bible which my mother had given me when I left my parents' home, and which later, when short of money, I sold for a small amount. My name was still in it, written in my mother's hand. Beneath my name was the verse she had selected for me. . . .

I need not add much more. Be it sufficient to say that the regained possession of my Bible was the cause of my conversion.

It was this man, Dr. W. P. Mackay, who later wrote the famous hymn *Revive Us Again:*

> *Revive us again,*
> *Fill each heart with Thy love*
> *May each soul be rekindled*
> *With fire from above.*
> *Hallelujah! Thine the glory*
> *Hallelujah! Amen.*
> *Hallelujah! Thine the glory*
> *Revive us again.*[1]

---

[1] Wilbur Konkel, *Living Hymn Stories* (Minneapolis: Bethany Fellowship, Inc., 1971), 15–20.

Date: _____   _____   _____
Place: _____   _____   _____
Occasion: _____   _____   _____

With Fire from Above

In his book, *The Secret of Christian Joy,* Vance Havner writes: "The greatest need of America is an old-fashioned, heaven-born, God-sent revival. Throughout the history of the church, when clouds have hung lowest, when sin has seemed blackest and faith has been weakest, there have always been a faithful few who have not sold out to the devil nor bowed the knee to Baal, who have feared the Lord and thought upon his Name and have not forsaken the assembling of themselves together. These have besought the Lord to revive his work in the midst of the years, and in the midst of the fears and tears, and in wrath to remember mercy. God has always answered such supplication, filling each heart with his love, rekindling each soul with fire from above."[1]

Date: _____   _____   _____
Place: _____   _____   _____
Occasion: _____   _____   _____

Satan

Someone Once Said . . .

- *The Adversary is not in the first two chapters of the Bible, nor is he in the last two.*—Vance Havner[2]
- *We must be careful not to advertise the devil by talking too much about him and his devices.*—Corrie Ten Boom[3]
- *There are two equal and opposite errors into which our race can fall about the devils. One is to disbelieve in their existence. The other is to believe, and to feel an excessive and unhealthy interest in them.*—C. S. Lewis, in *The Screwtape Letters*
- *[The devil exists and] is a cosmic liar and murderer . . . [who] has the skill in the world to induce people to deny his existence in the name of rationalism and of every other system of thought which seeks all possible means to avoid recognizing his activity.*—Pope John Paul II, in 1986, in the first papal pronouncement about the devil in 15 years[4]
- *I feel like Satan is almost everywhere when I'm alone. I get very afraid and I feel the presence of evil around me, like something trying to hurt me. I feel like I have a problem that will keep me from ever being close to another human being.*—Kirk, a student and wife-beater[5]

S

[1] Vance Havner, *The Secret of Christian Joy* (Old Tappan, NJ: Fleming H. Revell Co., 1938), 24.
[2] Vance Havner, *Day by Day* (Old Tappan, NJ: Fleming H. Revell Co., 1953), 249.
[3] Corrie Ten Boom, *Defeated Enemies* (Fort Washington, PA: Christian Literature Crusade, n.d.), 27.
[4] "Pontiff Addresses Satan in Sermons," *The Nashville Banner*, September 11, 1986, A12.
[5] James and Phyllis Alsdurf, *Battered into Submission* (Downers Grove, IL: InterVarsity Press, 1989), 54.

- *The prince of darkness grim, we tremble not for him; his rage we can endure, for, lo, his doom is sure, one little word shall fell him.*—Martin Luther

Date: _____   _____   _____
Place: _____   _____   _____
Occasion: _____   _____   _____

Belief in the Devil

The New York Times, in reporting on a survey by the Barna Group, noted the diminishing belief in the devil among Americans. Two-thirds of Americans do not believe in the devil as a living entity. In a nationwide telephone survey of 1,007 randomly selected people, pollsters asked whether they agreed that Satan is "not a living being, but is a symbol of evil." Sixty-two percent agreed with the statement, while 30 percent disagreed; the remaining 8 percent had no opinion.

"If less than one in three Americans seems willing to give the devil his due," reported the Times, "then that is a result of fundamental, long-term shifts in the nation's religious culture."[1]

Date: _____   _____   _____
Place: _____   _____   _____
Occasion: _____   _____   _____

The Biting Snake

According to doctors at the Good Samaritan Regional Medical Center in Phoenix, Arizona, rattlesnakes thought to be dead can still strike, bite, and kill you. Doctors in Phoenix said they have a large number of patients admitted each year suffering from bites from rattlers thought to be dead. Sometimes the snakes were shot and their heads cut off; but the snake head retains a reflex action, and one study showed that snake heads could still make striking-type motions for up to sixty minutes after decapitation.

Satan, that old serpent, was defeated at Calvary. His head was cut off. Hebrews 2 says that our High Priest, by his death, destroyed him who holds the power of death. But for a season he can still strike and wound us. He can still hurt us and poison our relationships and spread his deadly venom into our homes and lives.[2]

Date: _____   _____   _____
Place: _____   _____   _____
Occasion: _____   _____   _____

---

[1] Gustav Niebuhr, "Poll Indicates Diminished Role of Devil," The New York Times, Saturday, May 10, 1997.
[2] From a sermon by the author.

A Liar from the Beginning

In his intense study of the devices of Adolf Hitler, British Prime Minister Winston Churchill operated with one primary assumption: Any given foreign policy statement by Hitler was the exact opposite of the truth.[1]

Date: _____ _____ _____
Place: _____ _____ _____
Occasion: _____ _____ _____

Satan's Carnivorous Side

The Bible likens Satan to five different animals:

- He is a **serpent** trying to deceive God's people—Genesis 3:1; 2 Corinthians 11:3; Revelation 12:9
- He is a **bird** trying to despoil God's harvest—Matthew 13:5, 19
- He is a **wolf** trying to defeat God's flock—John 10:12; Matthew 10:16
- He is a **lion** trying to devour God's children—1 Peter 5:8
- He is a **dragon** trying to destroy God's Son—Revelation 12:1-9

Date: _____ _____ _____
Place: _____ _____ _____
Occasion: _____ _____ _____

The Counterfeiter

According to Isaiah 14 and Ezekiel 28, Satan desires to be like God. In his book about the devil, J. Oswald Sanders offers this interesting description of the counterfeit nature of his schemes:

- Satan has his own trinity—the devil, the beast, and the false prophet (Revelation 16:13)
- He has his own church—"a synagogue of Satan" (Revelation 2:9)
- He has his own ministers—"ministers of Satan" (2 Corinthians 11:4–5)
- He has formulated his own system of theology—"doctrines of demons" (1 Timothy 4:1)
- He has established his own sacrificial system—"The Gentiles . . . sacrifice to demons" (1 Corinthians 10:20)
- He has his own communion service—"the cup of demons . . . and the table of demons" (1 Corinthians 10:21)
- His ministers proclaim his own gospel—"a gospel contrary to that which we have preached to you" (Galatians 1:7–8)

S

---

[1] William Manchester, *The Last Lion: Winston Spencer Churchill, Alone* (Boston: Little, Brown and Company, 1988), 173.

- He has his own throne (Revelation 13:2) and his own worshipers (Revelation 13:4)[1]

```
Date:      _____    _____    _____
Place:     _____    _____    _____
Occasion:  _____    _____    _____
```

The Snake Inside the Shirt

Many years ago, a strong young Indian decided to climb to the summit of a nearby, snow-capped peak. He donned his buffalo-hide shirt, wrapped his blanket around himself, and set off. When he at last reached the summit and gazed over the endless panorama below, feeling the cold against him, he swelled with pride over his accomplishment.

—————◇—————
Lion or Worm?

Infidels fear the devil as a lion, but those who are strong in the faith despise him as a very little worm.
—ST. BERNARD
—————◇—————

Then he saw a motion at his feet. It was a snake, which promptly and pitifully spoke to him. "I'm about to die," said the snake. "It is too cold for me up here and I am freezing. There is no food, and I am starving. Please wrap me under your shirt and take me down to the valley."

"No," said the young man. "I know your kind. You are a rattlesnake, and if I pick you up you will bite and kill me."

"No," said the snake. "I will treat you differently. If you do this for me, you'll be special and I'll not harm you."

At last the youth gave in to the creature's pleading and tucked the snake under his shirt. Arriving down in the valley, he removed it and laid the snake on the ground. Whereupon the snake immediately coiled, rattled, struck, and planted his deadly fangs in the young man's leg.

"But you promised," said the young man, falling, feeling the deadly venom enter his bloodstream.

"You knew what I was when you picked me up," said the serpent, slithering away.

Paul wrote to the Corinthians, "I fear, lest somehow, as the serpent deceived Eve by his craftiness, so your minds may be corrupted from the simplicity that is in Christ (2 Corinthians 11:3).[2]

```
Date:      _____    _____    _____
Place:     _____    _____    _____
Occasion:  _____    _____    _____
```

Amazon Spiders

Along the banks of the Amazon River lives a species of large, colorful spiders. When one of these creatures spreads itself out, it looks exactly like the blossom of a

---

[1] J. Oswald Sanders, *Satan is No Myth* (Chicago: Moody Press, 1975), 35–36.
[2] *The Preacher's Illustration Service,* Volume 3, Number 4, July/August 1990, 5.

brilliant flower. Bees and other insects lighting upon it expect to find honey. Instead, the spider secretes a poison that drugs some of them and kills others.[1]

Date: _____   _____   _____
Place: _____   _____   _____
Occasion: _____   _____   _____

But Pulling His Hair . . .

A little girl was once disciplined by her mother for kicking her little brother in the shins and then pulling his hair. "Sally," said the mother, "why did you let the devil make you kick your brother and pull his hair?"

"The devil made me kick him," she said, "but pulling his hair was my idea!"

Date: _____   _____   _____
Place: _____   _____   _____
Occasion: _____   _____   _____

———————— Second Coming of Christ ————————

Someone Once Said . . .

- *Has not our Lord Jesus carried up our flesh into heaven and shall He not return? We know that He shall return.*—John Knox
- *The Spirit in the heart of the true believer says with earnest desire, Come, Lord Jesus.*— John Wesley
- *We must hunger after Christ until the dawning of that great day when our Lord will fully manifest the glory of His kingdom.*—John Calvin
- *Many times when I go to bed at night I think to myself that before I awaken Christ may come.*—Billy Graham
- *The coming again of Jesus Christ and the end of the age occupies some 1,845 Scriptural verses.*—John Wesley White
- *We are not just looking for something to happen, we are looking for Someone to come! And when these things begin to come to pass, we are not to drop our heads in discouragement or shake our heads in despair, but rather lift up our heads in delight.*—Vance Havner
- *Their eschatology saved them from utter despair.*—W. R. Estep, about the Anabaptists during intense persecution[2]

Date: _____   _____   _____
Place: _____   _____   _____
Occasion: _____   _____   _____

---

[1] *Our Daily Bread*
[2] W. R. Estep, *The Anabaptist Story* (Nashville: Broadman Press, 1963), 193.

"What You Saw Is the Second Coming"

Jimmy Modha, who was raised in a devout Hindu home in Leicester, England, enraged his family by coming to Christ and converting to Christianity. He told them his sins had been forgiven because he had found God.

"Which god?" shouted his father.

"It's Jesus Christ," replied Jimmy. "Actually He came and found me. He died on the cross for my sins; I am a Christian."

His mother fainted, his father threw him out of the house, and his brother Jay prayed for the gods to kill him. "We would mourn his death," said Jay, "but at least our family would not be dishonored."

Jay, a brilliant student working on his Ph.D. in parasitology at the London School of Hygiene and Tropical Medicine disowned his brother and refused to talk to him. In parting, Jimmy said, "Jay, if you are ever desperate and no one is there to help you, remember Jesus loves you, and His hand is on your life. Call to Him and He will save you."

Jay was furious, but Jimmy began praying earnestly for him.

Shortly Jay began having disturbing dreams. "It was as if I was awake in my bed at three in the morning when suddenly a blinding light broke through the roof and ceiling of my bedroom. In that light I could see a cloud descending from heaven, bearing three awesome, fiery men-like creatures. The first blew a trumpet so loud that I was sure the whole world could hear its thunderous sound. I knew whatever was coming was universal in consequence. The second creature cried out, 'Prepare ye, for the Lord is coming to reap the harvest!' Then the third swung a scythe over the earth and cried, 'Now is the earth ready for harvest!'

"I tried to wake up from the dream because I felt I was going to have a heart attack from sheer fright. But I could not. Then, in the middle of the cloud, I noticed a Person who looked completely different. The brilliant light was coming from Him. His face shone so radiantly that no features were clear except for eyes that looked like blazing flames of fire. A robe went from His neck to His feet, which were like white-hot metal. He was dreadful in His beauty and terrible in His splendor.

"As He descended, He looked at me. I was completely undone, absolutely terrified. I could not bear to look at Him any longer, so I turned my head. To my amazement, there beside me was my brother Jimmy, who was not scared at all. In fact, his face was joyous, and he was reaching out as if to embrace the figure.

"When I gained the courage to look at Him again, He addressed me saying, 'Jay, what are you going to do when this happens?' Then everything vanished, and I woke up."

It took Jay an hour to calm down, and he prayed for understanding.

A few days later, Jimmy called and, hearing of Jay's dream, said, "Jay, what you saw is the Second Coming of Christ. Can I send you a Bible so you can read about it?" Jay hung up. But more dreams disturbed his sleep, and one night he awoke horrified to realize that he had been dreaming of praying to Jesus. In time, Jay received his doctorate and was awarded a prestigious research fellowship in Japan. But in Japan, his mental state deteriorated and one night, standing on his balcony, he nearly leaped to his death. But at the last minute, he pushed himself away from the railing, vowing to find out if Jesus was, in fact, the living and true God. For two years, God pursued him and every waking moment Jay felt the wrath of God hovering over him. At length, he dug from a cupboard a dust-covered old Bible and began to read in the Gospels. When he got to the Lord's words from the cross, "Father, forgive them, for they don't know what they do," Jay realized that he was a sinner for whom Christ had died. He prayed for forgiveness and the burden of his guilt lifted.

Jay grew quickly and, moving to Glasgow, joined a church and in time began teaching and preaching. Concluding that God was calling him into the ministry, he enrolled in Reformed Theological Seminary to prepare to preach the Gospel he had once so fervently resisted.[1]

Date: _____ _____ _____
Place: _____ _____ _____
Occasion: _____ _____ _____

A. B. Simpson

Only the computers of heaven will be able to tabulate the number of Christians who will populate eternity because of the ministry of A. B. Simpson. Born in Canada's maritime provinces in 1843, Simpson became a powerful soul-winner and missionary statesman. He was a pastor, the editor of *Alliance Weekly,* and the author of more than seventy books and many poems and hymns. But Simpson is primarily remembered as the founder of two missionary societies which combined in 1897 as the Christian and Missionary Alliance, and for establishing a Bible and missionary training school in Nyack, New York, which is active to this day.

Matthew 24:14 fueled Simpson's energy.

In the early days of the Christian and Missionary Alliance, a reporter from the *New York Journal* called on Simpson for an interview. They discussed the hundreds of CMA missionaries who were spanning the globe and the hundreds of thousands of dollars going for their support. Then the reporter abruptly asked, "Do you know when the Lord is coming back?"

"Yes," said Simpson. "And I will tell you if you will promise to print just what I say, references and all."

The reporter nodded and readied his pencil.

"Put this down," said Simpson. "'And this gospel of the kingdom shall be preached in all the world as a witness unto all nations, and then shall the end come'— Matthew 24:14. Have you written down the reference?"

"Yes, what more?"

"Nothing more."

"Do you mean to say you believe that when the Gospel has been preached to all nations, Jesus will return?"

"Just that," said Simpson.

"Then," said the reporter, "I think I begin to see daylight."

---

[1] "Journey Out of Darkness," *Reformed Theological Seminary,* Winter 1998, 8–17.

"What do you think you see?"

"Why I see the motive in this movement."

"Then," said Dr. Simpson, "you see more than some of the doctors of divinity."[1]

Date: _____ _____ _____

Place: _____ _____ _____

Occasion: _____ _____ _____

The Great Disappointment

Jesus said, "No one knows the day or hour [of my Second Coming]. The angels in heaven don't know, and the Son himself doesn't know . . . So be on your guard. You don't know when your Lord will come" (Mt 24:36, 42). Those words seem clear enough, but the disregarding of them led to one of the most highly anticipated— and most disappointing—days in history.

The churches of northeastern America grew rapidly in the early 1800s, fueled by one revival after another. The new Christians had little theological education, yet many of them began to discuss details of biblical prophecy with great vigor. Speculation boiled over the exact day and year when Christ would return, and among the speculators was William Miller of New York.

Miller, when newly converted, had torn into the prophecies of Daniel, concluding in 1818 that Christ would return in 1843 or 1844. When he later began preaching, this became a keynote of his messages, and his listeners, finding him earnest, eloquent, and sincere, multiplied. He finally announced that Christ would return to earth on October 22, 1844.

The financial panic of 1839 contributed to the belief that the end of the world was approaching. Enthusiasm for Christ's return became so great that prophetic charts were added alongside stock market listings and current events in the newspapers. Miller's teachings swept through New England, and large numbers espoused Millerism.

As the morning of October 22, 1844, dawned, a sense of fear and foreboding fell over New England. People gathered on mountaintops and in churches. Normal activities ceased as everyone awaited the sudden rending of the skies and the end of the world. When the day passed uneventfully, many Christians grew disillusioned. The unsaved became cynical. The following years saw a decline in conversions, and the period of revivals came to an abrupt end. The event became known as "The Great Disappointment."[2]

Date: _____ _____ _____

Place: _____ _____ _____

Occasion: _____ _____ _____

[1] Robert J. Morgan, *From This Verse* (Nashville: Thomas Nelson Publishers, 1998).
[2] Robert J. Morgan, *On This Day* (Nashville: Thomas Nelson Publishers, 1997), October 22nd.

Who Is the Antichrist?

Throughout Christian history, various candidates have been put forward for the position of antichrist as speculation has abounded regarding the "man of lawlessness." Based on several sources, including a study by *Christian History Magazine*, here are some names proposed in the past:

- Nero. This suggestion is found in the *Martyrdom of Isaiah,* a late first-century apocalyptic text.
- Justinian. According to Procopius in *Secret History* (late sixth century), *Many men have been born who . . . have shown themselves terrible beings. But to destroy all men and to ruin the whole earth has been granted to none save . . . Justinian, Prince of demons.*
- Frederick II. This was the opinion of Pope Gregory IX, who said: *What other antichrist should we await, when as is evident in his works, he is already come in the person of Frederick?*
- Martin Luther. According to Pope Hadrian VI, *He has rejected the sacraments, repudiated the expunging of sins through fasts, and rejects the daily celebration of the Mass. . . . Does this sound to you like Christ or Antichrist?*
- Napoleon. A friend of Samuel Johnson's ". . . was always ready to cite evidence of (the French Revolution's) antichrist-like character, culminating in Napoleon."
- Leon Trotsky. *In Trotsky, into whose hands all power is already passing from the dying Lenin, is . . . the greatest Jew since Christ; behind those fierce black eyes lurks ever the demon of suspicion and mistrust . . . the coming god-emperor.*[1]
- Hitler. *I believe today that I am acting in the sense of the Almighty Creator. By warding off the Jews, I am fighting for the Lord's work.*—Hitler, in *Mein Kampf*
- Mussolini. *Hannibal, Charlemagne, Mohammed, Napoleon, the Kaiser, grasped at the world-scepter, and failed. Fascismo is a deep revival of Imperial Rome . . . a scarlet-colored beast, full of names of blasphemy, having seven heads. . . . (The) Premier of Italy . . . is known as "the man of mystery."*[2]
- Ronald Reagan. Robert Fuller, in *Naming the Antichrist,* wrote: *The beast recovers from a mortal wound, which, in the 1980s caused quite a stir in evangelical circles when Ronald Wilson Reagan—each name having six letters—was shot and yet survived.*
- Gorbachev. *Gorbachev! Has the Real antichrist come?*—title of a 1988 book[3]

Date: _____ _____ _____
Place: _____ _____ _____
Occasion: _____ _____ _____

A Bride for His Son

Dr. Thomas Lambie, veteran missionary to Africa and the Holy Land, was doing deputation work for the Sudan Interior Mission in Glasgow, Scotland. The work

[1] D. M. Panton, James McAlister, A. Sims, *Startling Signs of Great World Changes* (Toronto: A. Sims, Publisher, 1926), 28.

[2] Panton, McAlister, Sims, *Startling Signs of Great World Changes,* 34.

[3] "Hall of Infamy," *Christian History,* Issue 61, 2–3.

was hard and seemed unproductive. One evening, coming home tired and discouraged, his host met him at the door and said, "I want to tell you a story before you go to bed."

Though Dr. Lambie was exhausted, he paused to listen. It was a story he never forgot, and he found that it greatly encouraged him—and those to whom he later shared it.

There once lived a great nobleman whose wife was dead, and his only child was a beautiful young lady of marriageable age. The father invited all the young noblemen in the country to come for a whole week of entertainment at his castle. During this week, when the young men were in close proximity with her, surely a suitable match could be made with someone of equal rank.

Great preparations were made for the festivities. A band of strolling players was hired. Minstrels were engaged and clowns and jesters, and a great store of food and drink. Whole pigs were roasted along with capons, hares, and pheasants. A hundred appetizing foods were prepared, and vast quantities of nut brown ale and mead, wines of Oporto and muscatel. The whole castle was in a bustle of preparation for the notable guests.

Early on the morning of the day of their arrival a loud knocking was heard at the postern gate of the castle, and an apparently deformed man on crutches appeared. A few crusts were unceremoniously thrust at him and the gate slammed shut in his face. He refused the crusts but he continued to knock.

"Give him a few farthings, someone, and get rid of him." But these he refused and continued to knock.

"Go away, you varlet, or we will unleash the dogs on you." But he continued to knock and beat upon the oaken panel with his crutches.

"What is it you want?"

"Is not this the day appointed for the guests to come to seek for the nobleman's daughter? It is for this that I have come, to beg for her hand," and he edged his way into the cobbled courtyard.

"What, you?"

"Oh, do come and hear this poor deluded beggar." Peals of laughter echoed as cooks and servants and soldiers deserted their duties and gathered round to laugh and mock at the poor fool.

The daughter was being adorned for the guests and she inquired of her maid what all the noise in the courtyard was about. Between giggles the maid said, "It's a poor beggar who wants to marry you."

"I'll go and see him."

Down the winding stairs she went, through the deserted kitchen where meats were baking, out into the cobbled yard, and the crowd opened to let her pass.

"What is it you want?" she asked the beggar. He fastened upon her an earnest look.

"I have seen you while I myself was unnoticed, and I love you and have come to ask if you will marry me?" Groans and laughter from the crowd. She paused and gave him look for look.

"Yes, I will marry you." More shrieks of merriment from the crowd.

"When?" said he.

"In a year and a day."

"Very well, I will return," and he hobbled off.

"You are a clever girl, you knew what to say to get rid of him."

"I meant what I said." More laughter.

"Of course you didn't. What fun!"

The guests arrived in due course but she gave them no encouragement. The nobleman scolded and importuned, and finally was actually cruel to his daughter. The servants, taking their cue from him, were the same. Gloom descended on the castle even before the departure of the guests. Then ensued an unhappy year for the girl, for although she did her best to please her father, for she was a good girl, he was not to be appeased.

"You would marry a beggar," he said. "He will never come back, that's sure." She would smile gently, but even this would only infuriate him. A year passed and only one day remained if the beggar were to show up. The morning passed uneventfully, and high noon. Then something quite different took place.

Distant peals of music and the rumbling of drums was heard, and the sun flashed on spears and polished armor. A courier spurred to the gate with the astonishing news that the king's son, the royal prince, was arriving at once. There was not time for preparation. The nobleman, accompanied by his daughter, had barely time to reach the castle gate where he saw, riding between two rows of knights and squires that reached to the far horizon, the king's son. He was mounted on a magnificent white charger and was clad in golden armor while his face shone as the sun.

Swinging gracefully from his steed he stood in front of the nobleman to whom he gave no recognition. He took the girl by the hand and in a most endearing fashion said, "My love, I have come back for you, even as I promised." Her eyes filled with tears as she murmured, "I knew you would come." So he took her, his bride, to his royal kingdom far away. But before she left there was just time for one of the maids to ask, "How did you know that the beggar was the prince in disguise?"

"Ah," she said, "I looked into his eyes and something I saw there, I listened to his voice and something I heard there, made me know that he was indeed the son of the king."

It is like that. The Lord Jesus came in humility as the poorest of men. He came for His Bride. The Bride is being made ready. She is now scorned and made light of, misunderstood and rejected of men. You, if you are in Christ Jesus, are that Bride. What does it matter if men despise you? Remember you are His beloved Bride, His greater Rebekah. He loves you with an everlasting love, and one glad day He is coming to claim you to be forever His. Yes, a Bride for God's Son. He is coming soon.[1]

Date: _____ _____ _____

Place: _____ _____ _____

Occasion: _____ _____ _____

---

[1] Thomas A. Lambie, *A Bride For His Son* (New York: Loizeaux Brothers, 1957), 25–29.

Predictions

1. "Computers in the future may weigh no more than 1.5 tons."—*Popular Mechanics, forecasting the relentless march of science, 1949*

2. "I think there is a world market for maybe five computers."—*Thomas Watson, chairman of IBM, 1943*

3. "I have traveled the length and breadth of this country and talked with the best people, and I can assure you that data processing is a fad that won't last out the year."—*The editor in charge of business books for Prentice-Hall, 1957*

4. "But what . . . is it good for?"—*Engineer at the Advanced Computing Systems Division of IBM, 1968, commenting on the microchip*

5. "There is no reason anyone would want a computer in their home."—*Ken Olson, president, chairman and founder of Digital Equipment Corp., 1977*

6. "This 'telephone' has too many shortcomings to be seriously considered as a means of communication. The device is inherently of no value to us."—*Western Union internal memo, 1876*

7. "The wireless music box has no imaginable commercial value. Who would pay for a message sent to nobody in particular?"—*David Sarnoff's associates in response to his urgings for investment in the radio in the 1920s*

8. "The concept is interesting and well-formed, but in order to earn better than a 'C,' the idea must be feasible."—*A Yale University management professor, in response to Fred Smith's paper proposing reliable overnight delivery service. [Smith went on to found Federal Express Corporation]*

9. "Who the (blank) wants to hear actors talk?"—*H. M. Warner, Warner Brothers, 1927*

10. "I'm just glad it'll be Clark Gable who's falling on his face and not Gary Cooper."—*Gary Cooper on his decision not to take the leading role in* Gone With the Wind

11. "A cookie store is a bad idea. Besides, the market research reports say America likes crispy cookies, not soft and chewy cookies like you make."—*Response to Debbi Fields' idea of starting Mrs. Fields' Cookies*

12. "We don't like their sound, and guitar music is on the way out."—*Decca Recording Co. rejecting the Beatles, 1962*

13. "Heavier-than-air flying machines are impossible."—*Lord Kelvin, president, Royal Society, 1895*

14. "If I had thought about it, I wouldn't have done the experiment. The literature was full of examples that said you can't do this."—*Spencer Silver on work that led to the unique adhesives for 3-M "Post-It" Notepads*

15. "So we went to Atari and said, 'Hey, we've got this amazing thing, even built with some of your parts, and what do you think about funding us? Or we'll give it to you. We just want to do it. Pay our salary, we'll come work for you.' And they said, 'No.' So then we went to Hewlett-Packard, and they said, 'Hey, we don't need you. You haven't got through college yet.' "—*Apple Computer Inc. founder Steve Jobs on attempts to get Atari and H-P interested in his and Steve Wozniak's personal computer*

16. "Professor Goddard does not know the relation between action and reaction and the need to have something better than a vacuum against which to react. He seems to lack the basic knowledge ladled out daily in high schools."—*1921 New York Times editorial about Robert Goddard's revolutionary rocket work*

17. "You want to have consistent and uniform muscle development across all of your muscles? It can't be done. It's just a fact of life. You just have to accept inconsistent muscle development as an unalterable condition of weight training."—*Response to Arthur Jones, who solved the "unsolvable" problem by inventing Nautilus*

18. "Drill for oil? You mean drill into the ground to try and find oil? You're crazy."—*Drillers who Edwin L. Drake tried to enlist to his project to drill for oil in 1859*

19. "Stocks have reached what looks like a permanently high plateau."—*Irving Fisher, Professor of Economics, Yale University, 1929*

20. "Airplanes are interesting toys but of no military value."—*Marechal Ferdinand Foch, Professor of Strategy, Ecole Superieure de Guerre*

21. "Everything that can be invented has been invented."—*Charles H. Duell, Commissioner, U.S. Office of Patents, 1899*

22. "Louis Pasteur's theory of germs is ridiculous fiction."—*Pierre Pachet, Professor of Physiology at Toulouse, 1872*

23. "The abdomen, the chest, and the brain will forever be shut from the intrusion of the wise and humane surgeon."—*Sir John Eric Ericksen, British surgeon, Surgeon-Extraordinary to Queen Victoria, 1873*

24. "640K ought to be enough for anybody."—*Bill Gates, 1981*[1]

Date: _____ _____ _____

Place: _____ _____ _____

Occasion: _____ _____ _____

Why Should He Change?

Three preachers were discussing the question, "If Jesus Christ came back to earth what church would he go to?"

The Episcopalian said, "He would go to the Episcopal Church because of our line of Apostolic Succession."

The Holiness said, "He would go to the Holiness Church because of our enthusiasm."

The Baptist said, "Of course, He would go to the Baptist church. Why should he change after all these years?"

S

Date: _____ _____ _____

Place: _____ _____ _____

Occasion: _____ _____ _____

[1] < www.bible-reading.com >

Singles

Someone Once Said . . .

- *The truth is that life is always difficult, whether one is married or not.*—Paul Tournier[1]
- *In today's pro-family church, it's not surprising that single men wonder where they fit in. It's time for us to see the critical role that single men should play in the church, just as it was when the first church was formed.*—Bill Dyment[2]
- *With all my heart I am seeking to embrace my singleness not as a consolation prize, but as a high calling.*—Bill Dyment[3]
- *It's not a problem—it's a gift!*—Elisabeth Elliot
- *For far too long, singles have been relegated to special meetings somewhere in the basement of churches.*—Doug Murren

Date:	_____	_____	_____
Place:	_____	_____	_____
Occasion:	_____	_____	_____

Stats

- 22,580,420 people live alone in the United States.
- Households made up of singles ages 18 to 34 account for about 58 percent of all one-person households.
- In the 1990 U.S. Census, 83 percent of all American men between the ages of 20–24 are single; 25 percent between the ages of 35 and 65 are single, as are 19 percent of those between 55 and 65.

Date:	_____	_____	_____
Place:	_____	_____	_____
Occasion:	_____	_____	_____

Eating Alone

The Wall Street Journal, noticing the incredible increase of one-person households in the United States, ran an article on the "Unseemly Secrets of Eating Alone."

" 'The Dining Room is increasingly the least used room in the house,' says Dr. Saul Katz. Jean Williams, a writer in Chicago, doesn't eat at her dining room table unless she has company. The twenty-six-year-old eats sitting up in bed, or at the kitchen counter or in front of her computer. 'I have this elaborately made-up table

---

[1] Paul Tournier, *The Adventure of Living* (San Francisco: Harper & Row, 1965), 136.
[2] Bill Dyment, "Single On Purpose," *New Man,* January/February 1995, 77.
[3] Bill Dyment, "Single On Purpose," *New Man,* January/February, 1995, 77.

with a flower arrangement in the middle. If I sit there, I've got to move all that stuff,' she says.

"Other singles bypass the table to be near the television. 'Usually I have dinner with the news people,' says Alan Tu, thirty, a radio producer in Philadelphia. 'It's kind of like sitting down with your date, but it's on TV.' "[1]

Date:			
Place:			
Occasion:			

Meals Should Be Pleasurable

Writing in *Christianity Today*, Cheryl Forbes, a single, said, "Meals should be pleasurable no matter what your marital state. Tom Howard is quite right when he says in *Splendor in the Ordinary* that a meal, whether a cheese sandwich or a cheese soufflé, is an image of the eucharistic feast and ought to be treated thus. I am a better and more imaginative cook now than I was five years ago. I am free to experiment on myself and my friends. I have the time and the money to entertain people around the dinner table, something I might not want or be able to do if I cooked for a family three times a day every day."[2]

Date:			
Place:			
Occasion:			

Singles in Church History

Some of the greatest leaders of church history lived their whole lives as singles: Saint Francis of Assisi, Thomas Aquinas, Joan of Arc, Teresa of Avila, Thomas à Kempis, Bernard of Clairvaux. More recently, Protestant leaders such as Methodist circuit rider Francis Asbury, missionaries Amy Carmichael and Helen Roseveare, and German martyr Dietrich Bonhoeffer were all single. C. S. Lewis was a bachelor for most of his life, married at age fifty-seven, was married for only four years, and remained a celibate widower after his wife's death. British theologian John Stott, now in his seventies and never married, has had a significant worldwide ministry. Mother Teresa spent seven decades serving the poor in India as a single woman.[3]

S

Date:			
Place:			
Occasion:			

[1] Calmetta Y. Coleman, "The Unseemly Secrets of Eating Alone," *The Wall Street Journal,* July 6, 1995, B-1.
[2] Cheryl Forbes, "Let's Not Shackle the Single Life," *Christianity Today,* February 16, 1979, 17.
[3] Albert Hsu, "Singleness: A Biblical Perspective," *Discipleship Journal,* Issue 108, 36.

Amy Carmichael

In 1 Corinthians 7, the Bible recommends the single life, for unmarried people have more time for the Lord and fewer burdens to distract from his work. But it isn't an easy road, and remaining single requires special grace, as Amy Carmichael found out.

Amy Wilson Carmichael (1867–1951) was born in Northern Ireland and educated in a Wesleyan Methodist boarding school. Having a heart for missions, she spent fifteen months in Japan, but suffered there physically and emotionally. She traveled on to Ceylon, to England, then to India where she found her niche at last, working with girls whom she rescued from slavery and prostitution, raising them in her Dohnavur Fellowship. Her life touched thousands, her books have blessed millions, and her work remains to this day.

Like most young ladies, Amy, attractive and radiant, wanted to be married. But her great work would have been impossible as a married woman, and God gave her Psalm 34:22 as a special promise. Amy's struggle with this issue was deeply personal, one she was unable to share for more than forty years, when at last she said this to one of her "children" who was facing a similar dilemma:

On this day many years ago I went away alone to a cave in the mountain called Arima. I had feelings of fear about the future. That is why I went there—to be alone with God. The devil kept on whispering, "It's all right now, but what about afterwards? You are going to be very lonely." And he painted pictures of loneliness—I can see them still. And I turned to my God in a kind of desperation and said, "Lord, what can I do? How can I go on to the end?" And he said, "None of them that trust in Me shall be desolate" (Psalm 34:22). That word has been with me ever since.

Date: _____ _____ _____

Place: _____ _____ _____

Occasion: _____ _____ _____

Older Singles

For fifty years Agnes Frazier and her husband Emit had morning Bible reading and prayer at the breakfast table. On the day he died, she went to bed thinking that she could never again start the day with devotional exercises. But the next morning she bravely sat at the kitchen table and opened her Bible to the spot where she and her husband had quit their reading twenty-four hours before. The verse that stared up at her was: *For thy Maker is thy husband.*

She smiled and said, "Thank you, Lord."[1]

Date: _____ _____ _____

Place: _____ _____ _____

Occasion: _____ _____ _____

---

[1] Personal interview with the author.

The Freedom of Being Single

I read about one woman who, after many years of being single, accepted a man's proposal and married him. It terribly disrupted her life. Up until then she had freedom to go where she wanted to go, to do what she wanted to do. She had everything arranged in her house just the way she liked it. She had her cosmetics arranged in her bathroom just so. She could go to bed when she wanted, and she could get up when she wanted. She prepared what she liked to eat without having to bother with anyone's else's fussiness. She had the house empty so that she could pray and study her Bible and sing to the Lord. And she had nothing to distract her from pouring herself into her church and into the service of the Lord.

All that changed when she married, and she testified later, "I finally adjusted to it and I love my husband; I believe it was God's will to marry. But I gave up a lot of advantages, and I often miss being single. I had so much more freedom to serve the Lord as a single than I do now."

Which is better—being married or being single? Both, and neither! God leads us all differently, and there are advantages and disadvantages to both. But in 1 Corinthians 7:1, the Apostle Paul said in effect, "It is good to be single." And in verse 7 he said, "I love being single. I wish everyone could be single like I am. I wish all were as I am."[1]

Date: _____ _____ _____

Place: _____ _____ _____

Occasion: _____ _____ _____

John Berridge

Had John Berridge lived in London or Edinburgh, he would have been famous for his powerful preaching, but the Lord placed him in out-of-the-way villages where he became the "Whitefield of the countryside." John was quaint and eccentric, but his strange ways merely added to the appeal and power of his ministry. He preached to great crowds in rural England, in one year alone leading over four thousand people to Christ— and he evangelized nonstop for thirty years.

> ——◆——
> **Singular Thought**
>
> *Aloneness and Loneliness are not the same thing.*
> —ANONYMOUS SINGLE
> ——◆——

He insisted he could most effectively minister by remaining unmarried, and he worried that the Wesley brothers and George Whitefield didn't do likewise. George Whitefield had married a woman with whom he had spent less than a week; she died in 1768. And poor John Wesley had marital woes. Writing to Lady Huntingdon, patron of the English evangelists, Berridge observed: *No trap [is] so mischievous to the field-preacher as wedlock; and it is laid for him at every hedge corner. Matrimony has quite maimed poor Charles [Wesley], and might have spoiled John [Wesley] and George [Whitefield], if a wise Master had not graciously sent them a brace [pair] of ferrets. Dear George has his liberty again, and he will escape well if he is not caught by another tenterhook. Eight or nine years ago, having been*

---

[1] From a sermon by the author.

grievously tormented with housekeeping, I thought of looking out for a [wife] myself. But it seemed highly needful to ask advice of the Lord. So, kneeling down before the table, with a Bible between my hands, I besought the Lord to give me direction.

The Lord gave John Berridge Jeremiah 16:2—"You shall not take a wife, nor shall you have sons and daughters in this place . . ." Thus he relinquished all thoughts of marriage, and gave himself to pleasing the Lord "without distraction."

Date:	_____	_____	_____
Place:	_____	_____	_____
Occasion:	_____	_____	_____

Hope for Single Parents

When you, as a single parent, grow discouraged, just consider how many children in the Bible, raised in single-parent homes, proved successful in life:

- Hagar was forced to raise Ishmael alone, but according to Genesis 21:20, "God was with the lad, and he grew. . . ."
- After her husband's death, Naomi had to raise her sons alone, but in the process gained Ruth as a daughter-in-law.
- Moses was raised by the daughter of Pharaoh.
- The widow of Zarephath in 1 Kings 17 was a single mother whose needs were met by God.
- The widow in 2 Kings 4 was trying to keep her sons from falling into slavery through poverty. God miraculously provided for her needs.
- Josiah, one of the greatest kings of the Old Testament, was raised by his mother after his father was assassinated.
- Queen Esther was raised by her older cousin Mordecai, a man of steel nerves and steady faith.
- The story of the widow of Nain in Luke 7 is an example of the grace and love of Jesus Christ for single parents.
- Jesus and His half-siblings were raised by a single mother after the apparent death of Joseph.
- Timothy seems to have been raised primarily by his mother and grandmother, with little being said in Scripture about his father.
- The Lord, we are told, is a Father to the fatherless, a Mother to the motherless, a Husband to the widow, a Companion to the single parent. And his grace is sufficient.[1]

Date:	_____	_____	_____
Place:	_____	_____	_____
Occasion:	_____	_____	_____

[1] Robert J. Morgan, *Empowered Parenting* (Lifeway Press, 1996), 38–40.

Small Numbers

Someone Once Said . . .

- *Those empty benches are a serious trial, and if the place be large and the congregation small, the influence is seriously depressing.*—Charles Spurgeon[1]
- *Could we but see the smallest fruit, we could rejoice midst the privations and toils which we bear; but as it is, our hands do often hang down.*—Mary Moffat, missionary
- *The preacher who will not preach his heart out before a few people would be no good before a multitude.*—Vance Havner[2]
- *I do not believe there are any small churches. I am more and more convinced that we should be very careful what epithets we attach to the term "church."*—Joseph Parker[3]
- *We can often do more with less, and sometimes the scope of our impact is in reverse proportion to the size of our audience. Jesus had more success with one Samaritan woman than with all Jerusalem, and Gideon found three hundred committed men preferable to thirty-two thousand vacillators. God called Philip from a citywide revival to a congregation of one in the desert.*[4]
- *Watch for souls, not statistics. God keeps the books. Matthew Henry lamented over the poor response to his ministry and felt that his labors were done, since so many had left and few had been added. But he still feeds us with messages not too well appreciated in his own time. One of the many delusions from which the ministry needs to be delivered today is the notion that a preacher may be judged by the size of his crowd.*—Vance Havner
- *We dare not measure the quality of our sermons by the quantity of the statistics. If we do, we might become either too elated or too depressed, and both pride and discouragement are sins. One day our Lord gave a sermon on the Bread of Life and lost His whole congregation, and yet false prophets always seem to have a crowd.*—Warren Wiersbe

Date: _____   _____   _____
Place: _____   _____   _____
Occasion: _____   _____   _____

The Success Syndrome

In their book, *Liberating Ministry from the Success Syndrome,* Kent and Barbara Hughes describe their anguish when, early in ministry, they were given a promising church-planting work in Southern California. When the work floundered, Kent grew depressed. "If church attendance was up, I was up; if it was down, so was I. And the numbers had been going down for a long time." But gradually the Lord led the Hughes to ponder these questions: "Can a man be a success in the ministry and pastor a small church? What is failure in ministry? What is success in ministry?" From the experience, Kent learned that God defines success in ministry as being

---

[1] Charles H. Spurgeon, *Lectures to My Students* (Grand Rapids, MI: Zondervan, 1954), 311.
[2] Vance Havner, *Hearts Afire* (Old Tappan, NJ: Fleming Revell Co., 1952), 22.
[3] Joseph Parker, *A Preacher's Life* (London: Hodder and Stoughton, n.d.), 258.
[4] From an article by the author.

faithful, serving others, loving and trusting Him, praying, pursuing holiness, and developing a positive attitude. This liberating discovery enabled Hughes to plunge back into his work, despite its paucity, with joy and enthusiasm. "We saw how success was equally possible for those in the most difficult situations . . . as well as those having vast ministries."[1]

Date: _____ _____ _____
Place: _____ _____ _____
Occasion: _____ _____ _____

D. L. Moody's Numbers

According to A. P. Fitt, D. L. Moody never counted converts. "He depreciated the boastful use of statistics. People used to ask him what were the most notable conversions he had achieved, and the greatest meetings he ever conducted. They could not draw him out on such matters."[2]

Date: _____ _____ _____
Place: _____ _____ _____
Occasion: _____ _____ _____

Only One

After the Civil War, John Broadus, burdened for more preachers to heal the nation's wounds, prepared a seminary course on homiletics. To his dismay only one student, a blind man, enrolled in the class. "I shall give him my best and I shall pursue my lectures as planned," said Broadus. Day after day, Broadus gave his lectures conversationally to his solitary, sightless student—lectures so powerful they later became the classic, *The Preparation and Delivery of Sermons,* that has gone through countless printings and is inspiring young ministerial students to this day.[3]

Date: _____ _____ _____
Place: _____ _____ _____
Occasion: _____ _____ _____

As If to Hundreds

Mrs. William Butler and Mrs. E. W. Parker of India envisioned a women's missionary society for their denomination, the Methodist Episcopal Church. But on the day of its organizing, a pelting rain kept the women at home. Only six showed up. Mrs. Butler and Mrs. Parker, however, "spoke as eloquently as if to hundreds."

[1] Kent and Barbara Hughes, *Liberating Ministry from the Success Syndrome* (Wheaton: Tyndale House Publishers, 1987).
[2] Warren W. Wiersbe, *Listening to the Giants* (Grand Rapids, MI: Baker Book House, 1980), 313.
[3] Benjamin P. Browne, *Tales of Baptist Daring* (Philadelphia: The Judson Press, 1961), 106.

Out of that meeting came the Women's Foreign Missionary Society of the Methodist Episcopal Church.

Date: _____ _____ _____
Place: _____ _____ _____
Occasion: _____ _____ _____

Prophets to the Discouraged

The messages of Haggai and Zechariah were specifically given to encourage those whose work seemed small in their own eyes. "How does [your work for the Lord] look to you now? Does it not seem to you like nothing? But now be strong . . . and work. For I am with you . . . I will fill this house with glory . . ." (Haggai 2:2–3, 7, NIV). "Who despises the day of small things?" (Zechariah 4:10, NIV). We both walk and work by faith, seeing in this life only a small fraction of our results. We are doing more good than we know.[1]

Date: _____ _____ _____
Place: _____ _____ _____
Occasion: _____ _____ _____

Failed Service?

January 6, 1850, was bitterly cold in Colchester, England, a hard-biting blizzard keeping most worshipers at home. At the Primitive Methodist Chapel on Artillery Street only about a dozen showed up. When it became apparent that even the pastor would not arrive, an unlettered man rose and spoke haltingly from Isaiah 45:22, then the crowd dispersed, thinking the day's service a loss—not realizing that a fifteen-year-old boy had ducked into the room to escape the snowstorm, and, hearing the sermon, had been converted.

Years later that boy, Charles Spurgeon, wrote: "Don't hold back because you cannot preach in St. Paul's; be content to talk to one or two in a cottage. You may cook in small pots as well as in big ones. Little pigeons can carry great messages. Even a little dog can bark at a thief, wake up the master, and save the house. . . . Do what you do right thoroughly, pray over it heartily, and leave the result to God."[2]

—✧—
Reasonable Numeration

The reason we count numbers is because numbers count.

—ANONYMOUS
—✧—

S

Date: _____ _____ _____
Place: _____ _____ _____
Occasion: _____ _____ _____

---

[1] From a sermon to ministers by the author.
[2] Charles Haddon Spurgeon, *John Ploughman's Talks* (New York: Sheldon & Company, n.d), 160–161.

The "Small" Church

Carl S. Dudley wrote, *In a big world, the small church has remained intimate. In a fast world, the small church has been steady. In an expensive world, the small church has remained plain. In a complex world, the small church has remained simple. In a rational world, the small church has kept feelings. In a mobile world, the small church has been an anchor. In an anonymous world, the small church calls us by name.*[1]

Date: _____   _____   _____

Place: _____   _____   _____

Occasion: _____   _____   _____

Spurgeon's Small Audience

Even Charles Spurgeon faced a small crowd—once. At age nineteen, shortly after he had begun preaching, he was invited to the village of Isleham. The deacons hoped for such crowds that they borrowed the largest chapel in the neighborhood, but when the day came the congregation in the morning numbered—seven. Charles, nothing daunted, preached one of his best sermons, with the result that in the evening there was not standing room in the place.[2]

Date: _____   _____   _____

Place: _____   _____   _____

Occasion: _____   _____   _____

Cartwright's Small Audience

Peter Cartwright, the early American circuit-rider, once planned an evangelistic crusade in which, on the first night, only one person showed up. Cartwright nevertheless preached his best for 45 minutes to a one-eyed Presbyterian elder. "It was the greatest sermon I ever heard," said the elder, spreading the news all over town. The next night, the hillside was covered with horses and wagons, the hall overflowed, and revival came.[3]

Date: _____   _____   _____

Place: _____   _____   _____

Occasion: _____   _____   _____

George Matheson's Small Audience

George Matheson grew discouraged over his small crowd one winter's evening in Innellan, Scotland. He had worked hard on his sermon, but the sparse numbers

---

[1] Carl S. Dudley, *Making the Small Church Effective, NAE Action,* November-December 1988, 5.

[2] W. Y. Fullerton, *Charles H. Spurgeon: London's Most Popular Preacher* (Chicago: Moody Press, 1966), 51.

[3] J. Gilchrist Lawson, *Deeper Experiences of Famous Christians* (Anderson, Indiana: The Warner Press, 1911), 238.

and empty chairs nearly defeated him. He nonetheless did his best, not knowing that in the congregation was a visitor from the large St. Bernard's Church in Edinburgh, which was seeking a pastor. "Make every occasion a great occasion," said Matheson, who was to spend the rest of his career at St. Bernard's. "You can never tell when somebody may be taking your measure for a larger place."[1]

Date: _____ _____ _____

Place: _____ _____ _____

Occasion: _____ _____ _____

G. Campbell Morgan and Crowds

"All through his life Campbell Morgan was . . . acutely conscious of numbers . . .

"The consciousness of numbers remained always with him. From the earliest days he was in the habit of noting carefully the attendance at services. A large congregation inspired him; empty pews dampened his spirit. Some would call it a flaw or a weakness of character and perhaps it was, for he was known to have cancelled an engagement because people did not seem to want him, and even left a pastorate largely because of the fact that the empty seats were an indication to him that his work was not appreciated. 'Numbers are not everything, but they certainly are indicative,' he once wrote in a letter, and repeated it many times in one way or another during the course of his active ministry . . . However, when he once said, "Always I would rather address a thousand people than one," he revealed a basic feature of his character.

Date: _____ _____ _____

Place: _____ _____ _____

Occasion: _____ _____ _____

The Invisible Congregation

"Has not every preacher an invisible congregation? At every service, there is a dim, unseen, listening throng," wrote the inimitable F. W. Boreham.

Who are they? Christ is present, the angels gather, and don't forget those outside the church who will be touched by your sermon through its impact on your listeners. And there is yet another audience, said Boreham, a vast one who will be affected more than we can know: "There are generations yet unborn. Posterity is simply the invisible congregation, sitting a little farther down the aisle."[2]

Date: _____ _____ _____

Place: _____ _____ _____

Occasion: _____ _____ _____

S

---

[1] Warren W. Wiersbe and Lloyd M. Perry, *The Wycliffe Handbook of Preaching and Preachers* (Chicago: Moody Press, 1984), 192.

[2] F. W. Boreham, *The Crystal Pointers* (London: The Epworth Press, 1925), Ch. 1.

More F. W. Boreham

"I'm fond of *little* things. I like little flowers. I like little hills. I can't love anything that isn't a pocket edition. . . . Walt Whitman wrote:

> *I believe a leaf of grass is no less than a journey-work of the stars,*
> *And the pismire is equally perfect, and the grain of sand,*
> *and the egg of a wren,*
> *And the tree-toad is a chef-d'oeuvre for the highest,*
> *And the running blackberry would adorn the parlours of Heaven,*
> *And the narrowest hinge in my hand puts to scorn all machinery,*
> *And the cow, crunching with depressed head, surpasses any statue,*
> *and a mouse is miracle enough to stagger sextillions of infidels.*

"Therein lies the wonder of all really wonderful things. An acorn is a wonderful thing; it is a pocket edition of a forest. Time is a wonderful thing; it is the tabloid of eternity. The Bible is a wonderful thing; it is a pocket edition of the thought of God"—F. W. Boreham, in *The Crystal Pointers*

Date:			
Place:			
Occasion:			

Edward Payson's Small Audience

In the *Life of Edward Payson* it is recorded that, on a stormy Sunday, the famous preacher had but one hearer. Mr. Payson preached his sermon, however, as carefully and as earnestly as though the great building had been thronged with eager listeners. Some months afterwards his solitary auditor called on him.

"I was led to the Savior through that service," he said. "For whenever you talked about sin and salvation, I glanced around to see to whom you referred, but since there was no one there but me, I had no alternative but to lay every word to my own heart and conscience!"

Date:			
Place:			
Occasion:			

Hudson Taylor's Small Audience

When Hudson Taylor was once advised to cancel an appointment on a stormy night in Birmingham, England, he replied, "I must go, even if there is no one but the doorkeeper." Only a dozen showed up, but the meeting hummed with unusual spiritual power. Half of those present later became missionaries or gave their children as missionaries, and the rest were faithful supporters of China Inland Mission for years to come.[1]

---

[1] Warren W. Wiersbe and Lloyd M. Perry, *The Wycliffe Handbook of Preaching and Preachers* (Chicago: Moody Press, 1984), 242.

Date: _____   _____   _____
Place: _____   _____   _____
Occasion: _____   _____   _____

Only Three Showed Up

On September 14, 1898, at the Central Hotel of Boscobel, Wisconsin, John Nicholson arrived at 9 P.M., longing for a quiet room to write up his orders. To his disappointment, every room was taken. The clerk suggested he share Room 19 with a stranger, Samuel Hill.

Before crawling into bed, Nicholson opened his Bible. At age twelve, he had promised his dying mother he would read the Bible every night at bedtime. "Read it aloud," said Hill. "I'm a Christian, too." Nicholson read John 15 and the two knelt for prayer. Then they stayed up till 2 A.M. discussing the spiritual needs of Christians on the road.

Nicholson and Hill bumped into each other again the following May in Beaver Dam, Wisconsin. They soon announced plans for an association of Christian salesmen and set the first meeting for July 1, 1899. Only three showed up—Nicholson, Hill, and Will J. Knights. The men nonetheless launched their organization to mobilize Christian commercial travelers for encouragement, evangelism, and service. They groped for a name, but after they had prayed about it Knights said, "We shall be called Gideons." The Gideons have since distributed over seven hundred fifty million copies of Scripture in over one hundred seventy nations.

Date: _____   _____   _____
Place: _____   _____   _____
Occasion: _____   _____   _____

Never Mind

S

Once, just as an oratorio of his was about to begin, several of George Frideric Handel's friends gathered to console him about the extremely sparse audience attracted to the performance. "Never mind," Handel said. "The music will sound the better" due to the improved acoustics of a very empty concert hall.[1]

Date: _____   _____   _____
Place: _____   _____   _____
Occasion: _____   _____   _____

---

[1] Patrick Kavanaugh, *Spiritual Lives of Great Composers* (Nashville: Sparrow Press, 1992), 4.

Solitude/Friendship with Self

Someone Once Said . . .

- *I am always best when alone; no place like my own study; no company like good books, and especially the book of God.*—Matthew Henry[1]
- *It is a difficult lesson to learn today—to leave one's friends and family and deliberately practice the art of solitude for an hour or a day or a week . . . And yet, once it is done, I find there is a quality to being alone that is incredibly precious.*—Anne Morrow Lindbergh, in *Gifts from the Sea*
- *There is a lordly solitude which both giants and geniuses seem to find essential.*—Victor Hugo[2]
- *Seek a convenient time to retire unto thyself, and meditate often upon God's loving-kindness. . . . The greatest saints avoided the society of men, when they could conveniently, and did rather choose to live to God in secret*—Thomas à Kempis
- *We are a peculiar people who somehow feel that the final measure of a person's spirituality is to be gauged by their capacity to go, go, go . . . for God. On the contrary, our Father calls us to come apart and spend some time in solitude with him.*—W. Phillip Keller[3]
- *It is easy in the world to live after the world's opinion; it is easy to live in solitude after our own; but the great man is he who in the midst of the crowds keeps with perfect sweetness the independence of solitude.*—Emerson
- *I love to be alone. I never found the companion that was so companionable as solitude.*—Henry David Thoreau, in *Thoughts From Walden Pond*
- *The best remedy for those who are afraid, lonely or unhappy is to go outside, somewhere where they can be quiet, alone with the heavens, nature and God. Because only then does one feel that all is as it should be.*—Anne Frank, in her diary, February 23, 1944

Date: _____ _____ _____

Place: _____ _____ _____

Occasion: _____ _____ _____

Quiet Spots

How tough is it in America to find a quiet spot? According to nature recorder Gordon Hempton:

- The hum of power lines can be heard upward of two miles.
- A chain saw cuts the quiet for more than five miles.
- Road noise can travel eight to ten miles.
- A coal-fired power plant can be heard as far as fifteen miles away.
- A major airport can cast a "noise shadow" longer than fifty miles.

---

[1] Wilber Smith, *Chats from a Minister's Library* (Grand Rapids, MI: Baker Book House, 1951), 164.
[2] Charles Connell, *World-Famous Exiles* (Feltham, Middlesex, Great Britain: Odhams Books, 1969), 78.
[3] W. Phillip Keller, "Solitude for Serenity and Strength," *Decision*, August/September, 1981, 9.

706

Date: _____ _____ _____
Place: _____ _____ _____
Occasion: _____ _____ _____

A Reflective Arena

Management guru Warren Bennis writes in his book *Why Leaders Can't Lead:* "The leader should incorporate a reflective arena into his or her structure, so that time out for musing is mandatory. I'm not speaking here of the sort of retreats that organizations have recently become so fond of, because they are usually the same old routine in a new location. If people in authority stopped regularly to think about what they were doing, they would have the kinds of fresh insights they now pay consultants dearly for."[1]

Date: _____ _____ _____
Place: _____ _____ _____
Occasion: _____ _____ _____

Going Afoot

Mrs. Charles Cowman, noting in Acts 20:23 that the Apostle Paul had sent his companions along the shore by sea while he had chosen to go alone and "afoot" (KJV), pointed out how important bits of solitude are for the cultivation of the soul:

- It was in the eerie solitude of Beth-el, and in the gray dawn by the ford Jabbok that Jacob was granted visions of God.
- It was when he was alone in the silent desert that Moses was shown the burning bush.
- It was when Joshua walked unattended under the stars by the wall of Jericho that the Captain of the Lord's hosts stood before him.
- It was when Isaiah was alone in the temple that a live coal touched his lips.
- It was when Mary was alone that the angel brought to her the message of the Lord.
- It was when Elisha was ploughing his lonely furrow that the Prophet's mantle fell upon his shoulders.
- Abraham wandered and worshiped alone.
- Daniel dined and prayed alone.
- Jesus lived and died alone.

Ah, it is good to be "minded to go afoot" sometimes, said Mrs. Cowman.[2]

S

Date: _____ _____ _____
Place: _____ _____ _____
Occasion: _____ _____ _____

[1] Warren Bennis, *Why Leaders Can't Lead* (San Francisco: Jossey-Bass Publishers, 1989), 158.
[2] Mrs. Charles E. Cowman, *Springs in the Valley* (Los Angeles: Cowman Publications, Inc., 1939), 124.

The Solitude of Cells

J. H. Jowett, in his study of the epistles of Paul, writes about the apostle's imprisonments, "What a life Paul would have lived had he been free to do whatever he liked! It is notorious that when a man is made a bishop his days become so crowded that it is a rare thing for him to produce his greatest books! And who knows but that if this great apostle had had more temporary freedom we might have had less permanent fruit. Sometimes the Lord permits our seclusion in order that we may do a larger work."[1]

Date: _____   _____   _____
Place: _____   _____   _____
Occasion: _____   _____   _____

Alone with God

When storms of life are round me beating,
When rough the path that I have trod,
Within my closet doors retreating,
I love to be alone with God.[2]

Date: _____   _____   _____
Place: _____   _____   _____
Occasion: _____   _____   _____

Silence, Solitude, and Inner Peace

"The desert fathers of centuries ago," Henri Nouwen tells us, "understood the importance of a silent environment for the cultivation of the spirit when they called out to one another, *Fuge, terche, et quisset*—silence, solitude, and inner peace.

"Few of us can fully appreciate the terrible conspiracy of noise there is about us, noise that denies us the silence and solitude we need for this cultivation of the inner garden. It would not be hard to believe that the archenemy of God has conspired to surround us at every conceivable point in our lives with the interfering noises of civilization that, when left unmuffled, usually drown out the voice of God. He who walks with God will tell you plainly, God does not ordinarily shout to make Himself heard. As Elijah discovered, God tends to whisper in the garden.

"Recently I visited a missionary center in Latin America where workmen were constructing a sound studio for a radio station. They were taking careful measures to soundproof the rooms so that no noise from the city streets could mar the broadcasts and recordings that would emanate from that place. We must learn to soundproof the heart against the intruding noises of the public world in order to hear what God has to say. I love the words of Mother Teresa of Calcutta: *We need*

---

[1] J. H. Jowett, *Life in the Heights* (Grand Rapids, MI: Baker Book House, 1925), 16.
[2] Cowman, *Springs in the Valley*, 124.

to find God, and he cannot be found in noise and restlessness. God is the friend of silence. See how nature—trees, flowers, grass—grow in silence; see how the stars, the moon and sun, how they move in silence . . .[1]

Date: _____ _____ _____
Place: _____ _____ _____
Occasion: _____ _____ _____

The Withdrawals of Jesus

- Matthew 4:1: *Then Jesus was led up by the Spirit into the wilderness. . . .*
- Mark 1:35: *Now in the morning, having risen a long while before daylight, He went out and departed to a solitary place, and there He prayed.*
- Luke 4:42: *Now when it was day, He departed and went into a deserted place. . . .*
- Luke 6:12: *Now it came to pass in those days that He went out to the mountain to pray, and continued all night in prayer to God.*
- Matthew 14:13: *When Jesus heard it, He departed from there by boat to a deserted place by Himself.*
- Luke 5:16: *So He Himself often withdrew into the wilderness and prayed.*
- Mark 3:7: *But Jesus withdrew with His disciples to the sea.*
- Mark 6:31: *And He said to them, "Come aside by yourselves to a deserted place and rest awhile."*
- Luke 9:10: *Then He took them and went aside privately into a deserted place belonging to the city called Bethsaida.*
- Matthew 14:22ff: *Jesus made the disciples get into the boat and go before Him to the other side, while He sent the multitudes away. And when He had sent the multitudes away, He went up on a mountain by Himself to pray. Now when evening came, He was alone there.*
- John 6:15: *When Jesus perceived that they were about to come and take Him by force to make Him king, He departed again to the mountain by Himself alone.*
- John 7:53f: *And everyone went to his own house. But Jesus went to the Mount of Olives.*
- Mark 7:24: *From there He arose and went to the region of Tyre and Sidon. And He entered a house and wanted no one to know it. . . .*
- Matthew 17:1: *Jesus took Peter, James, and John his brother, led them up on a high mountain by themselves . . .*
- Mark 9:30: *They departed from there and passed through Galilee, and He did not want anyone to know it. . . .*
- John 10:40: *And He went away again beyond the Jordan. . . .*
- John 11:54: *Jesus no longer walked openly among the Jews, but went from there into the country near the wilderness. . . .*
- John 12:36: *These things Jesus spoke, and departed, and was hidden from them.*
- Matthew 26:36: *Then Jesus came with them to a place called Gethsemane . . .*
- Luke 22:41: *And He was withdrawn from them. . . .*

[1] Gordon MacDonald, *Ordering Your Private World* (Nashville: Thomas Nelson, 1985), 126.

Date: _____ _____ _____

Place: _____ _____ _____

Occasion: _____ _____ _____

Impelled to Solitude

"Nothing was more characteristic of Mr. Moody than his longing for retirement in the country from the press of his work. Though his life-work lay for the most part in great cities, he was born a country lad, and for him the everlasting hills possessed a wealth of meaning and a marvelous recuperative power. Some instinct drew him back to the soil, some mysterious prompting impelled him to solitude, away from the crowds that absorbed so much of his strength; then, after a little respite, he would return with new strength and vitality."[1]

Date: _____ _____ _____

Place: _____ _____ _____

Occasion: _____ _____ _____

In the Death Camps

Nazi Death Camp survivor Viktor E. Frankl spoke of the need for solitude experienced by prisoners in the Nazi camps: "There were times, of course, when it was possible, and even necessary, to keep away from the crowd. It is well known that an enforced community life, in which attention is paid to everything one does all the time, may result in an irresistible urge to get away, at least for a short while. The prisoner craved to be alone with himself and his thoughts. He yearned for privacy and for solitude. After my transportation to a so-called "rest camp," I had the rare fortune to find solitude for about five minutes at a time. Behind the earthen hut where I worked and in which were crowded about fifty delirious patients, there was a quiet spot in a corner of the double fence of barbed wire surrounding the camp. A tent had been improvised there with a few poles and branches of trees in order to shelter a half-dozen corpses (the daily death rate in the camp). There was also a shaft leading to the water pipes. I squatted on the wooden lid of this shaft whenever my services were not needed. I just sat and looked out at the green flowering slopes and the distant blue hills of the Bavarian landscape, framed by the meshes of barbed wire. . . .

"The corpses near me, crawling with lice, did not bother me. Only the steps of passing guards could rouse me from my dreams. . . ."[2]

◆

Frequent Aloneness

I know of no way to recover that which we have lost other than to cultivate the practice of being more frequently alone with Him.

—J. WILBER CHAPMAN

◆

---

[1] William R. Moody, *The Life Of Dwight L. Moody* (Murfreesboro, TN: Sword of the Lord Publishers, n.d.), 262.

[2] Viktor E. Frankl, *Man's Search for Meaning* (New York: Washington Square Press, 1959), 71–72.

Date: _____ _____ _____
Place: _____ _____ _____
Occasion: _____ _____ _____

Friendship with Oneself

- *If you are lonely when you are alone, you are in bad company.*—Jean-Paul Sartre[1]
- *Other than a few times when he gave me a good deal of trouble, I've had a good time living with J. C. Penney all my life.*—J. C. Penney
- *I do not care what others say and think about me. But there is one man's opinion which I very much value, and that is the opinion of James Garfield. Others I need not think about. I can get away from them, but I have to be with him all the time. He is with me when I rise up and when I lie down; when I eat and talk; when I go out and come in. It makes a great difference whether he thinks well of me or not.*—President James A. Garfield[2]
- *He was having a splendid time being Senator Harry Truman*—David McCullough, Truman biographer[3]

Date: _____ _____ _____
Place: _____ _____ _____
Occasion: _____ _____ _____

Take It Easy, Malcolm

A father was pushing a stroller though a city park. The baby was screaming at the top of his lungs. It was a summer day, and the park was filled with people, all watching.

As the embarrassed young man passed by, he was saying, "Take it easy, Malcolm. Just relax. No reason go get excited. Just calm down and everything will be all right. Come on, Malcolm. Just trust the Lord."

An older lady drew alongside and said, "My, what a nice baby. Do you say his name was Malcolm?"

"No, ma'am," said the father. "His name is Barnaby. I'm Malcolm."[4]

Date: _____ _____ _____
Place: _____ _____ _____
Occasion: _____ _____ _____

Tea Party

I had a little tea party this afternoon at three,
T'was very small—three guests in all,

[1] John-Roger and Peter McWilliams, *Do It!* (Los Angeles: Prelude Press, 1991), 173.
[2] "Dear Abby," *The Nashville Tennessean*, May 17, 1996, 2D.
[3] David McCullough, *Truman* (New York: Simon & Schuster, 1992), 281.
[4] *Our Daily Bread*, attributed to Paul Harvey.

S

Just I, myself, and me.
Myself ate all the sandwiches, while I drank up the tea.
T'was also I who ate the pie
And passed the cake to me.[1]

Date: _____   _____   _____

Place: _____   _____   _____

Occasion: _____   _____   _____

Stress

Someone Once Said . . .

- *Sometimes I get the feeling the whole world is against me, but deep down I know that's not true. Some of the smaller countries are neutral.*—Robert Orben
- *Our Lord's life was full of storm and tempest, yet in the darkest days of all He bequeathed to us His legacy of peace. His rest is no imaginary escape from reality . . . (but) that blessed consciousness that in the midst of trouble our real lives are beyond the reach of circumstance, hid with Christ in God.*—Vance Havner[2]
- *Be still and know that I am God.*—Psalm 46:10
- *Jesus, I am resting, resting in the joy of what Thou art.*—Jean S. Pigott

Date: _____   _____   _____

Place: _____   _____   _____

Occasion: _____   _____   _____

Stats

- 43% of all adults suffer adverse health effects due to stress.
- 75–90% of all visits to primary care physicians are for stress-related complaints or disorders.
- Stress has been linked to all the leading causes of death, including heart disease, cancer, lung ailments, accidents, cirrhosis, and suicide.
- An estimated one million workers are absent on an average workday because of stress related complaints. Stress is said to be responsible for more than half of the 550,000,000 workdays lost annually because of absenteeism.
- The proportion of workers who reported "feeling highly stressed" more than doubled from 1985–1990.
- 40% of all worker turnover is due to job stress.
- Job stress is estimated to cost U.S. industry $300 billion annually, as assessed by absenteeism, diminished productivity, employee turnover, medical insurance, etc.

---

[1] Clipped from my files. Source unknown.
[2] Vance Havner, *By the Still Waters* (Old Tappan, NJ: Fleming H. Revell, 1934), 11.

- Workplace violence is rampant. There are almost two million reported incidents of homicide, aggravated assault, rape, or sexual assaults. Homicide is the second leading cause of fatal occupational injury.[1]

Date: _____ _____ _____
Place: _____ _____ _____
Occasion: _____ _____ _____

Sources of Stress

According to *USA Today*, a survey of 501 adults conducted by Research and Forecasts Inc. for Mitchum antiperspirant and deodorant isolated the major sources of stress for typical Americans.

- Work is the biggest source of stress in our lives, cited by 36 percent of the respondents.
- Money was second (22 percent).
- Children was third (10 percent).
- Health (7 percent).
- Marriage (5 percent).
- Parents (5 percent).
- Only 5 percent say they have no stress at all in their daily lives, and 19 percent have a little.[2]

Date: _____ _____ _____
Place: _____ _____ _____
Occasion: _____ _____ _____

Gadgets and Gurus

The American Booksellers Association estimates that more than two thousand self-help titles are published each year, and produce sales of about $500 million. No data exists specifically about stress-relief books, but that is one of the largest subcategories of self-help books, and has provided steady sales for many publishers.

Also popular: Cassette tapes reproducing the sounds of forests, oceans, birds, and rainfall.

Yoga, eastern exercises, and meditation are practiced universally, just to escape the effects of stress.

Gadget companies are also cashing in, with sound-therapy devices, vibrating chairs and beds, massage machines, special lights, pseudo-aquariums, and an assortment of balls, beads, and body-rollers.

S

---

[1] < www.stress.org >
[2] "A Mess of Stress," *USA Today*, March 21, 1990, D1.

Date: _____ _____ _____
Place: _____ _____ _____
Occasion: _____ _____ _____

The Overspent American

Harvard economist Juliet Schor has written two books that have hit a nerve with Americans. *The Overworked American* described how many are living highly-pressured lives, teetering on the brink of exhaustion with devastating results. In a newer work, *The Overspent American,* Schor claims that the average American works 163 more hours now than in 1976. Yet, Dr. Schor insists, the additional work load is not the only reason most of us are coping with a profound sense of time pressure. Our sense of the necessary and our desire for goods, services, and experiences is expanding too fast. We live in such a rush that we no longer fully appreciate and experience the moments of our days. Life flashes by us in a blur, leaving us overworked, overspent, and overwhelmed.

Date: _____ _____ _____
Place: _____ _____ _____
Occasion: _____ _____ _____

Eagle's Wings

In Isaiah 40, we are told that by waiting on the Lord, we will mount on wings like eagles. Eagles are majestic birds with remarkable vision. Scientists believe their vision may be eight times sharper than that of humans. They have powerful feet with talons that can grip like a vise. Their beaks are butcher-like, designed to cut and crush and tear their food.

Troubling Inability

One of the ways in which man brings the most trouble upon himself is by his inability to be still.

—PASCAL

But most of all, eagles are built for flying. They have incredible speed, able to fly at sixty and eighty and one hundred miles an hour. They can do rolls and loops like an airplane doing tricks. Their wingspan extends to nearly eight feet.

But eagles do not fly like sparrows or robins. Most birds fly through the air by flapping their wings, but eagles cannot flap very long. They're built for soaring, and thus they can go much further on little energy.

God created our planet with invisible columns of hot air called *thermals* rising up here and there from the surface of the earth. Eagles find these thermals, fly into the invisible currents, stretch out their wings, and are lifted higher and higher into the sky as though ascending on an elevator.

They may rise as high as fourteen thousand feet, so high in the heavens they can not be seen with the naked eye from earth.

When they reach those heights, they emerge from the updraft, wings still spread, and they soar this way and that way, downwards and sidewards, traveling for miles with very little exertion of strength.

Isaiah seems to be telling us that God is invisible, but like the invisible uplifting thermal currents of this planet, he is present for his people. When we search him out, claim his promises and trust in him, spreading out the wings of faith, we are caught up to a higher plane. We mount up with wings like eagles. We can run and not grow weary. We can walk and not faint.

The strength we need for holy, effective, victorious living comes not from frantically flapping our wings like sparrows in distress, but from trusting in God and resting in Jesus Christ.[1]

Date: _____ _____ _____
Place: _____ _____ _____
Occasion: _____ _____ _____

How God Dealt with a Nervous Breakdown

At the very apex of his career, the prophet Elijah suffered something akin to a nervous breakdown. It is very instructive to see how God dealt with this malady in 1 Kings 19. The Lord's treatment program contained the following elements:

- God prescribed sleep and nourishment.—1 Kings 19:5-8
- Angelic assistance was dispatched.—verses 5-8
- Elijah was allowed to verbalize his frustrations honestly and openly.—verses 9-11
- God reminded Elijah of His power.—verses 11-12
- The Still, Small Voice of God was needed.—verse 12
- There was a recommissioning, a renewal of purpose was given.—verses 15-17
- Where God is concerned, Elijah learned, things are never as bad as they may appear.—verse 18
- A good friend was assigned to provide companionship.—verse 19

Date: _____ _____ _____
Place: _____ _____ _____
Occasion: _____ _____ _____

S

Pressed

Pressed out of measure and pressed to all length;
Pressed so intensely, it seems beyond strength;
Pressed in the body, and pressed in the soul;
Pressed in the mind, till the dark surges roll.
Pressure by foes, and pressure by friends—
Pressure on pressure, till life nearly ends.

---

[1] From a sermon by the author.

Pressed into knowing no helper but God;
Pressed into loving the staff and the rod.
Pressed into liberty where nothing clings;
Pressed into faith for impossible things.
Pressed into tasting the joy of the Lord;
Pressed into loving a Christlife outpoured.[1]

Date: _____ _____ _____
Place: _____ _____ _____
Occasion: _____ _____ _____

Through the Wringer

A little boy went to the grocery store and asked the clerk for a box of detergent. The clerk asked the boy why he needed detergent.

"I want to wash my dog," replied the lad.

"Well, son, this detergent is pretty strong for washing a little dog."

The little boy replied, "That's what I want. He's mighty dirty."

He took the box of detergent home, and about a week later he returned. The store clerk, recognizing him, asked him about his dog. "Oh, he's dead," said the boy.

"Oh, I'm sorry," replied the clerk. "I guess the detergent was too strong."

"I don't think the detergent hurt him," said the boy. "I think it was the rinse cycle that got him."

Date: _____ _____ _____
Place: _____ _____ _____
Occasion: _____ _____ _____

—————— Sunday/The Lord's Day ——————

Someone Once Said . . .

- *Our great-grandparents called it the holy Sabbath. Our grandparents called it the Lord's Day. Our parents called it Sunday. And we call it the weekend.*—Anonymous
- *Blessed be to God for the day of rest and religious occupation wherein earthly things assume their true size.*—British statesman William Wilberforce, in his journal, about his Sundays[2]
- *With peaceful Sundays, the strings would never have snapped as they did from over-tension.*—William Wilberforce, in his journal, about two political friends who committed suicide[3]
- *If all our days are to be holy, then we must keep the Lord's day holy.*—Stephen Winward

---

[1] V. Raymond Edman, *The Disciples of Life* (Minneapolis: World Wide Publications, 1948), 16.
[2] Gordon MacDonald, *Ordering Your Private World* (Nashville: Thomas Nelson, 1985), 162.
[3] MacDonald, *Ordering Your Private World*, 162.

- [*Christians*] *pretend to keep a Sabbath by Sunday churchgoing, and then stuff the day with meetings, responsibilities, committees, and concerns until it looks (and feels) tight as a German sausage. Pastors are usually in charge of the stuffing.*—Eugene Peterson[1]
- *Sabbath-keeping gets us into step with the rhythm of the Savior.*—Eugene Peterson[2]
- *The world and the church need genuinely rested Christians: Christians who are regularly refreshed by true Sabbath rest.*—Gordon MacDonald[3]
- *Some keep the Sabbath going to Church—/ I keep it, staying at Home—/ With a Bobolink for a Chorister—/ And an Orchard, for a Dome.*—Emily Dickinson

Date: _____   _____   _____
Place: _____   _____   _____
Occasion: _____   _____   _____

Stats

According to a 1999 survey conducted by the Barna Research Group of Ventura, California, conducted among senior pastors of Protestant churches, shows that in 1999 church attendance declined slightly from the previous years' level while donations to churches increased slightly and pastoral compensation was unchanged.

In their annual tracking study of Protestant churches, the Barna study found that median adult attendance at church services in 1999 was 90 people, which is slightly below the 1998 average (95 adult attenders). The figure is 10% below the 1997 average (100), and 12% lower than the 1992 level (102).

In terms of geographic differences, churches in the South (100) were larger than churches in the Northeast (85) and the West (85), and especially those in the Midwest (80).

In spite of the mass media attention devoted to megachurches (i.e., those attracting 1000 or more adults on a typical weekend), those congregations remain just 1% of the Protestant church landscape.

Despite the attendance decline, the annual operating budget of churches rose by 5% in the past year, to an average of $110,000 per church. The current median is 34% higher than it was in 1992, and 59% above the 1987 average. . . .

George Barna, president of the company that conducted the research, noted that to understand the reported statistics they must be placed in their proper context. "Since 1992 Protestant churches have lost 10% in average weekly attendance. During that same period, America's population has increased by almost 9%. Some of this attendance decline is attributable to the planting of new churches, which tend to start small and thus brings down the national average, and to the less frequent attendance of church-going adults. The bottom line, however, is that we are attracting fewer people than we used to."[4]

---

[1] Eugene H. Peterson, "Confessions of a Former Sabbath Breaker," *Christianity Today,* September 2, 1988, 25.
[2] Eugene H. Peterson, "Confessions of a Former Sabbath Breaker," *Christianity Today,* September 2, 1988, 28.
[3] MacDonald, *Ordering Your Private World,* 175.
[4] < www.barna.org >

Date: _____ _____ _____
Place: _____ _____ _____
Occasion: _____ _____ _____

Monday Blues

This interesting item appeared in *U.S. News and World Report:* "A recent long-term study of executive heart-attack victims show that 75 percent of those who died at work died on Monday," reports the Blue Cross-Blue Shield magazine, *Health Talk.* "Of those who died at home, 50 percent also died on Monday. A major factor in those deaths, says the magazine, was the 'Monday Blues' associated with returning to work after an exhausting weekend."[1]

Date: _____ _____ _____
Place: _____ _____ _____
Occasion: _____ _____ _____

Seven Brothers

Seven unmarried brothers lived together in a large house. Six went out to work each day but one stayed home. He had the place all lit up when the other six arrived home from work. He also had the house warm, and most importantly, had a delicious, full-course dinner ready for his hungry brothers.

——◇——
Hollow Praise

*One generation called
it a holy day;
the next, a holiday;
to the next,
it was a hollow day.*
—ANONYMOUS
——◇——

One day the six brothers decided that the one that had been staying home should go to work. "It's not fair," they said, "for the one to stay home while the others slaved at a job." So they made the seventh brother find work too. But when they all came home the first night, there was no light, nor was there any warmth, and worst of all, there was no hearty dinner awaiting them. And the next night the same thing: darkness, cold, hunger. They soon went back to their former arrangement."

[It's] the day of rest and worship that keeps the other six bright, warm and nourishing. When we desecrate the Lord's Day, we only hurt ourselves."[2]

Date: _____ _____ _____
Place: _____ _____ _____
Occasion: _____ _____ _____

Weekends in the Country

In the early days of the Nazi domination of Europe, the British Parliament still considered weekends their own. Britain's ruling class left London for their country

---

[1] "Danger of Returning to Work," *U.S. News and World Report,* January 21, 1985, 68.
[2] Leslie B. Flynn, *Come Alive with Illustrations* (Grand Rapids, MI: Baker, 1987), 23–24.

estates and didn't want to be bothered. It created no small problem, for crucial decisions could not be made in crisis because those in authority were unavailable. Winston Churchill, frustrated beyond words, complained, "that Britain's rulers continued to take its weekends in the country, while Hitler takes his countries in the weekends."

When we neglect God's business on Sundays to pursue our own leisure, it gives Satan a free hand.[1]

Date: _____ _____ _____

Place: _____ _____ _____

Occasion: _____ _____ _____

Why Sunday?

- In the Old Testament, the Sabbath day was thought of as Saturday, the seventh day of the week. There were extra Sabbaths and special Sabbath observances from time to time. But by and large, Saturday and the Sabbath were linked together in Jewish thinking, and over the years the Jews became very strict about their observance of the Sabbath.
- Many Christians believe this changed in the New Testament. Little is said in the gospels and epistles about observing the seventh day. The emphasis changed with breath-taking suddenness to Sunday, the first day of the week, the Lord's Day. All four Gospels tell us that Jesus rose from the dead at daybreak, Sunday morning. Early on the first day of the week, while it was still dark, Mary of Magdala went to the tomb and found the stone removed.
- On the evening of that first Easter, when the disciples were together with the doors locked for fear of the Jews, Jesus came and stood among them, saying, "Peace be with you!" The disciples were overjoyed.
- Thomas, who was absent, scoffed at the reports. On the following Sunday, Jesus appeared among them again, this time convincing even Thomas.
- In Acts 20, the disciples in Troas gathered to break bread. Paul spoke to the people throughout the night.
- In 1 Corinthians 16, Paul instructed the Christians, "On the first day of the week let each one of you lay something aside, storing up as he may prosper."
- Hebrews 10:25, without specifying an exact day for it, warned Christians not to forsake assembling themselves together.
- The last New Testament reference to Sunday worship gives us the special title—the Lord's Day. In Revelation 1:10, John wrote, "I was in the Spirit on the Lord's Day . . ."
- About A.D. 115, Ignatius wrote to the Christians in Magnesia about those who "ceased to keep the (Jewish seventh-day) Sabbath and lived by the Lord's Day, on which our life as well as theirs shone forth, thanks to him and his death." That quotation equates the Lord's Day, the first day of creation, with

S

---

[1] William Manchester, *The Last Lion: Winston Spencer Churchill—Alone* (Boston: Little, Brown, & Co., 1988), 483.

spiritual sunshine; for after all, it was on the first day of the creation week that God's said, "Let there be light."

- The *Epistle of Barnabas* (early second century) referred to Sunday as the day set aside by the early Christians for worship.
- The *Didache,* written in the late first or early second century, reminds Christians, "On the Lord's day of the Lord, come together, break bread, and hold Eucharist."
- About A.D. 110, Pliny, the Roman administrator, wrote about Christians: "They gather on Sunday, the first day of the week, to sing praises to the Lord Jesus."
- Justin Martyr told his pagan audience in about A.D. 155 that "we all hold this common gathering on Sunday, since it is the first day, on which God transforming darkness and matter made the universe, and Jesus Christ our Savior rose from the dead on the same day."
- Christians soon adopted the newly coined pagan term and compared Christ's rising from the dead to the rising of the sun. Christ rose from the tomb at daybreak even as the sun rises from the dark horizon. So the day came to be called Sunday.
- In A.D. 321, Emperor Constantine by royal edict proclaimed Sunday a special day of worship in the Roman world. There has not been a single Sunday from the day of Christ's resurrection until this one in which the church of Jesus Christ somewhere in the world has failed to meet. It's an unbroken chain.

Date: _____ _____ _____

Place: _____ _____ _____

Occasion: _____ _____ _____

What Sunday Is Good For

Entire books have been published in the last few years on the impact of stress, fatigue, and sleep deprivation on our society. But few if any books, articles, or reports have connected all of this with the loss of one day in seven as a day of rest.

But the fourth commandment is clear. Our bodies and souls are made to work six days and to rest on the seventh. We cannot persistently violate that law without breaking down at some point—either physically, emotionally, or in family relationships.

D. L. Moody said, "Saturday is my day of rest, because I generally preach on Sunday, and I look forward to it as a body does to a holiday."

There are three purposes: To Rest, Reflect, and Rejoice.

It was Socrates who said that an unexamined life is not worth living. Sabbath rest is not merely a time for rest or recreation. It's modeled after the activity of God himself, who, having worked six days, took a Sabbath. He ceased from his labors, not to go off and play, but to examine what he had done. Looking over the previous six days, he declared, "It is good."

Sabbath is designed to provide us an opportunity to pause and look at what we have done and to decide whether it was worth doing and, if so, whether it was done well. It also gives us an opportunity to prayerfully plan the week opening before us.[1]

Date: _____   _____   _____
Place: _____   _____   _____
Occasion: _____   _____   _____

So They Won't Go Blind

In the old days, ponies and mules were used to haul out the coal in the mining camps. A man asked a little boy why there were so many ponies and mules out in the fields on Sunday. The little boy answered, "They work all week in the mines. We bring them up on Sundays so they won't go blind."

Date: _____   _____   _____
Place: _____   _____   _____
Occasion: _____   _____   _____

Seeker Sensitive?

Alice Morse Earle, in her old book, *Home Life in Colonial Days,* devotes a chapter to the way the Sunday was observed in Puritan New England. After describing the cold buildings, hard pews, strict rules, and severe punishments associated with the keeping of the Sabbath, she writes:

"The services were not shortened because the churches were uncomfortable. By the side of the pulpit stood a brass-bound hour-glass which was turned by the tithing-man or clerk, but it did not hasten the closing of the sermon. Sermons two or three hours long were customary, and prayers from one to two hours in length. When the first church in Woburn was dedicated, the minister preached a sermon nearly five hours long. A Dutch traveler recorded a prayer four hours long on a Fast Day. Many prayers were two hours long. The doors were closed and watched by the tithing man, and none could leave, even if tired or restless, without good excuse."[2]

Date: _____   _____   _____
Place: _____   _____   _____
Occasion: _____   _____   _____

Who Was That?

"Who was that cussing so loudly when I passed your house this morning?" a minister asked a little boy one Sunday morning.

---

[1] From a sermon by the author.
[2] Alice Morse Earle, *Home Life in Colonial Days* (New York: Macmillan Company, 1941), 376.

"Oh, that was Daddy," came the reply. "He was late for church and couldn't find his Bible."

Date:	_____	_____	_____
Place:	_____	_____	_____
Occasion:	_____	_____	_____

--- **Tears** ---

Someone Once Said . . .

- *That long drip of human tears. . . .*—Thomas Hardy
- *From infancy to old age the record of every man's life is written in letters of tears.*—M. R. DeHaan[1]
- *A tear is a distillation of the soul. It is the deepest longing of the human heart in chemical solution.*—M. R. DeHaan[2]
- *Tears are liquid pain.*—Herbert Lockyer[3]
- *The tears . . . streamed down, and I let them flow as freely as they would, making of them a pillow for my heart. On them it rested.*—Augustine, in *Confessions*
- *Tears are the diamonds of heaven.*—Charles Haddon Spurgeon[4]
- *Tears win victories. A cold, unfeeling, dry-eyed religion has no influence over the souls of men.*[5]
- *Those who don't know how to weep with their whole heart, don't know how to laugh either.*—Golda Meir

Date:	_____	_____	_____
Place:	_____	_____	_____
Occasion:	_____	_____	_____

Tear Therapy

Gregg Levoy, writing in *Psychology Today,* reports that crying can actually remove chemicals that build up during emotional stress. According to Levoy, the amount of manganese stored in the body affects our moods, and the body stores thirty times as much of manganese in tears as in blood serum. Biochemist William Frey says the lacrimal gland, which determines the flow of tears, concentrates and removes manganese from the body. Frey has also identified three chemicals stored up by stress and released by crying.[6]

---

[1] M. R. DeHaan, *The Chemistry of the Blood* (Grand Rapids, MI: Zondervan, 1943), 138.
[2] DeHaan, *The Chemistry of the Blood,* 140.
[3] Herbert Lockyer, *All the Messianic Prophecies of the Bible* (Grand Rapids, MI: Zondervan, 1973), 118.
[4] Charles Haddon Spurgeon, *Spurgeon's Sermons,* vol. 1 (Grand Rapids, MI: Baker Book House, 1983), 173.
[5] Lockyer, *All the Messianic Prophecies of the Bible,* 118.
[6] Mildred Tengbom, *Letting Tears Bring Healing and Renewal* (St. Meinrad, IN: Abbey Press, 1990), 3.

Date:	_____	_____	_____
Place:	_____	_____	_____
Occasion:	_____	_____	_____

Stats

Women cry about four times as frequently as men. In an average lifetime, the average American man cries 1,258 times; the average American woman cries 4,764 times.[1]

Date:	_____	_____	_____
Place:	_____	_____	_____
Occasion:	_____	_____	_____

Tears in the Bible

- Joseph is said to have wept 8 times.
- David, 7 times.
- Paul, 4 times. He described himself as serving the Lord with all humility, with many tears. (Acts 20:19)
- Jeremiah compared his weeping to both a fountain and a river of tears. (Jeremiah 9:1; Lamentations 3:48)
- David's men wept until they had no more power to weep. (1 Samuel 30:4)
- The Psalmist wept until he drenched his couch and made his "bed swim." (Psalm 6:6)
- Peter wept "bitterly." (Matthew 26:75)
- There are three records of Jesus' tears: Over a doomed city, over a friend's death, and over a painful sacrifice. (Luke 19:41, John 11:33–35, and Hebrews 5:7)
- Hell is described as a place of weeping and gnashing of teeth. (Matthew 13:42)
- The last mention of tears is in Revelation 21:4, the promise that God shall wipe away all tears from the eyes of his redeemed.

Date:	_____	_____	_____
Place:	_____	_____	_____
Occasion:	_____	_____	_____

T

Helping

A little girl was once late coming home from play. When her mother asked her where she had been, she explained that her friend had fallen and broken her very special doll. "And," said the little girl, "I stayed to help her."

"How did you help her?" asked the mother.

"I just sat down and helped her cry."

---

[1] Tengbom, *Letting Tears Bring Healing and Renewal*, 3.

Date: _____ _____ _____

Place: _____ _____ _____

Occasion: _____ _____ _____

When Lou Holtz Saw Tears

In Lou Holtz's second season as head coach of the Notre Dame Fighting Irish, his team experienced a humiliating loss against Texas A&M in the Cotton Bowl. Holtz was utterly dejected as he walked into the locker room, but it seemed to him that most of his players didn't seem overly distraught. With one exception. A second-string sub named Chris Zorich sat in front of his locker, weeping deep, gut-heaving sobs. Holtz decided at that moment that next year's team would be composed of players who loved football as much as Zorich.

The next season this young man went from sub to starter to team captain, and helped the Fighting Irish win a National Championship. Chris Zorich had won the spot on the starting team because he had cared enough to cry.

Some things are worth crying over.[1]

Date: _____ _____ _____

Place: _____ _____ _____

Occasion: _____ _____ _____

The Last

In a *Choice Gleanings* calendar, Alex Ross told of an elderly woman who lay dying. Her broken-hearted husband sat beside her, tenderly holding her hand. They had been married many years, and both knew that the time for parting had come. As their eyes met, a tear flowed down the old woman's wrinkled cheek. Gently, her husband wiped it away. Then, with a quiver in his voice, he said, "Thank God, Mary, that's the last."[2]

Date: _____ _____ _____

Place: _____ _____ _____

Occasion: _____ _____ _____

The Meaning of Our Tears

Not now, but in the coming years,
It may be in a better land,
We'll read the meaning of our tears,
And there, sometime, we'll understand.

---

[1] "The One Minute Message."
[2] *Our Daily Bread.*

God knows the way, He holds the key,
He guides us with unerring hand;
Sometime with tearless eyes we'll see;
Yes, there, up there, we'll understand.—Maxwell N. Cornelius

Date: _____ _____ _____
Place: _____ _____ _____
Occasion: _____ _____ _____

Keep Up the Treatment

Country comedian Archie Campbell enjoyed telling about two sweethearts who were sitting on the front porch. The young man noticed the tears were streaming down his girlfriend's face. He said, "What's the matter with my little sweetheart? I'll kiss those tears away." After kissing a few times he noticed she was still crying. He said, "Won't anything stop those tears?"

She said, "It's hay fever, darling, but keep up the treatment."

Date: _____ _____ _____
Place: _____ _____ _____
Occasion: _____ _____ _____

Temptation

Someone Once Said . . .

- *Call on God, but row away from the rocks.*—Ralph Waldo Emerson[1]
- *Who would have thought to have found adultery in David, and drunkenness in Noah, and cursing in Job? If God leaves a man to himself, how suddenly and scandalously may sin break forth in the holiest man on the earth! "I say unto all, Watch." A wandering heart needs a watchful eye.*—Thomas Watson[2]
- *When I find myself assailed by temptation, I forthwith lay hold of some text of the Bible, which Jesus extends to me.*—Martin Luther, in *Table Talk.*
- *Every temptation is an opportunity for us to draw nearer to God.*—George Sweeting

Date: _____ _____ _____
Place: _____ _____ _____
Occasion: _____ _____ _____

---

[1] *The Book of Uncommon Prayer*, ed. Constance Pollock and Daniel Pollock (Dallas: Word Publishing, 1996), 62.

[2] Thomas Watson, *Gleanings From Thomas Watson* (Morgan, PA: Soli Deo Gloria Publications, 1995), 85.

Stats

The magazine *Discipleship Journal* asked its readers to rank the areas of greatest spiritual challenge to them. The results came back in this order:

1. Materialism
2. Pride
3. Self-centeredness
4. Laziness
5. (Tie) Anger/Bitterness and Sexual lust
6. Envy
7. Gluttony
8. Lying

The respondents also noted that temptations were more potent when they had neglected their time with God (81 percent) and when they were physically tired (57 percent). Resisting temptation was accomplished by prayer (84 percent), avoiding compromising situations (76 percent), Bible study (66 percent), and being account-able to someone else (52 percent).[1]

Date:			
Place:			
Occasion:			

Pictures of Temptation

- According to legend, there was an island dominated by an Iron Mountain that emitted such powerful magnetic force that it attracted every piece of metal brought within the range of its influence. Ships at sea, passing near the shore of that land, felt its force on their anchors and chains. If the ship drew closer, the attraction became stronger until finally the very nails flew from the vessel's beams and planks, and fastened themselves to the side of the mountain. The ship, of course, would then fall to pieces with great loss of life.
- In Greek mythology, the siren was a creature half bird and half woman who lured sailors to destruction by the sweetness of her song. According to Homer, the sirens on an island in the Aegean were particularly dangerous. Their song was so irresistible to sailors that every passing ship was lured toward the rocks and wrecked. The Greek hero Odysseus escaped this danger by stopping the ears of his crew with wax so that they were deaf to the sirens. He himself, wanting to hear the music, had himself tied to the mast so that he could not steer the ship out of course.
- Robert Browning's famous poem, the *Pied Piper of Hamelin,* was based on a story centuries old. Hamelin, a little German town in the duchy of Brunswick, was overrun with rats. Every home was full of rats, as were the shops and streets. According to Browning,

[1] *Discipleship Journal,* November/December 1992.

They fought the dogs, and killed the cats,
And bit the babies in the cradles,
And ate the cheeses out of the vats,
And licked the soup from the cook's own ladles.

An odd-looking stranger entered town, promising to rid the town of rats for the sum of one hundred guilders. He was quickly hired, and, pulling a small flute from his pocket, he began to play a shrill tune. As he played, the rats came tumbling out of the houses and shops. As the piper played, he marched toward the river and the rats followed him in an ever-increasing mass until they were all led into the River Weser and drowned.

But the mayor refused to keep his end of the bargain, not wanting to pay the guilders.

Without a word, the piper left the mayor's office, took out his flute, and began playing a different song. This time, the sound wasn't shrill, but sweet and low and dreamy. Instantly, the children of Hamelin came tumbling out of the houses and shops and schools, and, to the horror of the onlookers, they followed the piper to a mountain which opened up as though it were a door and all the children—one hundred thirty of them—trooped inside and were never seen again.

All but one little boy who was lame on one foot. Unable to keep up, he escaped the fate of the others and later told them what he heard. The pipers tune, he said, was about a land where all things were beautiful, the people were good, the rivers were clear, the flowers were brighter, and the sky was brilliant. In this land, dogs ran faster, bees didn't sting, horses flew with eagle's wings, and no one was ever sick.

Its lure was virtually irresistible, and with this sweet, subtle, soft delusion the piper led the crowd toward their doom.

Date: _____   _____   _____
Place: _____   _____   _____
Occasion: _____   _____   _____

How Do We Face the Tempter?

In his book, *Disciples Indeed,* Oswald Chambers gives this insight regarding temptation: *How are we to face the tempter? By prayer? No. With the Word of God? No. Face the tempter with Jesus Christ, and He will apply the word of God to you, and the temptation will cease.*[1]

F. B. Meyer made a similar point in *The Christ Life for Your Life:* Speaking of temptation in the life of a Christian, he wrote: *Remember further that His purpose is to deliver from the power of sin. The guilt is gone, but the power remains, and He can only deliver from that gradually. Now, understand me. . . . I do not believe in sanctification, I believe in the*

---

[1] Oswald Chambers, *Disciples Indeed* (London: Oswald Chambers Publications Association and Marshall, Morgan, & Scott, Ltd., 1955), 76.

Sanctifier; I do not believe in holiness; I believe in the Holy One. Not an it, but a person; not an attribute, but Christ in my heart.

Meyer continued, *Abide in Jesus. Let the Holy Ghost in you keep you abiding in Jesus, so that when Satan comes to knock at your door, Jesus will go and open it, and as soon as the devil sees the face of Christ looking through the door, he will turn tail. . . .*[1]

Date: _____ _____ _____

Place: _____ _____ _____

Occasion: _____ _____ _____

I Want That Understood

Sometimes the best way to deal with temptation is to rule it out in advance. According to Harry Truman's biographer, David McCullough, President Truman was under incredible pressure while attending the Potsdam Conference. One evening near the end of an arduous session at the palace, Truman prepared to leave for his nearby lodgings. A young Army public relations officer, seeing Truman about to leave in his car, stuck his head in the window and asked to hitch a ride. Truman told him to get in, and the two struck up a conversation, overheard and later reported by Truman's driver.

Tempting Fight

You may have to fight a battle more than once to win it.

—MARGARET THATCHER

In Berlin the black market was rampant, and everything was available—cigarettes, watches, whiskey, and prostitutes. The officer said that if there was anything the President wanted, anything at all he needed, he had only to say the word. "Anything, you know, like women."

Truman bristled. "Listen, son, I married my sweetheart," he said. "She doesn't run around on me, and I don't run around on her. I want that understood. Don't ever mention that kind of stuff to me again."

Truman's driver later recalled, "By the time we were home, he got out of the car and never even said goodbye to that guy."[2]

Date: _____ _____ _____

Place: _____ _____ _____

Occasion: _____ _____ _____

Trying Not To

"What are you doing, son?" the shopkeeper asked a little boy whose eyes were on a large basket of apples outside the storefront. "Trying to steal one of those apples?"

"No sir," replied the boy. "I'm trying not to."

---

[1] F. B. Meyer, *The Christ Life for Your Life* (Chicago: Moody Press, n.d.), 66, 72.
[2] David McCullough, *Truman* (New York: Simon & Schuster, 1992), 435.

Broken in Two Places

A man went to the doctor complaining that he had broken his arm in two places. The doctor's reply: "Well then, stay out of those places."

Ten Commandments

Someone Once Said . . .

- *The world is nothing but a reversed Decalogue, or the Ten Commandments backwards.—* Martin Luther, in *Table Talk*
- *One rabbi who survived the [death] camp summed it up well when he said that at Auschwitz it was as though there existed a world in which all the Ten Commandments were reversed.—*Ravi Zacharias, in *Can Man Live Without God?*

The Ten Commandments in Verse

Above all else love God alone;
Bow down to neither wood nor stone.
God's name refuse to take in vain;
The Sabbath rest with care maintain.
Respect your parents all your days;
Hold sacred human life always.
Be loyal to your chosen mate;
Steal nothing, neither small nor great.
Report, with truth, your neighbor's deed;
And rid your mind of selfish greed.[1]

T

---

[1] Elton Trueblood, *Foundations for Reconstruction* (New York: Harper & Brothers, 1946), 10.

Date: _____   _____   _____
Place: _____   _____   _____
Occasion: _____   _____   _____

The Discarded Answer

Just after World War II, Elton Trueblood wrote a book called *Foundations For Reconstruction,* telling the nation that the recovery and restoration of world order depended on the solid moral foundations embodied in the Ten Commandments. He warned:

We prize our democracy but, for the most part, we pay no attention to the deeper convictions without which our vaunted democracy is practically meaningless and without which it could not have been produced in the first place. The mandatory need of our time is the discovery or recovery of an ethical creed that can give Western man . . . steady moral guidance. Fortunately, we do not need to hunt for such an ethical creed. We already have it. The Ten Commandments constitute the most memorable and succinct extant formulation of the ethical creed of the West.[1]

Unfortunately, the post-war generation responded to the Ten Commandments by seeking to have them banned from America's classrooms and courthouses.

Date: _____   _____   _____
Place: _____   _____   _____
Occasion: _____   _____   _____

Distilled Wisdom

The ability to reduce profound ideas to simple statements requires great wisdom. The Unitarian clergyman, Robert Fulghum, became famous because of his essay, "Everything I Really Need to Know I Learned in Kindergarten." He suggests that the simple rules learned in kindergarten will do for life. Rules like: Share everything. Play fair. Don't hit people. Put things back where you found them. Clean up your own mess. Flush. Remember that warm cookies and cold milk are good for you.

When Ernest Hemingway graduated from high school his parents wanted him to go to college, but he left home instead to take a job with the *Kansas City Star* as a cub reporter. His editor told him to use short sentences, avoid slang, speak plainly, and shy away from adjectives. Hemingway later said that those were "the best rules I every learnt for the business of writing." Using them, he became one of the best writers of the twentieth century.

The ability to distill profound subjects into a handful of simple, easy-to-remember rules is a mark of profound wisdom. Consider, then, how profoundly wise is Almighty God—for he reduced all our obligations and responsibilities in life to ten simple rules called the Ten Commandments. Those ten can be further reduced

---

[1] Trueblood, *Foundations for Reconstruction,* 8–10.

into two: Love God and love your neighbor. The two can then be summarized into one four-letter word: Love.[1]

Date: _____ _____ _____
Place: _____ _____ _____
Occasion: _____ _____ _____

The Ten-Sided Portrait

Suppose you were given pen and paper, ten minutes, and this assignment: Describe the character of Jesus Christ in ten brief sentences. What would you write? Perhaps the simplest and most theologically correct answer would be to write the Ten Commandments. These Ten Commands in Exodus 20 flow from the character of God himself and perfectly describe the person of Christ.

He said, "Do not think that I came to destroy the Law . . . I did not come to destroy but to fulfill" (Matthew 5:17). Jesus himself fulfills the law. He himself is the embodiment of the Ten Commandments, and thereby sinless.

They are more than archaic laws given to an ancient nation. The Ten Commandments are a ten-sided description of the Lord and of his character—and, by extension, they are descriptions of the character of Christ being reproduced in his followers by the Holy Spirit.

Date: _____ _____ _____
Place: _____ _____ _____
Occasion: _____ _____ _____

Dear Abby

Dear Abby: Regarding your letter about the Ten Commandments: I am reminded of the church minister who told his deacon that someone had stolen his bicycle and he suspected that the thief was a member of his congregation.

The next Sunday he decided to preach a sermon about the Ten Commandments because he felt that when he got to the commandment that says, "Thou shall not steal," the thief would be shamed into returning the bicycle."

The next Sunday, his topic was the Ten Commandments, but about halfway through his sermon, he abruptly switched his sermon to another subject.

Later his deacon asked him why he had changed his sermon. "Well," the minister said, "when I got to the commandment that says, 'Thou shall not commit adultery,' I remembered where I left my bicycle."[2]

Date: _____ _____ _____
Place: _____ _____ _____
Occasion: _____ _____ _____

---

[1] From a sermon by the author.
[2] *Nashville Banner*, Saturday, March 29, 1997, 2D.

For Fast Relief

A recent church ad had a picture of two hands holding stone tablets on which the Ten Commandments were inscribed with a caption reading: "For fast, fast relief—take two tablets."

Date: _____ _____ _____
Place: _____ _____ _____
Occasion: _____ _____ _____

Impressed

One man was so impressed by his pastor's sermon on the Ten Commandments, he said as he left the chapel, "Pastor, I'm so impressed by your message that I've made up my mind that for the next ten weeks I'm going to keep one of them Commandments each week until I get through all ten of them."

Date: _____ _____ _____
Place: _____ _____ _____
Occasion: _____ _____ _____

The Problem with Number Seven

Cathy Powers wrote, "I asked the students in my religion class for a volunteer to recite the Ten Commandments. One boy raised his hand and began rattling them off accurately until he reached number seven: "Thou shalt not admit adultery."[1]

Date: _____ _____ _____
Place: _____ _____ _____
Occasion: _____ _____ _____

Thanksgiving

Someone Once Said . . .

- *If in his gifts and benefits [God] were more sparing and close-handed, we should learn to be thankful . . . . The greater God's gifts and works, the less they are regarded.*—Martin Luther, in *Table Talk*
- *A grateful mind is a great mind.*—Rev. William Secker[2]
- *The person who has stopped being thankful has fallen asleep in life.*—Robert Louis Stevenson[3]

---

[1] *Reader's Digest,* August, 1991, 85.
[2] William Secker, *The Nonsuch Professor In His Meridian Splendor* (Chicago: Fleming H. Revell Co., 1899), 21.
[3] Alan Loy McGinnis, *The Power of Optimism* (New York: Harper & Row, 1990), 69.

- *Be thankful, therefore, for the least benefit and thou shalt be worthy to receive greater. Let the least be unto thee even as the greatest, and let that which is of little account be unto thee even as the greatest. If the majesty of the Giver be considered, nothing that is given shall seem small and of no worth, for that is not a small thing which is given by the Most High God.*—Thomas à Kempis
- *There are 138 passages of Scripture that deal with the subject of thanksgiving.*—Larry Poland[1]
- *How sharper than a serpent's tooth it is to have a thankless child.*—William Shakespeare in *King Lear*

Date: _____   _____   _____
Place: _____   _____   _____
Occasion: _____   _____   _____

An Old Swedish Hymn

Thanks to God for my Redeemer,
thanks for all thou dost provide!
Thanks for time now but a mem'ry,
thanks for Jesus by my side!
Thanks for pleasant, balmy springtime,
thanks for dark and dreary fall!
Thanks for tears by now forgotten,
thanks for peace within my soul!

Date: _____   _____   _____
Place: _____   _____   _____
Occasion: _____   _____   _____

You Are a Rich Man!

Dr. Robert Hill, author of over forty books, tells of visiting Bangkok, Thailand, where he was invited to a special celebration given by the King and Queen. His Thai guide, a young man named Joseph, asked several questions as he drove them to the pavilion. He knew a little English and was delighted to carry on a conversation. When he asked where the Hills lived, they told him Richmond, Virginia.

"Oh, you are a rich man?" asked the boy.

Bob laughed and told him, no, he wasn't rich.

Bob recalled, "Then he asked if we owned an automobile and I told him we had two cars in our family. His next question was about the house where we lived. I told him it was a rather simple house with ten rooms. He was amazed at its size, especially when he related his and his family lived in just two small rooms.

---

[1] Larry Poland, "Thanksgiving: More than Turkey Day," *Worldwide Challenge*, November/December, 1983, 37.

"Then he asked about our family. We told him we had four healthy children, two in college and two still at home.

"Joseph was silent for a moment or so, then he replied, 'You *are* a rich man.' We laughed, but deep in our hearts we knew he was right, though we had never thought of it in those terms. We were rich. But were we thankful?"[1]

Date: _____ _____ _____
Place: _____ _____ _____
Occasion: _____ _____ _____

Frankl's Lesson

Among the lessons Viktor Frankl learned in the Nazi death-camp, Auschwitz, was to take time to be thankful and to count your blessings. He wrote that prisoners in the camp dreamed at night about a certain set of things more than anything else. Bread, cakes, and nice warm baths—the very things we take for granted every day.

And Frankl said that the prisoners around him began to appreciate beauty as never before. In one especially poignant paragraph, he wrote: *If someone had seen our faces on the journey from Auschwitz to a Bavarian camp as we beheld the mountains of Salzburg with their summits glowing in the sunset, through the little barred windows of our prison carriage, he would never have believed that those were the faces of men who had given up all hope of life and liberty. Despite that factor—or maybe because of it—we were carried away by nature's beauty, which we had missed for so long.*

Date: _____ _____ _____
Place: _____ _____ _____
Occasion: _____ _____ _____

The Flower

Gerta Weissman was among the prisoners in a Nazi death camp. She recalled an episode one spring when she and her fellow inmates stood at roll call for hours on end, nearly collapsing with hunger and fatigue. But they noticed in the corner of that bleak, horrid, gray place that the concrete had broken and a flower had poked its head through. And the thousands of women there took great pains to avoid stepping on it. It was the only spot of beauty in their ugly and heinous world, and they were thankful for it.

Later in a radio interview, she added: "When people ask me, 'Why did you go on?' there is only one picture that comes to mind. The moment was when once I stood at the window of the first camp I was in and asked myself if, by some miraculous power, one wish could be granted me, what would it be? And then, with almost crystal clarity, the picture that came to my mind was a picture at home—my father smoking his pipe, my mother working at her needlepoint, my brother and I doing our homework. And I remember thinking, my goodness, it was just a boring

---

[1] Personal interview with Dr. Robert Hill.

evening at home. I had known countless evenings like that. And I knew that this picture would be, if I could help it, the driving force of my survival."[1]

Two Attitudes

Thanksgiving is essential to personal magnetism. The famous stress researcher Hans Seyle claims that two attitudes more than any other influence the quality of everyday life, and on these two emotions "depend our peace of mind, our feelings of security or insecurity, of fulfillment or frustration, in short, the extent to which we can make a success of life." The most destructive emotion is revenge. But in contrast, "among all the emotions, there is one which more than any other, accounts for the absence or presence of stress in human relations: that is the feeling of gratitude."

Mike McAdams of Nashville, Tennessee, visited his wife Cheryl in the intensive care unit of the hospital. "How is she?" an anxious friend asked as he exited her unit.

"It's touch and go," Mike replied. "She recognized me. We prayed together and held hands. And then we quoted the passage about thanksgiving in the book of James that says, 'Consider it joy, my brothers, when you face trials of many kinds . . .'"

"You know," he added, "*it's impossible to be anxious and thankful at the same time.*"

Seeds of Discouragement

The devotional book *Springs in the Valley* tells of a man who found a barn where Satan kept his seeds ready to be sown in the human heart. He found that the seeds of discouragement were more numerous than the others and he learned that those seeds could be made to grow almost anywhere. But when Satan was questioned, he reluctantly admitted that there was one place in which he could never get them to thrive. "And where is that?" asked the man. Satan replied sadly, "In the heart of a grateful person."[2]

---

[1] Dr. Julius Segal, *Winning Life's Toughest Battles* (New York: Ivy Books, 1896), 60, 69.
[2] Mrs. Charles E. Cowman, *Springs in the Valley* (Los Angeles: Cowman Publications, Inc., 1939), 250.

Reverse Proportion

We exhibit a degree of thanksgiving in life in reverse proportion to the amount of blessings we've received. Martin Luther wrote in his book *Table Talk:* "The greater God's gifts and works, the less they are regarded."

A hungry man is more thankful for his morsel than a rich man for his heavily-laden table. A lonely woman in a nursing home will appreciate a visit more than a popular woman with a party thrown in her honor. A Russian who finally gets his own copy of the Holy Scriptures after seventy-five years of state-imposed atheism is more thankful for his little book than we are for all the Christian books and magazines and translations that overflow our shelves.

Ralph Waldo Emerson observed that if the constellations appeared only once in a thousand years, imagine what an exciting event it would be. But because they're there every night, we barely give them a look.

One of the evidences of the Holy Spirit's work in our lives is a gradual reversal of that twisted pattern. God wants to make us people who exhibit a thankfulness in proper proportion to the gifts and blessings we've received.[1]

Full Stockings

If my children wake up on Christmas morning and have somebody to thank for putting candy in their stocking, have I no one to thank for putting two feet in mine?

—G. K. CHESTERTON

Date: _____   _____   _____

Place: _____   _____   _____

Occasion: _____   _____   _____

Think and Thank

The words "Thank" and "Think" hail from the same root, reminding us that thanksgiving comes from thinking about our blessings.

Helen Keller once said, "I have often thought it would be a blessing if each human being were stricken blind and deaf for a few days at some time during his early adult life. It would make him more appreciative of sight and the joys of sound."

Senator Richard Neuberger once said the experience of contracting cancer changed him. "A change came over me which I believe is irreversible. Questions of prestige, of political success, of financial status, became all at once unimportant. In their stead has come a new appreciation of things I once took for granted—eating lunch with a friend, scratching Muffet's ears and listening for his purr, the company of my wife, reading a book or magazine in the quiet cone of my bed lamp at night, raiding the refrigerator for a glass of orange juice or a slice of coffee cake. For the first time I think I am actually savoring life. I shudder when I remember all the occasions that I spoiled for myself—even when I was in the best of health—by false pride, synthetic values, and fancied slights.

---

[1] From a sermon by the author.

Date: _____ _____ _____
Place: _____ _____ _____
Occasion: _____ _____ _____

What a Pity

Sigmund Freud suffered from a horrible cancer to his mouth, and in 1926, he also developed heart trouble and spent time in a sanatorium. He returned to Vienna with a yearning for morning drives, and for the first time, he said, he experienced the glories of springtime in Vienna. "What a pity," he wrote, "that one has to grow old and ill before making this discovery."

Date: _____ _____ _____
Place: _____ _____ _____
Occasion: _____ _____ _____

14,000 Things

Barbara Ann Kipfer began keeping a list of her favorite things as a shy teenager. Soon the list became second nature; she found herself making additions while riding the bus, eating breakfast, and even in the middle of the night. Twenty years and dozens of spiral notebooks later, her list was published as a book titled *14,000 Things To Be Happy About.* Why not write your own book?

Date: _____ _____ _____
Place: _____ _____ _____
Occasion: _____ _____ _____

Havergal's List

Near the end of her life, Frances Ridley Havergal jotted down every day on a little calendar something—often a little thing—for which she thanked God. It was her way of thinking about thanking.

Date: _____ _____ _____
Place: _____ _____ _____
Occasion: _____ _____ _____

What Now?

The seventeenth-century minister Jeremy Taylor was persecuted for his faith. His house was plundered, his family driven out, and his estate confiscated. He wrote: *I am fallen into the hands of publicans and they have taken all from me. What now? They have not taken away my merry countenance, my cheerful spirit, and a good conscience; they have still left me with the providence of God, and all His promises . . . my hopes of Heaven, and my charity to them, too, and still I sleep and digest, I eat and drink, I read and meditate. And he that hath so many causes of joy, and so great . . . (should never choose) to sit down upon his little handful of thorns.*

```
Date: _____   _____   _____
Place: _____   _____   _____
Occasion: _____   _____   _____
```

Traveling Mercies

One day, according to a time-honored story, St. Francis of Assisi longed to see his brothers. They agreed to meet in a remote monastery in the Umbrian mountains of central Italy. After arriving and enjoying their reunion, each reported what he had experienced on the road.

One Franciscan brother who had traveled on muleback said: "God protected me in a miraculous way. When I was crossing a narrow bridge over a deep mountain gorge, the mule jumped. I fell and narrowly escaped falling over the wall of the bridge into the gorge. God by his love saved my life."

A second brother said: "I had to cross a river and I slipped and fell. The waters carried me down the river. But God in his grace provided a tree which had fallen across the river. I could grasp a branch of that tree and pull myself ashore, thanks to God's miraculous mercy."

Then St. Francis said: "Let us thank God for his wonderful works. I did experience the greatest miracle of all on my way. I had the smoothest, most pleasant, completely uneventful trip."[1]

```
Date: _____   _____   _____
Place: _____   _____   _____
Occasion: _____   _____   _____
```

—————— Trials and Troubles ——————

Someone Once Said . . .

- *A faith that can't be tested can't be trusted.*—Warren Wiersbe[2]
- *By affliction, the Lord separates the sin that he hates from the soul that he loves.*—Rev. William Secker[3]
- *I dare say that the greatest earthly blessing that God can give to any of us is health, with the exception of sickness.*—Charles H. Spurgeon
- *If Joseph had not been Egypt's prisoner, he would have never been Egypt's governor. The iron chains about his feet ushered in the golden chains about his neck.*—William Secker

---

[1] John H. Townsend, *Pulpit Digest*, September/October 1979, 53.
[2] Warren W. Wiersbe, *Why Us?* (Old Tappan, NJ: Fleming H. Revell Co., 1984), 13.
[3] William Secker, *The Nonsuch Professor In His Meridian Splendor* (Chicago: Fleming H. Revell Co., 1899), 22.

- *God does not waste suffering. . . . If he plows it is because he purposes as crop.*—Isobel Kuhn, in *Green Leaf in Drought Time*
- *Smooth seas do not make skillful sailors.*—African proverb
- *A sickbed often teaches more than a sermon.*—Thomas Watson[1]
- *Times of trouble have often been times of triumph to a believer. Suffering seasons have generally been sifting seasons in which the Christian has lost his chaff, and the hypocrite his courage.*—William Secker[2]
- *God's rod is a pencil to draw Christ's image more distinctly upon us.*—Thomas Watson[3]

Date: _____ _____ _____
Place: _____ _____ _____
Occasion: _____ _____ _____

ABC

The ABC's of spiritual growth: *Adversity Builds Character.*

Date: _____ _____ _____
Place: _____ _____ _____
Occasion: _____ _____ _____

Lord of the Compost Heap

Lord of the compost heap
you take garbage
and turn it into
soil good soil
for seeds to root
and grow
with wildest increase
flowers to bloom
with brilliant beauty.
Take all the garbage
of my life
Lord of the compost heap
turn it into
soil good soil
and then plant seeds
to bring forth
fruit and beauty
in profusion—Joseph Bayly[4]

T

---

[1] Thomas Watson, *Gleanings From Thomas Watson* (Morgan, PA: Soli Deo Gloria Publications, 1995), 55.
[2] Secker, *The Nonsuch Professor In His Meridian Splendor,* 70.
[3] *Gleanings From Thomas Watson,* 141.
[4] Joseph Bayly, *Psalms of My Life, Christianity Today,* January 15, 1988, 35.

```
Date:          _____    _____    _____
Place:         _____    _____    _____
Occasion:      _____    _____    _____
```

J. I. Packer

In his book *Knowing God,* J. I. Packer writes: "We should not, therefore, be too taken back when unexpected and upsetting and discouraging things happen to us now. What do they mean? Why, simply that God in his wisdom means to make something of us which we have not attained yet, and is dealing with us accordingly. . . .

"It is often the case, as all the saints know, that fellowship with the Father and the Son is most vivid and sweet, and Christian joy the greatest, when the cross is heaviest."

Packer then suggests two ways of handling the trials of life when we cannot, for the moment, see God's purpose in them. "First, by taking them as from God, and asking ourselves what reactions to them, and in them, the gospel of God requires of us; second, by seeking God's face specifically about them. If we do these two things, we shall never find ourselves wholly in the dark as to God's purpose in troubles."[1]

```
Date:          _____    _____    _____
Place:         _____    _____    _____
Occasion:      _____    _____    _____
```

Only Thus Were We Prepared

About ten years after World War I, The German writer, Erich Maria Remarque wrote *All Quiet on the Western Front,* a book that portrayed the war with graphic, aching reality. The story is told through the eyes of Paul Baumer, who enlisted with his classmates in the German army. The early chapter of the book describes the rigor and hardships of boot camp and of their training. He was under the command of Corporal Himmelstoss, a harsh disciplinarian.

He was a small undersized fellow with a foxy, waxed moustache, who had seen twelve years' service and was in civilian life a postman . . .

I have remade his bed fourteen times in one morning. Each time he had some fault to find and pulled it to pieces. I have kneaded a pair of prehistoric boots that were as hard as iron for twenty hours—with intervals of course—until they became as soft as butter and not even Himmelstoss could find anything more to do to them; under his orders I have scrubbed out the Corporals' Mess with a tooth-brush. Kropp and I were given the job of cleaning the barrack-square of snow with a hand-broom and a dust-pan, and we would have gone on till we were frozen had not a lieutenant accidentally appeared . . .

---

[1] J. I. Packer, *Knowing God* (Downers Grove, IL: InterVarsity, 1973), 86–87.

With full pack and rifle I have had to practice on a soft, wet, newly ploughed field the "Prepare to advance, advance!" and the "Lie down!" until I was one lump of mud and finally collapsed. . . .

I have stood at attention in a hard frost without gloves for a quarter of an hour at a stretch, while Himmelstoss watched for the slightest movement of our bare fingers on the steel barrel of the rifle . . .

But a little later, Remarque's character, Paul Baumer, gave these telling comments: *Had we gone into the trenches without this period of training most of us would certainly have gone mad. Only thus were we prepared for what awaited us. We did not break down, but endured. . . .*

Date: _____   _____   _____
Place: _____   _____   _____
Occasion: _____   _____   _____

The Blessings of Illness

While illness is a hardship every person wishes to avoid, it comes sooner or later upon us all. The Bible teaches that suffering is not to be wasted. "What circumstances could have rendered the Word of God sweeter and the presence of God so real, the help of God so precious?" asked Hudson Taylor about a difficult period in his life.

Several Scriptures point to special blessings that can come from periods of illness, including:

- Awakening to us the sweetness of Scripture—Psalm 119:50, 71, 92, 143
- Driving us to prayer—Isaiah 38:1–2
- Deepening the prayer lives of others—James 5:13–15
- Leading us to spiritual introspection—Psalm 119:67
- Humbling our souls—2 Corinthians 12:7–10
- Developing the qualities of patience and endurance in us—James 1:2–4
- Developing maturity—Romans 5:1–5; Isaiah 48:10; Hebrews 2:10; 1 Peter 1:6–8
- Enabling us to empathize and comfort others who will later go through the same thing—2 Corinthians 1:3
- Heightening our desire for heaven—Job 19:25–29; Romans 8:18
- Providing an opportunity for us to witness to others—2 Corinthians 12:9–10
- Glorifying God—John 11:4; 2 Corinthians 12:7–10

Date: _____   _____   _____
Place: _____   _____   _____
Occasion: _____   _____   _____

T

Andrew Murray's Four Truths

South African pastor Andrew Murray once faced a terrible crisis. Gathering himself into his study, he sat a long while quietly, prayerfully, thoughtfully. His mind flew at last to his Lord Jesus, and picking up his pen, he wrote these words in his journal:

First, He brought me here, it is by His will that I am in this strait place: in that fact I will rest.

Next, He will keep me here in His love, and give me grace to behave as His child.

Then, He will make the trial a blessing, teaching me the lessons He intends me to learn, and working in me the grace He means to bestow.

Last, in His good time He can bring me out again—how and when He knows.

Let me say I am here,

(1) By God's appointment

(2) In His keeping,

(3) Under His training,

(4) For His time.[1]

Date:			
Place:			
Occasion:			

McQuilkin's Two Questions

Robert C. McQuilkin, first president of Columbia Bible College, wrote that when plagued by undone tasks, misunderstandings, troubles, and apparent failure, he stops and deliberately asks himself two questions:

First, am I surrendered to the Lord; Do I want only his will so far as my choice is concerned. . . .

The second question is: Is the Lord just now meeting all my need? The answer must be to take Him at His word though there are fightings without and fears within and though the circumstances of outward things and of inward life seem to say the needs are not being met. His grace IS sufficient.

So I go forward doing the next duty and resting in faith, not in feeling.[2]

Date:			
Place:			
Occasion:			

Sangster's Four Rules

In 1939, William Sangster assumed leadership of Westminster Central Hall, a Methodist church near London's Westminster Abbey. During his first worship service he announced to his stunned congregation that Britain and Germany were officially at war. He quickly converted the church basement into an air raid shelter, and for 1,688 nights Sangster ministered to the various needs of all kinds of people.

[1] V. Raymond Edman, *They Found the Secret* (Grand Rapids, MI: Zondervan, 1960), 97.

[2] Marguerite McQuilkin, *Always in Triumph: The Life of Robert C. McQuilkin* (Columbia, SC: Columbia Bible College, 1956), 230.

At the same time, he somehow managed to write, to preach gripping sermons, to earn a Ph.D., and to lead hundreds to Christ. He became known as Wesley's successor in London and was esteemed as the most beloved British preacher of his era.

Sometime after the war, Sangster was diagnosed with progressive muscular atrophy. For three years, he slowly died, becoming progressively more paralyzed, finally able to move only two fingers. But his attitude didn't falter, for when first learning of his illness, Sangster made four rules for himself. Many people have rules for living. Sangster composed four rules for dying: "I will never complain. I will keep the home bright. I will count my blessings. I will try to turn it to gain." He did all those things. And thus the work of God was displayed in his life, and in his death.

Date: _____ _____ _____
Place: _____ _____ _____
Occasion: _____ _____ _____

Which Verse?

In *A Turtle on a Fencepost*, Allan Emery tells of accompanying businessman Ken Hansen to visit a hospitalized employee. The patient lay very still, his eyes conveying anguish. His operation had taken eight hours, and recovery was long and uncertain.

"Alex," said Ken quietly, "you know I have had a number of serious operations. I know the pain of trying to talk. I think I know what questions you're asking. There are two verses I want to give you—Genesis 42:36 and Romans 8:28. We have the option of these two attitudes. We need the perspective of the latter."

Hansen turned to the passages, read them, then prayed and left. The young man, Alex Balc, took the message to heart. He later enjoyed full recovery.

Every day we choose one of these attitudes amid life's difficulties—to be beat-up, or to be up-beat.

To say with Jacob in Genesis 42:36: *All these things are against me.*

Or to say with Paul in Romans 8:28: *All these things are working together for good to those who love the Lord . . . .*[1]

Date: _____ _____ _____
Place: _____ _____ _____
Occasion: _____ _____ _____

Opportunities in Difficulties

The Chinese Christian Christiana Tsai suffered from a debilitating disease much of her life. In her book, *Queen of the Dark Chamber*, we find these words: "Once a great scholar in China said, 'A sage seeks opportunities in difficulties, and a fool

---

[1] Allan C. Emery, Jr., *A Turtle on a Fencepost* (Waco, Texas: Word Books, 1979), 110–113.

finds difficulties in opportunities. . . .' We are born to overcome difficulties through the power of the Holy Spirit."[1]

Date: _____ _____ _____
Place: _____ _____ _____
Occasion: _____ _____ _____

Problems = Opportunities

In 2700 B.C. Emperor Whing Tee asked his wife Ce Ling Shee to try to find out what was damaging his Mulberry trees. The Empress first noticed that a drab-colored moth was laying tiny eggs on a Mulberry leaf, each hatching into a caterpillar that ejected a thread for three days which it wrapped around its body until it formed a cocoon. She dropped the cocoon into hot water and saw a single thread begin unwinding itself. She had discovered silk. The Empress observed that fineness and beauty of the silk thread. She unbound it completely and found it to be 1/2 mile long from that single cocoon. And she thought that these fine threads might be made into cloth.

Soon a loom was developed on which they could be woven. That silk cloth that was woven on their loom was in such demand that later Romans are said to have weighed the silk before buying it and then paid an equal weight of gold for it.

For more than 3000 years only the Chinese knew the secret of silk. Then in A.D. 522 Roman Emperor Justinian sent two monks to buy silk from China. The monks brought back more than silk. They personally broke Chinese monopoly on silk by smuggling back into Europe two silkworm eggs and Mulberry tree seeds in their hollow monks' staff. They were apparently the first industrial pirates. From these two silkworm eggs the Roman Empire acquired enough silkworms to make it partially independent from China.

Like so many serendipitous events, the discovery of silk came while trying to solve a problem. Before long the business of growing Mulberry trees was for the sole purpose of providing moths with leaves on which to lay their eggs so that the production of silk could be increased.

Nothing like silk had ever appeared before in fine fabrics. It brought about a world of revolution in fashions. The very word silk brings to mind something that is soft, lustrous or luxurious. The wealthy of the world have always dressed themselves in silken clothes.

It's important to look for solutions instead of trying to avoid problems, so when you have a problem of some kind, remember that you also have an equal opportunity.[2]

Date: _____ _____ _____
Place: _____ _____ _____
Occasion: _____ _____ _____

---

[1] Christiana Tsai, *Queen of the Dark Chamber* (Chicago: Moody Press, 1953), 12.
[2] Frank Morgan "Rambling through Time," *Fort Lauderdale Tribune*. Retold by Earl Nightingale in a clipping in my files.

Problems or Gifts?

Eileen Egan, who worked with Mother Teresa and with the Missionaries of Charity for thirty years, described Mother Teresa's outlook like this:

"One day, after my conservation had been filled with a litany of problems, Mother Teresa remarked, 'Everything is a *problem*. Why not use the word *Gift?*' With that began a shift in vocabulary. Shortly thereafter, we were to fly from Vancouver to New York City. I was dismayed to learn that the trip had to be broken en route, with a long delay, and was about to inform her of the *problem*. Then I caught myself and said, 'Mother, I have to tell you about a gift. We have to wait four hours here, and you won't arrive at the convent until very late.' Mother Teresa settled down in the airport to read a book of meditations, a favorite of hers.

"From that time on, items that presented disappointments or difficulties would be introduced with 'We have a small gift here,' or 'Today we have an especially big gift.' "[1]

Date:			
Place:			
Occasion:			

What Are Problems?

Predictors—They will mold our future.
Reminders—We are not self-sufficient. We need God and others to help us.
Opportunities—They pull us out of our rut and cause us to think creatively.
Blessings—They open up doors that we usually do not go through.
Lessons—Each new challenge will be our teacher.
Everywhere—No place or person is excluded from them.
Messages—They warn us about potential disaster.
Solvable—No problem is without a solution.[2]

Date:			
Place:			
Occasion:			

T

No Business Here

Many years ago, a large American shoe manufacturer sent two sales reps out to different parts of the Australian outback to see if they could drum up some business among the aborigines. Some time later, the company received telegrams from both agents.

The first one said, "No business here. Natives don't wear shoes."

The second one said, "Great opportunity here—natives don't wear shoes!"

---

[1] Eileen Eagan, *Such a Vision of the Street, Christian Clippings.*
[2] John Maxwell, *Your Attitude: Key to Success* (San Bernardino, CA: Here's Life Publishers, 1984), 99.

Date:			
Place:			
Occasion:			

Dragged Through Sand and Sea

Barbara Brown Taylor tells of spending a few days on a barrier island where loggerhead turtles were laying their eggs. One night when the tide was out, she watched a huge female turtle heave herself up the beach to dig her nest and empty her eggs into the sand. Taylor didn't want to disturb her, but the next day she returned to try to find the spot where the eggs were hidden. What she found instead were tracks leading in the wrong direction. Instead of heading back out to sea, she had wandered into the dunes, which were already as hot as asphalt in the morning sun.

A little ways inland, Taylor found the mother turtle, exhausted and all but baked. Her head and flippers were caked with dried sand. After pouring water on her and covering her with sea oats, Taylor fetched a park ranger, who returned with a jeep to rescue her.

—◇—
Traceable Hand

When you can't trace God's hand, you can trust God's heart.
—CHARLES SPURGEON
—◇—

The ranger flipped the turtle over on her back, wrapped tire chains around her front legs, and hooked the chains to the trailer hitch on his jeep. Then he took off, yanking her body forward so fast that her open mouth filled with sand and then disappeared underneath her.

The ranger hauled her over the dunes and down onto the beach, and the woman followed the path that the prow of her shell cut in the sand. At ocean's edge, he unhooked her and turned her right side up again. She lay motionless in the surf as the water lapped at her body, washing the sand from her eyes and making her skin shine again.

Then a particularly large wave broke over her, and she lifted her head slightly, moving her back legs as she did. Every fresh wave brought her life back to her until one of them make her light enough to find a foothold and push off, back into the water that was her home.

Watching her swim slowly away and remembering her nightmare ride through the dunes, Barbara Brown Taylor noted that it is sometimes hard to tell whether you are being killed or saved by the hands that turn your world upside down.

Sometimes we feel that our world is being turned upside down, but according to Romans 5, when we're in his hands his only design is to develop perseverance, which leads to character, which leads to a hopeful attitude. He makes all things work for our good.[1]

Date:			
Place:			
Occasion:			

---

[1] Barbara Brown Taylor, "Preaching the Terrors," *Leadership Journal*, Spring 1992,, 45.

Mud

Why did Jesus send the blind man to the Pool of Siloam to wash his eyes? Jesus could have just said, "Be healed," and the man's sight would have come to him on the spot. But he wanted the man to do something, to exercise obedience, so he sent him to the Siloam Pool to wash his eyes. But there's an interesting little detail to the story. Before sending him off, Jesus smeared mud on his eyelids.

The intriguing question is: Why? Have you ever seen anyone spit it into the dirt, twirl it around with his finger, then take the mud and smear it over someone's eyes? How would you like it if someone did that to you?

It's obvious. The mud made the man want to obey. It was a nudging, an additional motivation for the man to go to the pool of Siloam to wash his eyes. The mud provided the motivation for the obedience Christ required.

We don't always understand why mud gets in our eyes, but sometimes if it weren't there, we would never bring critical areas of our lives into obedience to Jesus Christ. And without obedience, the work of God can never be displayed in us. God, in his infinite grace and wisdom, sometimes uses mud to restore our sight.[1]

Date:			
Place:			
Occasion:			

Typhoid Fever

While traveling through Europe in 1874, Frances Ridley Havergal, in her late thirties but always somewhat frail, contracted typhoid fever and arrived home ill. By November, she was hovering between life and death as prayer meetings were held all across England for her. For months afterward, she was confined to bed. But her recovery was marked by cheerfulness, optimism, and patience. A year later, this was her testimony:

I have just begun to work a little . . . after twelve months of "falling apart": typhoid fever, which, with relapses and results, kept me ill for eight months, and part of the time very suffering, and then four months of very slow convalescence. But it has been the most precious year of my life to me. It is worth any suffering to prove to oneself the truth of "when thou passest through the waters I will be with thee," and worth being turned back (as it seemed) from the very golden gates, if one may but "tell of His faithfulness."

Date:			
Place:			
Occasion:			

The Blessings of Buffeting

Philippians 1:12 is an illustration of Romans 8:28. Because of Paul's imprisonment:

---

[1] From a sermon by the author.

1. His captors were evangelized.
2. His colleagues were emboldened.
3. His critics were exposed.
4. His Christ was exalted.

Date: _____ _____ _____
Place: _____ _____ _____
Occasion: _____ _____ _____

Though He Slay Me

Shortly after the death of their daughter Robin, Roy Rogers and Dale Evans met a pale little boy who stuck out his hand and said, "Howdy, pahtnah!" He had been abandoned in a Kentucky motel, and was physically and mentally disabled.

Roy and Dale adopted him, calling him Sandy in honor of his hair. He was bright-eyed and good-natured. During a Billy Graham Crusade, Sandy became a Christian.

Roy and Dale enrolled him in military school and he loved it. At seventeen, he enlisted in the army "to prove myself." Sandy worked hard and won respect. He was sent to Germany, then volunteered for Vietnam. "Put your faith in the Lord," he wrote home, "because (as I have found out) he's always around when you need him. All he asks in return is your devotion."

Then one day Dale Evans, returning from a trip, was met at the airport. "It's Sandy, Mom. He's dead." Sandy had returned from 26 days of maneuvers, dog tired. His buddies had taken him out for the night, needling him to "prove you're a man." Sandy, who couldn't tolerate alcohol, had given in. They fed him hard liquor until he collapsed. He was found next morning dead in his bunk.

Dale Evans survived the sorrow only by drawing strength from Scripture, particularly from Job 13:15. "Tragedy in a Christian's life is a refiner," she wrote. "God has not promised an easy way, but peace at the center of the hard way. The clouds of sorrow have been heavy, but I have reached the point of no return in my Christian experience, and with Job I can cry, 'Though he slay me, yet will I trust him.' "[1]

Date: _____ _____ _____
Place: _____ _____ _____
Occasion: _____ _____ _____

It Was on Fire . . .

Robert Fulghum tells of reading a newspaper account of a small-town emergency squad, summoned to a house where smoke was pouring from an upstairs window. The crew broke in and found a man in a smoldering bed. After the man was rescued and the mattress doused, the obvious question was asked: "How did this happen."

"I don't know," replied the man. "It was on fire when I lay down on it."[2]

---

[1] Robert J. Morgan, *From This Verse* (Nashville: Thomas Nelson Publishers, Inc., 1998), February 24th.
[2] Robert Fulghum, *It Was On Fire When I Lay Down on It* (New York: Villard Books, 1990), 5.

Date:			
Place:			
Occasion:			

Encouragement

A Sunday school class was concerned about one member's mother, who was in the hospital. The teacher suggested that each child sign a get-well card to send the mother and write a Bible verse after his name. The children all started thumbing through their Bibles, looking for verses. One little boy opened his Bible and made his selection—Matthew 5:26: "Truly, I say to you, you will never get out till you have paid the last penny."

Date:			
Place:			
Occasion:			

——— Unrighteousness/Sin, Nature of ———

Someone Once Said . . .

- *Sin has ruined men, ruined women, ruined angels. Sin has occasioned every tear of sorrow, every sigh of grief, every pang of agony. Sin has withered everything that is fair, blasted everything that is good, made bitter everything that is sweet, dried up springs of comfort, rolled far and wide tides of sorrow. Sin has digged every grave, built every coffin, woven every shroud, enlarged every cemetery . . . that the world has ever seen.*—Robert G. Lee[1]
- *All the old primitive sins are not dead but just crouching in the dark corners of our modern hearts—still there, and still as ghastly as ever.*—Carl Jung, psychologist.[2]
- *Sin has many manifestations, but its essence is one. A moral being, created to worship before the throne of God, sits on the throne of his own selfhood and from that elevated position declares, "I AM." That is sin in its concentrated essence.*—A. W. Tozer[3]
- *Everything in the universe is good to the degree that it conforms to the nature of God and evil as it fails to do so.*—A. W. Tozer[4]
- *Most of us spend the first six days of each week sowing wild oats; then we go to church on Sunday and pray for a crop failure.*—Fred Allen (1894–1956), US comedian
- *So small a boy yet so great a sinner.*—Augustine's description of his youth, in his *Confessions*
- *Adam and Eve ate us out of house and home.*—Vance Havner[5]

U

---

[1] Robert G. Lee, *Heart to Heart* (Nashville: Broadman Press, 1977), 65–66.
[2] George Sweeting, "Talking It Over," *Moody Magazine*, September 1985, 2.
[3] A. W. Tozer, *The Knowledge of the Holy* (New York: Harper & Row, Publishers, 1961), 36–37.
[4] Tozer, *The Knowledge of the Holy*, 93–94.
[5] Vance Havner, *Playing Marbles with Diamonds* (Grand Rapids, MI: Baker Book House, 1985), 39.

Date:			
Place:			
Occasion:			

Where the Line Falls

It would be different, Aleksandr Solzhenitsyn notes, if there were "evil people somewhere insidiously committing evil deeds, and it were necessary only to separate them from the rest of us and destroy them. But the line dividing good and evil cuts through the heart of every human being."[1]

Time, in an article on the existence of evil, said: "Evil is a word we use when we come to the limit of humane comprehension. But we sometimes suspect that it is the core of our true selves."[2]

Date:			
Place:			
Occasion:			

Germs in the Water

When I was a child, my dad took us on vacation to another country. We stayed at a motel where, that evening, we went swimming. Another boy in the pool pulled me aside and told me, whatever I did, not to allow any of the water from the pool into my mouth. If I swallowed it, he said, I'd become deathly sick. He also told me I shouldn't drink water from the tap in our room.

I have some friends who went swimming in the ocean near a large city in South America. They didn't realize the sewage from the city ran into the ocean, and they became horribly sick with a long-lasting dysentery.

Who among us would like to swim in or take a drink of sewage?

Recently, I joined a hiking expedition through the pristine woods of the southern Appalachians. The springs of water bubbled from the sides of the mountains, trickling over rocks, dancing down the creeks, and feeding into crystal-clear rivers. But our guide said, "We mustn't drink the water unless we boil it. It contains microscopic bacteria, and it'll make us sick."

The pollution of our environment is so great that the same germs we find in the brackish waters of developing nations are also in the mountain streams of Tennessee.

In the same way, the germ of sin that we find in the most diabolical homicidal maniac is present in your life and mine, for all have sinned and come short of the glory of God. There is none righteous, no not one.[3]

---

[1] James and Phyllis Alsdurf, *Battered into Submission* (Downers Grove, IL: InterVarsity Press, 1989) 59.
[2] Lance Morrow, "Evil," *Time,* June 10, 1991, 51.
[3] From a sermon by the author.

Muggeridge in India

Malcolm Muggeridge, the famous British philosopher and journalist who converted to Christianity late in life, once told of working as a journalist in India as a young man. One evening he walked down to the river for a swim. As he entered the water, he saw an Indian woman from the nearby village who had come for her evening bath. Muggeridge immediately felt the allurement of the moment, and he was besieged by temptation. He had lived with this kind of temptation all his adult life, but until this moment he had fought it off out of respect for his wife Kitty. But tonight, he was weak and vulnerable. He hesitated just a moment, then swam furiously across the river toward the woman, literally trying to outdistance his conscience. But when he was just a few feet away from her, he emerged from the water and what he saw took his breath away. She wasn't a beautiful young maiden, but old and hideous, with wrinkled skin, and worst of all, she was a leper. He said later, "The creature grinned at me, showing a toothless mask." Muggeridge muttered, "What a dirty, lecherous woman!" But as he swam away from her, a sudden shock gripped him: "It wasn't just the woman who was dirty and lecherous," he said. "It was my own heart."

Honey with a Sting

There are some things which are pleasant, but not good, as youthful lusts and worldly delights. These bees carry honey in their mouths, but they have a sting in their tails.—Rev. William Secker, seventeenth-century British minister

U

Raccoons

Gary Richmond, a former zoo keeper, explains that raccoons go through a glandular change at about twenty-four months old. After that, they often attack their owners.

Richmond had a friend named Julie who owned a pet raccoon. Since a thirty-pound raccoon can equal a one-hundred-pound dog in a fight, he felt compelled to warn her of the coming change.

"It'll be different for me," she replied with a smile. "Bandit wouldn't hurt me. He just wouldn't."

Three months later Julie underwent plastic surgery for facial lacerations sustained when her adult raccoon attacked her for no apparent reason. Bandit was released into the wild.

Sin, too, often comes dressed in an adorable guise, and as we play with it, it's easy to say, "It will be different for me." The results are predictable.[1]

Date: _____ _____ _____
Place: _____ _____ _____
Occasion: _____ _____ _____

How Eskimos Kill Wolves

The consuming, self-destructive nature of sin is like the technique used by Eskimos to kill wolves. First, the Eskimo coats his knife blade with animal blood and allows it to freeze. Then he adds another layer of blood, and another, until the blade is completely concealed in a block of frozen blood.

Next the hunter fixes his knife in the ground with the blade up. When a wolf follows his sensitive nose to the source of the scent and discovers the bait, he licks it, tasting the fresh frozen blood. He begins to lick faster, more and more vigorously, lapping the blade until the keen edge is bare. Feverishly now, harder and harder the wolf licks the blade in the arctic night. So great becomes his craving for blood that the wolf does not notice the razor-sharp sting of the naked blade on his own tongue, nor does he realize that his insatiable thirst is being satisfied by his own blood. He just craves more and more until he drops dead in the snow.

We are consumed, the Bible warns, by our own lusts.[2]

Date: _____ _____ _____
Place: _____ _____ _____
Occasion: _____ _____ _____

The Pit and the Pendulum

The famous American author Edgar Allan Poe wrote the short story *The Pit and the Pendulum*. In the Spanish Inquisition, a man had been found guilty of heresy and condemned to death in the dungeons. He was to die by torture—not physical torture but psychological torture. He was thrown into a damp and blackened cell, so dark the blackness wrapped itself around him and almost suffocated him. He knew that he was to die in that dungeon, but he didn't know how. He shuffled around, trying to feel the outline of the room. He fainted, revived, and tried again. As he inched across the dungeon, he slipped and fell on the slimy floor. His hand felt around him,

---

[1] Bob Campbell, "Sin's Delusion," *Leadership Journal*, Spring, 1988, 47.
[2] Paul Harvey, submitted by Chris T. Zwingelberg, "Sin's Peril," in *Leadership Journal*, Winter, 1987, 41.

and just before him the floor ended at the edge of a deep, dark and deadly pit, filled with water and water rats.

By slipping prematurely, he had been saved from the pit. He fell asleep again, and when he awoke, he was strapped to a table, unable to move, except for very limited movement of his left arm. His hand could reach a little plate of spicy meat; otherwise, he was immobile. There was dim light in the dungeon now, and he noticed above him a gigantic pendulum, swinging in wide arcs above him. The bottom edge of the pendulum was sharpened like a razor, and every time it swung it descended a fraction of an inch. Minute after minute, hour after hour, he watched the blade swinging back and forth, lower and lower, coming closer and closer to his chest. Every time the steel passed, the rush of wind hissed, sending shudders through his soul.

The hissing, flying blade finally lowered to within inches of his skin. It started slowly slicing through the threads of his coat. It was designed to slowly cut, inch by inch, through his chest and into his heart. The man had noticed that hundreds of rats had crawled out of the pit and were surrounding him. He kept them away by waving his one free hand and squirming under his ropes. Suddenly, he thought of a plan. Taking his free hand, he rubbed the spicy meat into the ropes that bound him to the table. Then he kept himself still, as still as death.

Apple Tree

It wasn't the apple on the tree that ruined everything. It was the pair on the ground.

—ANONYMOUS

The rats crept toward him, and finally they swarmed over him, gnawing and biting until they had bitten through the ropes. With one gigantic effort at the very last moment, he lunged to the side and rolled from the path of the deadly blade. Instantly the blade was pulled up into the ceiling by some watching, unseen executioner.

The prisoner then noticed that the steel walls of the cell were growing hotter. They became red hot and started moving toward him. The dungeon suddenly became smaller and smaller, and the fiery walls were pressing him closer and closer to the pit.

Finally, his seared and writhing body had only an inch of foothold on the firm floor of the prison. He struggled no more, but the agony of his soul found vent in one loud, long and final scream of despair.

Suddenly there was a hum of voices. There was a loud blast of many trumpets. The fiery walls rushed back. An outstretched arm caught him. In the final paragraph of the story, we learn that General LaSalle and his army had entered Toledo, and had saved the victims of the Spanish Inquisition. At the last moment, the man was snatched to safety.

It is a picture of the Gospel. Our fiendish enemy has thrown us into his dungeon. He makes us godless, senseless, faithless, heartless, ruthless, worthless, and powerless. He ties us up. He tortures us with rats of addiction and abuse and despair and discord. He wants us in the bottomless pit of hell, to share in his destiny forever.

We are absolutely powerless to help ourselves or to save ourselves. The walls are closing in, and the world seems lost. But *when we were still without strength, in due time, Christ died for the ungodly. For scarcely for a righteous man will one die . . . But God demonstrates his own love toward us, in that while we were still sinners, Christ died for us (Romans 5:6–8).*

U

Date: _____ _____ _____
Place: _____ _____ _____
Occasion: _____ _____ _____

The Scotsman's Shirt

V. Raymond Edman tells of the Scotsman who had a dress shirt he wore only on special occasions. After he had used it several times he would question its cleanness and take it to the window for better light. His wife's words were very wise, "If it's doubtful, it's dirty."[1]

Date: _____ _____ _____
Place: _____ _____ _____
Occasion: _____ _____ _____

"Little Sins"

Little sins are not like an inch of candle, which soon expires, but they resemble a trail of powder, which takes the fire until at last the barrels burst asunder.—Rev. William Secker, seventeenth-century British minister

Date: _____ _____ _____
Place: _____ _____ _____
Occasion: _____ _____ _____

Perfectly Allowable But . . .

The queen is a pretty woman, but she is empty-headed . . . and wastes her days running from dissipation to dissipation, some of which are perfectly allowable but nonetheless dangerous because they prevent her from having the thoughts she needs so badly.—Joseph II, Holy Roman Emperor about his sister, Marie Antoinette[2]

Date: _____ _____ _____
Place: _____ _____ _____
Occasion: _____ _____ _____

Screwtape's Advice

You will say that these are very small sins, and doubtless, like all young tempters, you are anxious to be able to report spectacular wickedness. But do remember, the only thing that matters

---

[1] V. Raymond Edman, *The Disciples of Life* (Minneapolis: World Wide Publications, 1948), 107.
[2] Carolly Erickson, *To the Scaffold: The Life of Marie Antoinette* (New York: William Morrow and Company, Inc., 1991), 142.

is the extent to which you separate the man from the Enemy [God]. It does not matter how small the sins are, provided that their cumulative effect is to keep the man away from the Light. . . . Murder is no better than cards if cards can do the trick. Indeed the safest road to Hell is the gradual one—the gentle slope, soft underfoot, without sudden turnings, without milestones, without signposts.—Screwtape's advice to Wormwood in *The Screwtape Letters*.[1]

Date: _____ _____ _____
Place: _____ _____ _____
Occasion: _____ _____ _____

With the Pennant on the Line

The 1908 National League season saw a fierce struggle between the Chicago Cubs and New York Giants. When they met with the Pennant on the line, there was a last minute change in the Giant lineup. The Giant's first baseman had a sprained back, and substituting for him was an eager nineteen year old named Fred Merkle who was thought to be a rising star in baseball.

The game was tied, and in the bottom of the ninth, the Giants were at bat. There were two outs, and two men on base. The winning run was on third, and Fred Merkle was on first. The batter hit a single, and the runner on third lumbered home. The Giants had apparently won the game and the pennant. Jubilant Giant fans poured onto the field while Fred Merkle was still on his way to second. Alarmed by the crowd suddenly bearing down on him and convinced the game was over, he ran straight for the clubhouse.

He didn't go all the way to second base. The Chicago second baseman noticed that Merkle hadn't bothered to touch second. If he could get the ball and touch second himself, the winning run would be cancelled by the force-out. First he had to find the ball.

One of the New York coaches saw what was happening, and he ran for the ball and threw it into the stands. A fan in a brown bowler caught it and started home with his trophy. Two Cubs players chased the man through the mob and tried to take the ball away from him. When he resisted, they knocked him down, grabbed the ball, ran back to the field, and threw it to their second baseman, who, holding the ball, jumped up and down on the bag to make sure the umpire saw what he had done.

As a result, New York lost the game—and the pennant—and although Fred Merkle stuck it out for fourteen more years in baseball, he never got over the reputation of being the man responsible for what is still to this day called "Merkle's boner."

A lot of people think they're safe, think they're headed home, think they're going to heaven—but they haven't touched the base.[2]

---

[1] C. S. Lewis, *The Screwtape Letters* (New York: The Macmillan Company, 1961), 64–65.
[2] Geoffery C. Ward and Ken Burns, *Baseball, An Illustrated History* (New York: Alfred A. Knopf, Inc., 1994).

Date:	_____	_____	_____
Place:	_____	_____	_____
Occasion:	_____	_____	_____

I Guess It's People

Someone sat down beside Will Rogers once at a dinner, and in the course of the conversation asked the comedian this question: "What's wrong with the world, anyway?" Rogers drawled in reply, "Well, I dunno, I guess it's people."

And I guess it is, for there is no such thing as evil in the abstract.[1]

Date:	_____	_____	_____
Place:	_____	_____	_____
Occasion:	_____	_____	_____

What's Wrong with the World?

In response to an article in *The Times* of London entitled, "What's Wrong with the World?" Chesterton replied, "I am. Yours truly, G. K. Chesterton."[2]

Date:	_____	_____	_____
Place:	_____	_____	_____
Occasion:	_____	_____	_____

Why Do You Do It?

According to Thomas C. Reeves in his book about John F. Kennedy, *A Question of Character,* JFK became very promiscuous after the deaths of his brother and sister, Joe and Kathleen. Feeling that he hadn't long to live himself, he "accelerated his pursuit of pleasure. Especially after Eunice moved out of the Georgetown house in 1948, girls went in and out of Jack's bed in such numbers that he often neglected to learn their first names, referring to them the next morning merely as "sweetie" or "kiddo."

"Jack confided a bit in one woman who resisted his advances . . . (She later wrote): 'During one of these conversations I once asked him why he was doing it— why he was acting like his father, why he was avoiding real relationships, why he was taking a chance on getting caught in a scandal at the same time he was trying to make his career take off. He took a while trying to formulate an answer. Finally he shrugged and said, "I don't know, really. I guess I can't help it." ' "

He spoke those words with a "sad expression on his face. He looked like a little boy about to cry."[3]

---

[1] William M. Elliott, Jr., *The World's Only Hope.*
[2] Ravi Zacharias, *Can Man Live Without God?* (Dallas: Word Publishing, 1994), 145.
[3] Thomas C. Reeves, *A Question of Character* (New York: The Free Press, 1991), 95.

Date: _____ _____ _____
Place: _____ _____ _____
Occasion: _____ _____ _____

The Ugliest Sin of All

In a vivid, autobiographical article in *Moody Magazine,* Charles Colson compares an incident in his past with Augustine's famous story about stealing pears for the sheer joy of stealing. Colson wrote,

"Having been at the center of the biggest political upheaval of this century, I've had my sins—real and imagined—spread across front pages around the world, re-enacted in living color on movie and TV screens, and dissected in hundreds of books. As a result, I am often asked which of my Watergate deeds causes me the greatest remorse.

"My invariable reply is, 'None. My deepest remorse is for the hidden sins of my heart, which are far worse.' That response tends to puzzle or infuriate the media. But it is an honest answer. . . . The sins for which I feel the greatest contrition are illustrated by an episode from thirty years ago.

"I was a new Marine lieutenant, proud and tough. My spit-shined shoes reflected the sun like two mirrors, matched in brilliance only by my polished gold bars. In the midst of Caribbean maneuvers, our battalion had landed on Vieques Island, a tiny satellite of Puerto Rico. Most of the mountainous land was a Navy protectorate used for landing and target practice, but on one end a clan of poverty-stricken souls endured the earsplitting shellings to eke out a living selling cold drinks to invading Marines.

"We officers were instructed to buy nothing from these peddlers, who, though strictly forbidden to enter the military reservation, invariably did so. The order was given with a sly smile and wink—no one obeyed it.

"The second day in the field, I was leading my platoon of forty grimy, sweating riflemen up and over a craggy ridge when I spotted an old man leading a scrawny donkey that nearly collapsed under the load of two huge, ice-filled canvas sacks.

"We were panting, and our canteens were getting low, so I immediately routed my men toward the distant figure. When the men saw the elderly man and his loaded beast, they picked up speed, knowing I would blink at orders and permit them to buy cans of cold drinks.

"But when we were just a few yards from the grinning old man, I ordered my troops to halt. 'Sergeant,' I commanded, 'take this man prisoner. He is trespassing on government property.'

"The platoon sergeant, a veteran of a dozen or more Vieques landings, stared in disbelief. 'Go ahead,' I barked. The sergeant shook his head, swung about, and, with rifle at the ready, marched toward the old man, whose smile suddenly turned to stone.

"I then commanded my men to 'confiscate the contraband.' Cheering lustily, they did so. While the sergeant tossed cans of chilled fruit juice from the two bulging

U

sacks, the old man squinted at me with doleful eyes. His sacks emptied, we released our 'prisoner.' Shoulders hunched, he rode away on his donkey.

"Technically, I had observed military law. Yet I had not given a fleeting thought to the fact that those satchels of juice might have represented the old man's life savings or that my order could mean an entire family might go hungry for months.

"Instead, I was smugly satisfied, believing that my men were grateful to me for getting them something cold to drink (which they would have happily purchased) and that I had proven I was tough (though my adversary was defenseless). As for the old man: *Well,* I thought, *he got what he deserved for violating government property.*

"Although I quickly forgot the incident, it vividly came to mind years later, after my conversion, as I sat in prison and read from Augustine's *Confessions* about stealing pears as a youth from a neighbor's tree.

"Augustine records that late one night he and a group of youngsters went out to 'shake down and rob this tree. We took great loads of fruit from it, not for our own eating but rather to throw it to the pigs.' He then berated himself for the depth of sin this revealed: 'The fruit I gathered I threw away, devouring in it only iniquity. There was no other reason, but foul was the evil and I loved it.'"[1]

Date:			
Place:			
Occasion:			

Weeds

A young man had a terrible falling out with a neighboring farmer. One night, in an act of cruel vengeance, he crept through the neighboring fields, sowing the seeds of a persistent, virulent weed. The weeds sprang up, and no amount of effort would eradicate them.

Years passed, and eventually the young man fell in love with the farmer's daughter. He married her and, at length, inherited the farm. He later confessed that he was spending the rest of his life reaping what he had sown in that one act of angry folly.

Date:			
Place:			
Occasion:			

Neglected Corners

Many years ago the smaller farmers of Scotland, being superstitious folk, kept a corner of their fields uncultivated in order to pacify certain evil spirits. They believed that by sacrificing this one corner to the spirits, the remainder of the field would be left undisturbed and fertile. What really happened, of course, is that the weeds in the uncultivated corner went to seed, which was, in turn, carried by the wind and scattered across the entire field.

---

[1] Charles Colson, "The Ugliest Sin of All," *Moody Magazine,* January, 1985, 21–23.

So it is with Christians. The whole of a person's life and witness will be infected and ruined if he allows unrestrained sin to dominate even one small corner of his life.

Date: _____ _____ _____
Place: _____ _____ _____
Occasion: _____ _____ _____

Sins of Omission

"What are the sins of omission?" asked a Sunday school teacher.

One little boy raised his hand. "Those are the sins we should have committed," he said, ". . . and didn't."

Date: _____ _____ _____
Place: _____ _____ _____
Occasion: _____ _____ _____

If You Call Him a Saint

There were two brothers, well known around town for their crooked business dealings and underworld connections. They were as mean and cold-blooded as you could imagine. One day one of the brothers died, and the surviving brother wanted to give his dead brother a funeral fit for a king. He called the funeral home and made all the arrangements, then he called the town's minister and made him an offer, as they say, he couldn't refuse. He said, "I will give you $10,000 to put that new roof on the church if, in eulogizing my brother, you call him a saint."

The minister agreed. The whole town turned out for the funeral, and the minister began: "The man you see in the coffin was a vile and debauched individual. He was a liar, a thief, a deceiver, a manipulator, a reprobate, and a hedonist. He destroyed the fortunes, careers, and lives of countless people in this city, some of whom are here today. This man did every dirty, rotten thing you can think of. But compared to his brother here, *he was a saint.*"

Date: _____ _____ _____
Place: _____ _____ _____
Occasion: _____ _____ _____

V

—— Violence Against Christians/Persecution ——

Someone Once Said

- *The Church of Christ has been founded by shedding its own blood, not that of others; by enduring outrage, not by inflicting it. Persecutions have made it grow; martyrdoms have crowned it.*—Jerome

- *The church grows and increases through blood.*—Martin Luther, in *Table Talk*
- *Every time her blood was shed, each drop became a man, and each man thus converted stood prepared to pour out the vital current from his veins to defend the cause. . . . Christ's church never sails so well as when she is rocked from side to side by the winds of persecution. . . . Nothing has helped God's church so much as persecution.*—Charles Spurgeon[1]
- *Be of good comfort, Master Ridley, and play the man. We shall this day light such a candle, by God's grace, in England, as I trust shall never be put out.*—Hugh Latimer, to Nicholas Ridley as they were being burned at the stake.

Date: _____ _____ _____
Place: _____ _____ _____
Occasion: _____ _____ _____

The Bloodiest Century

On September 28, 1997, M. Craig Barnes, pastor of the National Presbyterian Church, Washington, D.C., preached a powerful sermon on the Persecuted Church. He began with this vivid picture:

One evening the soldiers talked about a girl they had raped many times in the course of the afternoon. Through it all, the girl sang hymns, strange evangelical songs, and she kept on singing, even after they shot her in the chest. She lay on the ground with the blood flowing from her chest, but she kept on singing—a bit weaker than before, but still singing. Then the soldiers grew tired of this and shot her again, but still she sang. And then the soldiers became afraid. Terrified of the girl, they fell upon her with machetes, and at last the singing stopped.

For the last two thousand years, someone has always been trying to stop the singing of Christ's followers. The report I just read sounds a lot like the accounts of early church persecution I studied in history books. But this report does not come from a history book. It comes from the New Yorker *magazine (December 6, 1993), and it describes contemporary events.*

More followers of Jesus Christ have died during [the twentieth] century than in any other time in history. About 150,000 each year are martyred. About two million are actively persecuted. And millions more are living with their religious freedoms severely restricted.[2]

Date: _____ _____ _____
Place: _____ _____ _____
Occasion: _____ _____ _____

Put Another Way

There have been more martyrs in the twentieth century than in all the previous nineteen combined. The Global Evangelism Movement reports the average number of people martyred for their faith each year is 160,000. There are currently an

---

[1] Charles Haddon Spurgeon, *Sermons, Vol. 2* (Grand Rapids, Mich.: Baker Book House, 1983), 157–8.

[2] < www.persecutedchurch.org >. The story of the girl on La Cruz is told in an article by Mark Danner in *The New Yorker*, December 6, 1993, 87.

estimated one million people in prison for religious reasons. World Evangelical Fellowship shares that more people have died in circumstances related to their faith in this century than in all the twentieth-century wars combined.[1]

Date: _____   _____   _____

Place: _____   _____   _____

Occasion: _____   _____   _____

Worst Offenders

According to the organization, International Christian Concern, the ten worst current offenders of religious rights in the world are:

1. **China**—The communist government has intensified repression against Christians by raiding unregistered private homes and house churches, imprisoning the leaders, imposing harsh fines, confiscating property, and publicly slandering house-church leaders.
2. **Sudan**—The militant Arab-backed regime in Khartoum is using every method possible to repress non-Muslims. Over 25% of the population of Southern Sudan is Christian. Suffering the most are the Christians of the South and the Nuba Mountains. Arab forces continue to enslave children, rape women, violently attack and bomb villages, and withhold food and medicines. There is also evidence of the use of chemical weapons. More than two million people have died in Sudan over the past ten years, mostly non-Muslim black Africans. Every attempt is made to force Christians to become Muslims.
3. **Saudi Arabia**—Perhaps the most oppressive of all countries when it comes to Christians practicing their faith. The practice of the Christian faith and the public display of any Christian symbol is forbidden. Christian workers from outside the country are forbidden from praying or holding Bible studies in their homes. Evangelism and conversion to Christianity is punishable by death by beheading.
4. **Burma (Myanmar)**—The government of Burma has been involved in a brutal campaign to eliminate Christians and other minorities. Suffering the most are the Chin and Karen people. Buddhist monks backed by the military have been entering villages and forcing Christians to recant their faith. Buddhist leaders recently declared all Christian radio programs a threat to Buddhism and published a document suggesting how to eliminate Christianity from the country. Many Christians have been killed or forced from their homes.
5. **North Korea**—In May 1999, the government issued an open warning to all citizens that missionaries are "tools of imperialism" and must be "ferreted out." The number of believers in North Korea has dramatically reduced as a result of years of harsh persecution. Between 1987 and 1992, former prisoner Soon Ok Yi says she witnessed monthly executions of Christians.

V

---

[1] < www.gospelcom.net/bibleleague >

6. *Indonesia*—Christians have come under increasing attack from Muslims. Over the past four years, at least three hundred churches have been destroyed. In East Timor, nineteen priests and seven nuns have been reported killed since September 4, 1999. Christians are victims of a carefully-planned Muslim holy war that has resulted in hundreds of deaths and destruction to scores of churches and property.

7. *Vietnam*—The Protestant denominations continue to face persecution and the communist government destroys places of worship. Thousands of Christians have suffered ill-treatment, aimed at forcing the minorities to give up their faith.

8. *Turkmenistan*—All religious groups under five hundred members are required to register, limiting religious activities to only the Orthodox church and Sunni Muslims. Evangelism and conversion is strictly forbidden. On August 4, 1999, Shagildy Atakov of the Evangelical Baptist Church in Turkmenbashi was arrested on false charges following his conversion to Christianity. He was beaten, fined $12,000, an amount impossible to pay, and sentenced to four years in a labor camp.

9. *India*—The rise in Hindu nationalism has resulted in over one hundred acts of violence against Christians since June 1998. This is more than all the years combined since India's independence fifty years ago. The escalation of persecution against Christians made headlines after Australian missionary Graham Staines and his two young sons were mercilessly burned alive. Catholic priest Father Arul Doss was killed by a gang armed with bows and arrows.

10. *Egypt*—Conversion of Christian girls to Islam is often coerced. Poor Christians are offered incentives to convert. One Egyptian organization claims that it has documented 218 cases of abduction. Muslims, however, are forbidden to become Christians. Churches cannot be built or repaired without special permission, but the construction of new mosques continues to flourish.[1]

Date: _____ _____ _____

Place: _____ _____ _____

Occasion: _____ _____ _____

Examples of Persecution

Thousands of heart-rending stories about persecution exist and untold thousands are known only to heaven. Here are just a few, given in chronological order:

- **Stephen, the first martyr**—*Then they cried out with a loud voice, stopped their ears, and ran at him with one accord; and they cast him out of the city and stoned him. And the witnesses laid down their clothes at the feet of a young man named Saul. (Acts 7:57–58)*

---

[1] <www.persecution.org>

- **The Apostles.** According to ancient traditions . . .
  - □ James the son of Zebedee was beheaded in Jerusalem, the first of the apostles to die, during the Easter season in about the year A.D. 44.
  - □ Matthew was slain with the sword in a city in Ethiopia.
  - □ Mark was dragged through the streets of Alexandria until he expired.
  - □ Luke was hanged on an olive tree in Greece.
  - □ James the Less was thrown from a pinnacle or wing of the temple.
  - □ Philip was hanged up against a pillar in Phrygia.
  - □ Bartholomew was flayed alive.
  - □ Andrew was scourged then tied to a cross where he preached to the people for two days before dying.
  - □ Jude was shot to death with arrows.
  - □ Thomas was run through the body with a lance.
  - □ Simon Zelotes was crucified.
  - □ Peter was crucified upside down.
  - □ Matthias was stoned and beheaded.
  - □ John was exiled to the penal island of Patmos and later became the only apostle to die a natural death.

- **Polycarp**—On February 23, c. 155, a Roman military officer publicly demanded that Polycarp, disciple of the apostle John and the aged pastor of Smyrna, renounce Christ. The old pastor's famous reply has echoed through history: "Eighty and six years have I served him and he has done me no wrong. Can I revile my King that saved me?"

  "I'll throw you to the beasts!" shouted the Roman. Polycarp told him to bring them on. "Then I'll have you burned," the man warned. Polycarp replied, "You try to frighten me with fire that burns for an hour and you forget the fire of hell that never goes out." An hour later his body was ashes, his soul with Christ.

- **David Hackston,** Scottish Covenanter, preached the Gospel openly, though warned against it by the Scottish authorities who eventually dragged him to the scaffold. There they hacked off his hands with an axe, pulled him into the air by a rope around his neck, dropped him gasping back onto the platform. Then, while he was still living, they sliced open his chest with a knife and cut out his heart. The executioner picked up the heart on the point of his knife and held it up to show the people. Witnesses claimed that it was still fluttering on the point of the knife.

- **Obadiah Holmes**—Visitors to America's Boston Commons with its graceful swan boats might be surprised to learn what once happened there to Obadiah Holmes. In 1651, Holmes was arrested for preaching Baptist doctrine in nearby Lynn, Massachusetts. He was taken to Boston Commons, stripped to the waist, and tied to a whipping post. He later wrote: *As the man began to lay the strokes upon my back, I said to the people, Though my flesh should fail, yet God would not fail. So it pleased the Lord to come in and fill my heart and tongue, and with an audible voice I broke forth praying unto the Lord not to lay this sin to their charge.* The suffering wasn't wasted. The whipping of Obadiah Holmes deeply impacted

V

Henry Dunster, president of Harvard, and led to the organization of Boston's first Baptist church.

- **Gideon Akaluka**—In late December 1994, a Nigerian Christian named Gideon Akaluka was accused of desecrating the Koran by using its pages as toilet paper. Although the local court found no evidence to convict him, they detained him anyway—for "security purposes." He was imprisoned in Bompai, in the northern city of Kano. On December 26, the guards at the prison were overpowered by Muslim fanatics, seeking vengeance for Akaluka's alleged blasphemy. The mob forced its way into the prison and dragged Akaluka out of his cell. As the prison guards watched helplessly, the terrorists beheaded him. After hoisting his severed head on a spike, they paraded it around town, ending their march at the residence of the emir, the local Islamic spiritual leader.[1]

- **Roy Pontoh,** fifteen, was among one hundred fifty members of Bethel Church in Indonesia attending a retreat on January 20, 1999, when a Muslim mob attacked. Roy was asked, "Are you a Christian?" Armed only with his Bible, the teenager proudly replied, "I am a soldier of Christ." The attacker then cut Roy's hand with a sword and asked again, "Are you a Christian?" Once again, young Roy bravely replied, "I am a soldier of Christ." Angrily, the Muslim attacker stabbed Roy in the stomach and killed him.[2]

- **Cassie Bernall,** seventeen, was in the library at Columbine High School in Littleton, Colorado, on April 20, 1999, studying the Bible as she did every day at lunch, when she heard shooting erupt. As the gunman entered the room, Cassie reportedly knelt and prayed which angered the attacker. He approached her, asked her sarcastically if she believed in God. She paused, then said one word: "Yes." The gunman asked her "Why?" but Cassie had no time to answer before she was shot to death. Cassie, who had been a Christian for two years, was known for carrying her Bible to school every day and wearing a "What Would Jesus Do?" bracelet. Three days before the shooting, she had skipped her prom to help with a Denver Area Youth For Christ banquet.

  "She is a martyr, the best martyr," Pastor George Kristen told two thousand mourners at the memorial service. "Cassie died a martyr's death. She went to the martyr's hall of fame." And at that service over seventy-five kids made first-time commitments to Christ.

Date: _____   _____   _____
Place: _____   _____   _____
Occasion: _____   _____   _____

An Ancient Prayer

This prayer was written by seven anonymous martyrs in 1528 just before their painful death. The youngest, a fourteen-year-old boy, refused to recant his faith despite being promised wealth for life.

---

[1] Paul Marshall, *Their Blood Cries Out* (Nashville: Word Publishing, 1997), 63.
[2] < www.persecution.org >

O Lord, Thou art our Shield,
We turn to Thee.
For us it is a minor pain
When they take our lives.
Eternity Thou has prepared for us,
So when we suffer shame and stress here
It is not for nothing, We will be amply repaid.[1]

Date: _____ _____ _____
Place: _____ _____ _____
Occasion: _____ _____ _____

The Story Behind Foxe's Book of Martyrs

John Foxe entered Oxford still a boy. He was eventually elected a fellow of Magdalen College, and from 1539 to 1545 he studied church history. He converted to Protestantism and was forced to resign his academic position as a result. In 1550 he was ordained by Nicholas Ridley, Bishop of London, and he became friends with Hugh Latimer, William Tyndale, and Thomas Cramner. But when Queen Mary ascended the throne, tilting England back into Catholicism, Foxe fled. In Switzerland, he heard horrible news filtering from England. Latimer, Ridley, Cramner, and countless others were being captured and burned.

An idea formed in Foxe's mind, soon obsessing him. He would compile a record of the persecution of God's people. Despite living on the edge of poverty, Foxe spent every spare moment on his project. He labored by day in Oporinus of Basel's printing shop to support his family, but by night he pored over his manuscript. He wrote vividly, giving details, painting word pictures. In 1559, Foxe published his book on the Continent—732 pages in Latin. Returning to England under Protestant Elizabeth, he resumed pastoral work and translated his book into English. John Day published it in London in 1563 under the title *Acts and Monuments of These Latter and Perilous Days Touching Matters of the Church.*

But Foxe wasn't finished. He spent four years traveling across England, interviewing witnesses, tracking down documents, finding letters. After long days of church ministry, he sat by flickering candlelight, continuing his writing. In 1570, a second edition appeared—two large volumes totaling 2,315 pages—then a third and a fourth.

Foxe's Book of Martyrs was one of the most important events in Elizabeth's reign, having an extraordinary impact on Britain. Copies appeared in every cathedral alongside the Bible. Vicars read from it during Sunday services. Francis Drake read it aloud on the western seas. It inspired the Puritans. It took the world by storm.

But it also took a toll on Foxe's personal health, and he never recovered. He died from weariness on April 18, 1587. But he had given us his life's crowning achievement.[2]

V

---

[1] < www.persecution.org >
[2] Robert J. Morgan, *On This Day* (Nashville: Thomas Nelson Publishers, 1997), April 18th.

Date:	_____	_____	_____
Place:	_____	_____	_____
Occasion:	_____	_____	_____

Apathy

Mona Charen is a former speechwriter in the Reagan White House and a frequent panelist on the CNN political roundtable show, "The Capital Gang." Recently she wrote:

Lai Man Peng was a twenty-two year old Chinese Christian evangelist. In 1994, at a meeting of one of China's "house churches" (a non-government-sanctioned prayer meeting), he and four other evangelists were seized by agents of the Public Security Bureau, China's KGB.

In front of the congregation, Lai and the others were beaten severely. The security officers next handed the truncheons to the congregants and ordered them to beat the preachers, on pain of being beaten themselves. Lai was so badly injured that the security team feared he would die in their presence (leaving too much to explain), so it released him. He hobbled for several miles, attempting to reach his house, but finally collapsed and died on the road.

═══════ ◇ ═══════
Blood and Seeds

The blood of the martyrs is the seed of the church.
—TERTULLIAN
═══════ ◇ ═══════

Such persecution is commonplace in China, where only a fraction of the estimated thirty million to seventy million Christians belong to government-approved sects. Amnesty International reports cases of Christian women hung by their thumbs from wires and beaten with heavy rods, denied food and water, and shocked with electric probes.

Elsewhere in the world, Christians face other tortures and persecutions. In Egypt and Pakistan, Christians have been imprisoned and tortured merely for preaching their faith. Pakistan recently passed a blasphemy law that forbids speaking or acting against the prophet Mohammed. The punishment for violators is death. A twelve-year-old Christian child was recently sentenced to death under this law and was freed from Pakistan only because of international pressure. He is now hiding in a Western country with a bounty on his head . . .

Sudan is perhaps the worst violator. Its Islamic government has engaged in a policy of forcible conversion . . . and has sold thousands of Christian children—some as young as six—into slavery.

Where is the international outcry? The silence of American Christians is particularly hard to understand . . .

Steve Snyder of International Christian Concern, a human-rights group, offers some insights. American Christians, he notes, have been sheltered from persecution for three centuries. While they have supported missionaries overseas, they have not necessarily kept faith with those whom they have succeeded in converting. There has been an unfortunate emphasis on numbers, Snyder believes. If Christians in one country begin to face persecution, missionaries tend to look elsewhere for converts rather than fight the persecution.

Putting it bluntly, Snyder says Christians have forgotten how to take care of their own. Almost too focused on loving their neighbor, they've lost sight of Christ's injunction that "the world will know you are my disciples by our love one for another. . . ."

But above all, American Christians are simply ill-informed. If one major TV magazine program aired a segment on what is actually happening to Christians in the late twentieth century, the apathy would be gone in a flash. Child slavery, false imprisonment, torture and murder are all happening to Christians in Islamic and other countries. How long will the world's largest Christian community stay silent?"[1]

Date: _____ _____ _____
Place: _____ _____ _____
Occasion: _____ _____ _____

Strangling the Baby

One of the reasons the church has been under renewed attack in Communist China is because of what happened in the former Soviet block, and the role of the church there in bringing down the Iron Curtain. In 1992, the Chinese state-run press noted that "the church played an important role in the change" in Eastern Europe and warned, "If China does not want such a scene to be repeated in its land, it must strangle the baby while it is still in the manger."[2]

———————— "Why?" ————————

Someone Once Said . . .

- *I cannot recall a single explanation of trial—we are trusted with the unexplained.*—Amy Carmichael[3]
- *God's people live by promises, not by explanations.*—Warren Wiersbe[4]
- *God marks across some of our days, "Will explain later."*—Vance Havner[5]
- *One day of green pastures and still waters is followed by dark valleys and miry swamps, and a thousand "whys" lie unanswered, tabled for future reference.*—Vance Havner[6]
- *When belief in God becomes difficult, the tendency is to turn away from Him, but in heaven's name to what?*—G. K. Chesterton

Date: _____ _____ _____
Place: _____ _____ _____
Occasion: _____ _____ _____

[1] Written by Creators Syndicate, 5777 W. Century Blvd., Suite 700, Los Angeles, Calif., 90045 and poster at < www.celebproject.org >
[2] Paul Marshall, *Their Blood Cries Out* (Nashville: Word Publishing, 1997), 10–11.
[3] Ruth Bell Graham, *Legacy of a Pack Rat* (Nashville: Thomas Nelson Publishers, 1989), 75.
[4] Warren W. Wiersbe, *Why Us?* (Old Tappan, NJ: Fleming H. Revell Co., 1984), 46.
[5] Vance Havner, *Day by Day* (Old Tappan, NJ: Fleming H. Revell Co., 1953), 54.
[6] Vance Havner, *Playing Marbles With Diamonds* (Grand Rapids, MI: Baker Book House, 1985), 94.

W

Questions

- *There are over three hundred questions in the book of Job.*—Warren Wiersbe[1]

Date: _____ _____ _____

Place: _____ _____ _____

Occasion: _____ _____ _____

The Place Where We Begin

In discussing Psalm 22:1, Denis Lane, director of Overseas Missionary Fellowship, wrote that when the roof caves in, the first question that often comes to us is the same question Jesus asked: My God, my God, why . . . ?"

Lane said: *Asking the question is perfectly natural. We all ask it. There is nothing wrong, but that is usually the place where we begin. . . . God does not always answer our "why" questions, but He does understand our asking them. Jesus was given no answering voice as He hung upon the cross. . . . The resurrection was still three days in the future.*[2]

Date: _____ _____ _____

Place: _____ _____ _____

Occasion: _____ _____ _____

Tempted a Thousand Times

After the death of his wife, North Carolina evangelist Vance Havner was inconsolable. In one of his last books, he described it like this: *I think of a year that started out so pleasantly for my beloved and me. We had made plans for delightful months ahead together. Instead, I sat by her bedside and watched her die of an unusual disease. She expected to be healed, but she died. Now, all hopes of a happy old age together are dashed to the ground. I plod alone with the other half of my life on the other side of death. My hand reaches for another hand now vanished and I listen at night for the sound of a voice that is still. And I am tempted a thousand times to ask, "My God, why . . . ?"*

"How-to's" of Life

If we have our own why of life, we shall get along with almost any how.
—NEITZSCHE

But Havner ends his book with this paragraph:

You need never ask "Why?" because Calvary covers it all. When before the throne we stand in Him complete, all the riddles that puzzle us here will fall into place and we shall know in fulfillment what we now believe in faith—that all things work together for good in His eternal purpose. No longer will we cry "My God, why?" Instead, "alas" will become "Alleluia," all question marks will be straightened into exclamation points, sorrow will change to singing, and pain will be lost in praise.[3]

---

[1] Wiersbe, *Why Us?*, 51.
[2] Denis Lane, *When the Roof Caves In* (Singapore: OMF Missionary Fellowship, 1985), 3–4.
[3] Havner, *Playing Marbles With Diamonds*, 94–95, 97.

Date: _____ _____ _____

Place: _____ _____ _____

Occasion: _____ _____ _____

Biblical "Whys"

- *If all is well, why am I like this? So she went to inquire of the Lord.*—Rebekah, in Genesis 25:22
- *Lord, why have you brought trouble on this people? Why is it You have sent me?*—Moses, in Exodus 5:22
- *Why did we ever come up out of Egypt.*—the Israelites, in Numbers 11:20
- *Why then has all this happened to us.*—Gideon, in Judges 6:13
- *They lifted up their voices and wept bitterly, and said, "O Lord, God of Israel, why has this come to pass in Israel?"*—the Israelites following the destruction of the tribe of Benjamin
- *I went out full, and the Lord has brought me home again empty. Why . . . ?*—Naomi, in Ruth 1:21
- *Why is the house of God forsaken?*—Nehemiah, in Nehemiah 13:11
- *Why did I not die at birth? Why did I not perish when I came from the womb?*—Job, in Job 3:11
- *Why have you set me as your target?*—Job, in Job 7:20
- *Why, then, do I labor in vain?*—Job, in Job 9:29
- *Why do the nations rage?*—Psalm 2:1
- *Why do You stand afar off, O Lord? Why do You hide in times of trouble?*—Psalm 10:1
- *Why are You so far from helping me?*—David, in Psalm 22:1
- *Why are you cast down, O my soul? And why are you disquieted within me?*—Psalm 43:11
- *Why does Your anger smoke against the sheep of Your pasture?*—Asaph, in Psalm 74:1
- *Lord, why do You cast off my soul? Why do You hide Your face from me?*—Heman the Ezrahite, in Psalm 88:14
- *O Lord, why have You made us stray from Your ways?*—Isaiah, in Isaiah 63:17
- *Why is my pain perpetual and my wound incurable?*—Jeremiah, in Jeremiah 15:18
- *Why do You show me iniquity, and cause me to see trouble*—Habakkuk, in Habakkuk 1:3
- *Why could we not cast it out?*—the disciples in Matthew 17:19
- *My God, My God, why have You forsaken Me?*—Matthew 27:46

Date: _____ _____ _____

Place: _____ _____ _____

Occasion: _____ _____ _____

W

I Lay My "Whys"

I lay my "whys"
before Your Cross
in worship kneeling,

*my mind too numb
for thought,
my heart beyond
all feeling.*

*And worshipping
realize that I
in knowing You
don't need a "why."*—Ruth Bell Graham[1]

Date:	_____	_____	_____
Place:	_____	_____	_____
Occasion:	_____	_____	_____

The Weaving

*My life is but a weaving
Between my Lord and me.
I cannot choose the colors
He worketh steadily.*

*Ofttimes He weaveth sorrow,
And I in foolish pride
Forget He sees the upper
And I, the underside.*

*Not till the loom is silent
And the shuttles cease to fly
Shall God unroll the canvas
And explain the reason why.*

*The dark threads are as needful
In the Weaver's skillful hand
As the threads of gold and silver
In the pattern He has planned.*—Grant Colfax Tullar

Date:	_____	_____	_____
Place:	_____	_____	_____
Occasion:	_____	_____	_____

Why?

Malcolm Muggeridge was once invited to speak at All Souls Church in London, and all the local atheists showed up. After the service, Muggeridge answered questions, and the last one came from a boy in a wheelchair who spoke only with great difficulty. In fact, the boy couldn't get the words out, but Mr. Muggeridge said,

---

[1] Ruth Bell Graham, *Sitting By My Laughing Fire* (Waco: Word Books, 1977), 88.

"Take your time. I want to hear what you have to say, and I'll not leave till I hear it." Finally the boy blurted out, "You say there is a God who loves us."

Muggeridge nodded. The boy said with a grunt and a gasp, "Then—why me?" The room was suddenly silent as a tomb as everyone waited to see how the great Christian would answer. Finally Malcolm Muggeridge stooped down and looked at the boy. "If you were fit," he asked, "would you have come to hear me tonight?"

The boy shook his head. Again Muggeridge was silent. Then he said, "God has asked a hard thing of you. But remember, he asked something even harder of Jesus Christ. He died for you. Maybe this was his way of making sure you'd hear of his love and come to put your faith in him."

"Could be," the boy replied. "Could be."[1]

Date: _____ _____ _____

Place: _____ _____ _____

Occasion: _____ _____ _____

Seven Questions

R. C. Sproul includes this interesting insight in his book, *Not a Chance:*

When a child asks why the rain falls, the simple reply he often hears is, "Because." The term because *is used to explain something. It seeks to provide a reason for things as they are. It seeks to answer the "why" questions of life. It has been argued that any person's knowledge can be exhausted by seven questions, as long as they begin with the question, "Why?" and are asked seriatim.*

Only moments ago, as I finished writing the above statement, a bone surgeon walked into the room. I decided to test the seven-question theory on him. I asked him, "Why do bones break?" He answered it promptly. By the fifth successive "why" question, he shrugged his shoulders and said, "I don't know."[2]

Date: _____ _____ _____

Place: _____ _____ _____

Occasion: _____ _____ _____

Elisabeth Elliot's Answer

Missionary author Elisabeth Elliot, whose husband Jim perished at the hands of the Auca Indians he was trying to reach, lists six scriptural answers she has found to the question "Why?"[3]

- 1 Peter 4:12–13
- Romans 5:3–4
- 2 Corinthians 12:9
- John 14:31

---

[1] Graham, *Legacy of a Pack Rat,* 191.
[2] R. C. Sproul, *Not a Chance* (Grand Rapids, MI: Baker Book House, 1994), 167.
[3] "No Cause For Bitterness," *Wheaton,* Autumn 1998, Vol. 1, Num. 5, 48.

- Romans 8:17
- Colossians 1:24

Date:			
Place:			
Occasion:			

Each Anxious Puzzled "Why"

The poet Annie Johnson Flint put it like this:

I know not, but God knows;
Oh, blessed rest from fear!
All my unfolding days
To Him are plain and clear
Each anxious puzzled "Why?"
From doubt and dread that grows,
Finds answer in this thought:
I know not, but He knows.

I cannot but God can;
Oh, balm for all my care!
The burden that I drop
His hand will lift and bear,
Though eagle pinions tire—
I walk where once I ran,
This is my strength to know:
I cannot, but God can.[1]

Date:			
Place:			
Occasion:			

Wisdom

Someone Once Said . . .

- *Wisdom is, in fact, the practical side of moral goodness.*—J. I. Packer[2]
- *Wisdom is seeing life from God's point of view.*—Bill Gothard
- *Wisdom is the ability to apply biblical truths to all life situations.*
- *For every pound of learning a person has, he needs ten pounds of common sense to know how to use it.*—Persian Proverb

---

[1] George Sweeting, *Discovering the Will of God* (Chicago: Moody Press, 1975), 14.
[2] J. I. Packer, *Knowing God* (Downers Grove, IL: InterVarsity, 1973), 80.

- *A wise man learns by the experience of others. An ordinary man learns by his own experience. A fool learns by nobody's experience.*—Anonymous
- *Many an institution is very well managed and very poorly led. It may excel in the ability to handle each day all the routine inputs yet may never ask whether the routine should be done at all.*—Warren Bennis[1]
- *If I could stand for five minutes at His vantage point and see the entire scheme of things as He sees it, how absurd would be my dreads, how ridiculous my fears and tears!*—Vance Havner[2]
- *[Biblical] wisdom is always associated the righteousness and humility and is never found apart from godliness and true holiness of life.*—A. W. Tozer, in *The Divine Conquest*

Date: _____ _____ _____
Place: _____ _____ _____
Occasion: _____ _____ _____

Professors and Janitors

Vance Havner once noted that many college professors are searching for wisdom while the janitors that clean their offices may have discovered it years ago.

Augustine wrote in his *Confessions* about his professors: *They saw many true things about the creature (creation) but they do not seek with true piety for the Truth, the Architect of Creation, and hence they do not find him.*

Date: _____ _____ _____
Place: _____ _____ _____
Occasion: _____ _____ _____

The Professor and the Bootblack

Alexander Grigolia had immigrated to America from Soviet Georgia, learned English, earned three doctoral degrees, and become a successful professor at the University of Pennsylvania. But despite his freedom and achievements, he had a misery in his heart that he couldn't dislodge.

One day while getting a shoeshine, he noticed that the bootblack went about his work with a sense of joy, scrubbing and buffing and smiling and talking. Finally Dr. Grigolia could stand it no longer. He said in his funny-sounding accent, "What always you so happy?"

Looking up, the bootblack paused and replied, "Jesus. He love me. He died so God could forgive my badness. He makes he happy."

The professor snapped his newspaper back in front of his face, and the bootblack went back to work.

W

---

[1] Warren Bennis, *Why Leaders Can't Lead* (San Francisco: Jossey-Bass Publishers, 1989), 17.
[2] Vance Havner, *Consider Jesus* (Grand Rapids, MI: Baker Book House, 1987), 80.

But Dr. Grigolia never escaped those words, and they brought him eventually to the Savior. He later became a professor of anthropology at Wheaton College, and taught, among others, a young student named Billy Graham.[1]

Date: _____ _____ _____
Place: _____ _____ _____
Occasion: _____ _____ _____

Doing Wrong Things Well

University president and "management guru" Warren Bennis spent several years researching a book on leadership. He traveled around the country spending time with ninety of the most effective and successful leaders in the nation—sixty from corporations and thirty from the public sector. His goal was to find these leaders' common traits. At first, he had trouble pinpointing any common traits, for the leaders were more diverse than he had expected.

But he later wrote: "I was finally able to come to some conclusions, of which perhaps the most important is the distinction between leaders and managers: Leaders are people who do the right thing; managers are people who do things right. Both roles are crucial, but they differ profoundly. I often observe people in top positions doing the wrong thing well."

The same can be said for most people.[2]

Date: _____ _____ _____
Place: _____ _____ _____
Occasion: _____ _____ _____

What Is the Question?

In 1946, author Gertrude Stein felt very tired and ill during a car journey. She was rushed to the American hospital at Neuilly, France, and an advanced state of cancer was diagnosed. The surgeon operated, but Gertrude passed away in the evening of July 27th. Her baffling last words were, "What is the answer?" When nobody replied, she laughed to herself and concluded, "Then what is the question?"[3]

Date: _____ _____ _____
Place: _____ _____ _____
Occasion: _____ _____ _____

The Cracked Pot

A water bearer in India had two large pots, hung on each end of a pole which he carried across his neck. One of the pots had a crack in it, while the other pot was

[1] Ruth Bell Graham, *Legacy of a Pack Rat* (Nashville: Thomas Nelson Publishers, 1989), 187.
[2] Bennis, *Why Leaders Can't Lead,* 18.
[3] Charles Connell, *World Famous Exiles* (Feltham, Middlesex, England: Odhams Books, 1969), 147.

perfect and always delivered a full portion of water at the end of the long walk from the stream to the master's house; the cracked pot arrived only half full. For a full two years this went on daily, with the bearer delivering only one and a half pots full of water in his master's house. Of course, the perfect pot was proud of its accomplishments, perfect to the end for which it was made. But the poor cracked pot was ashamed of its own imperfection, and miserable that it was able to accomplish only half of what it had been made to do.

After two years of what it perceived to be a bitter failure, it spoke to the water bearer. "I am ashamed of myself, and I want to apologize to you." "Why?" asked the bearer. "What are you ashamed of?" "I have been able for these past two years, to deliver only half my load because this crack in my side causes water to leak out all the way back to your master's house. Because of my flaw, you have to do all of this work, and you don't get full value from your efforts," the pot said. The water bearer felt sorry, and said, "as we return to the master's house, I want you to notice the beautiful flowers along the path." Indeed, as they went up the hill, the cracked pot

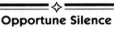

Opportune Silence

Never pass up an opportunity to keep your mouth shut.
—ELISABETH ELLIOT

took notice of the sun warming the beautiful flowers on the side of the path, and this cheered it some. But at the end of the trail, it still felt bad because it had leaked out half its load, and so again it apologized to the bearer for its failure.

The bearer said to the pot, "Did you notice there were flowers only on your side of the path, but not on the other pot's side? I have always known about your flaw, and I planted flower seeds on your side of the path. Every day while we walked back from the stream, you watered them. For two years I have been able to pick these beautiful flowers to decorate my master's table. Without you being just the way you are, my master would not have this beauty to grace his house."

Each of us has our own unique flaws. We are all cracked pots. But if we will allow it, the Lord will use our flaws to grace His Father's table. As we seek to minister together, and as God calls you to the tasks he has appointed for you, don't be afraid of your flaws. Go on boldly, knowing that in our weakness we find His strength. You, too, can bring beauty to His pathway![1]

Date:			
Place:			
Occasion:			

J. P. Morgan and the Great Depression

When the Great Depression hit Wall Street, according to Walter Lord in *The Good Years*, J. P. Morgan called in one expert after another, seeking opinions and advice. At length his secretary asked him, "Why don't you tell them what to do, Mr. Morgan?"

He replied, "I don't know what to do myself. But sometime someone will come in with a plan that I know will work, and then I will tell them what to do."

W

---

[1] Circulating on the internet.

Date:	_____	_____	_____
Place:	_____	_____	_____
Occasion:	_____	_____	_____

Dear Abby

These are actual excerpts from the "Dear Abby" column:

- Dear Abby: A couple of women moved in across the hall from me. One is a middle-aged gym teacher and the other is a social worker in her mid-twenties. These two women go everywhere together and I've never seen a man go into their apartment or come out. Do you think they could be Lebanese?
- Dear Abby: I have a man I never could trust. Why, he cheats so much I'm not even sure this baby I'm carrying is his.
- Dear Abby: I am a twenty-three-year-old liberated woman who has been on the pill for two years. It's getting expensive and I think my boyfriend should share half the cost, but I don't know him well enough to discuss money with him.
- Dear Abby: I suspected that my husband had been fooling around, and when I confronted him with the evidence he denied everything and said it would never happen again.
- Dear Abby: Will you please rush me the name of a reliable illegitimate doctor?
- Dear Abby: My forty-year-old son has been paying a psychiatrist $50 an hour every week for two-and-a-half years. He must be crazy.
- Dear Abby: Do you think it would be all right if I gave my doctor a little gift? I tried for years to get pregnant and couldn't and he finally did it.
- Dear Abby: My mother is mean and short-tempered. I think she is going through her mental pause.
- Dear Abby: I met this nice guy who was in the service. He's the chief petting officer.
- Dear Abby: I've been going steady with this man for six years. We see each other every night. He says he loves me, and I know I love him, but he never mentions marriage. Do you think he's going out with me just for what he can get?—Gertie
    Dear Gertie: I don't know. What's he getting?
- Dear Abby: My husband hates to spend money! I cut my own hair and make my own clothes, and I have to account for every nickel I spend. Meanwhile he has a stock of savings bonds put away that would choke a cow. How do I get some money out of him before we are both called to our final judgment? He says he's saving for a rainy day—Forty Years Hitched
    Dear Hitched: Tell him it's raining!
- Dear Abby: My boyfriend is going to be twenty years old next month. I'd like to give him something nice for his birthday. What do you think he'd like?—Carol
    Dear Carol: Never mind what he'd like. Give him a tie.
- Dear Abby: Are birth control pills deductible?—Kay
    Dear Kay: Only if they don't work.

- Dear Abby: Our son was married in January. Five months later his wife had a ten-pound baby girl. They said the baby was premature. Tell me, can a baby this big be that early?—Wondering
    Dear Wondering: The baby was on time, the wedding was late. Forget it.
- Dear Abby: Do you think about dying much?—Curious
    Dear Curious: No, it's the last thing I want to do.
- Dear Abby: I am forty-four years old and I would like to meet a man my age with no bad habits—Rose
    Dear Rose: So would I.
- Dear Abby: What's the difference between a wife and a mistress?—Bess
    Dear Bess: Night and Day.[1]

Date:			
Place:			
Occasion:			

Witnessing/Personal Evangelism

Someone Once Said . . .

- *We do not have a secret to be hidden but a story to be heralded.*—Vance Havner[2]
- *Evangelism is one beggar telling another beggar where he found bread.*—D. T. Niles[3]
- *God's evangelistic strategy in a nutshell: He desires to build into you and me the beauty of his own character, and then put us on display.*—Joseph Aldrich
- *Success in witnessing is simply taking the initiative to share Christ in the power of the Holy Spirit, then leaving the results to God.*—Bill Bright
- *I waited and watched fifteen long years to get my chance to speak with one man. Never a day passed in all those fifteen years that I did not speak to God about that man. At last my chance came, and it was my privilege to lead him to Christ.*—R. A. Torrey
- *Our great object of glorifying God is to be mainly achieved by the winning of souls.*—Charles Spurgeon[4]
- *I'm just a nobody telling everybody about somebody who can save anybody.*—elevator operator at a hospital in Nashville
- *The Gospel is not something we come to church to hear; it something we go from church to tell.*—Vance Havner

Date:			
Place:			
Occasion:			

W

---

[1] < www.mpinet.org >
[2] Vance Havner, *Why Not Just Be Christians* (Old Tappan, NJ: Fleming H. Revell Co., 1964), 43.
[3] Charles W. Colson, *Life Sentence* (Minneapolis: World Wide Publications, 1979), 69.
[4] Charles H. Spurgeon, *Lectures to My Students* (Grand Rapids, MI: Zondervan, 1954), 337.

Stats

According to nationwide surveys conducted by the Barna Research Group regarding evangelism:

- 9 out of 10 American adults (86%) cannot accurately define the meaning of the "Great Commission."
- 7 out of 10 adults have no clue what "John 3:16" means.
- Barely one third of all adults (31%) know the meaning of the expression "the gospel."
- 58% of born-again Christians claim they have shared their faith with a non-Christian during the past year. (1999)
- Busters (those between 18–33 years of age) are more likely than any other generation to share their faith with others. Barna's data show that 66% of Busters shared their faith in the last year, compared to 58% of Boomers (those 34–52 years of age), 52% of Builders (those 53–71), and 41% of Seniors (those 72 years plus). (1999)
- Blacks (76%) are much more likely than whites (52%) to report that they have shared their faith with someone in the past year. (1999)
- 66% of Protestant non-mainline attenders and 64% of Baptists report that they have shared their faith with a non-Christian in the past year, compared to 48% of mainline attenders and 43% of Catholics. (1999)
- Americans living in the South feel more of a responsibility to share their faith with others than do adults in other regions of the country, with 40% of southerners feeling a sense of responsibility to share their faith with others, compared to 25% of those living in the West or Midwest, and 23% of those living in the Northeast. (1999)
- Only about half (53%) of born again Christians feel a sense of responsibility to tell others about their faith. In other words, nearly half of born again Christians do not think that it is their personal responsibility to share their religious beliefs with those who do not know Christ. (1999)[1]

Date: _____   _____   _____
Place: _____   _____   _____
Occasion: _____   _____   _____

Evangelism and Gospel

- The word *evangelism* is *ev-angel-ism*, the prefix *ev* meaning *good*, and the word *angel* meaning messenger. So the word literally means *good-message-izing.*
- The word *Gospel* comes down to us from the Anglo-Saxon *godspell*, which signifies *God's spell*, or *God's Story.*
- The word *witness* is a translation of the Greek word *martus*, from which we get our English word *martyr*—one who witnesses with his or her life.

[1] <www.barna.org>

Date: _____ _____ _____
Place: _____ _____ _____
Occasion: _____ _____ _____

Bill Bright's Maxim

Although I have shared Christ personally with many thousands of people through the years, I am a rather reserved person and I do not always find it easy to witness.

But I have made this my practice, and I urge you to do the same: Assume that whenever you are alone with another person for more than a few moments, you are there by divine appointment to explain to that person the love and forgiveness he can know through faith in Jesus Christ.[1]

Date: _____ _____ _____
Place: _____ _____ _____
Occasion: _____ _____ _____

How Norman Geisler Began Witnessing

Some years ago, theologian Norman Geisler wrote a candid article in which he said: "I have a confession to make. I was a director for a Christian youth organization for three years, a pastor for nine years, a Bible college teacher for six years, and in all that time I did not witness for Jesus Christ. I scarcely ever shared my faith one-to-one with other people."

Geisler offered several reasons for this: He didn't think he had the gift of evangelism. He felt instead his gift was that of teaching the Word to those already Christians. He had read a book about evangelism and God's sovereignty that had turned away his zeal for personal evangelism. He had known someone who had practiced impersonal, cold-turkey evangelism, and Geisler had determined that "lifestyle" evangelism was more desirable. But as a result, he lived a Christian life but seldom vocalized his witness to an unsaved person.

Eventually, Geisler became convicted by the words of a little song that said: "Lead me to some soul today, / O teach me, Lord, just what to say." Those words became a sincere prayer for him, and his life began to change.

One day, having prayed that prayer, he was approached by a girl from the college where he taught. She had spiritual needs in her life, and he was able to lead her to Christ. (She later went to South America as a missionary).

Shortly afterward, Geisler volunteered to participate in a Monday night visitation program at his church. On his first outing, he found himself knocking on the door of a man who turned out to be an atheist. "Do you mind if we ask you a very serious spiritual question?" asked Geisler, when the man came to the door. After a long conversation and a couple of visits, the man prayed to receive Christ into his heart. (He is now a deacon in a church with his family committed to Christ as well.)

W

---

[1] Bill Bright, "How To Tell Others About Christ," *Worldwide Challenge*, April 1993, 17.

Now Geisler says: *The most rewarding experiences I've had in my Christian life have not come from teaching, pastoring, or ministering around the world. They have come from meeting with non-Christians and seeing one after another come to know Christ.*[1]

Date:	_____	_____	_____
Place:	_____	_____	_____
Occasion:	_____	_____	_____

Insight from Willowcreek

According to Mark Mittelberg, director of evangelism at Willow Creek Community Church of suburban Chicago, "God knew what he was doing when he made you. He custom-designed you with your unique combination of personality, temperament, talents, and background, and he wants to use you to reach others in a fashion that fits your design." For example, says Mittelberg, consider these six people in the New Testament:

- Peter's Confrontational Approach—He was direct, bold, and to the point.
- Paul's Intellectual Approach—He could be confrontational, but he was a well-educated man who could reason from the Scriptures, explaining and proving that Jesus was the Christ.
- The Blind Man's Testimonial Approach—The man in John 9 didn't know a great deal of theology, but he could say, "One thing I know: I once was blind and now I see."
- The Samaritan Woman's Invitational Approach—Leaving her water jug at the well, the woman in John 4 went into her village and invited her friends to come and hear the man "who told me everything I ever did."
- Matthew's Interpersonal Approach—In Luke 5:29 Matthew put on a big banquet for his tax-collecting buddies in an effort to expose them to Jesus. He relied on the relationships he'd built with these men and sought to further shore up their friendships, inviting them into his home and using his channels of friendship for evangelism.
- Dorcas' Service Approach—In Acts 9, we meet a woman who witnessed by serving others in Jesus name, making clothes for the needy and helping the poor.[2]

Date:	_____	_____	_____
Place:	_____	_____	_____
Occasion:	_____	_____	_____

He Gave Her a Bible

Dr. Doren Edwards, a surgeon in Erin, Tennessee, tells of a patient of his, Blanche Bennet, whose alcoholic husband had died. Her two children were giving her problems, finances were tight, and life was very hard. She wasn't a Christian.

---

[1] Norman L. Geisler, "Excuses," 1983.
[2] Mark Mittelberg, "Discover Your Evangelism Style," *Discipleship Journal*, Issue 95, September/October 1996.

One day she came to see Dr. Edwards with physical problems, and he diagnosed cancer, with multiple organs involved. No treatment was available, and she was very bitter. Dr. Edwards, a Christian and a Gideon, wanted to talk with her about the Lord, but she wouldn't allow him to share his witness. She did, however, accept a small New Testament.

A few weeks later, the doctor learned from the newspaper obituary that she had died. He sent a card to the family, telling them he had donated Bibles in her memory to the Gideons.

The woman's daughter called him. "Could you please send us a Bible like the ones you donated in memory of our mother," she asked. "We don't have a Bible in our home. The last six days she was alive, her whole life changed. She was no longer bitter, she wasn't afraid to die, and she said something about knowing Jesus. But she asked that her Bible be buried in her hand, and we couldn't keep it. Would you please send us a Bible so that we can find what Mama found in that book?"

Dr. Edwards sent them a Bible, and to date the daughter, the son, and one sister have been saved as a result.[1]

Date: _____   _____   _____
Place: _____   _____   _____
Occasion: _____   _____   _____

Naturally

At being requested to sing at a large gathering in London, hymnist Frances Ridley Havergal selected a sacred song. Later a young man, a stranger to Frances, opened conversation with her. He was soon surprised to find that she was quite easily drifting him from the playful banter with which he started into a serious talk about his personal soul-danger and his only hope of safety.

The ease with which Frances turned her conversation with others into spiritual channels was surprising even to herself. She always attributed the gift to an endowment from the Master. "I don't think anyone can say I force the subject," she wrote, "It just all develops one thing out of another, quite naturally, till very soon they find themselves face to face with eternal things, and the Lord Jesus can be freely 'lifted up' before them. I could not contrive a conversation thus."[2]

Date: _____   _____   _____
Place: _____   _____   _____
Occasion: _____   _____   _____

Conversational Evangelism

Try to turn the conversation to profitable use. . . . Be ready to seize opportunities adroitly, and lead on imperceptibly in the desired track. If your heart is in it and your wits are

W

[1] Personal conversation with the author.
[2] Anna Talbott McPherson, *Spiritual Secrets of Famous Christians* (Grand Rapids, MI: Zondervan, 1964), 36.

awake, this will be easy enough, especially if you breathe a prayer for guidance.—Charles Spurgeon[1]

Date:			
Place:			
Occasion:			

I'm Afraid They'll Sit Up

Pastor Wallace Hostetter of Rochester, Michigan, went for a haircut one day. His barber was a young Muslim woman. In the course of their conversation, he told her he was a pastor, that he believed in Jesus, and that later in the day he was going to perform a funeral.

She replied, "Once I was supposed to cut a dead man's hair. They were going to pay me $150, but I wouldn't do it."

"Why not?"

"I don't like to touch the dead. I'm afraid they'll sit up."

"I know one who did," said the pastor.

"Ugh! You're kidding."

"No, I'm not," he replied.

Then he told her about the resurrection of Jesus Christ. When his haircut was done, she asked, "Are you going to keep coming here?"

"Yeah, I'll come back."

She said, "I'd like to know more."[2]

Date:			
Place:			
Occasion:			

Maybe Not . . .

Robert Shockey doesn't believe in chance encounters. To him, every contact is an opportunity to evangelize. When he answers the phone, for example, and hears the person on the other end saying, "Sorry, I must have the wrong number," Bob responds: "Maybe not!"

Usually there is a pause on the line, followed by something like, "What do you mean?" That gives Shockey an opening to initiate a conversation about the Gospel. He has led more than one person to faith in Christ that way.

Evangelist Billy Graham once answered the phone in his hotel room. The person on the other end asked for so-and-so, and Mr. Graham told him he had the wrong number. There was a pause, and the person said, "You sure sound a lot like Billy Graham."

---

[1] Spurgeon, *Lectures to My Students,* 171.
[2] Wallace Hostetter, "Communicating to Contemporaries," *Leadership Journal,* Spring 1991, 23.

"This is Billy Graham," replied the evangelist. During the ensuing conversation, the caller gave his life to Christ.

> Date: _____ _____ _____
> Place: _____ _____ _____
> Occasion: _____ _____ _____

Celecca's Opportunity

Celecca Cutts of Nashville, while a nineteen-year-old nursing student in Florida, remembers sitting quietly in a church service. Her minister asked, "Will those of you who are willing to do anything necessary to lead others to Christ please raise your hands?" Celecca, concerned about her enfeebled testimony, cautiously lifted her hand.

A few days later while returning from nursing school, Celecca saw another driver coming toward her, trying to pass an eighteen-wheeler on a hill. She swerved, slammed into the truck, and her car rolled over three times before careening down an embankment.

For days afterward, Celecca hovered between coma and consciousness. Her mother sat by her bed, holding the girl's shattered hand and praying. In the same semi-private room sat another mother by her diseased daughter, listening.

By the time Celecca recovered, her mother had won both women to the Lord.

> Date: _____ _____ _____
> Place: _____ _____ _____
> Occasion: _____ _____ _____

Bearing Fruit

"As I reflected on the meaning of maturity," wrote Jerry White, "I realized that there is a central mark of maturity. In the human physical realm, maturity is gauged by when a person is able to bear or father children. A tree is mature when it bears fruit. A stalk of grain is mature when it can be harvested. In all creation, fruit-bearing is the preeminent mark of maturity.

"Certainly the spiritual realm differs little. A mature believer bears fruit of two kinds. The first is that of character and holiness of life. The second is becoming a spiritual parent either by leading others to Christ or by adopting a baby or growing a Christian."[1]

> Date: _____ _____ _____
> Place: _____ _____ _____
> Occasion: _____ _____ _____

W

---

[1] Jerry White, *The Power of Commitment* (Colorado Springs: NavPress, 1985), 130.

Cords of Evangelism

In his book *What in the World is God Doing?* Dr. Ted Engstrom relates a story told him by a veteran Korean Christian. In the early 1880s three Korean workmen, laboring in China, heard the Gospel and embraced the Lord Jesus. The three soon conspired about getting the message of Christ into their own country, an action forbidden by the government. Since the Korean and Chinese alphabets were similar, they decided to smuggle in a copy of the Chinese Bible. They drew straws to see who would have the privilege of bringing the Gospel into Korea.

The first man buried the Bible in his belongings and headed toward the border, a journey of many days by footpath. There he was searched, found out, and killed. Word reached the others that their friend was dead. The second man tore pages from his Bible and hid the separate pages throughout his luggage. He, too, made the long trip to the border only to be searched and beheaded.

The third man grew more determined than ever to succeed. He ingeniously tore his Bible apart page by page, folding each page into a tiny strip. He wove the strips into a rope and wrapped his baggage in his homemade rope. When he came to the border, the guards asked him to unwrap his belongings. Finding nothing amiss, they admitted him.

The man arrived home, untied the rope, and ironed out each page. He reassembled his Bible and began to preach Christ wherever he went. And when the missionaries of the 1880s fanned into the country, they found the seed already sown and the firstfruits appearing.[1]

Date:	_____	_____	_____
Place:	_____	_____	_____
Occasion:	_____	_____	_____

The Living Link

There have been several versions of this story, but according to research done by Warren Wiersbe, this is the official version: Britain's King George V was to give the opening address at a special disarmament conference, with a speech relayed by radio to the United States. As the broadcast was about to begin, a cable broke in the New York radio station, and more than a million listeners were left without sound.

A junior mechanic in the station, Harold Vivien, solved the problem by picking up both ends of the cable and allowing 250 volts of electricity to pass through him. He was the living link that allowed the king's message to get through.[2]

Date:	_____	_____	_____
Place:	_____	_____	_____
Occasion:	_____	_____	_____

---

[1] Ted W. Engstrom, *What in the World is God Doing?* (Waco, TX: Word Books, 1978), 161.
[2] Prokopé, 1988, the Good News Broadcasting Association, Inc.

Bringing Alice to Christ

Crotchety old Alice was a terror to neighborhood children, stray dogs, and delivery boys. Her face was sour and surly, and she waved her garden trowels and hedge-clippers like weapons in the faces of visitors.

When James and Jean Mader moved next door, they mustered their courage to speak to Alice one day about the Lord, but she cut them off. "I've been a member of the church all my life," she snorted. "I don't need the Bible to tell me what to do."

The Maders looked for ways of befriending Alice, and slowly the relationship thawed. Still, Alice wanted nothing to do with the Gospel.

During a community evangelistic campaign, the Maders became involved with a plan called "Operation Andrew," based on John 1:42, about Andrew's introducing his brother, Simon, to Christ. They listed ten people to pray for and to invite to the meetings. Alice's name was on the list, but she spurned their appeals. Still they prayed and looked for chances to share.

One summer returning from vacation, the Maders found Alice's house empty. She was in a nursing home, having suffered a stroke. They visited her regularly, bringing flowers and sharing news from the neighborhood. Alice was unable to speak, but one day when Jim asked if he could read Psalm 23, she nodded.

Jim visited regularly, always sharing Scripture, and they noticed that Alice began fixing her gaze on him as he read instead of staring straight ahead as she had previously done. One day Jim asked, "Alice, do you want the Lord Jesus to forgive your sins and give you peace with God?" Alice indicated that she did, bowing her head and praying silently as Jim led her. When she raised her head, her eyes were wet with tears.

It had taken over twelve years.[1]

Date:	_____	_____	_____
Place:	_____	_____	_____
Occasion:	_____	_____	_____

The Unending Chain

Edward Kimball was determined to win his Sunday school class to Christ. One of the boys, a teenager named Dwight Moody, tended to fall asleep on Sundays, but Kimball, undeterred, set out to reach him at work. His heart was pounding as he entered the store where the young man worked. "I put my hand on his shoulder, and as I leaned over I placed my foot upon a shoebox. I asked him to come to Christ." But Kimball left thinking he had botched the job. His presentation of the Gospel seemed halting, and he was downcast. Moody, however, left the store that day a new person and eventually became the most prominent evangelist in America.

On June 17, 1873, Moody arrived in Liverpool, England, for a series of crusades. The meetings went poorly at first, but then the dam burst and blessings began flowing. Moody visited a Baptist chapel pastored by a scholarly man named F. B.

W

---

[1]Jean Mader, "Alice," *Decision Magazine,* June 1990, 13.

Meyer who at first disdained the American's unlettered preaching. But Meyer was soon transfixed and transformed by Moody's message.

At Moody's invitation, Meyer toured America. At Northfield Bible Conference, he challenged the crowds saying, "If you are not willing to give up everything for Christ, are you willing to be made willing?" That remark changed the life of a struggling young minister named J. Wilber Chapman.

Chapman proceeded to become a powerful traveling evangelist in the early 1900s, and he recruited a converted baseball player named Billy Sunday. Under Chapman's eye, Sunday became one of the most spectacular evangelists in American history. His campaign in Charlotte, North Carolina, produced a group of converts who continued praying for another such visitation of the Spirit. In 1934, they invited evangelist Mordecai Ham to conduct a citywide crusade. It was during that crusade that Billy Graham was converted

And Edward Kimball thought he had botched the job![1]

Date:	_____	_____	_____
Place:	_____	_____	_____
Occasion:	_____	_____	_____

Witnessing by Walking

Christians are living witnesses who should "walk worthy" of the calling they have received.

In her biography of Marie Antoinette, Carolly Erickson tells about the queen's attempts to disguise herself and attend parties, dances, and balls incognito, but her walk gave her away. "When she walked, she strode like a man. Her swift, purposeful gait was her trademark. It was said that she could never successfully disguise her identity at masked balls, for no matter how she dressed, she still walked like an Empress."

F. W. Boreham reminds us of a story from the life of Francis d'Assisi. "Brother," Francis said one day to one of the young monks at the Portiuncula, "let us go down to the town and preach!"

The novice, delighted at being singled out to be the companion of Francis, obeyed with alacrity. They passed through the principal streets, turned down many of the by-ways and alleys, made their way out to some of the suburbs, and at length returned, by a circuitous route, to the monastery gate. As they approached it, the younger man reminded Francis of his original intention.

"You have forgotten, Father, that we went down to the town *to preach!*"

"My son," Francis replied, "we *have* preached. We were preaching while we were walking. We have been seen by many; our behavior has been closely watched; it was thus that we preached our morning sermon. It is of no use, my son, to walk anywhere to preach unless we preach everywhere we walk."

---

[1] Robert J. Morgan, *On This Day* (Nashville: Thomas Nelson Publishers, 1997), June 17th.

Date:			
Place:			
Occasion:			

What's Plan B?

According to a legend, when Jesus returned to heaven following his death on the cross and resurrection from the tomb, the angels gathered in amazement. They gazed at the wounds in his hands and feet, and shuddered to recall his suffering.

Finally Gabriel spoke: "Master, you suffered terribly down there. Do they know and appreciate the extent of your sacrifice."

"No," said Jesus. "Not yet. Right now only a handful of people in Palestine know."

"Then what have you done to let everyone else know?" asked Gabriel.

"I've asked Peter, James, and John, and a few others to spread the news. They will tell others who will tell others until the message spreads to the ends of the earth."

But Gabriel, knowing the nature of human beings, asked, "What is Plan B?"

"I have no Plan B," replied Christ. "There is no alternative strategy. I'm counting on them."

Twenty centuries later, he still has no other plan. He's counting on you and me.

Date:			
Place:			
Occasion:			

How the Gospel Spread

- *For four hundred years the Christian church had no great preacher by rhetorical standards. The first great preacher was Chrysostom. Yet during those centuries, Christianity conquered the Mediterranean world by the faithful witness of the common believer.*—Warren Wiersbe and Lloyd Perry[1]
- *While there were no professional missionaries devoting their whole life to this specific work, every congregation was a missionary society, and every Christian believer a missionary, inflamed by the love of Christ to convert his fellow men. . . . Every Christian told his neighbor, the laborer to his fellow laborer, the slave to his fellow slave, the servant to his master and mistress, the story of his conversion as a mariner tells the story of the rescue from shipwreck.*—Philip Schaff, about the early days of the post-apostolic church[2]

Date:			
Place:			
Occasion:			

W

---

[1] Warren W. Wiersbe and Lloyd M. Perry, *The Wycliffe Handbook of Preaching and Preachers* (Chicago: Moody Press), 5

[2] Philip Schaff, *History of the Christian Church, Vol 2: Ante-Nicene Christianity* (Grand Rapids, MI: Eerdmans Publishing Co., 1910), 20–21.

One on One

An old man, walking along the beach one dawn, noticed a young man picking up starfish and flinging them into the ocean. The boy explained he was afraid the stranded starfish would die if left until the morning sun.

"But the beach goes on for miles," said the man. "What difference will it make? There are so many starfish that nothing you can do will matter."

As the boy picked up another starfish and threw it into the sea, he said quietly, "It matters to this one."

Date: _____   _____   _____
Place: _____   _____   _____
Occasion: _____   _____   _____

The Touch of the Master's Hand

'Twas battered and scarred, and the auctioneer
Thought it scarcely worth his while
To waste much time on the old violin,
But held it up with a smile.
"What am I bidden, good folks," he cried,
"Who'll start the bidding for me?"
'A dollar, a dollar"—then, "Two? Only two?
Two dollars, and who'll make it three?
Three dollars, once; three dollars, twice;
Going for three—" But no,
From the room, far back, a gray-haired man
Came forward and picked up the bow;
Then, wiping the dust from the old violin,
And tightening the loosened strings,
He played a melody pure and sweet
As a caroling angel sings.

The music ceased, and the auctioneer,
With a voice that was quiet and low,
Said: "What am I bid for the old violin?"
And he held it up with the bow.
"A thousand dollars, and who'll make it two?
Two thousand? And who'll make it three?
Three thousand, once, three thousand, twice,
And going, and gone," said he.
The people cheered, but some of them cried,
"We do not quite understand
What changed its worth." Swift came the reply:
"The touch of a master's hand."

And many a man with life out of tune,
And battered and scarred with sin,

Is auctioned cheap to the thoughtless crowd,
Much like the old violin.
A "mess of pottage," a glass of wine;
A game—and he travels on.
He is "going" once, and "going" twice,
He's "going" and almost "gone."
But the Master comes, and the foolish crowd
Never can quite understand
The worth of a soul and the change that's wrought
By the touch of the Master's hand.—Myra Brooks Welch

Date: _____ _____ _____
Place: _____ _____ _____
Occasion: _____ _____ _____

Wonder

Someone Once Said . . .

- *I have never lost the wonder.*—Gipsy Smith
- *Wisdom begins in wonder.*—Socrates
- *Worship is transcendent wonder.*—Thomas Carlyle
- *I wonder as I wander out under the sky, How Jesus the Savior did come for to die.*—Appalachian Christmas Carol
- *O Lord my God, when I in awesome wonder consider all the worlds Thy hands have made . . .*—Carl Boberg
- *Wonder is a word to wonder about. It contains a mixture of messages: something marvelous and miraculous, surprising . . .*—Dr. Lewis Thomas, president emeritus of Memorial Sloan-Kettering Cancer Center
- *I remember the morning on which I came out of my room after I had first trusted Christ. I thought the old sun shone a good deal brighter than it ever had before. . . . As I walked out upon Boston Common and heard the birds singing in the trees, I thought they were singing a song to me. . . . It seemed to me that I was in love with all creation.*—D. L. Moody

Date: _____ _____ _____
Place: _____ _____ _____
Occasion: _____ _____ _____

W

Since I Know . . .

Heaven above is softer blue,
Earth around is sweeter green!
Something lives in every hue

Christless eyes have never seen:
Birds with gladder songs o'erflow,
Flowers with deeper beauty shine,
Since I know, as now I now,
I am His, and He is mine.—Wade Robinson

Date:	_____	_____	_____
Place:	_____	_____	_____
Occasion:	_____	_____	_____

Little Things

   Amy Carmichael writes of little joys, *like flowers springing up by the path unnoticed except by those who are looking for them. . . . Little things, like a quietly sinking sun, a friendly dog, a ready smile. We sang a little song in kindergarten which I've never forgotten: "The world is so full of a number of things / I'm sure we should all be as happy as kings." Simple, but such a devastating rebuke to the complaining heart. I am impressed with the joy that is ours in Christ, so that heaven above and earth below become brighter and fairer . . .*—Jim Elliot, in a letter to his wife Elisabeth[1]

Date:	_____	_____	_____
Place:	_____	_____	_____
Occasion:	_____	_____	_____

For the Wonder of Each Hour

For the wonder of each hour
Of the day and of the night,
Hill and vale and tree and flower,
Sun and moon and stars of light:
Christ our God, to Thee we raise
This our hymn of grateful praise—Folliott S. Pierpoint

Date:	_____	_____	_____
Place:	_____	_____	_____
Occasion:	_____	_____	_____

Ruskin and Wells

   The British actress Joan Winmill Brown once wrote: *Years ago John Ruskin, the English critic, wrote, "I would sooner live in a cottage and wonder at everything, than live in a castle and wonder at nothing." I have often thought of the statement that H. G. Wells made*

---

[1] Elisabeth Elliot, *Shadow of the Almighty* (Grand Rapids, MI: Zondervan, 1958), 85.

before his death, that his soul was no longer moved by the sight of the stars in the sky. The truth is, I cannot express to you all the wonder and joy that I have in my heart through Jesus Christ.[1]

Date: _____ _____ _____
Place: _____ _____ _____
Occasion: _____ _____ _____

How Charles Darwin Lost the Wonder

Late in life, Charles Darwin wrote in his autobiography: "I have said that in one respect my mind has changed during the last twenty or thirty years. Up to the age of thirty, or beyond it, poetry of many kinds . . . gave me great pleasure, and even as a schoolboy I took intense delight in Shakespeare. . . . I have also said that formerly pictures gave me considerable, and music very great, delight. But now, for many years I cannot endure to read a line of poetry: I have tried to read Shakespeare, and found it so intolerably dull that it nauseated me. I have also lost any taste for pictures or music. . . . I retain some taste for fine scenery, but it does not cause me the exquisite delight that it formerly did. . . . My mind seems to have become a kind of machine for grinding general laws out of large collections of facts. . . ."[2]

First Love

When I first trusted Christ, it seemed to me that I was in love with all creation.
—D. L. MOODY

Date: _____ _____ _____
Place: _____ _____ _____
Occasion: _____ _____ _____

The Dangers of Aging

• *We seem to lose our creativity, or at least let it atrophy, as we grow up. This is too bad, as every child under ten is not only creative but original, while most adults not only are uncreative but are copies of other adults. . . . To restore our creativity, we must restore our sense of wonder.*—Warren Bennis[3]
• *The older you get, the more it takes to fill your heart with wonder, and only God is big enough to do that.*—Ravi Zacharias[4]
• *You know you're old when you've lost all your marvels*—Merry Browne

Date: _____ _____ _____
Place: _____ _____ _____
Occasion: _____ _____ _____

W

[1] Joan Winmill Brown, "You Don't Walk Alone," *Great Reading from Decision* (Minneapolis: World Wide Publications, 1960), 166.
[2] Virginia Stem Owens, "Seeing Christianity in Red & Green," *Christianity Today,* September 2, 1983, 38.
[3] Warren Bennis, *Why Leaders Can't Lead* (San Francisco: Jossey-Bass Publishers, 1990), 119.
[4] Ravi Zacharias, *Can Man Live Without God?* (Dallas: Word Publishing, 1994), 89.

Familiarity Breeds . . .

- *Ralph Waldo Emerson said about the stars that if the constellations appeared only once in a thousand years, imagine what an exciting event it would be. But because they're there every night, we barely give them a look.*
- *Nothing is so deadening to the divine as a habitual dealing with the outsides of holy things.*—George McDonald[1]
- *Some of us grow so familiar with the Gospel, with the worship and ordinances of the church, that we lose our reverence.*—Vance Havner
- *One of the tragedies of life is that we get used to things. Those who live among the wild flowers rarely appreciate their fragrance. My own experience in the ministry ought to have taught me that no man is so apt to become deaf to the heavenly music, and blind to the heavenly vision, as the man who has every day of his life to stand in the presence of the sublimities of the faith and to take into his hands the eternal mysteries. No man is so apt to lose the reality and rapture of religion as the man who ministers in holy things every day of his life.*—F. W. Boreham[2]
- *It is easy to lose the wonder. The spirit of the age is against us. Iniquity abounds and the love of many waxes cold. We know too much. We have tried all the thrills. . . . A lot of religious activity today has lost the wonder. We engage in shop talk about men and methods and movement, but we do not exult in the wonderful news that Christ died and rose again.*—Vance Havner[3]
- *James Guthrie (seventeenth-century Scottish Covenenter, hanged for his faith) ever kept through his busy life his own personal fellowship with Christ, in the fresh bloom of his new birth, as if he had been but a young convert, and thus it wondrously was till his last day on earth dawned, and the summer sun streamed in through the iron bars of his cell windows. [He] rose at about four o'clock for worship, and was asked how he was. "Very well," said Guthrie. "This is the day that the Lord hath made; let us rejoice and be glad in it."*—Jock Purves, in *Fair Sunshine*[4]

Date:	_____	_____	_____
Place:	_____	_____	_____
Occasion:	_____	_____	_____

Huckleberry Finn

"I wish I had never read *Huckleberry Finn*," a man once told its author, Mark Twain. With a scowl, the great humorist asked the reason for such a remark. "So that I could have the pleasure again of reading it for the first time," came the reply.

Date:	_____	_____	_____
Place:	_____	_____	_____
Occasion:	_____	_____	_____

---

[1] Warren Wiersbe, "The Pastor and Prayer," *Prokopé*, November–December, 1985, 1.
[2] F. W. Boreham, *Shadows on the Wall* (New York: Abingdon Press, 1922), 146.
[3] Vance Havner, "Have You Lost the Wonder?" *The Alliance Weekly*, August 21, 1948, 532.
[4] Jock Purves, *Fair Sunshine* (London: Banner of Truth Trust, 1968), 17.

Toscanini

On the eightieth birthday of the famous musician and conductor Arturo Toscanini, someone asked his son what he considered to be his father's greatest achievement. He replied, "For him there can be no such thing. Whatever he happens to be doing at any moment is the biggest undertaking of his life, whether it be conducting a symphony or peeling an orange."

Date: _____ _____ _____
Place: _____ _____ _____
Occasion: _____ _____ _____

John Newton's Wonderment

How tedious and tasteless the hours
When Jesus no longer I see!
Sweet prospects, sweet birds, sweet flowers,
Have all lost their sweetness to me.
The midsummer sun shines but dim;
The fields strive in vain to look gay;
But when I am happy with Him,
December's as pleasant as May.

Dear Lord, if indeed I am Thine,
If Thou art my sun and my song,
Say, what do I languish and pine,
And why are my winters so long?
Oh, drive these dark clouds from my sky;
Thy soul-cheering presence restore;
Or take me unto Thee on high,
Where winter and clouds are no more.—John Newton

Date: _____ _____ _____
Place: _____ _____ _____
Occasion: _____ _____ _____

The Wonder of Wonders

There's the wonder of sunset at evening,
The wonder as sunrise I see;
But the wonder of wonders that thrills my soul
Is the wonder that God loves me.—George Beverly Shea

W

Date: _____ _____ _____
Place: _____ _____ _____
Occasion: _____ _____ _____

Everyday Wonder

- *Splendor in the Ordinary*—Title of a book by Thomas Howard
- *Hidden Art*—Title of a book by Edith Schaeffer on the joys of finding creativity in ordinary, everyday things
- *Enthusiasm Makes the Difference*—Title of a book by Norman Vincent Peale
- *It is a very rich and significant promise that the glory of the Lord is to rest "upon every dwelling," and all the commonest interests of life are to be lit up in its holy rays.*—J. H. Jowett[1]
- *The will of God—it gives joy, it gives dignity, it gives power, it gives glory to life. When we realize that everything in our daily affairs is included, in some way or other, in the will of God, what inspiration it gives us for what we are accustomed to call the most trivial and common of our duties.*—W. H. Griffith Thomas[2]
- *Divine Service Rendered Here Three Times Daily.*—Plaque over Ruth Graham's Kitchen Sink

```
Date:       _____   _____   _____
Place:      _____   _____   _____
Occasion:   _____   _____   _____
```

God's Photo Shoot

When a mother saw a thunderstorm forming in mid-afternoon she worried about her seven-year-old daughter who would be walking the three blocks home from school. Deciding to meet her, the mother saw her walking nonchalantly along, stopping to smile whenever the lightning flashed.

Seeing her mother, the little girl ran to her, explaining happily, "All the way home, God has been taking my picture."

```
Date:       _____   _____   _____
Place:      _____   _____   _____
Occasion:   _____   _____   _____
```

———— Working for Christ ————

Someone Once Said . . .

- *Neglecting my business? My business is to extend the Kingdom of God. I only cobble shoes to pay expenses.*—William Carey, as a shoe cobbler, when accused of neglecting his business because of his ministerial efforts
- *First, that all and every one who believes, being members of Christ, are in common partakers of Him and of all his riches and gifts; secondly, that every one must know it to*

---

[1] J. H. Jowett, *Life in the Heights* (Grand Rapids, MI: Baker Book House, 1925), 103.
[2] Warren W. Wiersbe, *Listening to the Giants* (Grand Rapids, MI: Baker Book House, 1980), 145.

be his duty readily and cheerfully to employ his gifts for the advantage and salvation of other members.—Heidelberg Catechism

- *It is lamentable, that we should live so long in the world, and do so little for God, or that we should live so short a time in the world, and do so much for Satan.*—Rev. William Secker[1]
- *I see a man cannot be a faithful minister, until he preaches Christ for Christ's sake— until he gives up striving to attract people to himself, and seeks only to attract them to Christ. Lord, give me this!*—Robert Murray McCheyne
- *It is possible to be homiletically brilliant, verbally fluent, theologically profound, biblically orthodox, and spiritually useless.*—G. Campbell Morgan
- *I don't believe that [a man breaks] down . . . with hard work, so much as with using the machinery without oil, without lubrication. It is not the hard work breaks down ministers, but it is the toil of working without power.*—D. L. Moody[2]
- *The only place where success comes before work is in the dictionary.*—Anonymous
- *Some of us are like wheelbarrows—only useful when pushed, and very easily upset.*— Jack Herbert[3]

Date: _____ _____ _____

Place: _____ _____ _____

Occasion: _____ _____ _____

Stats

According to the Barna Research organization, nearly 1 out of 4 adults (25%) volunteer some of their free time to help a church in a typical week. This statistic has remained relatively stable across the years. Those more likely than average to volunteer their time to help a church, according to Barna's 1999 study, are:

- evangelical Christians (46%)
- born again Christians (37%)
- Protestant mainline attenders (36%)
- political conservatives (34%)
- those age 72 or over (33%)
- Baptists (30%)
- Protestant non-mainline attenders (29%)
- married individuals (29%)[4]

Date: _____ _____ _____

Place: _____ _____ _____

Occasion: _____ _____ _____

W

[1] William Secker, *The Nonsuch Professor In His Meridian Splendor* (Chicago: Fleming H. Revell Co., 1899), 18.
[2] D. L. Moody, *Secret Power* (Chicago: Moody Press, n.d.), 53.
[3] Pat Riley, *The Winner Within* (New York: Berkley Books, 1994), 174.
[4] < www.barna.org >

Holy Ground in Washington

In January, 1995, according to Gary Thomas in an article, J. Robert Ashcroft had fewer than forty-eight hours to live, but he was holding on to life, hoping to see his son, John Ashcroft, sworn into the U.S. Senate the following day. As family and friends gathered in Washington for a small reception, J. Robert Ashcroft asked his son to play the piano while everyone sang, "We Are Standing on Holy Ground."

After the song, the frail old man spoke some powerful words: "John, I want you to know that even Washington can be holy ground. Wherever you hear the voice of God, that ground is sanctified. It's a place where God can call you to the highest and best."

Wherever we are in our vocation, if Jesus is Lord of our lives, that place is a holy place of service for him.[1]

Date: _____ _____ _____
Place: _____ _____ _____
Occasion: _____ _____ _____

Holy Ground

> *It may be on a kitchen floor,*
> *Or in a busy shopping store,*
> *Or teaching, nursing, day by day*
> *Till limb and brain almost give way;*
> *Yet if, just there, by Jesus thou art found,*
> *The place thou standest on is Holy Ground.*—M. Colley[2]

Date: _____ _____ _____
Place: _____ _____ _____
Occasion: _____ _____ _____

Your Spot

Executive Bob Shank wrote in *Total Life Management:*

Most everything I needed to know in life I learned in high school football. My team was a melting pot of ethnic flavors, coached by a similarly broad mix of committed men. My mentor was a 6'5", 260-pound persuader named Manny Penaflor.

As the giant on the defensive line (I weighed in at 172 pounds, minus gear), Manny would often start with me when demonstrating a point. One day as we lined up for scrimmage, Manny decided to capture a teaching opportunity. He had a peculiar way of seizing our attention—he grabbed your face mask and pulled you up real close, so you wouldn't miss a single word.

On this particular day, he grabbed my face mask and yelled in his distinctive accent, "Chank, you're a defensive tackle, not the whole team. I don't want you playing the whole field. Here's your job."

---

[1] Gary Thomas, "Working for All It's Worth," *Moody*, July/August 1998, 13.
[2] Mrs. Charles E. Cowman, *Springs in the Valley* (Los Angeles: Cowman Publications, Inc., 1939), 198.

He let me go and used his foot to scratch a ten-foot by ten-foot square around my spot on the line. "Chank, you see this square?" I couldn't miss it. "This square is yours. Anybody from the other team who comes into this square, it's you job to put them on their butt. You got that?"

When he was convinced I understood my assignment, he moved to the middle guard, Ernie Norton, and went through the same theatrics. Property rights were assigned in 100-square-foot increments to five linemen and two linebackers. None of us could ever say we didn't know what was expected of us. We knew our personal responsibilities.

I think of Manny often when I tense up over what needs to be done on a global scale. I have a tendency to become frustrated, then fatalistic, because I can't get my arms around all there is to do. It's at those moments that I need to remember I'm not assigned the whole planet. I've only been entrusted with a particular slice of it. This is the portion of the world for which God will one day hold me accountable.[1]

> Date: _____ _____ _____
> Place: _____ _____ _____
> Occasion: _____ _____ _____

The Winning Team

In his popular seminars on leadership, management guru William A. Cohen often asks his audience if they can think of any organization which has all these attributes:

- The workers work very hard physically, including weekends, with little complaint.
- The workers receive no money and little material compensation for their services.
- The work is dangerous and workers are frequently injured on the job.
- The work is strictly voluntary.
- The workers usually have very high morale.
- The organization always has more workers than can be employed.
- The workers are highly motivated to achieve the organization's goals.

The executives attending Cohen's seminars are frequently stumped, thinking there is no organization like this on earth. But Cohen knows of one such organization: A high school football team.

Christians know another: the church.[2]

> Date: _____ _____ _____
> Place: _____ _____ _____
> Occasion: _____ _____ _____

The Unseen Hand

There was once a famous German artist named Herkomer, born in the Black Forest, whose father was a simple woodchopper. Herkomer was a gifted artist, and

[1] Bob Shank, *Total Life Management* (Portland, OR: Multnomah Press, 1990), 153–154.
[2] William A. Cohen, *The Art of the Leader* (Englewood Cliff, NJ: Prentice Hall, 1990), 99.

as his reputation grew, he moved to London and built a studio there. He sent for his aged father, and the dad came, full of pride for his son, and lived with him.

The old man enjoyed creating things out of clay, and he learned to make very beautiful bowls and vases, items of which he was very proud. So the father and son were in business together as artisans. But as the years passed, the old man's abilities deteriorated, and at the end of the day, as he went upstairs, he would seem sad because he felt that his work was now inferior.

Herkomer's sharp eye detected this, and when his father was safely upstairs and asleep for the night, Herkomer would come downstairs and take in hand the pieces of clay that his old father had left. He would gently correct the defects and the faults, and mold them a little one way or the other. And when the old man would come down in the mornings, he would hold up the pieces in the morning light, smile, and say, "I can still do it as well as I ever did."[1]

> ### For Christ's Sake
>
> *I see a man cannot be a faithful minister, until he preaches Christ for Christ's sake.*
> —ROBERT MURRAY McCHEYNE

That's just what our Father does with us. We try to do for Him what we can. We visit the sick, teach the children, sing and usher and invite and take food to the bereaved. We send our missionaries and pray for them. But we're all frail and flawed, and our work for the Lord isn't as perfect and pure as we would like. Yet the Lord places His omnipotent hand on it, and shapes it, and uses it in ways far greater than we know.

Charles Spurgeon once said, *Don't hold back because you cannot preach in St. Paul's; be content to talk to one or two in a cottage; very good wheat grows in little fields. You may cook in small pots as well as in big ones. Little pigeons can carry great messages. Even a little dog can bark at a thief, and wake up the master and save the house. A spark is fire. A sentence of truth has heaven in it. Do what you do right, thoroughly, pray over it heartily, and leave the result to God.*

Date: _____   _____   _____

Place: _____   _____   _____

Occasion: _____   _____   _____

Everything We Do

Everything that we do should be advancing the Great Commission, and every one of us has our role to fill, our job to do, our part to play. It may be preaching or keeping the nurseries. It may be on a far-flung mission field, or teaching the children at home. Perhaps your role is counting the Sunday offerings, greeting visitors, visiting the sick, singing, or planning socials. But all of it plows into the Great Commission.

My father enlisted in the army during World War II. They didn't send him to Europe or the South Pacific, but into the mountains of East Tennessee as an agricultural specialist to help the farmers increase their crops for the war effort.

During the same World War, England needed to increase its production of coal, so Winston Churchill called together the labor leaders to enlist their support. He

[1] F. B. Meyer, *The Christ Life for Your Life* (Chicago: Moody Press, n.d.), 28.

told them to picture in their minds a parade that he knew would be held in Piccadilly Circus after the war. First, he said, would come the sailors who had kept the vital sea lanes open. Then would come the soldiers who had come home from Dunkirk and then gone on to defeat Rommel in Africa. Then would come the pilots who had driven the Luftwaffe from the sky.

Last of all, he said, would come a long line of sweat-stained, soot-streaked men in miner's caps. Someone would cry from the crowd, "And where were you during the critical days of our struggle?" And from ten thousand throats would come the answer, "We were deep in the earth with our faces to the coal."

Not all the jobs in a church are prominent and glamorous. But it's often the people with their "faces to the coal" who help the church accomplish its mission.[1]

Date: _____ _____ _____
Place: _____ _____ _____
Occasion: _____ _____ _____

The Challenge of Volunteers

Ted Engstrom, president emeritus of World Vision, points out: "A profit-making organization is the easiest to run. It's a business with a narrow measuring stick for success—profit. The next easiest to run is a nonprofit organization like World Vision. We pay our people. We can hire. We can release. There are more problems than with a profit company, but we still have a strong measure of control. Running a volunteer organization like the church is the hardest. The church accepts everyone, warts and all. Yet you're challenging these people to difficult ministry—without pay."[2]

Date: _____ _____ _____
Place: _____ _____ _____
Occasion: _____ _____ _____

Volunteers

Civil War general William Tecumseh Sherman discovered what pastors have found when he had to command forces consisting of available home guards and volunteers. "I never did like to serve with volunteers," he reflected later, "because instead of being governed, they govern."[3]

Date: _____ _____ _____
Place: _____ _____ _____
Occasion: _____ _____ _____

W

---

[1] From a sermon by the author.
[2] Kevin A. Miller, *Secrets of Staying Power* (Waco, TX: Word Books, 1988), 72.
[3] Miller, *Secrets of Staying Power,* 72.

God Doesn't Call Lazy People

It is observable that God has often called men to places of dignity and honor when they have busy and honest employment of their vocation. Saul was seeking his father's donkeys and David his father's sheep when called to the Kingdom. The shepherds were feeding their flocks when they had their glorious revelation. God called the four apostles from their fishing and Matthew from collecting taxes, Amos from the horsemen of Tecoah, Moses from keeping Jethro's sheep, Gideon from the threshing floor, Elisha from the plows. God never called a lazy man. God never encourages idleness and will not despise persons in the lowest employment.—D. L. Moody

Date: _____   _____   _____

Place: _____   _____   _____

Occasion: _____   _____   _____

What Are You Doing Here?

There is a story that when the famed English architect, Sir Christopher Wren, was directing the building of St. Paul's Cathedral in London, some of the workers were interviewed by a journalist who asked them, "What are you doing here?"

The first said, "I'm cutting stone for three shillings a day."

The second replied, "I'm putting ten hours a day in on this job."

The third replied, "I'm helping Sir Christopher Wren build the greatest cathedral in Great Britain for the glory of God."[1]

Date: _____   _____   _____

Place: _____   _____   _____

Occasion: _____   _____   _____

Three Blocks Down

A minister was approached by a man who wanted to join the church. "But," the man said, "I have a very busy schedule. I can't be called on for any service, such as committee work, teaching, or singing in the choir. I just won't be available for special projects or to help with setting up chairs or things like that. And I'm afraid I'll never be able to go on visitation, as my evenings are all tied up."

The minister thought for a moment, then replied, "I believe you're at the wrong church. The church you're looking for is three blocks down the street, on the right."

The man followed the preacher's directions and soon came to an abandoned, boarded up, closed church building. It was a dead church—gone out of business.

Date: _____   _____   _____

Place: _____   _____   _____

Occasion: _____   _____   _____

---

[1] Robert Fulghum, *It Was On Fire When I Lay Down on It* (New York: Villard Books, 1990), 74–75.

And I'm Getting Tired . . .

When he was pastor of the First Baptist Church of Dallas, W. A. Criswell wrote this in his weekly column:

The population of this country is 200 million. Eighty-four million are over 65 years of age, which leaves 116 million to do the work. People under 20 years of age total 75 million, which leaves 41 million to do the work.

There are 22 million who are employed by the government, which leaves 19 million to do the work. Four million are in the Armed Forces, which leaves 15 million to do the work. Deduct 14,800,000, the number of state and city office employees, leaving 200,000 to do the work. There are 188,000 in the hospitals and insane asylums, so that leaves 12,000 to do the work.

Now it may interest you to know there are 11,998 people in jail, so that leaves just 2 people to carry the load. That's you and me—and, brother, I'm getting tired of doing everything myself.

Date: _____ _____ _____
Place: _____ _____ _____
Occasion: _____ _____ _____

——————————— Worry ———————————

Someone Once Said . . .

- *Worry is a small trickle of fear that meanders through the mind until it cuts a channel into which all other thoughts are drained.*—Anonymous
- *Worry is putting question marks where God has put periods.*—John R. Rice
- *Worry is the interest we pay on tomorrow's troubles.*—E. Stanley Jones
- *Worry is a form of atheism, for it betrays a lack of faith and trust in God.*—Attributed to Bishop Fulton J. Sheen

Date: _____ _____ _____
Place: _____ _____ _____
Occasion: _____ _____ _____

Ulcers, Tumors, and Abscesses

Stress and worry break us down. They are the unseen source of our headaches, backaches, heartaches, and belly aches. They produce everything from obesity to obscenity, from constipation to diarrhea, and from impatience to impotence. They give us knotted stomachs, sleepless nights, high blood pressure, low morale. They make our tempers short and our days long. They cause indigestion, irritation, chest pain, and muscle strain.

W

"You do not get stomach ulcers from what you eat," said one doctor. "You get ulcers from what is eating you."[1]

"Those who are extremely anxious," said John Calvin, himself prone to anxiety, "wear themselves out and become their own executioners."[2]

Epictetus, the great Stoic philosopher, warned that we ought to be more concerned about removing wrong thoughts from the mind than about removing "tumors and abscesses from the body."

Date: _____   _____   _____
Place: _____   _____   _____
Occasion: _____   _____   _____

Word Pictures of Worry

Psalm 37 begins: *Do Not Fret,* and verse 8 repeats the advice: *Do not fret—it only causes harm.* The English word *fret* comes from the Old English *fretan,* meaning *to devour, to eat, to gnaw into something.* The Hebrew word David actually used as he wrote in his original language is *charah (ka-ra')* which has, at its root, the idea of *growing warm and blazing up.*

Put these two pictures together. Think of worry as a rat inside your soul, gnawing away. Think of Satan as an arsonist, setting little blazes of distress inside your heart.

King David is saying something like this in Psalm 37: "I have been young, and now I'm old (see verse 25). I've seen many things, suffered many burdens, and learned many lessons. Based on a lifetime of experience, my advice is: 'Kill off the rats and put out the fires. Do not fret, it only causes harm.'"[3]

Date: _____   _____   _____
Place: _____   _____   _____
Occasion: _____   _____   _____

More from Psalm 37

In one of his books, Methodist pastor Charles Allen tells of visiting a particular city. Being met at the plane, he was told, "We don't have time to wait for your baggage. Someone else will get it. You are to speak at the club in twenty minutes." Rushing from the airport, Allen learned he was to speak each morning on television at nine, at church at ten, and somewhere else each evening. He was also to address three civic clubs, two high schools, and one women's meeting. In all, he had nineteen speaking engagements in four days—plus a series of personal interviews.

---

[1] Dale Carnegie, *How To Stop Worrying and Start Living* (New York: Simon and Schuster, 1948), 19 & 96.
[2] William J. Bouwsma, *John Calvin, A Sixteenth-Century Portrait* (New York: Oxford University Press, 1988), 37.
[3] From a sermon by the author.

By Wednesday night Allen found himself wound so tightly he scarcely slept a wink. The worries and pressures got to him.

The next day he rebelled. After the morning engagements . . . *I told the pastor I would be gone for the remainder of the day. I started walking slowly down the street, going no place in particular and in no hurry to get there. A number of people spoke to me and stopped and talked awhile. It reminded me of living in a little town where you can enjoy visiting up and down Main Street.*

I walked on past the city limits until I came to a big bridge on the river. I found a comfortable place to sit down and I sat there for two hours watching the river . . . From the bridge I could see the point where two rivers flowed together. One of the rivers was almost clear, the other extremely muddy. For a short distance after they came together, you could distinguish the water of each, but a little farther on the clear water took on the brownish color of the other. I thought about how we let evil thoughts come into our minds and how the evil soon colors all our living. I made some mental notes for a sermon about that.

> **Epitaph of a Worrier**
>
> *Hurried, Worried, Buried!*

At the end of the bridge was a tiny hamburger place. I had one with onions; in fact, I asked for an extra onion. It tasted real good. I didn't care whether or not it left an odor on my breath. I had been so pious all that week that I was in the mood to do something daring.

I walked along the street until I came to a cemetery . . . (and) spent an hour walking among the graves. During that hour I was the only person there. I thought about how quickly someone is forgotten and how others take our places. It is not so important that we carry the world on our shoulders as we sometimes think.

I got back to the hotel for dinner before the preaching service that night. I felt rested and relaxed. When I got back to my room after the service, I went to bed. I picked up my Bible from the table and opened it to the Thirty-seventh Psalm. Next to the Twenty-third, that is my favorite Psalm. It was written for people who get disturbed and overly wrought-up.

The Thirty-seventh Psalm is gentle and tender; like a sweet kindly mother putting her hand upon the brow of a restless child, the Psalm begins, "Fret not thyself . . ." It goes on to say, "Delight thyself also in the Lord; and he shall give thee the desires of thy heart." Further on we read, "Rest in the Lord, and wait patiently for him . . ." All the way through, the Psalm leads one to a calm and triumphant faith. That night I slept easily and the next day I felt rested and strong.[1]

We weren't made for a nonstop, twenty-four-hour, frantic pace. We need to take time for ourselves, time to relax, time to walk by the still waters, time waiting before the Lord, for there alone can we renew our strength and overcome worry.

Date: _____ _____ _____

Place: _____ _____ _____

Occasion: _____ _____ _____

The Professional Worrier

"I have a mountain of credit card debt," one man told another. "I've lost my job, my car is being repossessed, and our house is in foreclosure, but I'm not worried about it."

W

---

[1] Charles L. Allen, *Prayer Changes Things* (Westwood, NJ: Fleming H. Revell Co., 1964), 62–64.

"Not worried about it!" exclaimed his friend.

"No. I've hired a professional worrier. He does all my worrying for me, and that way I don't have to think about it."

"That's fantastic. How much does your professional worrier charge for his services?"

"Fifty thousand dollars a year," replied the first man.

"Fifty thousand dollars a year? Where are you going to get that kind of money?"

"I don't know," came the reply. "That's his worry."

In a sense, the Lord's servants *do* have a professional worrier to do all our worrying for them. As 1 Peter 5:7 says, "You can throw the whole weight of your anxieties upon him, for you are his personal concern" (Phillips).

Date: _____   _____   _____
Place: _____   _____   _____
Occasion: _____   _____   _____

Antidote for Worry

Doing beats stewing.

When you are tempted to fret and worry, divert yourself. Don't sit around with the curtains drawn, wringing your hands. Throw open the windows, find something that needs to be done, and get busy. During the height of World War II, someone asked Winston Churchill if he worried about his tremendous responsibilities. He said, "I'm too busy. I have no time for worry."

Martin Luther gave similar advice: *When I am assailed with heavy tribulations, I rush out among my pigs, rather than remain alone by myself. The human heart is like a millstone in a mill; when you put wheat under it, it turns and grinds and bruises the wheat to flour; if you put no wheat, it still grinds on, but then 'tis itself it grinds and wears away. So the human heart, unless it be occupied with some employment, leaves space for the devil, who wriggles himself in, and brings with him a whole host of evil thoughts, temptations, and tribulations, which grind out the heart.*[1]

Date: _____   _____   _____
Place: _____   _____   _____
Occasion: _____   _____   _____

Martin Luther's Favorite Preacher

Speaking of Luther, the great reformer once described his favorite preacher: *I have one preacher I love better than any other; it is my little tame robin, who preaches to me daily. I put his crumbs upon my window sill, especially at night. He hops onto the sill when he wants his supply, and takes as much as he desires to satisfy his need. From thence he always hops to a little tree close by, and lifts up his voice to God, and sings his carol of praise and gratitude, tucks his little head under his wings, and goes fast to sleep, to leave tomorrow to look after itself.*

[1] Martin Luther, *The Table Talk of Martin Luther* (Grand Rapids, MI: Baker Book House, 1952), 290–291.

Date: _____ _____ _____
Place: _____ _____ _____
Occasion: _____ _____ _____

When J. C. Penney Worried

James Cash Penney, coming from a long line of Baptist preachers, grew up with deep convictions. He was unwaveringly honest. He never smoked or drank, and he was a hard worker. But in 1929 when the Great Depression hit, Penney found himself in crisis. He had made unwise commitments, and they turned sour. Penney began to worry about them, and soon he was unable to sleep. He developed a painful case of shingles and was hospitalized. His anxiety only increased in the hospital, and it seemed resistant to tranquilizers and drugs. His mental state deteriorated until, as he later said, *I was broken nervously and physically, filled with despair, unable to see even a ray of hope. I had nothing to live for. I felt I hadn't a friend left in the world, that even my family turned against me.*

> **Worried Thoughts**
>
> *Worry is a destructive process of occupying the mind with thoughts contrary to God's love and care.*
> —NORMAN VINCENT PEALE

One night he was so oppressed he didn't think his heart would hold out, and, expecting to die before morning, he sat down and wrote farewell letters to his wife and sons.

But he did live through the night, and the next morning he heard singing coming from the little hospital chapel. The words of the song said,

> *Be not dismayed whate'er betide*
> *God will take care of you.*

Entering the chapel, he listened to the song, to the Scripture reading, and to the prayer. *Suddenly—something happened. I can't explain it. I can only call it a miracle. I felt as if I had been instantly lifted out of the darkness of a dungeon into warm, brilliant sunlight.*

All worry left him as he realized more fully than he had ever imagined just how much the Lord Jesus Christ cared for him. From that day J. C. Penney was never plagued with worry, and he later called those moments in the chapel "the most dramatic and glorious twenty minutes of my life."[1]

Date: _____ _____ _____
Place: _____ _____ _____
Occasion: _____ _____ _____

Three Perspectives on Worry from a Well-Known Family

[A] When one of her sons was living a wild and dangerous life, Ruth Bell Graham, wife of evangelist Billy Graham, found herself torn apart by worry. One night while traveling overseas she suddenly awoke. A current of fear surged through

W

---

[1] Carnegie, *How To Stop Worrying and Start Living*, 253–254.

her like an electric shock. She lay in bed and tried to pray, but she suffered from galloping anxiety, one fear piling upon another. She looked at the clock and it was around three o'clock. She was exhausted, yet she knew she would be unable to go back to sleep. Suddenly the Lord seemed to say to her, "Quit studying the problems and start studying the promises."

She turned on the light, got out her Bible, and the first verses that came to her were Philippians 4:6–7. As she read those words, she suddenly realized that the missing ingredient in her prayers had been thanksgiving. ". . . in everything by prayer and petition, *with thanksgiving,* present your requests to God."

She put down her Bible and spent time worshiping God for who and what he is. She later wrote, *I began to thank God for giving me this one I loved so dearly in the first place. I even thanked him for the difficult spots which had taught me so much. And you know what happened? It was as if someone turned on the light in my mind and heart, and the little fears and worries that had been nibbling away in the darkness like mice and cockroaches hurriedly scuttled for cover. That was when I learned that worship and worry cannot live in the same heart. They are mutually exclusive.*[1]

[B] Compare those words with the slightly different perspective of Ruth's husband. In his autobiography, *Just As I Am,* Billy Graham describes these same difficult years when their sons were away from the Lord: *Ruth and I found out that for us, worrying and praying were not mutually exclusive. We trusted the Lord to bring the children through somehow in His own way in due time. On a day-to-day basis, however, we muddled through. But God was faithful. Today each one of them is filled with faith and fervor for the Lord's service.*[2]

[C] Franklin Graham once told a group, "If my mom has white hair, it's because of me!" To which Ruth replied, "Don't take all the credit, son. Age has something to do with it."[3]

Date:	_____	_____	_____
Place:	_____	_____	_____
Occasion:	_____	_____	_____

Wesley's Perspective

"I would no more worry than I would curse or swear."—John Wesley[4]

Date:	_____	_____	_____
Place:	_____	_____	_____
Occasion:	_____	_____	_____

---

[1] Ruth Bell Graham, *It's My Turn* (Old Tappan, NJ: Fleming H. Revell Co., 1982), 136–137.
[2] Billy Graham, *Just As I Am* (HarperSanFrancisco/Zondervan, 1977), 711.
[3] Franklin Graham, *Rebel With A Cause* (Nashville: Thomas Nelson, 1995), 314.
[4] W. Herschel Ford, *Simple Sermons on Prayer* (Grand Rapids, MI: Baker, 1985), 20.

Turn that Over to Me

The career of missionary E. Stanley Jones, who died in 1973, was nearly cut short by chronic worry. When he had first arrived in India, Jones wore himself out, working and worrying. "I was suffering so severely from brain fatigue and nervous exhaustion," he later wrote, "that I collapsed, not once but several times." Aboard the ship returning to America, he collapsed again and the doctor put him to bed. After a year's rest, he attempted to return to India, but became a bundle of nerves on the return trip and arrived in Bombay a broken man. His colleagues warned him that any attempt to continue ministering in such a state of anxious care would be fatal.

While praying one night, groping in emotional darkness, Jones seemed to hear a Voice ask him, "Are you yourself ready for this work to which I have called you?"

"No, Lord," replied Jones. "I am done for. I have reached the end of my resources."

"If you will turn that over to Me and not worry about it," the Voice seemed to say, "I will take care of it."

Jones answered, "Lord, I close the bargain right here."

A great sense of peace closed in over Stanley Jones, a rush of abundant life that seemed to sweep him off his feet. His energy returned, his enthusiasm bubbled over, and he plunged back into his work with a vitality he had never before known. Jones went on to spend a lifetime of ministry in India, writing numerous books, and ministering to multitudes around the world.

He later wrote, "This one thing I know: my life was completely transformed and uplifted that night . . . when at the depth of my weakness and depression, a voice said to me: 'If you will turn that over to Me and not worry about it, I will take care of it,' and I replied, 'Lord, I close the bargain right here.'"

Cast your burden on the Lord and He shall sustain you; He shall never permit the righteous to be moved. . . . Casting all your care upon Him, for He cares for you. (Psalm 55:22 & 1 Peter 5:7, NKJV)

The Worries of Life

We scarcely know when life will worry us half to death. Consider Pastor A. J. Jones in South Africa. Wanting to sell a television set, he ran a classified ad in a Pretoria paper. As first printed, the ad said: *The Rev. A. J. Jones has a color TV set for sale. Telephone 555-1313 after 7 P.M. and ask for Mrs. Donnelley who lives with him, cheap.*

The next day, the paper printed this correction: *We regret any embarrassment caused to Rev. Jones by a typographical error in yesterday's editions. It should have read, "The Rev. A. J. Jones has color TV set for sale, cheap. Telephone 555-1313 and ask for Mrs. Donnelley who lives with him after 7 P.M.*

The next day, the paper said: *The Rev. A. J. Jones informs us he has received several annoying telephone calls because of an incorrect advertisement in yesterday's paper. It should have read, "The Rev. A. J. Jones has color TV set for sale. Cheap. Telephone 555-1313 and ask for Mrs. Donnelley who loves with him."*

One day later: *Please take notice that I, the Rev. Jones, have no TV set for sale. I have smashed it. I have not been carrying on with Mrs. Donnelley. She was until yesterday my housekeeper.*

W

There was, however, one more ad the next day: *WANTED a housekeeper. Telephone Rev. A. J. Jones, 555-1313. Usual housekeeping duties, good pay, love in.*[1]

Date:			
Place:			
Occasion:			

Worship

Someone Once Said . . .

- *The world can be saved by one thing and that is worship. For to worship is to quicken the conscience by the holiness of God, to feed the mind with the truth of God, to purge the imagination by the beauty of God, to open the heart to the love of God, to devote the will to the purpose of God.*—William Temple
- *The most acceptable service we can do and show unto God, and which alone he desires of us, is, that he be praised of us.*—Martin Luther[2]
- *It behooves us to be careful what we worship, for what we are worshiping we are becoming.*—Ralph Waldo Emerson[3]
- *We tend by a secret law of the soul to move toward our mental image of God.*—A. W. Tozer[4]
- *Wash your face every morning in a bath of praise.*—Charles Spurgeon[5]
- *A drop of praise is an unsuitable acknowledgement for an ocean of mercy.*—Rev. William Secker[6]
- *Christian worship is the most momentous, the most urgent, the most glorious action that can take place in human life.*—Karl Barth

Date:			
Place:			
Occasion:			

Stats

In their surveys on the subject of worship, the Barna Research Group has found:

- The term "worship" means many things to many people. There is no single interpretation of the word that is common to more than one out of five adults in this country.

---

[1] *Paul Harvey's For What It's Worth,* ed. by Paul Harvey, Jr. (New York: Bantam Books, 1991), 9.

[2] Martin Luther, *The Table Talk of Martin Luther* (Grand Rapids, MI: Baker Book House, 1952), 66.

[3] *The Book of Uncommon Prayer,* ed. by Constance Pollock and Daniel Pollock (Dallas: Word Publishing, 1996), 61.

[4] A. W. Tozer, *The Knowledge of the Holy* (New York: Harper & Row, 1961), 9.

[5] Charles Haddon Spurgeon, *Spurgeon's Sermons,* vol. 2 (Grand Rapids, MI: Baker Book House, 1983), 184.

[6] William Secker, *The Nonsuch Professor In His Meridian Splendor* (Chicago: Fleming H. Revell Co., 1899), 25–26.

- The most likely definitions held by people related to expressions of praise or thanks to God (19%); praying to God (17%); attending church services (17%); having a personal relationship with God (12%); a particular attitude toward God (10%); or a way of living that reflects one's spiritual commitment (9%). (1994)
- The views of worship by born again Christians were not significantly different from those of other adults. (1994)
- Enjoying or appreciating worship is not synonymous with experiencing the presence of God. Nearly two-thirds of regular attenders say they have never experienced God's presence at a church service. (1997)
- 48% of regular church attenders have not experienced God's presence in the past year. (1997)
- When asked to identify the single most important responsibility of a Christian, the replies of born again adults show that worship is the top rated priority (listed by 34%). (1995)
- Two-thirds of church-going adults (65%) are very satisfied with the ability to worship God afforded by their church. (1994)

═══════◇═══════
Mirror, Mirror . . .

We always become what we worship.
—DAN DeHAAN
═══════◇═══════

- The terms most commonly selected from a list of one dozen terms offered to describe their worship experience at their church were inspiring (92%); refreshing (90%); Spirit-filled (86%); participatory (82%); and traditional (78%). (1994)
- Terms which are rarely used by the public to describe their worship activities at church include embarrassing (3%); disappointing (7%); boring (12%); just a performance (13%); and outdated (13%). (1994)

Date: _____ _____ _____
Place: _____ _____ _____
Occasion: _____ _____ _____

Worship from God's Perspective

There is an old story about a man who dreamed that an angel escorted him to church one Sunday. There he saw the keyboard musician playing vigorously, the praise team singing, the musicians playing their instruments with gusto. But the man heard no sound. The congregation was singing, but the sound was utterly muted. When the minister rose to speak, his lips moved, but there was no volume. In amazement, the man turned to his escort for an explanation.

"This is the way it sounds to us in heaven," said the angel. "You hear nothing because there is nothing to hear. These people are engaged in the form of worship, but their thoughts are on other things and their hearts are far away."

W

Date: _____ _____ _____
Place: _____ _____ _____
Occasion: _____ _____ _____

R. C. Sproul on Worship

"We see throughout the Bible that when someone in antiquity encountered the holy God, the experience was almost uniform. To a person they stood quaking in terror, trembling before the Most High God. They were frightened; they were humbled; they were disintegrated; but they were certainly never bored. How is it possible then that people say church is boring?"[1]

Date:			
Place:			
Occasion:			

A. W. Tozer on Worship

"Christian churches have come to the dangerous time predicted long ago. It is a time when we can pat one another on the back, congratulate ourselves and join in the glad refrain, 'We are rich, and increased in goods, and have need of nothing!'

"It certainly is true that hardly anything is missing from our churches these days—except the most important thing. We are missing the genuine and sacred offering of ourselves and our worship to the God and Father of our Lord Jesus Christ. . . .

"My own loyalties and responsibilities are and always will be with the strongly evangelical, Bible-believing, Christ-honoring churches. We have been surging forward. We are building great churches and large congregations. We are boasting about high standards and we are talking a lot about revival.

"But I have a question and it is not just rhetoric: *What has happened to our worship?*[2]

Date:			
Place:			
Occasion:			

More Tozer Quotes

- *Worship acceptable to God is the missing crown jewel in evangelical Christianity.*[3]
- *Jesus was born of a virgin, suffered under Pontius Pilate, died on the cross, and rose from the grave to make worshippers out of rebels!*[4]
- *I am of the opinion that we should not be concerned about working for God until we have learned the meaning and the delight of worshipping Him.*[5]
- *I would rather worship God than do any other thing I know of in all this wide world.*[6]
- *I wish that we might get back to worship again.*[7]

[1] R. C. Sproul, "Worship the Lord in the Beauty of Holiness," *RTS Bulletin,* Fall 1986, Vol. 5, No. 3, 2.
[2] A. W. Tozer, *Whatever Happened to Worship* (Camp Hill, PA: Christian Publications, 1985), 9–10.
[3] Tozer, *Whatever Happened to Worship,* 7.
[4] Tozer, *Whatever Happened to Worship,* 11.
[5] Tozer, *Whatever Happened to Worship,* 12.
[6] Tozer, *Whatever Happened to Worship,* 18.
[7] Tozer, *Whatever Happened to Worship,* 20.

- *Actually, the wisest person in the world is the person who knows the most about God.*[1]
- *I am going to say something to you which will sound strange. It even sounds strange to me as I say it, because we are not used to hearing it within our Christian fellowships. We are saved to worship God. All that Christ has done for us in the past and all that He is doing now leads to this one end.*[2]

Date: _____ _____ _____

Place: _____ _____ _____

Occasion: _____ _____ _____

Jim Elliot on Worship

On August 16, 1953, Jim Elliot, who would soon lose his life at the hands of the Auca Indians he was trying to reach, was recovering from malaria. He wrote in his journal:

The tent was too hot to rest in this afternoon. Bathed leisurely and alone in the Talac river. First time I've felt I could walk that far while in public.

This came to me as I was sitting on the cliff after a light supper of manoic, raw carrots, and tea:

Because, O God, from Thee comes all, because from Thine own mouth has entered us the power to breathe, from Thee the sea of air in which we swim and the unknown nothingness that stays it over us with unseen bands; because Thou gavest us from heart of love so tender, mind so wise and hand so strong, Salvation; because Thou are Beginning, God, I worship Thee.

Because Thou are the end of every way, the goal of every man; because to Thee shall come of every people respect and praise; their emissaries find Thy throne their destiny; because Ethiopia shall stretch out her hands to Thee, babes sing Thy praise; because Thine altars gives to sparrows shelter, sinners peace, and devils fury; because to Thee shall all flesh come, because Thou art Omega, praise.

Because Thou art surely set to justify that Son of Thine and wilt in time make known just who His is and soon will send Him back to show Himself; because the Name of Jesus has been laughingly nailed upon a cross and is even now on earth held very lightly and Thou wilt bring that Name to light; because, O God of Righteousness, Thou wilt do right by my Lord, Jesus Christ, I worship Thee.[3]

Date: _____ _____ _____

Place: _____ _____ _____

Occasion: _____ _____ _____

Brother Lawrence on Worship

Nicholas Herman (pronounced er-man´) (1611–1691) was a Carmelite mystic, born in France, who was converted at age eighteen. He became a lay brother of an

---

[1] Tozer, *Whatever Happened to Worship*, 62.
[2] Tozer, *Whatever Happened to Worship*, 94.
[3] Elisabeth Elliot, *Shadow of the Almighty* (Grand Rapids, MI: Zondervan, 1958), 208–209.

order of Carmelites in Paris where he worked in the kitchen as a "servant to the servants of God" until his death. He is best known for his little book of sayings, published under the name Brother Lawrence, called *The Practice of the Presence of God.*

When Brother Lawrence lay on his deathbed, rapidly losing physical strength, he said to those around him "I am not dying. I am just doing what I have been doing for the past forty years, and doing what I expect to be doing for all eternity!"

"What is that," they asked.

"I am worshipping the God I love!"

Date: _____ _____ _____

Place: _____ _____ _____

Occasion: _____ _____ _____

Vance Havner on Worship

- *God places high value on holiness, reverence, and worship. . . . He approved neither idol worship or idle worship but ideal worship in Spirit and truth.*[1]
- *Too many church services start at eleven o'clock sharp and end at twelve o'clock dull.*[2]
- *Most religious movements begin in a cave and end in a cathedral.*[3]
- *The living faith of the dead has become the dead faith of the living.*[4]

Date: _____ _____ _____

Place: _____ _____ _____

Occasion: _____ _____ _____

The Tide

"A rowboat in the sand is hard to move. But when the tide comes in, it is easy. The church is like that. When genuine worship is absent from the church she struggles to do her work, but when a tide of praise uplifts her heart everything goes better."[5]

Date: _____ _____ _____

Place: _____ _____ _____

Occasion: _____ _____ _____

The Lost Chord

Adelaide A. Procter wrote a famous poem (later set to music by Sir Arthur Sullivan of Gilbert and Sullivan fame) about a woman who sat down at the organ

[1] Vance Havner, *Don't Miss Your Miracle* (Grand Rapids, MI: Baker Book House, 1984), 57.
[2] Vance Havner, *Pepper 'n Salt* (Old Tappan, NJ: Fleming H. Revell Co., 1966), 11.
[3] Vance Havner, *Why Not Just Be Christians* (Old Tappan, NJ: Fleming H. Revell Co., 1964), 33.
[4] Vance Havner, *Playing Marbles with Diamonds* (Grand Rapids, MI: Baker Book House, 1985), 24.
[5] Frank L. Accardy, "Everything Goes Better With Worship!" *The Alliance Witness,* July 12, 1978, 6.

one autumn day just at twilight and struck a chord that swelled within the instrument with soft majesty. It flowed through the room and filled the whole house with melody. It also thrilled her heart with peace. It was the most beautiful chord in the world.

> *It quieted pain and sorrow,*
> *Like love overcoming strife;*
> *It seemed the harmonious echo*
> *From our discordant life.*
>
> *It linked all perplexéd meanings*
> *Into one perfect peace,*
> *And trembled away into silence*
> *As if it were loath to cease.*

The woman lifted her fingers from the keys and the sounds faded away. Something broke the spell, and when she tried again, she could not find that beautiful chord. She sought repeatedly to reproduce it, but in vain. It was a lost chord.

For many Christians and most churches, worship is the missing chord in their experience. It is the one thing that quiets pain and sorrow like love overcoming strife. It is the one thing that makes harmonious echoes from our discordant strife. But for many, it is a lost experience.

Date: _____ _____ _____
Place: _____ _____ _____
Occasion: _____ _____ _____

Magnifying the Lord

The Bible says that we should magnify the Lord and rejoice in Him forever. What does that mean?

One recent evening when the moon was full I studied it from my back porch. It seemed as clear and close as the globe on the lamp post. Finding binoculars, I steadied them against the railing and magnified the moon. In other words, I focused on it, made it larger in my eyes, and studied it until I was overwhelmed with its ivory plains and dimly outlined mountains, with its splotched craters and jagged edges.

What happens when we magnify the Lord? Just that. We focus on Him, make Him larger in our eyes, and study Him until overwhelmed with His brightness, His love, His grace, His care, His power. And when we do that, the next verb comes into play—we rejoice in God our Savior. Magnifying Christ brings joy to our hearts, joy that levels every mountain and fills every valley. *O magnify the Lord with me and let us exalt his name forever.*[1]

Date: _____ _____ _____
Place: _____ _____ _____
Occasion: _____ _____ _____

W

---
[1] From a sermon by the author.

Robertson McQuilkin's Act of Worship

Robertson McQuilkin, former president of Columbia International University of Columbia, South Carolina, wrote this testimony:

Life was heavy on me. My dearest friend and intimate companion, my delightful wife Muriel, was slipping away, one painful loss at a time, as Alzheimer's disease ravaged her brain. Just as the full impact of what was happening to us hit home, the life of Bob, our eldest son, was snuffed out in a diving accident.

Two years later, to care for Muriel, I left my life work at its peak. I was numb. Not bitter, let alone angry. Why should I be? That's the way life is, life in a broken world. But the passion in my love for God had evaporated, leaving a residue of resignation where once had been vibrant faith.

I knew that I was in deep trouble, and I did the only thing I knew to do—I went away to a mountain hideaway for prayer and fasting. It took about twenty-four hours to shake free of preoccupation with my own wounds and to focus on the excellencies of God. As I did, slowly love began to be rekindled. And with love came joy.

I wrote God a love letter, naming forty-one of his marvelous gifts to me, spotlighting eleven of his grandest acts in history, and exulting in ten of his characteristics that exceed my imagination. Surely he enjoyed my gratitude—who doesn't appreciate gratitude?

But I discovered something else. Something happened to me. I call it the reflex action of thanksgiving. My love flamed up from the dying embers, and my spirit soared. I discovered that ingratitude impoverishes—but that a heavy heart lifts on the wings of praise.[1]

Date:	_____	_____	_____
Place:	_____	_____	_____
Occasion:	_____	_____	_____

Being Preoccupied with God

Karen Burton Mains wrote these well-phrased admonitions about worship in the preface of the hymnbook, *Sing Joyfully:*

"Worship has been defined as *being preoccupied with God.* How do we learn to become preoccupied with God? By cultivating *intentionality.* By deliberately turning our minds toward divine preoccupation. By developing worship habits and working on them. Intentional worship means a worshipper is not going to church expecting that worship will just happen; but intentionality means that a worshipper is going to church determined to make worship happen . . .

"A church bulletin aptly (said): 'Too many Christians worship their work, work at their play, and play at their worship.' We must learn to work at our worship so that preoccupation with God becomes delightfully habitual.

"The biblical ethic regards worship as work. *Av'dh* in Hebrew, *dienst* in German, *leitourgia* in Greek, *service* in English all have the double meaning of worship and work. In fact, liturgy means 'common work.'

"We must remind ourselves, over and over, that the focus of Sunday worship

---

[1] A clipping in my files.

must be upon the living Christ among us. In truth, if Christ were bodily present and we could see him with more than our soul's eyes, all our worship would become intentional. If Christ stood on our platforms, we would bend our knees without asking. If He stretched out His hands and we saw the wounds, our hearts would break; we would confess our sins and weep over our shortcomings. If we could hear His voice leading the hymns, we too would sing heartily; the words would take on meaning. The Bible reading would be lively; meaning would pierce to the marrow of our souls. If Christ walked our aisles, we would hasten to make amends with that brother or sister to whom we had not spoken. We would volunteer for service, the choir loft would be crowded. If we knew Christ would attend our church Sunday after Sunday, the front pews would fill fastest, believers would arrive early, offering plates would be laden with sacrificial but gladsome gifts, prayers would concentrate our attention.

"Yet . . . Christ is present."[1]

Date:			
Place:			
Occasion:			

The Morning Song

Ruth Bell Graham once described a poignant experience that deepened her ability to worship the Lord:

"I had been getting up early, fixing myself a cup of coffee, and then sitting in the rocker on the front porch while I prayed for each of our children, and for each of theirs.

"One morning I awoke earlier than usual. It was five o'clock, with dawn just breaking over the mountains. I collected my cup of coffee and settled into the old rocker. Suddenly, I realized a symphony of bird song was literally surrounding me. The air was liquid with music, as if the whole creation were praising God at the beginning of a new day. I chuckled to hear the old turkey gobbler, that had recently joined our family, gobbling away down in the woods at the top of his voice as if he were a song sparrow!

"And I learned a lesson. I had been beginning my days with petitions, and I should have been beginning them with worship.

"When the disciples asked our Lord to teach them how to pray, He gave them what we commonly know as the Lord's Prayer. The very first line is one of praise: *Hallowed be thy name.*

"In the seventeenth century, John Trapp wrote: *He lets out His mercies to us for the rent of our praise, and is content that we may have the benefit of them so He may have the glory.*"[2]

W

---

[1] Karen Burton Mains, *Sing Joyfully* (Carol Stream, IL: Tabernacle Publishing Co., 1989), 3–6.
[2] Ruth Bell Graham, *Legacy of a Pack Rat* (Nashville: Thomas Nelson Publishers, 1989), 53.

Date: _____   _____   _____
Place: _____   _____   _____
Occasion: _____   _____   _____

Ruler of the Universe

One of England's most enduring legends involves the Danish King Canute who ruled Britain from 1016 to 1035. He was such an imposing and successful king that never-ending praise was rendered to him. His courtiers were afraid to mutter anything to him but flatteries, and Canute grew tired of it. One day in the year 1032, taking them down to the coast at Northhampton, he placed his throne in the sand as the tide was coming in. As his advisors stood around, he asked them, "You think I am the mightiest of the mighty?"

"Oh, yes, your majesty," they replied.

"You think I can stop the tide?" he asked.

"Oh, yes, your majesty," they again replied, a little doubtfully.

Looking at the ocean breakers, he said, "O sea! Stay! Come no further! I, Canute, ruler of the universe, command you."

But despite his commands, the tide continued to roll in until it was lapping at the feet of the men. It came to their knees, then, as the waves engulfed them, the king and all his men ran for safety.

"You see," said Canute, "how little I am obeyed. There is only one Lord over land and water, the Lord of the universe. It is to Him and to Him alone you should offer your praise."

Slowly the king and his courtiers walked back into town where, at the cathedral, King Canute removed his crown and hung it in the church.

Date: _____   _____   _____
Place: _____   _____   _____
Occasion: _____   _____   _____

Worth-ship

In *Worship: Rediscovering the Missing Jewel,* Ronald Allen and Gordon Borror question the use of the term "preaching service" to describe Sunday worship, saying: *Viewing the preacher's singular act of proclamation as significantly more important than the entire congregation's acts of adoration, praise, confession, thanksgiving, and dedication, is espousing an expensive heresy which may well be robbing many a church of its spiritual assets.*

The authors go on to define worship as *an active response to God whereby we declare His worth.*

"The English word worship is wonderfully expressive of the act that it describes. This term comes from the Anglo-Saxon *weorthscipe,* which then was modified to *worthship,* and finally to *worship.* Worship means "to attribute worth" to something or someone. When we say of someone that "he worships his money" or that "she worships her children," we are using the word a bit loosely. If, however, the supreme worth for him is in his money, or the highest value for her is in her children, then it is an accurate use of the term."[1]

Date:			
Place:			
Occasion:			

Distorted Worship

In her fascinating account of Marie Antoinette, *To The Scaffold,* Carolly Erickson describes a typical worship service attended by Marie Antoinette and her husband, France's King Louis XVI. An English visitor, Sir Samuel Romilly, wrote his impressions after having attended worship in the presence of the royal couple:

"The moment his majesty appeared," Romilly recalled, the drums beat and shook the temple, as if it had been intended to announce the approach of a conqueror. During the whole time of saying Mass, the choristers sang, sometimes single parts, sometimes in chorus. In the front seats of the galleries were ranged the ladies of the court, glowing with rouge, and gorgeously appareled, to enjoy and form a part of the showy spectacle. The King laughed and spied at the ladies; every eye was fixed on the personages of the court, every ear was attentive to the notes of the singers, while the priest, who in the mean time went on in the exercise of his office, was unheeded by all present."

Even at the elevation of the host, Romilly noted, the most solemn moment of the Mass, the crowd in the chapel paid attention to nothing but the King, everyone "endeavoring to get a glimpse" of him.[2]

Date:			
Place:			
Occasion:			

Praise the Lord

An expressive woman wandered into a liturgical service. As the pastor preached, she became so caught up in his message that she exclaimed, "Praise the Lord!" A fellow worshipper leaned over and whispered, "Excuse me, but we don't 'praise the Lord' in the Lutheran church." A man down the pew corrected him: "Yes we do; it's on page 19."

Date:			
Place:			
Occasion:			

W

[1] Ronald Allen and Gordon Borror, *Worship: Rediscovering the Missing Jewel* (Portland: Multnomah Press, 1982), 9, 16.
[2] Carolly Erickson, *To the Scaffold: The Life of Marie Antoinette* (New York: William Morrow and Company, Inc., 1991), 101.

———— Yieldedness to Christ/Commitment ————

Someone Once Said . . .

- *The Lord would rather have one person who is 100 percent committed to him than one hundred people who are only 75 percent committed.*—Anonymous
- *If I had three hundred men who feared nothing but God, hated nothing but sin, and determined to know nothing among men but Christ, and Him crucified, I would set the world on fire.*—John Wesley
- *I guess the reason is because God has all there is of me.*—William Booth, when asked by Queen Victoria for the secret of his ministry
- *The world has yet to see what God will do with and for and through and in and by the man who is fully and wholly consecrated to Him.*—Henry Varley, in a statement overheard by D. L. Moody with life-changing effect
- *Our Lord never put discipleship in fine print in the contract. He called on us to forsake all, take up our cross, deny self, love him more than anything else. We are not our own, we are bought with a price, the personal property of Jesus Christ with no right to anything. "Love so amazing, so divine, demands my soul, my life, my all."*—Vance Havner[1]
- *I want to remind the committee that within six months they will probably hear that some one of us is dead. Yes, is it at all likely that eight Englishmen should start for Central Africa and all be alive six months after? One of us at least—it may be I—will surely fall before that. When the news comes, do not be cast down, but send someone else immediately to take the vacant place.*—Alexander Mackay, missionary to Central Africa
- *I have dwelt forty years practically alone in Africa. I have been thirty-nine times stricken with the fever, three times attacked by lions, and several times by rhinoceri, but let me say to you, I would gladly go through the whole thing again, if I could have the joy of again bringing that word "Savior" and flashing it into the darkness that envelopes another tribe in Central Africa.*—Willard Hotchkiss, pioneer missionary[2]

Date:	_____	_____	_____
Place:	_____	_____	_____
Occasion:	_____	_____	_____

Life Slogans

- *Anywhere, provided it be forward!*—Mary Slessor, missionary to Calabar (located in present-day Nigeria)
- *The will of God: Nothing Less, nothing more, nothing else.*—Alan Redpath
- *No reserve! No retreat! No regrets!*—Bill Borden, young missionary who died in Egypt on his way to China.
- *If Christ isn't Lord of all, He isn't Lord at all.*—Stephen Olford

---

[1] Vance Havner, *Playing Marbles With Diamonds* (Grand Rapids: Baker Book House, 1985), 18.
[2] Quoted by Gordon MacDonald in *Restoring Your Spiritual Passion* (Nashville: Oliver Nelson, 1986), 21.

- *Resolved: To follow God with all my heart. Resolved also: Whether others do or not, I will.*—Jonathan Edwards

Date: _____ _____ _____
Place: _____ _____ _____
Occasion: _____ _____ _____

Never Give Up

- *Never give in! Never give in! Never, Never, Never, Never.*—Winston Churchill
- *With the help of God, I never gave up.*—President Herbert Hoover, when asked by Norman Vincent Peale the secret of his success in life as a Christian statesman[1]
- *Don't give up at halftime. Concentrate on winning the second half.*—Alabama Coach Bear Bryant
- *If you run into a wall, don't turn around and give up. Figure out how to climb it, go through it, or work around it.*—Michael Jordan
- *If I had to cram all my tournament experience into one sentence, I would say, "Don't give up and don't let up!"*—Golfer Tony Lema
- *When you get into a tight place and everything goes against you, till it seems as though you could not hang on a minute longer, never give up then, for that is just the place and time that the tide will turn.*—Harriet Beecher Stowe
- *My mother, a very poor woman in Columbus, Ohio, taught her kids to pray, to read the Bible, to follow Jesus Christ and never to give up.*—Captain Eddie Rickenbacker[2]
- *I . . . recollect that he was, from a boy . . . always resolutely determined never to give up any point or particle of anything on which his mind was set.*—Thomas Carey, about his brother William, the "Father of Modern Missions"[3]
- *I can do little; yet I am resolved through the grace of Christ, I will never give over the work, so long as I have legs to go.*—John Eliot, early missionary to the American Indians[4]
- *Men often give up at the very stage at which, most of all, they should keep on.*—F. W. Boreham
- *Many of life's failures are people who did not realize how close they were to success when they gave up.*—Thomas Edison

Date: _____ _____ _____
Place: _____ _____ _____
Occasion: _____ _____ _____

Lost Hope

In his book *Winning Life's Toughest Battles*, Dr. Julius Segal wrote: "Whether or not we respond to our crises with stiffened resolve can make a difference in our very

[1] Norman Vincent Peale, *The Positive Power of Jesus Christ* (Wheaton, IL: Tyndale House Publishers, 1980), 197.
[2] Peale, *The Positive Power of Jesus Christ*, 197–8.
[3] Mary Drewery, *William Carey: A Biography* (Grand Rapids: Zondervan, 1978), 25.
[4] Ruth Tucker, *From Jerusalem to Irian Jaya* (Grand Rapids, MI: Zondervan, 1983), 89.

survival. During the Korean War, hundreds of American captives of the Chinese communists perished in prison camps because of a condition later described as 'give-up-itis.' Unwilling to challenge the efforts of their captors to indoctrinate them, they accepted the enemy's verdict of guilt. Some actually curled up in their cells in the fetal position. They had lost a capacity found to be essential in any encounter with a crisis—the capacity of hope."[1]

Date: _____ _____ _____
Place: _____ _____ _____
Occasion: _____ _____ _____

All the Keys

Suppose you have rented or purchased a whole house, and the former owner comes to you with the keys. There are twelve rooms in the house and he gives you six of the keys. You say: "Where are the other keys?" "Oh," he says, "you can't have them! There is a room on the second floor you can't have, and there is a room on the third floor and a room on the fourth floor you can't have, and there is a dark place in the attic you can't have, but here are the keys for the others."

You say: "I purchased the whole house, and I want all the keys, or I don't want any of them."

[Christ] will take everything, from cellar to attic—all the keys to all your affections, all your hopes, all your ambitions, all your heart, all your life, or He will not take one key. . . .[2]

Date: _____ _____ _____
Place: _____ _____ _____
Occasion: _____ _____ _____

One Small Nail

While visiting in Haiti, Dale A. Hayes heard a Haitian pastor illustrate to his congregation the need for total commitment to Christ. He told of a certain man who wanted to sell his house for $2,000. Another man badly wanted it, but couldn't afford the full price. After much haggling, the owner agreed to sell the house for half the asking price with just one stipulation: he would retain ownership of one small nail protruding from just over the door.

After several years, the original owner wanted the house back, but the new owner was unwilling to sell. So the first owner went out, found the carcass of a dead dog, and hung it from the single nail he still owned. Soon the house became uninhabitable, and the family was forced to sell the house to the owner of the nail.

---

[1] Dr. Julius Segal, *Winning Life's Toughest Battles* (New York: Ivy Books, 1896), 94.
[2] From a sermon by T. DeWitt Talmage, in *The Authentic Life of T. DeWitt Talmage* by Rev. John Rusk, copyright 1902 by L. G. Stahl.

The Haitian pastor's conclusion: "If we leave the devil with even one small peg in our life, he will return to hang his rotting garbage on it, making it unfit for Christ's habitation."

Date: _____ _____ _____

Place: _____ _____ _____

Occasion: _____ _____ _____

Nailing Your Colors to the Mast

John Guest wrote in *Decision* magazine: When I went to hear Billy Graham at Harringay Arena in 1954, he spoke about nailing our colors to the mast. That is a phrase from the old sailing ship days. Your color was your flag flying from your mast. When the man in the crow's nest saw an enemy ship, he would often call to have the color lowered so that the enemy could not spot the color and blow the ship out of the water. When you nailed your color to the mast, you were in effect saying, "Come what may, this is who I am, this is my commitment. And if an enemy ship coming over the horizon wants to try to blow me out of the water, that is up to him. My colors are nailed to the mast." Billy Graham said, "I am asking you, those of you who for cowardly reasons have not accepted Christ, to do so this evening." And I did so that evening.[1]

His Great Sacrifice

If Jesus Christ be God and died for me, then no sacrifice can be too great for me to make for him.

—C. T. STUDD

Date: _____ _____ _____

Place: _____ _____ _____

Occasion: _____ _____ _____

The Jewel

The Koh-i-noor diamond is among the most spectacular in the world. Queen Victoria received it as a gift from a maharajah when he was a lad. Later as a grown man this maharajah visited Queen Victoria again. He requested that the stone be brought from the Tower of London to Buckingham Palace. The maharajah took the diamond and, kneeling before the Queen, gave it to her again, saying, "Your Majesty, I gave you this jewel when I was a child, too young to know what I was doing. I want to give it to you again in the fullness of my strength, with all my heart and affection and gratitude, now and forever, fully realizing all that I do."[2]

Date: _____ _____ _____

Place: _____ _____ _____

Occasion: _____ _____ _____

Y

---

[1] John Guest in *Decision Magazine,* March, 1984, 7.
[2] John Guest in *Decision Magazine,* March, 1984, 7.

Stand Up for Jesus

Dudley Tyng served as his father's assistant at Philadelphia's Church of the Epiphany and was elected its pastor when his father retired in 1854. He was only twenty-nine when he succeeded his father at the large Episcopal church, and at first it seemed a great fit. But the honeymoon ended when Dudley began vigorously preaching against slavery. Loud complaints rose from the more conservative members, resulting in Dudley's resignation in 1856.

He and his followers organized the Church of the Covenant elsewhere in the city, and his reputation grew. He began noontime Bible studies at the YMCA, and his ministry reached far beyond his own church walls. Dudley had a burden for leading husbands and fathers to Christ, and he helped organize a great rally to reach them. On Tuesday, March 30, 1858, five thousand men gathered. Dudley looked over the sea of faces and declared, "I would rather this right arm were amputated at the trunk than that I should come short of my duty to you in delivering God's message." Over a thousand men were converted that day.

Two weeks later Dudley was visiting in the countryside, watching a cornthrasher in the barn. Dudley's hand moved too close to the machine and his sleeve was snared. His arm was ripped from its socket, the main artery severed. Four days later his right arm was amputated close to the shoulder. When it appeared he was dying, Dudley told his aged father: "Stand up for Jesus, father; and tell my brethren of the ministry to stand up for Jesus."

Rev. George Duffield of Philadelphia's Temple Presbyterian Church was deeply stirred by Dudley's funeral, and the following Sunday he preached from Ephesians 6 about standing firm for Christ. He read a poem he had written, inspired by Dudley's words: *Stand up, stand up for Jesus, / Ye soldiers of the cross; / Lift high His royal banner, / It must not suffer loss.*

The editor of a hymnal heard the poem, found appropriate music, and published it. *Stand Up, Stand Up for Jesus* soon became one of America's favorite hymns, extending Dudley's dying words to millions.[1]

Date: _____   _____   _____
Place: _____   _____   _____
Occasion: _____   _____   _____

Matthew Henry's Creed

Matthew Henry, the famous Bible commentator, lived his whole life in the light of a little creed taught to him by his godly father:

I take God the Father to be my God;
I take God the Son to be my Savior:
I take the Holy Ghost to be my Sanctifier;
I take the Word of God to be my rule;
I take the people of God to be my people;
And I do hereby dedicate and yield

---

[1] Robert J. Morgan, *On This Day* (Nashville: Thomas Nelson, 1992), March 30th.

My whole self to the Lord:
And I do this deliberately, freely,
And forever. Amen.[1]

Date:			
Place:			
Occasion:			

Seeing the Stars

When missionaries Tom and Mabel Willey arrived in the village of El Valle, Panama, they moved into a mud hut with a thatched roof and dirt floor. Tom was often out and about, visiting the Indians, but Mabel found herself stuck at home, the center of attention of various villagers who examined her curiously but with whom she couldn't speak. The Willey children would come in from playing, covered with little brown insects which Mabel removed only with great difficulty, many tears, and liberal amounts of kerosene.

One evening after the children were in bed, Mabel was overcome with emotion. She ran outside, sat down on an old stump, and complained to the Lord.

"Lord, all I ever wanted was a beautiful home. Is this my beautiful home? This mud hut with a thatched roof and creatures falling from the ceiling? And what about my children? Can I bear this for them?"

Kneeling by the stump, she continued weeping and praying. Suddenly the Lord seemed to speak to her. He asked, "Can you not live in this mud hut for me? Remember what I have done for you."

Mabel's heart was touched, and she remembered the many blessings and gifts of love she had continually received from the Lord's hand. "Yes, Lord," she prayed, "I can live in this mud hut for you. I give my desire for a beautiful home, my children, my husband—all of us—to you. Do with me what you will."

She later recalled, *Suddenly, peace surrounded me. I rose from my knees and that mud hut might have been a mansion since my Lord had placed me there. It looked altogether different to my eyes. I saw what could be done to make it a home.*

I thought of the verse, "Two men looked through prison bars. One saw mud, the other saw stars." God had showed me the stars.[2]

Date:			
Place:			
Occasion:			

Smiling Bill

Civil war erupted in the Congo (Zaire) in the 1960s, and among the missionaries caught in the crossfire was a small sunbeam named William McChesney with World-

Y

---

[1] J. Oswald Sanders, *The Best That I Can Be* (Chicago: Moody Press, 1965), 23.
[2] Mabel Bailey Willey with Mary Ruth Wisehart, *Beyond the Gate* (Nashville: Randall House Publications, 1998), 64–65.

wide Evangelization Crusade (now WEC International). Though only 5'2" and 110 pounds, Bill had an outsized personality that radiated cheer wherever he went. His co-workers dubbed him "Smiling Bill."

On November 14, 1964, suffering from malaria, Bill, twenty-eight, was seized by Congolese rebels. Ten days later, he was beaten mercilessly, his clothing ripped off, and he was thrown into a filthy, crowded cell. Catholic priests gave him their garments, for he was shaking violently from malarial fever. The next day, he was dragged from the cell and killed.

Before leaving for Africa, Bill had written a poem explaining his desire for overseas missions. It said, in part:

I want my breakfast served at eight,
With ham and eggs upon the plate;
A well-broiled steak I'll eat at one,
And dine again when day is done.

I want an ultramodern home
And in each room a telephone;
Soft carpets, too, upon the floors,
And pretty drapes to grace the doors.

A cozy place of lovely things,
Like easy chairs with inner springs,
And then I'll get a small TV—
Of course, "I'm careful what I see."

I want my wardrobe, too, to be
Of neatest, finest quality,
With latest style in suit and vest:
Why should not Christians have the best?

But then the Master I can hear
In no uncertain voice, so clear:
"I bid you come and follow Me,
The lowly Man of Galilee."

If he be God, and died for me,
No sacrifice too great can be
For me, a mortal man, to make;
I'll do it all for Jesus' sake.

Yes, I will tread the path He trod,
No other way to please my God;
So, henceforth, this my choice shall be,
My choice for all eternity.[1]

Date: _____ _____ _____
Place: _____ _____ _____
Occasion: _____ _____ _____

---

[1] Morgan, *On This Day,* November 14th.

Zeal

Someone Once Said . . .

- *Come with me, and see my zeal for the the Lord*—Jehu, in 2 Kings 10:16 (KJV)
- *For the zeal of thine house hath eaten me up*—King David, in Psalm 69:9 (KJV)
- *I have been very zealous for the Lord God Almighty*—Elijah, in 1 Kings 19:10 (NIV)
- *Of the increase of his government and peace there shall be no end, upon the throne of David, and upon his kingdom, to order it, and to establish it with judgment and with justice from henceforth even for ever. The zeal of the LORD of hosts will perform this*—Isaiah about the Messiah, in Isaiah 9:7 (KJV)
- *Do not let your heart envy sinners, but always be zealous for the fear of the Lord*—Proverbs 23:17 (NIV)
- *Never be lacking in zeal, but keep your spiritual fervor, serving the Lord*—Paul, in Romans 12:11 (NIV)
- *It is fine to be zealous, provided the purpose is good*—Paul in Galatians 4:18 (NIV)

Date: _____ _____ _____

Place: _____ _____ _____

Occasion: _____ _____ _____

Giving Oneself to the Very End

In October, 1999, in a letter to his "elderly brothers and sisters," Pope John Paul II spoke candidly of his own "twilight years," and of his desire to remain zealous to the end. He wrote, "These are years to be lived with a sense of trusting abandonment into the hands of God, our provident and merciful Father. It is a time to be used creatively for deepening our spiritual life through more fervent prayer and commitment."

"Despite the limitation brought on by age," he continued, "I continue to enjoy life. It is wonderful to be able to give oneself to the very end for the sake of the Kingdom of God. At the same time, I find great peace in thinking of the time when the Lord will call me: from life to life!"

Date: _____ _____ _____

Place: _____ _____ _____

Occasion: _____ _____ _____

"My Zeal Inspire"

On an autumn day nearly 200 years ago, Ray Palmer met his friend Lowell Mason on a busy Boston street. Mason was a collector and publisher of hymns, and he asked Palmer if he had recently seen any good religious verse. Palmer thought a moment, then pulled out a little book in which he jotted down his own thoughts and poems. He showed Mason a particular poem he had earlier written as a personal prayer to the Lord.

Palmer, a theology student in his early twenties, had a passion for the Lord, and as he showed Mason his poem he recalled the night, two years previously, when he had sat alone at his desk on an early winter's evening and wept over the words he'd written. To him, this was a sacred text conveying the craving of his life, uttering his deepest prayer to the Lord, and he showed it to his friends hesitantly.

Mason, reading the lines, was immediately moved. Ducking into a store together, the words were copied and Mason put the copy in his pocket. Arriving home, he was so deeply touched by Palmer's verses that he immediately set them to music.

Two days later the two men chanced to meet again. "Mr. Palmer," Mason said, "you may leave many years and do many good things, but I think you will be best-known to posterity as the author of "My Faith Looks Up to Thee.""

Mason was right.

The words that had so moved the two men include this stanza which has worded the prayers of several generations of Christians since:

> *May Thy rich grace impart*
> *Strength to my fainting heart,*
> *My zeal inspire;*
> *As Thou hast died for me,*
> *O may my love to Thee,*
> *Pure, warm, and changeless be,*
> *A living fire!*

Date: _____   _____   _____
Place: _____   _____   _____
Occasion: _____   _____   _____

Henry Saulnier's Philosophy

Henry Saulnier headed up the ministry of Chicago's Old Pacific Garden Mission from 1940 to 1986, where he was a bundle of compassion and whirlwind of activity. Even into his 80's, Saulnier endured increasing arthritic pain to work late into the night at the mission. During Gospel meetings at invitation time, he regularly hobbled up and down the aisles of the mission auditorium, tenderly placing an arm on the shoulders of sin-ravaged men, nudging them to go to the prayer room for personal counseling to receive God's pardon and a new life in Christ.

What kept him going? How did he motivate others? He once summed up his philosophy of Christian work in one unconventional sentence: *Work like the blazes, but give God the glory.*

Date: _____   _____   _____
Place: _____   _____   _____
Occasion: _____   _____   _____

Topical Index

Scripture Index